Encyclopedia of
CREATIVITY

VOLUME 2
I-Z, Indexes

Encyclopedia of

CREATIVITY

Editors-in-Chief

MARK A. RUNCO
California State University
Fullerton, California

STEVEN R. PRITZKER
Luminescent Creativity
Greenbrae, California

VOLUME 2
I-Z, Indexes

San Diego   London   Boston   New York   Sydney   Tokyo   Toronto

Copyright © 1999 by ACADEMIC PRESS

Academic Press
a division of Harcourt Brace & Company
525 B Street, Suite 1900, San Diego, California 92101-4495, USA
http://www.apnet.com

Academic Press
24-28 Oval Road, London NW1 7DX, UK
http://www.hbuk.co.uk/ap/

Library of Congress Catalog Card Number: 99-61534

International Standard Book Number: 0-12-227075-4 (set)
International Standard Book Number: 0-12-227076-2 (Volume 1)
International Standard Book Number: 0-12-227077-0 (Volume 2)

PRINTED IN THE UNITED STATES OF AMERICA
99 00 01 02 03 04 MM 9 8 7 6 5 4 3 2 1

Contents

Contents of Volume 2

N

O

P

Contents of Volume 1

How to Use the Encyclopedia

The *Encyclopedia of Creativity* is intended for use by students, research professionals, and interested others. Articles have been chosen to reflect major disciplines in the study of creativity, common topics of research by professionals in this domain, and areas of public interest and concern. Each article serves as a comprehensive overview of a given area, providing both breadth of coverage for students and depth of coverage for research professionals. We have designed the encyclopedia with the following features for maximum accessibility for all readers.

Articles in the encyclopedia are arranged alphabetically by subject. Complete tables of contents appear in both volumes. The Index is located in Volume 2. Because the reader's topic of interest may be listed under a broader article title, we encourage use of the Index for access to a subject area, rather than use of the Table of Contents alone.

Each article contains an outline, a glossary, cross-references, and a bibliography. The outline allows a quick scan of the major areas discussed within each article. The glossary contains terms that may be unfamiliar to the reader, with each term defined *in the context of its use in that article*. Thus, a term may appear in the glossary for another article defined in a slightly different manner or with a subtle nuance specific to that article. For clarity, we have allowed these differences in definition to remain so that the terms are defined relative to the context of each article.

Each article has been cross-referenced to other related articles in the encyclopedia. Cross-references are found at the first or predominant mention of a subject area covered elsewhere in the encyclopedia. Cross-references will always appear at the end of a paragraph. Where multiple cross-references apply to a single paragraph, the cross-references are listed in alphabetical order. We encourage readers to use the cross-references to locate other encyclopedia articles that will provide more detailed information about a subject.

The bibliography lists recent secondary sources to aid the reader in locating more detailed or technical information. Review articles and research articles that are considered of primary importance to the understanding of a given subject area are also listed. Bibliographies are not intended to provide a full reference listing of all material covered in the context of a given article, but are provided as guides to further reading.

A select number of biographies have been included. These biographies discuss the lives of individuals famous for their creative endeavors. Only those individuals whose lives had already been studied by specialists in creativity were included. Hence, although there are many individuals famous for their creative pursuits, you may not find coverage of your favorite here. Inclusion is not intended to be a judgment on the impact or value of these individuals or their creations.

Imagery

John C. Houtz* and Cathryn Patricola

Fordham University

Creativity and/or Creative Thinking The cognitive processes that lead to the production of new, original ideas, processes, or artifacts that are judged to be useful or otherwise of some value. Many experts also recognize the importance and interaction of emotion and affective processes with cognitive skills in creativity and creative thinking.

Imagery An individual's internal mental representations of real objects, scenes, events, or symbols in the absence of the direct, external, observable, concrete experiencing (i.e., sensation) of the objects or events themselves or their symbols.

Perception The process of translation of sensory stimulation into meaningful concepts.

Problem or Problem Situation A set of conditions for which an individual has no satisfactory response.

Problem Solving and/or Creative Problem Solving The interplay of cognitive and affective skills and processes directed specifically to the resolution of a recognized difficulty, unresolved dilemma, or unsatisfactory condition.

Sensation Direct activation of the nervous system by external

*Correspondence should be addressed to Dr. John C. Houtz, Graduate School of Education, Fordham University, 113 West 60th St., Room 1008, New York, NY 10023.

stimulation of the sense organs. Many experts include activation through internal stimulation as well.

This article reviews the knowledge base and theory of **IMAGERY** *and creativity. It is divided into several sections, reflecting a step-by-step development of the basic concepts and information concerning the relationships among these two phenomena. First are presented definitions of creativity and imagery, then theories and characteristic research associated with imagery, and then specific efforts to connect the two phenomena.*

I. DEFINITIONS OF IMAGERY AND CREATIVITY

Creativity, creative thinking, and creative problem solving are closely related phenomena. There are those who would argue for important differences among these terms, but it does not appear that the imagery literature nor the knowledge base concerning imagery and creativity has made such distinctions. A most common definition of creativity is that it is a process which leads to the production of something that is both new and useful. Whether the creative process is considered primarily cognitive, involving particular creative skills, attitudes, or styles, or whether the resulting product leads to the solution of a particular problem is not an issue for this article. In simple fact, the numerous and colorful accounts of the effects of imagery on creativity, some of which will be described, typically involve individuals working on what they consider important problems, to which they have devoted considerable cognitive and affective energies, and for which they hope to achieve useful solutions. [*See* DEFINITIONS OF CREATIVITY.]

Imagery, on the other hand, requires more detailed definition and explanation. Generally, authors describe imagery as schematic representations of thought generated from internal cues or motivations as opposed to external sensations and perceptions. Imagery is non-verbal memory. Images can be of objects, events, or action scenes. They can be short-lived or long-lasting. They can occur spontaneously or be deliberately generated and manipulated by conscious effort. A commonplace description of imagery is "having pictures in one's head," although this metaphor is not thought to imply a directly analogous, physical, neural structure within the brain or central nervous system.

A few additional definitions are in order to help clarify the definition of imagery. For example, sensation generally refers to the impact of external stimulation on the sensory organs of the body, resulting in signals being sent along neural pathways to the brain. Perception, on the other hand, refers to the interpretation by the mind of those sensory perceptions—putting meaning to the information the senses send to the brain. Thus, imagery can be distinguished from both sensation and perception but, naturally, can be related to them. One does, after all, "sense" or "perceive" an image. As is discussed later, individuals can confuse sensation and perception of real objects that are external to themselves with imagined objects. Imagery, also, must be regarded as more than "visual," although that particular modality is what most people think of when they speak of imagery. There also can be auditory, olfactory, and gustatory imagery, and imaginings of such things as heat or cold, pressure, pain, and other qualities typically associated with our sense of touch. [*See* PERCEPTION AND CREATIVITY.]

There are many types of imagery that have been identified. For example, there is one's "body image," one's perception of one's own body and its shape, char-

acteristics, or actions. Individuals who have lost an arm or leg to amputation often continue to have sensations as if from the missing limb. Individuals under the influence of drugs, experiencing extreme stress or pain, or suffering from some form of mental illness may experience hallucinations. There are such things as "phosphenes," which are images of light patterns caused by retinal stimulation by other means than light, such as rubbing one's eye or otherwise putting pressure on the eyeball. During various laboratory experiments, individuals may continue to "perceive" an unconditioned visual or aural stimulus after it has been removed and only the conditioned stimulus is presented.

Other types of imagery include thought images, which are those internal "perceptions" or "sensations" that occur to us during deliberative, conscious thinking. Hypnagogic imagery refers to those images that occur while we are in a drowsy state, either just before sleep occurs or just as we are waking up (hypnapompic imagery). Eidetic imagery is a term used to refer to exceptionally vivid, strong images that persist and seem almost to be perceptions of real objects or events. Synesthesia refers to the experience of an actual real-object perception in one sense modality being accompanied by imagery in another modality, such as "colored hearing" or particular odors sensed with visual stimulation.

One of the most famous reports of the influence of imagery on creativity is August Kekule's discovery of the arrangement of atoms in the benzene molecule. During a drowsy, dreamlike state, by a roaring fire in the fireplace, Kekule imagined chains of smaller carbon-and-oxygen molecules dancing and wiggling like snakes until one of them turned completely around and began to chase its own tail. Kekule's insight was that the structure of the benzene molecule must be a closed, circle-like loop. This was an example of hypnagogic imagery. Albert Einstein, on the other hand, reported that he had great difficulty thinking with words and abstract symbols. He always "thought in pictures" (thought images), such as his image of himself riding a beam of light (or alongside a wave of light, depending on which account one reads). He attributed to such an image, repeated often during his work, some of his most important understandings that eventually led to his special theory of relativity. [*See* EINSTEIN, ALBERT.]

In their efforts to understand the creative process,

researchers have interviewed, observed, or read autobiographical accounts of many famous writers and poets, artists, mathematicians, scientists, and engineers. Many of these individuals report the frequent use of images of one kind or another. It is well known (but less publicized in polite circles) that before there were significant legal and social prohibitions, many of our most famous writers, poets, and artists were regular users of opium and its derivatives or other mind-altering substances, and to such they attributed a good deal of credit for the vividness, fluidity, or clarity of their inspirations and creativity. [*See* ALTERED AND TRANSITIONAL STATES; DRUGS AND CREATIVITY.]

Researchers have been intrigued by individuals who appear to demonstrate "photographic memories"—whose images are so clear and stable that they can examine them and recall from them the most precise and complex of details. Imagery is easily demonstrable with "average, everyday" problem solvers as well. For example, if you ask individuals to solve what are called "three-term series problems" (e.g., if Grace is taller than Carol, and Carol is shorter than Nessa, is Nessa taller than Grace?), often they report creating an image of a line and marking places along the line representing the relative positions of the three elements of the problem, based on the information provided.

II. THEORIES AND CHARACTERISTICS OF IMAGERY

As with definitions, there have been numerous theories of imagery advanced over the years and descriptions of the special characteristics of the imaginal process. To understand the relationship between imagery and creativity beyond the simple appreciation of anecdotal reports, a review of imagery theories is helpful. One of the earliest theories was developed by Donald O. Hebb, who focused attention on the possible neurological consequences of perception. He described what he termed "cell assemblies" in the brain, which were hypothesized to be bundles of nerve cells which become habitually "connected" to each other through repeated stimulation. Images were the reexcitations of these same bundles as a result of internal mental effort rather than as a result of external sensory perceptions.

Hebb's theory was structural in nature, responding

in part to the knowledge being gained by the advancing scientific study of human anatomy during the first half of the 20th century. Scientists had been learning about the specific areas or regions in the brain which appeared to process information from the different senses. For example, direct electrical stimulation of surgical patients' cerebral cortex in various regions resulted in their conscious reports of vividly recalled memories, including visual images, sounds, odors, and emotions.

Continual advances in our knowledge about the electrochemical processes in the brain and the relationship between neural structures and functions continue today. However, the predominant theories and debates about imagery processes concern the psychological or functional properties of imagery. In this regard, many of the prevailing viewpoints have been categorized into two approaches. The first approach argues that imagery is a symbolic coding system that is distinctive from that of a more abstract, linguistic mode. Imagery is regarded as a more concrete, holistic or global, parallel or simultaneous mode of information processing, whereas language is a more logical, analytic, sequential mode. Major proponents of this view have been Gordon Bower and Allan Paivio. Individuals recall words that are high in concrete imagery (for example, chair, tree, balloon, and house) far better than words low in concrete imagery (love, democracy, justice, truth, etc.). Paivio advanced the "dual coding" theory of imagery which postulated two separate and loosely connected means of encoding information from the environment into memory—one largely "pictorial" and one largely "verbal."

In contrast, there are those who argue that imagery is the result of the same cognitive processes that explain other types of mental experience. Images are reconstructions of experience from stored propositional knowledge structures. These "propositional" knowledges include coded descriptions of the objects that are perceived and "imaged" as well as the acquired rules or procedures for manipulating (scanning, rotating, changing, etc.) the images. There is no need to hypothesize a totally separate coding system. Zenon Pylyshyn describes imagery as an epiphenomenon—a by-product or corollary effect of mental process rather than a causative effect. He explains the type of imagery most often reported by individuals doing creative work as the application of their "tacit knowledge" about the problem and the larger domain of knowledge and experience that these individuals bring to the situation.

The dualism debate can be seen elsewhere as well. In theories of child development, Jean Piaget regarded imagery as a mainstay of early childhood thinking. Less abstract and symbolic than adult thinking, enactive and later concrete operational thinking were the means by which infants and children represented internally their experiences and interactions with the external world. For Piaget, intellectual growth proceeded gradually through stages toward the goal of more abstract, symbolic thought (that is, where symbols stand for things and the symbols themselves can be manipulated, classified, related, etc., apart from the things they represent). Growth comes as a result of constant challenge to the "status quo," so to speak. New experiences challenge old representations. Existing, less well-developed cognitive schema—the internal mental, functional representations of experiences—lead to mistakes in judgments about external reality and, thus, revisions to schema become necessary. As schemas enlarge to accommodate new experience, they combine with other schemas, thus accelerating intellectual development and increasing the level of abstraction possible. [*See* DEVELOPMENTAL STAGES.]

A full elaboration of Piagetian theory is not required here, but others, such as Jerome Bruner, also regard imagery as a critical stage of mental representations. With Bruner, however, the iconic (image-based) mode of mental representation is regarded as a more infantile, basic, limited stage, to be passed through on the way to more adult-like, abstract thinking. The dual hypothesis theory of imagery is reflected in the differences between Piaget and Bruner in that, for Piaget, imagery is as substantial a mental process as any other, and serves overall development in the same manner as the mental activity characteristic of any other stage. For Bruner, the symbolic processes, notably language development, conceptual thinking, etc., are much more important because of their "higher" level of development.

Psychodynamic and personality psychologists have joined the dualism debate as well. In classic psychodynamic terms, creativity springs from what is regarded as "primary process thinking." Primary process thinking is wish fulfillment and fantasy thinking focused on immediate, egocentric needs gratification.

Such thinking stems from the unconscious, libidinal forces that are part of our human nature, as described by Sigmund Freud. For example, artistic creativity was hypothesized to be one mechanism by which men could compensate for their inability to give birth to children or to safely express their needs for aggression, power, dominance, etc. In contrast, secondary process thinking describes thought which is influenced by the reality principle, not the pleasure principle. Socially accepted standards and procedures of civilized societies and cultures are internalized by individuals to hold in check or otherwise modify the expression of the basic urges of primary process thinking.

Imagery has been compared to primary process thinking and more abstract, symbolic thought to secondary process thinking, since symbols draw their meaning from the larger society or culture that agrees to assign particular symbols to particular experiences. Without such a social compact, everyone would use different symbols and no one would understand what the other person was talking about. The dualism argument arises among this theoretical approach because writers and philosophers throughout history have pointed to the apparent dualistic nature of the creative process.

Beginning with a common definition of creativity as the bringing together of disparate, often apparently conflicting ideas into a new, cohesive identity, other themes in the creativity literature evoke the dual processing viewpoint. One example is Ernst Kris' phrase translated as "regression in service to the ego," which implies that the creative process requires that the playful, unbounded, diverse, impulsive energies of the unconscious mind must be controlled or channeled by the reality-oriented, conscious mind. There is Silvano Arieti's view that a "tertiary" mental process explains creativity, a process situated in the "preconscious" mind—the place hypothesized between the unconscious and conscious mind where barriers are less rigid and more permeable. In the preconscious, both primary and secondary process thinking interact freely, yet within the "watchdog" view of the conscious mind.

There is the extensive literature on personality patterns of creative individuals which demonstrates a long list of apparently contradictory characteristics or predispositions. For example, creative persons can be aloof and apparently asocial, yet also demonstrate extreme sensitivity to others, empathy, and sense of humor. Men appear to score highly on "femininity" scales and women on "masculinity" indices. Creatives tend to be independent-minded and assertive, yet also withdrawn and overly critical of themselves and their ideas. Studies of creativity and intellectual ability suggest that the high creatives are above average in intelligence, but not the most superior. Of the decades of research on personality characteristics, one thing is clear: creativity requires both intellectual and affective characteristics—neither dimension is sufficient by itself. [*See* EMOTION/AFFECT; INTELLIGENCE.]

Another arena where the dual processing viewpoint receives support is the psychophysiology of the brain. The symmetry of brain structure belies substantial functional asymmetry. Research has demonstrated that the right and left hemispheres of the brain appear specialized for different functions. For example, language functions appear localized in the left hemisphere whereas visuospatial abilities appear localized in the right hemisphere. Instruments designed to measure preferred modes of information processing have been developed to identify individuals who have dominant styles favoring the right or left hemispheres. Some researchers have proposed, naturally, that creativity results from the successful integration of both styles. [*See* SPLIT BRAINS; INTERHEMISPHERIC EXCHANGE IN CREATIVITY.]

The dual processing theory of imagery was popularized by its intuitive appeal and by the numerous examples of imagery available from introspective accounts. But, the idea of a special, separate mental encoding mechanism, with distinct characteristics and advantages over a verbal symbolic system, has led to productive experimental research as well. Two of the most prolific experimental researchers have been Ronald Shepard and Stephen Kosslyn, who, with their students and colleagues, have demonstrated a number of important findings about imagery processes that support the dual processing viewpoint.

Largely as a result of Shepard's work and his 1978 paper, "The Mental Image," psychologists' and researchers' interest in imagery and its relationship to other cognitive processes was renewed after decades of apparent neglect. Shepard demonstrated in numerous experiments that individuals could "manipulate" images as if they were real objects. For example, subjects appeared to rotate complex figures in their minds (i.e.,

"turn them over and around") and examine them from different "viewpoints"—the greater the rotation, the more time required to perform the operation.

Kosslyn regards images as "depictive" of objects in a spatial medium. Each bit or component of an image corresponds to a bit or component of the real object being depicted. In his experiments, subjects "preserve" the spatial arrangements or "distances" between elements of the image. It takes them longer to scan things further apart in the image, for instance. Images have spatial limits. Figures can overflow their "boundaries"; when this happens, we compensate in our perceptions by "projecting" the image at greater distances to maintain the integrity of the image. It takes individuals longer to scan images of smaller objects, and details are less clear and more difficult to identify in "smaller" images.

These and other findings led to Kosslyn's "array theory." In other words, images are formed as temporary spatial displays which actually may have a psychophysical structure. According to this theory, images are generated from more abstract representations in long-term memory. They are not literally pictures but they function as such, and individuals can "look" at them, so to speak, and examine them as they would if they were holding a real picture-object in front of themselves. The array is the surface structure of the image—the screen or plate upon which the image is "projected" or "written."

But images also have a "deep" structure—additional, implicit knowledge about the real object conveyed by the image and knowledge about potential transformations of object-images possible in the real world. As a supporter of the dual code approach, Kosslyn imbues imagery with its own cognitive operations and mechanisms in addition to the simple "perceptions" or representations of objects. Images can be stored and retrieved from memory in chunks, added to, and improved. Images are not stored holistically, as when a photograph is made as light strikes a film of silver halide inside a camera; rather, images are constructed from memory using specialized, nonverbal, symbolic processes.

It is this principle—that imagery is a constructive process—that portends its importance for the study of creativity. Theories of the creative process have been as numerous and disparate as have those of imagery, but a common theme is the constructive nature of novel idea generation and invention. We now turn our attention to the functional effects of imagery (and imagery and language together) on cognitive and affective processes. A great deal is known about such effects and this information provides a basis for understanding the effects of imagery on creative constructions.

III. EFFECTS OF IMAGERY ON COGNITIVE AND AFFECTIVE FUNCTIONING

Imagery has long been of interest to philosophers and psychologists. Plato referred to imagery as if it were like imprinting on a wax tablet. Images were thought to direct behavior. Indeed, when scientific psychology—the study of mind—began in the late 1870s, the study of imagery was a major focus. Through the introspective method, individuals would talk about their images as they were thinking and working on problems. Thus, images were accessible to the scientist. Images could be described and recorded, and, it was hoped, relationships between imagery and action could be deduced.

By the 1920s, however, imagery was losing favor in psychology. So-called "imageless thought" experiments had demonstrated the prevalence of rather automatic (but appropriate and correct) responses that subjects would exhibit but could not explain. Without a conscious awareness of thought processes in some types of problem solving, it was realized that images were not the only (and perhaps not the major) way in which thought occurred. Thus disenchanted, psychology turned away from imagery as a topic and introspection as a method. In the early part of the 20th century, behaviorism was fast becoming the dominant approach to psychology and theories concerning human learning and memory, development, problem solving, and even creativity were to be reformulated in overt, observable stimulus–response terms, without the need for any consideration of unseen, so-called internal mental processes.

While behaviorism dominated, there were alternative theories available. Freudian psychodynamic theory, Gestalt theory, and other approaches were less influential in American psychology, and issues of imagery, perception, and cognitive process were of peripheral interest at most. It was not until the 1960s that imagery became an important topic in psychology again. Three factors led to its reentry and acceptance. First, the behaviorists themselves began to talk about internal, unseen mental operations, postulating invisible stimulus–response bonds interfacing between the external, observable stimuli and responses. Such admissions were essential to the survival of modern behaviorism. After 50 years, the behavioral approach still had not adequately explained, simply and efficiently, the development of complex human behaviors such as language and problem solving.

Second, cognitive psychology was gaining more and more attention. Cognitive psychologists had developed experimental methods to test their predictions based on their constructs about human memory and the processing of information. Cognitivism had the same inherent focus as the older Gestalt theories (how perception and meaning were related), but cognitive psychologists were able to extend their hypotheses about internal mental structures—schema, if you will—to behavioral consequences that could be observed. In other words, one might say the ancient Greeks were correct in their intuitions. Images (or internal mental operations) do affect behavior.

The third factor that renewed interest in imagery was the advance of computer technology. Even with the bulky, limited computer hardware in the 1950s and 1960s, as programmers wrote programs to play chess games and solve mathematical theorems or simple logic problems, they were forced to create concepts and constructs to guide their thinking about what they were doing. In other words, to get a machine to mimic human problem solving, programmers had to think about what it meant to think. The image, as a construct, became useful again as an explanatory device—as a model of cognitive processes for which they, the programmers, could then write instructions for the machine to follow to create what would be the machine analogue of a mental image.

The 1970s and 1980s were two decades of major research into imagery and its relationship to human cognitive and affective processes. By the beginning of the 1990s, imagery had clearly reestablished itself as a major topic of psychology. There is little doubt about the effects of imagery and useful applications of imagery to influence human thinking and feeling states. Indeed, applications of imagery have become widespread in education and mental health psychology, in creativity training for children and adults, and in other arenas where improvement of human performance is the goal.

For instance, as was mentioned earlier, Paivio demonstrated that concrete imagery was easier to generate than imagery of abstract words or concepts. Memory improved with more concrete words or ideas. Many researchers have demonstrated that learners who are practiced in and directed to create images recall more of the target material than those who do not make use of imagery. Children's books include more pictures than those of adult reading materials because it is thought that children require the concrete supports to aid them in learning about the more abstract material conveyed by words. In teaching mathematics, "manipulable" learning and teaching aids are part of almost all elementary grade classrooms. Children are able to see, touch, smell, or hear real objects, play with them, and otherwise manipulate them, in an effort to make connections between the abstract mathematical concepts and the symbols that are used to represent them and talk about them.

Researchers such as William Rohwer have demonstrated that learners who "elaborate" their images, that is, make active changes to or manipulations upon their images, learn more effectively. Rohwer's efforts also served to bridge an important gap in research on imagery—that of deliberate connections between imagery and verbal processes. As already mentioned, the dual code theory argues for substantial differences in the qualities or characteristics of information processing between verbal and spatial thought representations. Researchers have demonstrated that the two modes can interfere with each other. Young children, for example, may apply verbal information incorrectly to visuospatial problems because, presumably, they have not developed flexible abstract schema capable of resolving the inconsistencies. Classic perception and information processing experiments have demonstrated dual-input, cross-modality interference when verbal information concerns what is presented visually. When verbal information is irrelevant to the visuospatial information presented in another channel, interference is minimal. When the verbal information is relevant but conflicting, it dominates. The spatial information is not encoded.

Rohwer's training procedures demonstrated that even young children can learn to use verbal informa-

tion to enlarge and embellish visuospatial information. In other words, the two modalities, working together, can be highly effective in producing learning. For example, the modern Keyword method of memory enhancement is taught to many pupils learning to read and comprehend textbook material. It involves the selection of some concept or material that evokes a concrete image or series of images. The object that the image portrays may not have any direct connection to the material to be learned, but it becomes the key, so to speak, for unlocking the other material that is the goal of the learning activity.

The benefits of imagery are not exclusively cognitive. Imagery has been found to be an effective method in the affective domain as well. Images as well as words or behaviors may induce feelings and emotions. Patients suffering acute pain following surgery and individuals with chronic, long-term pain due to illness or injury have been able to improve their physical and mental well-being via imagery. Generally, the nature of their imagery is of some more pleasant, comforting, positive memories of past experiences that are created by the patient, using procedures that have been practiced under the guidance of a therapist or other health care professional who has been well trained in this intervention technique.

In other applications, counselors help individuals overcome common phobias (for example, fears of flying, of heights, of snakes, of speaking in public, or of taking tests) by teaching them to use imagery, of less fearful events, usually, before or during anxious moments. Often, the techniques include the individual picturing him- or herself in safe, relaxing, happy surroundings. The object of the fear or anxiety may be gradually introduced into this scene, first faintly and at a distance. As the individual adjusts to the presence of the fear-object, the therapist may encourage the individual to move closer and approach the object, even to touch it or hold it. This "desensitization" of the offending object can require much training. It can proceed as far and as fast as the individual can manage without overexcitation, withdrawal, or regression. Of course, despite many reported successes, systematic desensitization through imagery exercises and other visualization techniques does not help everyone.

Imagery can help us reduce stress, increase our mental stimulation, stretch our cognitive range and depth, develop richer images, and turn ideas into actions. The spatial or "holistic" character of imagery can facilitate our organization of information and the elaboration or embellishment of our ideas, and, in what may be especially important to problem solving and creative productivity, imagery may provide us with the means for "silent rehearsal" of our hypotheses and plans for action.

IV. IMAGERY AND CREATIVITY

A large literature exists relating creativity to imagery. Typically, research falls into three categories. The first consists of studies of creative individuals and their self-reports of imagery experiences during their work, and has been alluded to in earlier sections of this article. These reports, inherently interesting and of significant heuristic value, nevertheless are limited in their application. What is known about imagery and creativity in the general population, which has much greater potential for application to education and schooling, for example, comes from the second and third categories of research. The second type of study is that which attempts to show the correlation between the ability of individuals to generate images (most often visual) and their scores on measures of creativity or creative potential. Such research has indicated that scores on vividness of imagery correlate significantly with scores on acceptance of authority, environmental sensitivity, initiative, self-strength, intellectuality, individuality, and artistry.

Imaging ability has also been demonstrated to be an important predictor of performance on the *Torrance Tests of Creative Thinking* (TTCT) and a significant factor in actual creative production. Further, highly creative art and science high school students have reported strikingly different qualities to their imagery than low creatives. The image descriptions of the high creatives are longer and more detailed, vivid, multidimensional, and active. Further, the correlation between imagery and creativity has been shown to be more frequent and the correlation higher for individuals of a high-IQ.

The third type of study is that which attempts to show that the use of imagery affects creative productivity. Typically, such experimental studies provide training in imagery methods or techniques, or direc-

tions to subjects to use imagery when solving problems. There are comparison or "control" groups who receive no training, no instructions to use imagery, or some other procedure. Results of the groups are compared to determine the effectiveness of imagery. Research of this type has shown that imagination training enhances performance for individuals who are high imagers, but that such training makes a small impact on those without imaging ability. Research investigating the effect of imagery training given before or after a problem has shown that the effects of imagery depend on the nature of the problem as well as training conditions, as to whether imagery improves problem solving.

Research examining the effect of guided imagery practice on students' creative thinking, as reflected in their writings, has shown that guided imagery results in more original creative writing that when imagery is not utilized. Other studies have shown that imagery encouragement during instruction is helpful in science rule learning and can facilitate rule transfer.

Still other research has demonstrated positive effects of imagery training on responses to the *Torrance Tests* in the creative strength areas of movement or action and richness of imagery, and imagery training has improved creativity scores and other measures, including total affect, personal involvement, and risk-taking.

While studies have demonstrated positive relationships among imagery ability, imagery use, and creative problem solving performance, the reader is cautioned that the literature is large. Many studies have shown conditional, neutral, or even negative results. Imagery is not a guarantee of creative success. It may not even be one of the main predictors of creative performance. What may be reasonable conclusions to be drawn from the imagery literature may be the same as those offered by E. P. Torrance in his "Incubation Model of Teaching" when speaking of the research on the effects of incubation on creative problem solving. He stated the following conditions must apply:

1. States of consciousness other than the logical, wakeful state of consciousness must be activated, at least for brief intermittent periods
2. Intellectual, volitional, and emotional functions must all be brought into play together
3. There must be realistic encounters with a problem,

intense absorption, involvement, commitment, and heightened consciousness or awareness

4. Opposite, contradictory, or antithetical concepts, images, or ideas must be confronted simultaneously
5. Visual, kinesthetic, auditory, and other sensory modes of thought must be brought into play

It is likely that imagery, as with incubation or a number of other abilities, skills, procedures, or techniques, can be an effective aid to creativity, creative thinking, or creative problem solving under certain conditions. Those conditions are likely to include subjects who are well trained or well prepared and knowledgeable in their respective fields, problems which have concrete elements that naturally give rise to imagistic associations and/or require the use of information from multiple modalities, and settings in which prepared or trained subjects are directly instructed to use imagery and/or are deliberately made to do so.

There are two other individuals whose work may be singled out for discussion, Joseph Khatena and Ronald Finke. Khatena referred to imagery as "the language of discovery." Finke has stated that every person has the potential to make creative discoveries in their imagery. The careers of both researchers have led them to regard imagery as an "engine," if you will, of the creative process. It is not critical that creative persons use imagery in their respective domains, or that they are better imagers, even if these things are well documented in the literature. It is that imagery processes give rise to creative ideas because of the nature and qualities inherent in imagery, itself. There is something about imaginal processes that permits or propels the development of new ways of perceiving, understanding, feeling, or thinking.

Khatena focused his attention on what was defined earlier as imagination imagery—the imagery that occurs with deliberate, conscious thinking. But his testing results yielded examples of other imagery types as well, such as synesthesia, where sounds and words evoke color images, feelings, mood memories, and images of visual scenes and of action and movement. What explains the ability of imagery to lead to creativity? What is so special about the process of imagination that new ideas are discovered or generated? Khatena has argued for a "synthesis–destructuring–restructuring" process in creativity, which is quite in line with many classic and contemporary views of creativity, generally. New ideas come into being through a combinatorial process (synthesis), which is propelled because existing concepts and ideas are ineffective or unsatisfactory for one reason or another. But, before a new synthesis can occur, there is analysis (destructuring) and examination of problem parts or elements, obtaining new information, looking for alternative viewpoints and resources, breaking away from existing rules and functions, and testing possible hypotheses. This phase may be short or lengthy, and there is no guarantee of success. But, if there is a resolution, it comes in the form of a new arrangement—a new combination of elements that makes sense—and is integrative of key features and effective (a restructuring).

Khatena, however, did not describe specifically what enables imagery construction to aid the synthesis–deconstruction–construction process exactly. Like other writers and creativity theorists, he acknowledged that various transformational processes occur in imagery, as individuals create images from long-term memory (using visual- or verbal-coded memories or both) and actively or spontaneously manipulate them. He acknowledged, as have many others, the intuitive parallels between imagery activity and unconscious or preconscious thinking—less rigid, freer of restrictions, playful, spontaneous, etc.—and between imagery and right-brain thinking—holistic, global, inductive, etc. But these parallels could be just associative in nature. It could be that creative persons prefer right-brain thinking, and are more in touch with their own sub- or preconscious thoughts. Recall the claim that imagery is an epiphenomenon, not a causal agent.

For a more specific approach, we look to the promising work of Ronald Finke. As the decade of the 1990s began, Finke advanced what at first appeared to be an odd viewpoint—that creativity springs from using things we create, not from creating things we use. In other words, creative invention comes about less through deliberate seeking of the new and unusual, but more often from simple, undirected play and experimentation with what is familiar and interesting. Finke's program of research typically involves presenting figure drawings of simple shapes or objects and asking subjects to make something out of them. This method is certainly reminiscent of Guilford's Structure-of-Intellect test *Making Things,* a measure of divergent production of figural units. Many other creativity researchers have used similar tasks on their creativity or ingenuity tests or in their creativity training programs.

Finke also has used verbal stimuli, asking subjects to create inventions using various specified objects. The objects may be presented randomly or organized in some fashion, for example, categorized and classified according to some higher-level, abstract category. As with the visual stimuli, the goal is for subjects to generate new, interesting, worthwhile inventions. Finke defines creativity similarly to many others—creativity involves both originality and practicality or sensibility. [*See* INNOVATION; NOVELTY.]

Finke has obtained many and varied new inventions that exhibit the dual criteria of creativity. What he has added to the explanation of imagery's effects on creative process, however, is the view that the primary function of imagery is "mental exploration." It is because imagery provides a field for playful testing of combinations and arrangements of spatial elements that new ideas eventually may appear. Finke argues that the immediate goal of imagery is the creation of so-called "preinventive" forms, which are new combinations or shapes constructed from existing elements. Preinventive forms are, basically, new images, which the individual then examines for interest or application. Preinventive forms eventually give rise to creative ideas or inventions precisely because the individual considers them, toys with them, and tries them out. Most may lead nowhere, but some attract special attention, through intuition or effort, and lead the individual to see other new possibilities, relationships, and applications. The preinventive forms themselves probably are not the new invention; rather, they inspire continuing effort that leads to new forms. The individual searches his or her vast problem domain knowledge for applications of the preinventive forms.

Clearly, Finke admits his view of creativity and creative process is more spontaneous than deliberate. Individuals do better in his experiments when fewer restrictions are placed externally on solution goals or criteria. Individuals do much better when they have no preconceived notions about the forms with which they are to work. They do better with their own preinventive structures than with those offered from others. Finke allows that creative insights are largely accidental events and rejects the idea of unconscious or

preconscious processes determining creative outcomes. For him, unconscious or preconscious "incubation" in creative problem solving, for example, is simply another instance of preinventive forms being considered, elaborated, eliminated.

As for the famous reports of hypnagogic or imagination imagery contributing to discoveries by noted scientists or artists, these too are examples of the transformative generation of preinventive forms. In these cases, of course, the forms (e.g., Kekule's snake ring chasing its tail) are recognized by the individuals as interesting and useful for their particular problem. If these images had occurred to other individuals with different backgrounds and areas of interest, the same forms might have led to different creative ideas in their respective domains.

It should be noted that this reasoning takes full advantage of the current research and thinking from cognitive psychology regarding the development of expertise. It has long been accepted that a knowledge base was necessary for creativity (the moderate correlation between intelligence and creativity being one example), but only recently have cognitive psychologists estimated how long (possibly 10 years or more) it takes for an individual immersed in his or her field to develop an expert knowledge base. Furthermore, despite Lewis Terman's findings in his longitudinal studies of highly intelligent individuals that overall intellectual ability often is diffuse, leading to above-average school achievement across many subjects, modern cognitive theory argues that in adults, anyway, expertise becomes highly specialized. Generalized transfer of problem solving, for instance, from one subject domain to another is hard to demonstrate. This explains often disappointing findings from creativity and creative problem solving training activities that show immediate post-test gains but few transfer effects and long-term benefits. [*See* EXPERTISE.]

If one considers creativity to be a means, not an end, as Finke explains, then one need not look for imagery to equate with creativity. On the contrary, imagery merely is a process, not an outcome. Thus, when one looks at the extensive literatures relating creativity to information processing factors—such as brain lateralization; independent versus dependent, global versus analytic, or simultaneous versus sequential cognitive styles; introversion–extroversion; impulsivity–reflectivity; or complexity–simplicity—one need not look for underlying psychophysical or psychological iso-morphisms. A better use of our time would be to see if a particular style or preference complements the process of imagining a variety of preinventive forms or helps the individual to see applications of these forms to his or her domain. This would occur, Finke theorizes, by aiding a "perception-like" process whereby individuals note the importance or salience of particular elements, parts, or features of a form. What becomes "intuitively appealing," "potentially useful," or "personally relevant," to use Finke's descriptions, about the forms are precisely those features which lead on to creative applications of the new forms. With his colleagues Steven Smith and Thomas Ward, Finke has developed a comprehensive model of creative cognition, which has been termed the Geneplore Model, for "generate" and "explore." Imagery represents a large component of this model, drawing upon evolutionary history as well as modern psychological research, because imagery illustrates an essential spatial character of human thought. It is that special character which, while not the cause of creative thinking, nevertheless provides a mechanism, a "pathway," for invention to follow.

V. CONCLUSION

Imagery is a major topic of modern psychology. Systematic study of imagery processes has revealed that individuals can create, interact with, respond to, or otherwise manipulate images much as they would real objects. And, the mental processes by which we accomplish this activity share much the same psychophysical properties as those of our sensory perceptual processes. Imagery also shares a long history with creativity, which is evidenced by reports from both creative achievers and average persons that they use imagery in their problem solving and creative work. Some theories have stressed the special qualities of imagistic thinking—its nonlogical, global or holistic, spontaneous, inductive character—as an explanation for imagery's contribution to the creative process. Many researchers and trainers have demonstrated imagery's benefits in learning and creative problem solving. But, current thinking suggests that imagery's mechanism for new idea generation is its inherently spatial quality—that the "combinatorial, transformative" processes essential to creativity find a natural home in imagistic thinking. As individuals use objects in their imagery, they "see" new forms or arrangements that are possible, and from these "preinventive" forms, individuals see original and useful applications of these forms to their particular problems.

Acknowledgment

The authors thank Ms. Happy Berdugo for her research assistance in the preparation of this article.

Bibliography

Block, N. (Ed.). (1981). *Imagery.* Cambridge, MA: MIT Press.

Daniels-McGhee, S., & Davis, G. A. (1994). The imagery–creativity connection. *Journal of Creative Behavior, 28,* 151–176.

Finke, R. A. (1990). *Imagery and creative imagination.* Buffalo, NY: Bearly.

Finke, R. A., Ward, T. B., & Smith, S. M. (1992). *Creative cognition: Theory, research, and application.* Cambridge, MA: MIT Press.

Goff, K., & Torrance, E. P. (1991). Healing qualities of imagery and creativity. *Journal of Creative Behavior, 25,* 296–303.

Klinger, E. (Ed.). (1981). *Imagery. Volume 2: Concepts, results, and applications.* New York: Plenum Press.

Kosslyn, S. (1994). *Image and brain.* Cambridge, MA: Bradford/MIT Press.

Paivio, A. (1971). *Imagery and verbal processes.* New York: Holt, Rinehart, & Winston.

Parnes, S. J. (Ed.). (1992). *A source book for creative problem solving.* Buffalo, NY: Creative Education Foundation.

Piaget, J., & Inhelder, B. (1971). *Mental imagery and the child.* New York: Basic Books.

Rollins, M. (1989). *Mental imagery: On the limits of cognitive science.* New Haven, CT: Yale University Press.

Shaw, G., & DeMers, S. (1987). Relationship between imagery and creativity in high IQ children. *Imagination, Cognition, and Personality, 6,* 247–262.

Sheikh, A. A. (Ed.). (1983). *Imagery: Current theory, research, and application.* New York: Wiley–Interscience.

Torrance, E. P. (1995). *Why fly: A philosophy of creativity.* Norwood, NJ: Ablex.

Yuille, J. C. (Ed.). (1983). *Imagery, memory, and cognition: Essays in honor of Allan Paivio.* Hillsdale, NJ: Erlbaum.

Imagination

Jerome L. Singer

Yale University

Daydreams Shifts of our thoughts away from concentration on an immediate task to a range of images that may include "story-like" memories, wishful scenes, or fantasies of future realistic or improbable events that are more often positive but can be frightening, guilt-ridden, or vengeful.

Fantasy An imagined sequence of events that may be relatively remote from our daily reality but which may reflect long-standing or recent unfulfilled wishes, intentions, or current concerns.

Imagery The human ability to reproduce or mentally represent objects or events processed originally through our senses even when such external stimuli are no longer present.

Imaginative Play A form of play shown by children that emerges between the ages of two to five and involves creating miniature make-believe or pretending storylines. Such open play may be a forerunner of later private or internalized adult fantasy and daydreaming.

Schemas or Scripts Concepts employed in cognitive psychology to represent organized mental structures for storing and retrieving information efficiently using various categories or definitions. Scripts are special forms of schemas that relate to expected sequences of events in a variety of social or physical settings, for example, a restaurant, a barbershop or hairstylist, or a wedding.

Thought Sampling An important method for studying how imagination emerges in our normal stream of consciousness. Individuals may be regularly interrupted while performing a task or sitting quietly in a room, or by requiring them to carry paging devices which "beep" randomly during the day. They may then be asked to report as accurately as they can on the sequences of thoughts, images, and emotions they had just been experiencing.

Transitional Objects or Imaginary Friends Very young children who need to make a transition from clinging to parents toward more independence may at first cling to soft cloths or plush toys like teddy bears. They may use their early imaginative capacities to give "life" to those objects by talking to them or nurturing them. They may also create invisible companions to whom they give names and special identities.

TUITs Task-unrelated images and thoughts, which are measures used in experiments to capture the ways that our daydreams or fantasies intrude in our consciousness even while we are actively concentrating on performing a demanding signal-detection task. Such TUITs make up the "stuff" of our imagination.

IMAGINATION *is a special feature or form of human thought characterized by the ability of the individual to reproduce images or concepts originally derived from the basic senses but now reflected in one's consciousness as memories, fantasies, or future plans. These sensory-derived images ("pictures in the mind's eye," mental*

13

conversations, or remembered or anticipated smells, touches, tastes, or movements) can be reshaped and recombined into new images or possible future dialogues that may range all the way from regretful ruminations ("If I only had said or done it differently") to rehearsals or practical planning for upcoming job interviews or other social interactions and, in some cases, to the production of creative works of art, literature, or science.

I. IMAGINATION AND THE STREAM OF CONSCIOUSNESS

A. Definition

The great human capacity for imagery, that is, reproducing mentally an object, event, or face and associated sounds, tastes, touches, or smells even after they are no longer present in one's sensory field, is usually an important feature of imagination. The imaginative process as generally employed in psychological study is broader, however, than simply the imaging of a concrete stimulus. Imagination may involve elaborated verbal sequences conducted privately in consciousness or it may take on story-like forms such as reminiscences or wished-for future sequences of events. For individuals in particular vocational, scholarly, scientific, or artistic fields, imagination may involve elaborate potential activity. An automobile mechanic may mentally review the array of physical structures that are defective, imagine the repair manual or recall certain key words from it, picture mentally the kinds of tools required, and become aware of certain safety precautions inculcated in his training. He then may actually begin a series of movements based on what he imagined. A great composer such as Mozart has described how whole sequences of music appeared in his "mind's ear" and then were translated mentally into musical bars and note sequences. He often wrote out pages of musical notation which could then be printed with relatively few corrections or changes and distributed to musicians for performance. In one famous instance, the evening before the first performance of his great opera, "Don Giovanni," he realized he had forgotten to write the overture. While his wife kept him awake serving coffee, he stayed up all night writing out the piece and it was ready for copying and distribution to

the orchestral players the next day. That overture is one of the glories of the operatic repertory.

Some features of imaginative thought that must also be defined are fantasy, daydreaming, and night dreaming or sleep mentation. Much of imaginative thought takes the form of daydreaming, which usually involves shifts of attention away from an immediate task or concrete mental problem to seemingly task-unrelated images or thought sequences. Such daydreams may range from memories to wishful future events, or to playful story-like reshapings of current concerns of the individual or of long-standing desires. Daydreams may also involve mental experiences involving guilt, shame, or other dysphoric interactions with others, or they may also involve fearful or anxious mental scenarios, more or less realistic, of future events, for example, a natural disaster or an invasion from outer space by hostile aliens. While imagination can be utilized directly in a problem-solving mode as when a writer envisions various scenes to be used in a novel or movie scenario, daydreams are more commonly a feature of the naturally occurring stream of consciousness. Their adaptive function or practical utility may be harder to discern and often they may seem fleeting, even trivial, or else emerge as reactions to current emotions. Night dreams or the mental activity of which we become aware of shortly after awakening from sleep may be continuous with daydreams except that they occur (1) when our major task is to "stay asleep" and (2) when we have drastically reduced the processing of external stimuli by shutting our eyes, reducing light, and curling up in a bed to limit motion. [*See* DREAMS AND CREATIVITY.]

The term "fantasy" is used generally in two forms in psychology. It may reflect daydreams that are more likely to be considerably removed from the realities of individuals' lives, thus involving scenarios less likely to occur. Fantasies can be wishful or pleasant in content and tone but they can also involve frightening, hostile, or dependent scenarios. A fantasy of learning one is a long-lost relative of a billionaire may be positive and wishful but people also report fantasies about space invasions, nocturnal visits from vampires, or story lines in which they encounter teachers from childhood who humiliated them and on whom they now will be able to wreak terrible vengeance.

The term "fantasy" is also used by psychology when it is elicited through psychological tests, usually projective methods such as the Thematic Apperception Test (TAT). Here participants are shown ambiguous pictures and asked to make up stories about such pictures. The stories told are believed by clinical psychologists and personality researchers to reflect basic recurrent fantasies about important needs. When such stories from a given respondent are accumulated across a series of pictures as in the Thematic Apperception Test (or its variations), one can use these fantasy scores to represent needs of an individual such as power, achievement, or intimacy. Extensive research has shown that such accumulated solicited fantasies do indeed have behavioral predictive possibilities. The variety, complexity, and originality of fantasies produced to TAT-type pictures or related ambiguous materials like inkblots can also be shown to reflect a vivid or rich imagination generally with creative potential.

B. Imagination as a Special Feature of Consciousness

1. Some Early Theories of Imagination

While numerous references to the imagination can be found in world literature, it was not until the late Western European Renaissance, the 18th century period of Enlightenment, or 19th century Romanticism that one can find self-conscious efforts by scholars, scientists, or literary figures to examine imagination systematically. In the mid-1600s Thomas Hobbes moved from a passive to a constructive interpretation of imagination, stressing its capacity to engender desires or appetites and also strong emotion. In addition, Hobbes stressed the directional power of imagination as a means of exploring future events by extrapolating from our memories. In this explanation of the future we can consider the moral implications of various forms of action. In its constructive role, imagination may also play a significant part in the creation of new works of literature, art, or science.

By the mid-1700s, imagination was recognized as a part of the general human process of dealing with information.

It is only in recent decades that cognitive psychology has examined the process by which information generated through the senses becomes encoded and stored for retrieval and reshaping.

In his *Nouveaux Essais,* written originally in the beginning of the 1700s, Gottfried Leibniz outlined a viewpoint of imagination written in part to show that intrinsic qualities of mind were necessary for an understanding of human experience. All thought could not be attributed only to externally generated stimulation.

Leibniz proposed first of all that imagination is a bipolar system, one in which one relates oneself with external stimuli and makes connections through thought between oneself and others. At the same time the process also serves to distinguish oneself from others and to create a "private awareness." Thus, self-consciousness becomes an act of imagination. This view seems to anticipate Carl Jung's views of introversion and extraversion and David Bakan's polarity of community and agency, the striving for being part of a larger whole yet also for being a unique individual.

Leibniz further proposed that consciousness itself may lead to the active production of a specific image of oneself, a kind of "identity." This identity which unites one's past experiences with one's intended actions or wishes about the future can also be seen as a way of shifting passive receptivity of external stimulation toward actions engendered by intentions directed toward the future, certainly a view more in keeping with modern cognitive psychology. for Leibniz imagination was closely linked both to "suffering" and to "becoming," an existential view, indeed!

From Leibniz's standpoint the self-aware, imaginative person not only explores nature, which represents the external pole, but also through imagination comes to know more by recasting and reshaping externally generated experiences. Through imagination one re-experiences and reshapes so many different events that one in a sense is acquiring a vast additional source of knowledge. He suggested our greatest power for knowledge, wisdom, and personal identity and understanding emerges from an imaginative vision.

There was, of course, ambivalence about imagination among these early explorers. Shakespeare had praised imagination but also called attention to its dangers in leading to distortion and foolish hopes. Samuel Johnson, John Locke, John Keats, and Johann Goethe also expressed concerns about the "vanity of human wishes" and the distorting prism through which reality was reflected by elaborate imagery. The Romantic poets William Wordsworth and Samuel Taylor Coleridge gave imagination a central role in their work. The most extensive and elaborate formulations of imagination of that period are to be found in various works of Coleridge, who in his wide-ranging scholarship argued vigorously that the imagination must not be separated from "reality." Through its passive reception as well as its active reorganization, it influences all our human functions, and indeed becomes the source of language and communication.

2. William James and the Stream of Consciousness

The music, art, and literature of the 19th century are replete with examples of references to imagination. In music alone there are hundreds of compositions, such as Berlioz' Fantastic Symphony, Tchaikovsky's 1st Symphony labeled "Winter Daydreams," and the piano fantasies of Schumann, Liszt, Chopin, and Brahms. In art one can mention the paintings of Henry Fuselli or Eugene Delacroix, the combined engravings and poems of William Blake, or the joint paintings and poems of Dante Gabriel Rossetti.

With the publication in 1890 of William James' great two-volume *Principles of Psychology,* the study of the human imagination emerges from the first time as a central topic in the newly developing science of psychology. James brought out the central role of private thought in human experience and the ways in which the "pulsations" of the stream of ongoing consciousness reflected memories, fantasies, glosses on current stimuli, and anticipations of future events or personal actions. The critical feature of beliefs about the self in its presumed actual or ideal forms was closely tied in his view with the human imaginative capacity and with the formation of the personality, as well as with one's overt actions.

During the period of relative scientific neglect of William James, his influence was felt largely through literature. A genre of fiction called the "stream of consciousness style" appeared at the beginning of the 20th century and has continued to be employed ever since. Writers such as Dorothy Richardson, Virginia Woolf, Marcel Proust, James Joyce, William Faulkner, Ernest Hemingway (in *The Snows of Kilimanjaro*), and Saul Bellow have sought to portray the subtle workings of ongoing consciousness and the ways in which the individual narrator's imagination can be at the center of a well-told story. Words are, of course, limited in what they can do in describing a private experience that involves not only interior monologues in sequential form but also sensory-like representations such as visual or olfactory images. Perhaps the extremes of the possibility for the use of words to convey private experience and imagination are represented in james Joyce's *Ulysses* and *Finnegan's Wake.* Here the writer attempts first to capture the great range of conscious and preconscious experience by penetrating the consciousness of three characters, (*Ulysses*), and then to go beyond this to examining the dreaming experience of the sleeper in *Finnegan's Wake.* Joyce's final work represents an effort designed to capture not only the condensation, displacement, and symbolism of dreams through elaborate puns and word-fusions, but also to convey through sound and repetition, as well as verbal description, the deeper archetypes of the dreamer's cultural background and, ultimately, in keeping with the philosopher Vico's theory, the cyclical nature of all human experience.

Perhaps Joyce pushed words to their limits in his efforts. In the 20th century, the emergence of the art of film has opened the way for a further aesthetic exploration of the reality of imagination by making possible the use of visual images, auditory images, and interior monologues ("voice overs") in an effort to capture ongoing experience. The use of flashbacks, of quick cuts to presumed memory images intervening during ongoing behavior, by characters reflects such an effort. In Woody Allen's film *Play It Again Sam,* the "hero" carries on a running interior dialogue with his private version of a child's imaginary companion (Humphrey Bogart).

It remains to be seen whether the art of film, videotape, or related forms can begin to generate new possibilities for translating the very private functions of imagination into aesthetic form. We probably have not reached the limit of artistic possibility. Indeed, the far greater "diet" of visual stimulation that characterizes recent generations reared on film and, especially, television may actually be changing the ways we experience consciousness. [*See* TELEVISION AND CREATIVITY.]

3. Current Approaches to Imagination as a Feature of Normal Thought

A division of normal thought processes along two separate functional lines can be traced to the mid-19th century British neurologist Hughlings Jackson's distinction between "propositional" (abstract or logical) and "referential" (concrete or sensation-derived) thought, with the former more vulnerable to severe brain damage, toxic conditions, or great fatigue. Sigmund Freud extended this view into "primary process" and "secondary process" thought, the former involving imagery and fantasy reflecting the pressure of unconscious, erotic, or aggressive drives and being free of social constraints, while the latter form reflected more conscious, mature self-restraint and generally defensive or compensatory adaptiveness. More recent theory and a body of research suggest that Freud's emphasis on (a) the immaturity and (b) the drive-relatedness of his primary process is too narrow a view. Instead a growing number of investigators in psychology are proposing that human thought has evolved along two semiautonomous lines, both adaptive to special circumstances of the human condition. Two examples of such theorizing as they bear on imagination can be briefly summarized.

Jerome Bruner has proposed that human thought can be ordered along two dimensions, "paradigmatic," involving logical ordering of experience, and "narrative," constructing possible realities. The logical, sequential, paradigmatic mode is usually formulated in verbal terms in our own thoughts as well as in our communication to others; indeed, in its most advanced form it is expressed mathematically. This mode seeks for truth and is, as are all scientific hypotheses, ultimately falsifiable.

In contrast, the narrative mode, while sequential to the extent that it is communicated to others in a series of statements, may be thought of first in bursts of images, usually visual and auditory, but sometimes even olfactory, gustatory, tactile, or kinesthetic. It is expressed as a story and can also emerge as what cognitive psychologists call "episodic" or "event" memories, or as fantasies and daydreams. As Bruner has proposed, the object of narrative is not truth but verisimilitude or "lifelikeness." One can identify gaps in logic in a story sequence, but those very features (as in much poetry, in the novels of Franz Kafka and Thomas Pynchon, or in Philip Roth's recent Zuckerman series) are designed to communicate the sometimes comical or playful, but often sinister, irrationalities of the human condition.

Both of these models, formulating propositions about events into logical hierarchies and organizing our thou-

sands of experiences into believable or "acceptable" stories, must be mastered by children growing up in what we call the Western industrialized countries. It may be that some cultures place more emphasis upon narrative thought and communication than others, but it is hard to imagine societies that do not require the paradigmatic or logical sequential mode of discourse, even if only for economic purposes and business transactions. For Bruner, the narrative mode involves a subjunctive orientation, the formulation through images and remembered dialogues of possible personal life stories or of more or less realistic potential futures. The imaginative facet of human experience largely reflects Bruner's narrative process. For the production of a creative product—a fictional story, film script, or scientific theory or research study—both paradigmatic and narrative processes would have to be operative. [See CREATIVE PRODUCTS.]

A similar formulation, supported by a growing series of research studies, has been proposed by Seymour Epstein. His Cognitive-Experiential Self-Theory (CEST) also incorporates two modes by which people adapt to their physical and social milieus, a rational and an experiential system. A major extension of Epstein's approach is his linkage of the experiential system to human emotionality. The rational system is characterized by deliberateness and greater effort; it works through abstraction, verbal thought, or language and even may be a very recent evolutionary development. The experiential system involves the accumulation of concrete experiences ("episodic memories") into tentative emotionally nuanced story-like generalizations or models of one's life situation or of the world. At its lower or moderately complex levels of operation it proceeds rapidly and smoothly, seemingly without effort. Events are generally represented in images but can also be expressed in metaphors, prototypes, or stereotypes, and in stories. Epstein does point out that the more mature forms of the experiential mode (a reflection presumably of imagination), when functioning along with the rational system, may become the basis for intuitive wisdom or creativity. The excitement accompanying a scientific discovery may involve the emotions associated with concrete images that can then be formulated into a concise mathematical system. The image comes to mind of the ancient Greek scientist Archimedes watching the displacement of water as he lowers his body into his bath, reproducing those behaviors in an experiential or imaginative model, conceiving a mathematical proposition, and finally, in excitement at his discovery of a mathematical formula concerning displacement, running naked down the streets of ancient Syracuse shouting "Eureka!"

In an effort to integrate the "two mental processes" theories within a broader cognitive framework, Isaac Lewin has produced a three-dimensional table (Table I).

Lewin has proposed that cognitive processes vary not only in Imaginativeness and in Reality-boundedness, as well as in their specific Imaginal and Verbal features,

TABLE I

Examples of Some Cognitive Processes as Located within the Three-Dimensional Classificatory Space[a]

	a_1, imaginal		a_2, verbal	
	c_1, imaginative	c_2, reality and logically bound	c_1, imaginative	c_2, reality and logically bound
b_1	Majority of dream experiences	Spontaneous memory images	Associative thinking	Some verses of a known poem occur to the mind spontaneously
	Hallucinations, free-floating daydreaming of an imaginal, quasi-experiential nature	Recurrence of dramatic or traumatic experiences	Daydreaming of a verbal nature relaxing, meditating and thinking without any specific topic in mind	Obsessive thoughts and ideas
	Hypnagogic and hypno-pompic experiences			
b_2 Directed and controlled	Nonverbal (painting, sculpture) artistic creation in the nonrealistic artistic doctrine	Learning and problem solving by preverbal children and animals? (Tolman's "cognitive maps"?)	Writing of a science fiction	Problem solving in an abstract and well-organized way
	Effort to imagine the appearance of a legendary monster	Intentional eidetic experience	Invention of a new mathematic concept or area	Learning "facts" in school (history, geography, etc.)
		Nonverbal "realistic" artistic creation	Imagining argument that did not take place	Learning a foreign language
		An effort to "see" a friend's face and to "hear" her or his voice when he or she is not around		An effort to give a verbally accurate report of a dream
		Subject's task in "mental practice" experiment		

[a] Reproduced from Lewin, I. (1986). A three-dimensional model for the classification of cognitive products. *Imagination, Cognition & Personality*, 6(1). With permission of Baywood Publishing Company.

but also in the degree to which their occurrence in consciousness is Free-floating or Actively Directed and Controlled (one might almost say "willed"). In effect he is suggesting that while many of the features of an ultimate creative product emerge from images, fanciful or realistic, or language-focused thought (which can also be fanciful or realistic), an ultimate creative product (anything from a good business idea to a scientific or fictional literary product) requires an active and controlled stance. He seeks to make a distinction (supported by some research) between Imaginal processes, which may involve concrete sensory-derived and sensory imitative experiences (a mentally simulated picture, sound effect, taste, touch, smell or motion), and Verbal processes, which specifically involve lexical processes or word sequences in roughly grammatical form. A review of Table I makes it clear how the more free-floating features of the ongoing stream of consciousness may serve as the content sources for creative products but that final steps may call for deliberate effort and conscious integration. One might add, of course, that creative products emerge as a rule in a domain where an individual has already developed specialized skills through extensive practice.

In summary, imagination is currently viewed as a central feature of human cognition and information processing. It appears to reflect a key feature of human conscious experience. Evidence has shown that even in circumstances when a person is presented with a specific stimulus, there is a time gap between signal presentation and brain registration (as measured, for example, by the electroencephalographic or evoked potential recordings). This gap suggests that the processing of prior experiences and expectations as well as feature analyses of the presented stimulus continues even after the original signal or stimulus is no longer "objectively" present. Thus human conscious information processing necessarily involved "representations" of the stimulus or of environmental events. Once such representations are encoded for "storage" they may not only be retrieved by deliberate efforts at memory but may recur seemingly spontaneously as daydreams, fantasies, or nightdreams when external stimulation is reduced but when a moderate or high level of brain activation occurs. The "appearance" of such long-term memory material in focal consciousness, often in almost random combinatory forms, provides the "stuff"

or content that enriches or elaborates ongoing thought, and under proper conditions is a source for creative products or sometime simply for self-entertainment. When, however, there are dysfunctions in neurotransmitter activity at brain neuron synapses such material may seem to be out of control (as in schizophrenic or manic psychosis) and hallucinations or disorganized thinking may be observed in the individual. Under normal conditions the average person may ignore most of these "representations" as irrelevant to some currently undertaken task. Individuals who have defined themselves as striving for creativity in some particular domain may learn to be especially sensitive to these occurrences and to then seek in more deliberate fashion to use them to form creative products. [See BRAIN BIOLOGY AND BRAIN FUNCTIONING.]

II. CHILDHOOD ORIGINS OF IMAGINATION

A. The Forms of Play in Early Childhood

Although we do not have definitive longitudinal research on the origins of the adult imagination there is, however, good reason from studies of children's play to believe that adult daydreaming or fantasy emerges from the make-believe or pretending games of the preschooler. The early European investigations of Lewin, Piaget, and Vigotsky and much recent careful research indicates a very significant role in the 2.5–5 year old period for symbolic or fantasy play. [See PLAY.]

Children's play in the first year or two consists chiefly of purely sensorimotor activities engaged in seemingly for the sheer pleasure of physical contact. Soon we observe "mastery" activities by the baby such as repetitive dropping a bead into a hole or of solving puzzle-boards. Play continues through the lifespan in increasingly complex forms. By about 2.5 years of age children begin engaging in simple make-believe, for example, pretending to drink from an empty cup or to feed a toy animal from an empty dish. During the period between ages of 3 and 5 a significant portion of play involves the development of story lines—pretending to be different characters, pretending blocks are houses or sticks are astronauts, or using changed voices or sound effects to carry a plot along. Such play can be engaged in alone but research also shows that the more gifted or frequent pretend players among preschoolers are often leaders who initiate games with two or three other children. In the early elementary school years such play may continue but often in less open settings or, increasingly, it may be internalized in the form of private imagination.

Games with rules such as "hide and go seek" or "statues" or commercially marketed board games become a major focus of overt children's play in the early school years. While rule games become the prototypes for our later conceptions of law and order (and, indeed, persist in adult card games, gambling games, and mental skill contests from chess to crossword puzzles), symbolic play is expressed over the lifespan through one's playful use of one's own daydreams or fantasies as well as overtly through amateur theatricals or, vicariously, through our interests in literature, art, film, and television.

B. The Adaptive Role of Make-Believe Play

From a cognitive standpoint, play can be understood as a reflection of the necessity for the human organism from its earliest years to make sense of the complex environment. We must learn early to integrate signals (sounds, smells, sights, etc.) from the outside world with the signals we receive from our long-term memory or from the working machinery of our body (hunger pangs, aches, gurgles). Within this framework we organize sets of expectations about what new information to expect or preparatory thoughts to help filter new signals. For such expectations we build on organized mental structures that help efficient memory which are called "schemas" or "scripts." Such expectancies are part of a sequential process in accumulating and retaining information from the environment that goes beyond the narrower emphasis that prevailed in earlier stimulus–response psychology.

The key roles of information processing, curiosity, and expectancies are also closely linked to the emotional system. With respect to children we can see the early evidences of curiosity and exploratory behaviors in which the child strives to organize and integrate

novelty and complexity but also attempts to anticipate and to match prior learning with new material. When children can integrate new information or adjust the complexity of new information into preestablished schemas, they feel comfortable and indeed show a smile of familiarity. When new material is presented with great suddenness in a situation that was unanticipated, children will respond with startled reactions or fear. With prolonged periods of inability to assimilate such material into preestablished schemas, they will manifest emotions of anger, distress, and sadness.

From this standpoint, the early imaginative play of children can be understood as an effort of the growing organism to deal with the large objects and people around it by, first of all, trying to match such stimulus complexes with preestablished schematic structures. If this fails they may attempt to gradually reduce the negative affect by reshaping material into manageable sizes that can be explored and manipulated. A key feature of make-believe play, observable as early as 18 months in the child, involves an effort to enhance positive affect and to reduce negative affect by seeking to cut down the large things around it to manageable proportions. This can be done through the use of dolls, blocks, soft toys, and other manipulable objects that can be assigned meanings, roughly matching the real objects of the environment. Needless to say, such efforts also come into play when the circumstances confronting the child are not only properties of the physical world but are situations of a more social nature such as potential departure of a parent, arguments or fighting among family members, and situations involving teasing or humiliation.

In the course of attempts by children to incorporate such material into their previously formed mental organizations ("schemas" or "scripts"), the children are likely to experience the positive emotions of joy and laughter as they gradually, through repetition, link the novel material with familiar material in the fairly controlled setting of pretend play. Similarly in the course of pretend play they may find opportunities to express a full range of emotions, from excitement to fear, sadness, or anger, all in the make-believe games which they control. A child may pretend that a doll or toy cowboy is in danger, angered, or frightened but then may think of a way to resolve the situation by some previously learned "script" of heroic action or escape. Thus, the vicarious negative emotions may be followed by the excitement of discovery and the joy of a "solution." Make-believe play thus becomes a critical fashion by which children learn to make sense of their world: the nursery, the family, the neighborhood, television (an omnipresent feature of most children's environment today), and the ever-broadening social and physical settings that they confront as they grow older.

We have so far emphasized the structure of play. The content of pretend play often reflects the child's efforts both to demonstrate individual autonomy and mastery over specific content drawn from the family or the physical and social milieu and, at the same time, to demonstrate the child's desires for belongingness and affiliation.

It seems likely that all children (except possibly those who show the special form of brain disorder loosely called autism) demonstrate inclinations toward imaginative play by the end of the second year. There are considerable research indications that parental or other adult caregivers' influences play a critical role in sustaining, encouraging, and enhancing the likelihood that 3-, 4-, and 5-year-old children will continue and expand their imaginative play efforts. The parent's role is evident from research data that demonstrate that children who show greater spontaneous imaginative play in a laboratory situation or in daycare settings have parents or other caregivers who regularly read to the children at bedtime, tell them stories, or sometimes even directly engage in make-believe play with the youngsters.

Such adult intervention sets a tone for the child which allows the natural inclination to reduce larger complexities to miniaturized, story-like forms to come into full play. Here too one must credit the games sometimes introduced in daycare settings or even encouraged on particular television shows for children. In the United Sates, public television programs such as *Mr. Rogers Neighborhood* or *Barney and Friends* specifically emphasize for children the enjoyment and value to be gained through pretending and through make-believe games.

The concept of *transitional objects* first given special attention by Donald Winnicott has been now extensively studied from a research standpoint. It seems very likely that beginning with soft objects, teddy bears, and eventually invisible imaginary playmates, many children use their capacity for early storytelling and make-believe to create manageable companions or indeed even scapegoats.

It does seem very likely from the many training studies that have appeared that imaginative play may lead to specific increases in spontaneous language usage, imagery abilities, empathy, the capacity for self-restraint and for tolerance of delays, the enhancement of the child's acquisition of the distinction between reality and fantasy, and a number of other specific features. These may include, of course, the conflict-resolving or identity-forming aspects of what we find in the clinical applications of symbolic play.

Of course make-believe play is just plain fun. It has consistently been found that those children who played more imaginatively were also much more likely to be scored as showing more smiling and laughing, greater cooperation with teachers, and less evidence of the more negative emotions such as distress, anger, or lethargy.

Beyond this practicing of verbal skills, one can also consider the possibility that the making up of little plots and the transformation of blocks into space ships or nondescript rag dolls into parental figures or babies must call for some effort on the child's part to generate private images or to recombine earlier memories of individuals or scenes with new projected mental representations. While again such correlations between play and imagery or divergent production (a forerunner of creativity) might well be common to children who are imaginative players, there is good reason to believe from many training studies that increased opportunities to engage in imaginative play may actually enhance the later occurrence of divergent thought, imagery capacity, or storytelling abilities in children. In effect, then, we can see indications that imaginative play can have an array of adaptive benefits that might themselves lead to the kinds of imaginative leaps—a willingness to tolerate divergent mental operations—that often characterize adult creativity.

It may well be that playing at make-believe may help children to identify an entire dimension of possible human experience in which they can, in a playful manner and with enjoyment, reconstruct in simpler form the world's complexities. In this sense the play world may be seen as a prototype for our adult capacity for fantasy and daydreaming. In this mode we take our unfulfilled intentions or goals or the vicissitudes of our daily life and reduce them mentally into forms we can manipulate through imagery and interior monologues.

C. Imaginative Play
Internalized as Imagination

In the period between 5 and 8 years of age, the child, usually under the pressure of the formal school setting, learns to internalize its imaginative play tendencies so that they are carried out privately in the form of inner speech of imagery rather than through open vocalization and play on the floor. For the increasingly complicated world of middle childhood, the ability to use imagery is increasingly serviceable. It enhances the sense of individual privacy and personal control. Indeed, this sense of personal autonomy, the ability to mentally consider alternatives even while complying overtly with social demands, may be one of the great sustaining values of our ability to daydream and fantasize. Such imagery is central to children's thinking. A number of studies suggest it is the source for the tremendous richness of later biographical memories. Storytelling and pretending for children of this age group, carried out through reading and private fantasy, are not only forms of pure pleasure, but they also turn out to be useful communication tools for engaging the interests of peers and of teachers. And again, the gradual reduction in complexity and internalization of physical and social events to the manipulable form of private fantasies increases that sense of control. [*See* IMAGERY.]

Sometimes without completely recognizing it, children may actually find that their taste for pretending helps to master school content, to confront the novelty of the school setting, and to remember better and to think more clearly than peers who have already "put aside such childish things." Far from being a period of "latency," middle childhood is the age at which children begin to establish a sense of identity and uniqueness, some of this through identification with popular music or television figures, and some through recognition of salient components of their appearance or background which stand out from other classmates. It

is also during this period that children begin to speculate internally about dozens of alternative lives and about adventure and romance, research showing the former being more characteristic of boys and the latter of girls. There are more fantasies about heroism. Particularly now that there is a much greater sexual openness which characterizes comic books, novels, films, and television, there are increasing fantasies about sexual encounters. This is especially likely to emerge more strongly in puberty with physiological sexual changes and the emergence of masturbation, which is often linked to vivid fantasies that may have lifelong implications in terms of sexual appetite.

Play in the middle childhood and adolescence is sometimes characterized by contrariness, absurdity and maliciousness. Such behavior is an inevitable feature of the child's increased awareness in this age period of the limitations and flaws, first of all, of one's own parents or siblings and then, increasingly, of society more generally. One begins to try out in overt play and in fantasy these simple beliefs and hopes of childhood and then to turn them on their heads and look at them in a contrariwise fashion. The attraction of obstreperous, wrong-headed, or rebellious characters such as the recent American television figures like *Bart Simpson* or *Beavis and Butthead* exemplify this stage of development in which the child tries out absurdities and explores rebellious roles. This human capacity for tolerating ambiguities and playing and manipulating them in a miniaturized private world of thought allows children to sustain the inevitable disappointments and tragedies of growing up.

Many of the most creative features of human development are already being foreshadowed by elaborate middle-childhood fantasies. That period is also characterized by increasing awareness of personal identity and the anticipation of a range of possible selves which can become crystallized by the academic, social, athletic, or artistic successes and failure exposures of adolescence. Some of the more unusual human appetites, whether along sexual or aggressive lines, are also being formed through the repetitive fantasies of this period. The child who has, however, a rich elaborate earlier history of make-believe play and, in middle childhood, a rich and elaborate private fantasy experience, may be less given to monopolistic and single-minded focusing on bizarre fantasy. Instead, such children may be manifesting the potential for flexible thought that, coupled with special skills and effort, can emerge in dozens of useful original forms of artistic, scientific, business, and interpersonal creativity.

III. IMAGINATION, DAYDREAMING, AND ONGOING THOUGHT

A. How Imagination Is Studied Scientifically

Once symbolic play has been internalized, in the sense that children no longer speak their thoughts aloud, we must rely chiefly on the reports of adults about their private thought processes to study imagination. For the first half of the 20th century the major sources of evidence for the range and content of fantasies and daydreams (as well as nocturnal drams) came from the reports of patients in psychoanalysis or other forms of psychotherapy. Since the 1950s and 1960s, however, there have been significant advances in research methods for systematic study of imaginative processes. The following are some examples of the ways in which daydreams or related imaginative processes are investigated in a scientific approach.

1. Normative Studies through Questionnaires

A beginning step in identifying the range of use, frequency, and contingent conditions for daydreaming is by asking large numbers of normal (and, later, emotionally disturbed) adults to report on their imaginal processes through responses to psychometrically crafted questionnaires. Using factor analyses and related statistical procedures it has been possible to show that daydreaming seems an extremely general phenomenon that persists through the life span and is characterized by both positive-constructive and wishful content or by often dysphoric, guilt-ridden and anxious story lines. Daydreaming as measured by such questionnaire responses is also associated with overt behavior manifested in controlled laboratory experiments. Positive, wishful, or fanciful daydreaming is also linked to the major personality dimension of Openness to Experience, one of the so-called "Big Five Personality Traits" identified cross-culturally in current psychometric investigations. [*See* PERSONALITY.]

2. Laboratory Studies of Daydreaming during Signal Detection

Since daydreams have been defined as forms of thought that often intrude when one is thinking about or performing a specific task or chore, it has been possible to establish laboratory conditions that can pinpoint the spontaneous occurrence of such intrusive cognitions. By asking participants to sit in light-proof and sound-proof booths while processing rapidly presented auditory or visual signals and being rewarded for accuracy, one can interrupt individuals under controlled conditions and have them report on whether they have experienced *Task-Unrelated Images or Thoughts*. These reports, now labeled TUITs, have been shown to occur as much as 60% of the time even when the participants are highly accurate in their task performance. The content of such reports indicate that they reflect everything from memories to future plans or even bizarre fantasies. Normal persons who report a good deal of positive-constructive or wishful daydreaming on questionnaires also report more of such TUITs in the laboratory. Under specific experimental conditions one can decrease or increase the likelihood of TUIT reports but it is difficult to abolish them completely. In effect, then, the signal-detection studies point the fact that our brain is almost continuously generating daydream or fantasy-like materials that become the "stuff" of imagination.

3. Naturalistic Studies of Thought Sampling

Somewhat less rigidly controlled but still informative approaches, especially with respect to determining the content or motives for daydreams, have come from interruption methods during ordinary circumstances. These include having individuals carrying paging devices which "beep" them and ask them to report on their thoughts and on the contingent social circumstances. Such methods have shown, for example, that adolescents with a history of family stress are more likely to continue to ruminate more in fantasies after exposure to a simulated family conflict. Other research suggests that our ongoing TUIT processes reflect "current concerns," as yet unfulfilled intentions or short- or longer-term goals as yet unattained. Such reports of naturally occurring daydreams, especially those reported in relatively quiet, understimulated conditions, show considerable similarity tonight dream reports obtained in the sleep laboratory for these individuals, suggesting considerable continuity in themes and in the role of recent current concerns between daytime TUITs and mentation during sleep. Naturalistic thought sampling has also shown that measures of one's self-representations, for example, the closeness of one's beliefs about one's Actual Self to one's Ideal Self, are also reflected in one's ongoing thoughts and one's emotional moods as sampled over a week's time.

4. Psychophysiological and Brain Imaging Approaches to Studying Imaginative Thought

Early studies sought to determine whether one's daydream images were using the same neural pathways as one's sensory experiences. Exposing individuals to external visual or auditory stimuli indicated that processing such materials was impeded if one was engaging in visual or auditory fantasy or imagery. Subsequent extensive laboratory studies of imaging have confirmed that our imaginative processes do indeed draw on the same sensory-relevant brain systems as do our perceptions of the external environment. With the recent development of systems of physically imaging actual ongoing brain activity through positive emission tomography (PET) and functional magnetic resonance imaging (MRI), we may expect in the coming decades to be able to learn more directly what areas and systems of the brain are activated during imagination and daydreaming. For example, in a recent study at the National Institute of Neurological and Communicative Disorders, researches asked 12 normal volunteers to imagine their future behavior in either emotional or nonemotional situations. Using PET scannings they showed that the dorsolateral prefrontal and posterior temporal cortex were more activated during nonemotional situations. During emotional imaginations the medial prefrontal cortex and the anterior temporal cortex showed more activation.

In summary, psychologists and other mental science researchers now have available a range of systematic measurement approaches for studying imagination. The more physiological approaches may tell us about brain features and constraints of our fantasy capacities, and the psychological approaches may tell more about the contents as well as the adaptive or motivational features of imaginative consciousness.

B. Consciousness, Imagination, and Creativity

Many of the writers during the first half of this century seeking to link imagination and creativity followed Sigmund Freud in emphasizing the unconscious or preconscious features of the process. In more recent years there has been an increasing recognition that creative thought, rather than reflecting primarily the working out of unconscious childhood conflicts, can be better understood as a special feature of the complex nature of normal human consciousness and the operation of our cognitive system. It is clear that many human functions, from the formation of grammatical sentences to automatic stereotyping or the processing of information retrieval, are carried out unconsciously. At the same time, humans operate in dealing with novelty or in a variety of cognitive functions by relying on what Bernard Baars has called the "global workspace" or 'theater" of consciousness. As previously suggested, we work and reword new information in our working fantasies or night dreams and our brain seems to systematically reverberate or regurgitate such materials as the TUITs, the fleeting daydreams studied in the laboratory. Indeed as the choice of the acronym suggests, such TUITs are the building blocks for what is called "intuition," itself a precursor of the creative process. In effect, as we make mental glosses or associative connections about passing events, sights, or sounds, these are then formed into small-scale stories that recur to us in somewhat altered forms in our working thoughts or night dreams.

Students of dreaming like Carl Jung and Erich Fromm emphasized the creative as well as the defensive or conflictual features of night dreams. One can go further to argue that our presleep conscious fantasies or the fleeting TUITs that come to us as we push computer keys or lawn mowers all reflect a continuous reshaping of memories and anticipations that can, if we bring them to focal attention in our conscious workspace, become creative ideas. Such ideas can be put to use in our daily social relationships, in our business plans, or, for especially trained and gifted individuals, into the production of creative products of literature, art, or science. As Table I suggests, deliberation and planning along with special practiced skills must combine for the individual to produce a concrete creative outcome. The human imagination provides an essential and critical component of creativity, but even for those of us who do not deliberately seek to apply it in art or literature it can be enjoyed in itself as an enriching way of experiencing our world.

Bibliography

Baars, B. (1997). *In the theater of consciousness.* New York: Oxford University Press.

Bruner, J. (1986). *Actual minds, possible worlds.* Cambridge, MA: Harvard University Press.

Domhoff, G. W. (1996). *Finding meaning in dreams.* New York: Plenum.

Klinger, E. (1990). *Daydreaming.* San Francisco, CA: Tarcher.

Singer, D. G., & Singer, J. L. (1990). *The house of make-believe: Children's play and the developing imagination.* Cambridge, MA: Harvard University Press.

Singer, J. L. (1976). *Daydreaming and fantasy.* London: Allen & Unwin. (1986). New York: Oxford University Press.

Singer, J. L., & Bonanno, G. A. (1990). Personality and private experience: Individual variations in consciousness and in attention to subjective phenomena. In L. Pervin (Ed.), *Handbook of personality* (pp. 419–444). New York: Guilford.

Singer, J. L., & Pope, K. S. (Eds.). (1978). *The power of the human imagination.* New York: Plenum.

Implicit Theories

Mark A. Runco

California State University, Fullerton

*This article contrasts **IMPLICIT THEORIES** of creativity with the explicit theories which are held by scientists studying creativity. The implicit theories of parents, teachers, artists, and children are reviewed in this article, as are the personal explicit theories held by researchers themselves.*

Discriminant Validity The distinctiveness of creativity from related characteristics and talents (e.g., intelligence).

Explicit Theories Opinions and views held by scientists. They are explicit in the sense that they are shared with other scientists and testable.

Implicit Theories Opinions and views held by people other than scientists. They are often personal rather than shared, and they may not be in a form that allows testing.

Personal Explicit Theories These are the implicit theories that are held by scientists. They are personal and thus implicit, but because they can influence the research of the scientist, they are explicit as well.

Social Validity A psychometric technique relying on judgments given by parents, teachers, or others who are important in the lives of the research subjects (e.g., children). The assumption is that these judgments will have more ecological meaning than will test scores and judgments given by trained professionals.

Tacit Knowledge Personal understanding about the world. Often we know something about the world (e.g., gravity pulls objects toward earth), yet many of us cannot give a precise explanation for why this is the case. Our knowledge is in that sense tacit.

I. INTRODUCTION

Good scientific theories are testable. Hypotheses are easy to draw from them, and they are precise enough to know if data support or refute them. In this sense scientific theories must be explicit. They are made explicit to share, as well as to test. Scientists share ideas by publishing them, along with the results from their investigations. Other scientists can then attempt to replicate or utilize the research. Science is a social endeavor.

Implicit theories, on the other hand, reflect the opinions held by parents, teachers, children, managers, and others who need not articulate their views. Although implicit theories are manifested in opinions and expectations, they are largely personal. They reflect a kind of tacit knowledge, which is quite common. Often we know something about the world (e.g., gravity pulls objects toward earth), yet many of us cannot give a precise explanation for why this is the case (other than

27

referring to the mass of the earth or Newton's observation of an apple falling from a tree). Implicit theories allow us to judge creative behavior even if we cannot define creativity.

Implicit theories are important because they are related to the standards used in making many judgments—including judgments about creativity. They are also related to expectations, and a corpus of research has demonstrated the impact of expectations on development and behavior. Teachers' expectations, for example, may actually influence the rate of learning by students. Parental implicit theories and expectations are similarly important. If a parent has reasonable expectations for his or her child, for example, the child will be more appropriately challenged. The parent will give the child activities and tasks that require some effort, but they will not be so difficult that the child is frustrated.

Most of the research on implicit theories has focused on the opinions of teachers and parents. A few isolated studies have been conducted with other samples. Some research has, for instance, been conducted with managers in organizations. Their implicit theories presumably are important in that these will influence what expectations they hold for their employees. The most recent research has examined the implicit theories held by scientists who are studying creativity. These were labeled "personal explicit theories" because they are both implicit and explicit. The reasonable assumption here is that the implicit theories of scientists influence their thinking and the development of their explicit theories. This is analogous to what was noted above about parents' and teachers' expectations reflecting their implicit theories, only for scientists the expectations influence their work and research.

II. METHODS USED IN THE STUDY OF IMPLICIT THEORIES

The methods used to study implicit theories vary. One method utilizes social validity technology. Social validity was developed in the clinical setting as a means of ensuring that treatment outcomes would be meaningful in the natural environment. Treatment outcomes are frequently validated, but often this validation process relies on judgments of therapists. Social validation is

based on the judgments of parents, teachers, and individuals who are likely to be involved in the lives of the client in the natural environment. They are, then, based on implicit theories rather than on explicit theories.

Social validation requires two phases. First the sample whose implicit theories are of interest receive open-ended questions (e.g., what characteristics are shared by creative individuals?). The most commonly nominated characteristics are identified and placed on a questionnaire. This can be used in the second phase of the research to obtain ratings about particular individuals. The ratings on the questionnaire are usually categorical (e.g., Likert) but allow parametric statistical techniques to test group differences or relationships with other variables.

There is some subjectivity involved when the implicit theories of the individual are being compiled. Different individuals may express their implicit theories in different ways, so two individuals may both believe that creative persons are always original, but one of them describes this as being prone to novelty and the other as characterized by unusual behavior. The researcher attempting to identify the most commonly nominated characteristics may have difficulty determining which nominations refer to the same trait and which do not. Is "original" the same as "novel," "unique," and "unusual"? We cannot be certain, even if we consult a standard dictionary, because we are dealing with implicit theories. One person may say "original" and mean the same thing someone else means when he or she says "novel."

For this reason the first phase of social validation work may avoid open-ended questions. In Mark Runco's work with parents and teachers, the Adjective Check List was used in the first phase. This contains 300 adjectives, alphabetically arranged, and the individuals nominating traits simply choose which of those 300 are descriptive of creativity. The range of possible traits may be slightly truncated with this technique but it does avoid the subjectivity mentioned above. (Social validation using the Adjective Check List has not been conducted on anything other than creativity. Social validation is a part of some clinical assessments, but there the "significant others" are given the open-ended questions in the first phase of the research.)

Another advantage of the Adjective Check List is that it facilitates comparisons with explicit theories. This is because it contains several creativity scales. In fact, the Adjective Check List also has a social desirability scale, and this too has been used in the research examining the traits suggested by the implicit theories of creativity. This particular comparison is interesting because previous research indicates that teachers' views of the "ideal student" contain traits such as conforming, considerate, and so on—traits which may be unrelated to creativity. The creative student may daydream, only concentrate on intrinsically motivating tasks (rather than assignments), and do things in an original fashion.

One socially valid measure is the Parental Evaluation of Children's Creativity (revised). It was constructed from the traits parents most agreed on when asked to use the Adjective Check List to describe creative children. It contains 75 items, but only 24 of them (32%) are part of the scale that is relevant to social desirability. (The Adjective Check List scale used for social desirability is the "Favorable traits" scale.)

III. EMPIRICAL RESEARCH ON IMPLICIT THEORIES AND GROUP DIFFERENCES

Runco and colleagues have found that parents and teachers believe creative children to be active, adventurous, alert, ambitious, artistic, capable, curious, dreamy, energetic, enthusiastic, and imaginative. There were, however, differences between these groups. Teachers pointed to cheerful, easy-going, emotional, friendly, and spontaneous as characteristic of creativity. Parents chose enterprising, impulsive, industrious, progressive, resourceful, and self-confident.

Artists have been found to distinguish between artistic creativity, scientific creativity, everyday creativity, and "noncreativity." Imagination, emotion, and expressiveness were tied to artistic creativity, while "patient" and "thorough" were tied to scientific creativity. Clearly, the domain differences that are recognized in explicit theories of creativity are also recognized in implicit theories.

The social validation technique has also been used to empirically examine sixth- and seventh-grade children's implicit theories about creativity. In the first phase of the investigation the students were required to "list synonyms of creativity, behaviors they observed in peers they considered to be creative, and personality traits common to creative peers." Helen Miller and Janet Sawyers identified the most common items and placed them in their Students' Self-Evaluation of Creativity. They added several items (e.g., Conforming) to minimize the chance of response sets. These negative items were theoretically antithetical to creativity. As was the case with the implicit theories of artists, some of the characteristics nominated by the children (e.g., Imaginative and Interested in Many Things) are entirely consistent with explicit theories of creativity. Some of them reflect unfortunate biases. The item Artistic, for example, reflects the widely held but incorrect assumption that creativity is only possible in the arts.

Ratings from a second group of students (fifth-grade students) on this new instrument were correlated with originality scores on divergent thinking tests. They were also unrelated to the IQ, which gives the self-report some discriminant validity. Robert Sternberg has also reported evidence for the discriminant validity of implicit theories of creativity. He found differences among people's conceptions of creativity, intelligence, and wisdom. [*See* DIVERGENT THINKING; INTELLIGENCE.]

Creativity is associated with certain traits (e.g., originality and intrinsic motivation) and is inhibited by other traits (e.g., conformity and conventionality). For this reason those describing their implicit theories should be asked about traits that are related to creativity and those that are unrelated to creativity. The latter question may be asked something like, "what traits are uncommon in creative people," or "what traits are found only in uncreative persons?" Runco and colleagues did exactly this. They then constructed two indexes in the ratings obtained from mothers, fathers, and children. One was indicative of creativity and one contained contraindicative items. These showed good agreement among the groups. In particular, the indicative index of the mothers was positively related to that of the fathers, but negatively associated with both the mothers' and the fathers' contraindicative ratings.

In one study of personal explicit theories, Runco and colleagues asked creativity researchers to rate behaviors that were the most important for recognized creative achievement. Motivational behaviors received the highest ratings, with problem finding and questioning skills rated next most important, and adaptive cognition the third most important. The researchers were also asked about developmental influences on creativity. Here education and learning received the highest ratings, with Cultural and Social Factors and Family and Early Background receiving lower ratings. The final question to the researchers asked about important topics for future research. The rankings of these indicated that actual creative behavior, motivation and drive, imagery, imagination, and creative products are of critical interest. [*See* MOTIVATION/DRIVE.]

Interestingly, the differences in the ratings of researchers who had experience teaching creativity courses and those who had published a book or article, and of those who had not, were very slight. Additionally, only slight group differences were found for ratings of important research topics. There were a few differences in the interests (i.e., writing and music) of the researchers which were related to selected ratings of creative achievement variables and important research topics.

IV. CONCLUSIONS

Even with some group differences (including those implied by a comparison of characteristics across studies), there is some consensus about certain correlates of creativity. The characteristics Artistic, Capable, Clever, Curious, Imaginative, Individualistic, Intelligent, Wide Interests, Inventive, Original, and Resourceful are the most commonly recognized, for example. In a sense, these may be considered the core characteristics of the creativity complex.

The inclusion of Intelligence in that list may come as a surprise. Yet it may be that creativity does require some basic information processing skill. The relationship between creativity and intelligence is often described as a threshold, with some of the latter necessary for the former, but beyond a low level, the two are unrelated.

Alternatively, it may be difficult to justify the inclusion of Intelligence in the implicit theories of creativity. It does suggest a lack of discriminant validity (creativity being just another sign of intelligence). This is, however, an inherent feature of implicit theories: They differ from explicit theories. Moreover, explicit theories may not be able to justify implicit theories. If they could, there would be no reason to examine implicit theories. As it happens, implicit theories of creativity do differ from explicit theories in several ways, and they should be examined and respected. They tell us how people in the natural environment really think about creativity.

Bibliography

Domino, G. (1970). Identification of potentially creative persons from the Adjective Check Lists. *Journal of Consulting and Clinical Psychology, 35,* 48–51.

Gough, H. G. (1979). A creative personality scale for the Adjective Check List. *Journal of Personality and Social Behavior, 37,* 1398–1405.

Miller, H. B., & Sawyers, J. K. (1989). A comparison of self and teachers' ratings of creativity in fifth grade children. *Creative Child and Adult Quarterly, 14,* 179–185, 229–238.

Rosenthal, R., & Jacobson, L. (1968). *Pygmalion in the classroom.* New York: Holt, Rinehart & Winston.

Runco, M. A. (1984). Teachers' judgments of creativity and social validation of divergent thinking tests. *Perceptual and Motor Skills, 59,* 711–717.

Runco, M. A. (1989). Parents' and teachers' ratings of the creativity of children. *Journal of Social Behavior and Personality, 4,* 73–83.

Runco, M. A., Nemiro, J., & Walberg, H. (1993). Personal explicit theories of creativity. *Journal of Creative Behavior, 31,* 43–59.

Singh, R. P. (1987). Parental perception about creative children. *Creative Child and Adult Quarterly, 12,* 39–42.

Improvisation

R. Keith Sawyer

Washington University

Commedia dell'arte A popular form of theater in Europe in the 16th through 18th centuries. Although the basic plot was worked out in advance, most of the dialogue was improvised on stage.

Ethnography of Speaking A branch of linguistic anthropology that studies the improvisational creativity of folklore performers.

Method Acting A type of theater rehearsal that requires the actor to improvise a character's behavior, as a way of better understanding the character's psychology. Developed in New York City, method acting was based on the theories of the Russian director Konstantin Stanislavsky.

Motivic Improvisation In musical improvisation, the use of a set of motifs—melodic fragments between 4 and 10 notes in length—as the basic building blocks of an improvised melodic line. The same motifs may be used in many different songs, resulting in improvisations that have no necessary relationship to the original melody.

Oral Tradition In contrast to written tradition. Oral tradition includes all of the performances that are important to a society but are not written down. Oral tradition is particularly important in nonliterate societies, and can include religious rituals, stories, jokes, political oratory, and theater.

Paraphrase Improvisation In musical improvisation, an elaboration of a basic melodic line, using embellishments or rhythmic changes, such that the original melody remains recognizable.

IMPROVISATION is music or theater performance in which the performers are not following a script or score, but are spontaneously creating their material as it is performed. Improvisation can be as basic as a performer's elaboration or variation of an existing framework—a song, melody, or plot outline. At the other extreme, in some forms of improvisation, the performers start without any advance framework and create the entire work on stage. Improvisation can be performed by a group or by a solitary performer; this article will focus on group improvisation.

I. INTRODUCTION

Since the 1950s, creativity researchers have focused on product creativity—the creativity that results in the masterpieces of Western art, or the grand theories of science. Improvisation is a relatively new topic for creativity research, only beginning to receive attention in the 1990s. Two unique characteristics of improvisation have led to this increased focus.

First, in most creative domains, the creative process results in a product, such as a painting, a scientific article, or a musical score. Unlike product-oriented creativity, the goal of improvisational performance is to entertain an audience by exposing them to the creative process itself. Because the performance is live, in front of an audience, there is no opportunity for reflection or revision in the creative process. The audience observes the creative process in action. In a sense, the creative process *is* the creative product.

Second, almost all improvisations are performed by an ensemble, and require collaboration among all of the performers. For example, in a small jazz group with four to six musicians, no one musician can control or conduct the performance. Instead, all of the musicians have to listen closely to one another, responding to each other in a give-and-take that many jazz musicians call a "conversation." A jazz performance is a collaborative, group improvisation. Improvisational theater is also an ensemble art. An improvisational theater troupe typically has between five and eight actors. During a scene, no single actor takes on a director's role and guides the performance. Instead, the dialogue is collaboratively created, from line to line, as the actors respond to each other's words on the spot. Like jazz, improvisational theater is a collaborative, group improvisation.

These two unique characteristics make the study of improvisation potentially valuable for the study of creativity more generally. For example, improvisation gives the researcher an opportunity to observe the creative process in action, potentially providing insights about the creative process more generally. In creative domains that result in creative products—like art and science—the creative process usually takes place in isolation, in a studio or a laboratory. It can take months or years before the final product is completed. This isolation and the long time period make the creative process difficult for researchers to study directly. But with improvisational performance, the creative process is right there on stage, in front of the audience.

In addition, because collaboration is central to improvisational performance in both music and theater, improvisational performance can help creativity researchers understand how collaboration influences the creative process in all domains. For example, most modern scientific laboratories involve the efforts of many top scientists, Ph.D.-level researchers, and graduate assistants. Conducting a scientific experiment is a highly collaborative endeavor. In a broader sense, an entire scientific discipline evolves and grows as a result of collaborations—ideas and theories published, rejected, and elaborated in the pages of journals, constant e-mails across the country among leading researchers, and grant proposals accepted, edited, and revised by committees of experts. Although the collaborations of stage performers are obviously very different, some aspects of improvisational performance may be common to all collaborations. [*See* COLLABORATION AND COMPETITION.]

In recent European history, improvisational performance has been relatively unusual, because our performance traditions have emphasized the composer and the playwright. In Western music, we have a long tradition of scored music—written by a composer and later performed by a professional musician. This tradition extends at least back to the medieval period. In Western theater, we have an even longer tradition of scripts that are written by a playwright and then later directed and performed by professional actors. Since the 19th century, all of our serious, high-art performance forms have been scored or scripted, and improvisational performance has generally been associated with uneducated or rural subgroups. Examples include the fiddle dances of Ireland and the blues and jazz of African-Americans. Partly because of these cultural and economic associations, improvisational performance has faced an uphill battle to gain respect in mainstream culture.

The current predominance of scored music and scripted theater makes it hard to imagine a time when *all* performance was improvised. But of course, this was the case at the beginning of human culture, when writing systems had not yet been developed. The idea that a composer would write down a score for later performance is a relatively recent innovation in human history. Yet, human societies have always had musical and ritual performances, oral traditions that were passed from one generation to the next. In a society without widespread literacy, by necessity all performances have an improvisational element since there is no script for reference.

II. THEATER IMPROVISATION

All modern theater is rooted in ancient, prehistoric ritual performances. These performances, since they predate literacy, were essentially improvisational. Of course, some rituals are more structured and repetitive than others; nonetheless, all rituals that are not scripted display variation from one performance to the next. Contemporary anthropologists, who study verbal ritual performance around the world, have documented variations even in the most sacred rituals. For example, in many performance traditions only experienced elders have acquired the skills required to speak at important rituals. But even after a lifetime of performing prayers, incantations, and sermons, an examination of different audiotapes always shows differences between performances.

These observations have led to a revolutionary change in the way that folklorists conduct their research. For decades, until the late 1970s, folklorists were primarily concerned with discovering traditional folklore—stories, prayers, jokes, games, songs, and dances—and transcribing the words as they were told or sung. In many cases, there was a very real concern that this folklore would die along with the sometimes elderly people who were the only performers.

But there was always a problem with the approach of trying to identify *the* correct, official version of a song or a story. The problem is that these traditions are oral traditions; they are almost never written down. Every performance of a North Carolina tall tale or an Appalachian fiddle tune is a little different. Folklorists initially viewed this as an annoying problem. Their goal was to write down the correct version of the story, ritual, or game, but each time they observed a performance, it was different. In the 1970s, a branch of linguistic anthropology, called the ethnography of speaking, begin to accept that oral traditions are not fixed and verbatim, like the performances of a literate culture. Instead, these anthropologists realized that oral folklore is an improvised tradition. Trying to identify the source text was no longer the goal. Instead, these researchers began to study the improvisational creativity of the performer, and began to emphasize the ways that folklore was a living, practiced tradition.

A. History in Europe

These realizations have recently begun to change the way early European theater is analyzed. Modern theater is often traced to a popular form of entertainment, called the *commedia dell'arte,* a partially improvised genre of plays originating in 16th-century Italy and thriving for the next 200 years throughout Europe. The *commedia* is a classic example of an oral performance tradition. Some theater historians have hypothesized that the early actors were not literate, and no one has ever found a script for a *commedia dell'arte* performance. Instead, what historians have found are rough outlines of plot, with brief descriptions of the characters. The actors could easily memorize these rough outlines, called "scenarios," but all of the dialogue was improvised in front of the audience. The success of a *commedia dell'arte* performance depended on the actor's improvisational creativity.

The improvisations were guided by the scenario, which specified the characters of the play, an outline of the plot, the order of entrances and exits, the action for each scene, and summarized important conversations and monologues. These scenarios always used the same stock characters, and each character was always performed by the same actor. This allowed the actor to refine his performance, and allowed him to develop portions of speeches and dialogue that worked well. Each actor memorized particularly successful monologues, called *lazzi,* that he could fall back on if necessary.

Literacy became more widespread in Europe during the same years that improvisation was fading out of our performance tradition. Over the 200-year period that *commedia dell'arte* was popular, literacy became much more common among actors, and the scenarios developed into more highly scripted plays. By the 19th century, this form of early improvisation had been largely replaced by scripted theater.

In an interesting parallel development, during the same period, improvisation became less and less accepted in musical performance as well. Composers began to write much more detailed scores, leaving less room for embellishment and improvisation. Musicians were expected to stick to the score, and improvisation was restricted to an optional cadenza at the end of a piece. The influence of increasing literacy on these changes has recently received increasing attention from historians, literary theorists, and psychologists.

B. Recent History

Character improvisation was an important rehearsal technique for the Russian director Konstantin Stanislavsky. In character improvisation, actors improvise a monologue, going beyond the script to better understand the character. Influenced by Freud's psychology of the unconscious, Stanislavsky taught his actors to emphasize the feelings, moods, and expressions of a character, so that the performance would seem more authentic. Stanislavsky called this new technique "psychological realism." Stanislavsky's techniques have been influential for decades, leading to method acting and the New York school of actor training. Many contemporary theater and movie directors use character improvisation. But these improvisational techniques are used only in the privacy of rehearsal.

In a parallel development in France, the influential director Jacques Copeau began to transform French theater by drawing on improvisation and by reviving the techniques of the *commedia dell'arte*. His vision for *la comédie nouvelle* (the "new comedy") was based on improvisation, and his innovations in training and directing influenced almost every modern theater group, including those in England and the United States. In 1913, Copeau was the first to use semistructured improvisational games in rehearsals, drawing on his insight that children's games are fundamentally improvisational.

The first theater to improvise dialogue on stage was the "Theater of Spontaneity," created by Moreno in Vienna in 1923, and which performed to rave reviews in New York a few years later. Despite Moreno's initial success in New York, this innovation did not catch on. Contemporary American improvisational theater—using many techniques originated by Moreno in the 1920s—can be traced to Chicago in the 1950s. Rather than Stanislavsky or Copeau, Chicago-style improvisational theater has its roots in a series of games developed for children's peer play. These games were developed by a drama teacher, Viola Spolin, in the 1930s and 1940s. Her son, Paul Sills, used these games to found the first improvisational comedy group, the

Compass Players, at the University of Chicago in 1955. The Compass later evolved into the well-known improv group, the Second City, the model for the popular TV show Saturday Night Live.

Classic Chicago improv performances begin with the stage lights up and the ensemble standing on an empty stage. They ask for a suggestion from the audience—a location, a relationship, or a problem. After repeating the suggestion to be used, the actors immediately begin improvising a dialogue based on the suggestion. Nothing is planned in advance—they develop characters, plot lines, and dramatic tension as they go along.

Since its origins in the 1950s, improvisational theater has grown dramatically in Chicago and in other urban centers. With this growth has come a remarkable variety of styles and approaches to improvisation. These styles can be grouped loosely into two main approaches. The most well-known groups perform short "games," five minutes or less, which start from one or two audience suggestions. There are dozens of different games widely used by improvisational ensembles; each game is distinguished by a unique set of constraints on how the performance will proceed. A common game is Freeze Tag. After asking for an audience suggestion, perhaps a location or a starting line of dialogue, two performers begin to improvise a scene. The actors accompany their dialogue with exaggerated gestures and broad physical movements. The audience is instructed to shout "freeze" whenever they think the actors are in interesting physical positions. Immediately, the actors must "freeze" themselves in position. A third actor then walks up to these two and taps one of them on the shoulder. The tapped actor leaves the stage, and the new actor must take his place, in the same position, and then begin a completely different scene with her first line of dialogue, playing on the ambiguities inherent in the physical relationship of the frozen actors.

A second style of performance is referred to as "long-form improv." The ensemble asks for an audience suggestion, and then begins to improvise a one-act play which typically lasts for 30 minutes without interruption. These performances often are so good that many audience members assume a script is being followed. Yet this is never the case with authentic improv groups. The actors work very hard to avoid repeating even brief segments of a performance from a prior night. Long-form improv is less focused on comedy than are game performances, instead focusing on character and plot development.

C. Using Improvisation to Develop Scripts

Many directors and playwrights have begun to use ensemble improvisation in their rehearsals as a way of collaboratively developing new script ideas. Their belief is that by freeing the natural creativity of the actors, a more believable drama can result. They also believe that the "group mind" is capable of creative innovations that may be more inspired than even the most creative playwright's imagination. [*See* GROUP CREATIVITY.]

There are two parallel traditions. In Britain, the director Mike Leigh has been using improvisation to develop plays since the mid-1960s. He later shifted to movie producing, and his innovative technique has led to several award-winning and popular movies. For example, his 1996 film *Secrets and Lies* won the Best Director award at the Cannes film festival.

In 1959, the Second City theater formed in Chicago, and from the beginning they used improvisation during rehearsal to develop their comedy scripts. Although this group originated live improvisation, they no longer improvise in front of a live audience. However, they continue to teach and use improvisation as a technique for developing comedy scripts.

D. Conclusion

In conclusion, improvisation has always been an important component of theater performance. In a preliterate era, in the early roots of European theater, improvisation was a necessary skill for any performer. And since Stanislavsky and Copeau transformed modern theater, improvisation has become more and more central to theater training and performance. In historical perspective, the last few centuries of European theater have been perhaps the least-improvised theater performances that any society has ever created.

III. MUSICAL IMPROVISATION

For most of history and in all cultures, musical performance has been improvised. The style of musical performance that has been predominant in the West for several centuries—European art music like the symphony, which is elaborately scored by a composer and then performed by noncomposing musicians—is found in only a few cultures. A partial list of musical traditions in which improvisation is a key element would include, at a minimum, many genres of Indian music, the Arabic *maqam,* the Persian *dastgah,* African drum ensembles, Indonesian *gamelan,* flamenco, European baroque and organ music, American jazz and rock, and folk musics throughout Europe. In fact, almost all of the world musics that have been documented by ethnomusicologists and folklore researchers contain elements of improvisation. Unfortunately, most of Western musicology has focused on composition and written scores, and performance as a whole has been neglected.

Certain stereotypes follow from this bias toward composition: improvisation is spontaneous, primitive, and natural, while composition is calculated, sophisticated, and artificial. For example, a common misconception about improvisation is that the performers are playing without any preparation. But improvisation does not mean that "anything goes." There is always some musical structure, and "improvisation" can refer to many different types of music, ranging from relative freedom to relative fixity. For example, many people think that jazz musicians simply play whatever comes into their heads, in contrast to the years of training and practice that classical musicians go through. Recent research, by psychologists and musicologists both, is beginning to demonstrate what jazz musicians have known all along: playing jazz takes a lifetime of preparation, and requires incredible talents—not only some inborn instinct, but also discipline, rehearsal, and preparation.

Only a few cultures have the "composer–score–performer" division found in Western music. A relatively small percentage of musical traditions use any notational system. Even in musical traditions that have notational systems, the written notations are often only rough guidelines for a performance, with the expectation that a trained performer will improvise on the basic form of the piece. And in many musical traditions, these notations are not composed by anyone—they are transcriptions of traditional pieces that have been performed for generations.

Even early European composers did not have to write down every note, because they could assume that all performers were talented improvisers. Improvisation flourished in the music of the Baroque period. For example, most Baroque scores used a partially improvised system known as *basso continuo,* with a notated bass line and chords. The keyboard player was expected to use this shorthand notation to improvise the accompaniment. Along with this improvised accompaniment, the solo instrument that performed the melody was also expected to employ extensive variation and ornamentation of the written score. Even after the Baroque period, improvisation survived in the cadenza, a short section at the end of a movement where the composer would indicate that the performer should improvise. This provided the performer with an opportunity to demonstrate virtuosity. Improvisational and compositional creativity often went together—many famous European composers were also talented improvisers, including Mozart, Bach, Handel, and Beethoven.

Musicologists distinguish between two types of improvisation. The first is paraphrase improvisation, the ornamental variation of a written melody, such that the melody remains recognizable. The performer is allowed only minor embellishments on a standard melody, and the variations that are allowed are limited in number and must be placed in certain standard parts of the melody. An example of improvised embellishment is the performance of the melody of a Baroque composition, where the performer was expected to vary and embellish the written melody.

In paraphrase improvisation, we often say that the performer is improvising on the basic song. Although the song remains recognizable, each performance is clearly unique and different. But it turns out that not all cultures share this idea of improvisation; in some traditions that use extensive embellishment that we would call paraphrase improvisation, musicians of that tradition feel that they are performing the "same song" each time, even though tape recordings clearly show the differences. The ethnomusicologist Bruno Nettl wrote about a Persian *dastgah* performer, who was asked to comment on the differences between two performances of the same *dastgah.* He denied there was a difference. When the researcher played the two tapes for him, pointing out the differences, the musician admitted the differences, but claimed they were not

significant—that the essence of the song was the same. It seems that different musical traditions have different concepts of "sameness." These differences could be related to musical literacy—with our notational system, we believe that "the same" means note-for-note verbatim.

In the second type of improvisation, *motivic improvisation,* the musicians arrive at the performance with a repertory of patterns—called "licks" or "motifs"— stock phrases that the musicians then combine and draw on in each of their song performances. The set of patterns can be specified by the musical tradition, or may be the shared repertory of a single group or a single musician. For example, the jazz saxophonist Charlie Parker created his own repertory of about 100 motifs, each of them between 4 and 10 notes in length. In Javanese *gamelan,* a much smaller set of motifs is specified by the musical tradition, and the same patterns are used by many different groups.

In motivic improvisation, the creative challenge for the performer is to artfully combine and weave in the motifs, molding these fragments into a coherent whole. Different traditions vary in the rules for combining motifs, and in the degree of melodic creativity and variation that performers can use to connect motifs. Charlie Parker typically improvised completely new melodic material in between his standard motifs; the Javanese *gamelan* performer is not permitted to insert any new material, but must stick with the motifs specified by the tradition.

Within a culture's musical tradition, the motifs and their style of combination tend to be similar in both composed and improvised performance. Typically, the set of motifs used in a culture's improvised performances is less extensive than that same culture's composed music.

In the United States, improvisation is almost exclusively associated with blues and jazz. These are both examples of motivic improvisation. American jazz is one of the most highly developed genres of improvisation; musicians must go through years of intensive training and apprenticeship, and many do not reach their peak until middle age, with decades of performing experience behind them. Jazz requires of the performer a deep knowledge of complex harmonic structures, and a profound familiarity with the large body of "standards"— pieces that have been played by jazz bands for decades.

Standards are typically based on the 32-bar chorus of the song, with four subsections of 8 bars each. Usually one or two of the 8-bar sections is repeated, resulting in song forms such as "aaba," a song where the first 8 bars are the same as the second and fourth 8 bars. A standard is outlined on a *lead sheet,* a shorthand version of the song, with only the melody and the chord changes written. None of the musicians' parts are notated explicitly; all of the musicians have to improvise their own parts around the outline that is represented by the lead sheet. After playing through the chorus once or twice, the band then moves into the improvisational portion of the performance, taking turns soloing over the chorus form. Although these ensemble improvisations can diverge dramatically from the original melody, a virtuoso ensemble is always together and remains connected to the basic outline of the song.

There are other ways that preparation helps to structure a jazz performance. Most jazz performers use private rehearsals as an opportunity to develop "licks," personal motifs that can be inserted into a solo for a wide range of different songs. Still, the choice of when to use one of these motifs, and how to weave these fragments with completely original melodic lines, is made on the spot. In group rehearsals, jazz groups often work out ensemble parts that can be played by the entire band at the end of a solo. If you have never heard the musician or the band before, you will not know which portions of the song are completely new that night, and which portions have been rehearsed or played before.

These examples show us an important property of all musical improvisation: No performer ever makes up everything from scratch every time. There is a constant balance between preparation, tradition, and spontaneous creativity. No matter how spontaneous it sounds, there is always some structure that holds the performance together and guides the musicians. The completely spontaneous creation of new forms through free improvisation, without any preexisting framework, is quite rare in jazz and worldwide. Even the least-structured genre of jazz, called "free jazz," depends on themes, motifs, and other prearranged schemes such as the sequence of soloists.

Anthropologists have studied performance genres from around the world, and have found that there is no sharp line between completely scripted performance and completely free improvisation. Even cultures that have no notation system for music often have different genres of performance. Most cultures have genres that are quite rigid, and are supposed to be performed essentially the same way each time, as well as other genres that are extremely open to improvisational creativity, even demanding improvisation from the performers. Cultures with a range of genres include the Plains Indians, various Eskimo tribes, and Yemeni Bedouins. In these cultures, musicians and nonmusicians alike are quite aware of the different types of creativity required in each genre. The more structured genres generally require more preparation and memorization; the more improvised ones require more spontaneous skill. The worldwide existence of highly structured musical genres suggest that "composed" songs predated the first invention of written notation, although the origin of these traditional songs will never be known.

Jazz demonstrates almost all of the characteristics of improvisation. First, it depends on a complex balance of structure and free improvisation. Second, jazz is an ensemble art form. Perhaps the defining feature of jazz is the musical conversation on stage. Each musician must listen intensely to the other members of the band, both to coordinate with them, but also to draw inspiration from their last melodic phrase or rhythmic pattern, and to incorporate those musical statements into their own evolving part. In the best jazz performances, this conversation results in a constant give and take between the musicians. A collaborative performance emerges from the improvisations of all of the musicians working together, a performance that no one musician could have controlled or predicted. [*See* MUSIC.]

IV. SUMMARY

Improvisation is present in all creativity. For example, a painter is constantly responding to his canvas and oils as he is painting. More importantly, each step of the painting changes the artist's conception of what he is doing—the first part of a painting often leads to a new insight about what to do next. Fiction writers are constantly interacting with the story as they write. A character or a plot line frequently emerges from the pen unexpectedly, and an experienced writer will respond and follow that new thread, in an essentially improvisational fashion. [*See* ARTS AND ARTISTS, WRITING AND CREATIVITY.]

Improvisation is most essential in performance creativity, because unlike the painter or the writer, performers do not have the opportunity to revise their work. Where the improvisations of the painter can be painted over or discarded, and the writer has the power of a word processor to generate the next draft, the improvisations that occur on stage are exposed to the audience. As a result, the audience gets to see the creative process in action—they share in every unexpected inspiration, but also in those disappointing attempts that fail. Even the most famous artists often destroy or paint over a significant number of their canvases, but these aborted attempts are generally lost to history, and not available for study. Because it is "the creative process made visible," improvisational performance can teach us about the creative process in general.

The collaborative nature of improvisational performance also makes it a promising field of study for creativity researchers. Collaboration is important in most creative domains. In modern scientific research, these collaborations range from the group work that goes on in the laboratory to informal conversations over late-night coffee. The creative interactions of a jazz group are much easier to study, since the analyst can hear and transcribe how this interaction affects each musician's creative process. Studying improvisational performance could potentially help creativity researchers better understand all group collaborations.

Modern European performance traditions have been the least receptive to improvisation of all the world's cultures, and this bias against improvisation is found in both the theater and the musical communities. Impro-

visation has often been considered to be a less-refined, "popular" or "folk" genre, and all of these terms tend to devalue improvisational creativity, relative to composed or scripted performance. Because most creativity researchers are also European, they have tended to focus on these more highly valued performance genres. As anthropologists, ethnomusicologists, and cross-cultural researchers begin to join in the study of creativity around the world, improvisation will become an increasingly important part of the field of creativity research.

Bibliography

Berliner, P. (1994). *Thinking in jazz: The infinite art of improvisation*. Chicago: University of Chicago Press.

Byrnside, R. (1975). The performer as creator: Jazz improvisation. In C. Hamm, B. Nettl, & R. Byrnside (Eds.), *Contemporary music and music cultures* (pp. 223–251). Englewood Cliffs, NH: Prentice-Hall.

Ferand, E. T. (1961). *Improvisation in nine centuries of Western music*. Koln, Germany: Arno Volk Verlag Hans Gerig KG.

Frost, A., & Yarrow, R. (1990). *Improvisation in drama*. London: Macmillan.

Kernfeld, B. (1988). Improvisation. In B. Kernfeld (Ed.), *The new grove dictionary of jazz, volume 1* (pp. 554–563). London: Macmillan.

Monson, I. (1996). *Saying something: Jazz improvisation and interaction*. Chicago: University of Chicago Press.

Nettl, B. (1974) Thoughts on improvisation: A comparative approach. *The Musical Quarterly, 60*(1), 1–19.

Sawyer, R. K. (1996). The semiotics of improvisation: The pragmatics of musical and verbal performance. *Semiotica, 108* (3/4), 269–306.

Sawyer, R. K. (Ed.). (1997). *Creativity in performance*. Greenwich, CT: Ablex.

Sweet, J. (1978). *Something wonderful right away: An oral history of the Second City & the Compass Players*. New York: Avon.

Incubation

Steven M. Smith and Rebecca A. Dodds

Texas A&M University

Fixation A persistent block or impediment to successful problem solving.

Illumination A sudden insight into the solution to a problem.

Incubation A temporary hiatus in the creative problem solving process that precedes the realization of a solution.

INCUBATION *refers to a stage of creative problem solving in which a problem is temporarily put aside after a period of initial work on the problem. Incubation usually occurs after an impasse has been reached that blocks awareness of the solution, a situation referred to as fixation. An incubation effect results in illumination, the sudden realization of a solution that occurs either during the time away from the problem, or when one returns to the problem after the incubation period.*

I. HISTORICAL EXAMPLES

The best solutions to problems sometimes occur to people when they are not actively trying to work on the problems. Historically, there are numerous anecdotes about important discoveries that were made when the discoverer had taken a break from working on a problem, and was away from the typical workplace. These historically important cases, as well as more mundane ones that resulted in less momentous discoveries, are said to be the result of incubation, a stage of creative problem solving. [*See* PROBLEM SOLVING.]

Perhaps the best known case of incubation is that of Archimedes' discovery of the principle of displacement, the idea that the liquid displaced by an immersed solid is equal to the volume of the solid. For example, if you drop a brick into a tank of water, and the water level in the tank goes up by one cubic foot, that means that the brick has a volume of one cubic foot. Archimedes, a world-famous mathematician, had been trying to determine the volume of an irregularly shaped golden crown owned by his cousin, King Hiero of Syracuse. Laboring long and unsuccessfully to analyze the crown as a set of simpler solids, Archimedes did not remember even to bathe. When his friends forced him to put the work temporarily aside and go to the baths, Archimedes noticed that the bath water level rose when he immersed himself in it. Realizing that the crown in question would likewise displace an amount of liquid equal to its own volume, Archimedes rushed through the streets, still unclothed, shouting "Eureka!" in excitement over his discovery.

In another example of an historically important incubation effect, Kary Mullis, a biochemist, had been working on problems concerned with replicating segments of DNA molecules. One evening, having put his work aside, Dr. Mullis was driving through the hills of northern California, toying with images of molecules in his mind. Suddenly, he had an insight experience that was so stunning it forced him to pull his car over to the side of the road. Mullis had realized a method for duplicating and vastly increasing quantitites of entire DNA molecules, a discovery called the polymerase chain reaction (PCR). This discovery, another product of incubation, won Mullis a Nobel prize, and revolutionized the world of chemistry.

There have been many other historically important discoveries that were products of incubation effects, ideas realized when the discoverer was away from the typical workplace. These cases include Auguste Kekule's discovery of the structure of the benzene molecule as he dozed before a blazing fire, Henri Poincaire's formulation of fuchsian mathematical functions as he was stepping onto a city bus, and Beethoven's sudden discovery of a musical canon when he remembered a dream while riding in a horse-drawn carriage. Although these cases come from completely different domains of creative endeavor, they all have in common the fact that they occurred suddenly and unexpectedly, and they took place while the discoverers were away from their typical workplaces.

II. THEORIES

Several theories have been offered by psychologists to explain incubation. Whereas some of these have been supported by research findings, no single theory has been found to provide the sole correct explanation of incubation. There may be multiple causes of incubation effects, and there may be different causes in different cases. A list of theories of how incubation operates is shown in Table I.

The Conscious Work theory of incubation is that work on a problem is done intermittently instead of all at once. During automatic or repetitive tasks (such as driving, showering, or vacuuming), you may find yourself mulling over a problem. Although some attention is necessarily allocated to such simple tasks, the rest

TABLE I
Possible Causes of Incubation Effects

Conscious Work: Intermittent conscious work during the incubation period

Recovery from Fatigue: Recovery from fatigue built up during the preparation period of problem solving

Forgetting Inappropriate Mental Sets: Inappropriate initial strategies and responses are forgotten over time or with changes in one's mental set

Remote Association: Unusual responses emerge because common responses have been exhausted

Opportunistic Assimilation: Remaining sensitive to information related to unsolved problems, one assimilates chance environmental events into problem solving during the incubation period

Unconscious Work: Associations made among ideas in one's unconscious, or recognized in spontaneous environmental events

may be focused on unresolved problems. Why, then, does it seem that incubation seems not to involve conscious work? The explanation, according to this theory, is that one may forget the many brief episodes of work one has done on a problem, remembering only the last step leading to the final solution.

The Unconscious Work theory, like the Conscious Work explanation, states that the creative problem solver continues to work intermittently on problems outside of the problem solving context. Unlike the Conscious Work theory, however, the Unconscious Work theory states that the work that continues bringing one closer to a solution is done at an unconscious level, without the awareness of the problem solver. This theory further states that only after the solution to a problem has been unconsciously assembled does the problem solver suddenly become aware of the solution. It is from this Unconscious Work hypothesis that the term "incubation" derives its name. That is, when an egg incubates, the development of a chick occurs invisibly, beneath the opaque shell, before the new chick bursts into view. Likewise, according to the Unconscious Work theory, creative solutions to problems develop invisibly in the unconscious mind, bursting into view only when a solution has finished developing. As compelling as this theory is, however, it should be noted that there is currently no scientific evidence that supports the Unconscious Work theory.

The Recovery from Fatigue theory explains incubation in relation to preparation, a stage of creative problem solving that precedes incubation. According to G. Wallas, preparation involves a lot of hard work. The thinker takes time to learn about the problem situation. In the case of the scientist or mathematician, such study can last for years. An artist trying to create a still life drawing must first understand the techniques developed by the masters (e.g., drawing in perspective) and be familiar with an assortment of drawing tools from the softest charcoal for drawing heavy lines which smudge easily, to hard, fine points which can be used for detailed work. In everyday situations where such intense learning may not be necessary, problems must still be attacked from a variety of angles. When the first attempted solutions do not succeed, each separate piece of the puzzle must be picked up and examined carefully. The Recovery from Fatigue theory asserts that after such exertion during the preparation stage, the incubation period allows time to rest and recover. Once refreshed, the mind's normal processes can function better for solving the problem at hand.

Two other theories involve the construction of associations. Creativity involves putting old things together in new ways. These associations can be the result of mere chance where elements accidentally appear together in the environment or due to the similarity of one situation with another. During incubation, ideas stored in memory may be combined unconsciously to form solutions to problems. Another possibility is that the failure to solve a problem during preparation is stored in memory. When the missing idea, object, or experience is found in everyday life (like Archimedes encountering overflowing water), the failure is recalled, and the solution readily appears. This is the Opportunistic Assimilation theory, which states that the incubation period provides one with an opportunity to experience helpful stimuli in the environment and to assimilate those experiences into the problem solving process.

According to the Remote Association theory, information is retrieved from memory for use in problem solving. Only after dominant responses have been retrieved will new ideas be created. This process is very efficient. For most everyday problems there are proven solutions that usually work quite well. Such solutions are stored in memory where they can be quickly retrieved and applied. Therefore, incubation occurs only after such common solutions have already been tried without success.

The Forgetting Inappropriate Mental Sets theory states that incubation allows time for incorrect solutions to be forgotten. According to S. M. Smith, fixation in problem solving is the result of competition between responses. When a stronger response is incorrect, it must be forgotten before the problem can be solved. For example, if you were asked to name the object defined as a decorative glass vessel used for bringing wine to the dinner table, you might first think that the object is called a "carafe," which is not the correct answer. The correct answer, "decanter," might occur to you only after a period of incubation allows the incorrect answer, "carafe," to be forgotten. [*See* FIXATION.]

III. SCIENTIFIC EVIDENCE

As more mental effort is put forth, it seems only logical to expect solutions to appear. The results of C. Patrick's 1938 study appear to support this Conscious Work theory. She asked subjects to propose scientific methods to investigate effects of heredity and environment in humans. The control group worked on the problem immediately after it had been presented. Subjects talked through possible solutions aloud until making a final proposal. The incubation group was given a diary and asked to return within two to three weeks with their final proposals. Incubation subjects were asked to write down any thoughts or ideas they wanted in the diary. Patrick defined the incubation effect as an idea occurring early in the work process, reappearing several times, and being the chief topic of the final solution. Ninety-six percent of subjects in the study showed incubation effects. Additionally, more modification of ideas occurred in the diary group. Final proposals were rated for feasibility and excellence by a group of scientists. The proposals of the incubation group received higher scores overall than those of the nonincubation group. Subjects in the diary group were never directed not to work on the problem during the incubation period. The higher ratings of their proposals may be due to extra time which they were given to work.

R. Driestadt conducted an experiment to test the Opportunistic Assimilation theory. One set of subjects were to state how 10 trees could be planted in 5 rows so that each row contained 4 trees. Subjects were given paper and pencils to write or sketch their solutions. Some of the subjects worked on the problem continuously while others were allowed to take a break. In addition to being allowed to incubate, in some cases, subjects worked in a room with a tack board. On the board were pictures containing visual hints about the answer to the problem. Subjects with access to the pictures were more likely to solve (or come close to solving) the problem than those who did not see the pictures. Interestingly, many of the subjects who were successful reported after the experiment that they were completely unaware of the pictures of five-pointed stars or how they had been helped by those pictures. Planting the trees in a star shape—five lines making up the star with 4 trees per line—is the solution.

S. M. Smith and S. E. Blankenship tested the Forgetting Inappropriate Mental Sets theory using performance on rebuses as their creative task. The rebuses were presented with either helpful or misleading clues. Either a music perception task or unfilled free time lasting 5 or 15 minutes was used as the incubation period. The dependent variables were whether the rebuses were solved and the number of solutions generated after the incubation period. In the first experiment, the 15-minute incubation group solved more rebuses than either of the other groups, but did not differ significantly from the 5-minute incubation group. There was no effect for the music perception versus free time groups. The control group subjects who worked continuously showed greater recall of the misleading clue on a predetermined critical item than either of the incubation groups. The second experiment had a similar design, except the critical item was paired with a helpful clue. The results were essentially the same in performance and showed that the control group had more recall of the clue.

In the third experiment, the incubation groups worked on the entire block of rebuses for 30 seconds each, then performed the distractor, and then returned to work for 30 seconds on each, while the control group worked through the block with 1 minute on each rebus. The control group again showed less improvement than the incubation groups. In the fourth experiment, the distractor tasks used were work on math problems, reading stories, or no task. There was no difference between groups working on the story and math tasks. However, the story group significantly outperformed the control group. Smith and Blankenship concluded that the effects of incubation are due to forgetting incorrect solutions.

The Forgetting theory of incubation has also received empirical support from experiments that examined incubation effects in memory. S. M. Smith and E. Vela tested the effects of incubation on reminiscence, a memory phenomenon. Reminiscence refers to the situation in which a memory that is initially blocked from consciousness is suddenly remembered later, a phenomenon very similar to incubation in creative problem solving. Their study showed that an incubation period given after subjects' original attempts to remember events helped them recover memories that had been initially blocked from consciousness. Furthermore, keeping busy during the incubation period does not interfere with this incubated reminiscence effect, indicating that conscious work does not explain this memory recovery effect.

Little if any clear evidence has been published that supports other theories of incubation effects, such as the Unconscious Work theory, the Recovery from Fatigue theory, or the Remote Association theory. Whether this lack of empirical evidence is an indication of shortcomings of these theories, or merely demonstrates the need for research on incubation effects, cannot yet be determined.

IV. CONCLUSIONS

Incubation is defined as a stage of creative problem solving that involves putting a problem aside temporarily when initial attempts to solve the problem lead to an impasse. Several explanations were described that purport to account for incubation effects, including Conscious Work, Recovery from Fatigue, Forgetting Inappropriate Mental Sets, Remote Association, Opportunistic Assimilation, and Unconscious Work theories. Scientific evidence, however, supports only the Conscious Work, Opportunistic Assimilation, and Forgetting Inappropriate Mental Sets theories. Considerably more research is called for if the other theories are to be adequately assessed.

Bibliography

Driestadt, R. (1969). The use of analogies and incubation in obtaining insights in creative problem solving. *Journal of Psychology, 71,* 159–175.

Patrick, C. (1938). Scientific thought. *The Journal of Psychology, 5,* 55–83.

Smith, S. M. (1995). Fixation, incubation and insight in memory and creative thinking. In S. M. Smith, T. B. Ward, & R. A. Finke (Eds.), *The creative cognition approach* (pp. 135–156). Cambridge, MA: MIT Press.

Smith, S. M., & Blankenship, S. E. (1989). Incubation effects. *Bulletin of the Psychonomic Society, 27,* 311–314.

Smith, S. M., & Vela, E. (1991). Incubated reminiscence effects. *Memory & Cognition, 19,* 168–176.

Wallas, G. (1926). *The art of thought.* New York: Harcourt, Brace and Company.

Innovation

Michael A. West

Aston Business School

Tudor Rickards

Manchester Business School

Creativity In informal use, creativity can be regarded as the processes leading to the generation of new and valued ideas.

Emergent Innovation An innovation that arises in the course of a series of activities rather than as a consequence of a pre-planned innovation project.

Flow Intense absorption in a task, a state associated with peak performance, often of a creative kind.

Functional Fixedness A category of cognitive set or mental structuring that manifests in rigidity or lack of flexibility in disembedding components from a given field.

Innovation In informal use innovation concerns those behavioral and social processes whereby individuals, groups, or organizations seek to achieve desired changes or to avoid the penalties of inaction. Innovation is the introduction of new and improved ways of doing things at work. A more psychological or complex definition of innovation is the intentional introduction and application within a job, work team, or organization of ideas, processes, products, or procedures that are new to that job, work team, or organization and that are designed to benefit the job, work team, or organization.

Kaizen A production culture based on continuous improvement in both products and processes.

Organizational Slack Resources that are not already appropriated (claimed) for organizational use and that therefore might be claimed in order to support innovation. Absence of slack is believed to inhibit innovation. There may, however, be a U-shaped relationship between available slack and its effective exploitation within innovation projects.

INNOVATION *concerns those behavioral and social processes whereby individuals, groups, or organizations seek to achieve desired changes or to avoid the penalties of inaction.*

I. WHAT IS INNOVATION?

A. Definitions

A structure can be brought to the subject by distinguishing factors influencing innovation at different levels of social complexity. Psychological features are somewhat repeated at the individual, team, and organizational levels. However, innovation at a higher level of aggregation incorporates holistic features such that it cannot be understood as a simple aggregation of features identified at lower levels of aggregation.

B. The Multidisciplinary Appeal of Innovation

The topic of innovation has generated enormous interest and research activity in a variety of disciplines over many years. Sociologists, psychologists, economists, policy makers, managers, and organizational scientists have struggled to understand the factors that determine innovation in organizations and also to understand how innovations may be managed over time. This extraordinarily wide interest in innovation continues and, if anything, is increasing. Throughout the industrial world, there is great emphasis by central government, managers, and policy makers on the topic of innovation. The increasingly vigorous competition in global markets requires that organizations innovate and adapt if they are to survive and compete effectively in their environments. Indeed, vast amounts of money are now being invested by governments to promote understanding of innovation within organizations.

C. The Intentional Nature of Innovation

The term *innovation* is generally restricted to *intentional* attempts to bring about benefits from new changes; these might include economic benefits, personal growth, increased satisfaction, improved group cohesiveness, and better organizational communication, as well as productivity and economic gains.

D. Kinds of Innovation

Various processes and products may be regarded as innovations. They include technological changes such as new products, but may also include new production processes, the introduction of advanced manufacturing technology, or the introduction of new computer support services within an organization. Administrative changes are also regarded as innovations. New human resource management (HRM) strategies, organizational policies, or the introduction of teamwork are all examples of administrative innovations within organizations.

E. The Novelty Component of Innovation

Innovation implies novelty, but not necessarily absolute novelty. If teamwork is introduced into a government department, it is considered to be an innovation if it is new in that government department, irrespective of whether it has been introduced into other government departments. [*See* NOVELTY.]

Innovations may vary from those that are relatively minor to those that are of great significance. Innovation does not necessarily mean inventing the equivalent of the internal combustion engine! It is *any* new and improved product or way of doing things that an individual, group, or organization has introduced and that affects individuals, jobs, groups, or organizations. Some innovations can be introduced in the space of an hour, whereas others may take several years.

F. Planned and Emergent Innovations

Some innovations are unplanned and emerge by accident. One frequently cited example is the Post-It note developed in 3M. In contrast, some innovations are planned and managed, requiring an enormous amount of an organization's attention and energy to ensure their effective implementation.

G. A Distinction between Creativity and Innovation

The terms *creative* and *innovative* tend to overlap in much of the literature of change management. A distinction can be made by treating creativity as the generation of ideas for new and improved ways of doing things at work and innovation as the implementation of those ideas in practice. Aphoristically, creativity is thinking about new things, innovation is about doing new things. Note that the two types of activity do not occur in a simple linear sequence but interact and support one another.

H. Gaps in Innovation Theory

In 1996 the *American Academy of Management Journal* called for contributions summarizing state-of-the-art theory of innovation. The special-issue editors,

Robert Drazin and Claudia Bird Schoonhoven, concluded that innovation theory had failed to acquire a coherent and dominant theoretical perspective. They attributed this in part to the largely practice-driven nature of the subject, which had resulted in a great deal of prescriptive writing. Typically an assumption is made that innovation is a good thing for productivity and growth. Drazin and Schoonhoven also identified the difficulties in arriving at a fully integrated model of innovation across different levels of complexity, suggesting this to be an important challenge for future research. As a first step toward a fully integrated model, the best features of studies at individual, group, and organizational levels need to be examined.

II. FACTORS INFLUENCING INDIVIDUAL INNOVATION AT WORK

The undoubted variation in creative performance from individual to individual may sometimes have concealed universal capacities that lead to personal development and growth. The spontaneous creativity of the child, however, is inevitably restricted during maturation. What is unclear is the degree to which creative performance is *unnecessarily* inhibited or reduced by our experiences in educational systems and organizations, which tend inappropriately to devalue creative expression.

A. Resilience to Job Challenge

The resilience of the individual in responding innovatively to job challenges has been found in a range of studies. In a longitudinal study of more than 2000 managers and professionals conducted in 1988, Nigel Nicholson and Michael West found that people frequently changed the objectives of their jobs, the methods they use, scheduling, practices, procedures, and even who they deal with and how they deal with them. When people changed jobs, those moving into existing jobs were highly innovative and tended to mold and improve the jobs to fit their own way of doing things. Moreover, those who had the opportunity to be innovative at work—to introduce new and improved ways of doing things—were more satisfied with their jobs and better adjusted at work than those who did not

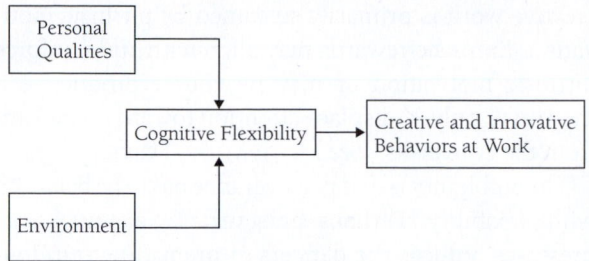

FIGURE 1　Factors influencing individual innovation.

have such opportunities. Among managers and professionals whose job moves led to reduced opportunities to be creative at work, the decrements in their mental health were greater than among those managers and professionals who became temporarily unemployed. Figure 1 summarizes the influencing factors most frequently reported.

1. Cognitive Features

Although intellectual abilities may be classified in various ways, a dominant characteristic associated with creativity is cognitive flexibility. [*See* FLEXIBILITY.]

Robert Sternberg's classification suggests three features relevant for innovation performance: *synthetic ability* to see problems or issues in new ways and to escape from conventional thinking, *analytic ability* to distinguish between those ideas that are worth pursuing and those that are not, and *practical contextual ability* to persuade others of the value of one's ideas.

A *legislative thinking style* is required or a preference for thinking in novel ways of one's own choosing. It also helps to be able to think globally as well as locally, to be able to recognize which questions are important and which are not.

At the perceptual level, an enthusiasm for the complex over the simple has been associated with creative capacity. Nevertheless, there may also be a tendency to seek elegant resolutions to problems.

B. Personal Characteristics

Creative people tend to be self-disciplined in matters concerning work, with a high degree of drive and motivation and a concern with achieving excellence. The emerging theories of creativity and flow suggest that creative work is primarily sustained by intrinsic motivation. Extrinsic rewards may align with and reinforce intrinsic motivation or may be counterproductive if they serve only to displace attention toward the reward from the core tasks. [*See* MOTIVATION/DRIVE.]

The ambiguity is that perseverance has to be balanced with flexibility. Perhaps perseverance against social pressures reduces the dangers of premature abandonment (stubbornness/ego strength/goal-oriented behaviors). Minority influence theory suggests that perseverance acts to bring about change in the views of majorities and is a necessary behavioral style among innovators. This is especially true where the innovators are seen as flexible enough to listen to alternative viewpoints, while not deviating from their position.

To bring about change in the status quo, people need to determine and pursue a course of action often in opposition to the views of those around them. This requires ego strength and independence of judgment.

People tend to feel some discomfort in situations that are uncertain and ambiguous. Creative people often respond positively to ambiguous situations, enjoying the process of sense making. Tolerance of ambiguity, widely associated with creativity, enables individuals to avoid the problems of functional fixedness and increases the chances of unusual responses and the discovery of socially unexpected novelties.

Creative people tend to be self-directed and less dependent on others, enjoying and requiring freedom in their work. They have a high need for freedom, control, and discretion in the workplace and often find bureaucratic limitations or the exercise of control by managers very frustrating. They create autonomy for themselves in the workplace and respond positively to such high discretion at work.

People who believe in their own domain-relevant creativity and are confident of their abilities are more likely to behave creatively in the workplace.

C. The Work Environment for Innovators

Organizations create an ethos or atmosphere within which creativity is either nurtured and blooms in innovation or is starved of support. Psychological research has revealed that supportive and challenging environments are likely to sustain high levels of creativity. Organizations also have to provide appropriate resources for creative efforts and encourage independent action in order to facilitate the creativity of those who work within them. Employees frequently have ideas for improving their workplaces, work functioning, processes, products, or services. Where climates are characterized by distrust, lack of communication, personal antipathies, limited individual autonomy, and unclear goals, innovation is inhibited. [*See* CREATIVE CLIMATE.]

The characteristics of the jobs that people do also have an impact on their creativity. Job characteristics can be objectively assessed. A recent empirical study in 1996 by Oldham and Cummings was able to account for a great deal of the variation by reference to five groups of factors as in Table I.

These examples indicate the complex manner in which environmental factors interact with individual factors to produce individual innovation. Further empirical studies are needed to clarify the overall view, even at the level of the individual innovator at work. [*See* CONDITIONS AND SETTINGS/ENVIRONMENT.]

III. FACTORS INFLUENCING TEAM INNOVATION AT WORK

As organizations become increasingly complex in response to environments that grow ever more changeable in their social, political, and economic character, isolated actions of individuals within organizations become decreasingly influential. Many organizations have responded to environmental uncertainties by making the team the primary functional unit. Individuals rarely bring about change within organizations; groups more often do. Teams have the resilience, range of skills, abilities, and experience to ensure that creative ideas are put into innovative practice. Societal changes, too, are often initiated through the activities of small groups of committed, persistent individuals whose values may well lie outside the acceptable social range. Within organizations there is a need for the integration of distributed knowledge and also for group acceptance of ideas in order for them to be implemented. Members who are present and involved in the creation of ideas are much more likely than otherwise to support their implementation. This is an under-appreciated rationale for interactive brainstorming, for example. Figure 2 illustrates the main factors associated with team innovation in work settings. [*See* TEAMS.]

TABLE I
Task Characteristics Affecting Innovation

Skill variety and challenge	The degree to which a job requires different activities in order for the work to be carried out, and the degree to which the range of skills and talents of the person working within the role is used. A nurse working with the elderly in their homes may need to use professional skills of dressing wounds, listening, counseling, being empathic and appraising the supports and dangers in the person's home.
Task identity	The degree to which the job represents a whole piece of work, or to doing a job from beginning to end. It is not simply adding a rubber band to the packaging of a product, but being involved in its manufacture throughout a meaningful part of the process.
Task significance	The importance of the task in terms of its impact upon other people within the organization, or in the world at large. This impacts the worker's creativity. Monitoring the inventory levels of stationery within an organization is likely to be treated socially as less significant than addressing the well-being of elderly people, and may therefore evoke less creativity.
Autonomy	This is the degree to which jobs provide freedom, independence and discretion for the people performing them in determining how to do their work and when to do it. The level of autonomy is generally regarded as a powerful influence on the extent to which people are creative and innovative in their work.
Performance feedback	Positive feedback on performance, from customers, clients, patients or even the task itself has a powerful impact on people's performance. Where the feedback relates to creative effort, it will increase the likelihood of further creative performance. Moreover, when people receive information about how well they are performing their job and on the effectiveness of their performance, they become aware of performance gaps and of the need to initiate new ways of working in order to fill the gaps.

From "Employee Creativity: Personal and Contextual Factors at Work," by G. R. Oldham and A. Cummings, 1996, *Academy of Management Journal, 39*, pp. 607–634.

A. Team Composition

Research on the relationship between team size and innovation shows that larger teams tend to be less innovative as the difficulties of integration and interaction become more important. However, there is also strong evidence that for creative decision-making tasks, team diversity (in terms of personality, training, background, and gender) is important for innovation. This may stem in part from the diversity of perspectives team members can bring to the decision-making process. To a considerable degree in practice, the complexity of the task and prevailing organizational structures dictate the composition of teams.

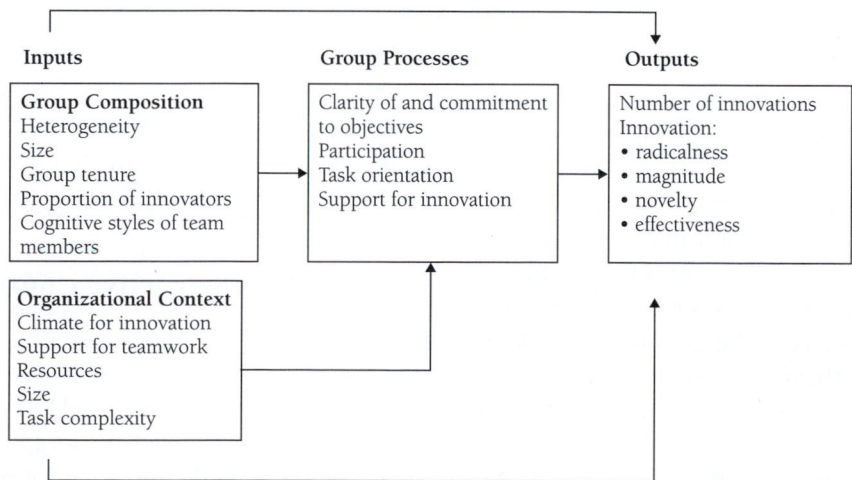

FIGURE 2   A model of team innovation.

B. Lifetime of the Team

There are innovation differences consequent on the team's tenure. Longer tenure is associated with increasing team homogeneity of knowledge, beliefs, and assumptions. This has deleterious effects on team innovation. Without changes in membership, groups may become less innovative over time. Project newcomers can enhance innovation within teams because they challenge and often broaden existing practices.

C. Characteristics of Team Members

Research evidence suggests that team innovation will be affected by the proportion of individuals contributing creatively within the team.

D. The Team Task

Key characteristics at the team level are similar to those found at the level of the individual: task identity, task significance, skill variety and challenge, feedback, and autonomy.

E. Resources

It is often assumed that the level of team innovation is determined by the resources available to the team and, by extension therefore, the slack, or unclaimed resources available within the organization. Earlier studies emphasized the damage to innovation resulting from absence of resources; organizational slack was associated with a capacity to innovate. More recent evidence suggests that slack may have an inverted U relationship with innovation productivity.

F. Team Processes

For a team to be innovative it must have clear objectives to give focus and direction to creative energies. The absence of clear objectives might be presumed to permit more innovation. In general, clear objectives are associated with successful innovation, when found in association with other innovation-enhancing factors. These objectives should be shared and negotiated with the team, perceived as attainable, and as an evolving representation of some valued future outcomes.

G. Team Participation

Participation implies a benign climate and some shared influence over decision making, information sharing, interaction, and safety. Team members who have influence over decision making are more likely to contribute their creative ideas. Such participation ensures that the views, experience, and abilities of the team members are used. This is the fundamental benefit of teamwork.

Frequency of interaction will necessarily determine the extent to which team members exchange ideas, information, and conflicting views. Conversely, when team members avoid one another to avoid conflict, they are essentially avoiding opportunities for creativity and creative consensus.

Team members are only willing to try out new ideas—and to risk appearing foolish—if they feel safe from ridicule or attack. In so many areas of human behavior the same phenomenon is found. We are likely to play with new and different ideas to the extent that we find that our team provides a sense of safety and support in the expression of those ideas.

H. High Task Orientation

High task orientation, which is critically necessary to team innovation, is characterized by constructive controversy, tolerance of minority ideas, and commitment to excellence. The more that teams take time to reflect critically on their objectives, strategies, and processes and then, crucially, to modify them, the more innovative and effective are they likely to be. Many teams believe that they are too overwhelmed by demands to take time for such reflection. Yet there is abundant evidence that doing so leads to more effective and innovative outcomes. This kind of reflexivity is fundamentally important in ensuring the appropriateness of team strategies, processes, and task outcomes.

I. Constructive Controversy

In innovative teams there is a high level of constructive controversy. Team members feel their competence is affirmed rather than attacked, and there is a climate of cooperation and trust rather than a climate of competition and distrust. Critical review is seen as an essential and constructive process rather than a destructive, aggressive conflict. In such teams there is a concern with excellence of outcomes and not with the individualistic ambitions of team members. The extent to which a team can tolerate within its membership a minority who adopt differing views is an important determinant of team creativity and innovation.

J. Support for Innovation

Support for innovation emerges as a significant predictor of the innovation and creativity of teams. Support has two distinct elements: espoused support and active support. If new ideas are accepted and encouraged verbally but team members do not also provide the necessary practical support, the platitudes of verbal encouragement soon lose their currency.

IV. FACTORS INFLUENCING ORGANIZATIONAL INNOVATION

The principal domains influencing organizational innovation are depicted in Figure 3.

A. Organizational Economic Performance

There is plenty of evidence that firms that fail to innovate risk decline and obsolescence. The successful introduction of new products is generally considered to be a powerful strategy for economic rewards, although the linkages between organizational activities and economic success are complex. Research in the United States and the United Kingdom seems to confirm that for originally matched firms innovators outperformed noninnovators in general, although unforeseen catastrophes still account for a proportion of firms, regardless of innovation stance.

B. Market Environment and Uncertainty

The literature suggests that there are generally positive correlations between R&D expenditure and industry concentration, with weaker support for the stimulating effect of monopoly on innovativeness.

A considerable consensus exists that companies op-

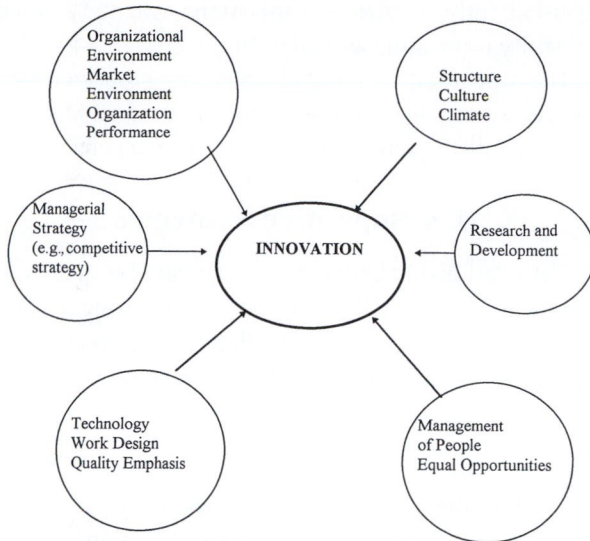

FIGURE 3   Factors influencing organizational innovations.

erating in uncertain environments will require flexible, decentralized, and informal work practices in order to respond effectively through innovation.

C. Organizational Size, Structure, and Age

Large organizations find it difficult to turn and change and to change their form to fit their changing environments. Yet organizational size has been found to be a positive predictor of both technological and administrative innovations. Innovative agility was a more a characteristic of smaller organizations. Size may be a surrogate measure of several dimensions associated with innovation, such as resources and economies of scale.

It is often popularly stated that centralization of decision making and many layers of hierarchy inhibit innovation. There is some support for the notion that high centralization is a negative predictor of innovation. However, in complex organizations, decentralization and specialization are not sufficient to ensure innovation. Integration across groups, departments, and specialisms is also necessary for communication and sharing of distributed knowledge.

The longer human social organizations endure, the more embedded become their norms and the more resilient to change become their traditions.

Consequently, mature organizations will have more difficulty innovating and adapting.

The sum total of research into the impact of size, structure, and age on innovation has to date failed to provide a clear picture of the underlying mechanisms.

D. Competitive Strategies

The relationship between organizational strategy and innovation is generally supposed to be strong. Strategies that direct a firm toward differentiating its competitive position might be expected to favor innovation.

E. Technology

Organizations invest in new technology to derive competitive advantage. A dominant theme in innovation studies is that of technological change. Currently the view prevails that a specific organization will be constrained to competencies largely dictated by its historical development and existing products and processes. This line of reasoning leads to notions of technological directions or trajectories along which firms may progress. That is not to say that a visionary leader or strategic team might not create a breakthrough vision and a switch to an unexpected trajectory.

F. Management of Quality

The total quality management (TQM) movement emphasizes the maintenance of high quality throughout the stages of manufacturing from product design to delivery. This philosophy of continuous improvement embodies a central commitment to innovation. A wide variety of methods and techniques are deployed by TQM adherents, including improvements in product and manufacturing design, upgraded technology, responsibility for quality at the point of production, statistical process control, and the development of a production culture based on continuous improvement in both products and processes (*Kaisen*). The more sophisticated and pervasive the management of Quality in the organization, the more innovative the organization will be in a wide variety of ways, such as the development of new products and adaptations of existing prod ucts, production processes, production technology, work organization and human resource management.

G. Human Resource Management (HRM)

The characteristics, skills, and abilities of those in the organization, how they are chosen, socialized, given feedback, and rewarded, will combine to create the products, services, and processes that arise from their interaction together. The research literature on high commitment HRM practices suggests that such practices lead to good interaction in organizational terms and high commitment among employees. The payoffs can include higher productivity and innovation as creative individuals are selected, trained, and rewarded for their activities. Much of the rhetoric of those advocating high commitment practices celebrates the notion that we can release the creative and productive potential of individuals, teams and organizations through such practices.

H. Research and Development (R&D)

R&D has become a surrogate measure of innovation in its own right. Another frequently used measure is the existence of an R&D department within organizations, considered to be a good predictor of levels of innovation or counts of patents. Evaluation of the cost/benefits of R&D go beyond simple accountancy exercises and seek to establish it as an essential component in knowledge management and strategy implementation.

I. Climate and Culture

The shared meanings, understandings, and perceptions people have of their social context exercise a powerful, mostly irresistible, influence over how they behave consciously and unconsciously in daily social interaction and directed work activity. The need for organizational climates supportive of innovation is often mentioned in the research and practitioner literature. However, as in other areas this research is rather inconclusive. Indeed it is safer to regard some climates as associated with innovation, rather than assume that there is a simple causal link between a so-called innovative climate and innovative outputs.

J. Supporting Innovation

In practice, companies use a wide range of schemes to support innovation, some of which are briefly described in Table II. Importing practices from other companies and cultures can stimulate innovation, but if these practices are not appropriately aligned with the organization culture, they are more likely to fail. There are various routes to encouraging innovation, each of which has its strengths and weaknesses. However, the four principles just articulated—clear vision and objectives, high levels of participation, commitment to excellence in task performance, and practical support for innovation—are central themes in any strategy for innovation.

TABLE II

Company Schemes to Support Innovation

Rewards	United Electric Control Company	A valued-ideas program. One hundred U.S. dollars are paid for every useable idea. Short-term action centers are also formed by employees to solve specific problems. Any employee can set up a center at any time and conference rooms are constantly available.
Resources	Frito-Lay, Inc.	Committees and researchers generate hundreds of new product ideas each year. These ideas are tested each night, five nights a week on 100 people, who sample up to 10 different products.
Best practice	PepsiCo	Senior executives regularly make field trips to observe companies renowned for innovation.
Organizational learning	Federal Express	45,000 customer-service staff in 700 locations across 15 countries keep abreast of 1700 annual changes to products and services through interactive video units installed in all locations, updated every 6 weeks. Savings amount to tens of millions of dollars. Each employee takes a job knowledge test every 6 months, after 4 hours of study time. The test provides a prescription for how areas of failure can be improved and workers who do not pass the test repeat the training via computer.
Structure switch rounds	The Philips Corporation	150 transient teams are formed once a year to brainstorm and problem solve. After 5 days the members revert to their normal organizational structure to implement the changes.
Innovative structures	Illinois Tool Works	A new division is formed every time a new product is developed. In the mid-1990s there were 90 product divisions, each controlling R&D, marketing and manufacturing. Closeness to customers is emphasized, and employees focus on organizational design as well as new product development.
Continuous improvement programs (CIP)	Cadillac	Programs designed to harness employee knowledge to improve products, services, and work practices. Elements of CIP include a plan to improve all operations continuously; bench marking company strategic plans against the world's best; close partnerships with suppliers and customers; a deep understanding of customers' needs; a focus on preventing, not just correcting, mistakes; and a commitment to improving quality throughout the organization.
Creative departments	Raytheon	Raytheon's New Product Center gives staff autonomy to develop new ideas while building close working relationships with other departments. Raychem (U.K.) has a top-level team specifically charged with developing creativity and innovation throughout the company.
Venture teams	Dow Chemicals	The venture team has total freedom to establish new venture projects for any department, operating like companies within a company. IBM's PC was developed by such a venture team.
Idea champions	Texas Instruments	Texas Instruments has concluded that its innovations that failed had no champions who believed passionately in the ideas and would fight to see them implemented. Now, only innovations with vigorous champions are supported.

V. MANAGING INNOVATION

A. Daft's Proposals for Participative Strategy

In 1992 Richard Daft suggested a variety of methods for developing a participative strategy for implementing innovation, outlined in Table III. Together the various strands of Daft's strategy provide a powerful behavioral approach to managing innovation.

B. Minority Influence Theory

One of the most exciting theoretical areas for understanding innovation is to be found in experimental social psychology. Minority influence theory provides an understanding of intragroup processes leading to creativity and innovation. It indicates the key processes while alerting us to ways of acting if complete consensus and shared visions are not present. It suggests the importance of dissent within organizations for independence and creativity. It implies that individuals in small groups can bring about change in organizational settings through consistency, persistence, and confidence. It suggests we not only should learn to tolerate but should encourage minorities and dissenting views in organizations to provide the seedbed for innovation and creativity. By drawing on this theory and research, powerful conceptual insights into innovation implementation strategy can be developed. To succeed the strategy depends on the commitment of a highly motivated team. The group members act to influence the views and orientations of significant others toward the innovation they are attempting to implement. The implications, summarized in Table IV, show parallels with Daft's proposals in Table III.

VI. CONCLUSIONS

A. The Challenge of Diversity

One of the key challenges for organizations is to learn to manage and harness the diversity of perspectives in modern heterogeneous organizations in ways that stimulate creativity and innovation. Diversity in the workforce leads to diversity of views, attitudes, skills, ideas, assumptions, and paradigms. Although it

---

TABLE III
A Participative Strategy for Innovation

Diagnose a true need for change.	Many innovations fail because the wrong focus for change is identified.
Find an idea that fits the need.	This means making sure that there is a match between the nature of the problem and the innovation idea which is generated or discovered.
Get top management support.	Innovation attempts are more successful to the extent that people with power and seniority support the change.
Design the change for incremental implementation.	The prospects for success for innovations are improved dramatically if teething problems can be managed one by one as they appear, rather than having to deal with a whole jaw full of problems at the same time.
Develop plans to overcome resistance to change.	The process of overcoming resistance to change therefore requires that the innovation meets the needs of those who are going to use or be affected by it. Other ways of reducing resistance include clear and persistent communication, extensive and early participation of those affected by the innovation, even (according to some practitioners and theorists) more unilateral coercive methods as a last resort.
Create change teams.	Organizational innovations are implemented more successfully if teams are created which carry responsibility for the successful implementation of the innovation.
Institutionalize the role of innovation champions.	Innovation champions are supporters who are deeply committed to a particular innovation. They assume responsibility for helping to ensure easier implementation through their influence and contacts.

From *Organizational Theory and Design* (4th ed.), by R. L. Daft, 1992, New York: West, pp. 248–282.

TABLE IV
A Minority Influence Strategy for Innovation

Clear vision	This vision should be coherent and have the commitment of all team members.
Effective small team	A powerful and effective group of no more than eight individuals.
A clear message	This message should be worked out and rehearsed in advance to ensure consistency in communication.
Communication skills for conveying its key message	The group will need to *present its message persistently* and repeatedly over a long period of time. It must develop the strategy for implementation of the innovation developed in consultation with other organization members.
Integrative listening skills	The group must be prepared to *listen flexibly* and to respond positively to the suggestions of those within the organization about innovation, but without diluting its intent to bring about a comprehensive change.
Constructive conflict-resolution skills	The group must use *consultation* processes and involve other organizational members wherever possible in order to anticipate and deal with potential conflicts.

may be uncomfortable initially to manage the consequent disagreements, such diversity offers great opportunities for creativity and innovation.

B. Innovation, Learning, and Reflexivity

Innovation involves calculated risk taking and requires courage, but "business as usual" no longer works. Organizations increasingly have to develop a deep reflexivity in their approaches to work. Reflexivity is the extent to which organizations, teams, departments, and individuals reflect on and challenge organizational objectives, strategies, and processes and adapt them accordingly. Organizations and teams that practice reflexivity develop a more comprehensive and penetrating intellectual representation of their roles and activities. They better anticipate and manage problems, and they deal with conflict as a valuable process asset within the organization, encouraging effectiveness, growth, and development.

C. Individuals, Teams, and Organizations

Our knowledge of innovation processes remains full of gaps. We cannot ignore the difficulties of integrating knowledge at the levels of the individual, the group, and the organization. For the innovative manager, the gaps have to be addressed through creative efforts in each specific case.

D. Everyone Has to Be a Creator and an Innovator

In the 21st-century world of electronically connected organizations, everyone will have a part to play as the creator and implementer of new ideas. In this respect, older notions of the exceptional individual as a creative genius and a top management chief innovator will become obsolete.

Bibliography

Daft, R. L. (1992). *Organizational theory and design* (4th ed.). New York: West.

Drazin, R., & Schoonhoven, C. B. (1996). Community, population, and organization effects on innovation: A multilevel perspective. *Academy of Management Journal, 39*(5), 1065–1083.

Nicholson, N., & West, M. A. (Eds.). (1988). *Managerial job change: Men and women in transition.* Cambridge: Cambridge University Press.

Oldham, G. R., & Cummings, A. (1996). Employee creativity: Personal and contextual factors at work. *Academy of Management Journal, 39,* 607–634.

Sternberg, R. J., & Lubart, T. I. (1996). Investing in creativity. *American Psychologist, 51,* 677–688.

West, M. A. (1997). *Developing creativity at work.* Leicester: BPS Books.

West, M. A., & Farr, J. L. (Eds.). (1990). *Innovation and creativity at work: Psychological and organizational strategies.* Chichester: John Wiley.

Insight

Robert J. Sternberg
Yale University

Janet E. Davidson
Lewis and Clark College

Associationism The idea that we learn new things by associating old ideas with each other or with new ideas.

Evolutionary View of Insight The notion that insight results from a process of blind variation and the selective retention of ideas.

Gestaltism The idea in psychology that the whole differs from the sum of its parts, and that, as a result, studies of components of a phenomenon could never adequately illuminate the phenomenon as a whole.

Ill-Structured Problems Problems for which a clear path to solution is not known.

Mystical View of Insight The view that insight cannot, and perhaps should not, be understood scientifically.

Nothing-Special Views of Insight Views that insightful problem-solving processes are just the same as any other problem-solving processes, even though they may be experienced as different.

Opportunistic-Assimilation View of Insight View that insights

results from people using the incubation stage of problem solving to search—largely at an unconscious level—for cues that are potentially relevant to the problem at hand, which then later allows solution of a problem when a cue fits the problem to be solved.

Selective-Combination Insight In one view of insight, the kind of insight in which reconceptualization of a problem depends on one's relating new information to old information whose connection to the new information is not readily apparent.

Selective-Encoding Insight In one view of insight, the kind of insight in which reconceptualization of a problem depends on one's seeing the relevance of information embedded in a mass of irrelevant information.

Special-Process Views of Insight Views that insight is a process that differs in kind from ordinary kinds of information processes.

Well-Structured Problems Views that insight is a process that differs in kind from ordinary kinds of information processes.

INSIGHT is defined in Webster's New World College Dictionary, *3rd ed., as "1. The ability to see and understand clearly the inner nature of things, esp. by intuition 2. A clear understanding of the inner nature of some specific thing." Psychologists, however, often go into somewhat more detail in their definitions. For example, Sternberg, in his introductory psychology textbook,* In Search of the Human Mind, *2nd ed. defines insight as a distinctive and apparently sudden realization of a strategy that aids in solving a problem, which is usually preceded by a great deal of prior thought and hard work; often involves reconceptualizing a problem or a strategy for its solution in a totally new way; frequently emerges by detecting and combining relevant old and new information to gain a novel view of the problems or of its solution; often associated with finding solutions to ill-structured problems [i.e., problems for which a clear path to solution is not known].*

I. INTRODUCTION

Before considering the theories of and empirical work on insight, it is worth unpacking the key elements of this expanded psychologically oriented definition, because it helps us understand some of the key aspects of just what psychologists mean when they talk about insight.

1. *Appearance of suddenness.* Insights typically feel as though they come in a flash. You may be thinking about a problem you have not been able to solve for a long time (e.g., how to afford a car, how to convince a partner to go along with a business deal, how to convince a spouse to change an annoying habit), when all of a sudden you see a strategy for solving what before had seemed like an intransigent problem. Notice two key features here. The first is the *appearance* of suddenness. Although insights often feel like they have occurred suddenly, they rarely do, a point to which we will return later. The second is that the insight does not guarantee solution to the problem. Sometimes the insight seems wonderful in theory but fails in practice. Or it may seem valuable when one first thinks of it, but its value seems to disappear as one thinks through its likely consequences. In fact, research by Janet Metcalfe has shown that the subjective experience of problem solvers solving insight problems is quite different from the subjective experience of problem solvers solving noninsight problems: In the former case, the solution feels as though it comes to them all at once, whereas in the latter case it does not.

2. *Importance of preparatory hard work.* Insights only appear to be sudden. Usually, they are the product of a great deal of prior reflection and perhaps action.

To produce an insight, sufficient preparation must be done to enable the insight to come into being.

3. *Importance of reconceptualization.* Insight differs from other forms of problem solving in its reliance on reconceptualization. An insight is not just another solution to a problem, but a solution that is somehow different in kind. For example, you may realize that the way to afford the new car is to sell some other kind of property you own that you no longer want. Or you may realize that the way to convince your spouse to let go of an annoying habit is to adopt the habit yourself and let your spouse see how it affects his or her life. Whatever the insight, it represents a reformulation of the "space" of possible solutions to a problem.

4. *Relevance of old and new information.* When we think, we typically combine new information with what we already know. An insight may feel totally fresh to us, but it often involves our utilization of prior knowledge that we had but whose relevance may not previously have been obvious.

5. *Association with ill-structured problems.* Some problems, such as how to get from a particular residence in Bloomington, Indiana, to the White House in Washington, D.C., are problematical because we do not immediately know the solution, but not because the route to solution is hidden from us. If we wanted to solve this problem, we could go through a fixed, largely prescribed set of steps that might have us looking in the Yellow Pages to find a taxi service to get us to the airport, calling a travel agent to find the best routing and airfare, looking into how to get from the D.C. airport to the White House, and so on. Insights typically apply not to such *well-structured problems*—in which the steps to solution are clearly discernible—but to ill-structured problems—in which the steps to take are far from transparent. For example, if we are talking more metaphorically in our effort to get to the White House—about how to be elected president of the United States—the problem is an ill-structured one because the steps are by no means obvious, as many potential presidential candidates have learned.

Insight is sometimes seen as one stage of several that occur in the course of solving a problem. The most well-known stage theory of problem solving goes all the way back to 1926 and the work of Graham Wallas. Many people still accept this view to the present day.

In his book, *The Art of Thought,* Wallas proposed that problem solving occurs in four steps: (a) mental preparation, (b) incubation, (c) illumination, and (d) verification. In Stage 1 an individual prepares to solve a problem, learning as much about the problem and its conditions as he or she can. In Stage 2 the individual puts the problem aside—lets it sit. The individual may continue to work on the problem unconsciously but does not do so at a conscious level. In Stage 3 the individual has the insight—the burst of illumination. Seemingly all of a sudden, out of the blue, the insight hits. But notice that even Wallas, writing more than 50 years ago, recognized that insights do not come out of the blue. They require mental preparation and perhaps incubation first. Finally, the individual verifies that the insight is correct. Whether one accepts Wallas's particular four-stage model or not, the major lesson it has to teach us is that insight is always part of a larger problem-solving process; it does not occur on its own or out of the blue. [*See* PROBLEM SOLVING.]

II. IMPORTANCE OF INSIGHT

There are many psychological phenomena that one could choose to understand. Why bother with something as difficult to understand as insight, when the nature of the phenomenon has largely eluded humankind for centuries? There are several reasons. First, insight is universal. Everyone experiences insights at multiple times during their lives, although the frequencies with which they have the experience may vary. To the extent a psychological construct is universal, it is more interesting than one limited to a particular time or place. Second, insight is interesting to almost everyone. Who has not suddenly come up with what seems like a great idea and wondered where the idea came from? Sometimes one can trace the source of the idea, and other times the source of the idea seems totally mysterious. But all of us have wondered, at times, how we (or others) came to what seems like a brilliant flash of insight. Third, many of the great discoveries of all times have emanated from insights. Of course, there are the classic cases, such as that of Archimedes bathing himself and suddenly realizing that the volume of a solid object can be measured by the amount of water it displaces. But there are many thousands of nonclassic

cases that nevertheless have made our world what it is. Finally, understanding of insight helps provide a key to the gateway of imagination, fantasy, and creativity. No understanding of creative thinking—thinking that produces novel task-appropriate ideas that are high in quality—would be complete without an understanding of the insights that seem to underlie such creative thinking. Thus, an understanding of insight is a prerequisite for understanding other interesting psychological functions. Such understanding might be seen as beginning with an analysis of what, if anything, can be understood about insight.

III. MYSTICAL VIEWS OF INSIGHT

There is a tradition in the study of insight and of creativity that attributes these phenomena to a kind of mystic power. For example, Plato argued that a poet is able to create only that which the Muse dictates, and even today people sometimes refer to their own Muse as a source of inspiration. It is as though some external power generates the moment of insight or inspiration. In Plato's view, one person might be inspired to create choral songs, perhaps imagining in a flash how one or more choral songs might go; another person might be inspired to create an epic poem. The mystical view did not go out of fashion with Plato—far from it. Rudyard Kipling, for example, wrote of the "Daemon" that lives in a writer's pen.

Colleen Seifert and her colleagues have referred to this view of insight as the Wizard Merlin perspective. Often we view great geniuses as having some kind of access to insights that others simply do not have. Seifert and her colleagues quoted a passage written by James Gleick that describes Murray Gell-Mann, a Nobel Prize–winning scientist, speaking of Richard Feynman:

> A physicist studying quantum field theory with Murray Gell-Mann at the California Institute of Technology in the 1950's, before standard texts have become available, discovers unpublished lecture notes by Richard Feynman. . . . He asks Gell-Mann about them. Gell-Mann says, "No, Dick's methods are not the same as the methods used here." The student asks, "Well, what are Feynman's methods?" Gell-Mann leans coyly against

the blackboard and says, "Dick's method is this. You write down the problem. You think very hard." (Gell-Mann shuts his eyes and presses his knuckles periodically to his forehead.) "Then you write down the answer." (1992, p. 315)

Perhaps the mystical view has the advantage that it leaves people with a sense of awe at the universe. But as science, it leaves much to be desired. The problem with the mystical view of insight is that it gives us no real understanding of insight at all, much less a scientific understanding. Thus, it is the one view that we dismiss out of hand. The other views of insight may or may not be right, but they differ from the mystical view in that they are attempts to understand insight scientifically rather than mystically.

IV. NOTHING-SPECIAL VIEWS OF INSIGHT

When we have an insight, we often feel as though something special has occurred. But has it? We sometimes feel like we are experiencing something but then realize it is something else, or nothing in particular. In dreams we feel like we are experiencing events that we are not really experiencing. Even when we are awake, we are easily deceived. We may see someone at a distance whom we think we recognize as our long-lost love. We feel the thrill of such a recognition. On coming closer to the person, we discover that it is not our long-lost love at all, but someone we know but would rather avoid. We did experience a thrill when we first saw the individual, but it was based on a false perception.

The view of insight as nothing special can be traced to associationist philosophers, who believed that we learn things by associating new ideas with old ideas or by associating old ideas that were formerly not associated. According to Richard Mayer, associationism involves four fundamental principles. The first—atomism—is that the elements of thinking are the specific ideas and the associations between them. For example, when a child gets bitten by a fierce dog, the child most likely learns to associate fierce dogs with potential pain

and suffering. The child has in mind three elements: the idea of the dog, the idea of potential pain and suffering, and the association that links these two ideas. The second principle—mechanization—is that the process of thinking involves our moving swiftly and automatically from one idea to the next by our following the strongest associative link. For example, a child may acquire, over time, a number of associations to fierce dogs, but what will determine the child's first thought when the child sees such a dog is the child's strongest association—perhaps that the dog can cause him or her potential pain and suffering. The third principle—empiricism—states that the acquisition of ideas and associations derives from our sensory experiences. This point of view was expressed most forcefully by John Locke, who argued that our minds are a blank slate when we are born and that experience imprints on the blank slate all it will ever need to know. For example, according to this view, we have no particular "hard wiring" that predisposes us to learn language or about fierce dogs or about anything else. We learn only by experience. The fourth principle—imagery—is that the experience of thinking involves the creation of mental images, which may be based on any of the senses. So a child may be able in his mind to see the fierce dog, hear the dog bark, and smell its odor, even though the dog is not even present. [*See* IMAGERY.]

A number of psychologists associated with the associationist tradition, or its successor, behaviorism (according to which the proper study of psychologists should be behavior rather than the mental or emotional states that underlie it), have argued that insight can be understood solely in associationistic terms—that is, in terms of the preceding four principles. Two such psychologists are Per Saugstad, a Norwegian psychologist, and Irving Maltzman, a U.S. psychologist. Their view is that an insight is a new combination of responses associated with an already existing problem. But all solutions to problems are of this kind, so there is nothing special about insight.

Consider a simple example. The child from the previous story is walking through the woods. He enters a clearing, and there in front of him is a gray, hairy quadruped with a longish snout. He does not recognize what kind of animal it is. But standing there staring at the animal, he has a flash of insight: This is an animal that potentially could cause him pain and suffering. He quickly makes tracks back where he came from. Afterward, when he discovers through consultations with a forest ranger that the animal he saw was a hungry wolf, he congratulates himself on his flash of insight, which may have saved his hide. According to the nothing-special view, however, nothing special occurred when he had that insight. Most likely, he saw the wolf and associated its physical characteristics with those of a fierce dog, even though he knew what he was looking at was not a dog. In turn, he associated the fierce dog with potential pain and suffering, which then established the link between the as-yet unlabeled wolf and potential pain and suffering. Although this example is simple, the basic principles behind it, according to associationists, can account for any insights we may have. We may feel like we have created something distinctly new, but what we have really done is to reconfigure what we already knew.

Today associationism and its successor, behaviorism, have nowhere near the impact on psychology they had in days of yore. But another variant of the nothing-special view of insight is alive and well, thanks to a transformation of this view to fit into more modern cognitive ways of viewing the mind. Today this view derives from an explanation that emphasizes not associative learning, but rather learning through the acquisition of knowledge and knowledge retrieval.

Consider a couple of examples and of how they might be explained by a nothing-special view of insight.

1. A stranger approached a museum curator and offered him an ancient bronze coin. The coin had an authentic appearance and was marked with the date 544 B.C. The curator had happily made acquisitions from suspicious sources before, but this time he promptly called the police and had the stranger arrested. Why?

Some people can look at this problem for a while, trying to figure out how the curator knew that something was wrong. They may then have a sudden "aha" experience, in which they realize that a coin could not be dated 544 B.C., because no coin-maker could know when Christ would be born or even that he would be born at all! Therefore, the coin must be a fake. But is

the "aha" experience any more valid than the false recognition of a former lover? According to Weisberg and others who adopt his point of view, nothing special has occurred. For one thing, the problem requires careful reading. Careless reading may prevent the solution. For another thing, the problem requires recognition that one cannot record an event as having occurred before it happens. People already know this fact. For example, neither they nor anyone else can record the date of one's death because they do not know the date on which it will occur. As soon as someone recognizes the applicability of this already known fact to the coin problem, the problem is essentially solved. It is just a matter of recognizing the applicability of the fact. No real restructuring of the problem—a critical component in our definition of insight—has occurred with this recognition.

2. Figure 1 shows three rows of three dots apiece. Without lifting your pencil from the paper, connect the nine dots by drawing four straight lines.

Figure 2 shows the solution to the nine-dot problem. Notice that the only possible solution to the problem is to allow the straight lines connecting the dots to leave the periphery of the nine dots. The "aha" experience that people who solve this problem have is the realization that nothing in the specifications of the problem required them to remain within the implicit borders of the dots.

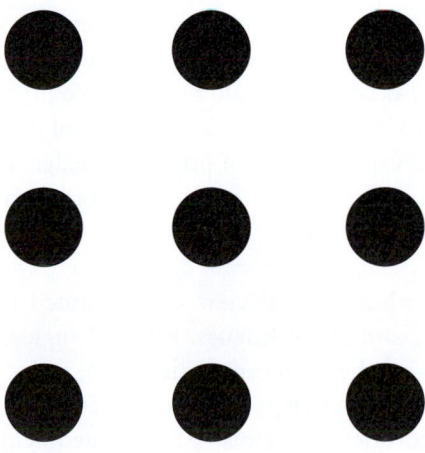

FIGURE 1   The nine-dot problem.

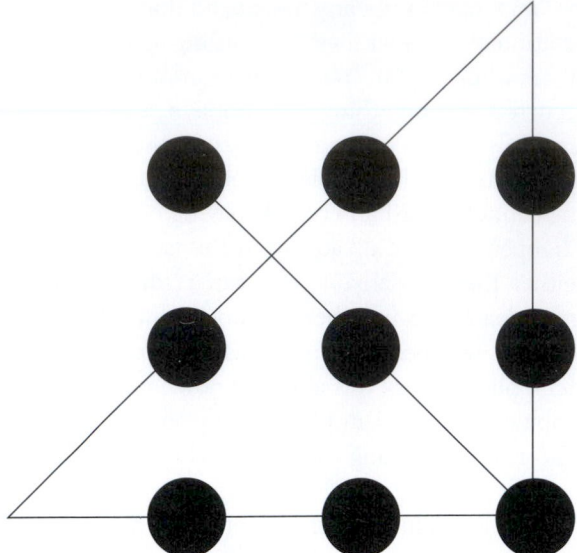

FIGURE 2   Solution to the nine-dot problem.

But is the solution to this problem really based on the insight that, in order to connect the dots, one has to go outside the periphery of the dots? Robert Weisberg and Joseph Alba tested this hypothesis by asking participants in an experiment to solve the nine-dot problem. In one group, participants were told simply to solve the problem. In another group, participants were told to solve the problem, but were also told that the solution would require their going outside the periphery of the dots. If solution of the problem hinged on the insight regarding the borders, then one would expect that telling people to go outside the dots would essentially solve the problem for them. But it didn't. Although telling them to go outside the dots was helpful, many people still could not solve the problem. According to Weisberg and Alba, solution of the problem draws on various kinds of prior knowledge, including but not limited to the fact that some borders are apparent but nothing more.

The nothing-special view is not limited to Robert Weisberg and his colleagues. Patrick Langley, Herbert Simon, and their colleagues devised a series of computer programs that reproduced several major scientific discoveries in chemistry and related fields. These discoveries all might have been viewed as stunning in-

sights that only great minds could have. But Langley, Simon, and their colleagues showed that a computer program could generate the same discoveries, and possibly the same insights that the great minds had, using the same kinds of problem-solving processes that could be used to solve any other problem. In other words, there is nothing special about insight.

The nothing-special view has at least two distinct advantages associated with it. First, it is parsimonious: There is no need to posit any special processes of insight. A good general theory of problem solving should be able to handle insightful problem solving as just one of many kinds of cases. Second, the view fits in with a widely accepted belief at the end of the 20th century that what distinguishes experts from novices is primarily knowledge and how it is organized. A number of researchers, including Micheline Chi, Robert Glaser, Jill Larkin, Alan Lesgold, Herbert Simon, and many others, have found that experts in a given domain seem not to process information in any special way; rather, they can draw on a vast and well-organized knowledge base to solve problems that novices cannot solve. Thus, what might appear to be insights in the solution of problems such as the nine-dot problem or even in the major scientific discoveries may be nothing more than the effective utilization of a vast, well-organized knowledge base.

Many psychologists studying insight do not accept the nothing-special view, however. They would question every one of the conclusions that nothing-special theorists would draw. Consider, for example, the solution of the nine-dot problem. According to these psychologists, it is naïve to believe that knowing one can go outside the periphery of the dots is *sufficient* for solving the nine-dot problem. Rather, this knowledge is *necessary but not sufficient*. Thus, giving participants this knowledge may facilitate their solution but it will by no means give away the solution. Indeed, several insights may be required to solve the problem. Consider as a second example the computer programs of Langley, Simon, and their colleagues. Are these programs really doing just the same things that the original scientific discoverers did? According to the critics, the programs are not doing the same thing at all. For one thing, when one rediscovers a finding rather than initially discovering it, one has the advantage of knowing just what the problem is, and that the problem is indeed soluble. For another thing, for a computer program to rediscover a scientific finding, its representations and organizations of information must be programmed by humans. The humans can cleverly do such programming to allow rediscoveries. But until computer programs start making their own discoveries of the magnitude of the rediscoveries they are making, one must be skeptical of whether they can come anywhere close to stimulating the processes that led to the discoveries in the first place. In fairness to the authors, however, they did not claim that their program was identical in its processing to human processing. Finally, it is difficult to refute nothing-special views. When people have the experience of insight, they may or may not be able to identify associations or prior knowledge of any kind that allowed them to discover the insight. But the fact that they cannot identify the associations or knowledge does not mean they do not exist. It is possible they exist but are inaccessible to consciousness. Thus, no matter what people may say, one can always argue that they used prior knowledge as the basis of their insights, whether they are aware of this knowledge or not. We might as well try to prove that little green men are not controlling our thoughts. No matter how hard we try to find them, there is always the possibility that they exist but are devilishly adept in hiding themselves.

V. SPECIAL-PROCESS VIEWS OF INSIGHT

According to special-process views, insight is a process that differs in kind from ordinary kinds of information processes. These views are most often associated with the Gestalt psychologists and their successors, who believed that one could not study psychological phenomena by decomposing them into their elements, because the whole often differs from the sum of its parts. Psychologists well known for this point of view included Kurt Koffka, Wolfgang Köhler, Max Wertheimer, and later, Norman R. F. Maier, among others.

In general, Gestalt psychology was a school of thought prominent in the middle part of the first half of the 20th century that arose in large part as a reaction to the atomism of associationism. Gestaltists believed that the attempt to reduce behavior in general and insight in particular to learned associations was futile. They believed instead that phenomena are better understood when they are comprehended holistically.

How might insight processes differ from other processes of thinking? Three possibilities were suggested by David Perkins, who is not himself a Gestalt psychologist. One possibility is that insight results from extended unconscious leaps in thinking. Another possibility is that it results from greatly accelerated mental processes. A third possibility is that it results from a short-circuiting of normal reasoning processes.

Richard Mayer has suggested other variants of the special-process view. One, based on the work of Otto Selz during the 1920s and 1930s, is that insight results from a person's completing a schema. so one is trying to understand some phenomenon, but there is a gap. The insight occurs when one fills in the gap. An example, provided by Selz, would be Benjamin Franklin's trying to retrieve the electricity of lightning and bring it down from sky to earth. Franklin worked with two givens: the sky and the goal of getting the electricity down to earth. He needed to fill in the middle part of the schema. He did so by attaching a wire to a kite and then letting it fly into lightning. In a set of studies (described by Richard Mayer and by Nico Frijda and Adrian De Groot), Selz had participants think aloud as they solved word-association problems, such as what would be a superordinate of *newspaper*? Selz found that his participants did not merely generate associations, but actively tried to construct meaning so that there would be some schema into which the word and its superordinate would fit. He took such thinking as evidence that participants were trying to complete a schema and not just generate simple associations to given words.

Another Gestalt view, adopted by Wolfgang Köhler in the late 1920s, was that insight involves a sudden reorganization of visual or other information. Köhler observed a chimpanzee, Sultan, confined in a cage with two sticks. Outside the cage and out of Sultan's reach with either stick was a banana. After trying to grab the banana with his hand and with each stick, the chimp took to tinkering with the sticks. Suddenly, he realized that the sticks could be attached to one another to form a new tool: one long pole that he could then use to roll the banana into range. In Köhler's view, the chimp's behavior showed that insight could be achieved through a sudden reorganization of the visual field.

Karl Duncker, another Gestalt psychologist, proposed a view of insight as a reformulation of a problem. Although Duncker was not clear on how this reformulation occurs, his general view of the importance of reformulation is still accepted by many psychologists today. Perhaps the most famous Gestalt problem for studying insight is one used by Duncker. The problem is called the radiation problem. It is still used in contemporary research. Here is the problem:

Given a human being with an inoperable stomach tumor and X-rays that destroy organic tissue at sufficient intensity, by what procedure can one free him of the tumor by these rays and at the same time avoid destroying the healthy tissue that surrounds it?

People's ability to solve this problem depends on exactly how they reformulate the problem and the goal of solving it. For example, if they reformulate the goal in terms of avoiding contact between the rays and healthy tissue, they are likely to arrive at an incorrect solution, such as sending rays through the esophagus (which is impossible). Another reformulated goal would be to desensitize healthy tissue, perhaps by immunizing healthy tissue with weak rays. But this solution also does not work. People do not become immune to X rays by repeated small exposures. Another reformulation would be to increase the intensity of the rays when they reach the diseased tissue, but, of course, it is not possible to change the intensity of X rays along their route. The best solution involves a reformulation of the goal of the problem as focusing many weak rays on one point. If the weak rays emanate from different points and converge on the diseased tissue, then the healthy tissue will receive only the weak rays but the diseased tissue will receive the converging rays at full blast.

Yet another Gestalt psychologist, Max Wertheimer, emphasized the role of finding a problem analogue in insight processes. Again, this view remains important today, although in somewhat more tightly specified forms. One of Wertheimer's most famous problems required participants to find the area of a parallelogram. (Wertheimer assumed his participants knew how to find the area of a rectangle.) Few people actually know

how to find the area of a parallelogram. Wertheimer showed his participants how to find the area, but he taught them by one of two different methods. He told one group to multiply the length of the base times the height of the parallelogram. This method gave participants a formula for finding the area, but it gave them no real understanding of what they were doing. Wertheimer showed the second group how the whole problem could be transformed. One would take the two right triangles that can be formed at each end of the parallelogram and combine them into a rectangle. Then one adds the area of this rectangle to the area of the rectangle in the center. The total is the area of the parallelogram.

Next one gives participants transfer problems— problems that are like the original problem in some ways, but different from the original problem in other ways. One then compares the performance of the participants in the two groups on the transfer problems. Wertheimer found that those who learned how to solve the parallelogram problem in a way that made sense to them did better on the transfer problems. In other words, they were able to have the insight that allowed them to see the analogy only if they were taught in a way that let them adequately organize and understand the original material.

The Gestalt special-process views have several strengths. The first is historical: Gestalt psychologists were among the first to take insight processes seriously and to study them in their own right. Second, although these psychologists may not have conducted the most elegant and rigorous experiments ever done, they did make a number of attempts to study insight processes via empirical methods. Thus, they contributed not only to theory, but to research. Third, the Gestalt theorizing served as a basis for later theorizing. In psychology as in other sciences, often the most one can ask for is that a line of work contribute to the progress of the field, which means contributing, ultimately, to its own demolition.

The weaknesses of the special-process views are fairly apparent in retrospect. First, although the Gestaltists did research, they never went much beyond labeling. For example, labeling Sultan's behavior as insightful is a far cry from understanding this behavior. Second, the ideas of the Gestaltists would have been very hard to test, in any case. It is not surprising that the Gestaltists did not much go beyond labeling. How could one really test the notion that insights represent short-circuited conventional reasoning processes? Finally, the Gestaltists suggested that the processes of which they spoke all connected to physiological processes, but they never made any progress at all in elucidating just what these connections were.

VI. THREE-PROCESS VIEW OF INSIGHT

We have proposed that a main reason psychologists (and others) have had so much difficulty in isolating insight is that it involves not one but three separate but related psychological processes.

Selective encoding insights involve sifting relevant information from irrelevant information. Significant problems generally present one with large amounts of information, only some of which is relevant to problem solution. For example, the facts of a legal case are usually both numerous and confusing: An insightful lawyer must figure out which of the myriad facts confronting him or her are relevant to principles of law. Similarly, a doctor or psychotherapist may be presented with a great volume of information regarding a patient's background and symptoms: An insightful doctor or psychotherapist must sift out those facts that are relevant to diagnosis of treatment. A famous example of what we refer to as an insight of selective encoding is Alexander Fleming's discovery of penicillin. In looking at a petri dish containing a culture that had become moldy, Fleming noticed that bacteria in the vicinity of the mold had been destroyed, presumably by the mold. In essence, Fleming encoded the information in his visual field in a highly selective way, zeroing in on that part of the field that was relevant to the discovery of the antibiotic. In the Duncker radiation problem, an insight of selective encoding can be seen as key. There are many potential pieces of information in the situation. The relevant piece is that the X rays need not be single-sourced but can be multisourced.

Selective combination insights involve combining what originally might seem to be isolated pieces of information into a unified whole that may or may not resemble its parts. Whereas selective encoding involves knowing which pieces of information are relevant, selecting combination involves knowing how to put together the pieces of information that are relevant. For example, a lawyer must know how the relevant facts of a case fit together to make (or break!) the case. A doctor or psychotherapist must be able to figure out how to combine information about various isolated symptoms to identify a given medical (or psychological) syndrome. A famous example of selective combination is Darwin's formulation of the theory of evolution. It is well known that Darwin had available to him for many years the facts he needed to form the basis for a theory of natural selection. What eluded him for those years was a way to combine the facts into a coherent package. Köhler's chimpanzee Sultan may be seen as having had a selective-combination insight: He saw how to combine the two sticks to reach the banana.

Selective comparison insights involve relating newly acquired information to information acquired in the past. Problem solving by analogy, for example—the kind of problem solving studied by Wertheimer—is an instance of selective comparison. One realizes that new information is similar to old information in certain ways (and dissimilar from it in other ways) and uses this information to better understand the new information. For example, an insightful lawyer will relate a current case to legal precedents; choosing the right precedents is essential. A doctor or psychotherapist relates the current set of presenting symptoms to previous case histories in his or her own or others' past experiences; again, choosing the right precedents is essential. A famous example of an insight of selective comparison is Kekulé's report of his discovery of the structure of the benzene ring. Kekulé dreamed of a snake curling back on itself and catching its tail. When he woke up, he realized that the image of the snake catching its tail was a visual metaphor for the structure of the benzene ring. (Some people believe Kekulé's report to be a fabrication.)

We have done a number of empirical studies testing and exploring the implications of our theory of insight. Typically, we use puzzle problems such as these:

1. One day you decide to visit the zoo. While there, you see a group of giraffes and ostriches. Altogether they have 30 eyes and 44 legs. How many animals are there?
2. George wants to cook three steaks as quickly as

possible. Unfortunately, his grill holds only two steaks and each steak takes 2 minutes per side to cook. What is the shortest amount of time in which George can cook his three steaks?

3. Heather and Lynn have three household tasks to perform.
   a. Their floor must be vacuumed. They have only one vacuum and the task takes 30 minutes.
   b. The lawn must be mowed. They have only one mower and this task also takes 30 minutes.
   c. Their baby sister must be fed and bathed. This too takes 30 minutes.

   How would Heather and Lynn divide the work so as to finish all three tasks in the shortest amount of time?

Of these particular problems, the first emphasizes selective encoding. The major key is realizing the relevance of the 30 eyes; giraffes and ostriches have the same number of eyes but not the same number of legs. This problem can be solved by simply dividing the number of eyes by two. The second example emphasizes selective combination; if the pieces of information are put together correctly, the problem solver discovers that the steaks can be cooked in 6 minutes. Although the third example also requires selective combination, it is used here as an illustration of how selective comparison was measured. In some cases, participants were taught how to solve sample problems, such as the steak problem used in the second example, that were similar to a few complex problems in the test booklet. Usually participants could solve the test problems only if they saw a connection between these items and the related samples. For example, if the problem solver saw a relation between the second and third problems just listed, then he or she would realize that Heather and Lynn need to divide one of the tasks.

In our studies, a number of findings have emerged. First, some adults and children have considerable difficulty knowing when to apply the three insight processes; others do not have such difficulty. Moreover, when children are classified as "gifted," the classification is only a weak predictor of an individual's ability to have insights of these kinds, presumably because whatever bases are used for classifying students as gifted has relatively little to do with their insight abilities. Second, the ability to apply the insight processes

is moderately correlated with scores on a general intelligence test, but the correlations are higher to the extent that the intelligence test emphasizes thinking in novel ways. Thus, insight abilities are related to, but not the same as, general intellectual abilities. Third, high-IQ individuals are slower, not faster, than lower-IQ individuals in analyzing the problems and applying the insights. The higher-IQ individuals see more into the problems and realize they are more complex than they appear, whereas the lower-IQ individuals may solve the problems rather quickly but incorrectly because they believe the problems to be simpler than they rally are. Fourth, insight can be developed through a training program, and the effects are both transferable to kinds of problems not specifically taught and durable over a period of as long as one year. Fifth, when students labeled as "gifted" and those not labeled as "gifted" are taught, both groups show improvement in their insightful-thinking skills. However, individual differences do not disappear. Rather, both groups improve about equally, so that the differences between them are largely maintained. Sixth, people who are good in having one kind of insight (e.g., selective encoding) tend to be, on average, good at having other kinds of insights (e.g., selective combination or selective comparison). Finally, people experience insightful problem solving involving the three kinds of insights in a way that is different from the way they experience noninsightful problem solving. As discussed earlier, the experience of difference is no guarantee that the processes are really different. But people experiencing the solving of the two kinds of problems as distinctly different.

Our research has shown us that testing for insightful thinking carries with it special difficulties that may not be as readily observable in other kinds of psychological testing. One of the problems we have used is the so-called water-lilies problem: Water lilies on a lake double in area every 24 hours. At the beginning of the summer there is 1 water lily on the lake It takes 60 days for the lake to become covered with water lilies. On what day is the lake half-covered?

We believed the problem to require insight, but otherwise to be relatively straightforward. If the water lilies double in area every 24 hours, then a lake that is fully covered at 60 days would be half covered the day before, that is, on day 59. The fact that there was 1 water lily on the first day is irrelevant (requiring a selective-encoding insight). After publishing an article that gave the water-lilies problem as an example of an insight problem, one of us received a page-and-a-half single-spaced letter pointing out that, if the water lilies really doubled in area every 24 hours, then the world would be more than entirely covered by water lilies by day 60. The recipient did not try to verify the mathematical calculations of the letter's author, because the conclusion would be the same regardless of whether they were correct or not (and they probably were, given the well-known mathematical distinction of the letter writer!): Sometimes the people being tested are more insightful than the people doing the testing. Thus one must be careful, in studying insight, not to disallow answers that may be more insightful than the one that was intended.

The three-process view, like the others we have discussed, has several strengths. First, it makes the useful point that insight is probably not a singular phenomenon: Insights can be of different kinds. Second, it is possible experimentally to separate out these different kinds of insights—at least to a first order of approximation—and then to test the theory empirically, something that has been done too infrequently in the study of theories of insight. Third, the theory has been useful in studying insight not only as a process but from the standpoint of individual differences in insightful-thinking abilities.

This theory also has some weaknesses. First, the three processes are specified at a rather global level. One can talk about distinguishing relevant from irrelevant information in selective encoding, for example, but exactly how do people make this distinction? The rather global level of specification leaves us without answers to questions such as these. Second, the theory does not specify how the processes of insight interact with the knowledge base. It is one thing to say that selective-comparison insights involve the utilization of old information. But how do people know which old information to use, and how do they access this information? The theory does not say. Third, one could argue that the three kinds of insights represent not psychological processes but a taxonomy of problem requirements. It has yet to be shown that there really are three distinctive psychological processes corresponding to the three kinds of insightful inferences that are

perhaps required when a person solves an insightful problem.

VII. THE OPPORTUNISTIC-ASSIMILATION VIEW OF INSIGHT

Colleen Seifert, David Meyer, Natalie Davidson, Andrea Patalano, and Ilan Yaniv have proposed what they refer to as an opportunistic-assimilation view of insight. This view builds on the model of problem solving proposed by Graham Wallas (described earlier).

According to Seifert and her colleagues, during the initial mental-preparation phase of problem solving, people sometimes discover that they just do not see how they are going to be able to solve a problem at hand. When they have this realization, the memory system marks the problem as unsolved. It is as though a red flag has been placed on the problem to highlight the fact that it has neither been solved nor even been understood in a way that suggests a path to solution. When people cannot see how to solve a problem, they are likely to go into Wallas's second stage of incubation. They stop thinking consciously about the problem and just let it sit. But the "red flag" associated with the problem results in their processing their environment in a way that is different from the way they processed it before. Now anything in the environment that might possibly be relevant to the solution of the problem gets special attention. Thus, features of the environment that before would probably not have been noticed now are noticed. In other words, people are opportunistically assimilating aspects of the environment. Finally, one of these features suggests a way to solve the problem. This feature enables people to leave the incubation phase of problem solving and to enter the illumination (insight) phase. They can later verify their solution at their leisure.

This model suggests that insightful problem solving is not quite like ordinary problem solving; it needs a period of incubation during which one lets the problem lie at rest. Thus the model is not a nothing-special type of model. Nor is it a special-process model, however, because the processes of assimilating the environment are the same as these processes always are. What has changed is exactly what is assimilated. In insightful problem solving, one uses the incubation stage to assimilate information that is relevant specifically to the problem at hand.

Seifert and her colleagues give an example of an insight problem, adopted from a book by Mosler, that illustrates their model of insightful thinking:

> Two men who were walking through a desert stopped when they saw an unusual thing. They had discovered a third man lying on a stretch of sand, and he was dead. They noticed the dead man had carried a small pack with fresh food and water still in it. The dead man also had a larger pack on his back, and on his index finger was a large ring. The two men pondered the cause of the third man's death, but they could not explain it, and so they proceeded onward.
>
> Later, while going along, one of the original two men accidentally dropped a handkerchief that he had taken from his pocket to wipe his brow. Then, he suddenly realized how the third man probably died. Overhead, the third man's parachute had broken, and he had fallen precipitously to earth. (1977)

This story illustrates opportunistic assimilation. Normally, the dropping of a handkerchief probably would have meant nothing to the man. But the dropping of the handkerchief resembled in some ways the dropping of a parachute, and the large pack on the dead man's back and the ring on his index finger could now be interpreted as a failed parachute. Seifert and her colleagues do not stop with this puzzle problem as an example of opportunistic assimilation. They describe the results of past research and show how it could be interpreted in terms of their model. They have also done their own research, which has been supportive of the model. In one experiment, for example, they showed that exposing problem solvers to relevant new information after an initial failed solution attempt promoted successful solution of the problem. In a second experiment, they showed that people have especially accessible memories of problems whose initial confrontation ends with a failure to reach solution. In both experiments, the positive results were consistent with the proposed model of insightful problem solving.

The opportunistic-assimilation view of insight has at least three distinct advantages. First, it is intuitively plausible. Second, it has empirical data to back it. Third, it is more well specified than some other models in which it is not really clear just what is going on. At the same time, the model has some disadvantages. For one thing, not all insights seem to arise during a period of incubation. Some insights occur while a person is actively trying to solve a problem. For another thing, the model does not make totally clear just how people zero in on the relevant information in the environment. What exactly is the mechanism that allowed the individual in the preceding story, for example, to see the analogy between the handkerchief and the parachute? On the whole, though the model is plausible and seems to offer promise for understanding at least some, but perhaps not all, insightful problem-solving processes.

VIII. EVOLUTIONARY VIEWS OF INSIGHT

Evolutionary views of insight, which have been proposed by Donald Campbell, David Perkins, and Dean Simonton, are based on the notion that the same kinds of principles that apply to the evolution of organisms can be applied to the evolution of ideas. The basic idea is simple. Ideas undergo haphazard recombinations in the mind. These recombinations are referred to as *blind variation,* much as would be mutations of genes in the evolution of species. The resulting blind variations in ideas then pass through a selective filter, meaning that only a subset of the combinations of ideas are retained for further cognitive processing. This selective retention of ideas is what may later be recognized as insights.

Dean Simonton gave as an example of this process a set of events that transpired with Henry James. One Christmas eve James was dining with friends. A woman next to James just happened to make mention of something. The something of which she made mention became the basis for his story, "The Spoils of Poynton." In other words, over the course of time, James probably heard many different bits of conversation. These blind variations of ideas came and went and most of them meant nothing to him and had no effect on him. But then somewhere along the line, one of them "took"— it was selectively retained. That idea provided the insight for his story.

The evolutionary view has several advantages. For one thing, it ties in the evolution of ideas with the evolution of organisms. It is certainly attractive to think of evolution as applying both to organisms and to ideas. For another thing, the mechanism seems to correspond, at some level, to what we all experience. We all hear and see much more than we can possibly pay attention to and process. But every once in a while something hits us in a certain way and gives us an idea. We are selectively retaining one of the blind variations of ideas that happen to assail us. For a third thing, ideas almost certainly do evolve, and evolutionary mechanisms are about as plausible and well worked out as any we have for explaining how this evolution might take place.

At the same time, the evolutionary view seems to have some disadvantages. For one thing, it is not at all clear how it could be tested. Although one can generate plausible instances, validation of the idea seems for the most part to rest on plausibility rather than empirical testability. For another thing, the idea that variation is blind seems somewhat suspect. Some people seem to place themselves in situations that promote generative ideas, whereas other people do not. Perhaps variation is not so blind after all, but rather, planned at least in part. Finally, the theory does not really explain the psychological mechanisms that give rise either to insight in general or to individual differences in insightful thinking in particular. Thus, for the time being, the evolutionary view is intriguing and enticing, but it is in need of further development and validation.

IX. CONCLUSIONS

At present, there are many more questions than there are answers when it comes to understanding insight. We can define the construct reasonably well, but we cannot say with any real certainty just what people do when they have insights. A number of alternative theories—reviewed in this article—have been proposed.

But at present, few tests truly discriminate among the models. Even those tests that have been done, such as the Weisberg-Alba work described earlier, do not provide a definitive comparison between models.

Although they differ in their language, some of the models are at least partially compatible. For example, some of the Gestalt special-process views are compatible with the three-process view. Both of these kinds of views can probably be reconciled with opportunistic assimilation. What may be needed most at this point is some kind of supermodel that integrates the best aspects of the different models now existing. Such a model only awaits one or more insights on the part of some individual investigating insight. Thus, what we need most in the study of insight are some new insights!

Bibliography

Gleick, J. (1992). *Genius: The life and science of Richard Feynman.* New York: Pantheon Books.

Langley, P., Simon, H. A., Bradshaw, G. L., & Zytkow, J. M. (1987). *Scientific discovery: Computational explorations of the creative processes.* Cambridge, MA: MIT Press.

Mosler, G. (1977). *The puzzle school.* New York: Abelard-Schuman.

Perkins, D. N. (1981). *The mind's best work.* Cambridge, MA: Harvard University Press.

Seifert, C. M., Meyer, D. E., Davidson, N., Patalano, A. L., & Yaniv, I. (1995). Demystification of cognitive insight: Opportunistic assimilation and the prepared-mind perspective. In R. J. Sternberg & J. E. Davidson (Eds.), *The nature of insight* (pp. 65–124). Cambridge, MA: MIT Press.

Sternberg, R. J. (Ed.). (1998). *Handbook of creativity.* New York: Cambridge University Press.

Sternberg, R. J., & Davidson, J. E. (Eds.). (1995). *The nature of insight.* Cambridge, MA: MIT Press.

Weisberg, R. (1986). *Creativity: Genius and other myths.* New York: Freeman.

Institute of Personality Assessment and Research

Ravenna Helson

University of California, Berkeley

Personality Assessment A method for the psychological evaluation of individuals that involves testing and observation in a group setting with a variety of tests and procedures by a number of staff members. The staff members pool test scores and subjective impressions to formulate psychodynamic descriptions of the individual that enable predictions to be made of future behavior in areas of special interest.

Q-Sort Procedure A set of rules for the scaling of a group of personality descriptors (Q items) as applied to an individual, so that the order of the Q items expresses the judge's formulation of the personality of the individual. In the construction of Q-sort prototypes, the descriptors are not applied to particular persons but to an ideal exemplar of a construct (e.g., a narcissist or a generative person). The correlation between the individual Q sort and the Q-sort prototype provides a score on the prototype for a given individual.

The **INSTITUTE OF PERSONALITY ASSESSMENT AND RESEARCH (IPAR)** *is known as the place where the study of creative personality emerged as a major* topic in the 1950s and where it has been carried on most extensively. After describing the origins, purposes, and procedures of IPAR, this article briefly reviews its research contribution in each of four periods from 1949 to the present.

I. ORIGINS, PURPOSES, AND PROCEDURES AT IPAR

IPAR was established at the University of California, Berkeley (UCB) in 1949 to develop and apply psychological assessment techniques in the study of effectively functioning persons. It supported at the start by the Rockefeller Foundation. Donald W. MacKinnon, a student of Henry A. Murray at Harvard University and chief of Station S in the Office of Strategic Services in World War II, was brought to UCB as the founding director. He held this position until his retirement in 1970. The group around MacKinnon at the beginning included two socially minded and psychoanalytically trained clinicians (Erik Erikson and Nevitt Sanford), a clinical psychologist with a strong interest in diagnostics (Robert E. Harris), a young proponent of the new empirical approach to test construction (Harrison Gough), a social perception specialist (Richard Crutchfield), and two graduate students (Frank Barron and Ronald Taft).

The IPAR group was dedicated to the objective study of effective and complex personality functioning. For this purpose, much information about many aspects of personality needed to be gathered. In a typical IPAR assessment about ten assessees would spend a weekend at the institute, being interviewed; taking tests of their intelligence, interests, and perceptual-cognitive functioning; filling out personality inventories; projecting their personality on Rorschach blots or into Thematic Apperception Test (TAT) stories; participating in group procedures of various kinds; and being observed by the psychology staff. After the assessees went home, the staff described each of them by means of adjective checklists, Q sorts, and a standard set of ratings. These procedures evolved through much group planning and individual effort to find or produce the measures that were needed. [*See* PERSONALITY.]

The publications from IPAR on creativity can be roughly grouped into four periods: tool and construct development in the 1950s; the assessment studies of highly creative persons in the 1960s; diverse topics including creativity in women, the encouragement of creative thinking skills in children, and the interrelations of creative product, process, and personality, all peaking in the 1970s or 1980s; and the longitudinal study of creative persons in the 1990s.

II. THE 1950S: DEVELOPMENT OF TOOLS AND CONSTRUCTS

The first years at IPAR were disrupted by the loyalty oath controversy at the university, which began in 1949 and led to the departure of Barron, Erikson, and Sanford for varying periods of time. Nevertheless, basic procedures for assessments were worked out, plans and hypotheses were drawn up, and assessment studies of effectiveness in graduate students and Air Force officers were conducted. During these years Gough developed the Adjective Check List (ACL) that was to become an essential IPAR tool and a widely used instrument. He also built the California Psychological Inventory (CPI). The CPI was modeled on the Minnesota Multiphasic Personality Inventory (MMPI), except that while the older instrument was used to assess psychopathology, the CPI assessed dimensions of effective personality functioning in society. Block produced the

California Q Sort, a third essential IPAR tool that became widely used by personality researchers. Hall developed the Mosaic Construction Test, valuable in assessments as a measure of aesthetic sensitivity and originality. Crutchfield's work on conformity appeared, and Barron (discussed next) conceptualized and developed measures of a number of aspects of the effective personality, including complexity of outlook, ego strength, independence of judgment, and originality.

The articles published by Barron in the early 1950s epitomize the IPAR approach in their concern with complex aspects of effectiveness, objective techniques of measurement, rich empirical findings, and intuitive elaboration. The first of these articles, published in 1952, described the somewhat accidental discovery of the complexity-simplicity dimension in a factor analytic study by Welsh of preferences for different kinds of figures, then the further development of this material into a scale of drawings differentially liked and disliked by artists and nonartists (the Barron-Welsh Art Scale), then the new work, based on the administration of the art scale to the IPAR sample of graduate students. Barron demonstrated differences in preferences for well-known paintings by high and low scorers on the Art Scale in this group, and he also reported differences in their self-descriptions on the ACL. On the basis of these findings, Barron conceptualized the complexity-simplicity dimension in terms of attention and perceptual choice, the preference for complexity allowing into the perceptual system the greatest possible richness of experience, even at the cost of discord, whereas the preference for simplicity allowed into the system only as much as could be integrated without great discomfort. The Art Scale has been used in many studies of creativity. The complexity-simplicity dimension overlaps considerably with what others now refer to as openness.

Early staff memoranda written in 1949 and 1950 by Barron and Gough show that originality was planned from the beginning as one of the three foci of investigation of the highly effective person, the other two being personal soundness and potential for seminal achievement. In 1950 Guilford gave an influential APA address on creativity, in which he suggested several ways to measure what he called divergent thinking. Some of these measures were used in assessments of the second IPAR sample, Air Force officers. In 1955, Barron offered a measure of originality that was a composite of eight free-response measures: three of the Guilford measures, three from the Rorschach and TAT, and two word-rearrangement measures. He tested the hypothesis that total scores would be correlated with a number of personality characteristics that he believed to be associated with originality: preference for complexity, independence of judgment, complexity as a person, self-assertion and dominance, and rejection of suppression. Due largely to his own work and that of his colleagues at IPAR, he was able to provide measures of these characteristics. The hypotheses were largely supported. [*See* DIVERGENT THINKING.]

Barron constructed a set of inventory items that he thought would test some of his hypotheses about attributes of the creative personality. These and other items from the CPI and MMPI were used to develop inventory scales differentiating high and low scorers on independence of judgment, complexity of outlook, and originality. They have been used in subsequent IPAR work on the creative personality.

III. THE 1960S: STUDIES OF HIGHLY CREATIVE PERSONS

In 1956 IPAR received funding from the Carnegie Corporation to conduct several studies of highly creative persons. Assessments were conducted in the late 1950s. There was strong public interest in creativity, so that much dissemination of findings took place through invited lectures, conference presentations, and journals not directed to professional psychologists. In 1962, MacKinnon gave a rationale for the approach taken at IPAR and reviewed the preliminary findings. True creativity, he said, included novelty, adaptiveness, and a development of the new idea to the full. This conception of creativity meant that it should be studied after it had been realized in identifiable creative products, and that criterion measures of creativity should be ratings by qualified experts. Because of known differences between artists and scientists, IPAR had undertaken the study of creative persons in each category and also in fields that pertained to both art and science. MacKinnon went on to review characteristics of the creative person as they were emerging in the IPAR studies.

Creative persons thought well of themselves, he said,

but were also more frank and critical of themselves than were others. On the MMPI and in interviews many of them appeared to have considerable psychopathology but also evidence of adequate control mechanisms. Male groups had high scores on measures of femininity, indicating an openness to feelings and emotions regarded in the American culture as feminine. On the Art Scale all of the creative groups showed a preference for complex and asymmetrical drawings, and in general the more creative the stronger the preference. On the Myers-Briggs Type Indicator, an inventory to assess Jungian typological dimensions, all the creative groups were preponderantly intuitive rather than sensing; three of the four samples were perceptive rather than judgmental, and two thirds of all of the groups were introverted rather than extraverted— though MacKinnon added that there was no evidence that the introverts were more creative than the extraverts. On the Strong Vocational Interest Blank, highly creative persons had a characteristic interest pattern, which MacKinnon interpreted as lack of interest in small details or facts for their own sake but concern for meanings and implications, cognitive flexibility, interest and accuracy in communication, intellectual curiosity, and lack of interest in policing either their own impulses or those of others. On the Allport-Vernon-Lindzey Study of Values, creative groups scored high on both theoretical and aesthetic values. On the CPI, creative persons had high scores on the scales for flexibility, psychological mindedness, and achievement via independence, and their scores were average or below average on measures of self-control. MacKinnon reported that within the range represented in the IPAR samples, there was little relation between creativity and intelligence. This finding aroused much controversy at the time, but additional data gathered by MacKinnon and Hall gave it further support, as did findings of investigators at other institutions. [*See* INTELLIGENCE.]

A. Individual Studies of Creative Men

The individual studies of highly creative persons were conducted by different IPAR staff members: Barron studied creative writers, Gough studied space scientists, MacKinnon and Hall studied architects, and Crutchfield and Helson studied male and female mathematicians. (The study of mathematicians was designed to provide data both about highly creative persons and about sex differences in creativity, which was another topic of interest, assigned to Helson.) Though all of the studies included the core assessment measures for at least the highly rated participants, each study was designed somewhat differently This fact has made it difficult to combine and compare studies except in an informal way.

1. Architects

The study of architects was the largest and most elaborate. MacKinnon chose a prestigious body of judges who drew up careful criteria for their nominations of creative architects, and later he obtained ratings of the creativity of the nominees from editors of professional journals, professors, and other experts. He collected considerable data not only from the 40 highly rated individuals who were assessed at IPAR but also from two other samples from whom data were obtained by mail: 43 architects who had worked in the firms of nominated architects and 41 representative American architects who had not worked in such a firm. Evidence for the validity of the criteria of creativity was strong, and correlations with a wide variety of personality measures were high.

Perhaps the most important theoretical contribution from the study of architects was MacKinnon's exposition of Otto Rank's theory of creativity, with its conception of creative, conflicted, and adapted types. This idea influenced several subsequent IPAR researches on personality types.

2. Space Scientists

The participants in the study of space scientists were 45 scientific employees in three industrial research laboratories. Later, 66 honor students in engineering were also assessed. This study was limited by a restricted range of creativity—most of the men fell into a high middle range. Nevertheless, Gough and Woodworth wrote an influential paper on stylistic variations in research style among the research scientists. They constructed a Research Scientist Q Sort, a set of 56 items that the scientists themselves used to describe their ways of working—their individual style of participation on the research team. The zealot, initiator, diagnostician, artificer, esthetician, and methodologist were some of the types that emerged. Gough also developed

a scientific word association test on which scientists, and later engineers, with high ratings on creativity were found to give infrequent but not bizarre associations.

3. Writers

Barron studied 56 writers, of whom 30 had been nominated by a panel of English professors, 10 were student playwrights, and 16 were competent professionals. The students and 20 of the creative nominees were assessed at IPAR. in an article describing the study, Barron said the writers were better than all other creative groups at his Symbolic Equivalents Test, which presents subjects with images (verbally) and asks them to write other images that have similar meanings. Their responses were rated for originality. He said that the writers reported more extreme experiences of emotion and fantasy life than the other samples. Most impressive to him was the importance of motivation in the writer's adoption of his calling and in the use of writing to serve a philosophic purpose.

4. Mathematicians

Helson and Crutchfield found that male mathematicians scored distinctively low in assertive self-assurance (extraversion) and distinctively high in adaptive autonomy (complexity, autonomy, and effectiveness), a pattern previously reported for adolescent males specializing in mathematics. Within the IPAR sample, creative and comparison groups had attended graduate schools of comparable quality, but the creative men had written more papers and held more prestigeful positions. In interests and personality the two groups differed in most of the ways described by MacKinnon as reported earlier. For example, the creative men had higher scores on the Art Scale and the Barron Originality scale but not on measures of intelligence. The creative mathematicians were found to have a more confident and assertive research style. They came from more advantaged backgrounds and described their mothers with more warmth, a fact that may be related to their greater breadth of personality.

5. A Common Creative Personality Profile?

The IPAR studies showed that highly creative persons differed from comparison subjects in a variety of domains. Did these creative groups have a common personality profile? Morris B. Parloff, Lois-Ellin Datta,

Marianne Kleman, and Joseph H. Handlon compared men rated higher and lower in creativity in four IPAR samples on factors of the CPI. They found the groups rated higher on creativity to show a common pattern of lower scores on disciplined effectiveness with higher scores on assertive assurance and adaptive autonomy. In other words, creative men, compared to other men in the same field, tended to be more flexible, assertive, and to show pursuit of complex tasks in a more vigorously independent and constructive way. However, there were large differences among samples and many exceptions to the pattern within samples.

These findings were compared with those from adolescent participants in a high-level science contest. High school scientists whose projects were rated as most creative, compared to those whose projects were rated less high, showed the high assertive assurance and high adaptive autonomy characteristic of creative adults, indicating that these characteristics were associated with creativity rather than eminence. However, they scored higher rather than lower on disciplined effectiveness. This fact suggested that a level of control conducive to creativity in adults may not be sufficient to support creativity in adolescents. In other words, personality characteristics associated with creativity may change with age.

Though IPAR researchers were interested in the creative personality in the abstract and across samples, they were also attentive to differences among creative persons. The investigation of creative styles and subtypes that had been initiated by Gough and Woodworth was continued in other IPAR work, such as studies of sex differences in creative style (see the following discussion).

B. Creativity in Women and Gender Differences in Creativity

Besides the study of highly creative persons, the proposal to Carnegie had noted as a problem of special interest that there were many more creative men than women, and that investigation was needed to clarify whether this fact was attributable largely to social and cultural factors or to more basic psychological and biological differences. In the late 1950s it was widely thought that women might lack ambition, ability in abstract thinking, and other qualities necessary for creative work. A creative woman mathematician was particularly hard to imagine. Therefore, Helson undertook a study of women mathematicians, collaborating with Crutchfield to attain samples of men and women matched in age so that sex differences could be examined. Later, she studied sex differences in personality and product among writers of children's literature, a field to which about equal numbers of men and women contributed. She also studied creativity in samples of college women, particularly at Mills College in Oakland, California. The Mills College sample has been followed several times subsequently, as reported in a later section.

1. Creativity in Women

These various studies showed that most of the characteristics attributed to the creative personality in the IPAR studies of men were fully as salient in women who were identified as creative (see Table I). The study of women mathematicians was unique in its combination of several important features: virtually the entire sample was assessed at the institute, the range of creativity represented was considerable, and because the staff had never heard of any of the women, there was no danger that their observations were biased by reputation. Staff perceptions of originality, autonomy, and other key characteristics yielded strong correlations

TABLE I

Highest Q-Sort Correlates of Creativity in Two Samples of Women

	Mathematicians N = 41	Mills women N = 105
Thinks and associates in unusual ways	.64	.59
Judges in conventional ways	−.62	−.52
Is an interesting, arresting person	.55	.60
Tends to be rebellious and nonconforming	.51	(.40)
Genuinely values intellectual and cognitive matters	.49	(.34)
Is uncomfortable with uncertainty	(−.35)	−.54
Has high aspirations for self	(.26)	.52

Note. Items listed are those from the California Q sort that had the five highest correlations with creativity in each sample. Correlations not among the five highest in a sample are in parentheses.

with the criterion creativity ratings. Even a woman's institutional affiliation was no clue to her creativity, because a striking finding was that some of the most creative women had no regular employment. Other findings were that a high proportion of the creative women were foreign born and that the women mathematicians as a group had fewer brothers than one would expect, especially the creative women. These results suggested that social opportunity, cultural factors, and parental socialization practices contributed to the scarcity of creative women mathematicians.

2. Gender Differences

Under conditions of social prejudice and perhaps for biological and cultural reasons as well, one might expect men and women to differ in the ways of working that would lead to creative products. To investigate this topic, Helson constructed the Mathematicians Q Sort, a set of 56 items based on the Gough and Woodworth instrument but adapted to include items suggested by mathematicians and also items designed to test hypotheses about differences between men and women. Using the Mathematicians Q Sort, creative men described their approach as more purposive, assertive, analytical, and masterful than all other mathematicians (male or female), whereas creative women, also differing from all other mathematicians, described theirs in terms of emotional brooding and reception of ideas from the unconscious. Both creative men and women were less orderly and more deeply interested in research than comparison subjects. Subsequent work with authors showed similar sex differences in the stylistic motive patterns of stories that were rated by expert judges as creative. The stylistic characteristics differentiating men and women were also found within each gender group. For example, among creative mathematicians, some men worked in a matriarchal way and some women worked in a patriarchal way. [*See* Gender Differences.]

C. Other Topics in the 1960s

Early in the 1960s Barron worked with Calvin Taylor in organizing conferences on creativity in science. He organized an assessment of innovative business leaders in Ireland, which was carried out by IPAR staff members in Dublin. Later he conducted a program of research in aesthetic education. Mendelsohn began a series of experimental studies of personality characteristics and other factors that affect the use of incidental cues in problem solving. Another line of activity in the late 1960s was the conceptualization of the skills involved in productive thinking by Crutchfield and the development of an educational program to encourage creative thinking.

IPAR was an important influence or context for a number of creativity researchers who spent extended visits there. Sarnoff Mednick developed the Remote Associates Test at IPAR and began work on his influential theory of the associative basis of the creative process. Morris B. Parloff and Lois-Ellin Datta worked at IPAR on their study of creativity across fields, and George S. Welsh, one of the originators of the Art Scale and known later for his theory of creativity and intelligence, visited on more than one occasion. Other repeat or long-term visitors with a special interest in creativity included William Schutz, who conducted and critiqued IPAR's group procedures and whose FIRO-B inventory was used in the study of architects; Robert H. Knapp, known for his work on the origins of American scientists, aesthetic preferences, and individual differences in sense of time; and Claudio Naranjo, a psychiatrist who studied new hallucinogenic drugs, personality types, and the spiritual quest. James Lester helped to organize an assessment at IPAR of the Americans who were to climb Mount Everest. Lester accompanied the expedition and wrote about it. These visitors helped to make IPAR a stimulating environment, as did the creative or innovative individuals who were assessed, the creative IPAR staff, and the shared task of exploring creative personality.

IV. THE 1970S AND 1980S: INDIVIDUAL PROGRAMS OF RESEARCH

A. Overview

Personality as a field of research came under a cloud in the 1970s, and funding was difficult. Crutchfield followed MacKinnon as director of IPAR in 1970, and after a brief period of poor health he was succeeded by Gough (1973–1984) and then Craik (1984–1988).

IPAR did not undertake any further assessment studies of highly creative persons. Several IPAR people pursued individual and less expensive ways of investigating creativity. For example, Mendelsohn continued his experimental studies of associative and attentional processes in creative performance, advancing the theory in 1976 that individual differences in how attention is focused are the key to differences in creativity. The wider the range of attention, he said, the more likely it is that one can make "the combinatorial leap which is generally described as the hallmark of creativity." [*See* ATTENTION.]

Craik and colleagues conducted research on humor, based on a Humorous Behavior Q-sort Deck. One of their findings was that overall "sense of humor" subsumes only a partial set of humor-related behaviors, in particular, socially constructive and competent forms of humorous conduct. Gough studied the progress of creative students in medical school, finding that they tended to drop out or go into psychiatry. Helson studied creative products (discussed later), and Feist for his dissertation taped interviews with a sample of West Coast scientists, also collecting supplemental data. Besides confirming the importance of intrinsic motivation, Feist found that an "arrogant working style" was related to scientific productivity. [*See* HUMOR; SCIENCE.]

B. Creative Product, Process, and Personality

According to MacKinnon, the IPAR program of research assumed that the product provided the essential evidence for creativity, but there was little articulation of how aspects of products might be related to creative process, personality, and social context. Helson conducted studies of carefully drawn samples of the published work of authors and critics. In each case she began with the development of coding forms, six to eight pages in length, that rater-analysts used to describe the themes, characters, motives, and stylistic features of the products. There was even a mini adjective checklist. She referred to this procedure as the personality assessment of products. The descriptions of the products—stories in the case of authors of imaginative literature for children and articles in the case of critics of children's literature—were cluster analyzed to identify stylistic-motive patterns. For example, the stories in-

cluded books such as *Charlotte's Web, The Hobbit,* and *Mary Poppins.* In a sample of about 100 stories, tender, heroic, and comic stylistic-motive patterns were found to be related in a complex but coherent pattern to gender and ratings of creativity (made by a separate panel of judges). In a historical study Helson reported that tender stories were popular in the Victorian period, animal and peer group stories in the Edwardian period, and heroic stories in the era after World War II. She gave a Jungian interpretation of this pattern: Creative imagination brought forth what was missing in the culture of the period.

In a second stage of this work, personality, life data, and professional Q sorts (to assess style and process) were obtained by mail from 54 authors and 59 critics, and the Q sorts were cluster analyzed. Thus tools were available to study relationships among product, work style, and personality. Authors of tender and heroic or comic fantasy, as well as authors differing in level of creativity, described their ways of working differently. Helson also studied differences in style among critics, using the Jungian functions of thinking, feeling, sensation, and intuition for this purpose. She analyzed criticism and gate keeping in children's literature during an era of transition from appreciation of imagination and fantasy to emphasis on the real-life difficulties faced by children. Critics who took the role of challenger (a stylistic-motive pattern based on a cluster analysis of the codings of articles by rater-analysts) scored lower in self-control (among other scales) on the CPI than critics who took the role of upholder of standards. On the Critics Q Sort, the challengers described themselves as more innovative and emotional and as less literary in values than the upholders.

V. THE 1990S: LONGITUDINAL STUDIES

Though the name of the institute was changed in 1992 to the Institute of Personality and Social Research (IPSR), some of the themes and values of the old IPAR continued. Among these were an interest in measures of creativity and in complex personological constructs. There have also been new developments: In the 1990s the longitudinal study of creativity began to take shape.

A. Tools

Gough published an article about the CPI creative Temperament Scale in 1992. He had published an ACL Creative Personality Scale in 1979, and both have been used in many studies. Helson and colleagues devised the Occupational Creativity Scale, intended to provide a measure of creativity in large heterogeneous samples of adults. Using the Mills sample (referred to later), they converted Holland's 1985 ranking of occupational interests in relation to creativity into a rough scale, which they extended in the creative direction on the basis of ratings of recognition accorded to individuals in artistic and investigative fields.

Q-sort prototypes to assess personality patterns associated with creativity were developed in the early 1990s. Autonomous narcissism was found to be related to creativity. Individuated, conflicted, and adapted types were additionally identified. Creative personality traits were positively correlated with the individuated type and negatively correlated with the adapted type.

B. Longitudinal Study of Creativity

Longitudinal study of creativity enables one to investigate problems such as what life outcomes are predicted by measures of creative potential, what factors predict creative productivity, the degree of consistency and change in creative personality, and how creativity is associated with personality development and personal growth through the life span.

A follow-up study of the IPAR architects, 25 years after the original study, found strong evidence for the persistence of creative style, motivation, and productivity into old age. Unlike many comparison subjects, the creative architects had not retired: They continued to be highly involved and successful in their work. [*See* PRODUCTIVITY AND AGE.]

Over a period of 34 years Gough collected personality data from graduate students in psychology, and later obtained ratings of their originality from faculty. These data provided the basis for the Creative Temperament Scale, mentioned earlier, and for identifying cognitive and personality characteristics related to creative work in psychology. Information on professional eminence was also gathered from a nationwide panel of raters. Preliminary findings suggest that unforesee-

able contingencies play an important role in the attainment of eminence in psychology. [*See* EMINENCE.]

The study of creativity in the Mills College classes of 1958 and 1960 became a longitudinal study of adult development. During their senior year, a total of 140 women were given tests and questionnaires, and 51 of these (women nominated for creative potential by the Mills faculty matched with comparison subjects) were invited in groups of 10 to the institute for assessment. The women were retested by mail at ages 27, 43, and 52, with further contact at age 60. As adults, some of the women were well-known novelists, choreographers, psychotherapists, journalists, and academics, whereas others were teachers, social workers, administrators, entrepreneurs, or housewives. The women's occupational creativity as scored at age 52 was predicted by many measures of creative traits at age 21. Thus, the data provided strong evidence for the enduringness of creative personality. However, there was also evidence of both sharp increases and decreases in creative temperament in individual women. These changes seemed to be associated with changes in their environments and relationships, which facilitated or interfered with their creative work. In the Mills sample, both creative potential (openness and unconventionality as assessed by four creativity measures at age 21) and creative achievement as assessed by the Occupational Creativity Scale were associated with intrapsychic personality growth—that is, an increase in characteristics such as tolerance of ambiguity and intellectuality. However, only creative achievement was associated with indicators of psychosocial development, such as achieved identity and generativity.

VI. CONCLUDING COMMENTS

The scope, richness, and vividness of the IPAR findings go beyond other early research programs. In 1953 MacKinnon said that theorizing and armchair model building had been pushed too far: What personality psychology needed was facts and hypotheses compatible with demonstrable empirical observations. The IPAR staff showed no lack of interest in theories, but the spirit of empirical exploration and the espousal of humanistic values were equally important. Theories were used to guide and interpret the research rather than to organize and dominate it. IPAR people never used the fewest possible measures; they reveled in the abundance and variety of measures that their procedures allowed, and they used this abundance to clarify important questions, such as the relation between creativity and psychopathology or the tension between self-expression and self-control in the creative process. The deficiencies in the IPAR studies of highly creative persons go along with the strengths. Their exploratory spirit was associated with a lack of the systematics expected today.

Today investigators in the field of personality tend to study motivational, cognitive, affective, or behavioral components of creativity rather than the creative personality as a whole. These studies have an important part to play in our understanding of creativity, and they are relatively inexpensive. In this low-budget era, does personality assessment have a future? It seems to have much to contribute to the study of creative lives through time. Personality traits and types are useful constructs for long-span studies, and longitudinal studies have a propitious set of economic realities: Because of the expense of studying the same individuals over time, it is practical to think in terms of many facets of the personalities and lives of participants and to collect measures of interest to different teams of individuals. To composite judgments of observers or raters remains a powerful way of describing personality. Thus longitudinal studies can maintain and extend at least some of the goals of personality assessment. Over the decades of its history, IPAR's researchers have studied creativity in both high-budget and low-budget ways. Their ideas, methods, and measures still have much to offer those who want to study personality in its complexity in quantitative ways.

Bibliography

Barron, F. (1965). The psychology of creativity. In T. M. Newcomb (Ed.), *New directions in psychology II*. New York: Holt, Rinehart & Winston.

Barron, F. (1968). *Creativity and personal freedom*. New York: Van Nostrand.

Gough, H. G. (1992). Assessment of creative potential in psychology and the development of a creative temperament scale for the CPI. In J. C. Rosen & P. McReynolds (Eds.), *Advances in psychological assessment* (vol. 8, p. 225). New York: Plenum.

Helson, R. (1982). Critics and their texts. *Journal of Personality and Social Psychology, 43,* 409.

Helson, R., Roberts, B. W., & Agronick, G. S. (1995). Enduringness and change in creative personality and the prediction of occupational creativity. *Journal of Personality and Social Psychology, 69,* 1173.

MacKinnon, D. W. (1962). The nature and nurture of creative talent. *American Psychologist, 17,* 484.

MacKinnon, D. W. (1975). IPAR's contribution to the conceptualization and study of creativity. In I. A. Taylor & J. W. Getzels (Eds.), *Perspectives in creativity*. Chicago: Aldine.

Intelligence

Robert J. Sternberg

Yale University

Convergent Production Production of a single correct or best response.

Crystallized Intelligence Intellectual skills that accumulate as a result of experience, such as vocabulary and general information.

Deliberate-Practice View of Creativity Elite levels of adult performance are the end result of a prolonged, deliberate effort to improve performance while negotiating motivational and external constraints.

Divergent Production The generation of a diverse assortment of appropriate responses to a problem, question, or task.

Factor Analysis A method of statistical decomposition that allows an investigator to infer distinct hypothetical constructs, elements, or structures that underlie a phenomenon.

Implicit Theories Constructions by people (whether psychologists or laypersons) that reside in the minds of these individuals. Such theories need to be discovered rather than invented because they already exist, in some form, in people's heads.

Investment Theory of Creativity The creative individual takes a buy-low, sell-high approach to ideas. In buying low, the creator initially sees the hidden potential of ideas that are pre-sumed by others to have little value. Once the idea has been developed and its value is recognized, the creator then sells high, moving on to other pursuits and looking for the hidden potential in other undervalued ideas.

Metacomponent A higher-order executive process used in planning, monitoring, and evaluating task performance.

Nonmetric Multidimensional Scaling A multivariate data-analytic technique that recovers the latent structure from a proximity or distance matrix.

Structure-of-Intellect (SI) Model The model specified that each ability had three components: the psychological operation, the content of the material dealt with, and the product configuration.

Theory of Multiple Intelligences A theory suggesting that intelligence comprises eight distinct constructs that function somewhat independently of one another but that may interact to produce intelligent behavior: bodily-kinesthetic, interpersonal, intrapersonal, linguistic, mathematical-logical, musical, naturalist, and spatial.

Three-Ring Model Joseph Renzulli has proposed a three-ring model whereby giftedness is at the intersection among above-average ability (as measured in the conventional ways), creativity, and task commitment. The circles for ability and creativity thus overlap.

INTELLIGENCE may be defined as the ability to purposively adapt to, shape, and select environments. Although there are many definitions of intelligence, they all

share at least some elements with this one. This defini-
tion immediately suggests that intelligence has at least
some connection to creativity. On the one hand, the
ability to adapt to the environment—to change oneself
to suit the environment—typically involves little or no
creativity and may even require one to suppress crea-
tivity, as when one realizes that adaptation to a school
or job environment means keeping one's creative ideas
to oneself at the risk of a low grade or job evaluation. On
the other hand, the ability to shape the environment does
involve creativity: Here, instead of changing oneself to
suit the environment, one changes the environment to
suit oneself. To do so requires a vision of what the envi-
ronment should be and of how this idealized environ-
ment can become a reality. Selecting a new environment
may also involve creativity, as when one realizes that a
given environment is not a good fit for oneself, and one
needs to imagine an environment that would be. Thus,
intelligence and creativity may be related but not identi-
cal constructs. Just what is the relation between the two
constructs? The five possible relations would seem to be
that creativity is a subset of intelligence, that intelligence
is a subset of creativity, that creativity and intelligence
are overlapping sets, that creativity and intelligence are
essentially the same thing (coincident sets), or that cre-
ativity and intelligence bear no relation at all (disjoint
sets). All of these relations have been proposed. The
most conventional view is probably that of overlapping
sets—that intelligence and creativity overlap in some
respects but not in others. But the other views deserve
serious attention as well. We shall consider each of the
relations in turn, realizing that these set relations are
idealizations that cannot possibly do justice to the com-
plexity and richness of extant theories of either intelli-
gence or creativity. We shall limit our consideration pri-
marily to theories and research on human intelligence,
although, of course, artificial intelligence also can pro-
vide key insights into the nature of creativity.

I. CREATIVITY AS A SUBSET OF INTELLIGENCE

One view of the relation between creativity and intelligence is that of creativity as a subset of intelligence.
Two very different theories seem to make such a claim.

A. Guilford's Structure-of-Intellect Model

J. P. Guilford had an enormous impact on the field
of creativity when, in 1950, he pointed out that creativity was a relatively neglected field of study, a claim
that has been made recently as well. Guilford almost
single-handedly created psychometric interest in the
study of creativity.

Guilford exemplified the view that creativity could
be understood as involving some of the facets of intelligence, and creativity could thus be seen as a subset of
intelligence, although Guilford, of course, recognized
other aspects as well. Guilford also pointed out the facets of his model of intelligence that involved creativity
were typically not measured by conventional tests of
intelligence (and, half a century later, still are not).

In his structure-of-intellect (SI) model, Guilford suggested three basic dimensions of intelligence, which
form a cube: operations (cognition, memory, divergent production, convergent production, evaluation),
content (figural, symbolic, semantic, behavioral), and
products (units, classes, relations, systems, transformations, implications). By crossing the 5 operations,
4 contents, and 6 products, one gets 120 factors (a
number Guilford increased in his later life). Most relevant for creativity is divergent production, which involves a broad search for information and the generation of numerous novel answers to problems (such as
finding unusual uses of a paper clip).

Guilford further broke down the kinds of abilities
involved in creative problem solving, including (a) sensitivity to problems (the ability to recognize problems),
(b) fluency, (c) flexibility, and (d) originality. These
abilities could be further broken down. For example,
Guilford distinguished among ideational fluency (the
ability to produce various ideas rapidly in response
to certain preset requirements), associational fluency
(the ability to list words associated with a given word),
and expressional fluency (the ability to organize words
into phrases or sentences). Similarly, flexibility could
be broken down into spontaneous flexibility (the ability to be flexible, even when it is not necessary to be
so) and adaptive flexibility (the ability to be flexible
when it is necessary, as in certain types of problem
solving). [*See* GUILFORD'S VIEW.]

Guilford devised a number of tests of creativity,

which were then adapted and expanded in the battery of Paul Torrance. For example, in the unusual-uses test, Guilford would ask people to think of unusual uses for common objects.

Guilford's approach has been enormously influential in the field of creativity, but today it has lost some of its appeal, in part because of studies by John Horn showing that the factor-analytic methods that Guilford used (or, to be more precise, his practice of rotating factor solutions in a way that maximized support for this theory) were probably invalid and grossly tended to capitalize on chance in favoring his theory. Tests such as Guilford's also seem only poorly to relate to other kinds of ratings of creativity.

Guilford's tests required people to do things (such as think of unusual uses of common items such as paper clips) that have seemed trivial to many investigators. Some investigators, such as Howard Gardner, have sought to look at what they believe to be more meaningful forms of creativity. [*See* APPENDIX II: TESTS OF CREATIVITY.]

B. Gardner's Theory of Multiple Intelligences

According to Howard Gardner, people can be intelligent in a variety of ways. For example, a poet is intelligent in a way that is different from the way that an architect is, who is intelligent in a way that is different from that of a dancer. What, exactly, is the nature of these differences?

Howard Gardner suggested in 1983 a theory of multiple intelligences (MI), according to which intelligence is not a unitary entity but rather a collection of eight distinct intelligences. These intelligences can be used in a variety of ways, including but not limited to creative ways. Thus, creative functioning is one aspect (a subset) of the multiple intelligences. The eight intelligences include (a) linguistic (as in writing a poem or a short story), (b) logical-mathematical (as in solving a logical or mathematical proof), (c) spatial (as in getting the "lay of the land" in a new city), (d) bodily-kinesthetic (as in dancing), (e) musical (as in composing a sonata or playing the cello), (f) interpersonal (as in finding an effective way to understand or interrelate to others), (g) intrapersonal (as in achieving a high level of self-understanding), and (h) naturalist (as in seeing complex patterns in the natural environment).

In 1993 Gardner analyzed the lives of seven individuals who made highly creative contributions in the 20th century, each specializing in one of the multiple intelligences: Sigmund Freud (intrapersonal), Albert Einstein (logical-mathematical), Pablo Picasso (spatial), Igor Stravinsky (musical), T. S. Eliot (linguistic), Martha Graham (bodily-kinesthetic), and Mahatma Gandhi (interpersonal). Charles Darwin would be an example of someone with extremely high naturalist intelligence. Gardner pointed out, however, that most of these individuals actually had strengths in more than one intelligence, and that they had notable weaknesses as well in others (e.g., Freud's weaknesses may have been in spatial and musical intelligences).

Although creativity can be understood in terms of uses of the multiple intelligences to generate new and even revolutionary ideas, Gardner's analysis goes well beyond the intellectual. For example, Gardner pointed out two major themes in the behavior of these creative giants: They tended to have a matrix of support at the time of their creative breakthroughs, and they tended to drive a "Faustian bargain" whereby they gave up many of the pleasures many people enjoy in life in order to attain extraordinary success in their careers. Gardner's theory thus underscores the importance of social and contextual factors in the expression of creativity.

Gardner further follows Mihalyi Csikszentmihalyi in distinguishing between the importance of the domain (the body of knowledge) and the field (the context in which this body of knowledge is studied and elaborated, including that of the persons working with the domain). Both are important to the development and, ultimately, the recognition of creativity. [*See* MULTIPLE INTELLIGENCES.]

II. INTELLIGENCE AS A SUBSET OF CREATIVITY

According to a second view, intelligence can be viewed as a subset of creativity. Creativity comprises intelligence plus other things, whatever these other things may be.

A. Sternberg and Lubart's Investment Theory

Creative people seem to have certain personal as well as intellectual attributes that distinguish them from noncreative people. But what might such attributes be?

A representative theory attempting to address this kind of question is Robert Sternberg and Todd Lubart's investment theory of creativity, proposed in 1995. According to this theory, creative people, like good investors, buy low and sell high. But their buying and selling is in the world of ideas. In particular, they generate ideas that—like stocks with low price-to-earnings ratios—are relatively unpopular or even openly disrespected. They attempt to convince other people of the worth of these ideas. Then they sell high, meaning that they let other people pursue their extant ideas while they move on to their next unpopular idea. [*See* ECONOMIC PERSPECTIVE ON CREATIVITY.]

Sternberg and Lubart argued that there are six main elements that converge to form creativity: intelligence, knowledge, thinking styles, personality, motivation, and the environment. Intelligence is thus just one of six forces that, in confluence, generate creative thought and behavior.

According to the theory, three aspects of intelligence are key for creativity: synthetic, analytical, and practical abilities. These three aspects are drawn from Sternberg's triarchic (three-part) theory of human intelligence, proposed in 1985. They are viewed as interactive and as working together in creative functioning.

Synthetic ability is the ability to generate ideas that are novel, high in quality, and task appropriate. Because creativity is viewed as an interaction between a person, a task, and an environment, what is novel, high in quality, or task appropriate may vary from one person, task, or environment to another.

The first key element of synthetic ability is what Sternberg referred to as a metacomponent, which is a higher-order executive process used in planning, monitoring, and evaluating task performance. This metacomponent is one of redefining problems. In other words, creative people may take problems that other people see in one way, and define them in a totally different way. In this sense, they defy the crowd. For example, they may decide that the fact that many of their friends are buying houses in a certain community in-

dicates not good value, but bad value, because houses in that community have already been bid up in price by high demand. Or they may take a problem they have seen in one way and redefine it. For example, they may decide that, rather than trying to make more money to meet expenses, they should instead lower their expenses. Redefining problems involves both an ability and an attitude—the ability to do it effectively, but also the attitude whereby one decided to do it in the first place.

Sternberg devised several tests of the ability to see problems in new ways. In one kind of problem, based on Nelson Goodman's so-called new riddle of induction, participants were taught about novel concepts, such as *grue* (green until the year 2000 and blue thereafter) and *bleen* (blue until the year 2000 and green thereafter). The participants were then tested on their ability to solve induction problems using these conventional concepts as well as novel concepts. Scores on these tests were moderately related to scores on conventional tests of fluid intelligence (i.e., tests of the ability to think flexibly and in novel ways, such as in solving geometric matrix problems). Most important, the information-processing component that seemed best to identify the creative thinkers involved flexibly switching back and forth between conceptual systems (green-blue, on the one hand, and grue-bleen, on the other).

Another type of item required participants to solve analogies and other kinds of induction problems, but with either factual premises (e.g., "Birds can fly") or counterfactual premises (e.g., "Sparrows can play hopscotch"). Scores on the counterfactual items were moderately related to scores on conventional fluid-intelligence tests, and the counterfactual items seemed to be the better measure of the ability to redefine conventional ways of thinking.

The synthetic part of intelligence as applied to creativity also involves three knowledge-acquisition components, or processes used in learning. These three processes, in the context of creativity, are bases of insightful thinking (*see* INSIGHT). They are called selective encoding, which involves distinguishing relevant from irrelevant information; selective combination, which involves relating new information to old information in novel ways. For example, Bohr's model of the atom as a miniature solar system was a selective comparison insight, relating the atom to the solar system, as was Freud's hydraulic model of the mind.

Sternberg and Janet Davidson tested this theory of insight in a variety of studies, including mathematical insight problems (e.g., "If you have blue socks and brown socks in drawer mixed in a ratio of 4 to 5, how many socks do you have to take out of the drawer in order to be assured of having a pair of the same color?"). They found that the three kinds of insights could be separated via different kinds of problems and that correlations between the insight problems and conventional tests of fluid intelligence were moderate. They also found that it was possible to teach elementary students to improve their insightful thinking.

The analytical part of intelligence—that which is measured in part by conventional tests of intelligence—is also involved in creativity. This ability is required to judge one's own ideas, and decide which of one's ideas are worth pursuing. Then, if a given idea is worth pursuing, analytical ability can further be used to evaluate the strengths and weaknesses of the idea and thereby to suggest ways in which the idea can be improved. People with high synthetic but low analytical abilities will probably need others to fulfill this judgmental role, lest they pursue their less rather than more valuable ideas.

The third intellectual ability involved in creativity is practical ability—the ability to apply one's intellectual skills in everyday contexts. Because creative ideas tend often to be rejected, it is very important for people who wish to have a creative impact to learn how to communicate their ideas effectively and how to persuade others of the value of their ideas. In essence, practical ability is involved in the selling of the idea, whether the idea is in the domain of art (where selling may be to a gallery or to potential purchasers or to critics), literature (where selling may be to a publisher or a public), science (where selling may be to relatively conservative scientific peers), or entrepreneurship (where selling may be to venture capitalists who are willing to fund only the most promising business innovations). Because creativity is in the interaction of the person, task, and environment, the failure to sell the idea properly may result in its never being dubbed creative or in its being recognized as creative only after the creator's death.

Sternberg and his collaborators suggested that because the analytical, synthetic, and practical aspects of abilities are only weakly related, students who are adept in one of these abilities might not benefit particularly from instruction aimed at another of the abilities, and in particular, creative students might not benefit particularly well from instruction as it is given in the schools, which typically emphasizes memory and analytical abilities. In an experiment, they found that high school students who were taught in a way that better matched their own pattern of abilities (e.g., analytic or synthetic) tended to achieve at higher levels than students who were taught in a way that more poorly matched their pattern of abilities.

It is important to say something of the role of knowledge in the investment theory, because knowledge is itself the basis of an important aspect of intelligence, sometimes called crystallized intelligence. According to the investment theory, knowledge is a double-edged sword. On the one hand, to advance a field beyond where it is, one needs the knowledge to know where the field is. Even reactions in opposition to existing ideas require knowledge of what those existing ideas are. On the other hand, knowledge can impede creativity by leading an individual to become entrenched. The individual can become so used to seeing things in a certain way that he or she starts to have trouble seeing them, or even imagining them, in any other way. The expert therefore may sacrifice flexibility for knowledge. There is actually evidence provided by Peter Frensch and Robert Sternberg that experts in a field may have more difficulty than novices adjusting to changes in the fundamental structure of the domain in which they are working.

Sternberg and Lubart tested the investment theory by asking people to generate creative products in four domains, choosing two from among a variety of topics they were given: writing (e.g., "The Keyhold," "2983"), art (e.g., "Earth from an Insect's Point of View," "Beginning of Time"), advertising (e.g., "Brussels sprouts," "Cuff links"), and science (e.g., "How could we know if there were extraterrestrial aliens hidden among us?"). They found only weak correlations across the four domains and moderate correlations of averaged ratings of creativity of products with tests of fluid intelligence, although the generality of creativity may depend in part on the population being tested.

III. CREATIVITY AND INTELLIGENCE AS OVERLAPPING SETS

Three basic findings concerning conventional conceptions of intelligence as measured by IQ and creativity are generally agreed on.

First, creative people tend to show above-average IQs, often above 120. This figure is not a cutoff, but rather an expression of the fact that people with low or even average IQs do not seem to be well represented among the ranks of highly creative individuals.

Second, above an IQ of 120, IQ does not seem to matter as much to creativity as it does below 120. In other words, creativity may be highly correlated with IQ below an IQ of 120, but only weakly or not all correlated with it above IQ 120. In 1926 Catherine Cox estimated the IQs of 301 "geniuses" in history, and found the IQs to be very high, averaging 165 (a value attained by only a small fraction of 1% of the general population). Ann Roe reached a similar conclusion in 1952 with regard to scientists. Of course, these estimates, based on ages of childhood at which the individuals had reached certain intellectual achievements, are suspect. Nevertheless, these estimates, even if correct, suggest that extremely highly creative people often have high IQs, but not necessarily that people with high IQs tend to be extremely creative.

Some investigators, such as Dean Simonton and Robert Sternberg, have suggested that very high IQ may actually interfere with creativity: Those who have very high IQs may be so highly rewarded for their IQ-like (analytical) skills that they fail to develop the creative potential within them, which may then remain latent.

Third, the correlation between IQ and creativity is variable, usually ranging from weak to moderate. The correlation depends in part on what aspects of creativity and intelligence are being measured, and how they are being measured.

A. The Three-Ring Model

These facts suggests another conceptualization of the relation between creativity and intelligence whereby the two overlap (e.g., creative people need a certain IQ level) but are nonidentical. Joseph Renzulli, for example, has proposed a three-ring model whereby giftedness is at the intersection among above-average ability (as measured in the conventional ways), creativity, and task commitment. The circles for ability and creativity thus overlap.

Renzulli distinguished between "schoolhouse" and "creative-productive" giftedness, noting that to be gifted in the one way does not necessarily imply giftedness in the other. Schoolhouse giftedness is conventional giftedness in IQ, whereas creative-productive giftedness is giftedness in the generation of creative ideas. The people gifted in the two ways are often different. We therefore need to be very careful in using conventional IQ tests to identify the gifted, because we are likely to miss the creatively productive gifted.

B. Implicit Theories

Another approach that has suggested an overlapping-circles model for creativity and intelligence makes use of people's implicit theories, or folk conceptions, of intelligence and creativity. Robert Sternberg asked laypeople as well as specialists in four fields (physics, philosophy, art, and business) to give information that, through a data-analytic technique called nonmetric multidimensional scaling, could yield their implicit theories of creativity and intelligence (as well as wisdom).

Sternberg found that people's implicit theories of creativity seemed to involve eight main components: (a) nonentrenchment (seeing things in novel ways), (b) integration and intellectuality, (c) aesthetic taste and imagination, (d) decisional skill and flexibility, (e) perspicacity, (f) drive for accomplishment and recognition, (g) inquisitiveness, and (h) intuition. Their implicit theories of intelligence involved six components: (a) practical problem-solving ability, (b) verbal ability, (c) intellectual balance and integration, (d) goal orientation and attainment, (e) contextual intelligence (i.e., intelligence in their everyday environments), and (f) fluid thought. The two constructs are thus seen to have some overlap, for example, in the importance of setting an reaching goals and in thinking in flexible (fluid) and nonentrenched ways. When people were asked to rate hypothetically described individuals in terms of their creativity and intelligence, Sternberg found moderate relations between ratings of the people's creativity and intelligence.

IV. CREATIVITY AND INTELLIGENCE AS COINCIDENT SETS

Some researchers have argued that the mechanisms underlying creativity are no different from those underlying normal problem solving of the kind involved in problems that do not seem, on their surface, to involve any need for creative thinking. According to these investigators, work is adjudged as creative when ordinary processes yield extraordinary results. David Perkins referred to this view as the nothing-special view. According to this view, if we want to understand creativity, we need look no further than to studies of ordinary problem solving.

For example, Robert Weisberg and a colleague had people solve the notorious nine-dot problem, in which people are asked to connect all of the dots in three rows of three dots using no more than four straight lines, never arriving at a given dot twice, and never lifting the pencil from the page. The problem can be solved only if people allow their line segments to go outside the periphery of the dots. Typically, solution of this task had been viewed as hinging on the insight that one had to go outside the periphery of the dots. Weisberg and Alba showed that even when people were given the insight, they still had difficulty in solving the problem. In other words, whatever is required to solve the nine-dot problem, it is not just some kind of extraordinary insight. [*See* PROBLEM SOLVING.]

V. CREATIVITY AND INTELLIGENCE AS DISJOINT SETS

Recently, some investigators, such as Anders Ericsson, have suggested that creativity and intelligence may be disjoint. According to this view, expertise of any kind, including creative expertise, develops as a result of deliberate practice, whereby an individual practices with a mind to improve his or her performance. Creative expertise thus is not really an ability at all but rather a result of deliberate practice in a domain, and particularly in doing creative work in a domain. Indeed, many researchers have spoken of the 10-year rule, whereby significant creative production seems to require ten years of active work in a field.

Ericsson and his colleagues have done a number of studies showing that expertise of various kinds does indeed seem to correlate with deliberate practice. In a variety of fields, deliberate practice is correlated with eminence. At the present time, however, the evidence is largely correlational, meaning that it is difficult to assess the causal chain. It may be, for example, that people with creative or other talent are more motivated to engage in deliberate practice than are those without such talent. Nevertheless, the deliberate-practice view of creativity cannot be ruled out, and clearly, deliberate practice facilitates creative work and may even be necessary for it, whether or not it is also sufficient. [*See* EXPERTISE.]

VI. CONCLUSION

At the very least, creativity seems to involve synthetic, analytical, and practical aspects of intelligence: synthetic to come up with ideas, analytical to evaluate the quality of those ideas, and practical to formulate a way of effectively communicating those ideas and of persuading people of their value. But beyond the basics, it is difficult to find substantial agreement among those working in the field.

Despite a substantial body of research, psychologists still have not reached a consensus on the nature of the relation between creativity and intelligence, nor even of exactly what these constructs are. All possible set relations between creativity and intelligence have been proposed, and there is at least some evidence to support each of them. The negative side of this state of affairs is that we can say little with certainty about the relation between creativity and intelligence. The positive side is that for those seeking an important, open research question, that of the relation between creativity and intelligence is worth considering. The question is theoretically important, and its answer probably affects the lives of countless children and adults. We therefore need elucidation of good answers as soon as possible.

Acknowledgments

The work reported herein was supported under the Javits Act program (Grant #R206R50001) as administered by the Office of Educational Research and Improvement, U.S. Department of Education. The findings and opinions expressed in this report do not reflect the positions or policies of the office of Educational Research and Improvement or the U.S. Department of Education.

Bibliography

Amabile, T. M. (1996). *Creativity in context.* Boulder, CO: Westview.

Boden, M. (1991). *The creative mind: Myths and mechanisms.* New York: Basic Books.

Boden, M. (Ed.). (1994). *Dimensions of creativity.* Cambridge, MA: MIT Press.

Csikszentmihalyi, M. (1996). *Creativity.* New York: Harper Collins.

Gardner, H. (1993). *Creating minds.* New York: Basic Books.

Ochse, R. (1990). *Before the gates of excellence.* New York: Cambridge University Press.

Simonton, D. K. (1994). *Greatness: Who makes history and why?* New York: Guilford.

Sternberg, R. J., & Lubart, T. I. (1995). *Defying the crowd: Cultivating creativity in a culture of conformity.* New York: The Free Press.

Weisberg, R. W. (1993). *Creativity: Beyond the myth of genius.* New York: Freeman.

Intuition

Emma Policastro

Harvard University

Combinatorial Explosion The outcome of an unlimited universe of combinations. With free rein, the number of possible combinations quickly becomes astronomical.
Divergent Thinking The ability to produce a large quantity of unusual associations in a short period of time
Tacit Knowledge Information that can influence thinking and acting without conscious awareness.

INTUITION *may be defined as a tacit form of knowledge that orients decision making in a promising direction. In the context of problem solving, a promising direction is one that leads to potentially effective outcomes. In the context of innovation, a promising direction is one that leads to potentially creative results.*

I. INTUITIVE DECISION MAKING

In recent years scholars have highlighted the role of intuition in complex decision making in various fields, such as chess playing, counseling, management, medical diagnosis, nursing, piloting, military leadership, firefighting, and operating nuclear power plants.

In fact, experts can size up situations quickly and accurately, while they react to patterns of subtle cues that together signal an effective course of action and while they tacitly consider the overall conditions and restrictions of a given context. For example, expert chess players can engage in masterful performances, even when they play at the rate of one move every 5 to 10 seconds. At that speed, they must rely mostly on intuition, because there is no time for analyzing and comparing options. Research on scores of American executives also shows that they frequently rely on intuition to make important decisions. As we all know, huge sums can be at stake in making such choices, and many successful executives state that in most circumstances their initial hunches prove to be right. Furthermore, top executives consistently show stronger intuitive skills than middle or low-level managers. [*See* EXPERTISE.]

Intuition may even have a biological basis. Researchers who compared brain-damaged patients to a control group of normal subjects demonstrated that normal subjects showed intuition—defined as a physiological reaction to the anticipated consequences of good and bad decisions—long before they were consciously aware that they had made a decision, whereas the brain-damaged patients did not show the same reaction. Other studies indicate that when people are asked to conduct an explicit analysis of the reasons for their preferences or to evaluate the potential options thoroughly, their decisions may end up being less effective.

As we all know, intuition is only one source, among others, to guide decision making. Thus, we may ask, under which circumstances is it most useful? Intuition seems to be most useful when there are high stakes, a high level of uncertainty, and pressure to make the right decision in a limited amount of time.

We may readily think of professional settings in which these conditions apply: a physician in an emergency room, a chess player participating in a world championship, a military commander in the midst of a heated battle, an entrepreneur seizing a unique opportunity in the run. Under such circumstances, if individuals had to carefully analyze each potential alternative before deciding what to do, they would not achieve their goals in any practical amount of time. In fact, sometimes the real dilemma may be limited to the following two options: (a) not to make the decision, because time will run out before the person can analyze each alternative thoroughly, or (b) to follow a hunch that provides some sense of direction toward promising results.

Intuitions, of course, are not infallible. They are more like rough estimates, which necessarily entail some margin of error. This is scarcely to say that they are worthless: Statistical predictions also entail various margins of error, yet we rely on them for important purposes. The difference is that we know little about how intuition works, under which circumstances it may (or may not) be useful, or how to reduce its margin of error.

II. CREATIVE INTUITION

Some individuals seem to have an intuitive sense, as they begin their creative work, about what their final product will be like. Indeed, evidence from several sources confirms the role of intuition in the creative processes of artists and scientists; among these sources are autobiographical testimonies, analyses of historical evidence, psychometric assessments, and experimental studies. In combination, this evidence supports the notion that early intuitions may guide decision making in the process of attaining creative results. But at least three issues remain. First, there may be various forms of intuition. Second, there may also be various forms of creativity. Third, it might well be the case that only certain forms of intuition are related to certain forms of creativity. It is important to develop a clear conceptual framework for distinguishing various forms of intuition as well as for explaining whether and to what extent they interact with one another and with various forms of creativity.

It is also relevant to distinguish intuition from insight, although the two phenomena sometimes overlap. Intuition entails vague and tacit knowledge, whereas insight involves sudden, and usually clear, awareness. In the context of creativity, intuition may precede insight. [*See* INSIGHT.]

Earlier intuition was defined as a tacit form of knowledge that orients decision making in a promising direction. In the context of innovation, a promising direction is one that leads to potentially creative outcomes. For example, Nobel laureates in physics, chemistry, and medicine refer to their own scientific intuition as "a metaphorical seeing of the phenomenon searched for, an anticipatory perception of its shape or its gross structure."

The time line between an early intuition and its final articulation might vary from a brief period to many years, depending on various factors, such as the nature of the problem or the subject's knowledge base. Jean Piaget, for instance, commenting on the creative process of Charles Darwin, said that he found two results most interesting: the time that Darwin needed to become aware of ideas already implicit in his thought, and the passage from the implicit to the explicit in the creation of new ideas. In fact, Darwin seems to have implicitly prefigured some of his most relevant ideas in his early writings. Highly creative individuals in other domains, such as Picasso (visual arts), Freud (psychoanalysis), and Cantor (mathematics), appear to have moved along their own creative processes in a similar sequence—starting off with generative intuitions and ending up with more explicitly ariticulated products after long periods of persistent work. [*See* FREUD, SIGMUND.]

This leads us to a further question. If some individuals have an early intuitive sense about what their final product will be like, why does it take them any longer to reach the ultimate goal? In other words, how can we explain a creative process in which the beginning is in a way also the end, given that we have a tacit estimate of the end state right from the start?

Perhaps the creative process unfolds as a developmental sequence of representational changes, from vague, syncretic, and implicit forms of knowledge into more differentiated, integrated, and explicit ones. In more technical terms, it is conceivable, at least, that the creative process might operate as a developmental translation—from an implicit code of associative strengths among neural units into an explicit code of symbolic rules. In this cognitive system, implicit neural networks might precede and constrain the generation of symbolic rules.

III. INTUITION AS CONSTRAINT

A number of scholars hold that divergent thinking (multidirectional and open ended) is the essential feature of the creative process. But, we may wonder, what prevents divergent thinking from becoming mere rambling as the person considers an infinite sequence of potential alternatives? [*See* DIVERGENT THINKING.]

As we all know, any creative process involves a long series of choices: each decision one makes will affect future options, and one's alternatives at any given point will depend on previous decisions. If individuals had to consider each option that arises in any creative search, the growth of alternatives would become astronomical. In other words, the sequence would lead to what cognitive scientists call a "combinatorial explosion," and it is very unlikely that the creative process would get to the desired result in any reasonable amount of time.

Creative intuitions may fulfill an important cognitive function: By setting the preliminary boundaries for promising exploration, these initial intuitions may keep the creator's divergent thinking from generating a combinatorial explosion. That is why creative intuition may be technically defined as a tacit form of knowledge that broadly constrains the creative search by setting its preliminary scope.

Although cognitive scientists have widely acknowledged the need to check a combinatorial explosion in a problem space, they have not considered intuition as a potential constraint for the creative search. Instead, they have focused on heuristics.

Creative intuitions may fulfill a similar role to that of heuristics by making the search for possible solutions more selective and efficient. Heuristics, however, are explicit rules of thumb, or particular strategies that, for example, deliberately move away from an old path and look for conflicts and resolve them. Conversely, creative intuitions appear to be implicit rough estimates of the final solution or goal, and advances in this problem space might be measured in terms of how close the subject is to achieving a clear symbolic representation. [*See* HEURISTICS.]

Creative intuition has always been difficult to define, explain, and measure. Conceptualizing it in terms of search in a problem space may be a valid and operational alternative for investigating this phenomenon. But it still leaves many questions unanswered.

IV. GENERATIVE COGNITIVE STYLE

Individuals with high levels of expertise are endowed with a rich, well-organized, and automatically accessible knowledge base, which allows them to perform intuitively and effectively in their own domains of expertise. The relationship between creativity and domain expertise has been consistently reported. In a general sense, this *has* to be true. Making a valuable contribution to any domain necessarily implies discerning what is important from what is not important within that same domain (knowing *what*). It also implies a skillful use of the tools and techniques that are available and permissible to particular disciplines (knowing *how*). Studies on human cognition indicate that experts tend to perform intuitively in their own domains of expertise. The question remains: "Why does domain-specific knowledge lead some experts to generate creative intuitions, whereas the same constraints lead other experts to generate performances that are competent, but not creative?"

Perhaps the response is that there are individual differences in cognitive style, which influence the way we encode, organize, and retrieve information. Thus, even if two subjects are experts in the same domain, they might each be responding to a different set of subjectively constructed parameters. More specifically, experts who show a *generative cognitive style* seem to be more likely to produce creative intuitions, compared to their peers. [*See* COGNITIVE STYLE AND CREATIVITY.]

The generative cognitive style involves three components: (a) imagination, (b) intrapersonal intelligence, and (c) sense of domain relevance.

A. Imagination

Imagination is a form of playful analogical thinking that draws on previous experiences but combines them in unusual ways, generating new patterns of meaning. Considerable evidence demonstrates that a playful approach to the task at hand increases the likelihood of producing creative results. [*See* IMAGINATION.]

Obviously, logical thinking with its rigorous rules does not leave room for free play, whereas imaginative thinking does allow for playful associations to occur within contextual constraints, leading to the generation of potentially creative intuitions.

It is important to distinguish imagination from fantasy, given that many scholars use both words interchangeably, generating unwarranted confusion. Imagination should denote the generation of new patterns of meaning that are contextually valid and that serve an adaptive function toward reality. Conversely, fantasy should denote the subjective expression of needs, conflicts, and wishes. It may also serve an adaptive function, but in a different way, because it contributes to the subject's intrapsychic equilibrium, in the Freudian sense.

Imagination may lead to creative intuitions. Fantasy may lead to illusory intuitions, and this leads us to intrapersonal intelligence, the second component of a generative cognitive style.

B. Intrapersonal Intelligence

Intrapersonal intelligence allows a person to understand his or her own intrapsychic life, effecting subtle discriminations among different aspects of it. Distinguishing creative intuitions from other psychological processes seems to entail a fine intrapersonal intelligence. If not, how can a person make subtle distinctions between imagination and fantasy, between intuitive tendencies and emotional reactions, or between generative intuitions and intuitive misconceptions? For example, a given subject may claim an intuition that "this will work out fine." Nevertheless, what this person may be in fact expressing is an illusion, a wish, or a feeling rather than a creative intuition, and without enough intrapersonal intelligence, he or she may be unable to tell the difference.

In other words, intrapersonal intelligence may help us to distinguish among "the lunatic, the lover, and the poet" inside ourselves, since they may appear to be "of imagination all compact", as Shakespeare pointed out.

C. Sense of Domain Relevance

Individuals who produce creative intuitions also seem to have a flair for distinguishing what is important from what is not, in generative ways. Henri Poincaré, for instance, says that "sterile combinations do not even present themselves to the mind of the inventor." And Albert Einstein is quoted as saying, "In physics I soon learned to scent out that which was able to lead to fundamentals and to turn aside from everything else, from the multitude of things that clutter up the mind and divert it from the essential."

Research shows that a special sensitivity for encoding, combining and comparing the most relevant information is associated with creativity. In fact, major scientists outperform their less able peers at (a) sifting out relevant information, (b) fitting the facts together in coherent ways, and (c) making generative connections between their own work and the relevant work of others in the field. Thus, the creative process of these very talented subjects appears to be informed by a special *sense of domain relevance,* or selective information processing.

In sum, experts tend to perform intuitively in their own domains of expertise, but they may differ in their propensity for developing creative intuitions. Experts who show a generative cognitive style may be more likely to produce creative intuitions, compared to their peers. This generative cognitive style involves three components: imagination, intrapersonal intelligence, and sense of domain relevance. Imagination leads to originality, a sense of domain relevance leads to high quality, and intrapersonal intelligence checks illusory or emotional interferences in the process of constructing a novel representation.

V. CONCLUSION

Some researchers consider the scientific study of intuition impossible; they view it as an esoteric phenomenon, a form of ESP, or just erratic nonsense. Dictionary definitions do not help the scientific cause, as intuition tends to be defined as the power of knowing something without reasoning or learned skill.

Contrary to such definitions, the current technical conception of intuition implies that it arises from knowledge and experience. It also implies that intuition involves a form of information processing that might be more implicit than explicit, but which is not at all irrational. Domain-specific expertise, generative cognitive style, and multilevel information processing may help us understand creative intuition from a scientific perspective.

It is important to disentangle intuition from overly mysterious connotations so that we can develop a scientific perspective for studying it. Further research into this phenomenon may have relevant implications for the field of creativity.

Bibliography

Agor, W. (1986). *The logic of intuitive decision making: A research-based approach for top management.* New York: Quorum Books.

Agor, W. (1989). *Intuition in organizations: Leading and managing productively.* Newbury Park, CA: Sage.

Bechara, A., Damasio, H., Tranel, D., & Damasio, A. R. (1997). Deciding advantageously before knowing the advantageous strategy. *Science, 275,* 1293–1295.

Bowers, K. S., Farvolden, P., & Mermigis, L. (1995). Intuitive antecedents of insight. In S. Smith, T. Ward & R. Finke (Eds.), *The creative cognition approach.* Cambridge, MA: MIT Press.

Davidson, J. E., & Sternberg, R. J. (1984). The role of insight in intellectual giftedness. *Gifted Child Quarterly, 28,* 58–64.

Dreyfus, H. L., & Dreyfus, S. E. (1986). *Mind over machine: The power of human intuition and expertise in the era of the computer.* New York: The Free Press.

Gardner, H., & Nemirovsky, R. (1991). From private intuitions to public symbol systems. *Creativity Research Journal, 4,* 1.

Klein, G. (1998). *Sources of power: How people make decisions.* Cambridge, MA: The MIT Press.

Policastro, E. (1995). Creative intuition: An integrative review. *Creativity Research Journal, 8,* 99–113.

Simonton, D. K. (1980). Intuition and analysis: A predictive and explanatory model. *Genetic Psychology Monographs, 102,* 3–60.

Wilson, T. D., & Schooler, J. W. (1991). Thinking too much: Introspection can reduce the quality of preferences and decisions. *Journal of Personality and Social Psychology, 60,* 181–192.

Invention

Michael Hertz*

University of Virginia

Evolutionary Invention The idea that all technological advancements have gone through a step-by-step change from an antecedent. A support of evolutionary invention would state that invention is nothing more than the coming together of known parts into new configurations.

Mental Model A representation of an object or how an object functions. It allows an inventor to break a problem up and work on individual sections of the problem space. A mental model is also dynamic, meaning that an inventor can manipulate parts and see if the object behaves differently. It can be incomplete in certain areas, suggesting where work needs to be done.

*In close collaboration with Dr. Michael E. Gorman.

Problem Space The space of all possible solutions to an invention problem. The problem space contains all the restrictions that must be filled by the new creation. The term is also generally used to represent any domain of expertise that an inventor or scientist might mentally go through in search of an answer to a specific problem.

Revolutionary Invention The notion that invention can involve radical changes. For a revolutionary invention to occur, it must be something more than the coming together of parts; it must be radically different from an antecedent.

Technological Momentum A term used by Thomas Hughes to illustrate how previous experience and applications cause society to be more willing to stick with an old idea than go with a new one. The longer an idea has been accepted as being true, the more momentum it has. The term also connotes the idea that technologies begin to define how inventors look at problems. This is one reason that technology progresses incrementally.

INVENTION, *as defined by Webster's dictionary, is a device, contrivance, or process originated after study and experimentation. Another definition of invention comes from the Patent Office, which states that invention is something that is novel and useful:* novel, *meaning something that someone skilled in the particular field would not know, and* useful, *meaning that it has some practicality.*

I. INTRODUCTION

The term *invention* can function as both a noun and a verb. In the verb form, the act of invention contains a much broader definition and is harder to give a concrete description than for the noun form. Invention as a verb can be described with additional terms: evolutionary and revolutionary. Evolutionary invention is invention by iteration; one step is followed by another one with a slight but definite change. Revolutionary invention, as the name implies, is the progress of invention in great leaps. Invention as a noun can be broken up into three basic types. The first type is probably the most obvious: the artifact. By artifact is meant an actual physical object. The next type of invention is a system. A system represents a manner of doing a certain activity. The last type of invention is a process. An example of a process would be the invention of factory automation by Henry Ford.

Operationally, invention can be defined as any object, idea, or process that is protected by a patent. The process of obtaining a patent is quite lengthy and it ensures that no two people can have a patent protecting the same idea. In a very basic and general sense, to obtain a patent one must show how the proposed object meets the Patent Office's definition of a new invention. The patent process ensures the holder of the patent that no one can use the ideas or processes without receiving some sort of permission from the patent holder. However, to obtain a patent, the person must provide written documentation of every aspect that goes into the object or process. The patent protection does not last forever either. There is a time limit at which anyone who wishes can use the patented object. Thus the patent system not only helps protect intellectual property, it stimulates development.

Thomas Hughes held that any invention or object is contained in a much larger framework. For Hughes, invention is a social process in which almost every decision is linked not only to the previous technology but also to the social aspects of the inventor.

Hughes argued that as systems grow, they start to develop momentum. This momentum makes changing the way a certain process is completed very difficult. He attributes the momentum of systems to why people are reluctant to change over to a new way of doing things. For instance, people were reluctant to

follow Einstein's understanding of the universe because it went against everything they had ever been taught. Hughes referred to the phenomenon of when people's previous knowledge is no longer valid as "deskilling" someone. Hughes gives the example of how in the 1920s an inventor developed a radical new method for refining gasoline. The major oil companies rejected the proposals because they went against everything they had learned and the technological momentum of the current way of refining gasoline was too great for them to simply abandon their current methods. However, when a company did start to use the new method, the increased yields, and therefore profit, caused the other major companies to change their methods of refining as well. The success of the new method deskilled those trained before and changed the course of the technological momentum from what it had been to a completely new direction.

II. INVENTION AND DISCOVERY

A primary distinction that must be drawn is between the terms *invention* and *discovery*. Invention can be described as something that is novel and that has not been done before. It is something that arises from existing objects. Discovery, on the other hand, refers to an object or principle that becomes known for the first time. To be sure, there are aspects of discovery in invention, and sometimes one must invent to discover, but in general they are separate and distinct. To invent something, one must simply uncover what is hidden in the physical world and use the newly acquired knowledge. Inventors sometimes have to discover. For example, when experiments with a glider in 1901 failed to meet expectations, the Wright brothers constructed a wind tunnel and refuted the widely accepted value for the coefficient of lift. To invent an airplane, they needed to discover new coefficients. In many ways, the Wright brothers did more than just disprove the coefficient of lift, they helped add evidence to debunk the myth that "science discovers and engineering applies." The Wright brothers showed that engineers must also discover if they are to be successful. Carl Mitcham may have said it best by observing that "invention causes things to come into existence from ideas, makes the world conform to thought; whereas science by deriving ideas from observation, makes thought conform to existence."

At the heart of the issue of the difference between invention and discovery is whether or not science precedes invention. The Wright brothers' example demonstrates that there are indeed instances in which science does set the precedent for an invention to follow. However, there are a number of instances in which an invention is created, and only then are the properties behind the invention discovered. In 1884 Paul Nipkow, a German inventor, was trying to develop a way to convert pictures to signals that could then be sent through a wire. What he discovered, in his failed attempt to make a scanning machine, was that light would not always act like waves but sometimes acted like little packets of energy. The packets of energy were not a function of the intensity of the light, but rather its frequency. It was not until Einstein's discovery of the photoelectric effect that this phenomenon was explained. By simple inductive reasoning, it can be concluded that while one sometimes has to discover to invent, it is not mandatory—science does not have to precede invention. [*See* DISCOVERY.]

III. INVENTION AND DESIGN

Another distinction that needs to be made is between invention and design. Arnold Pacey stated, "Invention is creation of a new form, while design is the adapting of existing forms to present constraints." In contrast, it has been stated that to design is to invent. Designing often entails taking objects that already exist and arranging them into some sort of useful object. It has been suggested that anytime someone looks at an object and thinks of how the parts could be arranged into different forms and therefore adopted into a "reasonably obvious alternative," they have both designed and invented an object. [*See* DESIGN.]

IV. EVOLUTIONARY PROGRESSION OF INVENTION

Because of the fact that inventions and designs are tied into the temporal realm, one can make easy assertions about how each one has a precursor that is modi-

fied to make the present object. George Kubler said, "All things and acts and symbols or the whole of human experience consists of replicas, gradually changing by the mind's alterations more than by abrupt leaps of invention."

One of the principal advocates of the evolutionary advancement of technology is George Basalla. He argued that technology is the summation of previously invented ideas. Basalla stated that one can "define invention as combining existing and known elements of culture in order to form a new element. The outcome of the process is a series of small changes, most of them patentable but none of them constituting a sharp break with past material." Basalla also felt that the speed at which technology proceeds is tied into the past developments. Not only is invention a successive line tying into all that has come before it, it is also speeding up because the amount of previous material is growing exponentially. This acceleration of invention development can be explained by the term *biassociation*. Biassociation is the unconscious coming together of previously disparate ideas. The more blocks one has to build with, the more new objects one can create.

Basalla acknowledged that there is some strong support of the idea of revolutionary invention. He stated:

> The source of this outlook is threefold: the loss or concealment of crucial antecedent; the emergence of the inventor as a hero; and the confusion of technological and socioeconomic changes. The theory boils down to the idea that the reason why objects appear to look revolutionary is because their antecedents are either not obvious, hidden or lost.

If those who study invention were able to have all previous antecedents, then it would become obvious that technology has moved in a straightforward and continuous fashion.

Another one of Basalla's ideas that is of considerable importance is the notion that there may be a tendency to think that technology is a process that cannot be stopped. Basalla wanted to emphasize that the role of the inventor is not removed from the situation. Basalla was not taking anything away from an inventor who makes something great; he was just arguing that great invention is an incremental process built on previous work. In other words, technological progression may be more a function of previous work and thought than of individual inventors.

V. REVOLUTIONARY PROGRESSION OF INVENTION

The notion of incremental inventions that is highlighted by Basalla is only one way to look at the process of invention. Thomas Kuhn believed that progress in science could occur in revolutionary fashion. He stated that a previous paradigm is replaced only when a competing paradigm is able to demonstrate that it is superior. This idea is substantially different from the evolutionary view, because that view held that a newer idea emerges incrementally from an older one; the old and new paradigms are incommensurable. An adherent of the older view cannot even understand the newer one. For Kuhn, this is unlikely in revolutionary science. Kuhn drew a distinction between revolutionary and normal science. Normal science, for Kuhn, is how most of science progresses. It is normal science that leads to the iterative look of a progression of artifacts. In periods of crisis, however, one does not give up on one idea and slowly move to another. Rather, one makes leaps from the old and now invalid ideas, to the newer ones. Kuhn stated "that scientific revolutions are here taken to be those noncumulative developmental episodes in which an older paradigm is replaced in whole or in part by an incompatible new one."

An example of this notion can be demonstrated by the revolution Einstein started with his theory of generalized relativity. Before Einstein, the scientific community thought that Newtonian physics was what governed the universe. Science had to accept that observations led to discrepancies with the predictions of Newtonian physics because there were no other theories that made predictions as well. However, once Einstein published his theories, there was a dramatic paradigm shift from Newtonian physics to Einsteinian physics. There were, of course, some people who did not immediately subscribe to the new theory, but eventually everyone held that Einstein was correct. Similarly, this was the case before the invention of the telephone was seen as the obvious, efficient way to send messages over wires.

VI. CORPORATE INVENTOR VERSUS THE HEROIC INVENTOR

It has been noted that solo inventors lead revolutionary inventions, whereas corporate inventors lead to secondary, evolutionary inventions. For instance, the telegraph companies did not invent the telephone. Nor did gas companies invent the electric light. The invention came from a man not familiar with the industry which displaced or improved the old industry. As outsiders, the innovators were not bound by any precedent or prejudice.

An outsider can effect the greatest deal of change in an industry. Large corporations are tied down by what they have already done and what they already know. Corporations often do not branch out from their core family of ideas; their inventions and innovations are relatively related.

However, to assume that corporations are unable to generate radical inventions is false. The development of the transistor is a good example how a corporation can work within its core business but still generate "world changing" inventions. The transistor was developed to replace vacuum tubes in electrical components. Bell Laboratories, to help the transmission quality of long-distance telephone wires, specifically developed the transistor to act as a repeater to boost signal strength. However humble the original impetus behind the transistor, it revolutionized electrical devices. It allowed for better reliability and for miniaturization of electrical systems. In the end, it can be stated quite firmly that this corporate invention was revolutionary in its field.

A. Heroic Inventor: Alexander Graham Bell

The relative freedom of independent inventors has been suggested as a reason why they so often are able to create radical changes in the way things are done. An inventor who works for a company generally creates inventions that will benefit the core products of the company. Independent inventors do not have to face this burden.

An archetypal example of an independent inventor who was able to risk pursuing a radical invention is Alexander Graham Bell. He was not an expert in electricity like a great deal of his competitors when he created the telephone. Neither did Bell have a huge research lab with numerous assistants. Instead, Bell was an expert in human speech and did most of his experiments himself. For his mental model of how the telephone would work, Bell used his expertise in human anatomy and tried to model the way nature functioned into a physical object; to direct his experiments, Bell used the "analogy of Nature." In the end, Bell's solo approach won out over others who may have exhibited expertise in more pertinent fields or who had more resources to devote to the task. For these reasons, Bell is often looked at as the archetypal heroic inventor. [*See* BELL, ALEXANDER GRAHAM.]

B. Corporate Inventor: Thomas Edison

To find an example of the "corporate inventor" one can look to one of Bell's contemporaries, Thomas Edison. Edison worked with a large research facility that was staffed by skilled workers and educated, competent assistants. An example of a corporate invention is Edison's Kinetoscope.

By the time that the Kinetoscope became a possibility, Edison was considered an inventor with no peer. Edison's research lab at Menlo Park is perhaps the most obvious and telling reason why one would call Edison a corporate inventor. His Menlo Park invention factory was funded in part by grants from large corporations like Western Union. For work on the Kinetoscope, Edison hired experts in fields related to photography to help work on the details of the invention. These experts did quite a bit of the work on their own with Edison stepping in to give assistance on several of the technical problems. For instance, Edison solved the problem of how to advance the film one frame at a time by modifying an earlier invention of a stock ticker. The whole development process took place within Menlo Park and the resources that a large group of creative and intelligent people afforded the project. It is hard to say if Edison should be credited with the invention of the Kinetoscope. His name is on the patents that protected the idea from other inventors, but he did not have the knowledge to produce the product without the help of others. The invention was truly the collaboration of many individuals toward a common goal. This is one of the obligatory facets of a corporate invention. The use of the affordances of Menlo Park is why Edison is considered a corporate inventor.

Historically, it could be argued that during the late 19th and early 20th century the heroic inventor led invention. Before the consolidation of technical know-how like Edison's labs, lone inventors were able to compete and create inventions before big corporations could. However, some would argue that currently this is not the case. Large corporations have the resources and the personnel that the solo inventor does not. This leads to an insurmountable advantage for the corporate inventor.

VII. MENTAL MODELS

It is common practice for inventors to use mental models or sets of heuristics to develop their projects. A mental model can be defined as "the ideas and concepts an inventor has about his or her invention. Mental models are often dynamic prototypes an inventor can run in the mind's eye." Mental models enable an inventor to break the problem that he or she is working on into smaller pieces. Take for instance the design of the internal combustion motor. If one looked at the whole problem and tried to build a motor from scratch, the task would be very difficult. However, if one instead broke the idea down into piston, cams, fuel injection, and so on, then the problem would become a manageable size. [*See* HEURISTICS.]

Another benefit of the mental model is that it allows the inventor to draw on previous knowledge to help solve a new problem. For instance, Bell had an expertise in human anatomy. He used this expertise to help guide him in developing the telephone. Edison also displayed the use of mental models. Edison made a career out of taking parts from one invention and fitting it together with a different invention to produce a third one. Edison's use of mental models also demonstrates one of the problems of using such techniques. When Edison was trying to develop the Kinetoscope, having the same mental model for motion pictures as he did for the phonograph hampered him. He saw the Kinetoscope as a single-use device, and in the end, his mental model of a "phonograph with pictures" had to be discarded. He may have saved time and effort if he had simply tried to look at the problem as a new one instead of trying to relate it to an old one. Other tools that the inventor often employs are the metaphor and analogy. [*See* ANALOGIES; METAPHORS.]

VIII. INVENTOR'S PROBLEM SPACE

An important aspect of invention that needs to be addressed is how an inventor constrains the problem. In general, the area that someone is working in is called the problem space. The problem space is represented by the area, either physical or mental, that the inventor is working in.

A. Goal Driven

Inventors may move through their problem space due to a goal-driven method. In other words, the inventor has some idea of what the object that should be created is and maybe how to go about making it.

B. Reverse Salient

The idea of a need-based invention is called a reverse salient. To illustrate what a reverse salient is, imagine a more or less straight line in which a portion is sagging behind the rest. The sagging portion of the line would be the reverse salient. Technologically speaking, a reverse salient is the part of any technology that is less advanced than the rest of the field. Reverse salients are the places in a technological field that hold the greatest opportunity for fame and fortune, because if one can fix a reverse salient, then one has added greatly to the existing technology. Of course there is also the idea of money and fame that drives inventors.

C. Search Method:
Exhaustive and Homing

To start the invention process, one must make what is called the ultimate assumption. This assumption is that there is actually a solution to the problem at hand. Once one has made this assumption, the role of how one defines the problem space comes into play.

One manner of going through the problem space requires an exhaustive search. Another method of search is called the "homing method." The idea is that there is a target gradient along which one can feel as if one is getting closer or further away from the solution one is seeking. An interesting aspect of searching methods is that the homing method may be more effective and take less time, but most often people have to start with the exhaustive method. Once one has gained enough skills and knowledge in a field, one naturally begins to shift from the exhaustive to the homing method. This shift is caused by the additions of more concrete knowledge and heuristics, or mental problem-solving methods, of the way things work.

IX. SERENDIPITY

It would be convenient if one could just work through the problem space and arrive at the conclusion that one was trying to reach. This idea probably happens to some extent in the invention process, but it does not happen every time. Sometimes the ultimate assumption is incorrect and the problem that one is dealing with is unsolvable. This notion is most easily illustrated with the idea of perpetual motion machines. Although many people have invested large amounts of time and money into this problem, it is fundamentally unsolvable.

Often serendipity plays a role in solving a problem or yielding a new discovery. Sometimes chance plays a role in the discovery of a planned objective, and sometimes chance leads to an unintended discovery. For example, the idea of solar panels to make electricity was discovered not by a scientist looking for alternative ways to make energy but by an observant telegraph operator. In 1873, at the transatlantic terminal on the Irish Atlantic Coast, the operator noticed that his instruments had a high level of interference during the times of the day that the sun was shining on his equipment. However, during the evening there was no interference at all. After numerous tests he discovered that the selenium metal resistors were creating electricity when they were in contact with solar energy. In other words, the foundation of photovoltaics had its beginning in a serendipitous event. [*See* SERENDIPITY.]

Another aspect of chance that often comes into play is the fact that one needs to be able to have an idea before someone else in order to receive credit. One needs to have the technical know-how in order to bring the idea to fruition and, in a very basic sense, one needs to be able to live in a time when the technology for the invention is available. The father of modern computers, Charles Babbage, was hindered not by the unfeasibility of his ideas but rather by the limitations of 19th century manufacturing. Babbage developed what he called the "difference engine," which was very much like modern computers. It had an input, output, and a store where numbers could be kept. However, no working version of the machine was ever built. If Babbage lived in a time where the parts could have been manufactured to meet his exacting needs, then the true first computers would not have been electronic, but mechanical.

Serendipity, it could be argued, does not exist to anyone except the person who is observing the process from the outside. To an inventor working through a design problem, a result must be interpreted. The result might represent some error, a disproof of a hypothesis, or it might be the foundations for a whole new line of thought. The successful inventor correctly interprets the result and plans accordingly. These seemly random or serendipitous events are, in fact, typically aspects of smart foraging. Scientists often work through the problem space in such a way as to draw conclusions that when viewed from the outside look like luck. Although sometimes these results are unexpected, they are surely not based on pure chance. Thus, in some instances, serendipity only exists in the eye of the beholder.

X. EPIPHANIES

One final characteristic of invention that needs to be addressed is the idea of epiphanies. The term *epiphany* connotes the coming together of the ideas that one has been working in such a way that the solution is suddenly reached. The idea is that what was at one time a complex set of related ideas in space are now a congruent group that form the solution to the problem space. This phenomenon is also characterized by a quick onset.

XI. IMPEDIMENTS TO INVENTION

One of the major hindrances to invention is the fact that new ideas are often rejected by the established organization. It is not just the struggling against the established norm that impedes invention. Some extremely bright people do not get good education or resources to further their talent which impedes advancement. Also, those who have received the schooling to make things happen must then try to sell themselves to people who will pay for the development of future inventions. [*See* BARRIERS TO CREATIVITY AND CREATIVE ATTITUDES.]

XII. CONCLUSION

In the end, what can be said about invention? It is, for many people, a source of hope that life will be better tomorrow compared to today; invention is the key to solving many of the problems that we face.

As an activity, invention is a complex process that tries to progress forward. Every novel artifact has an antecedent. The process may be smooth and punctuated by sudden developments or problematic and slow. One also can see that objectives are not the only things that drive inventions. Sometimes an invention is created by pure luck or some other odd occurrence. Invention, finally, is the creation and realization of a new object that one may reach through any number of possible ways.

Bibliography

Basalla, G. (1988). *The evolution of technology.* New York: Cambridge University Press.

Bijker, W. E., Hughes, T., & Pinch, T. J. (1989). *The social construction of technological systems:* London: MIT Press.

Bijker, W. E., & Shaping, J. L. (1982). *Technology and building society: Studies in sociotechnical change.* Cambridge, MA: MIT Press.

Burke, J. (1996). *The pinball effect.* Boston: Little, Brown and Co.

Ferguson, E. S. (1992). *Engineering and the mind's eye.* Cambridge, MA: MIT Press.

Friedel, R. D., & Israel, P. (1986). *Edison's electric light: Biography of an invention.* New Brunswick, NJ: Rutgers University Press.

Gorman, M. (1998). *Transforming nature: Ethics, invention and discovery.* Boston: Kluwer Academic.

Jewkes, J., Sawers, D., & Stillerman, R. (1969). *The sources of invention* (2nd ed.). New York: W. W. Norton.

Kuhn, T. S. (1970). *The structure of scientific revolutions* (2nd ed.). Chicago: University of Chicago Press.

Lindgren, M. (1990). *Glory and failure.* Cambridge, MA: MIT Press.

Pacey, A. (1972). *The maze of ingenuity: Ideas and idealism in the development of technology* (2nd ed.). Cambridge, MA: MIT Press.

Rossman, J. (1964). *The psychology of the inventor* (3rd ed.). New Hyde Park, NY: University Books.

Tenney, C. D. (1991). In H. M. Kaplan, R. E. McCoy, & L. E. Hahn (Eds.), *The discovery of discovery.* Lanham: University Press of America.

Weber, R. J. (1992). *Forks, phonographs, and hot air balloons: A field guide to inventive thinking.* New York: Oxford University Press.

Weber, R. J., & Perkins, D. N. (1992). *Inventive minds: Creativity in technology.* New York: Oxford University Press.

Wiener, N. (1993). *Invention: The care and feeding of ideas.* Cambridge, MA: MIT Press.

Janusian Process

Albert Rothenberg

Harvard University

Analogic Reasoning Drawing of inferences or conclusions based on likenesses and comparisons.

Cognition All processes of consciousness by which knowledge is attained.

Deductive Reasoning Making inferences or conclusions based on predetermined premises.

General Theory of Relativity The laws of physics are constructed as the laws of geometry in four dimensions, and these laws in turn are determined by the distribution of matter and energy in the universe. Postulates of the general theory have been upheld by measurements made during a solar eclipse, and the theory has provided the basis for developments of nuclear technology and of the field of cosmology in the 20th century.

Inductive Reasoning The process of drawing out or making inferences or conclusions based on facts and observations.

Kent-Rosanoff Word Association Test Psychological test usually composed of 100 stimulus words and requiring a response, usually timed, of the first word that comes to mind on exposure to each stimulus word. Developed by psychologists Kent and Rosanoff in the early 1900s and standardized on more than 1000 subjects.

Semistructured Research Interviews Use of predetermined questions and categories for eliciting interview information relevant to specific preconstructed hypotheses. These questions and categories are not presented in a set sequence but according to the flow and logic of the interview interaction.

Statistical Significance Method for assessing the operation of nonchance factors in an event or series of events.

The **JANUSIAN PROCESS** consists of actively conceiving multiple opposites or antitheses simultaneously. The term used for this process derives from the qualities of the Roman god, Janus, who had faces that looked in multiple (2, 4, or 6) diametrically opposite directions simultaneously. During the course of the creative process, opposite or antithetical ideas, concepts, or propositions are consciously conceptualized as simultaneously coexisting. Although seemingly illogical and self-contradictory, these formulations are constructed in clearly logical and rational states of mind to produce creative effects. They occur as early conceptions in the development of scientific theories and artworks and at critical junctures at middle and later stages as well. Because they serve generative functions during both formative and critical stages of the creative process, these simultaneous antitheses or simultaneous opposites usually undergo transformation and modification and are seldom directly discernible in final created products. They *are formulated by the creative thinker as solutions in working out practical and scientific tasks and as central ideas for an artwork.*

Data regarding the janusian process were derived from more than 2500 hours of semistructured recorded research interviews with 375 outstanding and neophyte creative persons and comparison subjects. Creative subjects were identified by independent judges. These interviews focused on the creative process in ongoing work in progress in art, literature, and scientific research. Hypothesis testing experiments with creative subjects in literature and art and matching controls were also carried out. Examples in the following text are derived from both interview studies and primary source investigations.

I. JANUSIAN PROCESS IN SCIENTIFIC CREATIVITY

While working on an essay for the *Yearbook of Radio-activity and Electronics* in 1907, Albert Einstein had what he called "the happiest thought of my life." This happy thought was the key to one of the most far-reaching scientific breakthroughs of the 20th century: the general theory of relativity. The unusual circumstances surrounding it were revealed for the first time in a 1919 document by Einstein, discovered after his death and still unpublished in its entirety, titled "Fundamental Ideas and Methods of Relativity Theory, Presented in Their Development."

Einstein had already developed the special theory of relativity, which holds that since the speed of light is constant for all frames of reference, perceptions of time and motion depend on the relative position of the observer. He had been forced to postulate the theory, he said, to explain the seeming contradictions in electromagnetic phenomena; that "one is dealing here with two fundamentally different cases was, for me, unbearable." Einstein was trying to modify Newton's classical theory of gravitation so that it could be encompassed within a broad relativity principle. He struggled for many years because he lacked a specific physical basis for bringing together Newton's theory and his own special theory.

Pondering those seemingly irreconcilable constructs, Einstein all at once reached a startling conception:

For an observer in free fall from the roof of a house, there exists, during his fall, no gravitational field . . . in his immediate vicinity. If the observer releases any objects, they will remain, relative to him, in a state of rest. The [falling] observer is therefore justified in considering his state as one of rest.

The general theory itself is highly complex, but the specific structure of the key step is clear: Einstein had consciously formulated the simultaneously antithetical construct that a person falling from the roof of a house was both in motion and at rest at the same time. The hypothesis was illogical and contradictory in structure, but it possessed a superior logic and salience that brought Newtonian physics and his own into the same overall conceptual scheme.

In another more recent example described in a semistructured research interview, Nobel laureate Edwin McMillan's formulation of critical phase stability, leading to his development of the synchrocyclotron (later called the synchrotron), was derived from a sudden realization involving simultaneous opposition. The synchrotron is a high-energy particle accelerator that has allowed for the discovery of a number of new particles and other nuclear effects. McMillan described the sequence of events in the following verbatim transcription:

It was in the month of July. I think it was the month of July. I didn't put down the date—I should record these things. It was night. I was lying awake in bed and thinking of a way of getting high energy and I was thinking of the cyclotron and the particle going around and encountering the accelerator field—the right phase each time around. And I thought of what will happen if the resonance is wrong, if the period is wrong, what will happen? And I sort of analyzed in my mind that it's going around and it's being accelerated, and it's getting heavier; therefore, it's taking more time to get around, and it will fall out of step. Then it gets behind and it gets the opposite sense. It gets pushed back again, so it will oscillate. It's going to oscillate back and forth, be going at too high and too low energy. Once I realized that, then the rest was easy.

If the timing is wrong, it's not going to fall completely out of step but it will overshoot and come back.

Phase stability, I call it phase stability. The very next day I called it phase stability. Phase is the relation—time relation—of what you're worried about. Stability implies that it clings to a certain value. It may oscillate about, but it clings to a certain fixed value.

As McMillan in detail described his sudden formulation of the critical concept leading to the construction of the synchrotron, he had conceived the simultaneously opposite states of too high and too low energy. Realizing that out-of-step particles would fall back in the accelerator field, he grasped the idea that these particles would be forced to accelerate. Consequently, they would oscillate and be both too high and too low in energy with respect to the overall accelerator field. They would be lower in energy because they were heavier and out of phase and would be also higher in energy because they would overshoot. Consequently, they would be stable overall with respect to the field. As McMillan reported in further elaboration:

> Once you have an oscillation, you have the element of stability. The things will stay put. They will wiggle around but they won't get away from you. Then all you have to do is to vary your frequency, or vary the magnetic field, either one or both, slowly, and you can push this thing anywhere you want. That all happened one night and the next day I started to write down the equations for that and proved that it would work.

Systematic study of notes and preliminary drafts of Niels Bohr's first presentation of his theory of complementarity, the theory that has been a foundation for modern quantum physics, revealed the operation of the janusian process at a generative phase. Stating in his notes—Bohr's characteristic way of thinking through a problem—that the physical nature of light consisting either of waves or particles, widely believed at the time to be completely conflicting alternatives, involved "no question of a choice between two different concepts but rather the description of two complementary sides of the same phenomenon," he then went on to formulate the full-blown complementarity theory stated as follows: Two descriptions or sets of concepts, though mutually exclusive, are both necessary for an exhaustive description of the physical situation. The key initial formulation of the complementarity idea was a janusian construct that light (later, including electrons) was a phenomenon with simultaneous antithetical wave and particle aspects.

II. SIMULTANEITY AND THE JANUSIAN PROCESS

Simultaneity of the multiple opposites or antitheses is a cardinal feature of the janusian process. Firmly held propositions about the laws of nature, the functioning of individuals and groups, or the aesthetic properties of visual and sound patterns are conceived as simultaneously true and not true. Or opposite or antithetical propositions are entertained as concomitantly operative. A person running is both in motion and not in motion at the same time, a chemical is both boiling and freezing, or kindness and sadism operate simultaneously. Previously held beliefs or laws are still considered valid but opposite or antithetical beliefs and laws are formulated as equally operative or valid as well.

These formulations within the janusian process are necessary way stations to clear-cut or high-level creative effects and outcomes. They interact and join with other cognitive and affective developments to produce new and valuable, sometimes breakthrough products. One of these developments may be a later interaction with unifying processes. [*See* HOMOSPATIAL PROCESS.] Others may be the use of analogic, inductive, deductive, and dialectic reasoning to contribute to production of uniquely structured theories, inventions, and artwork.

Unlike the janusian process, dialectic reasoning consists—as defined by Hegel—of separate opposites posited sequentially and then combined or otherwise reconciled or resolved (e.g., thesis, antithesis, then synthesis). In the formative janusian process, the opposites or antitheses are simultaneously brought together. Contradictory aspects are not reconciled but remain in conflict; opposites are not combined nor are oppositions resolved. Antitheses and opposites during the course of the janusian process are held in tense apposition; they operate side by side and lead to subsequent new and valuable constructions. Dialectic reasoning can sometimes be one of the late appearing modifying factors contributing to the final result.

III. THE JANUSIAN PROCESS IN ARTISTIC FIELDS

In art and literature, the janusian process usually begins with the recognition and choice of salient opposites and antitheses in a cultural, physical, or aesthetic field, progresses to the formulation of these factors operating simultaneously, and then proceeds to elaborated creations.

For instance, in a systematic long-term research exploration of the literary creative process, a Pulitzer Prize–winning novelist disclosed that he had developed the key idea as he sat in a lawn chair reading Erik Erikson's book on Martin Luther's rebellion. He thought of constructing a novel about another rebel, a revolutionary hero who, he said, "was responsible for the deaths of hundreds of people, but he himself would kill only one person with his own hand—and this was the one person who had been very kind to him and the one person he loved." Playwright Arthur Miller reported that he had come up with the specific idea for the play *Incident at Vichy* while travleing through Germany: "Driving on the autobahn, I suddenly felt amazed and overwhelmed at how beautiful Germany had become." He conceived of writing a play that would simultaneously express both the beauty of modern Germany and Hitler's destructiveness. "And then, I remembered a story I'd been told about a sacrifice made by an Austrian nobleman for a Jew in a Nazi official's waiting room." Later, the playwright incorporated the sacrifice into his play.

Poet Richard Wilbur reported that he had been walking on a beach and became interested in the quality of some rocks along the sand. As he touched the surface of the rocks, he noted that they seemed to feel like human skin. They were, however, also hard, heavy objects—violent weapons. The idea that the rocks were at once sensual objects and weapons led to a conception of the simultaneous operation of sex and violence in the world, and Wilbur elaborated those aspects separately in the final version of the poem.

On another occasion, Wilbur was sitting at his desk and thought of a poetic line connoting rest and movement as operating simultaneously in the action of long-distance running. The thought led him to write a poignant poem, titled "Running," about marathon racing and the ravages of time and age, which elaborated on, and modified, the initially conceived line.

Poet James Merrill had been home thinking about a past incident in which a horse had appeared at a lonely desert site, when it occurred to him that horses are animals who "renounce their own kind in order to live our lives." The idea that horses live human lives, that they are both beast and not beast and human and not human simultaneously, generated the poem, "In Monument Valley," with the central image and theme of a happy and intense relationship between a young person and a horse, followed by a sad, resigned separation.

Novelist John Hersey revealed that the earliest idea for his book *Too Far to Walk* was the concept in the verbal phrase, "love and hate are the same." The phrase had also guided the novel's whole construction. Another writer reported that her first idea for a poem was the line, "Cream of celery soup has a soul of its own." She had been thinking, she recalled, about the simultaneously formed and unformed qualities of both souls and soup. A creative playwright said that the earliest formulations in one of his works grew out of ideas and phrases that came to him while imagining that the white knight in a TV commercial was a black man.

Poet and novelist Robert Penn Warren recounted that he was doing his morning exercises when he thought of a series of poetic lines that, as he described them, would use the last word of each line as the first word of the next—a juxtaposition that sets one word to opposite functions, both ending and beginning a poetic thought. In the end, his poem implicitly retained that structure.

IV. EXPERIMENTAL ASSESSMENT

A tendency or capacity for the use of the janusian process among proven and potentially creative persons, manifested by rapid opposite responding on word association tasks, was identified experimentally by Rothenberg in 1983. Standard Kent-Rosanoff word association tests were individually administered to 22 Nobel laureates in science (physics, chemistry, medicine and physiology) and to rated-as-creative Yale college students. Control groups consisted of matched but rated-less-creative students and high-IQ psychiatric patients.

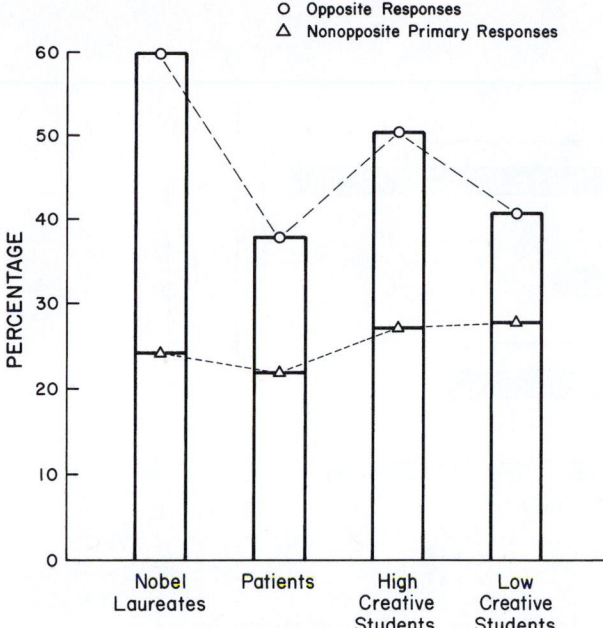

FIGURE 1 Percentage of opposite and nonopposite primary word association response by subject group. Reprinted with permission from A. Rothenberg (1983). *Archives of General Psychiatry* 40:937. Copyright 1983, American Medical Association.

Test instructions were to give the first word that came to mind in response to a standardized list of word stimuli and both speed and content of response were electronically recorded. As shown in Figure 1, after factoring out any tendency to give common and popular types of responses (lower broken graph line), results indicated that the statistically significant highest number of rapid opposite responses were given by proven creative subjects, the Nobel laureate group, and the next highest by the potentially creative Yale students. Speed of opposite responding among both these groups of subjects was extremely rapid (Figure 2), averaging 1.1 to 1.2 seconds from the time the experimenter spoke the stimulus word, suggesting the formulation of simultaneous or, virtually simultaneous, opposite associations.

V. PHASES OF THE JANUSIAN PROCESS

In scientific creativity, the janusian process has been empirically determined to operate over variable periods of time in four identifiable phases: (a) motivation to create; (b) deviation or separation; (c) simultaneous opposition or antithesis; and (d) construction of the theory, discovery, or experiment.

In the initial motivational phase, a person or agent deliberately sets out to create—that is, to produce something new and valuable. As determined by empirical investigation, both the intention to create and the area chosen for creation have emotional (including aesthetic) importance for the person him- or herself. Distinct cognitive abilities and proclivities are involved in the capacity to use the janusian process, and the emotional underpinnings interlock with these. Strong motivation provides the drive to consider and conceive the inconceivable; emotional significance and involvement, especially if it arises from and includes psychological conflict, jibes with the cognitive tendency to focus on opposites and antitheses and bring these together simultaneously. The simultaneous opposition and antithesis with its retained conflict among composing elements is isomorphic with emotional conflicts and other psychological processes.

In the second phase of conceptual deviation, one or both specific portions or poles of opposition (antitheses) are formulated. It is here that the initial breakaway from current scientific canons of approach and content occurs. This is the beginning of the necessarily radical departure from the known and accepted that ultimately constitutes newness in the creative discovery. Moreover, the gradual development of a specific thematic pole or aspect isolates a critical factor or number of factors in the area of consideration and exploration.

A third phase develops in which multiple opposites or antitheses are conceived as operating simultaneously. It is here that ideas constructed sometimes seem surprising to creative persons themselves. At first unthinkable and surprising are postulates that antithetical factors coexist or operate together, or that something in existence or known previously continues to operate validly together with its diametric and seemingly contradictory opposite. Also, one pole or portion of an opposite or set of opposites may earlier have been in conscious focus, whereas other portions as well as other oppositions were dimly held at the periphery. Conscious recognition and apposition of the full oppositions may become a sudden and surprising experience, producing a sense that is sometimes described as "something coming out of the blue." With respect to newness, the simultaneity of opposition is a phenome-

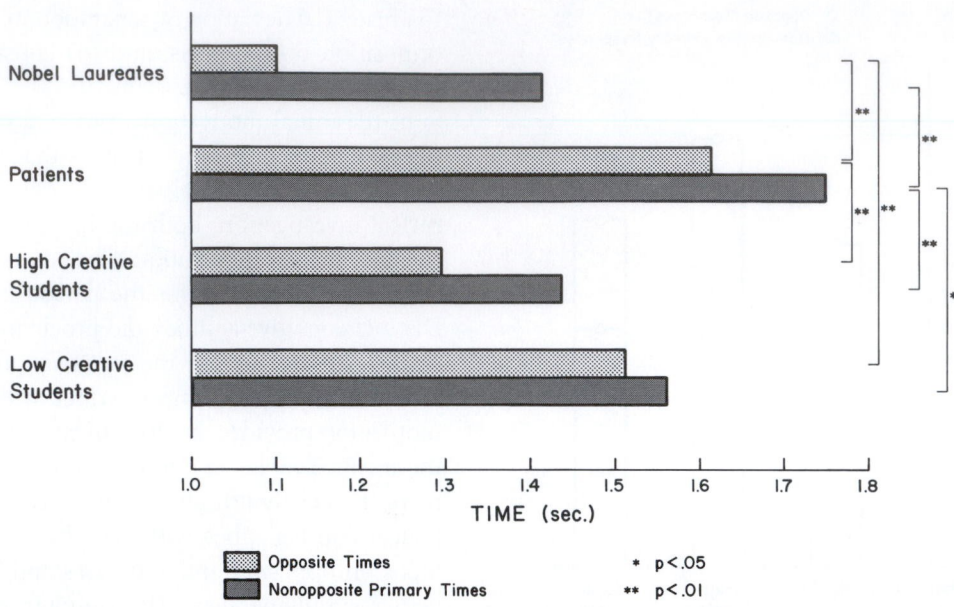

FIGURE 2 Latencies (response times) of opposite and nonopposite primary word association response by subject group. Reprinted with permission from A. Rothenberg (1983). *Archives of General Psychiatry* 40:937. Copyright 1983, American Medical Association.

non experienced as being out of time. As it is out of time, or out of temporal succession, it appears as discontinuous with previous factors and is therefore new.

The fourth phase consists of the making or construction of the full dimensions of the theory or discovery. In this phase, stepwise logical as well as constructive and unifying mental processes predominate. Not to be minimized in any way, scientific intellect, observational and deductive capacities, and scrupulous attention to canons of empirical validation are critically important in this phase.

Bibliography

Abler, W. H. (1992). Aesthetics and pragmatics in human ecological theory development and family therapy: Janusian, homospatial, articulation processes in theory and practice (Doctoral dissertation, Michigan State University). *Dissertation Abstracts International 53*, DA9302962.

Briggs, J. (1980). Unshrouding the muse: The anatomy of inspiration. *Art News, 79,* 52.

Einstein, A. (c. 1919). *The fundamental idea of general relativity in its original form.* Princeton, NJ: Princeton University, Institute for Advanced Study (Einstein Archives).

Grotstein, J. S. (1992). The enigmatic relationship of creativity to mental health and psychopathology. *American Journal of Psychotherapy, 46,* 405.

Handler, L. (1996). Object relations: Self, object and the space in between. *Contemporary Psychology, 41,* 385.

Rothenberg, A. (1979). *The emerging goddess: The creative process in art, science and other fields.* Chicago: University of Chicago Press.

Rothenberg, A. (1983). Psychopathology and creative cognition: A comparison of hospitalized patients, Nobel laureates, and controls. *Archives of General Psychiatry, 40,* 937.

Rothenberg, A. (1987). Einstein, Bohr and creative thinking in science. *History of Science, 25,* 147.

Rothenberg, A. (1996). The janusian process in scientific creativity. *Creativity Research Journal, 9,* 207.

Smith, G. J. W. (1981). Creation and reconstruction. *Psychoanalysis and Contemporary Thought, 4,* 275.

Jungian Theory

Keri Jones

Private Practice, Los Angeles, California

Analytical Psychology A psychological science, developed by Carl Gustav Jung, that grew out of psychoanalysis and includes theory, research, and practice.

Archetypal Image A representation, or motif, of an archetype that has infinite manifestations. The produced archetypal image gives a voice to the archetype itself and is commonly found in fairy tales, legends, religion, mythology, dreams, and art. Also referred to as a primordial image.

Archetypes Limitless instinctual forms, not yet ideas or representations, within the collective unconscious thought to be passed down through the ages and found in all cultures. Archetypes are not visible until an image is created.

Autonomous Complex An emotionally charged part of the psyche that usually includes material from consciousness as well as the unconscious. Forms the connection between the personal and archetypal parts of a person. Autonomous complexes, which are many, include the creative complex.

Collective Unconscious The second layer of the unconscious, preceding the personal unconscious, which houses the archetypes (often used interchangeably with the concept of archetypes, defined above). Considered the reservoir of great art.

Individuation The cornerstone of Jung's theory of personality development. The process is life long and the goal, which is attainable only in stages and not in total, is to become whole, complete, and truly individual. Making great art is linked to this process.

Personal Unconscious The first layer of the unconscious that stores traumatic memories, experiences, and ideas that are unique to the individual's past. This layer of the unconscious precedes the collective unconscious.

Symbol The greatest conceivable expression for an idea; the idea cannot be produced in a better way. Symbols can be recognizable connections to archetypes, but their actual meaning is unknown. Great art is truly symbolic.

Wholeness The ultimate form of expression of all parts of the personality to one's self, others, and nature. Being psychologically whole equates with health, and health equals creativity—the goal of individuation.

Carl Gustav Jung produced a plethora of work during his life, including a JUNGIAN THEORY of creativity. He was strongly opposed to seeing great art as a personal reflection of the artist; instead, he attributed great art as originating out of the collective unconscious. The artist is the vehicle of a message from the collective unconscious. Interestingly, Jung was quite influenced by his own personal experiences and his theories largely originate from his own self analysis, observations, and explo-

rations. The crux of his theory rests on the foundation of opposites. The awareness of oppositional forces were pronounced in his life and carried through to his ideas on human functioning. The following is a walk through Jung's history, his theoretical framework, and finally his theory of creativity. Although arduous at times, it behooves the reader to take the time to stroll through his theory of the mind in order to more closely understand his contribution to the world of creativity, as they are so closely linked.

I. CARL GUSTAV JUNG—THE MAN

C. G. Jung was born on July 26, 1875, in Kasswyl, Thurgovie, Switzerland (also spelled as Kesswil, Thurgau in other biographies). His family was economically poor. Jung's father, a doctor of philosophy, worked as a pastor in the Swiss Reform Church and was also an Oriental and classical scholar. His father was described as quite conventional in his religious beliefs, from which Jung later strayed. Kind, tolerant, reliable, and otherwise liberal were also reflective of his father. By some accounts, Jung believed his father was weak and unpowerful.

On the other hand, Jung's mother was thought to be inconsistent and divided in her thoughts. She often contradicted herself. He seemed to identify with her in many ways, especially regarding his intensely complex inner world and that she seemed to have two strong parts of her personality that opposed one another. This opposition was part of Jung's experience of himself (and later a central part of his theory of personality.) When Jung was 3 years old, his mother was hospitalized for several months, probably due to problems in her marriage that continued throughout his youth. Over time, Jung developed mixed feelings for his mother.

Jung was a highly sensitive, curious, and bright child who had several bouts of physical illness. He was acutely aware of his thoughts, feelings, and surroundings. Growing up in the country afforded him a great deal of pleasure and a place for exploration. He enjoyed the beauty of his homeland and was in a frequent state of discovery about the world around him. The beauty and brightness he experienced was contrasted by several dark experiences that followed him for much of his life. The dark experiences included

themes of death, religious activity, dreams, and fears. This duality serves as the cornerstone for much of his theoretical frame.

Jung took playing quite seriously, and playing alone became a constant for Jung as he was an only child until the birth of his sister when Jung was 9 years old (he had a brother who died 2 days after his birth, 2 years preceding the birth of Jung). He was quite interested in Eastern religion, mythology, and nature as a young boy. Being alone allowed him the space to ponder the many questions he had about life, especially religion. Some believe that the materialization of analytical psychology was his way of finding a replacement for religion. He did not have any companions that he trusted enough to share his meaningful ideas or questions, and thus he felt even further isolated.

School for Jung was wrought with ups and downs. At times he was strongly engaged and at other times he was disengaged. His interest varied depending on experiences he had with other students and his teachers, as well as their perception of him.

After much deliberation, Jung decided to attend medical school. He struggled with this decision because he originally wanted to study natural science or the humanities. His decision was largely based on practical matters of expenses and obtaining a reasonable income after college. Within the field of medicine he was inclined to choose surgery or internal medicine. Psychiatry, which became known to him late in his academic career, was his final choice. He found his university experience exciting and challenging. In addition to medicine he was able to continue his study and exploration of theology, philosophy, and Eastern theories.

After finishing school in 1900, Jung moved to Zurich, Switzerland, where he lived for the duration of his life. He began training at a psychiatric hospital in the city. For the first 6 months he lived in the hospital, immersing himself with psychiatric literature and learning firsthand what the experience was like. Here he became fascinated with the minds of patients with many disorders, including schizophrenia. Many of his theories originated from his work in the hospital. He became rather disillusioned by the way patients were treated and began to experiment with alternative therapies. This disillusionment led him to the work of Sigmund Freud.

Jung published his first paper in 1902 and began lecturing at the university in 1905, meanwhile building a private practice in Zurich. In 1907 Jung met Freud. From the beginning, Jung was reluctant to embrace many of Freud's theories, yet conversely he was intrigued with Freud and his work. At times Freud and Jung worked closely. Jung was beginning to formulate more of his own theories and had trouble accepting key ideas in Freud's theories. Yet he found himself unable to disagree overtly with Freud as Freud saw him as a loyal protégé. The final break between the two men occurred with the publication of Jung's book on libido (psychic energy) in 1913. Jung's work was met with a great deal of judgment, and he was rejected by many of his friends and colleagues leaving him isolated once again.

The next 4 years were wrought with a great deal of distress, mystery, and growth. Some reports indicate that Jung had a psychotic break, primarily because he was experiencing visions and emotional turmoil. Through these experiences he began to further understand the workings of his unconscious, which led him further along the path to the idea of the collective unconscious. He studied his dreams and fantasies, drew pictures of his visions, and began to create mandalas (circular drawings that become central to his theory of individuation). This creative and very dark period gave him the material to sort through and define for the rest of his life. He did not understand all that was occurring, only that it was significant, and later the meaning would be revealed.

From 1918 to 1919 Jung came out of his so-called darkness. He attributed the change to ending a relationship with a woman who continued to believe his fantasies were that of art. He adamantly opposed this assertion. Some writers point to the curious nature of his insistence on this matter. For when he was a young boy he derived great pleasure, and felt successful, making art. The second factor that released him from his darkness was his understanding of the mandalas he created. Mandalas will be discussed later, but for the sake of his story, Jung found them to be a way of journaling his internal growth.

Jung continued on this journey of understanding the psyche, especially that of the collective unconscious. He traveled throughout the world, which gave him greater evidence for his belief in the collective uncon-

scious and the role of archetypes. Everywhere he visited he was able to see connections to the archetypal and mythical world. The common images existed despite cultural, language, or age barriers. Jung spent the majority of his life writing about these experiences as well as maintaining an esteemed clinical practice.

Regarding Jung's family (which he rarely wrote about), he was married in 1903 and had five children. Jung's wife, Emma, also an analyst, contributed to the work of analytic psychology and wrote several works. At the time of his death in 1961 he had 19 grandchildren. Most of his life, he had a great number of students and people who worked with him. He was frequently sought after and deeply respected by most accounts. He received many awards throughout the world. He has contributed enormously to the field of psychology and continues to have a great number of followers with Jungian analytic institutes worldwide.

II. MODEL OF THE MIND

As mentioned earlier, Jung's theory of the mind rests on the concept of opposites and opposite forces, which is important to be mindful of as his theory unfolds. This section provides an overview of several key concepts of Jungian psychology, including the ego, consciousness, personal unconscious, collective unconscious, individuation, and wholeness. Whenever possible, the implication to the creative process associated with the corresponding structure of the psyche will be made. Psyche, or psychic material, refers to the entirety of both conscious and unconscious psychological processes. The psyche is very complex and works to keep itself in balance.

A. The Conscious Mind

The conscious part of the mind has the primary job of sustaining the relationship with the ego. The ego is a complex (see the definition of *autonomous complex* in the glossary at the beginning of this article and a further description following the archetypes) that contains a great deal of continuity and identity. For psychic material to be conscious, the ego must be aware of the material. Conversely, when psychic material is unknown to the ego, it remains unconscious. Awareness in this case is not merely intellectual but rather intuitive, emotional, and with meaning. Further, consciousness is thought of as the opposite of the unconscious.

B. The Unconscious Mind

The unconscious is the second psychic structure to which Jung referred. Consciousness is the unconscious' opposite and houses information that is not accessible to the ego but may later be accessible. The unconscious is vast in size and fluid in movement. The relationship, or link, between consciousness and the unconscious is referred to as compensation. Compensation means balancing or adjusting. In this case, compensation comes into play when consciousness is too one-sided, leading the unconscious to try and reach a balance.

The personal and the collective are the two substructures of the unconscious. Both substructures serve as a source of art, although in very different ways (which will soon be illustrated). First we take a closer look at the personal and the collective unconscious.

1. Personal Unconscious

The personal unconscious, the first layer, is that part of the unconscious specific to the individual. Included in the personal unconscious are repressed memories (memories that have been pushed down into the unconscious without one's control), ideas that are painful, and information without the strength, or the timing, to reach consciousness. Material in the personal unconscious was once conscious and may later be conscious again.

2. Collective Unconscious

The collective unconscious, the second and deeper layer, is that part of the psyche that is shared by all people, in all cultures, throughout the ages. Jung believed that the collective unconscious is much more important then the personal unconscious because it is the seat of power, wholeness, and internal transformation. The collective unconscious holds dreams, visions, religious experiences, and myths.

He arrived at the idea of the collective unconscious through his knowledge of mythology, anthropology, religion, and art. The collective unconscious concept was further materialized from Jung's work with patients who were diagnosed with schizophrenia (importantly, the collective unconscious is found in everyone, not just in psychotic patients.) Furthermore, in his work he realized that images in peoples dreams were not from their own personal experience, or life, but rather reminiscent of archaic symbols and images. He began to recognize these images in ancient works and religions that the patient who dreamed the material was not aware of. In many of Jung's original writings he unknowingly referred to the collective unconscious and the archetypes interchangeably. This confusion has led subsequent authors to speak of the collective unconscious and the archetypes together, not as separate structures.

Archetypes are universal structures in the collective unconscious that allow for the *potentiality* of ideas, but they are not ideas themselves. This point is often a source of confusion and the distinction is important to understand. Archetypes are known because of the archetypal image they represent in consciousness—in other words, how the archetypal images appear. The image is what gives proof of the existence of the archetype. You can not see an archetype; you can see an archetypal *image*.

Archetypes, and archetypal images, have a strong creative force along with many other qualities. Among the qualities present are that of favorability, emotion, number, intensity, and type. Archetypes are neither all bad nor all good. Rather, they simply exist, and understanding the importance of the structure is what is key. Intense emotion exudes from archetypal images. Experiences may be within the likeness of all human behavior, but the experiences that manifest within the category of archetypal are extraordinarily human. Going beyond the ordinary into the realm of the extraordinary, emotional response to an archetypal imagery is enthralling, bigger than life.

Because of the emotional magnitude of the archetypal image it acts as a communication device from the unconscious mind of the individual who produced the work, to the unconscious mind of the individual seeing or reading the work, through the symbolism inherent in the image. The communication is further enhanced by the image relating to mythological figures, or motifs, from ancestry. The manifestations of archetypal images change based on the current culture but are always linked to the past. When an archetypal image is seen or heard or read it evokes a great deal of emotion, power, and release. It is as though we are connected to our past and the *past of all mankind.*

a. Examples of Archetypes There are infinite numbers of archetypes and archetypal images. Some of the key archetypes that will be discussed are the anima and the animus, the shadow, the persona, and the self. Other archetypes are the mother, father, warrior, and wise old man, to name a few.

Unconscious archetypes of the opposite sex are referred to as the anima and animus, in Latin these words mean "the soul." The anima refers to a man's image of a woman; and animus refers to a woman's image of a man (which Jung viewed in traditional roles of the 19th century). The anima and animus are thought of as guides, primarily throughout the terrain of the unconscious creating a richer level of understanding of one's internal world. Another way of thinking about the anima and the animus is in their role of moderating between the conscious ego and the unconscious mind.

The anima was intensely studied by Jung as well as his followers. Less was written by Jung, and his followers, on the concept of the animus. The anima and animus are important for many reasons; especially in relation to the creative process. They are both portrayed continuously in fairy tales, myths, literature, film, and other art forms.

The shadow is another archetypal figure or image. The essence of the shadow is that part of everyone's personality that is disliked and incongruent with how one would like to be perceived. The part that harbors unacceptable feelings, thoughts, or wishes, distasteful impulses, and negative assessments of oneself. The shadow is actually the part of ourselves that we can only sometimes see and in varying degrees. Just as the sun creates shadows on all that catches its light, the shadow can be further thought of as the darker, uglier, and evil side of life (for example, violence, wars, and tragedy, as well as that part of the person who commits such crimes). Further, the shadow is the side of the personality that most people would wish to disown or pretend did not exist. The opposite, or counterpart, to the shadow is the ego. The shadow is often portrayed in movies, books, and art of all kinds.

Persona is the archetype Jung referred to as the mask that we *all* wear at times. The persona is thought of as the mediator between the ego and the outside world.

The concept of the mask suggests that we respond to the expectations of society by presenting ourselves in a certain light, even though the persona is not our true or complete self. In extreme instances, the mask, or persona, is represented in the person who cannot leave his or her professional identity aside. For example, the lawyer is always arguing a point; the preacher is always wearing his or her religious garb and reading from the Bible. The true personality, or person, of the lawyer or preacher is unknown to the people in their lives. A common example is that most of us have different roles in society, such as brother, sister, daughter, son, student, date, employee, and so on. We show different sides of our personality as we relate to others in those varying roles.

The self archetype is that of wholeness and completion. The self further refers to the ability of the conscious and unconscious to work together in order for an individual to be free to be her or his true self. The integration of all parts of the psyche allows the individual to live in a creative and symbolic fashion—to be truly an individual. The self archetype is the representation of individuation, which will soon be discussed.

Another concept often compared and contrasted to archetypes is that of the complexes (referred to in the section on consciousness). Jung suggested that there are many complexes in the psyche; unlike the archetypes that number is finite. However, like the archetypes they are neither all bad nor all good; rather they are a part of the psyche to be understood. The autonomy of the complex is such because the conscious mind does not regulate or control the information. In other words, information comes and goes on its own. The autonomous complex operates when there is enough energy to move information from the unconscious to consciousness. Even though the information is conscious it is only perceived, not known. The creative complex is one of the autonomous complexes. The autonomous complex is the *living* part of the creative process, the part that takes on a life of its own (which will be discussed in detail).

C. Individuation

The following section provides an overview of the concept of individuation including the concept of wholeness, the integration of mandalas, and the production of active imagination. The process of individuation is key to understanding Jung's theory of creativity. Individuation further includes the integration of the conscious mind, the personal unconscious, and the collective unconscious.

The cornerstone of Jungian, or analytic, psychology is individuation. The *process* of individuation, likened to his description of the creative process, is the road of integration between parts of the self that are conflicted—again, the notion of opposites. Bringing into harmony the parts of the psyche, both conscious and unconscious, that are at odds is the goal. In addition to the internal work required for individuation is the external work of increasing one's individuality. Thus, individuation includes both internal and external movement. Full individuation can never be reached, instead Jung believed that it was best to approach it as a lifelong process. Importantly, not everyone chooses or is able to travel down the road of individuation.

The *purpose* of individuation is to bring about wholeness in the individual. Wholeness suggests that one is able to fulfill one's destiny and vocation. Wholeness allows the individual to be authentic in the world, thereby avoiding using only the persona, or the mask. Being aware of one's own internal reality is at issue, *not* getting rid of a part of the self that is disliked. Coming to terms with the darkness and the painful images in the unconscious is a necessary part of individuation. Also included in the process is greater awareness of the collective unconscious and the collective world around each individual, thus avoiding isolation. A sense of wholeness further encompasses the spiritual aspect of life.

Through the process of individuation, with the hope of reaching wholeness, is the production of images, archetypal images. These images allow psychic material from the unconscious to become conscious, in varying degrees, thereby freeing difficult material in the collective unconscious. In the case of the artist, moving further along the path of individuation with the production of art subsequently provides the viewer or reader of the art with a similar experience—that of individuation.

One form in which individuation may be expressed is through the making of mandalas, which are a symbol of the psyche's center, or the self. The self, an archetype, is reflective of both conscious and unconscious parts of the psyche. The creation of mandalas was for Jung a tremendous experience of integration within himself, of unconscious and conscious experience. The mandala is a circular drawing usually divided into fourths, or derivations of four or eight. Mandalas are actually used in the East as a form of meditation, although at the time Jung began making them he was not aware of this historical element. He considered this work to be in the realm of religion as opposed to art. Others have considered the mandala to reside equally within the realm of art. The argument is that a work of art is also an integration of the inner world of the artist and the external world in which the artist lives—again, a representation of the unconscious and the conscious parts of a person.

Another route to individuation is through active imagination, a fantasy activity primarily used by Jung with his patients and with himself. Introspection or meditation is at the center of the activity. Active imagination allows the individual to have a dialogue between consciousness and the unconscious. Jung was not certain if the unconscious rules over consciousness or if consciousness rules over the unconscious during active imagination. The important note is the interaction between the two structures of the psyche, the conscious and unconscious, lead to a greater sense of wholeness and individuation.

The form of active imagination can take various shapes such as painting, drawing, writing, and so on. The end result is not what is of primary importance but rather the interplay in the psyche of the creator and the creative process. He found that during active imagination, people were able to tap into their unique creative potential. He did not regard this act as making art per se, but rather engaging in their own process of creation. [*See* IMAGINATION.]

III. ARTISTIC CREATION

This section provides an overview of Jung's conceptualization of the source and process of creativity, as well as his perception of the artist who creates. Jung was very cautious in his understanding and interpretation of artistic creativity, and he was primarily interested in literature, although he made references to all of the arts. He did not offer a complete theory of art primarily because he wrote on so many other topics, and because of his desire to resist overanalyzing art. As such, he was careful to identify the limits of his psychological study of art activity. In fact, he probably would not have touched the topic if he did not consider making art to be in the realm of psychology, which he did.

In general, Jung believed that the process of creation has a feminine quality and the creative work is that of the "mothers," an archetype, within the collective unconscious. As previously stated, much of Jung's theory emphasizes the role of obtaining balance regarding the opposite poles within the individual. The making of art follows through with this idea. When the artist is out of balance psychically, the archetypal image rises to the surface to restore harmony in the individual and, in turn, society, thus keeping in line with the concept of individuation.

Jung made a distinction between the artist and the actual work of art. Artwork may provide inklings to the artist's life but not reveal the unique qualities of the person who created it. Just as the artist's life may provide clues to understanding the work but not shed light on the meaning entirely, Jung felt strongly that psychology can never fully understand the causality of any work of art, largely because the creative urge originates in the unconscious. [*See* ART AND ARTISTS.]

A reductionist approach to understanding art was contrary to Jung's position. (A reductionist approach to art is attempting to trace all the elements of a work of art to the artist's past.) He was in favor of experiencing a work of art (poetry, paintings, literature, etc.) on its own terms instead of looking for the psychological reasons, or causes, of art. Even though the material of the work can be linked, or traced, to the artist's past, this does not allow others to then understand the actual meaning of the work. In this way, Jung saw the artist as quite separate from her or his creative work. In other words, a work of art in some cases transcends the person and is thus a separate entity. Jung was primarily interested in this type of work, later referred to as type two, or visionary, work.

A. Types of Artwork

Work that transcends the artist and work that does not was further described by Jung in the following typology. He identified two types of art: one derived from

the conscious mind and the second from the unconscious mind. The first type of art is controlled, conscious, and made with a specific intention. Jung later referred to this type of literature as psychological in nature. Psychological, in this case, refers to work that is derived from consciousness such as stories of love, family, crime, and society. These works are easily understood. Artwork of this type, whether literature or painting, is deliberate in that the artist knows exactly what he or she is intending to create. The artist and the creation are one; there are *no surprises*.

In contrast, the second type of art is unconscious, uncontrolled, and amazes the artist. The work produced takes on its own form and structure. Whereas the first type of literature is thought of as psychological, the second type is thought of as visionary. (Visionary does not exclude the psychological quality; rather it goes beyond the personal psychology into the suprapersonal realm). Visionary works are those that are unfamiliar, strange, gigantic, and superhuman. These works speak to the depths of the human psyche and the beginnings of our existence, holding ideas that transcend the words or images set forth. They are symbols of something unknown. Darkness surrounds them.

Visionary works are primordial, or archetypal, experiences and not personal experiences. The origins of the creative process are the primordial experiences, but the mythological figures give the work conformation. The primordial images, or archetypal images, are too dark (e.g., demons, spirits). The mythical figures bring lightness to the dark by appearing less frightful or intense and thus bringing harmony to the imagery in a way that is digestible for the current times. These works are extremely important because they originate in the collective unconscious and bring a message for future generations. Positive or negative, the message is ultimately of value.

The artist who produces the second type of work is astonished almost to the point of disbelief. In this experience the artist feels as if someone else has created the work. She or he must allow the process to occur, but not at his or her control. The artist is the vehicle for which the creative process transcends. The artist and the creative process are separate; there are *always surprises*.

A further distinction is made between the first and second type of artist. The distinction rests on the type of *activity* set forth by the artist. The first type of creative activity is thought to be introverted and sentimental. Here, Jung borrowed from the work of Johann Schiller in his conceptualization of sentimental and naive. Intraverted refers to Jung's idea that the artist consciously shapes and controls the art work. On the other hand, the second type of creative activity is extraverted and naive. Extraverted refers to the idea that the artist allows the work to control him or her. In other words, the artist's unconscious takes over.

The action of the unconscious is thought to be the creative urge or impulse that may, in a sense, take over the person. The creative urge arises out of the psyche and is extremely powerful. At times, the urge is so strong that everyday life goes by the wayside in order to create. The creative urge is different for all people and varies depending on the type of work produced.

The ability to *understand* both types of work is also different. The first type of work is intentional and comprehensible. The second type of work goes beyond our understanding to the same degree that occurred while the artist was in the process of creating it. The image, the poem, or the story can only be understood through intuition and always provides multiple meanings. However, within one piece of work there can be both types of expression.

Further, the second type of art produces a symbol or symbols. A symbol is an expression of an idea that cannot yet be discussed or stated in another, clearer way. The verbal expression is nonexistent. Works that are symbolic are difficult to understand and the meaning is not clear. They are challenging and stimulate the viewer or reader's thoughts and feelings. In contrast, the first type of creative work tends to be more appealing because it is complete, compared to the second type of work.

Symbols are produced for the culture and the spirit, according to Jung. They are a product of the collective unconscious. They are based on intuition and are never planned. Symbols allow for society and the individual to move energy from the psyche into valuable accomplishments found in art and science, among other disciplines.

Examples of symbolic, or visionary, art are found in the work of Paul Klee, Wassily Kandinsky, Carlo Carra, and Piet Mondrian. These artists were led by visionary images of their inner world that were indescribable. The inner world is secretive, even to the artists themselves. These artists brought art making to a new level,

that of the mystical and the spiritual, though not of a religious order. The manifestation of the spiritual and mystical visions were found in paintings, collages, and unusual figures made from stone, wood, metal, and glass.

The tracing of these prominent artists reaches to the time of pagan religions. A very dark nature permeated and was pushed into the unconscious psyche of humankind. Pushing away the darkness created more ugliness and evilness manifested in the form of obsessions, addictions, and so on. Artwork of the beginning of the 20th century (e.g., Kandinsky, Klee, Carra, and Mondrian) brought about a positive resurgence of the primordial spirit in the form of archetypal images.

The *part* of the unconscious where art originates was important to Jung. He believed that art derived from one's personal unconscious was more a symptom of a problem or situation rather than a symbol manifested from one's collective unconscious. Conversely, art, great art, that is produced from the collective unconscious, or with archetypal images, has a tremendous effect on the viewer. Our own collective unconscious is stirred up through the form and shape of the artist's work. In this way, art continues to revitalize our connection to the past in a way that is understood by today's culture. Jung believed that this effect revealed the social significance of art and held the artist in high regard. Thus, the creative process is the artists' abilities to manifest archetypal images from the depths of their collective unconscious (which is essential for the process of individuation to take place).

In this way the creation of art is what Jung referred to as participation mystique, which is the mystique, or veil, of great art. This movement is in the realm of the collective unconscious. Asking an artist to explain his or her work is unnecessary (largely because great art is beyond explanation), and learning of her or his life is inconsequential and nonexplanatory to the creation. However, he did write the following brief summary about attributes of the artist.

B. The Artist

Jung saw the artist as an extraordinary human being, one that is granted the benefit and the tragedy of creative vision. Those who create only, or primarily, from their personal experiences are *not* of this lot. They are expressing a symptom of their experience, as referred to earlier. In contrast, artists who are producing great art must transcend the personal and move into the realm of the collective unconscious, thereby speaking to the mind and heart of humankind. Jung saw the artist as a medium for producing work that speaks for all. He or she does not have conscious control to create or not create but rather is propelled by the collective force to create. The artist does not have a choice.

Not only is the artist a creator but also a human being with wants and desires for everyday happiness and experiences. Jung saw the artist as wrought with conflict if these opposing forces—existence as a human being and as an artist—are not reconciled. Primarily the creator who does not acquiesce to the divine power of creativity that has been granted to him or her will be quite conflicted. The creative force is so strong that there is little energy to do much more in life, namely the simple pleasures of the average person. The artist is laced with a burdensome existence, often resulting in a selfish, helpless, infantile, egotistical way of being in the world.

The following analysis of Picasso serves as one, if not the only, analysis of visual art written by Jung.

1. Picasso

Jung reluctantly and briefly approached the subject of Picasso's artwork, and stayed close to the psychology of his art rather then critiquing his art from an aesthetic point of view. He did so looking chronologically at Picasso's work. Overall, Jung described Picasso's work as nonobjective art, originating from inside, or from his unconscious (earlier referred to as type two artwork). There were a few exceptions, as will be illustrated. Again, work from consciousness, or outer experiences, produces images that are recognizable. The objects may be distorted but not to the degree that they are incomprehensible. Artwork created from the inside takes on a symbolic form, often producing works that are strange, unusual, and not understandable.

Jung viewed four periods of Picasso's work from the blue period to the post-Harlequin period. Picasso's blue period was described as objective, from consciousness. He then moved into a different period, which Jung described as moving into the unconscious, the inside. This period is very dark, characterizing the ugliness and evilness of life. Picasso's work then changed into another form and shape, that of the Harlequin, a tragic and ancient god—a very primitive im-

age. The Harlequin image was disturbing to Jung. The period that followed was Picasso's unconscious attempt at conquering his internal conflict—that of opposing forces. The use of piercing, relentless color reflects the strength of the unconscious to handle conflicts of violence.

IV. SUMMARY

Carl Gustav Jung provided a wealth of information to the field of psychology and the process of creativity. From his early days he was ever present to the subtle nuances of the world in which he lived. He was keenly able to integrate his own experiences with those of people around him, from his biological family, to his clients, to his created family. From the beginning he was astonished, amazed, and excited by the duality of life—the secrets of a world of opposites. This dualism continued to plague and interest him for the duration of his life, and through his own experiences, both internal and external, he developed a complex theory of the human mind.

Certainly his theory of the unconscious, with the division of the personal and the collective, was one of his greatest achievements. He has provided a legacy of imaginative, challenging, and intriguing ways of looking at oneself, especially in light of the creative process.

In his work, Jung provided a theoretical structure of two types of art. The first type is conscious, controlled, and within the realm of the personal. The second type is without limits and truly the work of the collective unconscious, or the archetypes. The second type of art was the focus of Jung's interest because it is the work of the primordial. The images that arise from the collective unconscious are symbolic. Symbolic images are the magical images that the viewer relates to with great emotion although not really understanding why. It is through this process that Jung's theory of individuation comes into play, both for the artist and for the viewer or reader. Again, bringing into play archetypes in the collective unconscious, giving them a voice, and allowing others to experience the transcendence into their own collective unconscious is the stuff of great art.

Jung held great regard for the artist. He believed that the artist was chosen, that the artist did not choose to become a creative agent. The artist's life was wrought with conflict over the unbearable creative urge, on the one hand, and the desire to live an everyday life, on the other hand. Jung believed the artist was a true visionary.

In closing, Jung believed that the creative process was central to having a sense of wholeness within oneself. The sense of wholeness provides the individual with an ability to be a true individual. The process of individuation is achieved through a number of different means with the end result, which is never wholly attainable, being that of an increased sense of self.

Bibliography

Hopcke, R. (1989). *A guided tour of the collected works of C. G. Jung*. Boston, MA: Shambala.

Jaffe, A. (1967). *The myth of meaning in the work of C.G. Jung*. London: Hodder & Stoughton.

Knapp, B. L. (1984). *A Jungian approach to literature*. Carbondale, IL: Southern Illinois University.

Knapp, B. L. (1988). *Music, archetype, and the writer: A Jungian view*. University Park, PA: Pennsylvania State University.

Neumann, E. (1959). *Art and the creative unconscious*. Princeton, NJ: Princeton University.

Neumann, E. (1979). *Creative man*. Princeton, NJ: Princeton University.

Philipson, M. (1963). *Outline of a Jungian aesthetics*. Evanston, IL: Northwestern University.

Sharp, D. (1991). *C. G. Jung lexicon: A primer of terms and concepts*. Toronto: University of Toronto.

Snider, C. (1991). *The stuff that dreams are made on: A Jungian interpretation of literature*. Wilmette, IL: Chiron Publications.

Storr, A. (1973). *C. G. Jung*. New York, NY: Viking Press.

Knowledge

Teres Enix Scott

Hampton University

Associative Gradient Mednick's representation (graphic) of a response probability curve based on associational thinking (e.g., word associations); it differs across stimuli and across individuals.

Convergent Thinking Thinking that narrows the available responses with the goal of identifying or selecting the single "best" response to a stimulus.

Divergent Thinking Thinking that seeks to generate multiple (more than one) appropriate and adequate alternative responses to a single stimulus.

Divergent Thinking Variables (Ideational) fluency, flexibility, and originality.

Domain-Specific Knowledge Base The organization of information and knowledge an individual has stored mentally regarding a particular concept or topic. It includes (but is not limited to) definitions, characteristics, facts, beliefs, and methods. A tree-like representation is a useful model of a domain-specific knowledge base.

Functional Fixedness The inability to perceive a tool or concept in any manner that is inconsistent with that typically assigned to it; for example, being unable to think of using a butter knife as a screw driver.

Knowledge Base Breadth The range of alternatives found at any one level of a domain-specific knowledge base.

Knowledge Base Depth The number of levels of stratification in a domain-specific knowledge base, exemplified in degree of detail possible.

Knowledge System The volume of information a person maintains, usually categorized and hierarchically organized.

Nodes and Links A network model where knowledge is represented as an interrelated set of concepts, each concept is a node, and the connections between them are the links.

Schema A mental model of knowledge about something involving an interrelated set of concepts, including attributes, contexts, and other schemata, for example, a schema for birds.

The role of **KNOWLEDGE** in creative thinking has long been a problem for creativity researchers and theorists. Several early theorists identified knowledge as an important component of the creative process. Guilford, who is credited by some with initiating the modern interest in creativity, pointed out in his 1950 presidential address to the APA that "no creative person can get along without previous experiences or facts. . . ," indicating that knowledge is an important resource in creative thinking. Currently it appears to be the consensus that some *knowledge about the area or domain in which the creative work is to be done is necessary. But which aspect of knowledge has what effect is still in question. Three knowledge characteristics are candidates for consideration, knowledge volume, content, and structure.*

I. THE KNOWLEDGE PROBLEM

The task for theorists regarding the knowledge problem is identifying just which creativity effects are the result of which characteristic of knowledge and which are desirable. An additional problem is determining how much of each knowledge characteristic is needed. That is, what type of knowledge structure would be needed to improve the probability of a novel and appropriate response?

Researchers have additional challenges to those of theorists. In order to research the role of characteristics of a knowledge system a researcher must be able to determine if there was any effect of the effort to tease apart the characteristics and to manipulate them independently. Therefore, first is the challenge of measuring people's knowledge (hopefully without adding to it). Because humans are adept learners and educated humans have developed automatic learning practices and habits, the measurement of an individual's knowledge may concomitantly enhance that knowledge. For example, we learn from probing questions and from the process of creating an answer.

A second challenge for the empiricist is manipulating reliably the knowledge base of research participants in experimental settings. This problem may be more technical. That is, how do we measure knowledge base parameters such as volume, content, and structure? Again, this challenge is sensitive to the ease with which knowledge is acquired and modified.

II. THE CONCEPT OF KNOWLEDGE

Knowledge is differentiated from intelligence and from information. Information is the objective body of conceptual and relational items (such as a newspaper, a lecture, or an observation) that forms the base on which an individual builds knowledge. Intelligence is the ability, enhanced by training and practice, to ma-

nipulate information. Knowledge development relies, in part, on both having information and the ability to manipulate it. Because knowledge is created within the individual, the same body of information and intelligence may lead to differing knowledge in different persons. That is, even when the intelligence of two people is comparable, knowledge may vary as a result of each assigning different weights to different units of information or of each having differing motivations or skill at manipulating the available information. [*See* INTELLIGENCE.]

Knowledge may be characterized as organized and systematized information and beliefs that are maintained in memory in a manner similar to a cognitive library. Our knowledge includes a great range of items such as the sum of 3 and 4 (called a "fact") and how to use strategies (a "process") to find the sum of much larger numbers. These two types of knowledge were characterized by John Anderson as "declarative knowledge" and "procedural knowledge." Facts are part of declarative knowledge, which is often the content of formal teaching in schools. Processes are referred to as procedural knowledge, which may be acquired through direct (such as how to add) or indirect instruction (such as learning to turn pages one-by-one for story continuity).

Our knowledge includes information we learned in formal school settings and things we learned informally from our life experience. Further, memory has placed markers on some items which tell us about the circumstances that prevailed (according to our perception) when we acquired that bit of knowledge. Markers can be the location we were in or the emotion we experienced in that learning episode.

Just as many libraries are organized by topics and cross-referenced, our knowledge systems appear to be similarly arranged and accessed, according to the evidence we draw from learning research. This topical organization is based on how we individually classify the things we know. A general topic, such as cars or vegetables, is referred to as a "domain." The content of an individual's knowledge in any specific domain is usually organized hierarchically and referred to as a "domain-specific knowledge base." [*See* DOMAINS OF CREATIVITY.]

The structure (hierarchical organization), volume (amount of information and relations), and content (items of information) of our domain-specific knowledge are important characteristics influencing how we access the information we have when performing cognitive tasks such as problem solving and creative thinking. This was exemplified by research on how "novices" and "experts" solve physics problems. The problems were relatively typical physics problems with well-known effective solution approaches. Novices used obvious or "surface" problem information to classify the problems into types they already knew, in preparation to select a solution strategy. "Experts," on the other hand, were more likely to identify problem attributes neglected by novices and use their greater experience-based knowledge to solve the problems directly, usually doing so faster and more accurately. The result was that novices had a lower probability of solving the problems, in part because they sometimes misidentified or misunderstood the true problem. In this case knowledge was important to recognizing the true nature of the problem, and thus enabling the selection of an effective solution strategy.

Other research on expertise reports that experts use forward solution strategies (starting with the problem and working straight through to a solution, often using an algorithm), which are more expedient, when faced with a familiar problem type. However, the same experts resorted to backward solution strategies (starting with a solution idea and trying to work backward to the problem to verify it) when confronted with unfamiliar problem types, behaving just like novices. The researchers noted that with unfamiliar problems the experts were no faster nor more likely to solve the problem than novices. [*See* EXPERTISE.]

A. Domain-Specific Knowledge Bases

As already stated, knowledge about a particular conceptual area is referred to as domain-specific knowledge. The volume of knowledge that can be identified as pertaining to a particular domain is referred to as a domain-specific knowledge base. Its contents include conceptual objects like facts (including beliefs, schemata, and prototypes) and methods (including strategies, algorithms, and heuristics). How we maintain information or knowledge in memory is a conceptually distinct question from the concept of knowledge discussed here.

Domain-specific knowledge has been conceptualized as having at least two partitions or divisions, the declarative and the procedural. The declarative knowledge partition holds the facts and the procedural knowledge partition maintains the methods that are necessary for the acquisition and verification of knowledge to be added to that knowledge base.

The contents of a domain-specific knowledge base represent a problem in the study of the functioning of a knowledge base because knowledge bases are mutable. Because humans are very adept at learning, whether we want to or not, a domain-specific knowledge base is highly susceptible to influence and change. Influences on domain-specific knowledge bases include addition, deletion, and reorganization based on, for example, the perceptual or conceptual context, learning, and memory. Figure 1 represents a generic graphical model of a small segment of a structured knowledge base.

B. Structural Aspects of Domain-Specific Knowledge Bases

The theory of M. T. H. Chi and her colleagues, about the structure of domain-specific knowledge and how it must be represented to function as it does, exemplifies one way to think about knowledge. In their research model, knowledge is conceptualized as being hierarchically organized and structured as networks or into tree-like systems around specific domains. Network models generally represent concepts as nodes in the structure with branches or links connecting the nodes with each other and with their shared attributes. Therefore the links represent the relational connections between concepts (see Figure 1).

Different knowledge bases within an individual vary in the volume or amount of information they contain, how internally related that information is, and how related it is to other knowledge bases maintained by the same person. The amount of information in any single knowledge base and its range of internal relatedness are evaluated as the "depth" and "breadth" of the knowledge base.

Knowledge is based in the relations within and among concepts. As semantic networks, the concepts of a single domain are hierarchically organized and this tree-like structural and organizational characteristic is the basis for conceptualizing the "depth" and "breadth"

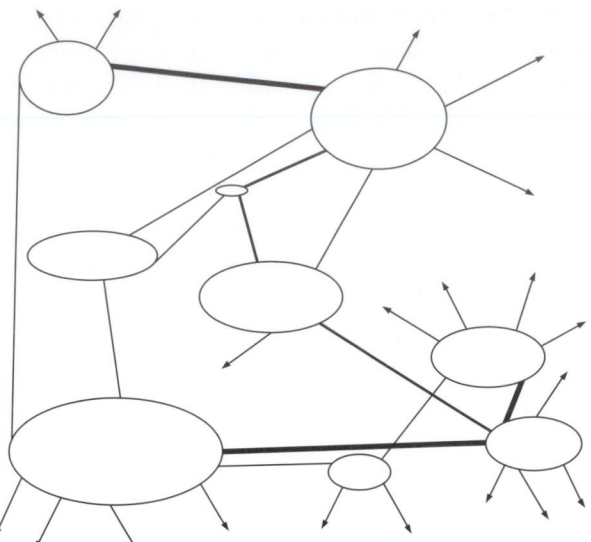

FIGURE 1 Nodes and links in a network. Each oval represents a concept and the lines represent the links between concepts. Concepts vary in size and importance relative to other concepts. Heavier links may represent importance or strength of association or more frequent use.

components of the knowledge base. The number of levels of nodes represent the depth dimension in the knowledge base and roughly correspond to degrees of detail in the organization of the knowledge contents. Similarly, the branching nature of the relations among nodes exemplifies the breadth dimension and represents the alternatives available at any nodal level (see Figure 2).

In a series of studies on children's knowledge bases, David Bjorklund adopted a modified semantic network model with knowledge units or "objects" being represented as nodes which are linked with each other by a variety of relations, including common relations like associative, categorical, and schematic. Bjorklund noted as well that each object has connections with features that characterize it (such as its color). In his research there was improvement on memory tasks in free recall as the children acquired more detailed information that helped in categorizing the stimulus words. He concludes that the effect of a detailed knowledge base is seen in the increased likelihood that relations among the items it contains will be activated. This activation,

in theory, would increase the probability of a creative response.

III. THE NATURE OF PROBLEMS

In the foregoing discussion there have been several references to problems and problem solving. While there is still debate about how to define it, creative thinking is often conceptualized as a problem solving process with certain defining characteristics. One important characteristic is that creative solutions frequently seem to arise from ill-defined problems.

Problems with clear, agreed upon solution strategies and specific answers are considered "well-defined problems." Such problems are successfully solved using convergent thinking approaches and the relevant knowledge base(s), where all bits of fact and strategy lead to a small number of "best" answers (usually just one). The set of physics problems attempted by Chi's experts and novices is an example of the use of knowledge in convergent thinking. The problems were well defined with solutions requiring selecting an appropriate algorithm. The solutions were required to be accurate but creativity was not considered. Apparently, both general and domain-specific knowledge are important to problem solving success and all three knowledge characteristics (volume, content, structure) contribute to the process for both novices and experts.

Problems that do not meet the clarity of strategy and answer criteria are called "ill defined." A problem is ill defined when the problem solver does not know the answer and does not know an infallible way of finding the solution. Because of this feature ill-defined problems are more likely to involve heuristic approaches rather than algorithmic solution strategies. Heuristic approaches send the problem solver in search through their knowledge storehouse for tools to try in the solution of the problem. This search has the potential of bringing a wider range of knowledge items or characteristics to bear on the problem, resulting in a higher probability of a creative solution. Many cognitive and creativity theorists have noted that ill-defined problems seem to be more effectively solved using divergent thinking approaches. This strategy is more likely to result in creative solutions. Many creativity theorists

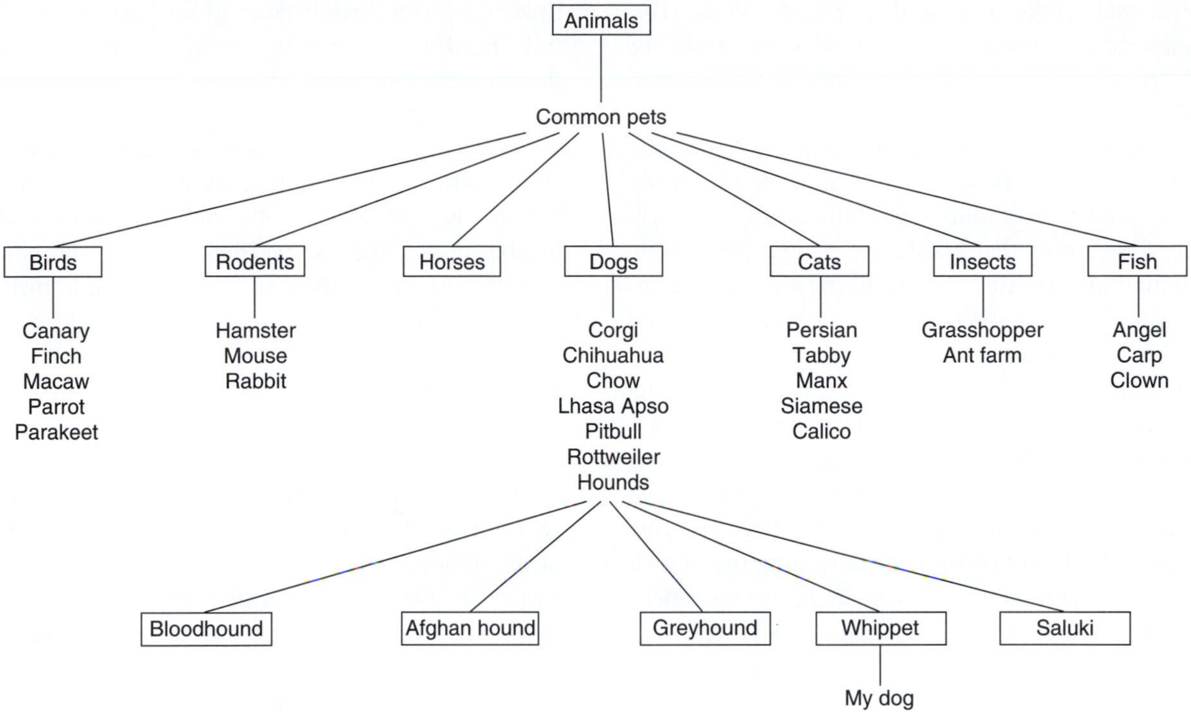

FIGURE 2 A stylized example of the author's knowledge system regarding common pets, indicating its hierarchical structure. Six levels of organization are displayed in this treelike structure. Items maintained at about the same level are assumed to be comparable in some way. Notice the breadth of types of animals the author includes in the concept "Common Pets" (from birds to fish). Would you have included insects in this concept? Note, also, there is greater depth as one proceeds from the general category "Animals" down to "My dog." The author apparently knows very little about horses.

suggest that often creative thinking includes divergent thinking, which is the process of finding multiple alternative solutions that satisfy the problem conditions. What is the role of knowledge in this case? And how must the knowledge be structured to be most functional in its role?

It is important to note at this point that anecdotal information and some research findings have suggested that a key component of the creative process is "problem finding." Problem finding refers to the process of identifying, selecting, or stating the problem to be addressed. Recognizing and identifying a problem that can serve as the substrate for creative problem solving may be a skill that is improved with practice or instruction. Problem selection may also be the way in which prior knowledge inhibits creative thinking, the habit of identifying problems in preconceived formats. [*See* PROBLEM SOLVING.]

IV. DIVERGENT THINKING

Divergent thinking and divergent thinking tasks are often used to evaluate creative potential. Typically they require the production of multiple alternatives in response to a single stimulus. These tasks traditionally give us at least three ways of measuring performance used in creativity research. The three variables, ideational fluency, originality, and flexibility have been demonstrated to be reliable and valid. Ideational fluency is the number of different ideas produced, originality is the number of unusual ideas given, and flexibility is the number of different categories represented in the responses.

Divergent thinking, by definition, requires the spawning of ideas, or the generation of many responses. In the study of creativity, the products of divergent thinking are also assessed using creativity criteria such as "novelty" and "appropriateness." Performance on divergent thinking tasks is currently one of the most widely accepted measures of the potential for creative ideation.

The act of thinking divergently includes the idea of generativity in the production of multiple responses. That is, it involves finding numerous alternative or divergent responses that satisfy the criteria inherent in the initiation of the divergent thinking activity. The criteria, therefore, are often either or both domain- and situation-specific.

The demands made by divergent thinking tasks suggest that the responses produced are the result of a search, for example, of the knowledge bases in memory. By requiring multiple alternative responses (each of which should satisfy some problem-related criteria), divergent thinking tasks initiate searching the knowledge base (assumedly using one or more heuristics). The nature of the demand and the criteria for responding help determine the course of the search, which, in turn, partially determines the extent of the search. For these reasons the multiple alternative response demand characteristic can lead to a relatively exhaustive search, when subjects are responding without known time constraints. [See DIVERGENT THINKING.]

A. Divergent Thinking and Knowledge

There have been few studies explicitly examining the functioning of knowledge in creative thinking or divergent thinking. One study found that more creative individuals, as identified by their peers, were influenced by a wider array of sources, both media and personal interactions, than less creative individuals.

An interpretation of knowledge base theory implies a parallelism between knowledge base structural characteristics and divergent thinking variables. It has been proposed that divergent thinking tasks may be a useful tool in the study of knowledge systems. The basic design of divergent thinking tasks mandates that respondents produce multiple exemplars of a case or multiple solutions to a problem. Because of their format, divergent thinking tasks are easily adapted, allowing the selection of a topic from a range of domains, while not changing the basic cognitive operations applied to the knowledge in a domain. Having respondents give mul-

tiple "uses" (the specification of the type of operation to be used) for a common object, for example, "fork," does not change when a different object is probed, for example, "paper."

Divergent thinking tasks have well-established evaluation methods—incorporating several measures which may be used as dependent variables such as fluency, flexibility, and originality. These measures are important because they appear to intersect with knowledge base depth and breadth, two key structural components of knowledge systems. Based on this analysis it has been suggested that divergent thinking tasks allow the examination of change in the structure as well as the content of a knowledge base. Several methodological constraints have been identified in the use of divergent thinking tasks to evaluate creative potential. Some of the important concerns are (a) the apparent elimination of time limits (from the respondent's point of view), (b) avoiding labeling the tasks as "tests," and (c) ensuring that in the structure and wording of the instructions there is an emphasis on the desirability of respondents producing multiple noncensored responses (sometimes with the stated goal that responses are to be "creative" or "unique").

In a study exploring the impact of the volume and structure of domain-specific knowledge in creative thinking, divergent thinking tasks were used to establish knowledge base volume in a pre–post four group design. The intervening treatments endeavored to manipulate specific knowledge base structural characteristics, particularly depth and breadth. Subjects responded to both problem solving and problem finding tasks. In a problem solving context, divergent thinking fluency and flexibility were enhanced by increasing the volume or depth of the knowledge base. However, uniqueness (originality) was increased only by adding to the knowledge base when problem finding. [See FLEXIBILITY.]

V. CREATIVITY THEORIES AND KNOWLEDGE

Theories of creativity differ in the position they take on the centrality and importance of a large volume of domain-specific knowledge and the effect such knowledge will have on the probability of creative production. For some theories, knowledge is essential to the process and central to true value in the creative product. Others suggest it may be helpful in some aspect of the creative process but it is certainly not required. However, the latter theories do tend to recognize the value of product-specific knowledge for the creative thinking process.

A statement that knowledge is important in creative thinking is hardly a theory of knowledge or of how knowledge works in creativity or in divergent thinking; however, it can provide a basis for empirical investigation. The following discussion considers a representative set of modern and historical theories.

A. Metaphor Models of Creativity

There is a set of current theories built on the role that metaphors have played in creative production. An anecdotal example of the metaphor as a process for creativity is found in the inspiration Friedrich Kekule found for the structure of the benzene ring. It has been reported that he credited a dream he had about a snake with its tail in its mouth taking a shape like a ring. [*See* DREAMS AND CREATIVITY.]

Metaphors, as a basis of creative thinking, are thought of as models which provide parallels for the creative connection. They usually function by making possible the reinterpretation of a concrete relationship in abstract form, thus allowing substitution of an abstraction for the concrete components. In the Kekule metaphor, the shape that the snake assumed was concrete, yet it represented the effective abstraction of "ringness." Kekule had only to remember the dream and identify the key salient features.

Metaphors generally embody multiple relationships. This is a consequence of their semantic structure and of their functioning, which involves symbolic representation in allowing one thing to stand for another, a paralleling process. Because there are multiple components of a metaphorical statement there are multiple possible internal relationships and multiple possible parallels. These multiple relationships mean the observer must identify specifically the effective parallel needed for creative reconceptualization of the components of the problem.

Therefore, metaphor models of creative processing have a knowledge need. In using metaphors one needs to recognize and understand the essential relationship in the metaphor that provides the parallels for the problem being considered—the parallel that models the creative function. Then one must establish the effective parallel. [*See* METAPHORS.]

B. Other Modern and Historical Theories

Many of the creativity theories which discuss knowledge can be assigned to one of two positions on the nature and functioning of domain-specific knowledge in creative thinking: they take either a "knowledge as necessary" position or a "knowledge as sufficient" position. Accordingly, some theories consider domain-specific knowledge to be essential to the development of novel responses. Others assume only minimal domain-specific knowledge is a prerequisite to creative solutions (where minimal is the theoretic minimum necessary to produce the actual product). Still other theories suggest that only a general domain structure is needed along with ability or technical facility in creativity or problem solving.

Theorists who believe that a significant depth of domain-specific knowledge is necessary to creative production suggest that a significant volume of domain-specific knowledge (beyond the common or general knowledge of the average educated person) is essential to the production of any truly valuable creative product. The reasoning of this view is that knowledge informs creativity in the following ways:

- By clarifying what has been tried, thus making it possible to avoid previously nonfruitful approaches
- By contextualizing the problem, thus making it possible to avoid pursuing irrelevant tangents
- By delineating the available tools and methods for addressing the problem

This approach may be called the "knowledge as necessary, essential, or required" perspective on the centrality of knowledge to creative production.

Other theorists believe that most creative products can be achieved in more than one way. That is, that there are multiple paths that can result in identical, similar, or comparable products. Evidence for this position has been drawn from a number of sources, not the least of which is the fact that throughout history there have been a number of incidents of parallel discovery or creation. If this idea that there are potentially multiple pathways to many creations is true, the possibility underscores the need for flexibility in creative thinking.

This view holds that, for any product *p*, the only knowledge which is therefore necessary is that knowledge which specifically supported the production of *p*, the observed creative product. Then, with respect to the general role of domain-specific knowledge, this second perspective may be considered the "knowledge as sufficient, important, or useful, but not necessary" approach.

Some of the latter theorists would include those who argue that it is possible to have *too much* knowledge. Their position is that too much knowledge would increase the probability of the establishment of some inhibiting or interfering cognitive process, such as functional fixedness, or the assumption of "knowing" what is *not* possible, or some similar form of psychological set. The "knowledge as necessary" versus the "knowledge as sufficient" characterization artificially categorizes the variety of positions held into a "strong" position—knowledge as necessary/essential/required—versus a more moderate one—knowledge as sufficient/important/useful.

C. Review of Theories

The following discussion reviews the suggested role of knowledge of several representative theories of creativity. This review provides a context for the consideration of the effect of knowledge in creative thinking. Thus, it allows the identification (or interpretation) of the "necessary" or "sufficient" position of these theories. The suggested "necessary/sufficient" determination has been based on the knowledge requirements imposed by the theory, either explicitly or implicitly. Some theories are more explicit than others in defining the centrality of knowledge to creative production.

1. Donald Campbell

Campbell proposed a theory entitled "blind-variation-and-selective-retention process in creative thought." Campbell's model requires knowledge resources that put him in the "knowledge as important" position. Campbell's theory implicitly suggests

that achieving the creative concept includes the conscious, though perhaps nondirected, search of appropriate knowledge resources by the creator. Without the knowledge resource base it would be difficult to perform Campbell's processing model. Even with the knowledge, there is no guarantee of creative problem solving success.

2. Graham Wallas

Wallas' theory suggests the "knowledge as necessary" position. Wallas suggests a four-phase model, labeling the phases preparation, incubation, illumination, and verification. The acquisition of knowledge is a primary component of Wallas' model of creative processing, in that it is the primary goal of his preparation phase of creative production. This level of importance implies that creativity is significantly involved with the volume of knowledge, Wallas clearly identifies the gathering of resources, including information, as a component of the preparation phase of the process. He conceptualizes the preparation phase in two ways: (1) lifelong learning stands as the backdrop providing context for (2) the gathering of problem-specific resources. Wallas' two-part preparation concept further suggests the "knowledge as necessary" position. [*See* INCUBATION.]

3. Sarnoff Mednick

Mednick expresses a "knowledge as important" position. Mednick suggests that creative responses are the result of associative processes bringing together remotely related elements. Mednick conceptualizes creativity as a form of problem solving that involves an associative search of the related memory or knowledge bases for possible solutions. He theorizes that a search using a flat associative gradient has a higher probability of bringing together remote associates and therefore potentially leads to creative responses.

The work of Mednick is notable as a theory about the role of knowledge in creativity. Mednick offers a general process model of creativity, in which he focuses on the processes involved in generating "new" ideas. He theorizes that creative responses are the product of "a flattened associative gradient" employed to find potential solutions to a problem. That is, according to Mednick, creativity is the result of an associative process where a "remote" association is found that creatively satisfies the problem.

He proposes that creativity operates through any of three component processes which he labeled serendipity, similarity, and mediation. Serendipity would account for relationships found by chance. It may be assumed that significant knowledge could increase the probability that the required knowledge elements are in the knowledge base while decreasing the probability of making the needed chance association. Similarity would be comparable to a metaphor model with the knowledge problems attendant thereto. Mediation suggests normal problem solving cognition and the related risks of psychological set. However, his focus on interacting elements of an associative gradient has more implications for structure of the knowledge base than for volume. [*See* SERENDIPITY.]

For Mednick the creative process is represented in the gradient of the associative hierarchy of the responses produced. A steep associative gradient with narrow breadth is representative of a narrow search along existing paths which usually leads to high levels of detail, specificity, and accuracy in a convergent thinking problem solving task. A flat associative gradient with wide breadth represents a broad search, slower solution speeds, less accuracy and detail, and a higher probability of examining the usefulness of peri- or extra-domain, "remote" material in the problem solving process. The type of thinking represented in the latter case is often referred to in the literature as divergent thinking and, according to Mednick, it represents the type of thinking needed to produce creative results.

Mednick suggests that it is the frequency with which the thinker has performed similar searches (which is a form of practice) that contributes to the development of a steep associative gradient and an automaticity in responding. His associative gradient model, coupled with his three operative components, suggests that Mednick would take a "knowledge as important" position.

4. M. T. H. Chi

Chi seems to take the "knowledge as necessary" position. Chi and her colleagues suggest that it is from the automaticity identified by Mednick that the expert's speed and accuracy arises in the manipulation of domain-specific material in problem solving. In a discussion of the functioning of knowledge systems, particularly with respect to creativity, Chi suggested the constraint that the definition of creativity be restricted to the type of conceptual change that is not necessarily between knowledge "trees" (domains) but instead is change that is unlikely to occur because of the distance between the creative concept and the initial concept in the knowledge structure. Thus, she supports the approach to knowledge use in creativity which suggests that domain-specific knowledge is necessary in the development of a creative response. Moreover, similar to Mednick, Chi suggests that the creative response is not the result of a significant reorganization of an existing knowledge structure, but rather the product of an extension of the knowledge base (based on a node and link network model; see Fig. 1). The extension results from following the pattern of concepts through links to a node–link–node point that satisfies the problem and is beyond the usual search parameters. That is, Chi suggests that creativity be defined as conceptual change which has a low probability because of the considerable distance between the starting concepts and the "creative" solution. This view of the creative process is similar to Mednick's associative gradient.

5. Robert Weisberg

Weisberg is representative of the "knowledge as necessary" position. Weisberg considers creative thinking to be problem solving and that all problem solving is based on knowledge. He concludes that solutions to novel problems require creative thinking. Thus, creative thinking in all domains requires extensive knowledge in those domains. He further points out that problem solving seems to require domain-specific expertise. In fact, according to Weisberg, there is little empirical support for "the occurrence of spontaneous, remote, analogical transfer . . . without overlap of surface information." (p. 120.)

Weisberg proposes that the creative solution develops out of the beginning attempts to solve the problem, that all solvers start at basically the same place, and that the ones who finally come up with the solution have no unusual insight to begin with. He goes on to state specifically that the development of the new solutions depends on the knowledge of the person. He suggests that straightforward knowledge application is used to attempt to solve the problem initially and that it is only after having difficulty with this approach that creative solution is possible. He notes that creative approaches often involve modifications of the initial attempts based on problem demands and that the modifications are in part the product of acquisition of additional information. He finally suggests that the volume of the individual's domain-specific knowledge predicts the probability of identifying relevant similarities between the current problem and the individual's past experience. Similarities allow the application of criteria or models that emanate from that knowledge to the development of a creative solution.

Based on his review of the literature, Weisberg concludes that the quality of detail from past experience determines efficiency in problem solving on a novel problem. He adds that developing expertise involves acquiring a significant volume of knowledge about specific situations, which can be applied to new situations based on the similarity to situations one has faced before.

With respect to expertise in problem solving, Weisberg agrees with Greeno, both emphasize the need for detailed domain-specific knowledge on the part of those who wish to make original contributions in any area. From this Weisberg concludes that all performances are based on knowledge and that the remaining question for him is how directly knowledge is applied. Therefore, for Weisberg knowledge is necessary.

6. Teresa Amabile

Amabile seems to support the "knowledge as useful" position. Amabile and her colleagues proposed a "componential model" that takes a social psychological approach to address a broad range of factors she found to be influential in creative production. Her model has three major components, with "knowledge about the domain" and "special domain-relevant 'talent'" as aspects of the first component called "domain-relevant skills." She suggests that this component is first in its fundamental relationship to the final product and that it is the basis of the cognitive behavior in the creative process. Amabile identifies both factual and procedural domain knowledge as important aspects of this component, together they establish a set of cognitive pathways that allow one to solve a given problem or do a given task.

This component includes all skills relevant to the general domain, rather than skills relevant to only a specific task within the domain. These "skills" function at an intermediate level of specificity with respect to the task demands. On the other hand, Amabile places

knowledge of heuristics for generating novel ideas in her second component labeled creativity-relevant skills.

Amabile concludes that performance will be "acceptable" if the requisite domain-relevant skills are present. However, ample domain-relevant skills will not result in creative work, if creativity-relevant skills are lacking. She takes the position that it is not possible to have too much knowledge about a task domain. This conclusion is based on research indicating that the important distinction is the way in which the available knowledge is stored and the ease with which it can be accessed, rather than the total amount of knowledge. This conclusion places Amabile in the "knowledge as useful" position.

7. Dean Keith Simonton

Simonton appears to express a "knowledge as required" perspective. Simonton, another social psychologist, is interested in "genius" and its relationship to creativity. He suggests the true measure of creativity is in the successful "persuasion" of viewers by the creative person of the value of his or her work. It is this view of the role of persuasion in the recognition of creativity that implies that the creator should be a leader, according to Simonton. His historiometric method and analyses led him to propose the "chance-configuration theory." He concludes that knowledge interacts with other creativity factors in such a way that the most personally directive, definitive, significant, and important creative contributions are made relatively early in careers, before peak knowledge attainment. Simonton's reliance on knowledge interacting seems to exemplify the "knowledge as required" perspective.

8. Robert Albert

Albert's position appears to be "knowledge is necessary." Albert conducted a longitudinal study on the relationship between giftedness and creativity in male adolescents. Albert believes that self-knowledge and self-directed world knowledge are the fundamental source of creativity because knowledge determines decisions and opportunities. Albert assumes that the decisions one makes on the basis of one's knowledge determine the opportunities one has.

Albert thereby identifies knowledge as the vehicle by which the opportunity to express creativity and have it recognized works. Yet, by comparing only comparably gifted persons who differ in creative production, he is still unclear about the role of knowledge in the generation of ideas. Albert's position appears to be "knowledge as necessary."

9. Howard Gruber

Gruber is representative of the "knowledge as sufficient or useful" approach. In the "evolving systems approach" theory of creativity developed by Gruber and his colleagues, creativity is a developmental process associated with a person's interests and work. The creative person is thought to be composed of three loosely related systems which have evolved coincidentally throughout the person's life. The three components are a system of knowledge, a system of affect or emotion, and a system of purposes.

Here knowledge is considered to be the individual's organization of self-selected cognitive structures. Gruber defines the term "creative" as accommodating all sorts of effective extraordinariness. Gruber claims insight comes to the prepared mind; but that this preparation is not done to the mind but by it. Thus, Gruber predicts that the processes of knowledge acquisition and use may be more important and influential than the knowledge base, volume, or contents. Therefore, Gruber is representative of the "knowledge as sufficient or useful" approach to creative thinking.

VI. CREATIVITY AND KNOWLEDGE

In the creativity literature there are several, either explicit or implicit, theoretical perspectives on the role of knowledge and the nature of the cognitive processes in creative thinking. Empirical investigation of these perspectives has been sparse. The divergent thinking paradigm may be an effective tool in this investigation. Theory and research suggest that a greater volume of general and domain-specific knowledge increases the resources available for problem solving and for divergent production, while individually or situationally determined characteristics of access and use of this volume of knowledge may influence the probability of a "creative" response.

It is suggested that, because of their structure and demand characteristics, divergent thinking tasks will effectively sample the essential structure and contents of a knowledge base without engendering significant change in it. This is consistent with theories which imply that sampling occurs because the task demand requiring multiple responses can be satisfied using an associative strategy with the problem as the stimulus and the initiating feature. The associative process, therefore, represents one method of covering the associative distance between conceptual nodes in a knowledge system.

Whether knowledge is "necessary, essential, or required," or is simply "sufficient, useful, or important," cannot be determined at this point. Whatever its role, how it functions to accomplish that role, and why it functions that way also remain to be determined. Further questions will address how information should be packaged to maximize the probability of creative thinking as compared to other kinds of thinking (e.g., critical thinking), and what knowledge management abilities and skills need to be developed to facilitate creative thinking when it is desired. Frontiers are created at the limits of knowledge—in invention, in discovery, and in all manner of creative function.

Bibliography

Amabile, T. M. (1983). *The social psychology of creativity.* New York: Springer-Verlag.

Chi, M. T. H. (1992). Conceptual change within and across ontological categories: Examples from learning and discovery in science. In R. Giere (Ed.), *Cognitive models of science: Minnesota studies in the philosophy of science.* Minneapolis: University of Minnesota Press.

Gruber, H. E. (1989). The evolving systems approach to creative work. In D. B. Wallace & H. E. Gruber (Eds.), *Creative people at work: Twelve cognitive case studies* (pp. 3–24). New York: Oxford University Press.

Runco, M. A. (1997). *The creativity research handbook, volume one.* Cresskill, NJ: Hampton Press.

Simonton, D. K. (1984). *Genius, creativity, and leadership: Historiometric inquiries.* Cambridge, MA: Harvard University Press.

Sternberg, R. J., & Lubart, T. I. (1995). *Defying the crowd: Cultivating creativity in a culture of conformity.* New York: The Free Press.

Weisberg, R. W. (1993). *Creativity: Beyond the myth of genius.* New York: H. H. Freeman.

Hans Adolf Krebs

1900–1981

Biochemist

Discoverer of the urea cycle and the citric acid cycle

Frederic L. Holmes

Yale University

HANS ADOLF KREBS was a German-born biochemist who settled in England after the Nazi takeover of Germany in 1933. Trained in medicine, Krebs learned in the laboratory of Otto Warburg the methods and style of biochemical research that he later pursued with great success. Two years after beginning independent research, Krebs discovered in Freiburg in 1932 the ornithine cycle of urea synthesis that marked him as a rising star in his field. In England he spent 2 years in the biochemical laboratory at Cambridge, then moved to the University of Sheffield, where he discovered in 1937 the cyclic reaction sequence of oxidative carbohydrate metabolism, later known as the "Krebs cycle," for which he was awarded a Nobel Prize in 1953. Together with numerous other publications on metabolic reactions, these two major landmarks made him by the beginning of World War II one of the leading architects of the emerging subfield of intermediary metabolism. In 1945 he became director of a Unit for Research in Cell Metabolism, later transferred from Sheffield to Oxford University, which became an international center for research and training in this field. Maintaining a steady scientific productivity for the remainder of his long life, Krebs continued to be a leader in his field for nearly 50 years.

The second of three children of Georg Krebs, a highly regarded otolaryngologist in the picturesque

Hans Adolf Krebs, Nobel Laureate in Physiology or Medicine, 1953. Copyright © The Nobel Foundation.

Hanoverian town of Hildesheim, and of Alma Davidson Krebs, whose family had been established there for many generations, Hans grew up in a comfortable, well-ordered, but strictly disciplined family. Hans deeply admired his father, a widely cultured, witty, but somewhat aloof figure in his life, who regarded Hans as less talented than his mathematically gifted younger brother, Wolf. Educated in the classical tradition of the humanistic gymnasium, Hans did well in all his subjects, but did not excel in any single area. Without close friends outside his family, he industriously pursued crafts such as bookbinding, read widely (especially in history), and practiced the piano assiduously, even though he recognized early his limited musical ability. Both of his parents were Jewish, but because his father believed in assimilation as the best course for German Jews, Hans was raised without any formal religion.

When he was about fifteen, Hans Krebs decided that he would enter medicine, assuming that he would eventually join his father's practice. Drafted into the army during the last months of World War I, he was released after receiving a few weeks of basic training, and immediately began his medical education at the nearby University of Göttingen. Following a long-standing German custom, he attended several other universities, including Freiburg, Munich, and Berlin, to hear the lectures of outstanding teachers in each of the basic science and clinical fields. Inspired by the discussions of their own scientific or medical discoveries that some of these teachers included in their lectures, Krebs became interested in the possibility that he too might go into research. At Freiburg he had an opportunity to carry out a project on the vital staining of cells, which led to a publication under his own name and reinforced his ambition to do further laboratory work. In emulation of some of his teachers, he envisioned that he might combine a clinical career in internal medicine with research in problems related to that field.

After receiving his M.D. from the University of Berlin in 1923, Krebs performed his mandatory year of clinical service at the Third Medical Clinic in Berlin. There he was able to undertake, nominally in collaboration with his supervising clinician, an experimental study concerning the passage of various dyes from the circulation into the cerebral spinal fluid of dogs. Essen-

tially unaided, he designed, carried out, and published the results of these relatively simple but soundly conceived experiments. Krebs then spent 1 year in a special course designed to teach chemistry to medically trained investigators.

Through chance personal connections, Krebs had an unexpected opportunity, at the beginning of 1926, to enter the laboratory of the eminent biochemist Otto Warburg as a paid research assistant. Spending 4 years there, Krebs learned the precise experimental techniques that Warburg had devised to study cellular metabolism quantitatively. Using an improved version of a micromanometer employed by physiologists since the beginning of the century to measure the rates of oxygen consumption and carbon dioxide formation in tissues, Warburg had found that thin slices of tissue placed in a fluid medium approximating that of their physiological environment could survive for several hours, maintaining their normal rates of gaseous exchange. Warburg applied these methods mainly to investigate the catalytic properties of what he called the *Atmungsferment*, or respiratory enzyme, and to compare the respiratory properties of cancer cells with those of normal tissue. While working on problems that Warburg assigned him, Krebs had the idea that these methods could be readily applied to study also the intermediary steps in the metabolic reaction sequences that connect foodstuffs with the final excretory products of organisms. One of his teachers at Freiburg, Franz Knoop, had impressed on him several years earlier that a central goal of biochemistry was to establish unbroken connections between the starting and end points of these reaction chains. Warburg did not permit Krebs to carry out such an independent project, but Krebs kept the idea in mind until he was able to begin research on his own. Then it became the guiding force in his early career.

Because Warburg informed him late in 1929 that he must leave his laboratory by the end of the following March, and then gave him little assistance in finding another job, Krebs concluded that his mentor did not consider him capable of a research career. Whether this was the case or only a subjective impression, Krebs did a "great deal of heart-searching" about the kind of career he could manage. His own doubts about his scientific competence were counterbalanced by his strong interest in continuing what he had learned to do under

Warburg. In a department of medicine in a hospital that encouraged research, he thought, he might be able to try for a research career, even while obtaining the clinical training that would enable him to fall back on medical practice if he did not succeed as an investigator. With the help of an older clinical friend in Berlin, he found a position at a municipal hospital near Hamburg. There he had time, despite heavy clinical duties, to begin his own research projects. One year later he moved to Freiburg, in a department of medicine headed by Siegfried Thannhauser. Here, too, he had clinical responsibilities, but entered a university environment conducive to basic research, where he had also the company of other able young scientists. In Freiburg Krebs took up an investigation of the synthesis of urea, using the methods he had learned from Warburg, that led him within 9 months to his first major discovery—the ornithine cycle (see Fig. 1). This auspicious success gave him a self-confidence that never again faltered. His research career thrived in Freiburg, where he soon began to attract a small group of young investigators, until it was abruptly interrupted by his dismissal, in April of 1933, under the terms of the Nazi Civil Service reform law that barred non-Aryans from university posts.

Invited by Frederick Gowland Hopkins to work in the biochemistry department at Cambridge, then one of the leading international centers of the field, Krebs was able to bring his manometers with him and quickly resumed his research where he had broken it off less than 3 months earlier. In England he did not reenter medicine. From then on he devoted himself tirelessly, 6 days a week, to his chosen science. After 2 years in Cambridge, he was offered a position as lecturer in the Department of Pharmacology at the University of Sheffield. Krebs left Cambridge for this much less prominent location largely because he anticipated that in Sheffield he would have sufficient laboratory space and other resources to begin to build a team of investigators. One year after settling there, he announced the discovery of the citric acid cycle (see Figs. 2 and 3). Many of the experiments were performed by his first graduate student, William Arthur Johnson. As Krebs's reputation grew, students began to come also from other countries to learn the techniques and to benefit from the leadership that he was now exerting in the field of intermediary metabolism.

During the war, Krebs was able to maintain his metabolic research, but he participated also in war-related investigations of human nutritional requirements with conscientious objectors who volunteered to serve as subjects. At the end of the war the Medical Research Council selected Krebs as one of the promising scientists that it would support by establishing a research unit under his direction. The additional funding thus made available enabled him to expand his facilities to make accommodation for the increasing number of young scientists who gravitated to his laboratory.

I. POST-WAR CAREER

Much of the work that Krebs and his associates carried out in the postwar years involved further exploration of the scope and function of the citric acid, or Krebs cycle. It was now seen not only as the pathway of oxidative carbohydrate metabolism, but as the final common pathway for the degradation of all classes of foodstuffs, as well as the source of the carbon skeletons for many cell constituents. Beginning in the mid-1950s, Krebs turned his primary attention from the identification of metabolic reaction sequences to the regulation of their pathways.

In 1954 Krebs received an offer to become the professor of biochemistry at the University of Oxford. After negotiating to bring his Medical Research Council

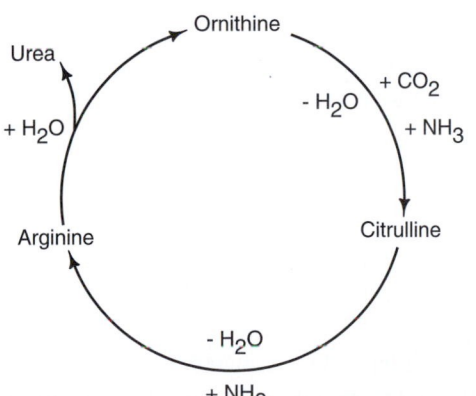

FIGURE 1 Ornithine cycle of urea synthesis. "The Discovery of the Ornithine Cycle of Urea Synthesis," by H. A. Krebs, 1973, *Biochemical Education, 1,* p. 21. Copyright 1973, with permission from Elsevier Science.

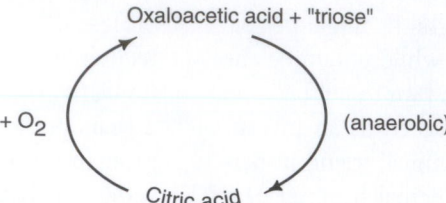

In this cycle "triose" reacts with oxaloacetic acid to form citric acid and in the further course of the cycle oxaloacetic acid is regenerated. The net effect of the cycle is the complete oxidation of "triose."

The conversion of citric into oxaloacetic acid passes through the following intermediate stages:

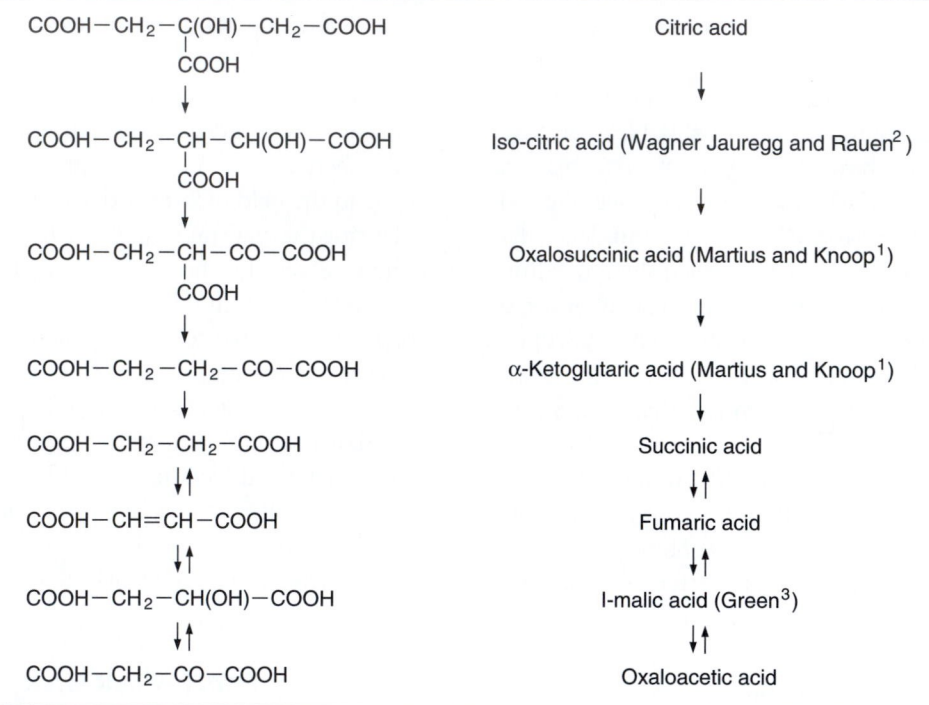

FIGURE 2 First schematic representations of Krebs cycle, redrawn from a sketch by Krebs in manuscript submitted to *Nature,* June 10, 1937. This paper was not published. A similar representation was published in 1937 in *Enzymologia, vol. 4,* pp. 153–154.

(MRC) unit with him, he accepted. At Oxford Krebs had responsibility, in addition, for the large existing department. Administrative duties and his efforts to introduce changes that would make it easier to attract and retain able scientists consumed much of his time, but he managed, with the support of his associates, to sustain his research productivity. Since the war, he had not personally performed experiments at the bench, but he kept in close daily contact with the students, technicians, and postdoctoral fellows who worked under his supervision. Unlike Warburg, Krebs also encouraged more experienced investigators to pursue relatively independent projects.

At the statutory retirement age of 67, it appeared that Krebs would be at last forced into research inactivity or else to leave England; but through the intercession of two prominent senior associates, he was able to obtain enough laboratory space at the Radcliffe Infirmary to

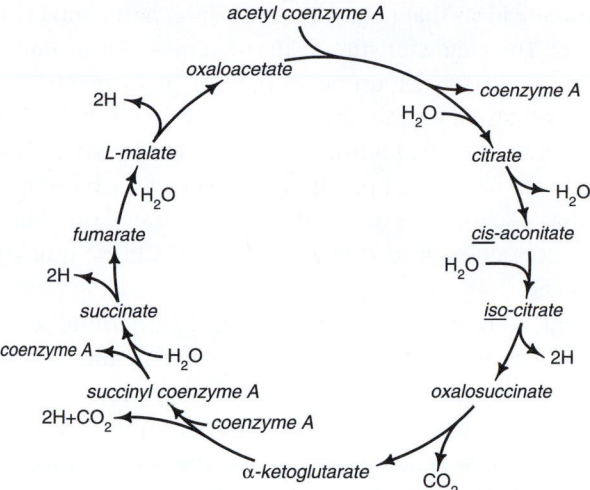

FIGURE 3   Krebs cycle as represented in *Energy Transforma-tions in Living Matter* by H. A. Krebs and H. L. Kornberg, 1957, Berlin: Springer Verlag, p. 215. The cycle was at that time called the "tricarboxylic acid cycle," rather than its original designa-tion, "citric acid cycle," because of doubts, later resolved, that citric acid itself lay on the main pathway.

continue, with the support of the MRC and a small core of his former research team. There he and his team fol-lowed the same lines of investigation that he had pur-sued for more than 30 years. Krebs stayed actively en-gaged in this work up until 2 weeks before his death, at the age of 81, in November 1981.

II. PATTERNS OF CREATIVE ACTIVITY

The general pattern of Hans Krebs's scientific activity displays characteristics that might appear at first sight disparate. Over the long trajectory of his career there were two peaks, attained during his first 7 years on his own, that tower over the field in which he specialized. The first, the ornithine cycle, marked, in the opinion of the distinguished historian of biochemistry Joseph S. Fruton, the beginning of a new era in biochemistry. The second, the citric acid cycle was, according to the influential recent textbook of biochemistry of Alfred Lehninger, "the most important single discovery in the history of metabolic biochemistry." Together these two discoveries formed the basis for a more general con-

ception of the metabolic cycle as a distinctive pattern of chemical reactions peculiar to life. To some observ-ers, Krebs brought to the field a deep creative insight that has given shape to this area of biochemistry.

The research on which these contributions were im-mediately based took place within surprisingly short periods of time. From the beginning of his investiga-tion of urea synthesis to the first publication announc-ing the outlines of the ornithine cycle, only 9 months elapsed. The broad problem of the oxidative metabo-lism of fats, carbohydrates, and several prominently identified intermediates occupied him intermittently for several years between 1933 and 1937. But after he obtained a crucial clue from a publication of Franz Knoop and Carl Martius in April 1937, it took Krebs less than 2 months to perform or direct the experi-ments and formulate the conclusions on which he based his proposal for the citric acid cycle.

These were not, however, isolated bursts of inspired activity. They were only highlights along a relentless course that Krebs pursued almost without interruption from the time he entered Warburg's laboratory in 1926 until the end of his life. From Warburg he acquired the habit of performing two sets of manometric experi-ments daily, 6 days a week, 11 months of the year, year after year. In no year from 1925 onward did Krebs publish fewer than 15 papers on work he had either carried out or supervised. Along the way there were other significant discoveries, such as the synthesis of glutamine; some steps in the synthesis of uric acid; a modification of the citric acid cycle—the glyoxylic acid cycle—which replaces the former in certain mi-croorganisms and plants; and in the later stages of his work, wide ranging explorations of the mechanisms that control metabolic pathways. There were also many papers that reported relatively minor refinements to the evidence for, or additional information on, the rep-ertoire of problems with which he concerned himself.

An unbroken run of the laboratory notebooks in which Krebs kept the daily record of his experiments from the time of his entry into Warburg's laboratory until beyond the publication of the Krebs cycle has sur-vived. With these documents and from extensive inter-views with Krebs during the last 5 years of his life, it has been possible to reconstruct his research pathway in fine detail through these years. The character of that pathway resolves the somewhat paradoxical contrast between the two summits of apparently extraordinarily creative activity that resulted in the two cycles that secured his fame, and the long stretches of strictly disciplined but seemingly more ordinary activity that connect them and that followed them.

As with other great achievements in science, the powerful integrations provided by the ornithine and citric acid cycles obscured the earlier progress made in the areas in which these discoveries impinged. Later biochemists tended to equate the work of Krebs, along with a few other landmarks in the 1930s such as the Embden-Meyerhof pathway of glycolysis, with the origins of intermediary metabolism. Because previous knowledge seemed afterward rudimentary and fragmentary, the new discoveries appeared to have fewer precedents than they actually had. It is true that, except for the sequence of fatty acid decomposition reactions, known as β-oxidations, proposed by Knoop in 1904, no extended sequences of metabolic reactions were firmly established before 1930. There had, however, been extensive investigations of these problems beginning at the turn of the century. By the time Krebs entered the field, a series of organic compounds, such as pyruvic acid, acetic acid, and several dicarboxylic acids, had been identified as important intermediates; certain types of reactions, such as dehydrogenation, hydrolysis and decarboxylation had been supposed to occur repeatedly in metabolic reactions; and strong rules for the criteria that a potential intermediate must meet were accepted in the field. Although the pathways along which foodstuffs are degraded to end products had initially been assumed to be linear, by 1930 there was reason to expect that they would be interconnected and branching. There had even been a closed circuit of reactions proposed during the 1920s to account for the oxidation of carbohydrates and fatty acids that received prominent attention. Some of its constituent reactions had been shown to take place enzymatically, whereas one critical step eluded efforts to confirm it.

Krebs came to these problems armed with the methods of Warburg, which enabled him to subject such proposed reaction sequences to critical, quantitatively rigorous scrutiny. His own training in organic chemistry was, on the other hand, too limited to allow him to reason as deeply as some of his contemporaries about possible reaction mechanisms. Consequently, he developed a style of research in which he kept closely in touch with current and recent literature in the field,

seeking ideas that he could test in his experimental system. The characteristics of his system—that he could perform many experiments quickly, with precise results that either encouraged or ruled out a given hypothesis—proved admirably suited to this style. Not given to long-range planning, he decided each evening what experiments to carry out the next day. When he became bogged down in one problem he quickly shifted to another.

Such an approach can easily lead to nothing more than the verification of existing views or the closing down of one possible lead after another. One can find many stretches along Krebs's investigative pathway that appear to be heading toward nothing very exciting or original. His style and methods were, however, well suited to notice something unexpected and to exploit with flexibility every hopeful lead. In the case of the ornithine cycle, it was his response to the unexpectedly large increase in the quantity of urea formed in a liver tissue slice when he added a combination of ornithine and ammonia to the medium that turned a routine investigation into a major discovery. In the case of the citric acid cycle, there was no single result so dramatically unforeseen, but there was a flexible approach in which his ideas were fluid, and fluctuating, and he tested a large number of current ideas before hitting on the fruitful ones that brought him quickly to a historic resolution of one of the central problems in his field.

Neither the ornithine cycle nor the citric acid cycle were revolutionary in the sense of breaking with existing norms, overthrowing current views, or introducing dramatically novel principles. They represented, in fact, the fulfillment of quests on which Krebs's predecessors and contemporaries were already engaged. He had not brought a new perspective or profound original insights to the field, but he had persevered, with a powerful method, great discipline, and commitment, further along the same general pathway that others had followed and were following. His creativity was not of the type that ranges far ahead of his times in lonely ventures. Rather, it resided in the quality of his responses to what turned up along his route. His optimistic temperament enabled him to keep going when nothing did seem to turn up, to try out many ideas without worrying about those that failed, and to exploit with great resourcefulness the breaks that came his way.

The peaks in Krebs's research career are, however, far

less than a full measure of his creative achievement. Too often scientific progress is measured only in prominent discoveries, especially in those for which Nobel Prizes are bestowed. The most remarkable aspect of Krebs's scientific pathway is the persistence with which he pursued, for half a century, a set of problems largely delineated within the first decade of his independent research, and the fact that over so long a time these problems never ceased to yield for him and his associates fresh increments of knowledge and understanding. No one did more over this whole period to shape the complex picture that we can see summarized in the intricate metabolic maps that frequently adorn textbooks of biochemistry or walls of biochemical laboratories.

III. LIFETIME PRODUCTIVITY

Dean Keith Simonton and others have recently focused attention on the lifetime contours of scientific creativity and productivity. Simonton has shown that there are characteristic curves of productivity as functions of creative potential and of the length of time in which one has pursued a particular field of creative activity. It is interesting to examine Krebs's life work within such a general analytical framework. Even without subjecting his output of publications to mathematical analysis, it is easy to see that Krebs's early productivity conforms in a general way with Simonton's curves. There is a rapidly rising output during the first 5 years and a further rise in the next decade. The "best work," the appearance of the Krebs cycle, comes at age 37, after 12 years of research activity, well within the ranges indicated by Simonton for the type of field within which Krebs worked. The most striking anomaly from the perspective of Simonton's analysis is that, whereas his curves predict a gradual decline in productivity from the point of best work to "last work," Krebs not only maintained but increased his productivity during that long phase of his career. Two dips in his output, between 1940 and 1945, and between 1955 and 1960, can be attributed, respectively, to wartime conditions and to the diversions attendant on his move to Oxford. Between the age of 60 and 65 he produced, or closely supervised, 33 papers, compared to 30 during the 5-year period in which he produced the citric acid cycle. After his official retirement, he produced at an even higher rate: 55 papers between 1965

and 1970, and 46 papers during the next 5 years. As his former associates and biographers, Hans Kornberg and Derek Williamson, have pointed out, the 100 papers published between his retirement and his death represent "a significant contribution to the field of physiological biochemistry. . . . Impressive is the range of subjects studied. . . . Here was no eminent retired scientist ploughing a well-trodden path but an active brain seeking the answers to new questions." [*See* PRODUCTIVITY AND AGE.]

How did Krebs evade the more standard trajectory of declining productivity? His own answer would be that he avoided the temptations that befall most eminent senior scientists to divert their energies in other directions. Although, like other Nobel laureates, Krebs too responded to some of the demands made on him by that accolade, he refused to allow himself to be drawn away from his laboratory. All the way until the final illness that preempted the last few days of his life, Krebs continued to show up at his laboratory every morning at the same early hour, just as he had been required to do in the laboratory of Otto Warburg as a young apprentice. Although he eventually allowed his associates to work a 5-day week, he himself was still at the time of his 80th birthday putting in an additional half day at his laboratory on Saturday. His mentor Otto Warburg had also worked regularly in his laboratory until the end of a long life, but Warburg had ended in isolation, pursuing old ideas and prejudices that were no longer acceptable to his younger colleagues. How did Krebs keep himself in closer step with changing times? Unlike Warburg, Krebs tempered his self-assurance with sufficient humility to realize that his ideas required control by the criticism of others. Impatient as he was with criticism that he considered ill founded or superficial, he nevertheless recognized also that he could only remain competent to carry on scientific research by keeping in touch with the views and the advice of the many colleagues to whom his distinction gained him access.

Long after he had discovered the ornithine and citric acid cycles, Krebs pondered over their meaning and over the question why organisms utilized such complicated pathways when shorter, linear reaction chains might appear to yield chemically equivalent results. During his 80th year, a chemist, Jack Baldwin, suggested to him that one reason for the necessity of a cyclic pathway for the final stage of oxidative metabolism was that acetic acid cannot be dehydrogenated without first combining with another molecule. That idea started Krebs on a quest to understand not only the citric acid cycle but other metabolic pathways, on the assumption that they could survive in evolutionary competition only if they provided the most efficient means available to perform their particular metabolic functions. At two symposiums held that year in honor of his 80th birthday, Krebs invoked these ideas to illustrate why he felt the deep satisfaction that he derived "from creative work" still far outweighed the pleasures that he might receive from the leisure time that he would gain if he were to retire. Krebs enjoyed his preferred form of satisfaction to the end of his life.

Bibliography

Primary Sources

Krebs, H. A. (1947). Cyclic processes in living matter. *Enzymologia, 12,* 88. (First paper by Krebs on meaning of metabolic cycles.)

Krebs, H. A., & Baldwin, J. (1981). The Evolution of Metabolic Cycles. *Nature, 291,* 381. (Last paper by Krebs on meaning of metabolic cycles.)

Krebs, H. A., & Henseleit, K. (1932). Untersuchungen über Harnstoff bildung im Tierkörper. *Klinische Wochenschrift, 11,* 757. (First announcement of the ornithine cycle.)

Krebs, H. A., & Johnson, W. A. (1937). The role of citric acid in intermediate metabolism in animal tissues. *Enzymologia, 4,* 148. (First announcement of Krebs cycle.)

Secondary Sources

Holmes, F. L. (1991). *Hans Krebs: The formation of a scientific life, 1900–1933.* New York: Oxford University Press.

Holmes, F. L. (1993). *Hans Krebs, Volume 2: Architect of intermediary metabolism, 1933–1937.* New York: Oxford University Press.

Kornberg, Sir H., & Williamson, D. H. (1984). Hans Adolf Krebs: 1900–1981. *Biographical Memoirs of Fellows of the Royal Society, 30,* 351.

Krebs, H., with Martin, A. (1981). *Reminiscences and reflections.* Oxford: The Clarendon Press.

Leadership

Michael D. Mumford and Mary Shane Connelly
American Institutes for Research

Leaders, under certain circumstances, can have a profound influence on the business, government, and social organizations that shape our lives. LEADERSHIP requires creativity, or the ability to solve novel, ill-defined organizational problems. Skills that leaders must acquire to solve these problems are discussed, along with the unique demands confronting leaders as they seek solutions to various organizational problems.

Charismatic Leaders who engender strong affective reactions in subordinates.

Discretion Amount of latitude granted in decision making.

Entrepreneur A leader who is establishing a new business or business direction.

Leadership Effective exercise of influence with respect to people or groups.

Mental Models Conceptions of how parts of a system interact together.

Organizational Systems Groups of people working together to provide products or services.

Roles A set of activities a person is expected to engage in by others or an organization.

Skills Developed capacities that promote performance.

Vision An image of what the organization should be doing now and in the future.

I. LEADERSHIP IN ORGANIZATIONS

Over the years, scholars have proposed a number of theories that are useful in understanding the nature and significance of organizational leadership. These theories typically focus on how leaders interact with their followers. More specifically, they hold that leaders influence people, or groups, in such a way that group tasks are accomplished and effective patterns of social interaction within the group are maintained.

At first glance, this description of how leaders function appears quite straightforward. However, it poses a subtle, yet important, question. Is leadership always necessary for effective group performance? Recent studies of leader substitutes indicate that leadership is not a crucial determinant of group performance if the task is well structured, goals are clear, members of the group are cohesive, and group members have the requisite expertise. Leadership counts, however, when groups confront turmoil, ambiguity, and change. [*See* GROUP CREATIVITY.]

In part, the prevalence of turmoil, ambiguity, and change in organizations ensures that leadership is virtually always an important influence on organizational performance. Although a number of models have been proposed that might be used to describe organizational behavior, sociotechnical systems theory represents the most widely accepted model. Systems theory views organizations as a collection of semiautonomous subsystems. These subsystems work together as loosely linked entities to produce certain products and services, transforming raw materials through a division of labor and judicious application of relevant technologies. Ideally, markets, subsystems, technologies, and people remain fixed, stable entities oriented toward rational goals. However, even as organizations seek stability, all these entities are constantly in flux, creating a dynamic, uncertain environment, one characterized by complexity, conflict, and change. [*See* SYSTEMS APPROACH.]

Under these conditions, goals and paths to goal attainment are uncertain. To cope with this uncertainty and adaptively respond to change, organizations create a set of boundary roles as part of the division of labor. Occupants of these boundary roles are expected to guide adaptive responses to change, coordinating and directing the activities of various people or subsystems. It is within these boundary roles that one finds organizational leaders—the managers, executives, scientists, engineers, marketing executives, and others who guide adaptive responses to change.

The concept of boundary roles is abstract, yet it makes an important point about the nature of organizational leadership. Change implies that leaders, the occupants of boundary roles, are confronted with novel, ambiguous, ill-defined situations where they must select goals and paths toward their attainment that will maintain the group and ensure that the work gets done. In this sense, leadership, as contrasted with routine management and administrative functions, represents an inherently creative activity, one calling for significant creative problem-solving skills.

II. LEADERS' CREATIVE PROBLEM SOLVING

This statement, however, should not be taken to imply that leaders' creative problem solving is inherently equivalent to other forms of creative ability. Leaders are not artists. In fact, organizational leadership roles impose a number of demands that make leaders' creative efforts a particularly complex phenomenon. To begin, leaders must solve problems in real group settings where time is short and demands are many. As a result, leaders must generate solutions to multiple, rapidly emerging problems using shortcuts and general heuristics. Accordingly, solutions to broader, more complex problems may be built up slowly over time as leaders, anticipating a vision, bring about integrated solutions through assembling smaller pieces rather than through one single grand project. [*See* HEURISTICS; PROBLEM SOLVING.]

Not only must leaders build solutions, they face some unique demands as they try to gain an understanding of the problems at hand. Organizations are highly complex entities operating in uncertain environments. As a result, leaders may have some difficulty obtaining timely, accurate information that enables them to diagnose the nature of the problem. Additionally, in complex, changing environments, it may not be clear exactly what the problem is in the first place or whether a problem is worth solving at all. Thus, problem construction may represent a key determinant of effective leader performance, particularly under conditions where others can be relied on to extend initial problem definitions.

In organizations it is often far more important to find a timely, workable solution than the single best solution. This observation underscores the rather pragmatic nature of leaders' cognitive problem solving. Leaders must attend to the restrictions imposed by the time frame, resources, finances, system demands, and conflicting goals and problems in generating and implementing potential solutions. Finding out how to work within these restrictions may, in fact, represent one of the more important manifestations of leader creativity. These solutions, moreover, must work within the context of other ongoing organizational activities. One implication of this statement is that leaders' creative efforts tend to rely on reorganizations of existing information, or material, rather than on the creation of fundamentally new combinations. Another implication of this statement is that leaders will exhibit a rather evaluative form of creativity, rejecting solutions likely to be associated with negative downstream consequences in a complex interactive system. By the same token, however, substantial creativity may be needed to identify potential downstream consequences, solutions that will prove workable within organizational constraints and the key variables that must be manipulated to bring potential solutions to fruition.

One set of restrictions, or potential assets, leaders must constantly come to terms with are the vested interests of various constituencies. In complex organizational systems, leaders must work with, and through, others to bring new ideas into being. Typically, solutions will be developed and implemented collaboratively—with the help of peers, superiors, subordinates, and representatives of other relevant organizations. Leaders' creative problem solving, as a result, is a highly social phenomenon that places a premium on consensus building, persuasion, and creation of a shared vision that can be accepted by the relevant constituencies. This distinctly social context not only places a premium on flexibility and social skills, it calls for people who can create conditions in which others can be brought together to work toward common goals.

A tripartite model describing the skills leaders need to solve novel, ill-defined organizational problems has been proposed by M. D. Mumford and colleagues. This model holds that leaders' creative problem-solving efforts, like creative thought in most other domains, begin with problem-focused cognition. More specifically, leaders must be able to identify and define significant organizational problems, gather more detailed information about the nature of these problems, formulate an understanding of the problem situation, and generate viable trial solutions. These activities depend on knowledge pertaining to both the problem and its relevance to the leaders' role in the organization. Thus, the problems likely to be addressed by first-line supervisors are typically quite different than those of concern to chief executives who must look after the long-term health of the organization.

Unlike many other forms of creative effort, the leader's creative work is not done with initial generation of a viable trial solution. Leaders must also be able to go outside themselves, and the immediate problem at hand, using experience, wisdom, and perspective taking to project likely outcomes, others' reactions, restrictions on solution implementation, external solution requirements, and ways of revising solutions to enhance workability and garner support. Leaders, moreover, must carefully plan solution implementation, developing a vision that will communicate the value of this solution to others. All of these efforts depend on sophisticated mental models, or complex knowledge structures, articulating the nature of the organization and how it operates.

Once leaders have formulated a workable implementation plan, they must communicate this plan to others. Not only must they communicate a viable vision that evokes the support of others, they must structure their activities, monitor their efforts, guide implementation, and point out the need for revisions. This direct interpersonal implementation requires an intimate knowledge of people, and their needs, as well as the capability to work with them while managing groups and requisite tasks.

The model proposed by Mumford and colleagues sees leaders' creative problem solving as involving three distinct components: (a) problem-focused cognition, (b) organizational cognition, and (c) social cognition. Although this model stresses the importance of these three distinct components, all three of these elements may operate in a highly interactive fashion as leaders attempt to solve novel, ill-defined, organization problems. Thus, leaders' understanding of subordinates may lead them to identify a series of organizational problems that result in poor subordinate motivation, just as the failure of an initial trial solution may stimulate a new cycle of problem-focused cognition.

III. PROBLEM-FOCUSED COGNITION

Research findings indicate that judgmental measures of creative problem-solving skills, such as problem construction and combination and reorganization, are related to indices of leader performance and their ability to solve organizational problems. Of course, the question remains as to whether these findings are tied to the use of judgmental skill assessments. However, more formal measures of these creative problem solving skills also evidence multiple correlations in the high .30s with indices of performance in leadership training courses.

IV. ORGANIZATIONAL COGNITION

There is a growing body of evidence indicating that the kind of cognitive skills required to generate new ideas and trial solutions are indeed important to successful performance in leadership positions. However, the model of leader performance proposed by Mumford and colleagues indicates that the effective exercise of creative problem-solving skills underlying solution generation is not sufficient for effective leadership. Leaders, additionally, must be able to tailor and shape initial trial solutions to complex organizational environments.

For example, leaders must be able to identify and find creative ways of working around various organizational restrictions. They must consider the positive and negative outcomes associated with various events. They must be able to identify long-term, downstream consequences of trial solutions using complex mental models reflecting a principal-based knowledge of the organization and how it operates.

Measures of organizationally based divergent thinking were correlated with indices on leader problem solving, performance indices, career achievement, and attained level in a 1998 study by Mumford and colleagues. As may be seen in Table I, attention to positive and negative consequences was not strongly related to these indices of leader performance. However, consistent with the notion that organizationally based creative thought plays an important role in leader performance, use of longer time frames in identifying consequences, generation of more realistic consequences, generation of consequences reflecting consideration of multiple elements, and generation of consequences based on principals all produced sizable positive relationships with the various indices of leader performance.

Other studies have extended this general line of research along two important avenues. One set of studies has tested this theory using open-ended scenario measures to show that leader performance indeed depends on organizational cognition. For example, the data suggest that leaders who are better able to identify organizational restrictions and find ways of working around these restrictions tend to be better performers. Other studies examined whether wisdom and perspective taking are related to leaders' ability to go outside the problem situation and attend to organizational demands. As might be expected, elements of wisdom and perspective taking that facilitate organi-

TABLE I
**Correlations of Leader Performance Measures
with Divergent Thinking Skills Drawn from Consequences Test**

	Criteria			
Divergent thinking skills	*Problem solving*	*Critical incidents*	*Organizational achievement*	*Attained rank*
Time frame	.45**	.24**	.32**	.41**
Realism	.39**	.22**	.33**	.42**
Complexity	.50**	.28**	.38**	.47**
Use of principles	.51**	.29**	.41**	.54**
Positive outcomes	−.05	−.03	.00	.04
Negative outcomes	.01	.03	.04	.09*

*p < .05
**p < .01

zationally based creative problem solving, including awareness of how well the solution fits the setting, understanding of social systems, judgment, and self-objectivity, are all related to various indices of leader performance.

V. SOCIAL COGNITION

The idea that leadership depends on both problem-focused and organizationally focused cognition is a key tenet of the model of leader performance proposed by Mumford and colleagues. This model, however, also indicates a third major form of cognition, socially focused cognition, that might play a role in creative leadership. Traditionally, studies of leadership have tended to focus on the social interactional component of leader performance. For example, some theories of leadership proposed that it is essential for leaders to clarify subordinates' paths to goal attainment. Other theories hold that effective leaders are capable of building subordinates' feeling of self-worth and positive affect among group members.

The importance of these and other insights arising from this social, interactional approach to leadership is not debated. However, it can be argued that the cognitive processes underlying the timely generation of these behaviors are also of some importance. Moreover, there is some reason to suspect that substantial creativity may be required as leaders seek to adapt to and direct others.

For example, in 1990 Simonton provided evidence indicating that effective leaders, like other highly creative people, tend to be unusually persuasive. In seeking to understand what makes leaders persuasive, other studies have examined the characteristics of charismatic or transformational leaders (e.g., Ghandi, Roosevelt, and Ford). Broadly speaking, these studies indicate that charismatic leaders are capable of communicating a vision, or an image of the organizational future, that both motivates and directs subordinates. It is not unreasonable that creativity may play an important role in both the creation and communication of high-impact visions.

At a somewhat more mundane level, however, leaders, ultimately, must, interact with followers. Fol-

lowers, however, are unique individuals who have different interests and may, at times, represent the interests of diverse constituencies. As a result, flexibility is required of leaders to help them to monitor the reactions of others and adapt their behavior to others' needs. This flexible, adaptive social behavior implies an ability to see alternative courses of action in social situations, and to choose actions that are likely to build consensus and resolve conflict in changing social settings. Thus, in their day-to-day interactions, leaders must be able to apply divergent thinking skills in social situations while using feedback from those interactions to identify emerging problems. [*See* FLEXIBILITY.]

VI. ORGANIZATIONAL INFLUENCES

These observations about leadership could be taken to imply that all leaders are constantly engaged in some form of creative thought. Although creative thought in its various manifestations may be a crucial determinant of leader performance, one must remember that organizational leaders are confronted with a number of routine management tasks that must be taken care of. Moreover, certain organizational characteristics set limits on the amount and type of creative activity that is possible. Leaders manifest creative abilities in the context of distinctly social roles. Thus, others' expectations for these roles, and the kind of problems that arise, restrict the nature and likely success of leaders' creative efforts. This point is nicely illustrated in Theodore Roosevelt's presidency during which many proposed new labor policies were summarily rejected by Congress and the public at large.

In organizations, furthermore, roles are defined with respect to authority, the amount of discretion granted someone holding a leadership role, and the duties this person is expected to perform. As a result, leaders' creative efforts tend to be channeled along certain avenues as a function of the work they are expected to accomplish. This inherent limitation on the kind of legitimate activities one can engage in is, in fact, one reason entrepreneurs often leave existing organizations to start new companies. Not only do organizations restrict the type of creative activity in which leaders can engage, they also restrict the breadth of, and potential for, creative activity by structuring roles hierarchically in terms of the amount of authority and discretion granted to leaders. Thus, the potential impact of leaders' creative problem solving is likely to be substantially greater for senior executives as opposed to first-line supervisors.

The organization's role structure is only one of many potential influences on leaders' creative efforts. The kind of work being done by the organization and the nature of the organization's operating environment represent two additional important influences. Typically, leader creativity is at a premium in the early phases of the organizational growth cycle when novel, ill-defined problems arise almost daily. In more mature organizations, however, where well-established procedures are available, creativity may have less influence on leader performance. Along similar lines, some industries, particularly those undergoing rapid changes in technology and markets, are more likely to call for leaders who are truly creative people. The need for leader creativity, however, may well decline as the technology is routinized and the industry begins to pursue a fixed market. Given these observations, it is hardly surprising that, at present, the software industry emphasizes creativity and innovation to a greater extent than the steel industry. Under certain conditions, the very nature of the work being done by the organization may require high levels of creativity and innovation. These conditions call for leaders who are not only creative problem solvers but who are also capable of encouraging subordinate creativity.

A number of scholars have examined the kind of environment leaders should create if there is a need for subordinate creativity. Broadly speaking, the results obtained in these studies indicate that the less tightly structured, less bureaucratic organizations facilitate creativity. Leaders, moreover, should try to encourage openness to new approaches; focus on process as well as outcomes; permit autonomy and risk taking; reward creativity and innovation; provide a demanding, intellectually challenging environment; and build feelings of self-efficacy in subordinates. There is also evidence available indicating that the kind of guidance leaders provide subordinates can influence their success in various creative efforts. Specifically, leaders who encourage subordinates to take more time in defining problems, to look at problems in different ways, to attend to the facts and identify anomalies, or inconsistent observations, are especially likely to be successful in encouraging subordinate creativity.

Leaders, however, are charged with looking out for the organization as a whole, not just subordinate creativity. A leader's responsibilities to the organization often necessitate channeling creative efforts along avenues that contribute to the work and continued adaptation of the group as a whole. As a result, leaders must *manage* subordinate creativity, not just encourage unrestricted creative thought. In fact, studies of innovative management indicate that effective leaders typically use an incremental, progressive change strategy often isolating creative efforts in certain offices or units to encourage creative thought while buffering more routine operations.

VII. CONCLUSIONS

This article has reviewed a number of studies concerned with leader creativity. Taken as a whole, studies indicate that creativity may be an essential component of effective organizational leadership. Not only do leaders need a set of complex creative thinking skills to solve novel, ill-defined organizational problems, they must be able to interact with followers in ways that encourage and manage subordinate creativity.

Although creativity appears to be an important influence on successful organizational leadership, it would be a mistake to arbitrarily equate leaders' creative efforts with the kind of creativity observed in more autonomous fields of endeavor, such as the arts and sciences. It is not enough for leaders to be able to formulate viable solutions to novel organizational problems, they must be capable of formulating workable solutions that can be implemented in dynamic social settings. As a result, leaders' creative efforts require organizationally based and socially based creative thought, as well as the kind of problem-focused cognition traditionally of concern in studies of creativity.

These observations are noteworthy, in part, because they indicate that new, more complex models may be called for in seeking to understand creativity in nontraditional fields such as leadership. These more complex models, however, may play an important role in advancing our knowledge of creativity as a general phenomenon. For example, it is quite possible that organizationally based forms of creative thought, such as the identification of restrictions and downstream consequences, may prove important in understanding creativity in a number of other fields aside from leadership.

Although the study of leader creativity may have some important theoretical implications, we should not lose sight of a more practical issue. Organizational leaders can have enormous impact on our lives—they may start and stop wars, they make possible a booming economy, they remind us of the importance of faith. By identifying the kind of skills leaders must acquire to steer their organizations through a turbulent, changing world, students of creativity may do much to enhance the quality of all our lives.

Bibliography

Bass, B. R. (1990). *Bass and Stogdill's handbook of leadership: Theory, research, and managerial application* (3rd ed.). New York: The Free Press.

Marshall-Mies, J., Martin, J. A., Fleishman, E. A., Zaccaro, S. J.,

Baughman, W. A., & McGee, M. L. (1996). *Developments and evaluation of cognitive and metacognitive measures for predicting leadership potential.* Alexandria, VA: U.S. Army Research Institutes for the Behavioral Sciences.

Mumford, M. D., Marks, M. A., Connelly, M. S., Zaccaro, S. J., & Johnson, J. F. (1998). Domain-based scoring of divergent thinking tests: Validation evidence in an occupational sample. *Creativity Research Journal, 12,* 152–164.

Mumford, M. D., Zaccaro, S. J., Harding, F. D., Jacobs, T. O., & Fleishman, E. A. (in press). Leadership skills for a changing world: Solving complex social problems. *Leadership Quarterly.*

Redmond, M. R., Mumford, M. D., & Teach, R. (1993). Putting creativity to work: Leader influences on subordinate creativity. *Organizational Behavior and Human Decision Processes, 55,* 120–151.

Simonton, D. K. (1990). *Pyschology, science, and history.* New Haven, CT: Yale University Press.

Tesluk, P. E., Farr, J. L., & Klein, S. R. (1997). Influence of organizational culture and climate on individual creativity. *Journal of Creative Behavior, 31,* 31–45.

Zaccaro, S. J., Mumford, M. D., Marks, M. A., Connelly, M. S., Threlfall, K. V., Gilbert, J. A., & Fleishman, E. A. (1995). *Cognitive and temperament determinants of army leadership.* Alexandria, VA: U.S. Army Research Institute for the Behavioral Sciences.

Learning Styles

Linda A. O'Hara and Robert J. Sternberg

Yale University

Abstract Theoretical, not practical or applied, considered apart from concrete existence.

Abstract Learning Learning in which relations between and among stimuli are more important than the physical features of those stimuli.

Concrete Practical, utilitarian; pertaining to the specific or particular instance as opposed to the general or abstract.

Intuition Act or faculty of knowing without the use of rational processes; immediate cognition, acute insight.

Learning A relatively permanent change in behavior or knowledge that occurs as a result of experience.

Learning Styles Characteristic cognitive, affective, and physiological behaviors that serve as relatively stable indicators of how learners perceive, interact with, and respond to the learning environment.

LEARNING STYLES are characteristic cognitive, affective, and physiological behaviors that serve as relatively stable indicators of how learners perceive, interact with, and respond to the learning environment. Thus, they *may influence the way people understand problems, generate ideas, and plan for action. They have been conceived as bridges between cognition and personality.*

I. WHAT ARE LEARNING STYLES?

Learning styles, cognitive styles, thinking styles, and *personality types* often have been used interchangeably. Much confusion results when some researchers use *style* to refer to a preference for thinking or behaving in a certain way with no more value attached to the preference than the value one places on crossing the right arm over the left or the left over the right, whereas other researchers use *style* to connote value judgments such as noting that a person has a creative or noncreative style. This issue has been referred to as the style-level or style-ability debate. An investigation of level asks, "How creative are you?" whereas an investigation of styles asks, "How are you creative?" Much criticism of theories revolves around whether or not what one calls a style is really an ability.

II. POPULAR STYLES IDEAS

It is not always clear why some psychological theories get picked up by the popular press and others do not. In any case, two learning styles ideas have become well known in the popular press. They are the modalities idea and the right/left brain idea. Sensory modalities refer to preferences to learn visually, auditorily, or kinesthetically, that is, by reading, listening to lectures, or through movement/doing.

The right/left brain idea, also known as hemispheric specialization, refers to the fact that parts of the brain have been shown to specialize in certain functions. Ned Hermann, a physicist-artist, has used this idea to create a whole-brain creativity model. He admits that his idea does not rely on whether or not the brain actually functions the way his model says. The value of his model is in the understanding of differences it provides; that is, the model may have started out as an intended physiological map but today it serves only as a metaphor.

According to Hermann, creativity is whole-brained activity. He relates Graham Wallas's four stages of the creative process (preparation, incubation, illumination, and verification) to four quadrants of the brain: structured/verbal (left), unstructured/nonverbal (right), cerebral (top), and limbic (bottom). Preparation and verification are on the left; incubation and illumination are on the right. In the upper-left quadrant are the fact-based, logical, rational, and quantitative processes. In the upper-right quadrant are the open-minded, visual, conceptual, and simultaneous processes. In the lower-right quadrant are the emotional, expressive, and interpersonal processes. And in the lower-left quadrant are the controlled, organized, sequential, and procedural processes.

Hermann's model has attracted more attention from management consultants than from researchers and it is one of the many ideas used by consultants to foster a climate that celebrates differences in people. Similar conceptions have categorized people as right, left, or integrated in their learning styles. A positive relationship has been reported between creativity measures and right-hemispheric learning styles and a negative relationship between creativity measures and left-hemispheric learning styles.

Another brain-specialization idea has been put forth by Edward de Bono, who has developed and promoted a course on lateral thinking. Lateral thinking is concerned with the making of new ideas and is contrasted with vertical thinking, which is concerned with the development and utilization of ideas. Vertical thinking has been called "digging the same hole deeper," whereas lateral thinking is "digging the hole somewhere else."

III. BUSINESS AND EDUCATION APPLICATIONS

A. Myers-Briggs Personality Types

The 16 Myers-Briggs types are based on Jungian typology theory and result from all combinations of four preferences: extraversion or introversion, sensing perception or intuitive perception, thinking judgment or feeling judgment, and judgment or perception. Extraverts are oriented primarily toward the outer world, people, and objects; introverts are oriented toward the inner world, concepts, and ideas. People with a sensing preference notice facts and detailed information through the five senses and seek the fullest experience of what is immediate and real; those with an intuitive preference notice meanings and relationships and seek the furthest reaches of the possible and imaginative. People with a thinking preference prefer to make judgments based primarily on logical, impersonal analysis; those with a feeling preference make judgments based on personal or social values. The judgment-perception preference refers to how one prefers to deal with the outside world. People with a perceptive attitude are attuned to incoming information, spontaneous, curious, adaptable, and open to new events and changes. People with a judging attitude are concerned with making decisions, seeking closure, planning operations, or organizing activities.

Studies have shown that intuitive types benefit more from a less structured, inductive teaching approach; sensing types, from a more structured approach. Intuitive types achieve higher grades and standardized test scores. Creativity and originality consistently have been shown to be associated with intuition and perception.

B. Kirton's Adaptors and Innovators

Michael Kirton's theory is included as a learning style because an important type of learning occurs through problem solving, more often on the job than in the classroom. Kirton argued in 1976 that everyone can be located on a continuum ranging from an ability to "do things better" to an ability to "do things differently," and the ends of this continuum are labeled adaptive and innovative, respectively. The Kirton Adaption-Innovation Inventory (KAI) has been used in numerous studies since then to distinguish people's preferred methods of bringing about intended change.

Adaptors are characterized by precision, reliability, methodicalness, and prudence. They seek to solve problems by incremental improvement and greater efficiency, with minimum disruption to the existing structure. Innovators, on the other hand, often challenge the existing structure, have little respect for past custom, and often suggest radical change and problem redefinition.

Kirton argued that although there is a relationship between style and behavior or ability, it is not perfect and the KAI measures a style and not creative behavior. He noted that a style is an essential element of the ego, whereas behavior is a compromise with the environment.

Although the theoretical argument for the difference between style and level is quite clear, empirical results are not. Some studies have shown no relationship between KAI scores and traditional creativity measures, but others have shown positive relationships such that innovators demonstrate higher fluency, flexibility, originality, risk-taking, and creative motivation scores. Correlations of .62 and .65 have been reported between the KAI and the combined Myers-Briggs intuitive and perceptive scales. The latter two scales have demonstrated relationships with creativity measures. The explorer-assimilator distinction is very similar to Kirton's. Explorers generally have higher creativity scores than assimilators, especially when they have little prior experience with the task. But assimilators can perform better when they have prior experience.

C. Kolb's Learning-Style Inventory

David Kolb's work is focused more on managerial learning than on childhood classroom learning. His 1971 circular model of learning consists of four stages: concrete experience leading to observations and reflections, which lead to the formation of abstract concepts and generalizations, which lead to testing the implications of concepts in new situations, which leads back to concrete experience. People prefer to gather infor-

mation either through concrete experience or abstract conceptualization and then to process it either through reflective observation or active experimentation. Kolb's learning-style inventory yields four styles—converger, diverger, accommodator, and assimilator—each with different relative strengths in the four stages of learning.

Convergers' strengths are in abstract conceptualization and active experimentation. They prefer to work on the practical application of ideas, like to work with things rather than people, are relatively unemotional, and have narrow technical interests. Engineers are a possible example.

Divergers' strengths are in concrete experience and reflective observation. They tend to be imaginative and emotional, to have broad cultural interests, and to specialize in the arts. Managers from humanities and liberal arts backgrounds are typical divergers.

Assimilators' strengths are in abstract conceptualization and reflective observation. They excel in inductive reasoning and in assimilating disparate observations into an integrated explanation or theoretical model. They are more concerned with abstract concepts and less interested in people or in practical implementation. This style is more characteristic of the basic sciences than the applied sciences and is often found in research and planning departments.

Accommodators' strengths are in concrete experience and active experimentation. They are best in doing things, carrying out plans, and involving themselves in new experiences and are often found in marketing or sales.

Research with the Learning Styles Inventory has clearly linked style to academic major and career choices as well as to decision-making strategies. From Kolb's theory, one would expect some relationship between creativity and the diverger style to exist. That relationship has been rarely tested, although one study of college freshmen found that 57% of John Holland's artistic vocational types (the most creative of his types) were divergers as compared with 40% expected by chance. Holland categorized careers as realistic, investigative, artistic, social, enterprising, and conventional.

D. Dunn, Dunn, and Price's Learning Style Inventory

A more encompassing theory that specifically addresses classroom learning has been proposed by Rita

Dunn and Kenneth Dunn. Dunn, Dunn, and Price's Learning Style Inventory contains 104 self-report items that ask to what extent the student prefers various elements when trying to learn difficult academic material. The elements are grouped into environmental, physiological, sociological, psychological, and emotional categories.

Environmental includes light, sound, temperature, and seating design. Physiological includes best time of day, snacking (which they refer to as intake), amount of movement, and modality (listening, reading, seeing, manipulating, or experiencing). Sociological refers to preferences about working alone, in pairs, or in groups of peers, with authoritative or collegial adults, and being motivated by a parent or a teacher. Psychological refers to global or analytical processing. Emotional includes motivation, interruptions, self–decision making or following others' orders, internal or external structure, and persistence.

Research indicates that across cultural groups and domains, gifted students are more highly motivated and have stronger tactile and kinesthetic learning preferences than do nongifted students. Very few gifted students prefer to work with other students. They prefer to work on their own and if necessary to receive direction from an authoritative adult. Although distinct learning-style patterns have been noted for gifted students within both their domain and culture, there are as many differences among individuals within cultural groups as between groups.

IV. THEORETICAL APPROACHES

A. Witkin's Field Dependence versus Field Independence

One of the earliest cognitive-style theories was proposed by Herman Witkin in 1949. It has sometimes been referred to as differentiation or global versus analytical perception. Someone with a global or holistic orientation sees the whole picture, whereas someone with an analytical orientation picks out the parts. An example of an extreme analytical type is someone who just does not understand pointillistic and some impressionistic paintings because of all the dots. Many studies have been conducted using the rod-and-frame and em-

bedded-figures tests, and have reported relationships between these test scores and a number of other constructs including academic achievement, social interaction, face watching, attitudes, and career choices, as well as learning and creativity.

The rod and frame test is conducted in a dark room in which the only visible things are a tilted rod inside a tilted frame, both painted with luminous paint. The object of the test is to determine how well a participant can reorient the rod to an upright position and to what extent the orientation of the frame interferes with the task. For example, at one extreme are people who need the frame and rod to be completely aligned for the rod to appear upright. If the frame is tilted, they will tilt the rod and say that it is upright. They are called field dependent because their decision depends on the surrounding field—the frame. At the other extreme are people who can orient the rod to an upright position regardless of the position of the surrounding frame. They are called field independent.

The embedded figures test involves finding a previously presented simple figure in a more complex design. Scores are based on the amount of time taken to find the figure. There is some debate about whether the embedded figures test measures something different than the rod and frame test.

It has been argued that it may be that field independence is a necessary but not sufficient condition for creativity; that is, all creative persons are field independent but not all field-independent persons are creative. However, creativity is not confined to field-independent students. After controlling for intelligence, field-independent people have been found to perform better than field-dependent people on creativity measures involving visualization, flexibility, math, and science. There are no differences on tests of verbal comprehension, redefinition, or symbolic fluency. There is considerable debate about whether measures of field dependence are measuring a style or a spatial-visual ability.

B. Sternberg's Theory of Mental Self-Government

The theory of mental self-government incorporates many elements from other theories of styles and summarizes them in a governmental structures metaphor that contains 13 different thinking styles. According to Robert Sternberg's theory, governments in society may be large-scale externalized mirrors of the mind such that governmental structures are external societal manifestations of basic internal individual psychological processes. Just as governments have many aspects, such as functions, forms, levels, scope, and leaning, so do our minds. And as some governments encourage or at least allow creative thinking among their citizens, whereas others actively repress such thinking, so people's thinking styles can either encourage or discourage creativity.

1. Functions

Three major functions of government are the legislative, executive, and judicial. The legislative function is to create new laws, the executive is to implement or execute the laws, and the judicial is to judge compliance with the laws. So, too, in any creative problem-solving effort, one's mind must first create the idea, then evaluate its value, and plan its implementation. People have preferences for which of these mental activities they like to engage in, regardless of their actual abilities in that area.

2. Forms

Governments come in four major forms: monarchic, hierarchic, oligarchic, and anarchic. Monarchies have one leader at a time until he or she dies or abdicates, hierarchies have multiple layers of leadership with differing levels of power, oligarchies are small committees of leaders with equal power, and anarchies have no formal leadership. People approach problem solving in similar ways. Those with a monarchic style prefer to do one thing at a time until it's done; they are very focused. Those with a hierarchic style like to do many things but in a prioritized order. Those with an oligarchic style prefer to do many things but give each of them equal importance. And those with an anarchic style prefer no order and no external control.

3. Levels

Levels of government range from the small town council up to the federal. So, too, a person's interest levels may vary from minute detail to a big picture. People with a local style prefer to be engaged in the details of very concrete, down-to-earth problems.

People with a global style prefer to deal with larger, abstract concepts. Globals prefer to see the forest, locals, the trees.

4. Scope

Governments deal with both internal domestic affairs and external foreign affairs. People with an internal style prefer to work independently on their own. People with an external style prefer to work with others.

5. Leanings

Just as governments can be characterized as conservative or progressive, right wing or left wing, so can people's thinking styles. People with a conservative style prefer to work within the existing rules, procedures, and structures. People with a progressive or liberal style prefer to step outside of the box and work in situations that allow substantial change.

The legislative style is the single style most conducive to creativity. People with a legislative style like to create their own rules and do things their own way. They prefer problems that are not prestructured. In school they prefer writing papers or doing projects to taking tests. They generally prefer discovery learning to expository learning, meaning that they would rather figure out how to do something than be told how to do it.

In contrast, people with an executive style like to be told what to do rather than figure it out for themselves. They prefer expository to discovery learning, like to follow rules, and prefer problems that are prestructured. In school they prefer memorizing for multiple-choice or short-answer tests. Schools and businesses often reward the executive over the legislative style because students or employees who want to do things their own way can be disruptive.

People with a judicial style like to evaluate things, people, and ideas. They prefer problems in which they analyze and evaluate. In school they like to write critical papers, such as ones comparing two novels or periods of history. This critical style can discourage creativity during idea generation but is necessary to select the best ideas generated.

All three functional styles are important for creativity, albeit at different stages in the creative process:

legislative during the idea-generation stage, judicial during the idea-evaluation and selection stage, and executive during the idea-implementation stage. Studies to date have been conducted primarily on the idea-generation stage.

Higher levels of creativity have been found to be associated with lower levels on the executive and conservative styles, which is consistent with the theory as a preference for conservative, rule-following behavior is opposed to creativity. Legislative students were found to perform better on independent projects that required some creativity, whereas judicial students performed better with the exam format in a study of a summer school psychology class. A positive correlation has been found between a legislative style and creative performance and a negative correlation between a judicial style and creative performance on an essay writing task. Both relationships are to be expected, as the legislative style is theorized to be most important for

creativity and an evaluative, critical style is discouraged by many creativity consultants who note that an absence of criticism is one of the rules in brainstorming for creative ideas.

V. INTEGRATION

One last theory to mention is Philip Holzman and Riley Gardner's concept of leveling and sharpening. Leveling refers to the leveling of differences and concentrating on similarities; sharpening refers to the sharpening of differences and concentrating on distinctions. At the risk of gross leveling to the point of decimating the niceties of the various theories discussed, we suggest that except for Dunn and Dunn's environmental preferences (light, sound, snacks, etc.) and modality preferences (visual, auditory, kinesthetic), five categories can capture the lot of them.

TABLE I
Mapping of Learning Styles Theories

Theorist	Holistic intuition	Subjective/ Interpersonal	Processing	Abstract thinking	Detail focus
Basadur	Generator		Optimizer	Conceptualizer	Implementor
de Bono	Lateral thinking		Vertical thinking		
Dunn & Dunn	Global				Analytic
Gregorc	Concrete-random	Abstract-random		Abstract-sequential	Concrete-sequential
Hermann	Cerebral right	Limbic right	Limbic left	Cerebral left	
Holzman & Gardner	Leveling				Sharpening
Kaufmann	Explorer		Assimilator		
Kirby	Global				Analytic
Kirton	Innovator		Adaptor		
Kogan		Impulsive		Reflective	
Kolb	Divergers		Convergers	Assimilators	Accommodators
Myers-Briggs	Intuitive/ perceiving	Feeling/extrovert	Judging	Thinking/introvert	Sensing
Pask	Holist		Serialist		
Pettigrew	Broad category				Narrow category
Sternberg	Legislative/ global/ progressive/ oligarchic	External/anarchic	Executive/ conservative	Judicial/hierarchic/ internal	Local/monarchic
Torrance	Right brained			Left brained	
Witkin	Field-dependent				Field-independent

In 1988 Ronald Schmeck reviewed a number of learning styles theories and concluded they could all be encompassed by one broad dimension labeled global versus analytic. However, from the work done since then there seem to be a few more distinctions to make. Table I presents a listing of the theories covered in this article as well as a few others reviewed by Schmeck and the five categories into which their style labels seem to fall: holistic intuition, subjective/interpersonal, processing, abstract thinking, and detail focus. Schmeck's global label has been divided into a cognitive/intuitive factor and an affective component. His analytic label has been divided into preferences for doing things in a sequential, controlled procedure (processing), what one values (abstract thinking), and what one notices (details).

Holistic intuition captures global, field-dependent thinking and attention that is impressionistic and imaginative rather than precise, and simultaneous rather than serial. Subjective/interpersonal captures styles that are more emotional and social, rather than independent and analytical. Processing captures a focus on operations, procedures, established ways of doing things in a controlled, step-by-step, sequential manner. Abstract thinking captures an interest in objective facts rather than feelings or impressions, in critical, logical, impersonal, and independent think-

ing. Detail focus captures an analytic attention that is field independent, detail and difference oriented, and grounded in concrete experience rather than imaginative ideation.

Bibliography

Furnham, A. (1995). The relationship of personality and intelligence to cognitive learning style and achievement. In D. H. Saklofske & M. Zeidner (Eds.), *International handbook of personality and intelligence* (pp. 397–413). New York: Plenum Press.

Grigorenko, E. L., & Sternberg, R. J. (1995). Thinking styles. In D. H. Saklofske & M. Zeidner (Eds.), *International handbook of personality and intelligence* (pp. 205–229). New York: Plenum Press.

Miller, A. (1991). Personality types, learning styles and educational goals. *Educational Psychology, 11,* 217–238.

Riding, R., & Cheema, I. (1991). Cognitive styles: An overview and integration. *Educational Psychology, 11,* 193–215.

Schmeck, R. R. (1988). *Learning strategies and learning styles.* New York: Plenum Press.

Sternberg, R. J. (1997). *Thinking styles.* New York: Cambridge University Press.

Treffinger, D. J., & Selby, E. C. (1993). Giftedness, creativity, and learning style: Exploring the connections. In R. M. Milgram, R. Dunn, & G. E. Price (Eds.), *Teaching and counseling gifted and talented adolescents: An international learning style perspective* (pp. 87–102). Westport, CT: Praeger.

Logic and Reasoning

Philip N. Johnson-Laird

Princeton University

Deduction The process of deriving a valid conclusion from premises, or evaluating whether a given conclusion is valid, that is, whether it must be true if the premises are true.

Formal Rules of Inference Rules that can be used to yield a conclusion from premises in a way that takes into account only the form (or syntax), not the meaning, of the premises. Logic relies on formal rules, and so do many psychological theories of reasoning.

Induction The process of deriving conclusions that are plausible, but not valid, from premises.

Logic The science of valid inference based on both formal systems for proof ("proof theory") and their accompanying semantics (or "model theory").

Mental Models Representations of the world that are constructed from perception or from discourse and that are postulated to underlie human reasoning.

Reasoning The process of deriving conclusions from premises. The two principal sorts of reasoning are deduction and induction.

Validity An inference is valid if its conclusion must be true if its premises are true. A valid inference from true premises yields a true conclusion; a valid inference from false premises may yield either a true conclusion or else a false conclusion.

LOGIC is the science of valid inferences. It is concerned with proofs, particularly of theorems in formal languages and mathematics. REASONING is the mental process of making inferences, particularly inferences that are logical. It is a central cognitive process, because without it, there would be no logic, no mathematics, no science, and no law (and no encyclopedias). It is also a major component of intelligence, and so tests of intelligence include problems in reasoning.

I. INTRODUCTION

Students of creativity sometimes claim that people are too logical to be creative; students of reasoning sometimes claim that people are too creative to be logical. In fact, no clear distinction exists between the mental processes of reasoning and the mental processes of creation. The two go together hand in hand. One criterion for reasoning, however, is that it should be logical, and so this article begins by describing logic. It then considers the psychology of reasoning. It describes the two main theories of reasoning, and it outlines some robust phenomena that elucidate them. Finally, it illustrates how reasoning in real life goes beyond logic and depends on creativity.

Consider this problem about a particular hand of cards:

If there is a king in the hand, then there is an ace
  in the hand.
There is a king in the hand.
What follows?

Nearly everyone responds with the correct conclusion:

        There is an ace in the hand.

This inference is of a form known as *modus ponens,* and
its conclusion is valid, that is, it must be true given that
the premises are true. Validity does not mean that the
premises *are* true, but only that *if* they are true then
so is the conclusion. Valid inference thus preserves
truth—it leads from true premises to true conclusions.

II. LOGIC

Logicians have formulated many different logical calculi. They can set up a calculus in two distinct ways.
The first way is purely formal, concerning patterns
of symbols, but not their interpretation. The propositional calculus, which concerns negation and sentential
connectives, such as "if," "or," and "and," can be specified using formal rules of inference, such as

      If A then B.
      A
    ∴ B.

This rule of *modus ponens* states that given a conditional
premise, if A then B, and the categorical assertion of A,
where A and B can be any propositions whatsoever,
then one can derive the conclusion, B. Formal rules
operate without reference to truth or falsity, or to the
meaning of the connective or of the propositions expressed by A and B. Such rules allow one to construct
a formal proof, leading from the premises to the conclusion. Thus, the inference about the cards can be derived in a single step with the rule of *modus ponens.*

Logicians sometimes formalize a calculus in the most
parsimonious way, using just the rule of *modus ponens*
and a set of axioms, which are assertions that are assumed to be true. But, the more intuitive method of
"natural deduction" dispenses with axioms and relies
instead on formal rules of inference for each of the sentential connectives. There are rules to introduce connectives, such as

A		
B	A	$A \vdash B$
∴ A and B	∴ A or B, or both	∴ If A then B,

where "$A \vdash B$" signifies that the assumption of A, for the
sake of argument, yields a proof of B. And there are
rules to eliminate connectives, which include the rule
for *modus ponens,* such as

	A or B, or both	If A then B
A and B	not-A	A
∴ B	∴ B	∴ B.

Natural deduction is easy to understand, and it had a
vogue in logic texts.

When logicians formalize a calculus, they bear in
mind the intended meaning of each sentential connective. But the formal rules themselves do not make use
of this meaning. They are rules for writing new patterns
of symbols given certain other patterns of symbols, and
the rules are sensitive only to the form of the symbols,
and not to their meaning. A formal system accordingly
operates like a computer program. When a computer
program plays a game of chess, the computer itself has
no idea of what chess is or of what it is doing. It merely
slavishly follows its program, shifting "bits," which are
symbols made up from patterns of electricity, from one
memory store to another, and from time to time displaying symbols that the human users of the program
can interpret as moves on a chess board. There is indeed an intimate relation between computer programs
and proofs, and programs have been written to implement various logical calculi in order to prove theorems.
The programming language PROLOG is itself closely
related to a logical calculus.

The second way in which logicians can characterize
a logical calculus is semantic. For the propositional calculus, this method depends on the meanings of assertions formed using the various sentential connectives.
Consider a disjunction of the form, "A or B or both,"
such as

      There is a king or there is an ace, or both.

Logicians assume that its truth or falsity depends only
on the truth of its constituent propositions. It is true
given that there is a king; it is true given that there is

an ace; and it is true given that there is both a king and an ace. It is false only if there is neither a king nor an ace. These conditions apply to many other disjunctions, for example,

> There's a flaw in the coil or the battery is dead, or both.

Natural language, however, is not always so tidy. Just as there is poetic license, so there is logical license— a need for logicians to make simplifying assumptions about the meanings of logical terms. Logicians lay out the truth conditions for disjunctions in a truth table:

A	B	A or B, or both
True	True	True
True	False	True
False	True	True
False	False	False

Each row in the table shows a possible combination of truth values for the propositions A and B, and the resulting truth value of the disjunction. The first row in the table, for instance, represents the case where A is true and B is true, and so the disjunction is true.

To complete the semantic characterization of the propositional calculus, definitions of each sentential connective need to be made. One tricky connective is "if." An assertion such as

> If there is a king then there is an ace

is true when there is a king and an ace, and false when there is a king but not an ace. But, what is its status when it is false that there is a king? This question has generated a large philosophical and linguistic literature. The simplest semantics, however, may be the one that governs usage in daily life. It treats the preceding conditional as equivalent to

> If there is a king then there is an ace, and if there isn't a king then there may or may not be an ace.

This semantics, which is known as "material implication," can be laid out in a truth table:

There is a king	There is an ace	If there is a king then there is an ace
True	True	True
True	False	False
False	True	True
False	False	True

One of the advantages of material implication is that it accounts for the meaning of biconditionals, such as

> If, *and only if,* there is a king, then there is an ace,

which is equivalent to

> If there is a king then there is an ace, and if there isn't a king then there isn't an ace.

Hence, the third row in the preceding table is false, because the biconditional is true in only two cases, where there is both a king and an ace, or neither.

Truth tables can be used to validate inferences. For the *modus ponens* inference about the cards, the conditional premise calls for the previous truth table. The categorical assertion that there is a king eliminates the last two rows in the truth table (in which this proposition is false), and so the only case in which the conditional as a whole is true is the first row, and in this row the proposition that there is an ace is also true. Hence this conclusion is valid.

Logicians have proved that any conclusion that can be proved using formal rules for the propositional calculus is also valid using truth tables, and vice versa. They have also shown that there is a decision procedure for the calculus; that is, the validity or invalidity of any inference can be established in a finite number of steps. But this happy state of affairs does not apply to all logical calculi. An important extension of the propositional calculus is known as the predicate calculus. It deals with proofs concerning quantifiers, such as "any" and "some," for example,

> Any of the hands containing a jack contain some clubs.
> This hand contains a jack.
> ∴ This hand contains some clubs.

The predicate calculus is only semidecidable; that is, any valid inference can be proved in a finite number of steps, but if an inference is invalid, there is no guarantee that its invalidity can be established in a finite number of steps. An attempted demonstration may, in effect, get lost in the space of possible derivations. The single most important logical discovery, however, is that logics exist in which not all valid inferences can be proved using formal rules. Thus, Kurt Gödel proved that there are truths in arithmetic that cannot be proved in any consistent formal system. Gödel's theorem has been used by some theorists, for example, Penrose, to argue that human creativity itself cannot be governed by rules, and so it cannot be modeled in computer programs. This argument is not decisive, however, and it remains an open question whether or not creativity depends on unconscious rules of some sort. [*See* COMPUTER PROGRAMS.]

III. DEDUCTION

Theories of deduction parallel the distinction in logic between formal rules and truth tables. On the one hand, your mind may be equipped with formal rules of inference. You are not aware of these rules when you reason, and so they must be unconscious. On the other hand, there may be no formal rules of inference in your mind unless you have learned logic. Instead, your inferences may be based on your understanding of the meaning of the premises. This idea lies at the heart of an alternative theory of reasoning—the theory of mental models.

Mental models have three essential characteristics:

1. Each model represents a possibility, just as each true row in a truth table corresponds to a possibility. Thus, the disjunction

> There is a king or there is an ace, or both,

calls for three mental models to represent the three possibilities,

> K
>   A
> K A,

where K denotes a model of a king, A denotes a model of an ace, and the third model integrates them into a single model of both a king and an ace.

2. In order to minimize the load on short-term working memory, mental models tend to represent only what is true, and not what is false. This assumption is so important it is dignified with a name: the principle of *truth*. The first model in the preceding set, for example, represents the possibility that there is a king, but it does not make explicit that in this case it is false that there is an ace. The set of models similarly does not represent the row in the truth table in which the disjunction as a whole is false. People can be aware of what is false, but usually soon forget it.

3. The parts of a model correspond to the parts of what it represents, and the structure of the model corresponds to the structure of what it represents. Thus, a mental model is like an architect's model of a building. It is also like a visual image, though many models are not visualizable.

The theory postulates that models can be based on the meaning of premises, on perception, and on general knowledge. Reasoners construct models that represent the complete content of each premise—though here we consider only sentential connectives—and they formulate a conclusion by describing something in the models that was not explicitly asserted by any single premise. The strength of the inference depends on the proportion of the models in which the conclusion is true. A conclusion that holds in all the models is *necessary* given the premises. A conclusion that holds in most of the models is *probable* given the premises. A conclusion that holds in at least one model is *possible* given the premises. The model theory accordingly provides a unified theory of logical and probabilistic reasoning.

To illustrate reasoning by model, let us reconsider the *modus ponens* inference:

> If there is a king then there is an ace.
> There is a king.
> ∴ There is an ace.

The conditional calls for a model of the case in which there is a king and an ace:

K　A.

People realize that there are other possibilities consistent with the conditional—in particular, those in which it is false that there is a king. But, according to the principle of truth, they do not represent them explicitly. The conditional therefore elicits two models,

K　A

. . .

where the ellipsis denotes a model that has no explicit content, standing for the cases in which it is false that there is a king. The premise that there is a king eliminates this second model, and the first model yields the conclusion that there is an ace.

There is a simple but robust phenomenon in reasoning which illuminates the difference between formal rules and mental models. *Modus ponens* inferences are easier than inferences in the following form known as *modus tollens:*

> If there is a king then there is an ace.
> There is not an ace.
> ∴ There is not a king.

People are slower to make this inference, and they often respond erroneously that nothing follows. For example, some engineers running an experiment knew these facts:

> If the experiment is to continue, the turbine must be rotating fast enough to generate emergency electricity.
> The turbine is not rotating fast enough to generate emergency electricity.

They went ahead with the experiment anyway, and this failure to make a *modus tollens* inference was one of the cognitive blunders that led to the Chernobyl disaster.

Theories based on formal rules explain the difference between the two sorts of inference by postulating that there is a rule for *modus ponens,* but not for *modus tollens,* which accordingly calls for a chain of inferences in its proof:

1. If there is a king then there is an ace.
2. There is not an ace.

3.　　There is a king. (An assumption)
4.　∴ There is an ace. (*Modus ponens* applied to 1 and 3)

There is now a contradiction between a premise ("There is not an ace") and a proposition ("There is an ace") that follows from the assumption. The rule of *reductio ad absurdum* entitles one to negate any assumption that leads to a contradiction:

5.　∴ There is not a king.

The mental model theory explains the difference between the two sorts of inference in terms of the principle of truth: people normally cope only with what is true, not with what is false. *Modus ponens* follows immediately from the models of the conditional, but *modus tollens* does not. Its premise,

There is not an ace,

eliminates the first model from the models of the conditional,

K　A

. . .

and nothing appears to follow from the remaining elliptical model. The correct conclusion depends on overcoming the principle of truth and representing explicitly the cases where it is false that there is a king. These cases are compatible with the presence or absence of the ace, and so the conditional calls for three fully explicit models,

K　　A
¬K　　A
¬K　¬A,

where "¬" denotes negation. The premise that there is not an ace eliminates the first two models to leave only the model

¬K　¬A,

which supports the valid conclusion:

There is not a king.

Do logically untrained individuals reason using formal rules or mental models? A recently discovered phenomenon may help us to decide. Suppose that you are playing cards with me, and I tell you that only one of the following assertions is true.

There is a king in my hand or there is an ace in my hand, or both.
There is a queen in my hand or there is an ace in my hand, or both.
There is a jack in my hand or there is a ten in my hand, or both.
Is it possible that there is an ace in my hand?

Nearly everyone responds, "yes," and the answer seems obvious. Yet, the inference is illusory. It is impossible for an ace to be in my hand, because then two of my assertions would be true, contrary to my initial stipulation that only one of them is true.

There are many illusory inferences concerning necessary, probable, and possible conclusions. They are predicted by the model theory's principle of truth; people go wrong because they cannot cope with what is false. But the illusions jeopardize current formal rule theories, because they rely only on valid rules of inference and so cannot explain systematically invalid conclusions.

IV. REASONING IN REAL LIFE

Reasoning in real life has at least three properties that distinguish it from logical deductions. First, it almost always depends on a knowledge of the meanings of words—beyond just sentential connectives or quantifiers—and on general knowledge and beliefs. For instance, if you ask someone why opera should be subsidized, they may tell you that art is good for business. There are some missing links in this argument, which we can spell out explicitly:

Art is good for business.
Anything that is good for business should be subsidized.
Opera is an art.
∴ Opera should be subsidized.

The second premise is presumably part of the speaker's general beliefs. The third premise is based on the speaker's knowledge of the meanings of words, which automatically, and unconsciously, establishes the link. A vast network of such semantic relations has been implemented computationally by George Miller and his colleagues in the WordNet project.

Second, reasoning in real life is often "nonmonotonic." In logic, if a conclusion follows from some premises, then no additional premises can invalidate it. Further premises lead to further conclusions, and nothing ever subtracts from them. Logic is therefore said to be "monotonic." Inferences in daily life do not always have this property; their conclusions can be withdrawn in the light of subsequent information. Researchers in artificial intelligence have developed a variety of nonmonotonic systems of reasoning, but the understanding of nonmonotonicity in human reasoning lags behind. Sometimes, you withdraw a conclusion because it was based on an assumption you made by default—an assumption that you can use only if you have no evidence to the contrary. For example, you use the assumption that dogs have four legs to infer that my dog Fergus has four legs. But if you learn that Fergus lost a leg in an accident, then you will withdraw your conclusion.

Sometimes, you withdraw a conclusion because it was based on an arbitrary assumption. Given

The desk is to the right of the cabinet
The table is to the left of the desk,

you make an arbitrary assumption about the relation between the cabinet and the table, which yields the following spatial model of the layout:

table   cabinet   desk

This model yields the conclusion,

The cabinet is to the right of the table.

But then you learn that the cabinet is to the left of the table. You must withdraw your arbitrary assumption, and construct a model that is consistent with all the information that you know:

cabinet   table   desk

Nonmonotonic inferences that call for the withdrawal of default or arbitrary assumptions are part of the mental model theory. There are more problematic cases, however. Suppose you know, for example, that

If Pat has gone to get the car, then Pat will be back to pick us up in five minutes.
Pat has gone to get the car.

You validly infer,

Pat will be back to pick us up in five minutes.

But, suppose 20 minutes elapse and Pat is still not back. You are in a typical situation in everyday life in which there is a conflict between what follows from premises that you believe to be true and what are the facts. Something has to give. At the very least, you have to withdraw your conclusion. This step is again nonmonotonic. But now the next distinguishing property of everyday reasoning is relevant.

Third, at the heart of real-life reasoning is the *creation* of possibilities. In the preceding case, you do not just withdraw your conclusion, you begin to make inferences about what can have happened to Pat. One possibility leads in turn to inferences about further explanatory possibilities, for example,

Possibly, Pat did not go to get the car.
∴ Possibly, Pat could not find the car.
   ∴ Possibly, Pat got lost walking back to the car.
   ∴ Possibly, Pat forgot where he had parked the car.

If one presents people with this problem, and rules out each of the possibilities that they generate, then they create a sequence of models that become more and more imaginative, for example,

Pat might have developed a severe amnesia.
Pat might have been abducted by aliens.
Pat might have been given a posthypnotic suggestion to abandon you.

In real life, you use your knowledge and any relevant evidence to rule out the more probable models before you entertain such improbable ones. Yet, as the example illustrates, inferences in real life are often not deductively "closed," that is, there is not enough information to draw a valid conclusion. The process of reasoning is just as much creative as logical.

Bibliography

Braine, M. D. S., & O'Brien, D. P. (1991). A theory of if: A lexical entry, reasoning program, and pragmatic principles. *Psychological Review, 98,* 182–203.

Brewka, G., Dix, J., & Konolige, K. (1997). *Nonmonotonic reasoning: An overview.* Stanford, CA: CLSI Publications, Stanford University.

Evans, J. St. B. T., Newstead, S. E., & Byrne, R. M. J. (1993). *Human reasoning: The psychology of deduction.* Hillsdale, NJ: Erlbaum.

Jeffrey, R. (1981). *Formal logic: Its scope and limits.* (2nd ed.). New York: McGraw-Hill.

Johnson-Laird, P. N. (1993). *Human and machine thinking.* Hillsdale, NJ: Erlbaum.

Johnson-Laird, P. N., & Byrne, R. M. J. (1991). *Deduction.* Hillsdale, NJ: Erlbaum.

Johnson-Laird, P. N., & Goldvarg, Y. (1997). How to make the impossible seem possible. *Proceedings of the Nineteenth Annual Conference of the Cognitive Science Society.* Mahwah, NJ: Erlbaum.

Miller, G. A., & Fellbaum, C. (1991). Semantic networks of English. *Cognition, 41,* 197–229.

Penrose, R. (1989). *The emperor's new mind.* Oxford: Oxford University Press.

Rips, L. J. (1994). *The psychology of proof.* Cambridge, MA: MIT Press.

Longitudinal Studies

Rena F. Subotnik

Hunter College

Karen D. Arnold

Boston College

Cross-Sectional Studies Data are collected comparing one set of individuals' responses to those of another set of individuals within a given population at a given time.

Longitudinal Research Methodology A form of repeated measures design in which a minimum of two data points are collected from the same individuals over some significant passage of time.

Predictive Validity The degree to which a measure is a good predictor of an outcome to take place at a later time.

Retrospective Studies Data are collected from individuals in the form of memories about their past including experiences, opportunities, feelings, or aspirations.

Threats to Validity Criteria for judging the degree to which the qualities of a method, design, or instrument may affect the accuracy of the study results.

Longitudinal research methodology illuminates the course of creative lives and the antecedents of creative productivity. Spanning quantitative and qualitative data sources, LONGITUDINAL STUDIES of creativity follow the same persons over time. In so doing, longitudinal in- *vestigations offer unique advantages to a field seeking to understand the conditions affecting the process of developing creative potential, the lasting impact of interventions, and genuinely meaningful indicators of mature creativity. A small but important body of longitudinal research has contributed to the knowledge base on creativity. This article will do the following:*

1. Discuss strengths and weaknesses of longitudinal methodology in studying creativity over the life span.
2. Describe the longitudinal research on creativity and assess the state of the longitudinal scholarship in the area.
3. Suggest future applications of longitudinal methodology for addressing the next generation of research questions.

I. WHY LONGITUDINAL METHODS ARE USED TO STUDY CREATIVITY

A. Strengths

The relationship of creativity test scores to adult creative behavior, the worth of educational efforts to increase creativity, and the life trajectory of recognized or unsuccessful innovators are concerns fundamental to scholarship on creativity. However, most research designs are ill-suited to address these topics. *Retrospective studies* of eminent creators blur events through selective memory and constructed life stories. Additionally, those individuals who appear to be equally promising but ultimately unsuccessful are omitted from the record. *Cross-sectional studies* compare individuals and groups but offer no demonstration of changes within individuals or the reciprocal interaction of persons and environments over time. Longitudinal designs can avoid these limitations.

B. Weaknesses

Longitudinal research studies also present some inherent *threats to validity:* subject attrition, historical and testing effects, and resource and logistical difficulties. First, some members of a longitudinal study cohort will discontinue participation as a result of relocation or perceived failure to meet researchers' expectations. The representative nature of the remaining participants comes into question when too many participants leave the cohort. Second, historical events or periods that affect given age groups will likely influence study outcomes. Such historical effects can confound maturation with educational interventions. Third, regular contact over long periods of time between participants and investigators and repeated exposure to research instruments constitute testing effects that can also threaten validity. Finally, maintaining sufficient connection to avoid subject attrition or following multiple cohorts to neutralize historical effects requires access to money and time. Many studies that are ideally suited to longitudinal methodology are not conducted because of the great expense and time commitment involved.

II. KEY LONGITUDINAL STUDIES OF CREATIVITY

A. Identifying Creativity in Children and Adults

Longitudinal studies of creativity are most often conducted to assess a measure's or a variable's *predictive validity* as a source of future productivity or innovation. These measures or variables can include tests, behaviors, personality traits, or a combination of the three. The classic predictive validity study of adult creative achievement was established by E. Paul Torrance more than 30 years ago. Torrance featured the key role

played by divergent thinking in the creative problem-solving process. Torrance's data also show that tests alone cannot predict high-level adult achievement, much less genius. Other variables such as personality characteristics and specific behaviors are essential to the equation.

1. Tests

The Torrance Tests of Creative Thinking (TTCT) were designed to challenge the central role played by IQ tests as predictors of high-level adult productivity. Torrance invested enormous efforts into establishing the reliability and validity of the TTCT and encouraging their use in educational and clinical settings. Seven, 12-, and 22-year follow-ups of elementary and secondary students who took the TTCT in three Minnesota schools were conducted to establish a connection between school age divergent thinking abilities and adult creative achievement. In 1993 Torrance introduced readers of the *Roeper Review* to Beyonders, those school-age Minnesotans who grew up to become outstanding achievers. In this 30-year follow-up, Torrance was able to feature the behaviors and personality characteristics that served as precursors to the Beyonders' eminence. [*See* APPENDIX II: TESTS OF CREATIVITY.]

2. Creative Behaviors

Identification methods targeting specific behaviors exhibited by adolescents have been used by several longitudinal researchers for predicting adult creativity. M. Csikszentmihalyi and his colleagues conducted a 5-year longitudinal study of 210 "talented teenagers" ages 13 through 17, selected on the basis of their creative products as well as their intense absorption and fascination with their chosen domains.

Milgram and Hong similarly focused on adolescents' intrinsic interests. Eighteen years after having gathered information about activities, school grades, and tested creative thinking in 48 Israeli high school students, Milgram and Hong found that adolescent leisure activities and creative thinking predicted adult life accomplishment far better than teenage academic performance or IQ. This finding was supported in a 15-year longitudinal study of 81 high school valedictorians and salutatorians. Superior high school academic performance predicted undergraduate scholastic success and advanced degree achievement, but not adult creativity.

3. Creative Personality

Everyday notions of creativity assume that creative people are somehow special in their individual traits and personality. A category of longitudinal investigations have followed individuals identified as having creative personalities. A 10-year study found that adults initially classified as creative thinkers accomplished significantly more than their peers in the domains of art, writing, science, and general achievement, and personality style and aspirations in college have been found to be strong predictors of occupational creativity at age 52.

4. Multimethod Identification

Given the different methods for identifying creativity—tests, behaviors, and personality traits—it is perhaps surprising that few longitudinal studies have attempted to devise an integrative, multimethod identification framework. An important exception is the Munich Longitudinal Study of Giftedness. This study began in 1986 with 25,000 German children and adolescents identified by teachers as exceptional in intelligence, creativity, or social, artistic, or psychomotor ability. Student data included ability and personality measures, school and extracurricular performance indicators, and environmental conditions such as family, classroom climate, and critical life events. Repeated measures over 2 years yielded a useful multidimensional model predicting achievement. A central finding of the massive study was that the profile of creatively gifted students differed dramatically from their academically talented peers.

The magnitude of the Munich study provides an ideal longitudinal research design, yet such projects are rarely conducted because of the vast amounts of resources and time they require. Consequently, studies of single identification criteria continue to be the primary vehicles for investigating the relationship between specific early indicators of creativity and later creative accomplishment.

B. Intervention Studies

A set of longitudinal studies of creativity reports on the efforts made by educators and researchers to elicit higher levels of creativity by way of specific interventions. Some of the intervention programs were designed with academically or creatively gifted children in mind. Others served more heterogeneous populations. Despite the acknowledged effect of either family support or pathology on creative productivity, only one study in the literature describes an intervention that can be employed by caregivers in out-of-school settings.

C. The Impact of Gifted Education Models on Creative Productivity

Several models of gifted education have been developed to serve children with exceptional abilities. One, the Enrichment Triad Model, was implemented in schools throughout the nation. The third of three components (Type III) of this model involves the production of original work in an area of student interest under the guidance of a resource room teacher or out-of-school mentor. Two follow-up studies were conducted to determine the degree to which participants in the elementary and high school versions of the program maintained their interests and pursuits of creative work. After 3 years and 10 years, respectively, participants attributed their ability to make satisfying academic and professional choices in college to their Type III experiences.

The Purdue Three-Stage Model is designed to generate creative productivity in academically gifted students. A longitudinal follow-up study reported that students who participated for at least 3 years remained highly accomplished at the end of secondary school. The researchers did, however, find gender differences in career and educational aspirations, with girls holding lower expectations for themselves than boys. [*See* GENDER DIFFERENCES.]

D. Instructional Innovations for Nonspecific Populations

Increasing children's creativity is not solely within the purview of gifted education. Three studies in the literature describe methods that were implemented in regular school settings with the goal of increasing children's creativity. In all the studies, teachers' feedback and nurturing of the children's creativity and personal styles were keys to advancement and growth.

Conversely, sometimes teachers need to set up rich environments and then step aside. A study conducted in Vienna explored the introduction of 4 hours per week of unstructured free play to the elementary curricula of 12 schools with growing academic and behavior problems. The authors believed that increasing structure and standardization of school life had led to reduced motivation and had hampered growth of creativity. Four years later, children were found to be happier in school, to have fewer behavior disorders, and to have increased their creative problem solving in classroom and schoolyard contexts. Taking 4 hours per week that might have been applied to academic pursuits did not appear to reduce scholastic achievement. [*See* PLAY.]

E. Domain-Specific Longitudinal Studies

Adult creative productivity occurs within a specific area or discipline: a *domain* of human endeavor. Most studies of highly creative and eminent individuals within a domain are cross-sectional or retrospective accounts of individuals' life courses, personalities, or correlates of achievement. A small set of longitudinal studies is available, however, that follows the career trajectories of individuals within specific disciplines. Most of this research concerns promising individuals who are getting closer to making a mark on their respective fields. The social context of a domain, particularly the "field" of gatekeepers and certifiers of achievement, emerges as a central factor in these investigations.

1. Art

The classic longitudinal study of mature creativity in a domain was an 18-year investigation of male visual artists at a prestigious art institute. After observing the students using a specified set of objects to create artistic problems, researchers classified the men into problem solvers and problem finders. Seven years later, those judged as problem finders were more successful artists according to experts such as gallery heads, art critics, and peer artists. Problem finding among art students predicted career recognition at the 7-year point in the life span better than personality traits. The value of a longitudinal study was further evidenced, however, when problem finding was discovered as less prominent in artistic career success than personality style 18 years after art school.

Other investigators have used longitudinal methods to explore the trajectories of fine artists. A study of 30 male artists indicated that the "starving artist" stereotype of low-level, intermittent employment fit very few artists. As compared at midlife to the more common cases of continuously employed artists, men with sporadic careers reported diminished marital stability and socioeconomic level but equal satisfaction with their careers and lives. Another 18-year longitudinal study followed 281 male and female art students beginning in 1963. In keeping with most of their generation, males were employed continuously while family and situational variables predicted women's more sporadic career patterns.

2. Music

A study of early musical creativity addressed fundamental questions about the comparative developmental pathways of normal and highly creative individuals. Investigators visited nine children in their homes bimonthly for 5 years, beginning shortly after the children's first birthday, and observed their natural progress in singing songs. Through careful analysis of children's mastery of musical tonal language and rhythm and pulse, researchers were able to conclude that musically gifted children are unique, not just accelerated in their development. Such children could bring to bear invention, nuance, and drama to musical interpretation. A musically oriented family context also characterized musically creative children. [*See* MUSIC.]

3. Science

Creativity in science is a staple of the literature on domain-specific productivity; however, as in other domains, longitudinal studies of creativity are few in number. One exception is a longitudinal follow-up of 1983 Westinghouse Science Talent Search winners. The Westinghouse prizes are awarded to high school seniors with outstanding individual research investigations. Researchers grouped students according to 1990 interview responses about the generation of research problems. The resulting typology classified students into problem finders (those continuing to generate their own research questions), problem solvers (those taking up problems posed by teachers and others), and nonresearchers (those no longer active in research). Problem finders turned out to be more likely than other Westinghouse winners to choose academic careers in research science and to have significant and intense relationships with mentors in their domain. This study points to the important interaction between an individual's talent and significant interaction with high-level experts in one's field. [*See* SCIENCE.]

4. Mathematics

The Study of Mathematically Precocious Youth (SMPY) is the largest-scale American repeated measure study of highly talented individuals. The planned 50-year project began in 1971 and involves 5000 individuals from several cohorts who were identified as mathematically or verbally talented on the basis of scholastic aptitude tests (SATs) administered at age 12 or 13. The focus of this project is not on creativity in mathematics per se, but rather on the transition from tested ability to high-level creative productivity in quantitative careers. Researchers have found that extremely high SAT test scores in early adolescence do indeed offer good predictors of engagement in such careers, particularly for males.

Gender differences found in the SMPY study of mathematics talent and in studies of scientific creativity show the importance of social context as it affects perceived and actual life opportunities. Similarly, a longitudinal study of creative Mills College women of the 1950s demonstrated the importance of family expectations in determining the fulfillment of high potential in creative careers for women.

III. AN ASSESSMENT OF THE CURRENT STATE OF THE LITERATURE

Lewis Terman, father of the Stanford-Binet IQ test, established the first modern and comprehensive longitudinal study conducted in the United States. His original objective was to demonstrate the *predictive validity* of IQ as a determinant of genius. From today's perspective, this investigation is considered flawed by the study sample's lack of representativeness, yet Terman's research remains vastly influential as a model of longitudinal methodology. In the same vein, Torrance established his 30-plus-year study of creative-thinking abilities to verify the notion that exceptional creativity in adulthood can be predicted from high scores on diver-

gent thinking tests taken in school. A wealth of investigations employing the Torrance Tests of Creativity were spawned by his work. [*See* DIVERGENT THINKING; INTELLIGENCE.]

As described in Section II, some admirable attempts have been made to evaluate the effectiveness of curricular or instructional models with theoretical underpinnings. The time is ripe for a ground-breaking longitudinal comparative study conducted by scholars who are not associated with any one of the theoretical models. Ideally, such an investigation would also address whether the interventions have differential effects on creatively or intellectually gifted children as opposed to more heterogeneous populations.

Although Getzels and Csikszentmihalyi included a battery of aptitude and achievement tests as part of their data collection process, they were far more interested in domain specific demonstrations of creativity, such as the problem formulation and problem finding that goes into making a still life drawing. Their study, like those of Terman and Torrance, established a new research direction for a generation of scholars, one in which the prediction of great creative performance was based on demonstrated talent in a domain rather than on tests of general potential.

Longitudinal research is capable of addressing some of the key questions in the creativity arena, yet most of the longitudinal scholarship reported in the creativity literature is single cohort in design. Replicating the results of current and future scholarship is essential to both alleviate the *threats to validity* that come from historical effects and to increase studies' potential for generalizability. Because replication is not viewed as an especially attractive option for most researchers, future scholars should look to the multiple cohort models (see the SMPY and Munich studies described in Section II). The multiple cohort design allows for the most rigor and therefore the most valid outcomes upon which to make policy.

The research literature takes two different tacks in defining the criterion variable of interest, creativity, and each suffers from imprecision and tremendous variability. The majority of longitudinal research concentrates on characteristics of the creative person and on everyday manifestations of novelty such as original, abundant, or flexible ideas and behaviors. Studies of everyday creativity shed little light on the process by which individuals make transformational contributions to valued societal arenas.

Csikszentmihalyi distinguishes brilliance and personal creativity from what he calls "Capital C Creativity," in which a person contributes an innovation to a specific cultural domain. This original contribution, when recognized and validated by a field of experts, subsequently enters into and changes the domain for all who follow. Person, domain, and field are all necessary, interactive components of the systems approach to creativity. This model draws the spotlight away from individual traits in favor of public, consensually valued novelty within a mastered domain. Once understanding of creativity broadens beyond individual qualities and sudden illuminating insights, longitudinal inquiry emerges as the ideal method for studying ongoing interactions of creative individuals with their disciplines and environments.

IV. FUTURE DIRECTIONS FOR LONGITUDINAL RESEARCH IN CREATIVITY

Retrospective studies bring us face to face with great creative thinkers. They provide some hints about the path to eminence through verifiable historical analyses. However, some important influences on the development of elite talent are lost to our observation if they are not caught along the way. Longitudinal studies designed to test the prediction of eminence from childhood potential can be inefficient because few productive adult creators will emerge from these groups. A more promising longitudinal approach is identifying cohorts of individuals in a domain who have already demonstrated achievements, which *retrospective studies* have suggested closely precede the emergence of creative eminence.

Future longitudinal studies on creativity should feature big C Creativity and the systems model to a much greater extent by attending to the interactions between talented individuals and the field, by examining domains and fields over time, and by carefully specifying the definition of creativity used. The systems view

and big C Creativity have three distinct advantages. First, this approach offers an empirical base on which to judge creativity—the incorporation of innovation in a domain. Second, it accounts for the social context of accomplishment. Third and finally, the person-domain-field conception focuses creativity research on the products of greatest significance to our lives.

Longitudinal studies of both everyday creativity and creative eminence are valuable, complementary endeavors—one improves daily life in our homes and schools, the other can attune us to recognize, value, and develop latent talent with the potential to reach beyond the individual to the transformation of society.

Bibliography

Arnold, K. D. (1995). *Lives of promise: What becomes of high school valedictorians?* San Francisco: Jossey-Bass.

Cramond, B. (1994). The Torrance Tests of Creative Thinking: From design through establishment of predictive validity. In R. F. Subotnik & K. D. Arnold (Eds.), *Beyond Terman: Contemporary longitudinal studies of giftedness and talent* (pp. 229–254). Norwood, NJ: Ablex.

Csikszentmihalyi, M. (1988). Society, culture, person: A systems view of creativity. In R. Sternberg (Ed.), *The nature of creativity,* (pp. 325–339). New York: Cambridge University Press.

Csikszentmihalyi, M., Rathunde, K., & Whalen, S. (1993). *Talented teenagers.* New York: Cambridge University Press.

Feldman, D. H., Csikszentmihalyi, M., & Gardner, H. (1994). *Changing the world: A framework for the study of creativity.* Westport, CT: Praeger.

Getzels, J. W., & Csikszentmihalyi, M. (1976). *The creative vision: A longitudinal study of problem finding in art.* New York: Wiley.

Milgram, R. M., & Hong, E. (1994). Creative thinking and creative performance in adolescents as predictors of creative attainments in adults: A follow-up study after 18 years. In R. F. Subotnik & K. D. Arnold (Eds.), *Beyond Terman: Contemporary longitudinal studies of giftedness and talent.* (pp. 212–228). Norwood, NJ: Ablex.

Oden, M. (1968). The fulfillment of promise: 40-year follow-up of the Terman gifted group. *Genetic Psychology Monographs, 77,* 3–93.

Schaie, K. W. (1983). *Longitudinal studies of adult psychological development.* New York: Guilford.

Subotnik, R. F., & Arnold, K. D. (Eds.). (1994). *Beyond Terman: Contemporary longitudinal studies of giftedness and talent.* Norwood, NJ: Ablex.

Mad Genius Controversy

Stephen D. Durrenberger

University of Kentucky College of Medicine

Affect The emotional feeling, tone, and mood attached to a thought, including its external or physical manifestations.

Bipolar Disorder An affective disorder characterized by the occurrence of alternating periods of euphoria (mania) and depression.

Delusion A fixed, false belief or wrong judgment held with conviction despite incontrovertible evidence to the contrary.

Depression A clinically discernible condition whereby the individual suffers a significant decrease in mood and energy level, and also usually experiences appetite and sleep disturbance (either an increase or a decrease in both). The person's outlook is hopeless; he or she does not see any positives in life, and may consider suicide as a "way out."

Flashback A past experience which manifests itself intrusively in the conscious mind as a hallucination or a reenactment taking place before the eyes of the victim. Often these past experiences are traumas, but can be past hallucinatory experiences as well.

Hallucination The apparent, often strong subjective perception of an object, event, or sound when no such stimulus is present.

Mad Suffering from or manifesting severe mental disorder; insane; psychotic; wildly foolish; or rash. Its origin is the Latin *mutare,* meaning "change," through prehistoric Germanic to Old English as "Gemad," meaning "insane," eventually shortened to "amadd," and then finally to mad.

Mania An emotional disorder characterized by euphoria or irritability, increased psychomotor activity, rapid speech, flight of ideas, decreased need for sleep, distractibility, grandiosity, and poor judgment; usually occurs in bipolar disorder.

Psychosis A mental and behavioral disorder causing gross distortion or disorganization of a person's mental capacity, affective response, and capacity to recognize reality, communicate, and relate to others to the degree of interfering with the person's capacity to cope with the ordinary demands of everyday life.

Schizophrenia A common type of psychosis, characterized by a disorder in the perception, content of thought, and thought processes (hallucinations and delusions), and extensive withdrawal of the individual's interest from other people and the outside world and the investment of it in his or her own.

Substance Dependence A condition whereby the absence of a drug or "substance" from the person's bloodstream produces a definite constellation of symptoms, where the returning of that substance to the body then alleviates these symptoms, and where a person spends a significant amount of his or her day consuming or attempting to obtain the substance in order to prevent this withdrawal syndrome from occurring.

In this article we will explore different approaches to MAD GENIUS CONTROVERSY. First, we will look at mental illness and our fascination with it as a society. Both our attraction to it and our fear of it will be explored. Then we will examine specific illnesses, schizophrenia, bipolar disease, substance abuse and dependence, and posttraumatic stress disorder. We will see how these illnesses may affect the world view and, thus, the creative output of those affected. We will take a brief look into the lives of some who have suffered mental illness and become famous enough for most to know their names. The concept of the "muse" will be explored. Finally we will look at research which has been conducted in pursuit of answers to the questions around creativity and "madness."

I. INTRODUCTION: THE CONTROVERSY

The question posed is, "is creativity like unto madness?" There is not a simple yes or no answer to this question. Debate has raged for centuries on this topic. The idea is woven into Greek mythology. Socrates and Plato considered creativity to be a "divine madness," whereas Aristotle believed it was a natural act of a rational mind. Even now, books and articles are written explaining it, refuting it, and declaring it true. Some individuals take offense to the very idea, while others embrace and flaunt their "madness." In retrospect we can look and see who is or has been a "madman." From this view we can make suggestions and theories about the nature of creativity with regard to sanity and mental illness. Some of the questions have been answered well in recent years; others remain the realm of the philosopher, wonderer, and poet, never to fall easily into the net of science.

II. THE STIGMA

If this thing called madness can be associated with notoriety through creativity, why then should there be some to whom the thought is detested that they as creative individuals, or their hero or idol, should ever suffer such a malady as mental illness? Joyce Carol Oates

is quoted in Kay Redfield Jamison's book, *Touched With Fire,* referring to Emily Dickinson: "(She) was not an alcoholic, she was not abusive, she was not neurotic, she did not commit suicide. Neurotic people or alcoholics who go through life make better copy, and people talk about them, tell anecdotes about them. The quiet people just do their work." There is indeed a heavy weight to bear upon the shoulders of one who suffers from such an illness. This is the isolating, degrading, and sometimes deadly stigma associated with mental illness.

Our fascination with maladies of the mind has always been strong. In the early years of the state mental institution, these warehouses for the insane were often the center of the local community. Many of the institutions constructed during the 19th century have not only large dormitories for patients, but, gathering places, such as ballrooms, for the well-to-do of society. Often events such as Madness Balls were held at these locations. The intentions may have been benevolent, such as raising money for the institution, but the draw was the chance to see the madmen and women paraded in front of the social elite. Morbid curiosity drew people to these events as much as beneficence.

Today we still view mental illness with caution. Patients often suffer from the isolating effects of their illnesses. Family members sometimes reject outright the disturbed individual. Jobs are hard to obtain once the knowledge of their histories is revealed. Insurance companies deny coverage for their illnesses and thus financial difficulties ensue. The institutions and homes which house these forgotten souls are often treated like prisons with public opinion being the cliche, "Sure we need them, but not in my backyard."

In cinema today we are inundated with visions of mental illness. Films have both contributed to, and attempted to demystify, false beliefs about insanity. From *One Flew over the Cuckoo's Nest* and *As Good as It Gets* with Jack Nicholson, to *Nuts* and *Prince of Tides* with Barbra Streisand, it is difficult to avoid the topic when going to the movies. Early films such as *The Snake Pit* with Olivia de Havilland showed disturbingly realistic views of mental institutions in a time when medications were not available to treat these individuals. Hitchcock embraced the subject as well, painting a portrait of repressed memory in *Spellbound.* Also, in *Gaslight* he has the protagonist being "driven mad" by her husband. Bipolar affective disorder is characterized in several movies including *Shine,* the story of David Helfgott, and *Mr. Jones,* starring Richard Gere.

Organizations such as the National Alliance for the Mentally Ill have formed with the sole intent of reducing or eliminating the negative public perception of mental illness. Indeed, now the battle is being fought in congress regarding giving equal coverage for mental health in medical insurance. The fact remains, however, that much of society continues to fear and misunderstand mental illness.

III. THE ROMANCE

Indeed, there is another view of mental illness. Many a poet has glorified his "divine madness." The rock star today, as the poet of yesterday, often partakes of mind-altering substances with a rebellious and defiant air, regularly resulting in drug or alcohol dependence. Blues artists write in their lyrics that one must live the blues to play the blues. Hollywood flaunts the excesses and passions of the creative genius. As in the movie *The Bar Fly* with Mickey Rourke, it often glamorizes the struggles of the mentally ill individual with his or her creativity. Ironically, many of the scientific "geniuses" portrayed in movies are clearly madmen. Yet, as will be shown later, this is a group of creative individuals remarkably free of mental illness, Nikola Tesla (eccentric inventor of alternating electrical current) not withstanding. We, in psychiatry, struggle to help patients for whom mania is a positive high, and who often refuse to accept treatment, even when it endangers their lives.

If we compare yesterday's poets and writers to rock-and-roll stars today we would find striking similarities—from the morbid depressions of Alfred Lord Tennyson and Edgar Allan Poe, to the mood swings, both high and low, of Virginia Woolf, Ernest Hemingway, and Vincent van Gogh. These mood problems were often coupled with substance use and abuse, including alcohol, laudanum (an opium-derived substance similar to morphine), absinthe (an anise flavored drink made from oil or wormwood used for its intoxicating effects, which, when consumed in quantity, can cause kidney failure and death, and is touted to have led to insanity in some users).

Today, of course, we often learn of the rock star or jazz musician who has died of drug- or alcohol-related causes or suffers from depression or another mental illness. Jimi Hendrix, the legendary guitar player and songwriter, died after an overdose of barbiturates (he actually choked to death on his own vomitus). Janice Joplin, noted blues singer, died of an accidental heroin overdose. The deaths via suicide in the 1990s of Michael Hutchence, lead vocalist for the pop/rock group INXS, and Kurt Cobain, lead singer of the rock group Nirvana, were further reminders of the personal suffering of these public figures. [*See* ALCOHOL AND CREATIVITY; DRUGS AND CREATIVITY.]

Thus, a few inspired individuals who have become well known to us fascinate us by the maladies they suffer. We want to look but not touch—to vicariously experience, yet remain distantly sterile from their madness. Many of us are voyeurs of this mysterious world. Just as we flock to movies displaying exaggerated violence, we too are drawn to the opportunity to see what it is like to live the life of the insane.

IV. THE REALITY

So, we stand looking and wondering, curious about these "outsiders." What are their lives really like? Here we will examine two potentially devastating mental illnesses which attract public curiosity. These are the "madmen" illnesses: schizophrenia and related psychotic disorders, and bipolar illness, formerly known as "manic depressive disease."

Schizophrenia is a disease characterized by a symptom complex that is defined in psychiatric literature. The primary components, according to the current definition, are the presence of both hallucinations and delusions. Secondary are the "negative" symptoms, or the absence of emotional or relational components of unaffected individuals. Of these are included lack of emotional expression, both verbally and physically, social withdrawal, slowed movement or reaction time, and impoverished speech (specifically, an inability to carry on normal conversation, giving only simple yes–no answers.)

This disease can have catastrophic effects on the lives of affected persons. Approximately half of all schizophrenia patients attempt suicide at least once in their lifetime. It is estimated that 10 to 15% of schizophrenics will die from suicide. These patients tend to slip slowly out of society and down the socioeconomic ladder. Because it is often impossible for them to hold jobs during a psychotic period, they are often excluded from jobs permanently. Many of today's homeless, estimates range from one- to two-thirds, are deinstitutionalized schizophrenic patients. Though schizophrenic patients receive much notoriety when they commit acts of violence, they are statistically no more likely to commit murder than the average member of society.

Living the life of a schizophrenic is often lonely and depressing. The decrease in use of hospitals to warehouse the mentally ill has overwhelmed underfunded social agencies, leading to the increased numbers of homeless schizophrenics. Those that are severely ill and do have homes often reside in group homes or boarding homes when families can no longer care for them. Society prefers to pay little attention to them. Money is not readily available to run programs which would enhance the quality of life of many schizophrenics. Fortunately, newer drugs on the market today do offer hope through decreased side effects and enhanced effect on the "negative" symptoms, helping some patients to move back into society as functioning, contributing members. [*See* SCHIZOPHRENIA.]

Bipolar illness, or bipolar affective disorder as it is called in psychiatric literature, is a disease of mood swings. As is suggested by the name, in its typical form, there are two distinct poles to the range of these swings. The one we are familiar with through movies and media is "mania." This is a period of exaggerated energy, sleeplessness which can last for several days, and often psychotic features such as delusions or hallucinations. More often the delusions are of a grandiose nature, with affected individuals believing they have unusual powers, or are famous persons. The other pole is the depression that often follows the "high." This is a period of hopelessness and lack of energy. Often patients will stay in bed for days, not eating or drinking. Patients will contemplate suicide and often attempt it during this stage.

A difficult struggle for many patients with this illness is whether to accept treatment. The medications offered to control and prevent the mood swings have significant side effects which make them uncomfortable for some to take. In addition, some patients resent having to be on medicine at all. Many bipolar patients enjoy the sensation of mania. This results in them stopping medication on their own without consulting their doctor. Unfortunately, mania is not without consequence.

Mania becomes more difficult to treat the longer it persists. Some believe there is damage to the brain caused by extended manic highs. Often manic patients will embark on spending sprees which will lead to huge debt and bankruptcy. Some will develop the desire to travel great distances with no destination planned. Manic patients have worked their way across many states aimlessly and furiously pursuing delusional intentions. Their inflated view of self may lead to sexual exploits with strangers and prostitutes with little thought of the risks involved. Their lives are often endangered by these irrational actions.

In between highs and lows, the manic patient struggles to make sense of what has transpired during a manic high. Often just coming to grips with the consequences of their actions can begin the cycle down into depression. Many end up addicted to alcohol and drugs due to either pleasure seeking, unrealistic expectations of their ability to "handle" substances, or attempts to "self-medicate" the depression or mania. Jail is another destination which awaits some patients, for their lack of insight and impaired judgment can lead to illegal activities. Fortunately, the patients who choose to stay in treatment are often productive, highly successful members of society. [*See* AFFECTIVE DISORDERS.]

Both of these illnesses are found at every socioeconomic level in society. Although there does tend to be increased numbers of schizophrenics as you look to lower levels, this is not true for bipolar disorder. Some of the stigma arises out of the false belief that anyone can spot a person with these illnesses. In truth, many of us may know someone who, without our awareness, is treated for one of these illnesses.

V. CREATIVITY AND MADNESS

After looking at the issues associated with "madness," we must now examine why the question is posed in the first place. Is creativity akin to madness? Does the creative process, at some level, mimic or come close to the state of psychosis or mania? Or, do the circumstances surrounding the life of the mentally ill person predispose that person to creative outlets. For instance, would a person who had lived a life in a well-supported family be able to write as Edgar Allan Poe wrote, having grown up in the shadow of a very ill mother, eventually witnessing her death?

It is true that not all creative people are mentally ill. It is also true that not all mentally ill people are creative. Also, not all creative people achieve notoriety for their creativity. As will be shown later, a higher percentage of notable creative individuals have a history of mental illness than would be predicted in the general population. Perhaps, the combination of intelligence, the elusive creative spark, and the often difficult existence of the mentally ill increases the likelihood one will put the creative spark to use in a medium which will gain public attention.

It is difficult to conceptualize a manner in which to study the creative process as it relates to psychosis or mania. The problem lies in the inability to show how creativity works. In addition, we lack a precise mechanism for psychosis and mania. We have multiple theories which are useful as models to explain the psychotic or manic states, but, at this point they remain difficult to prove right or wrong. We use the actions of medications which alleviate some of the symptoms of these conditions to help us decide which theories are closer to the truth. Unfortunately we do not have any probes for creativity.

Substance abuse and dependence is considered a "mental illness" for which diagnostic criteria exist in psychiatric literature. As stated earlier, it is a common affliction among certain creative groups. This is an illness which can serve as a model to examine the relationship between creativity and mental illness.

For instance, one could argue that hallucinogenic "street drugs" such as LSD and XTC have some effect on the creative process. If there is an effect, however, it does not appear to be significant enough to make a van Gogh out of a Charles Schulz. Some rock musicians in the sixties give the drugs credit for insights gained or experiences they had while using them. The Beatles' song, "Lucy in the Sky with Diamonds," describes a typical LSD "trip," and an anagram formed from the main words in the title would be LSD. Many more musicians have composed lyrics and songs when not under the influence of hallucinogens. Also, most of the people who have used these substances have not been known for their creativity. This points to the likely explanation that the individuals had a predisposition to creativity which may have been influenced by their drug use, rather than the drugs being the source of their creativity.

The legendary saxophonist Charlie "The Bird" Parker was addicted to heroin. His substance use became a model to be followed in jazz circles during his era. Many believed it was the source of his inspiration, and that using the same substance would push them into the realm of genius with him. Clearly, in retrospect, we can see that his work was more likely negatively influenced by his drug use, contributing, in part, to his early death.

The same can be said for the modern poet and singer Jim Morrison, lead singer of the sixties rock group, The Doors. He too abused substances, both alcohol and illicit drugs. He became a legend among his peers for his excesses in this area. The band was even named for the Aldous Huxley book, *The Doors of Perception,* a book about the hallucinogenic substance mescaline. Jim Morrison died of heart failure, likely secondary to his substance abuse. Even his wife later succumbed to the same and died of a heroin overdose.

If we look at psychosis and mania, we can postulate on another connection to creativity. There are aspects of the cognitive processes in both of these mental states which can contribute to the creative content of affected individuals. These states offer distortions of reality which are often translated into writing or painting. The world view as interpreted through the eyes of psychotic and manic patients/artists can be both bizarre and compelling.

In mania, the brain is moving at an accelerated pace. Many manic patients cannot handle this and decompensate. Occasionally one will meet a patient that is able to stay relatively intact during his or her manic state. This, when combined with enough intelligence, will lead to a patient who demonstrates lightning quick associations. Often the interviewer, when witnessing this, will only note connections when reviewing the content in retrospect. Indeed, some believe that this ability of a manic patient is what leads them to positions of power in large companies, especially when it is coupled with a decreased need for sleep.

When the manic puts pen to paper, or brush to canvas, he or she may describe things in a way we have never thought. We may be drawn into their world of fast pace thinking and moving. The visions they portray may be beyond our imagining, yet accessible enough to make it worth our time.

The reality view of the depressed bipolar patient, too, may be equally stimulating when translated into art. Examine the work of van Gogh. The miners and their families whom he painted are seen as human, touchable, remarkable people. The suffering they have endured is carved into their exteriors. His eyes saw what so many of us will never see.

In psychosis the process is different. Psychotic patients often use what is termed primary process thinking. This is a cognitive process we all used as toddlers, and continues in our adult dream worlds. Primary process is based on instinct, not logic. It is a process which forms connections between unrelated objects.

Salvador Dali demonstrates this perfectly in his surreal paintings. Landscapes which melt into faces, objects which do not hold their shape, changing into different objects, and sounds taking on visual meaning become the world in primary process thinking. Think of a dream you have had, one where you are in a familiar place which somehow is unfamiliar, too. Where people are known to you, yet strangely unknown. Where your efforts to move do not translate into the intended motion. You fly instead of walking. You think a thing and it happens. You begin to understand the unsettling world of a psychotic patient. Couple this experience with ability, and there might be a spectacular painting, a surreal novel, or a mystical poem.

Ultimately, however, the results of severe mental illness are a decrease in creative output. Research has shown that notable individuals in the throes of mental illness tend to have decreased creative output. However, these individuals have an overall increase in creative accomplishment when they are not in the midst of a psychotic, manic, or depressive episode. Also, it has been shown that the relatives of mentally ill individuals, who themselves may suffer from minor forms of mental illness, tend to have higher levels of creativity than the general population.

VI. PSYCHOLOGICAL TRAUMA

As a separate issue, trauma has had a profound effect on art and literature. Perhaps its greatest effect, however, has been on the world in total, through the acts of leaders who have been severely traumatized themselves as children. Society has been exposed to the re-enactments of traumas of many creative individuals through their work. The writing of Stephen King and Edgar Allan Poe, the movies of Hitchcock, and the paintings of Picasso and Magritte are all visions of the pasts of these talented individuals. Individuals such as Hitler and Stalin, and the great philosopher Friedrich Nietzsche, whose writing was used to justify slaughter by the Nazis, have had a profound and retraumatizing effect on the world.

A traumatic event, as it is defined in psychiatric literature, is an event outside of the realm of normal human experience, usually coupled with the imminent threat of loss of life or damage to the body. The after-effects of these events can have a profound influence on the life of the victim. Memories of trauma can reoccur in the form of flashbacks or nightmares. Some even report "body memories" whereby they experience sensations related to the trauma, years after the event. Trauma victims may suffer from post-traumatic stress disorder (PTSD). This is the name coined after the Vietnam war to describe a constellation of symptoms which have been noted throughout history in soldiers after battles. It has been known, also, in this century as "shell shock." Post-traumatic stress disorder also causes symptoms of hypervigilance, anxiety, and increased startle reaction. Trauma victims often have a foreshortened view of the future, meaning they cannot see or plan into the future because they do not believe they will live that long. These individuals will often tell others of their experiences in an effort to ease the pain, but, often in some sense, they traumatize the listener by doing this. Even when victims recover from PTSD, many, some say greater than half, suffer lifelong effects from the trauma.

When someone who has been traumatized has the talent to share their ideas and fantasies with us, we often are allowed to vicariously experience their trauma. Stephen King, author of many frightening novels, weaves themes of his personal trauma into his stories. He often represents large inanimate objects as having a mind of their own, and as destructive predatory forces. He himself allegedly witnessed an event similar to that seen in the movie *Stand by Me* where a friend was killed by a passing train. In the movie we see the clan of boys nearly struck by the train as it mindlessly, yet purposefully, drives past. He repeats this theme in *Pet Sematary* with the passing trucks being the monster. In *Christine* he has a car become the predator. One can find this theme in many of his books.

Alfred Hitchcock, too, exposes us to his traumatic past in nearly all of his movies. His experience of being falsely accused of theft as a young child, and subsequently locked in jail without being given the reason, left an indelible impression on him which he imparts to us through the plots of the movies he directed. Over and over we see the theme of false accusation repeated in his films. Gregory Peck's character in *Spellbound* was a patient who unconsciously assumed the identity of a man who had been murdered, fearing he would be accused of the murder. In *The Trouble With Harry,* a bevy of characters all believe they may have murdered "Harry" and spend the movie deciding how not to be caught. In *North by Northwest,* falsely accused Cary Grant spends the film evading capture in an effort to clear himself. *Rebecca* has the protagonist believing her new husband is guilty of murder. Nearly every film by the master of mystery and horror carries a theme of false accusation.

Many writers have vividly returned us to the scene of their traumatic past. Others have turned their aggressions from the perpetrators to the world. Edgar Allan Poe, having witnessed his mother's decline as a boy, later beds down with a dead woman in his haunting poem "Anabel Lee." Friedrich Nietzsche witnessed his father's mental decline, and lived with him through it for 11 months until his father's death. He was, at times, locked in dark closets as a form of punishment by his father. After his father's death, he was raised by women who took it as a challenge to make him the "man" they thought he should be. Nietzsche struck out at the women who raised him and at the religion they forced on him after his father's death, by taking on all women in his writing, and by his greatest act of vengeance, killing God. His writing was later used to justify slaughter by the Nazis and to support their fascist ideals in the time leading up to WWII.

Hitler was raised in a brutal totalitarian home. Joseph Stalin was reared in utter poverty, beaten regularly by his drunken father until his father's death, and witnessed the steady decline of his mother. Both of these men achieved status as leaders using both creative and deadly means of control. Each became the image of his cruel, tyrannical father to a nation and to the world.

In art the traumas of the artists can be found woven through their paintings. Picasso paints a startling vision of his earthquake shattered home village in Spain in his spectacular masterpiece *Guernica.* He was carried through the village as it crumbled, under the arm of his father, running for shelter. René Magritte exposes us to the intense loss he felt when his mother committed suicide while he was just 12 years old. She leapt from a bridge in the night, supposedly wrapped only in her night clothes. The story told by Magritte is that his brother and father found her at the river's edge, naked except for her nightgown pulled up over her head, occluding her face. In many of his paintings, he pictures a naked woman with her face covered by a garment or sheet.

These are but a few examples of how trauma can permanently and profoundly effect the creative output of those so gifted.

VII. THE MUSE

Who is this voice within, this silent inspiration? Can this be the madness in the man? Many writers and poets give credit to the muse. They speak of words that flow from some place unknown—of poems that write themselves. Painters describe entire paintings already complete within their mind, long before they put brush to canvas. Some musicians hear their music before they write it.

This muse is thought, by some, to be a real phenomenon which arises out of the redundant circuits in our brains. The two sides of our brains develop separately until about age 3 when they are joined by a large interconnecting structure called the corpus callosum. This structure serves as a two-way communication system between the sides of our brain.

The function of the hemispheres is well documented in medical texts. For most people, the left is dominant. It serves the function of logic, math, decision making, and speech. The right, nondominant side is credited with emotion and language. It makes speech interesting. It helps us to give meaning to life and not just to see it in black and white (figuratively).

We see proof of these theories in patients who have suffered a stroke in one side of their brain. Patients with left-side strokes may lose the ability to speak, but retain their comprehension of language, whereas right-side stroke victims may be able to talk, but not to understand. They may lose understanding of facial expressions or affect, or be unable to assign words to feelings.

The muse, it is believed, may arise from the nondominant hemisphere. It may be that the development of language may precede the connection by the corpus callosum. Thus, the nondominant hemisphere would learn its own language and develop its own dialogue. If this separate language center could persist even after the two sides are joined, we could then see a source for the voice within. [*See* SPLIT BRAINS: INTERHEMISPHERIC EXCHANGE IN CREATIVITY.]

VIII. THE NUMBERS

To approach this question from a scientific point of view, we will examine statistics determined in a recent study by Arnold Ludwig. He chose to look at creativity and madness by first selecting a large group of highly successful, "creative" individuals who have achieved significant notoriety and public acclaim for their achievements. He then reviewed biographies of these individuals and categorized them according to the type of creativity they displayed and the degree and type of mental illness they suffered, if any. Following this, he analyzed the groups statistically to determine if particular mental illnesses were more prevalent in individuals with particular types of creativity.

Ludwig divided the individuals he studied, based upon their careers, into two categories of creative pursuits, "creative arts" and "other." The "other" group included enterprising careers, such as public office, military, and business; investigative careers, including social and natural sciences; and social careers, such as sports, social figures, and activists. The creative arts group was further divided into categories including poetry writers, fiction writers, architects, performance arts, nonfiction, theater, art, and composition.

When he examined each of these groups for psychopathology, Ludwig found a definite correlation with career path and pathology. The group most likely to suffer from mental illness was the creative arts group. Within this group were specific patterns as well. He found that certain groups such as musicians suffered more problems with substance abuse. Poets tended to have more mania and psychosis. Suicide was highest among poets, musicians, and fiction writers, suggesting, perhaps, an increase in depression as well. Interestingly, the more precise fields of architecture, nonfiction writing, and the like suffered very little mental illness relative to the other groups.

Ludwig went on to compare the families of the subjects. He found that the same groups which suffer more mental illness tended to have problems within their families long before beginning their careers. They were much more likely to suffer from broken homes, difficulties in adolescence, and early emotional problems than those in the more precision-oriented fields. [*See* FAMILIES AND CREATIVITY.]

In a more recent article, Ludwig suggests we look at the distribution of mental illness among his cohort as though it were a figure created with fractal geometry. With fractals there is infinite resolution, in that the more we magnify, the more detail we see, and yet the overall structure remains the same. If one were to further divide his categories, one would find the distribution of mental illness to be similar. For instance, if one looks specifically at writers, and divides them as to be objective, or artistic, the artistic group would show the higher percentage of mental illness. One can do this for all of the groups he has designated and find that the pattern remains unchanged.

IX. CONCLUSION

The majority of creative individuals do not suffer mental illness. However, the high prevalence of mental illness in certain types of creative people points to a significant connection between creativity and madness. Perhaps it lies in the environment. Or perhaps this creative genius springs from the madness. Though these individuals suffering mental illness may be less creative when they are suffering the most severe symptoms of their respective illnesses, they tend, as a group, to have higher levels of creative achievement than is predicted for the general population. Also, the relatives of the mentally ill tend to show higher levels of creativity than the general population.

Bibliography

Jamison, K. R. (1993). *Touched with fire: Manic-depressive illness and the artistic temperament.* New York: Free Press.

Ludwig, A. M. (1995). *The price of greatness: Resolving the creativity and madness controversy.* New York: Guilford Press.

Ludwig, A. M. (1998). Method and madness in the arts and sciences. *Creativity Research Journal, 11*(2), 93–101.

Miller, A. (1990). *The untouched key: Tracing childhood trauma in creativity and destructiveness.* New York: Doubleday.

Richards, R., Kinney, D., Lunde, I., Benet, M., Merzel, A. P. (1988). Creativity in manic-depressives, cyclothymes, their normal relatives, and control subjects. *Journal of Abnormal Psychology, 97,* 281–288.

Spitz, E. H. (1994). *Museums of the Mind.* New Haven: Yale University Press.

Terr, L. (1990). *Too scared to cry: How trauma affects children . . . and ultimately us all.* New York: Basic Books.

Tinnin, L. W. (1991). Creativity and mental unity. *Perspectives in Biology and Medicine, 34*(3), 347–353.

Marginality

Mattei Dogan

National Center of Scientific Research, Paris, France

Hybridization Recombination of scientific specialties in new fields across formal disciplinary boundaries.

Hybrid, Marginal Scholar who works at the intersection of disciplines, where specialties are overlapping.

Innovation, Marginal The farther up the ladder of innovation a work is, the more likely it is to be accomplished at the margins of a given discipline, at its intersection with another.

Paradox of Density The tendency of densely populated subfields to produce less innovation notwithstanding the greater effort applied.

Status Inconsistency Incongruences of income, education, property, ethnic origin, occupational position, prestige of an individual; for example, high athletic talent and low education.

*The word **MARGINALITY** indicates the situation of an individual who belongs simultaneously by ascription, achievement, aspiration, or self-identification to two or more distinctive groups. The term was used first by the sociologist R. E. Park in 1928 to refer to the cultural hybrids sharing the traditions of two communities. Marginality is a polysemic concept, that is, has different meanings in different contexts. In economics, marginal analysis focuses on borders or limiting areas rather than on the entire phenomenon under investigation. In ethnology, marginality indicates maladjustment, and in cultural studies it means cultural duality. The term is frequently used in studies concerning societal pluralism. In the popular language marginality may have a pejorative meaning indicating the inferior margins of the society, but in sociology of science it has the opposite meaning, since it refers to the superior and advanced strata of scientific communities and research activities. In the history of sciences it signifies advanced frontiers, the vanguard, and distance from the mainstream, and it takes a noble sense. This article focuses on the social sciences, but the concept of creative marginality is equally important for the natural sciences.*

I. CREATIVITY, MARGINALITY, AND HYBRIDIZATION

Contemporary social sciences have experienced in recent times three major trends: a rapid expansion, a fragmentation of formal disciplines by increasing specialization, and a recombination of specialties in new hybrid domains. The third trend, hybridization of scientific knowledge, is essential for understanding scientific creativity in the social sciences today.

A hybrid scholar is a specialist who crosses the borders of his home discipline by integrating in his research factors, variables, theories, concepts, methods, and substance generated in other disciplines. Different disciplines may proceed from different foci to examine the same phenomenon. This multidisciplinarity implies a division of territories between disciplines. On the contrary, hybridization implies an overlapping of segments of disciplines—a recombination of knowledge in new specialized fields. Innovation in each discipline depends largely on exchanges with other fields belonging to other disciplines. An innovative recombination is a blending of fragments of sciences. When old fields grow they accumulate such masses of material in their patrimony that they split up. Each fragment of the discipline then confronts the fragments of other fields across disciplinary boundaries, losing contact with its siblings in the old discipline.

Why is scientific innovation so frequently achieved at the intersections of disciplines and their margins? A concrete example would be more appropriate than a theoretical discourse. How did Pasteur discover the microbe? In order to see a microbe you need a microscope. The essential elements of a microscope are the lenses. The study of lenses belongs to crystallography. Fortunately, Pasteur started his scientific activity as a crystallographer. If he had not been a crystallographer he would not have had the idea to use lenses in order to observe microbes. The history of sciences is full of examples of discoveries at the borders of formal disciplines. [*See* INNOVATION.]

Hybridization is a general trend across all disciplines. This is clear in the pattern of Nobel prize winners today. There are many combinations of subfields not officially represented within Nobel's framework. The most fertile of these hybrid subdisciplines include biophysics, biochemistry, mathematical physics, quantum biophysics, neurophysiology, neurochemical physiology, and so on. While not recognized as belonging to hybrids, scientists working at such interstices are the usual prize winners in the now-ancient fields of "biology," "chemistry," or "medicine." In fact,

the great changes that have occurred contribute to the growing conviction that the categorization of the Nobel prizes has become increasingly obsolete and that they no longer correspond to the contemporary contours of scientific fields.

In scientific research, most researchers are located at the margins of their formal discipline, in contact with other disciplines. This marginality appears in topological metaphors: overlaps, interconnections, interpenetrations, breaks, and cracks. In political science, for instance, mass behavior is related to social psychology, elite recruitment is related to sociology and history, urban politics is related to social geography, the welfare state is related to social economy and social history, values are related to philosophy, ethics, and social psychology, governmental capabilities are related to law and economics, poverty in tropical countries is related to agronomy, climatology, and economic geography, and development is related to all social sciences and to several natural sciences.

Many specialists are in the outer rings. They borrow and lend at the frontiers. They are marginal scholars. Scientific disciplines progress at their periphery, in contact with other disciplines by cross fertilization. The core of the discipline tends to stagnate. It is in this sense that the expression "creative marginality" should be read.

II. MARGINALITY AS A STIMULUS TO CREATIVITY

As Thorstein Veblen has observed, cultural marginality is frequently a stimulus for intellectual creativity. Veblen himself, as a son of immigrants, felt marginal to both American and Norwegian societies. He later concocted the concept of cultural marginality and applied it particularly to Jewish and Quaker families, in order to explain the success and the upward mobility of these two communities.

The concept of marginality is meaningful for the analysis of creativity where scientific disciplines are overlapping. Many scholars, among the most productive and imaginative, work at the intersections of disciplines, at their margins. Like prophets they exercise their influence in distant fields more often than in their nominal domain. They are hybrid marginals.

For instance, the economists Anthony Downs, Mancur Olson, and Albert Hirshman have a wider audience in political science than among economists. Sigmund Freud, the founder of psychoanalysis, was contested by his colleagues in medicine and classical psychology. The historian Arnold Toynbee, the criminologist Cesare Lombroso, and the mathematician-economist Augustin Cournot (the "Cournot equilibrium") were not "at home" in their own domain. Muzafer Sherif, one of the founders of social psychology, has explained how his Turkish background made him aware of the cultural biases of psychological theory. The list of stimulations by marginal position is long.

Examples of cultural marginality can be found in research on status inconsistency. Social stratification in advanced societies is almost never unidimensional. The various criteria and roles of individuals (education, occupation, income, prestige, social origin, ethnicity, physical appearance, intelligence, sex, seniority in the organization, and so on) are not ranked identically by all people. These characteristics are perceived as higher or lower, better or worse, and crucial or unimportant. The differences in perception of rankings generate status incongruences.

As Gerhard Lenski has observed, individuals with inconsistent statuses or ranks have the tendency to rank themselves in terms of the status or rank which is highest and to expect others to do the same. But other people, benefiting from a different ranking of statuses, tend to do just the opposite and to treat others in terms of their lowest rank or status. For instance, some rich businessmen would perceive famous professors or scientists according to their income (they would see their small house or old car), and reciprocally some brilliant scientists or artists would tend to perceive the low intellectual level of many owners of capital. The concept of status inconsistency is usually applied to individuals, not the groups. Incongruence of statuses is an individual feeling and perception, not a collective one. For the study of all kinds of minorities (ethnic, racial, religious, and cultural) others concepts are available in the sociological literature. Without the concept of status incongruence it would be difficult to explain the behavior and motivation of many revolutionary leaders, famous rebels, or radical politicians. This concept is indispensable in the writing of biographies of some of the most famous novelists and painters of modern times. This concept is also useful for the discovery of the sources of intellectual stimuli in general, and in social sciences in particular. Three examples among hundreds will suffice. Karl von Clausewitz, who proposed the changing of the Prussian class-based military establishment into an effective fighting force, had been dismissed from the Prussian army for not having been able to substantiate financially his title. The author of one of the most important books of the 20th century, Norbert Elias (*The Society of Individuals*), did not obtain a stable academic position until the age of 57. Lewis Carroll, the "father" of *Alice in the Wonderland* (alias Charles L. Dodgson), was a stutterer and a nonconformist professor. In some such cases, the concept of status incongruence is related to the concept of an inferiority complex.

Serendipitous discoveries are interesting cases of creative marginality. Serendipity, a word originated in a legend from Sri-Lanka, is an unplanned, unexpected, fortuitous discovery, which can steer the researcher to the margins of her domain. Robert Merton, in his book on *The Sociology of Science,* has given several examples. One of the most recent serendipitous discoveries was a molecule of nitrogen, for which three pharmacologists received the Nobel prize in October 1998. [*See* SERENDIPITY.]

III. MARGINALITY AND THE PARADOX OF DENSITY

Research in a given area is subject to the law of diminishing marginal returns. An important part of what scientists see as innovative work is in reality completed before the field has begun to mobilize a large number of specialists. The topic slowly becomes exhausted, and can be reinvigorated only by changing its basic parameters. The tendency of densely populated subfields to produce less innovation notwithstanding a greater effort is what has been called the paradox of density. Adding elements from outside to an overcrowded field can make a big difference.

In the domains where there is a high concentration of scholars, some negative practices can be observed. Too much density can result from teaching needs in particular subjects, like the American presidency and congress or the national history. Density can occur after important historical changes, like after the implosion of the Soviet Union and of the Communist regimes in Eastern Europe when some 800 Western sociologists and political scientists concentrated their attention on this region that they had previously ignored. In such areas overpopulated with scholars it is difficult to add something new to the scientific patrimony. Overcrowding facilitates the spread of opaque jargons, of verbosity, of theoretical hair-splitting, and of routine work. Such professional deformations are possible only where there is a large community of sinners. In densely populated fields, productivity per capita tends to decline notwithstanding the efforts applied. Then, density in the core opens up room for creativity at the margins. The higher the density of scholars in a given field the less likely is, comparatively, imagination and innovation. Marginality is the opposite of density and a good route out of its problems.

IV. TYPES OF CREATIVE MARGINAL SCHOLARS

In the history of modern social sciences, three basic types of scholars can be distinguished: the pioneer, the builder, and the hybrid. These three types are ideal types, the classification being in some cases arbitrary. The first and the third types are hybrid scholars located in the frontiers of disciplines; the second is a mono-disciplinary specialist. These types have been described in *Creative Marginality*.

The pioneer is the scholar who expands the territory of a given discipline, and who pushes forward the frontier of his or her discipline. This expansion moves into terra incognita, an area about which science was ignorant. The pioneer does not encounter resistance from other disciplines, but conquers empty territories and annexes them. Pioneers do not really cross the borders of their formal discipline: they push that frontier outward toward other disciplines, covering in most cases a no-man's-land. Even if closely associated with one discipline, their marginality means that each could be appropriated by more than one modern discipline. In fact, many of them never held university chairs in their fields: Adam Smith, Sigmund Freud, and David Ricardo, for example. The great historian of the Roman Empire, Edward Gibbon, had little formal education

and never held an academic position. The time of their appearance varies, but the pioneers are the first generation of specialists. They are marginals in the sense that they explore the boundaries of their growing field, claiming new ground in the direction of other fields.

After the pioneers come the builders, who follow in the footsteps of these frontiersmen. The role of the builders is to develop the land discovered by the pioneers. They exploit the same territory, developing the subject area of their discipline to the fullest. Once developed, there is less room for further research, and the paradox of density sets in. Then comes the time for a new generation, the hybrid scholars, who combine knowledge from a number of fields.

The hybrid scholar is a border crosser who penetrates the territory held by another discipline or who establishes a province carved out of the territory of two or more disciplines. The hybrid scholar's research takes place at the periphery of two disciplines, not at their core; it also occurs only along a specific part of the periphery, not the entire frontier. The hybrid scholar does not work in old fields. He borrows from his neighbors, and what he creates may be borrowed by both parent disciplines in turn.

Hybrids are, in a sense, pioneers at the intersection of two disciplines, and they may give rise to a second generation of builders within the hybrid field. Some hybrid fields are old by now. Social psychology and economic history are much older than psychological anthropology or sociolinguistics. Different fields are in different phases of growth and decline. Some develop in a spiral, such as political economy.

V. CREATIVE MARGINALITY AT THE SUMMIT OF THE SCIENTIFIC PYRAMID

Contrary to a misperception, scientific progress of disciplines has been achieved in the last three decades mostly by specialists, not by generalists. It is nevertheless true that most of the greatest scholars in the social sciences during the 19th century and until the 1920s were interdisciplinary generalists, from Auguste Comte to Max Weber. The hybrid specialist today may be in reality a "marginal" scholar in each of the disciplines from which he borrows, including his own original discipline. But he becomes central to the intersection of two or several disciplines. Dozens of examples could illustrate this proposition for the social sciences as well as for the natural sciences.

Major social phenomena cannot be explained in a strictly monodisciplinary perspective. They have to be comprehended transversally across the disciplinary borders. For instance, to explain the fall of the Roman empire we may choose between 15 theories belonging to as many specialties across disciplines. We have the agronomic explanation by Max Weber, the latifundia; the geographical explanation by Montesquieu, the extension of the territory; the demographic interpretation by Piganiol; the slave system by Mommsen; the economic factors by Rostovtzeff; the decline of the aristocracy by Ferrero; the military interpretation by Luttwak; the foreign trade by Rogowski; an ecological factor, the desertification of the land; a bacteriological factor, malaria; without forgetting Pareto, the only political sociologist to have contributed to the debate. But one of the most interesting interpretations, validated by empirical evidence, does not belong to the social sciences, because it is of chemical nature: the lead poisoning of the Roman ruling class over generations. Saturnism has poisoned a theory in vogue in political science: the circulation of elites.

Why is there no socialist party in the United States? A satisfactory response to this question necessitates a cross-disciplinary perspective: from history (absence of feudalism); from demography (permanent flux of immigration); from ethnology (vertical cleavages); from sociology (relatively high standard of living of the working class); from social psychology (weak class consciousness); from geography (the "open frontier" and the geographical mobility); and the rate of economic growth. We may count more than 20 factors spread across the entire spectrum of social sciences. Among these factors only 2 belong directly to political science: feudalism and the absence of proportional representation. This is a good example of a multiple hybrid causality of political phenomena at the margins of different disciplines.

Why have tropical countries, particularly black Africa and South Asia, lagged during the last two centuries in the process of economic growth, and why are the advanced pluralist democracies almost all in temperate zones? Such a question could be asked by political scientists, sociologists, geographers, or historians,

but in fact only economists like Galbraith, Kindelberger, Arthur Lewis, or Andrew Kamarck have emphasized the importance of ecological factors. To this important political science issue, the most pertinent and innovative questions have been asked and discussed by scholars belonging to other disciplines.

It is not possible to inquire into the major phenomena within a strictly monodisciplinary framework. Only by taking up a position at the crossroads of many branches of knowledge, at the margins of formal disciplines, can one try to explain the implosion of the Soviet Union, the proliferation of giant cities in the Third World, the economic decline of the United Kingdom, the economic growth of Japan, or how a child learns to speak. Whenever a question of such magnitude is raised, one finds oneself at the intersection of numerous disciplines and specialities. All major issues are crossing the formal borders of disciplines: war and peace, the breakdown of democracy, generational change, the freedom–equality nexus, individualism in advanced societies, fundamentalism in traditional societies, and ruling classes.

Political science, for instance, has contracted an enormous foreign debt, because politics cannot be explained exclusively by politics. Political phenomena are never produced *in vitro*, artificially in the laboratory. They are always related to a variety of factors behind politics. Dozens of nonpolitical variables are used to explain politics. This is one of the main reasons why political science is interwoven with the other social sciences. Most of the classical European sociologists and political scientists can be located at the intersections of sociology and political science: Max Weber, Karl Marx, Alexis de Tocqueville, Wilfredo Pareto, Roberto Michels, John Stuart Mill, Gaetano Mosca, and Joseph Schumpeter, for example.

VI. MARGINALITY AND SCIENTIFIC REPUTATION

The proportion of hybrids is much higher among the most visible scholars than among the rank and file. Such a stratification can be empirically validated by using the Social Science Citation Index and the reference lists of some important books. We can place the 800 most known scholars, the most cited in political science, into two categories: the monodisciplinary scientists and the hybrids. Such a distinction is not easy and is sometimes impressionistic, but in spite of the difficulties it appears that at the top of the scientific pyramid, hybrids predominate. Scholarly reputation and marginality are correlated.

In the cumulative index to the seven volumes of the *Handbook of Political Science,* edited by F. I. Greenstein and N. W. Polsby, more than 3,500 authors are listed. Among those who are cited at least 12 times, about half can be considered to be scholars working in hybrid fields. The same conclusion can be drawn from the alphabetical index of the *New Handbook of Political Science,* edited by Goodin and Klingemann. Among the hundred or so major innovations listed by Karl Deutsch and his colleagues in their *Advances in the Social Sciences,* two-thirds lie at the intersection of various disciplines or specialities. The higher one goes up the ladder of innovations, the greater are the chances that the boundaries between disciplines will disappear.

The proportion of hybrid scholars at the highest levels is not the same in all fields. In the United States it is low for the field of American politics. Conversely, comparative research is densely populated by hybrids. Some subjects are necessarily at the crossroads of multiple specialties, for instance, clientelism, nationalism, and socialization.

Marginality favors innovation: the farther up the ladder of innovation a work is, the more likely it is to be accomplished at the margins of a given discipline—at its intersection with another discipline.

While keeping one foot in their original discipline, most major figures in social science have operated at its borders. Many scholars are knowledgeable in a number of subfields of philosophy, history, economics, political science, cybernetics, and history of science, with their most important contributions coming from the juxtaposition of these subfields. V. O. Key applied two sociological methods, ecological analysis and survey research, to mass political behavior. Gabriel Almond has borrowed anthropological concepts to build several seminal theories in political science, particularly the theory of functional equivalence. Jurgen Habermas had the capacity for synthesis of a variety of subfields of sociology, philosophy, political science, and developmental psychology. Mancur Olson, Jr., used economic ideas to explore issues of relevance for political problems. Johan Galtung and Stein Rokkan were comparativists combining data from history and sociology, and concepts from economics, geography, and history, in their theories on "center and periphery" and on the genealogical tree of political parties in Western Europe. Several past presidents of the American Political Science Association came from other disciplines. Most of these individuals drew from the borders of economics, psychology, or sociology; a more extended list would include more cross fertilization from philosophy, history, legal studies, anthropology, and other fields. Some figures are unusual mixes: Quetelet, a professional astronomer and statistician, was an originator of quantification in the social sciences. Lewis Fry Richardson, a pioneer in the application of statistics to the study of war, was a meteorologist and applied mathematician.

Scientific disciplines progress at their periphery, in contact with other disciplines by cross fertilization. The core of the discipline tends to stagnate. It is in this sense that the expression creative marginality should be read.

Bibliography

Dogan, M., & Pahre, R. (1990). *Creative marginality, innovation at the intersection of social sciences.* Boulder, CO: Westview Press. [French and Spanish editions]

Dogan, M. (1994). Fragmentation of the social sciences and recombination of specialties. *International Social Science Journal, 139,* 27–42.

Dogan, M. (1997). The new social sciences: Cracks in the disciplinary walls. *International Social Sciences Journal, 153,* 429–444.

Klein, J. T. (1997). *Crossing boundaries.* Charlottesville, VA: University Press of Virginia.

Veblen, T. (1919/1943). The intellectual pre-eminence of Jews in modern Europe. *Political Science Quarterly, 34.* Reproduced in *Essays in our changing order.* New York: Viking Press.

Matthew Effects

Dean Keith Simonton

University of California, Davis

Cumulative Advantage A more technical and more inclusive term for the Matthew effect. According to the principle of cumulative advantage, those creators who are successful early will accumulate the resources that will enable them to be even more productive and influential. In contrast, those who are late in making contributions may never be able to overcome the handicap that results and may more quickly terminate their creative careers as a consequence.

Log-Normal Distribution The distribution of scores that would be normally distributed were the scores subjected first to a logarithmic transformation. Log-normal distributions are highly skewed right, with a long upper (right) tail. Moreover, rather than the mode, median, and mean being located at the same value, as is the case for scores distributed according to bell curve, log-normal distributions have a mode near the bottom of the distribution, a mean closer to the top of the distribution, with the median falling somewhere between.

Lotka Law An empirical generalization proposed by Alfred Lotka, a population geneticist and demographer. Stated in the most general terms, the law states that the number of individuals responsible for n contributions to a given domain is inversely proportional to n^2.

Multiplicative Functions In contrast to additive functions, which simply sum the separate influences of several independent determinants, multiplicative functions are founded on the product of the separate components. If the participating factors are normally distributed in the population, the scores produced by additive functions will also be normally distributed. But for multiplicative functions, the resulting scores will exhibit a log-normal distribution.

Pareto Law The empirical generalization first proposed by Vilfredo Pareto, an economist and sociologist. In simple terms, it states that the number of individuals making a certain income q is inversely proportional to some power of q.

Price Law An empirical generalization advanced by Derek Price, a historian of science. It states that if k represents the number of individuals who have made contributions to a given field, $\sqrt{k}$ is the number of individuals who are responsible for half of all of those contributions.

The term **MATTHEW EFFECT** derives from the passage in the Gospel According to St. Matthew that says, "For unto every one that hath shall be given, and he shall have abundance: but from him that hath not shall be taken away even that which he hath." The term itself was coined by the eminent sociologist Robert K. Merton, who used it to describe the reward and communication systems of science. In a nutshell, "the Matthew effect consists of the accruing of greater increments of recognition for particular scientific contributions to scientists *of considerable repute and the withholding of such recognition from scientists who have not yet made their mark." To borrow a common expression that makes the same point, "the rich get richer, and the poor get poorer." Subsequent researchers have greatly developed Merton's seminal idea. First, several sociologists have translated the concept of the Matthew effect into mathematical models of* cumulative advantage *and then tested these models against data describing the careers of scientific creators. Second, some psychologists have shown that the same process operates in other domains of creativity besides science, including the arts. In addition, Matthew effects have been identified in a wider range of phenomena than originally envisioned by Merton, such as talent development in children. This article begins with a synopsis of Merton's initial presentation. That summary will be followed by an overview of how the basic concept has been elaborated and extended. The final section provides an empirical and theoretical evaluation of this explanatory principle.*

I. ORIGINAL FORMULATION

Merton was one of the foremost founders of the sociology of science. He had already argued that science attains success as a knowledge-generating system because scientists subscribe to certain critical norms. The most important of these norms serve to ensure that the contributions of all scientists are judged by objective, unbiased standards. Yet Merton also observed that when it came time for scientists to receive special recognition for their scientific discoveries, the system did not always function according to an impartial manner. He provided three main illustrations:

1. Scientists at distinguished research universities apparently receive more recognition for their work than comparable work done by scientists at less prestigious institutions. In other words, at least a portion of the status attained by scientific creators is ascribed rather than achieved. Thus, two scientists who have published the same number of articles in top journals can be said to be roughly equal in achievement, but the scientific community will ascribe more importance to the output by the Harvard or Stanford professor than

to the output of the professor from some obscure liberal arts college.

2. When scientists collaborate on a single publication, the order of the names on the title page is supposed to reflect the relative contributions of each collaborator to the final product. Yet certain scientists will receive disproportionately more credit simply because they are already better known to the scientific community. For example, a Nobel laureate appearing last in a list of a dozen authors may be credited with being the brain behind the work, and thereby usurp the bulk of the credit. Indeed, occasionally an already eminent scientist will obtain all the kudos even when his or her name was not even included in the author list—simply because the work was done in the luminary's laboratory!

3. Sometimes two or more scientists will independently arrive at the same scientific discovery at about the same time. Such events are called "multiples," and these occurrences often provide the impetus for sometimes bitter priority disputes. The interesting question is who will finally receive the credit for the discovery. According to Merton, it is the better-known scientist who will get the lion's share of the glory. A good illustration is what happened to the theory of evolution by natural selection. Although this contribution was made independently by both Charles Darwin and Alfred Wallace, it was the older, better established Darwin who attained eponymic status as the author of Darwinism.

In all three illustrations, the lesser scientists receive less credit than they deserve, whereas the greater scientists receive more credit than they deserve, precisely as specified by the Matthew effect.

Merton discussed some of the reasons why this effect occurs. Perhaps the most interesting cause is psychological rather than sociological. With the exponential explosion of the number of scientific publications, it has become increasingly difficult for any scientist to keep up on everything published. Even within a single specialty, a researcher may feel compelled to read only a small percentage of the articles and books, the rest being covered by merely scanning titles and abstracts. To reduce the total quantity of material to a manageable size, researchers use certain guidelines for separating the wheat from the chaff. Among these rules of thumb is the following: Read first those publications by those who have already made a contribution, and then, if you have time, read publications by scientists who have not yet made a contribution. In practice, this heuristic means that the writings of the obscure scientists will remain largely unread, whereas the writings of illustrious scientists get read even when of lesser quality. In short, the Matthew effect constitutes a form of cognitive coping that simplifies the task of keeping up on the literature. The unfortunate cost of this selection strategy, of course, is that good work by unknown scientists often gets ignored. [*See* HEURISTICS.]

However, Merton also argued that the more famous scientists not only *appear* to grow richer—they actually *do* become richer. This happens because scientific creativity requires resources, such as libraries and laboratories, technical equipment, and research assistants. Those scientists who quickly make a name for themselves will find it easier to acquire these resources in the form of grant money and appointments at major research universities. In contrast, the scientists who have not yet made their mark will find more of their grant proposals rejected and will discover themselves relegated to lesser universities with poor research facilities and heavy teaching loads. The expanding inequality in resources then accentuates the initial disparity in accomplishment, producing a huge chasm between the most and least successful scientists in terms of their total contributions to science. Indeed, the top scientists will often end up in pure research positions, whereas the bottom scientists often finish their careers by taking on time-consuming administrative responsibilities.

II. MATHEMATICAL AND STATISTICAL ELABORATIONS

Merton's original formulation of the Matthew effect was qualitative rather than quantitative. As such, it did not lend itself well to empirical validation. However, several sociologists from the Mertonian school have attempted to provide a more precise formulation of the phenomenon that would circumvent this limitation. Sometimes this precision would be acquired by the derivation of mathematical models that would lead to exact predictions about creative productivity and influence in science. Even when that was not possible, researchers were often able to derive substantive hypotheses that could be tested against empirical data. In any case, these developments have tended to focus on two different aspects of scientific creativity, namely, individual differences and developmental changes.

A. Cross-Sectional Variation: Productivity and Influence

One of the most remarkable features about scientific creativity is the nature of individual differences in the number of contributions made by different workers. For example, according to the Lotka law, the number of scientists who produce n papers is inversely proportional to n^2. This function yields a distinctive curve where most scientists publish only one paper, and the predicted output declines very rapidly from that peak, approaching the zero frequency rate asymptotically. According to this curve, scientists who publish 100 or more papers would be extremely rare.

Another principle that describes this distributional peculiarity in a different way is the Price law. This law states that if k represents the total number of scientists actively publishing in a given discipline, the number of individuals responsible for producing *half* of all papers will be equal to $\sqrt{k}$. For example, if there are 100 scientists who have made at least one contribution to a field, a mere 10 of those will account for 50% of the entire corpus of contributions.

This cross-sectional distribution in total output is quite unlike what is more commonly seen in the behavioral sciences. Lotka and Price laws do not describe a normal distribution but rather an extremely skewed distribution. The upper tail of this productivity distribution is so extraordinary, in fact, that it cannot be said to represent merely the right-hand portion of the normal curve. The classic bell curve simply does not have tails long enough. Hence, the very existence of this distinctive distribution presents a genuine explanatory enigma.

The Matthew effect provides a possible solution. Several researchers have translated this process into mathematical models of cumulative advantage. While the models themselves are rather complex, the basic principle on which they operate is easy to comprehend at the intuitive level. To appreciate the broad concept entailed, consider the following scenario:

There are 100 aspiring young scientists who all want to make a name for themselves. All 100 have equal talent, and all graduated from comparable doctoral programs in the same year. All send off their first papers to the most prestigious journals in their field. But editors cannot accept all submitted manuscripts, owing to severe space limitations. Suppose that the journal editors can only accept 10%, and the editors mail rejection letters to the remaining 90%. In effect, the editors have reinforced manuscript-submission behaviors in the lucky few and punished the same behaviors in the unlucky many. Accordingly, the probability of submitting another paper will be enhanced for the 10% and weakened for the 90%. Now repeat this process over and over. Ever more would-be scientists become disheartened and drop out from the competition. The unfortunate will find that their grant proposals are turned down, and that their applications for tenure are denied. Ever fewer survivors come to dominate the output of scientific journal articles, as they emerge as the great scientists of their generation. The latter soon receive prizes and honors, making the rich ever richer. Meanwhile, their counterparts become ever poorer, as the gap between rich and poor becomes insurmountable in a career or a lifetime.

If this basic process is converted into appropriate mathematical models, the upshot is the highly skewed cross-sectional distribution seen in the empirical literature. Hence, the doctrine of cumulative advantage provides a viable theoretical interpretation for individual differences in total creative output.

Cumulative advantage operates not only on creative productivity but also on the amount of recognition received by that scientific output. After all, just because a paper gets published in a journal does not automatically mean that it will have an impact on the field. On the contrary, a very large percentage of published articles remain unread by anyone besides the authors, and even articles that are at least read by someone may have a low probability of being used by other researchers in their publications. The highly selective nature of the scientific enterprise is best documented in citation indices, which record how many times particular pub-

lications are cited in the bibliographies of subsequent publications. Typically, most papers do not earn any citations, and those that do are cited only very rarely. Only an elite group of papers will be cited frequently enough to be considered citation classics in a particular field.

Rather than examine the variation in citation rates for separate publications, it is valuable to investigate the cross-sectional distribution of the total number of citations that scientists receive to their entire life work. This distribution, like that of productivity, is highly skewed, a few scientists receiving a disproportionate amount of citations. Yet what is curious about this distribution is that it is far more skewed than the distribution of papers on which the citations are based. In other words, the most prolific scientists monopolize the citation indices even more than they dominate the tables of contents of journals. However, this more intense elitism makes a great deal of sense from the standpoint of the Matthew effect. Unlike the writing of journal articles, the receiving of citations is not constrained by how many hours a particular scientist can work per day. Citations are bestowed by the entire scientific community, which is far less bounded than a single laboratory. Each time a paper receives a citation, it increases the chance of further citation, because now the paper can come to the attention of other scientists who may have overlooked the original article. For the exceptional few papers, the citation process may snowball until a handful of papers (and their authors) will enjoy a hegemony in the citation indices. On the other hand, each year that goes by that a paper fails to get cited, the lower the probability that it will ever get cited at all. Once more the rich get richer, and the poor get poorer—only the disparity is more dramatic than that seen in counts of the actual number of publications.

It is worth pointing out that the metaphor of the rich getting richer and the poor getting poorer is more profound than first meets the eye. According to the Pareto law of income distribution, the number of individuals who earn q amount of money is also inversely proportional to a power of q (albeit the exponent is usually around 1.5 rather than 2, as in the case of the Lotka law). In other words, a very small percentage of a nation's workforce will earn a disproportionate share of the income. Moreover, there is ample reason to believe that this elitist cross-sectional distribution is the direct consequence of the economic equivalent of the Matthew effect. The more income a person makes, the more funds can be devoted to investments, so that money breeds more money. In contrast, those who cannot stay above the poverty line not only find themselves unable to accumulate surplus funds, but also discover themselves falling deeper into debt, so that they acquire negative wealth. Thus, the skewed distributions of creative productivity and economic income comprise a class of cumulative-advantage phenomena.

B. Longitudinal Changes: Career Development

The preceding discussion treated the end result of the Matthew effect. Taking a sample of scientists whose careers have terminated, and controlling for such extraneous factors as differential life span, the distribution of lifetime output will be described by the Lotka and Price laws because of the operation of cumulative advantage. Yet it is very clear that this principle actually operates in a dynamic, developmental fashion throughout the career. Hence, rather than examine the Matthew effect in terms of cross-sectional distributions of final output, investigators have sometimes examined its participation in career development. This research has concentrated on two aspects of the phenomenon.

First, some researchers have studied how creative productivity changes across the life span to determine whether it exhibits the pattern expected if the Matthew effect is influencing the process. For the most part, this research lends some support for cumulative advantage. For instance, those scientists who publish earliest in their careers are more likely to reach high rates of annual productivity than those scientists who are much older when they start publication. Indeed, one of the best predictors of a scientist's lifetime productivity is how early publication began, the really prolific scientists being those who tended to begin publication prior to receiving their Ph.D.s. Besides getting a quick start and attaining high output rates, the early bloomers are more likely to continue making contributions toward the very end of their lives. The late bloomers, in contrast, tend to always be slow producers, and will usually end their productive careers much sooner, for all practical purposes dropping out of the profession as a creative participant. These differential career trajecto-

ries make sense from the standpoint of the Matthew effect. [*See* PRODUCTIVITY AND AGE.]

Second, some investigators have examined the underlying mechanisms that are presumed to support the accumulation of advantage. According to the Mertonian theory, the contrasts in productivity are partly the result of the differential accumulation of the resources necessary to conduct scientific research. Those who start earning credit early will get a head start on winning grant support for their laboratories, and they will also more likely obtain positions at major universities where original research is more strongly supported. The evidence seems to support this view. For example, those young professionals who publish prolifically early in their careers do indeed have a better chance of securing positions at prestigious research institutions. Their less precocious colleagues, by comparison, are more prone to end up at liberal arts colleges or similar institutions where teaching has much higher priority than research. The early bloomers are therefore able to flourish even more, whereas the late bloomers often find their latent creativity nipped in the bud. Of course, initially promising young researchers may sometimes fall from grace, fail to attain tenure, and descend to the more instruction-oriented universities—if not remove themselves from academe altogether. And occasionally scientists who were obliged to begin their careers under less than auspicious circumstances may redouble their research efforts and eventually exhibit upward mobility in their institutional affiliations. But these exceptions are too rare to overthrow the general pattern of cumulative advantage.

In fact, the rarity of these exceptions is imposed by the Matthew effect itself. A scientist at a major university will receive more credit than a scientist at a lesser institution for work of equal quality, and hence the former will find it easier to publish, to win grant support, and to earn recognition. In this way, the Matthew effect can effectively generate a self-fulfilling prophecy.

III. SUBSTANTIVE EXTENSIONS

The Matthew effect has been extended beyond the original confines of the Mertonian school of the sociology of science. These extensions are of two types. First, the principle of cumulative advantage has been extended to encompass all varieties of creative behavior, not just the scientific. Second, the Matthew effect has been applied to developmental phenomena besides career development. In particular, the doctrine of cumulative advantage may actually provide a means for understanding the development of creative talent across the life span, including childhood and adolescence.

A. Generalization to All Domains of Creativity

Although the original research on the Matthew effect was directed at scientific creativity, it is rather apparent that the principle of cumulative advantage may apply to other domains of creative activity. For example, studies of individual differences in lifetime output have demonstrated that those individuals who constitute the top 10% of any field in terms of productivity will be responsible for roughly half of everything produced in that domain. In contrast, the bottom half of the productivity distribution, despite representing 50% of the total creators, can be credited with only about 15% of the entire output. So, again, the frequency distribution describing the number of persons making a specified number of contributions is extremely skewed, with an extremely long upper tail. Indeed, the modal number of contributions is one, and the frequencies decline monotonically from that mode. And, once more, these statistics only include those creators who have made at least one contribution to their domain. If all persons qualified to originate creative ideas are included as well—such as all living Ph.D.s in a particular field—the elitism becomes even more pronounced. Finally, the Price and Lotka laws apparently predict the cross-sectional distributions of output in the arts and humanities with the same precision that they predict the corresponding distributions in the sciences.

To offer one specific illustration, the Price law has been shown to apply to the cross-sectional distribution of contributions to the repertoire of classical music. Approximately 250 composers have contributed at least one work to the standard repertoire. According to the Price law, this means that about 16 composers should account for around half of the repertoire (i.e., $\sqrt{250} = 15.8 \approx 16$). In actual fact, the top 16 biggest contributors are responsible for 51% of the works performed in the concert halls and opera houses. Indeed,

the three most prolific contributors—Mozart, Beethoven, and Bach—together account for nearly 18% of the standard repertoire! The elitist distribution again reigns supreme.

Other cumulative-advantage effects found for scientific creativity have also been documented for other forms of creative behavior. In classical music, for instance, those composers who get their first musical success at an early age are also more likely to become highly prolific and to continue their productivity until late in life. The late bloomers, in contrast, seldom attain the same heights of output and usually end their careers earlier, despite the late start. This longitudinal pattern is compatible with what has been seen in the case of the scientific manifestation of the Matthew effect.

B. Application to the Early Development of Creative Talent

The initial research on the Matthew effect, besides concentrating on scientific creativity, also tended to focus on the adulthood career of the creative individual. Typically, the analysis would go back no earlier than graduate school, when a developing talent is already in his or her 20s. Yet there is also evidence that the cumulative-advantage process may begin much earlier than that. Indeed, it is possible to look at the entire development of creative talent as a progressive sequence of chained Matthew effects that begin in early childhood. Children who show special talents early will be more likely to be singled out by their parents for special encouragement and training. A subset of these will attract special attention from teachers or coaches, and as a result certain youths will receive more intense mentoring. As this process continues, the disparity between the highly talented and the average child or adolescent immensely widens. By the time these youths seek more advanced training, they may be heads and shoulders above their peers.

For example, this progressive process has been demonstrated in the development of creative genius in music. The greatest composers began to take music lessons at unusually young ages, which enabled them to begin composition at exceptionally young ages as well. Because they got a fast start on composing, the truly illustrious composers also tended to have their first successful pieces appear at precocious ages. Their career thus launched, they now enter a different world of adult rewards and honors. Hence, the accumulation of advantage began very early, and the advantage remains with these illustrious composers throughout the remainder of their lives.

IV. EVALUATION

Although the Matthew effect seems to be very persuasive in all domains of creativity, this explanatory principle also suffers from a number of severe limitations. The following four problems are especially noteworthy:

1. For some fields of creative activity, the Matthew effect would not seem to have the same force as it may have in the scientific enterprise. At least in contemporary times, scientific creativity often depends on impressive laboratory facilities that can only be found in institutions that can attract large extramural grant support. The most obvious example is high-energy physics, which cannot do anything without extremely expensive particle accelerators. In such domains, the accumulation of advantage may play a critical role in determining who are going to emerge on the top of the heap as the most productive and influential scientists in the field. Other domains of creativity, nonetheless, demand much less in the way of resources. The sole expense of a poet, for example, is the cost of pen and paper. In such domains, it is not immediately apparent that the Matthew effect has to operate in a manner as dramatic as seen in the big sciences. To be sure, one might argue that the selective nature of literary magazines and publishers may provide a window for the operation of cumulative-advantage effects. Yet even here the intrusion of Matthew effects will not be nearly so pronounced. The cost of printing poetry is far less than printing mathematics and numerical tables, permitting small publishing houses to proliferate with minimal economic constraint. Indeed, many poets will often publish their work at their own expense, and some will not feel the necessity of publishing their work at all. The sonnets of William Shakespeare were distributed in manuscript, while almost all of the poetry of Emily Dickinson only appeared posthumously. In instances such as these, it is difficult to discern what pressure is being asserted by the Matthew effect. Perhaps cumulative advantage only operates in those creative activities that consume exceptional material resources.

2. Even in those domains where the Matthew effect would seem to apply, many of the empirical results that lend support to the principle of cumulative advantage can just as well be explicated by alternative theoretical positions. Take the highly skewed cross-sectional distribution of lifetime output as a case in point. There exist at least two other mechanisms that can generate these characteristic individual differences in total productivity. First, some investigators have argued that the many and varied factors that underlie creative potential are combined according to multiplicative rather than additive functions. As a consequence, even if the diverse components that support creativity are normally distributed in the population (e.g., intelligence, originality, energy level, persistence, independence), the product of all these variables will exhibit a highly skewed, log-normal distribution quite similar to the empirically observed distribution. Second, other researchers have put forward combinatory models of creative potential that maintain that creative productivity is contingent on the total supply of ideas that are available for free recombination (e.g., Simonton's 1997 model discussed further next). Even if the number of combinatory elements is normally distributed in the population, the number of possible combinations will not be. On the contrary, because the number of combinations will likely increase exponentially with the amount of material variable for generating ideational combinations, the distribution of creative potential should again be approximately log-normal, with an extremely long upper tail. Given the existence of these two alternative theoretical accounts, the cumulative-advantage interpretation is not unique enough to adopt the cross-sectional distributions as the conclusive repercussion of the Matthew effect.

3. Sometimes alternative explanations not only exist, but in addition these rival accounts actually do a better job of handling the empirical data. One stark example concerns the problem of the continuity of creative productivity across the career. The number of creative products that emerge in consecutive decades of a career are highly intercorrelated. In particular, across a heterogeneous sample of creators in a given

domain, the output rate in the 20s correlates positively with the rate in 30s, the latter rate in turn correlating positively with that in the 40s, and so for each successive period of the career. This longitudinal stability in the individual differences in productivity is often taken as excellent evidence for the Matthew effect. Those individuals who are most prolific in the first decade of their careers will reap the resources needed to maintain a high rate of productivity in the next decade, and the process continues decade by decade throughout the career. This accumulation of advantage implies that the output in adjacent decades will be more highly correlated than in nonadjacent periods. In fact, the farther apart the two decades, the lower should be the correlations between the output levels. Yet Dean Simonton has proposed an alternative theory of creativity that argues that the output of contributions is a function of a single factor, namely, the latent variable of creative potential. According to the Simonton model, the correlations between contiguous decades should exhibit no systematic tendency to be more highly correlated that those between noncontiguous decades. So far, empirical research endorses the prediction of this second, rival theory. The continuity of individual differences in output across the career does not seem explicable in terms of the Matthew effect.

4. As specified by Simonton's theory, moreover, the creative potential that determines the total number of possible contributions is uncorrelated with the age of career onset. As a consequence, it is theoretically possible for individuals to exist who have a high level of creative potential but who get a late start in their careers. Such late bloomers will then exhibit the same career trajectories as the early bloomers with high creative potential, only with the whole age curve shifted over according to the amount of the delay in their career onset. The maximum level of annual output will be the same but will appear at a later age, and productivity will persist longer into the life span as well. This scenario is impossible according to the cumulative-advantage model because the early bloomers will have necessarily appropriated the resources and recognition. However, empirical data collected on the actual careers of creative individuals in both the arts and sciences lends more support to Simonton's rival theory.

What makes the Simonton theory of creative productivity most provocative is that it derives its predictions from a cognitive model of the creative process. Creativity thus is assumed to come from inside the individual. Therefore, both cross-sectional variation and longitudinal changes ensue from individual factors, such as the level of creative potential and the age at which the creator began to develop that potential. This theoretical framework departs dramatically from the doctrine of cumulative advantage, which holds that creative productivity is something generated by forces external to the individual. According to the Matthew effect, individual differences in total output and in career trajectories is determined by the reward structure of the discipline. The creative individual is like a rat or pigeon in a Skinner box, the operant under reinforcement being the creative product. The initial state of the organism is largely irrelevant to the impact of the reinforcement contingencies.

Of course, it is conceivable that both sets of factors are working during the development of creative personalities. Creativity may be rooted in the psychological capacity for generating novel ideas, but the manifestation of that creativity may be shaped to some extent by the rewards and resources bestowed by the sociological system. It thus remains for future research to determine how much the Matthew effect permeates creative behavior in various domains. Nonetheless, already the principle has stimulated a large amount of research that has greatly expanded our understanding of the careers of creative individuals, especially in the sciences.

Bibliography

Eysenck, H. J. (1995). *Genius.* Cambridge, England: Cambridge University Press.

Ludwig, A. M. (1995). *The price of greatness.* New York: Guilford Press.

Merton, R. K. (1968). The Matthew effect in science. *Science, 159,* 56–63.

Simonton, D. K. (1994). *Greatness.* New York: Guilford Press.

Simonton, D. K. (1997). Creative productivity: A predictive and explanatory model of career trajectories and landmarks. *Psychological Review, 104,* 66.

Memory and Creativity

Edward Nęcka

Jagiellonian University, Kraków

Encoding Assigning a specific label to the information that is to be stored in long-term memory in order to make it suitable for storage, retrieval, and further processing.

Long-Term Memory System able to hold large amounts of episodic or semantic information permanently, organized as a network.

Retrieval Activation of the information retained in long-term memory, presumably with the use of valid retrieval cues or specific mental strategies.

Short-Term Memory System responsible for maintaining restricted number of pieces of information for several minutes; also acts as an information processing unit responsible for the manipulation of symbols during problem solving and other types of cognitive activity.

Storage The intermediate phase of the memory process, which consists of keeping the memorized information in the latent form that potentially allows retrieval and further processing.

MEMORY *is a psychological structure that, apart from its many other functions, takes part in the cognitive mechanism of insight in creative problem solving and determines the specificity of information processing ob-*

served among creative individuals. The importance of memory phenomena to our understanding of creativity is enormous, for obvious reasons: creativity is an activity of the mind, and activities of the mind are executed through memory. Therefore, creativity cannot occur without the participation of memory processes and structures. However, the psychological theory concerning the relationship of memory with creativity has not been developed, and empirical results are rather scarce. For these reasons, the present article outlines the map of the problem at the very high level of abstraction and with large amount of speculation. The order of presentation is determined by the stages of memory processes, corresponding to the stages of information processing.

I. SHORT-TERM MEMORY AND CREATIVITY

Stimuli coming from the external world are first memorized for a short time by two structures: the sensory store and short-term store. The sensory store (e.g., iconic memory for images, or echoic memory for sounds) holds the information for less than 1 s. It performs the preparatory stage of stimulus elaboration, due to which the next stages are not overflowed with the surplus of information. There is no evidence whatsoever that sensory memory is connected in any way with creative processes or creative abilities. As to the short-term memory (STM) store, which is able to keep the information for several minutes, the situation is less clear. This system not only maintains information but also performs basic manipulations with symbols, synonymous with human information processing; for this reason, it is called "working memory" as well. It is therefore rather unlikely that the central processing unit of the human mind would not take part in the cognitive mechanics of creative processes. There is, however, little empirical evidence on how working memory affects creativity.

Characteristically, STM is very limited in its capacity, because it is able to manipulate less than 10 pieces of information (words, numbers, etc.) simultaneously. It has been convincingly shown that the STM capacity determines the general cognitive ability level (i.e., intelligence). Unfortunately, no evidence concerning the relationship of the STM capacity with creativity has been obtained, although in some studies both intelligence and creativity tests were used to check this hypothesis.

The difference is probably rooted in the particularity of cognitive mechanisms of intelligence and creativity as two distinct dimensions of human intellect. Intelligence is an ability to tackle convergent, well-defined problems of average complexity. Such problems are well described in terms of a number of separate "chunks" of information that have to be memorized and manipulated for a short time in order to let the problem solver reach the solution. In other words, an intelligent problem solver has to split the problem into separate portions of information, keep these portions in short-term memory, and manipulate them in order to achieve a suitable solution. In such cases, the more items a problem solver is able to keep in the short-term store, the more competent he or she is in tests consisting of convergent, well-defined problems of average complexity. On the contrary, if a problem solver's STM capacity is small by nature, or declines temporarily, he or she inevitably loses some part of his or her intellectual ability, because some tasks that are critical for one's intellectual level may surpass the actual limitations of STM. [*See* PROBLEM SOLVING.]

There seems not to exist anything like that in the case of creativity. It is usually assessed with tests consisting of divergent tasks of low complexity (e.g., un-

usual uses or alternative definitions), which do not exploit short-term memory thoroughly. As far as the limited capacity of STM is concerned, such problems may even be regarded as relatively "easy." No surprise, then, that creative abilities assessed with divergent thinking tests do not correlate with the STM capacity.

Of course, creativity is not reduced to the divergent thinking ability, particularly if real creative endeavors rather than basic cognitive skills are taken into account. However, there is no point looking for the short-term memory determinants of "real" creativity, either. The problems undertaken by exceptionally gifted creators and great achievers are usually divergent, too, but also ill defined and very complex in nature. In fact, problem finding and problem definition constitute the vital part of creative processes in real life, that is, outside the psychological laboratory. Finding, definition, redefinition, and solution of such problems usually take a lot of time, effort, and motivation, but they do not seem to rely on the extended capacity of short-term memory. Individual differences in STM capacity may matter in the case of problems of average complexity, because, for instance, if a problem needs 10 items to be kept and manipulated in memory, a person with the capacity of 10 is naturally endowed to tackle such a problem, whereas a person whose capacity is only 6 is naturally unable to deal with it. But both hypothetical persons are structurally unable to deal with a problem consisting of 100 or 1000 items of information, that is, with very complex, unclear, ill-defined problems that require a creative approach. [*See* DIVERGENT THINKING.]

This does not mean that such complex problems are unworkable for any human being, whose STM capacity—even when relatively large—usually does not exceed 10 portions of information. Rather rarely, a very complex and ill-defined problem is being solved by a very creative individual by means of his or her exceptional capacities—but not necessarily the STM capacity, as it seems. Such creative endeavors are attainable through specific strategies of problem solving, and through inventive manipulations with the problem structure and problem definition. Such manipulations are sometimes referred to as "metacognitive strategies." For instance, a creative person organizes his or her knowledge of the problem hierarchically: a relatively small number of higher-order, abstract portions of information may contain many lower-order chunks of information, accessible for processing only after having been "unwrapped." Another metacognitive strategy used by creative individuals amounts to simplification of the problem structure so that it could be workable by STM. However, such manipulations refer to long-term memory processes, mainly selective encoding and "familiarization." [*See* METACOGNITION.]

II. LONG-TERM MEMORY AND CREATIVITY

Stimuli formerly elaborated by STM proceed to the long-term memory system (LTM). Contrary to STM, long-term memory is able to keep the information for an unlimited period; it is also assumed to possess unlimited capacity. This does not mean that the human mind is able to remember everything; however, forgetting and other imperfections of memory do not result from the capacity of the LTM store but from other sources, such as interference or inefficient strategies of remembering.

Three basic categories of memory processes define the efficiency of operations in LTM: encoding, storage, and retrieval. These operations, or stages of the memory process, determine the way in which LTM performs its basic functions, including the ones connected with creativity, problem solving, and insight.

A. Encoding

Information cannot be placed in the long-term store without having been encoded. It is an operation analogous to labeling products in the department store or allocating new books in the library to appropriate shelves. Only after the information is encoded can it be stored in memory as a part of respective knowledge structures. In most cases, encoding amounts to categorization. For instance, we categorize the scene shown in headline news as a "street accident" and a portion of textbook knowledge as "the quantum theory of particles." The psychological function of encoding is obvious: it allows assigning of information to the appropriate parts of the LTM store. In this way, it makes it possible to arrange LTM as an organized system of knowledge. It is also the necessary condition of future

retrieval, because one cannot regain anything from the store without labeling it properly.

Creativity is probably connected with, and affected by, the specificity of encoding in three ways. First, we can encode information in a peculiar way, different from what other people do. For instance, a child can categorize the animals familiar to him or her into the categories of nice, shaggy, and awesome. This kind of categorization, though illogical and far from what biology offers, probably serves some important cognitive needs of the child. Such categorization is also unusual and different from how the majority of people think about animals and how they classify them. It is probably why small children perceive the world so originally. Children's originality is normally accounted for in terms of their being free from obstacles, conventions, and inhibitions typical of adult life. However, this phenomenon should also be regarded as a manifestation of the unusual way in which children categorize objects, and as a result of rather specific ways of encoding information that is stored in their LTM.

In the case of adult creative individuals, the instances of bizarre categorization are probably accompanied by the conventional, "uncreative" way of perceiving the world. In other words, an adult creative person is able to categorize the world in the "official," objective, commonly accepted way, as well as in an unusual, subjective, and personalized manner. This is the second exemplification of how the activity of this stage of the LTM operations affects creativity: alternative encoding. A person who encodes alternatively is able to take advantage of unusual encoding (e.g., making unpredictable associations, discerning similarities), while still being close to reality and conventions—a phenomenon recognized by Ernst Kris as "regression in the service of the ego." Some techniques of creativity training deliberately focus on the phenomenon of alternative encoding, with the conviction that divergent thinking and unexpected associations are more likely to result from the ability to memorize the same item of information in many different ways.

The third property of encoding found in creative persons is "selectivity." It is particularly important for the construction of the cognitive representation of the problem. Problems worth creative endeavor are usually too complex and ill defined to be memorized completely and categorized with the use of some clear-cut terms. Selection of information is therefore necessary; however, successful problem solvers are able to memorize only the important elements of the problem, while ignoring less important and superfluous ones. Less efficient solvers try to memorize everything, thus being unable to focus on the very gist of the problem situation. It is very unclear what are the origins and determinants of this ability to encode information in the selective way, as well as to what extent it is susceptible to development and training. However, the selectivity with which some people store information in their LTM store inevitably makes them more efficient solvers of complex, ill-defined problems; therefore, it makes them more creative.

Peculiar, alternative, and selective encoding are responsible for creative behavior in many ways. They help us to produce original associations, they are responsible for our "perceiving things" differently, and they allow simplification of the structure of too-complex problems through selectivity of encoding. In many instances, creative behavior is a result of natural, effortless use of specific encoding, although from the observer's perspective it may make the impression of being a result of rather difficult and complex processes. In other words, creative processes are sometimes less "exotic" than they seem to be from the point of view of somebody who normally does not encode information in a peculiar way.

Creativity also benefits from so-called "prospective encoding," which consists of setting up criteria for future acquisition of knowledge that might be relevant to a problem at hand. Careful examination of the problem and its requirements helps us to establish exact criteria of information needed for the continuation of creative problem solving. Such knowledge may not be available at the moment but it can be easily acquired upon the appearance of particular learning opportunities. The mental set established due to the prospective encoding induces highly selective acquisition of knowledge; consequently, it enhances the likelihood of sudden and insightful recognition of the new possibilities to deal with the problem.

B. Storage

Storage amounts to keeping previously encoded information for long time. Contrary to naive concep-

tions of storage, it is an active process, likely to impose unexpected changes on the seemingly dormant information kept in LTM. Three phenomena connected with storage are worth investigating from the creativity point of view: selective forgetting, familiarization, and spontaneous recovery.

Selective forgetting is apt to account for the phenomenon of incubation. According to the classical four-stage model of creative thinking, incubation is a stage of unconscious idea production following preparation but preceding illumination and elaboration. Modern cognitive approaches do not deny the empirical evidence that the incubational break sometimes helps with the creation of new ideas, though they usually do not accept the notion of subconscious incubation of solutions. Therefore, it has been suggested that, during the "incubational" break, we selectively forget the superfluous information, particularly the unnecessary elements of the cognitive representation of the problem. Our memory preserves only a part of the information that has been gathered concerning the problem: its definition, requirements, and context. After having forgotten a huge part of this information, we are more likely to "view the problem from a new perspective," that is, to experience sudden and holistic understanding of the problem, synonymous with insight. [*See* INCUBATION.]

"Familiarization" is another term introduced by Herbert Simon to account for the phenomenon of incubation. Simon assumed that problems worth creative endeavors are complex and difficult, requiring a lot of time and effort to be solved. During the long process of problem solving, almost all trials to seek for the solution are unsuccessful, except the final ones that result in solution. It does not mean that the former trials are worthless: Their function amounts to familiarization of the problem, that is, making it more and more understandable, clear, and simple. Simplification of the problem structure and definition makes it possible for them to be grasped with a small number of items of information. This, in turn, makes the problem possible to manipulate with the system of short-term memory, which has a very limited capacity to handle information. In other words, every instance of problem solving relies on the vital operations of working memory, which performs the basic operations of information processing. But to be suitable for such operations, the problem has to be simplified to great extent; otherwise, the working memory system is likely to be overflowed. Familiarization is a means to make the problem simplified enough to be dealt with by the system of working memory. Thus, numerous unsuccessful trials to find a solution have an important simplifying function, due to which problems originally too complex become more and more workable for the memory system of very limited capacity.

Spontaneous recovery consists of the increase in the likelihood of recalling information if it is kept dormant for some period of time, compared to the likelihood of recall at the beginning of the learning process. It is assumed that the vital information is blocked by other pieces of knowledge learned more recently or acquired with the learner's conviction about their importance. After some period of time, the blocking pieces of information lose their activation, thus giving way to the previously inaccessible knowledge. It is also assumed that the LTM store gets more and more organized with time, a process taking place without any intention or effort on the learner's side. Due to such hypothetical processes, we can sometimes remember more information if some amount of time has passed than at the beginning of the learning process—a phenomenon known as "reminiscence." These phenomena are important for creative thinking and problem solving because they may be responsible for elimination of mental sets, blocks, and other obstacles often preventing us from attaining original solutions. It is why incubational breaks probably help us to work out creative solutions, although there are other cognitive mechanisms apt to operate with similar results (e.g., selective forgetting and familiarization).

Selective forgetting, familiarization, and spontaneous recovery are possible mechanisms of insight, which—according to the modern cognitive theories—is basically a memory phenomenon. From the phenomenological perspective, insight is a sudden flash of understanding ("aha!" response). From the cognitive perspective, though, its mechanics is probably rooted in the operations taking place in long-term memory during the storage phase. However, the recognition of such a theoretical possibility requires that storage be viewed as an active, purposeful, and "creative" phase of the LTM operations. The spontaneous changes of the LTM structure during the storage phase do not guar-antee that insight will occur and be apt to help us solve the problem in a creative way, but without these cognitive operations the phenomenon of insight would be very difficult to account for beyond its purely phenomenological aspects.

C. Retrieval

Retrieval consists of recalling the information previously encoded and then kept in the LTM store. It is the reverse of encoding, and its efficiency mostly depends on encoding strategies used in the first stage of the memory process.

The main problem of retrieval amounts to accessibility of information stored in LTM. Creative ideas are often just recovered from memory, or they result from uncommon combinations of stored memories, although they may make an impression of being crafted out of nothing. In other words, a creative idea—or at least the very core of it—remains in the LTM store for a long time, "waiting" to be noticed and used. The difficulty lies in accessing such an idea or its bud, because it is not kept in memory in its ready-made, easy to retrieve form. If it were like this, it would probably be memorized and retrieved easily by many people; therefore, such an idea would rather frequently reappear and, by definition, could not be called creative. So, the act of creation consists, by and large, of the use of effective retrieval strategies, through which the vital information may be accessed and used in problem solving.

Hence, the problem lies in making the already stored information accessible, so that it can take part in the creative process. This aim is achieved in two ways: by the use of appropriate retrieval cues and by the application of effective strategies of search of the LTM store. The "retrieval cue" is a means to decode information kept in the LTM store, analogous to the operation of retrieving an item from the shelf of a real storehouse, library, or other kind of depot. Normally, the information is retrieved from LTM with the use of exactly the same code (e.g., a category or label) with which it had been put into the LTM store. These are the instances of the commonplace use of memory, resulting in uncreative behavior. However, the information may be retrieved with the use of entirely new codes, providing that a problem solver is able to recode the items constituting his or her knowledge, that is, to label the pieces of information kept in the LTM store in a new way, different from the initial encoding. Analogical thinking is enhanced in this way, since notions, memorized events, and other pieces of our knowledge can be retrieved on the basis of their similarity to other areas of our experience. It is a process particularly important for creativity if the analogies and similes are remote and unusual, which means that the pieces of knowledge utilized for the building of analogy have to be retrieved with cues other than those used during the acquisition of knowledge. [*See* ANALOGIES.]

As to LTM search strategies, the problem consists of making the search as global as possible. Our inability to use previous experience while solving a new problem, a phenomenon frequently described in the literature as mental "ruts," and other blocks to creativity, may result from a "local" memory search. This kind of search is limited to the narrow, well-defined areas of knowledge stored in the long-term memory, and does not apply to other areas of knowledge even though these regions could be highly relevant to the problem at hand. A problem solver is unable to use some fragments of his or her knowledge because they are "too distant" from the areas defined by the problem space, and as such they look "irrelevant" to the problem. Of course, the distance between the knowledge responsible for the problem representation and some potentially useful but neglected areas of experience may be superficial or seeming. Furthermore, the boundaries between different fields of knowledge and expertise are usually fuzzy and conventional, and sometimes artificial; however, they define the peripheries within which the memory search is normally performed. In consequence, the search is rather likely to be local, that is, limited to the knowledge base that is directly applicable to the problem being currently solved. To make the search global, that is, referring to the whole network of semantic memory and conceptual knowledge, as well as to the vast number of episodes stored in LTM, the problem solver has to cross the between-domain boundaries through analogy, metaphorical grasp, and mostly the redefinition of the problem statement.

The creative search of memory does not have to be entirely global; sometimes it suffices to make the search less local, that is, less limited to the narrow conceptual boundaries defined by the initial problem statement.

Redefinition of the problem statement naturally makes a problem solver more likely to cross the conceptual boundaries, as the newly defined problem requires a new set of information and provokes new associations. However, making the search "less local" may be a deliberate strategy used by the problem solver, utilized during the sessions of creative problem solving, not necessarily being preceded by problem redefinition. On the other hand, redefinition of the problem is rather unlikely to occur without the global (or "less local") search because only the truly uncommon information retrieved from memory is able to make us perceive the problem in a fresh way.

Creative individuals are more inclined toward a global memory search than less creative people. The semantic memory network of creative people is more compound and thus more apt to perform remote, unusual associations. The creative semantic memory is also more likely to get activated as a whole network rather than as restricted associative regions, if a priming stimulus is presented. The higher the general activation of the semantic network, the more likely it is that a person will perform the global search of the information needed during the problem-solving session. Contrarily, if the activation is limited to small areas of the semantic network, defined by the routine meaning of the priming stimulus, it is rather likely that a person will perform only the local search, with all its uncreative consequences.

III. CONCLUSIONS

Obviously, creativity is not just the proper use of one's memory. However, the purely creative phenomena known from the studies of creative problem solving, like insight, analogical transfer of knowledge, or unusual remote associations, probably result from the peculiarity of memory processes. It is therefore justified to conclude that memory of creative individuals differs qualitatively from memory of less creative people. The quantitative differences, for instance, the sheer amount of knowledge about some topic, are probably less important because there is no evidence that the more one knows the more creative one is. On the contrary, experts are frequent victims of rigidity and mental ruts, unless their knowledge is flexible and creative due to the specificity of its organization.

Bibliography

Eysenck, M. W., & Keane, M. T. (1995). *Cognitive psychology: A student's handbook* (3rd ed.). Hillsdale, NJ: Erlbaum.

Maruszewski, T., & Nosal, C. S. (Eds.) (1995). *Creative information processing: Cognitive models.* Delft, The Netherlands: Eburon Press.

Matlin, M. W. (1994). *Cognition* (3rd edition). Fort Worth, TX: Harcourt Brace.

Runco, M. A. (Ed.) (1994). *Problem finding, problem solving, and creativity.* Norwood, NJ: Ablex.

Smith, T. B., Ward, T. B., & Finke, R. A. (Eds.) (1995). *The creative cognition approach.* Cambridge, MA: MIT Press.

Sternberg, R. J. (Ed.) (1988). *The nature of creativity: Contemporary psychological perspectives.* Cambridge, UK: Cambridge University Press.

Sternberg, R. J. (Ed.) (1994). *Thinking and problem solving.* San Diego, CA: Academic Press.

Sternberg, R. J., & Davidson, J. E. (Eds.) (1995). *The nature of insight.* Cambridge, MA: MIT Press.

Metacognition

Norbert Jaušovec

University of Maribor

Epistemic Cognition Includes the individual's knowledge about the limits of knowing, the certainty of knowing and the criteria for knowing. It further includes the ability to identify and choose between the forms of solution appropriate for different problem types.

Feeling-of-Warmth (FOW) Judgments Method for studying problems solving. Subjects are asked to indicate how near they believe they are to the solution.

Metacognition Knowledge and cognition about cognitive phenomena.

Moderating Variables Activation parameters like heart rate, blood pressure, and electroencephalogram (EEG).

Monitoring Process Includes knowledge about oneself and others involved in the problem-solving process, knowledge about problems, and metacognitive experiences.

Procedural Knowledge How-to knowledge consisting of conditions specifying features that must be true to take a specific action.

Strategy A general plan of action in which the sequence of solution activities is laid down.

Thinking Aloud Methodology Respondents are asked to verbalize their thoughts as they work on a problem. The method is used for studying processes involved in problem solving and thinking.

Zone of Proximal Development The distance between what the child can do working alone and what he or she can accomplish with aid.

METACOGNITION *refers to knowledge and cognition about cognitive phenomena. This article presents a general overview of the definitions and methods of metacognition, and explains how metacognition is observed and studied. Research findings concerning the relationship between metacognition and problem solving are also discussed. The article devotes particular emphasis to the influence metacognition has in creative problem solving. Some suggestions for the development of more effective teaching methods are provided.*

I. DEFINITIONS OF METACOGNITION

Metacognition has had a major influence on the study of problem solving in the past 20 years. Despite its influence its definition has remained rather vague.

Metacognition has been referred to as knowledge about knowledge or executive processes that occur after cognition. However, most often the concept of metacognition is explained as metacognitive knowledge ("I know that I do not memorize names well"), and cognition about cognitive phenomena ("To facilitate remembering I will try some mnemonic technique"). The definition includes knowledge of general cognitive strategies, along with monitoring, evaluating, and regulating them, and beliefs about factors that affect cognitive strategies. The definition is extremely broad. In most cases, however, metacognition refers more narrowly to monitoring one's own cognitive processes and influences on them while one focuses on a specific task. The monitoring process includes three parts:

- Knowledge about oneself and others involved in the problem solving process
- Knowledge about problems
- Metacognitive experiences that lead to the reevaluation of strategies.

Some researchers have noted that the definition of metacognition overlooks the distinction between what is called Executive 1 strategies and Executive 2 strategies. Executive 1 strategies refer to knowledge about the particular task, whereas Executive 2 strategies refer to knowledge of whether a particular strategy is appropriate to apply in a problem-solving situation. An even more precise distinction can be made between knowledge about one's own cognitive processes and when to apply them on one hand, and knowledge about knowledge and the validity of truth claims in general on the other hand. A critical difference exists between knowing that a specific strategy is appropriate for solving a problem and knowing that for some problems we can never determine the absolute truth or correctness of a solution. This second aspect of metacognition relates to the meta-meta level of monitoring and was given the name *epistemic cognition*. It is important in creative problem solving, where no single and correct solution exists and where the criteria for evaluating a possible solution are limited.

Creative problems are solved on three levels of cognitive processing. On the first level individuals enter into problems by reading and perceiving them. On the second level, metacognitive processes are involved in monitoring the first level of cognition. These processes mainly include knowledge about problems, strategies that may be used to solve specific problems, knowledge of when and how a strategy should be applied, and the evaluation of these processes. The third level is epistemic cognition. It includes the individual's knowledge about the limits of knowing, the certainty of knowing, and the criteria for knowing. It further includes the ability to identify and choose between the forms of solutions appropriate for different problem types.

The ability to see the difference between problems that have only one correct solution and problems that have no absolutely correct solution but only better or worse ones is an important developmental characteristic of the late adolescent and adult years.

A more operationalized classification of metacognition was proposed by researchers involved in a psychometric approach in studying problem solving. These approaches distinguished between several metacomponents, such as selection of performance components for task solution, selection of one or more representations on which these components are to act, selection of a strategy of combining the components, decision about whether to maintain a given strategy, selection of a speed-accuracy trade-off, and solution monitoring— the keeping track of progress being made toward a solution. Loosely speaking, metacomponents are responsible for figuring out how to do a particular task or set of tasks and then making sure that the task or set of tasks are done correctly. Most of these metacomponents refer to Level 1 and Level 2 cognitive processes. This is understandable because the components proposed were used to analyze problem solving and reasoning in a psychometric way. It would be probably difficult to identify Level 3 processes with a psychometric approach. With the methods available in psychology it is possible only to describe them.

II. METHODS AND TECHNIQUES USED IN ANALYZING METACOGNITION

Another problem related to metacognition research is its estimation in the individual's cognitive process while solving a problem. The most frequently used approach is thinking aloud methodology, in which the respondents are asked to verbalize their thoughts as they work on a problem. This method was used by many early investigators. It gained popularity in problem-solving studies during the 1960s. Use of the method in information processing research led to its utilization in many related areas of psychological research. The thinking aloud method requires no more than that the subjects provide an account of what they are doing during their thinking activity. The subjects thus report problem-solving behaviors rather than mental states—the latter being the characteristic of introspection and retrospection, which require the subjects to analyze the composition of thought processes. The comparison of introspective and thinking aloud methodology revealed several characteristics in favor of the thinking aloud methodology. The thinking aloud protocols are more complete and contain more information than the introspective protocols. A second characteristic is that the thinking aloud protocols are more present oriented, have a more elliptical form, and contain more indefinite referents.

Although there is evidence to suggest that the instruction to think aloud does not significantly alter the sequence of cognitive process—some researchers interpreted it as merely the vocalization of inner speech—the method has its limitations: Verbal protocols include only the events and operations of which the subject is aware at the time; additionally, they are sensitive only to sequential operations. Another source of error could be the analysis of thinking aloud protocols with different taxonomies. No matter how carefully designed, the chosen scheme for both data collection and data analysis will influence not only what the investigator observes, but will to some degree determine the regularities and laws that might be identified.

It seems that these methodological shortcomings affect, above all research, into metacognition. Metacognitive processes occur infrequently in thinking aloud protocols (about 1% of all statements can be identified as metacognitive).

Recently a different method for investigating the individual's metacognitions during problem solving was introduced. The technique requires the subjects to give judgments repeatedly about how close they feel to the solution of problems—called feeling-of-warmth (FOW) judgments—in the course of the problem solving. These judgments are called "warmth" judgments after the searching game in which one person hides an object and then directs others to where the object is by telling them that they are getting warmer—closer to the object—or colder—farther away. Subjects are asked to indicate how near they believe they are to the solution. The "feeling of warmth" procedure was used to examine the subjective phenomenology of different problems. It could be shown that the patterns-of-warmth ratings differed for insight and noninsight problems. Noninsight problems showed a more incremental pattern in the course of being solved than did insight problems. The conclusion drawn from these findings was that insight problems were solved by some nonanalytic, sudden process, in contrast to an analytic process of reducing the difference between the initial and goal state, which characterized the solution of noninsight problems. Some researchers opposed this conclusion as being rather vague and speculative. The finding that subjects cannot predict their performance on insight problems does not logically necessitate that solutions to such problems occur as a sudden flash of illumination.

A similar technique to study metacognitive assessments subjects make about the likelihood that they know the answer to a question or will be able to solve a problem are feeling-of-knowing judgments (FKJ). This judgments are based on episodic memory which, for its optimal function, requires a subsidiary monitoring and control system that assesses the familiarity of incoming events and adjusts attention. Cognitive energy is assigned to events on the basis of novelty—devoting little energy to old and already well-known events and much attention to novel events. It is assumed that the values of novelty assessed by such a monitoring-control system are feelings that are available to consciousness and that they may be used for making feeling-of-knowing judgments. Many researchers have stressed the importance of such a judging system for creativity, especialy for problem finding. Identifying differences between a schema and the environment is also important for the process of conceptualization. However, as mentioned earlier, it is difficult to observe this processes, and defining them with FOW ratings and FKJs is a circular endeavor.

To overcome the mentioned methodological problems related to FOW, FKJ, and thinking aloud methodology some researchers suggested the use of moderating variables. Activation parameters like heart rate and blood pressure or even electroencephalogram (EEG) were used as moderating variables. The typical reaction to mental work or active coping is tachycardia and a redistribution of blood flow from skin and viscera to skeletal muscles. In contrast, passive coping is associated with an unchanged or perhaps lowered cardiac output. The characteristic of EEG patterns in a relaxed mental state is a higher amplitude in the alpha band (regular 7 to 14 Hz wave pattern). Some speculations exist that the so-called late components in event-related potentials (an ERP is a complex EEG wave form that is related in time to a specific sensory event), such as the transient wave in the range of 200 ms, 300 ms, and even the slow wave that develops 0.5 to 1.0 s after stimulus onset are related to an orienting response. This response was described as the consequence of a comparison between a sequence of neural events representing the incoming stimulus and stored neuronal models of past events. This explanation is similar to the assumptions on that are based FKJ, which can be observed on the behavioral level.

III. METACOGNITION AND PROBLEM SOLVING

From a theoretical viewpoint, metacognition seems to be an important aspect of cognition that can affect problem-solving performance, yet empirical studies have failed to give undivided support to the hypothesis. Experts in physics, for instance, give fewer metacognitive statements than do novices, the explanation being a more automatic process among the experts. On the other hand some of the strategic misfunctions of college students engaged in mathematical problem solving were described as failures of goal setting, monitoring, and the evaluation of plans, which is the essence of metacognitive proficiency. The majority of students so engaged embark on a course of action that can be described as "read a problem, pick a direction, and then work on it until you run out of time." Experts, by contrast, have metacognitive knowledge that leads them to ask themselves, and to answer, three kinds of questions:

- What (precisely) are you doing?
- What is the reason for doing it?
- How will the result be used later in the solution?

IV. METACOGNITION AND GIFTEDNESS

Some recent studies have tried to relate metacognition and giftedness. The findings differ considerably. It was reported that students who were high achievers were better able to describe their learning strategies. On the other hand, no superior metacognitive knowledge in gifted fourth grade students could be found. It was concluded that gifted students might possess some metacognitive knowledge, but they will not necessarily utilize it appropriately. [*See* GIFTEDNESS AND CREATIVITY.]

The results of several experiments utilizing FOW rating showed that able problem solvers differed in their FOW ratings when solving different problem types. These differences were less pronounced for average problem solvers. For low problem solvers no such differences were obtained. These findings suggest that able problem solvers have a higher ability to estimate their closeness to the solution and they use it to decide on the next steps in the cognitive activity.

A second characteristic of gifted individuals is their ability to better classify problems according to the way problems are solved. Thus, able problem solvers, because of their higher abilities in monitoring their own cognitive processes, are more successful in classifying problems according to the solution approach than are poorer problem solvers.

That high performers have a greater knowledge about cognitive phenomena was shown also by the comparison between the classification explanations given by high and low performers. The explanations given by able problem solvers were more abstract and reflected knowledge about the cognitive strategies that were involved in the solution process. In contrast, the explanations of poorer problem solvers were more oriented toward concrete features of the problems solved (the modality of the problem, whether the problem was difficult, etc.). Similar differences were reported for procedural knowledge among experts and novices in different domains. The procedural knowledge of novices appears to be clustered around concrete phenomena. In contrast, the procedural knowledge of experts is organized around higher-order principles. [*See* EXPERTISE.]

Support for the preceding conclusions comes also from EEG research. Gifted individuals, while solving different tasks, used processes that displayed a similar complexity of neural mass activity (EEG measures); by contrast, average individuals displayed a greater diversity in the complexity of neural mass activity. The differences were extremely pronounced over the right hemisphere. The problems used did not greatly differ. All of them could be classified as well defined, having one correct solution. Hence, there was no need for the strategy change displayed by the average individuals. It seems, further, that average individuals involved brain areas irrelevant for good task performance. Average individuals displayed the greatest complexity of neural mass activity over the right frontal and central areas for arithmetic tasks and lower complexity for the analogy tasks. From a theoretical viewpoint, the arithmetic tasks are solved in a more stepwise manner, in contrast to analogy tasks that require a more holistic approach. Research findings indicated that the right hemisphere specializes in holistic perception and is primarily a synthesist, dealing with information input. The speaking, left hemisphere, by contrast, seems to operate in a more logical, analytic, stepwise fashion. The pattern of EEG measure displayed by gifted individuals resembled this difference.

It can be concluded that metacognition is an important factor in problem-solving performance. Able problem solvers have higher abilities of estimating their closeness to the solution and they use them for deciding on the next steps in the cognitive activity. Capable students know much more about general cognitive strategies—how and when to apply them—than less capable individuals do. Poor problem solvers are also less efficient in monitoring their own cognitive process during problem solving than are able problem solvers. Poor students not only do not realize that they did not understand; in fact, they more frequently think that they had understood. Poorer college students are the ones who complain that they really knew the material but that they failed the examination. This may indi-

cate that students who do badly on tests are also poor at monitoring their comprehension and at predicting their future memory for material. [*See* PROBLEM SOLVING.]

V. EPISTEMIC COGNITION AND CREATIVITY

Epistemic cognition refers to the individual's knowledge about the limits of knowing, the certainty of knowing, and the criteria for knowing. Loosely speaking, individuals must know that some things can be known and others can not, or that they can be known only probabilistically, and that one knows the answer to a question if it can be conclusively verified scientifically. Furthermore, individuals must understand that problems do not always have one solution, that cognitive strategies are sometimes limited and even reasoning correctly about a problem does not necessarily lead to an absolutely correct solution. Epistemic cognition is important for solving ill-structured problems that require creativity. If a subject is not aware of these limitations, he or she will approach an ill-defined problem as if it were a puzzle. Average students approach creative problems in a similar way to that in which they solve the well-defined problems. In contrast, the thinking aloud protocols of gifted students reveal statements that indicate epistemic cognition. They evaluate a creative problem as being one of the problems in which no absolutely correct solution exists, in which the solution requires a lot of thinking that would not necessarily produce a correct solution, and in which there are no firm criteria that could be used to verify the answer scientifically.

VI. CAN METACOGNITION BE TRAINED?

A second approach to study the importance of metacognition for creative problem solving is to study the trainability of metaprocesses. In this way it is confirmed that these processes exist and that they are important for problem solving. Comparing training approaches aiming at different processes, such as flexible knowledge, contextual knowledge, and intuition, revealed that the greatest improvement in problem solving was achieved when students were instructed in the domain of metacognition. The greatest improvements were observed when metacognitive instructions aimed at the solution of well-defined problems; less effective were instructions that aimed at enhancing creative problem solving and analogic reasoning. This seems understandable, as much more is known about the domain of well-defined problems as is known about ill-defined problems.

Instructions used in metacognitive training usually aim at one or more of the following elements of metacognition:

- *Knowledge about problems.* Students are taught to distinguish among problem types. They are introduced to the main difficulties individuals are confronted with when solving a problem. Some suggestions about how to avoid perceptual and response set and how to increase the capacity of working memory by making chunks more abstract or by changing the modality of representation of the problem statement are provided.
- *Knowledge about strategies.* Students are introduced to strategies like modeling, subgoaling, working backward, making inferences, goal discovery, and analogies.
- *Knowledge of when and how the strategies should be applied is provided.*
- *Knowledge aimed at monitoring one's own cognitive processes during problem solving.* Students are asked to develop a plan of action, maintain their plan, and evaluate it while they work on a problem.

Research has shown that instruction aimed at monitoring had the greatest impact on problem-solving performance. Such instruction increases the likelihood that the learner will be able to transfer new knowledge to more difficult problems within a given domain.

VII. EDUCATIONAL IMPLICATIONS

The finding that instruction aimed at metacognition can improve the ability of respondents to solve prob-

lems has immense educational implications. Researchers have suggested some characteristics of teaching methods that could enhance students' metacognition.

The teaching methods are frequently based on Vygotsky's developmental theory. Even though Vygotsky's theory is mainly directed toward parent-child interaction and the influence it has on the child's development, it is also important for designing training and teaching methods. Two aspects appear to be significant:

- All higher psychological functions (e.g., perception, voluntary attention, intentional memory) have social origins. Vygotsky claimed that adults and more capable peers mediate the child's experience. Thus, knowledge and cognitive processes are socially transmitted.
- The distance between what the child can do working alone and what he or she can accomplish with aid was labeled the zone of proximal development. The zone of proximal development is a special kind of shared activity between the child and the adult in which their roles are complementary. The adult behaves as the child's extension, fitting into the child's autonomously motivated activity.

In the light of these theoretical aspects, the trainer or teacher should emphasize the following factors in his or her teaching approach:

- Teachers should express the knowledge and cognitive strategies involved in a problem solution. This externalization of skills could take several forms: telling the student what needs to be done, stepping the student through the problem, modeling appropriate strategies, and modeling while simultaneously explaining. In that way tutors provide a scaffold that enables a student or novice to solve a problem, that would be beyond his or her unassisted efforts. This modeling of thinking processes involved in expert problem solving is especially important for enhancing metacognition.
- The expert should help the student by reducing the cognitive workload. The teacher should do those parts of the task that the student cannot, while allowing the student to participate as fully as possible. In that way a true dialogue between the teacher and

student is developed. Loosely speaking, full contact between the teacher's mind and the student's mind is established.

- Teachers should take on less of the workload as students demonstrate increasing competence. This ceding of control encourages the student to complete more of the task on his or her own.

The described teaching methods and techniques are to some extent opposed to what is at present going on in schools. Two issues seem to be important:

- In schools more emphasis should be given to making children understand the world from different viewpoints, to integrating subject matters rather than to introducing them separately. It seems that our schools still prefer to teach children small units of knowledge, not only separated by the different subjects domains but also divided into chapters within each subject domain. To illustrate, children learn a lot about muscles, nerves, veins and other anatomical parts but know little about how they function together. They are far from seeing a roman-

tic picnic fire as an oxidation process, which is similar to the processes that go on in a working muscle. Only this type of knowledge makes analogic reasoning possible.

- It seems quite reasonable that education should pay more attention to teaching children general problem-solving strategies. However, it seems that this aspect of education is neglected in our schools. Only specific domain or task-related strategies are introduced. Such an approach can cause the rigid use of one strategy for all occasions.

Bibliography

Jaušovec, N. (1994). *Flexible thinking: An explanation for individual differences in ability.* Cresskill, NJ: Hampton Press.

Metcalfe, J., & Shimamura, A. P. (1994). *Metacognition: Knowing about knowing.* Cambridge, MA: MIT Press

Runco, M. A. (1994). *Problem finding, problem solving, and creativity.* Norwood, NJ: Ablex.

Sternberg, R. J. (1994). *Thinking and problem-solving.* San Diego, CA: Academic Press.

Weinert, F. E. & Kluwe, R. H. (1987), *Metacognition, motivation, and understanding.* Hillsdale, NJ: Erlbaum.

Metaphors

Raymond W. Gibbs, Jr.

University of California, Santa Cruz

Conceptual Metaphor A mental mapping in which knowledge from one domain of experience (the target) is understood in terms of information from a different, and usually more structured, domain.

Poetic Metaphor A linguistic expression that instantiates in some creative, novel manner, some metaphorical mapping between diverse domains of experience.

Speaking and Understanding The psychological processes of designing utterances for particular audiences and inferring what speakers intended to communicate.

Teaching Creativity Facilitating people's engagement in thinking about topics in new ways, often through trying to metaphorically relate ideas from one familiar domain in terms of a different aspect of experience.

Verbal Metaphor A linguistic expression that usually reflects some pre-existing conceptual metaphor.

METAPHOR *is traditionally defined as a literary or rhetorical device whereby a speaker refers to one domain* of knowledge (the target) in terms of a different domain (the source), as in "encyclopedias are gold mines." Metaphor differs from analogy in that the mapping from a source to a target domain is directional in metaphor, but is bidirectional in analogy (e.g., "The atom is like a solar system"). A widely held assumption about metaphor is that people produce and understand metaphor through the juxtaposition of disparate conceptual categories which themselves are fixed with objectively defined properties. Even though people can and do speak metaphorically, the ability to think, imagine, and speak metaphorically has historically been seen as a special human trait, requiring different cognitive and linguistic structures than those used in ordinary life. Metaphoric assertions are often thought to be distinct from true knowledge. Therefore, to think or speak metaphorically is to adopt a distorted stance toward the ordinary world, one that is held in disdain by many philosophers, scientists, and educators. Understanding metaphor is assumed to require special cognitive processes beyond those used to interpret ordinary, literal language, because of its heavy reliance on contextual, real-world knowledge.

These traditional views on the definition of metaphor are completely wrong in several major respects. Not only is metaphor an important part of everyday thought, particularly in relation to how we conceptualize abstract ideas and experience, and not just a special linguistic *device, but metaphor also has a fundamental role in creative thinking in both special and ordinary situations. Most generally, it is near impossible to characterize creativity without some consideration of metaphor.*

I. AN EXAMPLE
OF CREATIVE METAPHOR

Consider a typical use of metaphor in a literary text. The following is the opening verse of a poem by Elizabeth Bishop titled *Varick Street:*

> At night the factories
> struggle awake,
> wretched uneasy buildings
> veined with pipes
> attempt their work.
> trying to breathe
> the elongated nostrils
> haired with spikes
> give off such stenches, too.

Reading these first few lines, most readers get an immediate sense of Bishop's intention to draw a metaphorical comparison between the operations of a factory and the human body (i.e., a kind of personification). Our understanding of Bishop's intentions, and the underlying motive for her creating this poem in the way that she did, depends critically on our ability to think metaphorically about ordinary objects, events, and people in the world. One of the main ways we think metaphorically is through comparison to different embodied experiences in the sense that there is some tacit connection between human embodiment and how we think about different concepts and express ourselves with language in talking about, and understanding, important ideas. Creative artists like Bishop elaborate on these bodily-based metaphorical concepts in new, creative ways via their use of language (or art or music). The fact that we, as ordinary readers and observers, have similar metaphorical understandings of many abstract concepts, ones that arise from our own embodied experiences, allows us to make sense of creative works. Not all aspects of creativity are rooted in, and can be predicted by, bodily experience, but an important part of how we think, reason, and use lan-

guage in creative ways rests with our ability to think metaphorically.

II. SPEAKING AND
UNDERSTANDING METAPHOR

Speaking metaphorically is not just something that poets, or politicians, do to show off their creative talents, for metaphor is ubiquitous in oral speech, literature, poetry, and scientific writing. One analysis of different kinds of oral speech showed, for instance, that people use 1.80 novel and 4.08 frozen metaphors per minute of discourse. So speaking metaphorically, nevermind using other tropes, is a prominent part of everyday conversation. Even young children can, and often do, produce novel metaphors that illustrate their creative insights into the world around them. Most generally, people speak metaphorically to express ideas that are difficult to communicate using literal language, and to express thoughts in a compact and vivid manner.

Consider the metaphorical expression, "The thought slipped my mind like a squirrel behind a tree." It is difficult to literally predicate thought characteristics such as swiftness, suddenness, or ungraspableness. We might try to translate the metaphorical sentence into literal language, but we still end up with language that is essentially metaphorical (e.g., "The thought went away" and "The thought evaded me"). Metaphors enable people to express ideas that simply cannot be easily or clearly expressed with literal speech.

Metaphors also provide a particularly compact means of communication. For instance, the assertion, "My love is like a blossoming bouquet of roses," expresses a large amount of information about love (i.e., that it is sweet, delicate, beautiful, perhaps short in its life span, etc.) using relatively few words. Literal language simply does not enable speakers/writers to convey a great deal of information succinctly in the same way that metaphor does.

Finally, metaphors may help capture the vividness of our phenomenological experience. Because metaphors convey complex configurations of information rather than discrete units, speakers can convey richer, more detailed, vivid images of our subjective experience than can be expressed by literal language. These images seem to embellish what is communicated to listeners, providing them with subtle nuances that may be part of the speaker's subjective experience. Thus, "My love is like a blooming bouquet of roses" is likely to evoke various mental images in the listener that better reflect the speaker's vivid communicative intentions about the concept of love and his or her experience of love.

Does producing and understanding verbal metaphors require special cognitive and linguistic processes? The traditional view holds that literal language can be understood, for example, via normal cognitive mechanisms, but that listeners must recognize the deviant nature of a metaphorical utterance before determining its nonliteral meaning. For instance, understanding a metaphorical comment, such as "criticism is a branding iron," requires that listeners must first analyze what is stated literally, then recognize that the literal meaning (i.e., that criticism is literally a tool to mark livestock) is contextually inappropriate, and then infer some meaning consistent with the context and the idea that the speaker must be acting cooperatively and rationally (i.e., criticism can psychologically hurt the person who receives it, often with long-lasting consequences). This traditional view suggests, then, that metaphorical language should always be more difficult to process than roughly equivalent literal speech.

But the results of many psycholinguistic experiments have shown this idea to be false. These studies investigate the amount of time it takes people to read and interpret literal and metaphorical utterances in appropriate discourse contexts. Listeners/readers can often understand the figurative interpretations of not only metaphors, but irony/sarcasm, idioms, proverbs, and indirect speech acts as well, without having to first analyze and reject their literal meanings when these expressions are seen in realistic social contexts. People can read metaphorical utterances as quickly, sometimes even more quickly, as literal uses of the same expressions in different contexts, or equivalent nonmetaphorical expressions. Even without a defective literal meaning to trigger a search for an alternative nonliteral meaning, metaphor (e.g., "surgeons are butchers"), to take one example, can be automatically interpreted. Experimental studies also demonstrate that understanding metaphor requires the same kind of contextual information as do comparable literal expressions.

Listeners/readers may slowly certainly ponder the potential meanings of a figurative expression, such as

the literary metaphor from Shakespeare, "the world is an unweeded garden." It is this conscious experience that provides much of the basis for the mistaken assumption that metaphorical language always requires "extra work" to be properly understood. Nonetheless, experimental findings demonstrate that the traditional view of metaphor as deviant and ornamental, requiring additional cognitive effort to be understood, is incorrect.

III. METAPHOR IN LANGUAGE AND THOUGHT

Recent research in the cognitive sciences also questions many of the traditional views of metaphor by suggesting that metaphor is pervasive in everyday life, not just in language, but in an individual's structuring of experience. The way we think, what we experience, and what we do everyday are very much a matter of metaphors. Underlying many of the literary and conventional verbal metaphors found in literature and everyday speech are perhaps hundreds of conceptual metaphors that structure our everyday experience. Many literal expressions reflect metaphorical concepts, ones that are not merely dead, but very much alive and part of ordinary cognition. Consider the metaphorical concept, "time is money," as seen in the following utterances:

> "You're wasting time."
> "This gadget will save you hours."
> "You're running out of time."
> "How do you spend your time these days?"
> "Do you have much time left?"
> "The flat tire cost me an hour."
> "I've invested a lot of time in her."
> "I don't have enough time to spare for that."
> "He's living on borrowed time."
> "You don't spend your time profitably."

The systematicity of these conventional expressions for time illustrate how our understanding and experiencing of one kind of thing (e.g., time) in terms of another (e.g., money) gives rise to various linguistic expressions that seem quite literal despite their underlying metaphoricity. Each of the preceding expressions refers to specific metaphorical entailments of the "time is money" conceptual metaphor. Time, like money, can be spent, saved, wasted, borrowed, invested, budgeted, or squandered. Together these metaphorical entailments form a system of relationships that people find easy to talk about.

Consider another metaphorical concept that structures part of our experience in the mundane world: "anger is heated fluid in a container." This conceptual metaphor is actually one of the limited number of ways that people in Western cultures conceive of anger. Our understanding of anger (the source domain) as heated fluid in a container (the target domain) gives rise to a number of interesting entailments. For example, when the intensity of anger increases, the fluid rises (e.g., "His pent-up anger welled up inside of him"). We also know that intense heat produces steam and creates pressure on the container (e.g., "Bill is getting hot under the collar" and "Jim's just blowing off steam"). Intense anger produces pressure on the container (e.g., "He was bursting with anger"). When the pressure of the container becomes too high, the container explodes (e.g., "She blew up at me"). Each of these metaphorical entailments is a direct result of the conceptual mapping of anger onto our understanding of heated fluid in a container.

Some scholars believe that many conventional utterances, such as those just seen, are not really very metaphorical, or creative, but contain different "dead" metaphors. For example, we talk about "legs" of tables, and "arms" of chair even though we do not actively view tables and chairs metaphorically in terms of human body parts. In the same way, we might refer to anger as "bursting" or to time as being "wasted" or "borrowed" even though there are no longer active metaphors in our everyday conceptual system that motivate such language.

But there are plenty of basic conventional metaphors that are alive, certainly enough to show that what is conventional and fixed need not be dead. It is important to distinguish between conventional metaphors, which are part of our everyday conceptual system (e.g., "argument is war," or "time is money"), and historical metaphors that have long since died out. The failure to draw this distinction derives from an assumption that things in our cognition that are most active and alive are those that are conscious. On the contrary, those things that are most alive and most deeply entrenched, efficient, and powerful are those that are so automatic as to be unconscious and effortless. Our understanding of time as money or anger as heated fluid in a container is active and widespread, but these concepts are so deeply entrenched in our ordinary conceptual system that we tend to miss their metaphorical character. The unconscious part of conceptual metaphors provides the main reason why people fail to see the metaphorical nature of many literal expressions.

Finally, consider the following fairly mundane utterances that are often used to talk about various life experiences such as relationships and careers:

> "Look how far we've come."
> "It's been a long, bumpy road."
> "My career is at a crossroads."
> "We may have to go our separate ways."
> "My career is on the rocks."
> "We're spinning our wheels."

Why are each of these expressions acceptable ways of talking about, and understanding, life? All of these (and other) conventional expressions cluster together under one basic metaphorical system of understanding where our understanding of one domain of experience, life, is partly structured in terms of a very different, and more concrete domain of experience, journeys. This metaphorical mapping is tightly constrained such that entities in the domain of life (e.g., individual people, their personal and career goals, and their personal relationships) correspond systematically to entities in the domain of a journey (e.g., the traveler, the vehicle, and destinations).

One of the interesting connections between everyday metaphorical thought and more creative uses of language is found by looking at how creative poets use the same conceptual metaphors found in ordinary speech. There is empirical evidence that readers make sense of poetry, find poetry especially apt and meaningful, because they infer various underlying conceptual metaphors while reading poetry. Consider these lines from the poem titled, *Ode and Burgeonings,* by Pablo Neruda.

> My wild girl, we have had
> to regain time

and march backward, in the distance
of our lives, kiss after kiss,
gathering from one place what we gave
without joy, discovering in another
the secret road
that gradually brought your feet
close to mine.

These lines again illustrate how we conceptualize of our love experiences partly in terms of journeys. As was discussed earlier, various entailments arise when we think of life or love as a journey. These entailments are elaborated on in many poetic descriptions of love such as in Neruda's poem and people's individual love experiences. When ordinary college students read the fragment from Neruda's poem, they referred to entailments of the "love is a journey" metaphor such as the path (e.g., "They learned a better path to happiness," "They had to retrace their steps to find true love," or "They found a special road that they could travel together on in the same direction"), the goal (e.g., "The future of their love lay ahead of them," or "They had to catch up"), and the impediments to travel (e.g., "They managed to get over the rough places, rediscovering what was missed"). It seemed clear that readers were partially making sense of what the poems meant through their everyday metaphorical understanding of love. People's conscious, reflective interpretations of poetry appear to be strongly constrained by their ordinary metaphorical knowledge. Readers do not necessarily create novel metaphorical mappings to understand novel, poetic language. The vast majority of novel metaphors in poetry and literature reflect fixed patterns of metaphorical mappings between dissimilar source and target domains. Although poets may present novel instantiations for these preexisting, metaphorical mappings, people do not necessarily have to draw novel mappings in any algorithmic sense in order to understand poetic instantiations of conventional metaphors.

The conclusion to draw from this, and the previous, section is that metaphor is not just an ornamental linguistic device, but is a common scheme by which ordinary people think and use language. Part of our ability to understand the spectacular, creative efforts of artists and scientists rests with our ordinary metaphorical thought processes and common conceptual metaphors that are widely shared in any cultural community. One of the pleasures we derive from reading literary and scientific works is the metaphors we discover in these texts that somehow speak to us, or remind us of our struggles to find meaning and purpose in the chaos of ordinary living.

IV. METAPHOR IN ART AND SCIENCE

Much of the work in art and science is viewed as creative. Creative thinking is characterized by cognitive flexibility and the use of an active imagination. Metaphor has several possible roles in creative thinking, ranging from directly shaping thought (i.e., to draw connections between abstract ideas and concrete experience) to serving expressive, affective, or communicative purposes. Let us consider some examples of creative metaphor in art and science to illustrate some of the different ways that metaphor influences creativity.

Our enjoyment in reading literature very much depends on our ability to recognize and appreciate creative metaphors. In great works of literature, metaphors provide us with instruments for establishing imaginative connections between diverse emotions, ideas, and events. Consider as examples of metaphor the following passages from Vladimir Nabokov's novel, *The Defense,* about a genius chess-master, Luzhin, who suffers a nervous breakdown in the middle of an important match. Luzhin has so saturated his mind with chess that he sees his whole life in its terms. These passages describe his awkward courtship of the women who will become his wife.

Luzhin began with a series of quiet moves, the meaning of which he himself only vaguely sensed, his own peculiar declaration of love. "Go on, tell me more," she repeated, despite having noticed how morosely and dully he had fallen silent.

He sat leaning on his cane and thinking that with a Knight's move of this lime tree standing on a sunlit slope one could take that telegraph pole over there, and simultaneously he tried to remember what exactly he had just been talking about. (p. 97)

With one shoulder pressed against his chest she tried with a cautious finger to raise his eyelids a little higher and the slight pressure on his eyeball caused a strange black light to leap there, to leap like his black Knight which simply took the Pawn if Turati moved it out on the seventh move, as he had done at their last meeting. (p. 114)

Later on, Nabokov gives us a glimpse of Luzhin's mind soon after his breakdown.

He found himself in a smokey establishment where noisy phantoms were sitting. An attack was developing in every corner—and pushing aside tables, a bucket with a gold-necked glass Pawn sticking out of it and a drum that was being beaten by an arched, thick-manned chess Knight, he made his way to a gently revolving door. . . . (p. 139)

The power of chess over Luzhin's mind is not limited to the visual or spatial properties of chess. Much more pervasive is the discipline provided by the rules and tactics of the game. The abstract structure of chess obsessively drives much of Luzhin's thinking:

[He] presently would note with despair that he had been unwary again and that a delicate move had just been made in his life, mercilessly continuing the fatal combination. Then he would decide to redouble his watchfulness and keep track of every second of his life, for traps could be everywhere. And he was oppressed most of all by the impossibility of inventing a rational defense, for his opponent's aim was still hidden. (p. 227)

Nabokov's characterization of Luzhin is a wonderful example of how we live our lives via metaphor. Each of us may not be as psychologically fixated on one particular metaphorical theme in the way that poor Luzhin is, yet we still conceptualize of our everyday life in a whole system of metaphorical schemas that help us make sense of our inchoate experiences.

Scientists also use, and sometimes create, new metaphors to make sense of people and the world around them in their scientific work. Several case studies of scientists have examined the role that metaphor plays in creative scientific thought and practice. For exam-

ple, one study of Antoine Lavoiser's discovery of the chemistry of respiration demonstrated how Lavoisier shifted from a view of respiration as combustion to one of respiration as a kind of burning candle. Lavoiser's creative discovery can be described as employing metaphor in a series of 12 steps:

First, there was the problem and relevant observations. (1) The target domain was the chemical nature of respiration. (2) An observation relevant to the source domain was that respiration of animals results in oxygen being consumed and carbonic acid and water being formed. (3) An observation relevant to candle burning was that a candle burning in air consumes about half its oxygen and replaces it with carbonic acid and water.

Second, there is the formation of the metaphor, (4) respiration in animals is like a candle burning in air. (5) The source domain is a candle burning in air.

Third, there is relevant knowledge about chemistry of candle burning. (6) A candle is composed of carbon and hydrogen. (7) Candle burning consumes oxygen and produces carbonic acid and water. (8) Weight of candle burned + weight of oxygen = weight of carbonic acid + weight of air. (9) Oxygen can be converted to carbonic acid only by addition of "charbon." (10) Oxygen can be converted to carbonic acid only by addition of hydrogen. (11) This double combination can take place only with loss of "caloric" from the oxygen.

Finally, there is the solution to the original problem. (12) In respiration, carbon and hydrogen are extracted from the blood and replaced by a portion of "caloric."

What is important about this description is that once the metaphor was established, the relevant chemical fats surrounding the burning of a candle could be brought to bear on the problem at hand. Second, the conclusion or solution to the problem does not depend on the metaphor itself as the metaphor only served as the scaffolding that could be discarded once the conclusion had been drawn. Metaphors such as "respiration is like the burning of a candle" are not merely evocative because they serve as the bases for scientific explanations. These explanations are made feasible by the transfer of certain properties, aspects, attributes, or knowledge of the source domain to the target domain in a manner that allows certain conclusions to be drawn or explanations to be offered about the target subject. Metaphors work in this way to play a crucial role in discovery and invention.

Other case studies demonstrate that metaphors do not function in isolation, but blend together in certain key respects to form ensembles of metaphor. For instance, Charles Darwin used at least eight major metaphors in developing the theory of evolution through natural selection: tree, tangled branch, wedging, struggling, war, contrivance, and both artificial and natural selection. In his theory, the interplay between the forces of explosive growth, variation, and enrichment, on the one hand, and forces of selection, on the other, produce the evolving panorama of organic nature. Darwin's originality lay not in his creation of entirely novel metaphors. Rather, his creative contribution to science was in the way he assembled metaphors to paint a comprehensive picture of the evolving natural order. These metaphors were not simply expressive means for Darwin to communicate his ideas about evolution, but were theory-constitutive in that Darwin tried out different metaphors to work out the theory in the first place.

Many 20th century philosophers now contend that metaphors are in most respects constitutive elements of scientific theory rather than mere ornaments or dangerously misleading figures of speech. These revisionist theorists argue that metaphors play a significant role in science, even within highly specialized technical, mature sciences. A paradigmatic example has been found in contemporary physics. The mechanical models of 19th century physics described gases as collections of moving particles obeying Newtonian laws, and atoms as miniature solar systems. The conventional wisdom in the philosophy of science held that these metaphoric descriptions would give way to more direct, complete, literal descriptions of the primary system. In fact, many 19th century models have been replaced in modern physics, but not so their underlying metaphorical processes. When Bohr's model replaced the solar system model, the new model was not intended to be taken literally: electrons and nuclei were not seen as being exactly the same as small billiard or Ping-Pong balls.

One discipline where constitutive metaphors have been closely examined is experimental psychology. Metaphors abound in experimental psychology in theories about most aspects of human experience. For instance, the concept of memory has been described as a wax tablet, a dictionary, an encyclopedia, a muscle, a telephone switchboard, a conveyor belt, a storehouse for ideas, a computer, and a hologram. Descartes referred to memory as being like a riverbed through which sensory impressions flow. Freud talked of memory as a house full of rooms. Most modern theories of memory are variations of a metaphor theme of mental space with recall as a search through the contents of this space. Mental images are viewed as drawings, working spaces, blackboards, scratch pads, and cathode ray tubes. Metaphors employed in contemporary psychological texts are often related to new technology. For instance, the computer metaphor is the most important theory-constitutive metaphor in contemporary psychology. The computer metaphor, with its talk of inputs, accessing, retrieval systems, and the like, facilitates communication and verbal reasoning concerning human cognitive processes. The metaphor then organizes the phenomena for investigation and provides a vocabulary with which to carry out that investigation. Metaphor is clearly playing a critical cognitive role in science and does not simply serve as an ornament to communicate scientific ideas.

What is special and creative about the metaphors developed and used by artists and scientists? Both art and science spring from a heightening, widening, and deepening of attention to some phenomenon or human experience. People with special creative talents have the craft-sense to place this heightened attention into their work. An artist's or scientist's deepened concentration lets what may have previously been difficult to see enter the realm of the knowable and so be made available, to both artist, scientist, and others. Creative art and science mirror more closely than everyday thought the cunning, circuitous nature of our most basic mental strategies.

It seems very sensible to suppose that the ability to think metaphorically is positively related to creativity. Various research has considered whether people who frequently and effectively use metaphor may be similar to creative people in sharing a certain cognitive style that includes independence of judgment and complexity of outlook. Most generally, people who use metaphor a good deal tend to be flexible, personally open, and able to attend to several different things at once, and to effectively integrate and organize these dissimilarities. High producers of metaphor may also tolerate ambiguity and confusion quite well, are willing to experiment, and are able to regress and think in immature ways, but have the ego strength to respond in a logical, adult manner when the situation arises. People who use metaphoric language frequently and effectively demonstrate more flexible cognitive style than do people who use metaphoric language less frequently.

Empirical research has studied how people working in different creative professions (e.g., writers, artists, and scientists) differ in terms of their ability to think metaphorically. To give one example, the psychologist Frank Barron studied the transformation of images from the literal to the highly symbolic and metaphoric. His central concern in the psychology of creativity was on people's productive thinking ability or their "symbolic scope." He focused on the various ways that individual differences in creativity are expressed through the ways that images (in a variety of sensory modalities) and words are transformed to generate new insights, ideas, or images that are expressed in creative works. Barron's interest in the transformation of images originates from his observations of the British poet C. Day Lewis who in one lecture gave a nice example from his experience of the process by which an image that is drawn from one domain of experience is metaphorically mapped onto a dissimilar knowledge domain (Barron, 1988; p. 84).

> The poet was looking out of his bedroom window in blitzed London. A searchlight practice was on. The beams swung about the sky, then leaned together like the framework of a wigwam, and at the apex an aircraft could be seen, silver, moth-like, flying slowly, found, lost, found again by the searchlights. It was a common enough sight just then . . . but this time the poet saw it differently, as a dramatic paradox; it seemed to him that candle-beams were desirously searching for the moth.

This example offered by C. Day Lewis prompted Barron to consider the general problem of how images are metaphorically transformed and whether the resulting image is original, complex, or apt. Do some individuals have greater talent in transforming images? To answer these questions, Barron created the Symbolic Equivalence Test, an instrument designed to observe the process whereby a stimulus image is changed by design into a nonliteral or symbolic image that is recognizably another version of the original configuration. The Symbolic Equivalence Test presents participants with questions like the following:

> In this test, you will be asked to think of metaphors, or symbolically equivalent images, for certain suggested stimulus images. The task can best be made clear by an example. Suggested stimulus image: *Leaves blown in the wind.* Possible symbolic equivalents: *A civilian population fleeing chaotically in the face of armed aggression. Handkerchiefs being tossed about inside an electric dryer. Chips of woods borne downstream of a swiftly eddying current.*

Participants were asked to make up their possible equivalents for each of 10 images (e.g., the sound of a foghorn, a candle burning low, a ship lost in fog, and sitting alone in a drunk room). Participants' responses were scored in terms of their metaphoric originality and aptness. For example, a merely admissible response to "a candle burning low" would be "life ebbing away," while an original and apt response would be "the last hand in a gambler's last card game."

The Symbolic Equivalence Test has been administrated to hundreds of people working in different creative professions. The data, most generally, presented a clear rank ordering of creativity: (1) famous writers, (2) mathematicians, (3) successful entrepreneurs in Ireland, (4) expert mountain climbers, (5) research scientists, and (6) art students. Related work showed that originality in symbolic equivalence correlates with other personality measures such as independence of judgment and complexity of outlook. Even for ordinary adults, one study found a positive relationship between adults' score on Barron's Symbolic Equivalence Test and a test of ideational fluency (i.e., one test of creativity).

V. METAPHOR IN EVERYDAY CREATIVITY

Even though we applaud writers and scientists for their inventive uses of metaphor, a closer look at metaphor in everyday and literary language reveals that metaphor is not, as Aristotle once noted, "the mark of genius," but an essential part of how each of us thinks, reasons, and understands. At the deepest level, not just art and science but all forms of thought, even simple perceptions themselves, require the creative, metaphorical mind. So deeply is creativity a part of human experience that not only are great works of literature and science examples of creativity, but everyday objects such as furniture, baskets, cooking pots, and even the body's surface require creative spirals, colors, and patterns before they are considered ready for use. People of all types in all cultures cannot help but use metaphor because their conceptualization of everyday experience is primarily done via the metaphorical mapping from one knowledge domain (the source) onto another (the target). Scholars tend to miss the presence of metaphoric schemes of thought in everyday language and thought because of the mistaken assumption that metaphor is a special intellectual ability.

A wonderful illustration of metaphor in everyday creativity is seen in how Apache Indians in North America name the parts of automobiles. In metaphor, one thing stands for another, or a thing is called by a name for something else. For example, in the Coeur d'Alene Indian language, the tires of a car or truck become "wrinkled feet," a reference to the pattern on their treads. The new knowledge of automobiles is likened to the old knowledge of the body. Basso has described an entire system of naming the parts of motorized vehicles in the language of the Western Apache of east-central Arizona. The Western Apache have extended the names for the body parts of humans and animals to refer to the parts of automobiles and pickup trucks. In this structural metaphor, the hood became the nose (*bichih*), the headlights became the eyes (*bidaa*), and the windshield became the forehead (*bita*). The term for the face (*binii*) was extended to the whole area extending from the top of the windshield to the front bumper, so this term included the nose/hood and forehead/windshield as subparts. The front wheels became the hands and arms (*bigan*), while the rear wheels became the feet (*bikee*). All the items under the hood were classified as parts of the innards (*bibye*). Under the hood, the battery became the liver (*bizig*), the electrical wiring, the veins (*bit qqs*); the gas tank the stomach (*bibid*); the distributor, the heart (*bijii*); the radiator, the

lung (*bijii izole*); and the radiator hoses, the intestines (*bich'i*).

There is an underlying conceptual metaphor, "motor vehicles are human bodies," that motivates these correspondences between the parts of human beings and the parts of cars and trucks. In the "motor vehicles are human bodies" metaphor, the thing of which we speak (the motor vehicle), with its constituent parts and relations, is the target domain, while the thing with which we speak (human bodies), with its own constituent parts and relations, is the source domain. The naming of vehicle parts with the names of human body parts preserves the hierarchical cognitive structure of relationships among the parts so that both the car's body and the human body had "innards" that included, for instance, a "liver."

How people name the parts of automobiles may not seem to be the best place to find creative thinking. But the Coeur d'Alene names for automobiles reveal a deep-rooted, creative impulse to make sense of the world in terms of metaphor. By recognizing how parts of an automobile have a metaphorical relationship with human body parts, the Western Apache have created something new using the imagination to the fullest. The Western Apache have in a sense reordered their experience by looking at something differently than before.

Perhaps one of metaphor's great roles in ordinary creativity comes in how people think about and verbally express their complex emotional experiences. Consider the following narrative from a 45-year-old man, Sam, who was recently married and being treated for infertility. Sam describes the erosion of well-being in his marriage as a result of his infertility in a book by George Becker.

> It (infertility) became a black hole for both of us. I was so happy when I was getting married, and life for me, was consistently getting better. And she was continuously depressed. Everything was meaningless because she couldn't have a baby. And so it was a tremendous black hole, it was a real bummer. I mean, in the broadest, deepest sense of the term. It was very upsetting to me because it was like no matter what . . . it seemed like every time . . . I was, like, taking off and feeling good, and she was dragging me down. And it wasn't that she was dragging me down, but she was dragging

herself down. It was contrary to the overwhelming evidence of our lives, and it was very disturbing, to the point where I said to her that it was not tolerable anymore. And she went to a psychiatrist. She wanted to improve because she couldn't get out of it. I mean, she could not get out of it, and the Prozac (that was prescribed), made it worse. But it broke the cycle of depression, and she got out of it. But that was terrible. It ruined our sex life. It was just like everything was going down the black hole. . . . The notion of the black hole is that it's this magnet—this negative magnet in space through which all matter is irretrievably drawn—that was the image that I had of it. It was just sucking everything down out of our lives. Down this negative hole. It was bad (p. 66–67).

Sam depicts the black hole as a constricting force—the opposite of the life spiral—a negative force that was preventing him and his wife from experiencing the pleasures usually associated with the early stages of marriage. The black hole, which stands for infertility and its all-encompassing effects, sucks the life out of their relationship. Instead of the image of building that is frequently associated with early parts of relationships, Sam conveys an image of dismantling. Sam's narrative reveals both the embodied and cultural foundations of metaphor. He deals with a personal crisis in a creative way by embracing a new metaphor that allows him to replace an old structure with a new one, a personal transformation that allows Sam to take control over his life and deal with this life disruption.

VI. TEACHING CREATIVITY THROUGH METAPHOR

Educators have constructed different exercises to help students develop creative insights through metaphor. For example, one system has students engage in a metaphoric lesson to explore the concept of time as historical perspective. "Time" is an abstract concept that can be difficult for students to understand in all its complexity before the age of 12. Yet the notion of time is frequently seen in children's literature and textbooks. The goal of the metaphoric lesson is threefold; (1) To help students develop an increasingly sophisti-

cated conceptual understanding of the concept of time, (2) to help students gain insights into themselves and their life situation as related to the concept of time, and (3) to help students generate creative perceptions concerning the subject matter being presently taught and its relationship to the overall concept of time. [*See* TIME.]

The metaphoric lesson has four parts: the focus, the personal comparison, the metaphoric interaction, and the insight moment. The first three stages are designed to lead up to the final stage of concept mastery and insight.

In level 1, the focus level, students begin to explore the way they conceptualize the passing of time. After showing students several examples of "time" images (e.g., different clocks, watches, hourglasses, and sun dials), students are asked to state what all these images have in common. Following this, the word "time" is written on a blackboard and the students are asked what this word means to them personally. Once students have shared their personal reactions and experiences, teachers introduce some topic, related to some pertinent subject matter, and ask students to comment. For instance, in a class lesson looking at the effect of time on the monarchical power in Europe, the students might want to read some famous poem illustrating different views of time and then brainstorm about the different meanings of "time." Finally, at the end of the focus phase, students are again reminded that time itself is usually understood only in terms of their own experiences, that measures of time are human inventions, and that their understanding of time is limited by their need to know and understand other concepts.

In level 2, the personal comparison phase, the students are asked to compare themselves with the lesson's metaphor (i.e., time symbols). Students might be asked to say in what way they are like an hourglass, watch, clock, or sundial, or to choose the "time object" that most resembles their life and the way they are living it, or to specifically respond to a question like, "how is the burning candle, the four seasons, the calendar, the stop watch, and the metronome like you?" Students' different responses to these questions are shared and discussed. One eighth-grade student responded to the question of comparing his life with a "time line" by saying, "I keep going in one direction; I can't go backwards—I just keep getting older and older. And there's nothing I can do about it; just like time keeps going forward" (Sanders & Sanders, 1984, p. 77).

Level 3, the metaphoric intervention, provides students with the opportunity to interact with the lesson's metaphor, in this case with a "time movie." Students are guided through a fantasy journey through a "calendar" of the earth. To do this, students are shown slides or a real movie, or visit a museum (or some other interactive experience). Under this exercise, for example, the history of the earth is described in relation to a yearly calendar such that after watching the film for 11 months, 30 days, 23 hours, 59 minutes, and 40 seconds, we finally see Columbus discover America, while 17 seconds later the Declaration of Independence is signed, and so on. Afterward, students are asked a series of debriefing questions, ranging from, "How did you feel when it was March and still no change had happened in the world?" to "At 11:00 PM on the last day of the last month, the first Stone Age people can be seen. What were they doing/ How did you feel when you saw them?" Finally, if students exhibit a sophistication in answering the debriefing questions, they might be given further probes to help extend their experience (e.g., "If You could be represented by a grain of sand, how large do you think the pile of sand would have to be to represent all the human life we've had on this planet?").

The final level 4, the creative insight, links the experience of the time metaphors with the overall concept of the lesson, namely, a personal perspective on the passage of time. The students here are prompted to merge both images and concepts, to allow creative connections to emerge, and to view their experiences from a new point of view. Students are placed into small groups and asked to discuss a series of questions such as, "Time is a staircase for all our successes. Why?" "How do trees tell time? Rivers tell time? Rocks tell time? Birds tell time?" "Death is a sun dial for every generation. Why?" "Society is an alarm clock we need to wake us up. Why?" "Science is a process that tells time by exploring nature. Show this to be true." Teach-

ers and students report that these discussions produce different creative, conceptual insights that facilitate students' understandings of new information, skills, and values. As Sanders and Sanders (1984, p. 87) argue, the "ability to prompt simultaneous consideration of both fact and image, of both information and concept, is the essential, creative dimension of the metaphor."

The preceding method for teaching creativity through metaphor is just one of many possible ways that engaging in metaphoric thought can enhance learning in the classroom. One advantage of such programs is that they help students to not only think creatively, but also to value creative thinking through playing with metaphors. This type of program also supports claims that creativity reflects self-expression and is not dependent on problems. [*See* TEACHING CREATIVITY.]

Bibliography

Barron, F. (1988). Putting creativity to work. In R. Sternberg (Ed.), *The nature of creativity* (pp. 76–98). New York: Cambridge University Press.

Becker, G. (1997). *Disrupted lives: How people create meaning in a chaotic world.* Berkeley: University of California Press.

Bishop, E. (1967). *Selected poems.* London: Chatto & Windus.

Gibbs, R. (1994). *The poetics of mind: Figurative thought, language, and understanding.* New York: Cambridge University Press.

Lakoff, G., & Johnson, M. (1980). *Metaphors we live by.* Chicago: University of Chicago Press.

Leary, R. (Ed.). (1992). *Metaphors in the history of psychology.* New York: Cambridge University Press.

Nabokov, V. (1933). *The defense.* New York: Vintage.

Neruda, P. (1972). *The captain's verses.* Evanston, IL: Northwestern University Press.

Ortony, A. (Ed.). (1993). *Metaphor and thought: Volume 2.* New York: Cambridge University Press.

Pollio, H., Barlow, J., Fine, H., & Pollio, M. (1977). *Psychology and the poetics of growth.* Hillsdale, NJ: Erlbaum.

Runco, M. (1991). *Divergent thinking.* Norwood, NJ: Ablex.

Sanders, D., & Sanders, J. (1984). *Teaching creativity through metaphor.* New York: Longman.

Sternberg, R. (Ed.). (1988). *The nature of creativity.* New York: Cambridge University Press.

Wallace, D., & Gruber, H. (Eds.). (1989). *Creative people at work.* New York: Oxford University Press.

Mindfulness

Mihnea C. Moldoveanu and Ellen Langer

Harvard University

Causation The doctrine that events are linked by cause-and-effect relationships; a category of perception that structures our understanding of the world as a chain of causes and effects.

Construction of Knowledge The process of forming beliefs, theories, and models of the world that shape our perceptions of the world.

Discovery The act or process of articulating some new fact about the world that is true independently of the presence or mind of the observer.

Induction The process by which singular statements or statements about singular events are used to lend support to universal statements, or statements that are true for all events of a particular type.

Mindfulness A state of active cognitive and emotional engagement with lived experience, leading to the creation of new categories for structuring our understanding of the world.

Mindlessness A state of passive acceptance of concepts and observations, usually involving the categorization of new perceptions in entrenched categories that are not responsive to new experiences.

This article introduces and elaborates the idea of a **MINDFUL STATE OF BEING,** *and applies this idea toward a new understanding of the processes of creation and discovery. A mindful consideration of the world involves the conscious and continuous challenge of the categories and values we use to structure our experience, understand observations, and generate reasons for our actions, and the reconstruction of new categories, values, and concepts to replace old ones. We will show that the processes of creating new patterns of thought and breaking down old patterns are essential features of both processes of artistic "creation" and processes of scientific "discovery." The sharp line that is so often drawn between the ways in which the artist and the scientist approach and relate to the world needs to be reconsidered. Recognizing the elements of artistic creation present in what we now call the process of discovery leads to a new and useful reframing of the work of the scientist, as well as a new perspective of the relevance of the work of the artist in the evolution of knowledge.*

The article is structured in four parts. The first section introduces the concept of mindfulness and discusses its role in the way we use concepts to refer to objects, people, and events. It examines the implications of mindful consideration for the meaning, universality, and coherence of those concepts. The second section explores paths to mindfulness, in part by tracing the roots of the concept to the line of philosophical inquiry into the nature of our knowledge of the external world which began with the works of Hume and Kant. The third section reviews the phenomenology of mindful and mindless states, by reviewing the experimental record of mindfulness research, and establishing the relations which mindfulness enters as a dependent and independent variable. The last section argues that mindful involvement with a phenomenon is a property of processes of creation and discovery alike, and that the line used to distinguish these processes from one another sets forth a misleading distinction. The benefits of seeing discovery as a creative process—rather than a process of passive observation of a "new" phenomenon—are discussed.

I. PRELUDE

If the barber shaves all and only those who do not shave themselves, then who shaves the barber? It cannot be the barber himself, because then *he* would be shaving himself, and he is *only* supposed to shave those who do not shave themselves. Nor can it be someone else, since the barber shaves *all* those who do not shave themselves. By the law of the excluded middle, either the barber shaves himself or he does not (assuming that he is shaven to begin with). Since either statement seems to be excluded by the premises of the problem, we are left in a bind. The logician that we call on our cellular phone tells us the example represents a paradox—a problem whose solution process starts from true premises and reaches false or untenable conclusions by procedurally impeccable steps of reasoning.

To "solve" the paradox, which we can do by claiming that there is no such barber, requires us to step "outside" of the premises as stated and to question the assumptions inherent in the problem statement—to ask whether or not these assumptions are true or unique. To do so, we must resist the temptation to believe that what is said is more relevant or useful than what is left unsaid, as well as the temptation to mechanically apply the laws of logic in a repeated—but futile—search for an answer. Overcoming these temptations represents the step that takes us from a mindless to a mindful involvement with our experience.

II. MINDLESS AND MINDFUL STATES

Mindfulness involves the creation of new categories for organizing our awareness of the world. A precondition for the unfolding of this process is an awareness that the concepts which we currently hold to be coherent are only tentatively and therefore temporarily so. Just like the idea of phlogiston—which was held by 17th century chemists to be the substance given off by a burning object—turned out to be incoherent in view of subsequent stoichiometric analyses of oxidation, so the ideas we currently hold about the foundations of physics and chemistry, and the inferences we draw from these for biology and the social sciences, may turn out to have a far looser grasp on reality than we now think is the case. The predictive imperfection of physical laws may turn out to be related to the nature of the mental objects which we use to formulate those laws.

If concepts are tools with which the mind picks up and handles objects, people, and events rather than direct consequences of the availability of and involvement with certain sensory experiences, then there is no reason to think that these tools are not perfectible—that they cannot be continuously and perpetually improved upon. Improvement of these concepts is a continuous process in which the destruction of old ways of thinking and relating to the world must precede—or at least accompany—the creation of new concepts and ideas. Implicit in this process is an awareness that the categories we are currently using are fallible and potentially incoherent, and that their usage is potentially self-defeating, in the sense that using them leads us to undertake actions which diminish our well-being—by our own definition of it.

Seeing the height of a car as predetermined by constraints outside of our control deprives us of the possibility to navigate through a tunnel whose ceiling is too low for its passage—which we could have accomplished by letting the air out of the car's tires. Seeing a problem as an exercise in the application of the laws of logic prevents us from solving it by challenging its underlying assumptions. Seeing a lamppost as just a lamppost deprives us of a safe place to which we can chain our bicycle. Seeing a piece of chalk as a mere writing implement deprives us of a means to soak up the ink we have spilled on a manuscript. Seeing a dog as a domesticated animal subject to the commands of her owner prevents us from picking up the small child when a Rottweiler is charging with a bizarre look on his face. Seeing a screwdriver, a screw, and a pair of pliers found in the back of the car as a trio of implements with no apparent connection to each other deprives us of an elegant way to open a wine bottle while on a picnic to which we have forgotten the corkscrew. Seeing a wire coat hanger as just a wire coat hanger deprives us of a means of getting into the car in which we have locked our keys. Seeing a can of shaving cream as a mere bathroom implement deprives us of a quick and effective method of removing a fresh red wine stain from a beige carpet. Seeing the instructions for an assignment as given and undiscussable prevents us from proposing—perhaps successfully—to write an essay on a subject which we feel passionate about. Seeing a policeman as the robotic representative of an objectively formulated and immutable body of laws deprives us of the possibility to negotiate a lower penalty for our unwitting infraction. Seeing a cigarette lighter as something we light cigarettes with deprives us of the possibility of using the organic compound in its reservoir to set aflame some damp wood on a cold night. Seeing the apple in our lunch bag as a piece of food deprives us of a projectile with which we could have dislodged the badminton butterfly stuck in a tree.

A mindful state involves the active drawing of distinctions between different raw sense data, and therefore the active creation of categories with which we structure our experience. It involves an openness to new information about the world, especially to information which refutes inherent hypotheses and causal models, and which provides test cases for our concepts and ideas. It also involves an awareness of different perspectives or interpretations of the world—usually corresponding to different minds which "see" in different ways. By contrast, a mindless approach to experience involves a cognitive commitment to inherited categories and causal models of the world, which may be invested with properties like truth and absolute certainty. Necessarily, when we are in a mindless state, we are likely to discount new information, and especially information which challenges or does not fit neatly into the hierarchy of concepts and values we use to understand the world—or to "force fit" the new information into the inherited categories, by coding it, or committing to one understanding of it.

Alternative ways of "seeing" the world are threatening to our mindsets, since they directly challenge the conceptual framework used to categorize observations. Jon Elster's distinction between active and passive negation neatly applies here: a commitment to a rigid mindset represents a passive negation of an alternative point of view, which the subject implicitly—or passively—denies by virtue of not being aware of it. The transformation of passive negation into active negation is already a passage to a more conscious state—which acknowledges the existence and perhaps the threat of the alternative point of view, albeit in a negative sense. Active negation represents, relative to passive negation, an awakening to a more mindful state.

In the section that follows, we shall examine the characteristics which distinguish a mindful from a mindless state by discussing the nature and value of categories, with respect to their universality, verisimilitude, and communicability. We will seek to show that mindfulness and mindlessness are useful concepts for describing the evolution of concepts and categories, and can be used to predict the nature of the knowledge of the world which obtains at the end of an unfolding process of cognitive evolution.

A. On the Nature and Evolution of Categories

When speaking or thinking of our experiences and observations, we inevitably represent real objects, people, and phenomena by words or propositions which act as placeholders for these experiences in our minds. We refer to a person who periodically places some pieces of paper in our mailbox as the mailman; to a person who periodically brushes her teeth for at least 20 minutes while rolling her eyes at a mirror as an obsessive-compulsive; to a vast set of interactions between many people in which some end up with money and others end up with goods and services as a market; to a collection of events involving measurements of kinetic and potential energy in a small region of space as an electron: and to a beautifully shaped collection of viscera, bones, nerves, and muscles which is seemingly capable of thought and feeling as a self or a person. The names that we give our observations are the categories that we shall use to organize our experiences.

Categories have greater or lesser universality, depending on the sharpness of the criteria that we use for deciding whether or not an experienced object or event is an instantiation of a categorical class. Whether we consider the events of August 1991 in the former Soviet Union a coup d'etat or a debacle, for instance, depends on whether or not we define a coup d'etat by the intent of the protagonists or by the ultimate outcomes of their actions. Whether or not we consider a group of people who are sleeping in the same house a family depends on the properties of the relationships between them— genetic relatedness, mating behaviors, psychological closeness—which we choose to ascribe to members of a family.

We discover, by examining the levels of universality at which a category can be applied, that our commitment to various categories is contingent on the criteria that we use to include an observation or experience in a category. At one end of the spectrum, all observed behaviors may be examples of a particular category. Some economists, for example, find instantiations of the maximization of personal utility in all observed human behaviors. By definition, of someone undertakes an action, it is in virtue of some interest or intention which she has had prior to taking it. The action therefore is taken to further the actor's interest—and therefore it is an example of self-interest-maximization. At the other end of the spectrum, there are "categories" which contain a single element—the event or person or object from which they draw their substance. Barring time travel, there is only one initial charge of the French infantry at the battle of Waterloo.

It is only by maintaining a skeptical attitude toward the categories which we are currently using that we can retain the capability to improve upon them, and to make our own ways of expression more truth-like or verisimilar in nature. For example, once the momentum associated with a moving mass has been "defined" as the mass of the object times its velocity, we cannot speak of the "momentum" of a mass traveling at relativistically significant velocities, since the classical definition of momentum does not include a correction for the mass of the particle as a function of its velocity. Once we have settled upon an understanding of a person's actions as instantiations of the axioms of rational choice, we cannot accommodate phenomena such as weakness of will or susceptibility to biased perceptions and judgments.

The first essential feature of a commitment to a flexible and renewable—rather than immutable—set of categories is openness to new information, or the willingness to continuously test existing categories using data to which they purport to be relevant. Just as under a microscope of increasing power solid cells visible to the naked eye give way to intricate structures which in turn give way to more structures, so testing available categories by increasingly nuanced situations to which they are applicable will often reveal that the categories in question give way to fresh—and perhaps predictively more competent—ways of looking at the same information. For example, categorizing a person in terms of his or her personality profile will give way to new understandings of that person once we debrief her on the workings of her mind while she was answering the questions of a personality inventory. At risk, of course, are the categories used to identify various personalities, which may become meaningless or incoherent upon dialogue or reflection.

The universality of the categories we have devised creates the illusion that our thoughts are more communicable through language than is actually the case. People believe that others understand the same meaning that they have intended for a given word or concept, and that others use words the same way in which they use the same words. Deborah Tannen's work has documented important differences in the interpretation of the same situations by men and women. A woman's allusive references to the shortcomings of a project, when sandwiched between laudatory remarks, may be taken by a man to be wholehearted endorsement of the project, contrary to the expectations of the woman interlocutor. When many blind men give their separate accounts of a single elephant after feeling different parts of the animal, their accounts may give the semblance of the presence of many different animals. When clear-sighted people speak of the feelings and the thoughts that the sight of the same elephant arouses in them, they may be misled into thinking that they are experiencing the same feelings by the fact that they are looking at the same elephant and uttering the same words. It is therefore possible for them to find "corroboration" for the validity of the concepts they are using by confounding the phonetic similarity of their words with a similarity or identity of the experiences and thoughts on which those words are based.

An awareness of more than one possible perspective or interpretation of the world involves, therefore, a minimally presumptuous approach to the expressions of others. Our understanding of what someone meant when she said something must remain open to refutation by her subsequent expressions and actions. A mindful interpretation of others' expressions involves a continuous search for the meaning of their sentences, rather than an early commitment to a particular image, or "psychological profile" of that person, and is therefore closely related to a commitment to listening as part of the ethics of a conversation. By contrast, mindless interpretations of others' expressions involve a cognitive commitment to a particular set of motives or circumstances or properties which we impute to a speaker, and which is dispositive of any meaning that she gives her words. for example, we might say that it is in someone's best interest to take a particular view of the world, given her socioeconomic background (wealthy, well educated, never prospectively homeless). This "interpretation" thus provides an excuse for thinking of ways to rebut her arguments, even while she is still talking, instead of listening for new nuances or ways to interpretation.

III. THE PHENOMENOLOGY OF MINDFUL AND MINDLESS STATES

Experimental research by Ellen Langer and her colleagues has documented the precursors and effects of mindless states as well as the conditions that make possible a mindful approach to the world. This section reviews her experimental results by considering mindfulness and mindlessness in turn as dependent and independent variables. In this way, the precursors and benefits of mindful approaches, and the precursors and drawbacks associated with mindless states, can be considered side by side.

A. The Consequences and Precursors of Mindlessness

Mindless behavior can often be distinguished by its consequences and effects, which means that it is often available to scrutiny only retrospectively. Locking ourselves out of a car or throwing socks in the garbage can instead of the laundry basket jolts us awake. William James once told a story of starting to get ready for a dinner and ending up climbing into bed. Two routines that began the same became confused and he mindlessly followed the more familiar one. The phenomenon of mentally locking ourselves into routines and scripted behaviors is—by introspection—pervasive, and seems to have been so at least since the time of Henry David Thoreau, who despaired of the possibility of meeting someone who was truly "awake."

Langer argues from experimental and anecdotal evidence that mindless behavior can be induced by a commitment to a particular role or label given to a person by himself or by others. In a study that pretested the ability of participants to solve simple arithmetic problems, and then assigned participants to roles of "boss" and "assistant" for an impromptu set of interactions, the post-tested ability of the participants labeled "assistants" was significantly less than on the pretest. The label "assistant" undermined the participants' view of their abilities, which impacted performance.

Mindless behavior can also be induced by a commitment to a mindset, perhaps one that generated some good results in the past. Abraham and Edith Hirsch Luchins led participants of an experiment to the discovery of an optimal solution to an arithmetic problem, and then changed the problem so that the initial solution was no longer optimal, but could nevertheless be adjusted to give the required answer. They found that participants were reluctant to "let go" of the initial solution to the problem, even when that solution became nonoptimal. Janice R. Kelly and Joseph E. McGrath asked participants to solve two problems, the first under a significant time constraint and the second under no time constraint. They found that the time pressure experienced by the participants during the first problem carried over to the second problem. It seemed as if the participants had committed themselves to the requirements of the first task.

Mindsets that people use to prejudge a particular state of being or activity can influence their enjoyment of that activity. Labeling an amusing task—playing with the form and content of cartoons—as either "work" or "play" influences the self-reported enjoyment of the process of performing the task. Those to whom it was suggested that the activity was a form of play were more likely to report enjoying the activity than were those to whom it was suggested that the activity was a piece of work.

Cognitive commitments were also shown to influence people's performance on tasks designed to measure presence or awareness. Participants in an experiment were given a description of an imaginary perceptive disorder in which it was implied that they may be suffering from it without knowing it. Some participants were given information which suggested that it was likely that they were affected by the disorder, and others were given information which suggested that it was unlikely that they were suffering from the disorder. Participants who were led to believe that they were probably not subject to the disorder were more often subject to the (simulated) symptoms than were those who thought that they might have the disorder: people in the former group performed more poorly on a task of aural perception than did people in the latter group.

B. The Phenomenology of Mindful Awareness: Some Experimental Results

The most remarkable regularity that emerges from the experimental record is that people are sensitive and open to "awakenings" which challenge them to question their own assumptions and to break down their precognitions. As Langer points out, mindlessness is very different from Freud's conception of willful-not-knowing, which involves the will to actively repress or banish a particular thought. Langer's experiments point to some of the possibilities for opening up inherited categories and mindsets to new information and fresh perspectives. These range from mere promptings to avoid labels, to the conditionalization of propositions and hypotheses about the world.

It has been shown that the label given to a person sharply influences the evaluation of that person even by trained therapists. Participants in an experiment were asked to provide evaluations of a man whose interview was presented to them on videotape. Half the therapists were told that the man is a job applicant, whereas the other half were told that the man is a patient. Those therapists who had been trained on the use of labels saw the man as well adjusted, regardless of the label that he was given by the experimenter. Those therapists who had received no such forewarning were strongly influenced by the label they were given at the

beginning of the experiment: they found the "patient" to have serious psychological problems.

The direct exposure of a person to a concrete problem—as opposed to the exposure to a problem after a period of training in the use of a particular solution—was also found to increase the likelihood that the problem solver will arrive at several possible ways of solving the problem, relative to a person that has received training. College students asked to use a set of building blocks to build a bridge over an imaginary river, and who had no prior exposure to the use of the blocks, came up with a greater number of possible solutions than did students who were shown examples of how the blocks could be used.

The use of conditionalization of concepts and causal relations was also found to lead to a more mindful consideration of the information received. Students to whom a model of urban development was presented in a conditional way (i.e., in which concepts were presented using the construction "A could be B," rather than the construction "A is B" or "A is a model for B") were more successful in making use of the information presented to them than were students who were presented with the information in absolute terms (i.e., using either constructions like "A is B" or constructions like "A is a possible model for B").

In another study, students were given different versions of a typical examination given to stockbrokers. Some versions presented the information in deterministic and closed-ended terms. Other versions presented the information as a set of stylized facts, whose statistical nature was apparent. The students who were presented with the versions of the "facts" that were more open to criticism or to revision generated more creative answers—and reported enjoying reading the material to a greater degree—than did the students who were presented with the deterministically framed information. The implication is that the presentation of models of the world in ways that indistinguishably conflate objects with their representations—which underlies the vast majority of undergraduate curricula in the natural and social sciences—is self-defeating if the purpose of such a presentation is to encourage the creative application of the models to real-world situations.

Empirical investigations have also revealed some effects of mindful consideration on the attitude and motivation of people toward certain activities, other people, or states of being. People asked to engage in an activity which they initially thought of as unpleasant—such as listening to rap music—were more likely to find the activity pleasurable after performing it if they had been asked to notice several novel aspects of the activity than if they were not given instructions before engaging in it. These findings suggest that the myth of well-defined preferences which do not change over time—a staple of normative and positive economic theory for the past 50 years—may be the outcome of a self-fulfilling prophecy, which breaks down when people engage in the activities mindfully.

IV. MINDFUL APPROACHES TO THE WORLD: SOME LINKS TO THE PHILOSOPHY OF KNOWLEDGE

The "paradox" of mindfulness is that if the attainment of a mindful state could be enacted by following a prescription, an algorithm, or a program, then that state would cease to be mindful. Analogously to self-contradictory impulses like "be spontaneous" or "try to forget her," the injunction "be mindful by following these simple rules" is self-defeating, for it is precisely in the escape from rigid rules and rule-based behavior that the essential characteristic of a mindful state lies. The path to mindfulness must itself be created, and therefore is itself the outcome of a mindful state.

As noted previously, a precondition for the unfolding processes of cognitive creation and destruction is a skeptical or at least modest appraisal of the current concepts and ideas which we use to understand the world. Occasions for learning to be modest are to be found even in our daily experience. As Rupert Riedl has shown, a visit to the house of a new friend can throw doubt on intuitions about causes and effects which are so evident that they seem necessary or inescapable:

It is late in the day and the shadows have fallen. The house we enter is unknown to us, but the situation is familiar. It is too dark in the entrance hall to read the name plates. Where is the light switch? There—three buttons. It's probably the top one. We push it and immediately jump back: for as long as the finger was on the switch, a bell shrilled through the whole house

(and then the fluorescent light flickers on as well). Embarrassing! It must have been the doorbell (or did we also cause the light to come on?) A door opens behind us. Have we roused the tenants too? But no! It is the front door. "Excuse me" says the person coming in, "I thought the door was already locked." Did he then cause the bell to ring and did we turn the light on after all? Apparently. But why do we expect to be the cause of an unexpected coincidence, namely, the simultaneous occurrence of the touching of the switch and the sound of the bell?

Riedl has similarly shown that seemingly unimpeachable intuitions and expectations about causes that underlie our most indignant moral sentiments may turn out to be lamentably erroneous:

People are getting on a streetcar in Vienna. Among the passengers is a working class woman with her young son. The boy has an enormous bandage wrapped around his head. (How dreadful! What happened to him?) People give up their seats to the afflicted pair. The bandaging is not a professional job, it was obviously done at home and in a hurry; they must be on their way to the hospital (people secretly search the child's face for an explanation, and the bandage for traces of blood). The little boy whines and fusses (signs of sympathy from everyone). The mother seems unconcerned (how inappropriate!); she even shows signs of impatience (that is amazing). The little one begins to fidget; his mother pushes him back in his seat. The passengers' attitude changes from discrete observation to manifest concern. (The mother's behavior is disgraceful!) The boy cries and tries to climb the bench on which they are sitting. His mother pulls him back so roughly that even the bandage is beginning to shake. (The poor child! This is terrible!) The passengers' mood turns to open confrontation. The mother is criticized, but for her part rejects all interference. Now she is criticized again, and more openly. Thereupon she tells them to mind their own business and questions the competence of all those who criticized her. (That is too much! An outrage to human decency) Emotions run high, and things get noisy and turbulent. The child is bawling; his mother, red-faced and furious, declares she is going to show us what is the matter and begins (to everybody's horror) tearing off the whole bandage. What appears is a metal chamber pot that the little Don Quixote has pushed so tightly on his head that it is stuck; they are on their way to get help from the nearest plumber. People get off the streetcar in great embarrassment.

It is possible, and desirable, to go further and to seek an explanation of the very nature of causation, rather than merely challenge various proposed causal links. Philosopher David Hume criticized our knowledge of causal relations by first arguing that we are rationally justified in believing that one event (a B event) will follow another event (an A event) if we are justified in believing that nature is uniform—that the laws of nature are invariant across time. We are justified in believing that nature is uniform either by a priori reasoning (of the type, "axioms of real axis mean that (2 + 2) mod 10 = 4 could not possibly be false") or by our own experience. A priori reasoning fails because we can imagine a set of axioms which imply that nature is not uniform (one axiom could be, "nature is not uniform, although it seemed that way up to time = T"). We are left to our experience, which means that we are justified in believing that nature is uniform only if we are justified in believing that our past observations of uniformity imply that nature will be uniform in the future. But we are justified in believing this statement only if we are justified in believing that nature is uniform. So we are justified in believing that nature is uniform only if we are *already* justified in believing that nature is uniform, which we are not. Hume characterizes causation as a habitual construction of the mind.

Mindless approaches to choice involve the acceptance of inherited categories, either from one's own experience, or from other minds. These categories can be of the type, "an A event is of the type that causes a B event," given some inductive evidence for this relationship. This inductive evidence can be very scarce: a chance observation, the opinion of a person which the mind has labeled as an expert, and so forth. Therefore a mindless approach to choice is equivalent to the mechanical acceptance of a view of causation which Hume has criticized.

Another aspect of mindless approaches to choice which can be understood from a Humean perspective has to do with propositions of the form, "an A event in the world will cause a B event in the mind." This sort

of causal reasoning can lead to inferences of the sort, "being with person x has made me feel bad. I will feel bad next time I am with person x. Therefore being with person x is undesirable." Here "I" is using inductive evidence to predict her own affective response to a stimulus which she has experienced before. This is a form of mindlessness. One cannot "know" how one will feel, but can only suppose that one will feel in a certain way. By developing a cognitive commitment to that "guess," one may be precluding the possibility of feeling in a different way (or taking a different action).

Now let us turn to mindful approaches to choice. How do we draw distinctions anew? By referring to properties of objects, events, and phenomena. How do we know of these properties, and how do we know that these properties will "hold" in the future? By a mechanism akin to induction. We use spatiotemporal boundaries to categorize events, and we assume a Euclidean geometry of space, coupled with a Newtonian conception of time (flowing equably from an absolute past to an absolute future). How do we know that such a mechanism for categorization will work in the future? Because it has worked well in the past. What are the logical grounds for our belief in this regularity? Again, our experience. We reach the same sort of circularity which was reached by Hume in the case of causation, which requires some antecedent justification for the concept of causation not to be found in the elements or the temporal sequence of the elements of a presumed causal chain.

The idea of causation is also useful to an understanding of the nature of categories, and to their limitations and boundaries. Quite often, what makes the properties of objects or people what they are, and therefore what makes objects or people what they are, is their causal powers. The causal powers of a piece of chalk, for example, can be used to distinguish between properties that seem essential (like solubility in water and white color) and properties that seem inessential (like being in the left pocket of a person's skirt, or being 300 miles south of a Ford Pinto—these properties can be altered by a changing anything about the objects that they describe, for example, by shaking the skirt or moving the Pinto).

The category in which we place a person or an object has something to do with what we believe its properties to be—otherwise we would treat categories as mere conventions and would stop seeking to "make sense" to one another in a more than conventional sense. Queries about causation will therefore also be queries about categories, to the extent that we use the causal powers of an object to draw the boundaries of a category to which that object belongs. If we challenge the notion that causation is "objective," or that it reflects a property of reality that is independent of our minds, then we will simultaneously challenge the notion that the categories which we are currently using to organize our experience are objective, and accept the role of the mind in determining what we refer to as real.

In as far as the history of people's presence in the world is also a history of people's ideas about the world and therefore of the relationship between their minds and their experiences, we are interested in mindfulness as a way of looking at the evolution of ideas. Mindless approaches to experience map onto dogmatic perspectives, whose exponents seek to "prove," verify, or justify their theories by means of repeated confrontations of the theory and data sets that emerge from preplanned programs of empirical investigation. Mindfulness, on the other hand, does not entail a single approach to the evolution of consciousness or awareness of the world. A commitment to any particular epistemological program entails a commitment to a particular set of categories, and to a discursive form of referring to those categories. Such a commitment therefore runs contrary to an unconstrained way of knowing the world, and to a fallibilist approach to knowledge.

We shall consider, in what follows, the two most well-known approaches to the historical evolution of concepts: Karl Popper's description of the evolution of "objective" knowledge by a repeated process of trial and error carried out by many (like-minded, fallibilist) people over a long period of time, and Georg Wilhelm Friedrich Hegel's description of the evolution of consciousness through a dialectic process, by which ideas are refuted or negated, and expanded and turned upon themselves by confrontations with their antitheses and transformations into syntheses. These descriptions of the passage of the mind through the world are illuminating, but not unique or necessary. We will argue that they *describe* possible mindful approaches to the world—in the sense that they incorporate openness to new information and alternative points of view and

leave open the creation of new categories—but do not *define* or otherwise constrain such approaches. Furthermore, neither has a built-in mechanism for excluding a mechanical, automated, or mindless application of its form to the problem of reconciling our cognitions with our experiences. We shall explore—in order to illustrate this antinecessitarian point—some alternative descriptions of the evolution of ideas in time.

A. Popper and the Discourse of Trial and Error

Popper wanted to portray the evolution of human thought as a sequence of trials and errors, which leads to a "growth" of the knowledge we have of the world. The "scientific method," which his *Logik der Forschung* is credited with making explicit, is a process by which a person faced with a concrete problem offers, tentatively, a theory by way of a solution to that problem. He then proceeds to criticize that theory, most importantly from an empirical standpoint, by comparing the predictions and empirical statements of that theory with empirical observations of the phenomenon one is trying to predict, influence, or control. A theory withstands or does not withstand such criticism according to whether or not the empirical statements it generates are *logically* contradicted by the empirical statements generated by the experience of the person in question. The logical law of the excluded middle—by which a statement is either true or false, but not both, nor neither—is therefore the engine of progress in the history of knowledge, in Popper's model. Theories that have withstood the most vigorous criticism of this sort are accepted only provisionally. Their ultimate truth or falsity remains forever an open question.

The only apparent constraint which the scientific method places on the scientist is that of adherence to a particular form of criticism—that of empirical testing—which requires that theories be expressed in a falsifiable form, or a form which makes them refutable by empirical observations. The scientist is free to use any association of thoughts and ideas, any conceivable ontology, and any means of generating empirical statements from these thoughts, in order to arrive at the empirical statements required by Popper. Furthermore, one of the desiderata which the scientific method seems to strive for is that of openness to new information, which it accomplishes by requiring that theories be put through the most rigorous empirical tests, and accepted only provisionally when they have passed these tests.

It must be observed, however, that the application of the scientific method critically depends on the application of the law of the excluded middle in order to adjudicate between alternative hypotheses. The disappearance of this "engine of natural selection" among competing theories is what makes the dialectic, to Popper's mind, unappealing as a description of the evolution of knowledge. He argues that the simultaneous acceptance of thesis and antithesis via their incorporation into the synthesis, in the case in which they contradict one another, amounts to the acceptance of *any* proposition whatsoever, by a straight application of the laws of logic. This criticism, however, is based on the assumptions that the collective, shared consciousness of the world which is generated by the application of the scientific method is in fact an objective knowledge of the world—a knowledge whose truth-likeness is not dependent on the interpretative acts and thoughts of a person possessing it, and that the progress of objective knowledge is "powered" by the application of the law of the excluded middle for the purpose of criticizing theories. The first assumption is required because Popper makes knowledge itself—rather than the consciousness of the knower—the subject of his criticism. Describing knowledge as an objective, independent entity requires us to create a rule separating actuality from mere possibility, whereas saying that only states of consciousness—combining knowledge with the will to know—exist does not entail the rejection of contradictions on the grounds that they can generate any statement, unless we also assume that there exists the will to apply the laws of logic to that end. One must *want* to generate the universe of all possible statements from a contradiction in order for this universe to come into being. Accepting either of these assumptions is the outcome of an act of will—their acceptance is not required by any sort of precognition or ascertainably true precondition.

That such an acceptance of the assumptions underlying the scientific method *must* be the outcome of an act of will—rather than the inevitable consequence of the aim of arriving at truth-like descriptions of the world—is supported by the proof that Popper's definition of verisimilitude cannot be used to discriminate between two false theories so as to judge one theory to be more truth-like than another theory. In conjunction with Popper's fallibilist doctrine—which states that all theories are sooner or later shown to be false—the result entails that there is no "progress" in scientific knowledge—at least not to the extent that progress is defined by the evolution of more truth-like theories out of less truth-like theories.

B. Hegel and the Dialectic Process

The dialectic evolution of thought is based on the interplay of three concepts: The thesis is an idea or a proposition that emerges or is put forth; the antithesis is a refutation or negation of the thesis. It springs forth against the thesis, seeking to deny its substance. The synthesis represents the merging together of the thesis and the antithesis, perhaps with the aim of recognizing the merits and limitations of both. The synthesis then itself becomes a thesis, and the process begins anew.

Hegel introduces the idea of the dialectic by way of an example which suggests that he did not think of the thesis and the antithesis as propositions which may be connected by a logical relationship like mutual contradiction, and reminds us that he did not hold fast to the definition of truth as a correspondence between the content of a statement and the content of an observation.

> The bud disappears in the bursting-forth of the blossom, and one might say that the former is refuted by the latter; similarly, when the fruit appears, the blossom is shown up in its turn as a false manifestation of the plant, and the fruit now emerges as the truth instead. These forms are not just distinguished from one another, they also supplant one another as mutually incompatible. Yet at the same time their fluid nature makes them moments of an organic unity in which they not only do not conflict, but in which each is as necessary as the other. . . .

Whereas the scientific method assigns a predominantly *critical* role to the mind, Hegel's view assigns the mind a creative and generative role. Not only does consciousness of the world change over time, but the criteria for demarcation between illusion and consciousness also change. No such freedom is available to one who follows the scientific method, who must conform to a correspondence theory of truth and to the law of the excluded middle in order to keep the engine of criticism running.

C. Two Alternative Views of the Evolution of Mind

The processes of dialectic reasoning and of trial and error are two of several possible approaches to the evolution of thought. The following two are put forth as examples based on loosening two of the constraints which logical structure places on the method of trial and error proposed by Popper. Because Hegel's broader conception of the evolution of consciousness by a process of turning-upon-itself can be seen to subsume both the idea of the dialectic and discursive alternatives to Aristotelian logic, the two examples can be interpreted as workings-out of that conception.

1. Necessity, Possibility, and the Openness of the Past and Present

If we were to replace the relation of necessity or entailment in logic with one of possibility or enablement, we would achieve a discourse which highlights the role of the processes of imagination and interpretation, rather than that of calculation. The reason for this is that the number of possibilities—or options for action or belief—that we can generate increases with the number of interpretations that we can give to our current psychological states. If an experience is categorized unconditionally, in a way which inhibits further, playful consideration of its meaning, penumbra, or resonance, and if the categories we use are, in our minds, linked by relationships of logical necessity, then the states that we are led to by a single experience will be determined or fixed by the working of the logical apparatus we have at our disposal. Increasing the number of interpretations that we are willing to give to a single experience therefore will also increase the number of possible options for action or the number of possible psychological states which we can take on following that experience.

The replacement of the logic of necessity with the logic of possibility can be accomplished by an exchange of the will to know, or determine or control the future for the will to play with our relationship to the present and the past. Popper argued persuasively, in the context of his numerous lucid presentations of

the scientific method, that "the future is open" in the sense that our subsequent experiences may at any time refute our current beliefs. Loosening the bolts of logical argumentation can lead to psychological states in which the past and present are also open to creative interpretation—at the cost of a decreased sharpness of the relationship of denial or refutation.

2. Participation, the Interpretation of Events, and the Openness of Ontology

If we replace the process of constatation or "passive" observation that is supposed to provide the empirical tests of a theory with a process of participation or creative interpretation in the experience which we now describe as observation, then we will arrive at a "story" about the evolution of knowledge that is markedly different from that embodied in Popper's account of the scientific method. The approach that emerges is based on the relationship between the observer's observation of an event and his conscious participation in his observation of that phenomenon. For example, one could be observing an event, observing oneself observe that event, and observing the observation of the observation. The resulting state of mind can be reduced to a mere constative statement by the reductively minded scientist. However, such a reduction would prevent us from exploring the possibilities which the quality of reflexivity—or active participation in our own experiences—affords us. We could not, for example, gauge the effect of the observation on ourselves, or the effects of becoming conscious of that effect, and so forth.

A reductionist approach also truncates unnecessarily our representation of experience: if the essential properties of an object or person are connected to its causal powers, then the results of someone's experience of that object—her thoughts and actions, including the names she gives that object—are part of the causal powers of the object. Calling a facial expression a smile, for example, becomes part of the essential properties of that event—since a smile can be the cause of another smile or of a grimace.

Loosening the constraints we place on the link between experiences and statements about experiences leads us to an approach to descriptions which is reflexive as well as constative. In turn, this approach permits the incorporation of the process of interpretation and conscious participation of an event into the description of that event, and therefore makes the description open to revision after confrontation with additional information, or with the interpretations which others give to the same event. As in the case of the replacement of the logic of necessity with the logic of possibility, the replacement of descriptions closed to reflexive interpretation by descriptions open to reflexive interpretation must be the outcome of a will to replace a focus on predicting or expecting a particular future with a concern for an active participation in the present. The replacement of descriptions with reflexive interpretations leads to an ontology—a representation of what exists—that is itself open to evolution.

V. MINDFULNESS, CREATION, AND DISCOVERY

We are accustomed to thinking about the process of artistic creation in sharply different terms from that of scientific discovery. On this view, the artist creates new forms and images from inherent or given elements, whereas the scientist breaks down his perceptions and observations into elemental components and systems, in order to understand them. Whereas "reality" for the artist involves a component of active participation of her mind and is therefore created, enacted, or brought about by a conscious act of will, for the scientist "reality" is an object of passive observation—of discovery through repeated observations and criticisms of those observations. In all instances, "reality" stands independently of the will and imagination of the scientist, and his involvement in it is either passive or supposedly governed by the impersonal laws of rational discourse. Thus, just as reason and desire, or affect and cognition, are thought of as independent aspects of being, so the scientist's contemplation and analysis of reality is divorced from the artist's creation and interpretation of it.

We would like to show that this view is mistaken, by showing that the hypotheticodeductive method can be understood as one possible instrument of interpretation, whose application leads to intelligible results by an act of will and imagination very similar to the artist's activity. Testing a hypothesis by comparing its content with that of empirical statements is a process whose outcome depends on the choice of hypothesis and the interpretation of an observation used to produce an empirical statement. Even simple empirical attributes like "being red" are outcomes of an interpretation of a sense datum, rather than direct representations of that datum. Attempts to "depersonalize" observations by substituting "emitting radiation with a wavelength of x nm" for "being red" replace one act of interpreting a sense datum (i.e., interpreting a sensation by the proposition "is red") by another (i.e., interpreting a visual perception by the proposition "is equal to x nm"). When by "observation" we mean "intelligible empirical statement," there is no "immediate" access to our experiences: the mind participates, to a greater or lesser extent, in the creation of an intelligible interpretation.

The process of generating hypotheses that can be tested against a set of empirical statements or theories which inspire new programs of empirical inquiry can also be interpreted as a creative process. We have, to begin with, considerable freedom to choose the elementary propositions—or axioms—which will lead to a set of mutually exclusive and collectively exhaustive hypotheses that can be tested against our "intelligible empirical statements." Events—in and of themselves—cannot refute or corroborate one another. It is only statements about events that can stand in such logical relationships vis-à-vis one another, and then only relative to a system of self-consistent axioms. If we were to admit contradictory axioms to stand side by side in a logical system, then we would have to accept any hypothesis as following with equal logical force from those axioms, and therefore would have to accept any hypothesis as being corroborated by any empirical statement.

To see this, consider how we might produce equally logically impeccable proofs of the statements, "the president beat his wife" and "the president did not beat his wife," from the logically contradictory statements, "today is Tuesday" and "today is not Tuesday." First, from the premise "today is Tuesday," we can deduce the consequent, "either the president beat his wife or today is Tuesday" (since "$p \rightarrow p \land q$"). Second, from the two premises "today is not Tuesday" and "the president beat his wife or today is Tuesday," we can deduce the consequent, "the president beat his wife" (since $\sim p \ \& \ (p \land q) \rightarrow q$). By an analogous process, we can prove the proposition, "the president did not beat his wife," or any other proposition that we choose. It follows from this argument that the process of hypothesis testing only establishes the truth value of the tested propositions if the theory that generates the alternative hypotheses is self-consistent. If the theory contains a contradiction, then any hypothesis can be derived with equal logical force from it, and the test of a hypothesis will no longer provide an empirical test of the theory in question.

To illustrate the difference between creation and discovery, consider how we might describe the process of proving a hypothesis like "there are no more than 220 prime numbers in the set of the first 1,000 real numbers." (A prime number is a whole number which is divisible only by 1 and itself.) The aim of this example is to show that even cases of cognition that appear to sharply constrain the process of "knowing" and to leave little room for the mindful will of the "knower" can be thought of as creative processes, and leave room for the imagination of the "problem solver" or "innovator."

The argument, as given by Gabriel Stolzenberg, may go as follows:

> The number of primes that come up in the first 1,000 natural numbers already "exists," as a property of the system of whole numbers. Whatever this number is, it is only our imperfect computational powers and memory that is preventing us from knowing it at this instant. We can, given time and some computational resources, remedy this deficiency and produce an algorithm—like the sieve of Erathosthenes—which can produce the correct number of primes whose values lie between 0 and 1,001. This calculation will then provide an answer to the problem—an answer which already "exists," independently of our cognition of it. Therefore the act of producing that number is one of discovering the correct answer, just like we might discover an object hidden by a friend in a place known only to him in a crowded room.

This argument assumes that once we have constructed a logical structure, that structure has a series of properties which can be understood in a way which does not depend on the mind that is performing the process of understanding.

Stolzenberg further argues that the number of prime numbers lying between 0 and 1,001 is a state of knowledge, not an objectively existing quantity. We create, by our counting of those numbers, or by applying a particular algorithm for generating the number of primes within a certain value range, a state of consciousness or a state of mind corresponding to the representation of a number. Once we have created that state of mind, we can easily communicate it, by means of a written or spoken word, to another mind, thus creating an inexpensive "replica" of this state of mind. Without the will to create that state of mind—indeed, without the will which created the representation we know as the system of numbers—there would have been no "matter of fact" about the proposition, "there are at least 220 prime numbers lying between 0 and 1,001."

The argument can be developed further, and in a way which highlights the advantages of seeing the proof of the proposition as a process of creation. Whereas the outcome of a process of discovery is a finite number or fact, perfectly matched to the demands of the demonstration or the question asked, the outcome of the process of creating a state of mind is a complex mental object which has many qualities. For example, part of the state of mind that is created by computing the number of primes that occur between 0 and 1,001 may be the complexity of the algorithm used to calculate the number and the annoyance produced by the waste of time spent computing, or an appreciation for the aesthetic value of the algorithm. Part of that state of mind may also be a fresh insight into the distribution of primes in the natural number system, or an inspired guess at the proof of an "unsolved" problem of number theory. If the problem solver reflects upon the state of mind that she has created as part of the process of answering a question put to her, she will be aware of these qualities and heed the temptations packed in each of them: to refine the algorithm used or to attempt to create a proof of an unsolved theory. By contrast, if the process is understood as one of discovery, then the quest of the mind is "at an end" once it has reached an answer.

VI. CONCLUDING COMMENTS

If one grain of sand does not suffice to change something from a heap of sand into a nonheap of sand, and if a 10,000-grain pile of sand is a heap, then a 9,999-grain collection is also a heap. If we apply the process recursively 9,999 times, we arrive at the conclusion that a grain of sand is a heap. If we start from the premise that a 1-grain collection of sand is not a heap and apply our little logical machine in reverse, we discover that a 10,000-grain collection is not a heap, which means that it is a heap and is not a heap simultaneously, from a logical point of view. But, since any statement follows from this contradiction, referring to "heaps" presents a problem to those who want to test hypotheses about the properties of heaps.

Attempting to provide a logical justification "from first principles" for categories formed by the mind on the basis of experience and expectation, and thus to "ground" or even to constrain the process of forming categories, is a misguided enterprise: it is self-defeating by the standards of success of its own practitioners. The transition from a view of experience as the chronic instantiation of the same "forms" or categories to one which continuously creates new representations will most likely hinge on people's will to exchange the logic of necessity and the spirit of discovery for the discourse of possibility and the process of creation.

Bibliography

Bodner, T., Waterfield, R., & Langer, E. (1996). *Mindfulness in finance.* Manuscript in preparation, Harvard University.

Chanowitz, B., & Langer, E. (1981). Premature cognitive commitment. *Journal of Personality and Social Psychology, 41,* 1051–1063.

Hegel, G. W. F. (1977). *Phenomenology of spirit* (A. V. Miller, Trans.). Oxford: Oxford University Press. (Original work published 1807)

Kelly, J. R., & McGrath, J. E. (1985). Effects of time limits and task types on task performance and interaction of four-person groups. *Journal of Personality and Social Psychology, 49,* 395–407.

Langer, E. (1989). *Mindfulness.* Reading, MA: Addison-Wesley.

Langer, E., Hatem, M., Joss, J., & Howell, M. (1989). Conditional teaching and mindful learning: The role of uncertainty in education. *Creativity Research Journal, 2,* 139–150.

Luchins, A., & Luchins, E. (1942). Mechanization in problem solving: The effect of Einstellung. *Psychological Monographs, 54*(6).

Popper, K. (1940). What is dialectic? *Mind* (New Supplement), *49.*

Putnam, H. (1989). *Representation and reality.* Cambridge, MA: MIT Press.

Riedl, R. (1984). The consequences of causal thinking. In P. Watzlawick (Ed.), *The invented reality.* New York/London: Norton.

Searle, J. (1984). *Minds, brains and science.* Cambridge, MA: Harvard University Press.

Shoemaker, S. (1980). Causality and properties. In S. Shoemaker (Ed.), *Identity, cause and mind.* Cambridge: Cambridge University Press.

Stolzenberg, G. (1984). Can an inquiry into the foundations of mathematics tell us anything interesting about mind? In P. Watzlawick (Ed.), *The invented reality.* New York/London: Norton.

Misjudgment

Mark A. Runco

California State University, Fullerton

Associative History Creators may think their work is unoriginal because they know that they had other ideas that resembled the one that they eventually share. In other words, creators are aware of the associative history of their insight.

Consensual Assessment Uses judges to identify and rate the creativity of products.

Expert Bias A rigidity or inflexibility that follows from large investments, such as investments of time into a particular field or topic. Expertise thus may bias the expert, making the shifts of perspective that often lead to creative insight quite difficult.

Fundamental Attribution Error Applies to creativity when the potential creator focuses on the context to explain his or her own original actions. An audience or judge of the same original act will tend to focus on the creator him- or herself (and disregard contextual factors).

Misinformation Incorrect data that lead judgment astray.

Problem of circularity Who is to judge the judges? And the judges of the judges?

Representative Heuristic A cognitive tendency which may lead to misjudgment. It occurs when an individual relies on information that is not indicative of some large population or reality.

Reputational Path The change in a creator's fame that occurs through history. Some creators become more famous and some less, and some have reputations that remain fairly stable.

Whiggist Bias Historical misjudgments named after the Whiggists who judged predecessors using contemporary ideals rather than the values common to the historical period being judged.

Creativity requires some sort of judgment on the part of the individual creator him- or herself, and often by some audience. There are, however, a number of biases which may make accurate judgments difficult. Misinformation and ignorance also frequently distort judgments about creativity. This article reviews cases where **MISJUDGMENT** *has occurred, gives examples of biases and reasons for the use of misinformation, and explores the relevance to the research on creativity.*

I. INTRODUCTION

Creativity can be unequivocal and unambiguous. Sometimes it is ambiguous, however, and sometimes it must be inferred from indicators that are not entirely reliable. Many human behaviors can also be ambiguous, but uncertainties about creativity are especially acute. This is because creativity is inherently unpredictable. Creativity must be original, originality in turn assumes novelty, and this implies that the same behavior or product is different from what came before it. That ensures a level of unpredictability. [*See* NOVELTY.]

With this in mind it is not surprising that creativity is often misjudged. Sometimes this leads to assignments of incorrect labels, as is the case when children who tend to give original answers in school are labeled troublemakers or nonconformists. The implications are significant: the creativity of those children may never be reinforced and their potential unfulfilled. [*See* CONTRARIANISM.]

Misjudgment is not limited to the classroom. History is replete with examples of misjudged, overlooked, and ignored creative persons and works. Creative work is often misjudged in its own time and only later receives credit. Reputations are often lost, as well. When this occurs, who is to say which judgment is correct? Are contemporaries the best judges of creativity, or is a historical perspective the most accurate?

Judgments are necessary for several kinds of creativity research (consensual assessments, studies of the old age style, archival research), and accuracy is vital in each. Misjudgment is therefore an important topic of study. By recognizing the frequency of misjudgment, we may minimize bias and more accurately identify creative persons and creative works. [*See* ARCHIVAL INVESTIGATION; CONSENSUAL ASSESSMENT; OLD AGE STYLE.]

Bias is not the only cause of misjudgment. It may also result from general inattention or a misunderstanding of creativity. Historical misjudgments may occur from misinformation or ignorance (i.e., a lack of information). These influences will be explored after examples of misjudgment are reviewed.

II. EXAMPLES OF MISJUDGED CREATIVE PERSONS AND WORKS

The Beatles changed rock 'n' roll. Yet in 1963 the Decca Recording Company stated, "We don't like their sound. Groups of guitars are on the way out." Capitol Records also failed to recognize the appeal of the

Beatles, at least in 1964. They decided, "We don't think they'll do anything in this market."

Writers are often misjudged. The publisher of the Popular Library was, for example, certain that Richard Bach's "*Jonathan Livingston Seagull* will never make it as a paperback." A review of Lewis Carroll's *Alice in Wonderland* pointed out that "we fancy that any real child might be more puzzled than enchanted by this stiff, overwrought story."

The Editor of the *San Francisco Examiner* told Rudyard Kipling, "I'm sorry, Mr. Kipling, but you just don't know how to use the English language."

Sometimes misjudgment is directed at media or technologies. In 1910 the publication *The Independent* felt that the cinema was a "fad [that] will die out in the next few years."

Rembrandt was an unambiguously creative artist. He was, however, not that well respected in his own time. Other artists (e.g., Jan Lievens and Adrien va der Werff) were much more respected. Picasso's work was described as "the work of a madman" by the art dealer Vollard in 1907.

Leonardo da Vinci epitomizes a Renaissance man. But in his own time he was often seen as more of an eccentric than anything. He often worked in secret, because of possible negative public reactions. This says something about what may be required to do creative work. The creator may need to take a risk or disregard public reaction and rely on intrinsic values and motives. No wonder intrinsic motivation and an openness to risk taking are widely recognized correlates of creative work. Many of Leonardo's inventions (e.g., the helicopter) were not appreciated during his own time but were eventually revisited and completed.

The monk Gregor Mendel discovered some basic genetic tendencies in his research on peas. His work was completely overlooked for nearly 50 years.

Ben Franklin is often regarded as a brilliant inventor and statesman. Apparently his talents were not as well respected in his own lifetime. According to Bill Bryson, author of *Made in America,* many of Franklin's contemporaries had difficulty tolerating Franklin's involvement in the politics of the time.

Consider next the Gettysburg Address, now widely accepted as one of the greatest of the speeches by U.S. Presidents. It was not always widely respected. Immediately after the speech reactions were quite critical.

The *Chicago Times* referred to Lincoln's "flat and dishwatery utterances." Yet throughout most of the latter part of this century school children have been asked to memorize the words.

Inventions may be particularly difficult to judge. Their value and practical implications may be difficult to appreciate in the early forms. Franklin's genius may have been clearest in his inventions, and these may have required time so the implications could be explored. [*See* INVENTION.]

Franklin does seem to have been eccentric, and eccentricity is not uncommon among creative individuals. This eccentricity may be a cause or an effect of the creative work; but in any case this may itself elicit unfavorable judgments. [*See* ECCENTRICITY.]

One more example must be given of misjudged inventiveness. I am referring to the Wright brothers. Very few people working on the problems of flight believed the Wrights could succeed—they were bicycle makers. Even after the first few flights, the Wrights had trouble selling their ideas. The practical implications of flight were not at all clear, early on. The Wright brothers and their invention were both misjudged. The flights in Kitty Hawk were not formally acknowledged for decades. The first flight took place just after the turn of the century—in 1903, to be precise—but the Wright flier was in storage (in a small shed) for 25 years. The shed was in Dayton, Ohio, hometown of the Wrights. The Flier was eventually put on display in London. That lasted 14 years. It was not appreciated and showcased by the Smithsonian Museum until 1942, 39 years after the flight in Kitty Hawk.

III. INFLUENCES ON MISJUDGMENT

It may be that certain fields are more open than others to bias and misjudgment. As noted above, inventions may be particularly difficult to judge until implications have been discovered. Note, however, that the examples given above cover a range of domains.

Time can contribute to misjudgment. This typically occurs when someone looking at earlier eras uses his or her own contemporary perspective, rather than taking historical relativity into account. This kind of misjudgment has been labeled "Whiggest history." As Linda Joffee described the notorious Henry VIII, "if viewed according to the values of his own age, Henry's concern to produce an heir at whatever cost would have been seen by his contemporaries as a highly appropriate preoccupation for a man in his position" (1991).

Stephen Jay Gould gave the 18th century Dutch painter and physician Petrus Camper as an example. Apparently Camper was certain that particular facial angles characterized universal good looks. This is now refuted, but as Gould explained, "Camper lived in a different world, and we cannot single him out for judgment when he idly repeats the commonplaces of his age (nor, in general, may we evaluate the past by the present, if we hope to understand our forebears)" (1991, p. 238). Gould described inappropriate judgments as Whiggist "in dubious memory of those Whig historians who evaluated predecessors exclusively by their adherence to ideals of Whig politics unknown in their own time" (1991, p. 343).

Historical judgments are not always biased and inaccurate. In fact, the historical perspective is often highly respected. It is, for instance, seen as necessary in some areas of creativity research. In his article in the 1993 *Creativity Research Journal* on old age style, Martin Lindauer suggested that

> the age-old works of contemporary artists may be difficult to evaluate until after they have died, that is, until sufficient time has passed for some reconsideration. Contemporary critics may be highly critical of the older works of contemporary artists if their evaluations are biased in favor of the late-life characteristics of artists from previous generations. (p. 17)

Carl Rogers proposed much the same in his book, *On Becoming a Person*. He suggested that "no contemporary mortal can satisfactorily evaluate a creative product at the time it is formed, and this statement is increasingly true the greater the novelty of the creative product" (p. 351). Rogers also argued that the value of the creative product is in the eyes of the creator, rather than judges, experts, or audience.

IV. INTRAPERSONAL MISJUDGMENT

Creators themselves may misjudge their own work. Lincoln thought he failed with the Gettysburg Address.

Goethe believed his theory of optics was his most important work, rather than his poetry. Ben Franklin must have felt there was some value in his collection of American slang terms for drunkenness—or perhaps he was having fun when he researched it. He identified 228 such terms.

Creators may think their work is unoriginal because they know that they had other ideas that resembled the one that they eventually share. In other words, creators are aware of the associative history of their ideas. Moreover, an idea may seem quite logical, if you spend a great deal of time thinking about a particular topic; but to others who do not invest that much time, the same idea may seem quite unique. Not surprisingly, judgments of creators often differ from those of an audience or those given by judges. But who is to say who is correct? Who is to judge the judges? And the judges of the judges? This might be called the problem of circularity.

V. EXPERT MISJUDGMENT

Experts are far from immune to misjudgment. Indeed, some biases are more likely in experts than in others. One bias is especially relevant to creativity. It is a rigidity or closed-mindedness that may always accompany expertise. Experts invest heavily in their fields, but that means that they have a great deal to lose if their expertise is undermined. This parallels the idea of investment in economics. With a larger investment, more is at stake, so changes are resisted. In behavioral terms, experts will be biased toward their field or topic of expertise and resistant to alternatives. Such closed-mindedness and rigidity can make creativity difficult. It suggests that the creativity of experts tends to be of a particular kind—within their own field—and rarely if ever of the kind that involves synthesis, integration, or dramatic shifts of perspective.

Experts may also use inappropriate standards. Consider the use of expert artists as judges of student artwork. The experts may be judging the artwork based on its manifest quality rather than its potential. They may compare it to professional work rather than to other student art. (Of course, the question is really about what is being predicted. If artwork is to be evaluated in terms of the likelihood that the artist will eventually succeed as a professional, then professionals are probably the best judges. If artwork is part of a student

art show or the like, expert judges may not be the best choice for judges.)

The problem of expert misjudgment is not limited to the arts. In 1898 the U.S. Patent Commissioner claimed, "everything that can be invented has been invented." The "expert bias" mentioned above, which necessarily follows from heavy investments and expertise, will apply across fields.

VI. MISINFORMATION: GARBAGE IN, GARBAGE OUT

Misjudgment probably results primarily from misinformation as well as bias. This explanation exemplifies the concept of "garbage in, garbage out." The former is the misinformation; the latter is the resulting judgment. Cognitive scientists would explain the problem as unrepresentative information, which implies that the person is using information that is not indicative of a larger population or reality. Unfortunately, there is a tendency toward a heuristic which frequently leads people to make judgments using unrepresentative information. [*See* HEURISTICS.]

To make matters worse, much of the media and entertainment industries focus on unrepresentative (e.g., sensationalistic) information. That is what sells newspapers. In this light the problem is cognitive (the use of heuristics) *and* social (the available information).

Once again, historical examples show clearly how there may be a tendency to use misinformation and share it. Here is a short list of facts that are contrary to widely believed misinformation, presented by the historian Thomas Fleming in his book *Liberty: The American Revolution*.

- Americans of 1776 had the highest standard of living and the lowest taxes in the Western world.
- There were two Boston Tea Parties. The first, on December 16, 1773, is famous. The second, on March 7, 1774, is much less known. (Together the cost to the British was approximately $3,000,000 in today's dollars.)
- Nathan Hale was hanged for trying to burn down New York, as well as for spying.
- Without Benedict Arnold as general during the early part of the war, the Revolutionary War probably would have been lost. He was our best general.

- Cleopatra may not have been the wildly attractive woman she is often made out to be. She may have been more strategic than beautiful.

The "fundamental attribution error" may also contribute to misjudgment. This occurs because a creator explains his or her behavior by looking at the context. An audience or judge of the same creative act will tend to focus on the creator him- or herself (and disregard contextual factors). These divergent perspectives lead to predictable biases and occasionally misjudgment. [*See* ATTRIBUTION AND CREATIVITY.]

A distinction should be made between misinformation and ignorance. The latter reflects a lack of information. Ignorance may arise because judgments of creativity do change with time. For example, if a creative person is unrecognized during his or her lifetime, and only later is recognized as creative, there may not be much of a record nor much biographical material. Little is recorded unless contemporaries feel it is worthwhile to do so. Historians are understandably but regrettably ignorant about those persons whose reputations have improved.

The degree of change in the reputations of creative persons has been labeled "reputational paths" and is currently being quantified. This requires a comparison of the length of biographical and encyclopedic entries at several points (e.g., 1850 versus 1950). It may be that such changes in reputational paths will be predictive of eminence. The most outstanding creative persons may have the most stable reputations.

VII. MISJUDGMENT IN CREATIVE STUDIES

The field of creative studies has its own biases and misjudgments. As Madelle Becker pointed out in the *Creativity Research Journal,* most people discuss the field taking coherence in the 1950s, but a large amount of early thinking was done in the 19th century and very early in the 1900s. Becker reviewed the contributions of William James (1880), Sir Francis Galton (1869, 1882), J. Jastrow (1898), Binet (1896), Cattell (1903), Ellis (1904), Jevons (1877), Lombroso (1891), Ribot (1900), and Royce (1898). Becker identified a number of questions about creativity that these early scholars addressed and which are still raised in creativity re-

search—yet the early scholars are very infrequently cited. The 19th century treatment of the issues may be no longer relevant, but given how common it is to ignore and misjudge the work in earlier eras, it is also possible that the scholars of 19th century creativity research should still be consulted.

One trend in the field of creative studies is toward objective measurement. This can be seen in analyses of products and the social approaches to creativity. The assumption in these investigations and theories is that judgments can be accurate and trustworthy. One implication of this assumption was explored by Robert Albert in his seminal paper, "Toward a Behavior Definition of Genius." Simplifying some, Albert suggested that there is no such thing as a genius ahead of his or her time. This makes good sense from the objective, behavioral, product perspective. But if it is so common for creativity to be misjudged in its own era, and if it is so common for judgments to change and improve, it may be that there *can* be a creative genius ahead of his or her time. This is someone whose work was not recognized until after his or her death (e.g., Rembrandt). Admittedly, the individual may not be a recognized creative genius in his or her own time *and* be ahead of his or her own time. But if the person was not recognized in his or her own time but later proved to be a genius, is it not reasonable to say, from the current perspective, that the person was ahead of his or her own time?

VIII. CONCLUSIONS

Misjudgment takes many forms and occurs for several reasons. The two most obvious reasons are bias and misinformation. Cognitive tendencies, including our frequent reliance on shortcuts and heuristics, contribute to bias. Misinformation is probably used because we too frequently accept information mindlessly. Information is often a part of tradition or recorded history, but even that has its own biases.

Misjudgment works both ways. Sometimes inventions and insights are overlooked, and sometimes their creativity and value are exaggerated. Similarly, sometimes judgments improve with the passing of time (e.g., Rembrandt and Franklin), but not always. Sometimes a creator or inventor loses credibility.

The extreme case of bias and misjudgment has not

yet been mentioned. I am referring to censorship. Censorship most often acts on creative work either by disregarding its quality or by weighing other factors (e.g., social impact) more than the quality of the work itself. Even Mark Twain's books have been censored at some point, yet *Huckleberry Finn* has been called the Great American Novel.

The possibility of misjudgment has numerous practical implications. It implies, for example, that consensual assessments should be used very judiciously. These rely on social judgment; but as the examples reviewed here suggest, there are many biases that can lead to misjudgment. It may even be that the selection of "appropriate judges" leads to particular biases. Again, who is to judge the judges?

Judgments of some sort are involved in most contemporary models of creative thinking. Creativity requires more than originality—more than divergent thinking. It requires judgment, evaluation, and verification. Judgments are not, however, always objective.

Misjudgment is apparently quite common. Perhaps a recognition of its prevalence will remind each of us to carefully examine our own judgmental tendencies, biases, and information sources.

Bibliography

Albert, R. (1975). Toward a behavior definition of genius. *American Psychologist, 30,* 141–150.

Bryson, B. (1994). *Made in America.* New York: William Morrow.

Cerf, C., & Navasky, V. (1984). *The experts speak.* New York: Pantheon.

Gould, S. J. (1991). *Bully for brontosaurus: Reflections in natural history.* New York: Norton.

Joffee, L. (1991). Henry VIII: a revisionist look at a Renaissance man. *Los Angeles Times,* October 7, p. E8.

Rogers, C. (1961). *On becoming a person.* Boston, MA: Houghton Mifflin.

Runco, M., & Chard, I. (1994). Problem finding, evaluative thinking, and creativity. In M. A. Runco (Ed.), *Problem finding, problem solving, and creativity* (pp. 40–76). Norwood, NJ: Ablex.

Mood

Edward R. Hirt

Indiana University

Cognitive Tuning The view that moods serve an important evolutionary value in that they signal to an individual that the environment is either safe or threatening.

Demand Characteristics A threat to the validity of an experiment, whereby the participants figure out the hypothesis of the experiment and change their behavior to what they think is demanded of them (i.e., support the hypothesis) in order to please the experimenter.

Hedonic Contingency A mood management model which argues that positive mood individuals are particularly careful to scrutinize the potential affective consequences of their actions or behaviors in order to engage only in activities that will maintain or enhance their positive feelings.

Intrinsic Interest The extent to which interest in a task derives from one's personal enjoyment rather than from its ability to provide some extrinsic reward (praise, money, power, or prestige).

Mood as Information The view that individuals use their current mood as a source of information in making judgments and decisions (e.g., "How do I feel about it?").

Mood as Input The paradigm in which individuals are given different stop rules or processing goals (enjoyment-based versus performance-based) as they perform the task.

Mood-Congruent Retrieval The notion that moods facilitate or cue the retrieval of similarly valenced information from memory.

Mood Management The perspective that individuals seek to maintain a positive mood state or repair/improve a negative mood state.

Priming The notion that information currently activated in memory may influence one's interpretation or construal of the immediate situation.

Individuals in positive MOOD states have been reliably shown to be more creative on a range of tasks than are individuals in other mood states. This article will review evidence demonstrating the relationship between mood and creativity, and will discuss several possible explanations for this relationship. In addition, the role that creativity plays in modulating subsequent mood will be considered.

I. COMMONSENSE VIEWS

A commonly shared notion among many people is that mood states affect thoughts and behavior. On the one hand, we are familiar with the adage that happy individuals view the world through "rose-colored glasses." Many popular theories of motivation in the workplace believe that happy workers perform better and more effectively than those who are in more negative moods. However, the extent to which this view predicts that happy people would be more creative rather than simply more productive (in a quantitative sense) is somewhat unclear.

On the other hand, when people try to think of some of the most notably creative individuals—writers, artists, composers, theorists, etc.—many are struck by the fact that such individuals were particularly unhappy individuals. Biographies of the lives of such famous "tortured artists" such as van Gogh, Coleridge, or Mozart point out that often their most creative periods coincided with bouts of melancholy and depression. Thus, there are those who believe that creativity is borne out of times of negative mood.

II. EMPIRICAL EVIDENCE

Given the conflicting commonsense views regarding the effects of mood on creativity, researchers began empirical investigation of this relationship. In these studies, participants' moods would be either measured or manipulated (via a mood induction procedure) and then participants' creativity would be measured on a subsequent task. For example, research by Alice Isen and her colleagues has demonstrated that individuals induced into a positive mood tend to show enhanced creativity on a broad range of tasks. In one set of studies, individuals in various moods were asked to solve insight problems like the Duncker candle problem. The Duncker candle problem provides participants with a box of tacks, a candle, and a book of matches. Their task is to affix the candle to the wall and light it. The optimal solution is to use the tacks to fix the box to the wall, put the candle in the box, and then light it with the matches. However, many participants cannot solve this problem, for they see the box only as a container of tacks and fail to see its possible usage as a platform to support the candle. The inability to see novel or creative uses for objects is often called functional fixedness. Isen found that individuals induced into a positive mood by exposure to a 5-min comedy clip were more likely to solve this problem than were individuals in other mood states.

The effects of mood on other types of creativity tasks have been examined. Research has found that positive mood individuals provide more novel first associates to neutral words in a word-association task than do individuals in other mood states. Thus, for example, when given the task of writing down the first associate to the word "carpet," participants in a neutral mood overwhelmingly responded with the word "rug" (which norms established as the most common associate to carpet), whereas participants in a happy mood responded with words like "shag," "floor," and "soft." Research has also shown that positive mood individuals are better able to solve creativity problems like those on Mednick's Remote Associates Test. Items on this test provide individuals with three words (mower, atomic, foreign) followed by a blank space. Individuals are instructed to provide a word that relates to each of the three words given in the item (in this example, the solution is "power"—power mower, atomic power, and foreign power). Positive mood individuals were able to solve more of these items, again providing greater evidence of creative problem solving. In another set of experiments, researchers examined the creativity of individuals in different moods to category generation tasks (e.g., list as many different modes of transportation as you can). Again, these studies consistently show that individuals in a positive mood generate more novel and creative responses to these tasks, including such responses as "cannon," "broomstick," "email," and "imagination" as modes of transportation. [See PROBLEM SOLVING.]

Two comments are noteworthy at this point. First, one might wonder how moods are induced in these studies. A variety of mood induction procedures have been used, ranging from viewing selected video clips or listening to selected passages of music, to receiving free gifts of candy, writing about an event or events in one's own life in which one felt happy or sad, or reading positive or negatively valenced statements (e.g., "Some days I feel like I can accomplish anything"). The effects of mood on creativity appear to be remarkably robust both in terms of the mood induction procedure used and the range of possible creativity tasks that have been measured: Positive mood individuals demonstrate greater creativity of performance than do individuals in neutral or negative moods.

Second, one might wonder whether the effects of mood on creativity are due to the fact that people may be aware that their mood has been manipulated in the study. In psychological research, we refer to the problem of "demand characteristics" in experiments where participants may be able to figure out the experimental hypothesis being investigated and thus respond in a manner that confirms that hypothesis. In the studies already discussed, efforts were taken to make sure that people did not connect the mood induction procedure with the creativity task. For example, the two tasks were introduced as two separate experiments and often used different experimenters and were conducted in different rooms. Measures were taken at the end of the experiments to assess the extent to which participants (1) viewed the two "experiments" as connected in some way, or (2) could articulate the experimental hypothesis. Results from these experiments indicate that participants were not aware of the experimental hypothesis and effectively rule out a demand characteristics explanation of the findings. People are aware that they are feeling good or bad in the experiment, but they do not perceive these feelings as relevant to their performance on the creativity task. However, later in this article, we will discuss the importance of participants' awareness and interpretation of the source of their mood in understanding the effects of mood on many aspects of judgment and performance.

Thus, the literature on mood effects provides a consistent pattern of results indicating that positive mood leads to greater creativity. However, the question of why this pattern exists is one that is still being debated. Many different explanations of the effects of mood on various aspects of judgment and behavior have been offered and have been applied to explain the effects of mood on creativity. In the following sections, we will review these different explanations of mood effects, highlighting how each can explain the enhanced creativity of positive mood subjects. In the final section, we will try to integrate these various views together and summarize the current state of affairs regarding the role of mood in creative performance.

III. COGNITIVE EXPLANATIONS

One level of explanation that has been offered to account for the effects of mood on creativity focuses on the cognitive consequences of being in a mood. Research by Gordon Bower, Alice Isen, and others pro-poses that positive feelings serve as a retrieval cue for positive material in memory. Individuals in a positive mood are more likely to recall positive life experiences and words with positive connotations and meanings than are other individuals. Importantly, these differences in the content of what information is recalled have implications for judgments, evaluations, and expectations. People in positive moods have been shown to judge their satisfaction with their consumer products (televisions, cars, or dishwashers) as higher than people in other moods. People in positive moods also judge their current level of happiness and life satisfaction to be greater than people in other moods. Finally, people in positive moods express greater expectations of future success and other positive events, and perceive their likelihood of various risks to be reduced. All of these results are consistent with the notion that positive feelings cue positive material in memory, which is then brought to bear on current judgments and decisions.

Further research has emphasized the role that positive mood plays in the interpretation of information. Many studies have shown that priming can affect the way we interpret subsequent information. For instance, if I have just recently been watching a horror movie, I might interpret ambiguous sounds in my home (creaking floorboards, or the furnace turning on and off) as evidence that some intruder or monster is in the house. Similarly, positive mood can "prime" a positive interpretation or categorization of subsequent events. Individuals in a positive mood have been shown to categorize objects differently than individuals in other moods. Isen and her colleagues demonstrated that positive mood individuals are more likely to show increased category breadth and include more weak exemplars as instances of a category. For example, individuals in a positive mood would include "camel" and "elevator" in the category "vehicle," whereas individuals in other moods would not. Later research by Edward Hirt and colleagues has illustrated that people in positive moods are not always broader categorizers, but instead are more flexible in their categorization of information. In their research, they asked participants in different moods to note similarities and differences between sets of stimuli. Research on categorization indicates that seeing similarities requires broadening of categories to see areas of inclusion, whereas seeing differences requires narrow categorization to see areas of distinction.

Hirt's research indicated that positive mood individuals were better able to perceive both similarities and differences among stimuli, attesting to the greater flexibility in the way happy individuals can categorize and construe objects.

Proponents of this "mood-congruent retrieval" view would argue that the enhanced creativity of positive mood individuals is the result of the fact that a happy mood cues or primes positive material in memory. Isen and others have shown that positive material is more extensive and diverse than other material in memory, thereby creating a more complex cognitive context when a person is happy. Such a complex cognitive context may lead to diverse and multiple interpretations and organizations of material in memory, features essential to creativity. Thus, the mood-congruent retrieval view asserts that people in happy moods are more creative because positive mood leads to a broadening or expanding of associations. Indeed, Isen's findings that people come up with more unusual first associates during a free association task is consistent with this view. Other researchers like Klaus Fiedler and Joseph Forgas have similarly argued that positive moods lead to a general "loosening" of thought. People in positive moods are more willing to take risks, and are less inhibited than individuals in other mood states.

In summary, a mood-congruent retrieval view presents a cognitively based argument for the greater creativity of positive mood individuals. This view emphasizes the differences in the "content and organization" of information in memory resulting from being in a positive mood, differences that change the cognitive context accessible to individuals as they perform creative tasks. The broader and more diverse cognitive context associated with positive mood facilitates creative processing and problem solving, resulting in enhanced creativity on a wide range of tasks.

IV. MOTIVATIONAL EXPLANATIONS

The reader may have noticed that the preceding discussion of mood-congruent retrieval focused exclusively on the effects of positive mood on memory. One might ask whether similar mood-congruent retrieval effects are observed for individuals in negative moods. It would appear that negative mood should cue or prime negative material in memory, resulting in parallel effects to those of positive mood. However, the research that has examined mood-congruent retrieval effects with negative mood have found a mixed pattern of results. In some cases, individuals show facilitated retrieval of negative (mood-congruent) material, yet in other cases show facilitated retrieval of positive (mood-incongruent) material. Why might this be the case? An important consideration in understanding these effects is to consider the motivational as well as the cognitive consequences of being in a particular mood. Thus, our discussion will now turn to a consideration of the motivational consequences of mood and their implications for creativity.

When you are in a positive mood, how does it feel? Is it a state you want to perpetuate or one that you want to eliminate quickly? Certainly, we would all agree that a positive mood is a desirable state that we would like to maintain for as long as possible. Indeed, this is a fundamental premise of the mood management perspective. According to this perspective, happy individuals are interested in maintaining their positive mood state, and will engage in activities that are likely to accomplish this goal. Many researchers have found that individuals in positive moods are more helpful, and will readily perform acts of low-cost helping, since such acts can make one feel good and maintain one's positive mood state. Thus, happy individuals will approach tasks that have a high likelihood of resulting in a positive or hedonically rewarding outcome.

Interestingly, research has indicated that happy individuals are careful to avoid situations that could potentially threaten their positive mood state. Thus, if it is clear that a helping opportunity has a high likelihood of making us feel bad, positive mood individuals are less likely to help in these circumstances. Indeed, Duane Wegener and Richard Petty's hedonic contingency model specifically argues that, because more potentially mood-threatening tasks exist for individuals in positive moods, happy individuals are even more vigilant about the hedonic qualities of tasks they are contemplating performing than are individuals in other mood states. Research provides evidence that happy individuals are particularly attentive to information about how a task is likely to make them feel (e.g., when choosing a movie or story to read) relative to individuals in other moods.

Now, you might be asking yourself, how might this mood management perspective explain the greater creativity of happy individuals? According to this perspective, people might view being creative on a task as a way to maintain or enhance their mood. That is, happy individuals might see creativity at a task as a way to make it more fun and interesting, thereby maintaining their positive mood state. Thus, as is the case with helping, being creative might be a means toward an end for happy individuals, allowing them to sustain if not enhance their current positive mood.

Conversely, a mood management perspective argues that people in negative moods are interested not in maintaining their current mood state, but in improving their existing mood. Negative mood individuals are motivated to engage in "mood repair," choosing activities that are likely to improve or repair their current affective state. Thus, individuals in negative moods seek out activities and tasks that will make them feel better or at least distract them from their negative feelings. As a result, negative mood individuals are motivated to think about mood-incongruent rather than mood-congruent thoughts, a motivation that often counteracts any possible cuing or priming effect of negative mood states. This motivation is perhaps best illustrated by the words to the song "My Favorite Things" from the Rodgers and Hammerstein musical *The Sound of Music:* "When the dog bites, when the bee stings, when I'm feeling sad, I simply remember my favorite things, and then I don't feel so bad."

Similarly, negative mood individuals have been shown to engage in helping as a means to improve their affective state. If this is so, would not this perspective then expect that negative mood individuals should be just as likely to be creative at tasks as a means to improve their current affective state? Wegener and Petty's hedonic contingency model provides an answer to this question by pointing out that there exists a broader range of tasks that could potentially repair or improve the (negative) affective state of an individual in a negative mood than there are tasks that could maintain or enhance the (positive) affective state of an individual in a positive mood. Thus, they contend that it is the positive mood individual who must be particularly sensitive to and selective about the potential hedonic consequences of the tasks in which they engage. From their perspective, negative mood individuals can find a number of different avenues that will make them feel better, and thus are not as careful in scrutinizing the hedonic qualities of potential tasks. Wegener and Petty would therefore argue that positive mood individuals take a far more active role in ensuring that the tasks they engage in result in hedonically pleasing outcomes and thus are more likely to engage in creative processing in order to maximize their enjoyment of the task.

V. EVOLUTIONARY EXPLANATIONS

A third perspective regarding the role of mood in creativity derives from the evolutionary significance of mood to an organism. Norbert Schwarz's cognitive tuning view emphasizes the signal value conveyed by moods. According to this perspective, negative moods signal danger or threat to the organism, and evoke systematic, effortful problem solving to remedy the situation. Thus, when an organism is in a negative mood, it conveys to the organism that the current situation is problematic (danger is present, or needs exist that need to be met) and motivates actions designed to respond to or eliminate the problem. Positive moods, on the other hand, signal that the current situation is safe and satisfactory, and does not require response or action. Thus, when an organism is in a positive mood, it conveys to the organism that everything is fine, and the organism can relax and take it easy.

There is considerable evidence that these signal values of mood have consequences for the information processing strategies of individuals in different moods. Individuals in negative moods tend to engage in effortful, systematic processing of information. Negative mood leads to a narrowing of focus of attention, and leads to more careful and deliberate processing, resulting in longer response times. However, on a number of tasks, this style of processing produces qualitatively better performance. Indeed, individuals in negative moods have been shown to be more accurate in a variety of social and nonsocial judgments, and to rely more on the pertinent information and less on peripheral cues (e.g., the attractiveness of the communicator of a persuasive message) and stereotypes. Tasks that require more analytical processing (e.g., solving physics problems) are facilitated by being in a negative mood.

In contrast, individuals in positive moods tend to

engage in simpler, less effortful processing of information. Positive mood participants tend to use short-cuts or heuristics to solve problems, relying more on peripheral cues than message content when evaluating persuasive messages or relying more on group stereotypes than information about a specific individual when making social judgments. As a result, on a number of tasks, individuals in positive moods respond more quickly but show less accurate performance. [*See* HEURISTICS.]

However, recall that we indicated that positive mood individuals show enhanced creativity on a number of tasks, findings that appear to be at odds with the preceding results. Researchers who favor the processing strategy account point to the fact that many creativity tasks are facilitated by a "looser," more heuristic processing strategy (as opposed to a "tighter," more analytical processing strategy). According to Schwarz, the enhanced creativity of individuals in a positive mood is the result of their playful exploration of novel procedures, greater risk taking, and preference for simpler, more heuristic problem-solving strategies. This approach works well for positive mood individuals on many types of creativity tasks, which require the generation or consideration of novel or unusual associations or solutions to problems. Thus, this approach emphasizes the "processing strategy" differences between individuals in different mood states to account for the enhanced creativity of positive mood individuals.

VI. MOOD AS INFORMATION

A final view also emphasizes the informational value conveyed by mood. However, this view emphasizes the fact that individuals often use their current affective state at the time of judgment as information in rendering a judgment. Norbert Schwarz and Jerry Clore have proposed that people often use a "How do I feel about it?" heuristic in making judgments. For example, in one famous study, Schwarz and Clore called individuals and asked them to report their current levels of happiness and life satisfaction. Individuals were called on either sunny days or rainy days, given that we know that people's moods are affected by the weather. They found that people reported greater happiness and life satisfaction on sunny days as opposed to rainy days,

suggesting that individuals were using their mood as information in making these judgments.

Given our earlier discussion of mood-congruent retrieval, it may seem that these effects are simply the result of selective retrieval of mood-congruent memories at the time of judgment. That is, people in positive moods may be recalling more memories of positive events than negative events (and vice versa for the negative mood individuals), such that differential memory for past information may account for these effects. However, Schwarz and Clore argue for a different process, one which does not rely on selective retrieval from memory. Instead, they believe that individuals simply consult their current mood state and use those global feelings (rather than retrieval of specific memories) as a primary basis for making their judgments. Now, of course, the question remains as to whether one's mood is an appropriate source of information on which to base judgments. Research has indicated that people use this "How do I feel about it?" heuristic in making a broad array of evaluative judgments, ranging from judgments of self to judgments of others to judgments of consumer products and various activities.

An important assumption of the mood-as-information perspective is the mood should only influence judgments to the extent that one's mood is considered relevant or applicable to the judgment at hand. Indeed, in many cases, we feel that our moods are indeed relevant to a variety of judgments. If I am trying to decide whether to go to a movie or a party, I may consult my current mood. If I feel positive, I may decide to go; if I feel negative, I may decline to go. However, there is an important corollary to this assumption: To the extent that the diagnostic value of one's mood is called into question, individuals should fail to use their mood as a basis of judgment. That is, if someone or something informs you that your mood should not be used as a basis for judgment, then people will discount any influence of their mood in judgments and will rely on other sources of information in basing their judgments.

A number of studies have used a variety of procedures to test this assumption. For instance, in the earlier study by Schwarz and Clore in which individuals were asked to judge their life satisfaction on sunny versus rainy days, the experimenters ran a variation of that same experiment in which they first asked individuals what the weather was like there. This simple manipulation wiped out any effects of mood (i.e., the weather) on judgments of happiness and life satisfaction. Why? By calling people's attention to the weather there, and immediately following up that question with questions about life satisfaction, individuals were aware that the weather was not a reasonable or appropriate basis for judgments about their current level of happiness and life satisfaction. Thus, individuals corrected for any influence that these factors might play in their judgments, and therefore showed no effects of their feelings and moods.

Similarly, in other experiments, people who had previously undergone a mood induction procedure using film clips or music were in one condition given a simple reminder or cue that they might still be feeling some aftereffects from this earlier task, whereas participants in the other condition were given no such cue. The results indicated that those in the no-cue condition showed the classic mood-as-information effects on judgments; those in the cue condition, however, showed no effect of moods on their judgments. Thus, these findings illustrate that moods serve as information only to the extent that individuals view their current mood as relevant to the judgment at hand.

How then would the mood-as-information perspective explain the greater creativity of positive mood individuals? This perspective would argue that individuals consult their moods as a basis for judging whether to perform (or continue to perform) a task. For example, when introduced to a creativity task, the individual would ask themselves, "How do I feel about this task?" Individuals in a positive mood would use their mood as information and would be more likely to decide that the task looks interesting and fun, and would be more willing to expend the necessary effort to perform and persist at the task than would individuals in other moods. Individuals in a negative mood would likewise use their mood as information and would be likely to decide that the task does not look particularly appealing, and would expend less effort and show less persistence at the task.

Recent work by Lenny Martin and his colleagues put these predictions to empirical test. Martin had individuals (who had previously been induced into either positive or negative moods) perform an open-ended task (e.g., generating a list of birds) but explicitly manipulated the criteria that individuals should use

as a basis of deciding when to stop (what we will call their "stop rule"). Some participants were given an enjoyment-based stop rule, explicitly telling them to stop performing the task when they no longer enjoyed the task. Other participants were given a performance-based stop rule, explicitly telling them to stop performing the task when they felt they had done enough. The results indicated that when individuals were given an enjoyment-based stop rule, positive mood individuals spent a longer time on the task and generated a greater number of responses than did negative mood individuals. Subsequent research by Hirt and his colleagues has demonstrated that these differences in performance were due to the fact that positive mood individuals perceived the task as more interesting and fun than did negative mood individuals, evidence consistent with a mood-as-information perspective.

In contrast, when given a performance-based stop rule, Martin found that negative mood individuals actually spent a greater amount of time and generated more responses than did positive mood individuals. Again, Martin used a mood-as-information perspective to explain these effects. He argued that when judging the quality or adequacy of one's performance, people use their mood as information in making this judgment. A positive mood informs the person that "I feel good about my performance" and thus leads the individual to perceive that it is already sufficient and one does not need to continue performing the task any longer. A negative mood informs the person that "I do not feel good about my performance" and thus leads individuals to perceive that they need to expend greater effort and persistence at the task to get their level of performance up to par. Indeed, Hirt found that positive mood individuals perceive the quality of their performance as greater than do negative mood individuals, evidence consistent with the mood-as-information perspective.

Martin's results provide compelling evidence that moods can serve as input to decisions about task performance. Furthermore, the results obtained from his studies (which he calls his "mood-as-input" paradigm) can account for the fact that in some cases positive mood individuals perform better than negative mood individuals (i.e., when an enjoyment-based stop rule is operative), whereas in other cases negative mood individuals outperform positive mood individuals (i.e., when a performance-based rule is operative), while holding the task constant. But his results did not specifically address the creativity of participants' responses; rather, the focus was on the time spent and number generated, measures of quantitative as opposed to qualitative performance. Martin and his colleagues addressed this issue in a future set of studies in which they again induced participants into a positive or negative mood state and then gave them a free association task under one of two stop rules specifically designed to address the creativity of responses. In one condition, participants were told to ask themselves after generating their initial association, "Can I come up with a better response?" In another condition, participants were told to ask themselves, "Is my response a good one?" The "Can I come up with a better response?" rule was hypothesized to lead positive mood individuals to use their mood as information in answering this question, resulting in a greater tendency to respond "yes" and then generate a second response. Conversely, the "Is my response a good one?" rule was hypothesized to likewise lead positive mood individuals to use their mood as information in answering this question; however, here one's positive mood should lead one to again respond "yes" and believe that one's initial response was a good one, such that positive mood individuals would be unlikely to generate a second response under this stop rule. The results confirm their predictions and suggest that mood can indeed serve as input in judgments of the creativity of one's responses. Thus, it would appear from these results that the creativity of performance is also influenced by a mood-as-information process whereby individuals use their mood to determine how much effort they put into performing creatively at a task.

VII. MOOD AS A CONSEQUENCE OF CREATIVITY

Given all these different perspectives on the positive mood–creativity relationship, research is needed to address which of these perspectives account for or at least contribute to this association. It may be the case that a number of different perspectives contribute to the robustness of the link between positive mood and creativity, but it is important for researchers to begin to examine the processes by which positive mood leads to creativity. Recent research by Hirt and his colleagues has taken an initial step in this regard. Borrowing from Martin's earlier "mood-as-input" work, Hirt and colleagues gave individuals in positive or negative moods either an enjoyment-based or performance-based stop rule and examined not only quantitative measures of performance (time spent, number generated) but also qualitative measures of performance (creativity of responses). Results for the quantitative measures of performance replicated Martin's earlier findings, with positive mood individuals spending more time and generating more responses when given an enjoyment-based rule, but negative mood individuals spending more time and generating more responses when given a performance-based rule. However, the results for creativity were very different: across *both* stop rule conditions, positive mood individuals generated more creative responses than negative mood individuals.

Furthermore, in this study, participants were asked both before and after the task to report their level of intrinsic interest in performing this task. The results indicated that indeed positive mood individuals perceived the task as more interesting prior to actually performing the task, consistent with a mood-as-information view. However, the question still remained whether the effects of positive mood on performance were caused by or mediated by the greater task interest on the part of positive mood participants (positive mood → enhanced task interest → improved performance). These questions of mediation are particularly important in this context, because they allow us to distinguish among rival explanations for the effects of positive mood on performance. Questions of mediation are addressed by performing an analysis known as path analysis. Data are congruent with a mediational model when (a) the independent variable (here, mood) significantly predicts the final outcome variable (here, performance), (b) the independent variable also predicts the mediating variable (here, task interest), and (c) the mediator significantly predicts the outcome variable even when the independent variable is controlled for.

Path analyses performed on these data revealed that task interest mediated the effects of positive mood on the number of responses generated, but not on the creativity of those responses. In other words, people who were more interested in the task did come up with a greater overall number of responses, but their responses were not necessarily any more creative. Instead, these analyses revealed a different causal path—namely, that being more creative at the task led to greater subsequent task interest (positive mood → greater creativity → greater subsequent task interest). That is, people who performed creatively at the task reported greater subsequent task interest than did those who did not perform as creatively.

These results are important for two reasons. First, they suggest that the processes that underlie quantitative measures of performance (time spent, number generated) do not appear to be the same as those that underlie creativity. Thus, although it appears that a mood-as-information perspective can account for greater task persistence (as Martin found), it does not appear to account for the heightened creativity of positive mood individuals. Indeed, subsequent research by Hirt and his colleagues has shown that a cue manipulation (reminding participants of the earlier mood induction) designed to eliminate mood-as-information effects wipes out the effects of mood on quantitative measures, but has no effect on the positive mood–creativity link. Thus, it would appear that an alternative mechanism—perhaps a mood-congruent retrieval or mood management mechanism—may be a more viable account for the greater creativity of positive mood individuals.

Second, Hirt's work illustrates a mood–creativity relationship that we have ignored to this point. His results indicate that creative performance leads to subsequently greater interest and elevated mood. Indeed, this result makes good sense from a number of perspectives. The mood management perspective discussed earlier argued that positive mood individuals might choose to be creative in order to maintain or potentially enhance their positive feelings. These results attest to the fact that creativity makes one feel better about one's self and more interested in the task at hand. For years, researchers in the area of intrinsic motivation have pointed to the role that one's phenomenal experience while performing a task has on subsequent interest. Feeling involved or engaged in a task tends to promote continued interest. Although these researchers have tended to focus on variables such as evaluation, achievement motivation, desires to demonstrate competence, and competition on task interest, the present

analysis suggests that the perception or experience of being creative at a task also produces feelings of task involvement and engagement, which then translates into greater subsequent interest and elevated mood.

This new research suggests that it is important to look not only at the role of positive mood as an antecedent of creativity, but to also consider the fact that positive mood may be a consequence of being creative. The cyclical nature of how mood both influences and is influenced by creativity represents a more complete picture of the mood–creativity relationship than has been discussed previously, and represents an important avenue for future research.

VIII. CONCLUSIONS

The research to date provides compelling evidence that positive mood leads to greater creativity. Although several possible explanations for this relationship have been offered, the precise mechanisms that underlie the mood–creativity link are still unclear. It may well be the case that multiple mechanisms are involved, and researchers must turn their attention to studies designed to disentangle these rival mechanisms from one another.

It is important to also acknowledge that we have been talking about mood and creativity as if they were homogeneous constructs. However, research has demonstrated that there are critical distinctions among different types of mood and different types of creativity that have not often been taken into account. For example, mood researchers have been criticized by emotion researchers for talking about *positive* and *negative* moods, as if the valence of one's mood state is the only important dimension when considering one's affective state. Emotion researchers have shown that particularly with regard to negative moods, there is considerable variability in not only the nature of the affective experience of different negative emotions (such as sadness, fear, anger, and disgust), but that the cognitive and behavioral consequences resulting from these different emotions vary as well. In most of the mood research we have reviewed, the negative mood inductions have induced sadness in participants; however, whether the same consequences would be observed among angry, fearful, or disgusted individuals remains an issue for future research. In addition, one might wonder if there are conditions under which a sad or depressed mood might enhance creativity, consistent with the common-sense views espoused earlier. For example, might a sad mood enable an individual to be more creative with regard to negatively valenced material? To date, most of the research has focused on neutral or positively valenced stimuli. Thus, it remains an interesting avenue for future research to consider the role that the valence of the stimuli being considered has for creativity.

In addition, it is important to consider the many different aspects of what constitutes creative performance. Most of the studies we have reviewed have focused on tasks involving the generation of novel or unusual responses or associations, tasks that involve divergent thinking. Although positive mood has been shown to affect creativity on other tasks as well (e.g., the Remote Associates Test and insight problems), it is possible that a number of the effects of positive mood on creativity are restricted to a particular type of creativity task. Again, it would be important for researchers to assess creativity on a broader array of tasks, including tasks involving convergent as well as divergent thinking. Hirt and colleagues' recent work also suggests the role that perceptions of one's own creativity play. The extent to which an individual has the subjective experience that one is being creative during the task clearly appears to be essential to engendering subsequent interest in the task, but its role in affecting the overall creativity of one's performance is unclear.

Despite these limitations, the robustness of the effects of positive mood in enhancing the creativity of performance suggests that it will remain an important and fruitful avenue for future research. The interplay between affect and creativity has been noted by many researchers, and appears to play a pivotal role in creative performance and expression.

Bibliography

Forgas, J. P. (1995). Mood and judgment: The Affect Infusion Model (AIM). *Psychological Bulletin, 117,* 1–28.

Hirt, E. R., Levine, G. M., McDonald, H. E., Melton, R. J., & Martin, L. L. (1997). The role of mood in quantitative and qualitative aspects of performance: Single or multiple mechanisms? *Journal of Experimental Social Psychology, 33,* 602–629.

Isen, A. M. (1987). Positive affect, cognitive processes, and social behavior. In L. Berkowitz (Ed.), *Advances in experimental social psychology* (Vol. 20, pp. 203–253). New York: Academic Press.

Martin, L. L., Ward, D. W., Achee, J. W., & Wyer, R. S., Jr. (1993). Mood as input: People have to interpret the motivational implications of their moods. *Journal of Personality and Social Psychology, 64,* 317–326.

Schwarz, N. (1990). Feelings as information: Informational and motivational functions of affective states. In E. T. Higgins & R. M. Sorrentino (Eds.), *Handbook of motivation and cognition* (Vol. 2, pp. 527–561). New York: Guilford Press.

Wegener, D. T., & Petty, R. E. (1994). Mood management across affective states: The hedonic contingency hypothesis. *Journal of Personality and Social Psychology, 66,* 1034–1048.

Motivation/Drive

Regina Conti

Colgate University

Teresa Amabile

Harvard Business School

Drive Motivation produced by an excess or deficiency in the organism (e.g., a water deficiency raises the drive of thirst). A drive stimulates behavior directed toward restoring balance.

Intrinsic Motivation The motivation to engage in an activity solely for the enjoyment, challenge, or personal satisfaction that arises from the activity itself. Intrinsic motivation fosters creativity.

Motivation The energy underlying behavior. A person's motivation to initiate and persist in a specific action explains why the person chose that specific action given the circumstances.

Personality Trait An enduring characteristic of a person. Traits generally refer to a person's tendencies in social and emotional responding, rather than physical characteristics or cognitive abilities.

Psychic Conflict Results from opposing drives arising from different psychological sources. To resolve the conflict one drive must often be satisfied indirectly, perhaps symbolically.

Reinforcer Any consequence of behavior that increases the likelihood of that behavior occurring in the future. A consequence is thought to be highly reinforcing when it satisfies a basic drive.

Self-Actualization The need to maintain and enhance life; to develop one's full potential. Self-actualizing people are spontaneous, flexible, confident, trusting, creative, self-reliant, ethical, and open-minded.

Perhaps the most striking ingredient to creativity is the unyielding **MOTIVATION** *to create. The outstanding energy of great creators is described vividly by biographers and researchers in their accounts of highly creative lives. The motivation of highly creative persons is so intense that it has been thought to have a "driven" quality. Rather than engaging in work because they want to, many great creators feel a strong need to do the work that they do. Psychologists have wondered and investigated and debated where such a* **DRIVE** *to create might come from, if it exists at all.*

The study of personality traits established that highly creative persons are indeed different in some important ways: they are highly enthusiastic, they produce more ideas and more unusual ideas than their peers, and they have the courage to follow through with their ideas, even when their ideas are not popular. Some theorists believe that their energy and courage are so powerful because their creative work is satisfying a drive rooted in psychic conflict. Recent research has shown a relationship between mental illness (especially affective disorders) and high levels of creativity, providing support for this possibility. Another possibility, proposed by humanistic theorists, is that the need to create is a self-actualizing tendency that arises only in the most mentally healthy individuals. A simpler explanation comes from behaviorists, who propose that some people become more and more creative because they receive powerful reinforcers for their creative efforts. However, evidence from social psychological studies of creativity shows that intrinsic motivation fosters creativity, while extrinsic reinforcers such as reward can often inhibit it. Despite the clear differences between these attempts to explain the energy underlying creativity, taken together, an important message emerges. The motivation to create is most impressive when each of these forces supports the others. When our basic drives, our urge to self-actualize, and the social environment all contribute to the intensity of our work, we are likely to be highly creative.

I. DRIVING PERSONALITY TRAITS OF HIGHLY CREATIVE PEOPLE

Attempts to define the personality traits of highly creative persons must be interpreted with caution. Clearly, all kinds of people, from all backgrounds, with a variety of personality characteristics, have made creative contributions to all domains of endeavor. Nonetheless, systematic attempts to study the personalities of highly creative individuals have uncovered two categories of traits that they seem to share. One category includes descriptors such as spontaneous, playful, curious, and flexible. The second category includes traits like determined, independent, confident, and persistent. Clearly, creative persons are quite complex. At once, they are childlike in their ability to be open and interested in all possibilities, and exceptionally mature in the intense focus they maintain on their work.

Donald MacKinnon and Frank Barron were the first to attempt to capture this complexity in their landmark studies of creative lives at the Institute for Personality Assessment and Research in the 1960s. They conducted in-depth investigations of highly creative individuals from many disciplines; their participants included well-known mathematicians, architects, and

writers. By administering a wide range of personality inventories, interviewing and observing these people over several days, and using appropriate controls, researchers were able to describe these highly creative people with an impressive degree of clarity and depth. They found the highly creative to be more complicated, imaginative, flexible, and original in their thinking than matched groups of less creative professionals in the same fields. They were also more individualistic, courageous, independent, and confident. These qualities seem to propel their work in two directions. They are excited about new possibilities, and so generate a range of new ideas. They also have faith in the value of their ideas and are thus able to pursue them assuredly. [*See* INSTITUTE OF PERSONALITY ASSESSMENT AND RESEARCH.]

Most current theories of creativity include these two categories of personality traits. For example, Teresa Amabile's componential theory of creativity includes a "creativity-relevant processes" component. In part, creativity-relevant processes are personality traits that allow a person to generate and follow through with creative ideas. These include a high degree of self-discipline in matters concerning work; an ability to delay gratification; perseverance in the face of frustration; independence of judgment; a high degree of autonomy; an internal locus of control; a willingness to take risks; and a high degree of self-initiated striving for excellence. Robert Sternberg's investment theory also names personality as an important component necessary for creativity. The personality traits proposed would seem to facilitate unusual responses, such as tolerance for ambiguity and moderate risk taking, or encourage follow-through, such as willingness to surmount obstacles, perseverance, and self-esteem.

Recent research provides support for the notion that highly creative persons are highly energetic persons—both in generating ideas and in pursuing them. Although there are strong differences in personalities, especially across fields, these similarities emerge consistently. One study found highly creative persons to have a passion for autonomy, a high degree of self-sufficiency, and a heightened sense of identity. Another showed that the most creative individuals tend to be highly ambitious and confident in their views.

This self-assurance may allow creative individuals to focus on personal motives and goals, rather than be overly influenced by the opinions of others. In order to study this possibility, Teresa Amabile and colleagues recently developed the Work Preference Inventory, which assesses motivational orientation as a personality characteristic. They identified two primary directions for work motivation: intrinsic motivation, which is marked by a focus on the challenge and the enjoyment of the work, and extrinsic motivation, which is marked by a focus on external reward for one's work. Their research has shown that an intrinsic motivational orientation is positively correlated with creativity on a variety of tasks, in several different subject populations. Also, people involved in creative professions, such as artists, poets, and research scientists, were higher in intrinsic motivation and lower in extrinsic motivation than the general population.

This kind of research is important in that it extends beyond the basic personality traits of creative persons and begins to explore the motives that underlie these traits. Research on personality traits describes creative individuals, but does not explain them. How does the motivation that characterizes creative persons arise? Can creative work satisfy a drive that is not otherwise satisfied? Does creativity arise as a result of psychic conflict?

II. PSYCHOLOGICAL CONFLICT AND MENTAL ILLNESS

Sigmund Freud, the father of psychoanalysis, attributed creative energy to the motivating power of human drives toward sex and aggression. He described the process of sublimation as one that transforms the unacceptable impulses of the id into acceptable, even admired, creative expression. Freud proposed that, through creative work, people can resolve difficult psychic conflicts that arise from the repressive pressure that the ego and superego place on the id. The unique nature of creative expression simultaneously satisfies the untamed impulse to express emotion, the desire to maintain moral standards, and the need to be productive. Thus, creative expression is an effective means of coping with psychic conflict. The power of id impulses are thought to explain the impressive energy and enthusiasm that brings forth the plethora of ideas generated by highly creative individuals, while the restrain-

ing forces of the ego and superego may underlie the high standards and persistence that enable creative ideas to become creative products. According to the psychoanalytic view, strong psychic needs drive these seemingly opposite, yet complementary, tendencies.

Those with psychological disturbances might be especially likely to display high levels of creativity, according to this view. Because their psychic system is not in proper balance, those suffering from mental illness would have a higher level of psychic conflict than more psychologically healthy individuals. Indeed, several studies have shown that children and adults with psychological disorders are more likely to display high levels of creativity. Of the disorders studied, affective illnesses, especially bipolar disorder and cyclothymia, have shown the most consistent relationship with creativity. Other studies have uncovered differences between highly creative and less creative groups in the incidence of affective disorder. For example, a study of prominent poets, playwrights, novelists, biographers, and artists reported that 38% had been treated for affective illness (compared to a significantly lower percentage in the general population). In another study, a higher level of affective disorders was found in a sample of creative writers. Perhaps even more interesting was the finding that the highest levels of creativity were displayed by the first-degree relatives of those with affective illness. There is little debate that affective illness is associated with creativity. There is less agreement about the mechanisms that underlie this relationship. [*See* AFFECTIVE DISORDERS; FAMILIES AND CREATIVITY.]

One school of thought proposes that creativity is simply a desirable side effect of affective illness; the severe mood swings that cause such distress also fuel the creative work that these people intensely value. By increasing the variability and intensity of experience, mental illnesses could provide useful material for creative work, while promoting an intense need for self-expression. It has been suggested that, because writers and artists draw so heavily on their life experiences and emotions for inspiration, affective illness is an advantage. The strong feelings that affective illnesses impose can be injected into art and writing, making the work more vivid and potent. Because these feelings are so powerful, expressing them is natural and satisfying.

While experiencing emotion is crucial to producing

creative work in the arts, in math and the sciences emotions do not, in themselves, contribute to creative work. There is evidence, however, that the fluctuating periods of positive and negative emotion may support the development and refinement of creative ideas in any discipline. Those suffering from mood disorders experience manic states of energy, elation, and euphoria, balanced by depressive episodes. The mania may help creators to generate ideas. During manic periods people typically need less sleep, are more active, and engage in various kinds of excessive behavior. This excessive behavior may include working intensely for long periods. While productivity may be lower during depressive episodes, they may be a good time for the evaluation of creative work produced while manic. In those with bipolar disorder, the depression eventually becomes too severe to promote high-quality work. The benefits of experiencing mania and mild depression, though, may outweigh the costs of the severe depression suffered by those with bipolar disorder. The debilitating nature of major depressive episodes may help to explain why first-degree relatives of those with affective disorders display the highest levels of creativity. They may experience mood swings severe enough to support their work, but not so severe that they are debilitated. Another possibility is that the success of their creative work helps to make their mood fluctuations less extreme. The symptoms of affective disorders contribute to the vitality of creative work. Creative work may, in turn, contribute to a person's resources for coping with affective illness.

People suffering from mental illness may be attracted to creative pursuits as an opportunity to work through their psychic conflicts. In addition to having more psychological problems, creatively gifted individuals also have an enhanced ability to cope with their problems. Highly creative individuals may be those who are able to use self-expression in their work as a way to endure their mental illness. For example, when individuals write about emotional experiences their physical and mental health improve as a result. A crucial component of therapy is self-disclosure. While feedback of some kind is inherent in the therapy process, simply expressing painful emotions has a substantial beneficial impact on psychological functioning. The creative process, because it often involves self-expression, may be a useful means of working through psychological problems. In fact, various kinds of creative activities have been incorporated into recent therapeutic efforts. Clinicians have used artwork, music, and drama to encourage creative expression, and thus improve mental health.

Creativity might also support mental health by promoting feelings of self-worth and competence. A great deal of self-esteem can come from creative accomplishment. Those suffering from affective disorders, or any form of mental illness, may have a fragile sense of worth. A deep involvement in creative work may allow them to channel their anxieties into a valuable pursuit. The work itself may represent a part of the self that is valued and under the individual's control. The recognition that comes when the work is complete can be self-affirming. Of course, the criticism and failure that are also an inevitable part of efforts toward creativity may have the opposite effect. When creative work is progressing well, it may be wonderfully supportive. In times of difficulty, individuals may seek therapy as a way of coping with their symptoms.

Although the traditional psychoanalytic approach conceptualizes creativity as emanating from psychic conflict, it paradoxically proposes that creativity promotes psychological health. A greater incidence of affective disorders is observed in highly creative individuals, yet creative expression may be a positive means of coping with strong and conflicting emotions. Does creativity necessarily arise from psychic conflict? Or does it reflect a drive toward mental health? Rather than satisfying basic biological drives, could creativity perhaps satisfy human needs for personal growth and fulfillment? Humanistic psychologists have addressed these questions.

III. SELF-ACTUALIZATION: THE DRIVE TOWARD GROWTH

Humanism places a great deal of importance on respecting the potential of individual people. It is grounded in the belief that people have a great capacity for creativity. Humanists recognize that basic biological needs have an impact on behavior, but they focus on higher needs: needs for self-improvement, self-expression, spontaneity, humor, and love. They believe that creativity arises from a natural human tendency toward growth and self-actualization. Self-actualization represents the height of mental health. Self-actualized persons are comfortable with themselves and with others. Rather than focusing on themselves, they pursue important problems. They seek beauty, meaningfulness, and justice in their work. Self-actualization promotes experiencing and enjoying life fully, while producing valuable and creative work.

Abraham Maslow was one of the founders of humanistic thought. Starting with his two teachers, Ruth Benedict and Max Wertheimer, he studied the lives of highly creative persons in depth. His subjects included Eleanor Roosevelt, Abraham Lincoln, Albert Einstein, Jane Addams, Aldous Huxley, and, perhaps most revealing, himself! It was through this work that he was able to define the characteristics of self-actualizing persons, who are by definition highly creative. The picture that emerged was far from the mad genius that psychoanalytic theorists identified. Instead, these people were psychologically healthy, independent, happy, and highly productive. This work grew from Maslow's well-known theory of motivation.

Maslow's theory proposes a hierarchy of human needs. At the base of the hierarchy are the most pressing: physiological and safety needs. If basic needs for food, water, and safety are not met, the individual becomes exclusively focused on meeting them. Once they are met, the next steps of the hierarchy become important: needs for belonging, love, and self-esteem. When each of these needs is satisfied, the individual becomes consumed with self-actualization needs. Needs lower on the hierarchy are considered deficiency needs because they become stronger when they are not met. Thus, they operate as drives do. The need for self-actualization is a growth need; the more it is fulfilled, the stronger it becomes. Creativity emerges from the need for self-actualization. From Maslow's perspective, the motivation underlying creativity does not operate as a drive, but instead is a self-perpetuating process.

Carl Rogers, another prominent humanistic theorist, focused on how the social environment can promote self-actualization. He believed that in order to function fully, people must accept themselves as they truly are. This self-acceptance only comes from positive, accepting experiences with others. If children are loved unconditionally, they will accept themselves and develop the urge to self-actualize. Although self-actualization is the central life-promoting force, in Rogers' view, it is

also quite fragile. If children are loved only under certain conditions, their development will be impaired; they will focus on gaining love, rather than becoming their true selves. Experiences of love and acceptance throughout life can promote psychological growth, according to Rogers. With psychological growth comes the potential for creativity.

Mihaly Csikszentmihalyi has also explored the process that supports the self-actualizing tendency. More specifically, Csikszentmihalyi has studied optimal experiences or peak experiences, as Maslow called them. Self-actualizing individuals take great pleasure in their work. At times, they experience states of complete and utter absorption in the work. They lose all sense of time. Csikszentmihalyi has labeled this highly enjoyable state "flow." Work produced during flow is often highly creative. Through extensive interviews and field studies, Csikszentmihalyi has identified the conditions that facilitate flow. The most important appears to be an optimal level of challenge in relation to a person's level of skill at a task. If challenges are too great, the person becomes anxious, and his enjoyment and concentration is disrupted. If the task is not challenging enough, it is experienced as boring. One way that highly creative people maintain their motivation is by seeking optimally challenging work. As their skills develop, they will pursue more and more difficult problems. This process likely contributes to the self-reinforcing nature of the self-actualizing tendency.

While self-actualization is an appealing construct for explaining the motivation behind creativity, it does not seem consistent with the strong relationship between mental illness and creativity. Humanists might point to the finding that the highest levels of creativity were shown by the first-degree relatives of those with affective illness. Perhaps these persons had a tendency toward affective illness, but were loved, supported, and challenged, and thus able to pursue their self-actualization needs. Those actively suffering from affective illness may periodically be able to meet their deficiency needs and produce creative work. Humanistic theorists might deny that the highly creative were truly mentally ill at all. Or, they might not consider novel products produced by mentally ill individuals to be true creativity.

Celeste Rhodes provides a more satisfying answer. She proposes that both basic needs and self-actualization needs can motivate creativity. From these two categories of needs, Rhodes defined two types of creativity. The first satisfies the deficiency needs in Maslow's hierarchy. This type of creativity aids psychological functioning, can serve to work through psychic conflicts, and increases self-esteem. The work leading to this type of creativity has a driven quality. Such individuals *need* to be creative in order to be satisfied with themselves. The second type of creativity is motivated by growth needs. This type of creative work is pursued for the beauty of the work itself, in order to reach a higher level of understanding or to solve an important problem. The motive of the artist, according to Rhodes, has an important impact on the final product. The audience can appreciate the transcendent understanding expressed by the self-actualizing creator.

The personality traits that characterize highly creative persons can be viewed within the context of the motives that underlie them. Psychic conflict may drive the imagination, excitement, and persistence behind creative work. On the other side of the spectrum is the motivating force of self-actualization. This tendency toward growth brings with it the confidence, spontaneity, and commitment needed for creative expression. Although quite intense, self-actualization is a positive motivating force, not a drive. The self-actualizing creator loves to work and becomes deeply absorbed in it. the common personality traits of highly creative individuals are motivated by both basic drives and a tendency toward growth and fulfillment. [*See* SELF-ACTUALIZATION.]

Our analysis, thus far, has focused on the creative person. Are there factors outside the person that motivate creativity? Can creativity be encouraged or thwarted by the social environment? Behaviorists focus on efforts to encourage creativity with rewards.

IV. REINFORCING CREATIVE EFFORTS

B. F. Skinner championed the effort to develop the scientific study of observable behavior, an approach known as behaviorism. Because internal states could not be measured directly, Skinner focused on the influence that the external environment has on behavior. After years of carefully controlled experiments, Skinner became convinced that the most important principle underlying the control of behavior was operant conditioning. Operant conditioning is the process by which behavior is followed by consequences that influence the frequency of that behavior in the future. If a reinforcer follows a behavior, it will occur more frequently. If a punishment follows a behavior, it will occur less frequently. Because of the pain and fear that punishment causes, Skinner advocated the use of reinforcers to control behavior. His analysis of creativity followed this principle precisely. Creative behavior could be promoted, he argued, by following it with a reinforcer.

Reinforcers gain their motivating properties by satisfying a basic need or drive. Food is a commonly used reinforcer in animal experiments. Hungry people also find food reinforcing, but many other items have been used in experiments with children and adults including money, praise, awards, stickers, and small toys. When a person is behaving in order to obtain a reinforcer, that person is motivated by the need that will be met by the reinforcer. So, rather than the creative activity itself satisfying the need, as the psychodynamic and humanistic approaches propose, the need is satisfied by the consequence that follows the activity. The motivation to be creative, from a behaviorist view, is simply the tendency to seek reinforcing consequences and avoid punishing ones.

There is much support for the notion that rewards for creativity are essential for encouraging it. Even Freud once wrote that money, prestige, and sexual rewards were essential to maintaining creativity. Certainly, an environment where creative outcomes are followed by desirable consequences is likely to be an environment where creative efforts are frequent. Using the Torrance Tests of Creative Thinking, Mark Runco has shown that providing rewards for divergent thought can increase the fluency of responses. Robert Eisenberger and his colleagues have also demonstrated that reinforcing divergent thinking on word construction and picture drawing tasks can enhance future divergent thought. Teresa Amabile's work in business organizations has shown that when there are rewards for creativity in the work environment, work teams reach more creative outcomes. The reinforcement principle, applied in the most global sense, holds true.

Some behaviorist thinkers go a step further, and propose that creative responses can be shaped by contingencies of reinforcement. They conceptualize every creative behavior as a combination of simpler behaviors. If a creative behavior is broken down into the series of behaviors that compose it, a program of reinforcement could be devised to strengthen the likelihood of each component behavior. As Skinner explained it, some people will display true creativity, but before that can happen they need something to be creative with. Previously established behavior manifests itself in new situations in orderly ways. When the environment facilitates it, this order can result in high levels of novelty. Creativity, according to these theorists, is simply connecting previously learned behavior in new ways.

The practical problem with this approach, however, is that in order to develop a reinforcement plan, it is necessary to know all of the component skills involved in a creative outcome before the outcome occurs. Naturally, for truly original work, this is impossible. A second problem is the evidence that not all component parts of creative behavior are responsive to reinforcement. Kenneth McGraw distinguished between tasks that are algorithmic (clear and straightforward) and heuristic (require exploration and discovery). His research showed that algorithmic tasks are responsive to reinforcement while heuristic tasks are not. Amabile further developed this idea by proposing that some elements within creative activities are algorithmic and will, thus, respond very well to reinforcement. Reinforcing heuristic aspects of a creative task is more difficult; reinforcers may be effective if they are not salient, if the person is highly interested in the activity, or if the reinforcer provides useful feedback. Amabile's work points to the importance of considering the subjective experience of the creative person in order to determine the impact of a reinforcer.

The behaviorist approach represents an advance over previous work that considered only the individual's characteristics and motives in understanding the source of creativity. Research from this perspective highlights the importance of the external environment for supporting creativity. Yet, it also presents an incomplete picture. By considering only environmental variables, behaviorist thinking leaves the creator out of its explanation of the motivation underlying creativity.

How are an individual's motives influenced by the social environment? Is it possible to consider both the person and the situation in exploring the motivation underlying creativity? Several recent theories have attempted to do so.

V. INTRINSIC MOTIVATION AND THE SOCIAL ENVIRONMENT

Contemporary approaches to understanding the impact of the social environment on creativity propose that external factors, including reinforcers, influence creativity by the effect that they have on the individual's motivational state. Amabile, in her componential model of creativity, was among the first to advance such a proposal. According to the model, an individual's level of creativity is determined by three primary factors. The first is the person's level of domain-relevant skills, which include knowledge, developed talent, and special skills in the target domain. The second is the person's level of creativity-relevant processes, which include personality characteristics, styles of thinking, and styles of working that facilitate creativity. The third is the person's motivation toward the task. The model describes the impact that the social environment has on all three components, but emphasizes the role of the social environment in determining task motivation. The intrinsic motivation principle of creativity specifies that intrinsic motivation (derived from interest and enjoyment of the activity itself) is conducive to creativity, while extrinsic motivation (directed at a goal separate from the task) can be detrimental.

Thus, the intrinsic motivation principle considers the impact of the social environment on creativity, as the behaviorist approach does. At the same time, given its view that creativity emanates from natural human tendencies, the intrinsic motivation principle is compatible with the work of the psychodynamic and humanistic fields. Intrinsic motivation is the inherent satisfaction that we derive from productive, engaging activity. Perhaps a task is intrinsically interesting because it satisfies basic needs or allows the individual to resolve psychic conflict. To those whose basic needs have been met, a task may be intrinsically interesting because it is challenging, focuses on an important problem, or allows them to achieve a higher level of understanding. When a person's intrinsic motivation is supported, she is more likely to be highly creative. If she is pressured or constrained by extrinsic motivators, she is less likely to be creative.

Using similar reasoning, Mihaly Csikszentmihalyi proposed that creativity arises in "autotelic" activities, where rewards stem from engagement in the activity itself, rather than from an external source. A concern for extrinsic rewards, or reinforcers, could interfere with an individual's focus, and disrupt the fragile process of discovery.

There is considerable empirical support for the intrinsic motivation principle. When extrinsic constraints are imposed on individuals who are working on an intrinsically interesting task in the laboratory, the work they produce is, on average, less creative than when extrinsic constraints are not imposed. Amabile and her colleagues have shown this effect with several different kinds of creative activities, including making collages, writing stories, and building towers, and with a variety of subject populations, including preschoolers, elementary school children, college students, and creative writers. This effect has been observed when research participants expected their work to be evaluated, when they were being observed (surveillance), when they contracted to do the activity in order to obtain a reward, when they were asked to compete with other participants, when they were denied choice, and when they were simply led to focus on extrinsic motivators. Many of these same extrinsic constraints have been observed to undermine creativity in real-world settings. In one study, research scientists reported that strong extrinsic incentives interfered with the development of creative ideas in their laboratories. Another study found that professional artists were less creative when their work was commissioned, as compared with when it was not commissioned.

Although there is substantial evidence that extrinsic constraints can undermine creativity, recent experimental and nonexperimental evidence shows that in some circumstances, extrinsic constraints have no influence, or even enhance creativity. To explain the patterns of results that have been observed, Amabile has formulated a theory of motivational synergy. The central premise of the theory is that although intrinsic motivation is necessary for high levels of creativity, extrinsic motivation is not always detrimental. Some forms of extrinsic motivation may combine positively with intrinsic motivation, and thus boost overall levels of creativity. The theory proposes that this is most likely when intrinsic motivation is initially high and when the extrinsic motivators are perceived as supporting, rather than limiting, autonomy and skill development. The motivational synergy theory acknowledges the motivational potential of extrinsic reinforcers, while emphasizing the importance of maintaining the highest levels of intrinsic motivation in order to facilitate creative accomplishment.

Other social psychological theories consider the impact of the wider social environment. For example, in David Harrington's work on long-term collaborative groups, it has been proposed that a "creative ecosystem" must develop within the group, in order to support ongoing creativity. Because creative people tend to be curious and active, their ecosystems need to provide them with encouragement and opportunities for playful task engagement. These opportunities sustain their intrinsic motivation toward their work. Reinforcing creative effort is also important. A multifaceted reward system can capitalize on the variety of motivations that creative individuals bring to work. This work suggests that the principles of motivational synergy apply to work groups as well as individuals. Other theorists have considered the influence of the larger community in their analysis of the motivation underlying creativity.

Dean Keith Simonton considered the broad cultural, social, political, and historical influences on creativity. Findings from his program of archival research both support and go beyond those uncovered in experimental and traditional observational studies. In one study he found that musicians who had a higher number of contemporary competitors were less creative than those who faced less competition. This research demonstrates that factors in the wider cultural environment can impact creativity. Many of these factors are analogous to those identified as influencing creativity in the immediate social environment. Other researchers have adopted a perspective that incorporates the wider cultural climate, the physical surroundings, and the immediate social environment. These factors influence people differently depending on their past experiences and their personality characteristics. Thus, social psychological approaches to creativity motivation range from those concentrating narrowly on the influence of particular motivators on an individual to those broadly considering the full range of influences across the lifespan. [*See* CONDITIONS AND SETTINGS/ENVIRONMENT; CREATIVE CLIMATE.]

VI. CONCLUSION

Highly creative individuals are also highly motivated individuals. They stand out as curious and playful, yet persistent and committed. They appear to be driven, and in some cases, unstable or even mentally ill. Their energy seems self-perpetuating: a positive, growth-promoting force. Their efforts often pay off with those around them appreciating their work and generously compensating them for it. At the same time, they are devoted to what they do. Rather than being lured by fame, status, or wealth, highly creative persons often seem most excited about the pleasure of engaging in the work that they love.

The five approaches reviewed here start in very different places in their attempts to explain the energy behind creativity. The essence of each approach rings true, leading to a picture more complete and more complex than any single explanation could provide.

The social psychological approach comes the closest to recognizing the diversity of energy sources that support creativity. An understanding of how a person can become completely absorbed in creative activity emerges by focusing both on the individual's motives and on the enormous influence of the social environment.

Bibliography

Amabile, T. M. (1996). *Creativity in context: Update to the social psychology of creativity.* Boulder, CO: Westview Press.

Barron, F. X. (1969). *Creative person and creative process.* New York: Holt, Rinehart and Winston.

Csikszentmihalyi, M. (1996). *Creativity: Flow and the psychology of discovery and invention.* New York: Harper Collins.

Gedo, J., & Gedo, M. (1992). *Perspectives on creativity.* Norwood, NJ: Ablex.

Glover, J. A., Ronning, R. R., & Reynolds, C. R. (1989). *Handbook of creativity.* New York: Plenum Press.

Jamison, K. R. (1993). *Touched with fire: Manic-depressive illness and the artistic temperament.* New York: Free Press Paperbacks.

Runco, M. A., & Albert, R. S. (1990). *Theories of creativity: Contemporary psychological perspectives.* Newbury Park, CA: Sage.

Simonton, D. K. (1984). *Genius, creativity, and leadership.* Cambridge, MA: Harvard University Press.

Sternberg, R. J. (1988). *The nature of creativity: Contemporary psychological perspectives.* New York: Cambridge University Press.

Multiple Discovery

Amy Ione

Art and Science Writer, Berkeley, California

Abduction A logical operation that introduces an explanatory hypothesis by moving the form of inquiry from a universally recognized problem to a tentative, but nevertheless plausible solution.

Eponymy The practice of affixing names to all or a part of what someone has invented, discovered, or supported (e.g., Euclidean geometry, daguerreotype, Planck's constant, and Boyle's Law).

Parallel Discoveries Independent and similar discoveries.

Pluralism Grants a kind of equivalence to many possibilities, making them seem more or less equal.

Problem Finding The recognition, identification, and definition of an anomaly, obstacle, or problem that must be resolved in order for problem solving to begin.

Singleton Something only invented or discovered once.

Zeitgeist Spirit of the times. The actual spirit of a zeitgeist can only be understood in a long retrospect.

MULTIPLE DISCOVERY is typically defined as when two or more scientists or inventors simultaneously give expression to a similar theory, form, model, or invention.

That being said, it is necessary to consider the relationship between the words "multiple" and "discovery." Traditionally, the central meaning of discovery has been to gain knowledge or awareness of something previously unknown. Multiple, on the other hand, is defined as "more than one." When coupled with discovery, multiple is intended to denote that scientists operate within a community and that discoveries reflect an ongoing exchange and communication process. This means discovery is defined as contextual (rather than exceptional) and that multiple discovery is defined as the normal method by which science proceeds. It should be noted that (1) an invention or discovery is termed a singleton if it is only discovered once and that (2) parallel discoveries are defined as those that are independent of one another and simultaneous in time. Parallels will be considered multiples in this article and the two terms will be used interchangeably.

I. OVERVIEW

Contemporary research into multiple discovery reflects the changing nature of the scientific environment as well as the current interest in social science studies. Areas of primary interest and debate include: (1) how the discoveries of particular individuals are related to the broader community, (2) whether multiple discoveries are inevitable, (3) whether parallel discoveries show similar levels of completion, (4) how to evaluate a time lag between a discovery and the cultural acceptance of it, (5) the difficulty in defining creativity in a general sense when using definitions derived from a scientifically determined multiples framework, and (6) the ways we define creative products as compared to definitions applied to creative people and creative processes. This article integrates these areas with specific historical examples, as follows: Contextual issues related to scientific institutional practices, values, and unexpected discoveries will be presented in Section II. Section III explores the relationship between the individual and the community, focusing primarily on examples combining science and the visual arts. The final section integrates multiple discovery with cultural, philosophical, and educational issues of concern.

Before turning to specific examples, it needs to be stated that multiple discovery discussions are complex. On the one hand, the overall strength of the multiples argument rests on the evidence that scientists do work and interact within a community. This community, by definition, is a domain where several people are using similar methods and technologies in exploring problems of scientific interest. As such, the argument favoring multiple discovery is based on the evidence that shared ideas and shared instruments are an integral part of each individual scientist's biography. The evidence of information exchange is further supported by the evidence that many discoveries do share patterns of similarity. Moreover, the extensive number of parallel discoveries that have been documented support the idea that something critical is lost when discovery is simply reduced to psychological thoughts and subjective processes within the heads of creative individuals. Finally, the concept of community allows discovery to be broadly defined so as to include the products that are often needed for a discovery to be practical. For example, the invention of the telephone—be it attributed to Elisha Gray, Alexander Graham Bell, or both—necessitated the invention of switching devices, amplifiers, transformers, and transmission mechanisms.

On the other hand, the prevalence of multiples throughout scientific history has not convinced all that the idea of multiples is the best way to characterize creativity. Critics of multiples say that conceiving of scientific innovation simply in terms of community ex-

change pushes aside many unresolved issues in regard to what creativity actually is. These unresolved areas, the critics add, include the "art" of science, the evidence that chance only favors the prepared mind, and the particular kinds of education, focus, and passion creative individuals bring to their work. This article leans toward the latter view, this being that multiple discovery per se does not comprehensively address what human creativity is and what particular individuals contribute to their projects and to community exchange.

II. SCIENTIFIC ISSUES AND HISTORICAL EXAMPLES

A. Institutional Practices and Values

The ideal of science has always included the presupposition that humility is a part of a cooperative effort to reveal (and apply) universals. Yet, and despite the value placed on humility in scientific practice, proof of personal accomplishment is a critical component in gaining professional employment, prestige, promotion, and funding. Thus, a picture of dedicated individuals working toward human good is often contrasted with a picture of scientists working for the rewards associated with professional recognition within the institutional system. This contrast has had an impact on studies in multiple discovery. One issue the contrast has raised is whether it actually brings a contradiction into scientific institutions in regard to practices and values. From a creativity perspective this includes the question of whether these kinds of conflicting priorities leave room for work done for the personal reward gained in solving difficult problems as well as the rewards of professional promotion. In addition, if there is room for both kinds of rewards to coexist, does the practice of rewarding some individuals for research advances obscure that many hands and many minds work in tandem as science develops?

As will be presently shown, these are not easy questions. The diversity of scientific work allows one a great deal of latitude in formulating conclusions that both support and diffuse the idea of multiple discoveries. Before expanding on this statement, it should be noted that the literature on multiple discovery catalogs numerous parallel and independent discoveries. For example, an incomplete list of well-known parallel discoveries would include: (1) the independent invention of the differential and integral calculus by Isaac Newton and Gottfried Wilhelm Leibniz, (2) the discovery of the lightbulb by both Sir Joseph Wilson Swann and Thomas Edison, (3) the independent discovery of the fundamental principle of analytic geometry by Pierre de Fermat and René Descartes, (4) the discovery of Neptune, generally credited to the British mathematician John Couch Adams as well as Urbain-Jean-Joseph Le Verrier of France, and (5) the non-Euclidean geometries independently discovered by Nikolai Ivanovich Lobachevsky, Janos Bolyai, Karl Friedrich Gauss, and George Friedrich Bernhard Riemann. All show that parallel, independent investigation is possible.

Nonetheless, historical examples highlight four points of primary importance. First, a critical defining element of creativity has been the individual, heroic, "genius" model. One reason it has endured is that it is compatible with both theories of genetic determination and theories that suggest creative insight comes from out of nowhere, as if one is touched by something akin to the divine. Built on the image of God, the Creator, the model took form primarily in the Renaissance and has served as a means to glorify individual accomplishments. Still in use today, this perspective generally proposes that creativity is something particular to exceptional people. Second, despite the general acceptance of the genius model, people sympathetic to multiple discovery have always kept multiple discovery in the pool of cultural ideas. For example, philosopher Francis Bacon's (1561–1626) interest in multiple discovery establishes that the idea has a long history. Third, the practice of teamwork in 20th century science and the difficulty this creates in establishing the contributions of particular individuals have challenged the genius model, fostered interest in multiple discovery today, and generated investigations into "product" rather than "person"-based models. Finally, in a general sense, independent, parallel discoveries are hard to dispute. In light of this it should be stated that one fascinating element that highlights priority is of great importance to people is that discoveries tend to be credited differently from country to country, countries choosing to honor their own citizens. [*See* TEAMS.]

Contemporary consideration of the preceding four areas was initiated by sociologists, anthropologists, and historians of science. All convincingly cataloged a vast number of parallel discoveries and, in doing so, emphasized the role of context (rather than person), institutional practices, and values. Contemporary discussions continue to draw upon this work, and continue to keenly debate the conclusions. One significant area of debate is Robert Merton's idea of the "Matthew effect." According to *Matthew* (25:29), "Unto every one that hath shall be given, and he shall have abundance: but from him that hath not shall be taken away even that which he hath." Merton's point here was that whether position includes the commemorative use of eponymy or simply results in better funding, those who are credited with priority are given position and thus also have the leverage to disproportionately increase their stature on an ongoing basis. [*See* MATTHEW EFFECTS.]

While evidence can be offered in support of this view, as in all areas concerning multiple discovery, there is also evidence to temper it. Briefly, most do agree that parallel discoveries do exist in science, priority is often disputed, many of the disputes involve values, and it does help to be at the right place at the right time. Moreover, many of the disputes are acrimonious, long-standing, and aggressively pursued. But the wrangling appears to be oversimplified when characterized as the esteemed as opposed to the marginal. [*See* SCIENCE.]

For example, the controversy between Newton and Leibniz over the invention of the calculus is one of the best known examples of a priority dispute involving parallel discoveries. It did not involve an esteemed individual and one on the margins of science. Rather, the dispute involved two individuals of high repute. Thus the disagreement can easily be interpreted in many ways. One is that it is simply an example of how hard-fought some priority battles are. Although Leibniz published first, Newton developed his version of the calculus several years earlier. While it is now generally agreed that the two systems use different approaches and were developed independently, at the time each man accused the other of plagiarism. It was an emotional disagreement, to put it mildly, and when Newton became the President of the Royal Society he decided to appoint a committee to adjudicate the rival claims of Leibniz and himself on the matter of priority.

Historical records reveal Newton packed the committee, directed its activities, and wrote many of the published reports issued by the group. The second report (a draft of which was written in Newton's handwriting) is especially noteworthy because the anonymous author (Newton!) states that "no one is a proper witness in his own cause." Given the way the investigation was conducted it is not surprising that the committee voted in favor of Newton.

This is not to say that parallels are synonymous with animosity. When Charles Darwin first received a copy of Alfred Wallace's theory of evolution he spoke of the striking coincidence, for even Darwin's chapter headings used Wallace's terms. This striking coincidence illustrates that regardless of whether one wants to credit Darwin for the theory of natural selection or characterize the insight as a multiple discovery and then attribute it to Darwin and Wallace (they presented their work together in a joint paper at the Linnaean Society on July 1, 1858), it does not change the fact that the theories took form at a particular point in time. This "coincidence" has encouraged many to apply the idea of zeitgeist to parallel discoveries and to emphasize that parallels appear to reflect the spirit of a time. This correlation is not universally assumed to be correct.

The issue here is what, if anything, does the zeitgeist concept add. The arguments are complex. The philosophical debating points, discussed in more detail later, are whether a zeitgeist view implies inevitability and whether defining discovery in terms of a "spirit of a time" makes it difficult to explain discovery in a developmental way. Briefly, on the one hand, some arguments state that zeitgeist fails to contend with factors that are not a part of a culture per se, such as natural catastrophes and serendipity. Although these kinds of events significantly impact individual ideas as well as the broader community, they do not germinate from within a culture or even from within an individual. Specific concepts proposed to explain (or explain away) zeitgeist in light of the existence of inexplicable events include God, free will, fate, causality, chance, and determinism. On the other hand, there are also concrete, contextual debating points that are often a part of zeitgeist discussion. These turn on the evidence that some individuals within a specific cultural environment will see theoretical and actual possibilities their colleagues miss. Being an area that involves the community, this

area is of particular relevance to scientific multiple discovery. It is explored next. [*See* SERENDIPITY; ZEITGEIST.]

B. Unexpected Discoveries

The crux of the debate surrounding unexpected discoveries in science centers on why some choose to investigate anomalies in nature and theory that others noticed and did not pursue. In other words, often a scientist chooses to focus on more solvable or socially esteemed problems. Later, with the evidence that an important discovery touches on material he or she had seen and ignored the scientist is likely to acknowledge having seen a facsimile and put it aside. As such, the multiples issue is not just that history books, perhaps in error, tend to refer to discoveries in terms of individuals (e.g., we speak of Halley's comet, the Copernican revolution, and the Linnaean system). Rather, there is also evidence that a contextually defined focus for discovery can overlook that products are not generic and that the minds of particular individuals have made a difference.

Sir Alexander Fleming's discovery of penicillin and Wilhelm Conrad Roentgen's discovery of X-rays offer examples of investigations where individual attention did make a difference. In Fleming's case, for instance, he noticed a bacteria-free circle in a petri dish had been spoiled by a mold that killed the bacteria (in September 1928). Investigating, he found a substance in the mold that prevented growth of the bacteria and he termed it penicillin. Historical records indicate that similar observations had been made 50 years earlier, the primary difference between the earlier work and Fleming's is that only Fleming's work led to the discovery of antibiotics.

Roentgen, on the other hand, discovered the X-ray (in November 1895) when he found that invisible radiation could not only penetrate solid, opaque substances but was also capable of producing images of the interiors. The investigation began in full force only after Roentgen observed his bones were visible on a photographic plate during one of his experiments. At this time, Roentgen was working with cathode rays and a variation of a Crookes tube designed by a younger colleague, Philipp Lenard (who later demanded credit for the discovery). After Roentgen investigated the anomaly, he deduced that the rays created the image of his bones, which were easily discernable through his skin due to the different qualities of bones and flesh. The critical point here is that many scientists were working with Crookes tubes and cathode rays at this time. For example, A. W. Godspeed of the University of Pennsylvania and a friend, W. J. Jennings, had made similar pictures six years earlier and filed them away. In addition, Crookes, the inventor of the tube, had observed that photographic plates fogged when placed near a Crookes tube. The evidence of these earlier observations has encouraged some to argue that the discovery of X-rays was inevitable and thus a multiple. Critics of adopting this hard-line view note that the distinguishing element Roentgen brings to the picture is his willingness to investigate when he saw something that logically should not have appeared before his eyes (the image of his bones through his opaque skin). In Crookes' case, for instance, he did not ask what could be gleaned from the fogged plates. Instead, he returned the tubes to the manufacturer with the claim that they were defective.

In sum, these two discoveries are frequently cited because neither pristinely fits into a multiples category, despite the fact that both are often, correctly, classified as products of their time. These examples are also debated because they show that some discoveries are more complete than others. In addition, both examples raise the question of whether unexpected discoveries should be considered as equal to similar discoveries that were made earlier when the earlier "discoverers" decided not to pursue what they noticed. Finally, these examples raise the question of whether there is a contradiction regarding discovery embedded in the multiples definition. In other words, the multiples definition does not convincingly account for anomalies that were "seen" and ignored a number of times before the individual credited with the discovery recognized that he was seeing an event worthy of investigation. [*See* DISCOVERY.]

It should be emphasized that the preceding scientific examples do not dispute that multiple discovery is compatible with the idea that scientists are a community sharing a common stock of knowledge. Rather, they illuminate why some state that characterizing unexpected discoveries as multiples omits the importance of addressing problem finding in models of creativity. Problem finding, according to these critics, is why dis-

covery is not a social construction, a logical exercise, or even abduction. More specifically, problem finding is a critical part of discovery, and far-reaching creativity includes problem finding, attention, background, training, and interest. Attention, background, training, and interest also speak of the importance of the individual in discovery. Examples that focus on the individual in turn raise the question of how each individual is related to the broader community environment. This is explored in the next section by turning to examples that combine science and the visual arts. [*See* PROBLEM FINDING.]

III. SCIENCE AND THE VISUAL ARTS

The literature regarding visual art has always characterized multiple discovery somewhat differently from what is found in science and social science publications. Given this, a short introduction is needed before introducing multiple discoveries that include the visual arts. Briefly, the diversity of art and art as a practice show that the art within any particular culture has been compatible with ideas about multiple discovery in a general (contextual) sense. This is because art has been a part of all cultures and has also developed along with cultural traditions. Moreover, throughout most of history artistic styles have changed gradually, reflecting that subtle refinements were made by practitioners as the cultural wisdom passed from generation to generation. One result of this gradual evolution is that it has often been difficult to look at the art of a culture and identify the hand of any one particular artist. It has also been difficult to distinguish one hand from that of others. In part this can be explained by the fact that a good artist was not striving to achieve something new. Rather, the belief was that good art was art made according to time-honored formulas and, toward this end, artists generally used traditional tools and techniques. To state this in terms used in the scientific survey outlined earlier, the emphasis was on producing the product according to the community's standards, not a unique process or the individual's contribution per se. [*See* ART AND AESTHETICS; ART AND ARTISTS.]

Within this matrix, some cultural periods include process and individuals to a larger degree. They also stand out as exceptions to this statement. These periods thus offer benchmarks useful in bracketing the practice of art in relation to multiple discovery in science. Well-known benchmarks include (but are not limited to) classical Greece, Renaissance Florence, Elizabethan London, and the 19th century fin-de-siècle. The styles associated with these periods are distinct and thus capable of demonstrating how particular artists have invented new technologies, redefined long-standing formulas, and altered time-honored practices. In addition, in these periods of rapid cultural change we can pinpoint specific problems that were redefined, and these problems can be aligned with a multiples characterization to show that a larger cultural redefinition includes many domains. Overall, this generalized approach has convincingly shown that art forms differ from culture to culture and that social factors inform artistic motivation, opportunity, the choice of genre, and how the choices of one generation are transmitted to future generations.

Two points are critical here. First, when we approach the context in this way we find that discovery in the visual arts, as in science, can be defined using multiple and singleton perspectives. Second, retrospective analysis of art and science often excludes the fact that many elements of art practice are not scientific concerns. Questions particular to art include, is an artistic work intended to form a relationship with the viewer as well as the creator of the work, or is the product an objective statement? Should a work be characterized as more successful when many viewers identify with it? Why (and to what degree) have artistic traditions (especially in the West) benefited from the ways artists have conformed (and failed to conform) to the norm? In other words, it is precisely because artists produce a different kind of product than scientists, and have different intentions when engaged with the practical problems that govern art making, that it is harder to integrate art into the type of contextual presentation used for scientific discovery, including multiple discovery.

This suggests that when we address art and science together, the inquiry into mutliples must include additional questions as well. For example, how do artistic and scientific discoveries (be they multiples or singleton) compare? Why are artistic styles defined in different kinds of terms than those used for the contextual analysis of scientific theories? Why do artistic styles

represent some elements (e.g., aesthetic and democratic) science includes and other modes (e.g., political, sexual, and religious) scientists claim they attempt to remove from their investigations? Why have there been so many kinds of artistic practice and representational systems throughout history? And, finally, why does the idea of convergence in discoveries so evident in science seem inadequate and incomplete for the kinds of contextual (multiple) discoveries found in art?

This section cannot address these questions in detail. Therefore this article will turn to three case studies (the invention of oil painting, Galileo's illustrations of the moon, and the impact of photography on 19th century painting) to offer an overview of multiple discovery in science and the visual arts. Before proceeding to the specific examples, it should be noted that while art and science are often represented in terms of dichotomies (e.g., imagination and logic, objective and subjective, inner and outer), this article does not proceed in this way. While it is beyond the scope of this article to outline why these dichotomies have become popular, it nonetheless is important to state that scholarly work in the history of art has shown these kinds of dichotomies distort the many interactive elements that are a part of discovery in art. The use of dichotomies thus tends to obscure that visual artists and scientists alike grapple with concrete materials and subtle relationships. As they do so, their work combines theory with experiment and the individual, probing mind with the products that result.

A. Individual Contributions and Multiple Discoveries

1. The Invention of Oil Painting

Two early sources on the lives of artists, Giorgio Vasari's *Lives of the Artists* (1550) and Karel van Mander's *The Lives of the Illustrious Netherlandish and German Painters,* from the first edition of the Schilder-boeck (1603–1604), described oil painting as a sudden technical innovation that was discovered by Jan van Eyck (~1395–~1441) after much experimentation. In recent years extensive documentation has established that many painters were experimenting with oil, even as far back as the 8th century. What van Eyck (and other Netherlandish painters) did was see the optical possibility of using systematic glazing to make a painted surface look more realistic. Still, and despite the evidence that clearly documents the invention of oil paintings was a cultural (and thus a multiple) discovery, research has yet to explain why people continue to be drawn to agree with the attribution of priority to van Eyck. His paintings are often introduced in books with the statement that in viewing them one can see why van Eyck had long been credited with the invention. This tendency to attribute the discovery to van Eyck is then explained by looking closely at his work and at descriptions of van Eyck's virtuosity. For example, to demonstrate that van Eyck knew ways to make oil paint behave that no one had displayed before him, the eminent art historian Erwin Panofsky wrote that van Eyck's eye operated as both a microscope and a telescope. As a result, according to Panofsky, the beholder's eye is compelled to oscillate between a position reasonably far from the picture and many positions very close to it.

In sum, it is because the art establishes this complex relationship with the viewer that people are inclined to agree that van Eyck was not a technician. He had a style of application most of his contemporaries could not duplicate, even when using the same materials and approach. This evaluation highlights that something particular to van Eyck is evident in his paintings. His "eye," his attention to detail and color relationships, his patience in application, and the rich quality of his descriptive product cannot simply be reduced to his knowledge of painting techniques and the evidence that the invention of oil paint was actually a multiple discovery.

2. Galileo and the Moon

Galileo's illustrations of the moon expand on the van Eyck example. It is also an example that explains why many claim that what an individual contributes needs to be factored into multiple discovery conclusions, for individual contributions often show that discoveries can reflect a community larger than the particular field in which the multiple is generally explored. Briefly, the activity of looking at the moon and other planetary objects through telescopes excited many scientists early in the 17th century. What set Galileo apart from his contemporaries was that he had some training

in drawing and watercolor. He also had a relationship and ongoing correspondence with the artist Lodovico Cigoli. Thus, while research has convincingly shown that the telescope was a multiple discovery, a multiples explanation per se deletes that Galileo brought a cognitive advantage to the activity of looking through the telescope due to his background. This need not be defined as innate genius. Rather the advantage was environmental. His training prepared him to see that the three-dimensional sphere had a rough texture and to perceive how to translate the terrain onto a two-dimensional surface so that others could ascertain how to likewise see it.

Galileo's now well-known astronomical observations/illustrations were published in *Sidereus Nuncius*. In the text Galileo expands on what the painted images reveal, carefully explaining how he observed the geography of mountains, valleys, and craters. By making reference to how the light and shadows change their disposition as the moon moves from one phase to another, Galileo also shows how he brought his unique body of knowledge to the project of looking at the moon through the telescope. In sum, his background and contacts helped him perceive, illustrate, and forthrightly assert the difference between the terrain he saw and the long-standing Aristotelian belief that the moon must be a smooth surface.

This is not to say that no one else had glimpsed the moon's rough surface. The information was readily available even to the inquiring and thoughtful naked eye. In fact, William Gilbert, best known for his research with magnetism, had earlier produced naked-eye maps of the moon's geography. The outstanding element here is that Gilbert's maps did not draw upon the mathematically based perspective techniques known to artists, which were the techniques Galileo used to render a naturalistic picture. Given that Gilbert's studies did not contain an abstract component capable of translating the two-dimensional surface into a believable three-dimensional form, it was hard to decipher that the moon had a geography similar to that of the earth. Thomas Harriot offers a good counterpoint to Gilbert. He is now generally credited with making the first rendering of the moon as seen through a telescope and thus has the somewhat dubious distinction of being one of the first to fail to "see" the rocky surface until viewing Galileo's images. Having no previous cognitive understanding of how a rough three-dimensional image would appear on a lens, Harriot could not conceptualize that he was viewing ridges and shadows—until he had Galileo's work to reference. Like all scientists and natural philosophers, he simply accepted the idea the moon was smooth despite the evidence we see with the naked eye, for the rough surface is evident and has long been known as "the man in the moon." This was not the case with the painter Jan van Eyck. He had produced three paintings in the 15th century that included naturalistic depictions of the moon's rocky terrain. The paintings, however, were not included in the philosophical and scientific discourse, where it was unquestioned that the moon was smooth.

The differences among these images and the conclusions drawn from them explain why critics of multiple discovery say the multiples concept is overly generic. By reducing discovery to loosely defined products (like oil paint and the discovery of the telescope), the concept underemphasizes how attention, experience, and training inform discovery. In light of this, it should be mentioned that historians of science have long been interested in the community of science and multiple discovery complements this area of community by showing scientists compose a community in which all scientists participate. Galileo's illustrations likewise affirm the scientific valuation of community and add that the more communities connected to a particular scientist, the more potential there is to bring information outside of one's domain into one's creative ventures. Galileo's work also demonstrates that scientific discovery has often been fostered by cross-disciplinary exchange and that cross-disciplinary examples inform the shared problems/parallel product style of inquiry. History, however, also offers examples of multiple discovery that underline that a community tends to explore several lines of inquiry simultaneously, even when addressing one product or discovery. This accounts for the tendency to see products in zeitgeist terms.

B. Zeitgeist

The history of photography speaks directly to the zeitgeist issue, offering a classic case of how artists and scientists often work on problems in tandem. In this case, practitioners in both domains were interested in developing better methods for representing the world we see. This is not surprising given that representation has been an ongoing practical problem for both artists and scientists, and a practical problem easily separated from the philosophical arguments centered on "appearance" and "reality." Many of the prephotography solutions (the *camera obscura,* the *camera lucida,* studies of optics, and perspective) aided the hand and the eye tremendously. But what was wanted was something that would allow an individual to fix an image and forego the need for long calculations and/or systematic tracing. Eventually this problem was solved by determining a combination of light and chemicals capable of copying and fixing images. The exciting solution, photography, made it possible to permanently record visual images and offered a level of detail that led some to exclaim that it was like looking at nature with a telescope.

Many helped develop this exciting technology. As early as 1727 a German professor of anatomy, Johan Heinrich Schulze, had shown it was possible to render images using sunlight and silver salts. In England, as early as 1802, Thomas Wedgewood, the son of the famous potter Josiah Wedgewood, successfully recorded images on paper. In 1819 the chemist John Hershel, the son of William Hershel, the discoverer of the planet Uranus, likewise discovered how to fix images and by 1839 could print them on paper as well. Independently, William Henry Fox Talbot, an English scientist who became interested in the problem because he was unable to draw easily using a camera lucida, determined how to create a single negative from which multiple copies of positive prints could be made. Other independent investigations were conducted early in the 19th century by the Frenchmen Jospeh Nicéphore Niépce and Louis-Jacques Mandé Daguerre. Their experiments grew out of lithographic techniques and eventually, after Niépce's death, Daguerre fixed a single positive photographic image (a daguerreotype) on a metal plate coated with chemicals and exposed to light.

Assuming these examples represent parallel discoveries, and many think this is an incorrect assumption, does not explain why the mechanical representations of nature changed the cultural environment of art in ways quite unlike their influence on science. This aspect of multiples is of great importance to how one defines creativity and to how one applies the zeitgeist characterization to multiples. Some elements of disparity thus need to be briefly explored. This inquiry will clarify that multiples take form in a context and form a context as well.

In a general sense, the photographic image provided a means for both scientists and artists to quickly record information about nature. Many found the efficiency attractive and the camera was quickly adopted as a professional tool by astronomers and others in the natural sciences. They immediately saw the technology eliminated the bothersome tasks of drawing and were pleased to no longer have to bear the burden of tracing moving images (although early prints often included afterimages). In addition, the images satisfied several cultural demands. These included the desire for relatively inexpensive images for books (or as separate items) and the desire for cheap portraiture. The way in which the camera could record faces was a source of so much delight that some enthusiasts marveled at how the camera was able to make the fugitive images of the mirror permanent.

The excitement, however, was not all-embracing. Generally, there was some concern that a photograph could be staged to give the impression it was a snapshot and thus be used to deceive people about events. Moreover, especially in the arts, many still preferred something included in the cognitive exercise of rendering by hand and eye. Even those artists (e.g., Manet) who did choose to incorporate the possibilities the camera offered had reservations about the mechanical nature of photographic reproductions. This is not to say that artists were against reproduction per se. Art has always been reproducible in principle, and multiples had always been printed using various technologies (e.g., woodcuts and etchings). It was the mindless mechanical reproduction of the camera that was disdained. Critics felt the camera was only capable of rendering surfaces. This argument was not a "multiples" (Talbot's technique) versus "singleton's" (the daguerreotype) argument in regard to the multiple discovery of the photographic process per se, although the differences between the two processes were a part of the argument. Rather, the concern centered on the mindless nature of the mechanical images and whether mechanical images of surfaces could capture all that art and reality include. In other words, people believed, rightly,

that mechanically produced copies did not contain the history, the pulse, and the depth of understanding embodied in an original.

In terms of zeitgeist, the photographic images and the multiple reactions beg two questions. First, why did disciples of art and science have contrary reactions to the multiple discovery of photography? Second, how do we define a product of a time? The key point in evaluating these questions is that scientists were more likely to see photography as a tool. Painters, however, felt compelled to compare the nature of their images with those the camera produced. The overall conclusion of the painters was that the mechanical images were not a replacement for painting or a reason to deny that the so-called objective reality of nature was of painterly interest. It would be more accurate to say that 19th century painters continued to see an objective reality and to believe in the importance of rendering it. But the process of evaluating what images include also changed the nature of painterly problems. In sum, photography was one of many discoveries that reframed numerous 19th century ideas regarding invention, mechanism, discovery, the mind, appearance, reality, the artist, the scientist, nature, seeing, and knowing. Some other factors include the 19th century political situation and the turn toward romanticism at the end of the 18th and through the mid-19th centuries.

The details surrounding the entry of photography in the 19th century have been introduced to highlight a recurring question in discussions about creativity and multiple discovery: where do painters like Vincent van Gogh (1853–1890) and Paul Cézanne (1839–1906) fit? Both 19th century painters are hard to reconcile with multiple discovery in a generic sense, especially when a zeitgeist model is implied. Now deemed as superior artists, their work was considered virtually worthless when they lived. What must be stressed in considering how these men "fit" into models of creativity and discovery are, first, that the paintings done by van Gogh and Cézanne depicted the "objective" natural world and were thus deeply rooted in the 19th century tradition. This tradition, as noted, included the development of photography. Second, while both men were marginal in their time, each tried to integrate his work while he lived and failed to receive community acceptance. Finally, it is now said that the authenticity of their paintings and the way the forms conjure up a sense of presence that seems to go beyond the surface turned art in a new direction.

Putting these elements together raises the question of how we evaluate the contextual incongruence the discoveries of van Gogh and Cézanne present. Many have pointed out they were people of their time. Yet, it is hard to align their productive lives and the intrinsic motivation that guided them with the idea that community acknowledgment of one's efforts is an integral part of being a successfully creative individual. It is equally difficult to align their lives with multiple discovery as generally defined. The problem is best summed up by asking why and to what degree the individual and the culture are connected in the discovery process, be it multiple or singleton. While it is true that most highly creative people do achieve success in their fields and are well respected by their peers, in the visual arts we do find significant exceptions to this. As van Gogh and Cézanne attest, if we assume a discovery is contextually created, that the quality of a creator's work is evaluated by experts and institutions, and that only one who is "accepted" by the community can be justly deemed creative in a complete sense, we are left with examples where a person, who is not defined as creative during his or her life, has, nonetheless, left behind products that are deemed creative long after the person has died. This time lag is especially problematic if we want to define artistic and scientific creativity using similar terms and in relationship to one another.

IV. CULTURAL ISSUES AND CONCLUSIONS

As this article shows, various questions related to multiple discovery and creativity remain unresolved. The issues and debates include: (1) the fact that the contribution of one individual may be significantly more complete than that of another in parallel discoveries, (2) the question of whether multiples theories adequately address individual creativity, especially given the differences between artistic and scientific creativity, (3) the length of time that separates what are termed "multiple" discoveries, (4) the length of time that separates an individual's creative process of discovery and the community's acceptance of the work produced,

(5) whether it is useful to define all discoveries as inevitable products of a time, an idea that zeitgeist implies, (6) the individual priority disputes that have resulted from parallel discoveries throughout history, (7) the greater emphasis on teamwork in scientific research today, and (8) how the growth of teamwork makes it harder to recognize the contribution of any one individual. The complexity of these unresolved questions tends to give rise to philosophical explanations. Given this, and although philosophical theory has not been the primary concern of this article, some precedents related to multiples need to be mentioned.

Briefly, both Plato and Aristotle grappled with the "one" and the "many" and did so because each saw human development and education as key concerns. Moreover, despite their differences, both Plato and Aristotle were deeply committed to an inquiry premised on logic and reason. Both were also in agreement that scientific knowledge is universal knowledge and that it is the same for all people, for all times, and for all places. These points of agreement were to become the backbone of natural philosophy and science. As such, Platonic and Aristotelian ideas gradually set the stage for some of the ambiguities that have come to define the concept of multiple discovery today, as well as western views of creativity.

Since Plato and Aristotle have come to be defined more in terms of how they disagree, with Aristotle being seen to emphasize studies of the natural world to a greater degree, it is often overlooked that both men did adopt a language/logic prototype for inquiry. The western allegiance to this prototype is no doubt why the concept of multiple discovery per se works better in a scientific (or verbal) context than in the visual arts. This language/logic preference, moreover, has generally been adopted by cognitive science in its search for universals.

Presently this long-standing preference for logic-based explanations is being counterbalanced by contextual case studies, systemic studies, stochastic models, research into the psychology of history, cognitive-historical analysis, and multiple intelligences research. Within this broad range many possibilities coexist. One that might foster viable information connecting individual and community approaches is the evidence of brain plasticity now being generated in cognitive neuroscience, for it appears that new tools might offer ways to align the focus on universals with individual case studies. Even if bridging studies are pursued, however, social and cultural interpretations will still have to be judged on their own terms.

One powerful example of how critical interpretation is was expressed by Plato himself, albeit indirectly. Plato, who had a creative mind and was in awe of artistic inspiration in the sense that he saw it as divinely inspired, solved the problem of the one and the many with a philosophy premised on the idea that individuals could all discover the one Truth. In order to ensure it be the "right" Truth, Plato banned artists from his ideal Republic, arguing their facility for imitation could too easily turn people toward appearances and thus turn them away from a genuine engagement with moral purpose. As philosophers, sociologists, and others have often noted, societies that mold people in this way cannot be reduced to simple philosophical conundrums. Rather, manipulative social foundations pose numerous questions regarding education, individual growth, and governance. How people answer these kinds of questions, in turn, has a tremendous impact on what we discover in general—as well as conclusions pertaining to multiple discovery. The heart of the issue has two sides. On the one hand, how does a society differentiate between a discovery that is a "correct" product in the sense that it is in line with a culture's norms and the discovery of something that is actually new and unique. On the other hand, we find a dynamic challenge created by the fact that cultures are intergenerational. Each generation needs to be educated, and each educational process must align technological advances with ever-emerging cultural issues. Within this, one overriding problem is fostering excellence in discovery, be it multiple or singleton. How does a culture balance individual potential and honor models that include structure, cooperation, teamwork, pluralism, and the exceptional?

The exceptional is of exceptional importance within this—especially because exceptional people defy neatly packaged conclusions about multiple discovery. This is even more the case when an individual inverts the picture, having multiple discoveries to his or her credit. For example, recognized as one of the most creative people ever to have lived, Albert Einstein revolutionized scientific and philosophic inquiry in the 20th century. In his annus mirabilis (1905), Einstein published five papers and each shattered cherished scientific beliefs. Clearly, individuals like Einstein raise the question of whether the high points of one individual's achievement and the comprehensive nature of an individual's contributions can be fully addressed using a model highlighting communal influences. The response of those who defend the multiple viewpoint is that all of Einstien's discoveries would have happened even without an Einstein. From this perspective, the discoveries may have taken more time, and required more minds, but the climate was ripe for these problems to be solved and thus they would have been solved. This does not actually explain why Einstein, as an individual, was able to conceptualize so many ideas that were not yet directly a part of his culture. [*See* EINSTEIN, ALBERT.]

In sum, multiple discoveries can be defined as products that emerge from scientific exchange. Within this, definitional challenges exist due to the difficulty in precisely balancing the many variables that contribute to individual and communal change.

Bibliography

Gardner, H. (1997). *Extraordinary minds*. New York: Basic Books.

Lamb, D., & Easton, S. M. (1984). *Multiple discovery: The pattern of scientific progress*. Avebury, UK: Avebury.

Merton, R. K. (1974). *The sociology of science*. Chicago: The University of Chicago Press.

Simonton, D. K. (1988). *Scientific genius: A psychology of science*. Cambridge: Cambridge University Press.

Wallace, D. B., & Gruber, H. E. (Eds.). (1989). *Creative people at work: Twelve cognitive case studies*. New York: Oxford University Press.

Multiple Intelligences

Becca Solomon, Kimberly Powell, and Howard Gardner

Harvard University

Creativity The ability to solve problems, fashion products, or pose questions within a domain in a way that is initially unusual but is ultimately accepted by at least one cultural group.

Domain A discipline, craft, area of work, or system of symbols used in a cultural activity; a set of practices associated with an area of knowledge.

Field A construct denoting individuals and institutions that judge work in the domain at a given historical moment. In some domains, a few powerful individuals can dominate judgments about the quality of work.

Intelligence(s) The ability to solve problems or fashion products that are valued by one or more cultures.

In our rapidly changing world, creativity—once viewed as a rare quality possessed only by artistic and scientific geniuses—is now seen as vital to human learning, teaching, and working. Gardner's theory of MULTIPLE INTELLIGENCES (MI theory) offers one promising way to look at creativity. MI theory was developed in the late 1970s and early 1980s to counter theories of intelligence that are based purely on psychometric (i.e., test) evidence and that posit only a single form of intelligence. The theory stands out because of its synthesis of knowledge obtained from two usually contrasting sources: evolutionary and biological findings about the structure of knowledge in the human nervous system and anthropological and cross-cultural evidence about the kinds of abilities and skills that are valued in societies around the world, both historically and contemporaneously. In recent years MI theory has been extended to the study of creativity. According to this view, creativity, like intelligence, is multiple in nature, context sensitive, and culturally bound. In particular, creativity involves an original approach to a problem or product in a given domain of study. Through close examination of highly creative individuals in a variety of domains, Gardner put forth an interactive, developmental, and domain-specific model of creativity.

I. INTELLIGENCE: HISTORICAL PERSPECTIVES

The scientific study of intelligence dates back a century. It grows out of a desire to base psychology on quantitative data. Measures of intelligence highlight such capacities as abstract thinking and problem solving, believed by many to be the central components of intellectual competence. This psychometric approach was founded by such pioneers as Alfred Binet, Charles Spearman, and Lewis Terman. It continues to occupy a dominant position within academic psychology and is enormously influential in the selection and placement of students at several levels of education.

The psychometric approach exhibits a number of common features. Most intelligence testers believe that the bulk of intelligence is determined by a general factor (g), though they recognize that there are also specific (s) factors at work as well on particular tasks. Tests are so devised that they yield a bell curve, with the bulk of individuals arrayed near the center of the distribution (IQ = 100: standard deviation 15 points). The instrumentation focuses on the differences among individuals; at various times, special attention has been paid to those individuals who fall at the far end of the bell curve—those with significant learning disabilities (e.g., retarded individuals) and those who are exceptional performers in school (intellectually gifted students). For many years, there was also a tendency to conflate intellectually gifted individuals with creative ones.

In recent years, there has been a great deal of renewed interest in the theory and practice of intelligence. The aforementioned notions of g, intelligence as abstract problem-solving, heritability of intelligence, and the use of psychometrics continue to play key roles in Western conceptions of intelligence. Today, however, many psychologists and theorists have reconceptualized such views to include new developments in cognitive and developmental psychology and other disciplines concerned with human development, such as anthropology, artificial intelligence, biology, and neuropsychology. Extending beyond psychometrics, researchers have drawn on this range of disciplines. The field continues to debate whether intelligence is better thought of as monolithic or as pluralistic. Similarly, authorities disagree about whether faculties are best thought of as *horizontal*—extending across all kinds of mental content, or *vertical*—keyed to specific kinds of content, such as language, music, or the emotions. Some psychologists who propose pluralist or vertical faculty theories have moved away entirely from the idea that there is a central faculty responsible for intellect.

Among those who have put forth new conceptions of intelligence, Robert Sternberg has been especially influential. Sternberg's triarchic theory of intelligence included the componential subtheory (internal, basic information processes of intelligence), the experiential subtheory (how an individual deals with differing degrees of novelty in a given situation or task), and the contextual subtheory (cultural and environmental issues related to an individual's intelligence). Stephen Ceci's related work emphasized the role of contextual factors, including the domain of knowledge in which one has expertise; the influence of the workplace, school and other settings; and the historical conditions surrounding an individual's life.

In *Frames of Mind,* Howard Gardner introduced his theory of multiple intelligences. The central assertion of this theory is that human beings have evolved over the millennia to represent and analyze the world in a number of relatively autonomous ways, which are labeled the multiple intelligences. All human beings possess all intelligences; in that sense, the intelligences constitute a definition of what it means to be a human, cognitively speaking. On the other hand, because of the accidents of genetics and environment, each human being (even an identical twin) possesses his or her own peculiar blend of intelligences. [*See* INTELLIGENCE.]

II. MULTIPLE INTELLIGENCES THEORY AND ITS EXTENSIONS INTO CREATIVITY

Gardner was concerned with accounting for the wide range of performances and adult roles, or end states, that are valued in different cultures. Rather than a single, governing factor responsible for processing information and tasks, Gardner posed several autonomous yet interactive faculties, or intelligences, that are responsible for performing and carrying out various activities. From this perspective, cultural context is an important consideration in defining intelligence. Gardner thus defined intelligence as the ability to solve problems or fashion products valued by one or more cultures.

Except in cases of pathology, no intelligence functions in isolation. Rather, intelligences typically work interactively or in concert with one another. A politician, for example, requires strong linguistic (public speaking), interpersonal (communication with constituents), and perhaps even intrapersonal (clarity of personal motives and beliefs) intelligences to be an effective advocate and leader.

Gardner has emphasized the crucial distinction between an intelligence and a domain. As noted, an intelligence is a biopsychological potential to process information of a certain type in a certain way. Given a reasonable amount of exposure to language or to music, individuals will develop their respective linguistic or musical intelligences. In contrast, a domain is a discipline, craft, or other organized activity that is valued in a given culture. Every society features multiple domains, with the boundaries and practices within a domain shifting over time because of individual and cultural values and trends.

Although some domains typically emphasize certain intelligences and symbol systems, most intelligences do not map neatly onto a particular domain. For example, as Gardner has pointed out, there is no one-to-one correspondence between music as an intelligence (the capacity to create and perceive musical patterns) and music as a discipline (which, in addition to musical intelligence, might involve bodily-kinesthetic intelligence or spatial intelligence needed to play an instrument). An individual possessing spatial intelligence has a range of distinct domains in which to practice depending on complementary abilities and inclinations. The spatial intelligence required to be an airplane pilot is combined with logical-mathematical intelligence involved in understanding the physics of flight and linguistic intelligence for effectively communicating verbally with pilots, air traffic controllers, and passengers. Scuba divers, who also rely on spatial intelligence to determine ocean depth and their own physical orientation under water, depend equally on bodily-kinesthetic intelligence to manipulate their bodies and equipment, and perhaps engage naturalistic intelligence in observing sea life.

Although many human activities employ different combinations of intelligences, not all abilities can be defined as intelligences. The key to Gardner's MI theory lies in eight criteria employed to determine the existence of an intelligence. The criteria are based on an examination of empirical data from neurological, biological, and environmental studies, as well as a consideration of viable cultural roles or end states. A candidate intelligence earns the status of one of the multiple intelligences only if it fills each of these criteria reasonably well.

1. *Potential isolation of brain damage.* In brain-damaged patients, skills entailed in music, spatial reasoning, object manipulation, and linguistic functioning prove to be quite independent of one another; that is, a performance in one area does not predict performance in another intelligence.

2. *The existence of savants, prodigies, and other exceptional individuals.* Such individuals demonstrate that certain capacities operate in isolation of other capacities. For example, an autistic individual may be able to calculate a large list of numbers or perform other algorithmic functions yet cannot communicate or participate in activities with others.

3. *Support from experimental psychological tasks.* Experimental research reveals that certain intelligences are relatively autonomous. When subjects are asked to carry out two tasks simultaneously, musical, linguistic, and spatial tasks seem to involve noninterfering skills.

4. *Support from psychometric findings.* In general, when factor analyses are applied to these tests, verbal and spatial abilities fall into separate groups. At present, there is not reliable technology for assessing most of the other intelligences.

5. *Distinctive developmental history and definable end-state performances.* For each intelligence there is a developmental trajectory in which all people learn and manifest basic skills, while some progress to more expert, specialized end states.

6. *Evolutionary history and plausibility.* Evidence from evolutionary biology suggests sources of human abilities and capacities in earlier or less complex species.

7. *Identifiable core operation or set of operations.* Each intelligence exhibits several distinct modes of processing information, which, as Fodor noted, may be modular in nature. Performing a musical composition requires such processes as perceiving and differentiating tone, timbre, and intervallic relations; celestial

navigation requires perceiving and differentiating spatial relations among stars, planets, and geographic markers.

8. *The existence of a symbol system.* An intelligence must have an identifiable coding system, a culturally created system of meaning that conveys important information. Gardner argued that the existence of symbol systems and corresponding intelligences is not coincidental; it appears that humans have computational capacities for making sense of their culture and therefore have a natural predilection for encoding information in a symbol system. Examples of symbolic notation include written alphabets, musical notation, and numeric systems.

As these criteria suggest, intelligences have a distinctive developmental history. Although certain basic capabilities may be hard wired, proclivities develop over time with the onset of opportunity and the provision of end states that are available and plausible at a particular historical moment. Intelligences can also be enhanced through schooling in particular techniques. For example, as Gardner has observed, by virtue of a careful analysis of the conditions that lead to virtuosity, the Suzuki music method from Japan has successfully trained young musicians from all over the world.

As noted, Gardner originally posed seven distinct but interactive intelligences, stating that there could be fewer or more, depending on the degree to which end states could be supported by his established criteria for an intelligence. Since the original publication, Gardner has added one intelligence that fits these criteria. Examples of end states (cultural roles) exemplifying the use of each intelligence are also included.

1. *Linguistic intelligence.* The ability to communicate and make sense through language; sensitivity to the rhythm and sounds of language (editor, rap artist, or poet).

2. *Logical-mathematical intelligence.* The ability to use, appreciate, and discern abstract relations, logical or numerical patterns (mathematician or scientist).

3. *Musical intelligence.* The ability to communicate and create meaning from sound; to produce and understand pitch, rhythm, and timbre (piano tuner, composer, or violinist).

4. *Spatial intelligence.* The ability to perceive, use,

and transform visual and spatial information accurately (pilot, sculptor, or sailor).

5. *Bodily-kinesthetic intelligence.* The ability to use one's body, or parts of one's body, to produce movements or to handle and manipulate objects skillfully (dancer, surgeon, or carpenter).

6. *Intrapersonal intelligence.* The abilities to distinguish and discriminate among one's own feelings, to compose mental models, and to draw upon self-knowledge to guide one's behavior (writer or monk).

7. *Interpersonal intelligence.* The ability to recognize and distinguish among feelings and intentions of self and others and to discern and be sensitive to the needs, moods, and feelings of others (therapist, teacher, or actor).

8. *Naturalist intelligence.* The ability to distinguish among, classify, and build models of environmental features (biologist, astronomer, or botanist).

Gardner views these eight intelligences in two complementary ways: (a) as a definition of our species and (b) as a factor that differentiates among individuals. We each possess all of the intelligences, but individual profiles vary.

Paralleling his definition of intelligence, Gardner views creativity as the ability to solve problems, fashion products, or pose questions within a domain in a way that is initially unusual but that is ultimately accepted by at least one cultural group or field. Just as individuals can stand out in virtue of one or more intelligences, so they can use one or more intelligences to carry out creative work in a domain. Indeed, some creative individuals are characterized more by their unusual combination of intelligences than by particular strength in a single intelligence.

As in his work on intelligence, Gardner has reached outside of studies of processes "in the head" and those that flow directly from one's genetic inheritance. Rather, his stance has focused on the important role of historical and cultural factors, the necessary developmental milestones en route to expertise and originality, and the desirability of obtaining deep understanding of particular instances of creativity. Gardner also has proposed that each of the multiple intelligences harbors different kinds of creativity.

Gardner has sought to go beyond other cognitive approaches to creativity as well as theories that present creativity as a single, general faculty. He has approached the study of creativity through individual case studies, a developmental perspective, a focus on symbolic forms, and an examination of interaction among three aspects of a system. Gardner compared creativity across diverse domains and looked within particular points of history for examples of creativity. His view of creativity as multiformed and interactive propels understanding and research in this area.

III. APPROACH AND METHODOLOGY

Research in creativity parallels the trajectory of investigation into intelligence. In 1950 Joy P. Guilford argued that creativity is not equivalent to intelligence; he urged the same type of scientific focus pioneered by Binet and Terman to determine *which* individuals had the potential to be creative. The years of research following Guilford's initial foray suggest that, although related, creativity is not the same as intelligence and that creativity tests, although statistically reliable, do not indicate creativity in different domains. People viewed in their culture or discipline as creative do not necessarily demonstrate the divergent thinking skills measured on psychometric creativity tests. [*See* DIVERGENT THINKING.]

Subsequent research on creativity has tried to account for cognitive processes as well as personality and environmental influences. For example, cognitive researchers Margaret Boden, David Perkins, and Robert Sternberg have suggested that creative people identify promising problem and solution "spaces" in order to search for appropriate approaches to the particular problem, assess alternative solutions, determine an efficient investigation of options, and judge when to research further or move on to other questions. Innovative people also reflect on their own creating processes. Social psychologist Teresa Amábile stresses that creativity is sought for intrinsic reward. She notes that creative solutions to problems more frequently arise when an activity is practiced for enjoyment rather than for possible external rewards. [*See* MOTIVATION/DRIVE.]

In related work, psychologist Mihaly Csikszentmihalyi described, in 1990, a highly sought-after affective state as the "flow experience." These intrinsically mo-

tivating experiences happen in any domain, and people describe being completely engaged with the object or activity at hand. Those "in flow" are simultaneously unconscious of their activity and feel fully alive. To achieve periods of flow, individuals endure much practice, effort, and even physical or psychological pain. During this immersion, what was once too challenging becomes possible and enjoyable. In his 1996 study of highly innovative people, Csikszentmihalyi found that intrinsic motivation may explain why creative people persist in their activities, even heightening their challenges, despite frustrations and grave risks.

In 1990 Howard Gruber and his team used an idiographic method for understanding creativity: They looked for unambiguous examples of the creative processes as modeled in individuals working within domains. Gruber's proposed "evolving systems" approach of studying creativity is one in which organization of knowledge in a domain, the creator's purpose(s), and the affective experiences he or she undergoes are examined simultaneously. The interaction of these systems over time helps one understand the fluctuation of creative activity over the course of a productive human life. In direct contrast to Gruber, Dean Keith Simonton adopted a historiometric, or nomothetic, methodology. He put forth clearly articulated questions about creativity and examined large bodies of data to resolve them. This methodology can be applied to a variety of issues ranging from personality traits of creative individuals to features of their training. His focus on more general laws or principles provided useful assessments of individuals in a broader context.

Significant in Gardner's approach to creativity is his effort to bridge Gruber's idiographic and Simonton's nomothetic methods. Specifically, proceeding in the manner of a naturalist, through careful observation and case studies of a few highly innovative individuals deliberately chosen from diverse domains, Gardner searches for more general patterns. With further testing, these identified patterns may be bolstered or belied.

The individuals studied by Gardner possessed a range of intelligences and utilized them in work; but each seemed to highlight and exemplify one specific human intelligence and a sophisticated use of the symbols, images, and operations correlated with that intelligence functioning in a particular discipline or domain. For example, in the linguistic realm, revolts against classical verse and narrative structures were led by T. S. Eliot. In the logical/mathematical realm, Einstein challenged long accepted assumptions about the absolute status of time and space. And in the spatial realm, Picasso and Braque demonstrated that faithful representation was not of the essence in the arts: They created a genre (cubism) in which aspects of form were dominant and in the process laid the foundation for abstract art.

Extraordinary people like these are formed from the same building blocks as are all humans, though they are distinguishable from others in notable respects. As exceptional cases, they do not readily fit within developmental psychological frameworks such as Piaget's theory of human cognition. Unless we also come to understand where the musical and mathematical prodigies or geniuses fit in, researchers cannot construct a truly comprehensive theory of human cognition.

IV. FIVE FORMS OF CREATIVE ACTIVITY

As individuals' strengths in each intelligence vary, so do their predispositions to certain creative forms. The intelligences themselves do not necessarily predict the favored framework for expression. Rather, an inclination to a particular creative form is a combination of intellectual predisposition, opportunities in a particular domain in a given moment in history, and personality/temperament configurations. Within each domain, symbols and symbol systems contrast dramatically from one another, as do the mental skills needed to work with them and to communicate discoveries to others. Because of these extreme differences, Gardner has distinguished five forms of creative activity:

1. *Solving a particular problem.* Individuals use existing or innovative methods to solve problems already defined in a domain. Scientists often adopt this form of creativity—for example, Watson and Crick's original solution to the structure of DNA.
2. *Putting forth a general conceptual scheme.* A set of concepts and the interrelationships among them are explored, such as Freud's psychoanalytic theory of the human unconscious.
3. *Creating a product within an already established do-*

main or genre. The traditional genre is stretched in a new way, as exemplified by Balanchine's ballets or Picasso's introduction of cubism to painting.

4. *A stylized kind of performance.* The components of a performance are well planned and successfully executed, but some opportunities for innovation, improvisation, or interpretation exist. For example, jazz trumpet player Miles Davis's rendition of classic tunes may be somewhat different with each performance but is always recognizable as his.

5. *A performance for high stakes.* These presentations are not fully planned in advance, depend on time and the nature of the audience, and have no guaranteed outcome. Kennedy and Nixon's nationally televised presidential debate in 1960 serves as example, as do Mahatma Gandhi's nonviolent protests.

The forms of creativity may blend into one another. At crucial points in a person's career, perhaps a musical debut at Carnegie Hall, a production may be understood as being a high-stakes performance. Conversely, with much practice and repetition, a political speech or choreographed event can become a stylized exhibition rather than one for high stakes. Ultimately, the deciding factors are the experience of the performer and the response of the audience.

Although each of these creative forms has significant associations with particular disciplines, they are not immutable. Certain creators are attracted to certain forms of creation for a number of complex reasons including temperament, personality, and historical accident. Each variety does, however, have its own developmental history, and most creators seem to become involved in a favored form from the early years of childhood.

V. AN INTERACTIVE AND DEVELOPMENTAL MODEL OF CREATIVITY

Gardner has come to view creativity as contextualized, reflecting the cultures in which individuals live, and distributed, entailing the full spectrum of human and cultural resources available to an individual. By and large individuals are creative within particular domains rather than across domains; creativity requires not only intellectual proclivity but also expertise and mastery of the knowledge, concepts, and skills required of a particular domain.

In collaboration with colleagues Mihaly Csikszent-mihalyi and David Henry Feldman, Gardner has developed an interactive model that reframes creativity not as a single element or quality but as interacting among three core components:

- The *individual* creator
- A particular project or object in a specific *domain* in which the person is working
- The others—or *field*—working in a discipline or domain who render judgments of quality

With this conceptualization, we no longer ask, "What is creativity?" but instead, inquire, "Where is creativity?" The answer lies in the interaction over time among the three nodes.

Gardner's explanation departs from other definitions of creativity in several aspects: He focused equally on problem solving, problem finding, and the creation of products; he posited that rather than possessing general creativity, individuals are creative in particular *domains* of accomplishment and require expertise in these domains in order to carry out significant creative work; and he maintained that nothing (an individual, achievement, or product) is creative or noncreative in and of itself. Judgments of creativity rely on the *field*, the group of experts and other influential stakeholders within a domain. Additionally, he argued that creative individuals regularly exhibit their creativity at various points in their lives rather than experiencing a once-in-a-lifetime episode of creativity. He suggested no time limit—an idea, solution, or product may be recognized as creative immediately or not for many years.

A. The Individual

The single variety of creativity is a myth, but certain commonalties obtain across creative individuals. For example, creators exhibit self-confidence, attentiveness, disregard for convention, industriousness, and, as they age, an obsession with their endeavors. Less admirable traits include strong egocentric, masochistic, sadistic, and sado-masochistic tendencies. Self-promotion contributes to success across domains, but the degree varies among individuals. Creative individuals also seem to enter into a quasi-spiritual Faustian bargain with themselves or a higher power: They maintain that, with sacrifice of self or other, they will be able to pursue their creative work. [*See* PERSONALITY.]

The sources of this collection of characteristics may be examined by taking a lifelong perspective. Young children experience a phase of exploration of their environment during which they have the opportunity to discover principles governing the physical and social worlds, as well as their own personal worlds. This discovery of universals provides a base for future learnings. Perhaps even more important is that these processes of self and world discovery become models for examining newly encountered phenomena. What might distinguish the developmental trajectories of creative individuals are the ways in which they utilize their childhoods. Gardner identified eight developmental features that appeared across the creators he studied.

1. *Concern with the universals of childhood.* Innovators often preserve the child's worldview. Picasso, for example, consciously integrated the kinds of forms children instinctively create into his masterful, adult artwork. Adult creators also maintain childlike abilities of disregarding convention, pushing questions and inquiries to their limits, and directly probing the core of an idea. The creator's own childhood insights, feelings, and experiences are joined productively with the most advanced understanding and skills achieved in a domain. An individual's childhood is important as a reservoir for creativity in mature works but also as a determining factor for whether a person will strike out on his or her own. Individuals who make creative breakthroughs as adults have often been explorers in their own and other areas of expertise from an early age. A restrictive upbringing—without a role model or mentor who displays or encourages exploration—reduces the chances that a child will develop into a highly creative individual.

2. *Examination of original interest and its development into expertise in a domain.* Drawing on Feldman's notion of a "crystallizing experience," Gardner found that early in life, creators locate an area or object that is consuming. This initial instance is important, but creators must devote at least 10 years of continuous work to a discipline or craft before it can be mastered. Persistence

is crucial. Even Mozart, a child prodigy, dedicated a decade to musical study before he was able to compose mature works.

3. *The discovery or creation of new or divergent elements.* Many are fulfilled by mastery; few forge ahead to create new paths in a domain. The challenge for the prodigy is to continue beyond mastering the domain to generate something innovative. Creators often exhibit simultaneous and contrasting trends: a tendency to question every assumption and the press to learn everything about the domain. As the individual works, he or she locates problem areas in the domain and begins moving toward a new perspective. For example, Roy Lichtenstein, one of the most important contributors to the pop-art movement, pushed popular and established conceptions of art into a new direction. His paintings reconceptualized popular cartoons and cultural icons of the day. [*See* INNOVATION.]

4. *The creator's reaction to a discrepancy and subsequent initiation of a program of exploration.* Experimentation and exploration are important to the emerging creative individual. If creators did not reach a flow state as a result of their endeavors, it is doubtful that they would persevere. To master a domain and then extend it, the adventurer must embark on a more rigorous program. What may have appeared to be a local problem susceptible to easy repair may in fact call for a fundamental reorientation of the domain. Schöenberg's mastery of conventional Western harmonics, along with a recognition of its limitations, led to explorations of alternative tonal systems and his subsequent development of a 12-tone system. This in turn led to a complete reconceptualization of tonality and music theory.

5. *Supportive (emotional and intellectual) role played by other individuals during the secluded period.* Although creators might be imagined as working in seclusion, the role of other individuals actually proves essential throughout their development. As a developing novice in his or her domain, a creator often passes through an apprenticeship period during which a mentor or instructor proves critical. Particularly during crucial times of creative breakthrough, creators evince a strong need for both cognitively (intellectually) and affectively (emotionally) supportive individuals. Author Gertrude Stein's close, dependent relationship with her partner Alice B. Toklas serves as one example; Freud's friend-

ship with fellow physician Wilhelm Fliess is another prototype.

6. *The ways in which a new symbol system, language, or mode of expression is evolved.* The creator at first accepts and employs the established common language or symbol system of a domain but eventually this conventional means of expression becomes inadequate. Initially the creative individual may make minor adjustments to suit his or her needs; ultimately, a new symbol system must be created to address the problem or product effectively. For example, Picasso was not consciously trying to create cubism; because he was unable to capture what he sought by employing already established techniques (realism, impressionism, or expressionism), he and his close collaborator Georges Braque began to originate the vocabulary that led to cubism. With no reliable guides, an individual must rely on his or her own instinct and withstand severe disappointments along the course, with no guarantee of reward.

7. *Initial reactions of the relevant critics and subsequent alterations in the field.* Often when creators release innovative work, their efforts are met with criticism and disappointment. Withstanding such setbacks, some creators even extract enjoyment from the controversy. As creative individuals' work in turn becomes acknowledged by critics over time, their work becomes the establishment against which new innovators push. With its highly politicized lyrics about police brutality and cynicism about inner-city life, the rap music group Public Enemy initially met with harsh judgment and, indeed, censorship. Today, while still marginalized in some circles, the group is considered an important contributor to music and is played frequently on music video stations and radio stations. Public Enemy's style has been replicated by many others, and the group has even been the subject of music documentaries.

8. *Events related to a second, more comprehensive innovation that often occurs midlife.* Creators often have a second breakthrough occurring about a decade after the first. The second innovation is traditionally less extreme than the first but more synthetic or integrative in nature. Characteristically, Einstein progressed from the special theory of relativity to the more universal general theory of relativity. Depending on the energy level and health of a creator, and the domain in which an individual works, there may be opportunity for ad-

ditional breakthroughs at approximately decade-long intervals.

B. The Domain

Whatever the developmental trajectory and personality profile of the creator, he or she works within a recognized domain. To make drastic changes within a domain, a creator must have a sense of the evolution and possible development of a domain. The creative individual must be neither too enmeshed in the domain to strike out on his or her own nor too removed from the rules and language by which the domain operates.

The paths of highly creative individuals correspond, but particulars of each domain often vary. Notably, although the symbol systems with which individuals work in each domain may have similarities, their differences are equally significant. Where the poet uses words to provoke imagery and sensation, the naturalist uses them to describe the observed material world. Gestures made with the dancer's body are unlike the spatial schemas and mathematical equations engaged by the physicist. The intelligences do not map neatly onto disciplines, although some do fit more snugly than others. For example, logical/mathematical intelligence is unquestionably an element in the domain of mathematics. As noted, however, domains inevitably draw on a variety of individuals' intelligences. If the application of mathematics is in the service of designing architecture, for example, spatial intelligence will also be called on. The domain includes the symbol system, history, and body of knowledge of a particular discipline.

The nature of the domain itself also helps to determine and define the limits of a creative individual's contributions. With few exceptions, lyrical poets peak early in their lives. In contrast, novelists or essayists often continue to write increasingly complex and engaging works as they mature. Inevitably mortality will frustrate even the most innovative creators, but athletes and ballet dancers evidently face more rapidly the physical limitations of aging.

The historical moment exerts a great influence on a domain. If there is a well-entrenched paradigm in a discipline—for example, Western classical music in the middle of the 18th century—it may be more difficult for an individual to stretch the domain. Sometimes a paradigm is ripe for expansion, particularly after someone (or group) has mastered and fulfilled a domain to its limits. For example, at the beginning of the 20th century, impressionism's decline left the art world primed for the innovation of the post-impressionist movement. In the field of psychology, Freud offers an exceptional example by creating a new domain of psychoanalysis in the hitherto "pre-paradigmatic" area of psychiatry.

C. The Field

The collection of people who shape a domain may include a creative individual's rivals, colleagues, followers, critics, audience members, or patrons. Without a knowledgeable field that can effectively judge work, products may remain anonymous. The existence of the field ensures that the creative individual cannot rely on only those intelligences necessary to accomplishment in a given area of work (e.g., the linguistic intelligence called on for eloquent communication in journalism). For an individual's work to be recognized by others working within a discipline, some measure of personal intelligences must be called on; for a contribution to the domain to be recognized as such, acknowledgment by the field is integral. The aspiring creator must be able to share his or her ideas in order for them to be assessed and either discarded or celebrated. (In rare cases, someone else can represent the creator). Simultaneously, an individual must be resilient enough to continue working even in the face of repeated rejection.

As a group of changing individuals, the field is a fluid construct whose judgments may change over time. Thus, an individual's contributions may be judged differently by the field in one era to the next. Unfortunately for some, as in the case of the poet Emily Dickinson or the biologist Gregor Mendel, acknowledgment of the work may not take place during an individual's lifetime.

The individuals studied by Gardner realized the existence and importance of the field; they devoted time and effort to bringing their work to the attention of these judges. Their degree of self-promotion varied in intensity and may have affected their success. Of course, the field does not always judge well, as occurred in the case of painter Vincent Van Gogh. When the field evaluates inaccurately, it must either self-correct, be educated by others, or, ultimately, be replaced by a new field.

VI. CONCLUSION

Creative individuals are distinguished from the rest of the population by their focused pursuit of a goal, knowledge of the domain, and sensitive awareness to the workings of the judging structures. Without the exceptional individual, there is no creative work. However, such work is also context sensitive and culturally defined: It does not exist in isolation. Rather, it is always situated firmly within a domain of knowledge during the moment in the progression of human history during which a culture is ready to accept it and nurture its growth. It is also important to note that creative activity in general is not always accepted. Throughout most of human history, in most human cultures, the potentially creative individual or work is spurned. Florence in the 15th century and China in the T'ang Dynasty are exceptional in terms of the tolerance of creative activity during those historical eras.

Multiple intelligences theory opens up the study of creativity in a number of ways. First of all, it emphasizes that the different intellectual strengths (and combinations of strengths) of individuals may lead to innovations in disparate domains. Second, it points up the varieties of creative stances, ranging from problem solving to the creation of theories to the execution of ritualized or high-stake performances. Finally, it foregrounds the delicate interplay among individual talents and proclivities, the domains that exist in a culture at a specific historical moment, and the power and vagaries of the field.

Such a theory can be brought to bear in various ways on the study of creativity. It can be utilized in experimental research, in case studies, or in broad-based historiometric or nomothetic investigations. In the present instance, we have focused on findings obtained from the studies of individuals who have unquestionably effected change within one or more domains. So far, these findings are tentative and subject to revision as more case studies are added to the sample. Ultimately, we anticipate that it should be possible to discern firm patterns of human creativity: Only then will we know which features characterize all creative individuals and contributions, which features distinguish some individuals and contributions, and which features prove unique to particular creators or works.

Acknowledgment

We wish to thank the Louise and Claude Rosenberg Jr. Family Foundation for supporting some of the research described here.

Bibliography

Amábile, T. (1983). *The social psychology of creativity.* New York: Springer-Verlag.

Binet, A. (1916). *The development of intelligence in children (the Binet-Simon scale).* Translated by E. S. Kite. Baltimore, MD: Williams & Wilkins Company.

Boden, M. (1990). *The creative mind.* New York: Basic Books.

Cox, C. (1926). *Genetic studies of genius: Volume 2. The early mental traits of three hundred geniuses.* Stanford, CA: Stanford University Press.

Csikszentmihalyi, M. (1988). Society, culture, and person: A systems view of creativity. In R. Sternberg (Ed.), *The nature of creativity* (pp. 325–338). New York: Cambridge University Press.

Csikszentmihalyi, M. (1990). *Flow: The psychology of optimal experience.* New York: Harper & Row.

Csikszentmihalyi, M. (1996). *Creativity.* New York: Harper Collins.

Einstein, A. (1921). *Relativity: The special and general theory.* New York: Holt.

Feldman, D. H. (with L. Goldsmith). (1986). *Nature's gambit.* New York: Basic Books.

Feldman, D. H., Csikszentmihalyi, M., & Gardner, H. (1994). *Changing the world: A framework for the study of creativity.* Westport, CT: Greenwood Press.

Fodor, J. (1983). *The modularity of mind.* Cambridge: MIT Press.

Freud, S. (1954). *The origins of psychoanalysis: Letters to Wilhelm Fliess, drafts, and notes 1886–1902.* New York: Basic Books.

Gardner, H. (1983/1993). *Frames of mind.* New York: Basic Books.

Gardner, H. (1993). *Creating minds.* New York: Basic Books.

Gardner, H. (1993). *Multiple intelligences: The theory into practice.* New York: Basic Books.

Gardner, H. (1994). The creators' patterns. In M. A. Boden (Ed.), *Dimensions of creativity.* (chap. 6, pp. 143–153). Cambridge, MA: The MIT Press/Bradford Books.

Gardner, H. (1994). Five forms of creative activity: A developmental perspective. In N. Colangelo, S. Assouline, & D. Ambroson (Eds.), *Talent development: Proceedings from the 1993 Henry B. and Jocelyn Wallace national research symposium on talent development.* Dayton, OH: Ohio Psychology Press.

Gardner, H. (1997). *Extraordinary minds: Portraits of four exceptional individuals and an examination of our own extraordinariness*. New York: Basic Books.

Gardner, H. (in press). Are there additional intelligences? In J. Kane (Ed.), *Education, information, and transformation*. Englewood Cliffs, NJ: Prentice Hall.

Gardner, H., Kornhaber, M., & Wake, W. (1996). *Intelligence: Multiple perspectives*. New York: Harcourt Brace College Publishers.

Gardner, H., & Policastro, E. (1999). From case studies to robust generalizations: An approach to the study of creativity. In R. J. Sternberg (Ed.), *Handbook of creativity* (pp. 213–215). New York: Cambridge University Press.

Guilford, J. P. (1950). Creativity. *American Psychologist, 5,* 444–454.

Li, J., & Gardner, H. (1993). How domains constrain creativity. *American Behavioral Scientist, 37(1),* 94–101.

Perkins, D. N. (1981). *The mind's best work*. Cambridge, MA: Harvard University Press.

Piaget, J. (1983). Piaget's theory. In P. Mussen (Ed.), *Handbook of child psychology*. Vol. I. (pp. 103–128). New York: Wiley.

Simonton, D. (1994). *Greatness*. New York: Guilford Press.

Spearman, C. (1927). *The abilities of man: their nature and measurement*. New York: Macmillan.

Sternberg, R. J. (1985). *Beyond IQ: A triarchic theory of human intelligence*. New York: Cambridge University Press.

Sternberg, R. J. (1988). A three-facet model of creativity. In R. J. Sternberg (Ed.), *The nature of creativity*. (chap. 5, pp. 125–147). New York: Cambridge University Press.

Sternberg, R. (1988). *The triarchic mind: A new theory of human intelligence*. New York: Viking.

Terman, L. (1917). *The Stanford revision and extension of the Binet-Simon scale for measuring intelligence*. Baltimore, MD: Warwick & York.

Wallace, D., & Gruber, H. (1990). *Creative people at work*. New York: Oxford University Press.

Watson, J., & Crick. F. (1953). A structure for deoxyribose nucleic acid. *Nature, 171,* 737.

Music

Marc Leman
University of Ghent, Belgium

Context of Creation Set of infrastructural, professional, and paradigmatic conditions that constrain creativity.

Artistic Paradigm Set of strategies, methods, and stylistic convictions for the production of art.

Avant-Garde Modernist movement in Europe and North America after World War II.

Institutionalization Process by which human activities become structured into a fixed organization (often supported by the state).

Creativity in MUSIC, or musical creativity, is about the production and realization of new and valuable musical output, such as compositions, performances and improvisations. This article discusses the concept of musical creativity in relation to (a) the context in which creative activities take place and (b) the mental or brain processes that are involved in dealing with musical activities.

I. CREATIVITY IN MUSIC

Musical creativity is not a property of musical products but of persons that are involved with musical information processing. It is not a synonym for talent because talent is assumed to be innate whereas creativity can be partly acquired. Neither is it a synonym for intelligence because intelligent people are not necessarily creative, though creative people are in general intelligent (sometimes also talented). A composer, performer, or improvisor is considered to be creative when he or she does not merely repeat what has been learned or what others have done before but when a point of view is introduced that is unexpected and that adds new possibilities for further exploration. The latter means that it surpasses spontaneity and that it contributes to society.

Musical creativity is associated with notions such as novelty, originality, and flexibility but also with divine intuition, passion, and the courage to express personal emotions. The Romantic view of creativity assumes that creative composers and performers are extremely gifted people with an extraordinary talent to implement their passions into divine compositions or improvisations. The concept originates from the 19th century developments in musical reification and commerce. [*See* GIFTEDNESS AND CREATIVITY; NOVELTY.]

In compositional practice, the notion of creativity is

more related to strategies of ill-defined problem solving. Creative thinking in music is believed to display many similarities with creative thinking in science. Consequently, attempts have been undertaken to explore creativity from a rational point of view. In the 1950s, and since then, music institutes have been established whose aim is to foster musical creativity on a rational basis, often in connection with the development of new technology. Ultimately, this Rational view led to attempts in which formalized methods and automated processes share part of the creative process.

Since the 1960s, the concept of musical creativity has been popular in an educational context. In particular, in performance of classical music, jazz education, and improvisation training, musical creativity is believed to be related to the ability to make fast and unexpected decisions, given a learned repertoire of musical idioms and motoric skills. Education in musical creativity has a focus on the mental processes associated with creative production. Music educators are convinced that creativity can be learned by stimulating the personal viewpoint. Some also believe that the active involvement in fast (also understood as intuitive) decision making within an interactive musical environment is helpful.

The study of musical creativity as a process focuses on information processing and problem solving. A distinction can be made between behavioral studies that focus on issues of knowledge representation, learning, and memory structures for motoric actions, and brain science studies that focus on brain activity during creative tasks. Descriptive models of musical creation give a rather general but all-compassing view, whereas recent computational models give a more detailed but limited account of information processing during specific problem solving tasks. [*See* PROBLEM SOLVING.]

II. SOCIAL AND PSYCHOLOGICAL BASIS OF MUSICAL CREATIVITY

Musical creativity is a multifaceted concept and its analysis therefore implies a discussion of both the context in which creative processes take place as well as the perceptive, motoric, and cognitive processes that

subsume creativity in rapid decision making and in problem solving. Unfortunately, in much of the literature on musical creativity, the role of context is often neglected and authors tend to concentrate mainly on mental processes.

The analysis of the creative context for music aims to clarify the constraints in which music is composed and improvised. Musical creation, in general, is constrained by social factors that depend on global, cultural, economical, and political tendencies within a society. Social conditions have a determining effect on the organization of musical life and thus on the context in which creation takes place. Taking these aspects into consideration, it is important to keep in mind that the timescale in which the conditions of a cultural environment change are in general of a greater order than the timescale in which creative mental processes take place. The latter occur from a few milliseconds (rapid decision making) to a few years (incubation of creative thinking), whereas the contexts in general change from a few years to a few decennia or a few centuries. The fact that creative thinking in music often subsumes the constraints imposed by the social conditions is an effect of social interiorization, a transformation from social structure and constraints to mental structures and representations such that successful handling in the social environment is optimized. Nevertheless, creative individuals may be able to break some of the conventions imposed by the contexts.

The ability to internally process and imagine sound is a central feature of musical creativity both when different possible solutions are scanned in reaction to a given musical problem (so-called divergent thinking) as well as when making a decision for one of the possible adequate answers (so-called convergent thinking). Scanning and decision making rely on learned knowledge schemata that are acquired during a learning process by which brain structures adapt themselves to regularities and generalities of musical styles and repertoires. Problem solving and rapid decision making in music are trained and stimulated through musical education. Recently, studies of creative behavior and brain activity have been conducted and cognitive models of musical creativity have been set up.

In what follows, the concept of musical creativity is first situated within a social context. Then an analysis is given of musical creativity from the point of view of information processing.

III. THE ROMANTIC CONCEPT OF CREATIVITY

The Romantic view of musical creativity assumes that at the center of creation there is the famous inspiration that is independent from the machinery of reason or the compulsions of instinct. Musical creativity is believed to come from the muse. It is much like a gift or talent to extraordinary people who serve their lives as a medium for a supernatural being's immanent appearance in the world. Those, however, that do not believe in divine forces assume that the muse has its origin in an affective disease. Anyhow, creativity cannot be educated but must flow out of a natural drive and emotional engagement.

The Romantic view holds that there are—perhaps unfortunately—a number of side effects that stigmatize the elected artist. Creative artists are believed to display a certain tendency to unadapted social and often psychotic, extravagant, or bizarre behavior. Their creative talents exhibit diabolic powers (like the violinist Paganini), radiate sex appeal (like the pianist and composer Liszt), or are due to tormented minds (like the composers Berlioz and Beethoven), but the society has to accept this because it is in the very nature of being creative to be either possessed or mad. It led to the idea that derangements such as depression, mania, drugs, or personality disorder are important for having an unusual creativity. [*See* ECCENTRICITY.]

The Romantic view on musical creativity can be traced back to the works of J.-J. Rousseau (1712–1778) who defended informal education and the natural origin of creativity. Yet the typical Romantic picture became popular at the beginning of the 19th century. The Romantic view is said to be irrational both with respect to the origin of creation and with respect to the features associated. The origin of creation is situated either outside the individual, in a metaphysical reality, or inside as degeneration. In the first case, it is considered to be a matter of belief and hence beyond any reasonable understanding, effective exploitation, or education. In the second case, studies have pointed out that there is no compelling evidence that there is pathology in musical creativity. Obviously, the social behavior by which the creative artist distinguishes him- or herself from common people is often cultivated (both by the artist and his or her musical environment), and it is thus part of an image-building machinery that subsumes social factors of the way in which musical life is organized but that is disconnected from the actual creative processes.

The advent of the Romantic conception of musical creation goes hand in hand with the development of industrialization, liberalism, and nationalism in the late 18th and first decades of the 19th century. The revolutionary developments, both in politics and industrialization, inaugurated the decline of the *Ancien Régime* and its associated organization of musical life throughout Europe. It rapidly led to the installation of a new type of professional framework based on the principles of free market. In that framework, composers and musicians were no longer working in service of a court but became individual entrepreneurs that worked in free competition conditions with other entrepreneur-artists. The cults of the child prodigy, the virtuoso, and the tormented genius (whose work is first misunderstood and later hailed) are emerging effects of the dynamics that is inherent in this new organization of musical life. The free market was made for the bourgeois class minority and lower and middle classes were excluded from it. Nevertheless, it created a dynamics so powerful and all encompassing that its influence is still a dominant factor in the contemporary organization of musical life.

With the decline of the bourgeois society after World War I and the advent of mass media and mass movement in the United States and Europe, the organization of musical life became dominated by a music industry composed of major recording companies, state broadcasting companies, and impressario houses. Musical sound became materialized using recording media and this process of reification favored a tendency to consider music henceforth as a commodity whose return sales are in direct proportion to the success of commercial strategies to exploit Romantic musical creativity. Classical music, a main achievement of the bourgeois society, was no longer the dominant type of music. Instead, jazz music and, expecially, rock 'n' roll (in the 1950s) and popular music in general found their way to the masses. The market for musical commodities rapidly increased and the music industry became one of the most important industries of the postindustrial societies. Given this context, the Romantic concept of creativity was easily extended toward all forms of classical and popular music.

The music industry today is still perfectly aware of the force of the popular Romantic view on musical creativity. The vague ideas of the creative genius are now at the center of the mechanisms in which idolization and excess worship are subject to marketing strategies of major commercial companies. As a matter of fact, the very irrationality behind the Romantic concept of creativity makes it ideally suited to commercial exploitation. Extravagant behavior, sex appeal, and the use of religious symbols are associated features that contribute to image building. It fits with carefully planned strategies that favor idolatry and worship in consumption patterns. In many respects, therefore, the Romantic concept of creativity is an effect of musical reification and commodification, a process that started in the 19th century and that continues today.

IV. RATIONAL CREATIVITY

In contrast to the popularity of the Romantic view, some countercurrents offered an alternative view on musical creativity. In particular, during the 1950s and 1960s, the social conditions were present for the emergence of a professional subframework that was entirely different from the free market framework that dominated popular music and music of the classical repertoire. It is the achievement of the so-called institutional musical *avant-garde* to have explored a view on musical creativity that is in total contrast to the Romantic conception. The origin of this Rational view can be traced back to the 18th century period of Enlightenment where the first successes of the scientific methods (in particular, deduction, induction, and abduction) were taken as a model for a total worldview, in particular also for creation. A more detailed sketch of the sociological background of this development is important to understand the effects on creativity.

The concept of rationalized creation and the consistent way in which it was worked out in connection with new developments in technology formed the foundation of many new developments in musical creativity. The achievements of the avant-garde, given the growing impact of the music industry in all other fields of music, can only be explained by a combination of factors involving the development of new recording technology and mass media institutions, institutionalization within the context of broadcasting institutions and universities, and association with scientific research. From a political point of view too, it is now believed that, at least in Europe, the support for unbridled creativity played a role in an attempt to reestablish the European high culture after the calamities of World War II. Yet this was no isolated European phenomenon. The attention for unlimited creativity is much associated with the zeitgeist of the Golden Sixties, the successes of capitalism in social welfare, and the advent of the postindustrial society.

The avant-garde movement presented itself as the antipode of musical commodification, while at the same time it put forward the reification of music to the extreme. In particular, it neglected the developments in music industry and the free-market framework by a thorough institutionalization via electronic music studios supported by the state. It based the essence of musical creation on technology that transformed abstract sounds into real material objects. The latter is particularly evident in electroacoustic music productions in which the creative molding of sounds requires the knowledge of particular nonmusical skills in acoustics, psychoacoustics, electronics, and computing in order to record on magnetic tapes, to use techniques of cut and paste, stretching, compressing, and filtering, and to make many other sound manipulations.

A main effect of combining technology with musical creation is that musical creativity was no longer believed to lay outside the human being or inside an affective disease (as in the Romantic concept). The technological environment implies that creativity can be controlled and guided by rational thought. Machines become useful as extensions of musical creativity, just like electronic calculators are useful in taking over some parts of mathematical reasoning. Three aspects of this development deserve further analysis because they provide important aspects of the social conditions that enable creative thinking: (a) the role of institutionalization in the establishment of contexts for rational music creation, (b) the legitimation of creativity in the technological context, and (c) the impact of methodology and tendencies toward automated creation.

A. Institutionalization and Contexts for Rational Music Creation

To describe the context for rational musical creation it is useful to make a distinction between three types of frameworks: the infrastructure of creation, the professional framework, and the artistic paradigm.

The *infrastructure of creation* defines the production environment for music. It is typically a production or rehearsal studio, with all the equipment and assistance personnel. The infrastructure is composed of machinery for production, such as a set of magnetophones and sound generators. It imposes a methodology for creativity because the composition process often involves the planning and realization of musical ideas as a function of the available technology. It also entails a division of labor between the composer and the technical staff while at the same time it makes the boundaries between composition and realization more diffuse. As a matter of fact, creativity in the studio causes the composer to acquire engineering skills or to collaborate with other people who may influence the creative process. It is known, but rarely mentioned, that technicians often contributed to the creation process by finding new solutions to problems posed by the composer. In addition, it is often mentioned that creativity is constrained by standards imposed by the music industry. MIDI, an industrial standard for music instrument digital interfaces, has for example been criticized for being too focused on the traditional concept of music making. Alternative composer environments have been developed at universities and artistic centers.

The *professional framework* defines the way in which the organization of the artistic activities are socially worked out. This level thus pertains to the sociocultural conditions in which the infrastructure is embedded. In the 19th century it was based on private initiative and entrepreneurship of the artist. The support and commands of contemporary (nonpopular) music in the 1950s and 1960s was to a large extent taken over by state commands via radio broadcasting companies or universities. The role of the state in the organization of musical life can be compared with the roles of the church in the medieval times and the courts in the Renaissance and Baroque periods. The main difference, however, was its absolute tolerance with respect to creation. Creativity was assumed to be free from any constraint, even (or especially) the audience. The professional framework thus acquired a status of a pseudoscientific creative enterprise. In contrast to this, the advent of private studios and the integration of technology in popular music has to be situated in a framework of free-market conditions. In such a framework, musical creation is necessarily more functionally oriented and consumer dependent.

The *artistic paradigm* concerns the technical and stylistic aspects of music production. It entails a methodology that guides creative thinking and it often imposes a stylistic idiom, a sort of musical worldview. In the 19th century the artistic concept is typically called Romantic. It is characterized by a tonal syntax and causal deployment of musical ideas. Musical genres and forms, such as the sonata form, the concerto, or the symphony, provided schemata by which composers constrained their creative thoughts or added new extensions or ideas. The tonal syntax itself implied several rules for the generation of music. This too provided a thorough set of constraints that composers could follow or slightly change. The avant-garde artistic conception was strongly involved with the exploration of new possibilities of sound production, transformation, and manipulation using new technology (electronics and magnetophones) within an institutionalized infrastructure. The focus on novelty determined the peculiar conception of musical creativity as something that is directed on novelty. Avant-garde creativity tried to avoid the constraints of the tonal syntax and rejected most of the traditional musical forms. It focused instead on the use of timbre and noncausal structural principles. In some cases, however, novelty (and use of new equipment) was considered to be a more important category of musical creativity than musicality.

The three levels (infrastructure, professional framework, and artistic paradigm) obviously depend on each other and they reinforce each other. Together they provide the social framework within which creative actions take place. Very often it can be shown that the social context has a determining effect on musical creation.

B. The Legitimation of Musical Creativity

The avant-garde movement gave rise to the idea that, ultimately, musical creativity can be automated and taken over by machines. This idea emerged from the social conditions in which absolute freedom in creative thinking goes hand in hand with a thorough rational approach to musical research. This section goes deeper into the forces that facilitated the development of this idea, and the next section gives an account of the basic conception behind automated creativity.

First, the notion of music research was associated with radiophonic applications. It aimed at a *creative exploitation* of the hitherto unexplored new world of sound objects. The latter were conceived either as isolated objects (e.g., the sound of a train, of footsteps, or of water) or as sound objects in a context of other sound objects. The latter, of course, implies a musical environment. This exploitation was conceived of in a systematic and methodological way, interpreted as a solfège of musical objects. The above-mentioned context of institutionalization played herein a central role. Music research was originally meant to be an examination of the possibilities of new technology for artistic creativity. Later on, in the 1970s, the concept of music research became more involved with interdisciplinary scientific research, such as in acoustics, psychoacoustics, and informatics, and focused on the creation of new (electronic) musical instruments, less on the exploration of the composer's intuition.

Second, the integration of technology with music established a highly scientized context for musical creativity, both within the context of free-market conditions and in the context of state-supported institutions. It is characterized by *division of labor* (and creativity), by paradigmatic constraints and attitudes with respect to commodification. The division of labor means that the context of creation is maintained by a specialized crew of people. For example, the production of electroacoustic music implies both the composition and the realization process. It often turns out that part of the creative process is delegated or works in interaction with other people and with machines. The individual creative process thus becomes subsumed in a group creative process. This is the case in the free market as well as in the state supported framework.

A third factor that favored the development of automated music creation is the *artistic concept*. State-supported institutions are often associated with an artistic paradigm that imposes a set of aesthetic beliefs and methodological strategies. It implies a number of bounds and constraints that composers have to accept if they want to use the institutional infrastructure for creation. The free-market infrastructures, on the other hand, have no such ideological constraints, although the constraints are to be situated at the financial level. The amount of money needed to use the professional equipment for creative experimentation is often a major threshold for beginning pop musicians. In the state-supported framework, commodification is not a dominant factor because the institutes guarantee the quality, transmission, and preservation of the achieved results. In the free-market framework, commodification is the ultimate goal. In the free-market conditions, commodification is a driving force of the artistic creation.

The existence of the free market and the state-support framework has led to entirely different schematas for the legitimation of musical creativity. The state-supported framework is characterized by a form of *autonomous legitimation*. It means that no forces other than the inherent forces of the institution play a role in the creative process. Nonexperts, such as an audience, are not allowed to interfere. In the free-market condition, the creative context is characterized by a *heteronomous legitimation*. The ultimate justification of musical creativity is functional and the feedback is determined by the consumer market. In music history the creative contexts were mostly heteronomous. Musical creativity was directed to God or to the Church in medieval times, to the king or to the prince in Renaissance and Baroque times, or to Nature or to the Self in Romantic music. Consequently, the organization of musical life, and the particular implementation of a scientized context for musical creativity, has been highly dependent on the professional framework (market oriented or state supported). The state-supported framework of the 1950s and 1960s led to the view that musical creation can be fully automated.

C. From Methodology to Automated Creation

Automated musical creativity is a goal pursued in the contemporary exploration of creative thinking but it is by no means an entirely modern invention. For many centuries the composition and improvisation rules have been written down as recipes for practical music making (both in composition and in improvisation). Recipes facilitate the creation of new music, although the creative mind will often break the received rules as a function of an original and interesting new finding. In the 15th and early 16th centuries, one often encounters canonic riddles embedded within compositions that require the working out of a puzzle in order to perform the music. Dice music—composed by throwing a die iteratively and choosing, on the basis of the outcome, a possible motive from a table of musical figures—was quite popular in the second half of the (rational) 18th century. In short, recipes and methods in general offer the means to achieve a goal—if not automated—by going through a number of steps. Without a methodology, one is often lost in the complexities of ill-defined musical problem solving.

Music is one of the application domains in which the idea of automated creation has found its most persistent and perhaps oldest application. This is due to the fact that (a) musical signification has no denotational constraints and that it is entirely context dependent and (b) that the materialization of musical ideas can itself be automatically realized into sonorous objects. Trends toward automated creativity can be observed in all forms of music production that rely on technology. As discussed in the previous section the social context of the 1950s and 1960s was favorable to the rational development and quasi-scientific approaches to automated creation. In a quite different context, automated music production is now used for the generation of popular songs and dance music.

The ultimate achievement in automated music making, such as conceived by avant-garde composers in the 1950 and 1960s, was to compose a musical germ out of which a whole composition may follow by self-development. The self-creativity of music is based on the idea of letting music create itself out of a single kernel. It shifts the process of creation to a single thought out of which everything follows automatically. In that sense, the act of composing as unfolding music through time is carried out by an automated creator, while the creative insight, idea, or finding is reduced to its bare kernel. Some argue that the musical creativity is then a combination of the starting idea (the kernel) and the creation of a system that unfolds the kernel. Hence, the unfolding itself is automated, but the potentiality of the system is a human invention, although sometimes a highly scientized one. Examples of this type of thinking can be traced back to Beethoven. It is prominently present in the works of avant-garde composers such as Stockhausen and Boulez and in more recent computer music realizations.

V. PRAGMATIC CREATIVITY

The pragmatic concept of musical creativity states that we know little about the origin and nature of musical creativity. Yet the concept is useful in education and it can be studied and even measured. Educators deny the fact that creativity has a metaphysical or pathological origin and believe that creation can somehow be stimulated and learned. They recognize that some people are more talented and gifted than others and that creativity can be sometimes (though not always) associated with these features. The interest is in the development of tools that improve and enhance creative music making.

Much of the literature on musical creativity focuses on practice and deals with the teaching of strategies in composition and improvisation in the classroom. This literature stresses the pursuit of an active engagement in discovery learning. Educators focus on musical praxis and exercise and not just on the understanding of learned rules in composition and improvisation. Reference can be made to the Kodaly approach that starts from folk styles and corporate singing as appropriate avenues for musical literacy. It is also argued that children must develop a background of enriched sensory images and activities to accomplish creative musical thinking and affective decision making. It is believed that children can be stimulated to explore a broad range of musical possibilities and education in general stresses the arrangement of musical materials and a gradual increase in complexity of the musical material onto which musical creativity is trained.

In short, there is little doubt that the concept of creativity should be central in musical education, yet the approach is pragmatic and does not tell much about the origin and nature of musical creativity. Part of the education process is focused on the acquisition of rules and methods that allow one to understand the way in which sounds interact with human activities. The aim is to set up this interaction so that pupils scan a large range of possibilities and know how to apply musical knowledge to achieve fast and efficient results.

VI. STUDIES OF MUSICAL CREATIVITY

Most studies on musical creativity have focused on information processing. A distinction can be made among three fields of research: (a) behavioral studies, (b) brain studies, and (c) modeling.

A. Behavioral Studies

Behavioral studies of musical creativity are done either in a natural environment or in a controlled experimental environment. In both cases the aim is to observe behavior and to extract general knowledge about the creative process. Often the aim is to set up tests for measuring creative aptitude.

Studies have focused on subjects of all ages. The study of creative musical behavior in children typically involves gamelike tasks. Children are observed when they explore musical parameters such as high/low, fast/slow, and loud/soft. They are given tasks that involve sound imagination. They are observed when dealing with ill-defined musical tasks such as telling a story in sounds, using drawings as an aid, or making a composition with musical instruments. The tasks are recorded on videotapes and analyzed using scores for creative features such as originality, extensiveness, flexibility, and musical sensitivity. Results suggest that children follow consistent patterns in creative attitudes so that testing is appropriate. Other studies have focused on spontaneous creative exploration. Children

have been brought into a room in which there were musical instruments. Without any predefined task or interruption, they were observed. The aim was to study how children explore music instruments, to what extent they rely on learned patterns when producing music, and to what extent children develop spontaneous group activities. Several years later, the same group of children was observed under similar conditions and comparison with former observations were made. Creativity turned out to be less spontaneous and more based on learned schemata.

Creativity is often associated with intelligent problem solving. Strategies of problem solving are called creative when diverse pertinent ideas come out of ill-defined problems, when practical problems are recognized, when reference frameworks of different domains are combined, and when the solutions are original. Since the beginning of the 20th century, studies have also focused on compositional creativity in adults, asking subjects to compose music from a given poem. Studies are based on autobiographical records, the study of notebooks and sketches (of great composers), final scores, and direct observation of composers at work. These studies have led to a *basic framework* for setting up variables for creativity research. In this context, Wallas's conjectures of a subdivision of the creative process into different stages has been taken over by many authors. (a) The first phase of the creative process is called the *preparatory phase,* which is often accompanied by an internal crisis and questioning of old reference frames, taking into account the specificity and complexity of the task. (b) The second phase is the *incubation phase,* in which the germ for a solution is founded by letting things develop in their due course. There is a focus on different reference frames and application of metaphorical thinking. It is also assumed that the unconscious takes over from the conscious. (c) The third phase is the *illumination phase,* typically accompanied by the *Aha-Erlebniss* when a solution is found. (d) The fourth phase is the *phase of verification,* when the excitement has passed and the solution is tested. Bahle related empirical results to five states: the state of conception, the state of abstract ideas or images, the state of concrete ideas (such as musical motives), the state of realization, and the state of production. [*See* INCUBATION.]

Further behavioral studies concentrated on setting up specific variables for behavioral research in creativity. Guilford, for example, made a distinction between a *convergent* type of thinking, which tends to seek solutions unique to the posed problem, and a *divergent* type of thinking, which tends to scan all possible solutions for a given problem. *Musical fluidity* or the capacity to produce much (i.e., the amount of time invested in creative thinking), is related to divergent thinking. It is measured in terms of the number of events produced in comparison with creative responses. Other components include flexibility, originality, and elaboration. [*See* DIVERGENT THINKING.]

Musical flexibility is the aptitude to produce a diversity of ideas in ill-structured situations. It is also associated with the number of categories in which one may classify the given responses. This is worked out in terms of the diversity of pertinent musical solutions for a given task, the number of phrases that are musically different, the elaboration of musical parameters such as register (high, low), intensity (loud, soft) and tempo (fast, slow). [*See* FLEXIBILITY.]

Musical originality or production of uncommon but pertinent answers is often measured in terms of the rareness of musical content with respect to the ensemble of the experimental population.

Musical elaboration concerns the level of complexity of the musical phrases produced. Other components are concerned with aspects such as *problem sensibility* and the capacity to recognize practical problems, *redefinition* or the aptitude to change the function of an object or part of the object and to use it, *rhythmical certainty* or the capacity to follow a regular pulsation and to improvise on a rhythmic sequence, *musical expressive quality,* and so on.

The attempt to operationalize creativity in terms of distinguished components has inspired researchers to develop tests for the prognosis of creative ability. Some authors argue, however, that such tests, given their limited testing condition, do not give any valuable proofs of creativity because the tests are not embedded in a social environment. They do show, however, that one person is more skillful than another in solving particular tasks under constrained conditions.

Behavioral studies have led to a so-called *cognitive view* of musical activities. This view stresses schemata-based processing of musical information. Schemata are learned hierarchical knowledge structures. Creative performances and improvisations have been related to the existence of knowledge of large-scale groupings or patterns within music. The control of the performance, guided by those patterns, is hierarchical in that parameters that apply to a larger grouping determine the settings for elements within the group. In contrast to experts, inexpert performance seems to be based on superficial features of music. High-level hierarchical control is furthermore supported by highly flexible procedures for solving local problems, whereas inexpert performers are more committed to solving immediate local problems. Finally, creative performers have the means to monitor their own performances and to take corrective actions in addition to a number of automated actions. Their attention is not fully engaged in technical aspects of the performance. Compositional processes are based on unconscious resources such as general tonal and stylistic knowledge and constraints on form and direction, and conscious resources and processes such as using a repertoire of compositional devices to transform a theme, to extend and develop a theme, and to modify it. [*See* EXPERTISE.]

B. Brain Studies

Studies that relate musical creativity to the brain are quite diverse. One of the few studies of the biological basis of creativity reports that creative musical behavior is associated with very low values of testosterone in males and with high testosterone levels in females. The data suggest that among a complex interaction of biological and social factors, an optimal testosterone range may exist for the expression of creative musical behavior. Exceeding the range in the course of adolescence may be detrimental for musical creativity in boys. The hypothesis is that talented creative musicians of both sexes are psychologically androgynous. [*See* BRAIN BIOLOGY AND BRAIN FUNCTIONING.]

There exists a wide range of studies about brain damage and their behavioral effects in famous composers. It has been found, for example, that the loss of verbal functions (aphasia) is not necessarily accompanied by a loss of musical functions (amusia). Some composers that suffered from aphasia (mostly due to damage in the left hemisphere) were still able to compose music without loss of musical abilities. The French composer Maurice Ravel, however, suffered from an injury to the left hemisphere and had forms of agraphia, alexia, and aphasia. He retained critical capacities, recognized melodies, and could appreciate music, but he lost his creative musical abilities to perform and to compose. Yet he claimed to be able to hear the music that he composed in his head.

The development of sophisticated brain scan techniques, such as electroencephalogram (EEG), magneto-encephalogram (MEG), positron emission tomography (PET), and functional magnetic resonance imaging (fMRI), gave rise (in the 1980s) to the development of a new field called *cognitive neuromusicology*. The aim is to find out whether specific brain activity can be correlated with musical functions, in particular also with musical imagining and creativity. Recent findings show that acts of creative thinking seem to be characterized by coherence increases between occipital and fronto-polar electrode sites. This is different in other mental tasks. Some recent work has also focused on sub-aspects of creativity, such as musical imagery. The phenomenological impression of imagined sounds can be associated with the bilateral neuronal activity in the secondary auditory cortices. Although the question of the format of mental images is not addressed, data suggest that auditory images have perceptual origins. Given the enormous industrial interests and the possible medical applications, it is to be expected that cognitive neuromusicology will become a key science in our understanding of musical creativity.

C. Models of Creativity

If musical creativity is related to musical information processing, then aspects of it can be modeled. Thus far, however, most models have been descriptive in that they give a rather general overview of the different components involved. Some models are computational and are intended to carry out some specific creative task rather than to give a general account of creativity as such. Due to the fact that our knowledge of the physiological basis of creativity is limited (or almost nonexistent), no specific physiological models for musical creativity have been proposed to date.

1. Descriptive Models

Descriptive models of musical creativity may serve as conceptual guides in research and education. Most educators agree that creative activity relies on a repertoire of musical aptitudes that are partly innate but also subject to development and improvement with training. Webster, for example, proposed a descriptive model of creative thinking that is based on the distinction between convergent and divergent thinking on the one hand, and skills and conditions on the other hand.

Webster made a distinction between composition, performance/improvisation, and analysis. They can be considered as goals or intentions of the creator and they are therefore called *product intentions*. Once such an intention is realized it represents the final *product of creation*. The creative process is based on a set of skills called *enabling skills* and a set of conditions called *enabling conditions*. They form the basis of musical intelligence and interact with the thinking process in a rich variety of ways. First among the skills is a collection of *musical aptitudes* such as the ability to recognize rhythmic and tonal patterns, and musical syntax in general, the ability to imagine sounds, or the ability to apply a range of expressions in musical dynamics, tempo, or pitch. The musical aptitudes include convergent thinking skills, such as the ability to recognize rhythmic patterns, tonal patterns, and musical syntax, as well as the previously mentioned divergent skills such as fluidity, flexibility, or originality. It is assumed that a number of these aptitudes are innate, although they are subject to development and training. Other skills are based on knowledge of facts, such as the craftsmanship to apply composition rules in the service of a complex musical task and the ability to mold a musical work in accordance with aesthetic sensitivity.

Next to the skills are inner and environmental conditions. Motivation, for example, refers to the drives, both external and internal, that help to keep the creator on the task. Subconscious imagery is the presence of mental activity that occurs apart from the conscious mind and that may help to inform the creative process. Personality, according to Webster, describes factors such as risk taking, spontaneity, openness, perspicacity, sense of humor, and preference for complexity. Environmental conditions, such as financial support or family conditions, may have an additional effect on the creative process. [*See* CONDITIONS AND SETTINGS/ENVI-RONMENT; MOTIVATION/DRIVE; PERSONALITY.]

One may add to this the institutional contexts for musical creation that were discussed in the previous sections. A central aspect of the describing model, then, is the thinking process in which the distinction between divergent and convergent thinking is embedded within the classical four-stage distinction among preparation, incubation, verification, and illumination.

The describing models provide rather general conceptualizations of the creative process. They have the advantage that a lot of factors can be taken into account but the disadvantange that the creative information processing as such is described in rather vague terms.

2. Computational Models

Computational models of musical creativity aim at understanding the dynamics of creation in terms of computational processes. In the cognitive musicology literature, since the 1970s, several such models have been described. Most models, though rather restricted in scope, apply learning strategies to establish a repertoire of knowledge used for the generation of music. The type of modeling is related to research in artificial intelligence. [*See* ARTIFICIAL INTELLIGENCE.]

The early models rely on logic-based inference techniques such as rules or grammars. The set of skills that are needed to solve a specific task, such as a harmonization or a jazz improvisation, is typically implemented in terms of *declarative* and *procedural* descriptions. Declarative knowledge gives a description of musical objects in terms of facts (e.g., that the C-major triad consists of the notes C-E-G), whereas procedural knowledge gives such a description in terms of a method (e.g., that the C-major triad can be obtained by adding a major third and a fifth on top of the fundamental C). The latter method is more general in that it can be applied to get the major triads of other fundamentals as well.

In the late 1980s, computational models of creativity have been built using so-called connectionist networks rather than logic-based inference systems. The latter are inspired by the wiring of the neurons in the brain. The systems have to be trained by example. The kernel of innovation comes down to the manipulation of stored probability functions or controlled random variation.

Experiments with computational models of creativity have led to more refined general models of creativity. Pressing provides a model of improvisation in terms of *real-time* perceptivo-motoric connections and regularities. The sequential processing of musical information is crucial at three points: (a) the perceptive encoding of sensorial data, (b) the evaluation of potentialities and choice of a response, and (c) the execution and organization of the chosen actions. The automatization of certain learned motoric sequences in response to input may free up time to analyze incoming information simultaneously. A distinction is made between a memory of musical objects and a memory of potential actions that can be actualized. The first relates to a declarative long-term memory of musical configurations, whereas the second implies a procedural long-term memory for the learning of variation techniques and techniques of combination according to different contexts and reference frames. The application of both memories in real time relies highly on learning and automatization. Learning can extend and refine the perceptive encoding; it can elaborate the evaluation and make the execution of musical actions more rapid. The limitations of the creative thinking therefore rely on conscious action related to decision making and unconscious action related to automated processes such as perceptive analysis and expression of precoded motoric actions.

Computational models are obviously limited in scope in that they concentrate on enabling skills and related information processing. The computer models, up to now, have not been embedded in the sociocultural environment and therefore the enabling conditions are not represented. In recent years, however, attempts have been undertaken to represent emotions in machines and to build creative musical robots that are embedded in an environment. This provides a promising context for future creativity research.

VII. CONCLUSION

Musical creativity is associated with musical compositions, performances, and improvisations that are novel but sufficiently musical to make it valuable in a given sociocultural environment. Further questions therefore relate to the minimal amount of novelty needed to be considered valuable creativity, the different aspects of novelty that are required to be considered creative musical output, or aspects of musicality in relation to novelty and tradition. In answering such questions, it is necessary to approach the study of musical creativity from an interdisciplinary point of view—that is, one in which historical, sociological, psychological/neuropsychological, and computational methodologies are somehow combined. Musical creativity is context sensitive in that its production and its reception are determined by a number of social factors that need further study and analysis. It deals also with ill-defined problem solving and fast decision making. The study of musical creativity therefore needs further analysis from an ecological point of view—that is, one in which creative thinking is studied directly and interacting with different strata of the social environment. The study of paradigmatic (historical) examples of musical creativity may provide important cues for setting up a methodology that covers these aspects.

Bibliography

Loy, G. (1991). Composing with computers—A survey of some compositional formalisms and music programming languages. In M. Mathews & J. Pierce (Eds.), *Current directions in computer music research.* Cambridge, MA: The MIT Press.

Mialaret, J.-P. (1994). La créativité musicale. In A. Zenatti (Ed.), *Psychologie de la musique.* Paris: Presses Universitaires de France.

Pressing, J. (1988). Improvisation: Methods and models. In J. Sloboda (Ed.), *Generative processes in music—The psychology of performance, improvisation, and composition.* Oxford: Clarendon Press.

Sergent, J. (1993). Music, the brain and Ravel. *Trends in Neurosciences, 16*(5), 168–172.

Sloboda, J. (1985). *The musical mind—The cognitive psychology of music.* Oxford: Clarendon Press.

Webster, P. (1990). Creativity as creative thinking. *Music Educators Journal, 76*(9), 22–28.

Novelty

Patricia D. Stokes

Barnard College, Columbia University

Constraint Anything that precludes and promotes particular kinds of responses.

Creativity A kind of novelty that is useful, valuable, generative.

Novelty A kind of variability involving responses that are new, fresh, and unusual. Novelty increases as variability increases.

Problem Space How a problem is represented by a solver. The problem space has three parts: an initial state, a goal state, and a set of operators (or legitimate moves) to get from the initial to the goal state. Constraints serve to structure problem spaces.

Variability Quality of doing something more or less differently. Variability levels range from stereotypy to randomness.

NOVELTY is part, but not the whole parcel, of what we call creativity. However, in contrast to the other parts (value, usefulness), which have shifting criteria, novelty is more amenable to measurement and manipulation. This chapter considers how constraints have been used to preclude highly probable responses and thus to promote the production of novel ones.

I. RELATIONSHIPS BETWEEN VARIABILITY, NOVELTY, AND CREATIVITY

Variability can been represented as a continuum with, at one end, responses that are completely predictable, invariant, stereotyped, and, at the other end, responses that are entirely unpredictable, random. Most behaviors fall between these extremes, ranging from the reliable (painting a still life by number, reciting the alphabet) to the novel (painting a still life from life, writing a poem). Novelty is defined here as a way of being variable.

Let us quality this further. Both associative and more recent rule-based models of responding posit hierarchies in which low-probability, including novel, responses appear *after* higher-probability ones. As these models predict, novel responses occur after more likely ones have been exhausted. Thus, novelty can be more exactly defined as a way of being *highly* variable.

However, although painting in a new way may constitute a novel response, it is not necessarily a creative one. To be considered creative, the new way of painting would also have to be valuable or influential, useful or generative in its domain. For example, Braque and Picasso's novel depiction of the world from multiple perspectives was valuable and influential in changing the criteria for representational painting. It was useful and generative in producing its own stylistic variants among other artists like Gris and Leger.

Just as novelty is a particular way of being variable, creativity is a particular way of being novel. One thing more must be considered in this definition. Because the criteria for influential, valuable behavior are subjective and shifting, determined at different times by the current gatekeepers in a domain (would Piero della Francesca, exploiting perspective during the Renaissance, be considered creative if he were painting today?), creativity is a culturally defined way of being novel. [*See* CONSENSUAL ASSESSMENT.]

It is precisely the changing and highly subjective nature of its criteria that make creativity so difficult to measure and manipulate. In contrast, novelty—like other related variability measures that we will consider, originality and fluency among them—is easily and objectively defined, facilitating study of the conditions under which it can be maximized. In consequence, important aspects of creative behavior can be understood and enhanced, as we shall see.

II. GENERAL ROLE OF CONSTRAINTS IN GENERATING NOVELTY

A simple, but comprehensive, way to organize, relate, and understand different ways of incrementing novelty is to group them under the rubric of constraint. This may seem surprising, because constraints are generally seen as restrictive or, in problem solving, as ways of limiting search. This makes it important to consider what is being restricted and how limiting search can generate novelty.

Constraints here are defined as some things, any things, that preclude some responses and promote other ones. If a constraint restricts or precludes common, highly probable responses, it will promote unusual, low-probability ones, some of which may be novel. Reward or reinforcement criteria are exemplary constraints, promoting specific responses that increase in frequency and, de facto, precluding nonrewarded responses that decline.

To understand the idea of limiting search, a brief primer on problem spaces may be useful. A problem or search space is how a given problem is represented by

a solver. It includes a set of states (initial, current, goal), a set of operators (condition action rules of the form "If the situation is *X*, then do *Y*") for constructing a path through the search space from initial to goal states, and—if the problem is completely specified—a criterion for knowing when one has reached the goal.

Different degrees of specification in these parts allow problems to be arranged on a continuum. At one end are well-structured, completely defined problems that generate little variability, much less novelty, in their solutions. For example, a jigsaw puzzle provides clear operators ("If a side of Piece A fits into a side of Piece B, then join the two pieces"), as well as an unambiguous criteria for solution ("Match the picture on the box"). At the other end of the continuum are ill-structured, incompletely defined problems that generate higher variability and potentially novel, even creative, solutions.

In problem-solving terms, constraints include anything specified in the problem definition. Ill-structured problems are characterized by "open" constraints. For example, if a composer is writing a fugue, the initial and only constraint is that the form be fugal, with expositions interspersed with episodes, and concluding with a coda. For an architect, an initial open constraint might be to design a house.

Adding novelty to a goal criterion would preclude highly probable paths (reminiscent of prior pieces or designs) and promote search for unusual ones. A constraint could be more specific, precluding, for example, use of the instrument or materials in which the musician or builder is most proficient or promoting search in a particular space, perhaps a form in which the individual has rarely, if ever, worked. In a later section, we will discuss how many accomplished artists have used these kinds of constraints as strategies for generating novelty. Interactions between constraints and individual repertoires will be considered in the section on design and composition.

III. NOVELTY AND VARIABILITY CRITERIA AS CONSTRAINTS

There are several reasons for considering constraints on a number of variability measures related to novelty. First, as mentioned earlier, novelty tends to increase as variability increases. Second, highly creative people tend to be highly variable in their areas of expertise. Third, although strict novelty criteria reward only responses that are different from all prior responses made by an individual, most creativity training and testing measures are less stringent, using variability rather than novel criteria. For example, the Torrance Tests of Creative Thinking (TTCT) measure originality, fluency, and flexibility. The measures are derived from work on divergent thinking, which is characterized by the generation of multiple possibilities. Originality scores are based on response frequency in a given population and reflect unusual, not necessarily novel, responses. Fluency measures reflect the number of different responses; flexibility measures measure different kinds of responses. Elaboration reflects the amount of detail used in developing an idea. This section is therefore subdivided into constraints on novelty alone, on novelty and other kinds of variability, and finally, on variability per se.

A. Strict Novelty Criteria

Novelty criteria can be applied either across or within training sessions. *Across* means that to be rewarded a current response must differ from all responses in all prior training sessions; *within* means that the response must differ from all responses in a particular session. The constraints here clearly preclude old responses and promote new ones.

In a famous study on porpoises, novelty was defined across sessions. Animals were only rewarded for swimming and leaping topographies that were not part of their normal repertoires. To put this in terms of constraints, novel forms of responding were promoted, high-probability forms were precluded. As training progressed, not only did novelty increase, but new responses were observed closer to and, in sessions 31 and 32, even at the start of the session.

In contrast, when children are studied, reward depends on the first instance of a response within a session, regardless of whether it appeared in a prior session. In a 1977 study, Goetz and colleagues used praise, either alone or with a toy or token that could be exchanged for a toy at the end of a session, to reward the first instances of a painting, collage, felt-pen drawing, lego or block-building response in each session. An example of felt-pen coding is "Blended color:

any hue formed by mixing two or more pure or available colors onto the paper." Both form diversity (the first instance of a response in a session) and new forms (the first instance in all sessions) increased when rewarded. High variability in form diversity was maintained 2 months later. Other work with fifth and sixth graders has shown reward increasing novelty on the unusual uses and squares tasks, as well as in felt-pen drawings.

B. Novelty and Other Specific Variability Criteria

Many different rewards have been successful in selecting and incrementing specific kinds of variability. Praise for improvisation increased improvisation in tool usage by 3-to-6-year-old children. Similarly, tokens and praise raised fluency, flexibility, and elaboration scores in writing among 10-to-12-year old children. The drawings of 3-to-5-year olds became more diverse and creative when followed by cartoons. Unusual uses and squares scores increased among fifth and sixth graders rewarded with points. Comparing concrete and verbal reinforcers on the same task showed no differences. Children given either candy or praise for ideational fluency significantly outscored control groups.

It is important to notice that in all the above studies (including those with strict novelty criteria) participants were not told what aspect of responding was being constrained. Rather they learned this *via* reward, which has informational as well as incentive properties. Incentive is derived from the reward itself; information, from the fact that only specific responses (novel ones, fluent ones) were followed by reward. The informational aspect is critical and suggests strongly that failure to increase creativity in intrinsic motivation tasks, or fluency in divergent-thinking ones, follows precisely from ambiguity, nonspecificity in performance criteria. Compared to standard, nonexplicit instructions, explicit instructions regarding criteria on divergent thinking tests increase originality and flexibility scores. If a standard instruction were "List 6 different uses for this object," an explicit originality instruction might be "List 6 unusual and worthwhile uses for this object." The first instruction precludes neither the usual or the useless; the second precludes both.

A 1997 series of experiments by Eisenberger and

colleagues illustrate this point quite clearly. These studies followed work on learned industriousness, which shows first that reinforcing high effort produces a generalized increase in industriousness and second that the effect is specific to the rewarded aspect of responding. For example, students rewarded for speed in Task A do Task B faster, whereas those initially rewarded for accuracy perform more accurately later. If this kind of learning occurs in creative tasks, rewarding novelty on Task A should increase novel responding on Task B, whereas initially rewarding familiar, higher-probability responses should reduce novelty later.

To be rewarded, responses on an initial unusual uses task had to be novel. When the novelty requirement was clearly stated, a larger, salient reward generated more originality on a subsequent drawing task than a smaller, or no, reward, and increased the likelihood that the child would choose to make an original drawing instead of copying one. Without specific novelty instructions, students in the large reward condition were less original or more likely to copy in the second task. Another study showed that promised reward (like that offered in intrinsic motivation studies) for completing a drawing task increased creativity either when children were told that the drawing should be unusual or when they were first praised for generating unusual rather than common uses for objects.

Other experimenters have used instructions and points to raise scores on several creativity measures. Compared to a control group, college students who participated in creativity training scored higher on fluency, flexibility, and originality during training and, 11 months after, on the TTCT. Instructions and points also effectively raises TTCT scores among high school students, fluency, flexibility, and elaboration in writing among 9 and 10-year olds, and diversity and creativity in storytelling by fourth and sixth graders.

Interesting, the same results appear when individuals learn to reward themselves (with points or praise). Self-praise by 8- and 9-year olds increased diversity in story writing. Novelty, creativity and diversity increased in felt pen drawings among 5- and 6-year olds.

C. General Variability Criteria

In contrast to requiring specific kinds of variability, a criteria may simply specify that responses be infrequent or different from immediately prior responses. In such cases, the measures used—uncertainty, frequency of different patterns, Markov chain, and log analyses—are indifferent to kind of variability. Training of this kind is said to involve *explicit* criteria because reward is directly contingent on variability.

1. Lag Requirements

One procedure that reliably increases variability involves lags. A lag of 0 means that the current response does not have to differ from any prior response. As the lag increases, say to 5, reinforcement will only follow a current response that differs from 5 immediately prior ones. For example, imagine that reward depends on sequences of 4 presses made on a Right (R) or Left (L) key. With a lag-2 criteria, the current sequence (LLLL) would be rewarded if it were different from 2 prior sequences (LLLR, LLRR, LLLL), but not if it repeated one of them (LLLR, LLLL, LLLL). Repetition is precluded, and variability is promoted.

This basic lag contingency paradigm has been used to selectively reinforce variability in animals, college students, and children as young as 5. Variability significantly increases in pigeons when sequential lag requirements increase from 5 to 25. Pigeons are capable of producing right and left keypeck sequences that differ from as many as 50 prior sequences. The same pattern of results appears when college students are required to make right and left key presses to move a white box through a square grid from upper-left to lower-right corners. Sequence variability increases significantly as the lag requirements increase. Although 5- and 6-year olds can meet increasing lag requirements, incorrect repeated responses decrease with age, plateauing at around 14 or 15. Of particular interest to creativity researchers is Neuringer's finding that variability under a lag contingency increases as the speed of responding decreases. What this suggests is that responding *deliberately* can increase the likelihood of responding in novel ways.

Although earlier work produced opposite results— that is, relatively stereotyped responding—these can be explained on the basis of efficiency. For example, a lag-1 or lag-2 requirement can be easily met by alternating between a small number of stereotyped sequences. In contrast, with a lag-25 or lag-50 requirement, it is efficient to be highly variable.

2. *Frequency Dependent Selection*

Another variability procedure does not specify lags. Instead, its criteria target momentarily less probable or less frequent responses for reinforcement. In this procedure, as Response A increases, the probability of reinforcement for A decreases, whereas reinforcement probability increases for an alternative response, B. Depending on the relative probabilities specified by the reinforcement schedule, some stable alteration pattern will earn maximum reward.

Schedules that define patterns that are difficult to master—high lags, for example—generate high variability. In contrast, low variability is generated by schedules that define and reinforce easily remembered stable patterns, for example, switching between few stereotyped sequences to meet a low lag requirement (lag-O could be met with RRRR and LLLL) or varying sequences in an orderly way (say, RRRR, RRRL, RRLL, RLLL, LLLL) to meet a higher one.

In addition to lag contingencies and frequency-dependent selection, which explicitly target variability, there is a third, *implicit,* way to select variability levels. In this view, variability criteria may be embedded early in training procedures that explicitly reward other aspects of behavior. Because the explicit criteria that generate—and, importantly, maintain—high levels of variability involve large shifts in response requirements or challenges, they will be considered in the following section.

IV. CHALLENGES AS CONSTRAINTS

A. Implicit Variability Criteria

The critical word in implicit selection and maintenance of variability levels is *early.* As often seen in problem solving, when a challenge or shift in criteria occurs late in learning, variability increases, but only temporarily. However, if the challenge or large shift occurs early in training, high variability levels are maintained in both rats and people. For example, rats shaped to barpress with a bigger early challenge (press with the right paw only) were more variable than another group shaped with a lesser challenge (press any way). This was true in the initial conditions and was more revealing much later in training when the re-quirements were reversed. When the switch occurred, variability in the low-challenge first group increased, but then returned to its prior levels once the new criterion was met. High variability in key-pressing patterns was established and maintained when college students were initially rewarded and then faced with a big, early challenge, which caused a decline in reward. The hypothesis was that the decline focused attention on, and thus implicitly reinforced, those aspects of behavior—including variability—that served to restore reward to its earlier level. As with the bar-pressing rats, an identical challenge presented later in training resulted in significantly lower variability levels at the end of training. Strategic hints given before shaping with the early challenge served to reduce task variability, presumably by helping subjects master the challenge more easily, thus halting the early decline in reward and increase in variability.

An explicit criterion requiring high variability can also be used as a big, early challenge to implicitly select and maintain high levels of variability. For example, when separate groups of college students were exposed to a series of lag requirements in either increasing (lag-0 to 2 to 10 to 20) or decreasing (lag-20 to 10 to 2 to 0) order, two things happened. First, in both groups, variability decreased or increased with the explicit lag requirements. Second, the group that was implicitly reinforced for high variability by starting with the biggest lag was more variable at all lags than the group that began with the smallest lag.

In contrast to the lasting effects of early challenges, when difficult problems are introduced late in learning, variability increases are temporary. There are numerous examples of this in the literature on cognitive development. When young children, who are already counting, are given challenging problems to solve, variability in strategy use increases but then returns to each child's earlier level once the challenge is met. Likewise, temporary increases in variability are observed when children are acquiring new concepts in moral reasoning, object classification, conservation, or mathematical equivalence.

B. Ill-Defined Problems

In problem-solving terms, challenges would be classified as ill-defined problems, ones in which either the goal criteria (what is an acceptable solution) or the operators (condition-action rules) are incompletely specified to the solver. Such problems are difficult to solve because the search space, the space of all possible solution paths to the goal, is very large. In accord with our organizing hypothesis—that constraints can increase novelty—discovering the correct, novel, solution path is facilitated by constraints on search. This can be illustrated with a classic insight problem.

What is challenging in insight problems is that novel condition-action rules must replace commonly used ones. For example, the condition part of the rule "If tack box, then use to hold tacks" must be recognized as "If box" before the novel action part, "then use to hold candle," can occur. In problems of this kind, hints help in triggering the required recognitions. In the candle problem, if the box of tacks is labeled "box," the frequency of correct solutions increases. [*See* INSIGHT.]

Problems of design and composition are also challenging because they are ill-defined, but ill-defined in a different way from insight problems. Here, the goal criteria are incompletely specified with "open" constraints, like design a museum. To appreciate the openness of such constraints, just compare the novel design of the entrance court of the Louvre by Pei with that of the Guggenheim in Bilbao by Gehry. The differences in the designs follows from further constraints on their respective search spaces, specifically by the domain-relevant expertise of the two architects.

In problem-solving terms, all challenges are ill-defined problems. Hence, whether high levels of variability in a domain are sustained or temporary depends on whether such a problem is presented early or late in learning. Whether, and what, novel solutions are produced depends on ways in which a search space is constrained. In the following section, a number of specific constraints on problems of design and composition will be considered.

V. CONSTRAINTS IN PROBLEMS OF DESIGN AND COMPOSITION

A. Inventive Combinations

There is little experimental work on these kinds of constraints. However, work on creative inventions pro-

vides strong experimental support for the idea that constraints promote novelty. Compared to conditions in which students chose either a category (e.g., furniture or toys) or parts for combination (e.g., wheels or handle), the highest creativity ratings were given when both category and parts were randomly specified. It has been speculated that the restrictions discouraged conventional approaches to invention.

There is much real-world evidence that restrictions—either formal constraints imposed by a domain on its practitioners or informal ones imposed by individuals—do discourage/preclude conventional/high probability responses and promote novel ones.

B. Domain-Specific Constraints

1. Language

The domain in which most people are expert is spoken language. Every day everyone speaks in new, meaningful, appropriate sentences. Although these novel word combinations may not count as creative with a capital *C*, they are based on a number of constraints put to creative use by orators, poets, writers. The primary constraint is grammatical, that is, the set of combinatorial rules that allow a limited number of elements—words—to be organized and reorganized in an unlimited number of meaningful combinations.

An example of a poet expert in exploiting other stylistic constraints is Homer. In the Greek epic, many phrases are formulaic. Homer uses well-used words. A ship, here a Trojan ship, is described as well trimmed, curved, dark prowed, or black; Achilles, as fleet of foot, the great runner, fast as a lion in battle. Why, then, does the *Iliad* not read as repetitive? Because phase choice is constrained by a metric formula, hexameter, in which each line of 6 feet repeats a long phrase followed by two short ones. If the descriptive phrase has to fit the last two short feet of a line, the ship will not be well trimmed or dark prowed, but curved or black. The patterns of phrase choices is surprising because of the constraint, which in effect precludes any predetermined or set alternation.

2. Painting

In the history of art, thematic and stylistic constraints have together produced masterpieces. Consider, for example, the madonna with child painted in a multiplicity of ways by Raphaelo or Bellini during the

Renaissance. To a large extent, these constraints were not selected by the painters but rather by their patrons, the gatekeepers of art at the time. Nonetheless, there is a clear parallel with personally chosen constraints on subject, style, and media by modern painters.

Pursuing his "research" on color and light, Monet imposed a thematic constraint on his work during the 1890s. The motif—Rouen cathedral, a pair of haystacks—did not change but was painted at different times of day, in different light conditions, in a series that illuminate each other as well as Impressionism.

Matisse imposed a series of constraints, not on subject, but rather on media. The two-dimensional surface of the paper or canvas was maintained by restricting line to contour or outline, and paint to unadulterated, unmixed hues. Later, Matisse precluded use of brush or pen, replacing both with scissors and paste to produce the great cutouts, the culmination of his "research" into an of pure line and pure color. Mondrian tightly constrained the elements in his paintings (vertical and horizontal lines, primary colors) and produced an astonishing number of novel combinations, culminating in his masterwork, *Broadway Boogie Woogie*. Like Mondrian, Jasper Johns constrains the number of elements (e.g., numbers, ale cans, crosshatches, handprints) in a painting or print, although not so severely, and, like Monet, produces works in series that share elements. He also has described a strategy for generating novelty: "Take an object. Do something to it. Do something else to it."

C. Interaction of Constraint and Repertoire

Being able to do something else, having a large repertoire, is critical to successfully applying a constraint like John's. One issue here is what constitutes a large-enough repertoire.

Continuing to use art as our example, expertise involves not just what you can *do,* but also what you can *see.* Larry Rivers, a painter and jazz musician, says that for a representational painter, the "first chorus"—on which the current work "improvises"—is the history of painting. His advice is to paint your way through that history, a task that artists like Picasso accomplish at a very early ages.

Likewise, in professional art and design schools, rep-

ertoire expansion is early, intense, and accelerated. For example, at Pratt Institute, the first-, or Foundation-, year curriculum immerses students in drawing, color and light, 2-, 3-, and 4-dimensional design. Using a strategy like Monet's, subject matter is often constrained to emphasize the multiplicity of ways to represent or present the same thing. The goal is to learn how to do different things as well as the importance of doing things differently, of applying constraints that preclude getting or staying stuck in an old solution. In such a context, problem finding, an important component of creative behavior, can be seen as constraint finding.

Similar principles apply to children's art programs. At the Brooklyn Museum, repertoire expansion involves gallery visits to see multiple, diverse ways to deal with a subject. Afterward, in the studio, the thematic constraint is combined with constraints on materials. For example, a class will first visit the African and American Indian galleries to explore facial exaggeration in masks. In the gallery, faces are made using cut and pasted papers. The results are radically different from the circles with stereotyped features drawn in pencil before the gallery visit.

It is important to note that repertoire expansion, with a view to precluding currently successful solutions, is a strategy used by highly creative artists. Think of Degas, Matisse, and Picasso learning to sculpt after they had mastered painting.

VI. SUMMARY AND CONCLUSION

A. When Constraints Generate Novelty

In general, constraints generate novelty when they preclude high-probability, common responses and promote unusual, less probable ones. More specifically, this occurs when a constraint meets the following conditions:

1. Requires novelty
2. Requires high variability in general or of specific kinds, including originality, fluency, and flexibility
3. Introduces challenges
4. Restructures domain-specific responding

B. When Constraints Do Not Generate Novelty

Constraints preclude novelty when they are too narrow for novelty to occur. For example, the constraint on simple arithmetic problems is to produce a single, correct answer. A novel answer, (e.g., $2 + 2 = 5$) cannot meet this constraint.

Even when a constraint promotes novelty, an individual's repertoire may preclude variation within the constraint. Thus, constraints cannot be considered independently of their interaction with both the size and the structure of individual response repertoires. The size of the domain-relevant repertoire determines if the individual is capable of varying within a constraint. The structure refers to the relative strength, or likelihood, of a set of responses. If someone's most likely response meets the constraint, novelty will not result.

C. Training for Novelty

In light of the preceding discussion, programs designed to increment novelty should focus on skill acquisition of two kinds, domain-specific and strategic. First, the range of domain-specific skills must be broad enough to allow for the recombinations required to meet constraints. Second, the use of constraints as a strategy to increment novelty should be explicitly taught and practiced. Ideally, repertoire expansion should be early and accelerated so that students not only learn how to do things, but also acquire the habit of doing them differently.

Bibliography

Baer, J. (1993). *Creativity and divergent thinking: A task-specific approach.* Hillsdale, NJ: Erlbaum.

Eisenberger, R., & Cameron, J. (1996). Detrimental effects of reward: Reality or myth. *American Psychologist, 51,* 1153–1166.

Finke, R. (1990). *Creative imagery: Discoveries and inventions in visualization.* Hillsdale, NJ: Erlbaum.

Greeno, J. G., & Simon, H. A. (1988). Problem solving and reasoning. In E. C. Atkinson, R. J. Herrnstein, G. Lindzey, & R. Duncan Luce (Eds.), *Steven's handbook of experimental psychology, Volume 2: Learning and cognition* (pp. 589–672). New York: Wiley.

Reitman, W. R. (1968). *Cognition and thought: An information processing approach.* New York: Wiley.

Stokes, P. D. (in press). Creativity and operant research: Selection and reorganization of responses. In M. A. Runco (Ed.), *Handbook of creativity research.* Cresskill, NJ: Hampton Press.

Winston, D. S., & Baker, J. E. (1985). Behavior analytic studies of creativity: A critical review. *The Behavior Analyst, 8,* 191–205.

Georgia O'Keeffe

1887–1986

Painter

Paintings include *Evening Star* (1917), *Radiator Building—Night New York* (1927), *Summerdays* (1936), *An Orchid* (1941), *Ladder to the Moon* (1958), *Sky Above Clouds IV* (1965), and *Black Rock with Blue Sky and White Clouds* (1972)

Tobi Zausner

The New School for Social Research, New York

GEORGIA O'KEEFFE *was a quintessential American painter. Born in the Midwest, she moved to New York City and became a central part of the New York art scene with her husband, the art dealer and photographer Alfred Stieglitz. She then established her home in New Mexico, becoming one of the founding artists in the Southwest art world.*

I. THE EARLY YEARS

On November 15, 1887, Georgia O'Keeffe was the second of seven children and the oldest girl born to Ida Totto O'Keeffe and Francis Calyxus O'Keeffe, owners of a prosperous 640-acre farm in Sun Prairie, Wisconsin. The O'Keeffe family was musical and encouraged creativity; there was a strong interest in reading and her mother promoted education.

Although O'Keeffe preferred her fun-loving father to her stern mother, it was her mother, grandmothers, and unmarried aunts Lola, a school teacher, and Ollie, who worked for a newspaper, who became her role

Georgia O'Keeffe at an exhibition of her work "Life and Death." (Copyright UPI/CORBIS/Bettmann.)

models as capable, assertive, and focused women. Intense drive, independence, and a strong will characterized O'Keeffe since childhood. As she grew older, they formed the strengths necessary to maintain an artistic career, but in childhood they made her appear domineering to her siblings. Referring to a family photograph of the children where O'Keeffe was partly blurred, her sister Catherine, as noted by Robinson, said it was "probably because Georgia was giving orders."

O'Keeffe, who began drawing at an early age, was given art lessons on Saturday afternoons from a woman in Sun Prairie along with her younger sisters. Between lessons, O'Keeffe would practice at home and by the age of 12 had decided to become a painter. At 13, she was sent to a Dominican Boarding School and then to a public high school in Madison. At both places, O'Keeffe concentrated on art, but it was a high school art teacher who made her aware of the details of nature through examining the structure of a jack-in-the-pulpit. Later, flowers became an important aspect of her iconography.

When O'Keeffe was 15, the family moved to Williamsburg, Virginia, and she attended the Chatham Episcopal Institute, whose principal, Elizabeth Willis, was also an art teacher. It was Willis who encouraged O'Keeffe to apply to the Art Institute of Chicago, where in 1905–1906 she studied anatomy with John Vanderpoel. Afterward, she attended the Art Students League from 1907 to 1908, winning a prize in William Merritt Chase's still life class. During this period she began going to the 291 Gallery owned by Alfred Stieglitz (1864–1946) and saw shows by Rodin and Matisse.

To help her family with its financial difficulties, O'Keeffe worked as a commercial artist until 1910 when she began a career teaching art in high schools and colleges in Texas and Virginia. During her time as an art teacher, she continued her own education, studying at the University of Virginia with Alon Bement and then from 1914 to 1916 at Columbia Teachers College with Arthur Wesley Dow. At Columbia, O'Keeffe became friends with Anita Pollitzer, a fellow art student, and continued to visit the 291 gallery, seeing shows by Braque and Picasso.

When she left New York and returned to teaching art in college, O'Keeffe reviewed her work. Realizing that she needed to break away from her academic training, she decided to eliminate influences from previous teachers and make art she could call her own. Living

and teaching first in South Carolina and then in Texas, O'Keeffe abstracted her impressions of nature and began creating works, such as *Special, No. 15* (1916), *Blue Lines* (1916), and the 1917 watercolor series entitled *Evening Star,* in what would become her mature style. O'Keeffe's independence and originality extended to her way of dressing. In a time when women wore ruffles, corsets, and pointed shoes, O'Keeffe wore simple dark garments, no corsets, and men's shoes. Interested in comfort and mobility, she said women's shoes pinched her feet. Looking at photographs of the young O'Keeffe, she appears contemporary, but when her style is compared to other women of her time, the contrast is marked. O'Keeffe also avoided jewelry but later in life wore a broach with her initials made by the sculptor Alexander Calder.

II. THE NEW YORK YEARS

O'Keeffe had been corresponding with Anita Pollitzer, and sent her friend works of art to critique. In 1916, Pollitzer showed several pieces to Alfred Stieglitz, the photographer and owner of the 291 Gallery. He was extremely impressed and presented O'Keeffe's art in two group shows that year. In 1917, just before closing his gallery, Stieglitz gave her a solo show. When O'Keeffe arrived in June just after the exhibition was taken down, Stieglitz rehung it for her to see. It was at this time that O'Keeffe began to model for Stieglitz.

Returning to her teaching job in Texas, O'Keeffe kept up her correspondence with Stieglitz and in June of 1918, at his urging came to New York to paint. Stieglitz moved in with her in the 59th street studio and later that year they vacationed at the Stieglitz family summer home at Lake George. O'Keeffe and Stieglitz, who were married in 1924, made annual trips to Lake George until the 1930s when the family home was sold. It was there that O'Keeffe painted her studio, *My Shanty, Lake George* (1922).

Living together on 59th street, Stieglitz continued photographing O'Keeffe, a process that over the years generated an enormous variety of images. O'Keeffe was shown in different costumes, as facial portraits, as erotic nudes, and as a series of hand portraits. O'Keeffe said her hands had been admired ever since she was a child but 60 years later looking back at the variety of images of herself, she said she wondered who that person was; it seemed to her that in one life she had lived many lives.

O'Keeffe painted intensely and Stieglitz promoted her career, speaking to critics, walking with them through her exhibitions, and explaining the work. She showed at the Anderson Gallery in New York along with other well-known artists of the period such as Arthur Dove, Marsden Hartley, Charles Demuth, John Marin, and Paul Strand. In 1925 Stieglitz opened The Intimate Gallery and in 1930 The American Place Gallery, continuing to exhibit O'Keeffe's work.

In 1925, when O'Keeffe and Stieglitz moved to rooms on the 30th floor of the Shelton Hotel, O'Keeffe was so taken with the view of New York that she began to paint images of skyscrapers and industrial docks. The male artists in the gallery thought women incapable of doing cityscapes, but O'Keeffe, used to competition with her older brother, was also competitive in the gallery. In works such as *East River from the Shelton* (1927–1928) and *Radiator Building—Night New York* (1927) she demonstrated that a woman could successfully paint the City.

It was during this period that she also began exhibiting her large flower series containing works such as *Black Iris III* (1926) and *Two Calla Lilies on Pink* (1928). Although New York was an exciting place, O'Keeffe longed for the countryside; she said "distance has always called me" (Hogrefe, 1992, p. 369). In 1920 O'Keeffe began taking yearly trips to Maine and in 1929 made her first trip to the Southwest.

III. THE SOUTHWEST

As a child, O'Keeffe's favorite stories were about the West, and visiting New Mexico was like an experience of coming home. On her second trip there, she sent back a barrel containing bones and fabric flowers, which enabled her to produce Western themes such as *Cow's Skull: Red, White, and Blue* (1931) and *Summerdays* (1936) when she painted in the East. Eventually O'Keeffe divided her year between living with Stieglitz in Lake George and New York and her time in the Southwest.

During her early trips to New Mexico, O'Keeffe stayed at Ghost Ranch, a dude ranch in the eastern part of the Jemenez Mountains where the Mesozoic rock formations derive their intense color from iron oxide.

In 1940, O'Keeffe bought Rancho de los Burros and in 1945 bought a second house in Abiquiu. She spent the summer and fall at Rancho de los Burros and the winter and spring at Abiquiu, which O'Keeffe considered to be her main residence.

Although she continued to make flower paintings, such as *An Orchid* (1941), the New Mexico desert was a constant source of inspiration both in its landscape and in the objects she found there. Walking in the desert the artist took pelvic bones bleached by the sun and used them in a series of paintings, such as *Pelvis With Moon* (1943) and *Pelvis III* (1944), where their holes let in the sky. After the death of Stieglitz in 1946 O'Keeffe settled his estate, delegating his large collection of art to museums. She was also active in organizing two exhibits of his collection, first at the Museum of Modern Art in 1947 and then at the Art Institute of Chicago in 1948. Beginning in 1949 the artist lived in New Mexico throughout the year.

O'Keeffe's career continued to expand. Even in the Depression she had sold work, but during the 1940s her fame increased. She had retrospectives at the Art Institute of Chicago in 1943 and at the Museum of Modern Art in 1946, and received an honorary doctorate from the University of Wisconsin in 1942. Later, in 1973, O'Keeffe received a second honorary doctorate from Harvard.

The 1950s were a decade of travel for O'Keeffe, who had until then spent her entire life in the United States except for brief forays into Canada. In 1951, she made her first trip to Mexico and in 1953 made her first trip to Europe, to which she returned in 1954. In 1956 she traveled to Peru and in 1959 took a three and a half month excursion around the world. Although O'Keeffe continued to paint images of the Southwest, such as *Ladder to the Moon* (1958), a new imagery entered her art as the result of her travels. O'Keeffe became interested in the cloud formations she saw from airplane windows and began her series of cloud paintings, which included the largest canvas of her life, the 8 × 24-ft *Sky above Clouds IV* (1965).

IV. THE FINAL YEARS

O'Keeffe remained active and retained good health until close to the end of her long life. She made her first rafting trip down the Colorado river when she was 74, her second one at 82, and her final trip in 1970 at 83. In addition to rafting, she also returned to Colorado to paint. Eventually O'Keeffe's failing eyesight necessitated a change of medium in order for the artist to remain creative. Juan Hamilton, a potter and her studio assistant, showed her how to construct hand-coiled pots and O'Keeffe turned to pottery. Her pots echoed the shapes found in her late paintings such as *Black Rock with Blue III* (1972) and *Black Rock with Blue Sky and White Clouds* (1972). Before her death on March 6, 1986, at the age of 98, O'Keeffe had become the most celebrated woman artist in America. She was elected to the American Academy of Arts and Letters in 1962, given the M. Carey Thomas Award from Bryn Mawr College in 1971, and in 1979 received the Medal of Freedom from President Gerald Ford. It is the nation's highest honor awarded to a civilian.

V. GEORGIA O'KEEFFE AND THE CREATIVE PROCESS

A. Her Quest for Originality

After she finished school, O'Keeffe had an intense desire to find her personal method of expression, saying "I decided I wasn't going to spend my life doing what had already been done." She hung all her recent work on the wall and observed that each piece reflected the influence of one or another of the teachers with whom she had studied. Wanting to find her own voice, O'Keeffe (1976) said,

> I have things in my head that are not like what anyone has taught me—shapes and ideas so near to me—so natural to my way of being and thinking that it hasn't occurred to me to put them down. I decided to start anew—to strip away what I had been taught—to accept as true my own thinking. . . . I was alone and singularly free, working into my own, unknown—no one to satisfy but myself.

B. Painting from Nature

One of her favorite ways to work from nature was by painting in her car. For this O'Keeffe said the Model A Ford was best. Its high windows let in the light and she could take out the passenger seat, and after unbolting

the driver's seat, turn it around and have the car as her studio. This ingenious solution shows O'Keeffe used her capacity for what Ruth Richards calls "everyday creativity" in the service of her creativity in art. Sitting in the swiveled driver's seat, she could prop a canvas up to a size of 30 × 40 in. on the back seat and paint until about four in the afternoon when bees would invade the car. At that point, she had to close the windows and eventually the car became too hot to continue working. A very keen observer of nature, O'Keeffe would often remember events and images so clearly that she was also capable of painting them from memory. [*See* EVERYDAY CREATIVITY.]

C. Visual Memory

Artists are known for their excellent visual memories and O'Keeffe demonstrated the capacity at a very early age. She remembered, when she was 8 or 9 months old, sitting on a patchwork quilt and seeing her Aunt Winnie, accurately describing her aunt's blond hair and the details of her dress. Years later she told her mother, who also remembered that day. Her mother was at first incredulous, but then had to admit that O'Keeffe's visual memory was accurate.

O'Keeffe, who was very physically active, always liked the outdoors. All her life, she took long walks, and her observations formed the basis for later work. Her paintings *From the Plains I* (1919) and *Orange Streak* (1919) were memories of Texas, but created months later in New York. The habit of working from memory lasted her entire life. In her sixties, O'Keeffe began her *Cloud Series,* images of the world seen from the window of an airplane. She did small charcoal drawings on the plane but filled in all the details for the large works from memory.

D. Early Evidence of Creative Ability

Evidence of early creative ability, common among artists, is also found in the life of O'Keeffe. She began to draw as a young child, first making images of her dolls. Because she sewed well, O'Keeffe made them clothing and then also built them a house. When she and her sisters were given art lessons as children, they learned by copying pictures of their choice in the teacher's collection. At home, O'Keeffe practiced by copying a picture of a lighthouse from her geography book. When she was unsatisfied with her first effort, she made another variation, this time with greater success. She then made a landscape drawing of the night view from her window, again working until it was made to the best of her ability. Writing in her late eighties, O'Keeffe noted that the two paintings—the lighthouse with the cloudy sky and the night with the bare trees and snow—must have been important to her because she kept them for a long time.

E. Abstraction versus Realism

For O'Keeffe even if a painting was realistic, it was not successful unless it worked as an abstract arrangement of color and form. She never separated the objective from the abstract and did not believe that subject matter alone produced a good work of art. For her it was the way lines and colors came together that formed the expressive basis of a painting. She altered the forms she saw in nature to heighten the abstract drama of her work, saying, "the abstraction is often the most definite form for the intangible thing in myself that I can only clarify in paint" (1976).

It was not her intention to copy reality exactly as she saw it, but rather to convey her response in the hopes that the viewer would share her impression about a place or object. She said, "the color used for the paintings had little to do with what I had seen—the color grew as I painted" (1976).

F. Positive and Negative Space

A strong point in O'Keeffe's work is the balance of positive and negative space. An example of positive space may be a wall, while negative space may be an open door in that wall through which a vista or other intimation of depth might be seen. Walls and doorways form a repeated graphic element in her work and it was a specific adobe wall with a doorway that made O'Keeffe want to buy the house at Abiquiu.

A further example of positive and negative space is found in her depiction of pelvic bones within whose holes the sky shines through. Speaking about the pelvic bones and her emphasis on their holes, O'Keeffe (1976) said that she was always the kind of child "that ate around the raisin on the cookie and ate around

the hole in the doughnut either saving the raisin or the hole for the last and the best." She said that it was the holes in the bones that held her interest—the way they framed the blue sky in their contours. For O'Keeffe, the blue sky represented her idea of the eternal, lasting beyond the time of humans and bones.

G. Focus on Work

What characterizes successful artists is not only talent but their ability to work and their interest in working as a way of life. As O'Keeffe said,

> One works because I suppose it is the most interesting thing one knows to do. The days one works are the best days . . . (you) can get at the paintings again because that is the high spot—in a way it is what you do all the other things for. . . . The painting is like a thread that runs through all the reasons for all the other things that make one's life. (Messinger, p. 58)

Even with advancing years, O'Keeffe continued working and made efforts to break new ground. When she was 78 years old, she painted the largest canvas of her life, the 8 × 24-ft *Sky Above the Clouds IV* (1965). Because of its enormous size, the painting could not fit in her studio, so O'Keeffe worked on it in the garage. She mixed the paints in her kitchen Mixmaster and then brought them outside. Painting from 6 in the morning until 9 at night, she wanted to finish the canvas by winter because there was no heat in the garage. Still, in evening because the garage was warmer than the surrounding desert, O'Keeffe was afraid that rattlesnakes attracted by the warmth would come in behind her as she worked.

H. Painting Technique as Language

Early in her life O'Keeffe spoke about the various techniques, such as pastel, watercolor, and oil paint, as being languages. She saw the artist becoming proficient in the language of a given media and then being able to express herself creatively in that language. When she grew old and her eyesight failed, O'Keeffe could no longer see well enough to paint. She turned to pottery, saying "it could become still another language for me" (1976).

I. Symbolism and Communication

O'Keeffe insisted that her work was not symbolic, saying it just was what it was and that was an aspect of the world. Her flowers have been compared to female genitalia, but O'Keeffe admitted no such connection. When a seashell that she painted was also seen as sexual, O'Keeffe said it brought the ocean to her and that was its meaning.

Artists work on conscious and unconscious levels. An artist who consciously may not be aware of the symbolic content of a work may nonetheless be using symbolism on an unconscious level. For example, in her repeated imagery of skulls and flowers, there may have been an unconscious symbolism of death and rebirth, but O'Keeffe insisted on reading her work on a conscious level only. She saw her art not as symbolic, but rather as a depiction of the landscape of her world, an image of her perception and her method of communication. In speaking about the objects she painted—the flowers, rocks, trees, shells, pieces of wood, and bones—O'Keeffe said she had used these things to describe the wideness and the wonder of the world as she experienced it. And it is through these objects and her paintings that O'Keeffe transmits her world to us.

Bibliography

Hogrefe, J. (1992). *O'Keeffe: The life of an American legend.* New York: Bantam Books.

O'Keeffe, G. (1978/1997). Foreword in *Georgia O'Keeffe: A portrait by Alfred Stieglitz.* New York: Metropolitan Museum of Art.

O'Keeffe, G. (1976). *Georgia O'Keeffe.* New York: Viking Press.

Messinger, L. M. (1984). Georgia O'Keeffe. In *The Metropolitan Museum of Art Bulletin, 42*(2).

Robinson, R. (1989). *Georgia O'Keeffe.* New York: Harper & Row.

Old Age Style

Martin S. Lindauer

College at Brockport, State University of New York

Altersstil See Old Age Style.

Artists Painters, sculptors, composers, writers, and others working with different aesthetic materials and media. In this article, the focus is on painters in the Western tradition.

Arts See Artists.

Cognition Mental abilities related to perceiving, learning, remembering, and thinking.

Creativity Usually indicated by a reputation for making original and lasting contributions that are of the highest quality; the development of new approaches and ideas.

Empirical Research characterized by quantification, control groups, large samples, and generalizations supported by statistics and observations.

Humanities Includes art historians, critics, philosophers, and scholars who write about literature, the arts, and aesthetics.

Interdisciplinary Cross-disciplinary studies that contribute to the sciences, arts, and humanities by integrating quantitative and qualitative approaches.

Late-life Style Marked changes in the late works of creative artists who died young.

Old Over 60 years in age (especially applicable to historical artists).

Old Age Style Marked changes in the art of creative artists when they reach age 60 and older.

Questionnaires Self-completed reports in response to predetermined questions.

Style Collectively refers to technique, composition, subject matter, and affective tone, among other subtle characteristics.

The OLD AGE STYLE refers to unexpected changes in the late-life works of creative artists over 60, one of several phenomena that characterizes old artists. This article discusses a number of conceptual and methodological issues related to the old age style, but in particular, it identifies artists and works with this characteristic, for which empirical results are presented. Covered, too, are the implications of the old age style for old age in general, research in cognition, and interdisciplinary study.

I. INTRODUCTION AND BACKGROUND

A. Definition and Examples

A number of well-known painters—Cézanne, Goya, Mondrian, O'Keeffe, Rembrandt, and Titian—markedly changed their styles after they reached age 60. Michelangelo's two *Pietas*, for example, sculpted at ages

22 and 90, are drastically different. Late-life shifts are called the old age style (or *Altersstil*, the term coined by the German critic Brinkmann in 1925.) Less preferred is the label *late-life style*, which describes changes in the works of artists who died young (e.g., Jackson Pollock).

The old age style has been discussed mainly in connection with painters but also for aged sculptors (Michelangelo), composers (Verdi), and novelists (Cervantes, Goethe, and Tolstoy), and to the late work of any kind of artist that is distinguished from early efforts. Few claims have been made, though, for the special virtues of aging scientists, philosophers, and other professionals.

B. Scope: Creativity, Art History, and Cognitive Psychology

The old age style demonstrates that artistic creativity continues throughout life and could also account for secondary peaks late in life, thereby raising questions about creativity's generally accepted early and short span (from about 30 to 40 for most professions). The old age style therefore adds a new chapter to the course of creativity: Along with declines and losses late in life, new expressions are also possible, as well as stability and a late emergence (e.g., Mary Robertson, also known as "Grandma Moses"). [*See* PRODUCTIVITY AND AGE.]

The old age style is studied mainly by art historians, using case studies of individual artists and giving close scrutiny to specific works. The old age style is also pertinent to the study of cognitive development, for it demonstrates that aging is not necessarily a time of stagnation. Instead, the old age style, like wisdom, points to a positive outcome in old age, thereby supporting the concept of successful aging.

C. The Context of the Old Age Style: The Special Nature of Old Artists

The old age style is related to other characteristics of older artists in the Western tradition. Most have lived long (notable exceptions notwithstanding, e.g., van Gogh). Consider these facts: 65% of more than 200 artists of historical fame were 60 or older when they died; two-thirds of the artists given at least one paragraph in Arneson's popular text of world art were productive through their 60s, and of these, about 70 were 79 or older when they died; in Cattell's early compilation of the 1000 most eminent men who ever lived, 13 of the 17 artists listed (76%) were over 60 when they died; and of 233 recognized masterpieces, 76% were produced by long-lived artists. (Most of these artists lived when life was shorter.)

In addition, most older artists, despite physical and sensory problems, have remained productive (e.g., Rubens suffered from gout, Renoir arthritis, Goya had bad eyesight and hearing, and four or five of seven major Impressionists are said to have suffered from ocular disorders that affected their perception of color, shape, and space). In his survey of 344 older painters with severe physical infirmities and poor health, the historian Silbergeld detected no artistic decline.

In short, renowned Western historical artists as a group lived long, remained productive, and retained their creativity into old age, often despite physical and sensory difficulties. The old age style is another example of the extraordinary pathways taken by creative artists in their old age.

A similarly encouraging picture describes nearly 90 living artists in their 60s to 80s. According to self-ratings, the quality and quantity of their work increased with age; the 60s were the best years. Their ideas about art and their general approach to art also improved as they grew older. Standing out among some 15 major reasons given for these improvements were increased learning, knowledge, and skills about themselves, others, and their craft. Contemporary artists, like their historical counterparts, maintain their creativity into old age.

II. ISSUES IN THE STUDY OF THE OLD AGE STYLE

A. The Existence and Quality of the Old Age Style

Most art historians do not question the existence of a special kind of art in old age; few dismiss the old age style as an empty label. There is also general agreement on its significance, maturity, and value, and as indicating the enriching, beneficial, and deepening effects of old age.

Some artists, though, have been discouraged by their old age. However, pessimism over old age should not be confused with the quality of work done at that time. The contemporary old artists (whose reports on creativity were given earlier) interpreted positive changes in their work as evolutionary rather than revolutionary. The old age style is also difficult to discern because it is rare. From among about 300 long-lived historical artists of some note, about 10% had an old age style.

It is also difficult to judge contemporary artists' old age style because, compared to their youthful work, it is unexpected and unfamiliar and may therefore be seen as a breakdown, the result of a deterioration of skills, illness, and senility. Viewers may also fail to find an old age style because they are looking for qualities that characterized aging painters from an earlier era but that have since changed because today's artists are influenced by markedly different circumstances (e.g., a longer life span, better medical facilities, and different forms of patronage). Future critics, long after the artists' deaths and with a longer perspective, may be in the best position from which to appreciate works done in the old age style that were rejected in the artists' own time.

B. Explaining the Old Age Style

Simply being old, by itself, is not enough to explain the old age style. What happens with increasing age? A variety of explanations have been offered. Jung suggested that the aging artist turns inward to illuminate the self rather than the external world for others. Goethe had a simpler reason: "When one is old one must do more than when one is young." In other words, artists may feel they have to change in order to re-prove themselves to a younger generation of artists, as well as the public. Artists may also feel the need to break away from earlier styles because they see their later years as a time when they have to exceed earlier achievements. Successful artists may also have, for the first time, an opportunity to create art for their own pleasure and benefit, to do "pure" works of art unrelated to making money. Change therefore occurs because of lessened materialistic ambitions and a decreased concern with success.

Continued failure could also lead to changes. For Tietze, the old artist, despairing of acceptance, becomes aloof and uninterested in praise and the result is an Indian summer, an apotheosis, of his art. Applicable too is the possibility of an identity crisis, or a generative stage of development. Social, cultural, political, and economic events (wars, poverty, inventions) in the artists' old age could also contribute to the old age style, as could changes in responsibilities (familial, social) and unresolved personal, interpersonal, and spiritual conflicts.

Simonton has offered an interesting account of the last works ("swan songs") of composers that may be applicable to all artists. When composers realized how little time was left in their lives, there was a major reshaping of the content and form of their last compositions, making them qualitatively distinctive from earlier works. They became more concise, brief, melodically simple, and expressive of either resignation or contentment (rather than despair or tragedy). The way composers looked back on their lives and toward the approach of death may have initiated an old age style. In another context, Simonton considered the old age style a possible trade-off with wisdom—that is, as the former increases the latter decreases.

Explanations of the old age style may also be related to the opportunities given by old age generally, namely, as a time to express new ideas, to integrate a lifetime of observations, to summarize the themes of one's life, to make sense of one's experiences, and to resolve long-standing dilemmas. Alternatively, the old age style may be a compensation for losses in health, strength, vision, and mental capacities. Pathology in general, and depression, alcoholism, and suicide in particular, appear to occur at an above average rate among creative people, especially artists.

Yet creative individuals have transcended (or were transformed by) their misfortunes. If some artists do indeed "have to suffer for their creativity," others are creative "despite their suffering." The latter course was supported by questionnaires completed by contemporary old artists. Physical and sensory effects on creativity ranked third in importance, and their impact was felt mainly on productivity rather than on the quality, originality, or style of the artists' work. Poor eyesight, declining health, and lowered energy were most often mentioned by artists in their 70s and 80s, not those in the 60s—the age at which the old age style would emerge. And no matter at what age they occurred, compensations and adjustments were made as the artists worked around age-related difficulties. For example, as artists became more frail, they shifted to an easier medium, reduced the amount of time they worked during the day, varied the times at which they painted, changed the location of their work, and relied more on memory and photographs than on going out to a site.

However, all artists get old, sick, accumulate experiences, develop (or lose) certain skills, and probably suffer to some extent—but only a few have an old age style. Why these artists and not others? To answer this question, a control group is needed—that is, artists without an old age style against whom to compare those who have one. Otherwise, the key traits of the old age style (e.g., a rough brush stroke, a pessimistic outlook) cannot be distinguished from those common to all aging artists. Unfortunately, the identification of artists with an old age style has not been easy, in large part for methodological reasons.

C. Methodological Ambiguities

Art historians, working within the framework of the humanities, emphasize the uniqueness of an individual artist's life and art and pursue their inquiries through in-depth case studies. This focus and method is attractive to clinically oriented psychologists, psychiatrists, and psychoanalysts who have added another layer of analysis of the old age style to that of art historians, literary critics, and philosophers of art. These qualitative and discursive approaches have rich implications, but disagreements are the norm and are difficult to resolve. Thus, three authorities (Munsterberg, Rosenthal, and the text *Man and His Years*), which collectively review over 160 artists, discuss the old age style of only 15; of these, they agree on only four as having an old age style, with the remaining 11 being in dispute.

With experts differing on which artists have an old age style, it is impossible to arrive at generalizations about its distinguishing characteristics, to know what to look for when exploring the phenomenon in art, and to discern its personal and situational determinants. Experts differ for several reasons.

One is the way they define *change*. It could mean that earlier tendencies were broadened or concentrated, a new or radical facet was added while other aspects

remained the same, or changes were evolutionary or revolutionary. However *change* is defined, there has to be—and usually is not—a group of excluded artists against whom to make comparisons. To weigh the extent to which artists with an old age style relied on a broad brush stroke or suffered, let's say, these characteristics have to be absent among artists without an old age style. Knowing both the number of artists with and without an old age style, furthermore, also makes it possible to estimate the relative number of artists who changed (a few or a modest number).

The term *old* is also handled ambiguously in the case of artists who died young but had late-life changes; they are referred to as having a late-life style. To complicate matters even further is the formidable concept of style, which depends on an intuitive sense of highly subjective, subtle, and complex qualities. Not easy, too, is grasping an artist's lifetime of work and then making contrasts between youthful and old productions. Artists produce hundreds if not thousands of works—sometimes in more than one medium—and there are at least several hundred artists over the centuries with reputations for creativity. Which artists to choose? How many works to compare?

Examples of art, especially earlier ones, also have to be correctly attributed. Further, because most art is not easily accessible, examples can only be inspected in reproductions, and these are not the most detailed or accurate (in their colors). Even originals in museums deteriorate. The unavailability of historical artists for questioning is an obvious and insurmountable difficulty, whereas contemporary artists have to be long dead before their old age style can be recognized.

D. Identifiying Artists with an Old Age Style

Given these fundamental methodological problems, it is not surprising to find experts disagreeing over which artists had an old age style. The problem of identification has been approached in two ways. In one study, art historians selected names from a fairly complete list of 225 long-lived artists of historical repute. They agreed on as many as 38 (17%) having an old age style (the range depends on the criterion of consensus used). Most historians (10 of 12) selected Titian, followed by Cézanne, Constable, Degas, deKooning, and

Goya; about two-thirds chose Matisse, Michelangelo, Mondrian, Monet, Picasso, and Rembrandt; and half selected Braque, Corot, David, Kandinsky, Kokoschka, Renoir, and Turner. Somewhat fewer chose the following seven: Corinth, El Greco, Hals, Klee, Nolde, Poussin, and Rothko. Another 12 were marginal: Bacon, Botticelli, Chagall, Chirico, Dali, Delacroix, Derain, Eakins, Fragonard, Gainsborough, Homer, and Vuillard. In contrast, 68 artists were not selected by a single judge. Artists without an old age style included such well-known figures as Albers, Bingham, Cole, Giotto, Gorky, Orozco, Peale, Prendergast, Man Ray, Soyer, J. Strella, Trumbull, Uccello, Van Dyck, Warhol, and A. Wyeth.

The selection of artists with an old age style is sharpened when the choices made by art historians are compared against the three authoritative texts by art historians. All judged four artists as having an old age style (Cézanne, Goya, Michelangelo, and Titian) and three as not (Chardin, Hartley, and Manet). Another set of artists emerges when the survey results for art historians are matched against the Rosenthal text, the most recent and largest compilation of artists with an old age style. From this comparison, the following 13 artists had an old age style: Braque, Cézanne, Fragonard, El Greco, Gainsborough, Goya, Homer, Kandinsky, Monet, Rembrandt, Renoir, Turner, and Vuillard. Only Reynolds did not.

In another study, fifteen of 24 (63%) young and old pairs from the Rosenthal collection on the old age style were judged by several sets of viewers as differing in at least two of the following characteristics: style, amount of detail, authorship (appearing to have been done by a different artist), and age of production (seeming to have been produced in the artist's old age). The pair by Eakins differed on all four measures, followed by the works of Guardi, Kirchner, Klee, Mondrian, and Monet. The pairs by Bellows, Cole, Goya, Innes, Picasso, Pissaro, Reynolds, Sargent, and Tobey significantly differed on half of the measures. Most of the works with these indicators of an old age style were landscapes (seven), with the remainder divided equally between figurative and abstract art (four each). Artists whose works differed on one or none of the four key measures of the old age style were Hoffmann, Marin, and Tiepolo (who were distinguished on none of the tasks), followed by Copley, Corinth, Klein, Leger, Manet, and

Stuart. Works without an old age style were equally represented by figurative and abstract art (four each); the only landscape pair was by Stuart.

The artists chosen on the basis of their work overlapped considerably with the artists chosen for their reputations by the survey of art historians, reported earlier. The two studies taken together point to 10 artists with an old age style: Eakins, Goya, Klee, Mondrian, Monet, and Picasso, with the greatest overlap between the two sets of judgments, followed by Kirchner, Pissaro, Sargent, and Tobey. Both studies agreed on six artists as not having an old age style: Copley, Hoffman, Manet, Marin, Stuart, and Tiepolo.

With two sets of artists identified with some certainty, one with and the other without an old age style, it is now possible to examine and contrast their works with respect to, for example, the amount of detail or kind of brush stroke, or their display (or lack) of personal and temperamental qualities. Unfortunately, art historians' descriptions of the old age style, like that of the identification of its artists, are profuse and not in agreement. Different indicators are used to disclose its presence, and this is done without differentiating them from works without an old age style. Some focus on the work, either as a whole (bold) or on specifics (the brush stroke), whereas others emphasize the artist (mood). Because each expert has his own list, it is possible to have as many ways of describing the old age style as there are old artists with this characteristic.

E. Describing the Old Age Style

Thirty-five descriptors distinguishing works done in the old age style were agreed upon by a panel of art historians from an initial group of 79. Most (63%) referred to the work as bold, *complex,* economical, intense, passionate, *restrained,* rough, spontaneous, strong, and suggestive. (*Italicized* traits are terms that, in their original contexts, applied to youthful works.) Somewhat less agreement was found for the following descriptors: *complete,* serene, simple, *sophisticated,* subtle, and understated. Another handful referred to the work as a whole: the special quality of the colors, an execution that is free and rugged, the medium is treated with familiarity, skill and effort are not obvious, and the technique is impatient.

In contrast, 16 terms were rarely if ever thought to

be characteristic of the old age style, most of which (11, or 69%) were indeed youthful terms: *clear, composed, detailed, objective, precise, realistic, refined, skilled, stylistic, technically proficient,* and *well formed.* Several traits frequently associated in the literature with old age were not chosen: angry, depressed, detached, lonely, irritated, melancholic, pessimistic, and shows physical deterioration, remoteness, and solitude.

Much of what is therefore written about the old age style is therefore appropriate—and an almost equal number is not: 58% of the original terms used in the literature were chosen by the experts as descriptions of the old age style of art. The problem, of course, is knowing when the experts are right or wrong. In any case, the task of describing the old age style has been considerably simplified by reducing the number of applicable terms. That the list is limited to 35 indicates there is no single way to describe the old age style. Earlier, too, four measures were needed to distinguish young–old pairs with this feature of aging (e.g., a pair looked as if it had been done by a different artist).

Canvas size was another distinguishing characteristic of the old age style. Art done in old age is painted on large canvases. A big surface would be appropriate for an older artist disinterested in detail who uses a broad and rough brush stroke to achieve holistic and global effects—all indicators of the old age style. By not relying on small canvases, it also suggests that older artists do not have to compensate for reduced strength, limited motoric abilities, and other physical infirmities of aging (although large canvases might be a way of coping with failing eyesight). Irrelevant distinctions between older and younger works included the nationality of the artists, the time periods in which they worked, their longevity, and, most surprising, subject matter (e.g., younger or older persons were not favored in older works).

A standardized list of descriptors of the old age style can reduce disagreements between art experts in choosing works that depict the old age style, the ways in which they depict it, and the artists who have this characteristic. An objective set of terms also helps minimize biases based on expectations from art history, societal prejudices, and idiosyncratic intuitions.

In addition, the set of descriptors makes it possible to examine the old age style in other kinds of visual art (sculpture and architecture) and to make comparisons between different domains of artistic creativity (music and literature). The list can also be used to search for the old age style in activities unrelated to art. For example, "boldness and passion," and terms indicative of a broad perspective (comparable to a "rough brush stroke"), may describe some aging scientists' research and scholars' writing. The descriptors can also serve as a checklist with which to examine biographical accounts of artists with and without an old age style, such as whether they differed in serenity (but not depression). For psychologists, descriptors of the old age style also suggest personal, cognitive, and motivational traits that are maintained into or improve with age.

III. CONCLUSIONS

A. The Old Age Style, Creativity, and Old Age

The extraordinary qualities of the old age style and its artists, and more generally the ability of old artists to sustain their creativity, offers a positive perspective on late-life creativity and aging; growing old is not necessarily marked by precipitous declines. Some aspects of creativity remain stable, others improve, a few emerge, and, in the case of the old age style, they change direction. Successful aging is therefore a real possibility. Physical, sensory, and motoric losses are inevitable, but they can be coped with, compensated for, and overcome in accomplishing creative work in old age.

B. The Old Age Style in General

Much of the uncertainty over identifying artists with an old age style and the characteristics of their work has been reduced. Building on the assumption that creative people in the arts are similar to one another, studies of the old age style in architecture, as well as in literature and other art forms, can proceed using descriptors already developed for paintings. The assumption about the pervasiveness of the old age style can be extended to domains other than art as aging scientists and scholars can also reconceptualize their earlier work. Psychologists and art historians who have not retired from their labs and libraries, for example, might take a broader perspective on their studies, become more interdisciplinary, and take a more critical stance toward their accomplishments.

The old age style in artists and other professions also prompts a search for parallel processes in old people who are not considered creative in the ordinary sense. The old age style may account for the unusual ways in which some older people suddenly change their behavior in ways that are judged as "not acting their age." Not all of the eccentricities of the aged can be dismissed or interpreted as due to pathology, a mental breakdown, or senility. Some of the unexpected actions of the aged may express changes in the sorts of cognitive abilities that underlie the old age style. This possibility encourages the study of ordinary people who drastically change their lives in old age.

C. Optimism about Old Age

The interests of the general public are also served when the achievements of aging artists are highlighted, for it encourages a more positive outlook toward aging and the course of creativity. Imaginative and other cognitive capacities can be sustained into old age, reinvigorated, as well as appear for the first time. The old age style also encourages working beyond the normal age of retirement. A lifelong career has several advantages: more knowledge and practical experience are accumulated, opportunities to produce first-rate works are increased, past efforts can be improved on, enough time passes for others to learn about your work, and there are more occasions to receive encouragement (and overcome discouragement). A long working career also makes it possible for a revitalization of one's work to occur—an old age style—if there is to be one. [*See* IMAGINATION.]

D. Recruiting Old Artists for Psychological Research

The old age style also encourages the recruitment of old artists in studies of old age. In contrast to the typical nonartists who are the usual participants, old artists have continued to do creative work. Their thinking is therefore flexible, open-minded, alert to multiple pos-

sibilities, and capable of a variety of problem-solving strategies. Furthermore, a long-term involvement in a creative career is good practice in facing, compensating for, and overcoming the challenges of unyielding materials, unfamiliar procedures, unusual requirements, unnatural demands, and unexpected restrictions—features that often characterize laboratory studies. [*See* FLEXIBILITY; PROBLEM SOLVING.]

E. Interdisciplinarity

Studies of the old age style and the art of old artists concretely demonstrate the contributions of psychology and art history to each other's interests. The methods of empirical scientific inquiry can be usefully merged with the kinds of discursive inquiry characteristic of the humanities. Studies of the old age style are therefore interdisciplinary: They integrate empirical psychology's insistence on quantification and generalization with art history's preoccupation with qualitative information and individuality. Generalizations about the old age style that hold for most artists and their work complement scholars' in-depth studies of the uniqueness of artists and the singularity of their work. Research on art can be done under controlled conditions and the results can be meaningfully tied to both art history and the psychology of creativity.

Bibliography

Arnheim, R. (1990). On the late style. In M. Perlmutter (Ed.), *Late life potential* (pp. 113–120). Washington, DC: Gerontological Society of America. Also in Arnheim, R. (1986). On the late style. *New essays on the psychology of art* (pp. 285–293). Berkeley: University of California Press. (Original work published 1978).

Baltimore Museum of Art (1954). *Man and his years*. Baltimore, MD: Baltimore Museum of Art.

Bornstein, M. H. (1984). Developmental psychology and the problem of artistic change. *Journal of Aesthetics and Art Criticism, 43*, 131–145.

Brinkmann, A. E. (1984). Earliest and latest works of great artists. *Gazette des Beaux-Arts, 46*, 273–284.

Cohen-Shalev, A. (1989). Old age style: Developmental changes in creative production from a life-span perspective. *Journal of Aging Studies, 3*, 21–37.

Edel, L. (1979) Portrait of the artist as an old man. In D. D. Van Tassel (Ed.), *Aging, death, and the completion of being* (pp. 193–214). Philadelphia: University of Pennsylvania Press.

Lindauer, M. S. (1992). Creativity in aging artists: Contributions from the humanities to the psychology of old age. *Creativity Research Journal, 5,* 211–231.

Lindauer, M. S. (1993). The span of creativity among long-lived historical artists. *Creativity Research Journal, 6,* 221–239.

Munsterberg, H. (1983). *The crown of life: Artistic creativity in old age.* New York: Harcourt Brace Jovanovich.

Rosenthal, G. (Ed.). (1968). *From El Greco to Pollock: Early and late works by European and American artists.* Greenwich, CT: The Baltimore Museum of Art and the New York Graphic Society.

Simonton, D. K. (1990). Creativity and wisdom in aging. In J. E. Birren & K. W. Schaie (Eds.), *Handbook of the psychology of aging* (3rd ed., pp. 320–329). New York: Academic Press.

Organizations Interested in Creativity

Tudor Rickards

Manchester Business School

CEO Chief Executive Officer.

Creativity The processes generating new and valued ideas by individuals or groups within an implicit or explicit domain or environment. In the context of this article, unless stated otherwise, the term is used in an informal sense of a process within which new and potentially valuable ideas are generated.

Group Creativity The processes generating new and valued ideas within a coherent team or group. The criteria refer to the novelty and value of ideas intersubjectively agreed upon within the team.

Individual Creativity The processes generating new ideas and valued ideas by an individual, and rated as new and valued by that individual, according to individual value criteria.

Innovation The process of enacting or realizing the potential of the creative idea. Most commonly the term relates to a process of enacting ideas in a socioeconomic context, in which individual innovation is a special case.

Interest in Creativity A term used here without formal characterization to imply organizations that support creative performance to an extent that differentiates them from other organizations. Such a differentiation makes it possible to develop richer models of organizational creativity.

Intersubjective Evaluation A term implying an evaluative conclusion that is shared by a nominated group of individuals. The conclusion is not one which can be established as correct or incorrect on a set of rational and universally determined truth criteria. In this context it is a means of working toward a study of creativity, permitting a noncontradictory means of defining and empirically studying it. The consequence is that a creative idea may be rated as creative either on agreed and stated criteria, or on one or more implicit criteria such as aesthetic appeal.

Organizational Creativity The processes generating new and valued ideas within a coherent organization, and rated as new and valued by members of that organization according to shared organizational values.

The study of ORGANIZATIONS INTERESTED IN CREATIVITY *opens up promising possibilities for gaining deeper insights into the relationships between organizational actions and outcomes. At an anecdotal level, a small number of organizations are frequently presented as exemplars of organizations interested in creativity. The development of interest indicators provides a means of codifying interest in creativity. The emergence of online electronic databases in the 1990s offered a powerful tool for studying interest indicators and for discriminating between organizations with high or low interest in creativity.*

I. WHY STUDY ORGANIZATIONAL INTEREST IN CREATIVITY?

There is a powerful case for studying organizations that are interested in creativity. One line of reasoning might be as follows: The pioneering organizations in any field are likely to be those that show considerable interest and involvement in that field. We may therefore decide that information about organizations interested in creativity would have value as a starting point to studying the wider picture of creativity in its organizational and individual forms.

Some urgency has been injected into the topic, as interest in creativity, for so long centered on individuals, has shifted to creativity at the level of the group and the organization. This shift became noticeable in the 1980s, and by the mid-1990s had gained attention among social scientists and business practitioners.

The study of individual-level creativity continues to interest and intrigue many researchers. Most reviewers take the view that the uncertainties surrounding the dynamics of individual creativity become compounded as the focus of research attention moved to the level of the creative team and the creative organization.

Among the difficulties can be listed the aggregation problem and the temporal problem. The aggregation problem makes itself known in any effort at examining the characteristics of creative individuals and attempting to find some means of reexpressing these characteristics in a creative team. Similarly, a creative team may have some credibility yet operate in an unsupportive organization, so that it eventually is stifled, and the team fragments. [*See* TEAMS.]

This point connects with the second, temporal problem of possible changes over time of creative interest or outputs. Creative individuals are generally believed to have potential that expresses itself under given conditions. Creative teams, and organizations, however, tend to be judged by their repeated performance. A creative award-winning team may be judged to have lost its edge. There is evidence that organizations regarded as excellent in results and creative in achieving these results may become yesterday's flavor of the month. This was famously demonstrated in the rapid decline of many organizations lauded in the all-time best seller, *In Search of Excellence*.

Thus, the more direct phenomenon of interest is the nature of creative organizations, which in turn offers prospects of insights into effective, innovative, and successful organizations. The more indirect measure is the organization's interest in creativity. Its own value (or interest) lies in the prospects of obtaining some reasonably stable empirical data that can be taken as indicators of motivational features favoring creative productivity. It has been suggested that the most potent research is triggered by recognition that an observation or phenomenon is of interest: "That's interesting!" is an important and indicative exclamation in discovery processes. One added complication is that interest in creativity leads to meta-level concerns. These lead to the processes of reflection about one's own processes, the self-reflective processes believed to be involved in systems development and change. [*See* DISCOVERY.]

Creative interest indicators therefore may be taken as signals indicating the most promising exemplars of change (the individuals, groups, or organizations doing the changing). In identifying organizations interested in creativity we may open up prospects for learning more about these elusive topics.

II. ANECDOTAL EVIDENCE

There is a distinction in the minds of the general public between creative individuals and the organizations in which they are found. For example, British managers asked in the 1990s to name a creative business individual tended to suggest one name above others—Richard Branson. American managers in the 1980s tended to favor Steve Jobs as a creative business person, and subsequently Bill Gates. Yet, 3M was more often rated as a creative organization than was Virgin Airways, Apple, or Microsoft (the organizations dominated by the creative individuals).

A poll of CEOs to name visionary companies which had survived over lengthy periods of change and transition found that organizations were rated as creative if they produced creative outputs that were not too closely associated with charismatic founders. The creativity is directed toward renewal of the company. In a sense, the creative process is that of organizational learning and adaptation; the creative product is the reshaped organization, which is consequently able to generate new commercially viable products and pro-

TABLE I

Enduring Visionary Companies as Nominated by U.S. CEOs in the 1990s

3M	Marriott
American Express	Merck
Boeing	Motorola
Citicorp	Nordstrom
Ford	Philip Morris
General Electric	Proctor & Gamble
Hewlett-Packard	Sony
IBM	Wal-Mart
Johnson & Johnson	Walt Disney

cesses or innovations. The companies named were almost exclusively American, industrial, and mature, and are shown in Table I. [*See* CREATIVE PRODUCTS.]

Of note among the organizations are those who have consistently supported creativity education and training both in-house and as sponsors of creativity conferences. Proctor & Gamble and Motorola are recent examples; General Electric was among the earliest industrial organizations to encourage creative thinking programs (at AC Spark Plug). Sony is the only non-American organization listed. 3M, it has already been noted, has been one of the most-cited organizations for making innovation a core competence.

Another interesting point illustrated in the list is the wide range of corporate sectors represented. In some there have been direct technological discoveries and developments (3M, Boeing, Ford, GE, Hewlett-Packard, IBM, Johnson & Johnson, and Sony). Others have shown a capacity to create organizational innovations (Ford, Walt Disney, and Nordstrom) and service innovations (American Express, Marriott, Nordstrom, and Wal-Mart). Clearly the CEOs are not limiting the nominations to organizations that have pioneered technological innovations.

III. CITATIONAL EVIDENCE

More information on organizations interested in creativity has been collected into a database located at the Creativity Research Unit at Manchester, England. Archives there cover direct involvement internationally with companies over a period reaching to the 1960s. A database incorporating the archival material was begun in 1996. From these archives an international perspective can be formed. The first materials codified and available for study summarized the proceedings of annual European and North American conferences on creativity organized by the European association for Creativity and Innovation (formerly the Periscope group) and the Prism group (representatives from the Center for Creative Leadership, Greensboro, NC, and Center for Creativity Studies and the Creative Education Foundation, both at Buffalo, NY). Data were also added from a comprehensive historical review of creativity training covering the 1950s to the 1990s by Sidney Parnes, from records of the activities within the Creativity Research Unit at Manchester Business School; and from other published materials of creativity conferences and corporate interest in creativity from the Center for Creative Leadership and The University of Valetta, Malta (Table II).

An approach for exploring this kind of data is offered by signaling theory. We can model the various kinds of references to corporate interest in creativity as signals generated through the activities of a communicating network of organizations. The organizations can be combined in various ways to test for possible shared characteristics within groups of organizations. The signals can also be combined in various ways to test the characteristics of a multitude of aggregate measures of an organization's interest in creativity, or an interest index.

The simplest aggregate index would be to count the presence of some operationally defined signal within a data source as a hit, and to sum the hits obtained. A next refinement would be to determine some discrimination within each database for strong signals and weak signals, and then allocate some form of weighting that favors strong signals. These signals have been analyzed in this fashion, with strong signals weighted at twice the level as weak signals.

Selection of reliable aggregate measures of organizations within a communications network requires further trials. However, a database and preliminary analysis suggest this to be a promising approach for building knowledge of companies interested in creativity.

The large organizations achieving the strongest signals as indicated by the selected interest index are

TABLE II
Interest Indicators Derived from Archival Data Available for the 1950s to the 1990s

Source	Details	Signals High	Signals Low
Euroconf 1	1st European conference on creativity, 1987	30	7
Euroconf 2	2nd European conference on creativity, 1989	26	22
Euroconf 3	3rd European conference on creativity, 1991	7	19
Euroconf 4	4th European conference on creativity, 1993	12	21
Prism 1	1st North American conference on creativity, 1988	14	19
Prism 3	2nd North American conference on creativity, 1990	17	6
Parnes	Comprehensive survey of creative problem solving, 1940s to 1990s	107	10
Maltaconf	1st International Lateral Thinking Conference, 1993	12	8
CrArchives 70s	MBS Archives of creativity activities in Europe (1970s)	30	9
CrArchives 80s	MBS Archives of creativity activities in Europe (1980s)	22	14
CCL	Documents from Center for Creative Leadership, Greensboro, NC	15	7

largely convincing examples (Table III). For example, of the eight large and miscellaneous organizations with the strongest signals, four were also included in the far more exclusive list nominated by CEOs, namely, IBM, Proctor & Gamble, 3M, and Sony. The additional four are arguably equally strong candidates for any such list, comprising Eastman Kodak, DuPont, Polaroid, and the British-owned chemicals multinational ICI.

The group sharing the next strongest interest indi-

cator (Table IV) contains a greater proportion of non-American firms. The set still comprises well-known "household name" firms, and includes another nomination of the CEOs. These groups make up cumulatively approximately 14% of the 134 large organizations listed in the database as interested in creativity.

The database also includes a more miscellaneous collection of smaller industrial companies and various-sized service industry companies (Table V). The citational characteristics of large industrial firms and service firms show good statistical homogeneity. A second clustering of firms can be detected among the smaller service firms, including groups from academic insti-

TABLE III
Organizations Most Strongly Cited as Interested in Creativity
(from Archival Information, 1960s to 1990s)

Organization	Interest index[a]
Eastman Kodak	6
DuPont	5
Polaroid	5
ICI	5
IBM[b]	4
Proctor & Gamble[b]	4
3M[b]	4
Sony[b]	4

[a]Weighted score based on 2 for evidence of major interest on an interest indicator, and 1 for evidence of minor interest on an interest indicator.
[b]Indicates that the organization is cited as a visionary company (Table I).

TABLE IV
Large Organizations Moderately Well Cited as Interested in Creativity[a]
(from Archival Information, 1960s to 1990s)

Unilever (Anglo-Dutch)	Rank Xerox
Glaxo (UK)	Kirin (Japan)
Philips (Netherlands)	Kao (Japan)
Corning	NTT (Japan)
G.E.[b]	Ricoh (Japan)

[a]All companies had a total weighted citation index of 3. Weighted score based on 2 for evidence of major interest on an interest indicator and 1 for evidence of minor interest on an interest indicator.
[b]Indicates that the organization is cited as a visionary one (Table I).

TABLE V
Citation Index Differences by Types of Organization and Regional Locations[a]

Factor	Mean	SD	Min	Max	N
Industrial and miscellaneous large organizations	1.54	0.95	1	6	224
Type					
Large manufacturing	1.56	1.01	1	6	131
Large, miscellaneous	1.51	0.87	1	6	93
Region					
USA	1.49	1.04	1	6	97
UK	1.52	1.01	1	6	50
Other European countries	1.56	0.73	1	4	50
Service (academic, consulting, R&D) organizations	2.19	1.94	1	10	108
Type					
Academic	2.22	1.74	1	10	46
Other service	2.15	2.1	1	10	62
Region					
USA	1.96	1.84	1	10	51
UK	2.08	2.08	1	10	26
Other European countries	2.83	2.21	1	10	23

[a]All t tests on pairs of means within organizational type are not significantly different at the $p > .01$ level. The USA versus other European countries difference of means approaches significance at the $p \sim .05$ level. Weighted scores based on 2 for evidence of major interest on an interest indicator and 1 for evidence of minor interest on an interest indicator.

tutes, R&D departments, and management consultancies. Interestingly, the cluster of smaller firms have a rather higher citational index than the cluster of large firms. This should be interpreted with caution. The higher mean score may reflect different motivations among the service firms to become highly visible in publications and events concerned with creativity.

IV. CONCLUSIONS

The good, but not perfect, fit with a sample of visionary companies nominated by American CEOs offers promise that companies interested in creativity over a historically extensive period tend to be those firms perceived as dynamically successful. Here we have a further possibility for characterizing the creative organization—that is to say the organization in which awareness of creativity is linked with creative renewal internally, and innovative outputs externally. The database provides a valuable analytical tool and illustrates how future comparative studies might be carried out.

Bibliography

Collins, J. C., & Porras, J. I. (1994). *Built to last: Successful habits of visionary companies.* New York: Random House.

Davis, M. S. (1971). That's interesting! Towards a phenomenology of sociology and a sociology of phenomenology. *Philosophy of Social Science,* 309–344.

Parnes, S. J. (Ed.). (1993). *Sourcebook for creative problem-solving.* Buffalo, NY: Creative Education Foundation Press.

Peters, T., & Waterman, R. (1982). *In search of excellence.* New York: Harper & Row.

Rickards, T. (1998). Assessing organizational creativity: An innovative benchmarking approach. *International Journal of Innovation Management, 2,* 367–382.

Overexcitabilities

Michael M. Piechowski

Northland College

Developmental Potential A concept describing innate endowment composed of abilities and talents, intelligence, and overexcitabilities.

Overexcitability An innate tendency to respond with heightened intensity and sensitivity to intellectual, emotional, and other stimuli. Also called psychic overexcitability.

Theory of Positive Disintegration A theory of emotional development from lower to a higher level of psychological functioning, proposed by K. Dabrowski. The core idea of the theory is that structures of a lower level must be dismantled before structures of a higher level can be erected. The theory emphasizes the role of inner conflict, moral sensitivity, compassion, and self-judgment in the personal growth of creative people and spiritual seekers.

OVEREXCITABILITY (OE) is a translation of the Polish term nadpobudliwość *which means the capacity to be superstimulated. The term* overexcitability, *rather than just excitability, was chosen to convey the idea that the stimulation is well beyond the common and average in intensity and duration. Overexcitabilities are assumed to be innate tendencies that appear in five forms: psychomotor, sensual, intellectual, imaginational, and emotional. The difference in intensity, sensitivity, and acuity is not only greater than normal, it is also a difference in the very quality of experiencing. As enhanced forms of experiencing, overexcitabilities contribute in important ways to the individual's psychological development. Consequently, the strength of overexcitabilities is taken, in part, as a measure of developmental potential.*

I. THE CONCEPT OF OVEREXCITABILITY AND ITS ORIGIN

Gifted, talented, and creative people are known to be energetic, enthusiastic, intensely absorbed in their pursuits, endowed with vivid imagination, and strongly sensual, but they are also known to be emotionally vulnerable. Some are known to be aggressive, others to be morally sensitive. They tend to react strongly to aesthetic, intellectual, emotional, sexual, and other stimuli. Because of this intensity, creative people may not always be easy to be with. They are considered deviant—too different to fit the norm. The characteristic of enhanced experiencing is believed to be the property of the nervous systems of creative people. Therefore, overexcitabilities feed, enrich, empower, and amplify talent. In most cases they appear stronger with higher intelligence, and they are strongest in creative people.

Overexcitabilities are found across all talent domains. Writers, composers, dancers, actors, scientists, inventors, as well as civic and spiritual leaders, all have them. In artists, they are often as strong in adulthood as in childhood. Do they aid or impede development? In the first entry of her *Journal of Solitude,* May Sarton wrote, "I feel too much, sense too much, am exhausted by the reverberations after even the simplest conversation. But the deep collision is and has been with my unregenerate, tormenting, and tormented self." Such great intensity of feeling as well as an inner struggle and self-judgment used to be viewed as mental disturbance. Now they are understood to be essential to inner growth. The sculptor Malvina Hoffman said, "Language is a clumsy medium to express the pounding surge of intense feeling. . . . Music could drive my blood and suffuse my entire being."

We can find similar examples among scientists. Louis Pasteur was deeply emotional, though he did not show it outwardly. He suffered such acute homesickness when he went to study in Paris that his father had to bring him back home. A somewhat different manner of enhanced experiencing was Norbert Wiener's vivid memory of smells and tastes from his childhood trip to Vienna: "The smell of the alcohol lamp over which my parents prepared my sister's warm evening meals, the smell of rich European chocolate with whipped cream, the smell of the hotel and the restaurant and *café*—all these are still sharp in my nostrils." These examples show a rich and amplified range of experiencing. Let us now look at how it came to be explored.

In 1937 the Polish psychologist and psychiatrist Kazimierz Dabrowski published a study titled "Psychological Bases of Self-Mutilation." Examining biographies of creators and clinical cases, Dabrowski identified factors that were predisposing toward physical self-mutilation and psychological self-torment. These predisposing factors are different forms of what he called *psychic overexcitability.* This was the germ of his theory of positive disintegration.

Dabrowski studied how a person responds to stimulation and stress. Emotional tension requires an outlet. When it becomes unbearable it can lead to self-infliction of pain, the pain then brings relief. The pain may be sought in physical self-injury or in emotional

self-torture. The stronger the tension, the stronger the need to release it. Dabrowski saw that people prone to self-mutilation were more susceptible to being excited, tense, thrown off balance by their overstimulation and inner turmoil. In other words, they were high strung and subject to nervousness. He also noticed that they tended to have a rich inner life. He studied clinical cases of gifted and talented youngsters, and biographies of such creators as Michelangelo, Dostoevski, Tolstoy, and Nietzsche. In each case he pointed to clashes of opposing tendencies that created enormous inner tension resulting in various forms of self-torment. The ability to sustain great inner conflicts was to Dabrowski a sign of inner strength because rather than injuring others the person injured himself. He observed that an emotional crisis and mental suffering, so great that it could bring on a psychotic episode, at times resulted in personality integration at a higher level. Personality development toward a higher level through suffering and inner conflict is the leading idea of his theory.

Dabrowski emphasized the disequilibrating, disorganizing, and disintegrating action of overexcitability on many areas of psychological functioning. When this kind of disintegration fosters emotional growth, it is positive, hence the name *theory of positive disintegration.* Overexcitability was defined by the following characteristics: (a) the reaction exceeds the stimulus, (b) the reaction lasts much longer than average, (c) the reaction is often not related to the stimulus, and (d) the emotional experience is promptly relayed to the sympathetic nervous system (accelerated heartbeat, blushing, trembling, perspiring, headaches).

As Dabrowski kept developing his theory, the five overexcitabilities became components of the concept of *developmental potential.* This concept includes overexcitabilities, talents, and intelligence. It is the potential for emotional development to a higher level such as, for example, self-actualization. In fact, Maslow and Dabrowski began a friendship that was cut short by Maslow's premature death in 1970. The overexcitabilities are ways of experiencing with great intensity, aliveness, vividness, depth, and richness in the sensory, intellectual, imaginative, and emotional realms. They are also the means of processing emotional tension.

Each form of overexcitability can be looked on as a mode of being in the world or as a *dimension of mental functioning.* Thus, the *psychomotor* mode is one of movement, restlessness, action, excess of energy seeking an outlet; the *sensual* mode loves surface contact, sensory delight, comfort and hedonism; the *intellectual* mode favors analysis, logic, questioning, the search for truth; the *imaginational* mode celebrates vivid dreams, fantasies, images and metaphors, personifications, strong visualization of experience; the *emotional* mode centers on attachments and affectional bonds with others, empathy, the despair of loneliness, the joy of love, the enigma of existence and human responsibility. The overexcitabilities are modes of personal experience and personal action. Each mode can be viewed as a channel through which information flows in the form of sensations, feelings, experiences, images, ideas, hopes, and desires. The five dimensions are like color filters or interactive channels through which the world is perceived and felt.

The response is specific to the most dominant form, or forms, of overexcitability in a person. For instance, persons characterized by emotional overexcitability when asked what triggers in them the feeling of being incredibly happy may answer that the love of family and friends moves them to tears or that the feeling of oneness with all creation makes them ecstatic. If the answer to the same question is the speed and excitement of water-skiing, playing a hard game of racquet ball, or racing on a motorcycle to feel its roar, it indicates psychomotor overexcitability. In the latter case, although the question was asked in the emotional dimension ("What makes you feel incredibly happy?"), the response came in the psychomotor dimension.

These channels can be wide open, narrow, or operating at bare minimum. They are assumed to be part of a person's constitution and to be more or less independent of each other. If more than one of these channels have wide apertures, then the abundance and diversity of feeling, thought, imagery, and sensation will inevitably lead to dissonance, conflict, and tension. Consequently, experience becomes multidimensional, enriching, expanding, and intensifying the individual's emotional development. At times the inner tensions and conflicts may be overwhelming.

The five overexcitabilities, plus specific creative gifts, talents, and abilities constitute the original equipment with which a child enters life. Parental, peer, school, historical, economic, and cultural forces all influence how this original equipment will fare.

Today we can say that individual differences, such as heightened versus average excitability, lie in the speed of information processing, in the developmental experiences that stimulate the brain to grow denser and more efficient neural connections, in the extensiveness of cognitive and other networks, and in the excitability and rate of emotional processing by the brain. With current advances in tapping the activity of the living brain, the overexcitabilities could be tested directly by comparing the responses of individuals who score high on a given overexcitability with those who score low.

II. EXPRESSIONS OF OVEREXCITABILITY IN CREATIVE PEOPLE

The following illustrative examples come from biographies and from overexcitablity questionnaires obtained from writers, poets, musicians, fine artists, film makers, and dancers-choreographers. Responses marked (π) are from material collected by Jane Piirto for her study of creative writers.

A. Psychomotor Overexcitability

Psychomotor overexcitability describes the surplus of energy characteristic of gifted and creative people as well as the funneling of emotional tension into psychomotor forms of expression. As shown in Table I, the heightened energy of a person can find expression in speaking rapidly, outward gestures of excitement, intense athletic activity, physical work, pressure for action, and strong competitiveness. Emotional tension can be funneled into actions that help discharge it through compulsive talking and chattering, engaging in impulsive actions, displaying nervous habits, working compulsively, or acting out destructively. The higher energy level of creative people is readily noticed, though it is not universal.

Some creators were highly spirited and energetic when they were young but were not so in their adult years. Chopin did not have a strong constitution to begin with and it was later weakened by tuberculosis. Once she returned from boarding school, Emily Dickinson gradually became so agoraphobic and fearful of strangers that she never left her family house. Richard

TABLE I
Forms and Expressions of Overexcitability

Psychomotor

Surplus of energy
   Rapid speech, marked excitation, intense physical activity (e.g., fast games and sports), pressure for action, (e.g., organizing), marked competitiveness

Psychomotor expression of emotional tension
   Compulsive talking and chattering, impulsive actions, nervous habits (tics, nail biting), workaholism, acting out

Sensual

Enhanced sensory and aesthetic pleasure
   Seeing, smelling, tasting, touching, hearing, and sex; delight in beautiful objects, sounds of words, music, form, color, balance

Sensual expression of emotional tension
   Overeating, sexual overindulgence, buying sprees, wanting to be in the limelight

Intellectual

Intensified activity of the mind
   Thirst for knowledge, curiosity, concentration, capacity for sustained intellectual effort, avid reading; keen observation, detailed visual recall, detailed planning

Penchant for probing questions and problem solving
   Search for truth and understanding; forming new concepts; tenacity in problem solving

Reflective thought
   Thinking about thinking, love of theory and analysis, preoccupation with logic, moral thinking, introspection (but without self-judgment), conceptual and intuitive integration; independence of thought (sometimes very critical)

Imaginational

Free play of the imagination
   Frequent use of image and metaphor, facility for invention and fantasy, facility for detailed visualization, poetic and dramatic perception, animistic and magical thinking

Capacity for living in a world of fantasy
   Predilection for magic and fairy tales, creation of private worlds, imaginary companions; dramatization

Spontaneous imagery as an expression of emotional tension
   Animistic imagery, mixing truth and fiction, elaborate dreams, illusions

Low tolerance of boredom

Emotional

Feelings and emotions intensified
   Positive feelings, negative feelings, extremes of emotion, complex emotions and feelings, identification with others' feelings, awareness of a whole range of feelings

Strong somatic expressions
   Tense stomach, sinking heart, blushing, flushing, pounding heart, sweaty palms

Strong affective expressions
   Inhibition (timidity, shyness); enthusiasm, ecstasy, euphoria, pride; strong affective memory; shame; feelings of unreality, fears and anxieties, feelings of guilt, concern with death, depressive and suicidal moods

Capacity for strong attachments, deep relationships
   Strong emotional ties and attachments to persons, living things, places; attachments to animals; difficulty adjusting to new environments; compassion, responsiveness to others, sensitivity in relationships; loneliness

Well-differentiated feelings toward self
   Inner dialogue and self-judgment

Wagner, Antoine de Saint-Exupéry, Sergei Rachmaninoff, and Thomas Alva Edison are a few examples of the many creators who as children were impetuous, hard-to-control bundles of energy. Today highly spirited gifted children are often mistakenly labeled as hyperactive or having attention deficit/hyperactivity disorder (ADHD).

Saint-Exupéry as a boy was wild and fearless, fond of violent games in which he tyrannized over others. Edison was always getting into scrapes because of his inquisitiveness. One day, he attached wires to two large cats and then attempted to rub them vigorously to produce static electricity. The scratches and claw marks he got were deep. Rachmaninoff's favorite sport was to jump on and off horse-driven streetcars in motion, even in winter on icy pavement.

In response to the question "How do you act when you get excited?" a poet wrote, "I wave my hands, stumble over my tongue & yak at hyperspeed until my lips are ready to fly off" [π]. A dancer said, "I feel the most energy in the a.m. Or during or immediately following dancing. I try to 'stay with it,' ride the wave as long as it lasts." The question "What kind of physical activity gives you the most satisfaction?" evoked this response from a young writer/actress, "Swimming but most of all water skiing. It's the most exhilarating sport I've done—the feeling of movement, water and wind against my body all at once." These examples illustrate high energy that finds ways to be discharged physically.

B. Sensual Overexcitability

In sensual overexcitability the pleasures and delights offered through seeing, smelling, tasting, touching, hearing, and sex, as well as multisensory experiences, become enhanced. Persons so endowed immerse themselves in the delight of beautiful things, sounds of nature, sounds of words and music; they note the form, color, and balance in anything around them. Specific aversions to certain tastes, smells, or touch, and the like are also common. Hedonism is often sensual. Sensual pleasure tends to be relaxing and temporarily satisfying.

In contrast, when emotional tension is diverted to the sensual channel it may become excess in eating, smoking, shopping, sex, and a constant desire to be admired. For example, Tchaikovsky began smoking for the pleasure it gave him but soon found that it pacified his high-strung nerves—sensual pleasure combined with a reduction of emotional tension.

Painters smell paint, feel the texture of their material, feel the brush strokes in a painting, just as potters feel the clay being molded in their hands, with heightened sensibility in their whole physical being. Many poets are acutely sensitive to the sound of words and their rhythms, the touch of paper, and the look of print fonts. Musicians are supremely aware of timbres of instruments and the distinct color and timbres of voices, sounds of nature, and of their everyday surroundings (e.g., John Cage).

Chopin's description of Henrietta Sontag's singing—one of the greatest sopranos of the early 19th century—is extremely sensual: "You feel as if she was blowing at you perfumes of the freshest flowers and caressing you with the delicious pleasures of her voice,

but she rarely moves one to tears." Chopin was making a distinction between a purely sensual delight and being deeply moved emotionally. Charles Darwin derived such intense pleasure from listening to music that his "backbone would sometimes shiver."

The vividness of sensory experience and sensory imagination in highly creative people raises an interesting possibility of testing it. Recent reports show that the brain lights up differently when real memories are recalled than when imaginary memories are recalled. In real memories the sensory areas light up, in imagined memories they do not. Because people who have high overexcitability report experiencing their visualizations as real, one would expect their sensory areas to light up during their fantasizing. [*See* IMAGERY; IMAGINATION.]

C. Intellectual Overexcitability

Intellectual overexcitability encompasses the intensified activity of the mind as thirst for knowledge, curiosity, capacity for concentration and sustained intellectual effort, avid reading and precision in observation, recall, and careful planning. Questioning is the hallmark of intellectual overexcitability as the person is driven by the search for understanding and truth. Perceiving patterns and relationships leads to naming them; thus, new concepts are born. Solving problems, finding it difficult to let go of a problem, and finding new ones to solve is typical. Another trait is reflective thought, exemplified by watching one's own thought processes, delighting in analysis and theoretical thought, preoccupation with logic, moral thinking, introspection, and seeking integration of concepts and intuitions. People strong in intellectual overexcitability are independent thinkers and often highly critical of the thoughts of others. [*See* METACOGNITION.]

Although one would think that intellectual overexcitability is the prerogative of scientists and philosophers, it is also characteristic of artists and creative people in all domains. The more original an artist's work was judged by experts, the more facility for asking questions the artist had. Habitual or relentless inquisitiveness—pondering and puzzling over things—is one of the distinct characteristics of intellectual overexcitability. The *Allport-Vernon-Lindzey Study of*

Values similarly defines *theoretical value* as an interest in and pursuit of truth, a desire to gain knowledge, systematize it, and bring order to it.

A statement from Darwin illustrates curiosity, concentration, and the thrill of learning a logical principle. Recalling his youth, Darwin said:

> I had strong and diversified tastes, much zeal for whatever interested me, and a keen pleasure in understanding any complex subject or thing. I was taught Euclid by a private tutor, and I distinctly remember the intense satisfaction which the clear geometrical proofs gave me. I remember with equal distinctness, the delight which my uncle (the father of Francis Galton) gave me by explaining the principle of the vernier of a barometer.

In his autobiography, *Ex-Prodigy: My Childhood and Youth,* Norbert Wiener stressed that he was motivated by the ideal of service to truth rather than service to humanity even though his father exerted a strong moral influence on him to serve humanity. Wiener also described how when working on a problem "the unresolved ideas were a positive torture to me until I had finally written them down and got them out of my system." The excerpts from Darwin and Wiener show the crucial involvement of emotion in learning and solving problems.

These examples demonstrate several aspects of intensified activity of the mind that lead to ever more probing questions and search for understanding, shared by scientists and artists alike though their questions and their methods of inquiry may be quite different. They also show a strong emotional component in the process.

D. Imaginational Overexcitability

The role of imagination in creativity has been well documented in many sources. As a personal characteristic, the concept of imaginational overexcitability is broader. It looks at the creator's underlying predisposition, manifested in childhood, to engage in the free play of the imagination, to fantasize and daydream, but also to come up with unusual associations. To be able to convert experience into imagery depends on an exceptional ability to see analogies, which are facilitated by unusual associations to emerge as metaphors. When Edison was 10 years old he weighed himself on a scale and said to his mother, "I am a bushel of wheat now, I weigh 80 pounds." Imagination makes such analogies possible. The impulse to explore new possibilities and to change what is given into something else is ever present; it was delightfully illustrated in the film *Amadeus*. After hearing a court composer's piece, Mozart goes to the keyboard to play it and to show how to make it more interesting. All it took was imagination. [*See* ANALOGIES; METAPHORS.]

Imaginational overexcitability can be also noticed in a person's facility for visualizing, making elaborate dreams and fantasies, perceiving life experiences poetically and dramatically, and in animistic and magical thinking. Animistic thinking involves endowing inanimate objects with personality, character, and a will of their own. Magical thinking rests on the conviction that to think something is as good as making it happen. The private rituals and formulas to ensure that everything works out all right are examples of such thinking. The capacity for living in a world of fantasy often goes together with the need to spend certain amount of time daydreaming, reading fairy tales and stories, or even creating private imaginary worlds. Having several imaginary companions in childhood, and for some even into adulthood, is a telling sign.

Emotional tension is easily diverted into the theater of imagination where feelings and emotions find their form. It is helpful for understanding one's emotional life to be able to give an image to what is felt. Words are inadequate and limited, but an image carries the energy and felt quality that reveals the meaning of an experience. For people with overexcitability of imagination, spontaneous imagery is as natural as breathing; dreams are elaborate, illusions and mixing truth and fiction are possible. This does not mean that at other times such persons are not capable of sorting fantasy from reality. On the contrary, for them the difference is quite enhanced. The boundary may blur when intense emotions take over in a rush of vivid images. Frank Lloyd Wright once imagined that his mother was going to give a party for him. He started telling his friends in detail what would be served and how special this occasion was going to be. So they came, all dressed up. Wright's mother was surprised but knowing her son she improvised a party. Because he imagined it, he actually believed the party was going to take place.

Richard Wagner was so fascinated by Beethoven and Shakespeare that he created in his mind a vivid image of each one: "I used to meet them both in ecstatic dreams, saw them, and spoke to them; on awakening I was bathed in tears." His imagination was so graphic that whenever he thought of ghosts he was terrified. When as a boy he visited his relatives who lived in a big house, he was lodged in a stately guest room. The old portraits of young ladies "in hooped petticoats and white powdered hair" seemed to him to be ghosts. Alone in the room he was possessed by terror because they seemed to come to life. Every night of his stay he was drenched with perspiration, a victim to his frightening visions.

Creative people do not tolerate boredom well. They do not enjoy routine and unimaginative exercises. As a boy Rachmaninoff took up improvisation because the music he had to study was too dull for him. He said to his naive listeners that he was playing Chopin or Mendelssohn and no one realized he was playing his own music.

These are just a few examples of the free play of imagination, the capacity for visualization and for fantasy, animistic and magical thinking, and the ability to conjure up novel images and unusual analogies, responses typical of imaginational overexcitability.

E. Emotional Overexcitability

Emotional overexcitability is easily recognized. A person's feelings and emotions are frequently at a higher pitch. The person has a keen awareness and sensitivity to nuances of feeling both in oneself and in others. Because the vehicle for emotion is the body, there are distinctly recognizable psychosomatic signs of overexcitability, such as blushing, getting flushed with color, perspiring, trembling, feeling tension in different parts of the body, feeling hot or cold, and so on. Positive as well as negative feelings are experienced with great intensity, openly by extroverts and inwardly by introverts. We live in a culture in which being emotional is criticized and tampered with. Children are often told

what they should or should not feel rather than accepting what they do feel. When this happens, children with high overexcitability are intensely miserable and confused. Consequently, we have a much higher frequency in emotional individuals of a tendency toward depression, suicidal thoughts, feeling of being out of place, and not belonging. Feelings of profound alienation, even suicide, are often the result.

Highly emotional individuals make strong attachments to people, living things, and places. When they have to move they experience great difficulties adjusting to new environments. To pull up so many roots and strike them in new soil takes up much energy; it often takes a long time, or it fails to happen. This imparts compassion toward others, sympathy for the loneliness of others. Friendships are strong and enduring. Being emotional often means to judge oneself, to carry on an inner dialogue and self-judgment on how well one does toward others, how well one carries out one's responsibilities toward others. May Sarton, quoted at the beginning, wrote of the deep collision with her "unregenerate, tormenting, and tormented self."

Intensity, passion, and sensitivity to nuances of feeling are usually associated with creative people in the arts but not in science or mathematics. Herbert Simon, a Nobel Prize winner in economics, said in an interview that there is no emotion in his creative process—only hard cognitive work and hard problem solving. This, however, is not true of other scientists. Simon took for granted his wife's contribution to his emotional well-being and overlooked the obvious fact that the intense interest driving him is an intense emotion. Louis Pasteur and Norbert Wiener, to cite just two examples, were deeply emotional and highly sensitive people. Darwin and Einstein also had a strongly emotional aspect to their personalities. The spectrum of emotions and feelings is immense and exceedingly intricate. The portion of the emotional spectrum that is characteristic of each creator is probably unique.

In his autobiography Darwin made frequent observations on his friendships and their importance to him as personal relationships in contrast to scientific ones. In describing people he always noted the emotional impact each person had on him. Recalling his childhood, Darwin confessed to an act of cruelty. He beat a puppy and it troubled his conscience for a long time.

"The exact spot where the crime was committed" was engraved in his mind. It was all the more troubling to him because he loved dogs and they often preferred him to their masters. Darwin also recalled that he was more affectionate in his youth when he had many friends among the schoolboys whom he said he loved dearly. When as a student he attended the clinical ward of the hospital some of the cases distressed him and left vivid imprints on his mind. Two surgeries he attended were performed without anesthesia—it was not yet introduced—he could not bear to stay and see them completed.

Einstein said about himself, "I am not much with people, and I'm not a family man. I want my peace." In personal relationships he kept a distance. He concentrated all his energy on solving the riddle of how God created the universe. Yet he was also animated by deep emotions and sensibilities. He was close to his mother, to his sister Maja, and to his uncle Cäsar Koch. He was deeply honest and abhorred German militarism so strongly that from the age of 15 he sought to give up his German citizenship; a year later he became stateless; eventually he became a Swiss citizen. He cherished those few with whom he could discuss physics. Einstein said that he suffered nervous conflicts "at the very beginning when the Special Theory of Relativity began to germinate" in him. Similarly Max Planck described the 6 years of his own seminal work on the equilibrium between radiation and matter as "a process of despair" because the solution was eluding him.

As a boy Einstein had a great sensitivity to beauty and a deep religiosity. About the age of 12 he came to the conclusion that many Bible stories could not possibly be true. Religion lost its authority. This led him to suspect that all institutional authority was intentionally deceiving the young through lies. The resulting emotional crisis made him distrust every kind of authority. Einstein loved music and studied the violin but was making little progress with teachers who stressed mechanical practicing and accuracy without feeling. When he was 13 he fell in love with Mozart and his violin sonatas: "The attempts to reproduce, to some extent, their artistic content and their singular grace compelled me to improve my technique . . . I believe, on the whole, that love is a better teacher than sense of duty."

Pasteur as a boy liked to fish but abstained from trapping birds—a wounded bird was too much for him. The contact with his family and friends was vital to the young Pasteur. Away from home he constantly begged for more frequent and longer letters. Pasteur was also deeply religious and it pained him to see in the practice of religion so much controversy, intolerance, and lack of peace and love.

Wiener's account of his boyhood and youth is very emotional. He remembered his first sweetheart in kindergarten—charmed by her voice he loved to stay close to her. He described his fears of the dark, injury, violence, and death and his sensitivity to the injustice and cruelty suffered by others. He was quite shaken when at the age of 13 he was told that his mother had a second child who died at birth. It shattered his sense of security to realize that his own family was not immune to tragedy. Lacking religious upbringing he learned the story of Christ's crucifixion from his Catholic friends. The image of Christ's wounds and the crown of thorns filled him with pain.

Despite his extraordinary abilities and being radically accelerated in school—Wiener graduated from Tufts College at the age of 14½, spent a year at Cornell, and earned his doctorate at Harvard before he turned 19—his self-confidence was undercut by his father's demands for perfection. Even worse, his father stated publicly in print that all the boy's accomplishments were due to the training he gave him and none to his abilities. Wiener was devastated; he felt that all his successes were his father's but the failures were his own. He dreaded graduation, which forced him to leave the protection of childhood and face adult responsibility for himself. He seriously doubted he could succeed. "My achievement of independence during the year at Cornell had been incalculably retarded by the confused mass of feelings of resentment, despair, and rejection which had followed early in the year upon discovery of my Jewishness." The feeling of oneness with nature, or even with the universe, is also frequently expressed by creative people.

Studies comparing artists and scientists in regard to emotionality have shown that as a group scientists tend to be less emotional. But this comparison overlooks at least two things. First, the comparison is made of adults. The examples cited make it clear that as children scientists often are emotional and sensitive but later the involvement in research restricts their emotional range—recall Darwin saying that he was more affectionate as a boy. Second, there is a distinct difference in the artists' and the scientists' material. Scientists study phenomena outside themselves, which are analyzed, experimented with, and explained in objective terms. But the process of working out solutions to problems is often described as despair or torture. Whether the scientist approaches this work with passion or not does not enter the final picture. That's how science is usually viewed and portrayed. Objectivity is in fact the outcome of the collective enterprise of science in which replication of results and confirmation of theories are carried out by different people checking on each other's work. In art the very material is human subjectivity, the life of feeling to which an artist gives expression. Artists work with the complexities of human emotion and feeling. Before experience can be portrayed and expressed it has to be felt, whether in reality or in imagination.

In some cases emotional overexcitability is expressed negatively. For instance, Wagner was so self-centered that he believed that to be his friend a man had to be totally dedicated to him. Picasso, emotionally equally intense, was not far behind, being destructive in most of his intimate relationships. Somerset Maugham was often cruel to the boys procured for him. To understand what tips the balance toward a negative expression of overexcitability would require a close examination of the person's emotional development.

III. CONCLUSION

The overexcitabilities, according to Dabrowski's theory, are fundamental attributes of a creator's makeup. Without them a talent lacks richness and power. The model of developmental potential offers a way of examining the range of expressions and categories of any given overexcitability in a given creator as the palette of each overexcitability changes its spectrum from individual to individual. Advances in brain research present the possibility of examining the nature of overexcitabilities directly.

As a property of the nervous system, each overexcitability contributes significantly to the creative process by not only heightening the experience but by making it also more complex, especially when the emotions are engaged as they almost always are. *Psychomotor* overexcitability imparts a high level of energy and drive. *Sensual* overexcitability contributes a richer and more vivid sensory experience frequently in conjunction with emotional overexcitability. *Intellectual* intensity generates relentless questioning and searching for truth. Enhanced *imagination* brings the power to envisage undreamed of possibilities, to create new realities. *Emotional* overexcitability endows the creator with greater intensity and complexity of feeling in all dimensions.

Scientists have greater emotional intensity than it is generally believed. We know today that intellectual processes divorced from emotion are ineffectual. Damasio in his *Descartes' Error: Emotion, Reason, and the Human Brain* described cases in which damage in a very small frontal area of the brain disrupted the connection between reasoning and feeling. The patient was perfectly rational on all psychological tests and yet could not bring his reasoning to any practical conclusion. Without feeling he was unable to decide which of two rational alternatives was the better one. It is therefore not surprising that creative scientists show clear evidence of emotional overexcitability, even those who would deny the role of emotion in their cognitive processes.

The problems of science are difficult. The gaps and the contradictions in our knowledge are never obvious, they have to be discovered first before they are solved. The problems of art are also difficult. The artist has to discover what experiences or humanly significant trends need to be expressed. The artist may be aware of something pushing for expression yet may need years to express it just as a scientist working on a basic problem may go through years of despair and torment before the solution appears. Work of this order requires as a starting point extraordinary equipment: intelligence, talent, and overexcitabilities.

Bibliography

Dabrowski, K. (1937). Psychological bases of self-mutilation. *Genetic Psychology Monographs, 19,* 1–104.

Dabrowski, K. (1967). *Personality-shaping through positive disintegration.* Boston: Little, Brown.

Damasio, A. (1994). *Descartes' error: Emotion, reason, and the human brain.* New York: Grosset/Putnam.

Getzels, J. W., & Csikszentmihalyi, M. (1976). *Creative vision.* New York: Wiley.

Piechowski, M. M. (1979). Developmental potential. In N. Colangelo & R. T. Zaffrann (Eds.), *New voices in counseling the gifted.* Dubuque, IA: Kendall/Hunt.

Piechowski, M. M. (1991). Emotional development and emotional giftedness. In N. Colangelo & G. A. Davis (Eds.), *Handbook of gifted education.* Boston: Allyn & Bacon.

Piechowski, M. M., Silverman, L. K., & Falk, R. F. (1985). Comparison of intellectually and artistically gifted on five dimensions of mental functioning. *Perceptual and Motor Skills, 60,* 539–549.

Paradigm Shifts

Thomas Nickles

University of Nevada, Reno

Conceptual Framework or Conceptual Scheme A set of basic categories, concepts, variables, or even a language, together with some (possibly tacit) fundamental assumptions about the structure of the universe or of the particular domain in question. Some authors hold that we can justify a claim only relative to a conceptual framework but that no framework itself can be proven correct.

Convergent Thinking or Behavior Activity that conforms to social norms and conventions; inquiry that raises standard questions and produces orthodox answers.

Divergent Thinking or Behavior Activity that is flexible, opportunistic, and disregards established rules or conventions to strike out in new directions and that invents and plays with radical variants; nonconvergent, unorthodox, iconoclastic.

Holism Doctrine that the whole is more than the sum of its parts in the sense that the functional relation or organization of the parts is crucial in determining the nature of the whole. The emergent or holistic significance of a part derives from its relation to the other parts—its place in the organizational structure—rather than from its own intrinsic nature.

Incommensurable Paradigms Thomas Kuhn's idea that there is no neutral standard against which competing paradigms can be objectively compared, as can two competing theories within the same framework; nor is there a paradigm-neutral language. There has been much disagreement about what incommensurability is and whether it actually exists in the sciences and other disciplines. One issue is whether incommensurability precludes the full translation of statements of one paradigm into the language of the other.

Paradigm Literally, a model, template, or matrix for making or evaluating something. A paradigm is usually an object or item as distinct from a set of rules. In common parlance, *paradigm* is roughly equivalent to *conceptual framework, conceptual scheme,* or even *ideology.* A paradigm can also be either an *exemplar*—an exemplary concrete problem solution—or a *disciplinary matrix*—an entrenched point of view and a corresponding set of practices that organize the efforts of a community of investigators to emulate exemplars.

Relativism The view that there is no objective justification, no neutral way to justify a set of claims, that they can be established or at least stabilized only within a particular, unprovable conceptual framework that will be incompatible with other, competing frameworks. Crude relativism asserts that all claims are equally valid, that what is true for you need not be true for me even when we are seemingly making objective claims about the world.

Structuralism In its broadest sense the holistic view that meaning or intelligibility is not intrinsic to individual items (letters, words, atoms, etc.) in isolation but resides in their relations to one another, their functional place in a system (as a word's place in the structure of a language). Systems of relations among items at one level of description constitute new, more abstract levels of reality, as when an organized collection of components constitutes a computer—or a legal system. More narrowly, structuralism is the theory that many relational patterns of everyday human activity, including language, have a common structure explainable by postulating the existence of "deep structures" (either mental or nonmental) that generate the common patterns—a kind of cultural genetic code. These deep structures are theorized to vary from culture to culture and from one historical period to another.

*A **PARADIGM SHIFT** is a change from one paradigm to another by a professional group or community, institution, or even an individual. A paradigm shift occurs in a field of physical science when the community of investigators in that discipline abandons one paradigm in favor of another, incommensurable with it. This article examines the roles of paradigms and especially of paradigm shifts in creative thought and practice.*

I. PARADIGM SHIFT AS A THEORY OF CREATIVITY

The term *paradigm* derives from a Greek word meaning "to show side by side." In the wide sense, a paradigm is a model or ideal of something, a standard of comparison, something to be emulated or avoided as the case may be. Like its near synonyms *archetype* and *prototype, paradigm* is mildly ambiguous, designating either a particular or a universal. That is, a paradigm can be a particular, concrete item that is especially clear and instructive or at least typical (a "paradigm case"), or, more abstractly, it may be a general type, pattern, template, or matrix that the particular cases exemplify, embody, or copy. In manufacturing, a single, successful prototype or model may provide the basis for a decision to set up a mass-production process that will routinely produce good copies of the original. This process may employ a matrix, as when molten metal is poured into matrices, molds, or forms in a foundry.

Since the 1960s, *paradigm* and *paradigm shift* have been used in these senses to describe and explain the development, first, of the physical sciences, and then, by extension, of just about any creative activity or, indeed, any sort of regularized practice and major change

in practice. For example, the term has appeared in IBM advertisements and regularly occurs in U.S. political debate.

The paradigm idea is important to studies of creativity in two ways. Work within a paradigm is *convergent* thinking, while a paradigm change signals *divergent* thinking. Let us begin with convergent thinking. This can be work guided by a set of rules or by standard models, or both. The paradigm idea is often invoked to account for the nonrule aspects of convergent learning and problem solving (although in popular usage an established set of rules or procedures may be called a paradigm). The central idea is that we (sometimes, at least) learn by example rather than by rule. That is, we learn to handle new instances by directly modeling them on stored, concrete experiences of previously encountered cases. This seems to occur when we directly perceive something as a swan rather than a goose. We seem to apply stored patterns of what typical swans and geese look like rather than to apply rules or definitions that we have memorized. At least we are usually unable to articulate the defining rules (precise necessary and sufficient conditions) for being a swan and being a goose. Similarly, in problem solving we may attempt to solve a new problem by seeing it as like one or more problems (exemplars) we already know how to solve, rather than by trying to derive a solution from scratch by applying a method or set of rules, including definitions. Obviously, such work depends on perceiving resemblances among problem situations, on recognizing analogies. In both cases critics will counter that we are applying rules at a subconscious level. [*See* PROBLEM SOLVING.]

The classical example of a rule-based model of inquiry is Euclidean geometry. New theorems are proved by deriving them from axioms and from previously proved theorems by means of logical and mathematical rules. However, this requirement for geometrical proofs does not force us into a rules' account of what is going on when we think geometrically. Our discrimination of distinct geometrical and logical forms may depend on subconscious pattern matching rather than rules—although, again, the critic may propose a rule-based account of pattern matching. Be that as it may, even in Euclidean geometry we may discover how to do a proof by modeling the present problem on a proof we already know; so example-based or case-based reasoning (as it is called in artificial intelligence) can be valuable even when working within an explicitly rule-based system.

Paradigm *shifts* represent creative behavior of a more *divergent* variety—creative leaps that break away from conventional rules and standard ways of perceiving, thinking, and acting. What exactly a paradigm shift amounts to depends on the kind of learning system in which it occurs. Given a rules model of convergent learning and problem solving, a paradigm shift breaks out of the old system of rules and establishes new rules. Given an exemplar-based (non-rule-based) account of learning and problem solving, a paradigm shift installs a new set of exemplars (or at least transforms the status of those retained) and, more important, changes the network of similarity or analogy relations by which one item is perceived as sufficiently like another to be treated in the same way. [*See* DIVERGENT THINKING.]

In either case, a paradigm shift introduces a new classification system or taxonomic grid that lumps and splits items in the world in a different way than before. Such a scheme typically acquires an evaluative-appraisal role, because it introduces new models or rules. A paradigm shift is a shift in accounting system. Such a shift can be controversial because the new classification usually includes categories of items that did not exist in the old taxonomy, and vice versa. Accordingly, the world "looks" quite different through the new grid.

The two major kinds of reclassification through paradigm change are called *branch jumping* and *tree switching*. These terms stem from the fact that classification systems typically have a hierarchical or "tree" structure, in which one major type or branch divides into subtypes, each one of those in turn branches into subsubtypes, and so on. As familiar examples, think of a family tree or of the chart representing the power hierarchy of a large organization. Here the branches represent status in the family or the company. In the latter case, the highest authority may be labeled "president," with several vice presidents reporting to the president, several directors reporting to each vice president, and so on, down to the ordinary workers (the smallest branches or twigs) at the bottom of the hierarchy. Better yet, think of the hierarchical classification of

animals. The animal kingdom branches into distinct phyla, which in turn branch into distinct classes, which branch into orders, which split into families, which divide into genera, which branch into species. Human beings belong to the species *homo,* the genus *sapiens,* the *hominid* family, the primate order, the class of mammals, and so on.

Now branch jumping means reclassifying or relocating something thought to belong to one branch to another branch of the same tree, as when the whale, thought to be a fish, was reclassified as a mammal. Before the work of the meteorologist and chemist John Dalton, ordinary air was believed to be a solution of distinct gases. After his atomic theory of the elements was accepted, the atmosphere was reclassified as a mixture. Sometimes new branches are introduced, and sometimes old branches disappear completely. For example, scientists no longer believe in witches, phlogiston, caloric, or the ether. However, one person's branch may be another's tree (because the world of one's specialty area is defined as a branch of a larger tree); so the appearance or disappearance of whole branches provides a transition to the more pervasive kind of change termed tree switching.

In tree switching the entire tree (or what counts as the tree for one's own specialty) is replaced by another tree embodying a different principle of organization. Something of this sort occurred when Darwin replaced the static classification system of Linnaeus by a system of evolutionary classification, in which the branches now indicated causal relations of evolutionary descent (a kind of genetic pattern matching) rather than timeless logical relationships (definitional rules). Think also of Mendeleev's arrangement of known and unknown chemical elements into the modern table of the elements, replacing older organizing schemes. In both cases most of the old items were retained in the new arrangement or pattern, yet such a shift transformed our view of the world and ascribed old items a different value than before.

Our discussion so far suggests five different models or theories of creativity.

1. *Learning-by-example or case-based-reasoning.* Here creative behavior consists in seeing analogies or similarities of new problems to old problems and their so-

lutions, with no explicit use of rules. This account is exemplar-based and mainly convergent, involving no paradigm shift. [*See* ANALOGIES.]

2. *Exemplar-based, divergent thinking.* In this case creative behavior produces transformative (more than merely additive and subtractive) changes in the library of exemplars and fundamentally alters the similarity relations. The distinction between Model 1 and Model 2 is not sharp: Seeing a new way to model a single problem can be revolutionary enough to lead to a paradigm shift, as when Newton saw the moon as a falling apple.

3. *Convergent, rule-based thinking within a single system of rules.* Here creative behavior consists in finding new applications for the same set of rules. On this rules account of creativity, there is only a difference of degree between minor and major instances of creative behavior. A creative breakthrough is achieved by someone who achieves deeper insight into the consequences of the system of rules. Accordingly, some commentators fail to appreciate that very surprising and creative results can follow even from a simple system of rules, with no rule breaking. A famous case is Kurt Gödel's astounding proof that there is no system of axioms and rules that captures all the truths of simple arithmetic. More widely known are the dramatic results of chaos theory in which a system governed by simple, deterministic laws, such as the familiar desk toys, may yet exhibit amazingly complex behavior.

4. *Rule-breaking divergence.* This is the idea that genuine creativity requires daring leaps that break the rules and establish new rules. This theory of creativity is rule based and divergent and clearly involves a paradigm shift.

5. *The various mixed accounts of creativity that involve both direct modeling on exemplars and the use of rules.* Such an account may be either divergent or convergent, paradigm breaking or not. Talk of a paradigm shift usually invokes Model 2 or 4, or else a mixture of one of these with something else.

Does the fundamental innovation of paradigm change amount to recombining elements already available into a new pattern or does it replace the old elements by something altogether novel or possibly imported from another field? Is scientific progress basically additive or does scientific innovation transform previous results almost out of recognition, so that

progress is largely illusory? Thomas Kuhn's work lent an urgency to these questions.

II. THOMAS KUHN'S ACCOUNT OF PARADIGMS AND SCIENTIFIC CREATIVITY

Following the psychologist J. P. Guilford, educationists often operationally define creativity as divergent thinking, as if divergence is part of the very meaning of creativity. However, in his original model of creativity, Thomas Kuhn, a physics-trained historian and philosopher of science, rejected the dominant view that creativity in the sciences and the arts requires divergent thinking. At least in the physical sciences, he claimed, innovation is normally the product of convergent thinking and results in piecemeal extensions of the established framework. For only when a highly disciplined scientific community can take for granted basic aims, standards, and techniques can it focus research on the most esoteric but revealing details. The social sciences and philosophy, Kuhn said, are too undisciplined, too divergent, to build consensual structures of theory and practice because they expend too much energy debating fundamental questions. Kuhn's paradox is that (in the physical sciences at least) convergent research is the most efficient way to divergent results! The convergent conduct of normal science turns out to be the fastest way to a genuine revolution, because the detailed work made possible by the convergent framework is eventually bound to disclose anomalies that resist solution in terms of that paradigm, thereby provoking a crisis. [*See* INNOVATION.]

Kuhnian inquiry involves an "essential tension" between tradition and innovation, between convergent and divergent thinking. Creative inquiry clearly requires innovation, but if innovation is too divergent and too rapid, Kuhn contended, a field loses so much coherence that it is no longer clear how to evaluate or even to recognize innovation as such. Esoteric research becomes pointless, even meaningless, without a common basis of shared meaning. A well-defined problem presupposes established constraints on the solution, so constraint-free problem-solving becomes a contradiction in terms. To heed philosopher Karl Popper's call for "scientific revolution in perpetuity" as a way to speed up scientific progress would have precisely the opposite result, Kuhn said. It would destroy science as we know it. Margaret Boden furnished an example from a different sphere: An attempt to introduce atonal music in the 17th century would not have been recognized as music at all, and its composer/performer would have been dismissed as an irrelevant crank.

The previous remarks about the essential tension must be qualified. First, Kuhn did not mean that each individual researcher's work must express the essential tension by being equally convergent and divergent at all times. The tension is primarily a tension within the scientific community as a whole, some members of which will be more convergent than others. Second, in *The Structure of Scientific Revolutions* Kuhn changed the emphasis somewhat, so that the formerly pervasive essential tension of the creative act is now expressed most obviously in successive, alternating periods of highly convergent, tradition-bound, *normal* science, during which an entire scientific field is deeply committed to a single paradigm, and periods of divergent, extraordinary science, when the hold of the paradigm is broken. These latter are crisis periods. Sometimes the crisis can be resolved in favor of the old paradigm, but sometimes not, whence come the decisive, divergent breaks called paradigm shifts. [*See* SCIENCE.]

Kuhn held that a paradigm shift occurs when an old paradigm is shoved aside and replaced by another that is *incommensurable* with it. Members of each of the competing paradigm communities may reject the work of the other for its misguided aims and sloppy work ("That's not the way to do good physics!"). A reliable sign of incommensurability is communication breakdown, including failure to agree on what is a good problem and what counts as a solution. Lost is the "ease and fulness of communication" among practitioners and their "unanimity of agreement" over correct problem solutions—harmonies normally guaranteed by work within a common paradigm. Applied to the history of science, this means that the growth of scientific knowledge—scientific creativity—is not cumulative. Some of the most ingenious results of one paradigm may be dismissed as wrong headed by practitioners of its successor paradigm. Yesterday's scientific successes may be rejected or ignored today, and today's heretics may be tomorrow's heroes.

In short, Kuhn's essential tension between tradition and innovation now expresses itself chiefly in temporally separate stages. Normal science explores the one, orthodox viewpoint or form of practice in great depth until its potential appears to be exhausted. Further innovation requires scientists to break out of the old conceptual framework and establish a new one, a new research tradition fundamentally at odds with the first.

At first Kuhn was very unclear about the meaning of *paradigm*. In the second edition of *Structure* and in other writings, he responded to criticism by distinguishing paradigms in the "small" sense—*exemplars*—from paradigms in the "large" sense—*disciplinary matrices*. Contrary to rule-based accounts of scientific cognition advocated by philosophers, social scientists, and other proponents of scientific method, Kuhn insisted that normal research amounts to solving new puzzles by direct modeling on exemplars; and scientific education involves learning to use the exemplars as reference points in a network of "acquired similarity relations." Meanwhile, the disciplinary matrix more globally defines research within a single conceptual framework and a corresponding, rigid organization of community practices.

Philosopher Stephen Toulmin criticized Kuhn's theory of science and of creative development in general for positing an overly rigid and inflexible account of normal science and, correspondingly, being forced to introduce overly revolutionary breaks out of the old framework. A related criticism is that, like speciation in biology, we can only determine a genuine paradigm break retrospectively, because no one at the time could know where the current variations might lead. Kuhn claimed to find such sharp breaks only because he attempted to project in the forward direction of scientific work the intellectual shock he experienced as a novice historian of science trained in modern physics when he had to jump back across the centuries to make sense of the physics of Aristotle. Working scientists, the criticism runs, are never faced with such big jumps, nor are they as historically sensitive as professional historians are specially trained to be.

In *Human Understanding,* Toulmin defended an evolutionary model of scientific creativity in place of Kuhn's revolutionary model. Several other evolutionary models have been proposed since, such as that of Donald Campbell, who argued that all innovation, at bottom, must be the product of the biological evolutionary mechanism of blind variation plus selective retention of variants that happen to survive in the existing environment. On an evolutionary model of creativity, variation can have pretty ordinary sources (including everyday contingencies of research as well as conscious and subconscious mental play and simple misunderstanding); but it *cannot* be the result of genuine insight into what lies beyond the current frontier of knowledge, for the simple reason that we cannot know now what we shall only know later. Such an account, which, in effect posits a kind of brainstorming as the root of all creativity, sounds divergent, but the divergence can be so local and limited that it is part of an overall convergent process. In Kuhnian normal science, research puzzles are well defined by the established paradigm and scientists already know what sort of solution to seek, so any blind variation search process is heavily constrained. Once in a while, however, such variation opens up fruitful new ways of working that may lead to eventual revolution. [*See* BRAINSTORMING.]

III. PARADIGMS, PROTOTYPES, FRAMES, SCHEMAS, AND CASES

Paradigm is often used more or less synonymously with the terms *conceptual scheme, conceptual framework,* and the like. A paradigm shift therefore amounts to a change in conceptual framework. The idea of a conceptual scheme or framework originated with the philosopher Immanuel Kant, who held that all human beings (and to some extent all rational agents) represent their experience of the world in terms of a dozen underlying categories, such as substance and cause, plus two "forms of intuition"—space and time. The fact that we experience the world as physical objects moving and causally interacting in space and time is a fact about our cognitive systems, said Kant, a fact about the way we process raw data from the world, and not a fact about the way the world itself is. Although the real world does make a contribution to the content of our experience, the *form* of that experience is imposed by the human mind. The basic patterns that we perceive in nature, including basic scientific laws, reflect the structure of the mind rather than the structure of the world.

For Kant the system of categories and forms of intuition was absolute and unchangeable, innately prewired, so to speak. But once the idea of a comprehensive conceptual framework was formulated, it was not long before the philosopher G. W. F. Hegel (d. 1831) introduced the idea of *alternative* conceptual frameworks. In Hegel's grand vision the distinctive major epochs of human history are structured by different conceptual frameworks. The frameworks themselves are products of historical development and have an essential social dimension; they are not innately wired into our individual cognitive systems. They are products of nurture, not nature. In fact, Hegel postulated a kind of sociological reversal of the received views of mind and world: rather than society at large reflecting the structure of the individual human mind, we individuals acquire our cognitive apparatus from the social culture into which we are born. This was a radical idea, for it implied that (a) people living in different historical periods live in different worlds, at least different worlds of human experience; (b) the people are not aware of this historical variety and they mistakenly think that the truths self-evident to them are absolute truths about the structure of the universe rather than historical-cultural products that will probably go out of fashion during a future change in framework; and (c) therefore the permanent status of any conceptual system, including even logic and scientific method, is called into question.

In these radical consequences we find the major source of the problem of *relativism*. How can we justify the claim that our most basic truths (of science, morality, politics, religion, etc.) are really truths at all if other peoples can equally defend their own basic beliefs and practices? Indeed, if each conceptual system is underlain by basic principles that are beyond argument in this way, then how can proponents of distinct systems even rationally debate their merits? How can they reason together productively if they disagree about what is self-evident?

This background is important for understanding Kuhnian paradigm shifts, for Kuhn's idea of paradigm owes much to Kant's idea of a conceptual scheme, and Kuhn's move away from the position of positivism parallels Hegel's move away from Kant—and raises many of the same difficulties. The dominant 20th-century philosophy of science prior to Kuhn was logical positivism, which held, among many other things, that scientific concepts and principles have a timeless existence and validity. Once established, they provide a permanent, neutral framework for all future investigation, a permanent language of science—rather like an absolute, Kantian conceptual scheme. Kuhn, with his idea of paradigm, historicized the positivist view, much as Hegel had historicized Kant. A scientific field does not accumulate results within a single conceptual framework, over its entire history, Kuhn contended. Rather, it experiences a succession of paradigms and corresponding, dramatic, conceptual changes.

Unlike Hegel, however, Kuhn did not believe there is any absolute power (God or Reason) driving historical development toward a predetermined correct end, so Kuhn's problem of relativism is potentially worse than Hegel's. Kuhn repeatedly attempted to defend his controversial claims that (a) a paradigm shift is a change in world, so that scientists working under different paradigms literally live in different worlds; and (b) paradigm shifts are incommensurable, that is, the break is so severe that there is no way to make the transition rational, or even to avoid communication breakdown across the boundary. Kuhn, however, denied being a relativist and an irrationalist and called for a new, historically dynamic conception of rationality. Yet some critics have found his position hard to distinguish from T. S. Eliot's, that rational debate over fundamentals is impossible. To some readers, Kuhn's theory of science suggests the vaguely Romantic conclusion that there can be no rational account of highly divergent creativity.

As a conceptual scheme, a Kuhnian paradigm is something larger, more comprehensive, and more *holistic,* than an individual hypothesis or law or set of data. Kuhn and contemporaries such as Toulmin, Paul Feyerabend, Imre Lakatos, and Larry Laudan introduced into the philosophy of science some larger-sized units of analysis than the data statements, laws, and hypotheses of the positivists and Popper. They made this move to larger structures in order to handle the fact that the history of science does not display a scatter-gun effort of inventing and testing dozens of unrelated hypotheses in isolation but instead reveals the existence of ongoing research programs or traditions of thought and practice. Kuhn went further than most in seeing paradigms as demarcating deep *cultural* traditions in the sciences.

Recent cognitive science has fruitfully employed various counterparts to Kuhnian paradigms. Kant's work again provides some perspective. His idea of a conceptual framework introduced a cognitive turn into our theories of human cognition and action. No longer did the world simply present itself to us as it really is, as the old philosophical schools of empiricism and rationalism both held in some degree. Rather, the world as we experience it is the product of a great deal of human cognitive processing, with Kant's categories functioning as basic processing rules. Change the rules and you change the world of experience.

Although he abjured a rules account of cognition, as we have seen, Kuhn made a similar cognitive turn. He introduced his paradigms during the 1960s, a period that produced a major cognitive turn within psychology, against the narrow empiricism of behaviorism and positivism. The basic idea is that how we perceive the world depends not only on the (history of) physical stimuli impinging on our sensory surfaces but also on our internal state (our beliefs and desires and the elaborate cognitive processing mechanism itself, whether rule governed or not). For example, psychologists introduced "mental sets" to explain why we perceive things in one way rather than another—or fail to perceive them at all. The overall point is that the world is not just given to us as it is: what we perceive depends also upon our take on it. To Kuhn and many contemporaries, this implied that even scientific observation is influenced by theories to which we are deeply committed, and it challenged the positivist-empiricist view that observational data are theory neutral. This problem of the theory ladenness of observation connects with the relativism problem mentioned earlier, for if we cannot help observing the world in the light of our deepest theories (paradigms) and the corresponding deep-cognitive processes, then how can we test these theories fairly and objectively?

The field of artificial intelligence (AI) has introduced similar concepts in attempting to explain why our experience (or a computer's behavior) is organized into larger structures in the way that it is. *Frames, scripts,* and *schemas* are three prominent examples of structures postulated to explain how we recognize and classify items and situations. How do we make sense of our situation in a fast-food restaurant or in a bank, once we become familiar with these establishments? One suggestion is that we have acquired from experience cognitive structures that script the typical, complex sequence of activities in, say, a restaurant (enter door, walk toward counter, get in line, place order, receive order, pay for order, carry tray of food to empty table, etc.). These structures will have default values that can be overridden by local perceptual information such as that in this restaurant one is given a paper cup to fill one's own drink.

For reasons of cognitive efficiency AI researchers often provide their programs with contrast enhancers. To avoid bogging down the classification scheme by noisy data and borderline cases, the contrast enhancer cleans up (eliminates) much of the noise, enhances the similarity among the members of a particular category, and also exaggerates the contrast with items in other categories. Geese are made to resemble each other more than they actually do and to look more different from swans than they actually do. Thus can the demands of cognitive economy lead to stereotyping. Comparable mechanisms heighten the contrast between competing Kuhnian paradigms, perhaps making the break seem larger than it is. An interesting question is whether such enhancement affects our judgments of creative divergence in general.

There has also been much recent AI work in case-based reasoning, in which programs attempt to solve new problems by modeling them on one or more already solved problems stored in a case library rather than using rules to derive a solution from scratch each time. This seems close to what Kuhn had in mind with his idea of exemplars. Critics hold that human beings as well as computers must really be using rules at subconscious levels, for example, rules for finding similar cases. On the other hand, cognitive psychologist Eleanor Rosch and her associates have long contended that people recognize birds, chairs, and most everything else not by applying sets of necessary and sufficient rules or definitions of *bird* and *chair* but rather by matching the new item to a stored model or prototype. Rules tend to have an all-or-nothing character: Something is either a bird or it is not. However, human perceptual judgment seems to operate with something like a Kuhnian or Roschian similarity metric that admits of degrees of resemblance. For example, we judge a robin to be a more typical bird (and more easily recognized as a bird) than a penguin is. [*See* ARTIFICIAL INTELLIGENCE.]

Kuhn's work also revives part of the old debate between rhetoric and logic. For in stressing the importance of analogy, metaphor, and the network of similarity relations while abjuring rule-based models of cognition, Kuhn, in effect, contended that human cognition, including creative cognition, is rhetorical rather than strictly logical. Indeed, there would seem to be a continuity between ordinary, convergent cognition (e.g., recognizing the fact that raindrops are falling into the pond) and divergent cognition (e.g., describing the same scene in terms of polka-dots or visualizing light photons hitting a cathode as like raindrops striking the surface of a pond). Both involve pattern matching, but the more divergent behavior stretches the similarity metric, or it finds similarity at a higher level of abstraction.

We see, then, that deep controversies in cognitive psychology, artificial intelligence, learning theory, and sociology of knowledge lie at the heart of the debates over Kuhn's work on paradigms and over competing accounts of creativity. That human cognition works like a digital computer, applying rules to transform strings of symbols that convey information, is still the standard model in much cognitive psychology, although it faces increasing competition. According to this view, cognition is a logical machine and creative problem solving amounts to using logical rules and heuristic strategies to explore a space of possible solutions, as chess-playing computers do. An alternative, more Kuhnian sort of account holds that non-rule-based pattern matching is fundamental to cognition. Meanwhile, sociologists of knowledge deplore the cognitive psychologists' emphasis on individual cognition and stress the importance of social recognition for something to be accounted a discovery or creative success. Here we meet the essential tension again. After all, something will not count as a new kind of thingamajig if no one recognizes it as a thingamajig at all.

IV. WIDER IMPLICATIONS

Previous sections have alluded to several models of creativity that, for present purposes, we can organize into opposing pairs: (a) creative processes are divergent versus convergent; (b) novelty is the invention of totally new elements versus the rearrangement of already existing elements; (c) creative processes are revolutionary rather than evolutionary, that is, discontinuous and nonlinear rather than continuous and linear (a nonlinear change is one in which a small change can have a disproportionately large effect, like the straw that broke the camel's back); (d) creativity is the product of deliberate, insightful, conscious design (a goal-directed process) versus the product of blind variation and selective retention (evolution again). However, these apparently competing models can be reconciled as complementary, to some degree and in some contexts.

A major issue concerning the development of just about anything (including embryological development of biological organisms from a fertilized egg, the cognitive development of children and of individual adult scientists, and the development of human culture as a whole) is whether that development is continuous and gradual or discontinuous with abrupt transformations. Is a given development evolutionary or revolutionary? Does it follow a smooth trajectory from one point to another in development space or does it jump from place to place?

On the one hand, in the case of human cognitive development, the default position would seem to be evolutionary continuity. If Darwinian accounts of evolution are basically correct, then all plant and animal species, including human beings, have evolved gradually. A roughly similar, although more contentious, evolutionary story can be told about the history of human cultures as well as about the lives of individual persons. But if cognitive growth is evolutionary and if evolution is gradual and linear, then how could major discontinuities or nonlinearities even be possible? Such accounts would seem to call for special justification. The default position assumes that evolution is linear. How can mere quantitative changes produce the fairly rapid appearance of qualitative change?

On the other hand, discontinuity accounts of various kinds of development are quite common. After all, we often speak of political revolutions in the history of human societies, and major earthquakes and volcanic eruptions interrupt centuries of slow geological change. Even while stressing that scientific discovery has a historical structure and sometimes portraying scientific research in evolutionary terms, Kuhn himself, using stock expressions such as "the scales fell from his eyes," still spoke of sudden, almost religious conversions or "Gestalt switches" to a new paradigm.

Kuhn was not the first to hold such views. Roman-tic accounts of creativity have long insisted that new ideas frequently come to their ingenious discoverer in a flash of intuitive insight. German and English poets and painters in the early decades of the 19th century claimed that a sensitive soul could experience a momentary epiphany that revealed the truth about the universe with particular clarity. Later, philosophers of science such as Popper retained elements of this model in contending that there could be no logic of scientific discovery because the creation of a new hypothesis, like the composition of a new poem or sonata (*sic*!), is an irrational act, one often accompanied by an "aha" experience. [*See* INSIGHT; INTUITION.]

A second source of the discontinuity view is the so-called stage theory of development according to which the development of human culture, or a nation, or a person occurs in discrete stages marked by relatively sudden transitions from one to the next. (On most but not all theories, the stages represent progress.) We have already seen how Hegel turned Kant's ahistorical perspective into a historical succession of quasi-Kantian epochs. Then Karl Marx in turn transformed Hegel's idea of intellectual stages into stages of material, economic development. In Marx's theory of Western history, the ancient, Greco-Roman modes of economic production and exchange eventually yielded to medieval feudalism; then came the capitalist era, which will be supplanted by socialism at some future time. In the early decades of the 20th century, Sigmund Freud and the Swiss psychologist Jean Piaget each advanced stage theories of individual development. In Piaget's theory of cognitive development, a sensorimotor period is succeeded by a preoperational period that lasts from around age 2 to age 7. Then comes a concrete operations period, followed by a formal operations period, by which time the cognitively mature young adult can manipulate abstract symbols, think logically, and perform operations on other operations. Today, developmental psychologists such as Susan Carey debate whether children undergo Kuhn-like paradigm shifts. The educationist William Perry has developed a stage theory of intellectual maturation of young people (students) from an early absolutist perspective through various kinds of relativism to more sophisticated kinds of judgment. [*See* DEVELOPMENTAL TRENDS IN CREATIVE ABILITIES AND POTENTIALS.]

Twentieth-century French thinkers such as Gaston Bachelard, Georges Canguilem, and Michel Foucault also have theorized the existence of "ruptures" or "epistemological breaks" separating distinct periods in the development of science and society. Foucault used such terms as *discursive formation, regime of practices,* and *episteme* rather than *paradigm* for his long-term cultural formations. Kuhn's position has also been compared with *structuralism,* a position developed by Ferdinand de Saussure in linguistics and extended to anthropology and other fields by writers such as Claude Lévi-Strauss. According to structuralism, human activities have a symbolic or "semiotic" character and fall into repeating patterns underlain by systematic "deep structures" that vary discontinuously from culture to culture and from one period to another.

Insofar as the structures posited by these "discontinuity" accounts are rigid, it is difficult to see how there could be an easy, evolutionary transition from one to the other. This point is especially apparent for the various versions of structuralism, all of which hold, roughly, that the meaning of each element of the structure is determined not by its own intrinsic nature or essence but by its relations to all the other elements, that is, by its place in the overall, abstract structure. Thus structuralism is committed to a kind of holism: any change in the system structure or organization threatens to be nonlinear, because it will alter all the relations, at least somewhat.

We can now return to our old question: Given a relational system, should we say that novelty consists in introducing entirely new elements or only in altering the relations among the items already there? Surprisingly, there need be no incompatibility between these two ways of speaking, as long as we distinguish two levels of description. Consider these examples. The bricks taken from the walls of an old warehouse can be reassembled to build a new restaurant—or a home, or a city plaza, depending on their context and arrangement. Rearranging the order of the very same musical notes can result in a totally new song. Students from a school can be reorganized to form a debate team—or an army unit. Rearranging even a few letters or words in an important telegram can transform its meaning. Interestingly, many theorists now see biological evolution itself as driven more by the variations produced by recombinations of clusters of genes in sexual mating than by chance mutations of individual genes.

Philosophers and historians question whether Ein-

stein's theory of relativity merely altered the relations between the Newtonian concepts of force, mass, velocity, space, time, and so on, or whether Einstein's theory introduced novel, changed concepts. Kuhn's view was that the relativity revolution might become

> a prototype for revolutionary reorientations in the sciences. Just because it did not involve the introduction of additional objects or concepts, the transition from Newtonian to Einsteinean mechanics illustrates with particular clarity the scientific revolution as a displacement of the conceptual network through which scientists view the world.

A related question is whether relativity introduced genuine conceptual change or only changed beliefs about the old concepts. Can concepts themselves change? Perhaps not, but the meaning of words and technical symbols can certainly change over time. This is precisely Kuhn's point about the Einsteinean revolution. Critics complain that Kuhn exaggerated the problems of deep conceptual change and thereby created the difficulties about paradigms being incommensurable.

The idea of multiple levels of description provides a way to reconcile revolutionary with evolutionary models of creativity, in some cases. The elements and relations of a system may gradually evolve by means of hardly perceptible changes when, relatively suddenly, it becomes possible to reinterpret the complex as a quite different relational system. This frequently happens in detective stories and in historical and scientific work, in which investigators, upon reexamining a body of data and theory that may have grown slowly over the years, can now read into them a new pattern. Even if all creative activity is driven by an evolutionary process of blind variation followed by selective retention (mostly at subconscious levels), remarkable new complexes may occasionally emerge among the variants. A familiar example is that every work of English literature, from Shakespeare to science fiction, is expressed in terms of various combinations of the same, rather small set of letters and punctuation marks of the English alphabet. As noted earlier, a slight recombination can change the meaning totally—or render a piece completely meaningless. Consider the experience of translating a paragraph from a foreign language or of straining to make sense of the pattern of sounds heard over the telephone when the radio is playing too loudly.

The multiple levels view can therefore, to some extent, reconcile the Greek model of creative design, as bringing harmonious order out of a preexisting chaos, with the Judeo-Christian model, as creation from nothing. Actually, both models are suggested by the opening verses of Genesis. According to one tradition, God, the most creative being of all, created the world *ex nihilo*. Making an intricately designed piece of work from nothing is as creative as one can be! But this is not wholly incompatible with the other model of creation: imposing order on chaos. Consider that the emergence of meaningful form or design out of the rearrangement of preexisting elements does, in a sense, create something entirely new, at the design level of description. This, too, is creation from nothing in the sense that the present design or intelligible pattern does not necessarily derive from some previous pattern, nor does it reduce to the intrinsic nature of the basic elements themselves. It seems to appear out of nowhere. [*See* DESIGN.]

Sometimes this newly perceived order in things, the new take on things, presents itself quite suddenly. Indeed, evolutionary theory itself suggests that it must (although some would contend that Kuhnian revolutions, like biological speciation, can only be identified as such retrospectively). We must be able to size up situations quickly, as a matter of survival. We and the other animals possess a "rage for order": we must impose meaningful patterns on the world, and soon. Accordingly, we detect or impose patterns and jump quickly to new patterns that seem more reliable or more economical than the old ones. This forcing the world to make sense to us is accomplished by our, usually hurried, lumping and splitting practices. For example, we lump things together into handy classes, as we saw earlier with stereotyping. Human beings and other animals do not have the cognitive capacity to track each item they encounter as a distinct individual. We can handle only a limited variety of things and that, unfortunately, means that stereotyping is inevitable.

Kuhn's view of scientific research is rather similar. Paradigms are patterns that we impose on the world in order to make sense of it, but paradigms involve a kind of stereotypical lumping and splitting and are therefore almost certainly unable to handle the diversity of phenomena that will emerge when research discloses the esoteric detail. In response to these anomalies, one or more researchers may find another pattern that makes more sense to them and invite others to leap to it—and a new paradigm is born.

Finally, if Kuhn is right that paradigms demarcate distinct cultural communities, each with its own ethnicity, then teachers attempting to instill new paradigms in students are engaged in a form of cultural imperialism, at least insofar as the education is involuntary. So much for the ideal of the teacher as a neutral, objective presentor of established knowledge! A related cultural implication of Kuhn's view of paradigms is that genuinely interdisciplinary work is very difficult. The literary critic Stanley Fish has argued that no one can be fully at home in two or more distinct disciplinary communities, for such a person will speak each professional language with an accent, reflecting her other commitments. She will remain something of an outsider to each discipline from which she draws. And her disciplinary mixing of materials is bound to depart somewhat from the shared understandings of the full-blooded natives. Nor will she be fully aware of this unless prompted by the natives. A certain amount of ethnographic appropriation, or at least insensitivity, is unavoidable.

A similar problem arises for historians and for scientists themselves who claim to revive ideas they find in earlier work in their own field. Purists can rightly point out that their borrowings from the past are not fully authentic, for they bring to the subject understandings that previous generations could not possibly have possessed. Imposing our present perspectives on the past (and correspondingly evaluating our forebears as geniuses or idiots insofar as they anticipated our own ideas, or not) is another form of cultural imperialism. It is commonly called the "whig fallacy" or the mistake of "presentism," but Kuhn himself prefers to label it a form of ethnocentrism.

However, when it comes to creativity, does it really matter where the ideas or practices come from or how faithful they are to the culture from which they are borrowed? One may argue that what matters is whether the resulting network of relations works—whether it makes sense and is capable of solving new problems. Here, once again, we find continuity at one level, because we can in principle trace the sources of each element, and discontinuity at another level, as those elements, in their new cultural arrangement, are invested with new meaning and new creative power.

Bibliography

Gutting, G. (1980). *Paradigms and revolutions: Appraisals and applications of Thomas Kuhn's philosophy of science.* Notre Dame, IN: University of Notre Dame Press.

Hoyningen-Huene, P. (1993). *Reconstructing scientific revolutions.* Chicago: University of Chicago Press.

Kuhn, T. S. (1962/1970). *The structure of scientific revolutions.* (2nd ed. with postscript). Chicago: University of Chicago Press.

Kuhn, T. S. (1978). *The essential tension.* Chicago: University of Chicago Press.

Margolis, H. (1993). *Paradigms and barriers.* Chicago: University of Chicago Press.

Nickles, T. (1998). Thomas Kuhn, historical philosophy of science, and case-based reasoning. *Configurations, 6,* 51–85.

Runco, M. (1991). *Divergent thinking.* Norwood, NJ: Ablex.

Thagard, P. (1992). *Conceptual revolutions.* Princeton, NJ: Princeton University Press.

Toulmin, S. (1972). *Human understanding.* Princeton, NJ: Princeton University Press.

Perceptgenesis

Gudmund J. W. Smith

Lund University, Sweden

Creative Functioning Test (CFT) A method whereby a stimulus is first introduced in a perceptgenetic fashion with systematically prolonged exposure times until it is correctly recognized by the viewer, then again presented at systematically abbreviated times. CFT measures if the viewer is closely tied up with what he or she knows to be the correct meaning of stimulus or if he or she rather indulges in subjective interpretations as the support of stimulus is gradually eroded.

Perceptgenesis Alternatively termed microgenesis, a process of construction of reality, proceeding from subjective stages to more and more externalized impressions, partly unconscious, abbreviated and automatized after repeated confrontations with the same stimulus.

Reconstruction Refers to methods used to prolong perceptgeneses and make them available for observation.

Tachistoscope An apparatus facilitating reconstruction of perceptgeneses by means of controlled exposure times, starting below threshold levels. Old contrivances used camera shutters. Nowadays exposure times are electronically steered and swift TV screens used for showing the stimuli.

PERCEPTGENESIS *is a theory of perception that can be used to understand creativity and a concomitant methodology applied for its measurement. In orthodox perceptual theory a perception starts with a retinal pattern that is transmitted to the occipital lobe of the cortex and, secondarily, to other parts of the central nervous system (CNS) involved in the processing of that pattern. Perceptgenesis turns this model topsy-turvy by suggesting that primarily the phylogenetically old parts of the brain are involved in the appraisal of a stimulus and only secondarily the cortex. The main reason for this would be the fundamental importance for the individual of knowing the emotional significance of a new stimulus.*

I. PERCEPTGENESIS

The idea that reality is not immediately there when we look around us but has to be constructed was formulated long ago and was transferred to the United States by Heinz Werner. The process of construction, called Aktualgenese on the continent, was then rechristened microgenesis, a label later adopted by most Americans. The term perceptgenesis seems to have become more popular in Europe. But let us leave terminological considerations aside and go to the heart of the matter, the psychological face of perceptgeneses (PG).

A PG is assumed to proceed from chaos to order or, rather, from stages dominated by subjective representations to more and more externalized impressions. Most of this process is necessarily preconscious; attention must always be directed toward the final product. The use of the term *chaos* alludes to the dreamlike character of reconstructed early process stages (P-phases), their lack of logical structure and their emotional coloring, as opposed to the relatively ordered and autonomous character of late stages (C-phases), intersubjectively concordant. The PGs described here may have a duration of fractions of a second, shorter if the stimulus situation is well known to the perceiver (that is, often encountered). This contraction of PGs with repetition is called *automatization*.

In the efforts to reconstruct PG processes, to make them available for observation, care must be taken to avoid well-known stimuli or stimuli devoid of emotional meaning (e.g., geometric figures). The construction of suitable stimulus material can be very tricky indeed, even if such stimuli are avoided. Unimportant details, if wrongly emphasized, dark surfaces not meant to dominate the motif, may conceal the planned constellation of, for instance, two human beings in interaction, and erase expected interindividual differences.

Many techniques for reconstructing PGs have been tried. This article presents only the tachistoscopic variety. In the early days, stimuli were exposed by means of camera shutters, exposure times being prolonged as systematically as was possible with such primitive tools. The modern variety of a tachistoscope consists of a swift TV screen manipulated by means of a computer. Short exposures, close to the visual limen, are assumed to start the PG. When, at the next presentation, the exposure time is prolonged, the PG continues a tiny distance but has to be nudged forward again by means of a new, still longer stimulation, and so on. Presentations continue until the viewer has reached a correct conception of the stimulus, correctness being determined in relation to the dominant structures of the motif.

Critics of this technique of reconstruction have argued that it interferes with the natural PG, perhaps so much as to distort it and make it unrecognizable. However, everyday perception is also characterized by an analogous succession of interrupted fixations. The main defense of exploiting laboratory-produced PGs, however, points to the existence of meaningful associations between PG characteristics and an array of criteria gathered in research on children, adults, and patients with psychiatric pathologies. PGs could thus hardly be dismissed as methodological artifacts. Studies using PG experiments as tools for personality description date as far back as the 1950s and are still multiplying.

Reconstruction of a PG can be blockaded in many ways. The usual hindrances are caused by defensive operations against anxiety-provoking associations, operations pressed on by the threatening stimulus pictures used in diagnostic studies. The defense mechanism of isolation, for instance, may result in the total obliteration of most PG-phases. The viewer abstains from reporting until close to the C-phase. The obstacles to reconstructing very early P-phases may, however, also be mainly cognitive. If these phases represent very early developmental stages, they do not easily fit into an adult viewer's frame of reference, however flexible. They have no more meaning for the viewer than a blur impossible to make head or tail of.

Normally, a PG terminates in a stimulus-proximal impression. But to be fully integrated with personal experience, the PG must represent a dialectical interplay between subjective and objective factors. This implies open communication between early and late PG-phases. If this openness is not going to trigger defensive counter-operations, the individual must be tolerant of anxiety. Such a tolerance is typical of creative subjects.

II. A PERCEPTGENETIC CREATIVITY TEST

The empirical results presented next are based on the perceptgenetic Creative Functioning Test (CFT). A session with that test proceeds as follows: The test subject is seated before the tachistoscopic screen, told that pictures will be flashed on the screen, and asked to report what he or she has seen after each exposure.

Stimuli used in the test consist of still lifes with no human beings in them. The pictures are simple, built up of two or three main structures. Reports after the exposures may be rich, containing a variety of interpretations, or meager, with reports of nothing but light flashes or of incomprehensible objects. Number of subjective themes is recorded, particularly the presence of human themes. This first of the test series, the *straight PG,* terminates with the correct reporting of the stimulus—three times in a row.

Thereafter, the exposure series is continued with an *inverted PG,* starting at the level of correct recognition and continuing with gradually diminishing exposure values. After the viewer has been impressed by one of the most powerful perceptual clichés—correctness—the question is how snared he or she will be by that cliché. Will it dominate the rest of the inverted sequence, until nothing at all can be glimpsed on the screen, or will the successively diminishing power of exposure times be exploited by the viewer as a chance to again play with idiosyncratic interpretations?

According to the test constructor's original assumption, a return to subjective interpretations indicates creativity. In some instances the viewer may abandon the correct interpretation early in the inverse series, in other instances correct and subjective interpretations are entertained side by side or intermittently. Interpretations may be hesitant or concern only details. Finally, the correct meaning of the stimulus may be preserved while only distance and size are affected: "The motif looks closer to me now." This latter type of flexibility is called sensitivity. At the bottom of this ladder we find those whose inverted series contain nothing but "correct" reports, the presumed low-creatives.

III. VALIDATION STUDIES WITH ADULTS

A considerable number of studies have been performed to validate the claims of the test. An early study dealt with researchers ($n = 18$) who had recently absolved their Ph.D. degrees or were close to doing so. An array of criteria was collected from advisers who knew their students well and from the students themselves. Data were treated in an inverted factor analysis.

Three factors deserve to be specially mentioned. The first of them consisted of persons who were judged as intelligent and efficient but not particularly rich in ideas, not original in their thinking, not deeply engaged in research, and with relatively empty inverted PGs. People in the second factor were also judged as intelligent but not necessarily efficient. On richness in ideas, originality, and engagement, however, they received high scores. And both their straight and inverted PGs had many themes. Additional characteristics were interest in dreaming and closeness to childhood experiences (i.e., openness to their inner lives and personal histories). A third factor could be characterized as a group of mediocre students, neither very bright and efficient nor creative.

Even if the creative researchers reported many incorrect themes in their inverted PGs, they also held on to the correct interpretation, knowing that the stimulus motif had not really disappeared. It seemed a natural thing to do for researchers whose task was to always match deviant ideas against established notions. Evidently, creative students who did not anchor their ideas in physical reality were not likely to get high marks. But in a group of amateur artists and writers ($n = 43$), total immersion in subjectivity often dominated the last stages of the inverted PG.

Creative researchers, more often than low-creatives, revealed proneness to anxiety reactions. The amateurs took part in an experiment designed to reveal the effect of an anxiety provocation on creativity in the CFT. When the straight PG had reached its apex with a correct interpretation, the CFT stimulus was paired with either a threatening or a nonthreatening control stimulus, both of them subliminal, the pair being exposed another five times. Then the test continued with the inverted series as usual. By relying on a number of markers such as early childhood memories, color dreams, attitude to dreaming, and so on, subjects were judged as highly creative, medium creative, and uncreative. The threatening subliminal stimulation affected the medium creatives in particular, enhancing their scores relative to the controls. The high creatives were presumably too close to the ceiling to be really affected, and the low creatives were resistant. A study of psychiatric patients, in all probability with low tolerance of anxiety, using the same design, demonstrated, however, that in them the subliminal provocation could have an obstructing influence.

IV. CREATIVITY IN CHILDREN

Experiments with children from 4 to 16 years of age (altogether 277) produced an interesting picture of the frequency of various CFT scores at different ages. Creativity seemed to be peaking at the ages of 4 to 6 and 10 to 11 years. Low water marks were found around the beginning of regular school in Sweden (7 years) and at prepuberty (about 12 years). The children were also tested with the MCT (the Meta-Contrast Technique), a test aimed at elucidating anxiety and defensive strategies. It was obvious that anxiety surfaced more often in the MCT protocols of creative children than in the uncreative ones. Prepuberty, in particular, was characterized by a drying up of creative ideas, a strengthening of compulsive types of defenses, and low anxiety scores.

When testing the validity of the CFT in children, special care was taken to collect a variety of data to be used as criteria. The children were asked to draw, paint, and sculpt, and their products were assessed by professional artists. But they were also interviewed about their favorite games, about the toys they preferred, ready made or constructed by themselves, about their favorite books, and, above all, their own attempts at composing poetry and music. In order not to forget the young inventors, parts of the interview concerned technical interests. And as with the adults, attitudes to dreaming, and so on, were assessed.

Criterion correlations were obvious, often strong, up to high puberty (13 to 15 years) when they suddenly disappeared. The puberty youngster seemed to reflect group preferences rather than authentic ones. But criterion correlations returned after puberty, earlier in girls than in boys. It was also possible to predict performance in the CFT at age 10 to 11 on the basis of the child's CFT results 5 to 6 years earlier. The two sets of test results correlated .69 (G index of agreement). Even the professional artists' evaluations of the young children's products had a substantial predictive power, as had the child's report of a fantasy playmate.

V. PROFESSIONAL ARTISTS

Because artists are involved in so-called creative work, artists are often assumed, as a matter of course, to be creative. A study of professional artists ($n = 32$)

showed that they performed better in the CFT than other groups. But there were many exceptions. An art professor evaluated the subjects' products in a number of dimensions of which originality, expressiveness, and authenticity yielded the highest correlations with CFT scores. Artists with a formalized and highly structured art production were likely to get low scores. It could also be shown that those reporting human motifs in the straight PG were more inclined to be emotionally involved in their creative endeavors than those lacking such motifs, a finding substantiated in other groups of subjects.

The study of artists also included the MCT. Compulsive isolation and depressive stereotypy, as revealed by MCT signs, were the factors most prone to inhibit creative functioning. An additional negative sign in that study was grave anxiety. The more vague and open the defenses, the better for the outcome in CFT. These results were partly substantiated by another study using a variant of the Defense Mechanism Test called DMTm (*m* for modified) instead of the MCT. High creativity in CFT correlated with signs of introaggression in the DMTm. Evidently, self-destructive tendencies go together with attempts to repair the damage. What could be a more powerful motive for creative endeavors? When assessing creativity the researcher also relied on the number of themes reported in the straight PG arguing that it correlated rather substantially with the inverted PG, although less with independent criteria.

A tailor-made version of the Identity Test (IT) was also applied in the study of artists. Here the thematic stimulus depicted two human beings, quite similar and lacking obvious sexual attributes, who stand half facing each other. One of them is drawn against an open, diffusely structured background, the other placed inside a small room. This stimulus was projected on a screen in front of the viewer, the exposure time being just long enough to allow the viewer to perceive it correctly. A subliminal word *I* (JAG, in Swedish) was projected on one or the other of these figures according to the same design as described below in the aggression-victim version of the test.

The two main scoring dimensions were (a) The picture described in obviously positive words, the environment and the sex of the figures more clearly perceived than before, the subject's interest in the picture increasing, more contact reported between the two figures. (b) The picture described in negative words, the picture depreciated, the subject irritated and losing interest, the sex of the figures changed and the environment concealed or transfigured, attention shifting to the side where *I* is not presented.

The dominating subgroup among the 32 artists differentiated between the alternatives by reacting positively (ambivalently) to one alternative and negatively to the other. Typically, 14 subjects were more positive in the *I*-open series, 2 more positive in the *I*-closed series. Others were negative in both series or generally vague. An inverted factor analysis produced a first factor of 5 artists with low creativity scores, none of them preferring the open alternative. Moreover, subjects given a positive marking for both "form" and "articulation" by the art specialist—a description indicating a static production, dependent on a rigid internal order—also avoided the open alternative. Another low creativity factor of 3 artists showed severe anxiety and signs of depression.

VI. CREATIVITY AND AGGRESSION

Because creative people seem to be more autonomous and self-assertive than noncreative ones, it was assumed that they would rather identify with an aggressor than a victim of aggression. To test this presumption a variant of the Identification Test was used. Here, the second, thematic stimulus depicts two persons standing facing each other, one of them obviously looking like an aggressor and the other like the victim. After the viewer has been adapted to this picture, it is presented at a fixed, rather brief exposure level where the viewer can still deliver correct reports.

A second stimulus, just containing the word *I,* is thereafter exposed immediately before the thematic stimulus, the exposure time being brief enough to prevent it from being detected. This *I* is first directed at one of the two combatants in the picture five times, then at the other one another five times. The order between aggressor and victim series is rotated. Finally, the thematic picture is again presented five times, now alone. Subjects were 33 16-year-olds, 17 of whom were boys.

The protocols were divided in three main categories: (a) clear aggression or gradually increasing aggression reported in the series where *I* was presented on the aggressor, (b) no aggression in any series, and (c) evasive or no reports of aggression in the aggressor series,

but at least some indication of aggression when *I* was flashed on the victim.

By dividing the CFT signs according to the best possible median, we produced a four-field table yielding a *p*-value of .005. The G index of agreement was .71. Thus the most creative subjects saw clear aggression, and the less creatives saw no aggression or were evasive. When compared to MCT data, collected in the same testing session, high CFT scores were more often found in subjects with signs of repression (meaningful transformations of the threat) and sensitivity, less often in subjects with signs of compulsive isolation and depressive stereotypy.

A similar study was done with 33 10- to 12-year-olds. The scoring dimensions were slightly more elaborated than in the foregoing study: (1) more aggression reported by the subject when *I* was projected on the aggressor than when projected on the victim; (2) more signs of anxiety (increasing darkness or more diffuseness) or perceptual distortions when *I* was presented on the victim; (3) the inverse of (1); (4) the inverse of (2); (5) the subjects show obvious signs of fatigue (yawns).

The subjects were divided into three groups according to their IT scores: (a) those who responded as described in categories (1) and (2), (b) those who responded in the opposite way, and a middle group. In the entire sample, 18 youngsters had high or medium creativity scores and 15 had low scores. Of the 12 youngsters with (a) scores in IT, 11 were creative, of the 13 youngsters with (b) scores, only 3 were creative. The middle group of 8 divided evenly between creatives and noncreatives.

This experiment could be regarded as a cross-validation of the first experiment, although these younger children were more reluctant to identify with an aggressor. Even if the creative children did not readily recognize themselves as aggressive, they obviously avoided the role of passive victim.

VII. THE NEUROBIOLOGICAL BASIS OF CREATIVITY

Popular notions of the role of the brain for creative functioning seem to hold that it mainly depends on the right hemisphere, with a simultaneous moderation of the influence of the left hemisphere. To test this assumption, MCT was used in visual half-field situations, either stimulating the right or the left part of the retina, corresponding to the left- or right-brain hemisphere. The MCT was scored for anxiety and defensive strategies according to the 1989 manual. Eighty-four undergraduate students took part in the experiment, evenly divided between the two conditions. All of them were also tested with the CFT.

Low creative subjects, irrespective of visual half-field group, had less signs of sensitivity (or the stronger variant called projection) than more creative subjects. There were no laterality effects. Signs of the mature defense variants of isolation and repression and of the immature variant of regression seemed, however, to differ betweeen the two situations, the two former being more associated with the left hemisphere, the regressive variant with the right hemisphere.

But these differences were only typical of low-creative subjects, not of high-creative ones. In medium-creative subjects a tendency to differentiation remained. In combining the three defensive varieties, a significant difference was found between high-creative and low-creative subjects, the former more often responding with non-hemispheric defenses than the latter. In other words, high-creative subjects are characterized by cooperation between the hemispheres, low-creative subjects by hemispheric isolation. [*See* SPLIT BRAINS: INTERHEMISPHERIC EXCHANGE IN CREATIVITY.]

VIII. CREATIVITY AND PSYCHOSOMATICS

The key assumption behind the CFT is that the creative person keeps an open communication with the preconscious world in order to enrich ideation. If people with psychosomatic ailments suffer from alexithymia (i.e., an inability or unwillingness to find verbal expressions for emotionally tinged conflicts), there should be ample reason to assume that they would get low scores on the CFT. The typical case reports of alexithymia in psychosomatic people have lately been supplemented by more systematic studies with tests. One such study showed alexithymia to be a central characteristic of patients suffering from ulcerative colitis.

In a study of 128 subjects suffering from ulcerative colitis ($n = 24$) or Crohn's disease ($n = 61$) or serving as controls ($n = 43$), a special version of the Identity Test (IT) was employed. In this test a face is flashed on a screen in front of the viewer. Because the flashes are brief and the face indeterminate, the viewer is likely to project aspects of herself in her descriptions of what she has glimpsed on the screen. This projected identification is manipulated by the presentation of subliminal verbal tags like *I, I WELL, I ILL* just prior to the face. The presentations are varied in a systematic design.

Alexithymia did not show itself only in lack of emotional words for the description of the face. There were several strategies to avoid emotional themes. Patients with Crohn's disease often confined themselves to descriptions of details: hair-do, skin, and the like, whereas patients with ulcerative colitis preferred to detect well-known persons behind the face, both groups thus parrying the need to empathize. Sometimes the face was just seen as unintelligible or, because the patient could not describe shifts in the face from one presentation to another, she or he just reported "another person."

The psychosomatic subjects were generally less creative than the controls. A surprising finding was that creative subjects more often saw a positive face in the *I ILL* series and a negative face in the *I WELL* series, apparently resisting the attempts to manipulate their reactions. At the same time the reactions to *I WELL* were not only averse in creative subjects. They also reported active-aggressive persons. It was concluded that if the subliminal message agrees with the creative person's view of him- or herself the reaction can be straight-forward.

IX. CREATIVITY AND AGE

As the ambiguities of old age increase, creativity becomes successively more important to handle them in a constructive manner. But is it a romantic dream, cultivated in certain gerontological circles, that creative functioning is still possible in advanced age? This was tested using the CFT.

Subjects were obtained in collaboration with the Gerontology Research Center in Lund. One group had been subjects in a study of the effects of Selenium (the S group). Another group was recruited from a Pensioner's Association (the Pa group).

The S and Pa groups differed with respect to the proportion of highly creative subjects (15% and 4%). But the rank order was reversed in the medium creative stratum (24% and 44%). All in all, 10% of the elderly were highly creative and 33% medium creative; altogether 43% were identified as creative subjects. This should be compared with 10% highly creatives in a group of 70 individuals aged 24 to 62 years and 30% in 171 youngsters aged 10 to 16 years. Considering the importance of group selection, these data should be treated with caution. But they still seem to relate an important fact: Creativity abates long before old age sets in.

The decline of creative functioning in adult age, perhaps already in the twenties, has been illuminated from many points of view, psychological as well as neurobiological. In the latter perspective, the concept of *parcellation* was introduced to explain what happens in the aging brain (i.e., a thinning out of exuberant neural interconnections in order to achieve specificity). But apparently the juvenile state can be prolonged in some individuals (*neoteny*). Does this mean that creative elderly people have preserved a childish nucleus?

This question was elucidated in an experiment with the above-mentioned group of elderly people. The Identity Test presented a middle-aged face on a screen in front of the subject in a series of brief flashes. Did more creative than uncreative subjects report alternations between the middle-aged face and more youthful ones? This was true in the more highly creative Selenium subgroup but not quite significant in the Pa subgroup.

The previous study had been preceded by another study using subjects with a median age of 22 years. There was a clear correlation between creativity and regressions from adult to childish (< 12 years) or youngish (13–15 years) faces, the childish regression being more common. It is important to notice that creative people do not report only childish faces but alternate between adult and childish ones. To be creative is not to remain infantile but to be in dialectical contact with your childish past. This is what PG theory understands by open inward communication, the prerequisite for creative functioning.

X. CFT CREATIVITY AND SELF-REPORT DATA

Some researchers find it an embarrassment for the CFT that correlations with self-report questionnaires on creativity are usually low. It has been suggested that the CFT and self-reports illuminate different aspects of creative functioning. Moreover, CFT appears to be less affected by the influence of what curtails the usefulness of many self-reports, viz. the bias of social desirability.

XI. THE MEDIUM CREATIVES

Many students of creativity prefer to write about the geniuses of the past or to fraternize with Nobel Prize laureates. The group of medium creatives appear much less exciting, perhaps because they do not inflate the egos of the researchers to the same extent as Mozart, Picasso, or Einstein do. But the medium creatives are an important category. They could be described as people who appreciate and understand breakthroughs in science, poetry, and the arts but are unlikely themselves to initiate them. Highly creative people need the medium creatives in order to catch the attention of a wider audience. In the CFT the medium creatives intimate that subjective contents are again emerging in the inverted series. But their reconstructive efforts remain tentative.

The diversion of attention from the high creatives to the medium creatives was accompanied by a broadened definition of creativity. Perhaps creativity should not be regarded only as an ability to produce new products but more generally as an attitude to life. To be creative in this sense is to be open to change, both outward and inward, or, more precisely, to be able to detect, comprehend, and appreciate new signals from these two worlds. It is a question of creating one's own existence, apart from all the common clichés and stereotyped opinions about what life is really all about.

XII. OUTSTANDING CREATIVES

Subjects scoring high on the CFT have indeed proved themselves to be creative in various endeavors like research and the arts. At the same time most of them could not be described as really outstanding. Even if induced by the "anarchism" of early PG phases to break loose from prevalent rules for scientific or artistic conduct they still appear rather well behaved. It is apparently not enough to have access to early PG phases. Cognitive prerequisites aside, pioneering creative work would hardly be initiated but for a very strong motivational force. The early PG phases setting such creative endeavors in motion are likely to be highly emotionally charged (i.e., to represent crucial emotional problems). Some of the problems may be openly personal, others camouflaged as cognitive riddles. Many such problems seem to be attacked again and again over the life span of a creative person, apparently in attempts to restore a disturbed balance or heal an aching wound. Most fatal for the creative process under these circumstances would be a growing intolerance of rising anxiety and a concomitant sealing up of the reconstructive operations.

It does not seem enough, however, to associate emotionally charged PG phases with pioneering creative motivation. The depth of the reconstructive operations must also be taken into account. Perhaps a strong urge to create increases one's efforts to actualize early PG phases. Even if the hypothesis of a parallelism between ontogenesis and perceptgenesis has not been proved beyond doubt, and perhaps never will, early PG phases are by definition richer in content than late phases because a PG is generally eliminative or reductionistic, and the early phases thus closer to the child's infantile way of experiencing.

With increasing depth of the reconstructive operations the problems actualized by them are likely to become more urgent, more fundamentally humane, less specifically situational. It is instructive to note that so-called oceanic experiences are most typical of highly creative people—and of children. And these experiences imply, among other things, that the individual self merges with something beyond its narrow boundaries.

Bibliography

Brown, J. W. (1991). *Self and process: Brain states and the conscious present.* Englewood Cliffs, NJ: Prentice-Hall.

Carlsson, I. (1992). *The creative personality: Hemispheric variation and sex differences in defence mechanisms and creativity.* Lund, Sweden: Department of Psychology.

Draguns, J. G. (1983). Why microgenesis? An inquiry on the motivational sources of going beyond the information given. *Archives of Psychology, 135,* 5–16.

Hanlon, R. E. (Ed.). (1991). *Cognitive microgenesis: A neuropsychological perspective.* New York: Springer-Verlag.

Smith, G. J. W., & Danielsson, A. (1982). Anxiety and defensive patterns in childhood and adolescence. *Psychological Issues, Monograph 52.* Madison, CT: International Universities Press.

Smith, G. J. W. (in press). Trait and process in personality theory. *Scandinavian Journal of Psychology.*

Smith, G. J. W., & Carlsson, I. (1990). The creative process: A functional model based on empirical studies from early childhood to middle age. *Psychological Issues, Monograph 57.* Madison, CT: International Universities Press.

Perception and Creativity

Gerald C. Cupchik

University of Toronto

Bottom-up Processing The direct effects on perception of organized raw sensory qualities.

Deautomatization The process of recovering an awareness of sensation by arresting the habitual everyday tendency to identify objects and focus on their utility.

Grouping A concept from Gestalt psychology that implies the spontaneous tendency to perceive figures in organized systems.

Synesthesia The involuntary union of the senses in a single common experience.

Top-down Processing Perceiving and directing cognitive or behavioral actions in the context of plans or expectations.

The topic of *PERCEPTION AND CREATIVITY* has not received a great deal of attention in psychology, perhaps because perception is considered part of "hard" psychology whereas creativity is viewed as a "soft" area lacking clear operational criteria for defining either the process or the product. Broadly defined, perception involves responses that are associated with sense organs either directly (as in the case of observing natural scenes or artworks) or indirectly (as in the case of dreams). Four areas that interface with perception are artistic and scientific creativity, as well as unconscious projection and synesthesia. These interfaces will be considered in relation to top-down activity, in which expectations or plans control unfolding events, and bottom-up activity, in which raw materials—sensations, synesthetic experiences, and unconscious meanings—possess an inherent structure.

I. INTRODUCTION

Everyday perception has been characterized as an automatic information reduction process that produces stable representations through sensory transduction, feature extraction, and figural synthesis. Creativity, in the form of novel representations, can result when executively controlled (i.e., top-down) processes modify automatic ones. This is accomplished, for example, through selective spatial attention, controlled figural organization in response to ambiguous sensory data, equating of perceptual input from different sense modalities (e.g., synesthesia), and decoupling automatic processes, such as spatial transformation, from their normal source of data.

Reflecting a cognitive bias against spontaneous (i.e., bottom-up) creativity, the top-down approach suggests that internal neural noise and loosely guided consultations with memory might inadvertently yield useful percepts and images. Similarly, the spontaneous grouping of sensory qualities might lead to atypical (i.e., creative) representations of perceptual events through loose perceptual organization (i.e., a failure to group). From the viewpoint of a pragmatic cognitive psychology, executively controlled (i.e., top-down) processes are favored over spontaneous (i.e., bottom-up) forms of organization.

Clearly the role of executively controlled processes has to be acknowledged whether in the form of specific plans and expectations or in terms of focused attention that determines the kinds of information incorporated into the creative endeavor. But much is lost if bottom-up processes are restricted to the automatic information extraction kind in which decoding sensory features leads rapidly to object identification. Other kinds of bottom-up processes include, for example, the visual effects of natural scenes or artistic styles, unconscious projection, dreamwork, and synesthesia. The complementary roles of top-down and bottom-up processing should be considered in relation to the creative process. Sometimes the press of a stimulus configuration overwhelms perception, whereas at other times purpose guides the selection of stimulus features, but usually the two processes interact.

II. ARTISTIC PERCEPTION AND CREATIVITY

It has to be said at the outset that merely rendering a figure and producing a painting does not make someone creative. But engaging in artistic activity does set the stage for possible creative results because it leads the person to abandon the object recognition habit that is central to everyday life. The Russian formalists argued early on in the century that sensory processes are in fact deautomatized in aesthetic perception. This implies that attention is reinvested in the retinal image and the structure of sensory stimulation (a bottom-up process). The person who de-automatizes perception can notice the distribution of visual qualities, such as light and dark tonality, texture, color, and so on across

a natural scene or in an artwork. This presumes a holistic viewpoint and is formally associated with an abstracted gaze founded on distributed attention. An artist goes at least one step beyond the aesthetically skilled viewer by first understanding how these visual qualities interact to produce apparent objects (a top-down process) and then manipulating a medium in order to recreate the visual effects out of which objects emerge. The selection of a particular aspect of a natural scene or the imposition of a two-dimensional design onto an artwork are other examples of top-down (i.e., executively driven) processes. Art thus provides for a dialectic between the natural observation of a scene and the imposition of structure in accordance with the canons developed by schools of art. The emotionally expressive Venetian tradition of *colore* and the more composition-oriented Florentine tradition of *desegnio* represent extremes of bottom-up and top-down sensibilities, respectively.

The application of these aesthetic attitudes might yield interesting art, but they do not guarantee originality. Originality lies in the meeting of observational talent with careful planning and an ability to critically evaluate the emerging work. While the artist is able to closely observe a natural scene, he or she must still be selective when it comes to choosing which qualities of that scene, hue, tone, texture, and so on will be emphasized in the work. These qualities then become the focus of the piece, lending it coherence, and the artist lets this emerging image guide the unfolding work (a bottom-up process). The artist can also match the unfolding work against rules that determine the choice of subject matter and style (a top-down process). If the subject matter and style of a work are transformations of existing traditions, there is a basis for assessing its originality. Originality does not lie in any single work because it is not the work itself as a singular event that is original. Rather, originality is embodied in the choice of subject matter and stylistic qualities that become part of the artist's *signature* and these can only be discerned across a series of works. This emerging prototype can then be compared with styles that went before and understood as a transformation of them. Therefore, creative development in art is not an idiographic problem; it does not refer back to the life of the artist but to the discipline as a whole.

In sum, creativity in art is founded on an appreciation of the transformation that an emerging style effects in relation to that which went before, what has been called "structural connectedness" in relation to scientific creativity. Short-lived and banal stylistic developments simply represent inversions or exaggerations of recent styles and rely on mere novelty or an adherence to transitory values. A long time can pass before the genuine contributions of styles, such as 16th-century *Mannerism,* are appreciated. This analysis explains why Parisians strongly disliked Impressionist painting when it first appeared because the dominant aesthetic involved carefully finished paintings with historical references. They had to stop searching for particular subject matter and learn to "read" and experience the *tachiste* (i.e., broken) brush stroke characteristic of the Impressionist style. [*See* ART AND ARTISTS.]

III. PSYCHODYNAMIC PROCESSES AND CREATIVITY

The essential phenomenon here involves a relationship between unconscious processes and perceptual experiences of artworks, dreams, fantasies, and so on. It has been argued that a field (object or experience) with relatively little structure provides the individual with an occasion to project upon that field his or her way of seeing life. The results are *constitutive* when the subject imposes a structure or form upon an amorphous, unstructured substance such as clay; or they may be *interpretive* when the subject describes what a stimulus (e.g., picture) means to him or her; or they may be *cathartic* when the subject finds an emotional release toward life as represented by a stimulus-situation (e.g., as when he or she plays with clay or toys). This is a variation of the bottom-up process in which primitive material from the person's unconscious past is given material or quasi-material form in a medium or dream image.

Psychodynamic processes are unique in combining powerful energy with subject matter and loose principles of organization or transformation to produce meaningful images. In the case of dreamwork, significant childhood events or themes gain expression through the mediation of the transformational principles of condensation, displacement, symbolization, dramatization, and finally secondary elaboration, to create a more or less coherent private imaginal episode.

Of special interest is the richness of the unfolding visual image that can incorporate multiple meanings, some camouflaged and others richly evocative. This process yields an image that might inform the creation of art, literary, film, and other works, while providing the creator with a means for catharsis, the temporary release of pent-up emotion. The multilayered meanings of the subject matter generally refer back to the person's private life and are not relevant to original stylistic transformations found in art history.

Perception has a therapeutic effect in psychoanalysis. Just as the grouping process is fundamental in Gestalt psychology, making the unconscious conscious requires establishing contours that make new perceptions possible. In psychoanalysis, individuals experience figure-ground reversals as when background memory images are understood in a new way. This rearrangement of old elements into new Gestalts may be the essence of all productive, creative thinking. An important shift can therefore be noted between Gestalt formation in childhood and in the adult insight process. Early childhood perceptions follow the basic (and bottom-up) "natural" principle of Gestalt formation, *pragnanz,* whereby forms are perceived in terms of simple, regular, symmetrical, and complete closure. Therapeutic experience requires a restructuring of figure/ground relations as they apply to the person's life. This kind of creative Gestalt formation, which involves breaking down and reorganizing images, is a top-down process wherein experiences are understood in a new and meaningful context. The selection of an appropriate context is a creative (in the sense of unique) product of client-therapist discourse and in and of itself is an emotion-releasing act. [*See* INSIGHT.]

The issue of unconscious (bottom-up) and conscious (top-down) principles of organization has been underscored by many authors. A biphasic process has been proposed in which inspiration is followed by elaboration. The inspirational stage has access to primary process thinking, which is not bound by logic and is free of the traditional constraints of time and space, whereas elaboration is governed by secondary process thinking, which is logical and reality bound. Artists, for example, are able to access the more primitive mode of thought that permits novel imagery to emerge through a kind of intentional regression-in-service-of-the-ego. The syncretic images offered by the unconscious are sought out and then manipulated within the framework of artistic design.

One view holds that unconscious perception and vision are sufficiently undifferentiated that figure/ground boundaries become obscure, and outer perception and inner fantasy become indistinguishable, such that image-making yields imagery which is outward perception and inward fantasy at the same time. At this syncretic level of functioning, any objects, however different, can become fully equated with each other.

A more generic view of the primary/secondary processing distinction focuses on the mere associative quality of primary process thinking which can yield novel combinations. In this view, the basic principle underlying primary process or primordial thought is equation and discovery of similarity which, through free-association and undirected thought, increases the probability of novel combinations of mental elements. These combinations form the raw material for a work of art.

IV. SYNESTHETIC PROCESSES AND CREATIVITY

Cross-modal representation and synesthesia are phenomena that integrate perception with creativity, though they are understood within different frameworks. It has been demonstrated that subjects perceive a correspondence between the pseudowords *maluma* and *takete* and forms that are rounder or angular, respectively. In a study of synesthetic metaphors, subjects were able to set the loudness of a tone and the brightness of a white light in accordance with the levels implied in metaphors, thus showing a psychophysical correspondence between loudness and brightness. It has similarly been demonstrated that as vowel pitch moves from high to low, synesthetic colors move from lighter to darker. Cross-modal correspondence has been described as an example of an automatic (i.e., bottom-up) perceptual process that can facilitate the appreciation of (i.e., perceptually resonate to) creative synesthetic metaphors in poetry. [*See* METAPHORS; SYNESTHESIA.]

Synesthesia has been related to physiognomic perception (in which affect and dynamism are spontaneously perceived in inanimate and static stimuli) and

located in the context of primary process, regressed, or dedifferentiated states. Research has demonstrated that in relation to synesthesia, and specifically the colors of tones, highly creative subjects gave similarity judgments showing stronger associations and finer discriminations compared with less creative subjects. More creative subjects also showed greater correspondence between color and emotional associations (for words like *happy* and *sad*). This perceptual-affectual correspondence can be related to primary process cognition. Individual differences in creativity are understood in terms of relative sensitivity to basic synesthetic and cross-modal as well as affective relations. In a sense this reflects a kind of de-automatization, an ability to turn away from everyday, pragmatic perception and tune to more primitive perceptual processes (a bottom-up process). At the same time, artists and authors must learn to select from among these complex stimuli and integrate them into a unified work (a top-down process).

V. SCIENTIFIC CREATIVITY

Kekule's discovery of the hexagonal structure of the benzene molecule has provided a paradigm example for how dreams or hypnagogic imagery and unconscious processes can influence scientific creativity. In essence, the idea is that a scientist discerns the analogical structure that links two matrices, one an enduring problem in science and the other an imaginal structure embodying a principle the articulation of which lends insight for resolving the scientific problem. It has been argued that dreams provide an indirect rather than direct source of influence for the resolution of scientific problems. It has been proposed that Kekule engaged in *homospatial thinking* bringing *multiple* entities together in a single mental conception for the purpose of producing new and valuable ideas. [*See* ALTERED AND TRANSITIONAL STATES; ANALOGIES; DREAMS AND CREATIVITY; IMAGERY.]

Kekule himself agreed that he was actively involved in the creative process, had studied architecture, and could therefore readily engage in this kind of visualizing. It has been suggested that he was in an active and volitional mental state when he constructed a mental image of a snake superimposed onto the mental images of the atoms. In addition, he was actively involved in a janusian process, conceiving multiple opposites or antitheses *simultaneously*. Conceiving simultaneously of opposites, contradictions, or antitheses can bring surprises that solve scientific problems seemingly unexpectedly and serendipitously. This is a conscious (i.e., top-down) process as opposed to the unconscious spontaneous process assumed in the psychodynamic framework. [*See* JANUSIAN PROCESS.]

Another kind of top-down process is revealed in a deductive approach that seeks out predicted instances. Thus, expectations about the presence of a new particular can lead a scientist to carefully and purposively scan the image produced in a cloud chamber in search of a particular trail, a sign marking the presence of an expected particle. Similarly, a scientist can walk along a beach noticing fossil shells that fit into an emerging theory of evolutionary development. Viewers who lack these expectations notice nothing out of the ordinary or meaningful. These instances exemplify a way that executive processes can control the search for theory-relevant information or data. [*See* SCIENCE.]

VI. PERCEPTION AND CREATIVITY: A SYNTHESIS

In this context, creativity occurs when a novel and meaningful relationship is obtained between some kind of sensory-based structure (e.g., a visual, fantasy, or dream image) and another domain of meaning including art or literary work, unconscious memory, synesthetic experience, or scientific phenomenon. Creativity is bidirectional, integrating sensory-based (i.e., bottom-up) and intellectually based (i.e., top-down) processes in a complementary manner.

From a cognitive perspective, bottom-up processing tends to be "loose" and reflects a "failure to group." However, the spontaneity of bottom-up processing can be seen in a more positive light, particularly when the diversity of sources is acknowledged. Synesthesia involves the spontaneous perception of relations between sensory modalities and is centered in the midbrain. Primary process or de-differentiated thinking is not bound by logic and the constraints of rigorous time and space and is affectively driven. It is more primitive and tied to the syncretic thought processes

of the younger child. Bottom-up processing is accompanied by peripheral, distributed, or global attention, which helps to encompass the various domains involved in the creative act. In this manner, lower-order processes can spontaneously generate, without constraint, "structural connectedness" that links the symbolic matrix of sensory experience and various domains of meaning.

Top-down or higher-order processing is usually thought of as centered in the cortex and is associated with the formal operational (i.e., logical and hypothetical) thinking characteristic of adults. Higher-order processes can help articulate a problem in science and evaluate the potential value of an analogical solution involving intellectual and perceptual matrices of thought. They can also be used to evaluate the unfolding success of an artwork in accordance with the artist's ideas and goals. Focal attention is an executively controlled process that facilitates the discrimination of local features and events. It is purposive and can play a role both in the isolation of a problem (e.g., the way that a tree's shadow is cast on the ground) and the evaluation of a solution (e.g., the presence or absence of a trail in a photograph taken in a cloud chamber signifying the presence of a sought after particle).

Bottom-up and top-down processes have a complementary relation both in science and the arts. In a revision of Piaget's genetic model of intellectual development, it can be argued that scientific creativity requires the executive control of formal operational thinking combined with the syncretic and cross-matrix freedom implied by preoperational thinking. The adult scientist thus preserves the free imagination of the child but interprets meaning at a more articulated level of thought. In a similar way, poets can avail themselves of cross-modal associations that appear in literary constructions. But they retain the ability to critically evaluate the quality of the image in relation to the overall meaning of the unfolding work. Artistic creations, too, may spontaneously incorporate these lower-level phenomena (synesthesia from the midbrain and free association from the unconscious) but always against the background of the history of stylistic development so that relative originality can be assessed. Thus, both in art and science, perceptual processes can interact with creativity, but in such a way that the product can be meaningfully discussed in relation ("structural connectedness") to a thought or discourse matrix that goes beyond the context of discovery. The same goes for psychodynamic moments of insight. Whereas a dream might provide the material for a conversation between client and therapist, insight results when it is understood in an appropriate context. This figure/ground reversal reflects a shift from bottom-up to top-down processing.

In sum, whereas top-down focal attentive processes respond to or generate the salience of particular facts and match them against expectations, global attentive processes lend coherence to works by placing facts in context. In this manner, perception and creativity are unified by appreciating the structure underlying each matrix and generating a solution that accommodates the two domains. The parallel between this process and Piaget's notion of equilibration (a reconciliation of the known and unknown through a process of accommodation) or Kuhn's theory of paradigm change (a revolutionary shift from one way of seeing to another that involves a conceptual basis) cannot be avoided. This kind of *real* creativity should be distinguished from *pseudocreativity,* a concept developed by Jung, in that the latter may be a thematic representation of a person's life and not inform more general problems. It is not enough to create a symbolically rich painting if the meaning of the work refers back to idiosyncratic experiences of the individual. The distinction between art historical development and art therapy must be underscored.

Bibliography

Arnheim, R. (1971). *Art and visual perception: A psychology of the creative eye.* Berkeley: University of California Press.

Brzezinski, J., Di Nuovo, S., Marek, T., & Maruszewski, T. (Eds.). (1993). *Creativity and consciousness: Philosophical and psychological dimensions.* Amsterdam: Rodopi.

Deri, S. (1984). *Symbolization and creativity.* New York: International University Press.

Ehrenzweig, A. (1967). *The hidden order of art.* Berkeley: University of California Press.

Finke, R. A. (1995). Creative realism. In S. M. Smith, T. B. Ward, & R. A. Finke (Eds.). *The creative cognition approach* (pp. 303–326). Cambridge, MA: MIT Press.

Flowers, J. H., & Garbin, C. P. (1989). Creativity and Perception. In J. A. Glover, R. R. Ronning, & C. R. Reynolds (Eds.), *Handbook of Creativity* (pp. 147–162). New York: Plenum.

Frank, L. K. (1939). Projective methods for the study of personality. *The Journal of Psychology, 8,* 389–413.

Kris, E. (1952). *Psychoanalytic explorations in art.* New York: Schocken.

Marks, L. (1978). *The unity of the senses: Interrelations among the modalities.* New York: Academic Press.

Marks, L. (1982). Synesthetic perception and poetic metaphor. *Journal of Experimental Psychology: Human Perception and Performance, 8*(1), 15–23.

Martindale, C. (1990). *The clockwork muse: The predictability of artistic change.* New York: Basic Books.

Rothenberg, A. (1995). Creative cognitive processes in Kekule's discovery of the structure of the benzene molecule. *Journal of Psychology, 108*(3), 419–438.

Smith, S. M., Ward, T. B., & Vaid, J. (Eds.). (1997). *Creative thought: An investigation of conceptual structures and processes.* Washington, DC: American Psychological Association.

Personality

Ravenna Helson

Institute of Personality and Social Research,
University of California, Berkeley

Primary Process Cognition Dreamlike experience characterized by a drifting unorganized succession of images that may be fused or displaced from their usual context. Also, thought with affect-laden content, especially sexual or aggressive. Primary process cognition is contrasted with secondary process cognition, which is purposeful, rational, and guided by conventional restraints. These terms were first used by Freud.

Projective Test A test that requires subjects to respond not in terms of preselected alternatives but in terms of their imagination, individual motivations, and perceptual or cognitive style. A set of pictures about which stories are told or beginnings of sentences that are to be completed are examples of projective tests.

Q Sort Procedure A set of rules for the scaling of a group of personality descriptors (Q items) as applied to an individual, so that the order of the Q items expresses the judge's formulation of the personality of the individual.

PERSONALITY *is the relatively enduring organization of motivations and cognitive and affective resources*

(traits) that any person manifests or that distinguishes one individual from another. In the study of creativity, personality psychologists have been interested in learning how to identify creative persons and in the conceptualization, description, and measurement of cognitive-affective-motivational structures characteristic of these individuals. They are also interested in factors that affect the development of creative personality, the stability of creative traits over time, and how these traits vary from one field or setting to another. This article begins with an overview of early work on creative personality in the fields of psychiatry, archival studies of the eminent, and personality psychology, and then discusses contemporary issues and findings.

I. THREE ROOTS OF THE STUDY OF CREATIVE PERSONALITY

A. Psychiatry and Psychotherapy

The creative product has an aspect of surprise, and the creative insight often seems to come out of nowhere. Creative artists sometimes use the imagery of dreams and arouse us in mysterious ways. Since the late 19th century, the conceptualization of the not seen, the irrational, and the emotional in our personalities has come to a considerable extent from psychoanalysis. Perhaps for this reason a recurring idea in the study of creative personality has been that the primary source of originality is the unconscious, and that the creative person has more access to this source than other individuals. Many influential formulations of creative personality have come from psychotherapists, who deal daily with thoughts and emotions outside of ordinary awareness.

One division in the psychoanalytic literature on creativity was between those who conceptualized the unconscious as having positive features and those who saw its features as negative. According to Jung, the creative process consists in the unconscious activation of an archtypal image and in the elaboration and shaping of this image into the finished work. "The unsatisfied yearning of the artist," he wrote, "reaches back to the primordial image in the unconscious which is best fitted to compensate the inadequacy and one-sidedness of the present." Thus the unconscious was seen as having a valuable compensatory relation to the values of the artist's society.

In Freudian psychology, the unconscious was usually seen as negative. How, then, does something creative result from its influence? Freud described the writer as a trickster who could not satisfy his desires for women and fame but was somehow able to sublimate them in the form of disguised daydreams, using aesthetic form to entice the reader to share his fantasy.

Elsewhere Freud suggested that in the production of wit, which in its unexpectedness and aptness resembles the creative, a preconscious thought is "entrusted for a moment to the unconscious for elaboration." In this way it gains access to associations ordinarily repressed. This idea was taken up by Kris, an art historian and one of the early psychoanalysts who developed ego psychology. Unlike the psychotic, he said, the creative person has "flexibility of repression" and is able to "regress in the service of the ego." "Primary process" cognition (concrete, fluid, affect-laden, analogical) was conspicuous in the inspirational phase of creative work and "secondary process" cognition (logical, reality oriented) in the elaborational phase. The creative person is able to shift from one process to the other.

Kris's ideas, published in 1952, stimulated much research in academic psychology. For example, to study regression in the service of the ego, Wild in 1965 compared art students with teachers and schizoprenics on object-sorting and word-association tasks. She found that art students enjoyed the tasks much more than the other groups, gave more unusual and clever responses, and showed bigger shifts in responses under instructions to take the role of a regulated and then an unregulated person. Other investigators have built on Kris's ideas.

Psychoanalysts and psychotherapists have made many suggestions about motivations for creative work and the development of the creative individual. For example, self-actualization has been emphasized as a motive, and humanistic psychologists discussed qualities such as openness, courage, and the ability to make commitments. Still others included creative productivity as a form of the generativity described as the task of midlife. [*See* SELF-ACTUALIZATION.]

Psychoanalysts also contributed a large number of case histories or psychobiographies of creative individuals, ranging from Freud's study of Leonardo da Vinci (building on interpretation of a childhood memory or fantasy of a bird repeatedly thrusting its tail in his mouth) to Erikson's studies of the development of creative personality in leaders such as Martin Luther and Gandhi in cultural context and through the life span. [*See* DA VINCI, LEONARDO.]

B. Archival Studies

A second and very different contributor from the past to the psychology of creative personality was archival research. It began with Galton, often called the father of the study of individual differences, who was interested in proving the hereditary nature of genius. He made the first statistical use of biographical sources to demonstrate the extent to which eminence ran in families. His work, published in 1869, was studded with provocative findings, such as that the most illustrious men had more eminent relatives than the less illustrious, and that the mortality curves for eminent men were bimodal—the eminent tended to be either weak or long-lived. Galton's method aroused much interest, and several others used biographical material to support the thesis that genius was related to insanity, that genius was not related to insanity, and that there was more pathology among aesthetic types than among scientific and practical types. [*See* FAMILIES AND CREATIVITY; MAD GENIUS CONTROVERSY.]

In the early 20th century, James McKeen Cattell did numerous statistical investigations of the eminent. He measured eminence more carefully than Galton had done, and he worked out methods for assessing contemporary eminence through ratings by peers. Using Cattell's lists, other researchers estimated IQs of 282 people who were considered geniuses of the past, based on reports of their achievements in childhood. These estimated IQs were quite high. The most outstanding of the eminent came from advantaged home backgrounds and were characterized in childhood by personality traits that included not only intellectual power and energy but also originality, confidence, persistence, and ambition. Gifted achievers in the Terman longitudinal sample showed similar characteristics, though the creative achievements in this sample were below the level of genius.

Another question addressed in archival research was the relation between age and productivity. It has been reported that curves of creative productivity rise rapidly in early maturity and then decline slowly. The age of productivity of best work varies from one field to another. Older people are handicapped in fields that required new learning and unlearning of the old, but are at an advantage when the accumulation of experience is important. [*See* PRODUCTIVITY AND AGE.]

Beginning in the 1970s, archival methods were brought to a new level of sophistication and psychological interest. Archival data has been used to test a variety of complex and intriguing hypotheses about influences on creative individuals across time and culture. [*See* ARCHIVAL INVESTIGATION.]

C. Personality Psychology

The field of personality psychology was consolidated in the United States in the 1930s when several outstanding books appeared. In the 1940s two of the best-known projective measures of imagination were published, the Rorschach Inkblot Test and the Thematic Apperception Test (TAT). Two important self-report inventories appeared about this time: Strong's inventory of occupational interests and the Minnesota Multiphasic Personality Inventory, an inventory of psychiatric dimensions. These were among the instruments that proved valuable in the later descriptions of creative personality.

In 1950, J. Paul Guilford gave a presidential address to the American Psychological Association in which he contrasted convergent thinking, as assessed in the individual's ability to give the "right" answer to questions on intelligence tests, and divergent thinking, in which the goal is to think of many different and original ideas or solutions. He offered examples of how divergent thinking could be measured, such as by asking subjects to list as many unusual uses as they could think of for common objects, or as many consequences as they could think of from hypothetical events. Subsequent studies on divergent thinking in children found that teachers preferred "intelligent" children. [*See* DIVERGENT THINKING.]

Meanwhile, the Institute of Personality Assessment and Research (IPAR), founded in 1949, had begun a program to study originality, soundness, and potential for success. In the 1950s the IPAR staff developed many valuable tools and procedures for studying personality in its richness and interpersonal context. In a typical assessment, subjects would spend a weekend at the institute, taking a variety of perceptual-cognitive tests, being interviewed, and interacting with each other in group procedures and with staff members in informal conversation so as to enable the staff to describe their personalities later by means of adjective checklists, Q sorts, and ratings. Work at IPAR in the 1950s included the conceptualization and measurement of several aspects of creative personality: originality, complexity of outlook, and independence of judgment. For example, subjects taking the Barron-Welsh Art Scale indicated how much they liked each of a set of drawings, which varied in symmetry and complexity. A preference for complexity and assymmetry was thought to allow into the perceptual system the greatest possible richness of experience, even at the cost of discord, whereas the preference for simplicity and symmetry allowed into the system only as much as could be integrated without great discomfort. [*See* INSTITUTE OF PERSONALITY ASSESSMENT AND RESEARCH.]

II. DEFINING AND IDENTIFYING CREATIVE PERSONALITY

The creative personality is the personality of someone who is consistently creative, but there have been many ideas about what it means to be creative, and whether consistency in the traits of creative individuals can be demonstrated across situation, age, and field. [*See* DEFINITIONS OF CREATIVITY.]

A. Creativity as a Cognitive Ability

Some researchers have regarded creativity as a cognitive ability and proposed to measure it through instruments similar to intelligence tests. At first there was skepticism that creativity and intelligence were separate cognitive abilities, but evidence has been provided that they are separate. Divergent thinking tests along with the Remote Associates Test were widely used by researchers in captive classroom samples as criteria of creativity. However, a critique of this approach argued that there was no evidence that the divergent thinker in the classroom would actually create anything of social value. It was additionally argued that the creative personality should be conceptualized as consisting of traits that had been shown to characterize eminent creative individuals across fields. These might include not only divergent thinking but also intelligence, intrinsic task involvement, and preference for complexity. It was recommended that the study of creative personality be linked to real-life achievement criteria, especially the evaluation of creative products. [*See* CREATIVE PRODUCTS; EMINENCE.]

B. Creativity as Real-Life Achievement

One way of measuring creative achievement was to obtain ratings from experts who could evaluate the contributions of the individuals to be studied. This was the approach used in the IPAR studies of highly creative persons. Another method, familiar from archival studies, was to use some form of already existing recognition of creative performance, such as space allotted to individuals in biographical dictionaries. Or subjects might be asked to describe their own accomplishments. Another measure was a checklist with which high school students could report their creative activities and achievements, such as having won an award for a scientific paper or having published poems, stories, or articles in a magazine. This checklist predicted creative achievement in college better than aptitude tests, grades, or self-conceptions. Similar checklists have been used successfully in other studies.

The measurement of creativity in terms of achievements is not without limitations and problems. A major limitation is that creative achievement is not an appropriate criterion for studies of creative personality in children or disadvantaged adults. Other problems are in part definitional. Characteristics of creative achievers may be attributable to their originality and insight but they may also be attributable to achievement motivation or success skills. Should creativity be defined to include such traits? Another problem is that some characteristics of eminent creative achievers, such as confidence, may be attributable to their stage of life or experience of success. To evaluate the confound between creative achievement and eminence, researchers needed to show whether or how creative personality changes with age and success.

C. The Creative Product as the Criterion of Creativity

Some of the problems in using achievement as a criterion of creativity have been overcome by a focus on the creative product. Products can be those of high achievers, but they can also be drawings of children. Sometimes the creativity of products is easily and reliably rated, but in other cases the assessment of the creative quality or significance of products has been unreliable or has shown low correlations with other criteria of creativity. Results depend on factors such as the range of quality in the products to be rated, the qualifications and biases of raters, the relevance of the products chosen as reflections of the individual's creativity, and the demand of the rating task. It has been suggested that the most creative products are transformative (meaning that they made one think about something in a new way) and condensed (meaning that they had a multiplicity of compactly presented implications that rewarded repeated "savoring"). Agreement about transformation and condensation is difficult to obtain.

D. Creativity as a Personality or Behavior Pattern

Some theorists have conceptualized creativity in terms of open, self-actualizing attitudes that are not necessarily associated with either products or outstanding achievement. Ruth Richards's concept of the person who shows "everyday creativity" puts emphasis on original and appropriate actions in everyday life and creative leisure interests. Others have wanted to anchor their concept of the creative person in the outstanding creative achiever but to conceptualize and identify this person in terms of personality traits. This strategy has met skepticism from those who believe that creativity often lies in group activity rather than in individuals, and that the personality of the creative person most importantly depends on the social system. Before discussing the characteristics of the creative achiever, let us consider a final definitional claim that the creative individual needs to be conceptualized in interaction with an environment or as part of a social system. [*See* EVERYDAY CREATIVITY.]

E. Creative Personality as Embedded in a Social System

The idea of the creative genius emerged in the 17th century as a part of the recognition of individuality, an expression of deviation from the conventional order in society. In the mid-19th century, Galton thought that the true genius could not be defeated by social obstacles, and others showed the importance of the individual qualities of intelligence and persistence. Focus on these individual qualities continued. During the Cold War there was much interest in identifying creative potential, particularly that of future scientists. Thus the Cold War supported research on creative personality, though interest in the autonomy and unconventionality of creative personality also signified resistance to conformist trends within American culture.

However, in the past several decades, it has become increasingly emphasized that the creative personality is not well conceptualized without recognition that the individual is influenced by many networks of social and interpersonal factors. For example many gifted young people who later become eminent have received support from their families and social class position. Studies of creativity in women revealed many social barriers. However, some have maintained that it is not enough to study social influences on the creative individual. It has been suggested that psychologists would have a better understanding of who becomes creative and how creative people operate if creativity was studied as an ecological system, with attention to flow between creative processes and personal and ecosystem resources. In this sense, the important question is not who or what is creative but where is creativity as located in the social system. Creativity is not in the person or the work but in the eyes of evaluators, and traits of people vary with the creative system of which they are a part. Though artists of today have strong intrinsic motivation and low economic and social values to protect themselves from factors that they feel would compromise their vision, artists in the early Renaissance did not have these attitudes.

On the other hand, Dean Keith Simonton has devoted much of his career to showing social influences on creative achievement across time and culture, and he found that what he terms intelligence and aggressiveness characterize both eminent creators and leaders across fields and generations. He concluded that neither creativity nor leadership can be considered merely the result of situational or attributional factors.

In many worthwhile studies of creative personality, the social system or the ecosystem can be taken for granted. Nonetheless, these crititicisms of individualistic biases pose a challenge: How does one measure creative personality as a part of a social system? One approach is to measure fewer general personality characteristics and more situation-specific aspects of cognition, motivation, and behavior. Such measures may be combined with measures of aspects of environments that are relevant to creative work.

Another approach is to to conceptualize a social system broadly so as to show where and how creative personality fits into it. John Holland showed the occupational world to have six kinds of work conducted in six kinds of environment by people with six kinds of personalities. Competent functioning within an occupation offers its own brand of social interaction and involves particular interests, skills, rewards, and rhythms. People with particular personality structures seek out and develop in these environments. Creative work is most likely to take place in the artistic and investigative environments, less likely to take place in the social and enterprising environments, and least likely to take place in the realistic and especially the conventional environments. A composer or physicist is expected to come up with new ideas, and institutional arrangements support this goal, but a bus driver is expected to take the same route each day, and might even be punished for innovation. When creativity was measured in a heterogeneous sample of college-educated women at midlife on the basis of occupation plus amount of recognition for artistic and intellectual accomplishment, creativity had substantial correlations with childhood artistic and imaginative interests, faculty nominations for creative potential, and measures of originality, complexity, and other creative traits at age 21.

Particular characteristics of organizations, such as age and stability, may also be related to innovation or creative style. Individuals who do not find the values and work conditions of an organization congenial tend to go elsewhere, so that there is increasing person–environment fit over time. [*See* CREATIVE CLIMATE.]

Another approach to the study of personality and creativity within a social system is to select samples on the basis of different roles people play in relation to creativity or the different statuses they occupy. For example, originality as assessed by the Remote Associates Test was found to be related to technical contributions in scientists who were influential in the laboratory and able to initiate new activities. Among scientists in less favorable positions, however, there was no relation. Historical, sociological, and biographical methods are also valuable for the study of creative persons as members of social systems.

III. CHARACTERISTICS OF THE CREATIVE ACHIEVER

Studies of the creative personality raise a number of questions. One is to what extent the same characteristics are actually found across fields. Another is whether young people identified on the basis of originality or other creative traits have the same personality as creative adults. A related question, which may require longitudinal data (information from the same individuals at different ages) is the extent to which creative personality traits are consistent over time, and how they change with age. Perhaps the hardest question is whether the creative personality can be described in terms of structure, rather than as a set of characteristics that overlap more or less from study to study. The structure would clarify what is central to creative personality, how the components are related, and how they influence creative process and product.

A. Consistency of Creative Personality across Fields

The IPAR researchers studied samples of highly creative architects, writers, mathematicians, and space scientists. Across fields, highly creative individuals showed a characteristic pattern of interests which was interpreted as concern for meanings and implications rather than in small details or facts for their own sake, cognitive flexibility, interest and accuracy in communication, intellectual curiosity, and lack of interest in policing their own interests or those of others. They showed a preference for complex and asymmetrical drawings, as measured by the Barron-Welsh Art Scale. Males had high scores on various inventory measures of femininity, indicating an openness to feelings and emotions regarded in the American culture as feminine. On the Minnesota Multiphasic Personality Inventory many appeared to have considerable psychopathology but also gave evidence of adequate control mechanisms. Within the range represented in the IPAR samples there was little relation between creativity and intelligence. On the Allport-Vernon Study of Values, highly creative individuals tended to score high on both the Theoretical and Aesthetic scales. The creative individuals were also described as being highly invested in their work. The IPAR studies showed that highly creative individuals in different fields shared many personality characteristics. Other studies of creative achievers were narrower in range but reported roughly similar results.

The different IPAR studies used most of the same instruments and procedures, but research designs varied in ways that made it difficult to compare results in more than an informal way. In an attempt to compare samples systematically, factor scores were analyzed on the California Psychological Inventory (CPI) for creative and comparison males in the four main IPAR studies: writers, space scientists, mathematicians, and architects. Overall, the findings fit the idea of the creative personality as being relatively uninhibited and unconventional; having a greater need for independence, self-direction, and autonomy; and being more assertive, forceful, and seemingly assured. However, there were large differences among men in different fields and many exceptions to the pattern within samples.

B. Are Original Students Like Creative Achievers?

Many studies have identified young people as creative according to a criterion of divergent thinking or high scores on inventory or projective measures of originality. However, eminent creative individuals do not necessarily do well on the measures of originality that are used to study creativity in students. They may resist or resent devoting their abilities to artificial tasks, such as thinking of unusual uses for objects. Also, these individuals, perhaps even more than students, show specialization. Creative women mathematicians did not score higher than comparison women on Barron's scale for originality, probably because they lacked the impact-seeking characteristics tapped by this measure. The Rorschach and TAT have been found to be less useful for demonstrating originality across fields in eminent natural and social scientists than for differentiating scientists in different fields of endeavor. The characteristic found to be universally important was an enormous investment in creative work, which is seldom assessed in studies of students.

On the other hand, several studies show important overlap in characteristics of creative students and professionals, though there are also differences that seem to be associated in a reasonable way with age and success. Adolescent winners in a high-level science contest had the same advantage over comparison subjects as creative adults in assertive assurance and effectiveness in reaching self-chosen, complex goals. However, the creative adolescents scored higher than comparison subjects in self-discipline, whereas creative adults scored lower. It has been suggested that the creative individual requires a level of self-control that is higher than that of peers in adolescence, when control tends to be low or erratic, but lower than that of peers in adulthood, when control tends to be high.

Art students and established artists both scored higher on Adjective Check List scales such as Change and Creative Personality and lower on scales such as Affiliation and Deference than the sample that was used to provide norms for this instrument. Art students who were committed to a career in art scored higher on Favorableness of self-description and Self-confidence (among other scales) than those who were uncommitted, and established artists scored higher on the same scales than either student group. Evidence on whether original students become creative achievers as adults is included in the next section.

C. Consistency and Change in Creative Personality over Time

1. Longitudinal Studies

Some studies have found that ratings of creativity in professional students do not predict future recognition in their field in any impressive way. Introverted art students rated as highly creative in art school often lacked the skills to deal with gallery owners, critics, and the media, and disappeared from the art scene.

Of course, students admitted to a professional school have much in common. One might expect to predict creative achievement more successfully if one began with a more heterogeneous sample. A longitudinal study conducted of 125 women first studied as seniors at Mills College included several college-age measures of creativity, Q sort descriptions of the women by psychologists at age 43 (made on the basis of extensive open-ended questionnaire information obtained by mail), and a measure of occupational creativity scored in the women's early 50s. Scales measuring aspects of creative personality, such as the Creative Temperament scale of the CPI and the Barron Originality and Complexity scales, showed correlations as high as .48 with occupational creativity some 30 years later. Combining work ambition with creative temperament increased the prediction of occupational creativity to .55. Though creative temperament for the sample as a whole showed a high level of consistency over time, many individual women increased or decreased substantially from one time of testing to another on this scale. The changes seemed to be related to improvement or worsening of their work and interpersonal environments.

Findings from this study also contribute to an understanding of which aspects of the personality of the creative achiever are predicted by inventory measures of creative personality traits in college students. In the age-43 data, the Q sort correlates of several inventory measures of creative traits as scored at age 21, called creative potential, were compared to the occupational creativity measure as scored at age 52, called creative productivity. Common to both creative potential and productivity were strong correlations with Q sort items describing openness, originality, and unconventionality. However, only the creative potential scales were correlated with items such as "Needs tend to uncontrolled expression" and "Tends to be self-indulgent," and only creativity productivity was correlated with "Has insight into own motives and behavior" and (negative) "Is self-defeating." In this study, then, creative potential as assessed by inventory measures scored at age 21 predicted the openness and unconventionality of the creative achiever, but not the creative achiever's depth and commitment. These qualities seemed to develop through focus on work.

2. Creativity and Stage of Adulthood

Do creative traits such as originality and complexity of outlook decline as people get older? Scores of teachers between the ages of 20 to 70 on several Guilford measures of divergent thinking and the Barron-Welsh Art scale (a measure of complexity of outlook) declined with age. However, scores of artists and writers on the Art scale showed no relation to age. The artists and writers scored much higher than the comparison group. This is an important factor, because in another study of the change in creative abilities with age, divergent thinking abilities declined, but age was a much less important factor than stable individual differences in personality. A person high in divergent thinking would remain high in relation to others and also high in absolute scores.

In some fields and eras creative individuals maintain both creative traits and productivity in later life. Architects who had been rated as highly creative 20 years previously were continuing to win commissions and to be confident of their talents and energetically pursuing their work. Those who had been rated less high on creativity were more likely to have retired. On the other hand, in scientific fields, research productivity usually declines with age. Older scientists may play an important role in administration or as public policy advisers. [See SCIENCE.]

Though many creative individuals make important contributions at an early age, this is not always the case. Midlife is a time when many creative careers begin, end, or change character, often in relation to dynamics of personality questioning and resynthesis. Long-lived visual artists show great variability in career onset, timing of masterpieces, and peaks of productivity.

D. Structure of Creative Personality

If there is such a thing as "the creative personality," one would like to understand it as a structure, to know how its components work together to facilitate the creative process and product. Some researchers achieve a simple level of organization by emphasizing one trait as cardinal.

1. Originality as a Cardinal Trait

In many studies, originality has been taken as synonymous with creativity, though the consensus is now that creativity involves not only an original idea but the development of it, which requires elaborative skills and perseverance. However, Colin Martindale argued that in the art world, though change in both the level of primary process and in elaborative techniques has an important place in the cycles of artistic style, the emphasis is on being different from what came before. The creative personality is a structure for producing something original. [See ART AND ARTISTS.]

2. Openness as a Cardinal Trait

Factor-analytic studies of personality traits often yield a five-factor solution. Four of the factors may be labeled neuroticism, extraversion, conscientiousness, and agreeableness. The other consists of measures of what has been labeled as intelligence, culture, and, increasingly, openness to experience. Openness is manifested in a rich fantasy life, aesthetic sensitivity, awareness of inner feelings, need for variety in actions, intellectual curiosity, and liberal value systems. Measures of openness show much higher and more consistent relations to measures of originality and creativity than do the other four traits.

In another set of basic personality factors, a trait called absorption is related to creativity. Absorption involves a heightened sense of attention to feelings, mental images, or ideas. It is correlated with openness, but emphasizes active seeking out and engagement with certain kinds of experience.

Though the perspective offered by these theorists is valuable, attention needs to be paid also to motivational variables largely outside their scope.

3. Affective Involvement in Work

Many creativity researchers have emphasized the strong and continuing affective involvement of highly creative people in their own work. There is a distinction made between intrinsic motivation, an interest in actually engaging in a behavior, and extrinsic motivation, an interest in obtaining rewards such as pay or praise that are the results of the behavior. Intrinsic motivation is of primary importance in creative work. In a number of experiments, subjects put out more effort and were more creative when they were motivated by interest and challenge of the task itself than when extrinsic rewards were offered. However, extrinsic rewards are sometimes found to be effective; much depends on the procedures of the study. In a study of adolescents in various art fields, subjects described a wide variety of gratifications from their work, many of which did not reflect intrinsic motivation. Though the distinction between intrinsic and extrinsic motivation is important, these concepts need specification, elaboration, and qualification if they are to be applied to creative achievers. For example, many creative people have a hunger for fame that might be considered an extrinsic motivation. [*See* MOTIVATION/DRIVE.]

4. Relating Components to Each Other

Openness and affective involvement in work may be the most important creative traits, but they are very general constructs. Some psychologists try to specify motivational, affective, and cognitive components of creative personality and to show how they are related to each other or to global personality traits.

Some psychologists appreciate the idea of constructing the creative personality from specific part processes. However, others believe that these parts will never add up to the creative personality; they prefer broader concepts, involving deeper motives or conflicts, even if quantitative verification must be sacrificed.

5. Structures Based on Paradox

Sometimes the structure of creative personality has been approached in terms of important paradoxes in traits associated with creativity. For Otto Rank, a creative man is one who, faced with the conflict between the need to express his own will and the need to meet the will of parents or other social agents, transcends this conflict by producing creations of his own that are valuable to society. A somewhat related paradox is that the creative person must find a balance between respect for tradition and the need to challenge it. Before offering a transformative theory, a young scientist must spend years mastering an enormous body of accepted work. Views of creative personality built on paradox tend to portray the creative individual as complex and broad in scope.

6. Developmental Theories

Others have approached the creative personality in terms of developmental processes. Heinz Kohut, a psychiatrist, described two paths of development, one taken by other-oriented people and the other by self-oriented people, for whom self-esteem was a core concern. Many of his patients were of the latter group, sometimes referred to as narcissistic. Creative expression and productivity, Kohut said, was a major way for self-oriented individuals to develop integration, vitality, and, in time, wisdom.

7. Unique Structure

Though not without empirical support, attempts to simplify or structure the creative personality have been rough, tentative, and only partially successful. Case studies have been used to show how different the personality structures of outstanding creative individuals have been. In one view, significant creative achievement represents the slow development of a novel point of view and results from a lifetime organization of work and life. The creative person monitors and directs the evolution of his or her systems of knowledge, affect, and purpose. Each case is unique, but there are concepts useful for studying the individual case, such as the "network of enterprise," "ensemble of metaphors," and the "social web." [*See* ENSEMBLE OF METAPHOR.]

IV. DIFFERENCES AMONG CREATIVE INDIVIDUALS

A. Subtypes of Creative Personality

Some of the subtypes of creative personality that have been suggested are related to dimensions that underlie the paradoxes in creative personality discussed earlier. For example, the creative person is described as open to primary process but also able to give form to ideas. It has been suggested that creative romantics emphasize the first aspect and classicists the second. Artists and scientists are the best-known creative subtypes, and they differ in these same respects. Artists have been described as more emotionally sensitive, tense, and impractical than scientists, and several archival studies have found artists to have more psychopathology in their backgrounds. Within the artistic professions, those who relied the most on precision, reason, and logic (e.g., architects) suffered less emotional distress than those who relied the most on emotive expression, personal experiences, and vivid imagery (e.g., poets). This evidence is consistent with the theory that creativity in the arts tends to involve the expression of affect in the exploration of the self more centrally than it does in science.

Another dimension of importance is conventionality versus unconventionality. Although people often expect creative people to be bohemians, those studied at IPAR fit a "briefcase" syndrome better. Creative people have also been described as adaptor and innovator types, the adaptors liking to work within established procedures but to do things better, the innovators liking to reconstruct a problem and do things differently. Which type is more creative depends on the environment. Others have suggested a three-part typology: the adapted, who accept the will of socializing agents; the neurotic, who rebel and have creative interests but suffer from conflict or insufficient personality development; and the creative, who transcend the conflict between their own will and that of socializing agents. Several empirical studies have used this framework to show that subjects rated as less creative are more likely to be adapted or conflicted than those rated as more creative. However, among individuals rated as highly creative, all three types can be identified.

B. Creative Personality in a Social System

Another way to account for differences in creativity or creative style among individuals is to conceptualize their personalities as influenced by their position in different domains of the social system. For example, the differences between artists and scientists, discussed earlier, can be understood in part in terms of the differ-

ent ways that art and science are carried on in our society. Emotional characteristics that are useful to poets may prevent them from desiring or qualifying for the long and demanding training of a scientist. Within a field, individuals play different roles. One study found that authors of children's literature and critics who wrote articles about children's literature (professors, librarians, journalists, and editors in publishing firms) shared strong artistic interests. However, differences between the two groups were consistent with their respective social roles to produce original stories and to serve as gatekeepers who evaluated these stories for the consumption of children and parents. Authors generally worked in isolation at home, whereas critics worked with others in offices. In personality, authors were more impulsive, distractible, and individualistic than critics; critics were more goal-oriented, efficient, and conventional than authors.

V. CREATIVE PERSONALITY, PROCESS, AND PRODUCT

The study of creative personality includes analysis of the ways that motives, affects, and cognitive processes are involved in producing the creative work. These ways are often subtle and mysterious. A few quantified approaches to the topic are described here.

A. Creative Product and Personality

The creative product often serves as a criterion of creativity, but it can also be used to study relationships between product and personal style. For example, individuals with innovator traits described their products as more original, attractive, and transformational, whereas individuals with the traits of adaptors described theirs as more adequate, logical, well-crafted, and useful.

B. Goals, Process, and Product

Goals are an important part of personality, and the creative process includes the goals of individuals as they work toward completion of the product. Art students who took time to explore materials and find their own problem for an assigned composition produced more creative paintings than those who went to work quickly with a standard problem. In a 22-year follow-up, the problem finders were reported to have made more creative contributions. [*See* PROBLEM FINDING.]

Writers who rated extrinsic goals (e.g., being adopted by movies or television) high on a set of items used to assess their work style produced books that were judged to be less creative than those of writers who were more concerned with literary goals and their own autonomous creative process. The first group tended to mention formulas (e.g., "I decided to write a fairy tale with modern humor") or egocentric goals (e.g., "I didn't want to be known as a one-book author") in describing how they went about writing the book that had been included in the study. On personality inventories they scored higher on measures of extraversion and conventionality.

In experimental studies, goals can be manipulated. Increasing the level of extrinsic motivation (e.g., offering rewards of some kind) often decreased the creativity of products, and merely instructing students to be original led to higher scores on measures of divergent thinking.

VI. CONCLUDING REMARKS

This article attempts to convey the questions that have most centrally concerned investigators of creative personality. There is no doubt that the field is still beset with contradictions and anomalies, but there is increasing consensus about the need for clarity in use of terms, about the range of factors influencing creative achievement, and about the reasons for apparent discrepancies. Promising new directions of research include goals and emotional processes in creative work, the influence of practice on creative skill and personality, the development of creative personality in adulthood, relationships and creative personality, case studies of creative individuals, cross-cultural studies, and many others.

Bibliography

Albert, R. S. (Ed.). (1992). *Genius and eminence.* (2nd ed.). New York: Pergamon.

Barron, F. (1968). *Creativity and personal freedom.* Princeton, NJ: Van Nostrand.

Barron, F., & Harrington, D. (1981). Creativity, intelligence, and personality. In M. Rosenzweig, & L. Porter (Eds.), *Annual review of psychology* (Vol. 32, pp. 439–476). Palo Alto, CA: Annual Reviews.

Jung, C. G. (1966). On the relation of Analytical Psychology to poetry. In *Collected Works, 15,* pp. 65–83. New York: Bollingen.

Martindale, C. E. (1989). Personality, situation, and creativity. In J. Glover, R. Ronning, & C. R. Reynolds (Eds.), *Handbook of creativity.* New York: Plenum.

Ochse, R. (1990). *Before the gates of excellence: The determinants of creative genius.* New York: Cambridge University Press.

Runco, M. A., & Albert, R. S. (Eds.). (1990). Theories of creativity. Newbury Park, CA: Sage.

Perspectives

Mark A. Runco
California State University, Fullerton

*Many creative insights have resulted from shifts in **PERSPECTIVE**. Shifts may force an actual change in one's physical position and thus change one's perspective in a literal and sensory way, or they may stimulate a change in the way the individual thinks about or defines a problem. This article will review the benefits of perspective for creative work. Famous cases will be cited as illustrations, and strategies implying an advantageous change of perspective will be discussed.*

Creative License Analogous to artistic license but not limited to the arts. Behaviorally, the strength and willingness to bend rules, question assumptions, break with tradition, and act in an unconventional fashion in order to ensure originality.

Egocentricism Being stuck in one's own perspective; being unable to take another's point of view.

Fixity Occurs when an individual views a problem from one perspective and is unable to break a routine or change perspective.

Incubation Time away from a problem which allows a relaxation of effort and eases shifts of perspective.

Paradigm Shifts Dramatic changes in worldviews and assumptions which occur periodically in the sciences.

Sociocentric Thinking The ability to take someone else's point of view. It is a mature capacity; young children are egocentric.

Tactics Intentional efforts to increase originality and creativity.

I. THE ROLE OF SHIFTS IN PERSPECTIVE IN THE ARTS AND SCIENCES

Changes of perspective are related to creativity in the arts and the sciences. Many artistic styles develop, for instance, when an artist or group of artists recognize the need to change the way the world is viewed. The new style, in this sense, presents an alternative perspective.

Dramatic shifts also characterize the sciences. In Thomas Kuhn's well-known model, "normal science" involves the accumulation of factual information, which is collected with theories and methods that reflect a similar perspective of the world. At some point, however, existing theories are found to be inadequate to explain certain observations. A dramatically new perspective results from a paradigm shift. These are dramatic in the sense that they do not merely extend the thinking that came before but instead introduce a completely new way to view the world. Examples include the scientific revolutions of Copernicus, Darwin, and Einstein. [*See* PARADIGM SHIFTS.]

Albert Einstein seems to have developed some of his most significant insights using thought experiments. He imagined himself riding a beam of light, for example, or on a train moving in the opposite direction to another train. These thought experiments gave Einstein a unique and useful perspective on the relativity of our physical world. [*See* EINSTEIN, ALBERT.]

Picasso has often been quoted as saying that he learned to paint only after he remembered how to think like a child. Picasso was well aware of the assumptions and routines adults too often develop. More often than not an adult's perspective will differ from that of a child.

One of the most dramatic changes in literature occurred when Dorothy Richardson and James Joyce developed stream-of-consciousness styles. They shifted the perspective within the novel away from the observer or third person and to the individual or protagonist.

Richardson, author of *Pilgrimage,* seems to have been the first to use stream-of-consciousness in literature. Her insight was that a new perspective in literature was needed. This led her to reorganize her thinking and writing about the protagonist of *Pilgrimage,* Miriam Henderson. Rather than describing the character and her actions, Richardson began to take the character's point of view and describe the "inner psychic existence and functioning" for the reader. . . . This process of organization and reorganization reflects a type of problem finding, for no one before Richardson saw the need for a new perspective (Runco, 1994).

II. PERSPECTIVE SHIFT AS FUNDAMENTAL TO RELATED PROCESSES

As my discussion of paradigm shifts may suggest, shifts in perspective, like those of Copernicus, Einstein,

and Darwin, can lead to dramatic changes in worldviews. In this sense the shift is the mechanism which leads to the insight. Shifts of perspective may underlie other processes related to creative work.

Recall here that shifts in perspective may be literal or metaphorical. Consider the tactic (often used in research and programs designed to enhance creative potential) to "stand the problem on its head." The idea here is to turn the issue upside down—to obtain a different view. Programs sometimes suggest magnifying or minifying a problem. In the former the problem or its representation is enlarged. In the latter the problem or its representation is reduced. Again, this requires a shift of perspective.

Another recommendation for finding creative ideas is to stand back and change one's "level of analysis." Related to this is the suggestion to alter the medium being used to represent the problem (use words instead of numbers or pictures instead of words). There may be several benefits to these changes, but certainly one of them is that a change of perspective is involved.

There are various explanations of the incubation that is often tied to creative insight. There may be a preconscious relaxation of constraints, allowing alternatives to be found. Incubation may be effective precisely because it allows one individual to find a new perspective and to break away from an existing viewpoint. Most of us have probably had the experience of taking time away from some difficult problem, only to return and solve the problem easily because we saw something that was obvious after the break (the incubation) that we were overlooking or taking for granted before it. [*See* INCUBATION.]

III. MOOD SWINGS AND PERSPECTIVE

A large amount of attention has been directed to the affective disorders of creative persons. Typically these are bipolar disorders, which are characterized by mood swings. Such mood swings may be functionally tied to creative work, and here again it is possible to speculate that there are relevant changes of perspective. Put briefly the mood swing may provide the individual with more than one perspective of his or her own work.

This hypothesis is supported by anecdotal reports by

creative persons that they are (a) highly productive but not critical when they are experiencing the mania of a mood swing, and later (b) highly critical—an effective editor so to speak—when they experience the depression which characterizes the opposite extreme and polarity of the mood swings. [*See* AFFECTIVE DISORDERS.]

IV. DEVELOPMENTAL TRENDS

Individuals may intentionally change their perspective in order to increase the likelihood of a creative insight. There may, however, be developmental trends in the capacity for shifting perspective. These would suggest that changes of perspective are more difficult for younger individuals and perhaps should not be encouraged early on.

Most obvious here is the tendency for young children to be egocentric in the sense that they cannot take someone else's perspective. Only in adolescence do individuals recognize that others hold different perspectives from one's own. To the degree that these general cognitive tendencies relate directly to creative problem solving, we would expect age differences in the capacity for using changes of perspective in a tactical manner to increase one's originality and creativity. This certainly would be consistent with theories of metacognition, with younger children not recognizing that tactics and intentional efforts are necessary for problem solving. [*See* DEVELOPMENTAL TRENDS IN CREATIVE ABILITIES AND POTENTIALS.]

V. COGNITIVE AND EXTRACOGNITIVE INFLUENCES ON SHIFTS OF PERSPECTIVES

Shifts of perspective require particular cognitive capacities. Some shifts may require visualization or other sensory capacities, as would be the case when the individual literally imagines what another perspective would look like. Higher order abilities are also required. The shift may, for example, take the individual to a hypothetical perspective, and this requires formal operational thinking. The shift may require that the individual imagines him- or herself in someone else's shoes. That is a special kind of hypothetical reasoning that reflects sociocentric thinking. This too is cognitively demanding. Young children, for example, will be egocentric and unable to shift to someone else's point of view.

Extracognitive capacities are also required for shifts. Open-mindedness is required, for example, because the individual must acknowledge that there are other possibilities. A courageous attitude may be necessary so the individual is willing to try something new, and perhaps take a risk with it. Ego strength will certainly be necessary. This provides the confidence to actually use one's personal creative license. Ego strength may be especially important because creative ideas and insights are often unconventional, and if they are found by shifting perspective, that shift may be away from conventions, norms, traditions, and expectations. It is analogous to what has been called "artistic license" but it may not involve art; hence the term "creative license."

VI. BEAUTY IS IN THE EYE OF THE BEHOLDER: PERSPECTIVE DIFFERENCES INFLUENCE JUDGMENTS OF CREATIVITY

To the degree that creativity is a social phenomenon, it is dependent on interpersonal judgments—and these will very likely vary depending on the perspectives held by the different persons involved. As a matter of fact there is a principle in social psychology that predicts that two people will tend to form different hypotheses to explain their actions. The person doing the action will tend to explain it in terms of the immediate environment and context. An observer of the same action will focus his or her explanation on the person involved. This follows from the divergent perspectives of the two individuals. The person doing the action will tend to look away from him- or herself. His or her physical perspective will be oriented outward. The observer, on the other hand, will probably see the person doing the action as salient and spend most of the time viewing that actor. This may apply to creative work, and a creator may explain his or her work contextually while an audience will emphasize the creator. The most important point is that discrepant perspectives lead to different opinions.

No wonder that (a) different judges often disagree about the qualities of creative work, or even about the level of creativity in the work, and (b) opinions of creators often differ from those of audiences and judges.

VII. CONCLUSIONS

Shifts of perspective are fundamental to several facets of the creative process. Some tactics may work effectively because they force the individual to shift perspective. Even though perspective is not mentioned in some recommendations, a change of perspective may be implicit in what is explicitly suggested, and its occurrence may explain the benefits.

The benefits of change of perspective may be explained in several ways. A shift of perspective may, for example, break the individual's routine and allow him or her to find an approach that is uncommon or novel. Novelty is of course a correlate of originality, and originality is in turn vital for creative insights. Shifts of perspective may thus have their effect because they lead directly to novelty. The breaking of routine may be sufficient for the finding of creative ideas and solutions. Much research has demonstrated that fixity precludes originality, and that avoiding fixity or breaking one's mental set can lead to original problem solving. The benefits of changes in perspective are numerous. [*See* PROBLEM SOLVING.]

Bibliography

Kuhn, T. (1963). The essential tension: Tradition and innovation in scientific research. In C. W. Taylor & F. Barron (Eds.), *Scientific creativity: Its recognition and development* (pp. 341–354). New York: Wiley.

Runco, M. A. (1994). Cognitive and psychometric issues in creativity research. In S. G. Isaksen, M. C. Murdock, R. L. Firestien, & D. J. Treffinger (Eds.), *Understanding and recognizing creativity* (pp. 331–368). Norwood, NJ: Ablex.

Shlain, L. (1993). *Art and physics.* New York: Quill/Morrow.

Wallace, D. B. (1991). The genesis and microgenesis of sudden insight in the creation of literature. *Creativity Research Journal, 4,* 4–50.

Fernando Pessoa
(Alberto Caeiro, Alvaro de Campos, Ricardo Reis, Bernardo Soares, and many more)

1888–1935
Writer

Works include *Message* by Fernando Pessoa, *The Keeper of Flocks* by Alberto Caeiro, *The Tobacconist* by Alvaro de Campos, *Odes* by Ricardo Reis, and *The Book of Disquietude* by Bernardo Soares

Barbara Duarte Esgalhado

Duquesne University

FERNANDO ANTÓNIO NOGUEIRA PESSOA was Portugal's major 20th-century writer. Over the span of his lifetime, he produced a vast array of poetry and prose that included commentaries on literature, aesthetics, philosophy, religion, and politics. In addition to his wide range of subject matter, Pessoa was extraordinarily original. This originality manifested itself not only in the form and content of his work, but in the manner in which it was conceived. Pessoa devised a creative universe with and through the use of what he referred to as "heteronyms"—72 in all. Heteronyms were personas, devised by Pessoa, from which to write. Although it is not unusual for writers to make use of a nom de plume or pen name as a creative device, Pessoa's creation of heteronyms extended well beyond this approach—particularly with four of them under which the bulk of his work fell: Alberto Caeiro, Alvaro de Campos, Ricardo Reis, and

Fernando Pessoa. Used with permission.

Bernardo Soares. These four were assigned biographical details, physical descriptions, specific aesthetic sensibilities, ideological inclinations, and relationships to each other. The creation of Bernardo Soares possessed a further distinction—that of being a "semiheteronym"— part autobiographical, part fiction. It was under this particular semiheteronym that Pessoa wrote his most autobiographical work, The Book of Disquietude.

I. BACKGROUND

Fernando Pessoa was born on June 13, 1888, to Joaquim de Seabra Pessoa, a civil servant in the Ministry of Justice who wrote for Lisbon's leading daily newspaper, *Diário de Notícias,* and Maria Madalena Pinheiro, a well-educated woman who was well versed in music, languages, and the written word. Pessoa's young life, however, was soon to be disrupted by the death of his father in 1893—when Pessoa was only 5 years old— and by the death of his brother 1 year later. It was in 1894 that Pessoa invented his first heteronym—one Chevalier de Pas.

Pessoa's mother remarried in 1895. Her new husband, João Miguel Rosa, was a Portuguese consul in Durban, South Africa. In 1896, the family moved to Durban. Upon arrival, Pessoa was enrolled in the West Street Convent School. Three years later, he continued his education at Durban High School. Pessoa proved to be a successful student and proceeded to learn English and French in addition to his native Portuguese. This ability in languages allowed him to read extensively and to be influenced by British, American, French, and Portuguese authors such as Milton, Shakespeare, Shelley, Keats, Tennyson, Carlyle, Poe, Whitman, Baudelaire, Verde, and Pessanha, respectively.

In 1901, due to the death of his half sister, Henriqueta Madalena, Pessoa returned with his family to Lisbon. He was 13 years old at the time. One year later, the family returned to Durban, and Pessoa entered a commercial school where he learned business English and bookkeeping. Two years later, back in high school, he published an essay on the historian Thomas Babington Macaulay. In addition, he was awarded the Queen Victoria Memorial Prize for his performance on his university examinations. Already proving to be an excellent student, Pessoa had to decide where to continue his studies. In 1905, at the age of 17, Pessoa decided to return to Lisbon, where he would remain all his life.

However, despite the return to Portugal and a brief stint at the university, Pessoa had little or no formal academic training. His plans to attend a university were thwarted by a student strike against João Franco, who at the time was the dictator of Spain. Throughout his life, Pessoa would rely primarily on his previous commercial business training for his livelihood as a bookkeeper and translator of foreign correspondence. This work would provide him with nearly sufficient income to write.

II. THE WRITING PESSOA

And write he did. Pessoa wrote nearly all the time and on nearly anything he could find, including scraps of paper. Although some of these "scraps" were published during his lifetime, most of them remained in a wooden trunk he left behind. Recent inventories have established that well over 25,000 items remain—still to be sorted and published.

Although many persons live to write, only a select few write to live. Pessoa was one such person. Certainly, he lived an everyday life—eating, drinking, working, sleeping, and interacting with friends, relatives, and associates. However, for the most part, he spent his time writing. This approach to living and writing has earned him such enigmatic titles as "The Man Who Never Was"—precisely because it often appears that, despite the engagement in the gestures of everyday life, Pessoa seemed to have lived predominately through an imagination that unfolded in and through his writing (this title is from the title of an essay written by Jorge de Sena. See Bibliography for source.) Also, given that he wrote very little under his own name of Fernando Pessoa, a question emerges as to the precise relationship between the author and the written text. Even his most autobiographical work is written as a semiautobiography by a semiheteronym— as if his life's story was, in part, a fiction.

A. The Writing Pessoa as Social Entity

No person creates in a vacuum. Human beings are inextricably linked to a multitude of intricacies that constitute their social world. These intricacies, in turn, formulate the very person and the world in which they create. For this reason, it is important to examine the social, historical, and ideological circumstances of any person's day—creative or otherwise—that constitute the person's very world. In Pessoa's case, his writing—both thematically and stylistically—gave voice to a historical time full of change and misgivings about present and future circumstances.

Modernism, the period in which Pessoa wrote, was formed by the changes that took place in the late 19th and early 20th centuries such as the impact of industrialization, world war, advances in technology, communism, fascism, and the spread of Western imperialism. One of the results of events such as these has been an increased disparity between inner and outer worlds. In previous historical periods, such as the Middle Ages or the Renaissance, people are said to have experienced more congruity between their inner lives and outer worlds. Lives were organized typically around their God, ruler, community, and family. The work that was done was continuous with the satisfaction of everyday needs such as providing food, shelter, and clothing for themselves and their families. However, with modern developments such as the increased use of technology, for example, and the resulting period of industrialization, the machine replaced work that human beings had once done. Although this transition made work more efficient, it also altered the relationship between human beings and the fruits of their labor. Mass production ensued, and with it a new era of reproduction through replication. Urban areas became centers of a new, technologically driven, modern age. Individuals and families often were forced to relocate from rural areas to urban centers to benefit from new job opportunities. Suddenly, there was a demand on persons to relate to their work, themselves, and others in a very different sort of way than they had been previously accustomed. This demand was to contribute to a need to negotiate life in an alternate way—one that would include a stance toward the newfound circumstances being presented. In short, urban life called for an unprecedented pluralism.

Modernism was also somewhat idiosyncratic in that its shape and impact was contingent on the particulars of the context in which it flourished. In Portugal, for example, certain conditions were present as a result of specific social, historical, and ideological circum-

stances that contributed to the exigencies of modern times, including the threat of war by Britain unless Portugal abdicated rights to what is now Zimbabwe, the financial and economic crisis of 1890–1891, and the 1910 revolution against the Portuguese monarchy. These specific, culturally bound events are important to the understanding of the factors that constitute the context in which any person—creative included—develops.

Although the effect of global changes may have been felt by people throughout, writers and artists typically depicted the effects in their artwork. Many writers and artists, situated in the urban centers of the day (e.g., London, Paris, Berlin, Vienna, New York), began to explore new forms and themes in reaction to the rapidly changing social and political world in which they found themselves.

One such theme was that of representation. Writers, in particular, used language to experiment with the issues of representation, including authorship. Pessoa devised two strategies in keeping with the modernist project. First, he created a universe of heteronyms from which to write that necessarily called into question the notion of authorship. Second, he wrote his most autobiographical work as a self-reflective text. Both these strategies suggest a play with representation, specifically, the relationship between who one is and what one writes—previously assumed to be a continuous relationship—in keeping with the previous view and experience of the world and lived life. It was through the use of both of these strategies that Pessoa also addressed the pluralism called for in persons as a result of the magnitude of changes being experienced at the time—changes that contributed to an increased fragmentation of reality, one of the fundamental characteristics of modern consciousness.

B. The Writing Pessoa as Excess to His Social World

The creation of a multitude of personas as a creative universe in which to write is certainly one response to a call for pluralism. However, despite Pessoa's creative response to the social, historical, and ideological circumstances of his day, there was a uniqueness about his approach that was not shared by many of his fellow countrymen and women. Differences such as these point to the way in which the individual, along with being formulated in and through the context in which she or he creates, can come to formulate a vision or perspective that relies on, but clearly exceeds, the very context in which it has been formulated. This excess—along with the finely tuned relationship between the creator, her or his medium, and her or his world—are just a few of the elements that come to constitute a creative person's life.

Portugal was and continues to be somewhat of a paradox. On the one hand, it manifested a certain sophistication during the Age of Discoveries in the 15th and 16th centuries when it participated in the exchange of goods through trade with China and India. On the other hand, it was, and remains, a largely homogenous population with cultural traditions and practices that, for the most part, have remained untouched to this day. In his day, Pessoa commented on a certain Portuguese provincialism—one sensibility he did not share with his fellow countrymen and women—perhaps due to the influence of having lived, learned, read, and written in two, very diverse worlds (Portugal and South Africa). As a result, he developed a sensibility uncommon among most others from his country, which, in turn, has earned him the credit of nearly single-handedly bringing modernism to Portugal.

III. CONCLUSION

This article has attempted to demonstrate the continuous relationship between the creative person and her or his social world. However, even with this continuity, a creative person, regardless of the shared experience of social, historical, and ideological conditions, brings her or his participation in these conditions to light—through her or his medium and imagination—in a unique and original way. Pessoa was one such person who, through both his writing and the creation of his universe of 72 heteronyms, demonstrated the way in which one person—an extraordinarily creative person—gave voice to the times in which he lived.

Bibliography

de Sena, J. (1982). The man who never was. In G. Monteiro (Ed.) *The man who never was: Essays on Fernando Pessoa*. Providence: Gávea-Brown.

Honig, E., & Brown, S. M. (Eds. & Trans.). (1986). *Poems of Fernando Pessoa*. New York: The Ecco Press.

Gallagher, T. (1983). *Portugal: A twentieth century interpretation*. Manchester: Manchester University Press.

Lisboa, E., & Taylor, L. C. (Eds.). (1995). *A Centenary Pessoa*. Manchester: Carcanet Press.

Pessoa, F. (1991). *The book of disquietude* (R. Zenith, Trans.). Manchester: Carcanet Press.

Jean Piaget

1896–1980

Psychologist

Works include *Language and Thought in the Child, Biology and Knowledge: An Essay on the Relations between Organic Regulations and Cognitive Processes, The Equilibration of Cognitive Structures,* and *The Origins of Intelligence in Children*

Howard E. Gruber

Teacher's College, Columbia University

JEAN PIAGET was one of the two or three outstanding psychologists of the 20th century. He was most widely recognized as a developmental psychologist. But his life-long effort was guided by biological and philosophical concerns about the nature, origins, and transformations of knowledge. For this reason he coined the term genetic epistemology *to characterize his vocation. His published output was enormous, some 60 books and monographs and well over 1000 articles.*

Jean Piaget. © CORBIS/Bettmann.

I. BACKGROUND

Jean Piaget was born on August 9, 1896, in Neuchâtel. He had two younger sisters. His father, Arthur Piaget, taught literature and history. His mother, née Rebecca-Suzanne Jackson, had no profession and was considered, at least by her son, to be quite neurotic. But she was active in socialist causes and during World War I, although outspokenly pro-French, she went to the aid of German refugees and prisoners.

In Neuchâtel, during Piaget's early years, there was considerable interest in science, especially natural history. Piaget's first publication, a paragraph describing an albino sparrow, appeared in 1907,* before he was 11 years old, in *Le Rameau de Sapin* (*The Fir Branch*), published by one of two local natural history societies in which he was active. During his boyhood and adolescence he studied the mollusks of the region assiduously and passionately. He received his first doctorate from the University of Neuchâtel, with a thesis on mollusks. Piaget went on to study at the University of Zurich and Paris, moving away (but not completely) from his early interest in mollusks to studies in philosophy, theology, psychology, and psychiatry. Beginning in 1921, he taught and did research at the University of Geneva until his death in 1980. From 1929 to 1939 he was professor of psychology, sociology, and philosophy of science at the University of Neuchâtel. From 1929 to 1939 he was also professor of history of scientific thought at the University of Geneva. Among his other parallel appointments at the University of Geneva, he was professor of sociology (1939–1971), director of the Institute for Educational Sciences (1933–1971), and professor of experimental psychology. Meanwhile, he was professor of developmental psychology at the Sorbonne in Paris (1952–1963). Although he retired from his professorships in 1971, he continued as director of the International Center for Genetic Epistemology (1955–1980). Recognition came early and continued long. Among his many honors were more than 30 honorary doctorates, the Dutch Erasmus Prize, and the Distinguished Psychologist Award of the American Psychological Association.

Although he wrote relatively little about education, he was director of the International Bureau of education from 1929 to 1967, and on the international stage his ideas have been very important in shaping thought about child rearing and education. The direction of his influence on educational thought has been to advance the conception of the child as a self-constructing knowing system and the conception of the teacher as a person who understands the process of cognitive development and the structure of knowledge according to the tenets of genetic epistemology.

No single work of his can be cited as most represen-

---

* In this article publication dates are given for the first appearance in French. Titles of works are given as published in English translation, except where there is none.

tative because his interest was in the cognitive system as a whole, at all organismic levels. Although he considered himself to be also a philosopher and a biologist, the article primarily focuses on his work as a psychologist. Taking his work as a whole, we can say that his network of enterprise was distinctly multidisciplinary but not eclectic. In every field he touched—psychology, biology, philosophy, history of science, and logic—he expressed a consistent and unified point of view. Various facets will be discussed later, but here we might bring out the particular form his biopsychological interactionism took, the elaboration of the idea of an "epigenetic landscape," borrowed in part from the British biologist Conrad Waddington. Briefly put, this means that, although the organism is self-constructing, it functions in a setting that provides various constraints on development, thus guaranteeing that all knowing systems will share certain cognitive characteristics. Although this position is certainly genetic, it is not the deterministic genetics of Mendel and his intellectual descendants. For Piaget every developmental step opens the way to new possibilities: Human knowledge has an ever-receding frontier.

Taking his work decade by decade, as a youth he was much concerned with the relation between science and religion and the relationships among the sciences. These preoccupations were expressed in a long prose poem, *The Mission of the Idea* (1915), and in an autobiographical, philosophical novel, *The Search* (1918). As already mentioned, during the same period he continued his work, mainly fieldwork, on mollusks, receiving his doctorate from the University of Neuchâtel in 1921.

His first book, *The Language and Thought of the Child* (1923), gained wide recognition. In the 1930s he published a pioneering trilogy about the mental development of his own three children. In the 1940s and 1950s much of his work was centered on elaborating the stage theory of mental growth, with a major focus on the period of concrete operations (i.e., from about 5 to 12 years of age). Toward the end of this period he and Bärbel Inhelder published *The Growth of Logical Thinking from Childhood to Adolescence: An Essay on the Construction of Formal Operational Structures* (1955). In this work he characterized the well-functioning adolescent as being capable of abstraction, thinking not only about things but about thought itself; capable of formulating and testing hypotheses systematically and with considerable combinatorial skill; and capable of distinguishing between the conceptually possible and the real as a special case of the possible. In one experiment it was shown that adolescents could construct an experiment about the period of a pendulum to demonstrate that, among a number of variables, only the length of the cord made a difference. It is striking that adolescents could do that much. In the history of science, it took many centuries until in about 1600 A.D. Galileo made his celebrated observations about pendulum motion. These somewhat paradoxical findings suggest the need for careful reflection on the relations between empirical psychology and the history of science.

Between 1955 and 1956 Piaget founded the Centre International d'Epistémologie Génétique, which held its first international symposium in 1956. This led to a long series of monographs constituting a protracted effort to integrate the empirical and theoretical works of Piaget and his collaborators. Subjects taken up included the epistemology of space, time, causality, and chance; also included were works on child logic and on the relation between learning and development, and—going beyond childhood and adolescence—the history of science. Among many elaborations and overviews perhaps the most comprehensive and accessible in English is *Biology and Knowledge: An Essay on the Relations between Organic Regulations and Cognitive Processes* (1967).

In the 1960s and 1970s Piaget and others in his entourage moved away from the earlier emphasis on stages and structures toward a more functional concern with intellectual processes and the strategies and procedures subjects actually use. Perhaps the most important work of this period is *The Equilibration of Cognitive Structures: The Central Problem of Intellectual Development* (1975).

It should be mentioned that Piaget was primarily interested in the *epistemic subject*—that is, the characteristics that all knowing systems must develop. In contrast, most psychologists have been interested in the psychological subject—that is, the particularities of individual persons. These two perspectives are not contradictory but complementary. Piaget has often been criticized for his omissions: having neglected the study of affect and the study of interpersonal relations. In reply it might be said, first, that one person cannot do everything and, second, that the criticism is based on

an incomplete knowledge of Piaget's work, especially the following: *The Moral Judgment of the Child* (1932), *Play, Dreams and Imitation in Childhood* (1945), and his lectures in 1954 at the Sorbonne on "Intelligence and Affectivity," published later.

For his analysis of different forms of knowledge, Piaget borrowed descriptive categories from philosophers, such as Kant, and from the history of science. Thinkers in these fields either took these categories for granted a priori or explicitly attributed them to learning and association. On the contrary, Piaget believed that these categories develop through the child's interaction with the world, both in its physical and social aspects. Piaget and his collaborators found ways of observing and documenting this development. There are thousands of articles and monographs reporting this work. We can consider only a few examples here.

II. CONSERVATION

The idea of conservation permeates scientific thought. Nothing is destroyed: Change consists entirely in processes of transformation. In the history of science this perspective was not freely given but hard won, discovered and rediscovered in many settings. Each such rediscovery was a great intellectual victory. Sometimes the search for what was conserved was undertaken deliberately, to solve a particular problem. Sometimes the discovery occurred in the course of trying to solve some other problem. A few key examples follow.

William Harvey, in his studies of the functioning of the heart and the circulation of the blood, had to refute the notion that each pulsation of the heart expelled blood from the body so that the blood had to be continually replaced. He calculated the amount of blood that must pass any point on each pulsation and was able to show that if it had to be replenished the amount of blood required would weigh thousands of times the weight of the body, a *reductio ad absurdum*. Thus, by assuming the conservation of the weight of the blood as it circulates, he was able to support his general position that the blood moves through the body in a closed cycle.

Around the same time, 1600 A.D., Galileo was able to demonstrate the fruitfulness of the idea of the conservation of momentum. About 200 years later Lavoisier was able to demonstrate the conservation of the weight of matter as it is transformed through burning. About 50 years later several scientists were able to demonstrate the conservation of energy across a variety of transformations, both biological and physical.

In modern science the conservation principle is so well established that it can guide the search for understanding of puzzling phenomena. Faced with an unexplained transformation, the physicist may be heard to mutter, "Something must be conserved—what is it?"

Piaget drew on this history for his studies of children's thinking. At one point, around 1930, he asked one of his students to show a child a lump of sugar dissolving in a glass of water. When the sugar disappears, the question becomes "Where did it go? Does it still exist? Did the level of the water rise when the now-invisible lump was dropped into the glass and if so did it stay up as the sugar disappeared? Children of different ages give different answers to these questions as their conceptual development proceeds. These observations were followed, over the next 2 decades, by some of Piaget's most famous experiments. Let the child make a ball out of clay, then squash it down into a pancake: Does the amount of clay remain the same? Likewise, if you pour water from a tall thin vessel into a short wide one—or vice versa—does the amount remain the same? The person who worked with Piaget on this problem, and on many others, was Bärbel Inhelder. They became lifelong collaborators.

This work has been repeated in many countries and forms the basis for Piaget's account of the stage of concrete operations. By operations he meant the mental acts by which the child copes with problems of the type described.

For conservation of matter three main operations have been discerned: identity, reversibility, and compensation. That is, "You didn't add anything or take anything away." "You could pour the water back again and it would reach the same level." "It's taller, but it's thinner." To the uninitiated it comes as a great surprise that it takes about 5 to 10 years to move from grasping the elementary conservation of matter to grasping the conservation of volume (i.e., displacement volume when an object is submerged in a vessel of water). The work on the development of concrete operations was done mainly with school-age children. Development

within this period has been richly documented in varied social settings and variegated tasks focusing on a wide range of concepts. The preoperational period and the period of formal operations are less well understood. On the other hand, the sensorimotor period was beautifully elaborated in Piaget's study of his own three children, which remain irreplaceable classics.

Piaget liked to describe one child who was spontaneously exploring the idea of number. This boy had about a dozen objects, which he would arrange in some spatial configuration and then count. Then he would rearrange them in another configuration and count them again. After each observation, of course, he got the same result. Finally he exclaimed, "Once you know, you know forever!"

This child's optimistic attitude toward the growth of knowledge resembles the scientist who, committed to the task of discovery, persists in this work in the face of all obstacles. The person who worked with Piaget on the child's conception of number—a subject that can get very subtle and sophisticated—was Alina Szeminska, a Polish woman who spent many years in Geneva. When World War II threatened, she went home and was eventually imprisoned in a concentration camp, but survived.

In many areas, then, Piaget found that intellectual development moved forward in a stagelike way. There has been some confusion resulting from Piaget's use of *stage* in somewhat different ways. On the one hand, he speaks of the four great stages: sensorimotor, preoperational, concrete operations, and formal operations. Movement through these stages is thought to take about 12 years. On the other hand, because in describing the first 2 years of life, Piaget discerned six stages, it will simplify matters if we refer to the stages of infancy as substages. In *The Origins of Intelligence in Children,* Piaget recounted his observations of his own three children in the first 2 years of life. Some phrases from this account give the general flavor: the Third Stage—procedures destined to make interesting sights last; the Fifth Stage—discovery of new means through active experimentation; the Sixth Stage—the invention of new means through mental combinations. The similarity of these concepts used for describing the baby to things we might say about the sciences is apparent. In *The Construction of Reality in the Child,* Piaget's emphasis is less on the process of thought and more on the content. Piaget takes up the development in the baby of four basic concepts: object, space, time, and causality. Here again we encounter six substages in the development of each of these concepts.

Piaget rarely discussed the concept of stage. Rather, he used it to organize his observations. He took the position that stages are not general. Uneven development, or décalage, occurs often in Piaget's empirical work. Indeed, for disequilibration to be a powerful force in development, widespread décalage is essential.

Although Piaget referred frequently to stages in his empirical work, his emphasis changed over time to ideas of process, such as exploring the possible, discovering the necessary, coping with contradiction, and moving toward wider and more stable equilibrations.

Piaget has often been criticized for his supposed neglect of two important areas: the psychology of affect and social processes. In reply it can be said that this "neglect" was by no means total. With regard to affect, several of his early works are pertinent: *Language and Thought of the Child* and *The Moral Judgment of the Child*. Moreover, the idea of intense interest as a motivating force permeates Piaget's work. The twin ideas, that there is a universal thirst for knowledge and that disequilibrated cognitive structures are disturbing, are hardly devoid of affect.

With regard to social processes, the criticism is unjust. In addition to the works mentioned earlier, a collection of his sociological essays, which finally appeared in English in 1995, belies the objection. Also, his celebrated experimental work on perspective taking in children showed that the child must learn to grasp the consequences of looking at a scene from more than one position, in other words, how the other sees the world and how different points of view can be synthesized. More generally, Piaget's work shows the child as moving away from domination by authority and arbitrary convention and moving toward freely chosen, self-constructed social ideas. If so, it can truly be said that in each generation children rediscover the social contract. Obviously, this statement is idealized, even utopian. Among other things it provides no place for leaders or for other exceptional people—and for that matter, no place for evil. Piaget's whole oeuvre depicts an unbroken series of cognitive victories, a forward march of knowledge, always graciously inclusive, assimilating old knowledge into new schemas. The picture reminds one of the exchange, perhaps apocryphal, between the English painter Turner and a woman who objected that the sunsets she saw were nowhere near as glorious as the ones he painted. Turner's reply ran, "But, madam, don't you wish they were?"

Bibliography

Chapman, M. (1988). *Constructive evolution*. Cambridge: Cambridge University Press.

Ginsburg, H. P., & Opper, S. (1988). *Piaget's theory of intellectual development* (3rd ed.). Englewood Cliffs, NJ: Prentice Hall.

Gruber, H. E., & Vonèche, J. J. (1977). *The essential Piaget*. New York: Basic Books.

Inhelder, B., & Piaget, J. (1958). *The growth of logical thinking from childhood to adolescence*. New York: Basic Books.

Piaget, J. (1923). *The language and thought of the child*. London: Routledge & Kegan Paul.

Piaget, J. (1952). *The origins of intelligence in children*. New York: International Universities Press.

Piaget, J. (1954). *The construction of reality in the child*. New York: Basic Books.

Piaget, J. (1971). *Biology and knowledge: An essay on the relations between organic regulations and cognitive processes*. Chicago: University of Chicago Press.

Piaget, J. (1972). *The child and reality*. New York: Grossman.

Piaget, J. (1975). *The equilibrium of cognitive structures*. Chicago: University of Chicago Press.

Piaget, J., & Inhelder, B. (1974). *The child's construction of quantities: Conservation and atomism*. London: Routledge & Kegan Paul.

Piaget, J., & Inhelder, B. (1969). *The psychology of the child*. New York: Basic Books.

Sylvia Plath

1932–1963

Novelist and poet

Author of *The Colossus and Other Poems, Ariel, The Bell Jar, Crossing the Water, Winter Trees,* and *The Collected Poems*

David Lester

Center for the Study of Suicide
Blackwood, New Jersey

SYLVIA PLATH (Victoria Lucas) was a creative American poet who died at the age of 30 in 1963 in England by putting her head in a gas oven. She wrote several volumes of poetry and a novel. Her work was based on her life experiences and had a confessional quality common also to the poets Robert Lowell and Anne Sexton. Plath had a severe depression when she was an undergraduate student, during which she attempted suicide. She was treated with electroconvulsive therapy and psychotherapy. Her life provides an opportunity to explore how creativity and psychiatric disorder interact throughout the course of a life history.

I. BACKGROUND

Plath's father, Otto Plath, was born in 1885 in the German town of Grabow. He emigrated to the United States when he was 15 years old and earned a doctorate in 1928, specializing in the study of bees. He began teaching at Boston University where he met a student named Aurelia Schober who was 21 years his junior. After divorcing his first wife, he married Aurelia in

Sylvia Plath seated in front of a bookshelf. (Copyright CORBIS/Bettmann.)

1932. Sylvia Plath was born on October 27, 1932, three weeks ahead of schedule. She was somewhat frail because of a sinus condition that plagued her for the rest of her life. Two and a half years later, her brother Warren was born.

Plath's early years were uneventful. She apparently was quite bright and used her intelligence to please her father, as many firstborns do. She learned the Latin names for insects, and Otto would show off her skill to visitors. From the beginning, she earned straight As in school, impressing teachers with her intelligence and dedication. Aurelia read a lot to the children as they grew, and Plath's verbal skills were so advanced that she went to school at age 4 and excelled right away. By age 5, she was writing short poems.

Otto fell ill in 1935, and he deteriorated over the next 4 years. He decided that he had lung cancer and chose not to seek treatment so that he would die quickly. He, therefore, initially refused to consult with doctors. In 1940, he noticed weird symptoms and finally sought medical advice. He found out that he had diabetes, which was treatable at that time, but he had waited too long before seeking treatment. In October 1940 his leg was amputated, and he died of an embolism on November 5, 1940, 8 days after Sylvia's birthday. Early loss is common among those who later commit suicide, and it may make them less able to cope with loss later in life.

Aurelia moved to Wellesley where she could raise her children in an educated and middle-class community and give them high-achievement experiences. Plath's first poem appeared in the *Boston Sunday Herald* in August 1941, when she was 8½ years old, and she won a prize for a drawing in another contest. As she progressed through school, her work continued to be outstanding, and she received many awards. She quickly developed an interest in literature and in writing. In junior high school she received straight As and a perfect record of punctuality. Her poems and drawings continued to win prizes. Her IQ was about 160.

High school continued in the same vein. Plath took the advanced literature courses and edited the school magazine in her senior year. Her stories and poems appeared in magazines such as *Seventeen* and the *Christian Science Monitor*. She was also active in the local Unitarian church and in the community. She ranked first among the 158 graduates and was admitted to

Smith College on a scholarship. Her biographers do not mention psychological problems at this time in Plath's life, though she tended to suffer from depression whenever her sinuses or menstrual cramps bothered her. However, the frequency and severity of the depressions is unclear.

Plath's career at Smith was outstanding. From the first, she obtained mainly As, and her literary achievements steadily grew. Throughout her stay at Smith, she worked hard, often ending up fatigued and depressed.

She continued to write and submit her work for publication. Despite frequent rejections, she built up an incredible body of published works. Indeed, a $500 prize from *Mademoiselle* in the summer of 1952 led to an offer by Knopf and Dodd Mead asking her to consider writing a novel. However, not surprisingly, a run of rejection slips led Plath to question her ability and to fall into a depression.

Her junior year led to her most severe depression. She confided to her mother thoughts of suicide, and she saw a psychiatrist in December of that year. But she continued to study hard and work toward winning a guest editorship at *Mademoiselle* in the summer of 1953, which she indeed won.

The summer of 1953 is the focus of Plath's novel *The Bell Jar,* written mostly during 1961 and 1962. At *Mademoiselle* Plath worked for Cyrilly Abels, reading and judging manuscripts and participating in all of the social activities planned for the group of guest editors. Abels noticed Plath's distancing manner and tried to break through and relate to the real Sylvia, but she failed to penetrate Plath's social mask. Although the guest editorship was exciting, Plath came home depressed by the experience.

Back in Wellesley, Plath was rejected for a course on creative writing at Harvard summer school, which left her with two months to fill. She could not write, and her depression worsened. After she cut her legs in a suicidal gesture, her mother began locking up the sleeping pills in the bedroom that they shared and took Plath to a local psychiatrist who diagnosed a depressive disorder and recommended electroconvulsive therapy. (In the 1950s, effective antidepressant medications had not yet been developed.) The electroconvulsive shock therapy seemed to make Plath's condition worse, and she developed chronic insomnia.

Plath contemplated using a razor blade to kill herself

and she tried to drown herself in the sea. Eventually, on a Monday morning in August 1953, she took 40 sleeping pills from where her mother had locked them up, went into the basement of the house (after leaving a note saying that she was going for a hike and would be back the next day), and crawled behind some wood that was stacked there. (It appears that she threw up some of the pills, which possibly saved her life.) Her mother called the police that evening, and search parties were organized. Plath was not found until Wednesday afternoon when her grandmother went into the basement to do the laundry and heard Plath moaning.

After a week in the hospital, Plath was transferred to the locked psychiatric ward at Massachusetts general Hospital where Erich Lindemann examined her. He diagnosed an adolescent nervous illness, whereas another psychiatrist diagnosed an acute schizophrenic episode. Her depression did not lift, and so she was transferred to McLean Hospital where she received insulin shock therapy, then chlorpromazine, and finally electroshock therapy again. This treatment was supplemented by psychotherapy from a female psychiatrist, Ruth Barnhouse. Barnhouse observed that Plath first refused to talk much and was angry at her mother. Barnhouse saw Plath as an intuitive-feeling type in Jung's schema, and Plath said that she felt she had been forced into using thinking to the neglect of feeling. Surprisingly, this time the electroconvulsive therapy helped and during the Christmas holidays Plath's depression disappeared. Plath was released in January 1953. She told a friend that she had tried to kill herself because she feared she had lost her talent to write. She also told him that she had tried to slit her throat when she was 10 years old, and she did have a scar on her throat. Barnhouse had encouraged Plath to no longer suppress her sexual impulses, so Plath had sex for the first time. When she returned to college, Plath confided to another friend that she had both loved and despised her father and probably wished many times that he was dead. When he died, she imagined that she had killed him (a theme that later appeared in one of her poems).

Aurelia heard from one of Otto's sisters that Otto's mother, a sister, and a niece had all suffered from depression, raising the possibility that an inherited predisposition to depression ran in the family.

Plath spent another 1½ years at Smith and graduated in June 1955. Although Smith took away the scholarship for her first semester back, the college restored it for her final year. Graduation resulted in many prizes and awards, including Phi Beta Kappa and summa cum laude (one of only four students in her class so honored), and she was awarded a Fulbright scholarship to Cambridge University in England.

Plath had written at least 200 poems, short stories, newspaper articles, and magazine pieces, some of which had been published in national periodicals. Of course, she also received numerous rejection slips, but although the rejections often damaged her self-confidence they did not deter her from writing and submitting her work for publication.

II. CAMBRIDGE UNIVERSITY AND TED HUGHES

Plath spent 2 years at Newnham College of Cambridge University, where she eventually obtained her second BA. She hated the cold and rainy weather and the poor heating of the rooms. She fell ill frequently with sinusitis, colds, and the flu. She realized how much better prepared the British students were, and she abandoned plans to obtain a doctorate. She kept busy with course work, writing, and dating. Plath determined that she would be, at best, a minor writer and decided to settle down as a wife and mother who would write only in her spare time. Her depression worsened, and she saw a psychiatrist at the university.

Then in February 1956, she met Ted Hughes. Hughes, an aspiring poet and writer like Plath, had graduated from Cambridge in 1954 and had worked in various odd jobs. Plath met him at a party in Cambridge and was attracted "at first sight." They married in June 1956.

Plath began to work with dedication on their literary careers, typing up and sending off submissions of both Hughes's work and her own. Their publications grew more and more numerous, and Hughes's first collection of poems was accepted for publication in 1957. They came to the United States, and Plath taught at Smith College for a year.

At this time, Hughes was the more successful poet. He had soon completed a second book of poems and a book of children's stories. His poems appeared in *The New Yorker*. The couple decided to return to England, especially as Hughes was not happy in the United States. But first they spent a year in Boston, and they supported themselves with the money Plath earned working at odd jobs along with their income from writing. Plath audited a course at Boston University from Robert Lowell, during which she met Anne Sexton, and her poems were eventually accepted by *The New Yorker*. Plath went back into therapy with Ruth Barnhouse and dealt with some of the feelings she had toward her mother and, with Barnhouse's encouragement, visited her father's grave.

Hughes was awarded a Guggenheim fellowship, which eased the couple's financial worries, and they were invited for three months to Yaddo, an artists' colony near Saratoga Springs in New York. They spent 3 months touring the United States during the summer of 1959, and during this trip Plath found out that she was pregnant. They left for England in December 1959. Plath was twenty-seven, pregnant, and headed for permanent residence in a foreign country.

III. ENGLAND AND SUICIDE

The couple first rented an apartment in London. Plath gave birth to Frieda in April 1960. Visits to Hughes's family did not go well, as Plath and Hughes's sister Olwyn had severe conflicts. Later that year, Plath and Hughes looked for and found a house in Croton, Devon, with the help of loans from both of their families. Before moving, Plath found out that she was pregnant again. They rented their apartment in London to a Canadian poet, David Wevill, and his German-Russian wife, Assia Gutmann, and moved to Devon.

Their literary careers continued to progress, and Plath's first book of poems was published in 1960. They each won prize after prize and by 1961 were successful enough as writers that their finances were thereafter in good shape. In 1961, Plath was awarded a Saxton Foundation grant to work on *The Bell Jar*.

Plath gave birth to a son, Nicholas, in January 1962, but Hughes seemed unhappy to have a son and kept distant from the baby. He later admitted that he had not wanted any children. The cold winter made Plath ill and depressed, but life was full and busy with writing, the children, and a new house to fix up.

By the summer of 1962, another woman had entered Hughes's life. Hughes and Plath had invited poet David Wevill and his wife Assia Gutman to visit, and soon Hughes and Gutman were in love and having an affair. Hughes left Plath in July, but Plath maintained hope that he would return to her.

Her work did not go well at this time. Plath's *Colossus and Other Poems* had received poor reviews, and the poems written in her new style were being rejected. She was also finding it hard to write. On her 30th birthday in October 1962, she was in Devon with two children, deserted by her husband, and now writing poems furiously every morning. By December Plath had moved to an apartment in London and had rented the house in Devon to others.

The last few weeks of Plath's life were difficult. She corrected the galley proofs for *The Bell Jar* and was awaiting publication and comment. She was working feverishly, smoking heavily, hardly sleeping, and eating little. She had lost 20 lb. since the summer and developed influenza, after which the children came down with it. The winter was one of the worst ever, with frozen plumbing, strikes by the electrical workers, and snow and ice everywhere. The weather did not break until the end of January.

The reviews of Plath's book appeared at the end of January, and they were lukewarm. (She had published it under a pseudonym, which meant that reviewers would be less likely to give the work close attention that a work by Sylvia Plath would merit.) Her recent poems were being rejected, and her publishers could not sell *The Bell Jar* to an American publisher.

In the last week of her life, from February 4, 1963 to February 11, Plath had a fever and wildly fluctuating moods. She lost her au pair on February 7 after arguing with her, and the weather was still bad. Plath kept in close contact with her physician, John Horder, and after February 4 she saw him daily. He treated her depression on his own, but also tried to refer her to a regular psychiatrist. Horder put Plath on antidepressants (a monoamineoxidase inhibitor), and then, on February 7, searched for a bed in a suitable hospital so that Plath could be admitted. Two he approached were full, and one he deemed unsuitable.

Friends invited Plath and the children to come and stay that day. On the evening of Friday, February 8, she met Hughes briefly and then came back to her friends' home. However, on Sunday she decided to take the children home, despite the protestations of her friends. Horder called her that night. That night she put the kids to sleep, opened their windows, placed milk and bread and butter by their beds, left a note on her downstair's neighbor's door to call Horder, sealed herself in the kitchen, and put her head in the oven and turned the gas on.

Horder had arranged for a nurse to come on Monday morning, February 11. The nurse arrived at 9 a.m., but could not get in. She went to a public telephone to check on the address she was supposed to visit, and came back to see two children crying at the bedroom window. She found a workman who helped her break in, and they found Plath. The workman began artificial respiration, and the nurse took over. A police officer rescued the children, but when Horder arrived he pronounced Plath dead at 10:30 a.m. The gas had asphyxiated the downstairs neighbor too, and he did not regain consciousness until the late afternoon.

IV. DISCUSSION

The loss of her father when she was 8 years old looms large in Plath's life, especially because of the way she wrote about him. Plath seemed to be filled with anger over his rejection of her, both while he was alive (neglecting her for his research) and upon his death. Her poem written in the months prior to her suicide casts him as a devil, a concentration camp guard with her as a victim. She viewed Hughes as a father substitute. Yet she loved her father too and casts her suicide attempt years earlier as an effort to be reunited with him. (Interestingly, Plath eventually kept bees, as did her father, and she studied German, the language of her father. Her identification with him was strong.)

Plath was depressed throughout her life, and it is likely that she had an affective disorder. Her first major breakdown occurred when she was an undergraduate, and her suicide has partly been attributed to her fear of becoming psychotic again. On top of this, she lost her husband, whom she loved, and who provided her with

the environment to flourish as a mother and author. He not only left her, but he rejected her for another.

In her novel about her psychiatric breakdown in 1953, Plath shows a distrust of her ability. She had worked hard to get good grades and to publish, but she feared that the success was temporary. However, Plath seemed to be quite persistent in her writing career and sent off poems and stories despite rejections.

V. WAS PLATH'S WRITING HELPFUL OR HARMFUL?

Is writing therapeutic for creative writers or is it a stressor that can contribute to their psychological disturbance? Martin Silverman and Norman Will have argued that, although Plath tried to control her suicidal impulses by means of her poetry, she failed in this endeavor. Successful poetry, they suggested, must communicate between the inner worlds of the creative person and the audience. (Presumably they mean *critically* successful, for even poor poetry can serve a useful psychological function for the writer, even if it is merely cathartic.) To be successful, poetry must first achieve a balance between the writer's use of the audience to serve his or her own narcissistic needs (a type of exhibitionism) and the desire to give others a way of structuring the terrors and anxieties that afflict us all.

The writer must also achieve a balance between the potentially destructive conscious and unconscious forces motivating the writing and the constructive desires to harness these forces for the purpose of writing creatively. In terms of psychoanalysis, the writer must balance primary and secondary process mechanisms. The writer must also compromise between the fantasy permissible in writing and the acceptance of reality necessary for successful living.

When they applied their ideas to Sylvia Plath, Silverman and Will asserted that the successful creative process is successful only when the unconscious forces in the writer operate silently and remain hidden from view. This assertion represents a rather traditional view of creative writing. It would seem to express a preference on the part of Silverman and Will for a particular type of literature rather than expressing a universal truth. For example, the unconscious forces motivating

Ernest Hemingway may be under control in his writing, but they are certainly not hidden, and the confessional style of poetry developed by W. D. Snodgrass and Robert Lowell and pursued by Anne Sexton and Sylvia Plath is in direct opposition to Silverman and Will's view.

In Plath's later poems she revealed her deepest feelings, using her experiences to create the poem rather than to simply transform it. Silverman and Will noted that she described her early poems as "proper in shape and number and every part" but not alive. Her poems moved from being a reordering and reshaping of experience with a poetic purpose to becoming expressions of herself. She identified with her poems, which made their rejection even more painful, and Silverman and Will labeled this change as a "narcissistic regression."

The causal sequence that Silverman and Will propose for Plath is simply one reading of Plath's life. Other equally plausible alternative paths can be proposed. For example, it is quite likely that Plath's participation—along with Anne Sexton, with whom she became very close—in a poetry workshop run by Robert Lowell had a major impact on her writing style. Several members of his workshop adopted a more self-revealing content for their poems, and two received Pulitzer prizes for their work (Lowell and Sexton).

Furthermore, Plath, as she herself clearly recognized, was prone to recurring depressions. In all probability, Plath had an affective disorder, possibly bipolar, and her depressions were likely to reoccur periodically. It is evident from the severity of her depression in 1953, which led to a very serious suicide attempt, that she would likely become suicidal again with each new depression (much as Virginia Woolf had).

It is interesting to note that although her writing may not have helped her cope with the stressors, external and intrapsychic, with which she was confronted during the early 1950s, in the later 1950s her switch to a more revealing and personalized style of writing may have helped her survive. Silverman and Will claimed that her writing failed to prevent her suicide. Perhaps it may have postponed her suicide?

In the months prior to her suicide, Plath wrote feverishly, sometimes producing several poems in one day.

(This feverish activity in the months prior to a suicide was apparent also in Anne Sexton's life.) What would Silverman and Will suggest as a more appropriate strategy for a person confronting intrapsychic turmoil who is not under professional care? It is very likely that the writing helped Plath control her inner turmoil, and some commentators think that the poems she produced were among her finest.

David Lester and Rina Terry have argued that writing poetry can be useful with suicidal clients. They saw the construction and revision of poems as serving a similar function for clients as the journal assignments devised by cognitive therapists by giving the clients intellectual control over their emotions and distance from the traumatic memories.

Both Plath and Sexton showed manic trends prior to their suicides, writing poems furiously, poems with more emotional expression and less poetic crafting. Rather than arguing that writing poetry contributed in part to their suicides, it makes much more sense to say that, in their final breakdowns, poetry was no longer able to help them deal with the intrapsychic forces driving them as it had in the past. As their inner turmoil increased, both wrote feverishly, almost like a safety valve letting out the steam under pressure in a boiler, but to no avail because the pressure was building up faster than they could release it.

This final failure of the craft of poetry to keep Sylvia Plath alive may not signify total failure. She was an outstanding poet and functioned quite well given her psychiatric disorder. Perhaps the craft of poetry kept her alive for many years after her self-destructive impulses first manifested themselves.

Bibliography

Alexander, P. (1991). *Rough magic.* New York: Viking.

Butscher, E. (1976). *Sylvia Plath.* New York: Seabury.

Lester, D., & Terry, R. (1993–1994). Emotional self-repair and poetry. *Omega, 28,* 79–84.

Silverman, M. A., & Will, N. P. (1986) Sylvia Plath and the failure of emotional self-repair through poetry. *Psychoanalytic Quarterly, 55,* 99–129.

Wagner-Martin, L. (1987). *Sylvia Plath.* New York: Simon & Schuster.

Play

Jeffrey L. Dansky

Eastern Michigan University

Associative Fluency The tendency to produce numerous ideas in response to questions or other situations; associative fluency is an important dimension of the process of creative problem solving.

Object Transformation Treating one object as if it were another.

Pretense A type of play in which children act out everyday and imaginative activities; includes role taking and object transformations.

Representational Thought Mental activity involving symbols, images, and ideas about objects or situations that are not present at the time.

Sociodramatic Play Tutoring Teaching or encouraging cooperative make-believe play in which children adopt roles and enact real or imagined plots.

*Both theory and research link **PLAY** to creativity. However, many behaviors that are labeled or categorized as play have little or nothing to do with creativity. This is because the term has so often been used as a catchall for virtually every type of behavior that does not seem to* serve some immediate goal-directed purpose in the way that eating and sleeping do. Breadth is not the only obstacle to the meaningful use of this term. Consider the playing of games. Some games with rules allow for a bit of playful variation, and some games, such as chess, require a certain amount of creativity from the successful player (at least until IBM's Deep Blue computer program beat world chess champion Garry Kasparov in 1997). But most rule-governed games leave little room for playfulness. Therefore, this article focuses on links between creativity and playful behavior, with the term play being reserved for those free-play activities that are to some significant degree playful. Playfulness refers more to the quality of an activity than to any specific behaviors that may or may not occur. Activities are considered playful to the extent that they are intrinsically motivated and self-directed, that they are relatively free from externally imposed rules or constraints, and that the link between means and ends is loose and flexible. In addition to this relative sense of freedom from stimulus or task constraints, playful activity also tends to involve positive affective states such as pleasure, joy, excitement, or fun. This article first provides a conceptual framework relating play to creativity, then examines empirical studies of the relationship between play and creativity, and concludes by discussing practical implications of this research and issues that require further study. The dimensions of creativity to which play will be related are *flexibility and the ability to produce ideas and behavior sequences that are both novel and adaptive. It might be noted from the outset that the kinds of behaviors and psychological processes that have just been described as playful are frequently creative in and of themselves.*

I. CONCEPTUAL FRAMEWORK LINKING PLAY TO CREATIVITY

A. Theories about Play and Creativity

The idea that play contributes to human development, particularly children's development, is not a new one. It dates back at least to the time of the Enlightenment and was subsequently promoted by influential educational theorists such as Rousseau, Froebel, and Montessori. Twentieth-century theorists like Vygotsky, Piaget, Bruner, Singer, and Sutton-Smith have continued to emphasize the role of play in development. One reason for assuming that play contributes to behavioral adaptations, including the ability to respond flexibly to one's environment, is that play occurs so frequently in many mammalian species during early periods of development, while major cognitive and behavioral systems are both emerging and becoming organized. Play is also most common and complex among higher mammals who undergo extended periods of socialization and display considerable flexibility in the ways in which they adapt to their environments. Although possibly a coincidence of nature, most theorists consider these observations evidence of the adaptive, evolutionary significance of play, and of the many adaptive functions that have been attributed to play, enhanced flexibility or creativity is probably the most common.

In his essay, "Nature and Uses of Immaturity," Jerome Bruner referred to play as "that special form of violating fixity." He suggested that evolution has provided humans and the great apes with an extended period of immaturity during which they are protected by their mothers and left free to observe, imitate, and cultivate the complex skills that permit them to live in societies that are noteworthy for their relative lack of rigidity. Much of this flexibility is attributed to the prolonged opportunities for play that are afforded to the young. Bruner suggested that, because playful activity tends to occur in relatively safe contexts and without the pressure inherent in much goal-directed action, the player feels free to experiment with combinations of subroutines and emerging skills that would not be tried under other circumstances. He contended that one of the critical "uses of immaturity" is to provide opportunities for the young to acquire flexible repertoires of skills that can later be creatively combined during goal-directed problem solving. Both naturalistic observation and experimental studies tend to support Bruner's theorizing. For example, when preschoolers (or chimpanzees) are given opportunities to play with various objects, they subsequently perform better on divergent problem-solving tasks. Although Bruner wrote extensively about how the playful manipulation of objects might contribute to flexible tool use, combinatorial play is also observed as symbolic skills are emerging.

Brian Sutton-Smith and Jerome Singer are two other play theorists who have had major influences on contemporary thinking about play and creativity. Sutton-Smith characterized play as "an exercise of voluntary control systems" in which the player "can choose the arbitrariness of the constraints within which he will act or imagine." Although Sutton-Smith views play as more self-expressive than functional, he noted that the imaginative and fantastic possibilities that emerge during children's play are also likely to increase the player's repertoire of actions and ideas that may later be called on in more serious problem-solving contexts. Singer believes that children's play, and particularly their make-believe play, serves multiple short- and long-term functions. In his book, *The Child's World of Make-Believe,* Singer proposed that children practice imagery and rehearse imaginal and verbal skills through play. He also considers such play a source of adaptability, flexibility, and divergent thought. The theorizing of Bruner, Singer, and Sutton-Smith served as catalysts for the blossoming of empirical research on play during the 1970s and 1980s.

Two other seminal developmental theorists who proposed relationships between play and creativity were Lev Vygotsky and Jean Piaget. Although some of their beliefs about early cognitive development differed considerably, there is more than a little similarity in their views about the ways in which imaginative play may be linked to creativity. They differed most in their beliefs about the role that cultural practices and social interactions play in each individual's development. For Vygotsky, social interactions and language play an essential formative role in early cognitive development. He proposed that the preexisting concepts and symbols of a society are transmitted to children through interactions with their parents and other adults. Vygotsky also maintained that pretend play is initially learned under the guidance of parents and other caretakers, as children interact with them within the context of socially meaningful events. Piaget emphasized the role of each individual child in constructing his or her understandings of the world. He considered the earliest forms of pretense solitary constructions that emerge from more internal changes in children's symbolic capabilities. Despite Piaget's emphasis on individual origins and Vygotsky's emphasis on the social origins of symbols, when the two theorists wrote about play and creativity, they both made the following important points: Both emphasized that the imaginativeness of children's play is inextricably tied to their understandings (and misunderstandings) of daily events. Both maintained that play can itself be a source of creative imagination, and both theorists identified the object substitutions that occur during pretend play as the earliest source of creative imagination.

Object substitutions (or transformations) involve treating one object as if it were another. For example, in his book, *Play, Dreams and Imitation in Childhood,* Piaget described his 15-month-old daughter, Jacqueline, treating a fringed cloth as if it were her pillow and periodically blinking her open eyes in a playful allusion to sleep. On subsequent days she was observed using the collar of her mother's coat and then the tail of a rubber monkey to represent the pillow. Piaget suggested that, during such pretense, objects are imbued with purely subjective characteristics that are themselves determined by children's personal play interests. A box may be used to represent a car and a stone may represent its driver or, on another occasion, a cookie. As symbolic capabilities develop, both solitary and socially interactive pretense become more complex. The link from pretense to creative imagination is that as efforts to accommodate to the details of reality are relaxed during play, the child forms relationships and associations among objects, actions, and ideas that are typically unrelated in less freely assimilative thought. Although these playful constructions might be viewed as creative in their own right, Piaget took the position that symbolic play achieves its final form of creative imagination, provided that it is reintegrated in thought as a whole.

Like many contemporary theorists, both Piaget and Vygotsky emphasized this distinction between the imaginative and fanciful quality of children's pretense and the creative problem solving of mature artists and scientists. The make-believe play of preschoolers derives some of its fanciful (and occasionally fantastic) quality from children's misunderstandings and partial understandings of events. Because preschool-aged children are less critically evaluative of their impressions than adults, and because they are aware that their pretense is not "for real," they feel free to incorporate their uncensored impressions and feelings into dramatic play episodes. However, the contributions of imaginative play to real-world, creative problem solving are not typically immediate and direct. Francine Smolucha summarized Vygotsky's position on the delayed benefits of play as follows:

> Vygotsky proposed a developmental theory of creativity in which creative imagination originates in children's pretend play and develops into a higher mental function that can be consciously regulated through inner speech. In adolescence a new level of creativity is reached as imagination and thinking in concepts begin to collaborate, but it is not until adulthood that creativity fully matures.

This sampling of theories about play and creativity, while far from exhaustive, reflects the thinking of those developmental theorists who have had the broadest impact on research in this area. Although most developmentalists assume that playful thought and behavior can occur throughout the life span, this article's focus on children's play reflects the observation that play occurs most often and most prominently from late infancy through middle or late childhood. In their book, *The House of Make-Believe,* Dorothy and Jerome Singer speculated that the *impulse* for pretense and fantasy play may scarcely fade at all as years go by, but that society's constraints and expectations for children as they reach school age causes play to be internalized and "go underground." Nonetheless, most research on the relationship between play and creativity has involved young children.

II. RESEARCH ON PLAY AND CREATIVITY

A. A Developmental Perspective on Play and Exploration

The character and frequency of playful activity changes over the course of the life span; however, all forms of play involve intrinsically motivated activities that tend to increase or modulate the player's state of arousal. Early in infancy, babies appear to prefer familiar stimuli. During the first 2 months of life, infants who are given a choice will look longer at a familiar stimulus than a novel one. However, by around 8 weeks, infants begin to display a preference for novelty that is then manifested in the exploration and play of all healthy children and adults. The earliest playful activity observed in humans centers around the face-to-face games between infants and their parents that are particularly prominent from 3 to 6 months of age. Although the links between these activities and later creativity are distant and indirect, it is through these early interactions (e.g., tickling games and peek-a-boo) that infants learn about turn taking and social reciprocity. They also learn that mothers and fathers can be stimulating play partners who can also be used as secure home bases from which to explore their physical and social worlds.

Although some writers use the terms *play* and *exploration* interchangeably, these activities are actually quite different. The goal of exploration is to become familiar with the properties of objects or situations. Corinne Hutt suggested that, in exploration, the individual seeks answers to the implicit questions, "What is this?" and "What does it do?" However, because play tends to occur in environments and with objects that are already relatively familiar, the emphasis changes from "What does this *object* do?" to "What can *I* do with this object?" The striking changes in behavior and affect that occur as exploration evolves into play can be

observed, for example, by watching an infant interact with a mobile that has recently been placed over its crib. At first, the infant's senses and actions are intensely focused. Upon first discovering that touching the object causes it to swing, the infant's expression is one of concentration, as if he or she were studying the situation. Only after a period of careful observation and action will this businesslike exploration give way to smiling and laughing, as the infant playfully swats at the swinging object, knocking it this way and that.

Sensorimotor play, such as mobile swatting and rattle shaking, becomes increasingly complex and varied over the course of the first year of life, with a shift toward playing with more than one object at a time and a broadening of the repertoire of actions applied to various objects. Because infants' object play develops so similarly in children around the world, there has been little if any research linking this play to subsequent individual differences in creativity. However, complex forms of sensorimotor play persist throughout childhood and beyond, from playgrounds to ski slopes, and, as Jerome Bruner has suggested, the novel combinations of skills that emerge during such play may contribute to an individual's flexibility or creativity.

A uniquely human form of play that is often considered creative in its own right is pretense. In pretense, children simulate and transform the routine events of everyday life, as well as events from movies, television, and storybooks. They decontextualize objects and actions, treating one object as if it were another (e.g., using a token as if it were a cookie); they take on the roles of others (e.g., putting out an imaginary fire like a fire fighter); and they project their own behaviors onto other people and toy figures (e.g., feeding a doll or having it hide from an imaginary witch). Although the content and style of this play are significantly influenced by the families and cultures in which children are socialized, several consistent developmental trends have been identified. (Individual and cultural differences will be described in the next section of this article.)

Pretense initially appears toward the end of the first year or shortly into the second year, along with significant changes in representational capacities that contribute to the emergence of both pretense and communication through linguistic symbols. Pretense first takes the form of self-representation. In self-representation, children imitate their own behaviors, but do so playfully and outside of the contexts in which they normally occur (e.g., pretending to drink from an empty cup, or simulating going to sleep outside of a real going-to-bed context). When pretense is supported by the social context in which a child develops, self-representation evolves into various forms of dramatic and sociodramatic play. In dramatic play, a child adopts a role and pretends to be someone else, or projects roles onto dolls, stuffed animals, or small replicas of people and other creatures. Simple forms of playful role-taking are commonly observed in the second half of the second year and, by age 3, some children cooperate with peers in social interactive pretense. In general, older preschool-aged children are more likely to develop reciprocal roles, to sustain thematic enactments and to use complex language during these sociodramatic episodes. Some children may never participate in extended, elaborate sociodramatic play; however, it is most often observed between the ages of 4 and 6.

In her classic 1968 monograph on sociodramatic play, Sara Smilansky emphasized that, although the term *drama* might seem to imply a predetermined plot or outcome, dramatic and sociodramatic play are characterized by spontaneity, flexibility, and improvisation. Because of the complex and novel ways in which the real and the imagined are integrated in these episodes, Smilansky claimed that

> Through participation in sociodramatic play the child learns flexibility in his approach to various situations. . . . [T]he child learns how it feels to be a creator. He experiences himself as a creative being, forming his personal response to the world from his position in it and experiencing the world as a place responsive to, and inviting of, his creation. (p. 14)

From participating in such play, children also become aware of the possibility of acting and thinking from within the context of intentionally chosen roles. They become aware of what Gregory Bateson labeled the "as if" mode of behaving and thinking, in which they may step outside of the literal and into the imagined and even the contradictory. And relating the "as if" frame to the domain of creativity, it seems likely that becoming aware of the "as if frame" of play may open the door to a mode of problem solving in which it is legitimate to play with ideas and possibilities in ways that in-

crease the chances of arriving at creative solutions to real problems.

During their second and third years, most children engage in increasing amounts of pretense, which also becomes more flexible and decontextualized as representational skills develop and children become capable of using less and less realistic objects as symbols in their play. The child who previously pretended to feed himself or herself or pretended to feed a banana to a doll, now might use a banana as a telephone receiver or simply signify an imaginary telephone with gestures and words. As pretense evolves beyond self-representation, children also incorporate the actions, sounds, and speech patterns of adults, animals, and other creatures into their play. The roles and actions portrayed in dramatic and sociodramatic play frequently involve events far removed in time and space from the child's immediate environment. Children take on the roles of parents, teachers, and characters from stories or films. Imaginary monsters may be chased and slashed with imaginary swords.

This is not to say that the pretense of older preschoolers is always fantastic or bizarre. Catherine Garvey and Inge Bretherton have shown that the elaborate, integrated episodes of preschoolers' sociodramatic play are frequently organized around the shared action plans or scripts of familiar routines, such as going shopping or preparing and eating dinner. Scripts are generalized mental representations of sequences of events that typically occur in specific, real-world contexts. The emotions expressed during pretense also have their origins in the events that children experience in their daily lives. In fact, Greta Fein has maintained that the expression of "emotional-affective issues" is what pretense is really all about. However, Fein also emphasized the creative license exercised by children during play and contends that pretense relies less on internalized scripts than some theorists have claimed. In several articles and chapters, Fein has analyzed transcripts of children's pretense, which show that play sequences are sometimes far less orderly than common, real-world events. Within a given episode, there is not only a great deal of moment-to-moment improvisation, but new and unrealistic themes may suddenly replace prior ones without disrupting the flow of the play. According to Fein, one reason that children feel so free to exaggerate, distort, and transform reality in these episodes is that they know that pretense is not about representing the real world, She has suggested that, so long as the participants are able to understand the general emotional meanings that are being expressed, they simply improvise particulars of persons and things and events as they proceed.

Although there is not full agreement among contemporary theorists on the extent to which sociodramatic play revolves around the enactment of scripts, there is agreement that pretense is a medium in which children feel relatively free to ignore practical consequences and ordinary conventions. Bretherton, who emphasized the importance of children's shared understandings of the real world, also has distinguished low-level play from high-level play. In the latter, children create symbolic alternatives to reality through improvisation and by inserting unlikely actions into familiar scripts. Although much of this article focuses on the extent to which play may *contribute* to creativity, there can be little question that high-level pretense is *itself* creative. In pretense, children *create* imaginary roles and symbolic alternatives to reality. Ideas, objects, and events are flexibly combined and transformed in ways that do not occur in the real world. In fact, in high-level play, children display virtually all of the seven dimensions of original thinking that Roberta Milgram and her colleagues included in their multidimensional model of original thinking: associative fluency, imagery, curiosity, fantasy, problem finding, metaphoric production, and selective attention deployment. In an often cited test of inventiveness, one must think to tack a small box to a wall and then use the box as a candle holder. In pretense, a similar small box may become a vehicle for little figures to ride in, a television on which Curious George watches an imaginary television show, or a swimming pool in which an imaginary dragon is drowned under imaginary water. Children do not engage in pretense in order to sharpen their creative skills, but it is difficult to imagine a better apprenticeship for artistic creativity than the child's world of make-believe.

B. An Individual Differences Perspective

To the extent that children's play is related to their creative functioning, individual differences in play should have implications for individual differences in creativity. Contextual variables that contribute to individual differences in children's play include the behavior of their parents, teachers, and peers; the characteristics of their physical environments; the availability of books, films, and other media; and the values and customs of their cultures and subcultures. Nevertheless, noteworthy differences in children's play styles are typically not observed until well into the second year of life or later. With the exception of infants raised under extraordinarily restrictive or neglectful circumstances, sensorimotor skills and early object play develop similarly in children around the world. However, after these relatively universal beginnings, differences in sensorimotor play, constructive play, and symbolic play become substantial.

In 1966 Corinne Hutt observed significant differences in the inventiveness with which 3 year olds to 5 year olds explored and played with a complex novel toy. The object was something of a super-toy, a large red box on legs with a buzzer, bells, counters, and a large lever protruding from the top. Hutt found that vigorous investigation of all aspects of the object always occurred prior to play. But once the children had learned all they could about the object, their behavior became more varied and playful. Some of the playful activity involved sensorimotor repetitions and variations, analogous to an infant's swatting at a mobile. The more inventive children also displayed object transformations in which they used the box in nonliteral ways, for example, as a bridge or a seat. Hutt kept track of these children, wondering whether these individual differences in the inventiveness of children's play would be predictive of future behavior. When Hutt and Bhavnani reported a follow-up of these children (and others) 4 years later, their longitudinal data showed that children who had been inventive and imaginative in their interactions with the toy later achieved higher uniqueness scores on divergent-thinking tasks.

L. Alan Sroufe and his colleagues have conducted longitudinal research, which shows that children who are securely attached to their mothers at 18 months explore their environments more comfortably, problem solve more flexibly, and engage in more imaginative play during their toddler and preschool years than their insecurely attached counterparts. Arieta Slade observed 18 month olds to 30 month olds and their mothers in a play situation. She found that children engaged in higher-level symbolic play when mothers initiated play and actively participated in the play with their children. Other investigators have reported similar positive effects of mothers' involvement in their children's play; however, some of these same studies show that mothers differ in the extent to which they seem aware of their young children's skills and needs. When mothers are more attuned and involved, their children play at higher levels. A variety of gender differences has also been observed in children's play; however, these have not been associated with consistent differences in creativity.

The variations in play styles that seem most clearly linked to creativity are differences in the frequency, structure, and imaginativeness of children's pretense. Toward the more imaginative end of the continuum, Greta Fein has described the sociodramatic play of preschoolers that she labels "master players." Their pretend events seem more like inventions than script-related documentaries of real-world occurrences. Toward the other end of the continuum are those economically disadvantaged children who, according to Sara Smilansky, have "play deficits." Prior to the publication of Smilansky's 1968 monograph, *The Effects of Sociodramatic Play on Disadvantaged Preschool Children,* there was no body of literature indicating that many disadvantaged children engage in little, if any, make-believe play. Smilansky's report was based on a large-scale observational study of the 3- to 6-year old children attending 36 different preschools and kindergartens in Israel. Children attending half of the schools were from predominantly middle-class families. In the other classes, the children were from economically disadvantaged families with parents who had immigrated to Israel from the Middle East and North Africa. Smilansky had initially planned to use sociodramatic play as a vehicle to help prepare these children to perform better in school but was astonished to discover that the disadvantaged children engaged in almost no sociodramatic play and displayed very little pretense of any kind. Smilansky subsequently conducted a large-scale play tutoring project, which resulted in significant increases in sociodramatic play and also led to enhanced play-related verbal behavior.

Since the publication of Smilansky's study, many investigations conducted in Israel, Canada, Great Britain, South Africa, and the United States have yielded data indicating substantial decrements in both the quantity and quality of dramatic play of some preschool-aged children, particularly children from economically disadvantaged, minority families. Several of these same studies have also demonstrated that the frequency, complexity, and imaginativeness of dramatic and sociodramatic play can be increased through various play tutoring interventions involving modeling and verbal encouragement. These studies have also shown that play tutoring can enhance a variety of cognitive and social skills.

Whether cultural and class differences in dramatic play should be considered developmental deficits in need of remediation, or simply differences is a controversial issue that has become somewhat politicized. Helen Schwartzman has argued persuasively that, for many reasons, it would be more productive (and more accurate) to think in terms of children having *differences* in their repertoires of skills rather than *deficits* in their imaginative play abilities. Labeling certain groups as deficient in creative imagination may lead teachers to expect less from them, and lowered expectations can be self-fulfilling prophesies. It is also possible that the play skills of economically disadvantaged and culturally different children are underestimated when they are observed in schools and laboratory settings. However, even if some children's play skills have been underestimated, it is clear that many children engage in very little imaginative play during the daytime hours that they spend in day care, preschools, or kindergarten. In a study comparing the play of Korean American and Anglo American preschoolers, Korean American children were frequently either unoccupied or involved in simple forms of parallel social play. They engaged in far less pretense or sociodramatic play than their Anglo American counterparts. These differences cannot be attributed to the Korean American children's being uncomfortable in a context that was foreign to them. They had all been attending their Koreatown preschool for at least 4 months and the school was staffed by Korean American teachers.

These findings are better interpreted from a difference perspective than a deficit perspective. The children from both preschools behaved in ways that were compatible with the values and expectations of their parents and teachers. They were also acquiring the skills most emphasized within their respective subcultures. The Anglo American children displayed more social competence; the Korean American children scored higher on a standardized measure of cognitive functioning (which fit their parents' and teachers' emphasis on academic skills, task perseverance, memorization, and hard work). The play differences observed here reflect cultural values. As this study did not assess the imaginativeness of these children outside of their play, it is not known whether the play differences observed were associated with other differences in creativity. Research linking playfulness to creativity in other populations is discussed in the next section.

III. RESEARCH LINKING PLAY TO CREATIVITY

It has been suggested that both playful and creative activities disregard the familiar, and involve the creation of novelty from the commonplace. In their play, children feel free to modify and transform reality, to enact possibilities that are unlikely to exist in the real world. Creativity also requires the imagining and enacting possibilities. The strong impression that there are similarities between playful and creative processes has promoted a number of empirical investigations seeking specific evidence of these associations. Are some individuals consistently more playful than others? If so, are playful individuals more creative than others? Does engaging in playful activity contribute to one's potential for creative problem solving? The research summarized next indicates that the answers to each of these questions may be yes.

A. Correlational Studies

Findings from most correlational studies are consistent with theorizing that has linked play to creativity. Individuals judged to be playful under some circumstances also tend to display more imaginativeness, divergent thinking, and associative fluency when assessed under other circumstances. However, because of the correlational nature of the studies, they provide little basis for drawing inferences about either developmental mechanisms or causal relationships among variables. In fact, most correlational findings are just as compatible with the hypothesis that divergent thinkers

enjoy play or fantasy as they are with the assumption that play promotes divergent thinking. An exception is a 1-year longitudinal study of play and various convergent thinking skills reported by James Johnson and Joan Ershler in 1980. They assessed the play and convergent cognitive skills (e.g., IQ scores and conservation and classification skills) of 24 preschoolers and repeated those assessments with the same children 1 year later. The pattern of changes in play and cognitive skills that they observed was more consistent with viewing cognitive change as an antecedent contributing to the quality of play than of play leading to changes in the other skills they assessed. No analyses similar to Johnson and Ershler's have been reported for play and divergent thinking; however, contemporary theorists assume the existence of two-way reciprocal influences, with existing skills influencing the quality of play and playful activity contributing to cognitive development. Several studies employing experimental methods, which are discussed next, have attempted to shed further light on direction of influence issues. [See DIVERGENT THINKING.]

B. Experimental Studies

In 1967 Brian Sutton-Smith wrote an essay lamenting the fact that, despite a great deal of theorizing about the functional significance of play, there had been no parallel attempts to test hypotheses about the presumed role of play in children's cognitive development. Although Sutton-Smith has taken the position that much playful activity may be "of no utility except as self-expressive, self-rewarding exercise," he also hypothesized that it is probable that play increases a child's "repertoire of responses and cognitions so that if he is asked a 'creativity' question, he is more likely to make a unique, creative response." (p. 365) In that same essay, Sutton-Smith reported a correlational play-creativity study in which he employed an alternate uses test as the dependent measure. He found that the children gave more novel uses for toys with which they were most familiar and fewer uses for toys normally receiving less of their attention during free play. As in other correlational studies, Sutton-Smith's findings were consistent with the interpretation that play enhanced associative fluency, but other interpretations are possible. In a 1973 follow-up to Sutton-Smith's report, Dansky and Silverman conducted the first of a series of experimental studies designed to test the hypothesis that associative fluency would be heightened by a brief period of play with familiar objects. Because this study has served as something of a prototype for subsequent experimental studies conducted by various investigators, and because this experimental paradigm has become somewhat controversial, portions of the procedures will be described in some detail.

Dansky and Silverman's experiment was designed to eliminate certain potentially confounding variables that Sutton-Smith could not control in his correlational study. They randomly assigned preschoolers to one of three 10-minute treatment conditions: free play with a set of objects, imitation with the same set of objects, or a comparison condition in which children colored pictures unrelated to the play/imitation objects for the same length of time. Immediately after 10 minutes of either play, imitation, or coloring, each child was asked alternate uses questions for objects that had been present during play and imitation (e.g., paper clips, empty boxes, plastic cups). The researchers found that, after playing, children gave significantly more uses and more nonstandard uses (i.e., unusual uses) than children who had imitated or colored. The latter two groups did not differ on any measure. The ideas that the players provided also indicated a greater tendency toward broad attention deployment, which is a cognitive tendency that appears to contribute to ideational productivity.

Because playful activity is a highly reactive phenomenon that can inadvertently be prevented or disrupted by environmental conditions not conducive to play, Dansky and Silverman took a number of steps to enure that the children would be comfortable with the physical and social environment. Also, to prevent fostering the type of defensiveness that is often aroused in a formal testing situation, the transition from the play, imitation, and coloring periods to the assessment phase was conducted in as nondisruptive and comfortable fashion as possible, with the alternate-uses questioning being characterized as a "uses game." That the children in the play condition did in fact play was reflected in the investigators' observation that some of the novel uses that players gave for objects were reiterations of make-believe object transformations that they had displayed during the prior few minutes. Finally, it is im-

portant to note that unlike longer-term play tutoring investigations that will be discussed later, and unlike some educational interventions that have focused on enhancing creative abilities, the brief play period used in Dansky and Silverman's experiment was not designed to have any long-term impact on the creative tendencies of its participants. Nor was this line of research undertaken to identify the conditions that would necessarily *optimize* creative responding. The focus was on testing the theory-based hypothesis that if children's play can enhance their ongoing tendency to think in novel or creative ways, then even a relatively brief period of playful activity should temporarily enhance a child's associative fluency.

The results of a second play-fluency study, using procedures similar to those just described, were reported by Dansky and Silverman in 1975. Immediately after participating in 10 minutes of either free play, imitation, or convergent problem solving, preschoolers were asked alternate-uses questions about "generalization objects" that had *not* been present during the free play (or during comparison activities). Children in the play condition again gave significantly more standard and nonstandard uses than those in the comparison groups, indicating that, in addition to any particular associations that may have been formed while playing, playful activity had a generalized facilitating influence on associative fluency. Subsequent play-fluency studies have, with one exception, supported the finding that play has a general facilitating effect on associative fluency.

Dansky and Silverman's three-group design was later extended by adding a fourth condition in which children were specifically asked to engage in make-believe play. Immediately afterward, each child was asked to give uses for three objects that were present during the treatment phase, as well as a generalization object that had not been present. Although play did lead to higher fluency scores for most objects, make-believe was only modestly facilitative of associative fluency. This might be because make-believe does not play a unique role in enhancing associative fluency, or it may be attributable to the fact that the only difference between the free-play and make-believe conditions was an initial word of encouragement to make-believe. It is thus possible that the free-play subjects in this study engaged in as much pretense as the make-believe subjects.

Another study categorized 146 preschoolers as play-ers or nonplayers, based on two independent ob-servers' unobtrusive recording of children's activities during their daily free-play periods. Players were chil-dren who spent more than 25% of their free-play time in make-believe, nonplayers spent less than 5%. One week after the naturalistic observations, players and nonplayers were assigned in pairs to free play, imita-tion, or convergent problem-solving conditions. They were exposed to identical arrays of common objects (pipe cleaners, clothes pins, corks, etc.) during these 10-minute sessions, which were conducted by assis-tants unaware of either the hypotheses of the investi-gation or of the prior observational phase of the study. Observations made during the experimental sessions showed that players did in fact engage in make-believe and nonplayers did not. The make-believe activities included a variety of object transformations, which Vygotsky, Piaget, and Sutton-Smith have all linked to creativity. Immediate posttesting showed that players in the free-play condition gave significantly more uses than children in the other conditions, with no signif-icant differences among the other conditions. Thus, providing opportunities to play heightened associa-tive fluency, but only for those children who engaged in make-believe play. This finding is consistent with many theorists' contention that the object transfor-mations and other flexible combinations of ideas and actions that occur in pretense should have implications for creative functioning.

Brian Vandenberg has suggested that the link be-tween play and creativity does not depend primarily on specific subroutines or associations formed during the play itself. In 1980 he wrote that "play seems to develop a more generalized attitude and/or schema which predisposes the individual to creating and using novelty." (p. 64) Presumably this predisposition is strengthened over time in individuals who frequently engaged in playful activities. It also seems likely that an individual's *immediate* inclination to create and use novelty should be similarly heightened (or suppressed) by engaging in particularly playful (or serious and con-straining) activities. In the play-fluency experiments described earlier, players displayed heightened fluency when tested with generalization objects that were not present during the play itself. The results of several ex-periments support the proposition that playful activity

has a general facilitating effect on creative processes. One such study provided preschoolers with a variety of objects that could either fit into a form board (con-vergent play condition) or that they could play with-out a form board (divergent play condition). Although children in both conditions were simply asked to play with these free-standing animals, vehicles, and shapes, those in the convergent condition responded to the sit-uational constraints inherent in the materials by spend-ing most of their time assembling the puzzles. Children in the divergent play condition engaged in a variety of actions, including far more symbolic play than those in the form board group. Similar sessions were repeated three times over a period of 5 days. When these chil-dren (and children in two additional control condi-tions) were later given a variety of problem-solving tasks, the children who had had the divergent play experiences showed more imaginative responses and gave more unique responses on divergent thinking tasks. The divergent players' enhanced problem solving also generalized to tasks involving stimuli that were not present during the play sessions. The divergent players appeared to be more flexible in abandoning ineffective strategies in seeking problem solutions.

Additional evidence that play can have a general fa-cilitating effect on associative fluency was reported in a play-fluency study that added a pattern-meanings task to the assessment phase. In addition to replicating prior reports of more novel uses after play, the effects of play also generalized to the pattern-meanings mea-sure of associative fluency (in which the task is to think of multiple meanings and interpretations for abstract visual designs).

Anthony Pellegrini and his colleagues conducted a series of experiments in which they focused more on maximizing associative fluency than on the effects of play per se. In one such study, preschoolers were as-signed to one of the following three conditions prior to alternate uses testing: sequenced questioning, free play, or control. During sequenced questioning, the children handled objects while they answered a series of open-ended questions that were designed to stimulate active exploration of the objects. In this study and also in a follow-up experiment, Pellegrini found that children gave more unconventional responses after sequenced questioning than after the play or control situations. Nonetheless, children in the play groups gave approximately two to three times as many nonconventional uses as control subjects.

One further study supporting the generalized effects hypothesis was reported by Dansky in 1986. The primary focus of this investigation was on immediate versus delay effects. Although frequent participation in playful activity may contribute to an enduring disposition toward creative thinking, a single, short period of playful pretense should presumably have only a temporary facilitating effect on associative fluency. To test this hypothesis, Dansky had 108 preschoolers either play, imitate, or color for 10 minutes. Each child was then asked to give uses for two generalization objects. Half of the children were questioned immediately after these activities (as in prior studies). Half were tested after a brief delay, during which each child was occupied with a reverse digit-span task. This is a serious task that requires careful attention to the questioner's directions and a narrow focus on the specific numbers that must be remembered and then repeated in reverse order. This design permitted a comparison of the associative fluency levels of children with a playful set (assessment immediately after play) and a nonplayful set (assessment after the digit-span delay). As in prior studies, play significantly enhanced associative fluency when assessment occurred immediately after play. However, those play subjects who were tested after a brief nonplayful delay gave no more uses than imitation or control subjects. Dansky concluded that the short-term facilitating effects of play on associative fluency are mediated by the activation of a playful cognitive set (what Bateson has labeled the "as if" frame of mind) that is conducive to the generation of imaginative associations. Others have drawn similar conclusions about the short-term generalized effects of play on associative fluency. Miranda Hughes proposed that "the state of mind associated with playfulness is related to divergent thinking." Nathan Kogan has opined that "the intrinsic motivation and positive affect aroused by the play experience might well be maintained" into the assessment phase of these studies. Whether the processes involved are motivational or cognitive or both, what these proposals have in common is the presumption that some degree of playfulness is being carried over from the prior activity and then enhancing ideational fluency during assessment.

Peter K. Smith and Sue Whitney have offered a very different interpretation of the several experimental studies linking play to creativity (and to other forms of problem solving). They believe that the significant differences observed in all such studies may be attributable to unintended experimenter bias effects. In particular, they have suggested that experimenters' expectations may have caused them to elicit more ideas from play subjects (or fewer responses from children in other conditions). To test their hypothesis, Smith and Whitney conducted a play-fluency study closely patterned after earlier studies of this type. They randomly assigned preschoolers to four 10-minute treatment conditions: fantasy play, free play, imitation, and a control activity. Although all play-fluency studies have differed from one another in certain ways, a critical difference between Smith and Whitney's experiment and all others was the manner in which the alternate uses testing was conducted. To ensure that experimenter expectations could not contribute to their results, they had the experimenter who was present during the individual play sessions take each child to another room at the end of the session. The children were then tested by a second experimenter who was always unaware of their prior treatment experiences. The same blind testing procedure was used with children in all treatment groups. In contrast to prior studies, Smith and Whitney found no significant differences among the four groups in the number or kinds of uses given. The children in every group gave approximately the same number of standard and nonstandard uses as control subjects have given in other studies. Having found no evidence of play effects, they concluded that the play-fluency relationships that have been observed in all other studies are most plausibly attributed to experimenter effects.

Smith and Whitney's results are difficult to reconcile with the rest of the literature. Either the positive findings of numerous studies conducted by several independent research groups are all attributable to experimenter bias, or Smith and Whitney's findings are attributable to some limitation involving their own methods. Despite the rigor of their research, there are a few reasons for questioning their conclusions. First, it is possible that their subjects did not engage in enough playful pretense to heighten associative productivity. Children in Smith and Whitney's free-play condition engaged in make-believe during only 9%

of the allotted time; in the fantasy condition, make-believe occurred 38% of the time. Second, although insufficient pretense could have accounted for Smith and Whitney's findings, it was their procedure for assessing associative fluency that differed most from prior studies. Research has shown that when free play is followed by even a brief nonplayful task, play subjects do not score higher on the alternate uses test than control subjects. Thus, it is possible that any playfulness and "as if" thinking that had been established during the play portion of Smith and Whitney's experiment would have been disrupted by then taking the child from the play setting into another room to be tested by a second adult whom the child had only met once before for 20 minutes.

Although it is possible that experimenter bias could have influenced the results of other studies, there are three additional reasons to wonder whether this is an adequate explanation for the convergent results of several independent investigations. First, the potential for certain types of bias had been eliminated in prior studies. Some investigators used blind scoring procedures, and in some studies none of the researchers who observed, tested, or otherwise interacted with the children were aware of the research hypotheses. Second, the play-fluency experiments were derived from, and their findings are congruent with, much theorizing about connections between playful and creative processes. Finally, in addition to making theoretical sense, the observation that play enhances associative fluency is congruent with the findings of both correlational studies and the play-tutoring experiments discussed in the next section. Several of these tutoring studies, conducted by independent sets of research groups, were designed in ways that eliminated the possibility of experimenter effects.

C. Dramatic Play Tutoring

Differences in the frequency, complexity, and imaginativeness of children's dramatic and sociodramatic play are correlated with important differences in their social and cognitive skills. To test the hypothesis that pretense *contributes* to the development of these skills, investigators have conducted play-tutoring experiments. In studies of this type, children who engage

in less dramatic and sociodramatic play than most children their age are randomly assigned to either play-tutoring groups or control groups. Tutoring has typically involved 8 to 12 small-group sessions with an adult who models and encourages participation in sustained social interactive pretense. These 20- to 30-minute sessions have usually been spread over the course of 3 to 6 weeks. The pretense activities are either related to the children's everyday experiences (sociodramatic tutoring) or involve the enactment of fairy tales (thematic tutoring). Typically children enact roles themselves, although some interventions have involved projecting roles onto dolls or other small figures. Although such tutoring has been associated with improvements in a wide array of skills, only those studies assessing creativity-related outcomes will be discussed here.

More than a dozen studies have shown that play tutoring can increase not just the quantity of play displayed but also the richness and imaginativeness of children's pretense. For instance, in 1973 Joan Freyberg reported that eight 20-minute training sessions significantly improved the imaginativeness of children's play. She also found that this increase in imaginativeness generalized to the children's everyday free-play activities and persisted through the 2 months of post-intervention observations. Although play-tutoring effects have failed to generalize beyond the training context in a few studies, results like Freyberg's are more typical. Another study assessed the effects of play tutoring on children's divergent problem-solving performance. Compared with children in three control conditions, play-tutored children later displayed significantly more imaginative play and showed a significantly greater increase in originality scores on Torrance's Thinking Creatively with Pictures Test. Results for three other creativity-related measures were in this same direction but were not statistically significant.

In Dansky's 1980 investigation, 36 lower SES preschoolers received either sociodramatic play tutoring, exploration tutoring, or free-play time. Exploration tutoring was structured so that children in the two tutoring conditions would receive similar amounts of verbal stimulation and attention from an adult tutor. What differed most about the two tutoring conditions was that the exploration groups' activities involved no pretense. Children in the play-tutoring and free-play conditions had access to the same play materials, but the latter group received no tutoring. The tutor was unaware of the hypotheses of the study. After the 3-week intervention, blind observations of the children's daily free play revealed that only play tutoring resulted in a significant increase in the amount, complexity, and imaginativeness of pretense (which were initially low, as in other intervention studies). Blind posttesting revealed that the play-tutored group scored significantly higher than the other groups on four measures of imaginativeness. These measures included an alternate uses measure of associative fluency, an index of imaginative elaboration in retelling stories, evaluation of the imaginativeness of stories told about ambiguous pictures (based on Weisskopf's Transcendence Index), and fantasy scores based on responses to a curiosity box task. Because much of the evidence in this article indicates that playful activity enhances creativity, it might seem surprising that the free-play group performed no differently on these tasks than the exploration group. However, because little imaginative pretense was observed among these children prior to the intervention, there should be no reason to expect that additional free-play opportunities would improve divergent thinking (in the absence of some play tutoring). The fact that the free-play control condition did not enhance creativity in this study was in keeping with the previously noted finding that free play only enhances associative fluency when the children engage in pretense during the play period.

In 1983 Orlee Udwin conducted a play-tutoring study with 34 children in London who had been institutionalized to protect them from parental neglect and abuse. All observations and assessments were blind and were conducted by individuals unfamiliar with the hypotheses of the study. The play-tutored children were compared with controls who were given an equivalent amount of adult warmth and verbal input while they engaged in a variety of activities that involved no pretense. Posttraining assessment was conducted 1 month after the conclusion of the intervention. Compared to control subjects, the play-tutored children showed significant improvements in imaginative play, positive affect, and cooperation with peers during free play. Play tutoring also led to significantly greater increases in the following creativity-related measures: fluency, flexibility, and originality scores on

an unusual uses task and ratings of the imaginativeness of stories told about two picture cards from the Children's Apperception Test (CAT).

In 1985 Diana Shmukler and her colleagues reported the results of play tutoring with 116 economically disadvantaged south African preschoolers. All observations and assessments were blind and were conducted by individuals unfamiliar with the hypotheses of the study. Two play-tutoring interventions were compared with a no-treatment control group and an attention control group that was designed to provide the same quantity and quality of attention from an adult facilitator as the play-tutored groups, but within the context of various mastery games (e.g., ball games, puzzles, cutting and drawing). The structured play tutoring involved enactment of fairy tales. The unstructured group received sociodramatic play tutoring, similar to that in Dansky's and Udwin's studies. Posttraining assessment 1 month after the intervention yielded results similar to those of the tutoring studies described earlier. No significant differences were found between the control groups, or between the two tutoring approaches. However, compared with controls, play-tutored children showed significant increases in imaginative play and scored significantly higher on the following creativity-related measures: fluency, flexibility, and originality scores on an unusual uses task and ratings of the imaginativeness of stories told about three picture cards from the CAT. Shmukler and Naveh had predicted certain differences in the effects of the more and less structured play tutoring. Their explanation for their similar effects was that the two techniques share the following common factors; encouragement, endorsement of imagination, supply of materials and ideas, transformational use of props, modeling, and warmth. These are elements shared by the play-tutoring interventions of all of the studies just cited.

The only other play-tutoring experiments that have included a measure of divergent thinking were two studies conducted by P. K. Smith and his colleagues. Each experiment included one measure of divergent thinking as part of a battery of measures assessing a variety of skills. In each case, play-tutored subjects improved on this task from pretutoring assessment to posttesting. In one study, the improvement was statistically significant; in another, the change was not significant. However, these mixed findings do little to either support or detract from the findings of the other studies just cited. This is because both studies used only the dog-and-bone task to assess divergent thinking. This is a little-used measure of creativity with unknown psychometric properties. The skills required in the task itself also appear to be more closely related to some of the activities encouraged in the investigators' skills-training condition (e.g., practice at shape printing and games involving concepts of color, shape, size, and position) than to those addressed by play tutoring.

Smith and his colleagues' primary hypothesis was that the effects of play-tutoring interventions may have nothing to do with *play* but instead could be entirely due to the amount and kind of adult contact that children receive during play tutoring. In both studies, they compared the effects of play tutoring with skills tutoring. In skills tutoring, children were encouraged in various games and activities that involved no pretense. In addition to planning the two types of tutoring so that they would involve similar amounts of attention from adults, they observed the adult-child interactions in both tutoring conditions and found no substantial differences. Having then found that children who received skills tutoring improved about as much in their cognitive and linguistic functioning as those who received play tutoring, they concluded that differential attention and verbal stimulation may be assumed to explain the effects of play tutoring in all other investigations, unless systematic observations of the interactions between children and tutors indicate otherwise. However, at least with regard to the literature on play and creativity, it seems that Smith and his colleagues generalized far beyond their data when they made this inference. First, their dog-and-bone test results do not imply that sociodramatic play had no effect on divergent thinking, even in their own studies. More important, in the studies reported by Dansky, Udwin, and Shmukler and Naveh, there were comparison tutoring groups in which the children almost certainly received a similar quality and quantity of attention as children in their play-tutoring groups. To take just one example, the mastery games encouraged in Shmukler's attention control group were very similar to activities that were encouraged in similar ways in Smith and colleagues' skills control group. Although interactions during tutoring for one type of skill can never be identical to interactions in tutoring for other skills, it seems highly improbable that small differences in verbal attention could account for the sizable differential effects of play tutoring versus other tutoring in Shmukler and Naveh's study (or in the other studies mentioned earlier). What seems far more likely to have enhanced the imaginativeness of the stories these children later told and the originality of their answers to various questions was the fact that during tutoring they were successfully encouraged to engage in imaginative, fanciful, playful activity.

IV. CONCLUSIONS, UNRESOLVED ISSUES, AND PRACTICAL IMPLICATIONS

Empirical studies of play and creativity have been motivated and guided by the voices of numerous theorists suggesting that playful and creative processes are related to one another. In addition to the formal theorizing of cognitive, developmental, and evolutionary scientists, there is the fact that playful and creative activities share certain characteristics that make it *seem* like they must be related. For example, both are often or always intrinsically motivated, almost never occurring when one is anxious or narrowly focused on achieving a specified goal. Both involve transformations, possibilities, and out-of-the-ordinary combinations of ideas, actions, and situations. Furthermore, some playful activity is itself clearly creative; and many creative artists and scientists report that creative solutions require that one "play around" with ideas. The research of the past 30 years indicates that there is some truth to these intuitions.

Correlational studies show that playful individuals, particularly children, tend to score higher on tests of creativity and tend to be judged more creative by others. There is also evidence that preschoolers who engage in more imaginative make-believe play tend to be more creative a few years later. However, these correlations are modest in size, indicating that many variables other than play are related to creativity. Much of the impetus for conducting experimental studies of play and creativity has been that experiments can aid in resolving questions about cause and effect that are far more difficult to address with correlational methods. The one-session experimental studies reviewed earlier indicate that engaging in playful activity, especially make-believe play, has a temporary facilitating effect on associative fluency and other divergent problem-solving activities. Longer-duration play-tutoring studies, in which effects have been measured anywhere from 1 week to 2 months after tutoring, are clearly assessing somewhat different processes than those explored in the one-session play-fluency experiments; however, they also indicate that playful activity enhances creativity. Although the outcomes of play-tutoring studies in general have been somewhat mixed, those studies assessing the effects of play tutoring on creativity have yielded consistently positive results. These results include increases in associative fluency, flexibility, and originality; consistent evidence of more imaginative storytelling; and significant increases in the imaginativeness of children's spontaneous free-play behavior (and longitudinal findings indicate that imaginativeness and participation in pretense during the preschool years is related to higher scores on divergent-thinking tasks a few years later).

Although these various lines of research provide tangible support for theories linking play to creativity, some of the findings cited here raise as many questions as they seem to answer. For example, longitudinal findings converge with what is known about various developmental processes to suggest that most correlational findings reflect two-way reciprocal interactions between play and children's emerging skills. A child's existing social and cognitive skills (including creative abilities) will influence the character of his or her play. At the same time, participation in rich, imaginative play will also contribute to a child's developing repertoire of creative skills. More longitudinal studies of longer duration will be required to shed further light on these reciprocal processes. Such studies should include repeated observations of play made in multiple contexts *and* concomitant assessment of a variety of social and cognitive skills. Longitudinal research of this type will help to answer questions about the stability of individual differences over time and also answer questions about the antecedents and consequences of particular types of playful activities. As yet, there have also been no prospective longitudinal studies that tell us whether playful children become creative adults. Vygotsky believed that many of the effects of play on development are not fully realized until adolescence or adulthood.

The findings of several brief, play-fluency experiments demonstrate that playful activity can facilitate creative functioning. But questions remain about the nature of the psychological mechanism(s) that link playful activity to better performance on divergent-thinking tasks. Dansky's explanation is that play generates a cognitive set, which contributes to broad attention deployment and combinatorial flexibility. Kogan suggested that the mechanism could involve a carrying over of positive affect and intrinsic motivation from playful activity to the problem-solving situation. These explanations are clearly not mutually exclusive. To learn more about these mechanisms, it will be necessary to systematically observe the behaviors and interactions that occur during free-play sessions, during the transition to assessment of skills, and during the assessment process itself. Peter Smith and his colleagues have made progress in conducting such process observations; however, more fine-grained analyses of behaviors and the inclusion of ongoing ratings of playfulness and related emotions would be helpful. Developing such indicators and making the needed observations without distorting the behaviors being observed are significant challenges for the future.

Reports of the substantial positive findings of some play-tutoring interventions have raised questions about how a dozen (or fewer) 30-minute tutoring sessions could have significant effects on children's ongoing behaviors? The answer may be that the direct and observable impact of play tutoring can extend far beyond the time spent in the tutoring sessions. Because children tend to enjoy this kind of play, successful tutoring quickly leads to substantial increases in the amount of *spontaneous* sociodramatic play that occurs in their everyday lives. This means that for every hour spent in play tutoring, children will, over time, spend many hours in more imaginative play than the children who do not receive this tutoring. This time spent in spontaneous, self-initiated pretense may contribute far more to measured outcomes than the time spent in the tutoring sessions. A related issue that has not been resolved involves the extent to which tutoring actually *teaches* sociodramatic play or primarily serves a *disinhibiting* function for children who may play in some contexts but are reluctant to do so in the schools and other care centers where they spend their days. The fact that some children who already engage in simple pretense commonly display more elaborate and more socially coordinated imaginative play after tutoring suggests that tutoring scaffolds these children to higher levels of play. The hypothesis of self-sustaining effects could be tested in future research by making observations of children's free play and assessing divergent thinking skills shortly after intervention and then repeating these observations and assessments at 6-month intervals throughout the remainder of their preschool and kindergarten years. However, children are unlikely to reenact their fantasies and impressions of the world in supervised settings unless the parents and teachers of play-tutored children endorse sociodramatic play themselves and provide time, space, and materials for this play. In fact, tutoring is unlikely to be effective in the first place unless the tutors are both skilled at working with children and playful themselves. More research needs to be done to identify the characteristics of effective tutors and to observe adult-child interactions in play-tutoring studies to ensure that effective play tutoring is actually occurring.

Some psychologists and educators agree with Brian Sutton-Smith's position that play should be children's "area of freedom just as adult recreation is our area of freedom." He admonished well-meaning adults not to "manipulate children's play to fit their own preconceived purposes." However, a majority of professionals currently agree with the position taken by play theorist and educator James Christie that "This hands-off stance toward play has been seriously challenged by a growing body of research that indicates that classroom play can be greatly enriched through teacher participation." However, Christie also noted that, "If teachers interfere too often in children's play, the children lose control of the activity and it ceases to be play." Although the research of Christie and others indicates that play can

be a medium for enhancing literacy, social role taking, and various other skills, the most consistent finding in the literature is that play can promote imaginativeness and divergent-thinking skills.

Bibliography

Christie J. F. (Ed.). (1991). *Play and early literacy development.* Albany, NY: State University of New York Press.

Dansky, J. L., & Silverman, I. W. (1973). The effects of play on associative fluency in pre-school-aged children. *Developmental Psychology, 9,* 38–43.

Garvey, C. (1990). *Play.* Cambridge, MA: Harvard University Press.

Gorlitz, D., & Wohwill, J. F. (Eds.). (1987). *Curiosity, imagination and play: On the development of spontaneous cognitive and motivational processes.* Hillsdale, NJ: Erlbaum.

Johnson, J. E., Christie, J. F., & Yawkey, T. (1987). *Play and early childhood development.* Glenview, IL: Scott Foresman.

Klugman, E., & Smilansky, S. (Eds.). (1990). *Children's play and learning.* New York: Teachers College Press.

Roopnarine, J., Johnson, J., & Hooper, F. (1994). *Children's play in diverse cultures.* New York: State University of New York Press.

Runco, M. A. (Ed.). (1966). *Creativity from childhood through adulthood: The developmental issues.* San Francisco: Jossey-Bass.

Singer, D. J., & Singer, J. L. (1990). *The house of make-believe.* Cambridge, MA: Harvard University Press.

Smilansky, S. (1968). *The effects of sociodramatic play on disadvantaged preschool children.* New York: Wiley.

Smolucha, F. C. (1992). The revalence of Vygotsky's theory of creative imagination for contemporary research on play. *Creativity Research Journal, 5,* 69–76.

Sutton-Smith, B. (1967). The role of play in cognitive development. *Young Children. 6,* 364–369.

Vandenberg, B. (1980). Play, problem solving and creativity. In K. H. Rubin (Ed.), *Children's play: New directions for child development.* San Francisco: Jossey-Bass.

Poetry

Jane Piirto
Ashland University

Canon A body of literary works said to define the tradition.

Foot A group of syllables serving as a unit of meter, in verse—for example, *spondee* (two accented syllables), *iamb* (one unaccented syllable preceding one accented syllable), *trochee* (one accented syllable preceding one unaccented syllable), *anapest* (two unaccented syllables preceding one accented syllable), *dactyl* (one accented syllable preceding two unaccented syllables).

Free Verse Rhymed or unrhymed poetry composed without attention to conventional rules of meter.

Image and Imagery A figure of speech, especially metaphor or simile; a representation of a thing.

Line Phrase or words that make up a theoretical pattern of verse—for example, *dimeter* (two feet), *trimeter* (three feet), *tetrameter* (four feet), *pentameter* (five feet), *hexameter* (six feet).

Meter Measured, patterned arrangement of syllables in lines of poetry according to stress and length.

Mimesis Imitation or representation.

Muse One of the nine goddesses who presided, in Greek mythology, over art, literature, and the sciences. The spirit that inspires a poet.

Poesis Making, or invention.

Rhyme Correspondence of end sounds in lines of verse or in words.

Rhythm Regular recurrence of grouped strong and weak, stressed and unstressed, long and short, high-pitched and low-pitched syllables arranged in feet or cadences, in alternation.

Stanza A group of lines of verse forming one of the units of a poem.

Symbol A sign that refers to or stands for another thing, usually abstract.

Verse A sequence of words arranged metrically in accordance with some rule or design.

POETRY is an arrangement of words in verse, always rhythmical, sometimes rhymed, expressing facts, ideas, or emotions in a style that is concentrated, imaginative, and powerful. This article examines poetry and creativity.

I. INTRODUCTION

Poetry is the oldest form of literature. It is characterized by meter, rhythm, rhyme, or verse. Called by many the highest of the linguistic arts, it is written by poets. (The obsolete term *poetess* is no longer in use, as both male and female practitioners prefer to be called poets.) Both poetry and the other form of literature, prose, are distinguished in that they are written from the imagination. Poetry, however, is metrical or at least cadenced.

II. KINDS OF POETRY

A. Lyric Poetry

Lyric poetry has a strong emotional component, using imagery, especially of nature. The emotion is compressed with attention to sensuality. Lyric poetry has its origins in musical singing, chanting, and reciting to accompaniment. By the Renaissance, however, the bard (singing and strumming poet) gave way to the lyric poet who wrote to be read and not for a musical presentation.

The lyric poem came to have its own rules: (a) Edgar Allan Poe (1809–1849) said it must be brief; (b) Samuel Taylor Coleridge (1772–1834) said it must be unified and metrical; (c) William Wordsworth (1770–1850) said it must be "the spontaneous overflow of powerful feelings"; (d) Friedrich Hegel (1770–1831) said it should be subjective, personal, and intense; (e) Arthur Schopenhauer (1788–1860) said it should be "an inverted action of mind upon will"; (f) John Stuart Mill (1806–1873) said it should be concrete, like a brief overheard conversation; (g) Northrup Frye (1912–1991) said it is "an internal mimesis of sound and imagery"; (h) Herbert Read (1893–1968) said it is "the imaginative prehension of emotional states; and (i) James Joyce (1882–1941) said it is where the poet "presents his image in immediate relation to himself." The relation of the form to music is apparent in that the words of songs are still called *lyrics*.

Lyric poetry includes not only popular and folk songs, drinking songs, hymns, lullabies, and love songs, but philosophical poetry, dream visions, satire, odes, epigrams, sonnets, and elegies. Lyric poetry has its traditions in all cultures and geographical regions.

B. Narrative Poetry

Narrative poetry includes the epic poem, the romance, the ballad, the verse tale. The narrative usually tells a story of historical import. Narrative poems are difficult to categorize metrically, as sometimes they look like prose and sometimes they use strict meter and verse. An example of the former is John Clare's *The Badger*; an example of the latter is Byron's *Don Juan*.

C. Dramatic Poetry

Dramatic poetry imitates speech and is exemplified by the Greek tragedies, Shakespeare's plays, Molière's work, Goethe's *Faustus*, Pushkin's *Boris Gudonov*, Ibsen's *Peer Gynt*, Eliot's *Murder in the Cathedral*, and Shange's *For colored girls who have considered suicide / when the rainbow is enuf*.

III. HISTORY OF WESTERN POETRY

Each national and ethnic group has its own revered and special poetic heritage. Because this encyclopedia is written in English and published in the United States, within the sphere of the roots of that language, this brief history will concentrate on the history of Western poetry.

The first poet of the Western canon was Homer, who wrote the *Odyssey* and the *Iliad* circa 2000 B.C.E., yet poetry is much older than Homer, who wrote from oral traditions dating from as far back as the 8th century B.C.E. Poetry is older than writing. In the Judeo-Christian canon, much oral poetry was captured in the Old Testament, especially in such books as Psalms. One of the most common forms of poetry was the hymn, an ancient Greek liturgical genre. Hymns have been found in all cultures, including aboriginal, Oriental, and African. Hymns were religious verses that praised the gods, heroes, or patriotic or religious abstractions.

Poetry was the spoken form of hymns and songs. By the 5th century B.C.E., Socrates (470?–399? B.C.E.), Plato (c. 428–c. 347 B.C.E., and Aristotle (384–322 B.C.E.) were functioning as critics of poetry, and their works formed the first literary criticism. Poetry was described as being about heroes, gods, and common people; poetry was of concern to the public; poetry was itself a form of entertainment and delight to the people; poetry was touched with the divine, inspired by gods or Muses; poetry was both an art and a craft; the poet was secular, not a priest, prophet, or god. In Socrates's dialogue with Ion, Plato defined poetry's themes:

> Is not war his [Homer's] great argument? And does he not speak of human society and of intercourse of men, good and bad, skilled and unskilled, and of the gods conversing with one another and with mankind, and about what happens in heaven and in the world below, and the generations of gods and heroes?

In his dialogues, Plato viewed poetry as both inspiration and imitation. Poetry was a gift possessed by poets, and Socrates said it was not an art but "an inspiration; there is a divinity moving you." The divinity was like a stone magnet that attracted iron which in turn attracted other iron. The Muse inspires the poet who inspires others. "All good poets, epic as well as lyric, compose their beautiful poems not by art, but because they are inspired and possessed." Poets fall under the spell of music and meter. "For the poet is a light and winged and holy thing, and there is no invention in him until he has been inspired and is out of his senses, and the mind is no longer in him; when he has not attained this state, he is powerless and is unable to utter his oracles."

Yet Plato also thought that the poet was an imitator. That is, the poet committed these inspirations to written language, which is imitative, a *mimesis.* The language is referential, that is, representative of the emotion and captures the emotion through certain linguistic conventions such as metaphor, simile, and other figures of speech—as well as through imagery, rhyme, rhythm, and sound. Poetry as mimesis was inferior, as it was but an imitation, a copy, of the real form that existed in the ideal, nonmaterial world. Thus poetry was not truly creative, as it was written or oral representation and not original. This idea lasted until the time of the romantics in the 18th century, when poetry became *poesis,* or making. In Plato's *Republic,* the poet was to be relegated to a lesser height than the politician because of this imitative representation.

To Aristotle, however, poetry was more true than history because the poet could fabricate truth from the elements of history rather than exhaustively tell the facts. The poet is able to tell the truth on a deep level, being able to see the patterns and the overarching themes. Aristotle said,

> The distinction between history and poet . . . consists really in this, that the one describes the thing that has been, and the other a kind of thing that might be. Hence poetry is something more philosophic and of graver import than history, since its statements are of the nature rather of universals, whereas those of history are singulars.

Though Aristotle spoke of the forms of poetry called drama (tragedy and comedy) and the epic poem, subsequent critics and thinkers have credited Aristotle with denoting the true nature of poetry. Poetry can capture the inner essence of a situation whereas history cannot. This idea about poetry was not to resurface in any major way until the late 17th century. Until then, poetry was often viewed as a branch of logic. "Hence poetry is something more philosophic and of graver import than history, since its statements are of the nature rather of universals, whereas those of history are singulars."

The fact that poetry spoke of universal truth was the aspect of poetry that attracted the romantics in the 18th century and up to the present. Unlike the classicists of the Middle Ages and the neoclassicists of the 17th century, who produced poems in strict Platonic imitation, *mimesis,* the romantics and later poets did not focus so much on the prescribed forms with their prescriptive line lengths in certain kinds of syllabic meter (i.e., iambic, trochaic, anapestic, and the like) but instead focused on the Aristotelian idea that the poem speaks more truly of a situation than a historical text could. The poem defined the inner reality. It was constituted of inner truth and not outer conformity to verse standards.

The poet thus was thought of as a seer, someone who could probe to the inner depths. However, the poem was not mere psychological essay, but a form of art evoking the Aristotelian fear and pity, a sense of beauty and of awe in both the poet and in the audience with its wedding of words and the elements of rhythm, rhyme, and stanza. The purpose of the poem was not to persuade, for that is the purpose of rhetoric and not poetry. The very form of the poem combined with the elements of poetic syntax, and put together with the denotative "meaning" created something beyond meaning, inseparable from the form. The words of the poem form sound, a pure, nonintellectual substance heard by the ear and resounding within the throat or the breast. Mimesis was thus combined with poesis.

Nineteenth century romantic philosophers debated the meaning of the sense of beauty (fear and pity) evoked by the poem (imagination), the form of the poem (sense), and the moral influence of the poem (intellect). In Germany, Kant (1724–1804), Schlegel (1772–1829), von Schiller (1759–1805), Hegel (1770–1831), Schopenhauer (1788–1860), and Nietzsche (1844–1900) thought about and debated the aesthetics of poetics.

In England, William Wordsworth wrote a preface, which became classic, to the second edition of his *Lyrical Ballads.* The poems were written in common language and not in neoclassical diction. Meter alone distinguished poetry. Although meter is also present in prose, poetic meter has a regularity detectable in the line. Followed by poetic reflections by Samuel Coleridge (*Biographia Literaria*), John Keats (1795–1821), Percy Bysshe Shelley (1792–1822), and George Gordon Lord Byron (1788–1824) these English romantic poets asserted their own philosophy. They revered the noble poet standing alone against the vagaries of the world and sentimentalized the peasant and the savage. The solipsism of self-reference in some romantic poetry led to a backlash by postromantics such as Victorian critic John Ruskin (1819–1900) and poet Matthew Arnold (1822–1888).

In France, romanticism was personified in Jean-Jacques Rousseau (1712–1778), a prose writer who had great influence on poetic thought with his visions of oneness with nature. Lamartine (1790–1869), Vigny (1797–1863), and Hugo (1802–1885), among others such as Baudelaire (1821–1867), continued with pantheistic and magical realistic views of nature as the source of feeling and a guide to spiritual wholeness. They also advocated a return to common language and disavowed classical form. By the end of the century, the poet was regarded as having a special magical relationship with the unknown, and poetry was regarded as prophecy. The works of Arthur Rimbaud (1854–1891) and Stèphane Mallarmé (1842–1898) expressed this.

At the end of the 19th century the French symbolists such as Jules Laforgue (1860–1887), along with Mallarmé, Rimbaud, Paul Valéry (1871–1945), and Verlaine (1844–1896), asserted that poetry was overwhelmingly music and should capture from music the elements that belong to poetry. Poetic symbol shows a relationship between the thing and the readers. Prosody, or the ancient forms of verse, should be utilized in this attempt. Symbols expressed truth through suggestion rather than narration. Symbolist poetry also uses experimental grammar, many allusions that may make the poetry rather obscure. Paul Claudel (1868–1955) asserted that the symbol is metaphoric, that is, a relationship between two subjects. Each object is named and compared with another object, perhaps a divine object. For Claudel, the syllogistic nature of the old poetry should be replaced by the logic of the metaphoric and the symbolic.

In the dialectic of poetic history, Apollinaire (1880–1918) asserted a return to the lyric sensibility. His work and thought paralleled the rise of cubism, Fauvism, and the modern in the visual arts. Apollinaire coined the word *surrealism,* which signaled that the world of poetry was on the threshold, just outside the world of realism. The surreal deals with the ordinary and with the everyday and does not try to comprehend the divine or the spiritual. The poetry of the surrealists, especially Breton (1896–1966) and Eluard (1895–1952) dealt with love of the woman, seeing her as equal to man.

French poetry of midcentury was called *engagée* by Jean-Paul Sartre. Dealing with World War II, the Resistance, and the meaning of devastation, it tried to make sense of existence (*existentialism*). Poets separated from poetic movements, isolated themselves from current chic thought, and wrote as receptors of events around them. By the 20th century poetry was looked at as sign, for it had a dualism. Poetry was physical words on a page; the medium was ink on pulp. However, although prose was also physical words on the page, the medium was in the background. In poetry, the physical words are the foreground as well. This led poetic philosophers to contemplate the difference between signification and content.

T. S. Eliot (1888–1965) brought French symbolism to England. The romantic metaphysical way of looking at poetic subject matter and the symbolist way were similar, he thought. The comparison of poetry to music was essential. The subject matter was difficult, evoking religious symbols and obscure texts. American imagist Ezra Pound (1885–1972) was another influence on symbolist poetry, and on Eliot, who dedicated his poem *The Wasteland* to Pound. Pound defined the image as "an intellectual and emotional complex in an instant of time." The pentameter was to be broken and straightforward line similar to the sequence of the musical phrase was to ensue.

Irish poet William Butler Yeats (1865–1939) spanned the romantic and modernist era. His *A Vision* (1925) is a prose explanation of how he used symbolism and mythology in dealing with opposites: objectivity and subjectivity, art and life, soul and body. Postwar poets with competing theories—the Georgians (Walter de la Mare [1873–1956], Robert Graves [1895–1985; who advocated a return to nature and myth]); the soldiers who died (Rupert Brooke [1887–1915], Wilfred Owen [1893–1918], who argued a pacifist or patriotic vision of their experiences in World War I); the colonialists (Rudyard Kipling [1865–1936], who wrote of England's glory overseas)—dominated the poetry of the early 20th century. By the 1930s, English poetry had become concerned with leftist causes such as the Spanish Civil War (Stephen Spender, W. H. Auden [1907–1973]). In the postwar, Dylan Thomas (1914–1953) wrote on personal themes in formal and experimental verses. The movement of the 1950s was short-lived, and no theoretical schools of poetry have dominated British poetry since.

United States poetry was derivative or simultaneous with the movements in British and French poetry until the liveliness of post–World War II signaled an ascendancy. For example, Walt Whitman (1819–1892) acclaimed a romantic vision of poetry derived from Ralph Waldo Emerson (1803–1882) (who called for a transcendental vision whereby there is an association between the word, the thing, and absolute truth) and Edgar Allan Poe (1809–1849) (who argued for the importance of the imagination). Whitman's *Leaves of Grass* (1855) proclaimed the importance of the body as much as the soul. Whereas Whitman was representative of Emerson's call for a poetry of the democratic person in nature, Emily Dickinson (1830–1856) represented Emerson's call for a poetry hermetic and private. She became the most well-known woman among romantic poets on all continents. Other American romantic poets such as Henry Wadsworth Longfellow (1807–1882) and James Russell Lowell (1819–1891) were very popular but their works have not stood the test of time. Dialect poets such as James Whitcomb

Riley (1849–1916) and son of former slaves Paul Laurence Dunbar (1872–1906) and the late romantic poetry of southerner Sidney Lanier (1842–1881) signaled a regionalism and ethnic emphasis that was to continue in American poetry.

Premodernist poets such as Robert Frost (1874–1963) continued to write pastorals with the subject matter of nature. Frost began to use the speaking voice within poetic form, responding to the call of the romantics. He eschewed free verse, which was advocated by the symbolists and which contains lines of irregular length that evoke the cadence of music.

Modernism advocated that there is a connection between art and life. The construction of the verse was irretrievably linked to the meaning of the words. Verse did not serve to convey words, but was itself an irrevocable structure intrinsic to the meaning. Symbolism and imagism were two different ways to achieve this unity. Symbolism (Poe, Baudelaire, Rimbaud, Mallarmé, Valéry) advocated a turning in to the subjective with impressions of the external world expressed in implied emotions and sensations. Imagism (Pound) called for a visual flash, which stood for both the emotion and the thing. William Carlos Williams (1883–1963) sought to use the American idiom (a romantic precept) in a variable foot (the line as a musical bar) in an imagistic way (the word as thing). Hilda Doolittle, known as H. D. (1886–1961), Pound's fiancé, incorporated psychoanalytic concepts into her images. Eliot declared himself a British citizen, but his deep influences were from his childhood in St. Louis, Missouri. Wallace Stevens (1879–1955) wrote with affinity to the symbolism of Mallarmé and Valéry. If poetry is connected to nature, it is connected through figures of speech and relationship to music. Hart Crane (1899–1932) tried to take in modern industrialization with the symbol of the Brooklyn Bridge and a hearkening back to Whitman's romantic optimism.

Regional and ethnic Black writers also hearkened back to romantic visions in structuring their poems around spirituals—Langston Hughes (1902–1967) and Countee Cullen (1903–1946)—and images of small towns and large cities in the Midwest—Carl Sandburg (1878–1967) and Edgar Lee Masters (1868–1950). Women also followed romantic principles—Edna St. Vincent Millay (1892–1950) and Elinor Wylie (1885–1928)—in their lyrics and formal sonnets.

The influence of imagism, surrealism, and symbolism continued with poets such as Robert Bly (b. 1927)—who talked of the "deep image" that would psychologically take the reader into a formerly unconscious place—and Allen Ginsberg (1926–1996—who with the Beats looked to Whitman as well as to Pound in advocating a counter-cultural lifestyle with a poetic line that resembled jazz. The so-called Black Mountain poets—Robert Creeley (b. 1926) and Denise Levertov (b. 1923)—were allied with the abstract expressionists of the midcentury art world and they called for open form poetry with stresses more gestural than formal. The "confessional" poets—Anne Sexton (1928–1975) and Sylvia Plath (1832–1963)—took after Robert Lowell (1917–1977) in their frank autobiographical work. The New Critics called for an "objective" look, apart from autobiography, at the work as it stood itself, apart from personal history, geography, or culture.

Formal verse gave way to the ironic lyric. Modernism is giving way to postmodernism. Constructivism is giving way to deconstruction. By the end of the 20th century poetry was looked at as sign, for it had a dualism. The experimenting of early and mid-20th-century poets who aligned their work with movements in music and art shook the very Platonic and Aristotelian foundations of what poetry is. At the millennium we are left with these questions. Can poetry stand up to the creative imperatives of the other arts or is it merely a fundamentally poor imitation? Can poetry show truths through art that philosophy and religion cannot show? Can poetry continue to be a political force with a critique of bourgeois values? Can poetry align itself not with an obscure elite but with the common people? These questions continue to plague those who write poetry.

IV. POETRY AND CREATIVITY

Poetry is inherently creative in that it is a work of the *imagination*. Imagination is a faculty much discussed in creativity literature. The Romantic era of the 18th and 19th centuries began to view imagination as the primary criterion for writing poetry. Coleridge said it was the main power used in writing poetry: a "synthetic and magical power." Any writer can string images together, but the poet infuses the images with imaginative power and with passion and makes not an account of imagery but of emotional truth. The poet must have an innate sense of music. Coleridge noted:

> But the sense of musical delight, with the power or producing it, is a gift of imagination; and this, together with the power of reducing multitude into unity of effect, and modifying a series of thoughts by some one predominant thought or feeling, may be cultivated and improved, but can never be learned.

Even the intellectual deconstructionists and postmodernists say that imagination is necessary in uniting poetry with philosophy. In their discussions, imagination remains the creative force behind poetry. [*See* IMAGINATION.]

Although imagery is to be infused with the poet's imagination and sense of music in order to produce the truly creative poem (as opposed to the nonpoem, the "fancy"), the *image* is the organic heart of the poem to the 20th-century modernists. The image is the concrete metaphor for inner reality. The poem itself becomes the image, an energy field made corporeal. Pound said, "The image is not an idea. It is a radiant node or cluster; it is a . . . VORTEX, from which ideas are constantly rushing." The image is then both a description and a metaphor for the creative energy of a field surrounding the image. The image is a reference to a visual, aural, or kinesthetic semblance named to subdue or elaborate the unnameable.

To postmodernist deconstructionist Jacques Derrida, the image fills out the words. The reader, with imagination, completes the poem's empty spaces with the image. Thus figurative images—onomotopoeia, irony, metaphor, simile, and the like—the rhythmic conventions of poetry, function as rivers to complete the effervescent meaning of the poem. The poet as creator is at the mercy of the image created, for the references evoked by the images are uncontrollable. The reader in the physical act of reading, the eyes moving across the page, taking in the letters in type on paper combined into words and an evocative language, enters into a dark room, which is only illumined by images evoked by the words put into patterns created by the poet.

Images become symbols, icons, imagery. These also are creative, both in the spiritual sense of having been infused with import and meaning by centuries of thought and in the individual sense of resonance with an interior truth to which the reader (or hearer) gains access through the associations evoked by the aesthetic creation of the poet. Consider the imagery in this line from Whitman's "Song of Myself."

I hear the bravura of birds, bustle of growing wheat, gossip of flames, clack of sticks cooking my meals.

The reader is thrown to the auditory by the first two words, and the image of swaggering, bragging birds, chests puffed up, sitting in trees loudly chirping comes on the ear. To hear growing wheat "bustle" evokes the humming sounds of fussing, moving females, scuffling and scurrying, who more often "bustle" than men. With "bustle" comes a transition to "rustle," which is a sound evoked by the word, and perhaps to the taffeta dresses women wore at that time, which had appendages called "bustles." All these and many more images associate to the ear from the juxtaposition of "bustle" with wheat growing.

Whitman added the "gossip of flames" to his auditory images. Gossip has a sound that is quiet, as it is usually passed from one person to a trusted other in a hallway, a doorway, before a meeting. Gossip is hearsay, rumor, not truth. To associate "gossip" with fire makes the flame seem friendly, for gossip is usually exchanged between friends about other friends or acquaintances, and the person who gossips usually trusts the person to whom he or she is gossiping. Thus the auditory image is homey, friendly, but a little cruel and dangerous as well.

The "clack of sticks" also creates astonishing auditory imagery, as "clack" seems too loud for what sticks do when they hit each other. "Clack" is a sound word, but in the increment of sounds, sticks would not "clack" but would perhaps "click" or make a dull "thwack." That they "clack" enhances their flame-readiness, for they must be quite brittle and quite large. Yet they are "sticks" and not "logs" and so the imagery presented by the juxtaposition of the two words "clack" and "sticks" tells the reader—in that dark recess that creates imagery—exactly how big the sticks are. Big enough to

cook a meal, quite dry, but not logs. Thus the reader must be creative also in trying to understand the imagery created by the poet. [*See* IMAGERY.]

A third way that poetry is creative is in its connection to intuition. Poetry has recently (in the 20th century) been called a form of intuition. Though ideas can be deduced from a poem, the poem itself is the idea, and that is intuition. Phenomenological theories of poetry assert that the reader grasps the poem through a kind of "inseeing"—according to Henri Bergson (1859–1914), who advocated the importance of intuition over intellect, expounding the idea that there are two opposing forces; he promoted the idea of two opposing currents: lifeless matter in conflict with organic life as the vital urge (*élan vital*) strives toward the freedom inherent in the poet's and poem's intuitive creative action. [*See* INTUITION.]

V. CONCLUSION

Poetry is one of the oldest domains of creativity, practiced instinctually by humans throughout evolutionary time. Because of this, the future for poetry is assured; whether new forms will evolve through technology is immaterial, for the human creative instinct to produce poetry has always existed and will continue to exist.

Bibliography

Aristotle. *Poetics and Rhetoric.*

Ciardi, J., & Williams, M. (1975). *How does a poem mean?* (2nd ed.). New York: Houghton Mifflin.

Coleridge, S. T. (1872). *Biographia Literaria.* New York: John Holt.

Hutchins, R. (Ed.) (1952). The dialogues of Plato. *Great books of the western world. Plato, Vol. 7* (trans. B. Juwett). Chicago: Encyclopaedia Britannica.

Hutchins, R. M. (Ed.). (1952). *The great ideas: A syntopicon of great books of the Western world.* Chicago: Encyclopaedia Britannica.

Plato. *The Republic* and *Ion.*

Preminger, A., & Brogan, T. V. F. (Eds.). (1993). *Princeton Encyclopedia of Poetry and Poetics.* New York: MJF Books.

Political Science and Creativity

Jay A. Seitz
York College, City University of New York

Masterpieces are not single and solitary births; they are the outcome of many years of thinking in common, of thinking by the body of the people, so that the experience of the mass is behind the single voice.

Virginia Woolf

I. Legitimating Creativity: Individual and Community
II. Funding Creativity: Corporate Gifts, Subsidies, and Silicon Valley
III. Communitizing Creativity: Politics and Creative Inheritance

Capital Any accumulated asset or resource that may abet some goal or pursuit. For example, physical capital refers to buildings, land, and physical access to them (e.g., roads and sidewalks). Investment capital refers to the financial resources of an individual, group, or institution. Social capital refers to social bonds among individuals and group membership, as well as access to information and resources (e.g., access to the Internet). Human capital refers to the endowments of health and education that individuals possess.

Communitarianism A political theory that views persons as constituted within a community that shares common values, norms, and goals that each individual views as a good in itself.

Community A body of people marked by common social, economic, and political values and interests.

Liberalism A political theory that emphasizes the autonomy and freedom of the individual from arbitrary authority (e.g., government).

Market Economy An economic system determined by free competition for goods regulated by supply and demand.

Political Science An academic discipline concerned with an analysis of the distribution of power among individuals, groups, organizations, and institutions in society.

In investigating the relationship between **POLITICAL SCIENCE AND CREATIVITY,** *it is important to note that the political and social milieu and the differential distribution of power within a society constrains creative expression. Standard psychological theories view creativity as arising largely from the unique or extraordinary characteristics of individuals (e.g., mental processes or personality) giving credence to social attitudes and beliefs about the folklore of such terms as the* lone genius, brilliant inventor, estranged artist, or wayward entrepreneur. *In fact, any creative product emerges from a unique coincidence of individual intellective abilities; the nature and relative sophistication of a scientific, artistic, or entrepreneurial domain; the complexity and structure of the field of legitimization; and the distribution of power and resources within a group, community, or society.*

I. LEGITIMATING CREATIVITY: INDIVIDUAL AND COMMUNITY

A. The Genius View

The tension between individual creativity and the needs of the larger community are central to an understanding of creativity and political science. The prevalence of the genius view in contemporary American culture is instructive: It consists in the belief that (a) creative persons have unusual or phenomenal thought processes and (b) these thought processes are largely unconscious and operate through flashes of insight. Scientific studies of creative individuals, however, support just the opposite interpretation: that creative solutions are slow and incremental and involve the conscious testing and rejecting of ideas. Yet creative solutions are not conceived in isolation but are worked out through direct or indirect contact with others including the influence of previous historical developments in the field of inquiry. For example, science is the cumulative knowledge of many individuals, rarely, if ever, an isolated breakthrough. Indeed, one important view of the development of the sciences is a succession of revolutionary breaks in theory, method, or institutional structure set against a sustained background of tradition-bound periods. Shared scientific values held during these entrenched periods can be seen as a way of diversifying creative risk within the scientific community. Art and politics may follow a similar periodization with occasional revolutionary punctuations affecting artistic preferences or forms of political government— thus, Karl Marx's view that art and politics are the surface manifestations of the same underlying social order. To be sure, groups of artists regularly share artistic and social bonds that deeply influence emerging artistic developments; cubism in the beginning of the 20th century is a poignant example. The same holds true for government; politics involves power and privilege within a group over others through authority, coercion, and repression.

By the same token, artistic genius consists not in some extraordinary individual's effort at self-expression but in the interaction between a work of art and the receptivity of an audience at some particular historical point in time. For example, the premiere of Igor Stravinsky's "Rite of Spring" in Paris in the early part of the 20th century was initially greeted with overwhelming hostility. According to this view, genius is not a property of individuals but a characteristic that a community or society bequeaths on an individual in response to a work of art. It is a multidirectional relationship among political, cultural, and social forces and the individual that creates genius rather than a unidirectional one in which some extraordinary human creates the world anew. Nevertheless, uncommunitized personhood may be a significant source of creativity and transformation within the community, organization, or institution. The Swiss psychologist, Jean Piaget, in his advice to creative scientists, advocated solitary creative striving to avoid outside influences from the community.

Creativity is thus a confluence of the creative and intellectual potential of the individual, exposure of individual creative initiative to divergent social enclaves as well as the constraints of the surrounding political, cultural, and social milieu. Such a perspective goes beyond C. P. Snow's classic dichotomy of two creative cultures—art and science—to recognize the central importance of political and cultural constraints on individual creativity. This so-called third culture includes political or religious censorship (e.g., the defunding of the National Endowment of Arts) as well as large corporate bodies controlling access to resources and information exchange (e.g., corporate gifts to individual scientists) through copyright restrictions or through related economic constraints (e.g., monopoly, oligopoly, or cartel).

One substantive approach to the problem of constraints in the macroenvironment has been to conceive of individual creativity as an investment in a scientific, artistic, or entrepreneurial domain in which there is a chance of a significant creative payoff. Although intraindividual elements are important (mental processes, background knowledge, intellectual style, personality, motivation, and so on), these factors themselves are influenced by the social and cultural contexts that both nurture creativity and evaluate and legitimate creative ideas and their products. Because so many social and cultural forces must converge to promote creativity, few people are willing to invest in it. According to this view, creativity is conceptualized as the result of buying low and selling high. Creativity is the process of generating unpopular ideas—visual, political, economic, literary, and so on—and convincing others of their relative value. That is to say, creativity only functions within a larger social matrix in which ideas are commodities and their value in the intellectual marketplace is both galvanized and suppressed by extant social organizations and institutions. [*See* ECONOMIC PERSPECTIVE ON CREATIVITY.]

B. Arts

With regard to the arts, in as early as the 18th century art came to be increasingly viewed as reflecting national character or values, particularly as represented in national museums (e.g., French Louvre, British Museum, and Rijksmuseum in Holland) and schools of art (e.g., Italian, Flemish, Dutch, and French). Indeed, given the advancement of individual rights during the French Revolution, the Musée Napoléon in France was the first to exhibit art to the public at large. This democratization of art reflected the liberal political order that had begun to emerge during this period. According to the 19th century German philosopher Friedrich Nietzsche, art superseded religious belief and the artist became a symbol of the national spirit.

C. Business

Within the entrepreneurial field, the extraordinary development of computer hardware and software technologies, particularly in the United States, can be understood as the result of a confluence of variables at the individual, community, and national levels. Much of it has been centered geographically in the culture of Silicon Valley in northern California. This culture is distinguished by (a) webs of interlocking relationships among companies in close proximity, (b) collaboration, cooperation, and coordination in product development (e.g., the Intel–Microsoft alliance), (c) minimal bureaucracy and command structures resulting in flatter, more democratic organizations with diminished management hierarchies, and (d) a risk-tolerant culture in which failure is rewarded by others. Moreover, there is a rich ecosystem of diverse companies and individual talent, an entrepreneurial infrastructure of ancillary businesses and financial concerns (e.g., venture capital, banking, law, and real-estate firms), business-government partnerships (e.g., Internet access in com-

munity schools), and a synergy among executives, many of whom inhabit the same work environments, cafes, and outdoor surroundings that promote the cross-fertilization of creative ideas. Even the local universities provide more technologically savvy graduates to the region than any other area in the United States.

II. FUNDING CREATIVITY: CORPORATE GIFTS, SUBSIDIES, AND SILICON VALLEY

A. Sciences

Corporate and company influence on research is significantly leveraged in the natural sciences and exerts tremendous pressure on scientists in both what they study and how they study it. For example, in a 1998 study of academic-industry research partnerships in the life sciences it was reported that close to 50% of scientists had received corporate gifts. These gifts included biomaterials (e.g., viral cultures), research equipment, travel and discretionary funds, and student support. But companies often demanded acknowledgement and coauthorship, restriction of gifts in both use as well as transmission to third parties, prepublication review of articles and reports, mandatory testing of company products, and ownership of potential patents. Moreover, faculty members who received more gifts were more likely to publish in refereed journals as well as produce more patentable products and start-up companies. Indeed, in at least one case a company attempted to suppress research findings when it was found that a pharmaceutical drug worked no better than a less expensive generic drug. [*See* SCIENCE.]

B. Arts

On the one hand it has been claimed that access to art is a basic human right and thus government should not interfere with the exercise of artistic freedom. On the other hand there is a long history of artistic and intellectual censorship going back to the early Greeks who viewed art as dangerous to the community. In a recent controversy in the United States, a report from the National Endowment of the Arts (NEA) suggested that art institutions had become elitist, ethnic, and class-based as well as isolated from the communities they serve. As a result, the arts had been marginalized in American culture with a consequent decline of arts education in the public schools including support for modern art and artists. In fact, the report indicated that in 1997, 50 art organizations received 32% of all corporate and private funding of which only five states accounted for 65% of the total. Community-based (e.g., folk), experimental, underground, and cross-disciplinary art were almost entirely ignored by both public and private funding agencies. For instance, during this period individual federal grants for artists were eliminated by the National Endowment of the Arts. Similarly, private foundations began to increasingly fund art under guidelines and goals that advanced corporate interests at the expense of artistic and intellectual diversity. [See ART AND AESTHETICS; ART AND ARTISTS.]

C. Business

Within the entrepreneurial domain, the success of Silicon Valley strengthens the case for the value of social over human capital. Whereas human capital reflects individual endowments of education and well-being, social capital emphasizes access to information and resources, group membership, and webs of social relationships that reflect rich voluntary associations. This "new institutionalism" asserts that individuals in disparate institutional contexts define and pursue their interests in diverse ways. Moreover, rich voluntary associations facilitate independence, change, and promote novelty by increasing access and communication among individuals and institutions through open communication and information exchange. Studies of such "civic" cultures, cultures with strong voluntary associations, indicate that civic governments are less hierarchical and authoritarian as well as legislatively more creative in facilitating flexible specialization, decentralization, and integration among businesses and individuals. The tremendous creative and financial success of Silicon Valley has much to do with the horizontal integration of businesses, particularly the interlocking network of investment bankers, venture capitalists, real-estate brokers, and ancillary businesses that provide physical and investment capital to emerging hi-tech firms within the technological community. [See BUSINESS STRATEGY.]

III. COMMUNITIZING CREATIVITY: POLITICS AND CREATIVE INHERITANCE

Liberalism, a theory of government and society that became increasingly influential in the 17th century, (a) requires equal treatment of all citizens independent of any particular conception of the good life mandated by the state and (b) promotes representative democracy and a market economy so as to uphold the rights of individuals as well as economic and ethnic equality for all. According to this view, liberalism abets creative production by encouraging individual creative expression.

On the other hand, communitarianism, a contemporary political theory, maintains that self-determination develops through extant social practices, social roles, and cultural and political institutions. Thus the individual is seen as situated within a social matrix, and it is the influence of the latter that shapes citizen's unique preferences, personal choices, and individual creative pursuits. Creativity is posited to be not merely the result of intraindividual factors (e.g., individual creative expression or genetic endowment) but the consequence of the confluence of cultural domains and social and political institutions that directly and indirectly influence the development of individual creative expression.

Current research on creativity finds strong support for the communitarian view: (a) creative individuals engage in a broad, interconnected network of endeavors; (b) both childhood experiences including relations with siblings in the family and proximate and distal relationships with others in later life play a pivotal role, particularly interactions with formal and informal educational institutions; (c) both the micro-environment—the immediate creative context—and the macroenvironment—the social, cultural, and institutional context—facilitate creative production by enabling individuals to make connections across disparate domains; and (d) dominant elites within a society tend to suppress creative initiative in order to secure the advantages of the status quo. To be sure, the creator draws his or her creative nourishment from the vitality and richness of the community, which is no doubt why so many creative individuals are drawn to urban centers with their deep and extensive cultural and intellective resources. Moreover, creative accomplishments in any field stand atop the often unacknowledged, earlier labor of many distinct contributors. To wit, (a) technological accomplishments in computers and software in the last 20 years stand on a Gibraltar of scientific invention in the middle part of the 20th century, (b) advances in modern art arose as a result of the introduction of new technologies into the field (e.g., acrylic paints, computer graphics, and new kinds of architectural materials), and (c) the reinvention of the American corporate business sector in the 1980s had less to do with the magical leadership abilities of any particular CEO and more to do with the changing corporate institutional framework in reaction to technological and global challenges to American business.

Bibliography

Avineri, S., & De-Shalit, A. (1992). (Eds.). *Communitarianism and individualism.* New York: Oxford University Press.

Business Week. Silicon Valley: How it really works. (1997, August 25).

Chadwick, W., & de Courtivron, I. (1993). (Eds.). Significant others: Creativity and intimate partnership. London: Thames & Hudson.

Csikszentmihalyi, M. (1996). *Creativity.* New York: Harper-Collins.

Danto, A. (1992). *Beyond the brillo box: The visual arts in historical perspective.* New York: Farrar, Straus, & Giroux.

Feldman, D. H., & Goldsmith, L. T. (1986). *Nature's gambit: Child prodigies and the development of human potential.* New York: Basic Books.

Gardner, H. (1993). *Creating minds: An anatomy of creativity seen through the lives of Freud, Einstein, Picasso, Stravinsky, Eliot, Graham, and Gandhi.* New York: Basic Books.

Larson, G. O. (1997). *American canvas: An arts legacy for our communities.* Washington, DC: National Endowment for the Arts.

Sternberg, R. S., & Lubart, T. I. (1995). *Defying the crowd: Cultivating creativity in a culture of conformity.* New York: Free Press.

Sulloway, F. J. (1996). *Born to rebel: Birth order, family dynamics, and creative lives.* New York: Pantheon Books.

Weisberg, R. W. (1986). *Creativity: Genius and other myths.* New York: W. H. Freeman.

Postmodernism and Creativity

Glen R. Brown

Kansas State University

Appropriation The strategical borrowing of images, styles, or entire works from a variety of cultural and historical contexts and integration of them into a new configuration where they become ambivalent as representations but retain much of their original stylistic identity.

Autonomous Subject The Cartesian subject; a self-present being capable of thought before expression.

Deconstruction A method to demonstrate that human reality is constructed within language rather than given in experience of an absolute nature.

Language The all-encompassing symbolic system outside of which even the most basic cognitive functions cannot be performed.

Logocentrism The belief, characteristic of Western metaphysics, in a logos or transcendental signified that stands outside language and guarantees the truth of representation.

Signifier A sound/image corresponding to a signified or concept. In structuralist linguistics the signifier and signified form the sign; in poststructuralism every signified is always already another signifier.

The status of creativity has varied widely in theories of culture since the 1970s and the advent of what is frequently described as the postmodern era. Although there is by no means agreement on the definition of POST-MODERNISM, or even more than a general consensus that such a term is appropriate for describing contemporary culture, the majority of self-proclaimed theories of postmodernism have either rejected or significantly altered the idea of creativity as formulated in 19th- and early 20th-century modernism. Much of the critique of this modernist idea of creativity has manifested itself as the postmodernist rejection of the concept of the autonomous subject, a subject fully intelligible outside of or prior to language (in the broad sense of an all-encompassing symbolic system), which acts as an origin for content expressed through language. For many postmodernists, critique of the autonomous subject has necessarily given rise to a period of postcreativity in which the subject is no longer seen as capable of originating meaning but rather is conceived as merely a site through which language "speaks." Other postmodernists have taken up the less extreme position of arguing that creativity must be redefined from its associations with expression of original content toward the collagelike practice of arranging preexisting information in original configurations. Still others have argued that the concept of creativity promotes a sense of responsibility for one's actions and consequently is a socially beneficial

Copyright © 1999 by Academic Press
All rights of reproduction in any form reserved.

fiction that ought to be maintained through faith even if it cannot be supported through logic. Finally, some postmodernists have attempted to redefine subjectivity so as to allow for the critique of the subject's autonomy while maintaining the ultimate defensibility of originality and creativity.

I. CRITIQUE OF THE AUTONOMOUS SUBJECT

The concept of creativity in modernist theory of the 19th and early 20th centuries frequently found definition in biogenetic terms (one thinks of Maurice Vlaminck's assertion that art is a product of the loins rather than the intellect or Max Pechstein's even more telling proclamation on painting, "painful and joyful is the exultation of giving birth"). Such figures of speech betray a linking of originality to nature, implying that the source of literature, visual art, music, and other aesthetically creative productions is a primal experience that precedes any expression in cultural symbolism. Reversing the terms of science, in which culture gave meaning to nature, the modern artist sought to bring nature to bear on culture. Through art, it was argued, the humanizing aspects of nature could make culture endurable, could even influence social progress. The modernist theory of the avant-garde arose as a description of a dialectical process wherein the subject transcended the social by reverting to a private experience of the natural, then synthesized the work of art from these two discrete spheres. As a consequence, modern art was viewed as both original and critical, part of a process of reforming society toward the underlying, originative truths of human nature.

The modernist, humanistic vision of creativity could be maintained only so long as the subject was posited as an autonomous, natural being, a being whose experience in some manner preceded and exceeded the operations of language. By the late 1960s, however, the conviction had begun to form—principally among French theorists of literature and social history—that this description of the subject was no longer tenable. Proceeding from arguments in structuralist linguistics for the all-encompassing and self-referential character of language, intellectuals such as Claude Lévi-Strauss,

Roland Barthes, and Michel Foucault began to argue that the subject was not, after all, a natural being capable of coming to language from a space outside but rather a position always already inscribed within language. Having dismissed the possibility of a distinction between interior and exterior in relation to language, Barthes could reject the idea of creativity and even provocatively announce the "death of the author." What appeared to be expression, he argued, was not in fact the translation of an individual's private, inner experience into the public domain of language but merely language turning back on itself, a recourse to a "ready-formed dictionary." Foucault, arguing that the author was merely a concept that had emerged under specific historical conditions in the West, further suggested that one speak not of the author but of the "author function." Rather than a living being capable of originating ideas, he suggested, the author was a concept resulting from a tendency to attribute human psychology to certain operations of language.

Undoubtedly the most influential argument of this type was made by Jacques Derrida, whose method of "deconstruction" would not only put in question the concept of an autonomous subject but would apparently undermine all metaphysical theories of meaning. Suggesting that Western thought since Parmenides had been dominated by "logocentrism," a belief in a logos or ultimate meaning that in some sense transcended language itself, Derrida set about exposing the impossibility of any such externality. Although deconstruction is precisely not a method of establishing a new philosophy but rather of demonstrating the impossibility of traditional philosophy, some conclusions about meaning can be drawn from Derrida's practice. The most significant for any discussion of creativity is the conclusion that expression is never free of indication: that a content (a signified) cannot be separated from an element by which content is expressed (a signifier). As there can be no pure content, there can be no pure expression. Furthermore, because the signifier acquires its indicative meaning not in a positive sense but rather through its opposition to other signifiers within a larger system, the meaning of any expression is never present but rather is infinitely deferred through the play of difference in language. The subject, likewise, cannot be described as autonomous, because every attempt to represent the self, even in a supposed private voice, always already disperses the subject across language.

II. POSTCREATIVITY

In the 1970s, the critique of the autonomous subject initiated a serious reconsideration of the role of creativity in aesthetic practice. Within modernist theory, creativity had been intimately linked to originality, the critical capacity of the artist to introduce aspects of private experience into a shared language. If the subject could no longer be characterized as exterior and anterior to language, the concept of originality as the expression of an inner experience could no longer be maintained. Originality, in fact, could be viewed as a modernist fiction, a concept emerging in modernist discourse—as the art critic Rosalind Krauss suggested—only through repression of its negative counterpart, repetition. Under these conditions, the "original" work of art resulted not from expressing a unique vision but rather from masking the repetitive aspects of the work, all those elements that linked it not to a supposed private experience but rather to the conditions of repeatability endemic to language. From a postmodern perspective, in other words, pure expression had begun to appear possible to modernists only when the indicative aspects of the work of art were repressed.

The most frequent method of critiquing the modernist concept of creativity as pure expression could be roughly described as reversing the relationship between the terms *originality* and *repetition* in order to privilege the latter. Although such a reversal has characterized the practice of numerous postmodern artists, the strategy is epitomized by a series of photographs produced by Sherrie Levine in the late 1970s. Utilizing an extreme form of a practice that has come to be described as appropriation, Levine simply photographed the works of celebrated modern photographers such as Edward Weston, Walker Evans, and Eliot Porter. Her photographs were not manipulated in any way, for all practical purposes duplicating the originals. The point was to suggest that if the original photo and Levine's copy were visually indistinguishable, then any further distinction between original and copy could only be

maintained through recourse to conceptual rather than material criteria. But if a work of art could be described as original only if the concept behind it were original, in what sense could any work of art really be considered original? When Walker Evans photographed the interior of a West Virginia coal miner's shack, for example, he was not operating in an artistic vacuum. He drew directly from his knowledge of aesthetic composition—formal conventions of balance, rhythm, contrast, and harmony established in Western art history through multiple works from the past. These contexts determined how Evans's photograph would appear; in forming the composition, in other words, Evans only found what he was already conditioned to see. Consequently, he could not be described as a point of origin for the composition but rather as a conduit for preexisting information: precisely, in fact, what Levine was claiming to be her own role in photographing Evans's photograph. Furthermore, the viewer's recognition of Evans's (and Levine's) practice as art can only occur because of the indicative relationship of the photograph to the larger context of art history. For the postmodernist, just as every text indicates another text, behind every image lies another image. As a result, the modernist concept of creativity—of giving pure expression to the work of art from some inner realm of private and natural experience—no longer seems viable, and many postmodernists appear resigned to conditions of postcreativity.

III. COLLAGE/MONTAGE AND SCHIZOPHRENIA

Are there ways of defining creativity without invoking the concept of the autonomous subject? Some postmodernists have argued that the manipulation of preexisting information—the practice of collage or montage—is in itself a creative act, although what is produced is merely a new configuration of information. For such an argument to be maintained without reverting to the characteristics of logocentrism, however, the process of collage/montage must avoid positing an autonomous subject who initiates the new configuration and may be isolated as the origin of its meaning. The extreme difficulty of this practice lies in the reader, listener, or viewer's tendency—a historically specific tendency, as Foucault pointed out, but a powerful one nonetheless—to attribute any unity in a work to a unified subject, or author, behind it. Likewise, the perception of this unity appears to confirm the unity of the reader, listener, or viewer. How would it be possible to produce an original configuration of preexisting information without suggesting the autonomy of the work, an autonomous subject who initiates the collage/montage, or an autonomous subject who perceives it?

The strategy employed by many postmodernists is to appropriate recognizable styles, imagery, or even entire works from a variety of historical or cultural contexts and to render them ambivalent by inserting them into a new context shared with other appropriated elements. The appropriated style, image, or work, as a consequence, acquires a new meaning from its relationship to other elements in the collage/montage while simultaneously carrying with it the traces of its meaning in a previous context. The new configuration—the collage/montage—cannot, as a result, be mistaken for a pure expression; its unity is constantly deferred through its indication of other contexts. Nor can an autonomous subject be discerned behind the collage/montage; no single meaning can be attributed to the configuration and presented as evidence of a unified consciousness that created it.

In reference to the work of Gilles Deleuze and Felix Guattari the postmodern subject in this formula has often been characterized by the term *schizophrenic,* not to indicate a pathology or to comment negatively on the strategies of appropriation and collage/montage. Rather, the term *schizophrenic,* as the literary theorist Fredric Jameson has suggested, emphasizes certain aspects of postmodern practice that parallel an actual schizophrenic's relationship to language. According to the French psychoanalyst Jacques Lacan, whose work constituted a reformulation of Freudian theory in the terms of structuralist linguistics, schizophrenia is a condition resulting from an infant's incomplete acquisition of the principles of language. By failing to grasp the temporal aspect of language—the unfolding of a sentence across time—the schizophrenic fails to form a scene of the self's unity across time. As a result, a schizophrenic's discourse is characterized by discontinuity, the lack of a logical sequence between signifiers.

Because the schizophrenic's words or images do not appear to express a unified rationality, they take on a primacy of their own, heightening the material experience of language. The creative aspects of a schizophrenic's discourse, as a consequence, appear not to derive from an autonomous subject but rather from the potential configurations inherent to language. By mimicking these characteristics of schizophrenic discourse, some postmodernists would argue, it is still possible to engage in creative activity, to produce an original work, while apparently deferring indefinitely the impression of an autonomous subject in relation to it. [See SCHIZOPHRENIA.]

IV. CONSTRUCTIVE POSTMODERNISM

Although skepticism about the possibility of a unified self characterizes postmodern thought in general, not all postmodernists agree that the critique of the autonomous subject has been beneficial, especially in social terms. In the late 1980s, a movement described by its followers as "constructive" postmodernism, emerged as a challenge to the antihumanistic bent of much previous postmodern discourse. The crux of the constructive postmodernist argument has been the assertion that many so-called postmodern ideas and practices are actually detrimental forms of ideas and practices developed in modernism. Perhaps the most important example is the concept of the avant-garde, which in modernism pitted the individual against mainstream society as a radical voice against traditional values. Although the dialectic underlying the theory of the avant-garde and its aspirations to social progress may no longer characterize contemporary art practices, constructive postmodernists argue that radical social critique has in deconstructive postmodernism reached the extreme position of challenging the validity of society in general. If the "truths" that bind a social system together can be deconstructed as fictions, it is argued, society itself begins to unravel.

Although constructive postmodernists do not in general deny that truths are constructed within language—that values are produced socially rather than given in an absolute and unchanging world—their concern is for the consequences of deconstructing certain of these social fictions. For example, the concept of creativity as pure expression of an experience prior to language helps to form the basis for belief in the ability of the individual and community to effect positive social change. As the constructive postmodernist Suzi Gablik has argued, feelings of contingency brought about by the deconstruction of individuality have led to a general pessimism about the future of the earth and the human race. Problems such as rising crime, violence among youth, the destruction of the natural environment, and the proliferation of weapons of mass destruction seem inevitable and beyond the power of human beings to rectify through creative problem solving. Furthermore, without a sense of the ability of the self to make a meaningful impact on a larger reality, there can be little feeling of responsibility for any actions one might carry out. As a consequence, extreme forms of narcissism can develop without any attendant feelings of compunction.

David Ray Griffin, the chief advocate of constructive postmodernism, has argued that the pessimism endemic to contemporary society is essentially a problem of spirituality diminishing in favor of the materialism promulgated by modern science. By invoking the term *spirituality* and attaching to it positive connotations, however, constructive postmodernists do not mean to suggest that social and environmental problems can be effectively combated through recourse to traditional forms of organized religion. Rather, the spiritual is proposed as another way of describing faith in the transcendental signified, a logos or cosmological purpose giving meaning to human actions and events. It is for the constructive postmodernist unimportant whether such a logos is a fabrication within language or an absolute entity that actually transcends language, so long as it can be *experienced* as transcendental. The role of the artist, for the constructive postmodernist, is to make a cosmological purpose seem credible once more, to "re-enchant" the word by restoring belief in creative spirit. To attempt to do so in the wake of deconstructive postmodernism, however, requires a Kierkegaardian leap of faith that some admit may no longer be possible.

V. THE SPEAKING SUBJECT

Although the critique of the autonomous subject has prompted most postmodernists to reject or re-define the concept of creativity, some theorists have approached the problem from another direction and attempted to find ways of redefining the subject to preserve the concepts of originality and creativity. Their work neither accepts nor rejects categorically the conflicting arguments that the subject is, on the one hand, a fully intelligible consciousness outside of and prior to language or, on the other, that language is all encompassing and the subject merely a function within it. Treating these positions as extremes, some have argued that the subject should be redefined as equally a cultural being constructed through the operations of language and a natural being whose experiences extend beyond language. To support such a formulation without reinstating the autonomy of the subject, the natural being of the subject must not be conceived in terms of a unified rationality, a consciousness that possesses a complete meaning and then expresses it. Consequently, the most important attempts to redefine the subject in this manner have drawn heavily on theories of unconscious psychosomatic processes.

The most convincing model for a being perpetually split between language and natural experience has been offered by the psycholinguist Julia Kristeva. In elaborating a theory of the "speaking subject," Kristeva has argued that the self is not an a priori entity expressed through language but rather is only ever "present" in the act of enunciation itself. The self, in other words, is purely a "signifying practice," an experience that emerges and is sustained only within the actual employment of language. At the same time, this self is not entirely inscribed within language. The speaking subject emerges in the conflux of the symbolic operations of language and the preverbal activity of psychosomatic processes. Paralleling the Freudian description of parapraxis, Kristeva argues that preverbal distributions of energy such as the rhythms of the drives and stases continually erupt into language, disrupting and reordering its structural logic. An example of how this disruption might appear at its most extreme in an aesthetic context is the stream-of-consciousness writing of James Joyce.

The importance of Kristeva's model of the speaking subject for a discussion of creativity lies in its description of the subject's enunciations as motivated—even original—without implying the subject's self-presence prior to enunciation. The part of the self consisting of psychical activity is experienced as a pure motility or kinetic being which, although it constitutes a kind of unity, cannot be described as a rational, autonomous subject. On the other hand, the discourse produced by the speaking subject, because it is also inherently bound to the temporal aspects of language, can produce a sense of the unity of the self across time. As a consequence, creative activity can occur without implying on the one hand an autonomous subject that initiates it or on the other a purely schizoid subject whose sense of self is perpetually deferred. Creative activity, in fact, is necessarily implicit to some degree in any enunciation, because the speaking subject can no more exist wholly within the confines of language than entirely within psychosomatic processes.

VI. CONCLUSION

Even a brief survey of postmodern ideas on the concept of creativity is sufficient to reveal the diversity of perspectives that many consider to be a defining characteristic of postmodernism itself. With the decentering of the subject and the deconstruction of absolutes, empirical methodologies have come increasingly under attack and in their stead has emerged a theoretical discourse that posits all meanings as necessarily contextual and reflexive. As a consequence, what common ground exists between postmodernists has less to do with positive assertions about the objects of knowledge than with the rejection of the positivities informing modernist discourse. The modernist concept of creativity as pure expression, for example, has been widely discredited, but no central theory of postmodern creativity has emerged to take its place. As indicated earlier, postmodern approaches to the subject have ranged from attempts to redefine creativity or subjectivity to the denial that creativity is possible at all. From the postmodern perspective, in no case can there be recourse to an independent reality in assessing the merits of each perspective. A fundamental heterogeneity is inherent to postmodern discourse; as a consequence, from a postmodern perspective the status of concepts such as creativity must remain necessarily indeterminable outside the specific arguments in which they are addressed.

Bibliography

Foster, H. (Ed.). (1995). *The anti-aesthetic: Essays on postmodern culture* (9th ed.). Seattle, WA: Bay Press.

Lawson, H. (1985). *Reflexivity: The postmodern predicament.* London: Hutchinson and Co.

Leitch, V. B. (1983). *Deconstructive criticism: An advanced introduction.* New York: Columbia University Press.

Risatti, H. (Ed.). (1998). *Postmodern perspectives: Issues in contemporary art* (2nd ed.). Englewood Cliffs, NJ: Prentice Hall.

Sarup, M. (1989). *An introductory guide to post-structuralism and postmodernism.* Athens: University of Georgia Press.

Proactive Creativity

Thomas E. Heinzen

William Paterson University

Incubation The ability to maintain an interest or a work on a problem even when attention is not being directed toward that interest or problem.

Intrinsically Motivated Behavior Action performed because the action is its own reward; it is not instrumental in achieving some other goal.

Motivation Continuum The range of causes of creative behavior, anchored by the extremes of proactive and reactive creativity.

Positive Affect Refers simply to feeling good—any pleasant emotional state.

Proactive Creativity The process characterized by intrinsic motivation, positive affect, spreading activation, and focused self-discipline, which produces new, effective products that tend to be of enduring value.

Reactive Creativity The process characterized by extrinsic motivation, negative affect, limited mental associations, and desperate problem solving, which produces new, effective products that solve only a short-term problem.

Spreading Activation The set of mental associations engaged when memory stores are cued for recall and those associations trigger further associations.

The range of causes of creative behavior may be understood as existing along a continuum anchored by proactive and reactive creativity. **PROACTIVE CREATIVITY** *is often personality driven and characterized by positive affect and spreading cognitive activation, whereas reactive creativity is often situationally driven and characterized by negative affect and limiting cognitive activity. The mix between these two types of creativity represents the kind of everyday creativity that describes most individuals most of the time.*

I. A MOTIVATION CONTINUUM

One way of understanding human creativity is to place it along a continuum representing the instigation or causes of creative behavior. *Proactive creativity* anchors one end of this continuum and contrasts with *reactive creativity* at the other end. If we could survey the entire range of human creativity along this continuum, we would probably discover that it is normally distributed in the shape of the familiar bell-shaped curve. Although this *motivation continuum* represents the range of causes of creative behavior, research by Teresa Amabile and her colleagues suggests that the amount and quality of creativity closely correspond to the initial motivational cause of creativity.

Creativity is simultaneously multifaceted and holistic. The continuum of proactive and reactive creativity describes the motivational characteristics of creativity and represents just one repeating facet of this theoretical jewel. Mark Runco has clarified the multidimensionality of creativity along developmental lines; Amabile has redescribed the same phenomenon in an attempt to articulate social influences on creativity. Like other psychological constructs (such as intelligence), every attempt to cut this jewel, by experiment as well as by theory, produces a fascinating new insight without damaging our pleasure in the whole. Consequently, the description of proactive and reactive creativity presented here is with the recognition that this continuum is just one repeating facet of a larger, more compelling phenomenon.

II. AFFECT: PLEASURE VERSUS PAIN

Proactive creativity is *intrinsically motivated behavior* that eventually produces some new and effective product. As an affective process, proactive creativity is characterized by *positive affect* that receives its inspiration from within the individual personality. This is meant to imply more than simply feeling good, although simple manipulations of affect also appear to facilitate creativity. This experience is something akin to Mihaly Csikszentmihalyi's notion of "flow," in which the creator is caught up in the pleasure, fascination, and process of being fully engaged. For the creator, proactive creativity is desirable and exciting. [*See* MOTIVATION/DRIVE.]

Reactive creativity, by contrast, is externally motivated and characterized by negative affect. The individual feels desperate and anxious because he or she fears a solution may not be forthcoming and tends to be driven by situation and circumstances rather than inspiration and personality. The process still results in some new and effective product, but the process by which it appears is a miserable experience. Among humans, an unhappy marriage may result in separation or divorce. Nevertheless, those generally negative processes require, virtually force, new and effective life patterns for all the participants. Not infrequently, the miserable process eventually creates entirely new families. When this happens often enough, we may begin to socially reconstruct (i.e., re-create) our notion of what it means to be a family. Although the process is generally characterized by negative affect, it is nevertheless a truly creative process because it produces new and effective adaptations. Similarly, everyday evolution is also a process of reactive creativity. It produces new and effective adaptations but the process is certainly painful for any extinguishing species or the new prey on which an evolving predator might uniquely feed.

III. COGNITION: ACTIVATION VERSUS LIMITATION

The cognitive characteristics of proactive creativity are characterized by *spreading activation* in which multiple ideas, consequences, and benefits are quickly surveyed and assessed. This is especially true at an early stage of the creative process. However, to move beyond the pleasures of brainstorming and produce an eventual product, the cognitive characteristics of proactive creativity eventually become focused and disciplined. The creative process requires both types of cognitive abilities and is one reason that high creativity is a relatively rare event. Originality by itself is simply a schizophrenic-like phenomenon. When directed and strengthened by focused self-discipline, originality can become creativity. The ability to suspend a quality idea somewhere in consciousness, keeping it alive and at the ready yet without allowing it to unduly interfere in present tasks, is one form of *incubation*. The cognitive characteristics of proactive creativity are so fascinating as to be entirely distracting for some individuals. Perhaps this explains the emergence of cognitive science departments at so many colleges and universities to supplement such diverse departments as psychology, neuroscience, philosophy, and computer science. [*See* INCUBATION.]

The cognitive characteristics of reactive creativity also contrast sharply with those of proactive creativity. The desperate affective state corresponds to thought processes that severely limit any problem solving beyond the immediate crisis. In contrast to spreading activation, thoughts are narrowly focused on the immediate trouble. The ability to incubate and suspend useful ideas is ignored or not engaged in the first place.

IV. INDIVIDUAL DIFFERENCES: PERSONALITY VERSUS SITUATION

It is probable that the distribution of creativity among individuals varies along this continuum of proactive and reactive creativity. Over the past 10 years, Thomas Heinzen has been able to study the creativity of three fairly distinct populations. The first was represented by the Johns Hopkins Center for Talented Youth and comprised pre- and post-adolescent men and women identified as "gifted and talented." The second was government bureaucrats in New York State, several of whom were quite busy circumventing many of their own rules and restrictions in order to accomplish a specific goal. The third population has been nursing home residents, many of whom have debilitating physical and corresponding mental disabilities. Each of these populations demonstrated significant individual variation.

Proactive creativity was personality driven, whereas reactive creativity is situation driven. Some of the "talented" teenagers were keen to write short stories, test ideas scientifically, or become social leaders. Others, just as talented, simply wanted to complain about the food during their camp experience and spent their creativity on petitions for small goals. A handful of middle-aged bureaucrats were enjoying the game of circumventing a complex bureaucracy in its own self-interest so that more children would actually wear bicycle safety helmets. Unfortunately, many were seriously discouraged and exhibited symptoms similar to clinical depression. They spent their creativity figuring out ways to hide behind their union's protective cover. Many nursing home residents demonstrate remarkable courage and find a way to create pleasure, offer insight, and cleverly manipulate nurses, social workers, and administrators to get what they want. Others allow their creative impulses to shrivel up and spend their declining energy on what they themselves acknowledge to be unrewarding activities. All of these people are potentially creative. Those who chose to be proactively creative were generally more creative more often and in far more original ways than those who chronically reacted to events with random bursts of poorly aimed originality. The first demonstrated strong personalities, whereas the second succumbed to desperate circumstances.

Proactive creativity represents the kind of creativity that most aspire to. Reactive creativity represents the kind of creativity we often live with, whose temporary solutions often achieve an unwelcome permanence. Proactively creative people tend to find one another, network together, and enjoy the strength of shared experience and so become more creative. Reactively creative people tend to operate in isolation, hardly recognize their temporary solutions as even creative, and avoid problems. The mix between proactive and reactive creativity in our own lives describes the creative output that represents our own contribution across the life span.

V. SUMMARY

Proactive creativity is the process characterized by intrinsic motivation, positive affect, spreading activation, and focused self-discipline that produces new, effective products (broadly defined). Reactive creativity stands in contrast to proactive creativity, both affectively and cognitively. We look forward to being proactively creative—we stay up nights working on a favorite project and steal every hour to pursue our passion. We avoid certain tasks and exercise reactive creativity to get them out of our way. We create many new and effective adaptations simply to make better use of our time or as a result of the everyday frustrations of our lives.

Bibliography

Heinzen, T. E. (1994). *Everyday frustration and creativity in government.* Norwood, NJ: Ablex.

Runco, M. A., & Albert, R. S. (Eds.). (1990). *Theories of creativity.* Newbury Park, CA: Sage.

Shaw, M. P., & Runco, M. A. (Eds.). (1994). *Creativity and affect.* Norwood, NJ: Ablex.

Problem Finding

Mark A. Runco and Gayle Dow

California State University, Fullerton

Divergent Thinking Cognition that leads to a number of ideas, rather than one, some of which are original.

Evaluative Thinking Judging ideas, often for their originality.

Problem Definition Altering a previously identified problem, before solutions are attempted, to make it workable.

Problem Finding The umbrella term for activity that occurs before problem solving. Includes problem identification, problem definition, problem construction, and so on.

Problem Identification Recognizing that a problem exists before defining or solving the problem.

Recursion Interactions among stages of the problem finding and solving process, and in particular revisiting an earlier stage.

PROBLEM FINDING plays an important role in creative thinking. Many achievements in the past reflect creative problem definition more than they do creative problem solving, and in fact a creative solution to a problem may depend on first defining a creative problem. Even in everyday contexts problem solving may depend on prob- *lem identification and problem definition, two important kinds of problem finding. Very often the solution to a problem is extremely obvious once the problem has been properly defined and represented. In its original or conventional form the problem may have been exceedingly difficult; but a creative redefinition can make that same difficult problem an easy one to solve.*

Problem finding can be defined in general terms as the process or processes that precede problem solving. The specific processes under the term "problem finding" include problem discovery, problem construction, problem expression, problem posing, problem definition, and problem identification. Some of these are similar processes but different researchers have given the same process different labels.

I. BACKGROUND

Problem finding operations are frequently (but not always) included in models of creative thinking. Figure 1 presents one such model, with problem finding one of three primary components to creative thinking. The other two reflect ideational skills and evaluative skills. The model in Figure 1 differs from Graham Wallas' early model of problem solving, in that there is a second tier of components that influence problem finding, ideation, and evaluation. These reflect moti-

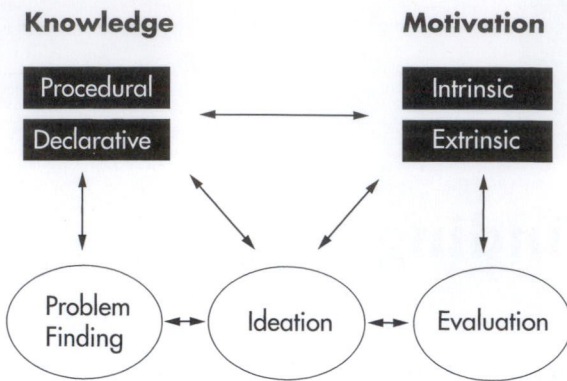

FIGURE 1   An example of one model of creative thinking.

vation (both intrinsic and extrinsic) and knowledge (both procedural and conceptual or factual). [*See* Mo-tivation/Drive.]

J. P. Guilford, who first distinguished between divergent and convergent thinking, recognized problem finding, though he referred to it as "sensitivity to problems," which may imply an affective tendency more than a cognitive skill. E. Paul Torrance, author of the other widely used tests of creative thinking, also recognized the importance of problem finding. He included "the process of *sensing gaps* or disturbing missing elements and formulating hypotheses" in his definition of creativity. [*See* Divergent Thinking.]

Many attempts to model problem finding and problem solving place them in a fixed sequence. This step by step explanation to problem finding and solving is unrealistic. It is reasonable to assume that there are stages of problem finding and solving; however, these stages are far from rigidly fixed and often recur during the various stages of the problem solving process. While some stages do follow a fixed order (e.g., what is known as data finding, which by its very definition must occur prior to the attempt of any solutions), the majority may be revisited several times. In the simplest case this recursion will occur when a person identifies a problem, attempts one solution, learns from the attempt, and returns to a problem definition position to redefine the problem.

The affective contributions to problem finding must also be acknowledged. These were implied by the model presented above, with motivation being a key influence on the process, and by Guilford's term "prob-lem sensitivity." In order to attempt any task or problem, there must be a degree of emotional involvement. This will allow the individual to attend to and invest effort in the task. Such an involvement is often referred to as "problem ownership." Curiosity, intrigue, and motivation are each ways of describing the affective influences on problem finding—and problem solving. The interesting thing is that there is a debate about which comes first: the cognitive basis of the problem (i.e., recognizing that there is a problem) or the affective basis for the problem (i.e., the interest in it). It makes sense that we do not attend to things which do not interest us, which implies that affect must precede the cognitive basis of problem definition, and yet if we have not defined the task, it is difficult to see how we would understand it well enough to be intrigued by it. This issue is far from resolved.

II. PREVIOUS RESEARCH AND IMPLICATIONS FOR EDUCATIONAL PROGRAMS

Some researchers have suggested that creativity is the outcome of discovered problem-solving. They distinguish between "discovered" and "presented" problems. The affective basis of problem finding has been referred to as "a concern for discovery." As an example, John Wakefield presented some standard tests of the potential for creative thinking to a group of fifth grade children. These children were asked to list all of the things a given line figure could represent. This was a kind of presented problem. Later the same children were asked to draw their own line figure, and then to list all of the things that their own figure could represent. This second was a discovered problem task. Statistical analyses confirmed that the responses given by the children to it were predictive of various criteria of creative potential. Mark Runco and Shawn Okuda extended this work to other students and to the verbal domain; adolescents generated significantly more responses to verbal discovered problems than to verbal presented problems, and discovered problems were more accurate predictors of creative accomplishment than presented problems. Discovered problems contributed significantly to the prediction of creative accomplishment above and beyond the prediction which used only scores from the presented problems. This research has been extended to more realistic tasks and again discovered problems were found to be more accurate predictors of creative achievement. The use of realistic problems is important because they may tap different strategies and different motivations than presented problems. This is another way of recognizing the affective basis of problem finding and creativity.

The use of realistic task and discovered problems is important for testing, if the most accurate predictions are desired. They are also important for programs which are designed to enhance creative thinking skills. This is because in the natural environment, most problems are not presented, or at least not presented in a clear-cut format. Some problem definition is often necessary. If that is what is common in the natural environment, then programs which are designed to enhance efforts in the natural environment should use ambiguous tasks as well. Participants should practice problem definition in these programs or the skills learned may very well not generalize to the natural environment. [*See* EN-HANCEMENT OF CREATIVITY; TEACHING CREATIVITY.]

III. THE ISSUE OF CREATIVITY AS A KIND OF PROBLEM SOLVING

The claim that problem finding is a key aspect of the creative process needs to be slightly qualified. This is because creativity does not always involve a problem. However, the separation of creativity from problems (and thus problem finding and solving) is controversial. One view is that creativity can be portrayed as independent of problem solving. Problem finding proficiency would thus not be required for creativity. Usually when creativity is viewed as independent of problem solving, the creativity involved is a kind of self-expression. The other view is that even self-expression can be viewed as a kind of problem solving. Self-expression may not have a concrete problem at hand, nor a well-defined problem, and it may be that the problem is an issue of finding the best expression for one's self or one's thinking. Clearly, creative effort that reflects the individual's self-expression, when the problem is personal and not explicit, could easily be conceived as dependent on problem definition.

IV. CONCLUSIONS

Although there are unresolved issues in this area, it is clear that problem finding plays a significant role in creative work. However, it is no longer adequate to discuss problem finding as unitary. It may be best to use specific terms such as problem identification and problem definition, which are more precise. It is also necessary to recognize the recursive nature of the specific processes subsumed under the problem finding label. Realistically, these may be used more than once as the individual attempts to solve a problem. Creative success may even be associated with the capacity to allow the recursions and redefinitions of the problem.

Bibliography

Jay, E., & Perkins, D. (1997). Problem finding: The search for mechanism. In M. A. Runco (Ed.), *Creativity research handbook*. Cresskill, NJ: Hampton Press.

Runco, M. A. (Ed.). (1994). *Problem finding, problem solving, and creativity*. Norwood, NJ: Ablex.

Problem Solving

Richard E. Mayer

University of California, Santa Barbara

Creative Problem A problem for which a problem solver must invent a novel solution method.

Insight A creative process in problem solving when a problem solver suddenly progresses from not knowing how to solve a problem to knowing how to solve a problem.

Problem A situation in which a problem solver has a goal but does not know how to achieve it.

Problem Representation A major process in problem solving in which the problem solver builds a mental representation of the problem.

Problem Solution A major process in problem solving in which a problem solver devises, carries out, and monitors a solution plan.

Problem Solving Cognitive processing aimed at figuring out how to move from a given state to a goal state when no obvious solution method is available to the problem solver.

Productive Thinking Problem solving that requires the invention of a new solution method.

Reproductive Thinking Problem solving that requires applying an already known procedure to a problem.

Routine Problem A problem for which a problem solver knows a solution method based on past experience.

*This chapter defines **PROBLEM SOLVING**, distinguishes between routine and creative problems, distinguishes between reproductive and productive thinking, analyzes the processes in problem solving, reviews the major theoretical approaches to problem solving, examines the role of insight in creative problem solving, and explores the teaching of problem-solving skills.*

I. DEFINITIONS

Problem solving is cognitive processing directed at transforming a given situation into a goal situation when no obvious solution method is available to the problem solver. This definition is broad enough to cover a broad array of directed thinking activities ranging from solving mathematics problems, to playing chess, to composing a poem, to discovering a new scientific principle, to resolving a personal dilemma. In particular, this definition includes four components. First, problem solving is cognitive, because it occurs in the mind (or cognitive system) of the problem solver. Cognition can occur in humans, nonhuman animals, or machines. Second, problem solving is a process, because the problem solver engages in some sort of mental computation such as applying a set of operations to knowledge in the cognitive system. The computational nature of problem solving places it squarely within the domain of cognitive science. Third, problem solving is directed, because the problem solver aims to reach a goal. Thus, problem solving can be conceived as directed thinking. Fourth, problem solving is personal, because it depends on whether or not the problem solver knows how to achieve the goal based on past experience. What is a problem for one person may not be a problem for another.

A *problem* occurs when a problem solver has a goal but does not have an obvious means for achieving the goal. In particular, a problem consists of a given state, a goal state, and a set of allowable operations. The given state is the current state of the problem, the goal state is the desired state of the problem, and the allowable operations are the actions that the problem solver can take. Thus, a problem solver has a problem when a situation is in the given state, the problem solver wants it to be in the goal state, and the problem solver does not have a plan for how to apply the allowable operations to achieve the goal. For example, given the problem "$3x - 5 = 10$, Solve for x" the given state is "$3x - 5 = 10$," the goal state is "$x = \_\_$," and the allowable operations include adding the same number to both sides of an equation, dividing both sides of the equation by the same number, and so on. If a problem solver does not know a method for solving the equation (e.g., add 5 to both sides and then divide both sides by 3), this constitutes a problem.

Based on this definition, it is possible to distinguish between well-defined problems and ill-defined problems. A well-defined problem is presented with a clear given state, a clear goal state, and a clear set of allowable operations. For example, an algebra problem such as "$3x - 5 = 10$, Solve for x" is a well-defined problem because the given state is clearly defined as an equation, the goal state is clearly defined as finding a value for x, and the allowable operations are clearly defined by the procedures of algebra and arithmetic. In con-

trast, an ill-defined problem includes a poorly specified given state, goal state, or set of operations. For example, "How can we improve the literacy of the world population?" is an ill-defined problem because what is meant by improvement in literacy is not clearly specified and the steps one is allowed to take (i.e., the allowable operations) are not clear.

II. DISTINCTION BETWEEN ROUTINE AND CREATIVE PROBLEMS

To better understand the relation between problem solving and creativity, it is worthwhile to distinguish between routine and creative problems. A routine problem primes a solution plan in the problem solver, such that the problem solver recognizes a way to solve the problem based on similar past experiences. For example, most computational problems, such as $223 \times 47 = \_\_$, are routine problems for an adult. In contrast, a creative problem does not prime a solution method in the problem solver, such that the problem solver lacks past experience on similar problems and must construct a novel way to solve the problem. For example, a question such as "What would happen if people had six fingers instead of five?" is a creative problem for anyone who is not already familiar with it. In short, a routine problem is one in which a problem solver applies a solution procedure that is already known based on past experience, whereas in creative problem solving the problem solver invents a solution procedure that is novel for that problem solver.

The distinction between routine and creative problems depends on the personal experiences and knowledge of the problem solver, so a problem that is routine for one person might be a creative problem for another person. For example, a simple arithmetic problem such as $5 + 3 = \_\_$ is a creative problem for a child who does not have the answer memorized. The child may reason as follows: "I can take 1 from 5 and give it to 3, so I have 4 plus 4, and I know that 4 plus 4 is 8."

A strict interpretation of the definition of problem solving would exclude the solving of routine problems and focus solely on the solving of creative problems. Similarly, the creativity research literature focuses on how people solve creative rather than routine problems, because creativity is commonly defined as the creation of an original and useful product. [*See* DEFINITIONS OF CREATIVITY.]

III. DISTINCTION BETWEEN REPRODUCTIVE AND PRODUCTIVE THINKING

Paralleling the distinction between routine and creative problems, it is useful to distinguish between reproductive and productive thinking. *Reproductive thinking* occurs when a problem solver applies an already known solution procedure to a problem, that is, the problem reproduces a method based on previous experience. For example, a student may learn that the procedure for finding the area of a parallelogram is to drop a perpendicular line, measure the height, measure the base, and then multiply height by base, using the formula area = height × base. Then, when the student is given a standard parallelogram with height of 3 and base of 5, the student can engage in reproductive thinking to produce the answer $3 \times 5 = 15$. According to the Gestalt psychologist Max Wertheimer, learning by rote leads to good performance on retention problems (i.e., problems that are very similar to the taught problems) but poor performance on transfer problems (i.e., problems that are somewhat different in appearance from the taught problems).

In contrast, *productive thinking* occurs when a problem solver invents a solution procedure that is novel for that problem solver. For example, by using a pair of scissors, a problem solver discovers that she can cut the triangle from one side of the parallelogram and place it on the other side to form a rectangle. Because she knows how to find the area of a rectangle by multiplying height by base, she now sees a general principle for finding the area of a parallelogram. Thus, she is able to solve a transfer problem involving finding the area of an unusually shaped parallelogram or other geometric shapes. According to the Gestalt psychologist Max Wertheimer, learning by understanding leads to good retention and transfer performance.

Creativity research focuses mainly on productive rather than reproductive thinking or, put another way, on creative problem solving rather than routine problem solving.

IV. PROCESSES IN PROBLEM SOLVING

It is customary to distinguish between two major phases in problem solving: *problem representation* and *problem solution*. In problem representation, a problem solver takes the problem statement and builds an internal mental representation of the problem. Cognitive psychologists have further analyzed the process of problem representation into the subprocesses of *translating* and *integrating*. Translating involves mentally representing each sentence or portion of the problem, whereas integrating involves putting the knowledge together into a coherent structure that can be called a situation model. In problem solution, the problem solver devises and carries out a plan for solving the problem. Problem solution includes the subprocesses of *planning, executing,* and *monitoring*. Planning involves devising a solution plan, executing involves carrying out the plan by engaging in action, and monitoring involves awareness and control of one's cognitive processing, including assessing the effectiveness of one's plan as it is put into action. Monitoring is an important aspect of *metacognition,* the awareness and control of one's cognitive processing. [*See* METACOGNITION.]

For example, George Polya analyzed the processes involved in solving a geometry problem:

Find the volume *F* of the frustrum of a right pyramid with square base given the altitude *h* of the frustrum, the length *a* of a side of its upper base, and the length *b* of a side of its lower base.

According to Polya, the first step is *understanding the problem,* which corresponds to the translating subprocess in problem representation. Here the problem solver asks, "What do I want?" and "What do I have?" In this case the goal is to find *F,* the volume of the frustrum, and the given information is *a, b,* and *h*. Polya's second step is *devising a plan,* which includes both the integrating subprocess in problem representation and the planning subprocess in problem solution. This is where creative insight occurs. To help build a coherent representation of the problem, the problem solver can ask, "What is a related problem I can solve?" and "Can I restate the goal or the givens differently?" In this case, the problem solver might know how to find the volume of a full pyramid. The major creative insight occurs when a problem redefines the goal as finding the area of the full pyramid (of which the frustrum is the bottom part) and subtracting the volume of the smaller pyramid (which is the top part of the full pyramid without the frustrum). This plan is based on a new way of representing the problem. Polya's third step, *carrying out the plan,* corresponds to the executing subprocess in problem solution. In this step the problem solver carries out the needed arithmetic computations. Finally, Polya's fourth step is *looking back,* in which the problem solver looks for the overall logic of the solution method. This step includes aspects of the monitoring subprocess in problem solution.

Although the subprocesses in problem solving can be neatly distinguished, problem solvers rarely engage in them in a linear order. In most complex problem solving the subprocesses interact such that a problem solver may begin by trying to represent the problem, then trying to plan, then going back and modifying the representation, then trying to execute the plan, then monitoring, then revising the plan, and so on. Most of the difficulty and need for creativity in problem solving concerns building a coherent problem representation (i.e., integrating) and devising and monitoring a solution plan (i.e., planning and monitoring).

V. THEORIES OF PROBLEM SOLVING

Over the course of its first 100 years as a science, the study of problem solving has produced three large-scale theoretical approaches: associationism, Gestalt psychology, and information processing.

According to the associationist approach, mental representations consist of elements (or ideas) and links (or associations) between them, so problem solving involves following a chain of mental associations. For example, solving an anagram that forms a common word (e.g., converting UGARS into SUGAR) is easier than solving an anagram that forms an uncommon word (e.g., converting OBRAC into COBRA), presumably because the associations leading to a common word are stronger than those leading to an uncommon word. Associationist theory does not emphasize creative processes, because problem solving mainly involves the use of preexisting associations. Dating back to the be-

ginning of the psychological study of problem solving 100 years ago, associationist theory lives on in some connectionist models and computer simulations of cognition. [*See* ASSOCIATIVE THEORY.]

According to the Gestalt approach, mental representations consist of organized structures, so problem solving involves mentally restructuring problems. For example, when a problem solver is asked to use six equally long sticks to construct four equilateral triangles, the student may first attempt to solve the problem on a table surface using only two dimensions. However, the flash of creative insight occurs when a problem solver realizes that the problem can be solved in three dimensions by constructing a pyramid with a triangle as its base. Gestalt theory emphasizes creative processes, such that the major creative accomplishment is to attain structural insight—that is, seeing how all the pieces of the problem fit together to satisfy the requirements of the goal. Gestalt psychology, which reached its peak in the 1920s, 1930s, and 1940s, no longer exists by this name but key ideas such as schema theory and learning by understanding continue to influence modern research on cognition.

According to the information processing approach, mental representations consist of procedures that can be specified as computer programs and isolated facts that can be specified as propositions, so problem solving involves applying a set of transformations to information. A problem is represented as a *problem space,* that is, a representation of the given state, the goal state, and all possible intervening states produced by applying allowable operators to each state. The problem solver must use a strategy for moving through the problem space from the given state to the goal state. In their classic book, *Human Problem Solving,* Alan Newell and Herbert Simon describe a computer simulation of problem solving based on a means-ends analysis strategy, in which the system establishes subgoals when larger goals cannot be directly achieved. Some scholars have argued that the classic version of information processing theory does not accommodate creative problem solving whereas a constructivist version does. Having begun in the 1950s, information processing theory is still a viable approach within the multidisciplinary field of cognitive science.

Major research areas in the psychology of problem solving include the nature of problem-solving expertise, the nature of intellectual ability, thinking by analogy, thinking in everyday contexts (i.e., situated cognition), problem solving in specific domains (e.g., mathematical or scientific problem solving), development of problem solving skill, and teaching of problem-solving skill.

VI. ROLE OF INSIGHT IN PROBLEM SOLVING

Perhaps the most important but least understood aspect of creative problem solving is insight. *Insight* is the process involved in creative problem solving in which a problem solver suddenly progresses from a state of not knowing how to solve a problem to a state of knowing how to solve a problem. More than 50 years ago, the Gestalt psychologists sought to understand the nature of insight. For example, in the late 1930s Max Wertheimer eloquently posed questions about the nature of insight that are still central to modern theories of problem solving (in Abraham Luchins and Edith Luchins' *Wertheimer's Seminars Revisited*):

> Why is it that some people, when faced with problems, get clever ideas, make inventions and discoveries? What happens, what are the processes that lead to such solutions?

Wertheimer and his fellow Gestaltists were not able to provide definitive answers to these provocative questions, and modern researchers continue to search for the mechanisms underlying insight. Today's cognitive psychologists have concluded that we do not yet understand insight.

In grappling with Gestalt psychology's great unanswered questions about the nature of insight, researchers have proposed six views of insight: insight as nothing new, insight as completing a scheme, insight as reorganizing visual information, insight as reformulating a problem, insight as overcoming a mental block, and insight as finding a problem analog. For a more detailed examination of these topics, see the source in the bibliography under Mayer, 1995.

A. Insight as Nothing New

According to the nothing new view of insight, what appears to be insight is nothing more than the problem solver using past responses to solve a current problem. For example, Robert Weisberg proposed that "people create solutions to new problems by starting with what they know and later modifying it to meet the specific problem at hand." Based on research in which problem solvers were more successful when they had previous experience with the solution behaviors than when they did not, he concluded that "there seems to be very little reason to believe that solutions to novel problems come about in flashes of insight."

The classic educational psychologist E. L. Thorndike was one of the earliest proponents of the nothing new view of insight. Based largely on observing how laboratory animals learned to escape from puzzle boxes, Thorndike proposed that animals possess a hierarchy of responses associated with any problem based on their past experience. When confronted with a problem, problem solvers work by trial and error in which they apply the response most strongly associated with the problem situation, then the next strongest response, and so on, until one works. Subsequent research with humans confirmed that problem-solving transfer occurred only when elements in a previously learned task were identical to elements in a new to-be-solved task.

However, even this classic version of the nothing-new view was challenged by researchers of the day. For example, evidence has been provided that students displayed better transfer when they learned general principles rather than specific responses. Evidence has also been provided for a distinction between rote learning and meaningful learning. In seeking to broaden psychology's view of human cognition, it has been suggested that the objection to the theory of one kind of connection as the basis of all learning, is it has prevented an unbiased study of other kinds of learning.

More recently, the nothing-new view has been challenged by modern research on insight. First, training problem-solvers how to make specific responses to solve a problem is less effective in promoting problem-solving transfer than helping problem-solvers learn about the general structural features of a problem. Second, new evidence for an "aha!" experience comes from studies in which people solving insight problems generally do not feel they are getting progressively closer to solving the problem before actually figuring out a solution. Five alternatives to the nothing-new view are described in the next five subsections.

B. Insight as Completing a Schema

According to the completing-a-schema view, insight occurs when a problem solver fills a gap in a structure—that is, when a problem solver sees how the givens and goals fit together within a larger system or complex. As articulated in the landmark work of Otto Selz, a problem is a potentially coherent set of information with a gap, and problem solving involves figuring out how to fill the gap in a way that completes the structure.

For example, when Selz asked subjects to give the superordinate category for newspaper, they did not always follow a chain of associations as predicted by the nothing-new view. According to Selz's analysis of the subjects' thinking aloud protocols, sometimes problem solvers engaged in *schematic anticipation* in which they mentally built a structure such as "____ is a superordinate of *newspaper*" and tried to fill it in a way that maintained its structural integrity. Selz (in Nico Fridja and Adriaan De Groot's *Otto Selz*) argued that the solution emerges "not through the senseless play of associations" but rather through building a new mental structure in which "new specific responses occur only as integrated members of a system."

What is the current status of the schema-completion view? Although Otto Selz was the first psychologist to propose a nonassociationist theory of thinking, his research is imprecise by modern standards and is not widely acknowledged by modern cognitive psychologists. Yet his ideas foreshadowed Gestalt theories of problem solving and, to some extent, are reflected in cognitive psychology's modern attempts to understand how schemas are constructed and used to support both human and machine cognition.

C. Insight as Reorganizing Visual Information

Building on Gestalt theories of perception, the reorganizing-visual-information view is that insight involves literally looking a problem situation in a new way. According to this view, insight occurs when a problem solver suddenly reorganizes visual information in a way that satisfies the requirements of the goal. In short, insight involves the mental restructuring of visual information.

For example, in what is perhaps the most well-known early study of insight, Wolfgang Köhler confronted chimpanzees with problems that required creative solutions. For example, in one problem, there are wooden crates on the floor of a cage and a bunch of bananas hanging overhead beyond the reach of the chimp. The chimp's problem is to get the bananas. The solution to the problem occurs when a chimp places the crates on top of each other to form a ladder, climbs up, and grabs the bananas. According to Köhler, the idea for this solution occurs suddenly and the specific responses were never practiced before. Instead of trying responses until one works, Köhler's chimps seemed to mentally reorganize the visual information in a way that attains the goal.

What is the current status of the reorganizing-visual-information view? Köhler's work can be criticized for lack of methodological rigor, for vagueness of theorizing, and for inconsistency with subsequent research showing that animals perform better if they have had previous experience using the objects in the problems. In spite of these shortcomings, Köhler's work sparked continuing interest in visual thinking, including visual representations in mathematical cognition and mental models in human and machine cognition.

D. Insight as Reformulating a Problem

The reformulating-a-problem view holds that insight involves conceiving of the givens or the goal in a new way that promotes solution. In short, insight occurs when the problem solver defines or formulates the problem in a new, more productive way. In what is widely recognized as the single most important publication on insight, Karl Duncker's *On Problem Solving* offered two ways to reformulate a problem: a *suggestion from below* in which a problem solver redefines the given state of the problem and a *suggestion from above* in which a problem solver redefines the requirements of the goal. Complex problem solving may involve a series of insights—that is, a succession of reformulations of the problem.

For example, in Duncker's radiation problem, problem solvers must think aloud as they grapple with the following problem:

Given a human being with an inoperable stomach tumor and rays which destroy organic tissue at sufficient intensity, by what procedure can one free him of the tumor by these rays and at the same time avoid destroying the healthy tissue that surrounds it?

Duncker found a problem solver might begin by reformulating the goal as "avoiding contact between rays and healthy tissue," leading to incorrect solutions such as sending the rays through the esophagus; subsequently reformulate the goal as "desensitizing the healthy tissue," leading to incorrect solutions such as immunizing the healthy tissue with weak rays; and eventually reformulate the goal as "lowering the intensity of rays on the way through the tissue," leading first to an incorrect solution such as turning the intensity from high to low as the ray enters the tumor, and finally to the correct solution of aiming several weak rays from different angles so that they converge on the tumor. According to Duncker's analysis of this protocol, the problem solver solves the problem by successively reformulating the goal and deriving some specific solutions based on the reformulation.

How has the reformulating-a-problem view fared in current theories of problem solving? Although Duncker's writings are vague and his research methods are imprecise, his work foreshadowed the constructivist revolution in which humans are seen as sense makers who actively seek to construct meaningful representations of their experiences. For example, Duncker's theory is consistent with modern research on the development of problem solving expertise in which creative problem solving progresses from general qualitative representations of a problem to specific quantitative solutions. The insight-as-reformulating-a-problem view lives on in modern research on how experts solve novel problems in rich domains such as medicine, physics, and computer programming.

E. Insight as Overcoming a Mental Block

This view holds that insight depends on a problem solver's ability to overcome a mental block by ignoring inappropriate past experience. In direct conflict with the nothing-new view, in which successful problem solving depends on past experience, the overcoming-a-mental-block view is based on the idea that past experience can hinder problem solving. This is the case when the solution requires using a given object in an unconventional way or using procedures other than those that would habitually be used.

Duncker used the term *functional fixedness* to refer to a situation in which a problem solver tends to think of using a given object only in its most common way rather than in a more novel way. For example, in a classic study on functional fixedness, Duncker presented students with a table that had a pasteboard box containing candles, a pasteboard box containing tacks, and a pasteboard box containing matches, and he asked them to mount three candles side by side at eye level for use in visual experiments. The solution is to tack each box upside down to the door as bases for the candles, to use the matches to lightly burn the bottom of three candles, and then stick one candle on each base. Duncker found that students had much more difficulty in solving this problem when the elements were presented in each box, but that the problem was much easier when the boxes were empty and the elements were simply piled next to the boxes on the table. According to Duncker, placing the elements in the boxes created functional fixedness in which the subjects conceived of the boxes solely as containers—the boxes' conventional function—rather than as bases—an unconventional function.

In another classic study, Abraham Luchins showed how previous experience in solving water jar problems by a particular method can create a mental set—called *einstellung*—in which students continue trying to use the same method on new problems even though much simpler methods are possible. For example, a problem such as "Given an unlimited supply of water and a 21-, 127-, and 3-qt jar, obtain exactly 100 qt of water," an appropriate solution is to fill the 127-qt jar, dip out 21 qt once and 3 qt twice. After solving five problems that could all be solved by this procedure (represented as $b - a - 2c$), students tended to be unable to find simple solutions to new problems, such as "Given an unlimited supply of water and a 23-, 49-, and 3-qt jar, obtain exactly 20 qt of water." Students who lacked previous experience tended to solve the problem by filling the 23-qt jar and taking out 3 qt (i.e., $a - c$), whereas students who had previous experience tended to use the longer procedure of 49 − 23 − 3 − 3. Luchins argued that the "blinding effect" of previous experience can result in "mechanized problem solving" that reduces the chances for creative solutions.

Does the overcoming-mental-blocks view have an influence on modern theories of problem solving? One area in which this approach continues to exert an influence is in the teaching of problem-solving skills. For example, one effective technique for fostering creative problem solving involves a sort of cognitive apprenticeship in which a novice models the problem-solving strategies of a more experienced problem solver in a particular domain. The teaching of techniques for overcoming mental blocks represents an important venue for modern research on insight.

F. Insight as Finding a Problem Analog

In contrast to the mental-blocks view in which inappropriate past experience is a culprit, the problem analog view depends on appropriate past experience. According to the problem analog view, insight occurs when the structural relations or principles in a previously solved problem (i.e., an analog problem) are applied to solving a new problem (i.e., a target problem). In thinking by analogy, a problem solver must focus on general structural features shared by two problems rather than the specific responses needed to solve the problems.

For example, Max Wertheimer provides an example in which he shows a child how to build a bridge using two short blocks as horizontal bases and a long block as a vertical cross bar. Then, he gives the child two long blocks and a short block, and asks the student to build a bridge. The incorrect solution involves giving the same behavioral responses as in the first problem—that is, using a short block as a base and a long block as a cross bar; the correct solution involves abstracting the general principle that bases must be equal in length and the cross bar must be perpendicular to them. Wertheimer (in *Productive Thinking*) describes the children's performance as follows:

Some . . . place the short block vertically, the long one horizontally, holding it in this position, and appear anxious to find another small block. I do nothing. Then they begin to try to put the third block in the horizontal position; it falls down. . . . After it falls down, they do it again, but most children, after about two trials, suddenly smile, and change the place and role of the blocks. Many of the children do this at once after a short pause, without any previous trials.

These results provide evidence of structural insight in which students grasp the structural relations of one problem (i.e., to build a bridge you need two equal bases and a perpendicular cross bar) and apply them to the solution of a new problem. A similar result was obtained by George Katona in which students who learned to solve puzzles based on structural principles were better able to transfer to solving new problems than were students who learned a series of specific responses. Wertheimer concluded that "the crucial question is not whether past experience, but what kind of past experience, plays a role—blind connections or structural grasp."

Modern cognitive psychology continues to examine problem solving by analogy including research on barriers to analogical reasoning and the role of concrete models in scientific reasoning. Reflecting Wertheimer's distinction between structural relations and arbitrary associations, current cognitive theory distinguishes between structural similarity and surface similarity between problems. If the mechanism underlying insight involves the use of problem analogs, then current research on analogical problem solving represents an important venue for research on insight. [See ANALOGIES.]

This brief review of conceptions of insight in creative problem solving demonstrates that the classic conflict between associationist and Gestalt views of cognition are still being played out in cognitive psychology. The nothing-new view is consistent with the idea that problem solving involves reproductive thinking about routine problems, whereas the other five views are based on the idea that problem solving involves productive thinking about creative problems. In short, the two classes of views were designed to explain different kinds of problem solving, and, hence, each may be successful. The mechanisms underlying insight—and, hence, creative problem solving—may eventually be clarified as researchers more deeply explore one or more of the views of insight presented in this section. [*See* INSIGHT.]

VII. TEACHING OF PROBLEM-SOLVING SKILLS

What is the best way to improve a person's creative problem-solving skills? This question raises four issues concerning the what, how, where, and when of problem solving skill. For a more detailed examination of these topics, see the source in the bibliography under Mayer, 1997.

A. What Is Problem-Solving Skill?

The first issue concerns whether problem solving should be taught as a single monolithic ability or as a collection of smaller component skills. The single-ability view—originally known as the *doctrine of formal discipline*—was dominant around 1900, when psychologists first began to empirically study this issue. The doctrine of formal discipline held that students' minds improved when they studied certain school subjects (or disciplines) such as Latin, geometry, and logic. For example, Latin schools were established based on the premise that studying these subjects would foster "proper habits of mind" in students. Early in the 20th century, however, research evidence was mounting that studying subjects like Latin did not help students learn or solve problems in other unrelated subject areas. In contrast, recent advances in the study of intellectual ability suggest that problem-solving skill is best viewed as a collection of small component skills as well as strategies for managing them. Thus, problem-solving instruction should target a select group of well-defined component skills rather than aim to improve the mind in general.

B. How Should Problem-Solving Skill Be Taught?

The second issue concerns whether problem-solving instruction should emphasize the product of problem solving (e.g., getting the correct answer) or the process of problem solving (e.g., figuring out how to solve the problem). The traditional answer to this question favors an emphasis on product in which students practice on problems and are rewarded for correct answers. However, early critics of the product-based approach provided evidence that an emphasis on product can lead to rote learning that does not transfer easily to new problems.

As reported in their classic book *Problem-Solving Processes of College Students,* Benjamin S. Bloom and Lois J. Broder taught unsuccessful college students how to answer examination questions by asking them to model the problem-solving processes of successful students. For example, in a typical training session a successful problem solver would think aloud as he solved an examination question—carefully articulating what he was thinking about at each step in the process; next, the unsuccessful student would do the same thing, and then compare his thinking process to that of the successful student. After several sessions like these, which emphasize the process of answering examination questions, the unsuccessful students improved dramatically on their examinations. Consistent with current research and theory in cognitive science, these results demonstrate the importance of focusing on problem-solving process rather than product.

C. Where Should Problem-Solving Be Taught?

A related question concerns whether problem solving should be taught in a general stand-alone course or be integrated within specific school subject areas. Early theories of problem solving favored a domain-general view, in which students were expected to learn general reasoning skills that could be used in a wide variety of domains. In contrast, recent ethnographic research has pointed to the domain-specificity of problem solving, in which skills learned in one context are rarely used in other contexts.

For example, *Street Mathematics and School Mathematics,* by Terezinha Nunes and colleagues, describes how street vendors could accurately carry out complex arithmetic computations within the context of selling their wares but made many errors when solving similar computational problems in a school setting. In a series of evaluation studies, elementary school students who learned how to solve problems using the Productive Thinking Program—intended as a general stand-alone course—excelled on solving problems similar to those in the course but did not show as much improvement in solving different kinds of problems. These results, as well as cognitive science theories, support the idea that problem-solving skills are often domain specific, so it makes sense to incorporate problem-solving instruction within authentic contexts.

D. When Should Problem Solving Be Taught?

The final issue concerns whether problem solving should be taught mainly to older, experienced students who have mastered the underlying basic skills in a subject area or also to younger, inexperienced students who are novices in a subject area. The traditional view—which can be called *prior automatization*—is that students must master basic skills before they can learn higher-order thinking skills. According to this view, for example, before a student learns how to compose an essay, he or she must first develop skill in handwriting, spelling, punctuation, and sentence grammar. In contrast, the *constraint-removal* view is based on the idea that students can engage in higher-level problem solving in situations that do not require complete mastery of lower-level skills. For example, in the case of composing an essay, the constraints of good handwriting, spelling, and punctuation can be removed by asking the young student to dictate the essay to an adult who types it into a word processor.

Research on cognitive apprenticeship demonstrates that students who have not yet mastered lower-level skills can benefit from participating in tasks requiring higher-order problem solving. In cognitive apprenticeship, beginners participate along with skilled practitioners on authentic tasks, such as students and teachers working together to make sense out of a text. The practitioners provide modeling (e.g., describing how they solve problems), coaching (e.g., offering hints, comments, and advice), and scaffolding (e.g., assisting the student on parts of the task that the student cannot do alone). For example, Ann Brown and Annemarie Palinscar found that a cognitive apprenticeship technique called reciprocal teaching helped elementary school children learn higher-order skills for text comprehension including how to summarize a text.

These kinds of results, coupled with other advances in cognitive science, suggest that problem-solving skills can be successfully learned by students who have not yet mastered lower-level basic skills. Of course, problem solving expertise depends on both kinds of skills.

VIII. SUMMARY

In summary, problem solving is a cognitive process aimed at figuring out how to move from a given state to a goal state when no obvious solution method is available to the problem solver. A problem exists when a problem solver has a goal but does not know how to achieve it. A well-defined problem has a clearly specified given state, goal state, and set of allowable operations, whereas one or more of these three components is not clearly specified in an ill-defined problem.

A routine problem is one for which a problem solver knows a solution method based on past experience, whereas a creative problem is one in which a problem solver must invent a novel solution method. Similarly, reproductive thinking involves applying an already known procedure to a problem, whereas productive thinking requires the invention of a new solution method.

The major processes in problem solving are problem representation and problem solution. Problem representation includes translating and integrating; problem solution includes planning, executing, and monitoring.

Three main theoretical approaches to problem solving that have developed over the past 100 years are associationism, Gestalt psychology, and information processing.

Insight occurs when a problem solver suddenly progresses from not knowing how to solve a problem to knowing how to solve a problem. Six conceptions of insight are insight as nothing new, insight as completing a schema, insight as reorganizing visual information, insight as reformulating a problem, insight as overcoming a mental block, and insight as finding a problem analog.

Teaching of problem-solving skills is enhanced when problem-solving skill is viewed as a collection of component skills rather than a single ability, instruction emphasizes the process rather than solely the product of problem solving, teaching takes place within the specific context of an authentic task rather than a general subject, and as the problem solver is developing basic skills rather than after all basic skills have been mastered.

Bibliography

Bloom, B. S., & Broder, L. J. (1950). *Problem-solving processes of college students.* Chicago: University of Chicago Press.

Duncker, K. (1945). On problem-solving. *Psychological Monographs, 58*(5). 270.

Gilhooly, K. J. (1996). *Thinking: Directed, undirected, and creative.* London: Academic Press.

Katona, G. (1940). *Organizing and memorizing: Studies in the psychology of learning and teaching.* New York: Columbia University Press.

Köhler, W. (1935). *The mentality of apes.* New York: Liveright.

Luchins, A. S. (1942). Mechanization in problem solving: The effect of einstellung. *Psychological Monographs, 54*(6), 248.

Mayer, R. E. (1992). *Thinking, problem solving, cognition* (2nd ed.). New York: Freeman.

Mayer, R. E. (1995). The search for insight: Grappling with Gestalt psychology's unanswered questions. In R. J. Sternberg & J. E. Davidson (Eds.). *The nature of insight* (pp. 3–32). Cambridge, MA: MIT Press.

Mayer, R. E. (1997). Incorporating problem solving into secondary school curricula. In G. D. Phye (Ed.), *Handbook of academic learning* (pp. 473–492). San Diego: Academic Press.

Newell, A., & Simon, H. A. (1972). *Human problem solving.* Englewood Cliffs, NJ: Prentice-Hall.

Nunes, T., Schliemann, A. D., & Carraher, D. W. (1993). *Street mathematics and school mathematics.* Cambridge, England: Cambridge University Press.

Polya, G. (1965). *Mathematical discovery, Vol. II: On understanding, learning, and teaching problem solving.* New York: Wiley.

Smith, E. E., & Osherson, D. N. (Eds.). (1995). *An invitation to cognitive science: Vol. 3, Thinking* (2nd ed.). Cambridge, MA: MIT Press.

Sternberg, R. J., & Davidson, J. E. (Eds.). (1995). *The nature of insight.* Cambridge, MA: MIT Press.

Weisberg, R. W. (1986). *Creativity: Genius and other myths.* New York: Freeman.

Wertheimer, M. (1959). *Productive thinking.* New York: Harper & Row.

Prodigies

Martha J. Morelock

Vanderbilt University

David Henry Feldman

Tufts University

I. Prodigy Research and Creativity Research: An Overview
II. Contemporary Research: Merging Prodigiousness with Creativity
III. The Relationship between Creativity and Prodigiousness
IV. Asking the Question, "Are Prodigies Creative?"
V. Filling a Gap: Capturing the Creativity of the Prodigy
VI. Hitting Middle C: Toward a More Comprehensive Domain of Creativity Research
VII. Finding Closure

Domain The structure and organization of a body of knowledge evolved to contain and express certain distinct forms of information.

Field The social and cultural aspects of a profession, job, or craft.

High C Creativity/Genius Unique reorganizations of knowledge resulting in substantial new contributions to bodies of knowledge. Some rare human beings produce creative contributions that are so significant that they utterly transform a domain of knowledge. These are considered works of genius. An example is Albert Einstein, who transformed the laws of physics with his theory of relativity.

Low C Creativity Everyday occurrences of creativity exemplified by original transformations in small products, thoughts or expressions. Examples might be a satisfying flower arrangement or a humorous play on words.

Middle C Creativity Creative products appreciated in terms of interpretive skill, mastery of technical forms, distinctive style, and success in achieving a technical, practical, commercial, or academic goal.

Nonuniversal Developmental Domains Organized bodies of valued knowledge that human beings can master by moving through levels of ever increasing competence, complexity, and subtlety of understanding. Examples include music, mathematics, chess, cooking, and surgery.

Prodigy A child who, before the age of 10, performs at the level of a highly trained adult in a cognitively demanding domain.

*Only within the past half century have there been efforts to operationally define **PRODIGIES** or the construct of creativity. Although not numerous, studies of prodigies have increased our knowledge about this remarkable phenomenon. Much more numerous are studies of creativity, defined in various ways. Both terms have gradually evolved, slowly crystallizing into meaningful concepts, until, in the past few years, it has become possible to systematically begin looking at the relationship between the two. This article traces that evolution and provides an understanding of the relationship between prodigies and creativity as reflected in contemporary research.*

I. PRODIGY RESEARCH AND CREATIVITY RESEARCH: AN OVERVIEW

During the two decades following 1950, creativity research explored cognitive processes and the creative personality. Taking its lead from the psychometric

Encyclopedia of Creativity
VOLUME 2

449

Copyright © 1999 by Academic Press
All rights of reproduction in any form reserved.

movement, which emphasized mental measurement and individual differences, creativity research focused on designing tests to isolate traits such as various forms of divergent thinking. [*See* DIVERGENT THINKING; APPENDIX II: TESTS OF CREATIVITY.]

In contrast, during that same period, prodigy research was essentially nonexistent. The term *prodigy* was used freely to refer to a broad range of types of precocious children. With the widespread use of IQ as the primary gauge of giftedness, prodigies were subsumed under the IQ umbrella, and children who could compose sonatas at the age of 6 were assumed, implicitly at least, to be very high IQ children with penchants for particular fields. [*See* GIFTEDNESS AND CREATIVITY; INTELLIGENCE.]

Prior to 1950, two major studies of prodigies had appeared in the literature. These were destined to remain the only large-scale scientific studies of child prodigies in the world literature until 1980. In 1925 Geza Revesz conducted an in-depth case study of a 7-year-old Hungarian musical prodigy, Erwin Nyiregyhazi. Five years later, Franziska Baumgarten studied nine child prodigies. Neither study focused on creativity as a central issue. However, Revesz did make a passing reference to the topic when he differentiated between the talents of young Erwin and those of what he referred to as infant prodigies. He observed that although infant prodigies were identifiable by their technical virtuosity, they generally suffered from a lack of musical sensibility. Any success they achieved in the interpretation of musical works was due to imitation. Erwin, on the other hand, possessed a real musical sense. Revesz insisted that the child would never belong to the class of infant prodigies because his interpretation was distinguished by a creative quality, which is a hallmark of the work of genuine performance artists. For Revesz, at least, prodigious performance did not necessarily imply creativity.

II. CONTEMPORARY RESEARCH: MERGING PRODIGIOUSNESS WITH CREATIVITY

In 1975 the contemporary study of child prodigies began; an effort that eventuated in the merging of two lines of research—on prodigies and creativity. A number of scholars believed that the field needed to shift its emphasis from the study of what they called Little C Creativity—the small incidences of creativity in everyday life—to the study of Big C Creativity—the achievement of something remarkable and new that transforms and changes a field of endeavor. In addition, they advocated a change in approach from the psychometric one traditionally adopted by the field to one which was more developmental and more domain specific (i.e., pertaining to specific bodies of knowledge). [*See* DOMAINS OF CREATIVITY; EVERYDAY CREATIVITY.]

A prodigy was defined as a child who, before the age of 10, performed at the level of a highly trained adult in a cognitively demanding domain. The age of 10 was selected as an arbitrary marker. The chosen marker just as easily could have been 11 or 12. The idea was to mark the shift from childhood to adolescence as being the boundary between childhood prodigiousness and extraordinary adult performance.

Research findings in this area shattered the myth that prodigious talent occurs effortlessly and spontaneously. Quite to the contrary, precocious mastery of a domain is the result of a fortuitous coincidence of a number of factors. These include the child's natural talent plus specialized resources and intensive efforts on the part of master teachers. There must be a domain that is distilled, distinctly structured, self-contained, and easily communicable such that it can be assimilated by a child. Tools, instruments, technologies, and techniques associated with performance in the domain must be accessible and manageable by young children. Moreover, supporting sustained development of prodigious talent requires tending to organizational details such as locating and accessing master teachers, arranging for transportation, and facilitating changes from one source of instruction to another as the children's needs change. These responsibilities generally fall to the family—the main early catalyst of the coincidence process.

Whereas the educational aspect of the research dealt with the ways in which instruction was orchestrated and delivered, the psychological piece dealt with the progression of the prodigy through the domain as ever higher levels of mastery are attained. It was proposed that in addition to universal cognitive development, there are also *nonuniversal developmental domains*. These are organized bodies of valued knowledge that human beings can master by moving through levels of ever-increasing competence, complexity, and subtlety of understanding. Unlike universal stages of development, nonuniversal development requires instruction, guidance, support, and prosthetics. Examples of nonuniversal domains are mathematics, music, art, chess, cooking, and surgery. The prodigy is a child who is so biologically pretuned to the requirements of a specific nonuniversal developmental domain, that movement through levels of mastery takes place at an exceptionally rapid rate.

Once the notion of nonuniversal developmental domains emerged as an organizing construct for understanding the achievement of prodigious performance, the next step was to describe the range of nonuniversal developmental domains. This was accomplished using a universal to unique continuum that characterizes domains in various ways. *Idiosyncratic developmental domains* consist of subareas of a discipline, craft, or profession—one's specialty or the particular work that one chooses to master in a particular way. Prodigies exemplify one form of idiosyncratic development because they connect with a domain in a very unusual way—almost as if they were naturally pretuned to express their individuality through one special field. Idiosyncratic specialties tend to reflect the particular subareas of a discipline practiced by adults, such as open heart surgery, Elizabethan music, or patent law. In the prodigy, what makes the situation idiosyncratic is an exceptional reciprocity and complementarity between the child and the domain rather than the domain itself.

Moving as far from universal achievements as possible, one arrives at the region of *unique developmental domains*. A unique developmental domain represents a form or organization of knowledge within a domain that has never before been accomplished in quite the same way. This is where individuals transcend the constraints of an existing discipline to establish a major new order. Within the theory, unique reorganizations of knowledge that result in substantial new contributions to bodies of knowledge are called creative. Those rare human beings whose contributions are so significant that they utterly transform a domain of knowledge can rightfully be said to have produced works of *genius*. An example is Albert Einstein, who forever changed the laws of physics with his theory of relativity. Whether or not a work of genius comes from a child prodigy is an issue to be studied rather than an assumption to be made. For example, it is clear that Einstein as an adult contributed works of genius. As a child, however, his work and thought was not such that he was identified as a prodigy. On the other hand, he may well have been recognized as a physics prodigy in childhood if there had been more of his work to assess. [*See* EINSTEIN, ALBERT.]

III. THE RELATIONSHIP BETWEEN CREATIVITY AND PRODIGIOUSNESS

With the advent of the universal to unique conceptual framework, the prodigy was placed in logical relationship to the construct of creativity—at least to Big C Creativity. Prodigies are noted for their precocious mastery of a domain, but they are generally not creative in a Big C way. They do not, while still children, transform their domain through a reorganization of knowledge that is widely recognized, enduring, influential on others who come after them, and transformational in scope. Why is this so?

The most obvious reason is that as children, prodigies are fully challenged to master the forms and techniques that are a part of their domain. Indeed, part of the developmental progress of prodigies consists of the exploration and mastery of different techniques contributed by those who previously mastered their talent domain. Writing prodigies may try their hand at writing Shakespearean verse or Japanese Haiku; child artists replicate the styles of painting most prevalent in their cultural tradition.

A second reason may relate to what is called the 10-year rule, first put forth by Herbert Simon and William Chase on the basis of their studies of chess players. This is the finding that it seems to take a minimum of nearly 10 years of concentrated, sustained effort to move from novice to master in any of the domains that have been studied so far. By the time a child prodigy spends 10 years mastering a domain, he or she is likely to be in transition to becoming an ex-prodigy because of age alone. Recently, a 10-year-old girl achieved the title of master in chess, perhaps challenging the number "10" in the rule. [*See* EXPERTISE.]

A third reason is that genius requires a broader stage on which to act than does prodigiousness. Exploration of instances of genius resulted in the positing of other confluence theories to explain Big C types of creative productivity. It is instructive to examine some of what has been found.

Three dimensions of analysis are required for the study of Big C Creativity. One of these is the *field,* referring to the social and cultural aspects of a profession, job, or craft. A second is the *domain,* referring to the structure and organization of a body of knowledge evolved to contain and express certain distinct forms of information. Finally, there is the *individual person,* the site of the acquisition, organization, and transformation of knowledge that has the possibility of changing domains and fields. Two of these factors, the domain and the individual person, are also factors in the emergence of prodigious performance. The third is not as much a factor in prodigious performance as it is in genius-level creativity. A brief comparison of the phenomena of prodigy and genius with regard to these factors is worthwhile.

The relationship of the prodigy to the domain, as has already been pointed out, is one of progressive mastery of already established techniques and forms. Natural proclivities seem almost perfectly matched to the domain as it currently exists, hence the relatively rapid progression of the prodigy to higher levels of mastery. However, prodigiousness is not synonymous with creativity. Indeed, precocious superiority may even cause difficulties and get in the way of ultimate achievement. Unlike the prodigy, the creative individual is marked not by a synchrony of forces, but by fruitful asynchronies—not by a perfect concordance of factors but rather by strategic mismatches or asynchronies that the creative individual turns to his or her advantage by reframing experience.

An example is Sigmund Freud, who dabbled in a number of fields before carving out his own domain of psychoanalysis. As a young man, Freud considered medicine, law, and academic scholarship as lifetime occupations. Although he was especially passionate about philosophical speculation, Freud decided that it would be more practical financially if he became a physician. He studied medicine in Vienna, began a research career in neurology, and served a succession of apprenticeships in several fields. Eventually turning away from the neurophysiological laboratory in order to understand patients displaying strange psy-chic symptoms, he ended up founding the domain of psychoanalysis—a perfect showcase for the introspective ability, interpersonal discernment, and emotional and philosophical insights that were his forte. Had Freud's abilities fit more seamlessly with the domains already in existence, he would have had little need to create his own. Indeed, a likely precondition for creating or reshaping a domain is one's dissatisfaction with or alienation from a domain as it exists. In addition to asynchronies between the individual and the domain, conflicts between individuals and their social or cultural surround may precipitate the emergence of some creative resolution to their alienation, the distillate from which might be the recasting or construction of a domain. [*See* FREUD, SIGMUND.]

In the world of the adult professional, it is the *field* which judges the merits of contributions and decides on whether they should be retained as a part of the evolving and perhaps transformed domain, or rejected. If retained, new contributions become a part of a transformed body of knowledge that is then passed down to succeeding generations of students to master. Prodigies strive to master a domain, generally doing so within the confines of a cocoonlike highly supportive and protective family environment. But would-be creative geniuses must master a domain, transcend it, have their creative offerings acknowledged by the wider field, and then have them incorporated back into a consequently transformed body of knowledge. Hence, a wider stage must be engaged for the emergence of genius than is necessary for the development of a prodigy. Thus, prodigies per se are not creative in the Big C sense unless they encounter and transcend the constraints of their domain. But are prodigies creative in some other sense? This question is addressed next.

IV. ASKING THE QUESTION, "ARE PRODIGIES CREATIVE?"

The history of ideas and evidence reviewed in the previous discussion has led the field of creativity research (as well as the reader, we hope) to the point where the question "Are prodigies creative?" has become meaningful. There are now quite clear operational definitions of *prodigy* as well as *creativity,* allowing us to respond based on the accumulation of knowledge about both. Perhaps the answer might be something like the following:

If, by *creative,* we are referring to Big C Creativity, the answer is no. If, by *creative,* we are referring to Little C Creativity, the answer is "most likely to some extent" because everyone possesses some capability for everyday creativity, though the degree and kind may vary from person to person and prodigy to prodigy. Whether divergent thinking is manifested in or relevant to the prodigy's performance in his or her special talent domain probably varies according to what the domain is and who the prodigy is. Little C Creativity may not necessarily improve the quality of, say, the performance of a piano concerto. [*See* DEFINITIONS OF CREATIVITY.]

But the forced choice between Big C and Little C may itself be limited. Harking back to Revesz's remark about Erwin Nyiregyhazi's musical interpretation as being distinguished by its *creative quality,* which is a hallmark of performances of great reproductive artists, one might well ask "Where does this fit into the Big C/ Little C dichotomy?" In 1997 two scholars suggested that the dichotomy is too limited and offered a third alternative.

V. FILLING A GAP: CAPTURING THE CREATIVITY OF THE PRODIGY

Ellen Winner, a specialist in child art, proposed a three-tiered view of creativity in the visual arts. Universal creativity is the creativity that characterizes all normal young children. Gifted creativity is the creativity that characterizes children who are particularly talented in the visual arts. Domain creativity is the creativity of adults who alter a domain.

The drawings and paintings of very young children (i.e., between 3 to 6 years of age) are universally creative in the sense that they are spontaneous, appealing, surprising, inventive, and playful. In their grace, charm, and simplicity, they are often strikingly similar to works produced by contemporary Western expressionists. The reason for this resemblance is that child art is typically *pre*conventional. Because children this age have not yet mastered the rules of drawing, they perforce cannot follow them. Consequently, their artwork appears creative. Normally, as children approach

the middle years of childhood, they begin to draw less and their drawings tend to lose much of the aesthetic appeal of the drawings produced at a younger age. The artwork begins to appear conventional and stereotyped. Although more accurate in depicting things the way they actually look, the drawings are also generally less pleasing to viewers and seem less creative.

Gifted creativity applies to the art of children who are particularly talented in the visual arts. The child prodigy in the visual arts falls into this category. A gifted child artist shows a precocious ability to draw realistically, to capture the illusion of depth, to depict contour faithfully and in one fluid line rather than in schematic formulae. Renderings of objects and people are often rich with detail. Gifted child artists demonstrate at an early age a sense of the adult art world of their cultures and master techniques that allow them to produce the kinds of artwork prized by this art world.

The ability to draw realistically can be argued to be an indication of creativity because, for children gifted in the visual arts, it tends to be self-taught. These children invent for themselves the rules and regularities that others with lesser talent would have to learn from a mentor. They see how to capture the three-dimensional moving world on the two-dimensional static page. In addition, they internalize the artistic style of their culture in such a way that they can make new paintings or drawings reflecting that style.

What child prodigies in the visual arts have, then, is technical mastery and facility. But to achieve domain creativity, they must go beyond what has already been done in their domain and develop a unique style that is valued by the field. Domain creators, unlike gifted children, are risk takers, because anything new is likely at first to be ignored or repudiated. They want to change the status quo—not just master it. Frequently, unlike more typical gifted children, they also experience with disproportionate frequency excessive stress in childhood and report mood disorders as adults.

VI. HITTING MIDDLE C: TOWARD A MORE COMPREHENSIVE DOMAIN OF CREATIVITY RESEARCH

Like Winner, but broader, David Feldman offered a way of reconceptualizing the full range of creativity. In

1997 he observed that the field of creativity studies had two mountains of research. One dealt with relatively modest cleverness and ideational productivity, whereas the other dealt with the greatest achievements of Western civilization. He suggested that one way to move the field forward would be to try to describe what lies between little and big creativity, an area that he dubbed "Middle C."

Middle C Creativity is a region falling somewhere between the kind of freshness of approach to everyday problems represented by making a lovely flower arrangement for the dinner table every evening on the one hand, and painting the ceiling of the Sistine Chapel on the other. Middle C refers to the middle levels of creative work, as represented by the commercial artist or the accomplished artist whose works are commissioned and purchased for display in fine hotels, offices, and banks. Possible distinguishing features of Middle C Creativity are the following:

1. Contributions of the Middle C sort at their best are more likely to enrich, extend, and deepen the experience within a domain or improve the effectiveness and efficiency of existing technologies and techniques rather than to transform domains and create radically new ideas, technologies, and techniques.

2. Middle C creative products are more likely to be appreciated in terms of interpretive skill, mastery of technical forms, distinctive style, and success in achieving a technical, practical, commercial, or academic goal.

3. Practitioners of Middle C Creativity will likely be experts in their various domains as well as share the distinctive qualities, talents, sensibilities, and skills of others practicing within their domains. For example, there are likely to be distinctive qualities that all experts share such as an unusually high degree of technical mastery or a 10-year period to achieve a high level of expertise.

There are also likely to be qualities distinct to each discipline, field, or domain; for example, becoming an expert dancer requires certain physical qualities of bone structure and musculature, whereas an expert air traffic controller must be able to tolerate having great responsibility for the lives of other people day in and day out.

4. The personal qualities that lend themselves to Middle C Creativity vary from field to field, but there may also be qualities that tend to be common across fields. These qualities are likely to include specific and identifiable intellectual, emotional, personal, and interpersonal strengths and weaknesses.

5. The Big C works of a great composer very likely depend on the Middle C contributions of many lesser known instrument makers, paper producers, impresarios, and orchestra members, as well as other composers.

To facilitate the inclusion of the Middle C construct into views of creativity, Feldman suggested that the terminology be shaped to correspond to a piano keyboard. Instead of referring to great creativity as Big C and less great creativity as Little C, the former would be called High C, the latter, Low C, and Middle C takes its place between the two. This new terminology is desirable for another reason: It tends to diminish the pejorative implications of the labels. The piano keyboard analogy with its horizontal layout of High C, Middle C, and Low C does not convey the same feeling of hierarchy as does Big C, Middle C, and Little C with their connotations of relative size. *Higher* on the keyboard does not correspond with *better*. Rather, all the notes work together to produce a harmonious whole that is greater than the sum of its parts.

The Middle C construct relates directly to expert performance in a given domain. In one sense any expert could be called Middle C creative because, by definition, an expert is someone who regularly produces works of excellent quality in a challenging field. In another sense, there are important differences between and among experts, and these also would be of interest to those who study creativity.

Within this framework, Revesz's differentiation between the performances of infant prodigies and those of Erwin Nyiregyhazi becomes more theoretically meaningful. Revesz's differentiation refers to the distinction between threshold expertise reflecting technical virtuosity and the more sensitive musical interpretation characteristic of a higher level of (Middle C) expert performance.

Thus, the question "Are prodigies creative?" can finally begin to be addressed in a satisfying way. Domain-specific prodigious performance falls in the realm of Middle C Creativity. However, it is conceivable that some prodigies could demonstrate Low C Creativity in their daily lives and go on as adults to make High C creative contributions in their domains.

Mozart is a particularly interesting case in point. Often cited as the greatest prodigy of all time, he began playing the clavier and the violin at the age of 3. By the age of 6, he was composing clever minuets. When he was 9 years old, he and his father and 14-year old sister Nannerl were invited to travel from their native Austria to the Hague because the Princess of Weilburg was eager to see this child about whom she had "heard and read so much." During the 8-month period while he was in Holland, Mozart produced a Symphony (No. 5 in B flat major, K. 22) for 2 oboes, 2 horns, and strings. The work was performed in Amsterdam with the child conducting his own composition. During this period, Mozart also composed the six violin and clavier sonatas of Opus 4 (K. 26–31) on commission from the court for the coronation of the Prince of Orange.

In addition to these extraordinary Middle C achievements, Mozart also demonstrated signs of Low C Creativity. He was given to making innumerable changes and transformations in speech, writing, and music. Indeed, he was an inveterate tinkerer—perhaps the greatest musical tinkerer of all time. His tendency to verbal transformation is exemplified in a postscript he added to his mother's letter to his father, written when Mozart was almost 23:

> I can't write anything sensible today, as I am rails off the quite. Papa be annoyed not must. I that just like today feel, I help it cannot. Warefell, I gish you good wight. Sound sleeply. Next time I'll sensible more writely.

What about Mozart and High C Creativity? No one can deny that Mozart's work was widely recognized and, over the past 200 years, has proved itself to be enduring. Certainly, it is unique in the sense that it perfects and epitomizes the style of music characteristic of the Classical period, and it continues to influence those who come after him. However, Mozart did not invent the Classical style, he perfected it. We cannot say that he transformed the domain of music in the way that Beethoven did some years later, although whether he might have done so had he lived past the age of 36 is

an interesting, but unanswerable, question. However, even if Mozart's work does not precisely fit the criteria for High C Creativity, it certainly comes close. On our metaphorical piano keyboard, it would lie somewhere between Middle and High C—perhaps only a note or two away from High C Creativity. This is not a statement of value, but rather a description of a particular form of creative contribution.

Happily for Mozart, the metaphor of High, Middle, and Low C on the piano keyboard allows shades of distinction between different genres of creativity without judgment as to comparative value. One might imagine an additive model in which some of the abilities of Low C Creativity are necessary but not sufficient for Middle C Creativity, and certain abilities of Low and Middle C Creativity are necessary but not sufficient for High C Creativity. Each genre is important in its own way. Although High C creative transformations may be crucial for revolution or transformation of domains and fields, Middle and Low C Creativity are equally important for the preservation, enrichment, and continuity of culture.

VII. FINDING CLOSURE

The great Russian developmentalist Lev S. Vygotsky once observed: A word is a microcosm of human consciousness. As consciousness evolves and changes, so does the meaning reflected in a given word. This is perhaps nowhere more applicable than when considering the relationship between prodigies and creativity. All considered, one might argue that efforts first to define these two constructs and then to explain the relationship between them may ultimately result in a reconceptualization of the field of creativity research itself. But that, of course, is for the field to decide.

Bibliography

Csikszentmihalyi, M. (1996). *Creativity: Flow and the psychology of discovery and invention*. New York: HarperPerennial.

Feldman, D. H. (with Goldsmith, L. T.). (1991). *Nature's gambit: Child prodigies and the development of human potential*. New York: Teachers College Press. (Original work published 1986)

Feldman, D. H. (1999). The development of creativity. In R. Sternberg (Ed.), *The handbook of creativity* (pp. 169–186). New York: Cambridge University Press.

Feldman, D. H., Csikszentmihalyi, M., & Gardner, H. (1994). *Changing the world: A framework for the study of creativity*. Westport, CT: Praeger.

Gardner, H. (1994). The fruits of asynchrony: A psychological examination of creativity. In D. H. Feldman, M. Csikszentmihalyi, & H. Gardner (Eds.), *Changing the world: A framework for the study of creativity*. Westport, CT: Praeger.

Howe, M. J. A. (1999). Prodigies and creativity. In R. Sternberg (Ed.), *The handbook of creativity* (pp. 431–446). New York: Cambridge University Press.

Morelock, M. J., & Feldman, D. H. (1993). Prodigies and savants: What they have to tell us about giftedness and human cognition. In K. A. Heller, F. J. Mönks, & A. H. Passow (Eds.), *International handbook of research and development of giftedness and talent*. New York: Pergamon.

Morelock, M. J., & Feldman, D. H. (1997). High-IQ Children, extreme precocity, and Savant Syndrome. In N. Colangelo & G. A. Davis (Eds.), *Handbook of gifted education* (2nd ed., pp. 439–459). Boston: Allyn & Bacon.

Radford, J. (1990). *Child prodigies and exceptional early achievers*. New York: The Free Press.

Winner, E. (1996). *Gifted children: Myths and realities*. New York: Basic Books.

Productivity and Age

Robert Root-Bernstein

Michigan State University

Effective Productivity The number of things created by an individual that have at least some given intellectual or other value.

Late Bloomer An individual who first displays their creativity at an unusually old age.

Novice Effect The phenomenon in which entering a new discipline by changing fields appears to provide an individual with a new burst of creativity.

Persister A continuously creative individual or one who continues to be creative within a discipline beyond the usual age of other people in that discipline.

Polymath An individual who displays creative ability in multiple disciplines.

Prodigy An individual who becomes creative at an unusually young age.

Swan Song The final and often benchmark work created by an individual.

Total Productivity The total number of things created by an individual over a given period of time.

Creative **PRODUCTIVITY** can be defined as the number of creative products generated by an individual in any given period of time. All available evidence indicates that creative productivity varies with age, but that the way in which it varies differs markedly from individual to individual and from profession to profession. Both professional and individual differences in age-related creative productivity suggest that strategies may exist to maximize creativity at any given age or career stage.

I. DEFINITIONS OF CREATIVE PRODUCTIVITY

To examine the relationship between aging and creative productivity requires a clear understanding of what is meant by creative productivity. One must begin by distinguishing between *total productivity* and *effective productivity*. Total productivity may be defined as the total number of things that a person generates during any given period of time. These things could be books or articles published, paintings painted or exhibited, musical pieces composed, sculptures completed, novel processes patented, or widgets manufactured. The assumption underlying the measurement of total productivity is that every product is of roughly equal value or importance. Effective productivity, in contrast, employs selective criteria to rate the value of the products. Not every painting by an individual is as good or as important (to them or to the art community) as every other, and a similar statement can be made of individual products in every field. Effective productivity is a measure of the most important contributions an individual makes, and thereby separates the metaphorical wheat from the chaff.

Another distinction is also important in considering creative productivity. The creative process has many facets and an individual may be more active in one facet at one time in her career and switch to another facet later on. A composer, for example, may invent a new musical form or a new tonal scale early in his career (the innovation) but produce the most developed piece using that innovation only late in his career (the exemplar). Thus, it can be important to distinguish between the age at which some types of creativity (such as problem recognition and inventiveness) are manifested and the age at which other types (such as applications or the production of exemplars) come to the fore.

II. ISSUES RELATING CREATIVE PRODUCTIVITY TO AGE

One of the standard remarks that all mathematicians and physicists hear when they enter college is that if they have not made an important contribution by the time they reach 30, they never will. The mathematical sciences are, it is said, a young person's game.

Most fields have their equivalent of the mathematician's dilemma, though the details may differ. Can a person who has never taken music lessons before the age of 15 ever hope to compete with individuals who began taking violin or piano at age 3? Conversely, does the child prodigy in mathematics or music have any advantage over her peers as an adult, or might early creative maturation actually be a disadvantage in terms of career longevity and impact? Having succeeded by age 30, is the mathematician then doomed to decades of fruitless puttering? Does the musical or chess prodigy flame brightly and then sputter out to spend his adult years in frustrated reminiscence?

All of us face some version of these issues due to the fact that aging itself is correlated with decreasing mental and physical competence. We reach the height of our physical development between our teenage years and our late twenties. On average, the human brain then shrinks 20% between the ages of 20 and 90. Although these changes do not result in noticeable declines in cognitive functions for most people, for a substantial portion of the population, they do. Whereas dementias affect a negligible number of young people, they affect almost 1% of those age 65 to 69, 10% of those 80 to 84, and nearly 25% of people 85 to 95 years old. Similarly, the incidence of mental illnesses such as manic-depression and schizophrenia increase with age eventually affecting about 2% of the population.

Meanwhile, physical energy, which is vital to beginning and carrying through almost any enterprise, fades. Even the most fit elderly person cannot compete with the average 20-year-old in almost any sport. For example, sprinter Duncan McLean (1884–1980) ran the 100-yard dash in 9.9 seconds in 1904 and set a world record for his age group in 1977 at 21.7 seconds when he was 92. Reaction times in general tend to diminish with age so that response times to sudden noises are often two or more times longer in the elderly than in the young. Moreover, health problems occur disproportionately in the very young and in people over the age of 65. Thus, one might expect that a window of creative opportunity exists between the late teenage years and late middle age. Since women tend to mature earlier than men and to outlive them by six or seven years, one might also suspect that some differences in productivity with aging might exist. These issues will become ever more important as current demographic patterns shift the relative proportion of the population toward an ever-older average age during the first decades of the 21st century.

Other age-related productivity issues are also of importance. If innovation is generally a young-person's game, then what will happen to the overall rate of innovation as the general age of the population shifts? Will the impact be the same in every discipline, or does age affect productivity differently in the arts and literature, say, than in science and engineering? How can an individual best make use of such information to traverse the productivity curve most effectively? [*See* INNOVATION.]

Some of these questions can be given tentative answers at present. Some cannot. One that cannot, for example, is how to measure effectively the productivity of teachers. Is the appropriate number the hours spent per week in the classroom most important, or is it the number of students taught per semester, some combination of the two, the number of new classroom exercises or demonstrations invented per year, the number of new courses sanctioned by the school, the number of successful students graduated, or some presently unquantifiable measure of impact on student thinking? Equally confounding is the question of how to measure administrative productivity. Is a manager more productive the more meetings she organizes, or the less? Are memos or reports a measure of administrative productivity? Are reorganizations? Does the size of the budget have the greatest impact or the number of employees? Indeed, one could ask how to measure the productivity of parents! Are parents who produce many children regardless of what role they grow up to play in society more productive than those who give birth to only one or two who grow up to become leaders in some field? Fortunately or unfortunately, these are questions without useful answers at present. The resulting lacunae are troublesome. Quality of product is clearly as important as quantity, if not more so, whether we are talking about children, teaching, or compositions.

We must also find ways to take into account changing careers. Many people, including some of the most successful, move from hands-on activities early in their disciplines to managerial or organizational roles later on. Because we are able to measure only their hands-on productivity but not their administrative productivity, we must consider the data concerning aging and productivity possibly misleading. The measurable productivity of younger people may actually owe a very large debt to the unmeasurable organizational productivity of their elders. Grandparents, while themselves effectively barren, may nonetheless provide leadership and guidance to multiple generations of offspring in ways that are totally divorced from their professions. With this caveat in mind, we can now look at the kinds of data that currently exist.

III. GENERAL TRENDS IN CREATIVE PRODUCTIVITY WITH AGE

Nearly all of the literature that exists concerning the relationship of productivity, whether total or effective, as a function of age agrees on several basic points. First of all, children are not (except as child laborers in some underdeveloped countries) productive. Creative productivity begins in nearly all disciplines only in the teenage years or during the twenties. Creative productivity then rises to a statistical peak sometime between the thirties and fifties for most individuals in most disciplines. Productivity then declines with age. Women have, historically, been less productive than men in terms of professional activities—undoubtedly due to social and cultural factors—but the productivity of women as they age follows exactly the same trend as that observed in men. The effect of choice of discipline has a greater influence on productive aging than gender, people in the arts and literature having longer effective careers than the typical person in the sciences. [*See* GENDER DIFFERENCES; WOMEN AND CREATIVITY.]

Without a doubt, the most comprehensive study of these phenomena was undertaken by Harvey Lehman in his 1953 book *Age and Achievement,* which remains a classic to this day. Lehman focused most of his attention on effective, rather than total, productivity. Most studies subsequent to Lehman's have validated his general findings although they clearly do not apply to overall productivity or to some particular disciplines.

One of the things that Lehmann clearly demonstrated was that although the effective productivity/aging curve is similar for nearly all disciplines, it begins, peaks, and tails off at different ages. Lehmann found, for example, that both mathematics and poetry are young peoples' games, with significant contributions beginning in early teenage years and peaking in the mid-twenties. Novel writing, playwrighting, and psychology however, are the domain of more mature individuals, with effective productivity peaking in the mid-forties. The overall number of papers published by chemists and the most significant papers published by chemists, on the other hand, begin to be manifested in their late teens, peak in their thirties, and tail off toward nil at around age 70. Similar measures of productivity in the biological and medical sciences tend to begin in the early twenties, peak in the late thirties or early forties, and tail off more slowly thereafter. Peak overall productivity is reached in art and architecture in the late thirties and early forties and a similar peak is seen in effective productivity, but effective productivity tends to be spread out chronologically much more evenly than overall productivity so that paintings by 45-year-old artists and 80-year-old artists are about equally likely to be considered exemplary. [*See* Art and Artists; Science; Writing and Creativity.]

Lehmann looked at productivity measures in other disciplines such as business and politics as well, showing that peak incomes tend to be achieved at around age 60 and highest political office in a person's seventies. It is important, as Lehmann himself points out, to adjust all data concerning productivity at older ages for the increase in mortality that occurs with increased age. Although mortality has little effect on productivity curves for disciplines in which the peak is reached very young, it has a very significant effect on disciplines in which the statistical peak is reached in later years. For example, the total number of 85-year-old millionaires is not much higher than the number of 25-year-old millionaires, but the probability that an 85-year-old will be a millionaire is many times greater than that of the 25-year-old simply because there are many 25-year-olds in the population and few 85-year-olds. Thus, an increasing number of studies have shown that age-adjusted productivity tends to remain reasonably constant in many fields. The phenomenon of apparently decreasing productivity with age can partially be accounted for by decreasing numbers of practitioners at older ages.

Indeed, a "swan song" phenomenon has been noted among composers, which Lehman documented in other disciplines as well but without noting its importance. The swan song phenomenon consists of elderly individuals, often those facing death, who create their final gift to humanity. This final creative effort more often than not results in an unusually important result, so that the final major work of a composer (consider Mozart's Requiem or Beethoven's Ninth Symphony) is remembered as his or her most important. Lehman's effective productivity curves therefore show a significant upturn past the age of 70 in many disciplines. These works are rarely innovative but often represent the best exemplars of a person's mature work. [*See* Old Age Style.]

Some of the loss of productivity with age appears, however, to be real. Studies of individual research careers in science and technology have clearly shown that total productivity peaks in the early decades and tends to diminish with age. Thomas Edison, for example, had his name on 1093 patents. He filed his first patent at the age of 20, reached the peak of his productivity at the age of 35 when he filed some 50 patents in a single year, went through a period in which he filed no patents during his late forties, and then reached two plateaus at about 10 patents per year during his fifties and early sixties and a handful of patents per year through his eightieth year. He filed his last patent at the age of 82. It is clear that Edison's most important patents in terms of their long-term impact on society also fall mainly during the peak of his total productivity. Many studies have confirmed that Edison's career is typical of most scientists and inventors. Economists and policy makers are justifiably worried that as the general age of the scientific population increases over the next few decades, both real and effective productivity will drop.

Existing evidence makes it reasonably clear that quantity of output is not directly related to quality, although limited evidence suggests that longer creative life spans may result in a greater probability of producing important work. Although Edison was the most prolific inventor in American history, and Picasso the most prolific artist in history, many prolific individuals are almost unknown. For example, the most published computer scientist in the world today has, according to citation analysis, never published a paper considered by is colleagues to be of any value. Georges Simenon published more than a thousand novels, but only a handful are considered by critics to be worth reading. Similarly, the most prolific composer of symphonies—Melchior Moltor (1696–1765)—left us 170 of these pieces, none of which are part of the modern orchestral repertoire. Franz Joseph Haydn, on the other hand, wrote 108 symphonies, many of which continue to be played today. At the other end of the productivity scale, Joseph Heller, author of the classic American novel *Catch-22,* experienced a 20-year period of writer's block following the extraordinary success of his novel. Borodin produced only a handful of orchestral and chamber works, yet all of these remain in the modern repertoire. Similarly, in science Gregor Mendel's total output was a mere seven papers written in a 10-year period as a young man, yet these papers sufficed to create a revolution in genetics. More recently, Nobel laureate James Watson produced only a couple of dozen research papers, all in his twenties, yet these sufficed to produce another genetics revolution by elucidating the structure of DNA. Effective productivity is often, therefore, completely different than total productivity and may be limited to extremely short periods of an individual's lifetime.

Mention of Mendel and Watson raises a final issue. Loss of productivity in one field is not equivalent to loss of productivity in general. Both men turned to administration after their early scientific work. Mendel became the abbot of his monastery, and Watson has held numerous posts as head of major scientific laboratories and organizations. In trying to analyze the productivity of a Mendel or a Watson, how does one evaluate these later years? Neither continued to be a productive research scientist, yet both continued to play important leadership roles in their respective communities. As noted earlier, until we have a way of evaluating the productivity of administrative and other problematic types of activities, the question of how to evaluate the effect of aging is unresolvable. [*See* LEADERSHIP.]

A similar problem confronts us with polymaths such as Aleksandr Borodin. Borodin was both a working chemist and a composer. His total output in both fields was low, yet it was of very high quality and impact. It is clear from reading his biographies that although each vocation interfered with the total productivity of the other, each activity in some ways also fed the other. This multidisciplinary interaction is particularly notable in the career of biologist Desmond Morris who has successfully integrated three vocations: research ethologist, science popularizer, and surrealist painter. Current approaches to measuring productivity would make Morris's carreer appear in any single vocation as a series of punctuated bursts of activity, whereas an examination of his overall productivity shows it to be very high and continuous. The metamorphosis of the child actress Shirley Temple into international ambassador Shirley Temple Black presents similar difficulties. Her productivity in any given field is totally distinct in nature and time from the rest, yet her lifetime achievement is extraordinary from any standpoint. Further theoretical and empirical research will be needed to properly come to terms with such multifaceted people. Indeed, because increasing evidence suggests that most college graduates can expect to have multiple careers, the future of age-related productivity studies may lie in understanding the ways in which career changes can modify standard aging curves.

IV. EXCEPTIONS TO THE GENERAL TRENDS

The examples of Borodin, Morris, and Black lead to the conclusion that exceptions to the general trends exist. Such exceptions are actually fairly numerous and provide interesting insights into the factors controlling age-related productivity. The most notable of these exceptions are prodigies, late bloomers, persisters, polymaths, and field changers.

Prodigies are people who exhibit unusually developed abilities at an unusually young age. Prodigies are clearly recognized in fields characterized by very rigid rules or techniques such as musical performance and composition, chess, mathematics, and logic. Children in these fields have been able to master them beyond the abilities of most adults and have sometimes been able to become productive in the sense of creating new compositions or proofs even before reaching adolescence. The existence of prodigies in other fields is more controversial. Although artistic and acting talent may appear early in individuals such as Picasso, Shirley Temple, and Mickey Rooney, it is unclear whether these represent true prodigies because every child can draw or imitate to some extent. In some fields the number of skills to be mastered is so high that it is not clear that prodigies are possible. Literature represents one example. Although very few people have written novels by the time they are sixteen, as both Jane Austen and Georges Simenon did, there are no examples of great literature being produced by children. Prodigies also seem to be absent from the experimental sciences, medicine, history, philosophy, psychology, and other humanities in which the peak age for effective contributions is middle age or later.

There is no correlation between status as a prodigy and overall productivity. The productivity over the lifetimes of prodigies ranges from extraordinary (e.g., Mozart, Herbert Spencer) to nearly nil. For example, in 1910, Harvard University was home to five infant prodigies: W. J. Sidis, A. A. Berle, Cerdric Wing Houghton, Roger Sessions, and Norbert Wiener. Sessions became an important and productive composer. Wiener, after many vicissitudes, went on to found the new science of cybernetics (feedback control systems). Berle and Houghton went on to have unremarkable careers. And Sidis, a brilliant mathematician, became one of the youngest professors in the country only to experience a total collapse shortly afterward. He spent the vast majority of his life in penury, unable or unwilling to hold a job. A more recent study of Science Talent Search winners, many of whom are extraordinary in publishing original scientific papers or obtaining patents as high school students, shows similarly diverse outcomes. Some go on (at unusually high rates) to become Nobel prize winners, but over half do not even remain in science through college. Thus, in terms of *scientific* productivity, their prodigious work is actually of lower predictive value than it is for college science majors. [*See* PRODIGIES.]

Late bloomers are at the opposite end of the age spectrum from prodigies. They are people who tend to find their life's work during middle or old age. Examples include Vincent van Gogh and Paul Cézanne, who only took up art in their thirties and forties; Louise Nevelson, who came to sculpture in her forties only after trying and abandoning half a dozen other arts; Grandma Moses, who took up painting only at age 76 and continued to produce paintings till her death at age 100; and Laurence Sterne and Edith Wharton, who began writing novels only in their forties. Even in science a few late bloomers have risen to stardom, including Sir Francis Crick, a Nobel laureate who received his Ph.D. at the almost unheard of age (especially for a physicist) of 36!

Persisters are people who make high-impact (effective) contributions to a discipline over an entire lifetime. They represent one of the most interesting exceptions to the general age-productivity trends. Playwright George Bernard Shaw exemplifies the persister. He died at age 94 having completed several well-known plays in his nineties. Other examples include Pablo Picasso, who was still innovating in his eighties, and Giuseppe Verdi, who composed some of his best operas in his seventies and eighties. The existence of persisters in fields such as composing, writing, poetry, the arts, and the humanities is not terribly surprising, given the generally sedentary and time-independent nature of the creative process in these fields. If it takes longer to write a play, novel, or symphony or to paint a painting at age 90 than it did at age 30, no one really cares, particularly as the quality and insights may be greater. It is much more surprising to find persisters in fields such as dance or music performance that require

highly trained bodies and lightning-fast reflexes. Nonetheless, notable examples exist. Martha Graham is one. She continued to perform her own dances up until the age of 76, when she finally decided that her body would no longer do what she required of it. Similarly, Felix Horowitz was still performing virtuoso piano pieces in his nineties as was jazz pianist Eubie Blake. The Romanian pianist Cella Delavrancea (1887–1991) gave her last public recital at the age of 103! One critical feature in these instances is the interesting fact that physical skills that are practiced regularly do not obey the general rule concerning loss of reaction time for reflexes. Pianists who practice regularly have been found to be able to perform trills and very fast passages just as quickly and precisely in old age as when they were young.

Persisters also exist in mathematics, the sciences, and engineering. Henri Poincaré, for example, is perhaps unique among 20th-century mathematicians in having made a major contribution to every major area of mathematics, an achievement that, not surprisingly, took him a lifetime. Perhaps the most amazing example of a persister is the 18th-century mathematician Leonard Euler who was so prolific that his novel contributions were still being put to press for the first time 50 years after his death. His total output consists of literally thousands of papers, each making a novel contribution to mathematics, and they will fill more than 75 volumes when his works are finally collected. Mathematical physicists such as Richard Feynman and S. Chandrasekhar and physical chemist Linus Pauling have also broken the mold by continuing to produce high-impact, innovative results into their seventies.

An analysis of persisters in the sciences has yielded the unexpected observation that such people tend to be either polymaths or field changers. Polymaths are individuals who excel in more than one field, often simultaneously, whereas field changers are people who commit themselves with great intensity to one discipline at a time, but only for a decade or so before moving on to another. Several studies have shown that the concurrent activities pursued by polymaths increase overall individual productivity as well the probability of achieving a high degree of effective productivity. Thus, scientists who work on several research projects concurrently, have multiple consulting jobs, and are actively engaged in one or more creative hobbies far outstrip their more focused colleagues in measures of both total and effective productivity.

Field changers also tend to have greater overall and effective productivity compared with individuals who stay within their area of expertise. Many very successful scientists have stated that they change fields regularly and on purpose to stimulate new ideas, and similar strategies are apparent in the lives of continuous innovators in the arts. Picasso, in contrast with many of his contemporaries, regularly changed styles or moved onto new media such as linoleum prints, sculpture, lithography, and so forth. Matisse created an entirely new art form with his paper cut-outs only as an old man when disease made it impossible for him to control a brush any longer. He could, however, use scissors. Similarly, in the sciences, Nobel laureate Luis Alvarez recounts in his autobiography that after an extended period during which he had no interesting research ideas, he finally took the unusual step of apprenticing himself to two of his graduate students in order for *them* to teach *him* the intricacies of a newly emerging field about which he knew nothing. He found that his creative energy and his ideas both returned. This phenomenon has been termed "the novice effect."

The principle behind the novice effect is that a person is allowed only one important insight per field or per artistic style and this insight is most likely to occur within a decade of entering the field. The novice effect therefore helps to explain why mathematicians must make a breakthrough by the time they are 30 or lose all hope of doing so. It also helps to explain why major innovations in the arts, such as Arnold Schoenberg's 12-tone scale or Wassily Kandinsky's nonrepresentational art, are usually made by youngsters while exemplary works are the products of maturity. The problem is that having made a breakthrough shows only that a person has the *ability* to discover or invent but guarantees nothing about future performance. Indeed, analysis of the careers of scientists who made a notable contribution in one area and stayed within that area for the rest of their careers showed that these individuals never made another significant breakthrough as measured by peer evaluation or citations to their work. This failure to be continuously *effectively productive* occurred even for scientists whose total productivity

remained high and despite obtaining awards such as Nobel Prizes that gave them high professional visibility.

Although exceptions such as these are often said to prove the rule, they also show that statistical generalizations concerning age-related productivity need not apply to individuals. The specific nature of the exceptions suggests further that individuals may be able to influence the ways in which they traverse the productivity curve by changing fields, utilizing the novice effect, or exploring new disciplines polymathically. The existence of persisters and late bloomers also proffers the possibility that, even as our population ages, the elderly can remain active and significant contributors to culture and economy. The critical question may be not whether they are capable but whether society is willing to let them.

Bibliography

Abra, J. (1989). Changes in creativity with age: Data, explanations, and further predictions. *International Journal of Aging and Human Development, 28,* 105–126.

Alpaugh, P. K., & Birren, J. E. (1975). Are there sex differences in creativity across the adult life span? *Human Development, 18,* 461–465.

Bayer, A. E., & Dutton, J. E. (1977). Career age and research-professional activities of academic scientists. *Journal of Higher Education, 48,* 259–282.

Dennis, W. (1966). Creative productivity between the ages of 20 and 80 years. *Journal of Gerontology, 21,* 1–8.

Finklestein, S. N., Scott, J. R., & Franke, A. (1981). Diversity as a contributor to innovative performance. In E. B. Roberts (Ed.), *Biomedical innovation* (pp. 135–143). Cambridge, MA: MIT Press.

Lehman, H. C. (1953). *Age and achievement.* Princeton, NJ: Princeton University Press.

Levin, S. G., & Stephan, P. E. (1991). Research productivity over the life cycle: Evidence for academic scientists. *American Economic Review, 81,* 114–132.

Root-Bernstein, R. S., Bernstein, M., & Garnier, H. (1993). Identification of scientists making long-term, high-impact contributions, with notes on their methods of working. *Creativity Research Journal, 6,* 329–343.

Simonton, D. K. (1984). *Genius, creativity, & leadership.* Cambridge, MA: Harvard University Press.

Simonton, D. K. (1989). The swan-song phenomenon: Last-work effects for 172 classical composers. *Psychology of Aging, 4,* 42–47.

Simonton, D. K. (1990). Creativity in the later years: Optimistic prospects for achievement. *The Gerontologist, 30,* 626–631.

Programs and Courses in Creativity

Sidney J. Parnes

Buffalo State College

Aha Sudden insight as a result of seeing something in a new way or making an unexpected connection of thoughts.

Brainstorming Group process following the principle of deferred judgment.

Convergent Thinking Evaluating and selecting from many possibilities.

Creative Problem Solving A process of sensing opportunities, challenges, desires, and problems, then creatively defining and resolving them.

Deferred Judgment Withholding judgment or evaluation while producing many thoughts, ideas, alternatives.

Divergent Thinking Focusing on expansion of thoughts, producing many ideas and alternatives.

Imagery Sensory experiences revived from memory and manipulated in the mind in whole or in part without the original sensory stimulation.

Incubation Process of deferring effort on a problem or creative project while resting, sleeping, or pursuing unrelated work or recreation.

Intuition Gaining answers or solutions through unconscious internal resources.

Synectics Process of joining together; creativity-development programs specializing in making new connections, especially by metaphorical thinking.

Visionizing From vision-actualizing; searching for imaginative visions of a bright future, then bringing as much as possible into reality by creative processes.

This article deals with what is known about the deliberate, systematic stimulating or developing of an individual's creative productivity or achievement. Creative is defined as conceiving and implementing ideas that are new and valuable to the individual or society. The article covers PROGRAMS AND COURSES IN CREATIVITY that help creative productivity in (or even in spite of) any environment or culture. The methods help people to release internal governors, such as habit or anxiety, which have cradled the person safely on most of his or her windy, twisty roads through life. But these governors often inhibit creative growth and accomplishment even when turnpikes are available to allow freer travel. The deliberate methods are designed to help people use their internal governors flexibly as they discover or design better roads on which to travel. The focus of this article is thus on deliberate methods and techniques for nurturing individual creativity rather than on the nature of creative people, their contributions, or the general environmental or cultural climates that encourage their creativity. Furthermore it emphasizes interdisciplinary programs rather than those in a specific discipline such as a particular level or subject in education, a specific aspect of business or industry, or a specific discipline of the arts.

I. HISTORY

In the early days, the concept of creativity was generally studied as to its *nature,* but not its *nurture.* The classic Graham Wallas model of preparation, incubation, illumination, and verification was generally accepted as the "way creativity works." The message people received from the literature was basically work hard, gather and analyze abundant data, then "sleep on it," get away from it, let it simmer, and hope for illumination—the "aha"—to rise up from the subconscious bombardment and resulting interconnections of memory data or new sensory input to the brain. Generally, this process was discussed regarding the genius, not necessarily the average person.

Whereas this activity is still extremely important to the birth of new ideas, an abundance of evidence— both scientific and anecdotal—now indicates that we can also use deliberate methods and procedures to *stimulate* that incubative activity and thereby increase the *probability* of new insights—"ahas"—occurring more frequently.

The first formal and lasting attempts to create programs for deliberate creativity development were offered by Alex Osborn and Robert Crawford in the 1940s and grew to maturity in the 1950s, along with William Gordon's and George Prince's Synectics. Osborn's efforts were institutionalized in the 1950s with the formation of the Creative Education Foundation and the annual Creative Problem-Solving Institute.

Second generation creativity development, stressing spontaneous imagery processes, grew up in the 1960s and 1970s. Lewis Walkup, Robert Eberle, George Eckstein, and Robert Adler were early advocates of the imagery processes in problem solving. Many programs and processes evolved. Examples are Win Wenger's psychegenics, Assagioli's psychosynthesis, Maharishi's transcendental meditation, Don Taylor's functional visualization, E. Paul Torrance's sociodrama process, Gary Davis's creative dramatics, Jean Houston's work at the Foundation for Mind Research, and other offerings in human-potential development. One might even consider the mind-altering drugs of the 1960s as an abberation or mutant of the natural imagery processes of the so-called second generation. Third generation processes came into being in the 1980s and 1990s, utilizing a background of the intuitive imagery process within a strong foreground of the logical creative problem-solving model.

II. SUBSTANTIATING THEORY AND RESEARCH

A. Theory

Long before research substantiation, a wealth of theory provided the framework for the structuring of creativity-development programs and processes.

Examples of theories pertinent to the deliberate development of creativity with examples of proponents of same are cognitive theories, J. P. Guilford; associative theories, I. Maltzman; Gestalt, M. Wertheimer; stimulus-response, B. F. Skinner; psychoanalytic, Sigmund Freud; preconscious, Laurence Kubie; collective unconscious, C. G. Jung; psychedelic, Jean Houston; humanistic, Carl Rogers; self-actualization, Abraham Maslow; biological growth, George Land; and motivation, Teresa Amabile.

It might be well to point out that practitioners like Alex Osborn advocated deferred judgment and brainstorming as ways of tapping the well of data we have and are acquiring and rearranging it and interrelating it for productive creativity. Freud and the introspective psychologists said creativity comes from the deep unconscious and used psychoanalysis to release the flow of related data. The humanistic psychologists emphasize openness of perception, being open to the environment, and so on. Behaviorists emphasize chance and reinforcement theories.

But we do not need to choose from among these diverse theories; instead we can integrate and synthesize them all toward the end of releasing, capturing, harnessing, and directing the greatest flow and interrelationship of data in the creative process.

B. Research

When Osborn founded the Creative Education Foundation (CEF) and the annual Creative Problem-Solving Institutes (CPSI) in the mid 1950s, psychologists were seeking ways to identify creative scientific talent. The nation's leaders were scurrying to find ways to keep up with the Soviets, who had shown their technological space superiority with the launching of the first artificial space satellite, *Sputnik*. The National Science Foundation sponsored a series of national research conferences on the identification of creative scientific talent. University psychology departments around the nation were contacted in an effort to find researchers who were involved in work along these lines.

By 1959 the search led to several investigators who were providing significant evidence that this critical talent could be deliberately developed. From then on, the interest focused both on means of identifying creative talent in the gifted invididuals among us, as well as cultivating it in all people, including the gifted. Since then, hundreds of scientific studies have confirmed Osborn's strong conviction that creativity can be nurtured. Many of them have shown evidence of gains by experimental subjects in their ability to solve real-life problems effectively after a creative problem-solving (CPS) course. The real-life criteria involve areas such as academic accomplishment, personal adjustment, and industrial problem solving. Some data have also started to appear on the relative effectiveness of various creativity techniques, but much more research is needed in this area.

One unique research effort, by Laura Hall Rose and Hsin-Tai Lin, regarding the deliberate development of creativity includes data from a wide range of research studies rather than from a single study. Through the statistical technique of meta-analysis it provides a comprehensive examination of the effects of creativity training and the resulting increase in creative productivity. It concludes, "Through education and training the innate creative ability of individuals can be stimulated and nourished." Besides the formal statistical research there are countless anecdotal reports, from all disciplines, of the effectiveness of creativity development.

III. GENERAL PRINCIPLES

A. The Essence of Deliberate Creativity Development

What we are attempting to develop through deliberate creativity nurturance is the greater imaginative use of both data already stored in the brain and external data we absorb through the senses. The essence of creativity—the aha—might be considered to be the association of thoughts, facts, ideas, data, and so on into a new and relevant configuration, one that has meaning beyond the sum of the parts—that provides a synergistic effect. The product, if one results, may be new and relevant to a group or organization, to society as a whole, or merely to the individual concerned.

B. Facilitating the Creative Process

Creativity-development programs attempt to remove two major blocks to creative achievement. First of all, they try to help individuals understand the influence of background, experience, and habits on present behavior. They are thus helping people to perceive themselves as creative beings and to get rid of internal blocks to creative functioning. This perception is analogous to removing a governor from an automobile: the horsepower remains the same but performance increases.

Second, these programs provide present conditions that encourage creative functioning. They thus remove external blocks to creative behavior, just as we might remove roadblocks from the path of an automobile. A driver on a freeway can use more of the car's potential than is possible on a narrow, obstructed road; the individual can use more of one's potential when in a receptive climate. Note, however, that the internal governor must be removed before the environmental freeway can effect a change in behavior. It is well to add that the individual must learn to be one's own governor. One must learn to adjust to a twisty, bumpy, obstructed road when it is necessary to do so. Cultural conditioning internalizes this governor, but culture has not done a satisfactory job of teaching a person how to use it with appropriate flexibility.

C. Overcoming Blocks

Effective programs can help us overcome the internal and external blocks to creative functioning by increasing new associations in our brains in two general ways: (a) by feeding our brain the fuel required for it to operate at full capacity and (b) by removing the brakes that stop our associative mechanisms from functioning naturally.

1. *Required Fuel*

The fuel for our associative mechanisms is the sensory impressions we bring to our brain from all sources—books, people, environments, experiences, and so on. The more data we supply the brain, the more interrelationships it can create. However, the quality of associations is dependent on both the quantity and richness of input. Therefore, the development of acute awareness and sensitivity is an important aspect in the cultivation of creative talent. It implies the development of a wide curiosity that will increase the likelihood of discovering connections between remote fields or areas of interest and activity. The more seemingly remote the relationship, the more the likelihood of originality in the idea.

2. *Removal of Brakes*

Here the elimination of the blocks is accomplished by providing the individual with complete freedom for mental exploration. What is done in creativity-development programs is to place individuals into environmental settings that allow for complete self-acceptance. This includes not only freedom from concern about the reactions of others, but also willingness to defer their own judgment of their own ideas during the exploration process. Furthermore, to use psychologist L. L. Thurstone's terminology, we show the individual the value of "inhibiting the impulse" to act on one's first idea. [*See* CONDITIONS AND SETTINGS/ ENVIRONMENT.]

D. Deliberate "Stretching" Processes

The many deliberate "stretching" processes used in divergent stages of effective creativity-development programs may be grouped under two main categories:

1. Processes that tend to "*let* thoughts flow"—such as deferred judgment (called brainstorming when used in groups) and meditation procedures. These processes are analogous to opening a spigot and thereby allowing the water to flow. Deferring judgment and meditating allow new thoughts to flow. [*See* BRAINSTORMING.]
2. Processes that tend to "*make* new thoughts flow"—such as forced relationships and checklist pro-

cesses explained in section V. These are analogous to placing pumps in the water line to start or increase the flow. Computers have been creatively applied to step up the flow. Some computer programs can become mental sledgehammers for a creative person.

We also might classify processes, methods, tools, and techniques as either verbal (so-called left brain) or nonverbal (so-called right brain). We might also group these many processes under those focusing on internal data (already stored in the brain) or those focusing on external data (available to the brain from the environment through the senses). The latter would include group processes like brainstorming, with its "quantity breeds quality" principle.

Quantity breeds quality is the fundamental principle behind the divergent stretching process. Dean Keith Simonton's work on high-level historical leaders, including American presidents, shows that those higher in creative productivity seem to be that way based on Osborn's *quantity* principle. They *attempt* more than low producers, and while their percentage of successes (good ideas) remains the same as for the low producers, their absolute number of successes is therefore higher. "Quantity breeds quality," in Osborn's words.

George Land shows biological evidence of the quantity breeds quality principle. He postulates psychological principles of growth and creativity to be a natural parallel of biological growth processes. As he explains it, nature combines bundles of genetic information into an enormous range of mutations (quantity). Environment selects the "fittest" (quality) to survive, while the rest die off. The brain, in a parallel process, collects bundles of data and can combine them into a variety of alternative patterns or ideas (quantity). However, the brain pretests by judicial processes (quality) rather than by trying out each idea. Thus, the tremendous waste occurring in the biological realm with its literal "survival of the fittest" does not exist.

E. Incubation

Incubation is not usually thought of as a deliberate stretching process. It is more typically looked on as something that happens after the deliberate effort stops. It is like the cartoon showing Dennis the Menace with folded arms, looking at a painting he is doing on a canvas, and declaring, "I'm waiting for an idea to hit me!"

The mental processes described earlier can be facilitated consciously and deliberately. As we focus on a problem and search for ideas, we may consciously defer judgment and allow full flow to our associative processes. We may increase the flow with the checklists and forced relationships processes described in section V. But associations may also occur in the preconscious, before awareness, as during incubation. In a sense, the deliberate, conscious efforts at making fresh associations may be considered an attempt to replicate what seems to be the unconscious or preconscious phenomenon of incubation; for incubation enables our minds to attend to items of our past experience while we focus consciously on other items in our present awareness. Links may thus be formed that are overlooked when we search consciously for relationships. The conscious mind is limited in the number of ideas it can attend to at one time. Subconsciously, however, the mind is capable of much additional activity.

Lawrence Kubie, in discussing the preconscious system, cites a phenomenon associated with hypnosis. A subject is brought into a strange room for a few minutes. When asked subsequently to list every item seen, the subject will reproduce 20 or 30 items. Thereupon under hypnosis he or she will go on to reproduce another 200 items. All of this indicates how much intake, registering, recording, and recalling can occur without participation of conscious awareness at any step in the process.

An incubation period actually provides for deferment of judgment about the problem and bombardment of the mind with the greatest variety of random input so as to increase the likelihood of a chance connection—a "lucky" observation. [*See* INCUBATION.]

F. Clarification

The previous principles underlie creativity-development programs. Many courses and programs exist that are designed solely to stimulate the imagination or to increase a person's divergent-thinking abilities. But in line with the definition of creative as *conceiving* and *implementing* ideas that are *new* and *valuable,* programs that stress only half of that definition are not covered in this article. [*See* DIVERGENT THINKING.]

IV. CREATIVE PROBLEM SOLVING

A. Introduction

Scholar Morris Stein puts Alex Osborn as grandparent and CPS and Synectics as parents "of most if not all existing creativity programs." CPS and Synectics are programs that have undergone constant research and development since the 1940s. Each provides fully for intelligent creating. As synectics emphasizes, making and breaking connections is the heart of both creating and learning. In creating we make the familiar strange; in learning we make the strange familiar.

Both CPS and synectics involve a wide variety of techniques within their total process. Key techniques will be discussed in the next section. Many of those found in the literature are variations of one another that are referred to by different names.

Let us now examine CPS in detail. Of the two "parental" programs, it is the one that is best known and most thoroughly researched. Synectics will be covered later with other major ongoing programs.

B. Orientation to Model

Over the years CPS has been explained in many ways. Whereas it is deceptively easy to understand logically, internalizing that understanding into problem-solving behavior is much more difficult because of the way most of us have been programmed by our education and experience.

Therefore, a course or workshop in CPS is frequently begun by providing a CPS "run-through"—an experiential introduction to the process. Participants then feel some of the nuances of the process as it unfolds.

In applying the steps of CPS, what you are really trying to do is to proceed from examining "what is" to exploring "what might be," to judging "what ought to be," to assessing "what can presently be," to deciding "what I will commit to do now," to action that becomes a new "what is."

What is refers to your awareness of the facts or data about a situation.

What might be implies the generation of multiple viewpoints, forward-thrusting definitions, approaches and ideas toward the realization of objectives.

What ought to be involves considered judgments about approaches and ideas.

What can presently be refers to your choices and adaptations of approaches and ideas into what seems to be a manageable solution for now.

What I commit to do now becomes your best plan for gaining acceptance and implementing.

Action becomes your actual *doing, implementing,* including checking results and making adjustments—all of which brings about the new "is."

Out of subsequent deeper examination of our action and its results—the new "what is"—grow new challenges and problems to be handled through the CPS process, culminating in further action that again becomes another *new* "what is" and so on.

Let us now relate this to the steps named in the Osborn-Parnes CPS process. Using this process instead of merely reacting in a habitual way to what you see as you focus on an "objective" or "mess," you do the following:

1. Reexamine for more facts (viewing data anew)—fact finding.
2. Redefine the situation in many ways from how you first perceived it (gleaning and devising interesting and fruitful opportunities from desires, messes, challenges, or problems)—problem finding.
3. Generate alternative ideas as responses to the situation as now viewed (restructuring, remaking the givens)—idea finding.
4. Evaluate against multiple repercussions and consequences (resolving in ways that are sensitive to more than the obvious)—solution finding.
5. Develop the best ideas as fully as manageable before putting them to use (devising effective plans for refining, testing, and implementing)—acceptance finding.

Fact finding (F-F), problem finding (P-F), idea finding (I-F), solution finding (S-F), and acceptance finding (A-F) are probably not as important as the extent to which the imagination is stretched as one alternates throughout the process. You react first with imaginative play, then with tempered reality to the new fact, viewpoint, or idea. The open-mindedness we are seeking to instill relies on how much imagination you use in approaching a thought before tempering it with re-

ality. CPS exercises people in faster and faster, wider and wider imaginative play as a prelude to each judgment they make. As a result of each exercise, you may tolerate a bit more ambiguity in a situation. In the end, you can take more and more factors into consideration *in a given unit of time* while making decisions. This was verified in an extensive research project.

As one learns to produce many more alternatives by *diverging* as stated earlier within each step of a creative process, one must also learn effective means of *converging,* or making choices to deal effectively with the increased mental output. This allows one to move smoothly from step to step into ultimate action.

1. Acting on Good Ideas

The end point thus involves *acting* on good ideas—ones that bring positive results to the person, the organization, the society. In doing so, you follow up by monitoring for and handling new challenges growing out of the changes introduced while striving toward the objective.

C. Eclectic Development of the Program

Over the years, CPS has become a very eclectic program for nurturing creative behavior. Starting with Osborn's original contributions, CPS has synthesized a variety of existing theories and programs, as well as many new approaches that were being developed concurrently over the past decades. This has been possible especially because of the continuing contributions of several hundred associated leaders in the creativity field. Fundamental principles of Osborn's model involve combining, adapting, modifying, and so on, and the development of CPS has applied these principles as fully as possible. Whereas some individuals or groups have constructed a particular program and developed it extensively in an almost independent manner, CPS developers have attempted to study and relate—even to force relationships—with all these areas and approaches.

This ongoing synthesis is demonstrated in a session of the CPS course titled "Putting It All Together." Each participant is led through an expanded and diversified experience of the six steps of objective finding, fact finding, problem finding, idea finding, solution finding, and acceptance finding regarding the participant's own desire, objective, or goal. This session capsulizes the kind of interactive programming created between Synectics, sensitivity programs, the arts, imagery, fantasy, meditation, body awareness and movement, and so forth in one experience that provides the participants with a montage of what the program was designed to accomplish. This is done through the vehicle of each participant's significant concerns or desires.*

D. Imagination Stretching throughout Process

As institutes and courses evolved over the years, there has been a steady growth toward more and more emphasis on imaginative exercises in evaluating and implementing ideas and in developing plans of action. Practice is provided in the stretching of the imagination in these phases of the problem-solving process rather than mainly in the idea-generation stage itself. In the matter of problem definition, there is likewise a great deal more effort now in using the imagination for acquiring a multiplicity of viewpoints of the problem.

E. Visionizing

Visionizing ("vision actualizing") is the latest way of emphasizing the "front end of the CPS process." Visionizing focuses on your dreams, your visions, and on making these come true. It focuses on goals and objectives—on opportunity making—on respecting your wishes and desires for yourself, your organization, and the society you live in. It focuses on expanding and amplifying these and then fulfilling whatever portions you can manage through CPS.

The visionizer, in pursuing dreams, discovers and effectively responds to new challenges, goals, and opportunities while simultaneously making new and effective responses to old problems or challenges.

1. Visionizing Model

Thus all stages of visionizing and CPS use the oscillating process depicted in Figure 1. "Stretch" is provided by deferring judgment in each step, as much as

Visionizing (1988). (pp. 259–263). Buffalo, NY: Creative Education Foundation Press.

time allows and circumstances warrant. At the conclusion of each stretch, judgment is applied in selecting from the output the most relevant and valuable items. The broken lines in the model are designed to signify possible feedback or feedforward at all stages.

In visionizing the process is started with *desires* rather than *objectives* or *messes*. *Desire* is the best word for the starting point of the process. Visions are full of desires—for self, for others, for the organization, for society, for the world. [*See* DREAMS AND CREATIVITY; IMAGERY.]

F. Developing a Balance

CPS programs always try to develop a balance in individuals—a balance between the open awareness of the environment through all of the senses and the deep self-searching into layer upon layer of data stored in the memory, between logic and intuition, between deliberate creative effort and incubation, between the individual working with the group and working alone, between gaining new insights (ahas) and acting on those insights. The underlying problem seems to become developing this balance between these extremes

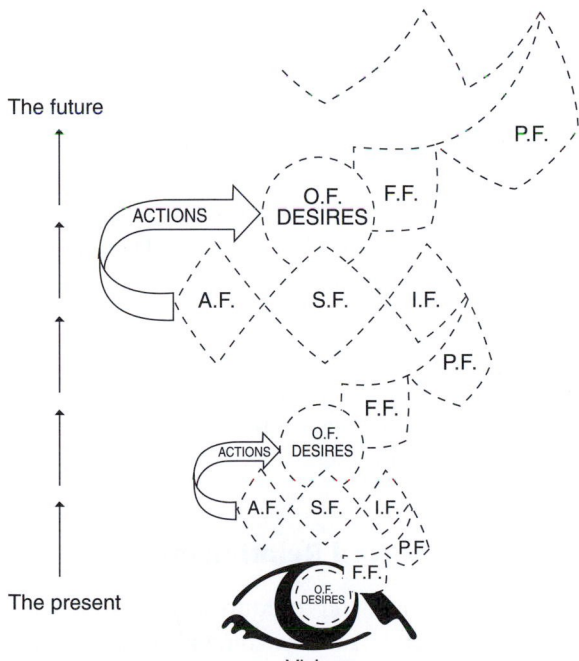

FIGURE 1 CPS/Visionizing model.

by strengthening the weaker aspect, not by stunting the strong side.

V. IDEA-STIMULATING TECHNIQUES

The turnpike of deferred judgment allows and encourages individuals to express ideas as they occur, whereas other procedures help to bring the ideas to mind; the following are some of the most universally applied processes to help do this.

A. Checklists

One of the most common and impactful checklists was devised by Alex F. Osborn in his book *Applied Imagination*. His checklist consists of a series of verbs that help to change an individual's mental set as he or she contemplates a problem or a situation. For example, three of the verbs are *magnify, minify,* and *rearrange*. Suppose a family were trying to generate ideas on ways to enjoy their meals together. If they were to think about the situation and apply the word *magnify,* they might come up with the following notions: "Invite more people occasionally—foreign students, teachers, local artists, and so on" or "Increase the number of courses (but decrease size of the portions) to provide more variety and interest to the dinner." Smaller portions relate to *minify*. Next might be the idea, "Eat around a very small table to make the whole dinner much more intimate" or "Eliminate the meal and feed a needy family instead." *Rearrange* might suggest "Eat in the living room or on the porch" or "Have a reverse meal with the dessert first."

These ideas may not be to your particular liking, but they illustrate the kind of thinking that might be sparked by Osborn's checklist. Furthermore, the new thoughts invariably trigger others that become more relevant, suitable, or interesting.

B. Forced Relationships

Another fundamental procedure is to make a "forced relationship"; that is, take anything in one's awareness and attempt to relate it to the problem at hand. For example, in the previous meal situation, suppose the

group were told to focus on a tree outside the window. Someone might spot the leaves and suggest decorating the table with leaves or serving some simple element of the meal on attractive leaves; another might see the bark and suggest the possibility of a small ice carving prompted by the groovings in the bark of the tree.

Forced relationships might involve other senses than sight. For example, the group might focus on a sound heard in common, such as a bird twittering outside; members might attempt to force a relationship between that sound and the situation. This could prompt ideas such as "play recordings of favorite songs during meal times" or "Bring the canary into the dining room when we have dinner" or "Play the music box, and pass it around from person to person to wind up and reset during the meal."

Aside from the use of current sensations as stimuli for forcing relationships, the participants can also be urged to use their imaginations for providing additional stimuli. For example, the group might imaginatively take a safari into Africa and bring back something that relates to the situation at hand. The following examples might result: "Monkey around with the way the food is served by placing the soup in glasses, the coffee in soup bowls, and the ice cream on large platters" or "Take a picnic meal out onto a canoe or rowboat and eat in the middle of the river or lake."

C. Attribute Listing

Another commonly used process to aid the flow of ideas is what is called *attribute listing*. This involves taking specific aspects of the situation and then focusing particularly on the aspect selected. The checklisting or the forced-relationship processes can then be applied to whatever specific aspect is the subject of focus. For example, in the meal situation, we might look at the question of dessert and examine everything we know about it—the shapes, colors, tastes, and so on of each specific dessert that we might think of. We might then vary any one of those attributes or connect something else to that specific attribute. Suppose the item focused on was orange jello, cut into squares. One attribute might be that it was "soft and shimmery." If we focused on a brick in the fireplace and applied something about the brick to the soft and shimmery quality of the jello, it might lead to the idea of freezing the jello and making it into a semi-icy dessert. The mental trip to Africa might suggest an animal-carving contest out of each one's jello before eating it.

D. Morphological Approach

The morphological procedure applies the notion of attribute listing together with forced relationship in a matrix approach. It speeds the production of countless ideas. In our meal illustration, we might list some of the following attributes: people involved, place, time, foods, or special effects. Under each heading we would list a number of alternatives. For example, under "people" we might list family, friends, strangers, needy people, and celebrities. Under "place" we might list different parts of the house, outdoors, picnics, and campgrounds. Under "time" we might list breakfast, lunch, dinner, snacks, and evening snacks. Under "foods" we might have all kinds of different food items listed. Under "special effects" we might list music, TV, odors, and incense. Then the group would take items at random from each of the headings (attributes) and connect them into a novel meal idea. For example, we might select celebrity, basement, breakfast, hamburger, and incense as random elements, one from each attribute list. The group would then put these together or adapt them in different ways, such as "incense" the "head of the house" by serving the kids hamburger for breakfast in the basement game room; then surprise (him or her) with a special breakfast in bed. This example illustrates the point that we do not necessarily take the word literally. *Incense* suggested something different from a "special effect." So did *monkey* in the earlier example.

E. Special Emphases about Idea-Stimulating Techniques

These processes can help to break us away from some of our habitual thinking—some of our rigidity—into new connections of thoughts. It is also important to emphasize that these new ideas are often just a starting point in the creative process. A great deal of refinement and development are usually necessary to make the ideas workable within the realities that exist.

It is well to emphasize that these processes can be used during any one of the steps of the problem-solving process. In the problem-finding step, while trying to develop many "how to" definitions of the problem, we can use the same triggering stimuli to generate new viewpoints; likewise, these processes can be utilized in each of the other steps.

The procedures mentioned are only samplings of some of the main categories of methods used to help stimulate the imagination. In the divergent stage of each step of creative problem solving, the main concern is *flow*. At each such stage of the process, everything is done to maintain a constant flow of thoughts, whether these be the facts, problems, ideas, criteria for solution finding, or the means of implementing and gaining acceptance. Research and practice have shown that the greater the number of thoughts at each of these stages—the greater the flow—the greater the likelihood of some new insights, some ahas, some new connections that become relevant as they are developed through the balance of the process.

F. And Then Judgment—Convergence

Because of the emphasis placed on the generation of more and more thoughts—flow—it would be well to reemphasize that divergent production—the creation of many alternatives at each stage—is not an end in itself but only a means to an end. The goal is to produce an effective, viable course of action.

Thus CPS over the years has emphasized convergent processes such as creative evaluation. Here a deferred-judgment flow produces criteria beyond the obvious for judging ideas one has already produced divergently. This is followed by selection of the most important criteria by which to then evaluate.

The creative stretch for criteria ensures that potential consequences, repercussions, and effects of ideas are carefully considered before implementation. The value of this stretch is usually demonstrated by examining the chosen criteria to see if they came from early or late in the divergent list. In most cases, one finds that some of the important criteria chosen came from the latter part of the list.

Evaluation matrices are often used to measure and rate ideas against selected criteria. Those on which a preferred idea rates low are used as focal points for finding new ways to strengthen the idea.

Emphasis is provided in clustering ideas for greater strength and in considering openly and broadly an idea's advantages and disadvantages.

G. Conclusion

With an understanding of the concepts about creative behavior discussed in this article, one would be potentially able to invent most if not all of the prevalent methods or techniques for enhancing creative behavior, as well as to create a variety of new procedures. Remember that underlying all of these CPS methods and approaches is the basic objective of getting you to interrelate more freely and effectively both what you already know and what you acquire through the senses so that you are able to find relevancy where you did not see it before.

VI. SYNECTICS AND OTHER MAJOR ONGOING PROGRAMS

A. Introduction

Now that the CPS process and program has been examined in some detail, as well as specific techniques used therein, we will consider Synectics. We then will highlight some of the other major continuing programs, mentioning special features of each. All of the programs use many of the processes and techniques covered under CPS and in the previous section, or adaptations of same.

B. Synectics

This process deals with the two core problems, influence of background/habits and providing a present environment or field of stimulation with a series of steps as CPS does. W. J. J. Gordon and George Prince experimented over decades with ways of liberating the creative talents of individuals and groups. Beginning in the 1950s they used audio and later videotapes of the action to discover what helped and what hurt the production and development of ideas.

Osborn's insight into the destructiveness of negative comments was reinforced by Synectics experiments. It

became clear that most people were unaware that many impulsive words, tones of voice, and gestures can make a field that is toxic to the development of new thinking. Synectics created a brief conditioning experience to help participants appreciate this. The group is asked to organize to solve a problem and then is given a problem to solve. The proceedings are videotaped for a few minutes and then played back. Each action is focused on and the question is asked, "Will this increase or decrease the probability of success?" Then, "How can we get the benefit of the good intention behind the action without the drawback?"

Over the years, Synectics learned to differentiate content from process and three well-defined roles evolved: the facilitator—the person in charge of the process who stays out of content—does not contribute ideas but runs the session; the client—problem owner, who makes decisions about content; and the participants—who contribute their thinking.

The facilitator protects ideas and participants and assures interpersonal security so participants can think adventurously without anxiety. The facilitator has a number of strategies to provide the group with a wide variety of connection-making material. Where the original focus of "excursions" was metaphor and the "force fitting" of them to the problem, experience has produced many other ways of creating the safe "chaos and mind-play" that nurtures new, unexpected connections.

Another contribution of Synectics is a "forced" open-minded way of evaluating ideas realistically while keeping the idea and the originator safe from put-downs. It is called the itemized response and requires one to focus first on what is positive about the idea and only after that to bring up concerns in the form of "How might we (overcome this concern)?"

C. Synectics—CPS Comparison

Figure 2 is provided to relate the Synectics process to the CPS process. It shows how the CPS steps and deferred judgment principle fit within an example of a Synectics group run-through. In Synectics there are many variations of the particular pattern outlined; but with the specific outline presented, you may better understand how the two programs work and the strong relationships between them. Informal experiments have

L. = Leader of session
G. = Group
C. = Client ("owner" of problem)
D.J. = Deferred Judgment (divergence)
J. = Judgment (Convergence)

Fact-Finding
L.   Call on client for brief explanation of h/sr problem or challenge ("mess" or objective)
G.   Everyone listens for
     information
     possible solutions ("purge")
     goals

Problem-Finding
G.   List goals ("How to's") (D.J.)
C.&L. Pick (J.) a "How to" and its essence

Start Excursion—Idea-Finding
G.   List (D.J.) direct analogies from a "world" (leader chooses "world" for "stretch")
L.   Pick (J.) a direct analogy
G.   List (D.J.) personal analogies
G.   List (D.J.) essential paradoxes (symbolic analogies)
L.   Pick (J.) essential paradox and a "world" (for "stretch")
G.   List (D.J.) direct analogies from the "world"
L.   Pick (J.) a direct analogy
G.   Examine analogy (D.J.) (fact-finding with respect to the analogy)
G.   Fantasy force-fit (D.J.)
G.   Practical force-fit (D.J.)

Solution-Finding
C.   Itemized response (D.J.) (what like about idea, followed by concerns) toward possible solution (may be a new and valuable "How to")

Acceptance-Finding
G.   Achieve "viewpoint" (overcoming concerns and gaining acceptance for doing) (D.J.) or start new excursion
C.   Make plan of action (J.) unless decision to start new excursion

FIGURE 2   Synectics/CPS process comparison.

been conducted at Buffalo State College in which one group followed the Synectics model specifically while another followed CPS specifically. The resultant solutions presented by the two groups were remarkably similar.

D. Project Renaissance

Win Wenger, head of Project Renaissance, is a breaker of boundaries in the field of creativity study. His research in visualization and especially in spontaneous imagery has led him to devise several effective programs for personal creative development, invention, and problem solving. In all his work he is constantly being creative *about* creativity. A key process

that Wenger has developed through his research is image streaming. He deals especially with spontaneous imagery and teaches its power in creativity and problem solving.

E. Whole Brain Problem Solving

Whole-brain problem solving has been emphasized by Ned Herrmann, physicist/artist and head of the Ned Herrmann Group, Inc. He incorporates significant right-brain (nonverbal) emphasis into his whole-brain training. To do this, he draws from his demonstrated ability in engineering at General Electric (GE), as well as his accomplishments in art and music. He describes himself as having "one foot in the world of big business, the other planted just as solidly in the world of art and music." GE was among the first companies to establish formal training programs in creativity development some 50 years ago. Herrmann's own work at GE brought about a revived interest in the subject. In his programs, Herrmann uses his four-quadrant concept of the human brain and the Herrmann Brain Dominance Instrument.

F. Lateral and Vertical Thinking

Edward de Bono, a British physician, attracted worldwide attention with his approach to convergent and divergent thinking. "Vertical thinking is concerned with digging the same hole deeper. Lateral thinking is concerned with digging the hole somewhere else." He further explains, "Vertical thinking is concerned with the development and utilization of ideas. Lateral thinking is concerned with the making of new ideas." de Bono concentrates on thinking skills. The Edward de Bono Programme for the Design and Development of Thinking at University of Malta has announced a master of arts in creativity and innovation.

G. German Creativity Development

Horst Geschka spearheaded creativity development in Germany, where he reports that 80% of German companies showed a positive response to introducing creativity techniques. He has conducted research and development work for several decades, first at Battelle Institute, Frankfurt, and more recently in private consulting practice. Geschka has developed adaptations of many existing creativity techniques to make them suitable for specific management situations in companies in Germany. His visual confrontation method provides ideas through pictures. His processes have spread well beyond his native land, and he has conducted extensive international surveys on their use.

H. Japanese CPS Methods

On an international basis the Japanese were among the first to show intense interest in the early CPS processes and have continued developing programs ever since. The quality circle is a well-known adaptation of the brainstorming process. The Japanese are less known, except perhaps among some creativity trainers, for the Kawakita, Jiro and Nakayama, Masakazu methods that were developed and popularized in Japan. These appear to be largely based on CPS and Synectics principles, but have evolved into their own systems for idea generation and problem solving.

I. Other Efforts Internationally

A number of efforts have been made internationally with creativity development. Two nations have provided impressive current case studies of intense applications of creativity development programs over many years. Brazil's work is spearheaded by Jose Leao de Carvalho and his "ILACE" organization. South Africa's work has been developed by Kobus Neethling, president of the South African Creativity Foundation. In Europe, China, and Japan, large creativity societies have been furthering the work.

J. Computers and Mechanical Aids

Some of the computer programs and mechanical aids are elaborate extensions, with gamelike materials, of the old dictionary technique of finding a word at random and then trying to force associations between the word and the problem in order to make fresh connections. Despite their simplicity, they are useful, productive, and enjoyable for people who like working with computers and mechanical devices. Other programs provide a computer-presented version of creativity-development programs such as Synectics or CPS. Still others provide computer-assisted processes for group ideation (brainstorming) and even for use as group de-

cision-making support technology. Arthur VanGundy has provided an analysis and evaluation of the wide variety of software programs available for individual and group use for computer-aided creativity. [*See* Computer Programs.]

K. Styles of Learning

Understanding individual differences in creative styles of participants in a creativity training program has become an important part of such programs. Many instruments have been developed to measure these differences. When these are used at the start of a program, participants gain understanding and appreciation of each other's strengths and weaknesses. They learn to better appreciate and support one another. Instructor/facilitators can group people effectively to build better learning and problem-solving teams.

England's Michael Kirton focused attention on styles of creativity with his widely used Adaptation-Innovation Inventory. The Myers-Briggs Type Indicator is also an early instrument that has been used for determining styles of creativity. Ned Herrmann's Applied Creative Thinking Workshop focuses strongly on styles, applying his Herrmann Brain Dominance Instrument. Min Basadur, head of Center for Research in Applied Creativity in Canada, developed the Creative Problem-Solving Profile Inventory. Stan Gryskiewicz of the Center for Creative Leadership, as well as faculty of the Buffalo State College's Center for Studies in Creativity, have also given heavy emphasis to the styles question. So has William Miller of Global Creativity Corporation. All of these efforts provide help in understanding and applying knowledge about individual differences in creativity styles. [*See* Appendix II: Tests of Creativity.]

1. Mentoring

Instruments measuring styles of creativity can be used effectively by mentors helping individuals in their creative development. Ruth Noller and Barbara Frey (Buffalo State College) put strong emphasis on the many values of mentoring. It can actually provide a type of individual creativity development. Many counselors and others try to solve people's problems for them. Mentors who understand creativity development can provide processes for people to resolve problems on their own.

L. Noteworthy Centers and Programs

The longest-standing university center for teaching and research in creativity development is the center for Studies in Creativity at Buffalo State College. Following up major research in the late 1950s and 1960s, its Creative Studies Project in the late 1960s and early 1970s, in cooperation with the Creative Education Foundation, was the most extensive and comprehensive study on the development and the impact of college creativity courses. Its design and follow-up included the input from a national advisory board of eminent creativity scholars. The Project's positive results ultimately made possible the approval of an undergraduate minor and a master's degree in creative studies at the college. For full details, see source in bibliography under Parnes, 1987. Three other noteworthy centers of long-standing and continuing productivity in English-language publications and programs are Stanford University, Center for Creative Leadership in North Carolina, and Manchester Business School in the United Kingdom. Three examples of cutting-edge programs adapting CPS for executive leadership are George Land's Leadership 2000, Robert Johnston's IdeaScope Associates, and Clothier Rapaille's Archetype Discoveries Worldwide.

1. Master's Degrees

Three universities currently offer master's degrees in creativity. They are Buffalo State College, Universidade de Santiago de Compostela in Spain, and University of Malta.

Bibliography

Creativity Research Journal. M. Runco (Ed.). Mahwah, NJ: Erlbaum.

de Bono, E. (1992). *Serious creativity.* New York: Harper Collins.

Gordon, W., & Poze, T. (1981). *The new art of the possible: The basic course in synectics* (2nd ed.). Cambridge, MA: SES Associates.

Herrmann, N. (1988). *The creative brain.* Lake Lure, NC: Applied Creative Services.

Isaksen, S., Dorval, B., & Treffinger, D. (1994). *Creative approaches to problem-solving.* Dubuque, IA: Kendall-Hunt.

Journal of CREATIA. P. Sung (Ed.). Seoul, Korea: CREATIA Management Consulting. (printed in English, Korean, and Japanese)

Journal of Creative Behavior. D. Simonton (Ed.). Buffalo, NY: Creative Education Foundation.

Journal of Creativity and Innovation Management. T. Rickards & S. Moger (Eds.). Oxford, England: Blackwell Publishers.

Parnes, S. (1987). The Creative Studies Project. In Isaksen, S. (Ed.), *Frontiers of creativity research: Beyond the basics.* Buffalo, NY: Bearly Limited.

Parnes, S. (1992). *Source book for creative problem-solving.* Buffalo, NY: Creative Education Foundation.

Prince, G. (1973). *The practice of creativity.* New York: Collier.

Shallcross, D., & Sisk, D. (1986). *Intuition: An inner way of knowing.* Buffalo, NY: Bearly Limited.

Torrance, E. P. (1972). Can we teach children to think creatively? *Journal of Creative Behavior, 6*(2), 114–143.

Wenger, W. (1996). *The Einstein factor.* Rocklin, CA: Prima Publishing.

Psycholinguistics

Albert N. Katz

University of Western Ontario

Conceptual Metaphor The claim that the conceptual system consists of a set of mappings from one conceptual domain (e.g., IDEAS) to another (e.g., FOOD), leading to tacitly held relation (e.g., "IDEAS ARE FOOD"). Evidence for the underlying metaphor is seen in various seemingly unrelated sentences (e.g., "He swallowed the argument whole" or "It took her a long time to fully digest the novel concept"). It is argued that natural languages presume and express these conceptual mappings.

Head The part of a linguistic expression that gives the main part of the meaning to an expression. In a noun phrase the head would be the noun. As an example, in the noun phrase "red sky," the phrase is about skies (and not redness) and thus sky would be the head noun.

Linguistic Creativity The fact that natural languages are open-ended in the sense that new meanings can be given to already existing words, that new words can be created as required and novel word combinations formed. Also used to describe the fact that, even in the absence of direct experience, people can understand and produce an infinitely large number of syntactically appropriate sentences.

Linguistic Relativity If thought is determined by the structure of language, then the differences between languages should be reflected in differences in thought patterns. That is, people in different linguistic communities would represent reality differently. A weaker version now generally supported holds that the differences in languages predisposes to differences in thought.

Literal (versus Nonliteral) Language A traditional argument is that words and therefore sentences built from them, have at least one fixed meaning that is always evoked by them. Such meaning is termed "literal," an example of which would be the following sentence: "The cat is on the rug" when used to describe a type of animal located on a specific object. Many words or sentences cannot be described in that way and are labeled nonliteral language. Some examples being metaphor (e.g., "my love is a rose'), idioms (e.g., "He kicked the bucket"), and metonomy or using one term to talk about another (e.g., using the term "White House" to refer to the president, such as "The White House isn't saying anything").

Overgeneralization of Language The observation that when children learn language they go through a stage in which they treat irregular words as if they were regular. It is as if one had learned a rule (e.g., add *s* to make a word plural) and were now applying it in a novel instance inappropriately (e.g., when applied to the word *sheep* produces the overgeneralization, *sheeps*)

Protolanguage A hypothesized stage in the evolution of language in which reality is internally represented by linguistic symbols but in which the rules that govern the relations in a sentence are not represented; these rules of syntax govern who does what to whom. Evidence of this primitive system is arguably seen with various brain injuries, in ape language, and in pidgin languages. True language leads to the syntactic representation of reality.

Standard Pragmatic Theory A theory that proposes that one attempts initially to understand a sentence literally, and only if that fails does one attempt to find a nonliteral sense that is consistent with context.

Universal Grammar A theory about what constitutes a possible grammar of any human language; the initial state of the language facility that would permit the specification of the grammar of any natural language.

PSYCHOLINGUISTICS is the study of how linguistic knowledge is acquired, represented, and used by the human mind. As such it lies at the intersection of two disciplines: linguistics and psychology. A heuristic distinction is that the former is more concerned with linguistic competence *(characterizing the knowledge of language possessed by an ideal speaker-hearer), and the latter is more concerned with* linguistic performance *(the actual use of language in concrete situations). Both competence and performance models of language have to explain* linguistic creativity, *the open-endedness found in all natural languages that permits the creation of new words, the creation of new meanings to existing words, the novel but meaningful combination of words into larger units, and the ability of people to understand the meaning of sentences that they have never heard. Language also serves as a means of representing the world and, as such, creates a* problem space *in which creative thought occurs. The discussion here will consist of four sections: (1) linguistic approaches to language creativity, (2) language as a representational format, (3) the creativity of nonliteral language, and (4) selected individual differences in language performance relevant to creative performance.*

I. INTRODUCTION

The study of language is important to creativity because, arguably, language is the quintessential human creative activity. People can, in principle, produce and comprehend an infinite number of utterances. Thus, even in the absence of explicit prior experience, virtually any person can understand or produce a given novel sentence in their native language. Current linguistic theory emphasizes the commonality shared by the structures of every known human language and, as such, suggests that work in language theory can provide insights into the basic workings of the human mind, including the structures and processes required for linguistic creativity. Language also serves as a means for representing events and actions in the world and, consequently, serves a vital function in creating the problem space within which people perceive and understand reality.

II. LINGUISTIC CREATIVITY AND THE STRUCTURE OF LANGUAGE

A. The Design Features of Language

Charles Hockett attempted to identify the characteristics of language shared by all human languages that are not universally shared by the communication systems of other animals. Over the years some of these so-called design features have been called into question, but, in general, the list he provided is accepted. Examination of these features is instructive to students of creativity inasmuch as the features not only describe language but also describe characteristics important to creative thought, suggesting a close link between language and creativity. In this regard it is illustrative to consider some of these linguistic design features and the parallel to creative thought.

1. *Interchangeability.* Adult members of a linguistic community are both transmitters and receivers of linguistic signals (the analogue would be that people both produce and appreciate, or aesthetically respond, to creative products).

2. *Semanticity.* Words and larger linguistic elements mean something beyond themselves, that is, they refer to object, events, and relations in the world.

3. *Arbitrariness.* Semantic relations are independent of any physical or geometric relationship between the linguistic element and its referent.

4. *Displacement.* Linguistic messages can refer to ob-

jects and events that are not in the here-and-now, that is, they are displaced from the perceptual field.

5. *Prevarication.* Linguistic messages can be false or even logically meaningless. These features, taken together with the previous features, are essential building blocks of creativity: symbols that can be freely manipulated in the mind, regardless of constraints of environmental reality.

6. *Productivity.* Language is open in the sense that new linguistic messages can be created freely, so that one can say something that has never been said before and this message can be understood by someone else. Creativity occurs at various levels of language, including semantic creativity in which new words or word combinations are formed or in which the meaning of a given word changes over time.

7. *Reflexive.* One can communicate about communication, that is one can talk about anything we experience, including language itself. That is, one can use language to critique someone else's language, a characteristic with obvious relevance to literary analysis, scientific reasoning, and other aspects of artistic and scientific creativity.

The contrast of these design features with the characteristics of nonhuman communication is striking. Whereas other animals communicate with one another, they do so in a limited, fixed, and context-bound manner. Thus a chimpanzee call might warn others in the troupe about the presence of an eagle, but that call could only be used in the here-and-now (when the danger is perceived) and is fixed in the sense that the troupe could not get together and decide the meaning of the call should be changed to now convey danger from, for instance, lions. Despite the critical differences in nonhuman and human communication, one must be cautious in the interpretation one gives to these differences. First, one should not conclude that nonhumans are incapable of creative thought: There is ample evidence that animals can solve problems in novel ways. Arguably, language provides a medium that extends creativity in ways that are not available to other animals. Second, the close analogue between language and creative activities might reflect either of two possibilities, both of which are reflected in the literature: language is a medium of thought and the charac-

teristics of language shape creative thought or, alternatively, that creative thought occurs autonomously and language merely expresses (and the analysis of which can elucidate) the thought processes.

B. The Structural Components of Language

Language has a hierarchical structure. At the lowest rung of the hierarchy are the basic sounds (*phonemes*) from which larger units, such as words, are built. Phonemes can themselves be decomposed into a finite set of features (such as where and how a sound is produced); each phoneme can be characterized by a unique set of features. Groups of sounds (or written counterparts) that convey meaning are called *morphemes*. Morphemes can be combined into words (such that, for example, the word *boys* would consist of two morphemes: *boy* = young human male; *s* = more than one). Words are combined into phrases and phrases into sentences. Thus the sentence "The boy hit the ball" consists of two phrases: (the boy) (hit the ball). In most linguistic analyses the sentence is at the top of the hierarchy: a coherent combination of words that express the intended meaning of the speaker. Naturally even larger units of analysis can be considered: the linguistic discourse and the extralinguistic contexts in which the sentence is embedded.

Creativity can occur at various levels of the hierarchy. Morphemes can be combined to create new words (e.g., in this century, *television*), words can be combined into novel phrase (e.g., *black hole*) and phrases combined to produce an infinite number of novel sentences. In each case the combinations deemed linguistically acceptable are constrained. It is tempting to appeal to rules that permit acceptable combinations and prohibit others; these rules are called the rules of syntax. Syntactic rules determine whether a sequence of words is grammatical, that is, conforms to the acceptable linguistic patterns of a given language. Syntactic rules also specify the role of each word within the sentence, such as which word signifies the actor, the action, the recipient of the action, and so on.

Not surprisingly each component of the hierarchy has been the subject of independent inquiry and one can identify separable literatures on phonology (how speech sounds are produced and combined), *syntax* (the nature and rules that underlay the production and comprehension of acceptable word combinations), lexical semantics (understanding the meaning of basic expressions, such as words), compositional semantics (characterizing how the meaning of complex expressions depends on the meaning of their component parts), and pragmatics (characterizing how language is used in specific contexts).

Ultimately a fully developed model of language creativity would require the link between each of these components of language. The links need not be intuitively obvious. For instance, one might think that the syntactic acceptability of a sentence is governed by the meaning that it generates. Data from judgments of grammatical acceptability suggest otherwise. To illustrate, consider the sentence "Colorless green ideas sleep furiously." One would deem this meaningless word combination as grammatical but would reject some other meaningless combinations of the same words (e.g., "Sleep furiously idea green colorless"). Thus, semantic acceptability or pragmatic factors per se cannot be the basis for syntactic acceptability. One can find numerous reactions to this claim in both the linguistic and psycholinguistic literatures, resulting in a wide range of theoretical positions, from those who still generally support the autonomy of syntactic processing to those who argue that semantic and pragmatic factors are involved at all levels of the hierarchy.

C. The Generativity of Language

Noam Chomsky has been the most influential figure in the 20th century in examining the creative aspects of language. Although his specific theoretical arguments have changed since the publication in 1957 of his book *Syntactic Structures,* the emphasis on linguistic creativity has remained a central concern. Any model (descriptive grammar) of language he argued must be capable of predicting which combination of words is acceptable and which is not. Because natural languages are infinitely large, the model must be generative in the sense that from a finite set of principles one can characterize an infinite set of sentences. He argued further that the model must be represented mentally as a system of rules and principles. Moreover, Chomsky and others have noted that humans rapidly become com-

petent in handling language in all its complexity even though one experiences meager linguistic input. Rapid acquisition in the presence of poverty of the stimulus has led Chomsky to argue that linguistic competence is biologically based, and as such there must be universal principles governing the structure of all languages. Competing models with different principles are represented in the technical linguistic literature. Despite the differences in these models, all share a commitment to accounting for linguistic creativity and a concern for uncovering linguistic universals and thus, presumably, commonalities in the human cognitive apparatus.

D. Abstract Rules and the Role of Experience in Linguistic Creativity

Chomsky championed a view of the mind that is *modular,* in the sense that the mind consists of a number of autonomous processing units, each one with its own set of rules specialized for handling domain-specific information. Processing within a module is informationally encapsulated, and as such information processing proceeds independent of activity in other areas of the mind, though, of course, the output of the module is available to general intellectual capabilities. This position would lead to the argument that language is autonomous from other intellectual activity and, within language, that syntactic processing proceeds independent of semantics or pragmatics. This claim has been extended to various domains other than language and, if correct, would lead to the argument that creative activity in different domains are served by different modules, each with their own rules of processing. The linguist Ray Jackendoff has suggested separate modules exist for music, language, and dance-related activities; there is some evidence as well that different domains of creative activity are mediated by different brain structures, a position consistent but not necessary for modularity. Chomsky also posited that the internal workings of the language module is multi-layered (e.g., between an abstract d-structure level, in which the thematic relations of a sentence are represented, the actual final representation of the sentence, or s-level, and transformation that permit movement from d-level to s-level structures). These layers can be described in abstract, formal terms. Along these lines, some mechanical, computational models of creativity have been recently advanced, such as in describing the characteristics of scientific discovery. Finally, the internalized rules are innate. In more recent writings Chomsky has argued that *universal grammar* consists of a set of principles, each of which can be set to one of a number of parameters. Through exposure to a given language (even the impoverished experiences that one faces) the various parameters appropriate for that language are set.

Beginning in the late 1980s, a new approach to linguistic creativity has emerged that does not accept the modular, abstract, rule-based assumptions of Chomskians. Construction grammarians take as a starting point that all statements judged as grammatical have to be explained by a full model of generative grammar, including certain linguistic expressions that have been problematic to the rule-based approach. Some such expressions are "in her own right," "been there, done that," and "you're not Jack Kennedy." To explain these, and the more traditionally studied syntactic forms, *construction grammarians* argue that language consists of a network of form-meaning pairs—that is, a pairing between conceptual and linguistic information such that through convention one learns that certain linguistic patterns have associated meaning. To give one example, a pattern might be "P however Q," where P and Q stand for linguistic input, such as phrases. For instance, one might hear "Many Americans think that FDR was a great president, however . . ." We have expectations about the nature of Q that follows from the form, namely some comment contrary to the proposition expressed by P. Some perfectly syntactic sentences compatible with the common meaning of *however* do not fit this expectation, such as the continuation ". . . however, let's not talk about that." Judgments that the former is a better sentence than the latter are taken as evidence of the psychological reality of constructions and in a more general sense argue for experientially based models of language creativity.

Construction grammarians, while maintaining an interest in explaining linguistic creativity, do so by eliminating much of the theoretical structure of the Chomskians and replacing it with a model in which language and thought are intrinsically paired. The approach is quite new and it remains to be seen how it will fare in the long run. The elimination of syntactic modularity and the integration of semantic, pragmatic, and syntactic properties has also been championed by some experimental psycholinguists. For instance, experimental psychologists often study language comprehension online—that is, they track mental processing while the processes are occurring. Many studies are now emerging that indicate that pragmatic and semantic knowledge are both available for use at the earliest stages of language comprehension, even for the access of the meaning of individual words and for settling on an appropriate grammatical structure.

III. LANGUAGE AS REPRESENTATION: IMPLICATIONS FOR CREATIVITY

A. Language and Protolanguage

The linguist Derek Bickerton has argued that language is primarily representational and not communicative in nature. The characteristics of the representation was described earlier in the design and syntactic features of language. Accordingly, language provides a symbolic medium through which humans internalize and can manipulate their knowledge of the world. Given that how one represents a problem constrains how one goes about solving it, this position has obvious implications for creative problem solving. Bickerton went further and, on the basis of pidgin and Creole languages, ape language learning programs, and other sources of evidence, he has argued that language evolved to its present form by first passing through a *protolanguage* stage in which concepts might be represented lexically but in which true syntactic properties are missing. Thus via protolanguage one might be able to understand and communicate complex thoughts such as "Man woman sit," but in the absence of direct experience one would not be able to disambiguate the various causal and other relations that these words might invite (such as "The man and woman are both sitting," "The man is sitting on the woman," or "The man is with the sitting woman"). True syntactic language thus frees one from the here-and-now and allows for the representation of causal agents, their actions, and the recipients of these actions. According to this view, language is the medium through which creative thought occurs. Based on the evolutionary evidence of the growth of hominid brain size coupled with the *artifacts* created by different hominids (such as the tools they invented), Bickerton concluded that proto-language might have evolved with *Homo erectus* but that true syntactic language (and the rich creative possibilities it supports) only can be found in *H. sapiens.*

B. Linguistic Determinism and Reality

Edward Sapir and Benjamin Lee Whorf are the main proponents of the view that language determines thought and that the structure of different languages predisposes different linguistic groups to represent reality in different ways. This position has been most studied in the lexical domain in which different languages have different number of words to describe the same physical input and in the grammatical domain in which languages differ in the type of information that one is obligated to give. The evidence for this hypothesis from psycholinguistic experiments of the 1950s to the 1980s is mixed; beginning in the mid-1980s a set of methodologically improved studies has appeared that in general support the Sapir-Whorf position.

There is clear evidence that the representational aspects of language play a role in specific aspects of creativity. For instance, a classic block to creativity is labeled *functional fixedness,* the difficulty in conceptualizing objects or events in other than standard ways. Psycholinguistic experimentation has shown that how one labels the objects presented for use in productive problem-solving situations influences the likelihood with which fixedness will be overcome. As an example, if in a task one requires the use of a box to solve a problem creatively, and if this box is filled with tacks, one is more likely to find this unique solution if the stimuli are labeled "box and tacks" rather than "box of tacks" because the former invites separate representation of the box whereas the latter does not.

IV. NONLITERAL LANGUAGE AND CREATIVITY

A. The Processing of Nonliteral Language

A special problem for psycholinguistic models of language are certain linguistic forms in which the con-

ventionally expressed meaning of a phrase or sentence differs from what the speaker intends. The use of such so-called nonliteral language is pervasive; some common examples are metaphor (e.g., "Juliet is the sun," "my car is a lemon"), idioms (e.g., "kick the bucket," "blow one's stack"), and indirect requests ("Do you have a dollar?"). These linguistic forms have proven problematic both linguistically and psycholinguistically. Because the syntactic and semantic characteristics of nonliteral language cannot be readily explained by many models of language processing, a suggested solution has been the theoretically disquieting position that these ubiquitous forms of speech are marginalized as not being representative of real, core language. [*See* METAPHORS.]

The most traditional processing model, labeled the *standard pragmatic model,* has assumed that processing priority is given to attempting a literal interpretation of any sentence. Only if this fails will a person attempt to find nonliteral sense compatible with the context in which the sentence is embedded. Psycholinguistic research has demonstrated that, contrary to the claims of the standard pragmatic approach, the comprehension of nonliteral language is not optional and dependent on a prior failure to find a literal sense in which the sentence is true. Rather, given sufficient context, in many cases (1) it is as easy to understand nonliteral language as literal language and (2) one cannot avoid processing the nonliteral sense, even if the sentence is also sensible when taken literally. These and related findings suggest that the difference between literal and nonliteral language may be minor and that similar principles underlay the creative mapping of one concept onto another (as occurs in a nonconventional or novel metaphor) and language use in general.

Metaphor is especially important not only because of the theoretical issues it poses for standard models of language comprehension but because it is so closely associated with creative thought. Metaphor is a means through which novel meanings of words occur, may be one of the major ways in which novel concepts are communicated, is an important tool in creative writing, has been implicated in creativity training programs, and, in a general sense, the metaphoric ability to juxtapose unrelated concepts to produce a novel insight has been taken as a fundamental characteristic of creative people.

B. Conceptual Combinations

A simple version of linguistic creativity occurs when two words are juxtaposed to create a novel concept. Thus, "peeled apple" possesses features (e.g., "is white") that are not predictable from either constituent word but emerge only as a consequence of the juxtaposition. Two basic types of psychological theories have been proposed. In one, the *head noun* in the case above, *apple*) is assumed to consist of a *schema* consisting of a set of dimensions, with each dimension (such as color) having slots that can be filled by specific attributes. According to this theory, pragmatic and semantic knowledge facilitates the identification of relevant slots and is also used to modify dimensions other than just the one selected by the modifier. The alternate theory argues that combination depends on identifying a *thematic relation* that links the modifier and head noun. Example relations are "noun caused modifier" (e.g., flu virus), "noun located modifier" (mountain cloud), "noun made of modifier" (chocolate egg). In one version, selection of a relation is based on the frequency with which the modifier has been used in different relations. For instance, the concept "mountain" is typically used with a locative relation (such as mountain cabin or mountain goat) and much less rarely with a made of relation (as in mountain range). It remains to be seen which class of model will prove eventually more successful in predicting combinational creativity.

C. Metaphor as a Linguistic Issue

The notion that the mechanisms underlying metaphor are language based can be traced back to the writings of Aristotle who claimed that the act of metaphorizing was the creative act of giving one thing a name that belonged to something else. The traditional class of model that has attempted to implement this has assumed that the concepts juxtaposed in metaphor possess features in common, and that the act of metaphorizing involves finding this similarity. The common terminology has the concept being described as the "topic," the concept being used for the comparison is called the "vehicle," and the emergent similarity the "ground." Several psychological models based on finding or creating similarity have emerged in the 20th century, some of which are somewhat similar to Ar-

thur Koestler's notion that creativity involves *bisociation*. Several psychological testable variants are available: those that argue that metaphors involve mapping a salient feature of the vehicle to a low salient feature of the topic (salience imbalance theory), those that argue that mapping involves maintaining systems of relations between topic and vehicle (structure mapping theory), and those that argue that mapping occurs across semantic space in a manner similar to that found in analogical reasoning (domain interaction theory). Each of these theories can explain some, but not all, of the available experimental data on metaphor comprehension. In recent years, an alternate has emerged, which makes the claim that metaphor processing does not involve identifying similarities but rather involves treating metaphors as class-inclusion statements. To give one example, in the Shakespearean metaphor "Juliet is the sun," the concept "sun" is assumed to act as an indicator of a class (of which the sun is a prototypical example). Comprehension thus involves the act of classifying Juliet as an instance of this class.

D. Metaphor as a Conceptual Phenomenon

A growing number of scholars have argued that metaphor is not a linguistic problem at all because the mechanisms underlying metaphoric thought exist independently of language. George Lakoff made the clear distinction between metaphor (mapping in the conceptual system from one domain of knowledge to another domain of knowledge) and metaphoric expression (the language-based realization of the cross domain mapping). Nonetheless, much of the evidence for this distinction is based on the analysis of language. The classic work was by George Lakoff and Mark Johnson, who argued that both literal and nonliteral language is governed by a set of *conceptual metaphors,* that is, mappings from one conceptual domain (e.g., LOVE), to another (e.g., JOURNEY). In the conceptual metaphor LOVE IS A JOURNEY, the correspondences would include lovers = travelers, love relationship = vehicle, lovers' goals = destination, and so on. Conceptual metaphors are experientially based and allow for the understanding of the relationship between quite diverse sentences. Thus, the intuition that a sentence such as "the relationship is going nowhere" is related to quite a different sentence (e.g., "I think we are moving too fast") is motivated by the presence of a conceptual metaphor to which both sentences can be mapped. Creativity is directly explained as an inferential process in which we can reason about one domain (e.g., LOVE) using the knowledge that we use to reason about the other domain (JOURNEYS). Psycholinguistic research has now shown that concepts, idioms, proverbs, polysemy, and other linguistic expressions are grounded in conceptual metaphors. Mark Turner has extended the analysis to poetry and has demonstrated that the same relations hold in that prototypical instance of creative writing. One issue that remains contentious is whether or not conceptual metaphors are automatically engaged as a sentence is being comprehended, or whether the observed effects are only obtained at some later stage of discourse understanding.

E. Conceptual Blending and Integration

A processing model compatible with construction grammar and with the conceptual basis of language is emerging that is directly relevant to creative thought. The position holds that small conceptual packets (called *mental spaces*) are constructed as one thinks and talks for the purposes of local understanding and action. Conceptual blending is taken to be a general cognitive process that operates over mental spaces as inputs; structure from two input spaces are projected to the blend, a separate space. The blend inherits partial structure from the input stage and has emergent structure of its own. Once a blend is established, one can work cognitively within that space, permitting the manipulation of the various events as an integrated whole. Thus, blends provide a cognitive representation and processing mechanisms wherein and whereby creative synthesis occurs. Evidence for the presence of blends has come largely through analysis of spoken language and creative writings. The creation of blends has been taken as a central process of grammar. It has also been used to explain the difference in literal and nonliteral language as a function of the relative status of the counterparts in the mapping between inputs, and not as a function of different cognitive operations. The claim that the creation of blends occurs on-line has yet to be demonstrated.

V. SELECTED INDIVIDUAL DIFFERENCES IN LANGUAGE PERFORMANCE AND CREATIVITY

Recall the distinction between linguistic competence and performance. The former refers to knowledge held about ideal speaker-hearer interactions, whereas the latter is the study of actual language use, which is subject to differences in attention, motivation, memory, personality, developmental experiences, and so on. Some instances in which actual language use has relevance to the study of creativity follow.

A. Verbal Creativity Tests

The measurement of creativity is often intrinsically related to language. Many tests involve the manipulation of verbal stimuli in one way or another. Examples include finding a common remote associate for various sets of three seemingly unrelated words, divergent thinking in which one is asked to generate verbal associates to a stimulus word, and by checking descriptors from a list of adjectives. Although verbal stimuli are employed and the task involves the use of semantic or syntactic knowledge, the tests have not been constructed with linguistic characteristics in mind. There is quite a large psychological literature on performance factors that influence the generation of verbal associates and on the role that semantic relatedness plays on checklist type of stimuli. Nonetheless, these factors have not played a role in either the construction of most of these tests or in the manner in which they are interpreted, and as such many of these tests have questionable internal validity. Psycholinguistic factors also play a role in the verbal instructions given to participants, even for tests in which the stimuli are nonverbal. There is growing evidence that pragmatic factors, also largely ignored, might influence how one completes a creativity test. For instance, instructing participants to complete the test by "being creative" has been shown to increase the creativity score on verbal divergent thinking and self-report checklists measures. These data indicate that some portion of the test score reflects differences in the pragmatic knowledge about when it is appropriate to display oneself as creative. [*See* TESTS OF CREATIVITY.]

Pragmatic effects can also be seen more widely. The term "being creative" is applied differently to school-aged students compared to adult artists or other experts in a specific domain. The use of the same lexical term in different contexts indicates that pragmatic factors have to be considered in how the concept "creative" is mentally represented and used. Pragmatic principles include those that are necessary for successful communication between speakers, assuming a shared context between members in communication and following tacit rules of conversation, such as "follow topic," "be relevant to context," "say as much as necessary to be informative but no more." Such factors have not been considered in the verbal instructions provided to participants in experimental studies of creativity. This failure would most clearly threaten the validity of those tests that depend on asking participants to generate descriptors or acts that exemplify creative people, such as those used to construct creative personality scales.

B. Developmental Issues

Because humans learn to speak and understand the language of their community, it may be reasonable to assume that performance factors known to influence learning in general should be reflected in language acquisition as well. What is noncontroversial is the observation that children acquire language, a very complex system, very rapidly. By the age of about 6, most children are capable of using language, with all its complexities. The speed, and way, with which the complex system of language is mastered has led to the argument that children are biologically preset to acquire language and that language learning is substantially different than learning to ride a bike or play a musical instrument.

Among the many findings in the developmental literature is that linguistic creativity follows a pattern wherein children learn to associate a word with some object or event in the word (e.g., foot refers to a part of body) and learn some rules of language (e.g., to make plural add *s*). Application of these rules can lead to errors of *overgeneralization* (e.g., saying "foots"). This creative generation of concepts occurs in the absence of any experience with the produced form. By early

school-age years these errors drop out and are replaced by the irregular forms (e.g., feet) that the children actually hear in their environment. Studies have also shown that children also are sensitive to the grammatical structure of language and not merely to the linear order of words that they hear. Also, in a variant of conceptual combination, experiments have shown that children as early as 3 years of age constrain what concepts get combined. Thus, a child would call an animal that likes to eat a mouse "a mouse eater," one that likes to eat a rat is called a "rat eater," one that likes to eat mice is called a "mice eater," but one who likes to eat rats is rarely called a "rats eater." Instead, and consistent with a prominent linguistic model of word construction, even the young children employed the adult form: rat eater. The willingness to say "mice eater" and unwillingness to say "rats eater" does not appear to be based on the linguistic input a child experiences, suggesting that at some level this type of constraint on creative combinations is innate. The actual role of innate factors is, not surprisingly, controversial with some arguing that child language acquisition reflects universal grammar whereas others argue that at least some of the acquisition data can be explained by a pattern-recognition mechanism sensitive to the frequency with which different linguistic forms are experienced.

The acquisition of nonliteral language also shows some regularities at the level of discriminating intended from expressed meaning. Children understand metaphor before they understand irony. Children as young as three or four have been shown to use and understand some instances of metaphor, but the understanding that someone is talking ironically does not appear until six years of age or later. Note that in both metaphor and irony the expressed meaning differs from the intended meaning, so the differences cannot merely be that understanding nonliteral meaning involves developing the ability to distinguish what one says from what one intends. Some argue that the developmental differences are a function of conceptual growth. For metaphor, one has to somehow perceive one concept in terms of another and arguably the ability to do this is present quite early in life. Irony on the other hand involves knowledge about another person's belief system, which requires the acquisition of social awareness and a theory of mind.

C. Pathology of Language

Language can be disrupted in several ways.

1. Deafness

Those who are born deaf do not possess a functioning vocal-auditory channel and, in the original list of Hockett's design features, could not demonstrate true language. This claim is no longer held to be true and sign languages are recognized as real natural languages. An additional claim has been made that the nature of sign language would not permit for creativity. This claim too has now been shown to be false.

2. Genetic Disorders

Examination of various genetic-based disorders have been taken as evidence for a dissociation between intellectual abilities and language. A general argument in the creativity literature is that creativity and intelligence are correlated and that for exceptional creativity a threshold IQ level has to be reached. There are some genetic disorders in which cognitive functioning is severely limited and yet high level performance can be reached. Howard Gardner described the case of an autistic child with limited linguistic skills who produced impressive artwork. There are reports of people who have limited language but who nonetheless exhibit impressive (albeit limited) abilities in one specific domain, usually in mathematics or music.

In recent years several psycholinguists have examined two genetically based disorders because of the differences in language and cognition. In Down's syndrome language development lags behind cognitive development, whereas in Williams syndrome cognitive performance lags behind linguistic skills. Some have taken these differences to reflect modularity—namely, the independence of language from cognition in general. However, the evidence is not as clear as some have described it, and one should be cautious in drawing the inference that comparison of these disorders necessarily indicates that linguistic abilities are independent of cognitive abilities.

3. Psychopathology

It has long been argued that some psychopathologies are related to creativity, both as measured by creativity tests and by observation of those with notable creative achievement. Even with nonpathological populations, reliable relations are observed between creativity and measures of psychopathological predispositional tendencies, such as *psychoticism*. One notable characteristic is found in verbal output of these people: on word association tests people high in psychoticism produce more responses in general and more unusual or deviant responses than those low on the dimension. These data have been taken as suggesting either that, in some people, the boundaries of concepts are overextended or that some people cannot adequately filter out irrelevant thoughts. That is, the verbal data are taken as indications of conceptual disorders when found in a pathological population. When similar language characteristics are found in productive people they are taken as indicative of greater unusualness of thought processes and mental content, and less inhibition and freer expression of impulses. With respect to language per se, these data are further indications regarding how personality characteristics influence linguistic output.

4. Brain, Language, and Creativity

The two halves (hemispheres) of the *human brain* are specialized for different cognitive tasks. Creativity involves the integration and coordination of the cognitive activities subserved by both hemispheres. The importance for creativity of the coordination of cognitive activities by both hemispheres has been demonstrated in studies of people who have lost the major nerve pathway joining the two hemispheres and by experimental studies that selectively engage each hemisphere. Nonetheless the special contribution of each hemisphere is also apparent.

The left is the dominant hemisphere for language. A stroke, head injury, or brain tumor damage to parts of the *left* cerebral hemisphere will, in most people, lead to severe impairment of linguistic functioning (what is called *aphasia*). The precise location and extent of the brain damage determines the nature of the linguistic disorder. The impairment is often very selective: a person may demonstrate failures to comprehend language but be able to speak or may demonstrate inability to comprehend and carry on conversational speech but be able to repeat long strings of words. Aphasia is clearly related to the loss of literary creativity. The evidence with other creative domains is not as obvious. There is evidence that artistic (figural) creativity is spared for aphasic patients; for musical creativity the evidence is mixed. There is evidence of continued musical creativity despite significant aphasia (as seen, for instance, in the continued creativity after suffering a stroke of the Russian composer V. Shebalin), though it is clear with some musicians (e.g., M. Ravel) that the loss of language was accompanied by a loss in musical creativity.

The right hemisphere also has been shown to play an important role, both in language and creativity. There is growing evidence that the right hemisphere plays a role in the processing of language, as seen, for instance, by the presence of semantic priming and other evidence that *right hemisphere* supported processes are sensitive to word meaning. Moreover, there is ever growing evidence that the right hemisphere is sensitive to the processing of nonliteral creative language. Damage to the right hemisphere is associated with impairments in pragmatic aspects of language comprehension and with impairment in understanding metaphoric, idiomatic, and other forms of speech in which the expressed and intended meanings differ. These effects have been attributed to the disruptions of right hemisphere mechanisms sensitive to context and use of general knowledge. Such mechanisms play a special role in comprehending nonliteral language and in creativity. [*See* SPLIT BRAINS: INTERHEMISPHERIC EXCHANGE IN CREATIVITY.]

Bibliography

Fauconnier, G. (1997). *Mappings in thought and language.* New York: Cambridge University Press.

Gardner, H. (1982). *Art, mind and brain.* New York: Basic Books.

Gibbs, R. (1994). *The poetics of mind.* New York: Cambridge University Press.

Katz, A. (1997). Creativity and the cerebral hemispheres. In M. Runco (Ed.), *Creativity Research Handbook,* Volume 1 (pp. 203–226). Cresskill, NJ: Hampton Press.

Lakoff, G., & Johnson, M. (1980). *Metaphors we live by.* Chicago: University of Chicago Press.

Pinker, S. (1994). *The language instinct.* New York: Penguin Books.

Turner, M. (1996). *The literary mind.* New York: Oxford University Press.

Wasow, T. (1989). Grammatical theory. In M. Posner (Ed.), *Foundations of cognitive science,* (pp. 161–205). Cambridge, MA: MIT Press.

Quantum Theory of Creativity

Amit Goswami

University of Oregon

Collapse The discontinuous transition of converting quantum possibility waves into manifest actuality.

Consciousness The ground of all being.

Creativity The discovery or invention of something new of value having new meaning in a new context or in an old or in a combination of old contexts.

Inner Creativity The discovery of new contexts of being beyond the ego-identity.

Quantum Discontinuously discrete.

Quantum Leap Discontinuous transitions in quantum physics.

Quantum Self The self (or subject) experience in primary awareness.

Unconscious Processing Processing in which consciousness is present but awareness (or subject–object split) is not.

Creativity is our greatest gift and some of our best moments in life are those spent in creative acts. In every field of human endeavor, we now generally recognize that real change comes from the creativity of individuals such as Georgia O'Keeffe, Albert Einstein, Rabindranath Tagore, Martha Graham, Wolfgang Amadeus Mozart, and Thomas Edison. We marvel at creative individuals, we

acknowledge their creative achievements, and questions swarm in our heads: What is creativity? Can we ever understand the nature of creativity and the creative process? Would such understanding help each of us individually to fulfill our creative potential? Can everyone be creative? Can we educate our children optimally for creativity? Heretofore we have addressed these questions in a piecemeal manner but finally, thanks to quantum physics, we have a comprehensive theory that can satisfactorily address all these issues. This article will examine the **QUANTUM THEORY OF CREATIVITY.**

I. DEFINITIONS AND A NEW TAXONOMY

A. What Is Creativity?

Creativity is one of those subjects for which we have quite a developed field of research yet no consensus definition. The definition of creativity seems to depend on the worldview and the corresponding nature of the theory to which the proponent subscribes.

Creativity researchers serve three different worldviews: mechanistic, organismic, and idealist. Mechanists hold a materialist worldview in which all things are made of matter and are mechanically deterministic, objective, continuous, and local. Creativity to them is a brain (computer) phenomenon. Organismic theorists believe there is, in addition to mechanism, significance in the whole organism and how it develops. Because there is purposiveness and discontinuity in the development of the organism, organismic theorists of creativity define creativity with that in mind. Idealists believe that consciousness, not matter, is primary in the world and that creativity is fundamentally subjective.

An important development in science, although not yet quite a consensus, is that quantum theory permits us an integrative worldview that brings together all three disparate worldviews. Accordingly, we can develop an inclusive definition that responds to the needs of all three camps of creativity theorists.

So what is creativity? Everyone agrees that creativity is the discovery or invention of something new. It is the definition of *new* that theorists cannot agree on. To the mechanist, there is nothing entirely new under the sun, so the definition follows this line of thinking. Mechanists include a novelty or surprise element in the definition to account for the seeming discontinuity. The organismic theorist, on the other hand, insists on including purposiveness or value in the definition. Idealists insist that creativity is the discovery or invention of something of new meaning that is perceived by the creative; thus consciousness is involved. Using the quantum worldview, we can find a definition that is inclusive of all of these perspectives. [*See* DISCOVERY; NOVELTY.]

The quantum worldview conceives of all things, matter and thought, as waves of possibility. The question arises: Who or what collapses the waves of quantum possibility into actuality, the actual events that we perceive? Clearly, when we observe, we never see a material object spread around or a thought simultaneously carrying multiple meaning; we see a unique actuality. Thus, conscious observation, consciousness, is a sufficient condition for collapsing quantum possibility into actuality. The mathematician John von Neumann argued long ago that consciousness is also a necessary condition for collapse. Because all material objects, such as mechanical machines (including the brain), are made of quantum possibility objects, they cannot resolve the quantum possibility of an object with which they interact. The interaction just makes bigger and bigger entanglements of possibility, ad infinitum; this is called the infinite von Neumann chain. The agency of collapse, said von Neumann, must be

consciousness, because consciousness is nonmaterial and is outside the jurisdiction of quantum mechanics.

One can raise objections against von Neumann's resolution of the quantum measurement problem. The first objection is dualism. But that objection is refuted by noting that if both matter and mind are quantum possibilities within consciousness and that, in the event of collapse, consciousness is just recognizing and choosing one of the possibilities, which becomes actuality, then there is no need for any intermediary or any energy exchange.

The second objection is a little subtle: If collapse is conscious choice, then what happens if two observers look simultaneously? Whose choice counts? The answer here (arrived at independently by Ludwig Bass, Casey Blood, and Amit Goswami) is that consciousness is one; there are no two choosing-consciousnesses in the world to cause the paradox. Our perceived separateness from the unity of consciousness comes entirely from our conditioning (discussed later).

A third objection is this: Would not a transcendent, all-encompassing unitive consciousness be omnipresent, collapsing every possibility always? We can resolve this dilemma by noting that in every event of quantum measurement, an observing brain (or at least, a living cell) is involved. Furthermore, the act of observation itself creates the (apparent) subject–object split out of the unity of consciousness and its possibilities.

So there is no need to limit ourselves to the narrow definition of creativity that mechanistic theories propose, because consciousness *is* involved in *all* the affairs of the world. Instead, we recognize creativity as an act of collapse by consciousness of possibility into actuality (downward causation) in which a new meaning in thought is seen, one that leads to a new product of value. This way of defining creativity clearly incorporates the organismic and idealist views and, as you will see below, also validates the mechanistic view as a limiting case.

B. Fundamental and Situational Creativity

There are still more issues to sort out because meaning depends on the context. The easiest way to see this is to consider the difference between lexical meaning and contextual meaning. Consider the two sentences:

The ass is an intelligent, useful animal.

Anyone who does not appreciate the importance of context for meaning is an ass.

Here, context is obviously important. Just so, we are led to differentiate between creativity in which new meaning is perceived in a new context and creativity in which new meaning emerges from an old context or a combination of old contexts. The first kind of creativity we will call fundamental creativity and the second we will call situational creativity. The naming is obvious because you can build situational creativity on acts of fundamental creativity, but not the other way around.

Now, finally, some actual definitions:

Fundamental creativity involves the creation of a new product of value in a new context of meaning.

Situational creativity involves a product of value based on the perception of new meaning in an old context or a combination of contexts.

Notice that what we ordinarily call discovery fits into the first category of fundamental creativity, and what we call invention fits into the second category of situational creativity. Discovery opens new contexts for investigation. Examples are found in many fields: Newton's discovery of universal gravity that began the paradigm of classical mechanics; Picasso's discovery of cubism, which revealed a new way to paint an object that shows its multidimensional character; Martha Graham's discovery of modern dance. Invention further explores the meaning of already discovered contexts: Marconi invents the radio on the basis of Maxwell's theory of electromagnetic waves.

Notice also that situational creativity is, in some ways, similar to situational problem solving. In both cases, the creator starts with a "problem space" of known contexts and finds various solutions to the problem. The only difference is the perception of meaning. A computer may be able to write a poem of new meaning combining old poems, but it would not know it. Only a conscious human can see the new meaning of the poem. In the limit that we take such "seeing the new meaning" for granted, we may be tempted to say that computers occasionally can be creative. What we mean is that *we* can use computers to occasionally accomplish acts of situational creativity. [*See* PROBLEM SOLVING.]

C. Outer and Inner Creativity

There is a further refinement in the taxonomy of creative acts. Mechanistic models of creativity ignore the subjective component of the world. Thus in these models, talk about creativity makes sense only in fields of external endeavor, such as science, literature, music, and art. But because we are starting with an ontology based on the primacy of consciousness, the definition of an act of creation can and must be enlarged to include the subjective component of our being as well.

Mahatma Gandhi made an impact on the entire world culture through his discovery of the effectiveness of nonviolent struggle for freedom against oppression, but his act of creation was intimately connected with his own personal transformation; he himself became nonviolent to the core. In such acts of personal transformation, when a new context of being is discovered and is manifested into a product (the personality of the creative), we can and must recognize an act of creation. To distinguish from acts of creation in the outer arena (*outer creativity*), this kind of creativity is called *inner creativity*.

With this definition—inner creativity is the discovery (and manifestation) of new contexts of living—we can see that growing from childhood to adulthood falls in the category of inner creativity. Other examples of inner creativity occur in acting and in spirituality.

Within inner creativity, also, we can discern acts of fundamental creativity (discovery of new contexts of living) and situational creativity (discovery of new meaning in other people's discovered contexts). The founders of the world's great religions, people such as Moses, Buddha, Jesus, and Lao Tsu, are fundamental creatives. People who have followed in their footsteps, St. Paul, for example, are situational creatives.

II. THE QUANTUM NATURE OF CREATIVITY

There is a Sidney Harris cartoon that depicts Einstein standing, baggy pants and all, before a blackboard. He has written $E = ma^2$ on the board and crossed it off.

Below that, $E = mb^2$ is written and crossed off. The caption says, "The Creative Moment."

Why does this cartoon evoke our laughter? We laugh because we know implicitly that creative insights do not occur through such reasoned steps as this but are, instead, discontinuous leaps. [*See* INSIGHT.]

On closer look, researchers (first stated clearly by Graham Wallas) have found that the discontinuous act of creative insight is part of a protracted process that consists of four stages: preparation; incubation, or unconscious processing; sudden insight; and manifestation. (The stages are not as linear as this sounds.) It is easy to make mechanistic models of two of these steps, preparation and manifestation, but unconscious processing is as mysterious as discontinuous insight. Creativity is expressed as an action; why should inaction—that's what unconscious processing is—be important for it? [*See* INCUBATION.]

Organismic theorists insist that there is purposiveness in creativity, to which mechanists rightly object. The material world, in the classical worldview, evolves causally. There is no room in this worldview for teleological purpose or final cause. So, how could there be purposiveness in creativity?

How important is development, another tenet of organismic theorists, in creativity? Genetic determinism, subscribed to by many mechanistic theorists, proposes traits as the principal determinants of who is creative and who is not. Can we settle this debate of development versus trait? Can anyone be creative?

The following section shows that all these controversial questions and issues find answers when we recognize the quantum nature of creativity within a consciousness-based worldview.

A. Creativity and the Quantum Leap

Is creativity continuous, or is there discontinuity in a creative act, in the so-called aha experience that creatives themselves refer to as sudden, "like lightning," and so on? Three famous instances of sudden arrival at creative insight, the cases of the "bath" (Archimedes discovered the law of buoyancy force in hydrostatics while taking a bath), the "bed" (Kekule's insight about the ring-shaped nature of electronic bonding in the Benzene molecules came while he was dreaming), and

the "bus" (Poincaré arrived at one of his important mathematical discoveries unexpectedly while stepping onto a bus) all support the idea of the sudden and discontinuous nature of creative insight.

Computer scientists cannot accommodate discontinuity in their models of creativity simply because computing machines are Newtonian in nature; they operate continuously, on the basis of algorithms. The case for the assumption of continuity seems reasonable enough because in the macro-nature around us, it is hard to find any example of discontinuity. But quantum physics, from the outset, has recognized discontinuous movement.

Consider the Bohr model of the atom. In this model, the electrons orbit around the nucleus; this movement is continuous. But when the electrons jump from one orbit to another, they never pass through the intervening space, giving us a model for discontinuity. The famous phrase "the quantum leap" for discontinuity comes from the Bohr model.

When quantum mechanics was discovered to replace Bohr's stop-gap model of the atom, it was confirmed that there are two kinds of movement of objects. In the continuous movement, quantum objects spread as waves of possibility, acquiring more and more facets. But their collapse to actuality is discontinuous movement, a quantum leap.

The continuous movement of quantum objects is caused by material interactions—upward causation. The cause of movement travels upward from elementary particles to atoms, to molecules, to cells, and, finally, to the brain. In a quantum measurement, which every act of perception or thinking is, the brain ultimately offers macroscopically distinguishable waves of possibility from which consciousness chooses. This choice results in the downward-causation event of collapse, which is discontinuous. Thus the idea of quantum measurement in the brain gives us a model of discontinuous creative insight.

Is creativity a discontinuous quantum leap of the brain, then? Creativity is the quantum leap in meaning, but it is easily seen that the brain, being a material machine, cannot process meaning. Like all material machines, brain processes symbols, not meaning. And you cannot reserve some of the symbols to process meaning, because you would need more symbols for keeping track of the meaning symbols, ad infinitum. So we must face it. The carrier of meaning, thoughts, do not belong to the brain. They originate in the mind, of course, but we must recognize that mind is not brain.

This need not raise the specter of dualism. Because if the mind is quantum, if thoughts are quantum movements of possibility waves of the mind, then consciousness can simultaneously collapse the possibility waves of the brain and of the mind. This is a new, dualism-free form of psychophysical parallelism in which the mediation of consciousness maintains the parallelism between the brain and the mind.

So, a creative insight is a quantum leap of thought. Is there evidence that thought is quantum in nature? There is plenty of evidence. In a book on quantum mechanics written in 1951, David Bohm said that thoughts obey an uncertainty principle: We cannot simultaneously ascertain both the content and the direction of thought as anyone can verify directly via observation. Ambiguous words carry ambiguous meaning in thought when we do not measure them (that is, process them without awareness, which is called unconscious processing); that is, thoughts do become superpositions of possibilities between measurements. But when we measure them, we find only one meaning; the superposition of multiple meanings collapses. This has been verified in a cognitive experiment by Anthony Marcel in 1980.

A telltale sign of the quantum nature of objects is their nonlocality—a mutual influence via phase relationship that extends beyond space and time and does not involve signals. The evidence of nonlocality of creative thought may be found in many events of multiple creativity, that is, simultaneous discoveries by noncommunicating scientists. An example is the nearly simultaneous and independent discovery of quantum mechanics by Werner Heisenberg and Erwin Schrödinger.

B. The Creative Process and the Importance of Unconscious Processing

As mentioned before, the creative process consists of four stages: preparation, unconscious processing, insight, and manifestation. Preparation is widely regarded as the acquisition of existing knowledge, and manifestation is the finishing of the product based on the insight. These two stages can be seen to be mainly algorithmic. But the middle two stages, unconscious processing and insight, require the quantum in order to understand them.

The suddenness of insight is due to the discontinuity of the quantum leap of thought. But why is unconscious processing important and how is unconscious processing different from conscious processing or preparation?

We address the second question first. Quantum collapse requires brain-mind awareness. When there is no awareness, there is no collapse, and this is the situation when the processing is unconscious—there is no awareness of the processing. In contrast, preparation is processing with awareness. To put it another way, preparation is doing; unconscious processing is nondoing. Preparation is active work; unconscious processing is passive relaxation.

Why is unconscious processing important? Quantum waves of possibility spread between measurements. If we do not collapse thoughts through conscious striving to solve our problem and, additionally, if we feed on ambiguity, we can accumulate quite a lot of uncollapsed superpositions of possibilities in the brain and in thought. The materialist assumption is that uncollapsed superpositions collapse by chance. But in the quantum-within-consciousness model, no collapse can occur until consciousness so chooses. So when does consciousness choose? When there is a Gestalt of possibilities that combine to present a solution to the problem. This is similar to what Walters and Gardner called the crystallizing experience. [*See* UNCONSCIOUS.]

There is only a small probability of hitting the correct combination of ideas from the plethora of possibilities. First, the creative must make many attempts, so striving is as important as relaxation and unconscious processing. Second, we must remember that fundamental creativity is discovery; the solution is already in consciousness as a theme, what Plato called an archetype. When there is a resonance between the theme and the Gestalt, collapse takes place. Resonance, as when soldiers march in unison on a bridge, enhances the probability of collapse.

A word about purpose here. Consciousness collapses

the creative insight according to a purposive theme that it recognizes, but this is not teleology.

Do probabilities really wait uncollapsed until consciousness chooses? There is now experimental evidence for this. The physicist Helmuth Schmidt, in an experiment reported in 1993, uses random radioactive quantum decay to generate random sequences of the binary numbers 0 and 1; psychics then try to influence the random number generator to behave in a nonrandom manner, for example, to produce more zeros than ones. Over the years, Schmidt has obtained some positive data in favor of such psychokinetic (PK) influence on random number generators. In a more recent twist, Schmidt had the radioactive events stored in computers and even printed out, but nobody looked at either the computer data or the printout. The sealed printout was sent to an independent observer who, after 3 months, chose an arbitrary direction for the psychic influence on the random number generator. Now the experimenter told the psychics to look at the data and do their PK with that direction in mind. Amazingly, even though 3 months had elapsed, psychics were able to influence the data by three standard deviations in the chosen direction as verified by the independent observer who now looked at the printout for the first time.

Were the psychics changing the past? No. The quantum explanation is that before the psychics looked at the data the decays were mere possibilities and, therefore, susceptible to influence. Such a quantum explanation is further supported by a control experiment in which, unbeknownst to the psychics, someone had thoroughly examined the computer printout, in which case the psychics were unable to influence the data.

C. The Quantum Self, the Creative Encounter, and the Flow Experience

Who creates? At the most superficial level, this is easy to answer: the creative, of course. But the creative insight is a phenomenon in which the player is unitive consciousness, the only collapser of quantum possibilities there is. Yet, at a subtler level, the role of our conditioned identity, the ego, cannot be denied either. In this way, it is clear that we need to explore further the quantum measurement process(es) via which the one consciousness becomes many.

Consciousness chooses quantum waves of possibility but only in the presence of brain and awareness. But this leads to the chicken or the egg question: which comes first, choice or awareness? The answer is dependent co-arising. In the event of collapse, the choosing self/subject and awareness (of objects) arise simultaneously. Quantum collapse is self-referential.

The example of the self-referential sentence *I am a liar* will make this clear. In this sentence, the predicate qualifies the subject, as usual, but then the qualification reverberates because the subject also qualifies the predicate: if I am a liar, then I am telling the truth, then I am lying, and so forth. This is called a tangled hierarchy in contrast to the simple hierarchy of ordinary sentences in which the predicate qualifies the subject. But the tangled hierarchy is also our creation, we are its cause; it is we (the unity), from a transcendent level, who see that the subtlety of English grammar is responsible for the paradox. In the process, the sentence acquires self-reference, it talks about itself, it becomes isolated from the rest of the world of discourse.

The infinite von Neumann chain is a tangled hierarchy that the brain simulates in the process of amplifying the submicroscopic quantum possibilities in the brain, an amplification that begins every experience. Transcendent consciousness collapses actuality from the macroscopically distinguishable quantum possibilities that the tangled-hierarchical machinery of the brain offers, but within the tangled hierarchy, there is dependent coarising of the subject and object of self-reference.

The self of this self-reference is universal, and its choice is free (constrained only by the quantum dynamics of the possibilities that are offered). It is also tangled hierarchical. I call this self-identity the *quantum self*. The reflection in the mirror of memory that precedes our ordinary experiences of repeated, learned stimuli converts the creativity of free choice into conditioning and the tangled hierarchy into a simple hierarchy; this was demonstrated in a paper by Mark Mitchell and Amit Goswami in 1992. The resultant self-identity is our conditioned and simple-hierarchical ego.

But the conditioning never reaches 100%, which is the behavioral psychology limit. In that limit all responses are conditioned, the concept of the self is no longer needed, and there is no creativity.

We all operate in the intermediate situation; we are never 100% conditioned with any stimulus, we can always say no to conditioning as demonstrated in experiments by the neurophysiologist Benjamin Libet. We acquire an extensive conditioned repertoire in the process of growing up, but on occasion we are able to jump out of it to engage in creativity. This process of engagement must be looked on as an encounter (as Rollo May has emphasized) between our two self-identities: the ego and the quantum self. This encounter is beautifully depicted by Michelangelo on the ceiling of the Sistine Chapel with Adam (the ego) and God (the quantum self) reaching out to each other.

In response to every stimulus, learned or new, the quantum collapse produces the primary event of the quantum self-experience. For a learned stimulus, the reflection in the mirror of memory produces a series of secondary-collapse events of progressively increasing conditioning that is responsible for the experimentally observed time lag of half a second between the arrival of the stimulus and our verbal response to it. Normally, the primary-collapse event and the intermediate secondary-awareness events remain preconscious in us. In the creative encounter, we literally enter the preconscious and experience ourselves as freer and freer as we move toward the primary awareness event. In this encounter, there is what Csikszentmihalyi calls flow, and there is joy.

Considering this encounter, we can understand why the creative process is not a linear progression of the four stages. In truth, all creatives know that creativity does not begin with preparation; it begins with intuition, an invitation from the quantum self to investigate, an intimation that we can barely hear. Creatives also know that the journey to the creative insight is best served by alternate striving (preparation) and relaxation (unconscious processing). Striving is dominated by our ego modality, whereas relaxation takes us toward the unencumbered being of the quantum self. In the process of this alternation between doing and non-doing, suddenly we are able to quantum jump beyond our conditioned repertoire into new recognition and insight.

The quantum leap, as previously mentioned, is a quantum leap of thought, a quantum collapse in our mental body. Simultaneously, a brain state is collapsed

that makes a representation of the insight. The brain process in creativity also involves a chaotic system and its chaotic destructuring and restructuring.

D. Creativity and Development

Developmental theorists have made important contributions to our understanding of creativity. The quantum theory helps us to integrate all the developmental ideas into a coherent whole.

First, let us briefly consider Piaget's theory, based on his study of child development, with which the quantum view is in complete agreement. Piaget found that ego development is a result of a series of alternate creative and homeostatic stages. In the creative stage, quantum leaps of insight (Piaget called this reflective abstraction) and hierarchical equilibration lead to new contexts in the growing repertoires of the child. During the homeostatic period, the new addition to the child's repertoire is further extended and assimilated through acts of situational problem solving and occasional situational creativity (simple and reciprocal equilibration).

Essentially, developmental theorists try to answer this quintessential question for all of us: Why are some of us creative as adults and others not, whereas all of us are creative as children? Mechanistic trait theorists posit that special traits (for example, the ability of divergent thinking), ultimately traceable to genetic endowment, are responsible for the creativity of the adult. But nobody has ever found any special creative trait gene, and there is some evidence that creatives may acquire the traits that serve their creativity while on the job, as there is no one-to-one correspondence between early traits and later-life creativity. Developmental theorists like Howard Gruber and Howard Gardner say that the individual and his or her development is the crucial thing, and indeed developmental theorists have found some plausible developmental answers to the question of adult creativity.

People who become creative in later life have an early match between their talent and their field of activity. One has to be careful here because there is the phenomenon of burnout. The crucial factor, in addition to talent, is curiosity in a field of activity. Where does curiosity come from? [See TALENT AND CREATIVITY.]

John Briggs has suggested that lifelong curiosity

results from early experiences of *nuance,* a special kind of sensitivity to the universe. Einstein had such an experience in his childhood, as did the novelist Virginia Woolf (read Briggs, in 1990, offered many other examples). What is nuance? In the quantum-within-consciousness view, nuance is a primary-awareness experience of the quantum self in which one wakes up to the creative purpose of the universe, which is for consciousness to see itself in manifestation.

Creative people are also those people who can transform danger into opportunity, an evil cadaver into "something rich and strange" to quote Shakespeare. This is because in our quantum modality even evil is not perceived as separate from us, thus we can transform it.

Developmental theorists make good points, but the points they make are not necessarily contradictory to the idea that anyone can be creative. Just as helpful traits can be learned on the job, the quantum self can be experienced at any age, and with that experience all of us have the ability to wake up to our creative potential.

E. The Role of the Unconscious

The psychologists Sigmund Freud and Carl Jung have emphasized the role of the unconscious as crucial to creativity. Freud believed that creative people put their childhood repressed material to creative use. Mona Lisa's smile came from Leonardo's repressed childhood feelings about his mother. Jung, on the other hand, saw creativity as a drive from the collective unconscious to make repressed archetypal themes conscious.

In the quantum view, childhood trauma may well lead to the exclusion of certain states from conscious collapse in later life. These states then contribute (via unconscious processing, of course) to fantasies and play, which all creatives use.

We can understand Jung's repressed archetypal themes in the same way. For example, males would tend to repress mental states that pertain to the experiences of a female body, for which they have no context. This is the origin of the anima archetype. The repressed-male archetype, the animus, in females can be understood in the same way.

But ultimately we are the whole, and we are capable of collapsing the mental states of all human individuals—past, present, and future. Creativity liberates us from conditioned preferences, personal and collective.

III. INNER CREATIVITY

Creativity researchers have begun to take notice of inner creativity only recently. However, as a culture, we still tend to exclude inner creativity unless we are in spiritual pursuits.

The quantum view of creativity developed here should help change our attitudes toward inner development. As children we are all creative until we reach a homeostatic stage consisting of a repertoire of learned contexts that is sufficient for life's tasks—making a living, romancing a partner, being parents, and so on. But the ego does not have to be the terminus of our creative journey. Self-development can continue beyond ego.

The process of inner creativity is similar to the process of outer creativity, but there are also differences. This is part of the subject of this section.

We have polarized the outer and the inner so much that an entire culture, the East, is identified with explorations of inner creativity, and similarly the West is identified with exploration of outer creativity. But is this polarization necessary or welcome? The final section of this article points out that continuing the journey of creative growth beyond ego through inner creativity enhances our potential for outer creativity. Conversely, engaging in outer creativity puts expressions of inner quantum-self explorations into the outer arena, enriching civilization.

A. The Process of Inner Creativity

The ego presents two basic obstacles to our further growth: conditioning and simple hierarchy. In outer creativity, we temporarily rise above these ego tendencies, encounter the creative and tangled-hierarchical quantum self, and then return to our ego homeostasis. In inner creativity, we learn to stabilize our self-identity beyond ego.

So we may begin with a self-discovery process: What is my pattern, really? What defines my ego? Meditation, watching our thought processes, is, therefore, part and parcel of inner creativity in all of its stages.

Once we uncover the pattern of our conditioning, how do we deal with it? The spiritual traditions of the world have developed four different paths in the journey beyond ego: the path of wisdom, the path of love, the path of right action, and the path of the body.

The path of wisdom is the closest in spirit to outer creativity because we are trying to discover new mental contexts beyond the repertoire of the ego, but they are contexts of social living. We want to transform our being; we cannot do so by trying to live the contexts, true as they may be, discovered by other people. This is what exoteric religions preach; they teach us the moral formulas to live by but do not give us techniques. But the mystical core of all spiritual traditions is different; it fully appreciates the need for a creative approach to wisdom.

The path of the body is also similar to outer creativity, but now creativity of the body is emphasized. Like the mind, our body also settles down in conditioned homeostasis, but most of us in modern times do not identify with the body. Our ego identity is tied almost entirely to our mind. So the strategy here is to shift our identity beyond our mental ego to a more general one that includes the body. The East Indian *hatha yoga* and the Asian martial arts are examples.

The path of love has no parallel in outer creativity. However, it is still a path of inner creativity because it serves the objective of shifting our identity beyond ego. The path of love achieves its objective by practicing tangled hierarchy in relationship with other humans; the object is to undermine the ego's simple hierarchy at its base. So we follow ethical rules to extend our behavior with others beyond our selfishness. Kant gave us the idea of ethics as a categorical imperative; but it is a categorical imperative only to those who are committed to inner creativity. By practicing ethics, by practicing love, neither of which can truly be done within the simple hierarchy of the ego, we discover the "otherness" of others, we become truly tangled hierarchical, and we fall into an identity beyond ego.

The path of action is similar to the path of love, only the emphasis is not on relationship but on action. By pursuing right action, action that emanates from ethics, not from our desires, we discover that our ego is not the cause of our action. In this path, we discover the transcendent inviolate domain beyond our tangled-hierarchical subject–object world.

Within each path, though, we still have to go through the four stages: preparation, unconscious processing, insight, and manifestation. We still have to engage in alternate striving and relaxation. The sudden insight is now given exotic names such as *satori* or *samadhi,* or seeing the inner light. Notice, however, that during manifestation, in outer creativity, we strengthen the ego; in inner creativity, we weaken our ego identity with the ego.

B. Polarization and Integration

As mentioned before, the culture in the West is highly polarized in valuing outer creativity, whereas Eastern culture still values inner creativity over outer. Is this polarization necessary? Not only is the polarization unnecessary but also an emphasis on both inner and outer creativity helps us to actualize our creative potential in both arenas as never before.

No polarization is necessary because both inner and outer activities are aspects of the play of consciousness to see itself, and both are important in this play. When we do not value inner creativity, outer creative actions are often destructive without ethics to guide them. When we do not value outer creativity, the material structure of societies suffers.

In actuality, the techniques of inner creativity can help outer creativity. Anyone who has meditated knows that it helps us both to concentrate and to relax. Being aware of the body makes us more complete and healthy human beings. If we engage in outer creativity motivated by love for humanity, only good can result. Similarly, if we learn to engage in acts of outer creativity with humility (we are not the doer) and without big ego postures, it will only be easier to make the creative quantum leap.

Likewise, we can look forward to the time when people of inner creative wisdom will engage in outer creativity, science, arts, music, and so forth. Music, art, and science, dedicated toward the whole and flowing from the inspiration of wholeness and not just from social accomplishment orientation, will reach unprecedented levels of greatness.

What is the way to educate our children optimally toward creativity? It is to instill in them the idea that creativity, both inner and outer, is important and that it is a lifelong endeavor. Thus, in addition to teaching children how to labor and reason, let us also teach them the value of discontinuous insight and the unconscious processing that precedes it. The three *R*s (reading, writing, and 'rithmetic) are no more important than the three *I*s (insight, intuition, and inspiration).

Bibliography

Goswami, A. (1993). *The self-aware universe: How consciousness creates the material world.* New York: Tarcher/Putnam.

Goswami, A. (1994). *Science within consciousness: Developing a science based on the primacy of consciousness.* Research Report. Sausalito, CA: Institute of Noetic Sciences.

Goswami, A. (1996). Creativity and the quantum: A unified theory of creativity. *Creativity Research Journal, 9,* 47–61.

Goswami, A. (1999). *Quantum creativity.* Cresskill, New Jersey: Hampton Press.

Libet, B. (1985). Unconscious cerebral initiative and the role of conscious will in voluntary action. *The Behavioral and Brain Sciences, 8,* 529–566.

Marcel, A. J. (1980). Conscious and preconscious recognition of polysemous words: Locating the selective effect of prior verbal context. In R. S. Nickerson (Ed.), *Attention and Performance VIII.* Hillsdale, NJ: Erlbaum.

McCarthy, K., & Goswami, A. (1993). CPU or self-reference?: Discerning between cognitive science and quantum functionalist models of mentation. *Journal of Mind and Behavior, 14*(1), 13–26.

Mitchell, M., & Goswami, A. (1992). Quantum mechanics for observer systems. *Physics Essays, 5,* 526–529.

Schmidt, H. (1993). Observation of a psychokinetic effect under highly controllable conditions. *Journal of Parapsychology, 57,* 351–372.

Schizophrenia

David Schuldberg

The University of Montana

Louis A. Sass

Rutgers University

Affective Disorders Mental disorders characterized by disturbances in mood or emotion, either depressed affect or "high," manic emotions. The affective disorders include bipolar affective disorder, characterized by the presence of episodes of mania or hypomania, often with shifts between depressed and elevated or mildly elevated mood. Mania refers to an "up," elated, or irritable mood also marked by energy, grandiosity, and a variety of other characteristics. Milder mood elevation is referred to as *hypomania*.

Modernism The highly innovative and, in many respects, antiromantic movement of literary, artistic, and general cultural endeavor that began around 1900 and extended at least into the early 1950s. Major figures include Kafka, Virginia Woolf, T. S. Eliot, Proust, Picasso, and Matisse.

Negative Symptoms A term coined by the neurologist Hughlings Jackson to refer to neurological symptoms characterized by behavioral deficits. The term has now been expanded to refer to clusters of psychiatric symptoms, and negative symptoms are being given increasing attention in the study of schizophrenia. Examples are anhedonia (lack of pleasure), avolition (lack of will or initiative), social withdrawal, and apathy.

Positive Symptoms Symptoms characterized by "too much" of a certain behavior or aspect of cognition. Examples of such behavioral excesses are hallucinations, delusions, and unusual or bizarre behavior.

Postmodernism The cultural epoch and sensibility of the last 2 or 3 decades, characterized by a philosophical rejection of the primacy of any particular frame of reference and an exaggeration of some aesthetic aspects of modernism (e.g., self-consciousness and irony) and by rejection of other aspects (such as modernism's glorification of aesthetic values and individual genius). Major figures in the arts include Andy Warhol, John Cage, and Thomas Pynchon.

Romanticism A literary, artistic, and philosophical movement whose heyday was during the first half of the 19th century but whose influence continues to be profound. It is characterized by emphasis on individuality, imagination, and the emotions, and often by exaltation of nature and the "primitive."

Schizoaffective Disorder A class of mental disorder defined by the presence of both symptoms of schizophrenia and disturbances in mood that are similar to those in the affective disorders.

Schizophrenia A severe mental disorder defined by disturbed functioning in a number of areas, including perception, behavior, and emotion. The disorder is primarily characterized by disturbances in the form and content of thought, as well as by hallucinations and flat or inappropriate emotional responses.

Schizotypal Personality Disorder A mental disorder less severe than schizophrenia characterized by more mild disturbances in cognition, affect, interpersonal relationships, and behavior. It is often observed in relatives of schizophrenic patients and thus is apparently etiologically related to schizophrenia.

Thought Disorder, Formal Thought Disorder Disturbances in how ideas are generated and linked together, *how* a person thinks. It is distinguished from disturbance in the *content* of thought, which refers to *what* a person thinks or believes. Formal thought disorder is often assessed with the Rorschach inkblot test.

In the past 20 years the role of **SCHIZOPHRENIA** *in understanding creativity has been questioned, and recent attention has turned to the role of emotional states and the affective disorders in creative functioning. This article reviews theoretical and empirical approaches to the study of creativity and schizophrenia; it argues for the relevance of the connections between creative functioning and symptoms in the areas of thought, affect, perception, and behavior. The article emphasizes the importance of specific subtypes of schizophrenia, focuses on the so-called negative schizophrenic symptoms and creativity, and argues that schizophrenia-like characteristics should be viewed as continua rather than as defining dichotomous diagnostic categories. The article also discusses the fit between specific subtypes of schizophrenic symptomatology and specific types of creative endeavor in particular creative domains.*

I. SCOPE OF THIS ARTICLE

This article describes the current status of studying the role of schizophrenia in creativity. It covers differential diagnostic and subtyping issues, including the distinction among the so-called Kraepelinian subtypes of schizophrenia, the role of positive and negative symptoms, and the distinction between schizophrenia and other psychiatric disorders, notably the affective disorders. Brief mention will be made of the possible role of impulse control disorders and antisocial personality disorder. Another issue concerns whether there are additional, healthy psychological factors that distinguish the artist from the schizophrenic individual.

II. THE GENIUS–MADNESS CONNECTION

The pairing of creative genius and insanity goes back at least as far as the ancient Greeks. Plato speaks of divine madness or *enthusiasmos,* and Aristotle believed that "all extraordinary men . . . in philosophy, politics, poetry and the arts are evidently melancholic." It is important not to equate these specific ancient notions of divine mania and melancholia with modern clinical conditions; yet it is clear that since ancient times greatness, especially creative greatness, has been viewed as extraordinary, unusual, sometimes irrational and beyond usual ways of life, somewhat alien, and out of reach of ordinary conscious understanding, in a way akin to madness. This article will argue that this conjunction also has particular relevance in the context of the modern and postmodern era.

The associating of insanity and creativity is also linked to more general philosophical, spiritual, and empirical questions regarding the relationship between illness or suffering and creativity. This connection was explored by Sophocles in *Philoctetes,* the story of a master archer who possesses a bow that cannot miss, whose presence is essential for the well-being of the Greeks, but who is also afflicted with a chronic injury, a horribly wounded foot that causes intense suffering and leads his comrades to abandon him on a remote island. This story has become a central metaphor for the link between disorder and creativity, a connection developed in Edmund Wilson's essay "The Wound and the Bow," where he argues that wound and bow cannot be separated. As will become clear, this metaphor can be given either a romanticist reading, where the primary experience of suffering is the stuff of art, or a more modernist one, in which genius is based on social disjunction, isolation, and alienation. (In this article *modernism* refers to the innovative art, literature, and thought of the first half of this century, and *postmodernism* refers to the cultural productions of the past few decades.)

A. Why the Connection with Schizophrenia?

As noted, the earliest formulations of the connection between creativity and madness appear to have focused on what were then termed *melancholia* and *mania,* conditions that might loosely be classified as related to affective disorders. Historically, the systematic study of links between creative activity and mental disorder goes back to the early part of this century. It was in the 1960s that the emphasis of the "genius and madness" question shifted more decisively to schizophrenia. This focus was abetted by the broad and lax American diagnostic criteria and practices then in use. [*See* MAD GENIUS CONTROVERSY.]

There are indeed strong conceptual, phenomenological, as well as empirical reasons for focusing on schizophrenia. Theory and research have emphasized the similarities between the thought processes of creative individuals and of persons diagnosed as schizophrenic or with less intense and pervasive *schizotypal* symptoms. A primary reason for this is that a hallmark of creativity is originality, the thinking of new ideas—sometimes unusual, at variance with cultural norms, or even shocking—and the combining of these ideas in new and surprising ways. For its part, schizophrenia's core symptoms involve disorders of either the form or the content of thought. The fluent generation of new and possibly useful ideas in creative divergent thinking, a central feature of creative intelligence in Guilford's theory, is difficult to distinguish conceptually from the novel productivity of thought disorder, cited as a defining characteristic of the schizophrenia syndrome. However, Guilford himself argued that creative thinking is essentially rational. [*See* DIVERGENT THINKING.]

Difficulty in making distinctions between the products of art and madness reflects the social embeddedness of such judgments. To complicate the issue, much creative work is like "outsider art" and not appreciated in its own time. Van Gogh is often cited in this regard, and a similar case can be made for revolutionary innovation in science and other fields.

Schizophrenia is also characterized by disorders of perception, predominantly auditory hallucinations. Until recent clarifications in diagnostic practices, there was also a tendency to associate visual and even tactile hallucinations with schizophrenia, even though it is now well known that these are more likely to be indicative of an organic mental disorder. In this way, schizophrenia was also linked conceptually to visual imagination.

B. Recent Interest in Affective Disorders

Dating from the pathbreaking work published in the 1970s by Nancy Andreasen and Kaye Redfield Jamison, the study of creativity and psychopathology's emphasis has shifted from schizophrenia to the affective disorders, particularly bipolar affective disorder. It is not uncommon to see eminent individuals from various historical eras who were diagnosed with putative schizophrenia on early lists of diagnosable creative individuals appearing on later lists as having suspected affective disorder. This shift is partially due to changing nosological fashion, increasing diagnostic sophistication, the use of narrower, more specific criteria for schizophrenia and the broadening of the category of bipolar illness, and a general shift in interest among clinicians and psychopathology researchers toward bipolar affective disorder. Part of this change is tied to the demonstrated efficacy and availability of Lithium as a treatment for bipolar disorder. [*See* AFFECTIVE DISORDERS.]

C. Schizophrenia and the Romantic Vision of the Creative Process

Images of schizophrenia have appealed to specifically romantic conceptions of both creativity and madness. Psychoanalytic approaches have emphasized the primary process thinking of the person diagnosed with schizophrenia, the supposedly regressed quality of the schizophrenic subject's thought and feeling, the primitive character of schizophrenic reasoning and ideas, and the apparent breakthrough of unedited free fantasy uncontrolled by a watchful ego. This psychodynamic formulation recalls romanticist notions of primitivism, naturalism, direct access to experience, porous ego boundaries, union and communion with the environment, solitude, and the glory of suffering; its adequacy as a characterization of schizophrenia is questionable at best, for it fails to reflect the centrality of the schizophrenic individual's sense of inner fragmentation and lack of attunement with emotions, bodily existence, and the social world, and it also contains questionable assumptions about returning to earlier stages of development. Romanticist notions of creativity and the arts came to dominance in the 19th century and continue to be influential up to the present day, not only in psychology and psychiatry but more broadly in the public mind and in the more traditional pockets of artistic and literary endeavor.

D. Romanticism and Affective Disorder

Romanticist notions are also present in our conceptions of mood disorders, but here there is a closer fit to the actual phenomenology of the disorders. The romanticist vision of the creative process fits well with the temperament and cognitive style of persons who suffer from affective disorders or who have a predominantly cyclothymic temperament, consisting of alternating states of relatively mild mania and depression. The latter sort of temperament is described in the classic work of Ernst Kretschmer as characterized by spontaneity, ready emotional reactivity, and a harmonious sense of unity both with the world and within oneself. Postromantic notions of the creative process, as well as increasingly sober appraisals of the painful reality of the experience of mental disorder, have suggested a revision of the genius-madness connection and a reconsideration of the roles of bipolar disorder and schizophrenia.

E. Schizotypal Characteristics, Negative Symptoms, and Antiromantic Sentiment

One might well expect a romantic vision of the creative process to overlap more either with symptoms of the affective disorders or with the so-called positive psychotic symptoms (e.g., delusions, hallucinations, disordered thought, bizarre behavior) emphasized until very recently in the diagnosis of schizophrenia, rather than with the less dramatic characteristics that are more noticeable in schizoid, schizotypal, or negative-symptom schizophrenic individuals. However, recent criticisms of romanticism suggest a reevaluation of these latter attributes and their possible connections with creativity.

Note that in this article the terms *negative* and *positive* symptoms are meant only to refer to syndromal clusters of psychotic-like experiences and behaviors roughly characterizable as behavioral deficits and excesses. We do not mean to endorse a model of degeneration or disinhibition of the nervous system as ex-plaining schizophrenic behavior and phenomenology, a model that is implied by the original neurologists' usage of the terms *positive* and *negative* symptoms.

F. Antiromanticism: Modernist and Postmodernist Conceptions of Creativity

For more than a hundred years many of the most influential and innovative artists, writers, and critics have been sharply critical of the organicism, personalism, and emotivism central to the romantics, with their valorizing of nature, process, and spontaneity over calculation and self-consciousness and their yearning to overcome the Cartesian separation of subject from object. Neither Baudelaire nor Mallarme, the key proto-modernists (or proto-postmodernists) of the 19th century, considered spontaneous, irrational processes of free fantasy to be the key to artistic creativity.

Baudelaire emphasized instead the role of dispassionate deliberation and conscious craft, placing artifice above nature in his hierarchy of aesthetic worth. Mallarme called on the poet to "cede his initiative to words," to eliminate his own, personal contribution and signature by standing back and letting words clash and interact like objects independent of the poet's intentions. Both of these artists and theorists were precursors to the sometimes virulent antiromanticism of T. E. Hulme and Ezra Pound, key formulators of a modernist aesthetic that recoiled from what they saw as the mushy emotivism inherent in the pathetic fallacy of romantic subjectivism.

Antiromanticism is, if anything, even more prominent in so-called postmodernist art and theory, where thinkers and theoreticians such as Jacques Derrida and Paul de Man and artists such as Andy Warhol have banished every vestige of romanticism, rejecting any aspiration toward the ideals of authenticity or unity of the self, passionate spontaneity, or immediate contact with the world. Instead, they have come to view forms of alienation or detachment as the sine qua non of significant aesthetic achievement. Included among the targets of the postmodern critique is, in fact, the very notion of creativity itself, which is seen as overemphasizing the flawed and even sentimentalized notions of spontaneity, originality, and individual genius.

Both the possibly mad person and the possibly mis-understood artist are often viewed as outsiders, in some sense antisocial, and as deviants existing on the fringes of society or conventional, dominant culture. This image is also a component of the individualism in the romantic vision of the artist. The parallel is especially strong for artists or scientists working with genre-breaking forms or originating new movements.

Later this article will consider the implications of modernist and postmodernist conceptions of art and aesthetics for the traditional connections drawn between schizophrenia and creativity. We shall argue for a revival of interest in the implications of schizophrenia-like experience for a variety of fields and creative endeavors and for a reexamination of the roles of social and perceptual detachment and alienation, as well as of the negative symptoms of withdrawal, apathy, and anhedonia.

III. PROBLEMS WITH SCHIZOPHRENIA AS A DIAGNOSTIC CATEGORY

Clarifying the connections between schizophrenia and creativity has been hampered by loose diagnostic criteria and clinical practices for assigning the label of schizophrenia. For example, until relatively recently, American clinicians could and did diagnose schizophrenia even when a patient evidenced prominent symptoms of affective disorder, thus mixing together groups of patients that would currently be considered bipolar or perhaps schizoaffective with those that would be considered schizophrenic. In addition, schizophrenia also served as something of a placeholder for generic or unclassified forms of madness, deviance, or bizarreness.

A. The Spectrum Concept

Similar problems arose from the use of the term *schizophrenia spectrum* to refer to a variety of disorders presumed to be syndromally or etiologically related to schizophrenia. Much work on genetic and other etiological factors has used an overly broad concept of the schizophrenia spectrum, one that refers to a variety of psychotic and psychotic-like syndromes including bipolar disorder. Choices regarding how much is included within the spectrum can be very important for the results of research on such topics as genetic versus environmental contributions to the disorder. Such diagnostic lumping obscures the issue of whether cre-

ativity and creative cognition are associated more with affective disorders or with schizophrenia.

The term *spectrum* can have two meanings. One implies that there is a continuum of severity ranging from normality (however defined), through subclinical symptoms, to less severe psychopathology (for example, schizotypal personality disorder), to the severe mental disorders. In this *vertical* spectrum of degree of severity, more severe and less disabling disorders are seen as being on a continuum with each other and with normality. The second meaning of *spectrum* suggests that different kinds of psychopathology lie in a continuous dimensional space of classification, that diagnostic groups are not rigid or exclusive. In this *horizontal* view of the spectrum, different disorders (e.g., bipolar disorder and schizophrenia) are seen as related and sometimes overlapping.

This notion of a horizontal schizophrenia spectrum, like the category of schizoaffective disorder, may actually reflect the reality and prevalence of mixed types of mental disorder evidencing several classes of symptoms. Some researchers in psychopathology do believe that a common factor is responsible for a broad variety of severe mental disorders; H. J. Eysenck, for example, stated that schizophrenia and the affective disorders should not be separated. In addition, the notion of a vertical schizophrenia spectrum allows a focus on symptoms as continuous traits and helps in the understanding of psychological processes underlying both creativity and psychopathology.

IV. RESEARCH ON SCHIZOPHRENIA AND CREATIVITY

Conceptual linkages of creativity and mental disorder have pointed to a variety of different possible causal relationships, including psychopathology causing creativity, creativity leading to psychopathology, a third variable causing both, as well as other plausible models involving multiple factors. Such models are not specific to any single form of psychopathology. Without even considering causal relationships between different factors, the same cognitive variables may be viewed either as problem-solving processes or evaluated negatively in clinical terms. This can make it difficult to separate them as independent and dependent variables. [*See* FIVE-PART TYPOLOGY.]

This section reviews the literature on creativity and psychopathology then focuses on studies of clinical and creative traits. It then turns to the role of disordered cognition. Many traditional views of schizophrenia, especially in psychoanalysis, have viewed it as a primitive and essentially Dionysian state, as a return to infantile forms of irrationality and symbiotic union, and as an overwhelming of the ego by the polymorphous passions of the id. Such a vision is, in fact, more applicable to certain phases of affective, especially manic, disorders; schizophrenia's relevance to creativity is likely to include other types of symptoms and experiences.

A. Empirical Studies

1. Studies of Eminence

Empirical studies of the connection between creativity and psychopathology have used a number of methodologies. This first looks for evidence of diagnosable mental disorders in populations of eminent individuals. The occurrence of psychopathology in creative individuals, as well as their relatives, has been documented extensively, both historically and in contemporary populations.

For individuals who lived in the past, the person is generally assessed via biographical materials, and creativity is defined with reference to achieved fame or well-recognized achievement; contemporary individuals may be nominated by mentors, teachers, or peers. Psychopathology is evaluated, often retrospectively, by categorical diagnosis of mental disorder or *spectrum* disorder, or by the presence of specific psychiatric symptoms; with living individuals, scores on psychological tests that measure symptoms are often used (the latter approach will be discussed further under trait approaches to research). This research has found symptoms of affective disorders and schizophrenia, unconventional or antisocial behavior, and alcohol and substance abuse in eminent and creative individuals and also sometimes in their relatives. Clearly not all of these symptoms are related to schizophrenia or the schizophrenia spectrum.

Eminence studies and biographical research suffer from several methodological problems. First, psychopathology is often assessed at a distance, through contemporaries' reports, analysis of biographical materials, and sometimes the subject's own productions. Such assessments are vulnerable to selectivity and retrospective biases. Secondly, the diagnostic criteria employed are often loose and inconsistent. Finally, there is a problem of lack of controls. With whom is the historically eminent or contemporarily celebrated individual to be compared? Relatively little work has been done on base rates of psychopathology, symptoms, odd behavior, family problems, and environmental tribulations in noneminent people, and, with some exceptions, few study biographies of so-called ordinary people. Thus, it is often unclear whether the sometimes lurid, dramatic behaviors and histories of the creative and eminent set them apart from the noncreative, whose histories may be unknown. Nevertheless, there is some controlled research in this area that has found elevated rates of mental disorder in both creative individuals and their relatives when contrasted with comparison groups. [*See* EMINENCE.]

2. Family Studies

It is well known that relatives of patients—and sometimes patients themselves—can achieve greatly, despite (or perhaps because of) a presumably inherited predisposition for schizophrenia not expressed at clinical levels in the "well" relatives. Family study research explores creativity and eminence in relatives of psychiatric patients or of schizophrenic subjects in particular. This research has been conducted in Iceland and Denmark, Massachusetts and Oregon, using case registers or a search for patients or relatives. In some studies adopted-away children are examined as part of studies of the heritability of mental disorders.

Along with a higher incidence of spectrum disorders, relatives of schizophrenic patients have shown greater degrees of creativity and attainment than comparison groups. Heston found that nearly half of the foster-home raised offspring of a group of schizophrenic mothers not only had successful adaptations but demonstrated imaginative and artistic talents not found in control children. Similar research has examined the accomplishments and activities of adult relatives.

This research also has potential methodological problems. Although blind assessment is generally maintained for the diagnosis of relatives, it is not clear that blindness continues during the assessment of creativity or eminence, which has sometimes been evaluated after the core parts of a study have been conducted. As with other research, this work has generally used broad diagnostic categories for the assessment of relatives and leaves open the criticism that the research is not specific to schizophrenia. [*See* FAMILIES AND CREATIVITY.]

3. Shared Trait Research

A third methodological approach examines stylistic similarities and shared characteristics in members of creative and psychiatric populations. It relies on the psychometric assessment of personality traits, patterns of interests, and motivational, affective, cognitive, and behavioral styles rather than on diagnostic categorization or the assessment of symptomatic behaviors alone. Characteristics found to be prominent in both creative and pathological groups include psychoticism, impulsivity, various forms of affect, and different types of clinical and subclinical psychopathology, including schizotypal traits, narcissistic features, hypomania, depression, aggression, and substance use.

Research on personality traits overlaps with diagnosis-related categorical research on schizotypy and schizotypal symptoms; some of the characteristics assessed are similar to the defining features of schizoid or schizotypal personality disorder. There are continuities between schizophrenia, less severe syndromes, and subclinical styles representing what Paul Meehl has termed *schizotypy,* less pronounced than either schizophrenia or generally schizotypal personality disorder, and hypothesized to express a genetic predisposition to schizophrenia.

Schizotypy is often measured using pencil-and-paper psychological tests, including scales from the Minnesota Multiphasic Personality Inventory (MMPI), the Wisconsin Scales of Hypothetical Psychosis-proneness developed by Loren J. and Jean P. Chapman and their colleagues, the Psychoticism ("P") scale from the Eysenck Personality Questionnaire, and other measures. A number of investigators have found associations between psychometric indices of schizotypy and assessments of creativity based on actual activities or scores on creativity tests. H. J. Eysenck has centered a theory of the origins of creativity on psychoticism; unfortunately, the definition and measurement of this trait is broad and contaminated with self-reported impulsive and antisocial characteristics.

Some researchers have noted that, unlike some members of clinical groups, creative individuals show both signs of strong health and signs of psychopathology,

providing support for a two-factor theory. Aristotle himself felt that for a melancholic individual to be a genius required a delicate balance of different humors or types of bile. It is important to attend to disjunction as well as overlap, to possible mitigating and differentiating factors that can lead to creativity or exemplary functioning. One candidate for such a healthy characteristic is Frank Barron's measure of ego strength, which he has found to distinguish members of some creative groups from schizophrenic subjects, despite both groups' average high scores on a psychometric indicator of schizotypy.

A weakness of trait studies is that they often use a shotgun approach, looking for creative subjects' elevations across a broad range of scales. This atheoretical methodology leaves it unclear whether trait differences are centrally related to creativity or reflect possibly irrelevant or secondary additional factors. There are also concerns about how these characteristics are defined and measured. Nevertheless, in evaluating the relative strength of the eminence, family, and shared trait studies, it appears that the research on schizophrenia and creativity most strongly supports a specific connection for traits related to schizophrenia, rather than for categorical diagnosis.

4. The Continuum Point of View

An important implication of shared trait studies is their grounding in continuum views of health and psychopathology. It is also important to treat creativity as a dimensional, nondichotomous variable and to look at everyday, noneminent creativity. This approach has been advanced greatly by Ruth Richards and her collaborators. An additional advantage of continuum approaches is that they lead naturally to dynamic conceptualizations of the vicissitudes, the ebb and flow of creativity—as well as psychopathology and normal functioning—in individuals over time, in the course of daily life. [*See* EVERYDAY CREATIVITY.]

The remainder of this section emphasizes cognitive characteristics relevant to schizophrenia. With some important exceptions that emphasize disjunctions, research has uncovered overlap in the cognitive styles of creative and schizophrenic individuals. The cognitive symptoms of schizophrenia are roughly divided into two main categories: disorders in the content and the form of thought.

Disordered thought content refers to ideas or beliefs generally considered false or delusional, deviant, unusual, or bizarre. However, schizophrenia is not the only disorder with delusions; grandiose and self-referential delusions, more limited in scope, can appear in such disorders as DSM-IV delusional disorder. Delusions can occur in affective disorders as well, where they are congruent with the mood that is the central symptom of the disorder.

Disorders of the form of thought have traditionally been viewed as the hallmark of schizophrenia. This *formal thought disorder* refers to reasoning, how ideas are linked together, combined, occur in sequence, follow from one another, and are communicated linguistically via peculiar language. Formal thought disorder has also been documented in affective disorder patients; a current research question concerns the specificity of certain types of thought disorder to certain classes of psychopathology.

This article makes two main points regarding thought disorder and creativity: First, both positive-symptom and negative-symptom thought disorder are important in the creative process, and differentiating types of unusual cognition may illuminate the understanding of varieties of creative activity as well. Second, positive-symptom thought disorder can be separated into subtypes characteristic of bipolar disorder or schizophrenia.

Formal thought disorder is assessed in several ways. Probably the oldest is via the clinical interview, sometimes augmented with structured questions and accompanying ratings. It is also assessed with psychological tests, both clinical ones and laboratory procedures. A good deal of research on deviant thought and language employs the Rorschach inkblot test. This work, originating with Rorschach himself, owes its greatest debt to David Rapaport who, working with colleagues at the Menninger Clinic in the 1940s, developed a list of deviant verbalizations that form the basis for today's Rorschach thought disorder scoring systems.

B. Types of Cognition: Schizophrenic and Creative

1. So-called Primitive Cognition

As noted, psychodynamic theories of schizophrenia have emphasized the role of instinctual, primary process thinking—which also occurs in the dreams, fantasy, and free associations of normal subjects, is rich in sexual and aggressive content and obeys its own nonrational laws of combination and symbol formation. It is noteworthy for its independence of secondary process logic and mediation by language commonly associated with waking life.

Creative individuals' hypothesized and observed access to nonrational modes of producing and synthesizing novel concepts has been explained in terms of "regression in the service of the ego," a phrase that implies that return to primitive modes of experience is the sole source of inspiration and that the creative individual—in contrast to the person diagnosed as schizophrenic—accesses primary process material in a controlled way, rather than as an involuntary or unremitting experience. Research that has coded primary process content in both Rorschach responses and in other tasks has noted elevated levels of such material in members of creative groups.

2. Loose Associations

Some of the most enduring descriptions of schizophrenic thinking have been framed using associative theories of how ideas are generated and connected. Thus, the ideas that schizophrenic individuals generate, either as responses to external stimuli or in reaction to their own previous ideas, are seen as odd, unusual, and statistically uncommon. Research has indeed demonstrated that schizophrenic subjects have more unusual and nonnormative responses to word association tests and appear to lose the regulative link between ideas in conversation. "Loose association" is sometimes contrasted with "derailment" and "flight of ideas" (described next), generally observed in the thought and language of manic patients.

Creative thinking also involves forming new ideas and progressing from the old and ordinary to the new and original. Unusual and original associations have been observed in creative individuals, and Mednick's theory of creativity focuses on the generation of remote or distant associates.

3. Flight of Ideas and Derailment

Related to the idea of loose association is the concept of *flight of ideas,* which has to do with productive richness, rapid generation of new ideas, and fluent, pressured speech, generally assessed through clinical interviews. A related concept is *derailment,* a conversation's jumping the tracks and leaving a topic. Work in psycholinguistics involves the coherence and cohesion of speech, discourse's adherence to a topic and use of linking elements.

Although flight of ideas, derailment, and deficits in cohesion have been documented in the speech of schizophrenic patients, some researchers now believe that flight of ideas and derailment are more characteristic of mania. Similar rapid generation of ideas is also observed in creative brainstorming.

4. Logic and Reasoning

It was long thought that schizophrenic patients were deficient in the ability to employ if-then reasoning, instead using *paleologic,* or *primitive* logic. However, normal subjects have similar difficulties in using syllogisms correctly. Peculiar-sounding forms of reasoning, often having a non sequitur quality (and often referred to as *autistic logic*), are not uncommon in schizophrenia, but it is difficult to say whether these reflect disorders of thinking per se as opposed to disturbances of language or communication. Unusual and unconventional logic or sequencing of ideas may also be observed in some creative genres, for example, in the flow of poetic images and language and in creative brainstorming in search of solutions to seemingly insoluble problems. However, there is disagreement regarding the similarity of poetic and schizophrenic language.

5. Category Formation: Overinclusive Thinking

Some research has found that schizophrenic subjects form concepts that are too large and overgeneralized, with loose or fluid conceptual boundaries. Subjects will include in their classifications items that others would consider too different to belong, overly personal, or unrelated to the rules for membership. This is also referred to as *allusive thinking,* which has been linked to creativity. So-called overinclusion may, in many cases, best be understood as resulting from an extreme perspectivism or relativism characteristic of many schizophrenics. Other research has found that manic subjects may also be overinclusive in their thinking and that some schizophrenic subjects are underinclusive; styles of category formation appear to differ in different subtypes of schizophrenia.

6. Set Formation and Set Maintenance

Some theories, such as David Shakow's theory of loss of "segmental set," emphasize schizophrenic subjects' difficulties maintaining a consistent cognitive or attentional set toward a task. This may be related to more recent cognitive and neurobiological theories of core deficits in the biological substrates of information processing, resulting, for example, in disturbances of immediate or working memory or of the so-called comparator function. It is possible that such loosening of sets is related to originality in the creation of new styles.

7. Use of Contextual Information

There is evidence that schizophrenic individuals show impaired ability to attend to important and potentially useful incidental information; other research also shows that they are distracted by irrelevant and peripheral information and incorporate it inappropriately. Still other research suggests that their awareness of peripheral information may sometimes facilitate creative problem solving. These contradictory types of responding, both related to set maintenance, may point to different subtypes of cognitive style, with negative-symptom subjects perseverative and positive-symptom subjects having difficulties forming and maintaining consistent sets. Both distractibility and exaggerated focus are also relevant to creative activity and may correspond to the inspiration and consolidation phases of creative work.

8. Personalized Thinking and Interpretation

Responses of schizophrenic individuals tend to include personal material and are sometimes self-referential, as if the subject takes the test materials as somehow meant for him or her. This represents a place where formal thought disorder (personalized reasoning) can lead to disordered thought content (delusions). Similar humanizing of the meaning of environmental stimuli can be related to artistic production, for example in anthropomorphic or animistic approaches to the physical world.

9. Concrete and Abstract Thinking

Kurt Goldstein's influential theory asserts that schizophrenic thinking is concrete; subjects become "hung up" in the perceptual aspects of a stimulus and are also unable to generalize to abstract categories. Concrete thinking contrasts in some respects with overinclusive category formation, although overinclusive categorizing can sometimes include inappropriate objects based on concrete perceptual or functional attributes.

Attention to the raw sensory appearance of an object can assist in artistic vision and is related to a number of specifically modern philosophical endeavors that seek the nature of immanent or unmediated experience. However, persons prone to these sometimes literalist modes of perception need not be incapable of abstraction. Indeed, schizophrenic subjects' ideas may sometimes be *overly* abstract or cosmic, and this may obstruct common-sense or everyday forms of thinking more than their literalness does.

10. Autistic Thinking

Finally, starting with Bleuler, schizophrenic thinking has been described as autistic, private, alone, unshared, and perhaps unsharable. The picture of the misunderstood genius or the thinker whose ideas are out of step with his or her time is parallel to this.

C. How Specific Is Thought Disorder to Schizophrenia?

Recent work with both laboratory and Rorschach measures of thought disorder has found comparably high levels in bipolar manic and in schizophrenic patients. As noted, manic patients are more characterized by pressure of speech, derailment, combinatory and overinclusive thinking, as well as a tendency to engage the examiner interpersonally. It is precisely fluent and overproductive disturbances that are most akin to the processes of creativity. In contrast, specifically schizophrenic thought disorder is more likely to include the categories of poverty of speech, poverty of content of speech, underinclusive reasoning, absurdity, confusion, and loss of conceptual boundaries in "contamination" and "fluidity," as well as use of unusual and highly idiosyncratic language. An unresolved issue involves evaluating the degree to which these different types of thought disorder are present or absent in different types of creativity. It has been suggested that specifically schizophrenic forms are not primitive or regressive in nature, but rather have a hyperreflexive

quality; they have a special affinity with the highly perspectival and often hyper-self-conscious and detached modes of thought characteristic of the modernism and postmodernism of the past hundred years.

V. DIAGNOSTIC CONTRASTS

A. Subtypes of Schizophrenia

1. Kraepelinian Subtypes

The original subtypes of schizophrenia, first introduced by Emil Kraepelin, have been very influential and are carried into the DSM-IV. These subtypes include the paranoid form, characterized by hypervigilance, delusions, and relatively intact intellectual functioning; the catatonic subtype, characterized by disorders of movement and behavior; the hebephrenic or disorganized subtype, with silliness, inappropriate and often seemingly ironic affect, and bizarre behavior; and the simple or undifferentiated subtype, traditionally defined by what are now called negative symptoms of apathy, withdrawal, and paucity of speech.

The grandiosity and odd ideas of paranoid schizophrenia overlap with the image of the creator who is self-absorbed, concerned with grand themes, and possibly tortured by personal involvement with big ideas. The hebephrenic or disorganized subtype corresponds to images of the archetypal "fool" and also to the giddy and nonconforming creator who behaves in highly unusual ways, finding wisdom in unconventionality, irony, or silliness. Catatonic and simple schizophrenia have—until now—seemed less relevant to the creativity and schizophrenia question. The symptoms that characterize these two Kraepelinian subtypes are discussed in more detail next.

2. Positive versus Negative Symptoms and Creativity

As noted, the schizophrenia-creativity connection has emphasized the sometimes flamboyant positive symptoms of hallucinatory perceptual experience, bizarre ideas, unusual content of thought, and positive formal thought disorder, not the withdrawal and apathy of negative symptoms. However, there are also important negative-symptom forms of thought and language disorder, which include poverty of content, concreteness, literalness, and contamination or super-imposition of concepts. There are also schizophrenic affective symptoms, notably flat affect (absence of visible emotions), anhedonia (lack of experienced pleasure), and inappropriate affect. The latter refers to affect that seems self-contradictory or unrelated to what the subject is actually experiencing or describing (often involving a kind of irony) and is especially prominent in disorganized schizophrenia. There is also a developing interest in the possible contributions of "schizoid" characteristics and lifestyle, including detachment and social disengagement, to creativity in certain realms.

The study of negative symptoms represents a very important area and is congruent with current interests of schizophrenia researchers and new interest in pharmacological treatment of this subset of symptoms, often formerly considered treatment resistant. Negative symptoms can also be connected with characteristics of gifted or high-functioning autistic or Aspberger's syndrome individuals.

How one views the possible affinities between creativity and disorders in the so-called schizophrenia spectrum will depend on how one envisions these clinical disorders. The romantic vision of madness does not capture the distinctive features or overall qualitative feel of schizoid or schizophrenic existence, whose central characteristics actually include flattened or peculiar affect, apathy, withdrawal, or seeming indifference to real-world events, a general sense of inner disharmony or discordance, and what the French psychiatrist Eugene Minkowski aptly termed "loss of vital contact with reality" or what the German phenomenological psychiatrist Wolfgang Blankenburg called the "loss of natural self-evidence." These features are indeed closely bound up with the negative symptoms of schizophrenia.

Generally, these symptoms have been understood as defects or deficit states and rather straightforward losses or absences of psychological processes or capacities. On such a view, they hardly seem conducive to creative production or sophisticated forms of mental life. But negative symptoms can also be viewed as positively contributing to and even defining a form of life that has important implications for the creativity question. As we shall see, they may have a special affinity with characteristically modern and postmodern forms of creativity.

3. Interpersonal Symptoms

Any form of psychopathological symptom will have interpersonal ramifications. John Strauss and William Carpenter, who have elaborated the construct of positive and negative symptoms, have also argued for a separate interpersonal cluster. Factor analytic work on symptoms has suggested an interpersonal and a "bizarreness" cluster, both relatively independent of positive and negative symptom clusters. These considerations also lead back to the relational and social embeddedness of both creativity and psychopathology. Despite the romantic view of the artist as solitary misfit, art and other creative endeavors clearly have cultural implications and are highly dependent on social contexts.

B. Schizophrenia versus the Affective Disorders

Recent work within psychopathology has emphasized the prognostic utility and treatment implications of the symptoms of bipolar disorder and questioned the predictive validity of schizophrenic symptoms. At the same time empirical research by Andreasen, Jamison, and Richards has demonstrated strikingly high levels of association between affective disorders and symptoms and indices of creative potential or achievement, along with surprisingly low associations with the schizophrenic disorders.

The relatively weak association between schizophrenic symptoms and creative functioning may hold true at a general level, particularly if one focuses on romantic and postromantic styles, emphasizes literary work of a narrative or lyrical sort, and treats worldly success and widespread public endorsement as a prime criterion of creative achievement. Success and recognition, after all, depend in large measure on a number of factors extrinsic to the inherent cogency or originality of one's work, including the instinct to deviate just enough but not too much from social expectations and norms, the ability to share the concerns of one's audience, and the skills to promote oneself by networking. At most of these tasks schizophrenic and schizotypal individuals are likely to be at a disadvantage.

However, despite the methodological problems and sometimes inconclusive findings noted earlier, the evidence for creative potential or originality in schizoid, schizotypal, or schizothymic individuals, as well as in individuals who might best be diagnosed as schizoaffective as opposed to schizophrenic per se, is in fact reasonably strong; this evidence comes both from family studies and from biographical work focusing on modern and postmodern creators. Moreover, schizotypal traits have a fairly strong statistical association with creativity, although it admittedly may be difficult to separate the variance in creativity accounted for by schizotypal as opposed to hypomanic or sometimes impulsive characteristics. Researchers have studied the correlation of schizotypal and hypomanic traits, measured at subclinical levels by such instruments as the Wisconsin scales of hypothetical psychosis-proneness and the MMPI. The Wisconsin scales of Perceptual aberration (measuring distortions in perception, particularly involving the body) and Magical ideation (tapping superstitious and subclinical minidelusions), as well as the Hypomanic traits scale, are correlated with both paper-and-pencil and interview indices of creative traits and real-life activities. In addition, conceptual analysis of achievement in specific areas strongly suggests the relevance of schizotypal and schizoid symptoms to certain forms of creativity. Finally, cognitive and affective disorders may not represent neatly separable categories; this argues both for the continuum view and for increased attention to schizoaffective disorders.

VI. SUBTYPES OF CREATIVITY

The relationship between creativity and the schizophrenia spectrum needs to be reexamined in light of the diversity of what is considered creative in different fields, using different media, in various genres, separate stylistic traditions, across divergent settings and cultural contexts, and during particular historical epochs. Creativity seems to be an instance of what Wittgenstein termed a "family resemblance" concept, a grouping based on an open set of overlapping features, no one of which need be present in all instances. What merits the honorific "creative" will vary according to the context of production and the perspective in which it is seen, interpreted, and judged.

This article will not deal with all the relevant forms of diversity, but it is worth noting that the notions of creativity dominant in contemporary psychological re-

search and theorizing remain highly derivative of conceptions of the "creative imagination" that crystallized in European, especially English and German, romanticism in the first decades of the 19th century. This tradition viewed art and literary productivity as both the paradigm of creative endeavor and the epitome of human worth. This is also associated with an expressivist conception of art, in contrast to the mimetic or didactic conceptions more common in previous centuries in the West. This romantic view is also distinct from the objectivist conception that came to prominence with 20th-century modernism, involving a focus on the artwork itself rather than its message, audience, or the artist's inspiration. Creativity need not, then, be understood in a romanticist way; other conceptions of creativity may have closer affinities with the central features of the schizophrenic condition.

In *Madness and Modernism,* Louis A. Sass argued that most persons diagnosable in the schizophrenia spectrum are, in fact, characterized by a pervasive alienation or detachment from the lived body, their emotions, and the social and practical world, an alienation that is combined with forms of introversion involving hyperintense and often dysfunctional forms of self-consciousness (hyperreflexivity). As he pointed out, these features are also characteristic of the modernist and postmodernist sensibility. Seven interrelated features of the modernist and postmodernist stance have close parallels in both the experience and the expression of schizophrenia-spectrum individuals:

1. An adversarial stance, a tendency to defy authority, flout or ignore convention, and in general go against the grain of natural habit. This is also related to antisocial and impulsive symptoms characteristic of other disorders.

2. Perspectivism and relativism, sometimes having a disconcerting or dizzying effect as one perspective collapses into the next. This is apparent in the fluidity, slippage, or contamination of schizophrenic thinking and perception and may overlap with both positive and negative-symptom thought disorder.

3. A fragmentation and passivization of the ego, a loss of the self's sense of unity and of its capacity for voluntary action or effective interaction with the objective world—a feature overtly present in many of Schneider's first-rank symptoms of schizophrenia and

also implicated in the apathy and avolition of negative-symptom schizophrenia.

4. A sense that the external world is somehow subjectivized and unreal or else devoid of value and significance for the observer. This is parallel to the psychiatric symptoms of derealization, withdrawal, and interpersonal disconnection (autism).

5. Rejection or loss of a sense of temporal flow or narrative unity in favor of more static or spatialized ways of organizing the world. The critic Joseph Frank speaks of "spatial form" in modern art and literature, the psychiatrist Minkowski of the "morbid geometrism" of schizophrenic experience and expression, which tends to lack both the dynamism and the forms of narrative progression and organization characteristic of normal individuals.

6. Forms of intense self-reference that move the formal structures or underlying presuppositions of thought and action to the foreground, sometimes at the expense of more normal, worldly commitments and concerns. The art critic Clement Greenberg identified modernism with "the intensification, almost the exacerbation of [the] self-critical tendency that began with Kant," with a cultural tendency "to turn around and question [one's] own foundations." Analogous tendencies are manifest in schizophrenic hyperreflexivity, self-questioning, preoccupation with cosmic meaning, concern about ultimate ends, and dysfunctional intellectualizing.

7. Extreme and pervasive detachment or emotional distancing, sometimes accompanied by an all-encompassing, often disconcerting irony; this is also manifest in the flatness, incongruity, or inappropriateness of affect found in schizophrenic patients. An example is provided by the hospitalized patient quoted by Forrest, Hay, and Kushner who concluded a classically thought-disordered definition of *cigarette* by stating, "You can use them for trade with natives, so I believe, or . . . in this country you can use them for smoking."

The importance of features such as these may help explain an observation made by Karl Jaspers, namely, that it appears that a remarkable number of schizophrenic individuals have had a significant influence on Western culture since around 1800, whereas hardly any seem to have been of comparable cultural importance in earlier centuries. The recent empirical research on the mania-creativity association is impressive, but it does not minimize the profound influence on modern culture and sensibility that has been exerted by individuals with probable schizophrenic diagnoses such as the poet Holderlin, the writer and man of the theater Antonin Artaud, and the dancer Vaslav Nijinsky, and by severely schizotypal (or possibly schizophrenic) individuals such as Alfred Jarry and Raymond Roussel. Others seem to have had schizoaffective disorder, such as Strindberg and Gerard de Nerval, or to have had markedly schizoid or schizothymic temperaments, for example, Baudelaire, Nietzsche, Giorgio de Chirico, Salvador Dali, Kafka, Beckett, and Wittgenstein. In none of these cases can the contribution of the individual be said to have occurred *in spite of* these personal tendencies; in each the distinctive aesthetic or philosophical contribution actually reflects one or another aspect of what can be termed schizoid or schizotypal propensities and worldview.

VII. TOWARD SPECIFICITY IN DEFINING CREATIVITY, PSYCHOPATHOLOGY, AND HEALTH

In conclusion, it is crucial to consider issues of match or fit in studying psychopathology and creativity, fit between cognitive and emotional styles and types of creative endeavors or forms of eminence. Creativity and leadership have been studied in writers, poets, and architects, in people working in the graphic arts, performance and the theater, science, mathematics, philosophy, business, and in positions of political and military leadership. However, despite notable contributions by authors such as Arnold Ludwig, relatively little is still known about the precise factors differentiating among those who do creative work in different fields, nor about the cognitive and affective processes involved in their activities. Recent conceptualizations of both creativity and psychopathology have focused on increased specificity in defining both healthy and pathological characteristics, on better measurement and methodology, and on seeking the psychological processes underlying the functioning of both normal and disturbed individuals.

Both theoretical and empirical work in these areas holds promise of providing better understanding of the innovative and improvisational activities that play such a central part both in the large-scale development of human culture as well as in more mundane ways in people's everyday healthy responses to setback and stress.

Bibliography

American Psychiatric Association. (1994). *Diagnostic and statistical manual of mental disorders* (4th ed.). Washington, DC.

Barron, F. (1972). *Artists in the making.* New York: Seminar Press.

Engell, J. (1981). *The creative imagination: Enlightenment to romanticism.* Cambridge, MA: Harvard University Press.

Eysenck, H. J. (1993). Creativity and personality: Suggestions for a theory. *Psychological Inquiry, 4,* 147–178 (as well as responses in the rest of this issue of *Psychological Inquiry*).

Goodwin, F. K., & Jamison, K. R. (Eds.). (1990). *Manic-depressive illness* (especially chaps. 11 and 14). New York: Oxford University Press.

Prentky, R. A. (1989). Creativity and psychopathology: Gamboling at the seat of madness. In J. A. Glover, R. R. Ronning, & C. R. Reynolds (Eds.), *Handbook of creativity* (chap. 15, pp. 243–270). New York: Plenum.

Richards, R. L. (1981). Relationships between creativity and psychopathology: An evaluation and interpretation of the evidence. *Genetic Psychology Monographs, 103,* 261–324.

Rothenberg, A. A. (1990). *Creativity and madness: New findings and old stereotypes.* Baltimore: The Johns Hopkins University Press.

Sass, L. A. (1992/1994). *Madness and modernism: Insanity in the light of modern art, literature, and thought.* New York: Basic Books. (Harvard University Press edition, 1994)

Schuldberg, D. (1990). Schizotypal and hypomanic traits, creativity, and psychological health. *Creativity Research Journal, 3,* 219–231. [Reprinted in M. A. Runco & R. Richards (Eds.) (1997), *Eminent creativity, everyday creativity, and health,* chap. 9, pp. 157–172. Greenwich, CT: Ablex.]

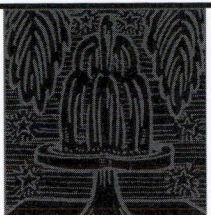

Robert Schumann

1810–1856

Composer and writer of 148 published works

Works include compositions for piano: *Papillons, Carnaval, Fantasie*; piano and orchestra: *Concerto in A minor*; vocal music: *Liederkreis, Dichterliebe, Frauenliebe und Leben*; orchestral music: *Spring Symphony, Rhenish Symphony*; chamber music: *Quintet in E flat major for piano and strings*

Lise Deschamps Ostwald

University of California, San Francisco

ROBERT SCHUMANN was a German pianist, founder and editor of the Neue Zeitschrift für Musik *(New Journal for Music), a conductor, and a composer. His published works range from miniature pieces for piano to virtuoso works on a grand scale. He composed powerful symphonic works and song-cycles of great depth and beauty. He wrote compelling chamber music for various instruments, oratorio, and operas. Schumann was one of the great figures of the Romantic era, a contemporary of Mendelssohn, Wagner, Chopin, Verdi, and Liszt, composers of such diverse style yet all born within four years of each other in the German, Polish, Italian and Hungarian principalities. However, Schumann fought against serious mental problems all his life. While he experienced surges of creativity, both musical and literary, his recurring depressions, inner turmoil, and episodes of madness led to a suicidal attempt to drown himself in the Rhine and a final incarceration in an asylum near Bonn.*

Robert Schumann. Used with permission from Scala/Art Resource, NY.

I. BACKGROUND

Robert Schumann was born June 8, 1810, in the small town of Zwickau, Saxony, halfway between Dresden, the artistic court capital, and Leipzig, the scholarly center of Germany. Robert's mother, Johanne Christiane Schnabel, was the daughter of a military surgeon. His father, August Schumann, the son of a Lutheran minister, was a prolific author and founder of Schumann Brothers Publishing Company. The year Robert was conceived, 1809, was a stressful time as August was mourning the death of both his father and his newborn daughter. August and Johanne Christiane had a daughter nine months after their marriage, then three sons in 1799, 1801, 1805, followed by a baby girl who was either stillborn or died soon after birth, a year before Robert was born. His mother, close to menopause and severely depressed by the loss of this infant daughter, may have wished for another girl. Schumann's father was also prone to melancholia and suffered from chronic abdominal problems.

In 1813, the province of Saxony experienced famine and devastation. A typhus epidemic broke out and eliminated 9% of the population. Schumann's mother was one of the survivors. As she had to be quarantined, Robert was separated from his mother for 2½ years and was placed with a surrogate mother. In his autobiography written at age 15, Schumann vividly recalled nights fraught with fear and nightmares.

Schumann began music lessons at age 7 with a church organist, Johann Gottfried Kuntsch (1775–1855). He soon assimilated all the rudiments of harmony and keyboard technique this teacher possessed. Schumann's creative awakening was manifest as early as 1817–1818 in both literary and musical compositions.

II. FLORESTAN AND EUSEBIUS—LITERATURE OR MUSIC

Schumann was an isolated child in a middle-class family with no tradition for musical professionalism. He was endowed with a wonderful talent for improvisation, which he used to capture people's manners and idiosyncrasies. Robert's education was enhanced by his father's private library, which contained approximately 4000 books, a definite stimulus to intellectual development. He discovered a passion for literature comparable to his love of music. It created a lasting conflict, trying to achieve verbal mastery to please his father while striving to communicate with his mother through musical sounds. This duality was later expressed when, at the age of 21, he created two imaginary companions, "Florestan" representing Schumann's masculine, outgoing self, and "Eusebius" the shy, withdrawn, and sensitive alter ego.

Two traumatic events contributed to Schumann's first serious depression at age fifteen, the death of his sister followed by that of his father. Schumann's sister, Emilie, 14 years older than Robert, suffered from a chronic skin disease as well as from emotional problems. It is believed that she either drowned herself or jumped from a window. This seems to have precipitated in Robert an inescapable "longing to throw myself into the Rhine." Later, in his early twenties, Schumann attempted to leap out of a fifth-story window, which led to a fear of heights as a possible self-protective mechanism. In August 1826, 10 months after the suicide of his sister Emilie, Schumann's father died suddenly at the age of 53. As a way to alleviate his sorrow and emulate his father's literary proficiency, Schumann began to keep daily records in his diary. He also wrote poetry and novels, but most of these adolescent works remained unfinished.

III. JURISPRUDENCE AND DEBAUCHERY—STUDENT YEARS IN LEIPZIG AND HEIDELBERG

In 1828, Schumann decided to join his friend Emil Fleichsig at the University of Leipzig. After much inner torment, he chose to go into jurisprudence, despite thinking it cold and dry. In this setting Schumann, shortly before his 18th birthday, experienced his first dissociative attack. "I seemed to be losing my mind: I did have my mind, yet I thought I had lost it. I had actually gone mad." This momentary disorganization could have been caused by overwhelming stress. At 18, he discovered the euphoric state of alcoholic intoxication and got "high" not only from alcohol but from other substances such as nicotine and caffeine. Schumann became aware of inner voices, or auditory expressions of diverse emotions often of a sensuous nature. Homosexuality is a frequent topic in his diary.

In Leipzig, Schumann wrote songs based on poems by Justinius Kerner (1786–1862). He was more and more drawn to music and to the charismatic piano teacher, Friedrich Wieck. This well-known pedagogue guaranteed his piano method, citing as best evidence his highly proficient 9-year old daughter, Clara, whom he wished to mold into the world's foremost pianist. Clara was an unusual child who did not use words until the age of four. When she first encountered Robert in 1828, the childish 9-year old was obviously smitten by the handsome yet taciturn 18-year old pianist.

Schumann's lessons with Wieck were not altogether satisfactory. Wieck was a demanding task-master who expected the aspiring pianist-composer to practice hours of technical exercises. The recalcitrant student's strange way of composing is vividly described by his roommate Fleichsig, "He always puffed on cigars, and the smoke irritated his eyes . . . he liked to whistle the melody of the songs, or rather hum them through his lips, and whistling with cigar in mouth was just about impossible." In 1829, Schumann's most daring composition was a quartet for piano and strings, which he performed in weekly chamber music evenings. Discussions and animated conversations followed the performances, but Schumann did not participate. His lack of verbal communication often perplexed his colleagues.

To alleviate his restlessness and recurring bouts of depression, Schumann decided to move to Heidelberg. In letters to his mother, he expressed growing concerns, "My lodgings face the insane asylum on the right and the Catholic church on the left, so that I'm really in doubt whether one is supposed to go crazy or become Catholic." Though he wrote glowingly about his law studies, in truth he was relying on drinking beer to cope with loneliness and frustration. Twice he fell asleep with a cigar, setting his bed on fire.

IV. EARLY PIANO COMPOSITIONS— RETURN TO LEIPZIG

After vacationing in Italy, Schumann's motivation to study law seemed to have totally disappeared. Piano playing constituted his main occupation, and improvisation never ceased to elicit his peer's admiration. Young Schumann did best as a composer of miniature pieces which he appropriately called "*Papillons*" (*Butterflies*). Tonal analogues between words and music will be found in several of Schumann's later compositions. This work's brilliant virtuoso style may reflect Schumann's way of playing at the time. He may have changed the tonality of his "Toccata" to make the double-notes and stretches easier, for he later acknowledged numbness in a finger of his right hand, a psychophysiological problem which would hamper and finally destroy his career as a piano virtuoso. Deeply perturbed, sounds haunted him during the night creating auditory hallucinations which would become an inherent part of his lifelong battle with madness. For the first time on March 18, 1830, he admits to hovering in a suicidal frame of mind, "longing to throw myself into the Rhine."

Schumann, dissatisfied with his musical progress though recognizing his superiority over Heidelberg pianists, wished to renew contact with his former teacher Friedrich Wieck. He pleaded with his mother to intercede with Wieck on his behalf. Music seemed his only mode of salvation. The response from Wieck not only surprised Schumann's mother but added to her confusion as to her son's chosen career, "I give my pledge to make your son Robert, with his talent and his fantasy, into one of the greatest living pianists within three years."

With limited means, Schumann relocated to Leipzig, where Wieck rented him space in his large house and placed him on a 6-month probation. Schumann diligently practiced 6 to 7 hours a day, although he felt depressed and constrained in this environment. Wieck's alternating crude contempt and exorbitant praise toward Schumann and his cruel behavior to his children were most disturbing.

V. MUSIC CRITIC— HAND PROBLEM

Schumann's two imaginary friends, Florestan and Eusebius, gave voice to musical as well as literary ideas. A product of his vivid imagination, they are suggestive of a latent psychotic tendency. As he neared his 21st birthday, music was relegated to second place and literature absorbed him more and more. He relished the works of E. T. A. Hoffman, and wrote poetry in the style of Schiller and Petrarch. Schumann began his career as a music critic with a startling and now famous review of Chopin "Hats off, Gentlemen, a Genius!" which was published by the *Allgemeine Musikalische Zeitung* in December 1831. His novel approach to music criticism aroused much attention from his readers while composers gained publicity and greater recognition from Schumann's writings.

Though Schumann made progress in his creative work—studying counterpoint, publishing his writings—a regressive pull toward states of terror and confusion held him back and contaminated his level of interaction with people. His speech was scant and constrained. It is interesting to note that Schumann's hand problem coincided with the rising fame of his young friend, Clara Wieck. Schumann possibly had a case of tendonitis, and perhaps nerve entrapment, a result of long hours of strenuous practice, known as overuse injury which often afflicts musicians who overtax their musculature. This resolved his conflict between becoming a pianist or a composer. As his state of mind improved, he composed a set of *Intermezzi* (opus 4), published in 1833. While improvising at the piano he kept playing with a four-note sequence, C F G C, a theme suggested by Clara which he incorporated in his *Impromptu on a theme by Clara Wieck* (opus 5). This marked the first of many musical references to Clara in his compositions.

VI. ACUTE BREAKDOWN

In July 1833, Schumann contracted malaria, had to be quarantined, and lost a good deal of weight. His letters show an unmistakable yearning for Clara, "a chain of sparks now attracts us." This was the beginning of a long, romantic, and stressful relationship for both Schumann and Clara. It alienated Schumann from Wieck for years to come. While Schumann lay ill with malaria, his brother Julius was dying from tuberculosis. Schumann could not overcome his fear of death and did not even go home when his brother

died, in August 1833. He withdrew into social isolation, immersing himself in creative work. In a self-therapeutic manner, he decided to consolidate all his previous writings in what would become a New Journal for Music, *Neue Zeitschrift für Musik*. Instead of the usual introspective entries in his diary, he began writing for the public at large. This journal gained universal recognition.

Two months later the death of Rosalie, his favorite sister-in-law, shattered his precarious equilibrium and caused an acute breakdown. Suicide and madness were his constant thoughts. Fortunately, another regenerating idea lifted him out of his depression, the founding of the Davidsbund, a fraternity of artists and musicians.

VII. ROMANTIC RELATIONSHIPS

As Clara Wieck's devotion to Schumann intensified, her father's vigilance escalated. He sent his daughter to Dresden for 6 months to study composition. Meanwhile, Schumann was ostensibly attracted to another of Wieck's students, Ernestine von Fricken. Clara took notice of this affair when she returned from Dresden, feeling sad and disheartened. Ernestine's father, Baron von Fricken, was an amateur flutist, and sought Schumann's advice on a *Theme and Variations* he had written. Schumann gallantly incorporated the Baron's theme in a magnificent piano work which he called *Etudes Symphoniques* (opus 13). This simple theme, beautifully harmonized, is succeeded by numerous etudes or variations suggesting orchestral instruments. The scope and texture of this gigantic work is reminiscent of a large orchestra, and the tonal resources of the piano are used by Schumann in ways previously unheard of. It remains one of the most astounding musical compositions of the 19th century.

After introducing Ernestine to his mother in Zwickau, and even though Frau Schumann clearly favored Clara, Schumann gave an engagement ring to Ernestine. However, when the Baron approved the wedding plans, Schumann bluntly rebuked her. This was another manifestation of his ambivalence toward the women he loved. It has often been thought that Robert rejected Ernestine after the disclosure of her illegitimacy. In reality, Schumann abandoned Ernestine long before he found out that she was an adopted, illegitimate daughter, and might not become the baron's heiress. She remained a loyal and helpful friend during Schumann's subsequent legal battle over another woman, five years later.

Schumann became the sole proprietor and main contributor of the now biweekly publication *Neue Zeitschrift für Musik*. During this period he created some of his most important musical works including his *Carnaval* (opus 9), a work of impressive originality and immediate appeal. Schumann had hoped that Clara would love and play his *Carnaval*, but she maintained a cool distance until his affair with Ernestine ended. Schumann noted in his diary, "disengagement from Ernestine, beautiful hours in Clara's arms."

VIII. SEPARATION AND CREATIVITY

Deeply alarmed by Schumann's change of affection, Wieck hurriedly dispatched Clara to Dresden in early 1836. An exchange of letters was futile, as Wieck intercepted and eliminated all of their correspondence. Shortly after his mother died, Schumann went to visit Clara during her father's absence, and both declared their loyalty and desire never to be separated from each other. Schumann began to picture Wieck as a future benevolent father-in-law. This was not a role Wieck intended to assume. On the contrary, he threatened to shoot Schumann if he came close to his daughter. Clara, the submissive child-pupil not yet 17, obeyed her father for a year and a half. She did not perform Schumann's works in her recitals, and there was total silence until August 1837. Schumann, deeply hurt, intensified his allusions to her in his compositions, quoting her own themes, using letters of her name in descending patterns, transforming thoughts into tones. This resulted in the birth of four transcendental works conceived in a period of great upheaval, the *Sonatas* (opus 11 and 22), *Fantasie* (opus 17), and *Grand Sonata* (opus 14).

Sustained by his faith in the value of these last works, Schumann hoped that Wieck would finally acknowledge his merit as a composer and potential son-in-law. On Clara's 18th birthday, September 1837, Robert gathered the courage to send his marriage proposal to her father who responded in negative and cruel terms. At the height of despair, Schumann produced another masterpiece, his most autobiographical composition, the *Davidsbündler Dances* (opus 6), which are individually signed Florestan, or Eusebius, or both. Schumann attached a motto on the title page:

At all times
Pleasure and grief go together
Keep faith in pleasure, and
Meet grief with courage.

At age 27, Schumann finally entered the road to maturity, and now he wished to pursue this road with his betrothed. During Clara's absence, Schumann reviewed as music critic no less than 81 compositions for his *Review of Leipzig's Musical Life in the Winter of 1837–1838*. His *Phantasiestücke* (*Fantasy Pieces*) (opus 12), for piano, have a remarkable structural symmetry and soon became favorites of Clara who often performed them to great acclaim. After which Schumann created *Humoresque* (opus 20), *Novelletten* (opus 21), *Kinderszenen* (*Scenes from Childhood*) and *Kreisleriana* (opus 15 and 16), *Faschingsschwank aus Wien* (*Carnival of Vienna*) (opus 26), and *Nachtstücke* (*Night Pieces*) (opus 23). He left Vienna on April 5, 1839 and arrived in Zwickau four days after his brother Eduardo's death.

IX. LEGALISTIC DISSENTIONS— THE FIGHT FOR CLARA

Friedrich Wieck, writing secretively to a good friend of Clara in Paris, disclosed plans to instigate legal proceedings against Robert and Clara. Using his legal background, Schumann prepared an affidavit. He would request legal permission to marry Clara if Wieck persisted in his refusal to settle out of court. After unsuccessful attempts to negotiate, Schumann filed his complaint on July 16, 1839.

In the courtroom, Clara was quite distraught and rather sympathetic to her father. Schumann escalated his defense, and obtained documents from the town council and local police asserting his good, honorable and decent citizenship. When the court reconvened, all charges were dropped except that of drunkenness.

X. SONGS AND POETRY

After a decade of writing essentially music for piano solo, Schumann embarked on a year of song writing of the highest caliber, placing him alongside his revered Schubert. The literary skills Schumann acquired from his father could flow comfortably with the sensitivity for vocal sounds nurtured by his mother. Schumann continued to express both his romantic genius and his emotional disturbances through his Lieder.

His first *Song-Cycle Liederkreis* (opus 24), reflect Schumann's fears, dreams, and melancholic state. The next cycle *Myrthen* (*Myrtles*) is a collection of 26 *Lieder,* one for each letter of the alphabet, mostly dealing with brides, grooms, flowers and marriages, intended to be a wedding present for Clara. After a brief reunion in Berlin, where Mendelssohn sang Schumann's songs accompanied by Clara, another lengthy separation from Clara gave birth to the most celebrated songs, the sublime *Liederkreis* (opus 39) and the *Dichterliebe* (opus 48), written in isolation. While Schumann's pen continued to produce an array of incredible songs, such as *Frauenliebe und Leben* (*Woman's Love and Life*) (opus 42), Wieck was on the verge of capitulating. When he finally renounced further legal proceedings, Schumann was jubilant.

XI. MARRIAGE AND SYMPHONIES

Awaiting the verdict of the high court in Dresden, Schumann chose the day before Clara's 21st birthday, September 12, 1840 for their marriage in the village church of Schöenefeld, near Leipzig. They began writing a household and marriage diary together and collaborated on *The Springtime of Love* (opus 37).

Soon Clara became pregnant, and this incited Robert to a flurry of creative activity. In four days he wrote the first draft of his *Symphony in B-flat major* (*Spring*), (opus 38). A month later, the score was completed. The premiere of this exultant symphony, March 31, 1841, was an immediate success and later that year, their daughter, Marie, was born on September first.

In 1842, Schumann began composing three string quartets in a frenzy of enthusiasm. Clara followed suit by becoming pregnant again. This may have inspired

Schumann to create one of the pivotal chamber music works of the 19th century, the grand *Quintet for Piano and Strings in E-flat major* (opus 44), followed by *Quartet for Piano and Strings* (opus 47).

Looking back on Schumann's productivity since his marriage, the years 1840 through 1843 are most impressive for their musical creations, notwithstanding other significant responsibilities such as a newspaper to publish, and a family to provide for. On July 24, 1843, Elise, their second daughter was born. She was christened on the day that Schumann started teaching at the new Conservatory of Music, founded by Mendelssohn in Leipzig. His teaching was unsuccessful and lasted less than a year. The end of 1843 also marks the invitation from Wieck for a reconciliation in Dresden.

XII. TRAVELS TO RUSSIA— RELOCATING IN DRESDEN

In 1844, Schumann and Clara embarked on what would be a triumphant concert tour of Russia for Clara, but a demeaning experience for Schumann. He was mainly acknowledged as Clara Schumann's husband. At social events, he remained silent and reserved. Schumann was a poor traveler and 4 months of horrendous schedules soon affected his moods. He was incapable of working under those stressful conditions. Following the trip to Russia, Schumann experienced one of his most severe depressions. A move to Dresden seemed advisable and Schumann, no longer interested in publishing his *New Journal,* decided to sell it. In December 1844, the Schumann household moved to Dresden. Schumann consulted a physician to treat his "violent nerve attacks," also his blurred vision and nearsightedness.

A third daughter, Julie, was born on March 11, 1845. As the voices increased in his home, Schumann wrote more and more contrapuntal music, including six "Fugues" based on the name of Bach (opus 60). Though Schumann lived only five years in Dresden where he had to endure daily visits from "the old man" (Wieck), and despite a massive depression, this was one of his most productive periods. His social demeanor, however, was deteriorating and he became more and more withdrawn. There was a halt in musical inspiration until shortly before Christmas when new ideas surfaced in Schumann's mind with great speed and intensity. In three days he completed the first movement of his C major *Symphony*. Afterward, Schumann felt much better.

In February 1846 Schumann's first son and fourth child, Emil, was born. Four days later, Schumann attempted to orchestrate his symphony; it progressed at a snail's pace. The full score was completed by the end of the year, despite a constant ringing in his ears. Concerts in Vienna, Prague, and Berlin were poorly attended and Schumann's conducting was so frustrating for the musicians that Clara rehearsed them from the piano.

Upon returning to Dresden in 1847, Schumann's creative thoughts turned to opera. The orchestral overture to *Genoveva* is one of Schumann's most successful works. However, the death of their 16-month-old son, the fatal collapse of Mendelssohn's sister while playing the piano, followed by the loss of their friend and mentor, Felix Mendelssohn, plunged both Schumann and Clara into a deep state of mourning. Nevertheless, Schumann was able to compose two *Piano Trios* (opus 66 and 80), interrupted by the birth of another son, Ludwig, on January 20, 1848.

In 1849, an abundance of works emerged from Schumann's creative genius, instrumental works for clarinet and piano, horn and piano, horns and orchestra, violoncello and piano, vocal works for chorus, women's voices, vocal quartet and piano, and *Song Album for the Young* (opus 79), a counterpart to his pianistic *Album for the Young*.

XIII. POLITICAL UPHEAVAL— ESCAPE FROM DRESDEN

In 1848 and 1849 political uprisings in Germany aroused Schumann's feelings and may have contributed to what was a most prolific period. He wrote many patriotic songs for chorus and organized a choral society. When the revolution broke out in Dresden, Schumann and Clara were forced to hide in the house until they managed to escape through the garden gate with only their eldest daughter. Later, Clara, 7 months pregnant, walked several kilometers in open fields during the night to rescue the other children. Concealed from the upheaval, Robert composed *Five Hunting Songs*

(opus 137) for double male chorus and four horns, and "Motet" (opus 93).

On June 12, the Schumann family headed back to Dresden where soon Schumann wrote sketches for the *Requiem for Mignon* (opus 98b) from poems by Goëthe. July saw the completion of three scenes for his Faust opera and the birth of their sixth child, Ferdinand, and in August Schumann completed *Four Songs for Soprano and Tenor* (opus 78), which included a tender lullaby. In September, Schumann wrote *Twelve Four-Hand Piano Pieces for Little and Big Children* (opus 85) closing with Schumann's favorite, a hauntingly beautiful and hushed expression of nocturnal repose, "Evening Song."

As this incessant flow of lyrical and powerful music continued, Schumann's fame was on the upsurge.

XIV. DÜSSELDORF— THE DECLINING YEARS

In November 1849 Schumann was offered and accepted the post of music director in Düsseldorf. The Schumann family was warmly welcomed to Düsseldorf and serenaded by the Choral Society. In the midst of directing orchestral and church concerts, Schumann managed to write one of his most compelling works, the *Concerto for Violoncello and Orchestra* (opus 129), followed by his *Rhenish Symphony no. 3* (opus 97). Perhaps as an antidote to his unrewarding work with his orchestra, his interests shifted to chamber music. In 1851 he wrote *Fairy-Pictures for Viola and Piano* (opus 113), *Sonatas for Violin and Piano* (opus 105 and opus 121), and *Trio for Violin, Cello, and Piano* (opus 110). He also produced new music for the piano, five four-handed pieces for children, and wrote 23 songs plus a number of longer choral works. If these were declining years, they were far from unproductive as Schumann created one-third of his total compositions in Düsseldorf. His ineptness as a conductor became more apparent, and the musicians began voicing their discontent. Another daughter, Eugenie, was born on December 1, 1851.

While vacationing in the Rhineland, and following a strenuous walk in the mountains, Schumann fainted, and a physician was consulted. Dr. Müller, also a director of the Music Society, advised Schumann to restrict his conducting and allow his assistant Julius Tausch to direct more concerts. He recommended 18 riverbath treatments in the cold Rhine. In mid-September 1852, the Schumanns moved into a spacious townhouse, the last residence they shared in Düsseldorf.

XV. BRAHMS, JOACHIM, AND THE SCHUMANNS

On September 30, 1853, a young man of 20, blond and blue-eyed, stood like an apparition on the threshold of the Schumann home. His name was Johannes Brahms, and he came from Hamburg for a brief visit that extended to 1 month. Schumann and Clara were both immensely taken by the angelic young man and his creative talent. In November 1853, Schumann, exhausted and demoralized, relinquished all of his responsibilities as music director. On the brink of a breakdown he was able to produce the *FAE Sonata* for Joachim, a set of *Fairy Tales* (opus 132), and *Songs of Early Morning* (opus 133), inspired by Brahms.

On their last journey together, in Hanover, the Schumanns wanted to visit their "two young demons" Joachim and Brahms. While Clara had great success playing at the court of George V, Schumann's new works for violin, the *Fantasy* and the *Sonata,* were badly criticized and contributed to "anger and restless nights." They were back in Düsseldorf in February 1854. On February 12, constant hallucinations of glorious and unearthly music threatened to "destroy his mind," wrote Clara. In his psychotic delirium Schumann wrote variations on a theme that he believed Schubert had sent him.

XVI. DESCENT INTO MADNESS

On February 26 Schumann, fearing he might harm Clara, suddenly announced that he had to go to the insane asylum. The next morning, a worried Clara pleaded with Schumann not to leave her. While consulting with two physicians, she asked their 12-year-old daughter, Marie, to sit with her father. The child, not realizing how sick her father was, let him leave for his bedroom. Schumann slipped out of the house unnoticed, threw himself into the Rhine River. The disoriented and water-soaked Schumann was forcibly brought home and five days later, on March 4, 1854, Schumann entered a private asylum in Endenich, near Bonn. This separation from home and family would

last 2½ years until his death. Clara, who was in the late stage of her ninth pregnancy, gave her husband a bouquet of flowers for this last journey. She never saw him again until two days before he died.

XVII. OBSCURITY AND DARKNESS

Few friends visited Schumann at Endenich except for Joachim and Brahms. While Schumann was hospitalized, Clara gave birth to their eighth and last child, a boy called Felix in memory of Mendelssohn. Missing the stimulating presence of his family, Schumann hallucinated an imaginary community of his own. In a deplorable psychotic state, Schumann declined rapidly. He became bedridden and refused to eat, and was unable to control his twitching limbs. On July 29, 1856, Schumann took leave of this world.

An autopsy was performed by Drs. Richarz and Peters with inconclusive findings. The limitations of brain dissecting technique in 1856 made it difficult to affirm if Schumann suffered from temporal lobe epilepsy, syphilis, or some other organic disease. However, no inflammatory cells are mentioned. The medical reports of Schumann's last years in the mental institution, previously thought to have been lost or secretly guarded, have been made available in January 1994 by Professor Reimann. The notes written by Dr. Richarz emphasize the decline of Schumann, his violent behavior and loss of control. The report mentions the composer's belief in the destruction of Düsseldorf, his ordained burning in hell, his being poisoned and his infection with syphilis in 1831. Delusions, hallucinations and lucid observations were noted by Dr. Richarz, as well as the patient's burning of letters from his wife, which he denied. According to the research of Dr. Peter Ostwald, the most comprehensive diagnosis for Schumann's psychiatric illness is that of "a major affective disorder." His extreme mood fluctuations stemmed from hereditary as well as environmental factors. A "narcissistic personality" describes other aspects of his disturbance—isolation, divided self, and withdrawal. In analyzing the problems leading to his hospitalization, the *schizo-affective disorder* is most probable. These are simply words to describe an illness, but we must look to the sublime music of Robert Schumann to do justice to the 19th century's greatest tone-poet, a quintessential romantic who transcended the tragic events of his life.

Bibliography

Academie der Künste, Archiv-Blätter 1, (1994). *The last years of Robert Schumann's life.* Berlin.

Escande, M. (1985). *Aperçus sur la vie, la création musicale et les troubles psychiques de Robert Schumann.* Sem. Hôpital, 61, no. 14, 948–955, Paris.

Ostwald, P. F. (1985). *Schumann, The inner voices of a musical genius.* Boston: Northeastern University Press.

Schumann, R., & Clara. (1993). *The marriage diaries of Robert & Clara Schumann.* (P. F. Ostwald, Trans.). Boston: Northeastern University Press. (Originally published in German, 1987, as *Robert Schumann: Tagebücher, 1836–1854,* G. Nauhaus [Ed.]. Deutscher Verlag für Musik, Leipzig)

Science

Kevin Dunbar

McGill University

Confirmation Bias Confirmation bias is the tendency that people have to seek evidence that confirms their hypothesis rather than to seek evidence that could disconfirm their hypothesis.

Distributed Reasoning Distributed reasoning is when different components of a reasoning episode are conducted by different people rather than being conducted by one person.

In Vitro/In Vivo Cognition In vivo refers to investigating scientists as they think and reason in naturalistic settings such as lab meetings. In vitro refers to investigating scientific thinking abilities of subjects in controlled experiments. The in vivo/in vitro distinction is borrowed from biology. In biology, in vivo usually refers to investigating a biological process in the live organism, whereas in vitro refers to investigating some aspect of the organism, often in a test tube or petri dish.

Problem Space A problem space is all the possible states that a problem could have as well as all the operations that can be applied to get from one state in the problem space to another state.

*Most researchers see scientific creativity as being composed of the same mental processes that guide all other forms of creativity. What makes **SCIENCE** different is that there is a vast theoretical, technical, and experimental knowledge that creative scientific ideas must either extend or more rarely supplant. Furthermore there are sets of norms and scientific practices that any new scientific discovery must abide by before it is accepted by other scientists as being a discovery. Roughly speaking, contemporary research on scientific creativity falls under the four following headings: historical analyses of great discoveries, in vivo analyses of scientists as they reason in their laboratories, cognitive analysis of people performing scientifically challenging tasks, and creative reasoning of groups of scientists. These different types of approaches are a microcosm of the different ways that creativity in general is investigated.*

I. OVERVIEW

Scientific creativity has been of central concern to all who work on creativity, and it is a topic that has been tackled by almost every major area in psychology ranging from psychoanalytic accounts of creativity, to Gestalt, social, cognitive, and psychometric approaches. Why is there this great interest in the creativity of scientists? One part of the reason is that scientists speak of their research and discoveries in the same terms that are used by other creative thinkers such as poets and artists. We hear of sudden flashes of insight, accidental discoveries, lone scientists striving against their peers, and so forth. Like most creative processes, scientific creativity is shrouded in mystery. The other part of the reason for the vast interest in scientific creativity is that science is highly regarded in our society and by discovering the key components of scientific creativity it should be possible to foster scientific discovery. One political event that generated much research on scientific creativity was the race between the United States and the former Soviet Union to put a man in space. The politicians turned toward psychologists and asked them to devise ways of identifying and fostering scientific creativity that could help the United States be first in the space race. This resulted in a renaissance in the psychometric approach to creativity. More recently, the cognitive approach to creativity has uncovered many of the important components of scientific thinking and creativity through experimentation, historical analyses, and in vivo investigations of live scientists.

II. HISTORICAL INVESTIGATIONS OF THE CREATIVE SCIENTIST

One of the most common ways of investigating scientific creativity has been to analyze either the life of a creative scientist or how a scientist made an important scientific discovery. The goal of the analyses is to determine the mental processes that a particular scientist used to make a discovery or discoveries. Researchers use autobiographies, lab notebooks, and interviews with scientists and attempt to determine the strategies that the scientist used to make a discovery. For example, many researchers on scientific creativity have used James Watson's autobiographical "Double Helix" to build an account of scientific creativity. Another common figure used in research on scientific creativity has been Albert Einstein. Early work using this approach was initiated by Gestalt psychologists such as Max Wertheimer. In his studies of Einstein, Wertheimer concluded that the way Einstein restructured the problems in physics were critical to his discoveries. Although this approach was innovative, one of its main problems was that Gestalt psychologists did not have

a detailed theory of how knowledge is represented in the mind or an account of the specific mechanisms by which knowledge changes over time. The more recent cognitive approach to scientific creativity made it possible to propose specific models of both the conscious and unconscious components of knowledge representation that form the basis of contemporary accounts of thinking and reasoning. Others have provided historical accounts of scientific discoveries that give detailed models of how creative scientists represented and changed their knowledge while making a discovery. [*See* DISCOVERY; EINSTEIN, ALBERT.]

Nancy Nersessian has conducted extensive analyses of Faraday's notebooks and has argued that the key to understanding his discoveries is in terms of his use of mental models. These mental models are mental representations that have spatial and temporal relationships to objects and processes in the real world. By mapping out the types of mental models that Faraday used and showing how these types of models shaped the discoveries that Faraday made, it is possible to give a precise account of the mental processes that underlie scientific creativity. Other researchers such as Ryan Tweney, Mike Gorman, David Gooding, and Arthur Miller have used this approach to analyze the discoveries of many eminent scientists and have provided a detailed account of the cognitive processes underlying the creative scientific mind.

One influential theory of scientific creativity that is based on an analysis of historical figures in science is Dean Keith Simonton's chance-configuration theory in which he argued that scientific creativity begins with the chance permutation of mental elements. He argued that from time to time these chance permutations coalesce to produce a configuration that is a new scientific idea, hypothesis, explanation, or experiment. This can then lead to a scientific discovery. The idea that a core mental process underlying scientific creativity is the random permutation of ideas is at the root of many theories of scientific creativity; it was used by Donald Campbell in his evolutionary model of creative thought.

Another approach to historical analyses of scientific creativity is exemplified by the work of Herbert Simon and his colleagues. They used historical records, such as diaries and notebooks, to identify the creative strategies that the scientists, such as Kerbs and Copernicus, used in making a discovery. Having identified the creative thinking strategies that the scientists used, Simon built computer programs that use these strategies and then conducted simulations to determine whether the program could make the discovery.

Yet another way of using historical data to test hypotheses regarding scientific creativity is to take a real scientific discovery and bring subjects into the psychological laboratory, provide them with information, and let them conduct simulated experiments similar to what the original scientists discovered. Using this approach, Kevin Dunbar took Monod and Jacob's Nobel Prize–winning discovery of the inhibitory mechanism of genetic control into the psychological laboratory. He found that one of the key aspects to making a discovery is to switch from a goal of testing a favored hypothesis to a goal of accounting for unexpected findings. Again, being able to focus on and use unexpected findings is a key component of scientific discovery. [*See* HISTORIOMETRY.]

III. SCIENTIFIC CREATIVITY IN VIVO

Although much has been learned about scientific creativity using detailed historical analyses of scientists' lives, much of what scientists really do and how creative scientists really think is difficult to determine from notebooks and interviews. Recently, Kevin Dunbar proposed that to gain a fuller insight into scientific creativity it is necessary to collect data on scientists as they think and reason in their laboratories as they are working and use this type of data to formulate theories and models of scientific creativity. It is necessary to investigate *live* scientists, as many of the important thought processes that the scientists use are forgotten by the scientists and do not make it into their lab books or notes. Dunbar has argued that it is possible to use this *in vivo* data to build models of the ways that creative scientists think and reason. Models built using the in vivo method can be tested and further elaborated by conducting controlled experiments in the psychological laboratory—in vitro research. Thus, he has proposed a general methodology of going from real-world in vivo data collection back to in vitro research in the

psychological laboratory. Using this approach, Dunbar has identified analogy, distributed reasoning, and focusing on the unexpected as key components of scientific creativity. The findings on analogy and distributed reasoning will be discussed in other sections of this article. We first focus on unexpected findings.

One of the most frequently mentioned aspects of scientific discovery is that a finding was due to chance or was unexpected. The recent discoveries of naked DNA and buckyballs are among the many significant discoveries that have been attributed to unexpected findings. Given that claims of unexpected findings are such a frequent component of scientists' autobiographies and interviews in the media, Dunbar decided to investigate the ways that scientists deal with unexpected findings. He spent 1 year in three molecular biology laboratories and one immunology laboratory at a prestigious U.S. university. He used the weekly laboratory meeting as his source of data on scientific creativity as a number of discoveries and much creative thinking occurred at the meetings. When he looked at the types of findings that the scientists made, he found that over 50% of the findings were unexpected and that those creative scientists had evolved a number of important strategies for dealing with such findings. Thus, what Dunbar found is that rather than the unexpected being a rare event scientists must deal with unexpected findings virtually all the time. One of the most important places that they anticipate the unexpected is in designing experiments. They build many conditions and controls into their experiments. These multiple conditions allow unknown mechanisms to manifest themselves. Thus, rather than being the victims of the unexpected, they create opportunities for unexpected events to occur, and once these events do occur, they have specific reasoning strategies for determining which of these events will be a clue to a new discovery. They focus on the method, using analogies to very similar experiments on the same types of organisms, and only after repeated demonstration of the unexpected event will they switch to the use of new theoretical explanations using more distant analogies and generalizations. Creative scientists are not passive recipients of the unexpected, but they actively create the conditions for discovering the unexpected and have a robust mental tool kit that makes discovery possible.

IV. EXPERIMENTAL WORK ON SCIENTIFIC CREATIVITY

Experimental cognitive research on scientific creativity has tended to fall into two broad classes of investigations. The first class is concerned with the types of reasoning that lead scientists astray and block scientific creativity. A large amount of research has been conducted on the potentially faulty reasoning strategies that scientists use, such as considering only one hypothesis at a time, and how this prevents the scientists from making discoveries. The second class is concerned with uncovering the mental processes underlying the generation of new scientific hypotheses and concepts. This research has tended to focus on the use of analogy and imagery in science as well as the use of specific types of problem-solving heuristics. [*See* HEURISTICS; TACTICS AND STRATEGIES FOR CREATIVITY.]

Turning first to investigations of what diminishes scientific creativity, philosophers, historians, and experimental psychologists have devoted a considerable amount of research to a type of creativity block known as *confirmation bias*. This occurs when scientists only consider one hypothesis and ignore other hypotheses. This important phenomenon can distort the design of experiments, the formulation of theories, and the interpretation of data. Psychologists have repeatedly shown that when subjects are asked to design an experiment to test an hypothesis they will design experiments that they think will yield results consistent with the hypothesis. This confirmation bias is very difficult to overcome. Even when subjects are asked to consider alternate hypotheses, they will not conduct experiments that could potentially disconfirm their hypothesis. The precise reasons for this type of creativity block are still widely debated. Researchers such as Michael Doherty at Bowling Green University have argued that working memory limitations make it difficult for people to consider more than one hypothesis. Consistent with this view, it has been shown that when subjects are asked to hold irrelevant items in working memory while testing hypotheses, the subjects will be unable to switch hypotheses in the face of inconsistent evidence. Although working memory limitations are involved in the phenomenon of confirmation bias, even groups of scientists can also display confirmation bias. For example the recent controversies over cold fusion and whether a meteorite that landed on earth shows signs of life having existed on Mars are examples of confirmation bias. In both these cases, large groups of scientists had other hypotheses available to explain their data, yet they maintained their hypotheses in the face of other more standard hypotheses. Clearly, factors such as motivation and commitment to hypotheses are at work here.

Turning now to processes that have been claimed to enhance scientific creativity, one of the most widely mentioned psychological processes is analogy. Many scientists have claimed that the making of certain analogies was instrumental in their making a scientific discovery, and almost all scientific autobiographies and biographies feature an important analogy that is discussed in depth. Coupled with the fact that there has been an enormous research program on analogical thinking and reasoning, we now have a number of sophisticated models and theories of analogical reasoning that show exactly how analogy can play a role in scientific discovery. Accounts of analogy distinguish between two components of an analogy: the target and the source. The target is the concept or problem that the scientist is attempting to solve or explain. The source is another piece of knowledge that the scientist uses to understand the target or to explain the target to others. What the scientist does when he or she makes an analogy is to map features of the source onto features of the target. By mapping the features of the source onto the target, new features of the target may be discovered, or the features of the target can be rearranged so that a new concept is invented and a scientific discovery is made. One frequently mentioned analogy in the history of science is the analogy of the structure of the solar system and the structure of the atom. In this case, the target was the atom and the source was the solar system. Ernest Rutherford ostensibly mapped the idea that the planets revolve around the sun onto the atom and argued that the electrons revolve around the nucleus. Thus, a number of historians have argued that by drawing an analogy to the solar system, Rutherford was able to propose a new account of the structure of the atom. By mapping the feature of the planets revolving around the sun, Rutherford was able to align his data with those predicted by a solar analogy. According to this view, the analogy resulted in a major restructuring of his knowledge, and a scientific discovery was made.

The process of making an analogy involves a number of key steps: (a) retrieval of a source from memory, (b) aligning the features of the source with those of the target, and (c) mapping features of the source onto those of the target. Scientific discoveries are made when the source highlights a hitherto unknown feature of the target or restructures the target into a new set of relations. Interestingly research on analogy has shown that subjects in psychology experiments do not easily use analogy. Subjects tend to focus on the sharing of superficial features between the source and the target rather than on the deep structural features, such as the feature of revolving around in the Rutherford analogy. The difference between the scientists and the subjects in experiments is that the scientists have deep structural knowledge of the processes that they are investigating and can hence use this structural knowledge to make analogies. Subjects in psychology experiments rarely have the structural knowledge and instead focus on superficial features of problems.

Most accounts of the use of analogy in science have focused on situations in which the source and the target are from radically different domains. However, using the in vivo approach outlined earlier, Dunbar has found that most analogies that scientists use, even when they are making an important discovery, are from related domains rather than widely different domains. Dunbar found that few analogies were made to radically different domains. These data show that analogy is indeed important, but that the ways that analogies are used vary, both as a function of the goals of the scientist and their current state of knowledge. Dunbar found that when scientists are formulating hypotheses, they tend to make analogies to related domains. However, when they initially attempt to account for unexpected findings, they use analogies to highly similar experiments. Their use of analogy changes when they receive patterns of unexpected findings. Here they draw analogies to related domains. Dunbar also found that many different analogies are involved in a scientific discovery. Thus, rather than one analogy restructuring the scientists' knowledge, a whole series of analogies could be used. A further aspect of analogy was that the scientists usually forgot the analogies that they had made, even when these analogies resulted in a scientific discovery. In fact, in postlab interviews the scientists rarely remembered the analogies that were generated during the meeting. Thus, analogies often serve as a scaffolding that the scientists use in the construction of new theories and methodologies. Once the new concepts and methods have been advanced, the analogy can be discarded. [*See* ANALOGIES.]

One important goal for accounts of scientific creativity has been to provide an overarching framework. One framework that has had a great influence in cognitive science is that scientific thinking and discovery can be conceived as a form of problem solving. Herbert Simon argued that both scientific thinking in general and problem solving in particular can be thought of as a search in a problem space. A problem space consists of all the possible states of a problem and all the operations that a problem solver can use to get form one state to the next. According to this view, by characterizing the types of representations and procedures that people use to get from one state to another it is possible to understand scientific creativity. Thus, scientific creativity can be characterized as a search in various problem spaces. As discussed earlier Simon has used this approach to describe the ways that Krebs discovered the urea cycle. This approach has been extended to propose that scientific thinking can be thought of as a search in both an hypothesis and an experiment space. In a similar vein, other researchers have argued that another important problem space that scientists search in is a data space. Each problem space that a scientist uses will have its own types of representations and operators used to change the representations. The contribution to creativity research that this approach has made is to identify the strategies or heuristics that are used to generate new theories, models, and explanations. [*See* PROBLEM SOLVING.]

V. BEYOND THE LONE SCIENTIST

The classic image of science is one lone, balding white male peering into a test tube. Scientists often pose for photographs alone, and their biographies usually stress their individual contributions to a scientific discovery; the contributions of other collaborators take a secondary role. Along with other areas of creativity, this story of the lone genius is now being called into question. Thus, just as in other areas of creativity, the scientist is now seen as part of a social group that has a very important role in the creative process. In his in vivo investigations of groups of scientists reasoning at lab meetings, Kevin Dunbar found that many of the creative aspects of science, such as the generation of new concepts and theories, takes place in groups and that the reasoning in these creative moments is distributed among different individuals rather than residing in one individual. One way distributed reasoning works is for one scientist to perform one type of cognitive process such as an induction and another scientist performed another cognitive operation such as a deduction to build a new theory or model. Sometimes one scientist will add one fact to an induction, another scientist will add another fact, and yet a third scientist may make a generalization from the two facts. This type of distributed reasoning frequently occurs when a series of unexpected findings is obtained and can be key to many creative moments in contemporary science. Dunbar found that the composition of the group can have radical effects on distributed reasoning. When all members of a group are from the same background, the group is little better than the lone scientist. What happens in distributed scientific reasoning is that many different representations of an issue are generated, allowing the scientists to look at problems from multiple perspectives. This helps ameliorate one of the major problems that lone scientist suffer from—generating alternate hypotheses and models to the ones that they currently have. [*See* COLLABORATION AND COMPETITION; GROUP CREATIVITY; TEAMS.]

VI. WHERE IS RESEARCH ON SCIENTIFIC CREATIVITY HEADED?

Although much is known about certain components of scientific creativity, much remains to be discovered. In particular, there has been little contact between cognitive, social, personality, and motivational accounts of scientific creativity. Clearly these different aspects of the creative process need to be combined to produce a truly comprehensive picture of the creative scientist.

One way that a comprehensive account of the creative scientist can be achieved is by using the in vivo/in vitro method outlined earlier. Yet another way of achieving more comprehensive models of scientific creativity is through cognitive neuroscience investigations of creative scientists. The emergence of the field of cognitive neuroscience is already having an impact on creativity research as a number of studies have examined the brain activation of creative pianists and conductors using brain scanning techniques such as PET, *f*MRI, and ERP. Similar studies of the important components of scientific creativity, such as the use of analogy, hypothesis testing, and deductive reasoning, are currently taking place. Rather than being the latest attempt in reducing creativity into a physiological process, these new techniques may make it possible to understand how cognitive, motivational, personality, and even social processes combine in the living brain to produce scientific discoveries. This new synthesis has the potential to not only give a more complete picture of scientific creativity but to educate future scientists in ways of making scientific discoveries.

Bibliography

Amabile, T. M. (1983). *The social psychology of creativity.* New York: Springer-Verlag.

Boden, M. (1993). *The creative mind: Myths and mechanisms.* New York: Basic Books.

Csikszentmihalyi, M. (1997). *Creativity: Flow and the psychology of discovery and invention.* New York: HarperCollins.

Csikszentmihalyi, M., & Sayer, K. (1995). Creative insight: The social dimension of a solitary moment. In R. J. Sternberg & J. Davidson (Eds.), *Mechanisms of insight* (pp. 329–363). Cambridge, MA: MIT Press.

Dunbar, K. (1993). Concept discovery in a scientific domain, *Cognitive Science,* 397–434.

Dunbar, K. (1995). How scientists really reason: Scientific reasoning in real-world laboratories. In R. J. Sternberg & J. Davidson (Eds.) *Mechanisms of insight* (pp. 365–395). Cambridge, MA: MIT Press.

Dunbar, K. (1997). How scientists think: Online creativity and conceptual change in science. In T. B. Ward, S. M. Smith, & S. Vaid (Eds.), *Creative Thought: an Investigation of conceptual structures and processes* (pp. 461–493). Washington, DC: APA Press.

Dunbar, K. (1999). *Beyond the myth of the unexpected: Are scientists the victims of chance?* Manuscript submitted for publication.

Holyoak, K. J., & Thagard, P. (1995). *Mental leaps.* Cambridge, MA: MIT Press.

Klahr, D., & Dunbar, K. (1988). Dual space search during scientific reasoning. *Cognitive Science, 12,* 1–48.

Kulkarni, D., & Simon, H. A. (1988). The processes of scientific discovery: The strategy of experimentation. *Cognitive Science, 12,* 139–176.

Nersessian, N. (1992). How do scientists think? Capturing the dynamics of conceptual change in science. In R. N. Giere (Ed.), *Minnesota studies in the philosophy of Science. Vol. XV: Cognitive models of science.* Minneapolis: University of Minnesota Press.

Roe, A. (1952). *The making of a scientist.* New York: Dodd Mead.

Simon, H. A. (1977). *Models of discovery.* Dordrecht-Holland: D. Reidel Publishing.

Simonton, D. K. (1988). *Scientific genius: A psychology of science.* Cambridge, England: Cambridge University Press.

Thagard, P. (1992). *Conceptual revolutions.* Cambridge, MA: MIT Press.

Tweney, R. D., & Chitwood, S. (1995). Scientific reasoning. In S. E. Newstead & J. St. B. T. Evans (Eds.), *Perspectives on thinking and reasoning: Essays in honour of Peter Wason* (pp. 241–260). Hove, England: Erlbaum.

Tweney, R. D., Doherty, M. E., & Mynatt, C. R. (Eds.). (1982). *On scientific thinking.* New York: Columbia University Press.

Weisberg, R. W. (1993). *Creativity: Beyond the myth of genius.* New York: Freeman.

Self-Actualization

Mark A. Runco

California State University, Fullerton

Intrapersonal Intelligence One specific domain of talent, increasingly recognized in creative studies, which in many ways parallels self-actualization.

Self-Actualization Openness to and acceptance of one's true self. Leads directly to openness to experience and creativity and epitomizes psychological health.

*Several humanistic theories have suggested that **SELF-ACTUALIZATION** and creativity are strongly related. Recent empirical support for this relationship has recently been reported. This article reviews the theory and the research. It also explores the issues. One issue reflects the fact that self-actualization is the epitome of psychological health, and yet creative persons are often unhealthy. A second issue is methodological. It concerns how to best operationalize creativity (as personality or as problem solving).*

I. THEORIES OF SELF-ACTUALIZATION

Self-actualized individuals are thought to be creative. Abraham Maslow, for example, felt that self-actualization and creativity are interdependent. He described how creativity facilitates self-actualization and self-actualization facilitates creativity. In 1971 Maslow even concluded that creativity and self-actualization "may turn out to be the same thing" (p. 57).

Carl Rogers, another leading humanistic psychologist, argued that "the mainspring of creativity appears to be the same tendency which we discover so clearly as the creative force in psychotherapy—man's tendency to actualize himself, to become his potentialities . . . the individual creates primarily because it is satisfying . . . because this behavior is felt to be self-actualization" (1961, pp. 351–352).

II. EMPIRICAL RESEARCH ON CREATIVITY AND SELF-ACTUALIZATION

Rogers and Maslow developed their theories of self-actualization by drawing from their experience conducting psychotherapy. Such work gave them extensive information about individuals; however, generalizations from clinical observations are often questioned. This is because (a) generally a small number of persons are observed, and (b) those observed may be atypical in many ways—after all, they are involved in psychotherapy. Fortunately, other more rigorous research has also examined the relationship between self-actualization and creativity.

Some of this research has failed to support the relationship between creativity and self-actualization. For instance, nonsignificant (and low) correlations have been found between four measures of creativity and self-actualization, the former operationalized with the Remote Associates Test (RAT), and the latter with the Personal Orientation Inventory (POI). The RAT may, however, be verbally biased. Moreover, its reliability was in the range between .51 and .67, which is marginal at best. Convergent validity coefficients were similarly marginal ($.01 < rs < .48$), which can be indicative of dubious construct validity. The point is that the lack of a relationship between creativity and self-actualization may reflect the measures employed.

Some researchers have operationalized creativity with the Torrance Tests of Creative Thinking (TTCT), which is quite widely recognized as a reliable estimate of the potential for creative problem solving. Note the emphasis on potential; no test of divergent thinking guarantees actual creative performance. Divergent thinking tests are predictors rather than criteria of creativity. Note also the emphasis on problem solving. Some creativity may be more self-expression than problem solving—and this may be especially true of the creativity that is related to self-actualization. Creativity was also operationalized with the Similes Preference test. [*See* DIVERGENT THINKING.]

Murphy and colleagues found that POI scores were significantly and positively correlated with the elaboration index from the TTCT. They did not provide the actual correlation coefficient, so it is impossible to really interpret the relationship. POI scores were unrelated to the originality fluency TTCT scores, and were unrelated to performances on the Similes test.

Mark Runco and colleagues suggested that the relationship between creativity and self-actualization could only be accurately assessed if creativity was operationalized in terms of personality and process. These reflect two common perspectives on creativity. The personality approach posits that there are core characteristics or traits that are functionally associated with creative behavior. The process orientation posits that creativity may not result in tangible products but should be understood as a perspective on life.

Maslow was explicit about the distinction between personality and product. In his words,

> SA creativeness stresses first the personality rather than its achievements, considering these achievements to be epiphenomena emitted by the personality and therefore secondary to it. It stresses characterological qualities like boldness, courage, freedom, spontaneity, perspicuity, integrity, self-acceptance, all of which make possible the kind of generalized SA creativeness, which expresses itself in the creative life, or the creative attitude, or the creative person. I have also stressed the expressive or Being quality of SA creativeness rather than its problem-solving or product-making quality. (1968, p. 145)

Maslow gave these traits when defining self-actualization: acceptance of self, others, and nature; detachment; a desire for privacy; autonomy; resistance to enculturation; problem-centering; and democratic character structure. Most of these are also characteristic of the creative personality.

In their research, Runco and colleagues used two well-respected measures of the creative personality: the How Do You Think Test (HDYT) and the Adjective Check List, which has a Creative Personality scale. They also administered the Self-Actualization Scale (SAS). Four scores were derived from the HDYT responses, and each was significantly and positively correlated with the SAS scores. It thus appears that the relationship between creativity and self-actualization does indeed depend on the measures employed. Importantly, although the findings of Runco and colleagues were contrary to the other two empirical studies on this topic, the findings were consistent with the observations of Rogers and Maslow. This suggests that the findings are trustworthy because they were predicted first by theory and then confirmed with empirical tests.

Lynne Buckmaster and Gary Davis also reported a positive and significant correlation ($r = .73$) between creativity and a measure of creative personality traits. In particular, Buckmaster and Davis uncovered a creativity factor that accounted for a significant portion of variance in an eight-factor factor analysis. This analysis included the Reflections of Self and Environment (ROSE) measure, which is a self-report focusing on self-actualization. There are two questions with this factor analysis: First, the creativity factor accounted for only 18.9% of the variance in the scores, perhaps because it was a fairly select sample of subjects. The subjects were all students in a creativity course. This may have restricted the range of scores. It was also a relatively young sample of subjects, which is an issue because self-actualization might require some experience and maturity. There is a debate in the psychological literature about the possibility of self-actualization in young persons. The second question concerned the ROSE index, which was more correlated with the creativity scores than it was with the POI scores ($r = .26$). The low correlation with the POI raises the issue of construct validity. Still, by and large these results were consistent with those of Runco and colleagues. Thus in the two studies that relied on personality measures a positive and significant correlation was found between creativity and self-actualization.

Runco and colleagues used the Adjective Check List. This is a self-report containing 300 adjectives. Respondents indicate which are self-descriptive. The vast majority of persons whose SAS scores were in the top 25% of the sample used these adjectives to describe themselves: Adventurous, Alert, Appreciative, Clever, Dependable, Friendly, Helpful, Honest, Loyal, Active, Adaptable, Capable, Easy-Going, Formal, Humorous, Intelligent, Interests Wide, Kind, and Mature. None of them described themselves as Commonplace, Conceited, Cruel, Despondent, Distrustful, Dull, Gloomy, Queer, Slipshod, Stolid, Sulky, Unintelligent, Unkind, or Unstable.

III. CREATIVITY AND HEALTH

Both creativity and self-actualization are indicative of psychological health. As is the case with most signs of health, however, it is not easy to determine which comes first. It is possible that self-actualization allows the individual to be creative, or that the creative tendency supports self-actualization. It is also possible that both are results of a third variable. This third variable might be the capacity for effective coping, adaptability, or intrapersonal intelligence. Recall here that Rogers said, in the quotation earlier, that self-actualization and creativity both reflect an underlying motivational force.

It does appear that some creative persons are not self-actualized. Some are certainly not healthy. In fact, creativity can be downright destructive. The dark side may be seen in creative but destructive discoveries and inventions, such as thermonuclear weapons, and in the not uncommon self-destructive behaviors of creative persons. This self-destruction may take the form of suicide or alcoholism. [*See* DARK SIDE OF CREATIVITY.]

IV. CONCLUSIONS

There is evidence that creativity and self-actualization are related. This relationship follows from the theories of Carl Rogers and Abraham Maslow, and was apparent in both clinical observations and some correlational studies. As is the case with all correlations studies, however, there is some uncertainty about the direction of effect. Creativity may lead to self-actualization, or self-actualization may support creativity. They may both reflect a third variable, such as coping or adaptability. And neither guarantees the other. There are many cases of unhealthy creative persons. This is not much of a surprise, if we keep in mind that there are different ways to be creative. Some individuals are creative in their work, and some in their leisure. Some are creative when they solve problems; others are creative only when they are not threatened by problems. Although some creative persons may be self-actualized, and that self-actualization may in fact be necessary for their creativity, other individuals may be creative without self-actualizing. Both creativity and self-actualization are multifaceted constructs, and this gives them any number of possible intersections.

Bibliography

Buckmaster, L., & Davis, G. (1985). ROSE: A measure of self-actualization and its relationship to creativity. *Journal of Creative Behavior, 19*, 30–37.

Maslow, A. H. (1968). *Toward a psychology of being* (2nd ed.). New York: Van Nostrand–Reinhold.

Maslow, A. H. (1971). *The farther reaches of human nature.* New York: Viking.

Mathes, E. W. (1978). Self-actualization, metavalues, and creativity. *Psychological Reports, 43,* 215–222.

Murphy, J. P., Dauw, D. C., Harton, R. E., & Fredian, A. J. (1976). Self-actualization and creativity. *Journal of Creative Behavior, 10,* 39–44.

Richards, R. (1990). Everyday creativity, eminent creativity, and health: Afterview for CRJ issues on creativity and health. *Creativity Research Journal, 3,* 300–326.

Rogers, C. R. (1961). *On becoming a person.* Boston, MA: Houghton Mifflin.

Runco, M. A. (1990). Creativity and health. *Creativity Research Journal, 3,* 81–84.

Runco, M. A., Ebersole, P., & Mraz, W. (1991). Self-actualization and creativity. *Journal of Social Behvior and Personality, 6,* 161–167.

Self Processes and Creativity

Paul Wink

Wellesley College

Archetype Primordial image expressing the inherent potentiality of the human mind. Archetypes are the product of the collective unconscious, part of the psyche that an individual shares with all humankind.

Humanistic Psychology An approach to personality and clinical psychology that emphasizes personal uniqueness, responsibility for shaping one's life, and potential for growth and self-fulfillment.

Object-Relations Theory Variant of psychoanalytic theory that emphasizes the motivational power of internalized human relations as opposed to biological drives.

Persona A mask that reflects the conscious intentions of the individual. According to Jung, the persona comes into existence for reasons of adaptation or personal convenience and it should not be identified with the entire self.

Psychodynamic Theory An approach to understanding the person that emphasizes the conflictual and unconscious aspects of the psyche.

Transitional Object An object that is an intermediary between the inner and the outer worlds. A one-year-old child uses a blanket or teddy bear as a way station between hallucinatory omnipotence and the recognition of objective reality.

William James distinguished between the self as I and the self as me, or the subject and object of our experiences. The self as I is the part of us that does the experiencing and, therefore, it can only be discerned indirectly in the process of being and acting. The I provides us with our sense of identity and cohesion. The self as me consists of all the attributes of the I. It includes our thoughts and feelings, our personal possessions, and our social roles and reputation. This article focuses primarily on the relation between creativity and the self as I. In particular, it will explore the relation between SELF-PROCESSES AND CREATIVITY. That is, it will consider the role played by creativity in maintaining a sense of psychic equilibrium and in the development of the self. The article draws primarily on psychoanalytic and humanist theories because these theories emphasize the dynamic nature of the self and its potential for growth. The article begins by exploring the phenomenology of the creative experience and then considers the role played by creativity in the process of self-realization and self-cohesion. Conversely, the article also looks at how the lack of self-cohesion contributes to the creative process.

537

I. THE PHENOMENOLOGY OF A CREATIVE EXPERIENCE

What does it feel like to be involved in the act of creation? According to Mihaly Csikszentmihalyi, the state of creativity is characterized by a feeling of total absorption in the task, an obliviousness to the passage of time, a lack of self-consciousness (i.e., an absence of self-awareness and self-monitoring), and feelings of vitality and exhilaration. This condition of *flow* is similar to experiences described by mountain climbers, tennis players, and others that engage in activities that pose a challenge to their skills and abilities. In all these instances, individuals merge with the activity and thereby becomes oblivious of the self or of the *I*.

Heinz Kohut took a somewhat less benign view of the creative experience, although he shared Csikszentmihalyi's contention that creativity involves feelings of merger. According to Kohut, the relation between the creator and the object of creation resembles that between a young child and its primary care giver. Both involve a projection of feelings of perfection onto an object (other), which then needs to be controlled and forcefully shaped in order to meet the harsh standards of idealization. If the child could verbalize the process of idealization it would say something like: "You my parent are perfect but I am part of you and therefore I expect you to do what I want you to do. After all, if I decide to raise my arm, the arm goes up and if I decide to say a word my mouth produces a sound and so if I decide that you should jump you better jump my beloved one." In other words, Kohut conceived of the creative merger as serving a narcissistic function aimed at satisfying the need for being soothed and for maintaining self-esteem. There is something inherently comfortable in the feeling that one is part of another being, a being that is predictable and within one's control. Hence, the creative object tends to be treated as a self-object; that is, it is infused with fantasies and desires and lacks autonomy. In this sense a relation based on idealization is very different from the more altruistic and empathic merger that occurs in a mature love relation (such as that between the primary care giver and the child). The childlike and self-directed nature of a relation based on idealization is illustrated, Kohut argued, by the behavior of Enrico Fermi (one of the creators of the atom bomb) while witnessing the first atomic explosion. According to his wife, Fermi tore a piece of paper into small bits and, as soon as the blast had been set off, dropped them one by one, watching the impact of the shock wave rise and subside.

The fact that, as argued by Kohut and Csikszentmihalyi, the creative relation is based on merger explains its addictive property and its tendency to energize the self. This does not mean, however, that the creative process leads inevitably to a sense of happiness or satisfaction. Relations based on merger are frequently volatile, and idealization can turn easily into devaluation. Because no human being is totally good or totally bad, conceiving of someone as **perfect** is bound to produce disappointment, just as portraying someone as totally bad will inevitably lead to feelings of guilt and attempts at reparation.

The next three sections describe the relation between creativity and the actualized self as well as the role of creative behavior in the process of self-integration and that of alleviating pathology and maintaining self-cohesion. This discussion is complicated by the fact that definitions of creativity tend to shift from one domain to another. For example, writers on the psychologically healthy process of self-actualization tend to view creativity in quite general terms as a state of being that is characterized by playfulness and vitality. In contrast, those who are interested in the role played by creativity in dealing with negative states of mind and adversity tend to focus on more narrowly defined creative achievement or productive creativity that meets external standards of excellence. In trying to understand the relation between creativity and the self it may be counterproductive, however, to draw such a sharp distinction between these two types of creativity.

II. CREATIVITY AND THE ACTUALIZED SELF

According to the humanist tradition, all people have the potential as well as the need to self-actualize and thus become fully functioning. In real life, nonetheless, various obstacles invariably impede strivings toward self-fulfillment. These include the need to overcome a sense of conditional positive regard (Carl Rogers) and the necessity to satisfy more basic needs such as security and love (Abraham Maslow). Once these inhibitory forces are overcome, the individual reaches a stage of self-actualization characterized by a creative and vital engagement in the world. According to Maslow, creativity associated with self-actualization is a state of being that expresses itself in the kind of spontaneity, effortlessness, and freedom from stereotypes that is typically found in a happy and secure child. The self-actualizing creativeness shows itself widely in the ordinary aspects of life such as cooking or housekeeping. It also allows the individual to develop a sense of perspective on life that manifests itself in a kind of humor. [*See* SELF-ACTUALIZATION.]

For Maslow, the creativity of everyday life is secondary to the process of self-actualization. In other words, it is an expression of the self-actualized person's boldness, freedom, spontaneity, and integration. In this sense creativity does not play a role in the journey toward self-actualization but rather is its by-product.

Similar to Maslow, the psychoanalyst D. W. Winnicott construed creativity as a way of being that permeates the daily activities of an individual with a true (as opposed to a false) sense of self. According to Winnicott, creativity resembles the state of play. Both occur in a transitional space where the person is able to fantasize about the external world without losing sight of its reality. In this sense, the creative object is very much like the favorite teddy bear or blanket of a 1-year old child; it is real but also possesses a magical capacity to soothe and comfort. In this example the fantasized or magical aspect of the teddy bear is its capacity to provide comfort because, after all, a toy is just a toy and its soothing capacity is the result of a projection. The ability to move in and out of a transitional space requires both a regressive quality that allows for play and good ego strength that prevents the play from turning into madness. According to Winnicott, this combination of characteristics typifies individuals who have experienced good enough (adequate) parenting. Winnicott argued that a good enough parent is able to provide a psychological space within which the child can become himself or herself.

III. CREATIVITY AND SELF-INDIVIDUATION

Carl Jung shared with the humanists the belief in our natural (inborn) propensity to strive toward self-realization. (Throughout this section my use of the word *self* differs from that of Jung who identified *the Self* with the totality of our conscious and unconscious experiences.) Unlike Maslow, Jung saw creativity as playing a vital role in the process of attaining wholeness. The task of adult life is to develop and integrate the many and varied potentialities of our mind. During the first part of our life, these capacities typically remain dormant as individuals adapt to the world using the most familiar and best-developed aspects of their personalities. According to Jung, this one-sided approach to life creates a psychic imbalance that needs to be compensated for by the development of the opposite tendencies. Hence, an extrovert may suddenly find solace in solitude, just as a retired business executive may turn to painting. As suggested by Anthony Storr, the prolonged process of human socialization results in psychic fragmentation and a state of "divine discontent" that propels people toward creative activity aimed at integration. Storr's point is similar to one made by Freud in his work *Civilization and Its Discontents*. To become part of a family and the society at large we have to give up some of our basic impulses and wishes. This produces a state of alienation (disengagement from one's "true" self) that in adulthood can become a motivating force for creative endeavor aimed at recovery of the lost self.

Following his break-up with Freud, Jung's own experience of playing with pebbles on the shore of a lake taught him the importance of creativity in the process of individuation. According to Jung, the creative process activates unconscious, primordial images (archetypes) that pave the way toward wholeness and self-realization by exposing us to hitherto unexplored potentialities of the mind. But creative activity alone does not guarantee psychic growth. The large number of famous artists and scientists who remain psychologically troubled throughout their lives attests to this fact. Jung argued that many artists adopt a rather passive attitude toward the object of their creation. In other words, the artists are a medium or conduit for the expression of the archetypes. This makes for good art, but does not help the process of redressing psychic one-sidedness. To benefit from encounters with the unconscious one must take an active stance and engage the images, visions, and symbols coming from the unconscious in a way that makes them personally relevant, understandable, and self-enriching. (In Jung's case this process of engagement took the form of trying to talk to the figures emerging from his imagination in order to discover their meaning and significance for the self.) Such an endeavor poses considerable perils and requires the kind of ego strength that many artists and writers lack. For as Jung suggests "great gifts are the fairest and often the most dangerous fruits on the tree of humanity. They hang on the weakest branches, which easily break." Some artists, moreover, wrongly believe that psychic integration might strip them of their creative powers.

In sum, Jung believed that creativity plays a pivotal role in the process of self-realization. For in order to individuate, we need to actively construct our selves in the same manner as we create objects of art and science.

IV. CREATIVITY AND SELF-COHESION

Contrary to popular belief, severe psychopathology does not enhance creativity. For instance, August Strindberg was able to become a great playwright despite his schizophrenia, and alcoholism destroyed Malcolm Lowry's ability to write. Nevertheless, many highly creative individuals appear to be odd and eccentric. They frequently exhibit such contradictory characteristics as maturity and childishness, vulnerability and ego strength, flexibility and organization. This raises questions about the relation between creativity and self-cohesion. Is there something about the lack of self-cohesion that contributes to being creative? Conversely, does creativity play a positive role in maintaining self-cohesion and preventing self-disorganization? Answers to these questions are complex and vary in part depending on the type of personal eccentricity or vulnerability that is involved. I will illustrate the role played by creativity in the maintenance of self-cohesion with the example of the schizoid character structure, a construct first introduced by the psychoanalytic object-relations theorist Melanie Klein and subsequently elaborated by W. R. D. Fairbairn.

Schizoid individuals face the unenviable predicament of believing that their love (the most precious gift a human being can offer) is destructive. In this sense they differ from depressive individuals who experience the more easily understandable conflict over the destructiveness of their hate. In other words, schizoid individuals tend to shy away from interactions with others because of a deep sense of personal vulnerability to slight, rejection, and abuse. In contrast, depressive individuals are not afraid of interactions with others. Their main concern is guilt over aggressive feelings and behavior, which then leads to a need for reparation or restitution. According to Klein, the fears underlying both the schizoid and depressive positions are unconscious and vary in intensity. It is, therefore, not easy to identify an individual with a schizoid character. For example, Anthony Storr argued that Albert Einstein showed schizoid traits based on the fact that he appeared to care more about humanity in general than about individual people.

Individuals predisposed to a schizoid character structure in adulthood are typically raised in families where parents are unpredictable and not attuned to the needs of their children. (The consequences of such a style for creativity and pathology is eloquently described by Alice Miller in her book *The Drama of the Gifted Child.*) Confronted with a family environment that lacks empathy, schizoid individuals learn quickly to seek out the relatively secure and predictable world of inner experiences and fantasy in preference to the pain and anguish of human contact. This coping strategy comes at a price. Forced into premature self-reliance, individuals with schizoid characteristics develop a strong sense of insecurity and vulnerability that is subsequently covered up with feelings of omnipotence, superiority, and disdain. The unpredictability of human relations contributes to the perception that the world is lacking in meaning and order. The writings of Franz Kafka, full of characters who are exposed to random, senseless, and brutal experiences, illustrate movingly the deep sense of anguish and alienation experienced by schizoid individuals.

Yet, as argued by Anthony Storr, schizoid characteristics fit many of the demands of creativity. Creative work is frequently solitary and this suits the schizoid individual's strong interest in inner-life and their deep-seated misgivings about human relations. A somewhat exaggerated sense of destiny and invincibility can be invaluable in overcoming the inevitable obstacles and adversities that accompany the process of creation. Misgivings about the meaning of life can become a strong motivating force to create as a way of imposing order into the world. But just as schizoid character traits facilitate creative endeavor, the act of creation plays an equally important role in maintaining self-cohesion and regulating the well-being of schizoid individuals. The ability to merge with the creative object, for example, provides an important substitute for human relations and love and becomes a vital source of self-esteem and comfort. As will be discussed in the next section, the role of a creator can also provide the means of relating to others without endangering the vulnerable inner-self of the schizoid individual. [*See* SCHIZOPHRENIA.]

V. CREATIVITY AND THE SOCIAL SELF

According to Freud, the creative artist is motivated by fantasies of fame, fortune, and romantic love. Yet this claim does not seem to apply to the majority of individuals who embark on creative careers or endeavors. As indicated by John Gedo, there are many easier ways of attaining external rewards than pursuing a career as an artist or a research scientist. In most instances, a life devoted to creativity entails substantial financial sacrifices rather than rewards, and it exposes the self to rigorous criticism and peer review. Nevertheless, Freud's claim highlights the social aspects of the creative process. After all, the self is largely a social construct and it is responsive to the external world. In the most basic way, creative individuals can derive self-esteem, support, and a sense of meaning from others who share their goals. The history of art and science attests to the power of avant-garde movements in nourishing and sustaining the creative flame against obstacles and adversity. This phenomenon is well described by Roger Shattuck in his book *The Banquet Years,* which deals with world of art in Paris at the turn of the 20th century. [*See* MOTIVATION/DRIVE.]

Some creative individuals develop a persona or cultivate an interpersonal style that reflects their vision or fantasy of what an artist or scientist ought to be. Paul Gauguin and Salvatore Dali are good examples of impression management in the service of the ego. Such attempts at cultivating a persona have the advantage of allowing these individuals to reap rewards from social interactions without, at the same time, exposing their more private and vulnerable selves to public scrutiny. For example, the mask of an artist or scientist can allow individuals with a depressive character structure to voice their anger (or just be appropriately assertive) without raising concerns about the destructiveness of their negative affect. In the case of persons with schizoid traits, the creative persona protects the vulnerable inner-self from feelings of slight and abuse. It therefore allows for interacting with others without threatening to annihilate the damaged self. Although the ability to create and identify with a new persona aids the process of maintaining psychic equilibrium, it is not necessarily conducive to personal growth and integration.

VI. CONCLUSIONS

The self and creativity are mutually entwined. Creative activity—big or small—provides us with feelings of cohesion and vitality and tempts us with the prospect of self-realization. Because our adult sense of the *I* is inevitably fractured and lacking, it finds the tune of the creative muse particularly alluring.

Bibliography

Csikszentmihalyi, M. (1996). *Creativity: Flow and the psychology of discovery and invention.* New York: Harper Collins.
Freud, S. (1957). *Civilization and its discontents.* London: Hogarth Press. (Original work published 1930.)
Gedo, J. E. (1996). *The artist and the emotional world.* New York: Columbia University Press.
Jung, C. G. (1966). On the relation of analytical psychology to poetry. In H. Read, M. Fordham, & G. Adler (Eds.), *Collected works* (Vol. 20, pp. 65–83). Princeton, NJ: Princeton University Press. (Original work published 1922.)
Kohut, H. (1966). Forms and transformations of narcissism. *Journal of the American Psychoanalytic Association, 14,* 243–272.
Miller, A. (1981). *The drama of the gifted child.* New York: Basic Books.
Ochse, R. (1990). *Before the gates of excellence.* New York: Cambridge University Press.
Shattuck, R. (1968). *The banquet years; the origins of the avant garde France, 1885 to World War I: Alfred Jarry, Henri Rousseau, Erik Satie and Guillaume Apollinaire.* New York: Vintage Books.
Storr, A. (1985). *The dynamics of creation.* New York: Atheneum.

Serendipity

Cora L. Díaz de Chumaceiro

Simon Bolivar University, Caracas

Dual Serendipity True and pseudo- serendipity play roles in a discovery process.

Pseudoserendipity Discovery through accidental means of things sought for.

Serendipity *Walpole:* Discovery by accidents and sagacity of things not in quest of. *Current:* Accidental discovery of the unsought for.

Serendipity Analog Alternative term for pseudoserendipity.

Serendipity Pattern Observation of unanticipated, anomalous, and strategic data.

This article presents an overview of the origin and general uses of the term **SERENDIPITY** *in this century. Applied to the unsought for accidental discovery, it increasingly appears today in the scientific, technological, and popular literature. Categories of usage of the term* chance *in the past and recent theories suggesting differentiation and clarification of different types of serendipitous events; applications of evolutionary theories to the creative process in general and specifically to the incubation phase; models of cognitive processes of discovery; and conclusions.*

I. ORIGIN AND USES OF THE TERM

Serendipity is a term coined by Horace Walpole (1717–1797), a British writer and fourth Earl of Oxford (1791), on January 28, 1754, in a letter to his friend Horace Mann, the British diplomat resident in Florence. He derived this new word from remembering once having read "a silly fairy tale" titled "The Three Princes of Serendip" (ancient name for Ceylon, or Sri Lanka) and considered that its meaning would be better understood by derivation rather than by definition: During their travels the three princes

> were always making discoveries, by accidents and sagacity, of things which they were not in quest of: for instance, one of them discovered that a mule blind of the right eye had travelled the same road lately, because the grass was eaten only on the left side, where it was worse than on the right—now do you understand *Serendipity*? (Lewis, 1960, p. 407)

Walpole stressed that *no* discovery of something being searched for is included in his description of "accidental sagacity." On March 8, 1754, Mann answered that he understood Walpole's serendipity "perfectly," as everybody must have experienced seeking for one thing and finding others of great significance. Nevertheless, over time, for many serendipity has merely meant "accidental sagacity" excluding "accidental discovery," as the term is usually applied today.

A. Dissemination of the Term

The word *serendipity* was printed in 1833 with the publication of Mann's correspondence. The *Oxford English Dictionary* notes its introduction in literary circles in 1880 with its appearance in the *Index Titles of Honour,* Pref. 5, authored by E. Solly, the British bibliophile, antiquarian, and former chemist.

In the United States, in this century, the term slowly spread from the literary milieu to the field of medicine. In 1940, the Harvard physiologist Walter B. Cannon, in "The Role of Chance in Discovery," discussed making a major discovery accidentally, due to the serendipity phenomenon; in 1945, he dedicated a chapter to "Gains from Serendipity," in *The Way of an Investigator.* The term continued to appear sporadically in professional writings, and its acceptance was accelerated in 1957 with the publication in *The Journal of the American Medical Association* of two articles on serendipity and an editorial; the next year a convention was held in the Bahamas to discuss this subject.

Following Cannon's leads, the social theorist Robert K. Merton argued that empirical research that is fruitful, besides testing hypotheses that are theoretically derived, also originates new ones. "This might be termed the 'serendipity' component of research, i.e., the discovery, by chance or sagacity, of valid results which were not sought for." Later, Merton described the *serendipity pattern* as the common enough experience of observation of datum that is "unanticipated, anomalous and strategic" which creates the opportunity for the development of a novel theory or for the extension of one in existence. It was introduced in social theory and then spread to allied fields.

In 1949, with serendipity's entry into the *New York Times*—in the science section, then in a book review, and finally on the front page on July 5—the term surpassed academic communities and gained social acceptance. Users included collectors, writers, scholars, lexicographers, medical humanists, social scientists, science writers, and researchers in applied sciences.

B. Definitions

Before the term eventually appeared in dictionaries with variations and deviations from Walpole's original definition, Irving Langmuir, 1932 Nobel Prize winner in chemistry, had defined serendipity as "the art

to profit from unexpected occurrences," disregarding Walpole's distinction of whether the goal was a desired one or not. Thus, over the years semantic confusion ensued. Initially, some dictionaries stated that Walpole wrote the fairy tale on which the term was based and many repeated this error in print. Others omitted the element of sagacity, or the accidental; and some described it as a faculty or gift to make happy, fortunate, or desired discoveries. Many have argued that the main element of serendipity is sagacity (highly intelligent reasoning powers) instead of "lucky accidents."

This phenomenon has also been called in the sciences *scientific serendipity.* Serendipity is characterized by *unintentionality;* misused phrases include "automated serendipity," "planned serendipity," and "serendipity on demand," among others.

II. CHANCE AND SERENDIPITY

Walpole coined the term serendipity for an aspect of chance phenomena. Since antiquity, however, many have written about chance from different vistas. The 1952 edition of the Encyclopaedia Britannica's *The Great Ideas: A Syntopicon of Great Books of the Western World* classified reflections about chance as (a) conceptions of chance as coincidental causes as well as total fortuitousness, spontaneity, or acausal; (b) existence of chance or fortune and its relation to causality (philosophical and scientific determinism) and to fate (providence and predestination); (c) chance, need, and design (purpose) in origins and world structure; (d) causality and chance linked to knowledge and opinion (probability theory); (e) control of chance or contingency by art; and (f) chance and fortune in human affairs (mythology of fortune) in the individual's life as well as in politics and history.

A. Late 1980s to Late 1990s

During the past decade, several proposals emerged calling for differentiation of types of chance events. In 1988, Albert Rothenberg objected to the use of "so-called serendipity" in the popular and scientific literature. He proposed to instead use the terms *articulation of error* and *conversion of error*—based on the Freudian theory of parapraxes, repression, and unconscious conflict—to differentiate this type of discovery from those of the broad range of purely accidental events in the sciences, psychotherapy, and the arts. Focusing on the popular examples in the field of medicine, of Fleming and the discovery of penicillin, Roentgen and the discovery of the X-ray effect, and Pasteur in immunology, he argued that in all these cases, the scientists understood what had happened and developed an error that had occurred. In each case, a link existed between the error's substance and the accumulation of knowledge to date in that field. Consequently, rather than only making a correction of a mistake or turning elsewhere toward a presumably more correct avenue, instead the clarification and separation of the fact of nature by the error was preserved by these scientists who then linked this datum with other data or facts. The word *error,* instead of chance, appeared to better represent discrepancies between the researcher's intent and execution.

In the field of psychological treatment, during the creative process that occurs in psychoanalytic psychotherapy, articulation of error specifically refers to transference and countertransference. The presence of transference in therapy is clarified to the therapist precisely due to such errors. *Erroneous actions,* both in therapy and in art, are another route for the revelation of unconscious material.

Pseudoserendipity, a term coined by Royston M. Roberts in 1989, was defined as the discovery through accidental means of things sought for, as a differentiation from true serendipity—accidentally finding something *not* sought for. In 1995 C. L. Díaz de Chumaceiro and Guillermo Yáber suggested that the term *serendipity analog* for this type of discovery might be more acceptable in academic and scientific communities. Díaz de Chumaceiro also proposed the term *dual serendipity* for cases when individuals recognize both types of serendipity during a creative process and focused on articulations of errors versus purely accidental events in the creative arts therapies; the term *serendipitous parapraxis* underscores the fortuitous aspect of having made an error that in hindsight proves to be favorable for treatment.

Also in 1989, Aharon Kantorovich and Yuval Ne'eman proposed that serendipity was a source of evolutionary progress in science, based on a modification of the Neodarwinian scheme of blind-variation and selective-retention (as represented by Popper and Campbell in the mainstream version of evolutionary

epistemology). Serendipity events can be separated into two main classes: (a) solving-explaining B when intended to solve-explain A and (b) solving-explaining B plus A when only intended to solve-explain A. Implications of this theory for the philosophy of science are that the principle of serendipitous discovery is descriptive and explanatory (i.e., science advances by serendipitous steps, based on an evolutionary theory of science) as well as normative (based on this theory's basic assumptions, only by serendipity can science obtain significant progress). Presumably, discovery by serendipity of new phenomena will be more frequent in sciences that do not yet have a fully developed theoretical system.

Ne'eman later extended the above two classes to the following tracks: (a) to explore/search but not for anything specifically and to find B, (b) to search for A and, as a by-product, to find B, and (c) to search for A and instead find B. B may be an answer for an open question that was not sought for, or it also be a new problem or a new phenomenon. For unexpected reasons, in some strange cases B is A. Thus, for anything to occur—a mutation, an accidental finding, or serendipitous discovery—there must be an ongoing program searching for A.

These classes or tracks of serendipity proposed, however, exclude the concept of pseudoserendipity. The omission of this complementary phenomenon creates confusion instead of intended clarity. Searching for A and accidentally finding A, as in the case of insulin, is an example of pseudoserendipity; another is the vulcanization of rubber, often presented erroneously today as an example of serendipity.

III. SERENDIPITY AND THE CREATIVE PROCESS

There are many theories of creativity. Some models that particularly refer to serendipity, presented in different decades, theoretically are differentiated as associative, evolutionary, and cognitive.

A. Associative Model

In 1962 Sarnoff A. Mednick presented an associative interpretation of creative thinking processes and suggested that the cultivation of serendipity was a desirable trait. Creative solutions could be achieved by serendipity, similarity, and mediation. In general terms, conditions or states of the organism that tend to bring the required associative elements into mental (ideational) contiguity will incrementally increase probability and speed of creative solutions. The required associative elements can be evoked in a contiguous manner: (a) with serendipity, by appearance of the milieu (accidental contiguity), (b) with similarity of associative elements or of the trigger stimuli that elicit them, and (c) with mediation of common elements. An individual's associative hierarchy influences the probability and speed of arriving at a creative solution.

B. Evolutionary Models

In 1988 Dean Keith Simonton proposed a theory of the mechanisms of the incubation stage that occur in the mind of scientific geniuses. This theory of the creative process in science is based on the blind-variation and selective-retention paradigm by Donald Campbell, which has two personal and social components. The first component is intrapsychic (individual) process, with two stages: (a) mental elements' chance permutations and (b) stable configurations formed by internal selection. The second component is interpsychic (interpersonal) processes, which are communications and social selections (social acceptance and sociocultural retention of selected configurations). In synthesis, a natural selection process occurs in the mind of the scientist, drawn from mental elements (including cognitive entities; e.g., rules, laws, facts, formulas, principles, relations, and images), which can be evoked from memory deliberately or involuntarily through associations. These do not have to be entertained consciously as they can be processed beyond immediate awareness. The basis of the creative process is that chance plays a role in the formation of new combinations of mental elements in the mind—termed by Simonton *chance permutations* (drawn from probability theory). The process of selection happens at intrapsychic and social levels. At the intrapsychic level, *stable configurations* (the most stable permutations) are drawn from mental aggregates that were formed during the process of chance permutation. Only stable permutations, which may be inventive and imaginative, can be processed consciously; nonstable permutations are beyond the

discoverer's awareness. Configurations are relatively stable and thus can be seen as new mental elements that can be used as a unit to form new combinations.

The principle of selection is as follows: If sufficiently coherent to a community of scientists, a permutation is considered stable; a shared sense of coherence (context dependent on prevailing worldview, internalized standards of scientific explanation, and individual preferences) leads to wide acceptance. *Stable permutations are fully imaginative when they arise by chance—unrestricted by logic or experience.* By contrast, inventive configurations are formed intentionally by the application of logic or mathematical rules (although inventions can also be generated unwittingly). In a genuine creative process, new configurations are generated by chance. *A priori configurations* are formed governed by rules through mathematical or logical procedures; *a posteriori configurations* are reached through experience; neither are genuinely creative. In Simonton's view, the programmed human intellect self-organizes its contents into structures that are hierarchical so that knowledge is distributed in the most efficacious way. The creative process in science is driven by self-organization instead of by truth as a goal.

With respect to interpsychic processes and social selections, not all configurations thus formed in individuals' minds will gain acceptance as scientific discoveries. For such to occur, two conditions are necessary. The first is linguistic or mathematical expression of the configuration (acceptable language in the specific discipline, that is, conversion into a *communication configuration*). An example of creative articulation is Newton's discovery of calculus to express physical ideas. The second necessary condition is that the configuration should lead to mental self-organization of other members in the particular community (i.e., recognition of a problem as a genuine one, for which a solution is proposed by the new configuration; mental elements are commonly shared by other members).

For Simonton, "in a loose sense, genius and chance become synonymous." Serendipitous discovery fits into chance-permutation theory: First, it must be recognized "that serendipity is nothing more than a special case of the more universal chance-permutation procedure that underlies scientific genius." Its only distinction is that an external experience provides at least one of the elements of the new stable permutation. After a scientist has initiated an incubation process about Problem X, new elements may be introduced into the permutations by extraneous environmental stimuli, directly or indirectly via divergent associations. Second, "the importance of configurations in making chance events pertinent to self-organization" needs to be taken into account. This is exemplified in Pasteur's observation that "in fields of observation, chance favors only the prepared mind." How many times were things *seen* yet not *noticed* until someone made the fortuitous discovery? (Consider Archimedes and the bathtub overflowing, Newton and the falling of an apple, or Fleming and a contaminated petri dish.) Scientists who are creative, even when self-confined to specific experimentation paths, are forever looking out, however subliminally, for the needed links. More recently, in 1995, after repeating Pasteur's famous quote, Simonton added, "Serendipitous insights are not dispensed indiscriminately on all, for only the most creative see their world as a busy and buzzing world of intellectual and asethetic opportunities."

When Kantorovich reviewed Simonton's theory of creativity in 1992, he reacted to the comment on genius and chance being synonymous considering that it gave a definite blow to the discoverer's heroic vista: "The discoverer is equipped with merely an efficient gambling machine." Instead, he proposed that Simonton's theory also was applicable to the intrapsychic creativity process in general rather than just limited to the special population of scientific geniuses, which he then described in more detail the following year in *Scientific Discovery*. The prototype of a serendipitous discovery occurs when trying to solve Problem A, then, unintentionally, Problem B is solved. In this case, the external stimulus for the generation of the new configuration that solved B was provided as a by-product of the efforts to solve A. In science, it is very common to find one solution when attempting to solve another one—a very specific kind of serendipity. Chance permutation theory provides an explanation for this occurrence: while engaging in current scientific research, it is more likely for the discoverer to focus on mental elements with intrinsic affinities to elements being considered to solve Problem B. Serendipity, however, is a social process and discoverers are blind as to how later researchers will vary their work. While Simonton considers the process of permutation to be blind—that

is, lacking a priori knowledge of the best direction for the search of combinations—Kantorovich makes the point that no process takes place *in vacuo*. The prepared mind is equipped with mental elements and associations that are the raw material for the process of chance permutation, and they are the a priori component of the discovery process.

1. Science versus Art

According to Kantorovich, the main difference between scientific creativity and artistic creativity is (a) scientific creativity intends a description of the world, whereas artistic creativity does not and (b) scientific creativity is constrained by experimental results and by the zeitgeist, whereas art is only constrained by the zeitgeist. Although both types of creativity may be based on the chance permutation process, the selection procedures are different. In scientific discovery, the selected configurations must be in accord with observational data and with the picture of the world. Although observational data may be partially dependent on the zeitgeist, they also are dependent on nature. Another difference is that the practice of science consists, generally speaking, of inferences and arguments, and several individuals or groups, independently, may make the same discovery; by contrast, in artistic creativity, the role of logic is different.

2. Cultivation of Serendipity

For this objective, Kantorovich recommended that after the arrow has hit the spot, encircle it as a target (e.g., Fleming, Kepler). From the former it follows that it is preferable to be engaged in solving several unrelated problems at a time rather than only one and to have awareness of as many problems as possible. Freedom of research needs to be encouraged in the scientific community, as preconceived goals should not control it. To understand the role of serendipitous discoveries contributes to the understanding of science's epistemic role and its character of evolution. The blind edge of science is supplied by serendipity: Human minds chart plans with a chance of producing successful results merely in terrains of familiar nature, whereas serendipity forces science toward deviations from charted courses in the direction of virgin, unexplored domains. Serendipity is essential for the advancement of science.

C. Cognitive Models

How does serendipity fit into the broader picture of discovery in science? In 1997 Paul Thagard outlined four models of cognitive processes of discovery: search, questioning, blind variation, and serendipity.

1. Search

The most prevailing model in computational and psychological work on scientific discovery uses the idea of "search in a space of possibilities." It is based on a model originated in 1972 by Newell and Simon's problem-solving theory that involves "a set of states and a set of operators for moving from state to state. Search is the process of finding a sequence of operators that leads from the initial state of knowledge to the goal state in which the problem is solved." A new model of discovery with search in four spaces was proposed by Schunn and Klahr in 1995: The old "space of hypotheses" is now divided into *datarepresentation space* and *hypothesis space* (drawing hypotheses about the data's casual relations by utilizing the current representation's set of features); the old "space of experiments" is now divided into *experimental paradigm space* (a paradigm is selected that identifies the varying factors and the constant components) and *experiment space* (within this paradigm, the parameter settings are selected).

2. Questioning

For scientists who lack well-defined problems, goals, or operators, search is hardly the best way to describe their discoveries. Authors in the fields of philosophy, psychology, and artificial intelligence have stressed the significance of the generation of questions and answers to inquiry. The three major sources of really original questions seem to be surprise (it happens when what is found is not coherent with knowledge to date), practical need (practical goals such as technological or medical), and curiosity (general interest has been aroused, not due to practical need or surprise).

3. Blind Variation

Campbell and others have defended the argument that discoveries occur due to a process of blind variation analogous to genetic mutation. Powerful genetic algorithms have been devised by computer scientists, modeled on mutation and recombination. That such algorithms form part of human cognition is unsupported by psychological or neurological data.

4. Serendipity

In science, many discoveries are accidental, resulting in ways unplanned by those scientists who created them. Roberts' differentiation between serendipity and pseudoserendipity (noted earlier) is cited, with Goodyear's discovery of vulcanization of rubber seen as a pseudoserendipitous example because he had been searching for years for this goal, and George deMestral's discovery of Velcro as a serendipitous one. The discovery of X rays by Roentgen and penicillin by Fleming, however, were also viewed as serendipitous (see Rothenberg's contrasting articulation of error, stated earlier). As there is no problem to be solved, in this sense, serendipity is hardly well characterized as search. "Pseudoserendipity is also not well characterized as search, since the solution comes by accidental introduction of an operator (e.g., drop the rubber on the stove) that was not part of the initial problem space."

5. Integration of the Four Models

These models are potentially complementary rather than in competition with each other. Within the model of discovery as search (model 1) can be included discovery as blind variation (model 3), if blind variation is viewed as a search strategy that is not heuristic. From the viewpoint of computation, it appears likely that blind variation "be slow and ineffective: cognition operates much more efficiently than biological evolution which has myriad organisms and vast stretches of time." Crossover (with the combination of two strong representations) is the most powerful operation in present computational work on genetic algorithms— not mutation. It can also be argued that questioning can be assimilated into the search model of discovery, though excluding problem generation. In similar fashion, a contribution to the questioning and search models can be made by serendipity. Events that are surprising, or that induce curiosity or trigger questions, may be provided by serendipity. Furthermore, when a search has begun, "serendipity may provide a representation or operator that was not part of the original problem space." For Kantorovich serendipity is a type of blind variation, but what is varied is vague.

IV. CONCLUSIONS

Walpole's imaginative term *serendipity* has transcended time. It is permanently linked with the origins of many scientific and technological discoveries and has been applied in most if not all fields of human endeavor—from the sciences in pure and applied research; to the humanities, business, and the arts; to the most mundane and banal aspects of human existence. It has been defined in different ways, used and misused in most fields, and has more recently inspired theory construction. Serendipity is usually associated with successful discovery at all levels of accomplishment—from unexpected, positive findings that enrich daily life to the heights of the Nobel Prize. Its role in the different stages of the creative process merits further study from different theoretical perspectives so that a clearer understanding of this human phenomenon can emerge.

Bibliography

Díaz de Chumaceiro, C. L. (1995). Serendipity's role in psychotherapy: A bridge to the creative arts therapies. *The Arts in Psychotherapy, 22,* 39–48.

Díaz de Chumaceiro, C. L. (1996). Freud, poetry and serendipitous parapraxes. *Journal of Poetry Therapy, 9,* 227–232.

Díaz de Chumaceiro, C. L. (1997). Serendipity citations in the biomedical sciences. *Creativity Research Journal, 10,* 91–93.

Díaz de Chumaceiro, C. L., & Yáber, O., G. E. (1995). Serendipity analogues: Modifications of the traditional case study for a psychotherapy research with music. *The Arts in Psychotherapy, 22,* 155–159.

Encyclopaedia Britannica (1952). *The great ideas: A syntopicon of great books of the western world* (Vol. 2). Chicago: Encyclopaedia Britannica.

Kantorovich, A. (1993). *Scientific discovery: Logic and tinkering.* New York: State University of New York Press.

Lewis, W. S. (Ed.). (1960). *Horace Walpole's correspondence.* (The Yale Edition, Vol. 20, pp. 407–408. New Haven, CT: Yale University Press.

Merton, R. K. (1949). *Social theory and social structure.* (1968 enlarged edition.) New York: Free Press.

Roberts. R. M. (1989). *Serendipity: Accidental discoveries in science.* New York: Wiley.

Rothenberg, A. (1988). *The creative process of psychotherapy.* New York: Norton.

Simonton, D. K. (1988). *Scientific genius: A psychology of science.* Cambridge, MA: Cambridge University Press.

Anne Sexton

1928–1974

Poet

Author of *To Bedlam and Part Way Back* (1960), *All My Pretty Ones* (1962), *Selected Poems* (1964), *Live or Die* (1966), *Love Poems* (1969), *Mercy Street* (1969), *Transformations* (1971), *The Book of Folly* (1972), *The Death Notebooks* (1974), *The Awful Rowing Toward God* (1975), *45 Mercy Street* (1976), *Words for Dr. Y* (1978), *Collected Poems* (1981), *Selected Poems* (1988)

Cathy Sanguinetti

Independent Writer/Producer

Susan Kavaler-Adler

Object Relations Institute for Psychotherapy and Psychoanalysis, New York

*With a high school diploma in one hand and no college degree in the other, **ANNE SEXTON** became one of the most famous and respected contemporary poets of her time. She began writing poetry in 1956 after watching a lecture on television about writing a sonnet. She propped up a typewriter and confidently began to write. From then on, Dr. Martin Orne, with whom she had just started psychiatric treatment following a suicide attempt, cultivated her identity as a poet as a way of recovering from the emotional instability that had led her to attempt suicide. Soon she would bring dozens of poems into her therapy sessions where she obtained the strength and encouragement she had lacked in her upbringing. Throughout her lifetime, Sexton received accolades from the most prestigious universities in the world such as honorary doctorates and Phi Beta Kappa keys from Harvard, Radcliffe, Tufts, and many more. She was praised by a myriad of literary societies including the most notable—the Pulitzer Prize for her book* Live or Die. *She received travel grants, Radcliffe fellowships, and even-*

Anne Sexton in Library. Used with permission from CORBIS/Bettmann.

tually became a regular instructor at Boston University—an accomplishment she was very proud of. She performed and read her poetry at readings all over the United States and England. Sexton spoke before Auden in a British event and with the most noted poets of her day. She took workshops with Robert Lowell, W. D. Snodgrass and John Holmes; and she was privately tutored by notable mentors. She had her own musical group backing up her rhymes, called Anne Sexton and Her Kind. When she took her life in 1974, Sexton was only 45 years old. A previously scheduled reading at Town Hall in New York City turned into a memorial service for the poet. In her eulogy, Adrienne Rich said, "We have had enough suicidal women poets, enough suicidal women, enough self-destructiveness as the sole form of violence permitted to women." Later, Denise Levertov wrote the Boston Globe*'s obituary of Sexton: "Anne Sexton's tragedy will not be without influence in the tragedies of our lives. We who are alive must make clear, as she could not, the distinction between creativity and self-destruction. The tendency to confuse the two has claimed too many victims."*

I. CHILDHOOD

Anne Gray Harvey was born on November 9, 1928, in Newton Massachusetts. She was the third of three girls; Jane was born in 1923 and Blanche was born in 1925. Her parents were Ralph and Mary Gray Staples Harvey, whom biographer Diane Wood Middlebrook described as a couple "out of a Scott Fitzgerald novel." They lived life at the fullest in the height of the roaring 1920s. Anne's father, Ralph was a successful businessman in the wool industry and traveled extensively. Later when Anne would meet her husband Kayo, he too would work in the wool business and spend many days traveling—a separation that was devastating for Anne. Ralph had but one sibling, a sister named Frances. Interestingly enough, Frances tried to commit suicide when she was in her twenties. She eventually married and lived a normal life with her husband on their horse farm. But in 1975, a year after Anne had taken her own life, Frances shot herself to death at the age of 69. Middlebrook noted that Anne's own suicide had affected Frances profoundly. Anne's mother, Mary Gray Staples, was an only child and, as such, was raised

as a little princess. She came from a prominent and popular family. As the only daughter, Mary Gray was very close to her father, Arthur Gray Staples, whom everyone called AGS.

While Anne was growing up she and her sisters did not form strong emotional ties with one another, probably because they were constantly competing for their parents' attention. Growing up, the eldest, Jane, was Ralph Harvey's favorite. Blanche, on the other hand, was recognized as the studious one in the family. She was the only one who went to college and who had a stable life. Tragically, Jane and Anne would both commit suicide during middle age.

As the baby of the family, Anne loved to be cuddled. She recalled feeling very lonely as a child. Family life was formal. The "girls," as they were commonly called, had to be formally dressed and ready to entertain at any time. Ralph and Mary Gray led a self-serving and self-absorbed life, full of parties, drinking and excessiveness. It did not help matters that Anne was fidgety, messy, and loud. She hated mealtimes and would often take her food to her bedroom. Her physical appearance and attire did not meet Ralph's demanding and impeccable expectations. She was a chatterbox and very active.

Some of Anne's happiest times were spent on Squirrel Island during the summers when the family would vacation there. It was during this time that Anne was nurtured by the women in her family other than her own mother. Her favorite great aunt was Anna Ladd Dingley, whom she called Nana. They became very close. When Anne was 12, AGS died and the houses on the island were sold. Thus, the summers at Squirrel Island ended.

During this time also, Anne's parents' drinking became worse, especially her father's drinking. Their behavior was unpredictable. They could be sweet at times, but at other times they would lash out in a rage. But it was her father's drinking that most seemed to affect Anne. He was like Dr. Jekyll and Mr. Hyde. One moment he could be very attentive. At other times he would insult Anne by telling her she disgusted him with her acne scars.

Nana actually came to live with the Sexton's when Anne was eleven. In 1940 Anne had a severe constipation problem and was hospitalized at the Lahey Clinic. Anne later told her therapist that this was a traumatic time because her mother had threatened to take her for a colostomy if she did not make an effort to put an end to her elimination problems.

It was also during this time that Mary Gray was away from home a lot taking care of her dying father. At some point, someone suggested that Anne be taken for psychological evaluation—probably as a response to her elimination problems and to her problems at school. But her parents ignored this suggestion. As usual, her parents displayed more interest in keeping up with their social activities rather than attending to the needs of their children.

When Anne was 13, she became interested in boys and would spend more and more time on the phone and out with her friends. This meant less time spent with Nana. One day, Nana's ear closed up and she became disoriented. She eventually was taken to a mental hospital for shock treatment.

By this time, Anne was fifteen. Her grandfather Louis Harvey had a second nervous breakdown and Ralph, Anne's father, was drinking heavily. Mary Gray spent a great deal of time trying to hide her husband's problem.

Finally in 1944, Nana was taken to live in a nursing home and she eventually died in 1954 when she was 86 years old. Anne would mark the departure of Nana for the rest of her life—feeling guilty that it had been her fault, that Nana got sick because she had abandoned her. This perspective was Anne's way of showing loyalty toward Nana. This guilt would resurface when Anne herself would become a mother.

II. ADOLESCENCE

Although in adulthood Anne recalled her adolescence as painful and uneventful, much information suggests otherwise. She had a couple of early relationships with boys that she recorded in her scrapbooks. Her first kiss came from Michael Bearpark who would later become a psychiatrist and see Anne again in the early 1960s during one of her visits to England. Although this first kiss was special, it would also be associated with Nana's breakdown in Anne's memory. So the kiss was also associated with betrayal.

Her other good friend from adolescence was Richard Sherwood. She later ran into him while on honeymoon with Kayo in Virginia Beach. Sherwood recalls Anne as being fun to be with and very talkative. When he saw Anne again with Kayo, he remembered how happy and full of sexual energy they were.

During the eighth grade, Anne had a steady boyfriend, Jack McCarthy. He was very much liked by Mary Gray and Sherwood and they hoped that she would eventually marry him. McCarthy remembered Anne as an extraordinary person—open about her feelings and energetic. They socialized a great deal and Anne was very flirtatious with other boys around him. Although McCarthy remembered Anne as pretty normal he did recall one incident that he found somewhat disturbing.

One night, the couple had a date to go sledding behind Anne's house. McCarthy was late, but when he arrived at the house, Anne was not there. He found her at the bottom of the hill unconscious and bleeding. When he brought her inside the house, he realized that the blood was Mercurochrome and that she had faked passing out. She had dramatized her own death and rationalized it by telling him that it was a good joke on him. Early on, Anne displayed an obsessive curiosity with death. This incident marked the beginning of a long trail of experiments with death.

During her teens, Anne was seen as "boy-crazed." So her parents sent her to Rogers Hall, a boarding school. Again, while Anne would recall a lonely past, her yearbook portrayed a normal and even popular teenager. She was captain of the cheerleaders and was on the swimming and basketball teams. Most important, she directed a school play and starred in all the others. It appears that it was here at Rogers Hall that poetic seeds were planted in Anne's memory that would later save and serve her. She even published some of her poetry in the school's literary magazine called *Splinters*.

III. EARLY WRITINGS

But it also seemed that early on in her life, her parents did not encourage her writing abilities. The first episode that scarred Anne for life was when her mother investigated the originality of one of her poems. The poem was going to be published in the school's yearbook. Prior to this, Anne's sister Jane had plagiarized and one of Anne's friends had been expelled from school for doing the same thing. Mary Gray, distrustful that her daughter Anne was also plagiarizing, sent the poem to a professor in New York for validation. The professor said that it looked like an original piece and that it showed a lot of promise. Anne was devastated and discontinued writing poetry for the next 10 years. It was clear from the scrapbooks that Anne kept during her high school years that she was expected only to find a husband and not to achieve academic success.

Later on when Anne started publishing her first poems, she thought again about becoming the writer in the family. Her mother, Mary Gray, had the reputation of being the family writer—a reputation which perhaps led her to envy her daughter's achievements in high school. But Mary Gray was no writer.

Anne's second great parental disappointment came when she published poetry in the *Christian Science Monitor* and her father compared her writing to that of Mary Gray's. He said that the "girls" were creative, but that Mary Gray was brilliant.

IV. MARRIAGE AND MOTHERHOOD

In May of 1948, while planning her wedding to a young man, Anne met Alfred Muller Sexton II, better known as Kayo. Three months later, the couple eloped. They married on August 16 in Sunbury, North Carolina and honeymooned on Virginia Beach.

Kayo came from a wealthy Bostonian family. His parents were George Sexton and Wilhelmine Muller, whom everyone called Billie. He was born the same year as Anne Sexton, in 1928, and Kayo's younger sister, Joan, was born in 1931. It is perhaps of no surprise that Kayo would marry Anne. As children and into adolescence both Kayo and Anne lived with alcoholic fathers and with mothers who desperately tried to control their husbands' addictions.

In the beginning, Anne Sexton's relationship with Kayo was intense, happy, and sexually fulfilling. Sexton tried hard to become a good housewife while Kayo continued taking premedical courses at Colgate University. But he dropped out of school in order to begin a more serious and mature life with Sexton. He got into the wool business as a salesperson. Sexton became good friends with Joan, her sister-in-law. They eventually moved in to Kayo's parents' house where Sexton

began to display some interesting personality traits, such as throwing temper tantrums when her mother-in-law would ask her to do something simple. But from the start, Sexton had not made a good impression on Kayo's mother Billie. The first time they met, right before the couple was married, Sexton shocked Billie with her bright red lipstick and chain-smoking.

Motherhood and couplehood presented a variety of complications for Sexton. In 1953 Sexton had her first daughter, Linda Gray. In 1955 she had Joyce (Joy) Ladd. She found it impossible to care for her children and herself while Kayo traveled on business. She would go into deep depressions and rage at her eldest, Linda. After Linda's birth, she was diagnosed with post-partum depression. Shortly after Joy's birth, Sexton tried to commit suicide. This led her to Dr. Martin Orne who became a major player in Sexton's life.

V. EMOTIONAL DISORDERS AND TREATMENT

When Dr. Orne first met Sexton, he asked her what she could do to have an identity in the world. Sexton could not think of anything to say except that she could possibly become a prostitute.

In the 1950s when Anne Sexton first showed dramatic signs of mental disturbance, the treatment of emotional disorders was rudimentary in the United States. When Sexton first resorted to mad suicidal gestures to display a formerly hidden anguish, the treatment available to her was limited.

When she first entered treatment with Dr. Orne, she had been a housewife and mother, living in the suburbs of Boston. She was embedded in the Massachusetts conservatism that in the 1950s was at its height of sexism. Sexton with her constant agitation was never noted as in any way out of the ordinary until she overdosed with sleeping pills. Her first suicidal gesture seemed like a hysterical play. Soon after marriage to Kayo, who became a traveling salesman like her father, Sexton unleashed her frenetic and manic temperament while her husband was on the road. She had brief sexual affairs in which she sought to have her hand held through the night. Being alone was intolerable. She commented that she didn't particularly like having affairs but that she needed "action." She manically defended against an inner emptiness generated by a sealed off early abandonment trauma. During her husband's regular absences, Sexton would stay up all night and listen to music, drink, and have drunken sex. After Kayo returned from his trips she would be temporarily all right. But she could not even cook a simple dish when he was away.

One of Sexton's romantic infatuations led her to precipitous wish to leave Kayo. Both her mother and mother-in-law told her to drop her newfound love and commit to Kayo. It was then that Sexton grasped control through masochistic self-destruction. She, who feared her mother-in-law and who craved the attention of her own narcissistically self-absorbed mother, struck out in the mode of the impotent. Sexton very dramatically took a load of pills and began to vomit. This was a defiant reaction to the two mother figures. Her suicide attempt was impulsive—like a tantrum. This dramatic gesture was to be the precedent for a long line of suicidal acts that ultimately ended in the last and fatal deed.

The family wished to forget, but Sexton's entrance into motherhood caused new seismic tremors. Sexton began to act totally out of control toward her older daughter, Linda. One day, at the sight of Linda putting feces in the back of a toy, Sexton threw Linda across the room. Later in a fight with Kayo, it would be her typewriter that she heaved across the room. Both Linda and the typewriter were extensions of herself. Sexton attacked Kayo by attacking herself, the writer in her who was symbolized by her typewriter. Sexton may have attacked Linda to disown that recalcitrant part of her inner being who wished to smear feces on her own mother when she had been so rigid about Sexton's constipation problem as a teenager.

Despite all the years she would spend subsequently seeing therapists, nobody was ever to inquire into all this in an effective way. Sexton could rage at Linda like she could never have raged as a child because it would have been too threatening to her bond with her narcissistic mother. If Sexton didn't risk revealing her rage as a child, perhaps it was because she feared that her mother would turn away from her with contemptuous indifference. Sexton's terror of abandonment from a mother who was competitive, self-absorbed, and emo-

tionally distant must have been incessant. Sexton's inability to form a healthy emotional and psychological bond with her mother must have severely impacted her ability to mother her own daughters.

From an object relations perspective, Sexton did not receive the proper treatment to her mental illness, which ultimately led to her own death. In a world without object relations theory and Melanie Klein, Anne was an example of the borderline personality.

When Dr. Orne first treated Anne for her suicide attempts, he did not practice the standard psychiatric approach to hospitalization of those days. Due to him, her 8-year treatment stands as a fortunate contrast to that of Sylvia Plath, who received multiple volleys of electric shock. Sexton's treatment was the exception to the rule. Dr. Orne prescribed some electric shock and a five times a week psychotherapy regime—an extreme exception for American psychiatry. At that time, Orne had been influenced by some education in psychoanalysis. Although not trained as a psychoanalyst, Orne had knowledge of Freudian psychoanalytic theory and of some clinical theory that enabled him to think in terms of the interaction of genetic history and transference. He also knew about the standard defense mechanisms.

Dr. Orne's five times a week engagement with Sexton during her early hospitalization at the Weston Lodge allowed Sexton to experience his presence, no matter how closed off she was by her dissociated and unintegrated psychic state. It is unfortunate that during later hospitalizations, Dr. Orne would not be with Sexton in this way. It appears that his counter-transference anger had by then got the better of him, as he did not know not to use and process such interactions in order to enable him to understand Sexton's internal world and its compulsion to perpetually repeat its drama. It appears that Dr. Orne gradually began to use hospitalization as a punishment.

But at this early stage of their contact, Dr. Orne was quite involved with observing all of Sexton's manifold incarnations. She was a chameleon becoming whomever she conversed with. Viewing this as a hysterical dynamic, Dr. Orne was not totally out of his depth when Sexton began to speak schizophrenic language. Not believing that she had a thought disorder, Dr. Orne removed Sexton from the schizophrenic ward and her language transformed back to normal. He noted her schizophrenic language induced by imitating others, as she merged with others to find an identity. He viewed this as part of Sexton's hysteria. Sexton's ability to so purely imitate, to model herself on others so quickly and thoroughly, can be related to a border-line hysterical dissociation, not to a neurotic hysteric's mode of repression. Dr. Orne did not make these distinctions. Sexton lacked the subjective *I*. She was not in herself, not in her body. She inhabited the paranoid-schizoid state of mind most of the time, a state of mind in which reactive reflex and reenactive reflex dominate the scene, rather than reflective thought. Dr. Orne did not understand the core schizoid level of Sexton's hysteria—the borderline preoedipal condition and its need for in-the-moment contact in treatment. He didn't understand that Sexton's chameleon mode of identification with anyone near her indicated a core lack of subjective self-identity and a borderline dissociation process as differentiated from neurotic hysteric's mode of repression that is founded on adequate preoedipal development.

Dr. Orne attempted to uncover her memories and history as in sessions in which she reported incest and sexual abuse from her father. He helped her discuss her lies and distortions, in relation to her memories. Yet the true memory lived in the moment—he did not tune into this.

One common aspect of Sexton's behavior was to go into trances. With Dr. Orne these trances would occur at the end of many sessions. Her sealed-off yearnings for connection, often manifested by body cravings or by an incorporation process in her mind, threatened to emerge through a pressured trance state, but they were warded off by emotional distancing during the therapy session. She became paralyzed at the end of each session, unable to leave and separate. She had not gotten what she needed in the session, the emotional contact and connection she required. The terror, need, blocked rage, and pain were contained in the state of trance.

During one session, this splitting process threatened to form a multiple personality. Unacquainted with borderline splitting, Dr. Orne was unequipped to deal with the phenomenology of a split-off personality appearing in the therapy session. Hoping to prevent Sexton's transition into a multiple personality, his response was to ignore the created personality whom Sexton

called "Elizabeth." He said that when he ignored Elizabeth, she went away. Dr. Orne thought he had stopped a pathological process. According to Sexton, however, Elizabeth was a little bitch. This bitch-witch part of her was the one that was erotically engaged in a sado-masochistic struggle with her father. Her father had become her demon lover when he spanked her and aroused her erotically. She wrote a poem for Dr. Orne titled "The Royal Strapping." Through the poem, Anne told him how her father had stripped her naked on his marriage bed and beat her behind with her own riding crop, just after she had returned from horseback riding. But the poem was never consciously experienced in the session, neither by Dr. Orne nor by Anne Sexton.

One of Sexton's best friends was the poet Maxine Kumin, whom she met at a poetry workshop by John Holmes. The two women had many things in common and they quickly became good friends—sharing poetry as well as dresses. Kumin, however, was well recognized in the poetry scene by the time she met Sexton. It appears that Kumin's successful status as a poet served Sexton well in terms of motivation and good role modeling. The first time Sexton shared a poem with Kumin—the poem "Music Swims Back to Me"—Kumin praised and encouraged Sexton.

Sexton eventually became a published and well-recognized poet herself. In her personal life however, she did not make progress. The mere presence of her daughters living at home with her disrupted and threatened her emotional well-being. As a result, Joy lived most of her early years with her paternal grandmother, Billie. Linda lived for a short while with her Aunt Blanche and Blanche's husband Ed. Although Linda lived with them a short while, she remembers this period of her life as an eternity. Unfortunately, Linda continued to suffer physical and emotional abuse from her Uncle Ed who would torture her with his leather belt and his lashing tongue.

As a result, Sexton spent very few years with her daughters, which affected the entire family. Billie seems to be the rock that kept the family together, but at a great cost. Having Billie pick up the pieces meant that Sexton had the freedom to manipulate and control as much as she wanted. Middlebrook noted that Joy was grateful for Billie's presence and mothering, however. Linda Gray made the same observation in her own autobiography.

Soon problems with Kayo began to arise due to Sexton's compulsion with poetry. Conferences, workshops, and trips would interfere with Kayo. Mixed in with her mental instability, Kayo found Sexton's new life intolerable. When he was around, they would get into horrible drunken fights in which they would both physically attack each other. Many of these happened in the presence of their daughters who would later have to explain to the police what had transpired.

No doubt that Sexton lived with a horrible fear of abandonment, which had existed since her childhood days. The feelings of being abandoned continued into adulthood. Anne lost Dr. Orne who took a job out of state. She eventually divorced Kayo, and her daughters went away to boarding schools or college.

Sexton's psychiatric treatment continued with a series of other doctors who just could not seem to help her. She became addicted to sleeping pills and alcohol. One of the most documented and alarming situations was Sexton's affair with one of her therapists, Dr. Ollie Zweizung. Breaching one of the cores of the patient-doctor relationship, Dr. Zweizung did not seem to understand the damage he would cause Sexton with his breach of boundary.

The last therapist Sexton saw was Barbara Schwartz. Nine months after she started seeing Schwartz, Sexton went to her scheduled appointment. It was October 4, 1974. She brought with her a poem she had written for Schwartz about a female therapist who took a young schizophrenic patient through a symbolic gestation and rebirth. Sexton had apparently felt a sense of gratitude toward Schwartz for the 9 months of therapy she had given her. Schwartz did not see the poem or Sexton's behavior as a form of saying good-bye until she noticed that Sexton had deliberately left her cigarettes behind—something Sexton would never do.

Later that day, Sexton had lunch with Kumin who was getting ready to take a long trip with her family to Europe. After the lunch, Sexton went home. After having a drink of vodka, she took off all her rings, and put on her mother's fur coat. She went to the garage; got in her car; turned on the radio and started the engine. On this night Anne Sexton experimented with suicide for the last time and ended her own life.

It was evident from the amount of documentation that Sexton left behind that she led a troubled life. Unable to cope with the demands of motherhood, Sexton lived torn between being a bad mother and wife, and being a great poet. The two lives could not coexist. She had once told Dr. Orne, "You see, I've taken care of that 'life' part by writing poems." This quote could not better describe Sexton's feelings for wanting to be a complete human being with a unique talent. But amid all the turmoil in her life, she was able to work every day. She was able to love her daughters as is depicted in Linda Gray Sexton's own autobiography *Searching for Mercy Street* where she quotes a song that her mother had written for her: "Night-night time has come for Linda Gray, Night-night time, the same time every day, It's night-night time, It's night-night time, night-night time has come."

Bibliography

Kavaler-Adler, S. (1993). *The compulsion to create.* New York: Routledge.

Kavaler-Adler, S. (1996). *The creative mystique.* New York: Routledge.

Middlebrook, D. W. (1991). *Anne Sexton: A biography.* Boston: Houghton Mifflin.

Sexton, L. G. (1994). *Searching for Mercy Street.* New York: Little Brown and Company.

William Shakespeare

1564–1616

English dramatist, poet, and actor

Author of 37 plays and 154 sonnets

Dean Keith Simonton

University of California, Davis

WILLIAM SHAKESPEARE created a body of plays and poems that are considered among the greatest in English literature. The plays include tragedies, such as Hamlet, Othello, *and* King Lear, *comedies, including* Much Ado about Nothing, As You Like It, *and* Taming of the Shrew, *and histories, such as* Richard III *and* Henry IV, *Parts I and II. Besides the collection of sonnets in Elizabethan form, Shakespeare wrote two heroic narrative poems,* Venus and Adonis *and* The Rape of Lucrece. *Often given the byname Bard of Avon or Swan of Avon, Shakespeare's literary creativity has shaped immeasurably the vocabulary, imagery, metaphors, and modes of expression in the English language. His best plays are often judged as among the greatest in any language, ancient or modern. Shakespeare is frequently seen as the prototypical literary genius.*

I. LIFE

For a creative genius of his stature, the biographical information about Shakespeare's life is surprisingly meager. We know that he was born in Stratford-upon-Avon, on April 23, 1564, where he presumably was educated at the local grammar school. At 18 he married Anne Hathaway, from the same town, who bore him three children, a daughter Susanna and the twins Judith and Hamnet. A couple of years later, he began to attain success as a playwright in London, where he became a member of the Lord Chamberlain's Company, London's leading theater group. Shakespeare prospered sufficiently that he could retire to his birthplace, living

William Shakespeare. Used with permission from The Folger Shakespeare Library.

out his final years as a country gentleman. He died in Stratford-upon-Avon on April 23, 1616, and was buried in the parish church. Only a month before, Shakespeare had made out his will, famous for the passage in which he left his wife the "second-best bed" in the house. Only a handful of largely impersonal legal documents and miscellaneous notices add any further details to this biographical sketch.

The sparseness of the biographical information has led a number of dissenting scholars to argue that Shakespeare was not the true author of the works that currently make up the canon. Among the candidates put forward are the essayist and philosopher Francis Bacon, the dramatist Christopher Marlowe, Edward de Vere, the 17th earl of Oxford, and William Stanley, 6th earl of Derby. These rival claims are often predicated on the belief that the true author must have had a higher social standing and a better education than that enjoyed by Shakespeare—an assumption that may reveal more class prejudice than a genuine understanding of creative development. Moreover, advocacy of these alternative candidates must overcome a host of factual difficulties of their own. Marlowe, for example, was killed in a tavern brawl in 1593, before Shakespeare began to produce the major plays on which his reputation rests. Just as important, more than four dozen contemporaries testify to Shakespeare's authorship, including his fellow actors as well as his fellow playwright, Ben Jonson. It is always possible that some authentic document will someday be found in some dusty archive that proves once and for all that someone else wrote the plays and poems. But until that day arises, the best conclusion to draw is that the traditional attribution is the correct one.

In any case, given how little is known about the man, it is clear that if we wish to understand Shakespeare's creativity we must turn from biography to the creative products that have earned him such an exalted place in world literature.

II. WORKS

Shakespeare's two large poems, *Venus and Adonis* and *The Rape of Lucrece,* were both written relatively early in his career, the first appearing when he was 29 and the second when he was 30. Although not without con-

siderable literary merit, Shakespeare's reputation rests most firmly on his sonnets and plays. Furthermore, these latter two manifestations of his genius are those that have attracted the most empirical research by psychologists who study creativity.

A. The 154 Sonnets

Shakespeare's sonnets were published in 1609, when the poet was in his mid-40s, although most of the poems probably date from when he was in his 30s. There has been considerable scholarly speculation about the autobiographical significance of these sonnets. The poems contain many cryptic references to various persons, including a rival poet, a dark woman, and a handsome young man. Whether or not these persons were real or imagined may never be determined. But what can be expressed with confidence is that Shakespeare managed to express strong feelings and universal themes within a tightly regulated literary framework. Almost all sonnets follow the same Elizabethan form of three quatrains and a couplet, all 14 lines in iambic pentameter and restricted to the rhyme scheme of *a b a b, c d c d, e f e f, g g.*

Although many of these poems represent some of the highest accomplishments in the history of the English sonnet, it remains true that the collection contains creations of uneven merit. Research on creativity has shown that even the greatest geniuses have days when their muses seem to abandon them, and Shakespeare was no exception. This variation in aesthetic success is evident in the differential frequency that the 154 sonnets are included in anthologies or cited in books of quotations. Content analytical studies have shown that the more popular sonnets differ in identifiable ways from those that remain in relative obscurity. In particular, the more successful sonnets treat a greater variety of themes, employ a richer vocabulary, and display much more primary-process imagery. These investigations have also demonstrated that the more popular sonnets tend to manipulate linguistic expression across the consecutive lines in highly distinctive manner. Particularly notable is the way Shakespeare designs the concluding couplet so that it provides enriched associative linkages with the preceding three quatrains. Remarkably, these characteristics of the most accomplished sonnets have been discerned by computer programs designed to tease out the content and style of literary text.

Unfortunately, it is not yet known whether these enhancing aesthetic attributes apply to other poems besides those attributed to Shakespeare.

B. The 37 Plays

Shakespeare wished to stake his fame on his poetry. Crafting plays, in contrast, is what he did to earn a good living—roughly analogous to writing film scripts today. Yet it is one of the ironies of his life that the dramas now probably represent his most pervasive and influential legacy to world civilization. Needless to say, not all of Shakespeare's dramas have received the same praise from posterity. Like the sonnets, the plays are not all of equal quality. For example, *Hamlet* is by far the most highly acclaimed, whereas his *Henry VI* trilogy could disappear off the face of the earth without damaging Shakespeare's reputation whatsoever. Accordingly, to appreciate better the basis for Shakespeare's creative genius, researchers have tried to fathom why some plays are more successful than others. The starting place for such empirical inquiries is the information exhibited in Table I. This lists all of the plays in the traditional Shakespeare canon (omitting only *The Two Noble Kinsmen*, which most scholars ascribe largely if not entirely to John Fletcher). Alongside each play are two key data. First are the estimated dates based on a statistical analysis of the many tentative datings of the plays advanced by Shakespeare scholars. Despite the presumed disagreements, these amount to no more than "tempests in a teapot," for an extremely impressive consensus prevails (i.e., the internal consistency alpha reliability of the datings is .999). Second are the ratings of the 37 plays according to their frequency of performance, recording, and quotation, the number of single editions and film versions, the number of operatic versions, subjective evaluations by Shakespeare experts, and so forth. These summary scores, too, are highly reliable (i.e., the internal consistency alpha is .88). To facilitate comparisons, they have been put in the form of standard scores (viz., z-scores with means of zero and standard deviations of 1). Thus, plays with negative scores are below average in merit, whereas those with positive scores are above average in merit. It is obvious, for example, that *Hamlet* stands at the very

TABLE I
The Shakespeare Dramatic Canon: Production Dates and Dramatic Popularity

Play	Date	Popularity
King Henry VI, Part 1	1591	−1.51
King Henry VI, Part 2	1591	−1.41
King Henry VI, Part 3	1591	−1.62
The Comedy of Errors	1592	−0.37
The Tragedy of Richard III	1593	0.23
Titus Andronicus	1593	−1.13
The Two Gentlemen of Verona	1593	−1.13
Love's Labour's Lost	1593	−0.81
The Taming of the Shrew	1594	0.58
Romeo and Juliet	1595	1.34
The Tragedy of Richard II	1595	−0.02
A Midsummer Night's Dream	1595	1.00
The Merchant of Venice	1596	0.98
The Life and Death of King John	1596	−1.13
Henry IV, Part 1	1597	0.27
Henry IV, Part 2	1598	−0.27
Much Ado about Nothing	1598	0.31
The Life of Henry V	1599	0.48
Julius Caesar	1599	0.55
As You Like It	1599	0.82
The Merry Wives of Windsor	1600	−0.07
Twelfth Night (or What You Will)	1601	0.90
Hamlet, Prince of Denmark	1601	2.19
Troilus and Cressida	1602	−0.74
All's Well that Ends Well	1603	−0.68
Measure for Measure	1604	0.34
Othello, the Moor of Venice	1604	1.19
King Lear	1605	1.36
Macbeth	1606	1.53
Antony and Cleopatra	1607	0.31
Timon of Athens	1607	−1.51
Coriolanus	1608	−0.81
Pericles	1608	−1.31
Cymbeline	1610	−0.17
The Winter's Tale	1610	0.19
The Tempest	1611	1.00
The Famous History of the Life of King Henry VIII	1613	−0.89

top, while *Henry VI, Part 3*, sits at the very bottom. The play *Richard II*, in contrast, may be said to represent the typical level of quality for a Shakespeare drama.

These two columns of data immediately suggest an interesting question: How did Shakespeare's dramatic success change over the course of his creative career? At first there may seem to be no clear pattern, because successful and unsuccessful plays seem to be interspersed throughout his career. Yet closer inspection suggests that many of his greatest plays appear when he was in his late 30s and early 40s, a career peak well in accord with the findings of research on the relation between age and achievement. In fact, when we fit a curvilinear age function, we obtain the results seen in Figure 1. The inverted-U curve accounts for 27% of the longitudinal variation in dramatic merit, a highly impressive percentage.

Of course, there still exists considerable fluctuation around this trend line. Hence, most of the differential impact of Shakespeare's plays cannot be attributed to age alone. Nonetheless, as in the case of the sonnets, empirical investigations have managed to isolate some of the factors that discriminate the masterpieces from the also-rans. One predictor is the thematic material that is featured in the play. For instance, those dramas that treat strong human feelings—especially those that verge on madness or emotional excess—tend to gain in popularity. *Othello, Lear,* and *Hamlet* are fine illustrations of this effect. In addition, certain stylistic devices also make a contribution to aesthetic impact. For example, Shakespeare's output shows evidence that he skillfully employed puns in order to enhance the effectiveness of his plays. Especially fascinating is his use of puns to provide comedy relief, such as the famous Porter Scene in *Macbeth.*

Thus far we have been concentrating on the deter-

minants of the comparative popularity of the 37 plays. But this has not been the only aesthetic attribute worthy of investigation. In fact, much research has concentrated on the factors that shape the form and content of these same dramas. Shakespeare's age, for instance, is linked with the themes scrutinized in his plays. As a young man, love themes tended to relatively conspicuous, especially when he was in his early 30s, but gradually this preoccupation yielded to more weighty issues, such as conflict in human affairs. The contrast between *Romeo and Juliet* and *Hamlet* exemplifies this change. Other developmental shifts may be seen in his use of primary- and secondary-process imagery, incongruous juxtapositions of images, and various linguistic devices, such as the use of rhymes, prose, and run-on lines. Clearly, Shakespeare's mode of creative expression was far from static, but rather displayed a dynamic progression over the course of his long dramatic career. In this respect, the Bard behaved just like other geniuses of the highest rank, such as Beethoven and Michelangelo. Creative geniuses seldom sit still.

The plays reveal Shakespeare to be like other great creators in yet another respect. The creative genius, no matter how grand, does not work in isolation from the external milieu. On the contrary, Shakespeare's dramatic output betrays many signs that he was ever responsive to the zeitgeist, especially in the political realm. Conspiracies against the throne, internal rebellions, and military threats from foreign powers all left their imprint on the thematic material found in his plays. For instance, when England found itself under attack by foreign military forces, Shakespeare was inspired to devote more lines to the discussion of war, conquest, and empire. The political circumstances could even exert a more direct effect on a play's aesthetic success, for the more popular works tended to come shortly after a major rebellion or conspiracy shocked the nation. The less popular dramas, in contrast, were more likely to emerge after the times had been more politically tranquil. This is also a consequence that has counterparts in the careers of other creators.

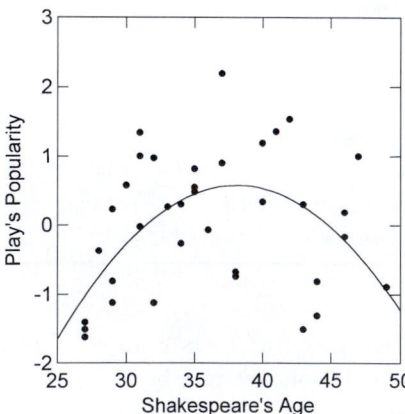

FIGURE 1 The curve best describing the relation between Shakespeare's age and a play's dramatic popularity. The quadratic function explains 27% of the longitudinal fluctuations.

III. CONCLUSION

The foregoing review could only present the highlights of what has become a very rich research literature on the Shakespeare canon. These empirical findings have not only given us insights into Shakespeare's life and works, but have also shed some light on how creativity may operate in other writers. Indeed, if we had to pick one genius as the starting point for a more general understanding of literary creativity, it is hard to imagine a better place to start than with the Bard. He is arguably the most influential of all literary creators. After all, Shakespeare's plays are still produced on stages all over the globe and in all of the world's major languages. They have been recorded on records, cassettes, compact discs, videotapes, and full-length feature films. The plays have also been adapted, extended, or transformed in a great diversity of ways, such as Akira Kurosawa's movie *Ran* (from *King Lear*), Leonard Bernstein's musical *West Side Story* (from *Romeo and Juliet*), and Tom Stoppard's play *Rosencrantz and Guildenstern Are Dead* (from *Hamlet*). Additional reverberations of his dramas show up in cartoons, comic books, and children's storybooks as well as in tone poems, songs, modern dance and ballet compositions, puppet shows, and even kabuki theater. Shakespeare's dramatic genius has inspired more operas than any other author, classic or modern. A partial list of the operatic composers inspired by his greatness include Adam, Barber, Bellini, Berlioz, Britten, Bruch, Goldmark, Gounod, Halévy, Holst, Nicolaï, Purcell, Rossini, Smetana, Vaughan Williams, Verdi, Wagner, and Wolf-Ferrari. Even the Bard's poetry has continued to sustain his posthumous reputation, albeit in a more quiet way, such as a booklet titled *Sonnets* gently tucked away in a traveler's suitcase. As Ben Jonson declared in the 1623 *First Folio,* Shakespeare "was not of an age, but for all time!"

Bibliography

Derks, P. L. (1989). Pun frequency and popularity of Shakespeare's plays. *Empirical Studies Arts, 7,* 23.

Derks, P. L. (1994). Clockwork Shakespeare: The Bard meets the Regressive Imagery Dictionary. *Empirical Studies Arts, 12,* 131.

Simonton, D. K. (1986). Popularity, content, and context in 37 Shakespeare plays. *Poetics, 15,* 493.

Simonton, D. K. (1989). Shakespeare's sonnets: A case of and for single-case historiometry. *Journal of Personality, 57,* 695.

Simonton, D. K. (1990). Lexical choices and aesthetic success: A computer content analysis of 154 Shakespeare sonnets. *Computers & Humanities, 24,* 251.

Simonton, D. K. (1997). Imagery, style, and content in 37 Shakespeare plays. *Empirical Studies Arts, 15,* 15.

Simonton, D. K., Taylor, K., & Cassandro, V. (1998). The creative genius of William Shakespeare: Historiometric analyses of his plays and sonnets. In A. Steptoe (Ed.), *Genius and the mind: Studies of creativity and temperament in the historical record.* New York: Oxford University Press.

George Bernard Shaw

1856–1950

Writer

Author of many works of fiction and nonfiction; most noted for
his plays such as *Pygmalion, St. Joan,* and *Major Barbara*

Laura Tahir

Correctional Behavioral Solutions
Mount Laurel, New Jersey

GEORGE BERNARD SHAW *is one of the most quoted
writers of the past 2 centuries. He was born in Dublin in
1856. Never a good student, he quit school at age 15
and worked as a clerk in a real estate office. His self-
education in the arts flourished, and in 1876 he emigrated to London where his mother and two sisters had
gone 3 years earlier. In London he made friends with a
wide range of artists and intellectuals. He began writing
music and art criticism, and in 1878 wrote his first
novel,* Immaturity. *After writing another four novels in
4 years, he gave up this genre. He was greatly influenced
by the work of Marx and other socialist writers. During
the 1880s he was active in the Fabian Society, a middle-
class socialist group in which he learned to debate and
lecture. There he met Sidney and Beatrice Webb, as well
as Charlotte Payne Townshend, whom he married in
1898. Shaw's plays became a means to express his ideas
about class and his criticism of Victorian and romantic
attitudes. He became well known for the polemical prefaces that he wrote to his plays. A Nobel Prize winner,
Shaw wrote more than 50 plays during his long lifetime.
As a playwright, critic, public speaker, and even as a
politician, his influence has spread worldwide.*

George Bernard Shaw in the study at Shaw's corner, 1946. Used
with permission from Popperphoto/Archive Photos.

I. EARLY LIFE IN DUBLIN

George Bernard Shaw was born in Dublin on July 26, 1856, to George Carr Shaw (1814–1885) and Lucinda Elizabeth Gurly Shaw (1830–1913). George Carr Shaw was the second cousin of a baronet, and this status as a gentleman gave him certain privileges and invitations; however, he had no inheritance, no particular skills, and an unfortunate drinking habit that soon alienated the whole Shaw family. George Carr Shaw eventually became a teetotaler, a practice his son would later assume. Although the younger Shaw often described his father (as well as his mother) in disparaging terms, he nevertheless acknowledged the gift of humor he received from him. In his autobiographical *Sixteen Self Sketches*, written when he was 93, Shaw described his mother as "the daughter of a country gentleman," "brought up with ruthless strictness to be a paragon of all ladylike virtues and accomplishments by her grand aunt." He attributed his imagination to Lucinda Elizabeth Gurly, an accomplished musician who apparently took care not to squander any passion on her family. The capacity for (or perhaps pose of) emotional coolness for which Shaw is often criticized must have been learned from his mother. George and Lucinda were not a happy couple and their home life was lacking in warmth. Given this type of upbringing, Shaw's self-reliance was learned early.

Fortunately for young Shaw there were a few maternal uncles who helped provide some nurturance and guidance. But perhaps the most important influence on him was that of George John Lee (1831–1886), his mother's singing teacher and close friend of the family. Lee was an eccentric man, short, dark, and crippled since childhood by an accident to his foot. He was a well-established orchestral and operatic conductor in Dublin who had created a method of singing that Shaw claimed preserved his mother's voice perfectly until her death at over age 80. Lee offered music to the Shaws, as well as the vitality of fresh ideas. Lee and the Shaws united households in 1863 when the two families moved into a four-storey house at Number One Hatch Street.

Shaw loathed school. He quit school at age 15 and became a junior clerk in the Charles Uniacke Townshend land-agency office. Meanwhile, the household was filled with music rehearsals and lessons of Lucinda Shaw and George John Lee, and young Shaw had an excellent ear for music. He also spent hours studying the masterpieces at the Dublin National Gallery and enrolled in freehand classes in the Royal Dublin Society's School of Art. He was an avid visitor of the Royal Theatre, and he read Dickens, Scott, Shakespeare, Bunyan, the Bible, and much of the contemporary popular literature.

Shaw's work at Uniacke Townshend was a source of boredom for him, but he did his job well. In *Sixteen Self Sketches,* he wrote that "my desk and cashbox gave me the habit of daily work, and taught me that I must learn to do something instead of daydreaming, and that nothing but technical skill, practice, efficiency: in short, mastery, could be of any use to me." Thus, we see the beginnings of a most remarkable self-discipline that would result in Shaw's prolific output through his long career.

In 1873 the Shaw-Lee household broke up when Lee's musical career became so successful that he changed his name to George John Vandeleur Lee and ambitiously left Dublin for London. One month later, Mrs. Shaw sold the Hatch Street House, sent her husband and son to a nearby boarding house, and with her two daughters followed Lee to London. Young Shaw soon became restless in Dublin, and in 1876 he resigned from his job at Uniacke Townshend and moved to England.

II. SHAW'S APPRENTICESHIP IN LONDON

Shaw arrived in England just 4 days after his sister Agnes died of consumption on the Isle of Wight. He stayed there with his mother and sister Lucy for a month before the three of them then moved to London. Shaw notes in his diary that he was "unoccupied" during his first months in London. He was shy and awkward at this time. Although he was not certain where his talents would take him, he claimed many years later in the preface to his first novel, *Immaturity,* that "as the English language was my weapon, there was nothing for it but London." He began to ghost-write articles for *The Hornet* and he continued to study music, French, and Italian.

In 1878 Shaw undertook three serious literary efforts. He began *My Dear Dorothea* in January. This short piece (approximately 4200 words) is a fictional letter of advice to a 5-year-old girl, Dorothea. It was intended to be the first of a series of letters on moral education, but no other letters of the proposed series have ever been found. *My Dear Dorothea* was published posthumously in 1956. Shaw's most important advice to Dorothea is that she "always strive to find out what to do by thinking." He warned that thought will bring self-insight, and that this insight may be disappointing. In this early effort one can see the emergence of Shavian form and content: humor, paradox, moralizing, the use of the letter as a means of expression, a female as the main character, and many inchoate ideas that would later become major themes of Shaw's work. *Passion Play,* a satirical drama in verse form, was begun in February 1878 and never finished. In this play Shaw continued to develop some of the themes from *My Dear Dorothea.* Also written in 1878 was an outline for a novel, which Shaw never completed, called *The Legg Papers.*

In March 1879 Shaw began his daily habit of writing every day. He submitted about a dozen essays to numerous publications. Two were accepted: "Opera in Italian" and "Christian Names." He read books at the British Museum on etiquette so that he could accept invitations from his sister's friends (as well as from associations he met through Lee). Gradually, he developed self-confidence. During this same year he began working for the Edison Telephone Company at a position that required him to persuade reluctant people in the east end of London to erect telephone poles on their property. He was promoted twice, but he eventually gave up the job in order to devote all efforts to writing. During the next 5 years he completed five novels, none of which were successful.

London in the 1880s was a good place to stimulate Shaw's curious mind. The ideas of such thinkers as Darwin, Marx, Spencer, and the Mills created an intense intellectual climate in which people could discuss and argue scientific, social, philosophical, and political issues. During this time Shaw became a lifelong believer in vegetarianism. He joined the Land Reform Union and the Fabian Society, both of which were middle-class socialist groups.

In 1885 Shaw began writing *Widower's Houses,* in collaboration with his friend William Archer. Archer,

who had known Ibsen personally, had translated some of the Norwegian playwright's work, and around that time Shaw became familiar with and deeply impressed by Ibsen's social criticism. In 1891 Shaw wrote *The Quintessence of Ibsenism,* championing Ibsen's plays of social purpose. *Widower's Houses,* which Shaw would later complete on his own, was an attack on the practices of slumlords in Victorian England. It was produced in 1892, with little success, and eventually published in his *Plays, Pleasant and Unpleasant* (1898). Shaw had come to feel that people should attend the theater in order to face unpleasant facts rather than to be entertained. The four "pleasant" plays in this collection, comedies with serious themes, are *Arms and the Man, Candida, The Man of Destiny,* and *You Never Can Tell.* The "unpleasant" plays (in addition to *Widower's Houses*) that deal with class injustice and sexual morality are *Mrs. Warren's Profession* and *The Philanderer.*

III. SHAW IN THE 20TH CENTURY

Shaw went on to write *Plays for Puritans* (1901), which included *The Devil's Disciple, Caesar and Cleopatra,* and *Captain Brassbound's Conversion.* Declaring himself a puritan in the broad sense of adhering to the dictates of conscience, he wrote these three plays as studies of conscience. In these plays he continued to see the stage as a means of social criticism on which he could broadcast his belief in the evils of capitalism, romanticism, and traditional morality. Other famous plays include *Major Barbara* (1905) and *Pygmalion* (1913), both of which were eventually made into motion pictures. Shaw's *Heartbreak House* (1917) is a somewhat pessimistic portrayal of disillusionment and ends with the outbreak of World War I. His monumental *Back to Methuselah* (1921) is a five-play collection that explores human progress from Eden to a science fiction future. In *Saint Joan* (1923), Shaw created a heretical Saint Joan of Arc whose brilliant monologues make the play one of his most popular. He was awarded the Nobel Prize for literature in 1925.

Shaw continued to write plays and prefaces, as well as other works of fiction and nonfiction, into his 90s. His *Common Sense about the War* (1914) and *Everybody's Political What's What?* (1944) are critiques of society in general and Britain in particular. *The*

Intelligent Woman's Guide to Socialism and Capitalism (1928) echoed many of the feminist themes of his earlier plays. The novella *The Adventures of the Black Girl in Her Search for God* (1932) describes Shaw's creative evolution and the idea of the "life force," or the energy of progress. According to Shaw, the life force was a metaphor for a universal will that each individual has and that strives to improve the human race. Shaw died on November 2, 1950, in his country home at Ayot St. Lawrence.

IV. THE EVOLVING SYSTEMS APPROACH TO CREATIVITY AND GENERALIZATIONS ABOUT THE DEVELOPMENT OF A CREATIVE SYSTEM

One way to study creativity is the evolving systems approach, a method constructed by Howard Gruber and his associates. A creative individual is an evolving system that regulates creative activity, which in turn regenerates the system. Creative thought is a product of such a system and occurs as a constructive process involving a series of changing and growing structures. The creative system evolves through the interaction of three interrelated subsystems: purpose, knowledge, and affect. Organization of purpose refers to the way a person orchestrates his or her activities to achieve optimal work. The creative person pursues a network of enterprises that is crucial to his or her productive life. Organization of knowledge refers to the structures of the creative individual's thought—that is, creative thought does not imply one great moment of insight. Rather it involves a stable, repetitively functioning system whose thoughts evolve over time in many enterprises. A third subsystem, organization of affect, refers to the feelings that occur when a person is being creative or functioning optimally.

Can any generalizations be formed from the life of George Bernard Shaw and the lives of other creative people like him? One generalization may be that creative people at some time early in their careers set up a scaffolding on which to further develop their ideas. For example, *My Dear Dorothea* shows that the style and content of Shaw's later work was present in his early work. This short work may have provided for Shaw what Gruber and Davis have called an "initial sketch—

the rough draft or early notebook to which the worker can repair from time to time—that serves as a sort of gyroscope for the oeuvre."

An initial sketch should not, however, be mistaken for the later work. The sketch provides a direction for the creative system, perhaps a reminder of or commitment to the initial sense of purpose. For instance, Shaw did not simply discover the idea of creative evolution by reading Samuel Butler, nor did he somehow pick up ideas about class injustice by reading Marx. These ideas were constructed through repetition and variation of structures, beginning with such early works as *My Dear Dorothea* and progressing through the novels, plays, letters, and essays. In *My Dear Dorothea,* the rudiments of Shaw's life philosophy are many and stimulating, but a close look shows this work to be a first draft, an experiment of the life force, with tenuous arguments to be developed and perfected by the author for the rest of his life. The construction of a creative work, for instance, Shaw's *Back to Methuselah,* was a result of years of struggling with and debating about some of the themes in *My Dear Dorothea.* Gruber and Davis cited the examples of Darwin, Piaget, and Picasso, in which each of these creative people made initial sketches that provided a guide for later work.

Another generalization may be what Gardner and Wolf call "asynchrony" in the life and work of a creative person. They define several levels of creativity: neurobiological, cognitive, affective, domain, and field. The neurobiological, cognitive, and affective levels have been more thoroughly researched than the levels of domain and field. Domain refers to one's organization of knowledge within a particular area, craft, or discipline. Field is a sociological concept that refers to the people who work in a particular discipline, and the agencies, institutions, and reward systems that motivate and govern the discipline. Outstanding examples of creativity tend to emerge not when there is synchrony between or among these different levels, but when there is an asynchrony. The asynchrony may be a discordance or tension, some kind of conflict that motivates the system to construct something new. Gardner and Wolf hypothesized that the lives of creative individuals may be characterized by asynchrony not because it *plagues* them, but rather because they *seek* it. This notion is similar to Hudson's (1966) finding that crisis seeking is characteristic of original thinkers and the correlation that Barron (1963) found between attraction for disorder and originality. Arlin (1984) described a postformal process by which problem-solving operations are replaced by problem-finding operations.

There are many examples of asynchrony in Shaw's life. His family were Protestants in a predominantly Catholic country. George Carr Shaw's adequate income was asynchronous with the high social rank that he claimed. Bernard Shaw was motivated to leave Dublin at the age of 20 and spent the rest of his life as an Irishman in England. His organization of knowledge was characterized by constructive opposition in which he created asynchronies. Gardner and Wolf hypothesized that "perhaps [creative people's] temperament is such that, constitutionally dissatisfied with the status quo, they are perennially predisposed to up the ante, to stir up troubles, to convert comfortable synchrony to tension-producing asynchrony."

In *The Quintessence of Ibsenism,* Shaw wrote that "every step of progress means a duty repudiated, and a scripture torn up." How does a creative system know when to construct from a foundation by modifying an earlier work and when that foundation should instead be "repudiated" or "torn up"? In other words, if a creative system seeks asynchrony, when is this asynchrony appropriate to creative work and when does it become counterproductive? A meaningful life is guided by a network of enterprises that enables the system to make the best use of time and energy. A purposeful life is guided by a network of enterprises that regulates the important need to tear down and rebuild. Thus, Shaw's iconoclasm was not destructive, because he did not randomly annihilate but instead carefully chose his targets and offered solutions. For instance, his disgust with poverty and the economic system that he felt created it should be replaced by socialism. The mindlessness of organized religion should be replaced with a belief in creative evolution. Rather than intoxicating theater goers with romantic escapism, he offers the realism of moral fiction.

Another generalization derived from Shaw's life is that creative people are likely to be creative in more than one domain. Shaw attended art school in Dublin and was a self-trained musician. He was fascinated with photography, and his last completed work is a small book of photos he took and rhymes he made about his home at Ayot Saint Lawrence, *Bernard Shaw's Rhyming Picture Guide to Ayot Saint Lawrence.* Shaw saw the advent of cinema as an opportunity to transfer his plays to a medium that would be available to a larger audience. (But Shaw did not appreciate the fact that cinema has a dramatic technique of its own and insisted that motion pictures must be filmed theater.) Hjerter (1986) has compiled a picture book of the art of more than 50 writers—for example, William Blake, Charlotte and Emily Bronte, Ibsen, Faulkner, and Harriet Beecher Stowe—who were also talented visual artists. A creative system again depends on a network of enterprises that is organized for optimal use of time and energy. A creative system intelligently chooses which talents, or enterprises, to pursue and which he or she may not have time or energy to pursue.

Finally, it is apparent from work with the evolving systems approach that creativity must be seen in a larger system, that a creative person does not function in a vacuum. Collaboration was an important theme in Shaw's life. A prolific writer, he wrote thousands of letters. Many of these were published, for example those to the English actresses Ellen Terry and Mrs. Patrick Campbell. Shaw was well aware that creativity does not spontaneously generate itself. As he wrote in the preface to *Major Barbara*:

> The body of thought is the slowest of growths and the rarest of blossomings [and the] conception of clever persons parthenogenetically bringing forth complete original cosmogonies by dint of sheer 'brilliancy' is part of that ignorant credulity which is the despair of the honest philosopher, and the opportunity of the religious impostor.

Bibliography

Arlin, P. K. (1984). Adolescent and adult thought: A structural interpretation. In M. L. Commons, F. A. Richards, & C. Armon (Eds.), *Beyond formal operations: Late adolescent and adult cognitive development* (pp. 258–271). New York: Praeger.

Barron, F. (1963). The needs for order and for disorder as motives in creative activity. In C. W. Taylor & F. Barron (Eds.), *Scientific creativity: Its recognition and development* (pp. 153–160). New York: Wiley.

Gardner, H., & Wolf, C. (1988). The fruits of asynchrony: A psychological examination of creativity. *Adolescent Psychiatry, 15,* 96–120.

Gruber, H. E., & Davis, S. N. (1988). Inching our way up Mount Olympus: The evolving-systems approach to creative thinking. In R. J. Sternberg (ed.), *The nature of creativity* (pp. 243–270). New York: Cambridge University Press.

Hjerter, K. G. (1986). *Doubly gifted: The author as visual artist* (Forward by John Updike). New York: Harry N. Abrams.

Hudson, L. (1966). *Contrary imaginations.* New York: Schocken Books.

Works by George Bernard Shaw

The Bodley Head Bernard Shaw, Collected plays with their prefaces, Volume VII. (1974). London: the Bodley Head.

Shaw, B. (1932). *The adventures of the black girl in her search for God.* London: Constable & Co.

Shaw, B. (1949). *The complete plays of Bernard Shaw.* London: Odhams Press Limited.

Shaw, B. (1944). *Everybody's political what's what?* New York: Dodd, Mead, & Company.

Shaw, B. (1931). *Immaturity.* London: Constable and Company, Limited.

Shaw, B. (1956). *My dear Dorothea.* London: Phoenix House.

Shaw, B. (1891/1979). *The quintessence of Ibsenism.* In J. L. Wisenthal, *Bernard Shaw's The Quintessence of Ibsenism and related writings.* Toronto: University of Toronto Press.

Shaw, B. (1949). *Sixteen self-sketches.* New York: Dodd, Mead, & Co.

Split-Brains: Interhemispheric Exchange in Creativity

Joseph E. Bogen

*University of Southern California,
University of California, Los Angeles,
and California Institute of Technology*

Glenda M. Bogen

Pasadena, California

Brain Stem The continuation upwards of the spinal cord.

Callosotomy Operation in which the fibers of the corpus callosum are cut—usually done to prevent seizure activity from spreading from one cerebral hemisphere to the other.

Cerebral Hemisphere One of the two halves of the cerebrum, each hemisphere sitting on top of one limb of the Y-shaped upper end of the brain stem.

Cerebrum The greatly expanded top of the nervous system, overhanging and largely hiding the brain stem.

Corpus Callosum A large collection of about 200 million nerve fibers that directly connects the two cerebral hemispheres.

Hemispherectomy Removal of one cerebral hemisphere by combining a complete callosotomy with transection of the nerve fibers connecting the hemisphere with the brain stem. Usually done to treat medically intractable seizure disorders that are spreading from a badly scarred nonfunctional hemisphere to a relatively intact hemisphere.

Split-Brain The result of a complete callosotomy; the two hemispheres still remain in communication via their connections through the Y-shaped upper end of the brain stem.

*Explanations of creativity in terms of brain function are rare. One brain-based theory was advanced by the authors in 1969 and expanded by others. The theory arose from observations of humans who had the **SPLIT-BRAIN** operation. This surgery successfully treated their epilepsy and made it possible for them to join in laboratory experiments, which led to a Nobel Prize for Roger W. Sperry, with whom the authors collaborated for more than 30 years. This article first offers some observations on creativity, emphasizing its development through several stages. Then a brief description of split-brain behavior is presented. Third, two implications of the split-brain research are considered: (a) each cerebral hemisphere can function to a significant extent independently and (b) the two hemispheres function differently. The article concludes with the authors' views on both creativity and a lack of creativity.*

I. STAGES IN CREATIVITY

Creativity provides a workable approach to an unsolved problem or a previously unrecognized opportunity. Often, the essence of the approach appears rather suddenly and further details are then filled in. Many people have pointed out that creativity occurs through several stages.

Hermann Helmholtz, the great physicist, described the way in which his most important new thoughts had come to him. He said that after a period of lengthy investigation, "happy ideas come unexpectedly, without effort, like an inspiration. So far as I am concerned, they have never come to me when my mind was fatigued, or when I was at my working table. . . . They came particularly readily during the slow ascent of wooded hills on a sunny day."

Henri Poincaré, in his book *Science and Method,* described in vivid detail the successive stages of his great mathematical discoveries. They came to him after long preparation and a period of incubation during which no conscious mathematical thinking was done. He wrote, "I went away to spend a few days at the seaside and thought of entirely different things. One day as I was walking on the cliff the idea came to me."

Such stories are not restricted to scientists. Supreme Court chief justice Rehnquist wrote, "I began to realize that some of my best insights came not during my enforced thinking periods in my chambers, but while I was shaving in the morning, driving to work or just walking from one place to another."

To result in a successful creation, an inspiration must next be verified to see that the idea really works. This verification phase is similar to the preparation phase in that the process is often logical, mathematical, or literary and is consciously deliberate. Graham Wallas suggested in 1926 that creativity proceeds in four distinct phases: preparation, incubation, illumination, and verification.

To produce something both novel and meaningful one must have a period of preparation. This involves acquiring a large fund of information. Following preparation is a period of incubation during which time the information is rearranged, typically while one is *unaware* of the process. Next is illumination. Almost everyone is familiar with the cartoonist's use of a lightbulb to symbolize the instant illumination of an idea. Last is necessary a phase of deliberate reorganization and refinement, readily describable by the creator, to test and polish the final product.

What can be the physiologic basis for this succession of stages? During incubation, some very productive thinking goes on, which is inaccessible to verbal output (in that one cannot tell how it went on) and whose re-

sult can become available in a sudden insight. Where does this thinking take place? To say that it comes from the heart describes the quality rather than the origin. To say that it comes from intuition is merely to rename it rather than to give it a physiologic source. It surely requires an elaborate neuronal system, of a size, complexity, and activity level comparable to that organ—namely, the left hemisphere—that produces the richness of human language. It is likely that much of the thinking that goes on during incubation takes place in the human right hemisphere. [*See* INCUBATION; INTUITION.]

By contrast, the preparation and verification phases seem more left hemispheric. One sees the likelihood of a greater than usual interhemispheric communication during an individual's more intuitive moments, an interaction dependent on the corpus callosum.

II. THE SPLIT-BRAIN

The corpus callosum, with more than 200 million nerve fibers, constitutes a system larger than the sum of all systems ascending to and descending from the cerebral hemispheres. The central location and the large size of the corpus callosum, especially in humans, have for centuries suggested an important role in mentation. During the past 30 years, a large number and variety of experiments have made it clear that the corpus callosum can transfer high-level information from one hemisphere to the other. Moreover, we now know that the hemispheres are not so much "major" and "minor" as they are complementary and that each hemisphere is capable of thinking on its own, in its own way. Much of this information has come from cutting the corpus callosum, that is, the split-brain operation.

The term *split-brain* has several meanings. Applied to the human, it denotes complete callosal section—an operation that has been performed for medically intractable epilepsy to stop the spread of seizure activity from one hemisphere to the other. Our own split-brain patients had complete cerebral commissurotomy, including anterior commissure, and dorsal and ventral hippocampal commissures, as well as complete callosotomy. But it is now common to use the term *split-brain* to refer to cases of complete callosotomy alone, because they show most of the same signs and symptoms. When patients who have had a complete callosotomy have recovered from the acute operative effects and reach a fairly stable state, they show a variety of phenomena that can be grouped under four headings.

A. Social Ordinariness

One of the most remarkable results is that in ordinary social situations the patients are indistinguishable from normal in spite of the cutting of more than 200 million nerve fibers. Special testing methods are needed to expose their deficits. These usually involve restricting the input to only one hemisphere—for example, by putting an object into one hand, with vision occluded.

B. Lack of Interhemispheric Transfer

A wide variety of situations have been developed to show that the human subjects are in this respect the same as split-brain cats and monkeys. A typical example is the inability of the split-brain person (or monkey) to retrieve with one hand an object palpated with the other, although same-hand retrieval is normal.

C. Hemispheric Specialization Effects

The hemispheric specialization typical of human subjects results in phenomena not seen in split-brain animals. A typical example is the inability of right-handers to name or describe an object in the left hand, even when it is being appropriately manipulated and can be reliably retrieved from a collection when the subject has previously felt it with the same, retrieving hand.

D. Compensatory Strategies

Split-brain subjects progressively acquire a variety of strategies for circumventing their interhemispheric transfer deficits. A common example is for the patient to speak out loud the name of an object palpated in the right hand; because the right hemisphere can recognize many individual words, the object can then be retrieved with the left hand.

III. THE FUNDAMENTAL FINDING

The fundamental finding from the split-brain is that the two cerebral hemispheres can function independently and simultaneously, in parallel. This point has been confirmed in dozens of human patients in several different institutions (unlike those famous, individual cases on which so much neurologic theorizing has been based). Moreover, the fact of hemispheric independence has been repeatedly confirmed in experiments with cats and monkeys that never had epilepsy or the other qualifying factors that have been recurrently pointed to by persons unwilling to recognize the fundamental finding because of its startling implications.

IV. CREATIVITY

If learning can proceed simultaneously, independently and differently in each hemisphere, so may problem solving. This contributes to a less predictable—that is, a less stimulus-bound—behavior. In other words, specialization of the hemispheres for different trains of thought greatly increases the flexibility of the ensemble. Such differentiation necessarily produces a concomitant decrease in stability. The successful expansion of the human species (so far) suggests that the loss of stability is less important than the gain in flexibility. [*See* PROBLEM SOLVING.]

Creativity has not only made the human species dominant (and dangerous) on the earth; what may be more important for each of us is that it gives value and purpose to human existence. Creativity requires more than the propositional skills and logical thought of the left hemisphere; it also needs the cultivation and collaboration of the other side of the brain. There is as yet no clear consensus on how best to describe the cognitive differences between the hemispheres. Whatever terms are used (e.g., propositional versus appositional), what is essential for our theory is the well-established fact that in most humans the two cerebral hemispheres function quite differently. We believe that this involves, indeed requires, a significant degree of hemispheric independence, such that the interhemispheric exchange is much of the time incomplete.

No one supposes that *all* creativity involves the corpus callosum. The left hemisphere alone, either following right hemispherectomy or isolated from the right by callosotomy, is capable of a full range of verbal expression, including generation of an unlimited number of novel sentences. But when a solution requires combining of "dual memory codes, verbal and imaginal" (as Brenda Milner put it) one readily recognizes an important role for the corpus callosum.

V. THE LACK OF CREATIVITY

If some kinds of creativity are dependent on a transcallosal interhemispheric exchange, there are three obvious explanations for its absence. There may be first of all a deficiency of technical competence in a suitable medium; in the case of literary as well as mathematical creativity this is easily seen as a lack of propositional skill.

Second, many persons possess technical proficiency in music, drawing, or writing whose production is devoid of those innovative and informative values that distinguish an artist from a performer. We are accustomed to hear, these days, of the "culturally disadvantaged," usually referring to persons whose propositional potential has remained undeveloped for lack of proper schooling. There is likely a parallel lack of appositional development in persons whose education has narrowly emphasized reading, writing, and their concomitants. Third, there must be the possibility of a heightened communication between the two hemispheres, overcoming temporarily the ongoing lack of transfer that has allowed independent processing.

The foregoing considerations, especially the extent of hemispheric exchange, led to a series of experiments by Warren TenHouten and colleagues in which split-brain patients (and controls) were studied by interview and EEG with respect to their reactions to a short movie containing symbols highly loaded with affective significance respecting separation and death. These experimental results, as well as the similarity between split-brain patients and persons who have experienced, with psychosomatic or addictive disorders, an impoverishment of their fantasy life without being bothered by it, led to the hypothesis of "functional commissur-

otomy" by Klaus D. Hoppe. That is, alexithymic patients appeared to be deprived, as were the split-brain patients, of what Hoppe has termed "hemispheric bisociation," which facilitates symbolexia, the verbal expression of empathic identifications with symbolized affective states.

The conditions for a fluctuation in callosal transmission have yet to be adequately explored. One consideration is that inspiration occurs not only in repose but often in striving under pressure. In any case, variations in hemispheric exchange are clearly contingent on appropriate affective states.

VI. SUMMARY

A duality of mind is readily demonstrable in split-brain humans, and evidence is steadily accumulating that ongoing interhemispheric communication is incomplete in the intact brain. It is now certain that the corpus callosum can transfer high-level information from one hemisphere to another. When we take into account the well-established principle of hemispheric specialization, the alexithymia in spite of the impressive normality of split-brain humans in ordinary social situations, a physiologic explanation for at least some forms of creativity seems close at hand. What is required is a partial (and transiently reversible) hemispheric independence during which lateralized cognition can occur and is responsible for the dissociation of preparation from incubation. A momentary suspension of this partial independence could account for the illumination that precedes subsequent deliberate verification. From this point of view, we can understand better the observation of Frederic Bremer, who wrote years ago that the corpus callosum subserves "the highest and most elaborate activities of the brain"—in a word, creativity.

Bibliography

Benson, D. F., Zaidel, E. (Eds.). (1985). *The dual brain: Hemispheric specialization in humans.* New York: Guilford Press.

Bogen, J. E. (1977). Further discussion on split-brains and hemispheric capabilities. *British Journal for the Philosophy of Science, 28,* 281–286.

Bogen, J. E. (1997). Physiological consequences of complete or partial commissural section. In Apuzzo, M. L. J. (Ed.), *Surgery of the third ventricle* (2nd ed.). Baltimore, MD: Williams and Wilkins.

Bogen, J. E., & Bogen, G. M. (1969). The corpus callosum and creativity. *Bulletin of the Los Angeles Neurological Society, 34,* 191–220.

Hoppe, K. D. (1988). Hemispheric specialization and creativity. *Psychiatric Clinics of North America, 11,* 303–315.

Hoppe, K. D. (1989). Psychoanalysis, hemispheric specialization, and creativity. *Journal of the American Academy of Psychoanalysis, 17,* 353–369.

Sperry, R. W. (1974). Lateral specialization in the surgically separated hemispheres. In Schmitt, F. O., & Worden, F. G. (Eds.), *Neurosciences: Third study program.* Cambridge, MA: MIT Press.

TenHouten, W., Hoppe, K., Bogen, J., & Walter, D. (1986). Alexithymia: An experimental study of cerebral commissurotomy patients and normal control subjects. *American Journal of Psychiatry, 143,* 312–316.

Trevarthen, C. B. (1984). Hemispheric specialization. In *Handbook of physiology—The nervous system,* III (chap. 25). Washington, DC: American Physiological Society.

Van Lancker, D. (1997). Rags to riches: Our increasing appreciation of cognitive and communicative abilities of the human right cerebral hemisphere. *Brain and Language 57,* 1–11.

Sports and Creativity

Jock Abra

University of Calgary

Gordon Abra

University of Arizona

works. Terrifying events hidden in the unconscious are indirectly released by expressing them in works of art.

Symbols Vague forms that carry many possible interpretations and that supposedly only human beings produce.

Existentialism A philosophy propounded by Albert Camus and Jean-Paul Sartre, among others, that sees existence as incomprehensible. People are free to interpret it however they wish, with any and all answers being equally valid.

Imagination A presumed psychological ability that allows the creation of possibilities not found in actual experience.

Libido A general psychic life energy, largely sexual, that for Freud gave rise to many human activities.

Peak Experiences (also called **flow**) Moments of intense euphoria or "highs" when we lose our sense of time, place, and individuality and that, according to Maslow, we may experience while deeply involved in activities. Peaks are supposedly one reason for undertaking such activities.

Repression According to Freud, one defence against undesirable experiences and desires. We force them into an unconscious mind of which we are unaware so that they are no longer threatening.

Reticular Formation An area in the brain that keeps other areas aroused so they can function efficiently.

Self-Actualization According to Maslow, a basic, uniquely human need to reach our maximum potential as individuals. Attempting to satisfy this need supposedly leads to creativity.

Sublimation For Freud, the mechanism that results in creative

This article explores similarities and differences between **SPORTS AND CREATIVITY.** *Creativity to most people suggests the arts and sciences, but it actually occurs in many other fields as well, including sports. There are many similarities between creative and athletic activity, between the greatest achievers in each—a Michael Jordan shows many of the personal qualities of a Beethoven—and the experiences they report during peak performance. Great athletic contests produce experiences in onlookers that resemble aesthetic ones. In short, the division between athletic and creative pursuits is far from clear, with sports such as gymnastics shading into physical art forms such as dance. Because of its similarities, sport is then exploited as an analogy to overcome some difficulties and puzzles that creativity poses, notably about its motivation. Many creative activities, especially in the arts, offer few apparent survival or material benefits and produce many negatives such as frustration, so the question arises, why do people indulge in them? Some likely motives for participating in sports are considered as possible answers. Finally, it is suggested that* *sports and creativity may both stem from one nonspecific energy pool.*

I. SPORTS AND CREATIVITY: SOME SIMILARITIES AND DIFFERENCES

As their first similarity, both sport and creativity are uniquely human activities. Lower animals do display related activities. They are capable of sophisticated problem solving, and as the evolutionary doctrine of survival of the fittest indicates, they must deal with competition, a major element of sports. That said, the human versions of these preliminaries differ enormously. Animals have produced nothing comparable to *Hamlet* nor become obsessed with winning Olympic Gold. Yet virtually every human culture features athletic and creative endeavors of some sort, although their forms vary greatly, so within our species such activities are almost universal.

As another similarity, neither activity, when viewed from a strictly rational or utilitarian angle, makes a great deal of sense. As aids to survival, both are at best mixed blessings. Creativity has provided advances in medicine and control over the environment but also weapons of mass destruction. Likewise, the drives for dominance and competition so evident in sport could facilitate either survival or annihilation, as witness the role of such drives in fighting and war. Moreover, neither activity offers realistic prospects of material reward. Regarding creativity, building the proverbial better mousetrap can lead to great wealth, but those who profit from inventing are few, and no one would take up, say, poetry or astronomy in order to get rich. Similarly, several sports nowadays do hold out immense, some would say obscene, possibilities in this regard. However, most elite athletes deny that this explains their readiness to make the endless sacrifices of time and energy that excellence demands—if anything, they contend, an excessive preoccupation with money can damage performance—and it certainly does not explain the far greater numbers who labor in poorly paid obscurity, to say nothing of the countless driveway two-on-twos, 2 a.m. shinny sessions in freezing arenas, or marathons where the main rewards, participants know full well, are exhaustion and shin splints. Furthermore, as these examples suggest, the two activities provide many seeming deterrents. The agonies of creating, the frustration, anxiety, and sleepless nights and very real risks of failure and ridicule by others are equaled by the physical pain and risk of injury that are part and parcel of most sports and, at higher levels, by the psychological traumas due to constant pressure to perform well and win or face boos and unemployment. In short, one necessary quality for both creators and athletes may be healthy doses of masochism.

But despite their enigmatic sources, these are pursuits that many people take very seriously and pursue with immense passion. Great achievers in the arts and sciences vary appreciably in other respects, but almost without exception they display a single-minded (if not obsessive) dedication to their work. A lazy genius is a contradiction in terms! Likewise the greatest athletes, as many themselves assert, are set apart from others of comparable ability in good part by their willingness to put in longer hours of practice and training. In a similar vein, both domains do include one-shot geniuses who actually gain the 15 minutes of fame that Andy Warhol promised everyone, and are never heard from again; examples include Banting, the discoverer of insulin for treating diabetes, and Bobby Thomson, whose dramatic home run in 1951 won a pennant for the New York Giants. However, they are exceptions. By and large, the label "great" describes those who achieve at a consistently high level over a long term. [See EMINENCE.]

As another similarity, although again there is no apparent reason why this should be so, both activities provoke similar amounts of passion in observers. The emotions may not be identical in quality—sports, unlike many creative works, invoke tension and suspense—but the emotions aroused by a superb concert or work of literature equal in intensity those from great contests such as the epic collisions between Canada's best hockey players and the Red Machines of the late Soviet Union.

The similarity that most vindicates connecting these activities, however, is in the personal qualities of their great achievers. One of these has already been mentioned: a persistence in the face of every frustration or discouragement. Before describing others, however, it must first be emphasized that every observation about the stereotypic athlete or creator must be prefaced by the qualifier "as a rule," for there are always exceptions. As well, there is little empirical evidence available to support those for athletes in particular, and what there is allows few firm conclusions.

As the first of these similarities, *creative* in part implies a propensity for originality, and great athletes too are distinguished not only by their successes but the means by which they attain them, a talent for innovation that supplies instant replays and Plays of the Day. Bobby Orr changed the hockey defenseman's historic role of preventing goals into that of a force for producing them as well. This directly implies a second likeness. Innovations by definition cannot be learned from others—yet another unprecedented Michael Jordan concoction led a commentator to observe, "You can't teach that, but you should sure try to draft it"—and this strongly suggests that someone who produces them must possess unusual qualities, a mysterious but crucial commodity summarized in the concepts of talent or genius. These rare gifts for activities that most people have tried at least casually produces in the rest of us powerful feelings of admiration and wonder *cum* hero worship, (sometimes mixed with envy). [*See* INNOVATION.]

Another similarity is considerable self-confidence and ego strength. It may not be attractive when it shades into the arrogance of a Mohammed Ali or Babe Ruth or, in the creative sphere, of a Newton or Wagner, but it is crucial. Both fields offer genuine possibilities for devastating failure, so those who aim for the heights must be willing to risk it, which presumably requires confidence that it is unlikely to happen. This suggests another shared quality: a desire to put one's abilities on public display. Few creators are content to finish their work to their own satisfaction and then keep it private. Novels must be published, paintings shown in galleries, or new theories shared with others, although the hassles and risks of rejection involved in this stage are many. Great athletes also seem to enjoy the limelight. One quality that sets a Jack Nicklaus or Joe Montana apart is an uncanny ability to save their best for when the stakes are highest and all eyes are on them. To take these risks too, one must be confident that one will succeed. Both stereotypic creators and athletes also have marked Peter Pan demeanors. A cluster of related attributes all associated with children—lack of discretion, impulsiveness, intense enthusiasm for their callings—when taken together suggest a refusal to grow up. [*See* MOTIVATION/DRIVE; PERSONALITY.]

Finally, we might mention two similarities whose applicability to creativity is in dispute. The first is a decline with age. Few would deny that in sport, youth will usually be served, but Lehman's conclusion that most creators produce their seminal work during their 30s and 40s (although the specific age peak varied somewhat across fields), with both quality and quantity decreasing thereafter, not all authorities accept. As for the second, just as athletic excellence has until recently been largely a masculine affair, there is no denying that men have produced most of the creative work that for whatever reason has been judged as great. This sex difference also varies across fields—women have accomplished much in literature, for example—but eminent female music composers, oil painters, or scientists have been rare. The debate here, however, concerns not the sex difference per se but the reasons for it, for there are a myriad possible explanations. Moreover there is every indication in both bailiwicks that with recent changes in sex roles and environment experiences, a different picture will emerge. [*See* GENDER DIFFERENCES; PRODUCTIVITY AND AGE; WOMEN AND CREATIVITY.]

The final shared quality, although it contradicts the confidence mentioned earlier, may be the most important in motivating achievement of any kind: considerable personal insecurity and self-doubt. Freud persuasively observed that people who are satisfied with themselves do not create. Neither, we suspect, do they become great athletes. This insecurity has several likely sources. Great achievements always seem mysterious and beyond personal control, so regardless of one's past record of success, fears must always lurk that one's ability to have them might disappear. Nor are these fears unwarranted, for many creators suffer dry spells such as writer's block, and athletes undergo the agonies of slumps when putts refuse to drop or passes fall just beyond receivers' or into opponents' hands. In addition, those who achieve great things in any domain presumably must set high standards for themselves; to conquer Everest, one cannot be content to tackle anything less. Unfortunately, in a less than perfect world, perfectionists must be eternally dissatisfied. In Browning's phrase "Ah, but a man's reach must exceed his grasp / Or what's a heaven for." Why are some people perfectionists? Benjamin Bloom's studies of great athletic and creative achievers provide some answers and in so doing suggest still another similarity. Parents of those in both groups had instilled beliefs that it is important to do your best at everything you do and be the best you can be. It was less that they preached this outlook than practiced it themselves, which presumably encouraged the child to internalize and copy it. Furthermore, neither group of parents were of the pushy kind who dragged their offspring kicking and screaming toward excellence. According to both parents and children, the initiative to pursue excellence had come from the latter.

It would be remiss, however, not to mention some evident differences between sporting and creative domains—indeed, these help explain why different people may express the same source of motivation in different ways. The most obvious is that sport usually connotes physical activities, creativity the realms of intellect and emotion; so unlike sport it supposedly requires a presumed psychological faculty, *imagination,* that allows one to expand on and conceive alternatives to reality as experienced. As well, creative work typically results in tangible products such as paintings, whereas athletes' deeds are of the moment, so in this respect they have more in common with creative interpreters such as musicians and actors than with those who, say, compose music or write plays. [*See* IMAGINATION.]

This difference suggests another. Creativity has a powerful thrust toward the future in that many innovations drastically alter life as we know it, whereas sports are set largely in the here and now. Great moments remain, but only in the memory of witnesses, and records endure only until they are broken, as most are. Thus athletes and spectators may momentarily savor a great victory or accomplishment, but soon it has no more interest than yesterday's newspaper, and athletes who fervently cling to past successes become pathetic. Baseball's Yogi Berra famously observed that "It ain't over till it's over." He might have added, "But after it's over, it's over."

In addition, creative people, with their unusual interests and priorities, tend to feel alienated from general society, misunderstood and unappreciated. Great athletes, on the other hand, garner immense adulation and hero worship. Over the long run, however, the situation may reverse. Many creators, van Gogh for one, have labored in obscurity while alive only to become immortalized once they die, while athletes, once retired, must adjust to the reduced status of yesterday's hero. Some personal qualities also differ. Creators tend

to be introverted and also androgynous, that is, to display interests and attitudes more typical of the opposite sex, and in stereotype are temperamental. Most athletes, however, are emotionally stable and those of both sexes score high on measures of masculinity. One intriguing difference whose reasons are unclear is in birth order; creators are more often firstborn than are athletes. In the same vein, family backgrounds seem to differ; athletes, unlike creators, by and large come from underprivileged backgrounds (although this is more true of basketball, say, than tennis). [*See* BIRTH ORDER.]

II. MOTIVES FOR SPORTS AND CREATIVITY

Why do we involve ourselves in these activities with such passion? Because they are uniquely human it seems reasonable to consider motives that are unique as well. Susanne K. Langer claimed that we experience vague but intense feelings that we cannot put into words—as we say, "Words fail me"—but like itches they demand attention. Therefore, people try to express them in the tangible form of *symbols,* because these ambiguous forms possess many meanings and so are peculiarly suited to capture ambivalent feelings. It is obvious that symbols are used frequently in creative work, especially in the arts, but they also play an overlooked but seminal role in sports. A defenceman passing the puck ahead to a speeding forward, a well hit ball heading for a distant fence—such moments have that hypnotic appeal, that sense of varied and vague meanings, that as Jung pointed out is the hallmark of a true symbol. Thus for participants such events may represent all manner of other experiences. Furthermore, team logos and uniforms also have mystic qualities, not only for fans (their marketing has become a huge business) but players. Those who don the hallowed bleu, blanc, et rouge of the Montreal Canadiens are expected to continue that storied franchise's tradition of success, a strong motivator to perform. A particularly intriguing symbol is the *home team.* Taken as individuals its members, because they are oftentimes less than admirable people and have as a rule come from somewhere else, resemble nothing so much as hired guns; in Jerry Seinfeld's words, "You're basically cheering for a jersey!" Nonetheless, their bumbling exploits torture their followers beyond all reason.

Another possible motive is suggested by beliefs of existentialists such as Albert Camus that people desperately want to understand existence, but this is impossible. Such questions as "What is the meaning of life?" or "Who am I?" offer many possible answers among which each of us is free to choose and it is these choices that, by establishing what someone makes of things, define them as a person. Unfortunately, no answer is certifiably correct, so uncertainty and therefore anxiety inevitably follows. Each choice tries to reduce that anxiety by discovering an answer that seems valid at least to the person. Since a work of art, like a personality, evolves through a series of arbitrary choices, it too can be seen as seeking in concrete form a statement that has such validity. Thus Camus asserted, "if the world were clear, art would not exist." The same might be said about sports. Their wonderfully precise universes—playing fields with definite boundaries, rules that are arbitrary but inviolate, and most of all the prospect of clear-cut results, winning and losing—offer another solution to life's ambiguities: sweep them under the rug. Is it the very simplicity and clarity of sports that makes them so attractive?

One powerful source of existential anxiety suggests another motive. Death, it is said, is one of life's two certainties, a fact of which human beings alone seem aware. Creating may reflect attempts to deal with this potentially terrifying realization. For Otto Rank, creative people aim to defeat death by becoming immortal. If one's work is admired by generations yet unborn, then one remains symbolically if not physically alive. Similarly, great athletes are referred to as immortals, as in "the immortal Babe Ruth." Their deeds, like those of great creators, live on to set ultimate standards of excellence. For Ernest Becker on the other hand, creativity reflects a denial of death. Freud attributed creativity to events so threatening that people consigned them to a hidden, unconscious part of the mind, but whereas he saw most of these fears as revolving around sex, for Becker they involve death. Certainly, most people seem to suppress this supreme fact of life—few of us can truly imagine ourselves dead, it only happens to others—and it is this denial, Becker has suggested, that lays the groundwork for creativity. Sport also suggests denial mechanisms at work. During physical activity we feel supremely alive, and great athletes personify vitality and youth, so as we watch them, mortality never crosses our minds. Except when serious injuries strike. Now a hush falls over onlookers that indicatively is called "deathly." Does this reflect a realization that we all, even the most physically capable, face the same ultimate fate?

The final possible motives involve the interpersonal needs, to relate to other people not only physically via sex but psychologically via intimacy—needs that, according to several authorities, are far more important to people than animals. These needs are expressed either through cooperating or competing with others. This reveals one advantage of the sports metaphor—to bring home competition and cooperation in creativity. In practice these two elements are by and large not mutually exclusive but accompany one another. [*See* COLLABORATION AND COMPETITION.]

III. THE MOTIVATION FOR SPORTS AND CREATIVITY: A COMMON SOURCE?

The sports analogy offers several other advantages for understanding creativity. First, a persistent problem in studying the latter is that there is no way to establish beyond the shadow of a doubt that some person, or product, is creative. It is in the last analysis a matter of opinion, so an investigator must constantly wonder whether those being studied actually qualify, because, if not, this must call any conclusions drawn into question. In most sports, however, as Daniel Chambliss has pointed out, great achievement is beyond dispute. It is verified by objective indicants such as victories in ultimate competitions such as the Olympics or measures such as times in track events or batting averages. Similarly, he continued, the stratification between levels of achievement, for example, local, national and international success, is clear-cut, so the attributes needed to succeed at each can be precisely determined. Thus he showed that progress from one level to the next requires not doing the same things, only more often, but a different approach, a qualitative rather than quantitative change.

As a second advantage, Robert Weisberg and others deny that there is anything special about creative achievers and so imply that everyone can do it, given the necessary environmental experiences. Although we certainly do not deny the importance of such experiences—genius, so called, is probably only a potential that remains dormant without them—in our view no amount of environmental advantage can lead to seminal achievements where that potential does not exist. Silk purses do not come from sows ears! Most people can accept the concept of natural athletes, that is, persons who because of fortunate genetic or biological endowments accomplish with ease (and sometimes with remarkably *little* practice) feats of which most of us can only dream. If such a concept is accepted for athletes and it is admitted that they seem to be cut from much the same cloth as great creators, then the importance of rare inborn gifts for the latter may be more readily accepted. For the belief that everyone can do it may appeal to our sense of fair play, but it is a misconception that can encourage harmful practices, notably in education.

Which raises a third, related advantage. Knowledge gained about educational and training practices that affect achievement in one domain may offer helpful suggestions for the other. For example, the suspicion is growing that sports have placed too much emphasis on skill and technique training as a necessary preliminary for achievement of not only the competent, but also the genius variety. It may be that the latter is actually harmed by learning too much about "the right way to do it," as opposed to discovering what is right for oneself. The skill training trend may have fostered a steady stream of very competent athletes who are also as indistinguishable as peas in a pod and lack the spontaneity and individuality that are the hallmarks of genius. In hockey, for example, the current emphasis on teaching youngsters the rudiments of skating, passing, and positional play, as opposed to just throwing a puck on the ice and letting them play shinny, has produced a far higher level of general competence than in days of yore, but in today's NHL, the innovative flare of an Orr is rarely seen. Oftentimes, genius goes about its business in a way that prevailing expert opinion sees as wrong; even in swimming, a sport that at first glance seems to allow little room for individuality, Mark Spitz, the winner of the most Olympic gold medals in history, broke many accepted principles about effective technique. All of this suggests a similar danger regarding creative domains. Recall the story of "The Emperor's New clothes." Sometimes, only someone unaware of prevailing beliefs can see the truth. The philosopher Kant claimed that "genius gives the rules." Rather than slavishly copying orthodoxy, it introduces new, unprecedented possibilities of which the merely competent never conceive.

Finally, creativity's parallels with sport suggest a possible answer to a perplexing problem. The motives discussed are not only uniquely human but to all intents and purposes universal within our species—to be human is to experience them—yet most people devote little attention to the arts and sciences even as onlookers, let alone as active participants. How do they satisfy these motives? We propose that creative work is only one of many possible outlets for a general, nonspecific motivational energy that can also be released in other ways, one of which is sports. That the two activities display so many similarities, including the motives that presumably drive them, is because they are different expressions of the same source. Where does this energy come from? All of the aforementioned motives, we suggest, contribute to it, like many rivers that replenish the same sea, so strictly speaking they should be called not *motives* (which implies that they are separate and independent), but *sources of motivation*. Most people shun creativity, therefore, because they are releasing the energy in other ways, very often in sports. Various activities are different means to the same end, so presumably energy expended on one depletes that available for others.

Several other accounts imply a similar scenario. Freud hypothesized a general life energy, the *libido*, that could be released in many ways, and also stressed various experiences and desires, real or imagined and usually involving sex, that are so threatening that we cannot face them. They are therefore obliterated, or *repressed*, pushed into a purported unconscious mind of which we are unaware, and thus are out of sight, but hardly out of mind; they still greatly influence behavior and conscious mental life. They exert constant pressure to be released overtly, but because this would be too devastating to the person, they are expressed indirectly in symbols, notably in dreams, which are hidden messages in code that, if interpreted, can reveal the dreamer's unconscious.

Creative works supposedly reflect a similar mechanism. By way of *sublimation*, these unacceptable tendencies are subtly expressed in the symbols in such works, so these too can be interpreted. Although Freud himself subjected the works of several artists, notably Leonardo da Vinci, to this exercise, he seems never to have done the same for sports, but his followers have corrected this oversight by providing remarkably ingenious, if completely arbitrary, interpretations involving hidden sexual elements for countless other endeavors in both domains. It is not entirely implausible that part of our admiration for a great athlete's grace and power might have a sexual aspect, and a number of sports phenomena—for example, throwing a pass to a receiver or completing a double play—suggest promising fodder on which doctrinaire Freudians could have a field day. Indeed, it is widely believed that athletic excellence may stem partly from sexual sources and therefore that sexual activity may impede performance. In a recent soccer World Cup, the Italian team was denied female companionship to conserve their energy for the soccer pitch (although the team's disappointing performance calls the reasoning into question).

Donald Hebb's account proposed another possible common source. The *reticular formation* in the brain stimulates other areas to keep them aroused and thus responding efficiently to incoming information, but to perform this important task, the reticular formation itself needs stimulation that has novelty and variety. This, Hebb contended, explains why we involve ourselves in activities such as sports, hobbies, and creative work that on the face of it do little to promote survival. In fact, they all serve the same, crucial purpose, to keep the reticular formation, and in turn the rest of the brain, functioning effectively.

Finally, Abraham Maslow proposed that people have a unique need for *self-actualization,* to fulfill their potential and become the best person they can be. Creativity follows automatically from trying to satisfy this need. Because each of us is different, becoming who we truly are must yield unique results. However self-actualization, and therefore creativity, can be achieved in many domains besides the arts and sciences, including athletic ones. In addition, Maslow asserted that, as we seek self-actualization in an activity, we periodically have *peak experiences.* We become so completely involved that we momentarily lose our awareness of time, place, and individuality. United in a mystic oneness, we now feel most supremely alive and sense in-tuitively what it means to be human. These highs are so exhilarating that for many people the prospect of experiencing them is the main reason they involve themselves in activities. They are seeking not so much a result, be it a creative product or athletic accomplishment, as a process. [*See* SELF-ACTUALIZATION.]

However, another problem remains. If sports and creativity are two means to the same end, what decides the choice of outlet? Howard Gardner's notion of independent cognitive abilities provides a promising answer. Supposedly, everyone has some amount in each of several abilities such as music, math, or language, but the amount of one has no relation to another, so there is no general, overriding cognitive ability, such as creativity, that determines one's capability in every pursuit. Rather, one has the potential to be creative in certain specific domains and may be quite untalented in others. The choice of outlet, then, probably depends on where ability is most pronounced, because most people prefer activities at which they feel competent. Thus someone gifted in the kinesthetic domain is more likely to concentrate on sports than, say, writing poetry. [*See* DOMAINS OF CREATIVITY.]

Bibliography

Abra, J. C. (1997). *The motives for creative work: An inquiry.* Cresskill, NJ: Hampton Press.

Becker, E. (1973). *The denial of death.* New York: The Free Press.

Camus, A. (1969). *The myth of Sisyphus and other essays.* New York: Knopf.

Gardner, H. (1983). *Frames of mind: The theory of multiple intelligences.* New York: Basic Books.

Hemery, D. (1986). *The pursuit of sporting excellence: A study of sport's highest achievers.* London: William Collins Sons.

Langer, S. K. (1951). *Philosophy in a new key.* New York: Mentor Books.

Maslow, A. H. (1962). *Toward a psychology of being.* Toronto: van Nostrand.

Weisberg, R. (1986). *Genius and other myths.* San Francisco: W. H. Freeman.

Suicide

David Lester

Center for the Study of Suicide
Blackwood, New Jersey

Affective Disorder A severe psychiatric disorder characterized by periods of extreme depression and extreme excitement known as mania.

Attempted Suicide Suicidal actions that the person survives. This is also called parasuicide and deliberate self-injury by some suicidologists.

Completed Suicide Suicidal actions that result in the death of the person.

Gifted People People who typically score high on tests of intelligence.

SUICIDAL BEHAVIOR encompasses a wide range of behaviors, including both fatal suicidal behavior (commonly called completed suicide) and nonfatal suicidal behavior (including attempted suicide, suicidal threats, and suicidal ideation). In addition, some scholars view other forms of self-destructive behavior as suicidal in nature. Alcohol and drug abuse have been viewed as chronic suicidal behavior and behavior such as self-mutilation and self-castration as focal suicidal behavior. This article focuses on fatal and nonfatal suicidal behavior and creativity. A discussion of suicidal behavior in creative people is intimately related to the issue of psychiatric disorder in creative people, because the majority of suicidal individuals have a diagnosable psychiatric disorder, over 90% in some studies. People who have been psychiatric inpatients have higher suicide rates subsequently than people who have been psychiatric outpatients who, in turn, have higher suicide rates than the general population. Suicide is especially common in those with mood disorders and schizophrenic disorders, disorders which are also associated with creativity.

I. IS SUICIDAL BEHAVIOR MORE COMMON IN CREATIVE PEOPLE?

Anecdotally, it has often been claimed that creative individuals are at high risk for suicide. For example, writers in the former Soviet Union, Great Britain, Japan, and the United States have committed suicide in large numbers during this century. The suicides of the Soviet Union writers have been attributed to the oppressive Soviet regime and the suicides of the British writers to poor sales and high taxes. It is more likely, however, that it is the profession of writing rather than local conditions that leads to this apparently high suicide rate in writers.

Estimates of the percentage of deaths from suicide in eminent people range from 0.3% to 13.3%, with a median of 2.9%. The percentage seems to be higher among literary figures. A study of 1000 eminent people of the 20th century found that a suicidal death was more likely among artistic individuals in general (especially poets). Other studies show that suicide was more likely also among the less creative and among those who were bisexual and homosexual; suicide was least common among public officials, explorers, architects, and social figures. (Gender, race, and religious affiliation were not associated with the likelihood of suicide.) Attempted suicide was more common among women, artistic types, blacks, bisexuals, homosexuals, and those from broken homes (but was not associated with religious affiliation or creativity). [*See* EMINENCE.]

II. RESEARCH ON WRITERS

Nancy Andreasen compared 30 creative writers at the University of Iowa workshops with 30 controls, two of the writers and none of the controls committed suicide, and 3% of the primary relatives of the writers committed suicide (versus none of the relatives of the controls).

David Lester has examined the lives of 13 famous novelists and poets who killed themselves. He noted that two of them had fathers who completed suicide. Three others lost parents during childhood while another lost the grandmother who had raised him. Two others lost siblings. Six of the writers had engaged in prior nonfatal suicidal acts. Five were judged to be alcohol abusers, three had been hospitalized in order to receive electroconvulsive therapy, and seven were judged to have suffered from a mood disorder. Only one writer was judged to be schizophrenic, although five showed signs of paranoia. Problems associated with their writing appeared to be present in the majority of

them and may have contributed to their suicides. There were many factors at work in these suicidal careers.

III. CREATIVE WOMEN

Lester also examined the lives and deaths of six creative women who killed themselves, comparing them with six creative women who died natural deaths and with six creative men who killed themselves. For the women, the suicides and natural deaths did not differ in birth order, substance abuse, or loss of parents early in life, but the suicides were younger at the time of their death. The suicides were more likely to be divorced or separated at the time of their death. Not surprisingly, more of the suicides had made nonfatal suicidal actions in the past. The most striking finding, however, was the presence of psychological disturbance among the suicides. Five of the six suicides had a mood disorder or depressed mood versus none of the natural deaths. [*See* MOOD.]

Comparing the suicidal women and men, Lester found no differences in age at death, prior suicide attempts, or birth order. Like the women, the majority of the men were experiencing marital problems (separation or marital discord). The men seemed to have more experience of early loss than the women, though the numbers in the sample were small. Both the men and women had a high incidence of mood disorders, but the men appeared to have a greater incidence of alcohol abuse. As with the women, problems with their creative work was common.

IV. SUICIDE AND AFFECTIVE DISORDER

Kay Jamison has documented the association between manic-depressive disorder (and suicide) and creativity. In a sample of 36 British and Irish poets born between 1705 and 1805, she found that 27 had clear signs of depressive and psychotic disorders and two had committed suicide, both manic-depressives.

Rather than the depression and mania simply increasing the risk of suicide in creative people, the greater incidence of suicide may be a result of a greater lack of impulse control since recent research has indicated that serotonergic dysfunction in the central nervous system may lead to impulsive behavior rather than depressive syndromes.

V. ATTITUDES TOWARD SUICIDE

George Domino has compared samples of creative and noncreative college students nominated by their professors. The two groups were similar in age, gender, college major, and vocabulary level. The creative students did perform significantly better on objective tests of creativity. When given an inventory to measure attitudes toward suicide, the creative students differed significantly from the noncreative students on seven of the eight scales. The creative students perceived suicide as more associated with mental illness and less as a cry for help, felt more strongly that people have a right to die, disagreed more that a lack of religious values was associated with suicidal behavior, perceived suicide as both a more normal behavior and as a greater reflection of aggression, and judged suicide to be less of a moral evil. Domino concluded that creative students, therefore, perceive suicide as a less readily available behavior and efficacious solution to life's problems, but my reading of his results suggests the opposite.

VI. ARE SUICIDAL PEOPLE CREATIVE?

Several studies have explored whether suicidal people are good at solving problems. The general conclusion seems to be that they are impaired in their problem-solving skills. [*See* PROBLEM SOLVING.]

VII. SUICIDAL BEHAVIOR IN THE GIFTED

Gifted people are not necessarily creative, although they may be. Typically giftedness is measured by intelligence tests, which penalize creative responses by scoring them as incorrect. However, there is some overlap between the gifted and the creative, and a review of research on suicidal behavior in the gifted is relevant here. [*See* GIFTEDNESS AND CREATIVITY.]

The academically gifted have been thought to be more susceptible to depression and suicide, not only because of the typical suicidogenic risk factors (such as psychiatric disturbance, drug and alcohol abuse, and dysfunctional family backgrounds), but also because of factors associated with their giftedness.

1. Gifted adolescents may be prone to perfectionism, a trait that has been linked to suicide.
2. They may be more sensitive to the world in general and to the stressors encountered in adolescent life.
3. They may have greater problems adjusting to the school system, which is not usually designed to meet the needs of gifted and creative students and often lacks appropriate educational resources and support for their abilities. As a result they may feel bored and alienated.
4. They feel more pressure from others to achieve, which may result in unrealistic expectations for themselves.
5. They may feel frustrated by their impotence to produce real-world change.
6. They may find themselves more socially isolated and alienated, partly because they prefer solitary and single-friend activities, which may result in poor relationships with their academically average peers.
7. Their development may be more uneven, particularly their emotional development, which often lags behind their intellectual development.

Methodologically sound studies of suicidal ideation and behavior in gifted children and adolescents have not found that the incidence of these is greater than among average people. At the college level, however, there is some evidence to suggest that suicide rates are higher at the most prestigious universities.

One of the most important samples of gifted children studied is that formed by Lewis Terman in California in 1921, consisting of 1528 children with a mean age of 9.7 years and an IQ score of over 140. By 1987, twenty-five men and nine women had killed themselves. The proportion of deaths due to suicide up to 1987 was 8.7% for the men and 5.2% for the women.

The strongest predictor of suicide in this sample appears to be poor mental health, although the suicides may have more often lost their fathers as children, had problems with alcohol abuse, experienced more stress in their family of origin, and had worse physical health.

Edwin Shneidman looked at the files of five of these suicides, ten people who had died naturally, and fifteen who were still living, all men, and was not informed as to which person fit into each category. He rated them for life success, perturbation (or disturbance), and lethality (likelihood of completing suicide). The five suicides were ranked first, second, fourth, fifth, and sixth by Shneidman as candidates for suicide.

VIII. THE ROLE OF OTHER FACTORS

It has been noted that there is a high incidence of alcohol abuse in creative individuals, such as artists and writers. This association may mean that alcohol intoxication (and perhaps abuse) increases creativity (perhaps by providing inspiration), that the creative lifestyle makes alcohol abuse more likely (alcoholism may be a disease of loners and individualism), or that some third factor (childhood experiences or psychosocial influences) increases the likelihood of both creativity and alcohol abuse. Regarding the first possibility, there is some research evidence indicating, for example, that alcohol intoxication does *not* increase creativity in average individuals.

Whatever the reasons, the association of creativity and alcohol abuse does provide a possible explanation for the association between creativity and suicidal behavior because alcohol abuse has been shown clearly to be associated with the likelihood of both fatal and nonfatal suicidal behavior. [*See* ALCOHOL AND CREATIVITY.]

IX. TREATMENT

Andrew Slaby has argued for the early recognition and treatment of depressive disorders in creative people in order to decrease their suicidal risk. He argued that electroconvulsive therapy (ECT) and medications were useful in this regard and claimed that creativity is not affected by these treatments. However, though hard data are not available, anecdotal evidence suggests that these approaches may not be the best. Both

Anne Sexton and Abbie Hoffman were diagnosed as having bipolar affective disorders and given lithium. Both disliked the side effects of the medication so much that they stopped taking it and both completed suicide. Sexton, in particular, found that the lithium affected her ability to write poetry. Ernest Hemingway tried to commit suicide while being taken to the Mayo Clinic for a second course of ECT and killed himself the day after his release. In those days, psychiatrists suppressed the knowledge that ECT led to memory loss (sometimes permanent), and memory loss may have contributed to Hemingway's motivation to kill himself.

Slaby also urged that society take pains to reduce the stigma of being different, including being creative, bright, or sensitive. Although this is desirable, it is far from clear how society can remove this stigma.

X. DOES CREATIVE WRITING HELP SUICIDAL PEOPLE?

Is writing therapeutic for creative writers or is it a stressor that contributes to their psychological disturbance? Although there may be merit in both positions, David Lester and Rina Terry have argued that writing poetry can be useful with suicidal clients. Writing poems per se may not be helpful to the client, but the revision of the initial drafts of poems may be therapeutically useful. Revising poems may serve a similar function for clients as the journal assignments devised by cognitive therapists, which give the clients intellectual control over their emotions and distance from the traumatic memories. The researchers illustrated their thesis with Anne Sexton's life and suicidal death.

Sexton revised her poems extensively and, in the process of revision, had to concentrate on form rather than content. This allows for both the action that therapists deem to be therapeutic and the distancing of the self from one's problems. Because Sexton ultimately chose the moment of her death, one should not discount the therapeutic help her writing afforded her.

Anne Sexton illustrates the dialectic in poetry as therapy, between expression and catharsis on the one hand and cognitive control on the other. Sexton, as long as she was able to stay psychiatrically stable, applied the craft of poetry to her creative productions.

Both Sexton and Martin Orne, her first therapist, believed that her poetry had helped her recover. Only toward the end of her life, as her ability to craft her poems declined, did her mental stability dissipate.

Interestingly, Sexton showed manic trends prior to her suicide. She would write poems furiously, poems with more emotional expression and less poetic crafting. Rather than arguing that writing poetry contributed in part to her suicide, it makes much more sense to say that, in her final breakdown, poetry was no longer able to help her deal with the intrapsychic conflicts as it had in the past. As her inner turmoil increased, she wrote feverishly, almost like a safety valve letting out the steam under pressure in a boiler, but to no avail. The pressure was building up faster than she could release it.

But this final failure of the craft of poetry to keep Anne Sexton alive does not signify total failure. She was an outstanding poet and functioned quite well given her probable affective disorder. The craft of poetry may have kept her alive for many years after her self-destructive impulses first manifested themselves and so signifies success.[1] [*See* SEXTON, ANNE.]

---

[1] Plath's life and suicidal death also can be used to illustrate this thesis.

XI. CONCLUSIONS

Suicidal behavior appears to be more common in creative people, particularly writers. It has not been proved that creativity per se is responsible for the increased risk of suicide. The most likely explanation for the association of suicidal behavior with creativity is that creative people are more likely to have an affective disorder, typically manic-depressive disorder, and to abuse alcohol, characteristics which are associated with a higher risk for suicide.

Bibliography

Andreasen, N. C. (1987). Creativity and mental illness. *American Journal of Psychiatry, 144,* 1288–1292.

Delisle, J. R. (1986). Death with honors. *Journal of Counseling and Development, 64,* 558–560.

Domino, G. (1988). Attitudes toward suicide among highly creative students. *Creativity Research Journal, 1,* 92–105.

Jamison, K. R. (1993). *Touched with fire.* New York: The Free Press.

Lester, D. (1993). *Suicide in creative women.* Commack, NY: Nova Science.

Ludwig, A. M. (1995). *The price of greatness.* New York: Guilford.

Shneidman, E. S. (1981). Suicide among the gifted. *Suicide and Life-Threatening Behavior, 11,* 254–281.

Slaby, A. E. (1992). Creativity, depression and suicide. *Suicide and Life-Threatening Behavior, 22,* 157–166.

Synchronicity

Jane Piirto

Ashland University

Formative Causation A hypothesis, proposed by biologist Rupert Sheldrake, which states that all biological and chemical systems at all levels of complexity are organized by morphic fields. Under standard conditions anywhere in the world, permutations in one morphic field will occur more readily over time in similar organisms through inheritance of habits. According to Rupert Sheldrake, "Formative causation is the kind of causation responsible for form, structure, and pattern, and the causal influence on this is the morphogenetic field" or "morphic field" (from the Greek word *morphi* meaning "form").

Implicate Order A theory by physicist David Bohm. The universe is organized from within as well as from without. The implicate order underlies and enfolds all matter. The external world is called the explicate order, and this was the concern of classical physics.

Morphic Resonance An influence of similar things on subsequent similar things. Fields have a kind of inherent memory within them that is nonmaterial but physical. The gravitational field is physical in that it has physical effects as is part of nature, but it is not material in the sense that it is made of matter.

Trickster A mythological character, found in many cultures, who transforms aspects of the world and who plays pranks. Often in the form of the raven, the coyote, the spider, the mink, the bluejay, or the rabbit in North American Indian cultures; in the form of the monkey in Asian cultures; in the form of Hermes and Prometheus in Greek mythology; and in the form of Loki in Norse mythology.

SYNCHRONICITY *is the simultaneous or near-simultaneous happening of coincidental events that have no cause. The odd events, because of their occurrence so close in time, are instilled with meaning by those who recognize them. This article examines the relationship between synchronicity and creativity.*

I. INTRODUCTION

Synchronicity has applications in several domains. In psychology, synchronicity is defined as the occurrence of meaningful coincidences that seem to have no cause; that is, the coincidences are *acausal*. The underlying idea is that there is unity in diversity. In biology, Rupert Sheldrake's work on morphic resonance has been concerned with principles similar to synchronicity. In systems theory, Ernst Laszlo's work on chaos theory has also affirmed the idea of synchronicity. In

591

modern physics, Bohm's work on the holographic cosmos is most consonant with the concept of synchronicity. Creativity and synchronicity have to do with these four concepts.

II. SYNCHRONICITY AND PSYCHOLOGY

Carl Jung, in his 1955 monograph on synchronicity, cited Kammerer's work on multiples, Schopenhauer's work on the first cause, the work of Davies, Richey, and Hammerian on probability calculus, the work of Wilhelm Von Scholz on how lost or stolen objects come back to their owners, Herbert Silberer's work on how chance functions from a psychological angle, and J. B. Rhine's experiments with extrasensory perception as evidence of a force called synchronicity. He focused on Rhine's work, saying the experiments show that events may be meaningfully correlated but not causally correlated, and therefore meaningful coincidences have archetypal roots. Jung also worked closely with physicist Wolfgang Pauli, who was interested in synchronicity as an explanation for the behavior of atoms in quantum mechanics. Jung defined *synchronicity* in several passages thus:

- Simultaneous occurrence of two meaningful but not causally connected events.
- A coincidence in time of two or more causally unrelated events which have the same or a similar meaning.
- The simultaneous occurrence of a certain psychic state with one or more external events which appear as meaningful parallels to the momentary subjective state and in certain cases, vice-versa.
- Synchronistic events rest on the simultaneous occurrence of two different psychic states. One is the normal, probable state (the one that is causally explainable) and the other, the critical experience, is the one that cannot be derived causally from the first.

Synchronicity does not only show its effects in the present; it shows its effects in the past and the future. Synchronicity has to do with the physical principles of time, space, and causality. That people who are able to perceive in the present, events in the future, with what

is called "extrasensory perception" or "precognition" is proof that such events are *synchronistic,* having to do with a relationship across time, and not *synchronous,* taking place at the same time. They fall into the same category whether they are separated by space or separated by time. Jung gave three examples that he said showed that space and time are, in their essence, one and the same:

1. A woman in therapy dreamed of receiving a scarab pin. While she was describing the dream, Jung heard a buzzing rap at the window. There, simultaneous with the woman's story, was a golden beetle, similar to the Egyptian scarab beetle, which is a symbol of rebirth in Egyptian mythology. This was an example of synchronicity in which a psychic state simultaneously occurs with an external event that coincides with the content of the state.

2. A woman saw birds gathered outside the rooms in which her grandmother and mother died. Jung was treating her husband for a neurosis. The man seemed to exhibit signs of heart trouble. Jung sent him to see a doctor. The man was given a clean bill of health. On the way back home after his appointment with the doctor, with the papers in his pocket, the man collapsed of a heart attack. The woman reported that soon after her husband had gone to the doctor, she saw a flock of birds land on their house. She remembered what had happened at the deaths of her mother and grandmother, and was very fearful. Her fears were justified. Jung said this was an example of synchronicity where the woman's unconscious had already perceived the danger to her husband. The first two incidents of birds landing were coincidences that set up a correspondence in her that could only be proved when the man's dead body was brought home.

3. A man in Europe dreamed the death of a friend in America. The next morning he received a telegraph that the friend had died an hour before the dream occurred. Jung said that such experiences commonly happen almost simultaneously with the event, just before, or just after it happens. The person had unconscious knowledge of the event.

The two necessities for synchronicity to take place are (a) the presence of emotion and (b) an unconscious image that comes to consciousness either directly or indirectly. The melding of space and time are crucial and how the energy is transmitted is not known and is perhaps unknowable. Jung said that there is no explanation for the transmission of energy in these cases.

He conjectured about three different ways of understanding synchronicity, focusing on how intuition has worked in a way that is statistically significant.

1. One could look at the ESP experiments that provided statistical empirical evidence that such events exist. In the ESP experiments, the subjects did better when the tasks were fresh and their emotion and interest was focused. As the tasks repeated, boredom set in, and they did not do as well. This shows that emotion is indeed necessary for synchronicity to occur.

2. If we look at the Chinese way of holistically seeing the world, rather than the Western way of seeing the world by analyzing small parts and generalizing to the whole, we can see that the concept of synchronicity is more explainable. The ancient Chinese practice *I Ching,* based on the concept of the Tao, where one throws stalks of yarrow (or, in the West, three coins) in order to grasp the meaning of an event or to predict the future, is based on intuitive principles. (Jung did much work with the *I Ching* and first used the word *synchronicity* at the funeral of his friend Richard Wilhelm, who had translated the *I Ching.*) When an intuitive person who understands the 64 mutations of Yin and Yang interprets the tosses, the interpretation taps into the inner knowledge of the person, which is the same as the person's psychological state at that time. This state is synchronous with the chance falling of the coins or sticks. Thus the results are meaningful but there is no cause or explanation for the meaning.

3. Jung settled on another intuitive technique based on ancient science, and that was astrology. He conducted an experiment with 80 married couples and found that their signs were compatible to a degree that was statistically significant. A mathematician colleague of Jung's looked at the data and found that 25% of the couples had signs that were compatible. Of course, the other 75% did not. Jung said such astrological coincidence has little chance of being proved by mathematical law and that astrologers would argue that probability mathematics is not subtle enough to decipher the many permutations that influence the married couple's charts and signs.

Jung reviewed historical antecedents to the idea of synchronicity, cautioning that the rationalistic view of people in the West is not the only possible explanation for events, and, in fact, the rationalistic view shows short-sightedness, prejudice, and bias. He cited the Western practices of astrology, alchemy, and mantic practices such as tarot and *I Ching* as being open to synchronicity.

Jung referred to Schopenhauer's idea of the unity of primal cause, Leibniz's idea of preestablished harmony, and Kepler's idea of a geometrical principle that underlies the physical world. Jung said there must be some girding idea or principle that can explain these seemingly coincidental happenings. Noting that both primitive and medieval people did not doubt the existence of synchronicity as explanation for seemingly acausal events, Jung asserted that it is the role of psychology and parapsychology to take into account the fact that synchronicity might explain such events.

Jung pointed to dream analysis and focused on his principle of the collective unconscious, which is an underlying species memory, common to homo sapiens, that is expressed in archetypes, overarching mythic figures that appear similar in myths and fairytales in all societies. They are primordial images that exist in the unconscious and surface in dreams, images made in art forms such as poetry, painting, and music, and in fantasy, delusions, and delirium states of people alive today. In 1961 Jung stated that the form of archetypes is comparable to the form of a crystal, which is preformed in the liquid from which it rises, even though it does not exist materially by itself.

Jung worked with physicist Wolfgang Pauli, who postulated that synchronicity is the fourth pole in a unity of time, space, and causality. Pauli pioneered with his explication of the exclusion principle, which stated that electrons cannot share the same path of orbit in an atom. This led Pauli to assert that quantum physics did not uphold the idea of universal principles and thus began the era of new physics. Pauli and Jung proposed an addition to classical physics, that of synchronicity (see Figure 1).

In 1980 Arthur Koestler described synchronicity as even more enigmatic than ESP such as telepathy and precognition. Humans have been infatuated with such riddles since the beginning of mythology. These riddles contain the perhaps accidental and coincidental

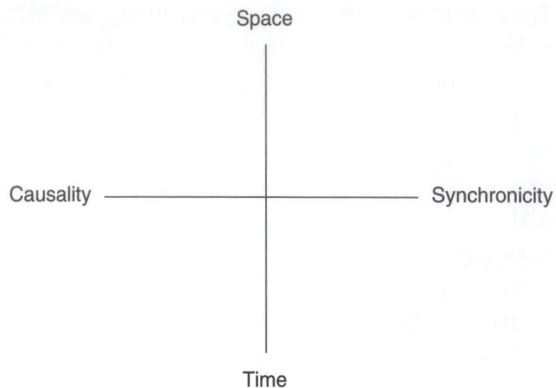

FIGURE 1   The four elements of the physical world.

meeting of unrelated events, which seem to have no cause but which also appear to be very important and significant. Koestler felt that Jung's relating synchronicity to the idea of the collective unconscious was a mistake. Koestler applauded Jung for working in concert with the physicist Pauli as he developed his theory. Whereas Jung used Pauli as a "quasi" tutor in theoretical physics, Koestler faulted Jung for not following up on Pauli's ideas but rather descending into the obscure by attributing synchronicity to the collective unconscious and to archetypes. Koestler said, "This was sadly disappointing but it helped turn synchronicity into a cult word."

III. SYNCHRONICITY IN BIOLOGY

Synchronicity is expressed by the principle of morphic resonance in formative causation described by Rupert Sheldrake. According to Sheldrake in 1994, "the hypothesis of formative causation suggests that self-organizing systems at all levels of complexity—including molecules, crystals, cells, tissues, organisms, and societies of organisms—are organized by 'morphic fields.'" These fields include morphogenetic fields that have to do with the how organisms, molecules, and even crystals inherently remember what previous bodies have done.

The case of the blue tits is an example. Over time, ornithologists noticed that small blue tit birds learned to pierce the tops of milk bottles left on the doorsteps in the morning in Great Britain. The phenomenon was first reported in 1921. By 1947 the behavior had been noticed throughout Europe. Blue tits do not usually travel far from their homes and live only 2 or 3 years. In the Netherlands, milk delivery had been all but stopped during World War II. When milk delivery resumed in 1947 and 1948, the blue tit behavior also resumed. Sheldrake used this as an example of how organisms remember habits established by previous generations.

Sheldrake said that space and distance do not matter to morphic resonance, for information and not energy is exchanged. That is, the universal principles of space and causality do not apply. The hypothesis of morphic resonance explained by formative causation explains the patterns and events in nature to be "understood as regulated by inherited habits and not by universal and eternal underlying principles."

Mechanistic science after Descartes took for granted that there were universal principles that were inviolable and that the task of science was to discover these principles. Thus memory was "stored" in cells in the brain or body; Sheldrake said this was not true; memory is part of a collective memory of the species inherited from former members of the species. In 1994 Sheldrake said that this is a concept similar to Jung's concept of the collective unconscious: "The hypothesis of morphic resonance enables the collective unconscious to be seen not just as a human phenomenon but as an aspect of a far more general process by which habits are inherited through nature."

Sheldrake commented that these two hypotheses—of formative causation and of morphic resonance—may seem mysterious, but the mechanistic idea that there are laws of mathematics that transcend nature are more mysterious, as they also rely on a metaphysical explanation for what happens in nature.

IV. SYNCHRONICITY IN CHAOS THEORY

In 1987 Ervin Laszlo formulated a hypothesis about mathematical wave functions that assemble themselves into forms and nested patterns or psi-fields. Laszlo theorized that once patterns are made, they probably will occur again. This is an expression of creativity in the universe, or cosmos.

V. SYNCHRONICITY IN THE NEW PHYSICS

In physics, the principle of correspondence was cited by Niels Bohr to illustrate the discontinuum between the particle and the wave. Bohr later changed the term to *argument of correspondence.* The idea of correspondence is related to the concept of the natural philosophers of the Middle Ages, who talked of the "sympathy of all things" and to the Greek philosophers such as Plato who postulated an underlying ideal form.

David Bohm expressed the theory of the implicate order, which is the order that underlies what is external, or the explicate order. The implicate order is part of and contains the explicate order. Bohm saw the universe as a hologram, where each part is enfolded into each other part. The synchronicity in this theory is that locality disappears. Time, space, and causality are not evident in events that happen. What may seem to be creativity may instead be the expression of synchronicity. Bohm also proposed a superimplicate order, which may contain a unifying principle. Intuition may be an expression of the superimplicate order functioning to perceive the implicate order and therefore the explicate order. The notion of the "sixth sense" is similar to the notion of synchronicity.

VI. SYNCHRONICITY AND CREATIVITY

These and other theories evolving simultaneously from many branches of knowledge converge in the root definition of creativity, which means "to make." The root of the words *create* and *creativity* comes from the Latin *creātus* and *creâre.* This means "to make or produce" or literally "to grow." The word also comes from the Old French base *kere,* and the Latin *crescere* and *creber.* The Roman goddess of the earth, Ceres, is an example, as is the Italian corn goddess, Cereris. Creativity as a word has roots in the earth. Other similar words are *cereal, crescent, creature, concrete, crescendo, decrease, increase,* and *recruit.*

The *Dictionary of Developmental and Educational Psychology* in 1986 defined creativity as "man's capacity to produce new ideas, insights, inventions or artistic objects, which are accepted of being of social, spiritual, aesthetic, scientific, or technological value." In 1988 the *Random House Dictionary of the English Language, Unabridged Edition,* noted that creativity was an ability to "transcend traditional ideas, rules, patterns, relationships or the like, and to create meaningful new ideas, forms, methods, interpretations, etc." [*See* DEFINITIONS OF CREATIVITY.]

Synchronicity has thus two relationships with the concept of creativity. First is that seemingly acausal coincidences may jar a person to have new ideas, to see the old in new ways, and may force a person to pay attention and perhaps change the old ways of behaving, acting, doing, making. Second is that in the new cosmology, where universal principles have been shown not to exist (except perhaps in Jung's concept of the collective unconscious and in Bohm's of the superimplicate order), creativity is found in the constantly evolving and perhaps accidental forms and patterns that are being developed.

The former may be illustrated with the following: A woman wakes up. Last night she dreamed about a coyote coming out of a cave and licking her hand. At the dentist, she flips through a fashion magazine and sees a new perfume called Coyote, in which the model is dressed in Indian fashion, petting a coyote. She goes to work and receives a letter from a man called William Coyote who wants her to give a speech at his school. At lunch she tells her friend about these unforeseen coincidences. Her friend pulls from her purse a novel she is reading. It is called *Coyote Justice.* By the fourth coincidence, the woman has a strong feeling that there is something going on. She and her friend talk about the coyote as trickster in American Indian mythology. This begins a search that leads the woman to a life change as she begins to embrace the significance of the trickster figure in her life. These coincidences with no seeming cause are called *synchronicity.*

An example of the latter is the following, as explained by Sheldrake. When random mutations occur, organisms must react in new ways. Organisms adapt to the genetic mutation by making a creative leap, which synthesizes into a new pattern. These patterns are instituted by morphic fields, which get more powerful and instill habits into the organism if the organism is preserved through natural selection. Sheldrake said:

> Thus the creativity that gives rise to new bodily forms and to new patterns of behavior is not explained by the random mutations alone. It involves a creative response upon the part of the organism itself and also depends on the ability of the organism to integrate this new pattern with the rest of its habits.

Thus synchronicity is basically creative whether at the level of the atom, the molecule, the cell, the organism, or the system. Enigmatic, inscrutable, mysterious, seemingly acausal, playful, and funny, synchronicity makes us laugh, cry, pay attention, and shake our heads in amazement. In 1996 Allan Combs and Mark Holland stated it well: "Nothing is closer to the heart of the experience of synchronicity than the feeling that the world itself expresses creativity in synchronistic co-incidences. Such coincidences often have more the feel of poetry than physics."

Bibliography

Bohm, D., & Hiley, B. J. (1993). *The undivided universe: An ontological interpretation of quantum theory.* New York: Routledge.

Bolen, J. S. (1979). *The tao of psychology: Synchronicity and the self.* San Francisco, CA: HarperSanFrancisco.

Combs, A., & Holland, M. (1996). *Synchronicity: Science, myth, and the trickster.* New York: Marlowe & Company.

Jung, C. G. (1961). *Memories, dreams, reflections.* (Richard & Clara Winston, Trans.). New York: Vintage Books.

Jung, C. G. (1973). *Synchronicity: An acausal connecting principle.* (R. F. C. Hull, Trans.). Princeton, NJ: Princeton University Press.

Koestler, A. (1972). *The roots of coincidence.* New York: Random House.

Koestler, A. (1980). *Bricks to babel.* New York: Random House.

Laszlo, E. (1987). The psi-field hypothesis. *IS Journal, 4,* 13–28.

Progoff, I. (1973). *Jung, synchronicity, and human destiny.* New York: The Julian Press.

Sheldrake, R. (1994). *The rebirth of nature: The greening of science and god.* Rochester, VT: Park Street Press.

Synesthesia

George Domino

University of Arizona

Chromesthesia (or Chromatic-Lexical Synesthesia) A type of synesthesia in which words elicit colors.

Eidetic Imagery A vivid type of imagery, in which the subject can "see" an object even though the object is absent.

Physiognomic Perception A type of perception in which cognition is suffused with emotion—for example, seeing the wind as angry.

Synesthesia (or Synaesthesia) A phenomenon whereby perception of one class of stimuli, such as sounds, is linked to images from another sensory mode, such as colors.

Synesthete A person who possesses synesthesia.

SYNESTHESIA is an interesting phenomenon, potentially related to creativity. This article looks at the nature of synesthesia; a brief history; some theories to account for synesthesia; synesthesia as related to psychology, the arts, and neurology; some case studies; and finally the evidence of a link between synesthesia and creativity.

I. NATURE

One of the most interesting and strange phenomena of human behavior linked to creativity is that of synesthesia, in which the aspects of sensation from one sensory domain are applied to another sensory domain. The word *synesthesia* comes from two Greek words— *syn* meaning "union" and *aisthesis* meaning "sensation." If you have ever attended a multimedia concert where music and colored lights are presented simultaneously, you have an understanding of what synesthesia is all about. If you enjoy walking in the rain and have discovered that "rain is the sound of motion," and that wetness is linked with the "feeling of shimmering rays of light and color," then you have an understanding of synesthesia—even though neither example is an example of synesthesia. A major problem with trying to understand synesthesia is that synesthesia is a nonverbal, intuitive, and sensuous phenomenon that can only be explained by a discursive, deductive, and intellectual approach.

What is synesthesia? If a person is presented with a stimulus in one sense modality, for example, a musical tone, but experiences sensations or images in another modality, such as seeing colors, then that experience is called synesthesia.

Synesthesia however, is not simply the association of colors to sensations or emotions. Thus for example, it is part of our linguistic heritage to associate certain colors with temperature; there are "cool" colors such as blue and green, and there are "warm" colors such as orange and red. Similarly, most of us have learned that envy is green and anger is red. But that is not sufficient to define the occurrence of synesthesia.

Synesthesia can be viewed as one category of a major class of perceptual phenomena termed *syncretic*. Syncretic phenomena involve a fusion of perceptual qualities in subjective experience. They include such aspects as physiognomic perception (which is a fusion of perception and feeling) and eidetic imagery (which is a fusion of imagery and perception). There in fact seems to be a relationship between these perceptual phenomena, such that for example, synesthesia and eidetic imagery tend to occur in the same person. [*See* IMAGERY.]

Theoretically, all of the five senses can blend with each other, but in fact there seem to be few combinations that exist. One of the more common types of synesthesia is that between vision and audition, specifically between visual lightness and auditory pitch. Auditory stimuli that are lower in frequency typically evoke visual sensations of stimuli that are darker, and conversely auditory stimuli higher in frequency typically evoke visual sensations of stimuli that are lighter. Another type of synesthesia is where visual images are produced by taste, but this seems to be relatively rare.

The most prevalent form of synesthesia is *colored hearing,* more formally called chromatic-lexical synesthesia or chromesthesia, in which sounds result in specific colors. Colors can also be seen not just with words, or specific sequences like the days of the week, but also with temperatures, pressure, taste, smells, and pain. In the literature, there is a report of a synesthete who saw specific discrete colors for everyone that she met and claimed that people with similar colors had similar personalities. Although chromesthesias are particularistic for different individuals, there are also some interesting communalities. This is particularly true of vowel-color associations, where for example the vowel *a*, sounded as in "ah" usually produces red and yellow images. This relationship apparently reflects the relationship between pitch and brightness. High-pitched

sounds produce white or bright images, whereas low-pitched sounds produce dark images. In addition, the pitch of the sound seems to be related to other visual aspects—for example, high-pitched sounds tend to produce images that are smaller, angular, and have sharp edges.

A number of characteristics have been associated with synesthesia. Sir Francis Galton (1822–1911), for example, believed that synesthetes (people who exhibit synesthesia) were imaginative and sensitive, often quite intelligent, and frequently musically or artistically gifted. Others have described synesthetes as having excellent memories, and many have *eidetic imagery,* the ability to perceive clear and detailed visual images of something seen previously. Still other researchers have linked synesthesia with good imagination, as well as internal conflicts. Many synesthetes report that their ability was present as far back as they can remember, but that when they mentioned their ability to others they were met with disbelief and ridicule. Although no formal studies have been done, synesthesia seems to run in families, thus suggesting a genetic basis. However, the responses of same family members are rather idiosyncratic.

Some synesthetes possess a *number form;* that is, they perceive numbers—or days of the week, months, or other concepts that involve time or magnitude—as organized in space. For example, a subject studied in our laboratory perceived numbers as indicated in Figure 1.

Is it possible that lower animals also can exhibit synesthesia? We really don't know, but from an evolutionary and physiological point of view we can make a compelling argument. After all, "simple" animals do not have highly differentiated sensory organs, so that their sensory experiences could easily cut across categories. In a study exploring this, an experimenter trained fish to discriminate between bright and dark

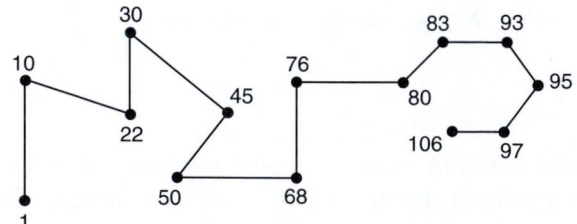

FIGURE 1 Drawing of a number form by a synesthete.

chambers, with half of the fish taught to prefer the lighted chamber and half the darkened chamber. The fish were then presented with two smells: musk and indol. In humans, musk is thought of as a "bright" smell and indol as a "dark" smell. If there is cross-modal matching (i.e., synesthesia) in animals, the predicted outcome would be that fish trained in the light chamber would choose musk more often, and those fish trained in the dark would choose indol more often. That is exactly what happened.

If synesthesia is not merely an associative process, how can we distinguish the kinds of experiences most people report (such as associating the color black with funerals and death or seeing fireworks when the national anthem is played) from true synesthesia? In general, researchers agree that synesthesia can be defined according to nine criteria: (a) synesthesia is involuntary and cannot be suppressed. (b) The sensation of color or other response appears not in the mind, but is usually perceived as external and as real. (c) The synesthetic response is specifiable along its various dimensions, such as brightness and saturation. (d) The synesthetic sensations are few in number and tend to be categorical or generic in nature; that is, the color response is simple and generic. (e) The response should cut across a range of stimuli; that is, a colored response should be available to all the numbers, not just the number 6. (f) The color sensations are highly memorable. (g) The response is often accompanied by strong emotion and a sense of conviction. (h) Synesthesia is reproducible over extended periods of time. If one perceives the number 6 as purple and green, that perception will remain unchanged over time. (i) Synesthesia should occur reliably and spontaneously, not as a result of outside stimuli such as drugs or a blow to the head.

Most experts on the topic agree that synesthesia is a real perceptual phenomenon, not explainable by metaphorical learning, mnemonic devices, or other associative aspects. At the same time, even though we may wish to distinguish between true synesthesia, in which the cross-modality experience occurs involuntarily, and the associate experiences that most people have, in which the experience is deliberate, there is some communality between the two. Thus a number of investigators have administered tests of synesthesia to non-synesthetes and have found that the process in both groups is reliable and similar. A useful analogy

here is that most of us do not hallucinate—we do not hear voices as a severely mentally ill person might. We can hear such voices, however, when instructed to do so, when fatigued, when under the influence of certain drugs, when in specific physical settings such as a large, quiet library room, or when self-instructed.

How prevalent is synesthesia? Unfortunately, the answer to that deceptively simple question is strongly influenced by the theoretical stance of the investigator, as well as the actual operational definition used in collecting the data. Some investigators have argued that synesthesia is basically an associative process, a way of thinking analogically, and therefore not a special ability, but potentially available to everyone. Others agree with the notion that everyone potentially has synesthesia, but that individuals forget how to use this ability as they become adults, just as many adults "forget" their dreams. Most studies that have taken a more discriminating approach—that is, synesthesia can be defined according to some or all of the criteria reported here—report incidence figures of between 10 to 15% in adults, with somewhat higher figures in women than in men, and even higher percentages in children. In one study done with a large sample of college students, 7% reported spontaneous and consistent synesthetic experiences, and another 18% reported nonspontaneous, nonconsistent, or drug-related synesthesia. In another study, completed recently with U.S. college students who were enrolled in courses that emphasized artistic and personal creativity, the incidence of true synesthetes was 23%.

Is there a gender difference? In one report from Britain, the author gave a radio interview on synesthesia. Following the radio program, 210 women and 2 men wrote to the radio station claiming to also have synesthesia. As the author indicates, the gender ratio was astonishing, as this was a science program with an equal number of men and women listeners. In the two studies of college students mentioned earlier, the number of females was greater than the number of males identified as synesthetes. [See GENDER DIFFERENCES.]

Why should children have a higher frequency of synesthesia? One answer is that synesthesia is a precursor to abstract language, as well as an aspect of imagery. For many adults, imagery diminishes as language increases—that is, the word *ice cream* can represent for an adult all of the joyous sensations embodied in the childhood experience of licking an ice cream cone, and we thus use a word that stands for a multitude of sensory experiences.

II. HISTORY

Synesthesia has been known within the fields of medicine and psychology for well over 200 years. In the early 1700s for example, Sir Isaac Newton (1642–1727) tried to relate mathematically the energies of sound and of color, which eventually resulted in an organlike instrument that could play sounds and lights simultaneously. Erasmus Darwin (1731–1802), the grandfather of Charles, also produced a harpsichord that could do the same. In 1710 an English ophthalmologist, Thomas Woolhouse, described a patient, a blind man, who perceived sound-induced colored visions. Sir Francis Galton (1822–1911), one of the pioneers in establishing psychology as an empirical and experimental science, studied synesthesia, and in 1883 gave us some of the first psychological characteristics associated with the phenomenon.

As psychology developed in the late 1800s and early 1900s as an empirical science, many investigations of synesthesia were conducted, and they repeatedly reported a relationship between auditory pitch and visual brightness, such that the higher the frequency of a sound the greater the brightness of the associated color. This was especially true of vowels: *a* was associated with the colors red and blue, *e* and *i* with yellow and white, and *o* tended to be red and black.

The topic became so popular that in the 1890s a committee of seven prominent psychologists was formed to standardize the terminology and to advance our scientific understanding of the phenomenon. By the 1930s however, the topic had run its course, and—partly because there were so many other topics to be pursued in the new science of psychology and partly because knowledge of the brain-behavior relationship was severely limited by the lack of appropriate methods of inquiry—the topic of synesthesia was almost abandoned. It was seen as a psychological quirk, something that did exist but could not be readily explained. Even now it is seen by many as an oddity, a psychiatric disturbance, and is rarely mentioned in most textbooks of psychology.

Currently, however, there seems to be a revival of interest in the topic, in large part due to the work of psychologist Dr. Lawrence E. Marks of Yale University and that of Dr. Richard E. Cytowic, a neurologist in private practice in Bethesda, Maryland. We now have a much better understanding of the physiology of the human body and the possibility of studying the living brain without intrusion, through magnetic resonance imaging and other noninvasive procedures. The possibility that synesthesia may play a part in creativity also adds an exciting dimension to this interest.

III. THEORIES

Many theoretical explanations have been given as to the nature of synesthesia. Some of these are historical curiosities no longer held by researchers. Others require an understanding of complex psychological principles and even more complex neurological structures of the brain. Still others are quite convoluted and would take us far afield. For the purposes of this work, and at the risk of introducing serious distortions due to oversimplifications, we can consider the various theories about synesthesia as falling under one of these nine categories:

1. *Synesthesia equals pathology.* These theories view synesthesia as an aberration, a reflection of psychological pathology, or perhaps related to neurological conditions such as seizures and a more developmentally primitive response. There are cases reported in the literature of synesthesia occurring in patients with neurological conditions, but that does not prove that synesthesia is therefore pathological. In fact, the majority of synesthetes seem to be well-adjusted individuals.

2. *Synesthesia reflects language.* Colors are symbolically related to other stimuli, and thus synesthesia is a linguistic phenomenon, illustrated by such phrases as "seeing red" when one is angry and "seeing green" when one is jealous.

3. *Synesthesia reflects the physiological fact that both colors and sounds are mathematically related.* This is the position of Sir Isaac Newton and others, and indeed there are mathematical relationships between the properties of colors and those of sound. Synesthesia, however, can be a broader phenomenon, and the responses

given by synesthetes do not necessarily follow these mathematical principles.

4. *Synesthesia represents a compensatory response.* Here synesthesia is seen as an alternative response used to compensate for a defect. The primary focus of this approach is based on the observation that a significant percentage of blind subjects show colored hearing, often developed after the loss of eyesight.

5. *Synesthesia is learned, typically early in life.* The famous French psychologist Alfred Binet (1857–1911), for example, taught himself to be a synesthete by repeatedly associating letters to sounds, and he believed that chance pairings of colors and sounds produced synesthesia. Other attempts to teach people to be synesthetic have, however, failed.

6. *Synesthesia is the result of chance associations.* For example, many children are given alphabet books, where each letter is illustrated in different colors. Synesthesia is thus seen as a learned response, but one based on chance associations.

7. *Synesthesia is the product of emotions.* The relationship between colors and sounds is mediated by emotions—If I like a sound, I will associate that sound with a color I also like.

8. *Synesthesia is caused by defective physiological processes.* In the "normal" person, the nerve pathways for each sense are separate; in the synesthete, they are somehow connected or there is "leakage." Variants of this theory postulate that synesthesia is caused by an immature nervous system or by some defect in the circuitry of the brain.

9. *All of the senses have common dimensions, and synesthesia is a reflection of this unity.* Associated with this view is typically the hypothesis that synesthesia reflects an "incomplete" differentiation and is therefore a phenomenon that occurs early in development, both from an individual point of view and an evolutionary perspective. Synesthesia is seen as a developmentally primitive way of making sense of the world, one that disappears in most people as language develops.

IV. PSYCHOLOGY OF SYNESTHESIA

A substantial number of empirical studies exist within the discipline of psychology that are relevant to synesthesia. Unfortunately most of these studies were done in the early 1900s when psychological methodology was rather primitive and experimental sophistication rather restricted. For example, many of these early studies simply asked subjects to report any associations they had between color or forms and letters, numbers, and so on. Thus it is not clear whether synesthesia or simply associative learning was being identified.

A number of experiments have shown that the visual-auditory correspondence found in synesthetes is very similar or identical to that found in normal individuals when such a correspondence is elicited experimentally—for example, when a person is asked to match musical tones with color chips. In part the explanation may lie in the physiognomic aspects of language; that is, words are not typically assigned arbitrarily to objects but often reflect some aspect of that object (this is seen most clearly in onomatopoetic words such as *buzz* or *tinkle*). In fact, experimental evidence indicates that sounds themselves, as found in words, are judged to have different properties (e.g., high-pitched words typically describe small objects) and to vary in size and brightness. In addition, physiognomic perception has affective connotations—that is, we often associate emotions to words. Although synesthesia and physiognomic perception seem to be intrinsically related at least at a theoretical level, the two are rarely investigated as related phenomena.

Many personality and cognitive variables have been ascribed to synesthetes, but very few empirical studies exist to support or disprove such relationships.

V. THE ARTS

It is not surprising that there is a great deal of writings on synesthesia in the arts, especially music, poetry, and literature.

To the extent that emotions can be considered a sensory modality, the relationship of emotions to music might well represent a subtype of synesthesia. A common experience, present in probably all cultures, is that musical passages elicit specific emotions. Certainly, the fiery music present in the opera *Carmen* is emotionally quite different from Debussy's "Claire de lune," and the love ballads of Frank Sinatra are, emotionally at least, a world apart from Roger Miller's "You Can't Rollerskate in a Buffalo Herd."

Are the emotions evoked by specific musical fragments consistent across people? The scarce available research evidence shows that the general answer is a guarded yes, that such consistency is greater in adults than in children, and that it varies for different emotions—for example, anger and fear are often confused.

It is not at all unusual for musical composers to display synesthesia, typically associating colors with musical tones. Athanasius Kircher (1602–1680), a Jesuit musical theorist and mathematician, proposed that each musical sound has an objective and necessary correspondence to a certain color. Both Beethoven (1770–1827) and Rimsky-Korsakov (1844–1908) reported specific colors as related to specific tones. Alexander Scriabin (1871–1915), a Russian composer, wrote some of his compositions to be performed with both music and light. In 1911 he wrote a composition titled "Prometheus," which was performed in Carnegie Hall in 1915. The concert utilized a specially equipped color organ, in which colors were played on a keyboard and projected onto a screen. Specific musical tones were accompanied by specific colors—for example, E and F-sharp were accompanied by blue.

One way to induce synesthesia is through the use of drugs such as hashish and mescaline. Poets like Theophile Gautier (1811–1872) and Charles Baudelaire (1821–1867) wrote of their synesthetic experiences under the influence of hashish and emphasized in their poetry the correspondence between sounds and colors.

A lot of poetry, of course, contains visual images, analogies, and various literary devices that might be described as "intersense" analogies. Using such analogies and being a synesthete are not the same. This seems to be true, for example, of the well-known poet Percy Bysshe Shelley (1792–1822), who frequently and effectively used intersense analogies, but apparently was not himself a synesthete.

A number of writers have also shown evidence of synesthesia. For example, Vladimir Nabokov (1899–1977), best known for his novel *Lolita*, in a 1949 *New Yorker* article described colored hearing where "the color sensation seems to be produced by the very act of my orally forming a given letter while I imagine its outline." He went on to give examples, such as the *a* of the English alphabet as having the "tint of weathered wood," but the *a* of the French alphabet "evokes polished ebony"; *s* has a "curious mother-of-pearl," whereas *t* is pistachio.

Even some well-known personalities are said to have been synesthetes. One such example is Jacqueline Kennedy Onassis (1929–1994) who, if not a synesthete, had a strong interest in synesthesia. When she traveled to China with architect I. M. Pei, she was taken with two calligraphy sayings "see fragrance" and "read paintings." In one of her writings, she cited the work of the poet Baudelaire on the magic power of colors, sounds, and perfumes to elicit each other.

Even in the realm of the arts, synesthesia has not been looked on in a favorable manner. For example, the critic Irving Babbitt (1865–1933) was rather perturbed by the use of intersense analogies in 19th century French literature and wrote that such analogies were trivial at best, interesting and curious but nothing more; at worst, they reflected psychological and spiritual "disorder" and were the province of alienists and nerve specialists.

VI. NEUROLOGY

One study on neurology attempts to empirically relate synesthesia and brain functioning. In this study, six women synesthetes, aged 45 to 64, were studied both psychologically as well as neurologically by magnetic resonance imaging scans of the brain while the subjects were presented with single words to evoke color responses. The authors of this study concluded that color-word synesthesia is generated by an interaction between the brain areas for language and for higher vision. In fact, there was activity in the visual areas of the brain that occurred in the absence of any direct visual stimulation, suggesting an unusual anatomical connectivity between language and visual areas in synesthesia.

Most experts currently assume that synesthesia has a neural basis and an organic cause, and that eventually as our ability to study the brain directly increases we will find a neurological explanation.

VII. CASE STUDIES

Perhaps the best-known case study of synesthesia is one presented by the Russian physiological psychologist Aleksandr Luria (1902–1977) in a little book titled

The Mind of a Mnemonist. This is the case of a most unusual man, originally a newspaper reporter who had an amazing photographic memory. This man could repeat long series of numbers or words in reverse order as easily as in the order in which he heard the items, even if asked some 15 or 16 years later. The man eventually became a professional mnemonist and gave public performances to show his amazing memory.

One of the interesting aspects of this subject was that he also exhibited synesthesia. He described how as a child of 2 or 3 he was taught the words of a Hebrew prayer, which he did not understand. The words "settled" in his mind as "puffs of steam or splashes." Luria tested this man in his laboratory and presented him with a variety of sounds. For example, when presented with a tone pitched at 200 cycles per second and an amplitude of 113 decibels, the subject replied "It looks like something like fireworks tinged with a pink-red hue. The strip of color feels rough and unpleasant, and it has an ugly taste—rather like that of briny pickle." This man had an extremely vivid imagination and could alter his own body processes simply by imagining certain situations. For example, he could alter his pulse rate from a restful 70 to 72 to a high of 100 by imagining he was trying to catch a train. He could raise the temperature of his right hand while at the same time lowering the temperature of his left hand by imagining touching hot and cold objects.

One recent case study reported in the literature is that of a 76-year-old British widow who was an artist and experienced colors whenever she heard a word. This experience was automatic and the colors appeared rather quickly. Each letter of the alphabet had its own color, as well as each word, although the color of a word was not necessarily related to the colors of the individual letters in that word. The colors were experienced "inside her head" and were described as images. This woman felt that such an ability helped her memory, because, for example, she could recall a person's name by the person's color. At the same time, she experienced some interference in memory if, for example, two people had the same color. She remembered having such an ability since age 7, and probably earlier. Psychological testing showed her to be of superior intelligence, with excellent color discrimination ability, no psychiatric features, and a normal EEG.

Her color perceptions associated with specific words were rather complex; for example, the word *Moscow* was seen as darkish grey, with spinach green and a pale blue in places. She was given a set of 103 words to which she indicated her color reactions. These words, which were presented in a random fashion, included the days of the week, names, letters of the alphabet, and various types of words. She gave detailed descriptions of the colors she saw with each word, and when she was retested 10 weeks later with no advance notice, she gave identical responses to all 103 items. A control subject, who was not a synesthete and who was explicitly told she would be retested, could only give 17 identical responses.

Words that were semantically related, such as *man* and *masculine,* were not related in terms of the colors they evoked, nor did words that sounded similar, such as *man* and *moon,* elicit similar colors. Nonsense syllables, such as *jik* and *xot,* were perceived with the colors of the individual letters, and numbers above 10 were combinations of the colors of the individual numbers—for example, the color of 46 was a mixture of the colors of 4 and of 6.

The same researchers who studied this woman also studied a sample of nine synesthetic women. All of the subjects reported that they had synesthesia for as long as they remembered, certainly as far back as age 4. They all reported that the colors were automatic and unsuppressible. When asked if anyone else in the family experienced colored hearing, only female relatives such as mothers and sisters were mentioned, possibly suggesting a gender-linked genetic basis. For these subjects the color experienced at the sound of a word was typically dictated by the dominant letter of the word, usually the first. Thus if *bat* triggered red, so did *ball* and *best.* Five of these subjects reported that the color was not in a particular part of the visual field, and two subjects reported that it was just above the center of gaze. Six of the subjects reported that the color had the shape of the word, and one said it had no particular shape. In all these women, colored hearing was a one-way phenomenon—words elicited colors, but colors did not elicit words. One interesting finding is that across the nine subjects, the colors evoked by the words were highly idiosyncratic. The same was true for the colors of the letters of the alphabet, but there were some notable exceptions; for example, eight of the nine women reported that *o* was white.

VIII. CREATIVITY

One of the most interesting aspects of synesthesia, in the present context, is that there seems to be a relationship between synesthesia and creativity, although most of the evidence is anecdotal, based on case studies, literary products of highly creative individuals, and semi-scientific evidence.

As we have seen, synesthesia seems to be part and parcel of many creative individuals. Yet if one were inclined to do so, we could probably find many creative poets and composers who did not have synesthesia. Case studies can be interesting and provocative, but also quite suspect. At the same time, they do provide us with some tantalizing evidence. For example, in one study of 42 adult synesthetes, 11 were artists or in artistic professions; this certainly seems to be a rather high percentage, not likely to be produced by the random laws of chance.

There is at present only one study of empirically obtained evidence that synesthesia and creativity are related. In that study, conducted in our laboratory, we first surveyed 358 fine arts college students at three large universities and found that 84 individuals (23%) reported experiencing synesthesia in a spontaneous and consistent manner. From this subject pool, we created two samples, 61 synesthetes and 61 controls, that were equated on gender, college major, year in school, and verbal intelligence. These subjects were then asked to complete four measures of creativity: one a personality scale, another a measure of artistic aesthetics, a third a measure of innovative ability, and a fourth a measure of creative analogical thinking. The synesthete group scored significantly higher than their control peers on all four measures, with their average scores comparable to those obtained by other creative groups.

Bibliography

Baron-Cohen, S., Harrison, J., Goldstein, L. H., & Wyke, M. (1993). Coloured speech perception: Is synaesthesia what happens when modularity breaks down? _Perception, 22,_ 419–426.

Cytowic, R. E. (1989). _Synesthesia: A union of the senses._ New York: Springer-Verlag.

Domino, G. (1989). Synesthesia and creativity in fine arts students: An empirical look. _Creativity Research Journal, 2,_ 17–29.

Lindauer, M. S. (1991). Physiognomy and verbal synesthesia compared: Affective and intersensory descriptors of nouns with drawings and art. _Metaphor and symbolic Activity, 6,_ 183–202.

Luria, A. R. (1968). _The mind of a mnemonist._ London: Basic Books.

Marks, L. E. (1978). _The unity of the senses._ New York: Academic Press.

Paulesu, E., Harrison, J., Baron-Cohen, S., Watson, J. D. G., Goldstein, L., Heather, J., Frackowiak, R. S. J., & Frith, C. D. (1995). The physiology of colored hearing: A PET activation study of colour-word synaesthesia. _Brain, 118,_ 661–676.

Rader, C. M., & Tellegen, A. (1987). An investigation of synesthesia. _Journal of Personality and Social Psychology, 52,_ 981–987.

Shindell, S. (1984). Personality characteristics associated with reported synesthesia. (Doctoral dissertation, University of Arizona, 1983) _Dissertation Abstracts International, 44,_ 3207A.

Systems Approach

Kevin Rathunde

University of Utah

Circular Causality A process of causation such that one part of a system affects another part and, in turn, is affected by that part.

Domain A set of symbolic rules and procedures nested in the shared knowledge of a culture (e.g., the domain of mathematics).

Emergent Properties Attributes of a system that emerge or make their "appearance" on the level of the whole system, depending on the particular arrangement of the parts.

Equifinality Ability of a system to achieve the same goal through different routes.

Feedback The return of the output of a process or system to the input, especially when used to maintain performance or to control a system. Negative feedback operates to maintain homeostasis, or to attenuate variation in a system. Positive feedback amplifies variation.

Field All of the individuals in a culture who, through their selective actions as gatekeepers, can affect the structure of a domain.

Network of Enterprise The pattern of projects and activities, broadly defined, that gives identity to the creator's working self and provides structure and organization for his or her life.

Nonsummativity The principle that the whole is greater than the sum of its parts, and the parts cannot be studied in isolation.

System A group of interacting or interdependent elements forming a complex whole.

*A **SYSTEMS APPROACH** views creativity as a process shaped by multiple forces, including, but not limited to, the contributions of the creative person. Systems theory reorients the study of creativity by placing the person within a sociocultural context, rather than isolating him or her from it. Creativity is seen as a time-dependent, emergent property resulting from the interactions between key systemic components (e.g., interactions between persons, fields, or social institutions that select worthwhile variations, and domains, or cultural repositories that preserve and transmit selected variations to future generations). A systems approach makes no attempt to pinpoint a single cause or origin of creativity; instead, attention is paid to describing the relationships within and between key subsystems.*

I. BASIC CONCEPTS OF SYSTEMS THEORY

A systems theory approach is a way of looking at the world wherein objects are seen as interrelated with one another and with the environment. Evolving from a diverse set of disciplinary influences, including biology,

Copyright © 1999 by Academic Press
All rights of reproduction in any form reserved.

robotics, mathematics, anthropology, and sociology, what we now call general systems theory represents a major theoretical paradigm in the social and physical sciences. Only a few theorists have explicitly applied systems thinking to creativity research; however, it is fair to say that current interdisciplinary and ecological approaches have benefited from the growth of systems theory in the 20th century.

A system is a group of interdependent elements forming a complex whole. The notion of interdependence is central to the theory. Interdependence suggests that causation within a system is not linear, or proceeding in one direction from element to element. The notion of circular causality, instead, suggests that one part of a system affects another part and in turn is affected by that part. Thus, a systems approach turns attention toward the pattern of relationships or feedback loops between elements.

The assumption of circular causality necessitates a reorientation of perspective. It becomes meaningless to search for a phenomenon of interest, such as creativity, by isolating a few elements of a system (e.g., separating the person from his or her sociocultural context). Because the whole system is greater than the sum of its parts (i.e., the principle of nonsummativity), and the path to creativity can proceed from many different routes (i.e., the notion of equifinality), creativity is viewed as a property that emerges on the level of the whole system.

One of the hopes of systems theorists was the unification of science around a set of principles that could be applied universally, whether speaking of planetary systems or social systems. An important distinction, however, was introduced to differentiate nonliving from living systems. Whereas physical systems tend to follow the second law of thermodynamics and exhibit increased states of randomness (entropy), living systems tend to increase in order (negentropy). This distinction has important implications for the study of human creativity. Living systems get better organized over time, and they proceed from the simple to the complex.

The qualitative distinction "complex" introduces a way for creativity researchers to compare persons or social systems with an eye toward understanding more or less favorable conditions for the appearance of creativity. A complex system is more flexible or permeable and thus has a greater capacity for self-organization. For instance, it can solidify its boundaries when adaptation requires the attenuation of variation; and it can open its boundaries when it is necessary to change and amplify variation. This dynamic balance of conservative homeostatic and expansive morphogenetic forces makes a complex system more viable and more likely to find an adaptive fit within a particular environmental niche. Therefore, complex social systems, or complex psychological systems, have advantages in creative production. The following section elaborates on this idea.

II. CREATIVITY RESEARCH AND THE SYSTEMS APPROACH

Over the past 40 years, a great deal of research attention has been invested in understanding qualities of the creative person. While not always consistent with a systems perspective, such approaches are not antithetical to it. What is known about individual differences that affect creative production can be incorporated in systems models that integrate persons with their sociocultural contexts. Several contemporary researchers have begun to do this by investigating creativity in the context of social processes. Most researchers, however, have not imported systems terminology into their theories.

One approach that explicitly adopts a systems view is the work of Mihaly Csikszentmihalyi. Many studies of creativity start by asking the question, "What is creativity?" Csikszentmihalyi asked, "Where is creativity?" In light of historical evidence that indicated flashes of insight were but one step in a creative process that often took years, and judgments of creativity were related to social attributions within specific contexts, Csikszentmihalyi proposed that creativity "resided" in a systemic process. Creativity was the result of three main shaping forces: a field that selects from the variations produced by individuals those deemed worthy of preserving; a symbolic domain that incorporates the selections of the field and transmits the selected information to following generations; and finally, the person, who after gaining familiarity with the domain brings about some novel change in it (see Figure 1). [*See* DOMAINS OF CREATIVITY.]

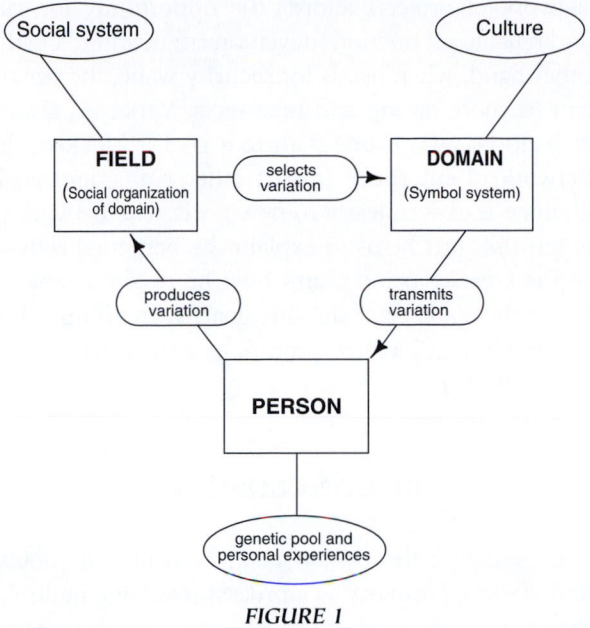

FIGURE 1

Consistent with systems theory, these three subsystems—person-field-domain—are seen as related through circular causality. Each subsystem affects the other and in turn is affected by the other. Thus, creativity cannot be located inside the individual or inside any of the other subsystems. The system of interrelationships is greater than the individual parts of person, field, and domain; therefore, it is impossible to study these parts in isolation. Without a symbolic domain, a person would have nowhere to start; without a field to evaluate an individual's ideas, there would be no way to differentiate what is creative from what is banal or bizarre.

Each subsystem provides an important "moment" in the process of creativity. The domain provides the set of rules and procedures that comprise a specific symbolic context (e.g., the domain of mathematics). Each domain, in turn, is nested in the shared knowledge of a culture. Domains provide patterns of order, or ways of making meaning. For instance, a psychological theory provides a way to think about the self; a musical style provides a way to organize rhythm and melody. These patterns of order expand the reach of our biological existence, but they are not programmed into our genes. They are passed extrasomatically between generations through the mediation of symbols. The

potentially creative person must therefore become immersed in a domain before the possibility exists to change it.

When an individual introduces a novel variation, members of a field act as gatekeepers of the domain. It is their job to decide if the new idea is worthy to be selected and preserved. For instance, when a scientific article is submitted for publication in a journal, it competes with other submissions through a process of peer review. If selected for publication, the article competes with other recent publications for a field's attention. If the author's ideas are ever going to be recognized as creative, they must be noticed. Moreover, the selection processes of the field were long at work before the article was written. The scientist/author would not have been in the position to offer a contribution if he or she was not shepherded through various levels of education and career by the recognition of teachers and other relevant individuals.

Csikszentmihalyi's systems approach views outputs from one subsystem as inputs to the other subsystems. In all of these transitions time plays an essential role. For instance, after a field selects a particular idea, it may take several years before the idea appears in the domain (e.g., in an encyclopedia). This focus on interconnections also emphasizes the principle of equifinality, or that the goal of creativity can be achieved through different routes. It is not necessary to start with the person in order to understand the creative process; it may be that in some historical epochs, conditions in the field, such as available resources or a well-organized group of colleagues, provide the most compelling starting point for the investigation of creative accomplishment.

The fact that domains and fields are essential to the process of creativity does not mean that efforts to understand the creative person are unimportant. It is the person's novel idea, after all, that gives members of a field the opportunity to include it in the domain. Much has been written about personal qualities that make innovation more likely. Such a person is thought to have aesthetic sensibilities that help in finding problems, broad interests and openness to new ideas, the drive to bring order and meaning to experience, unique life experiences and reflective insight, disciplined work habits, the ability to have deep emotional experiences and get absorbed in tasks, relatively high intelligence, and flexible cognitive styles that negotiate tensions between various needs, such as for social contact and solitary reflection. In 1998 Csikszentmihalyi and Rathunde discussed these personal attributes in relation to complex systems. [*See* INNOVATION.]

Other approaches have highlighted systems principles within the "person" subsystem. For instance, Howard Gruber's evolving systems approach examines the creative process by asking the question, "How does creative work work?" With attention to the details of the lives of extraordinary creators (e.g., Darwin), Gruber showed how momentary flashes of insight are continuous with thousands of past and future insights, all taking their place within the evolving system that is the creative person at work. Understanding the unique configuration of a system is the goal of Gruber's research. Thus, a cognitive case study method is used to carefully reconstruct each life. [*See* EVOLVING SYSTEMS APPROACH.]

Within the system "person," Gruber tries to uncover the pattern of organization underlying three loosely coupled subsystems: knowledge, purpose, and affect. His approach is developmental (i.e., examines how the person builds on his or her own past and the past of others), pluralistic (i.e., examines numerous factors relevant to creativity), constructionist (i.e., assumes that the creative person actively participates in building skills, finding problems, and shaping his or her milieu), and phenomenological (i.e., reconstructs experiences from the person's point of view, and takes seriously their beliefs, intentionality, emotions, and awareness).

The evolving systems approach attempts to understand creativity through an examination of a person's network of enterprise or pattern of projects and activities broadly defined. A network of enterprise gives identity to the creator's working self and provides structure and organization for his or her life. Through exploring the multifaceted and durable network, one can grasp the dynamics of the person system. The network of enterprise gives the person some measure of control and self-regulation over the rhythm and sequence of work. In systems terms, it allows the person some control over negative and positive feedback and thus some control over deviation-attenuating and deviation-amplifying processes. For instance, depending on the person's current moods and needs, if the risk of innovation (deviation-amplifying) is too great, the

network of projects affords the opportunity for safe and reliable production (deviation attenuating). On the other hand, when needs for security wane, the person can be more daring and take risks. Variety is always at hand because if one path to a goal is blocked, the network of enterprise reveals other paths, and goals attained lead seemlessly to new goals. The network of enterprise thus helps to explain the perpetual activity of the creative person, and how he or she is able to blend the stability of durable goals with an openness to variation and a slow process of growth with unexpected detours.

III. CONCLUSIONS

By situating the person in a sociocultural context and viewing creativity as a process involving multiple, dynamic shaping forces, a systems approach reshapes the study of creativity.

1. A systems approach changes the way creativity is defined and recognized. Creativity cannot be defined fully by references to personal qualities. Attributions of creativity are given in specific sociocultural contexts, and these attributions may be constructed and deconstructed depending on many circumstances. Who is deemed creative is largely a matter of faith in the experts that comprise a field, and the possibility exists that attributions of creativity can be influenced by political ideology, power, and the capricious tastes of uninformed critics. Creativity may be easier to recognize in some domains and fields because of the centrality of the domain to the culture and its clear and rational organization (e.g., mathematics). The complex nature of information in some domains (e.g., social sciences, philosophy) may make it more difficult for attributions of creativity to emerge through social consensus, thus making it difficult to recognize creative accomplishment early in life.

2. A systems approach alters traditional questions about the creative person. Studies of the creative person focus less on momentary insight and more on the developmental history of insight as sustained by a network of enterprise. This longer time frame permits an in-depth study of goals and subgoals, themes and metaphors that cut across projects, chance detours, and,

most important, the dynamic processes that open and close the boundaries of the person system in order to maintain and create order and meaning. By placing the study of personal qualities in a sociocultural context, a systems orientation suggests that the person should not be seen as the sole cause of creativity or the starting point of every investigation. Traditional questions about personal qualities are related to new questions about domains and fields. For instance, how do differences between domains (e.g., type or organization of information) affect a person's motivation? How do domain differences affect the person's accessibility to the domain or his or her capacity to change it? Likewise, how does a field's size, the quality of intercommunication between its members, available resources, or tolerance for ambiguity affect a person's potential for creative achievement?

3. A systems approach reorients attention toward interdisciplinary studies of creativity. Examining the circular relationships and feedback between person, domain, and field requires an expanded, interdisciplinary repertoire of methodological and theoretical skills. Adequate examination of these three subsystems requires an account of psychological, cultural, and social processes. Therefore, in addition to a psychologist's toolbox, disciplines with broader sociocultural perspectives have much to offer the creativity researcher. Interdisciplinary studies can investigate the synchrony or asynchrony between the subsystems and thus help explain configurations that facilitate or negatively impact creativity (e.g., when a field dominates a domain that it does not understand, or when there is a mismatch between individual skills and the structure of a domain or field).

In conclusion, as the systems approach is used with more frequency it will present new and demanding challenges. Systems models and metaphors are helpful for seeing the big picture and representing dynamic processes, but they are sometimes faulted for describing more than explaining. Systems models also elevate so many variables for consideration that a researcher can be overwhelmed. The need for interdisciplinary skills adds to this burden. Nevertheless, despite these challenges, the systems approach sets an agenda for creativity research that is consistent with contemporary social science perspectives that increasingly emphasize ecological validity.

Bibliography

Bertalanffy, L. von (1968). *General systems theory: Foundations, development, applications.* New York: Braziller.

Csikszentmihalyi, M. (1988). Society, culture, and person: A systems view of creativity. In R. Sternberg & J. Davidson (Eds.), *The nature of creativity.* New York: Cambridge University Press.

Csikszentmihalyi, M., & Rathunde, K. (1998). The development of the person: An experiential perspective on the ontogenesis of psychological complexity. In R. M. Lerner (Ed.), *Theoretical models of human development: Vol. l. Handbook of Child Psychology* (5th ed.). New York: Wiley.

Gruber, H. (1988). The evolving systems approach to creative work. *Creativity Research Journal, 1,* 27–59.

Tactics and Strategies for Creativity

Mark A. Runco

California State University, Fullerton

Accommodation One kind of tactic, used when the individual him- or herself changes. New information might be obtained, expanding the individual's knowledge base, or the creator's perspective on the problem or topic might change.

Assimilation A second kind of tactic, used when the individual changes the problem or representation of the problem.

Metacognition Thinking about thinking; the recognition that we can control our own thinking.

Overjustification Occurs when the person changes his or her opinion such that some activity that was initially intrinsically motivated becomes extrinsically controlled.

Procedural Knowledge "Know-how," information about how to get something done. It is distinct from declarative, conceptual, and factual information. Tactics are the actions prescribed by procedural knowledge.

Social Loafing One explanation for the superiority of working alone over brainstorming. It occurs when people assume that someone else in the group will complete the task at hand.

Children are spontaneously original on a regular basis. Adults, on the other hand, rely on routines and assump- *tions. For adults, creativity may require some effort. It certainly is an intentional activity during adulthood. When intentional actions are themselves routinized, they are said to be* **TACTICS.** *They are often called* **STRATE-GIES,** *but that is not strictly accurate. The intentional efforts to enhance creativity are technically more tactical than strategic.*

I. INTRODUCTION

Tactics are useful only if an individual is mature and interested in being creative. Maturity is necessary because tactics are metacognitive; they require the recognition that we can control our own thinking, and this is not apparent until early in adolescence. An interest in being creative is necessary because tactics are intentional, and the individual would not expend the effort unless he or she is interested in the potential result.

They are also metacognitive in the sense that they are not dependent on effortless cognitive processes. Very importantly, then, they are relatively distinct from the processes that underlie traditional intelligence and general ability. This provides some optimism; it means that everyone, at all levels of ability, can enhance their creativity if they find, develop, and practice the right tactics. [*See* METACOGNITION.]

Procedural knowledge is necessary for tactical

behavior. Procedural knowledge is "know-how." It is information about how to get something done. In this light it is distinct from declarative, conceptual, and factual information. Tactics are the actions prescribed by procedural knowledge. If that knowledge depends on traditional intelligence, the distinction between tactical behavior and general ability is blurred. This is why I suggested that tactics are *relatively* distinct from traditional intelligence and general ability.

Tactics are not entirely dependent on procedural knowledge. Certainly they are influenced by attitudes. In fact, attitudes may be the easiest way to enhance creative behavior. Attitudes are relatively easy to change. Attitudes are related to tactics in the sense that individuals must believe they are capable of creative thinking. They must be interested in creative ideas; they must be willing to take risks and try something new.

Tactics are often used in the classroom and the organizational setting. Educators, parents, and managers and supervisors often attempt to facilitate the creativity of their charges. Research has confirmed that such efforts pay off. There is, however, some question over the actual creativity of the results. Individuals can become more original in controlled settings, but skeptics question such efforts. Perhaps the originality learned from a training program does not easily or often generalize to the natural environment. A related question concerns attitudes: What is actually learned from training? Are new tactics learned, and learned in a manner that will generalize to the natural environment, or does the training simply change the attitudes of the participants such that they are more willing to try new things? Further research must address this question, but in some ways the answer does not matter. If behavior becomes more original, it does not really matter if that is a reflection of just tactics, or if it reflects tactics *and* attitude working together. [*See* ENHANCEMENT OF CREATIVITY; TEACHING CREATIVITY.]

II. CLASSIFYING TACTICS

Tactics for creativity and originality have been classified in several different ways. These classification schemes are reviewed here; they will structure the list of tactics reviewed.

One useful distinction between the different kinds of tactics was presented by Sidney Parnes. He referred to "let-it-happen" tactics and "make-it-happen" tactics. Incubation is an example of the former. Incubation cannot be forced, but it can be made more likely by taking a break from one's work, and perhaps by taking a walk or finding some optimally distracting activity. Let-it-happen tactics also include (a) being open to change and serendipity and (b) trusting your intuition and hunches. In these cases the individual is not directing the process but instead allows it to occur and simply appreciates the results. Individuals may go as far as to put themselves in a position where incubation, serendipity, and the like are more likely to happen. [*See* INCUBATION; INTUITION; SERENDIPITY.]

Make-it-happen tactics are more numerous in the creativity literature. Unlike let-it-happen tactics, make-it-happen tactics are usually more detailed step-by-step procedures. "Be a contrarian, think of things no one else will" is an example of a make-it-happen tactic. It is fairly operational, although it also suggests that all tactics allow information processing below the level of consciousness and assume that at least part of the benefit is beyond control. In other words, let-it-happen tactics may involve letting natural (e.g., intuitive) processing take place.

A second way to distinguish among tactics involves stages of the creative thinking process. Certain tactics may be used within one particular phase or stage of the creative process. There are different stage models of the process but most follow from the model presented by Graham Wallas in 1926, with preparation, incubation, illumination, and verification stages. Let-it-happen tactics are well suited to incubation, for example, just as tactics to "seek out reliable information" and "change perspectives" are well suited to the preparation stage.

Each of the four stages can be divided into two subcategories. For preparation, illumination, and verification this division reflects a separation between the subjective and the objective, or between the individual and everything else—the problem, the relevant information, the possible or tentative solutions, the setting, and so on. This subdivision follows from cognitive theories which divide information processing into assimilation (whereby information is changed to fit into an individual's existing personal cognitive structures) and accommodation (whereby the personal structures are changed to take advantage of the new information).

(This subdivision for incubation may not reflect subject and object, but this is understandable because incubation is largely personal and subjective.)

Assimilatory strategies are those with which the creator changes the problem or representation of the problem. He or she might turn the problem on its head, for example, or work backward from the desired objective or solution to the initial state. This tactic works especially well for scheduling and travel arrangements.

Strategies using accommodation are those with which the creator him- or herself changes. New information might be obtained, for example, expanding the individual's knowledge base, or the creator's perspective on the problem or topic might change.

Changes of perspective represent what may be the most general kind of tactic. This is because such changes underlie a variety of more specific tactics. Turning a problem on its head, taking time away from the problem, travel, seeking out criticism or input, and many other tactics rely on some sort of change in perspective. [*See* PERSPECTIVES.]

Problem finding is a kind of preparation and can be easily modified to identify and define problems such that creative solutions are more likely. Many problem finding tactics involve information or other resources; just above I alluded to a "seek out reliable information" tactic, which is a good example. "Question assumptions" is another example of a tactic that applies well to problem finding. [*See* PROBLEM FINDING.]

The tactic "question assumptions" can also be worded, "do not make assumptions." This rewording is only noteworthy because it highlights the last distinction that can be used to classify tactics. On the one hand there are tactics that suggest learning new behaviors. "Seek out challenges" is an example of this kind of tactic. "Do not make assumptions," on the other hand, is an example of what can be called an avoidance tactic. This kind of tactic suggests what should be avoided, like assumptions, routines, and conformity.

James Adams' excellent volume, *Conceptual Block-busting,* reviews many different kinds of avoidance tactics. What he suggests we avoid are conceptual blocks.

- Perceptual blocks occur when we define a problem too closely or too generally, or we ignore important information or a useful perspective. We need to avoid preconceptions and stereotypes.

- Cultural blocks occur when we fail to utilize fantasy, play, daydreaming, and humor because, in our culture, they are not associated with serious work. Taboos can create blocks.
- Environmental blocks occur when we are distracted by our immediate environment, including people with whom we live or work.
- Emotional blocks occur when we are afraid of taking risks or are not comfortable tolerating the ambiguity that may be necessary while we incubate or think further about a problem. We may also be uncomfortable postponing a decision or solution or with challenges.
- Intellectual and expressive blocks occur when we are inflexible or do not consider alternative media for representing a problem. We might also fail to obtain the most useful information. We might find a solution but fail to record it.

Each of these ideas can be translated into a recommendation. The last idea, for example, concerning the recording of our ideas, implies that we keep a pencil and paper next to the bed, in case we wake up with a good idea. We might take a small piece of paper and short pencil when we jog, and a small tape recorder when we drive.

David N. Perkins and Robert J. Weber described the role of tactics in their work on invention. They listed "search strategies," which are used to seek out information and options. They identified the following.

- Sheer chance
- Cultivating chance (searcher deliberately exposes self to wide semi-random input)
- Systematized chance (survey of a number of possibilities within a defined set)
- Fair bet (prototypes a possibility with expectations that it will work with modifications)
- Good bet (prototypes from principle and experience)
- Safe bet (derives by formal methods something that almost certainly will work) (1992, pp. 321–322).

Weber individually described the invention and refinement of inventions such as the Swiss army knife and the chair. He listed the following tactics:

> Finding ideas in nature
> Assemble (the parts or components) for complexity
> Fine tune what you have
> Repeat or duplicate a feature
> Add a feature
> Delete a feature
> Rearrangement of a feature
> Joining independent inventions
> Transform and change the scale

Although Weber's work was focused on invention, several of these strategies apply to all kinds of creative work. In fact, several parallel tactics are elsewhere recommended specifically for creative activities. Finding ideas in nature, for example, has been regularly suggested in the creativity literature. It is similar to other tactics as well, including "borrow and adapt" ideas from others, and even "find an analogy."

The use of analogies may be particularly powerful. Eli Whitney developed the cotton gin after seeing a cat trying to catch a chicken through a fence; Samuel Morse apparently put stations in the telegraph after thinking about stagecoaches changing their horses periodically; Pasteur used an analogy of grapes and human skin; the benzene ring may have been suggested by a dream of a snake biting its own tail; George Bissel used an analogy of a brine pump being used as an oil pump; James Watt was inspired to design the steam engine after observing a tea kettle; and Sir Marc Brunel borrowed from a worm for his work on underwater tunnels. Velcro and hundreds of other creative insights have resulted from the creative person finding apt analogies. [*See* ANALOGIES.]

Many famous insights have resulted from a more direct borrowing strategy. Freud borrowed heavily from neurology and the medical model when describing the psyche; Piaget borrowed from biology in his theory of cognitive development; Darwin drew from geology in his theory of evolution. Musicians often borrow from various styles, the result being an original integration. Elvis Presley, for instance, apparently borrowed from gospel and country music.

III. INTERPERSONAL TACTICS

Tactics can be interpersonal. As noted earlier, certain tactics can be used by parents, teachers, or supervisors to facilitate the creative work of their charges. Parents and teachers in particular should encourage children and students, but should be careful to avoid overjustification. This occurs when a person changes his or her opinion such that some activity that was initially intrinsically motivated becomes extrinsically controlled. Incentives and rewards are common extrinsic controls, and when individuals see them, they often assume that they are the reason for their actions—even if those same actions were intrinsically motivated moments earlier.

Parents and teachers should shape confidence and ego strength. This is especially important because original ideas are often unconventional, and children become quite sensitive to peer pressure in preadolescence. During that period they may shy away from their own original insights. If they have ego strength, they may maintain their originality and avoid common slumps that occur in childhood. [*See* FOURTH GRADE SLUMP.]

Another interpersonal tactic is part of brainstorming programs. Participants in brainstorming groups are asked to generate as many ideas as possible and to postpone criticism. The participants are required to be careful of what they say to one another in an effort to maximize ideational output and minimize constraint. The tactic here is best summarized as "postpone evaluation."

The empirical evidence suggests that brainstorming may not be the most effective use of time. Working alone may be better. When people are in groups there is a tendency toward social loafing, and people may assume that someone else in the group will complete the task at hand. [*See* GROUP CREATIVITY.]

Furthermore, it may be very difficult to postpone criticism, as required for brainstorming. In fact, it may not be a good idea to postpone certain kinds of evaluation. More likely a balance of divergent thinking and convergent thinking will benefit the process. With this in mind James March recommended a balance of play and reason. He suggested several tactics for finding a balance, including treating (a) goals as hypotheses, (b) intuition as real, (c) hypocrisy as a transition, (d) memory as an enemy, and (e) experience as a theory. The last of these—experience as a theory—is another way of suggesting that we question assumptions. [*See* BRAINSTORMING.]

March suggested that the five tactics be used alternatively, with a temporary suspension of "reasoned intelligence." In his words,

> play and reason are functional complements. . . . They are alternative styles and alternative orientations to the same situation. . . . Our design problem is either to specify the best mix of styles or, failing that, to assure that most people and most organizations most of the time use an alternation of strategies rather than perseverate in either one. (1987, p. 77)

One uncommon tactic was used by the Wright brothers when they worked on the first flier: they argued. Wilbur and Orville would take opposite sides of some technical problem, debate the issue, then switch sides and debate some more. It was, then, an intentional, tactical technique that the brothers used to help solve the problems of flight. Very likely the argument tactic led to a questioning of assumptions and a consideration of alternative perspectives.

One kind of tactic is interpersonal but focused on avoiding rather than collaborating with others. I am referring to the contrarian strategy. Here the creator does what others are not. This works some of the time because creativity requires originality, and a contrarian will be original because he or she is doing what others are not. Examples include Jean Piaget, Sigmund Freud, Duke Ellington, and Pablo Picasso. This is, however, a difficult tactic because it requires discretion and careful moderation. If someone relies on contrarian tactics they could reinvent the wheel. Sometimes there is a good reason others are not doing something. Originality is not sufficient for creativity, so contrarianism is not in and of itself adequate. It can be taken too far. [*See* CONTRARIANISM.]

IV. CONCLUSIONS

Tactics can be defined by (a) distinguishing them from strategies, which are general plans rather than specific techniques; (b) distinguishing procedural information from conceptual and factual information; and (c) distinguishing cognition from metacognition. Tactics take various forms and can be of the let-it-happen or the more structured and effortful make-it-happen variety, although here there is some blur and the distinction is imperfect. Make-it-happen strategies may involve some relaxation and preconscious processing, in which case there is a let-it-happen component to them.

Tactics can be personal or interpersonal; they can focus on the problem, as a kind of assimilation (e.g., "turn it on its head"), or on the person who is dealing with the problem, as a kind of accommodation (e.g., "change your perspective").

Tactics involving shifting one's perspective seem to be the most general. Some perceptual shift underlies many other tactics. The contrarian tactics, on the other hand, may require the most tact. This tactic did not always work effectively and might be best when used in moderation. Otherwise the result might be extreme but inappropriate originality, which is not synonymous with creativity. Very likely all tactics are best used with moderation and discretion.

Bibliography

Adams, J. (1982). *Conceptual blockbusting*. New York: Norton.

March, J. G. (1987). The technology of foolishness. In J. G. March & J. P. Olsen (Eds.), *Ambiguity and choice in organizations* (pp. 69–81). Bergen, Norway: Universitets-Forlaget.

Root-Bernstein, R. (1988). *Discovering*. Cambridge, MA: Cambridge Univ. Press.

Weber, R. (1996). Toward a language of invention and synthetic thinking. *Creativity Research Journal, 9,* 353–367.

Rabindranath Tagore

1861–1941

Poet, essayist, playwright, musician, painter

Author of *Gitanjali, Sandhya Sangeet,* "Sheshlekha," *Gora, Ghare-Baire, Nrityanatya Chitrangada,* "Kalantar," *Arogya, Janamadine,* "Nationalism," "Personality," "Religion of Man," and "Sadhana"

M. K. Raina

National Council of Educational Research and Training
New Delhi, India

Described as a "world poet," *RABINDRANATH TAGORE* is considered a puzzling ecumenical figure, a paradigm of human possibility, a mystery, and a complex challenge of creativity who exemplified total creativity, unique and rare. As "Rabindranath" he was an Indian writer, as "Tagore" he was an international figure. He is known for his poetry, particularly "Gitanjali" (Song Offerings), which made him suddenly famous and brought him the Nobel Prize for literature in 1913, the second writer in English to be thus awarded after Kipling. One of the greatest literary figures in history, Tagore was a master of several literary forms. He experimented with many forms of art and sought an outlet first in music, then in drama, opera, and ballet and toward the end of his life in painting. Tagore was a consummate histrionic artist, a playwright and producer of plays. He also inspired and directed the revival and full development of the art of dance in modern India. Tagore is remarkable for his versatility, extraordinary range, and complexity of creative perspective. As a high priest of internationalism and the author of the national anthems of two countries, his spirited protests against the inequities and cruelties

Rabindranath Tagore.

of British and other forms of imperialism and repression have a permanent place in history.

I. BACKGROUND

Rabindranath Tagore, the product of history and of the social environment, was fortunate that at the time of his birth currents of three movements had met in the life of the country. He was born in Calcutta on May 6, 1861, and was the fourteenth child (of 15 children), eighth son of his parents. The youngest child, however, died in early infancy, making Tagore both the youngest child and the youngest son of the family. Neither of the parents established any personal intimacy with him and early in life he lost his mother. There had never been that clinging affection between the mother and the son that would leave a void behind. But the thirst for mother's affection, never quenched in childhood, was to survive in the son as a constant longing for feminine affection and care. However, his father, known for contemplative inwardness, had the most abiding influence over the son. The influence had obvious manifestations later.

Tagore grew in a lonely and somewhat isolated family where literature, music, and painting were prized. The family was notable for the extraordinary concatenation of a variety of talents in its members. The house where he spent his childhood as a lonely outcast, a shy and quiet child, was to him tranquil and secluded.

The family provided the right environment for Tagore to discover two of the major motives of his creative life: joy and mystery. The sense of wonder and mystery that for him pervaded the world of nature and men—the yearning for that mysterious world, the instinctive delight in the smallest and most common place things experienced in childhood—became for him a lifelong spiritual treasure.

Though he attended several schools, Tagore was allergic to formal schooling, which distressed him. His education remained desultory and ultimately he became a dropout. The education that he received at home was quite thorough. More valuable than what he was taught, was what he breathed in, as it were, from the atmosphere of the house, where Vedic chants could be heard along with readings from Shakespeare and Marlowe; where Indian classical music, vocal and in-

strumental, was seriously practiced while European music was also studied, where the family had its own drama group and compositions and collections of costumes; where a lively intellectual and spiritual endeavor was pursued with easy grace. Therefore, it is no surprise that this solitary and sensitive truant proved a recalcitrant boy who became a rebellious youth without the modicum of respect for tradition that normal systematic schooling imposes on an average adult.

Tagore admitted "the torn and the incomplete" in his makeup. He had a spate of bereavements and private and public disappointments, which could not stigmatize his work. Creative in crisis, the magic of his creativity hides the fact that it came out of a matrix not unaware of the tragic and the terrible.

II. THE COMPLEXITY OF TAGOREAN CREATIVITY

When Tagore began his career, he was, as he put it, ridiculously young; in fact, he was the youngest of that band who had made themselves articulate. He had neither the protective armor of mature age, nor enough English to command respect. So in his seclusion of contempt and qualified encouragement he had his freedom. As he grew in years, he steadily cut his way through derision and occasional patronage to recognize that the proportion of praise to blame was very much like that of land to water on our earth. The Nobel Prize, which he was awarded in 1913, brought to him "an immense burden of loneliness." This was not only the recognition of his literary achievements but was also evidence of the impact of his personality on western contemporaries. During the World War I and for more than a decade thereafter, Tagore was hailed by the West and the East alike as a seer and a sage. Receiving the Nobel Prize was a turning point of his life.

His career and creative enterprises were largely conditioned by many influences and traditions, indigenous and foreign. His reason, personal will, and psyche only determined the form and character of this conditioning. Besides being influenced by *Upanishads,* Tagore was influenced by Buddhism, classical Sanskrit and English literature, Sufism, the *Vaishnava* poets, the submerged cultures of the rural agricultural folk and the *Bauls,* the itinerant singers who observed no formalities and were untouchables wandering from village to village, singing and dancing and taking delight in the ever-changing play of life. Tagore's subconscious identification with the *Baul* credo was almost perfect. These influences, in addition to the Indian reality, moulded his worldview. Tagore's life pattern was essentially melodic and his creative genius had many facets, permeated with the idea of national liberation, of the struggle for the spiritual and political liberation from the yoke of colonialism and feudal survivals. Tagore's multiple creative dimensions, issued from the same source and together formed an organic whole.

While not denying the usefulness of expressions like "Tagore the poet," "the essayist," or "the playwright," we must recognize that they overlap and interpenetrate and refer fundamentally to one unvariable reality. However, studying Tagore in a holistic framework involves risks and challenges not only of one man's astonishing career but of a vast and intricate network of intercultural relationships. To compress Tagore's versatility into a relatively brief account is to risk leading the reader with diffuse impressions that do the subject less than full justice.

Tagore's complexity and extraordinariness was not of one kind, nor did he satisfy the demand for continuous development. It was a devious and diverse development, which defeats the too systematic critic at every turn. It has been noted that a paraphrastic, chronological account would be tedious and little more than a catalog. Tagore's growth was not linear. Tagore was many poets in one, and not easy to track or label. His development did not have straightforward continuity and in fact overflowed the logical pattern of growth—it was instead a stage-wise progression. In short, Tagore's development was not unilinear.

III. THE CREATIVE PURPOSE

Tagore's purpose in undertaking creative enterprises emerged out of his concern for celebration of spirit and the infinite. He wrote that the desire we have to keep our uniqueness intact is really the desire of the universe acting in us. It is our joy of the infinite in us that gives us our joy in ourselves. Therefore, we must express ourselves strenuously in our life and work in "outward excursions." The joy, which is without form, must cre-

ate, must translate itself into forms. He, therefore, was sovereignly aware of the fact that "from joy are born all created things etc."

Though multitudinously various, Tagore gave a touch of completeness, an enormous unity, like the unity of a lyric, to his life. His life, it has been noted, was in fact, Tagore's greatest work. When his other works are forgotten, his life will remain unforgettable because it is a true and silent answer to the most inward question of humankind: "How am I to live?" It has been noted that everything Tagore did and wrote bore the mark of his obsession with the maturing of the body and soul, toward the extension and intention, or renewal, of his own personality as a human being. He always aimed higher and higher, "The song that I came to sing remains unsung to this day." His long life was densely packed with growth, activity, and self-renewal. He believed that in his creativity, one realized the supreme person (*Jivan—Devata*) who has made the universe so personal to humankind.

IV. THE TAGOREAN PEAKS

"Thou who are the spirit of manifestation, manifest thyself in me." This Upanishadic prayer was one of Tagore's favorite quotations. This prayer, in Tagore's case, was answered through diverse, multiple, continuous, and simultaneous literary enterprises. Poetry and the poetic consciousness was, of course, the animating principle in his extraordinary variety.

In 1893, Tagore wrote:

> The moment I begin to write poetry, I enter into my true self: true for all time. I distinctly feel that there lies my true home. Poetry is the sole refuge of all deepest truths of my life.

In May 1892 he wrote that the joy of writing one poem far exceeds that of writing sheaves and sheaves of prose. "If I could only write one poem a day." He almost did that.

Tagore, even before he was 20 years old, had published approximately 11,000 lines of verse which, with real good sense, he never reprinted. Before Tagore was 18 years old, he had published nearly 7000 lines of verse, and a great quantity of prose.

Closely related to poetry, another creative enterprise that distinguished Tagore's uniqueness was his incomparable songs. It was natural that he was attracted by a form of music that stressed the union of verse and melody. In the diversity of their mode and theme, these formed a class apart. The creative delight he discovered in his early musical experiments stayed with him until the very end of his life. When he was nearly 16 years old, he took liberties with the classical tradition and composed more than 2000 songs. From early boyhood onward his music had the quality of profundity not inferior to the quality of his poetry.

In Tagore's career as a composer of music, the last 20 years of his life—from 1921, when he started composing his life series of songs on the seasons, to a few weeks before his death—were the richest, both in quantity and quality. Indeed this was the period when Tagore built the edifice that has now come to be known as *Rabindra Sangeet* or the Tagore school of Indian music. This was also the period when Tagore effected a perfect integration of music and dance, one interpreting and contributing to the other and thus expanding the horizon of both, which opened up new possibilities and generated new enterprises. During the 1925 and 1931 phases, his songs came to have a wide thematic range, variety, innovation, and the creation of new beat—rhythms or *tala*.

Tagore's prose was as much a poet's work as was his verse. In him the poet and the prose writer were inseparable and mutually complementary, which means that we cannot assess the one without considering the other. The dramatic form interested Tagore very early in his career as a writer. He wrote more than 40 works of drama.

Tagore wrote several novels but this work, it is felt as a whole, may not claim to have attained the stature of his best poetry. Yet the novels are no less trendsetters in the unconventionality of themes, complexity of characterization, and poetic, often symbolic, language. The poet, the singer, and the teacher constantly meddled with the novelist and lured him away from concentration on one plot or one set of characters. Tagore wrote an infinite variety of stories: comedies, tragedies, fantasies, and parables. Some are short novels, others long short stories.

Apart from fiction and drama, Tagore's prose falls into a number of formal dimensions: belles letters, lit-

erary criticism, essays on subjects other than literature, travel writing, autobiography, and finally letters. These divisions, however, are far from being rigid, for Tagore had a way of transcending rules and definitions. These kinds of writings are thus interrelated, and the relation between them and Tagore's poetry is regarded as quite palpable. The letters by Tagore that have so far been published in book form comprise 11 volumes. He wrote thousands of other letters, which served very well as an effective means of expressing his personal and private musings and thoughts, his dreams and visions on a variety of subjects and issues that interested him. He also wrote a large number of essays and addresses on a variety of subjects, kept a diary of his extensive travels, and even wrote several textbooks for the boys and girls of his *asrama* schools. As if all these were not enough, in 1912 he completed a series of essays that were later delivered as lectures at Harvard University and published as *Sadhana* (The Realization of Life). In 1917 *Nationalism* and *Personality* were published, which contained his lectures and addresses delivered in Japan and the United States in 1916; and in 1922 *Creative Unity* was published containing his occasional essays and other lectures delivered abroad.

During the stretch of six decades, Tagore had interludes of stagnation as well. Many times the poet's muse started to falter, but not for long. He had comparatively few sterile periods, though he had produced enough to make a writer famous. Constant travel, intense financial struggles, public addresses, and a ceaseless crusade for a new outlook were distractions hardly conducive to meditative or creative moods. Besides these preoccupations and pressures, it has been noted that at times the poet lost to the prophet, the singer to the preacher, and thus the resultant cyclicity.

The last 10 years of Tagore's life opened a new phase of creativity: new but not inherently unconnected from his earlier phases.

Tagore felt certain that for him poet-nature was not his sole function in life. It was through painting that Tagore found the release that he could not quite achieve in poetry. Tagore recalled the Indian theory of creation as play (*leela*) and claimed that he was beating the creator at his own game and creating forms that missed their chance in actual existence since God did not provide a place for them. Thus his recourse to another aesthetic medium helped the poet fill in the lacunae in his poetical work. From 1928 to 1940 he painted more than 2000 pictures apart from his other work, his travels, the ever increasing calls on his time, and the darkening crises of the 1930s.

As if Tagore could not have achieved permanence through his ceaseless creative activity in literature, music, and painting, his energy found expression in the experimental work that he undertook in the field of social reconstruction and the ideas and ideologies that inspired and motivated them. Rehabilitation of village and rural economy, the cooperative movement, working out new principles and methods, and evolving a national system of education, ideas and speculations on the contemporary political life in India and on nationalism and internationalism—these were again a part of his mind and personality. His creative vision prompted him to ask questions about God, life, and death, and to answer them by evolving a religion of man. Tagore sought to give tangible form to his ideas on education and socioeconomic reconstruction by establishing and funding institutions like *Santiniketan* (Abode of Peace) and *Sriniketan* (Institute for Rural Upliftment). For Tagore, this enterprise was not unrelated to that of the creative writer and artist. It was intimately related to his total creative personality and spiritual being. He described *Vishvabharti* (World University) as his "tangible poem."

From 1912 to 1932 Tagore undertook 10 foreign tours and lectured in major cities of Europe, Asia, and North and South America. He lectured on the problems of power, militarism, war, and the decay of civilization through the human search for comfort and a consumer culture. A considerable part of these travels and sojourns was taken up by his attempts to collect funds for his school at *Santiniketan* (Abode of Peace), which had become a financial worry to the poet. Tagore's lecture tours abroad were an economic necessity for his school, but they were also a psychological necessity for Tagore. Like his many other creative endeavors, his travels also provided him opportunities to "know the full meaning of my birth as a human being in this world."

Tagore had other reasons to travel, which made some observe that he was not only a constant international traveler but a traveler in internationalism, which he had adopted as his most cherished cause. It is not surprising that Tagore has been called "conspicuously bicultural."

Tagore's progression toward selfhood and an attempt at the realization of the infinite was not smooth. From 1878 to 1941, he continuously worked at full pressure, and though we may not enjoy all his works, we have to note the flagging of his inspiration on occasions. We cannot trace the growth of his genius only up to a certain point, but have to discover the peaks scattered all over those 60 years. Tagore scholars feel that even his failures are more worthwhile than the success of many writers. The poet in Tagore grew slowly, stage by stage, and not in a flash. Years of formal discipline and layers upon layers of experience would have to follow before he could articulate himself convincingly.

Mahatma Gandhi called Tagore *Gurudev* (Revered Master) and he attained a certain classicality. His works have universal appeal and that illuminates his complexity and "myriad-mindedness." His unique humanism is reflected in a statement Darwin's granddaughter made to a friend after meeting Tagore: "I can now imagine a powerful and gentle Christ, which I never could before."

Bibliography

Das, S. K. (1988). Keynote address. In B. Chaudhuri & K. G. Subramanyan (Eds.), *Rabindranath Tagore and the challenges of today*. Shimla, India: Indian Institute of Advanced Study.

Dutta, K., & Robinson, A. (1995). *Rabindranath Tagore: The myriad-minded man*. London: Bloomsbury.

Ghose, S. (1986). *Rabindranath Tagore*. New Delhi, India: Sahitya Akademi.

Kripalani, K. (1961). *Tagore: A life*. New Delhi, India: Malancha.

Lago, M. M. (1976). *Rabindranath Tagore*. Boston: Twain.

Mukherjee, D. P. (1944). *Tagore: A study*. Bombay, India: Padma.

Raina, M. K. (1997). Most dear to all the muses: Mapping Tagorean networks of enterprise—A study in creative complexity. *Creativity Research Journal, 10*, 153–173.

Ray, N. (1967). *An artist in life*. Trivandrum, India: University of Kerala.

Thompson, E. (1991). *Rabindranath Tagore: Poet and dramatist*. Delhi, India: Oxford University Press.

Talent and Creativity

John F. Feldhusen

Purdue University

Ability General capacity for cognitive or motoric behavior.

Aptitude Predisposition for learning.

Creative Problem Solving A metacognitive set of steps or procedures that can be used to systematically achieve creative thinking and problem solving.

Creative Productivity Creative thinking that yields products such as stories, plays, and inventions.

Creative Thinking Cognitive activity that yields ideas.

Creativity Ability to produce new ideas, conceptions, alternatives, solutions, inventions, designs, schemas, or theories.

Gifted Having the genetic component that underlies superior ability.

Talent Superior aptitude or ability in any worthwhile line of human endeavor.

TALENT is superior aptitude or ability in any worthwhile line of human endeavor. It emerges early in childhood in a very general form such as verbal aptitude, mathemati- *cal skill, or artistic ability. It manifests itself in the child who speaks and reads early, who learns math more rapidly than other children, or who demonstrates leadership capability in first or second grade. Creativity is the ability to produce new ideas, new conceptions, alternatives, solutions, inventions, plans, designs, schemas, or theories that are accepted and viewed as having value by some people or audience in the world around the creator. There is a wide range of levels of creative functioning, from the 3-year-old child designing the layout for a tea party, to the teen writing a short story, to the college student writing a sonata, to the adult planning a new home, to the physicist synthesizing a new conception or theory of nuclear fusion.*

I. THE ORIGINS OF TALENT AND CREATIVITY

Talents are learned but some children are endowed with the ability to learn more rapidly and earlier than others. They have the potential to go on learning more and more rapidly and to grow more and more precocious if home and school provide the nurturing and stimulating experiences that motivate and challenge them to learn and develop their talents. Talents build on interest and curiosity. Highly talented children develop skills of curiosity, observation, inquiry, and questioning. They respond more powerfully to the world around them than do other children and thereby enhance the growth of their talents all the more.

Creative cognitive processing is also learned behavior. Some special divergent thinking skills can be learned, modeled, or mastered, such as fluency and elaboration. Creative processing also requires a knowledge base of information that is both declarative and procedural. Declarative information is knowledge and meanings about the world around us, whereas procedural information is knowing how to behave, perform, or produce. Desire or motivation to create as well as a sense of self-efficacy in creative functioning are also fundamental psychological components of creativity. [See Divergent Thinking; Motivation/Drive.]

As children reach middle school and high school their talents become more specific and are more career oriented. Their talents are in physical science, home economics, creative writing, agriculture, foreign languages, business subjects, drama, trade or industrial subjects, and so on. Their talents and interests find increasing focus in particular areas of the school curriculum.

Talent and creativity interact with one another in that well or highly developed talents serve as procedural and declarative springboards for creative production. Like creativity, talent comes to fruition with the acquisition of a knowledge base and a particular set of procedural skills. In itself, talent may simply denote functional proficiency in a particular career or occupational line of endeavor, but the proficiency paves the way to creative production. It is also the case that the environment, people, and workplace of the talented individual provides the stimulation or problem situations that motivate and give rise to creative cognitions.

It is beneficial for children to learn and understand what their talents are at a fairly early age so that school, home, and community experiences can be sought out to foster growth and development in the talent areas. As they mature children should take more and more responsibility for their own educational progress and talent development while still getting help from their parents. Those who go on to high level creative achievement become autonomous learners, independent and self-directing.

It is not helpful to simply learn that a child is gifted without finding out about the child's special talents. As researchers have noted, when we know about the special talent or talents possessed by a child, teachers and parents can make special efforts to provide experiences that will facilitate continuing growth in the talent areas.

Special classes and learning experiences can be designed to provide specialized kinds of academic stimulation of talents, to give children abundant opportunities to exercise and develop their emerging creative abilities, and to give them opportunities to discover their talent strengths. Through a wide variety of academic activities across the grade levels, children can learn about the academic base of knowledge in their talent area, begin to see career options related to the talent, have opportunities to explore and investigate ideas in the talent domain, become motivated for continuing development of their talents, and develop their divergent thinking abilities.

By the time talented youth reach the college or university level, their talents should be well defined, and they should be close to defining the specific profession, field, or occupation they will pursue. By this time they should know well the educational requirements for high-level creative positions in their talent areas. Their goals should be lofty and commensurate with their special talents. They should seek admission to the best colleges or universities and aim for excellence in their career aspirations. Highly talented youth can go on to be the discoverers, inventors, writers, and leaders of the 21st century.

II. THEORIES OF TALENT DEVELOPMENT

In his retrospective study of talent development among world-class mathematicians, neurologists, pianists, sculptors, swimmers, and tennis players, Benjamin Bloom isolated three relatively distinct stages. First, in childhood there was rapid progress in learning in one or a few specific talent areas. Supportive parents, highly stimulating teachers, and peers provided guidance, instruction, and motivational support. During the middle years of junior high school and high school the second stage emerges. Now that the child is precocious in one or several talent domains, parents begin a quest for the best schools and teachers and the talented youth becomes increasingly motivated and committed to the development of his or her own talents.

The third stage, the high school and college years, emerge with a strong commitment on the youth's part to the areas of his or her budding talents and expertise. The young person makes a career commitment to the talent field, develops a style of operating and working in the chosen field, and forms a clear understanding of the chosen field and its demands. The youth becomes acquainted with leaders in the chosen field and sets high-level creative goals. An emerging mastery enables the talented person to look beyond the defined knowledge and procedural base of the chosen career field and to envision creative new directions, styles, or theories to pursue. The talented individual is now ready to launch into the field both as expert or artistic practitioner and as creative leader.

Movement or development throughout these three stages often differed a great deal among the six disciplines that Bloom studied, and it should be noted that age in itself was often not the determinant. Teachers, coaches, and mentors were the critical influences.

François Gagné proposed a model for talent development that is not specific in designating ages and stages but does suggest that the child begins with aptitudes or abilities that are probably genetically determined. These aptitudes are stimulated by, are evoked by, and interact with environmental and intrapersonal catalysts surrounding the child and result in increasingly specific talent strengths. The intrapersonal catalysts are focused in personality and motivational characteristics of the child and later the youth. The environmental factors include people, the environment, the zeitgeist, physical resources, and chance encounters. [See CONDITIONS AND SETTINGS/ENVIRONMENT; ZEITGEIST.]

The Gagné model has been widely recognized in the fields of gifted education and talent development as providing a new and uniquely productive way of conceptualizing the processes of talent development in gifted youth, but it has far less to offer in explaining the role of creativity in the development of gifts and talents.

One of the most explicit descriptions of the development of talent and creativity was formulated by David H. Feldman, a research scholar whose work traverses both areas. Feldman proposed that creative talent grows through a series of six stages and ages:

1.	0–18 months	Basic intelligence emerges.
2.	18 months to 4 years	Symbolic representational cognitive systems emerge.
3.	4 years to 10 years	Growth occurs in cognitive control through exploration and observational experiences.
4.	10 years to 13 years	Specific talents develop through experiences and mentors, role models, contests, apprenticeships, and schooling.
5.	13 years to 18 years	The young person makes commitments to the development of her or his own talents, develops ideals and values, and the talent itself, as well as talent development, become part of the youth's self.
6.	18 years to 22 years	The talent is fully crystallized as the young person settles on a career choice and aspirations.

Like the Gagné model, Feldman said little about how creativity develops in tandem with talent. However, he explained that those individuals who possess or develop high-level talent and creativity have also developed attitudes and beliefs that career areas, disciplines, and fields of human endeavor can be changed for the better. Creativity, he argued, is the ability to discern needed changes, gaps, or problems and to produce solutions, improvements, or new explanations for phenomena.

Fully developed talents culminate in careers that help young people become experts and play major creative roles in their chosen careers or fields of endeavor. Simonton suggested that it takes about 10 years and 50,000 units of information, gained through intensive study, to achieve the status of expert. However, the role of expert does not, in itself, imply creative productivity. The expert may function chiefly convergently. However, when experts go beyond proficiency and pioneer new ideas, paradigms, systems, inventions, or styles for a field, they are operating in the creativity realm.

III. RECOGNIZING TALENT

A combination of tests, rating scales, behavioral observations, and case analyses can all be used to identify children's talents, but it is probably best to provide educational experiences and instruction as a stimulation for emerging talents to manifest themselves. The field of gifted education has been extremely concerned about precision in the identification process and in labeling children as "gifted" or "ungifted", processes that have many undesirable aspects. It seems far more profitable educationally to engage in identification procedures that discern emerging aptitudes and talents as well as interests in children, to provide a variety of educational experiences to foster the emerging talents, and to forgo labeling or categorizing youth as "talented" or "untalented."

Test instruments and scales for assessing gifts and talents and rating scales are also available for a wide variety of academic and vocational talents. Finding youth who will develop their talents and creative abilities to high levels of creative achievement is still an inexact science. The evidence indicates that it will be much more profitable to focus efforts on identifying a youth's specific talents and emerging creative abilities than simply searching for generally gifted youth who, although they may excel academically, do not go on to high-level creative achievement. By identifying specific talent strengths and creative abilities, we can design educational programs that will help youth excel in creative careers that grow out of their specific talents.

IV. NURTURING TALENT

Talents emerge and grow through diverse learning experiences. Intelligence alone is not a sufficient predictor of creative achievement. Creativity represents the highest level of achievement in a field of occupation. There are three indispensable elements in the lives of creatively productive people: (a) appropriate cognitive skills, (b) a large knowledge base in a field, and (c) a set of personality traits. The personality traits include flexibility, intrinsic motivation, sensitivity to details and essentials, intense independence, and a sense of creative power. [*See* FLEXIBILITY.]

We can nurture both talent and creativity by providing a variety of educational experiences from which youth can, with guidance, select those classes, courses, and extracurricular activities that relate most directly to their emerging talents. The experiences should be rich, in-depth, and accelerated to fit the precocity of talented youth. To foster creative skills, the school learning opportunities should focus on purpose, mobility, objectivity, and intrinsic motivation of students. The learning experiences of talented, precocious, and creative youth should also relate to the real world and its imperatives, processes, and pathways.

Finally, it seems that some metacognitive planning skills should be a part of the armament of the emerging creative and talented youth. There should be a growth planning process in which talented and creative youth are led in an effort to help them pull together and understand information about themselves. This process should include test scores, rating scales, interest analyses, and learning styles. Youth should use the information to set short- and long-term goals for themselves in the academic, career, personal, and social areas. They can then use these goals as guides in selecting classes and courses in school, extracurricular activities, and learning and mentoring experiences in the community outside the school. Students are urged to take advantage of offerings from museums, colleges, universities, and so on. Results of trials of growth planning with youth from Grades 4 to 12 indicate that they can take the initiative in setting their own educational and career goals.

V. MODELS AND MENTORS

Models and mentors can play significant roles in the development of talent and creative abilities. Children with special and high-level talents are especially able to relate well to adult models and to emulate some aspects of the model's or mentor's behavior, particularly those that are in the domain of shared talents. Models and mentors can also vary in the intensity of the relationships with protégés, ranging from intense, close, and personal to remote, vicarious, and impersonal. Mentors and models often help talented youth learn or acquire knowledge and skills that are not included in regular school curricula and help them acquire attitudes, beliefs, and theories as well as social skills that characterize experts and high-level achievers in a career that relates to a youth's talents. Models and mentors may be particularly effective in eliciting the motivation to create that must characterize those who rise to the highest level of productivity in a field.

A review of research related to modeling and its impact on creativity and talent development concluded that the presence of eminent people early in one's life can facilitate creative achievement, but extended involvement with a prestigious model may undermine creativity. The major function of a model in the life of a child or youth may be to evoke intrinsic motivation in the domains of children's and youth's talents. Rising talented youth are inclined to seek out highly creative and achieving adults, and highly creative and achieving adults are often eager to receive and work with promising youth who are already exhibiting high-level creativity and talent. A great benefit of such alignments for talented young people is access to labs, libraries, and other resources of the model or mentor.

The most general guidance for the role of modeling in the development of creativity and talent can be derived from social learning theory, which is also often called observational learning. Creative and talented youth can observe specific behaviors in models and mentors and thereby repeat, practice, and learn the behaviors that characterize a highly creative and achieving adult. The youth can also modify the behavior of the model or mentor in ways that are productive for both the youth and the mentor, a process called reciprocal determinance. Modeling involves attentional processes in which the youth discerns in the mentor critical behaviors to be emulated, retention processes in which the youth remembers and develops mental schema of behaviors observed, motor reproduction processes in which overt responses and behaviors are displayed based on the observations of a model, and motivational processes that lead to selectivity in discerning what is worth emulating in a model.

Modeling undoubtedly plays a significant role in the lives of creative and talented children. Although much necessary knowledge is acquired in school and from books, teachers, parents, and other significant adults exhibit and teach the behaviors necessary for high-level talent development and creative achievement.

VI. CONCLUSION

We have abundant evidence that human abilities are multifaceted and that we can best meet the educational needs of children and youth by helping them come to know and understand their specific talents and creative abilities and by providing opportunities for challenging learning experiences in which their talents and creative abilities can come to life, manifest themselves, and grow to full fruition in adulthood.

Bibliography

Amabile, T. M. (1983). *The social psychology of creativity.* New York: Springer-Verlag.

Csikszentmihalyi, M., Rathunde, K., & Whalen, S. (1993). *Talented teenagers.* New York: Cambridge University Press.

Feldhusen, J. F. (1995). Creativity: Teaching and assessing. In L. W. Anderson (Ed.), *International encyclopedia of teaching and teacher education* (pp. 476–481). New York; Pergamon Press.

Feldhusen, J. F. (1995). *Talent identification and development in education (TIDE)* (2nd ed.). Sarasota, FL: Center for Creative Learning.

Feldhusen, J. F., & Jarwan, F. (1993). Identification of gifted and talented youth for educational programs. In K. A. Heller, F. J. Mönks, & A. H. Passow (Eds.), *International handbook of research and development of giftedness and talent* (pp. 233–251). New York: Pergamon Press.

Feldhusen, J. F., & Wood, B. K. (1997). Growth plans for gifted and talented youth. *Gifted Child Today, 20*(6), 24–26, 48–49.

Feldman, D. H. (1992). Intelligences, symbol systems, skills, domains, and fields: A sketch of a developmental theory of intelligence. In H. C. Roselli & G. A. MacLauchlan (Eds.), *Proceedings from the Edyth Bush Symposium on intelligence: Theory into practice* (pp. 78–99). Blueprinting for the future. Tampa: University of South Florida.

Gagné, F. (1993). Constructs and models pertaining to exceptional human abilities. In K. A. Heller, F. J. Mönks, & A. H. Passow (Eds.), *International handbook of research and development of giftedness and talent* (pp. 69–87). New York: Pergamon Press.

Gardner, H. (1992). If teaching had looked beyond the classroom: The development and education of intelligences. *INOTECH Journal, 16*(1), 18–35.

Pleiss, M. K., & Feldhusen, J. F. (1995). Mentors, role models, and heroes in the lives of gifted children. *Educational Psychologist, 30*(3), 159–169.

Simonton, D. K. (1994). *Greatness: Who makes history and why?* New York: Guilford Press.

Teaching Creativity

Richard E. Ripple

Cornell University

Brainstorming A group problem solving method based on Alex Osborn's belief that all people have creative potential. The method involves deferring judgment, eliminating criticism, and valuing idea quantity.

"Capital C" Creativity Involves bringing into existence something genuinely new that receives social validation and is valued enough to be added to the culture. Also referred to as H-creative (historical).

Divergent Thinking One of the components in Guilford's Structure of Intellect model. Divergent thinking is a mental activity performed in situations where there is no prior correct solution or answer. Fluency, flexibility, originality, and elaboration of thought are components of divergent thinking and are likened to creativity.

Incubation One of the four stages in the Wallas four-stage process of creativity. The other three are preparation, illumination, and verification. Incubation is an unconscious process where direct efforts to solve the problem are abandoned and the problem is allowed to sink into the unconscious to "cook."

Lateral Thinking Associated with Edward de Bono, lateral thinking is intuitive, generative, provocative, nonsequential, and flexible. It involves looking for alternative ways of defining or interpreting a problem. It is contrasted with vertical thinking—direct problem solving efforts.

"Small c" Creativity Involves ideas or products which are new to the person, but only to the person. Also referred to as P-creative (psychological).

Synectics An extension of brainstorming associated with William Gordon. It is taken from the Greek word meaning the joining together of different and apparently irrelevant elements. The use of metaphor is important in "making the strange familiar and the familiar strange."

Creativity is a combination of abilities, skills, motivations, and attitudes. Much like athletic ability, which is really a combination of many different abilities, it is more useful to think of many "creativities." Many scholars affirm that creativity can be improved through instructional training programs, materials, techniques, and/or procedures, but much controversy surrounds this claim. In order to sort out claims about the TEACHING OF CREATIVITY it is instructive to examine a brief history of the ideal, leading to differing concepts, definitions, and approaches. A consideration of ways to enhance creativity follows. Specific approaches to its improvement through procedures, methods, techniques, and programs are identified.

I. INTRODUCTION

Creativity is one of the most ambiguous terms in the social sciences. It is a multidimensional concept, open to differing views and definitions. That creativity is a complex concept resistant to definition need not be overly bothersome. Conceiving of creativity as a single ability is unlikely to be any more productive than thinking of intelligence as unitary in nature. Both involve a combination of abilities, skills, motivations, and attitudes. Much like athletic ability, which is really a combination of many different abilities, it is more useful to think of many "creativities." Distinctions among various creativities involve different approaches to its study and generate differing views of how to improve it. In sum, creativity is a many splendored concept. Few concepts in social science are more elusive of definition. All approaches to its definition and study have merit. [*See* DEFINITIONS OF CREATIVITY.]

Can creativity be improved through instructional training programs, materials, techniques, and/or procedures? Many scholars affirm that it can be, but much controversy surrounds this claim. It is premature to support the claim definitively. The response to the question posed is closely related to the view of creativity. Some conclude that it is possible to teach creativity directly through the systematic use of instructional materials, procedures, and techniques. Others argue that creativity cannot be enhanced. The best we can do is to avoid inhibiting its development and expression. Similar to the Hippocratic dictum, "First, do no harm," all we can really do is avoid destroying creativity.

In order to sort out claims abut the teaching of creativity it is instructive to examine a brief history of the idea, leading to differing concepts, definitions, and approaches. A consideration of ways to enhance creativity follows. Specific approaches to its improvement through procedures, methods, techniques, and programs are identified. In conclusion, a model linking creativity to problem solving is offered in a systems context.

II. A BRIEF HISTORY OF CREATIVITY

A. Divine Inspiration

For most of human history creativity was held to be the prerogative of supreme beings. Ancient views attributed the power of creativity to the muses. The gods were the source of creativity, endowing human beings with their transcendental powers. Creativity bore the elitist mark of divine ancestry, closely related to the concept of "genius." And geniuses (like gentlemen) were born, not made.

Allied to this perspective was the view that some form of madness was needed for creativity to become manifest. But the form of madness required was not one of a disabling psychosis. Instead, it was thought of as a "divine" madness, again inspired by the muses. [*See* MAD GENIUS CONTROVERSY.]

Such views are not supported by the evidence from research and are no longer respectable as the dominant model of human creativity. They are consigned to the realm of interesting mythology. Although there is a stream of thought that regards subsequent scientific approaches to the understanding of creativity more as a threat than a promise, it is clear that attributing creativity to divine intervention suffers from a paucity of ideas.

B. Wallas and the Four-Stage Process

Although social scientists have demonstrated an interest in creativity for over a century, the beginnings of a more direct approach to its study is credited to Graham Wallas and his proposal of a four-stage process theory in 1926. Influenced by Freud, Wallas gave the unconscious a central place in his theory. But Wallas attributed much influence of the conscious over the unconscious. This partnership of the conscious and the unconscious is revealed in the four-stage process. In the first stage, preparation, the conscious mind does all the heavy lifting. It does the background work to decide what the problem is. In the second and third stages, incubation and illumination, the unconscious takes over. During incubation direct efforts to solve the problem are abandoned. The problem is allowed to sink into the unconscious to "cook." Illumination is the third stage (also unconscious), in which the problem solution appears often with suddenness, clarity, and certainty. The conscious mind becomes dominant in the fourth stage, verification, to evaluate and refine the solution.

The Wallas theory contained the markings of a good first effort, clearly improving on previous notions. It retains classical popularity and continues to have adherents. Clues are present as to how one might intervene to enhance the creative process, even though it is a passive process for the most part. But the theory is not without its weaknesses. The theory is based on the self-reports of universally accepted creative people. More recent controlled studies have failed to verify the theory. One major problem seems to be that incubation is a passive process, and alternative explanations exist for what happens when conscious attention is turned away from the problem. [*See* INCUBATION.]

C. Guilford: Divergent Thinking and the Psychometric Movement

The Wallas theory revealed the paucity of ideas associated with attributing creativity to divine inspiration. It remained for J. P. Guilford to launch the beginning of a new era in the scientific study of creativity. He is generally credited as doing this in his 1950 presidential address (entitled "Creativity") to the American Psychological Association. Guilford challenged researchers to study creativity as a unique characteristic of human beings. Fueled by Guilford's challenge, a series of studies were made into various aspects of creativity (e.g., tests and measures, characteristics of creative people, and efficacy of educational interventions). After a stagnant period of languishing activity the scientific study of creativity was born with Guilford's seminal effort.

Guilford's conception of creativity is embedded in the larger context of a structure of intellect. One of the components in the structure of intellect is termed divergent thinking. Divergent thinking is a mental activity performed in situations where there is no prior correct solution or answer. Instead, a range of more or less appropriate solutions are sought. Divergent thinking is contrasted with convergent thinking, in which solutions for problem situations are identified in advance. [*See* DIVERGENT THINKING.]

A host of paper and pencil tests of creativity was spawned by the concept of divergent thinking (which was considered implicitly as a definition of creativity). Aspects of divergent thinking such as fluency, flexibility, originality, and elaboration of thought were likened to components of creativity. These measurement efforts had two significant attributes. First, they introduced the psychometric movement into the scientific study of creativity. Components of creativity were thought to be quantifiable and measurable. And they arranged respondents in a continuous score distribution (as opposed to an all-or-none dichotomy). It would be difficult to overestimate the implications of these influences on subsequent inquiry into creativity. [*See* APPENDIX II: TESTS OF CREATIVITY.]

A half century later, although divergent thinking has not altogether been discredited as one approach to the definition and measurement of creativity, neither divergent thinking nor the psychometric approach has enjoyed consensual acceptance in the social science community. However, one residual legacy of these efforts is the concept of levels of creativity differing in degree. This concept underlies the view of creativity as a normative process available to everyone. As well, the idea that creativity could be improved as a result of direct efforts grew in popularity. Creativity has become a household word and the term "creative" enhances any noun that it modifies. The development of various instructional materials, procedures, methods, techniques, and programs to improve creativity has proliferated. They are used in homes, schools, business, and government organizations, and the like. The following ideas have taken root: creativity is an identifiable phenomenon; it can be measured; its characteristics and development can be described; and it can be improved through intervention efforts. Within the context of these ideas, controversy rages. The field of creativity is alive and well with ferment.

III. CONCEPTS, DEFINITIONS, AND APPROACHES

A. Concepts and Definitions

To create implies to bring into being—to cause to exist. The demystification of creativity involves some new combination of previously existing elements. Thus freed from the constraints of divine inspiration, there are many different senses of the term "creativity." This, in part, was the basis for referring to "creativities" earlier. Distinctions among these uses or senses of the term creativity are crucial in determining how and if it can be improved.

The primary distinctions among concepts of creativity involve a two-category definition. These two categories differ in terminology from one investigator to the next, but they all revolve around whether the creativity is unique to the person or to the culture at large. In addition to the initial dichotomy, another distinction emerges in conceptions of creativity resulting from ordinary or extraordinary thought processes. Again, attempts to improve creativity hinge on these distinctions.

The genius view of creativity sees it as the special province of special individuals at rare moments in historical time. Some refer to this as "Capital C" creativity. It involves bringing into existence something genuinely new that receives social validation and is valued enough to be added to the culture. Creativity with a small c is specific to the individual. It involves ideas or products which are new to the person, but only to the person.

Other proponents of this distinction refer to P-creative (psychological) and H-creative (historical), defined with respect to ideas, concepts, and styles of thinking. P-creative is the sense of creativity in which the idea is novel for the person, no matter how many other people may have had the idea. H-creative refers to ideas that are new in the context of the whole of human history.

Still another twofold definition of creativity is based on the degree of influence on others. Personally creative acts or ideas are limited in such influence, while universal creative acts or ideas affect large numbers of people in significant ways.

Each side of these two-category definitions is defensible, and is passionately defended by its adherents. Several implications arise. In the C-creativity, H-creativity, and universal creativity senses of the term, creativity is largely beyond our control. At best we can take pains to avoid undermining its expression, a variant of the "First, do no harm" dictum.

According to these views it is unlikely that children can be regarded as creative. Creativity involves changing a way of doing things or a way of thinking in a domain. Too much time for mastery of the old ways of doing or thinking is required for children to be creative. Use of creativity with a small c, psychological creativity, or personal creativity allows for improvement intervention attempts and for childhood creativity. Of course, big C advocates question whether this is "real" creativity. Still, it is an important and potentially enriching ingredient of everyday life.

Another set of distinctions among definitions and concepts is made by Edward de Bono (vertical and lateral thinking) and E. Jaques (sculpted versus "hot-from-the-fire" or precipitate creativity). According to de Bono the distinction between lateral and vertical thinking is critical. Vertical thinking involves mental operations which move in a straight line between lower and higher level concepts in defining and attempting to solve a problem. Lateral thinking means looking for alternative ways of defining or interpreting a problem. To de Bono, problem solving requires fresh viewpoints, different from logical thinking. Lateral thinking is intuitive, generative, provocative, nonsequential, and flexible. It moves "laterally" to find new ways of looking at and solving a problem. These views are consistent with training for creativity and, indeed, de Bono is one of the leaders of this movement. [*See* PROBLEM SOLVING.]

E. Jaques' distinction between sculpted and hot-from-the-fire creativity calls attention to the life span developmental aspects of the phenomenon. Sculpted creativity is domain specific and is usually manifest in middle age or extended maturity. It is a function of the distilled experience, wisdom, and judgment of an individual in a domain of inquiry over a long period of time. Hot-from-the-fire or precipitate creativity, on the other hand, is more insightful and is characterized by spontaneous inspiration. Each has its merits, but contain different implications for nurturance.

B. Thought Processes: Ordinary or Extraordinary?

Related to the differing concepts and definitions of creativity is the issue of the nature of the underlying thought processes. Is creativity the result of the same sort of thought process ordinary people use to solve ordinary problems? Or are the thought processes different, rare, and extraordinary? Is creative thinking a normative process, available to everyone? Are we all creative to some degree? Or is creativity an elite, mysterious, all-or-nothing ability confined only to genius?

Based on the evidence from research there is no reason to believe that creativity is the result of processes different from what goes on in ordinary thinking. This does not mean that creative thought is simple. But it does demystify the concept of creativity and render it capable of being analyzed, understood, and improved. And this seems to hold true for the creative process across domains, in the arts and the sciences.

The marked democratization of thinking processes underlying creativity is a recent phenomenon, dating from the psychometric approach to its study. The mental testing movement led by J. P. Guilford, and based on his structure of intellect model, gave rise to the notion of creative thinking as a normally distributed variable with a continuous distribution. The implication was that the potential for creative thinking and behavior exists to a greater or lesser degree in everyone. Implicit in this implication is that it can be improved through training.

C. Approaches to Studying Creativity

Given the historical relationship between testing for creativity and the training of it, it seems somewhat ironic that even more recent approaches to the study of creativity have taken a marked turn. The shift is away from quantitative psychometric testing and theory-based efforts to construct nomothetic nets with accompanying generalized principles. Current emphases in method tend toward the idiographic, biographical, case study qualitative mode. Inquiry has focused on domain-specific creative activities and away from notions of generalized creative abilities.

In part this shift in approach is consistent with the ascendancy of qualitative methods in the social sciences generally. And creativity cannot be properly understood in isolation from the methods used to study it and the social-historical context in which it is embedded. Yet, the shift in approach seems, at least in part, a retreat from the democratic view of human creativity and back to a more elitist, aristocratic view. Creativity is seen as still extraordinarily rare: possessed by few, absent in most. Attempts to improve it are futile and ineffective. Given the penchant for individuals to seek self-improvement, this change in approach to the study of creativity is all the more ironic.

IV. IMPROVING CREATIVITY

A. Approaches to Improving Creativity

There are two fundamentally different models used among strategies employed to improve creativity. One set of strategies is aimed at adding something; the other, subtracting something. Both strategies are included in methods, techniques, materials, programs, and procedures. In addition, emphasis is put on constructing environments conducive to the development and expression of creativity.

The deficit model assumes that creative skills and abilities are not present in the individual's behavioral repertoire. They must be learned through instruction and training. Efforts are made at the direct instruction of cognitive abilities and processes. This involves identifying components of creative ability (e.g., fluency, flexibility, and originality in thinking), and then packaging techniques to improve these skills in instructional programs, exercises, and the like. At the conclusion of the use of these instructional sequences, the individual will have abilities and skills that were not previously present. Abilities and skills have been added.

The barrier model assumes that the potential for creativity is inherent in the individual's behavioral arsenal. Procedures are targeted at sensitizing persons to their own creativity, and removing barriers to the expression of their creative nature. More often than not, instructional procedures are aimed at elements in the affective domain (e.g., attitudes, interests, or motivation), attempting to remove factors that might be blocking or inhibiting the expression of their activity.

B. Abilities, Attitudes, and Motivation

Whether we are parents, teachers, work-group leaders, or organizational managers, if we are interested in promoting creativity in our children, students, workers, or colleagues, the focus of our efforts is best directed at cognitive abilities, attitudes, and interests, and motivating environments. Historically, emphasis has been placed on cognitive ability variables. However, recent focus has shifted to the affective domain, working on attitudes, interests, and motivational factors.

Most systematic instructional efforts are designed to enhance three dimensions of thinking that are generally held to be fundamental to creativity: fluency, flexibility, and originality of thought. Fluency refers to the quantity of ideas produced in thinking. Techniques are aimed at encouraging individuals to produce as many ideas as possible. Flexibility refers to different kinds of ideas. For any given problem stimulus, techniques focus on rewarding the expression of alternative categories of ideas that are produced. Originality refers to the uniqueness of ideas. Although this is judged on the basis of the statistical rareness of the idea, an additional requirement is that the idea be adaptive of reality. It should be related to problem solution rather than rare in some bizarre sense of unusual. [*See* FLEXIBILITY.]

Implicit in these cognitive ability improvement efforts is the idea that they operate within a domain. The acquisition and mastery of learning in a domain of subject matter is critical for other cognitive abilities to flourish. How such domain-specific knowledge is learned becomes very important. Stressing analogies and metaphors within subject matter appears to have special significance for creative thinking. The disposition toward intuitive perception and thinking is additionally important. Exercises in imaginative play, retreating from specific facts in order to see them in the larger perspective of the subject matter domain, searching for transfer possibilities from one domain to another on the basis of common principles, and seeking symbolic equivalents across domains all seem to be supportive of increasing the probability of creative thinking. [*See* ANALOGIES; DOMAINS OF CREATIVITY; METAPHORS.]

Current thinking on the role of motivation in fostering creativity assigns a prominent place to intrinsic motivation. Intrinsic motivation (e.g., enjoying an activity for the sheer joy of it) contributes to increasing creativity, while extrinsic motivation, as represented by external rewards for behavior, actually impedes it. Evidence from research supports the view that at home, school, or in the workplace the arranging of environments over long periods of time that enhance high levels of intrinsic motivation (and downplay extrinsic motivation) maximize the possibility that creativity will flourish. [*See* MOTIVATION/DRIVE.]

In addition to focusing on internal rather than external rewards, other practices associated with affective factors that optimize creativity include valuing and expecting creative behavior, allowing the freedom to take risks, providing time for creativity to emerge, and avoiding premature judgment and evaluation of ideas. These practices are incorporated in the systematic intervention efforts used to foster creativity.

Clues to providing environments conducive to creativity can be found in research on people judged to sustain high levels of creative behavior. As it turns out these environmental conditions vary according to the particular characteristics of the creative individual. As one might suspect, creativity is a highly individualized characteristic. Some common elements include gaining sufficient control over one's immediate environment in ways that transfer routines into patterns leading to rhythms of behavior that enhance personal creativity. Ordering a personal pattern of action into a rhythm seems to promote creativity by freeing up the mind from expectations that might inhibit the concentrated thought required for creative problem solving. This rhythm includes the structuring of time schedules, activities, and place constraints in ways that are in harmony with the particular characteristics of the individual. Procedures that lend themselves to approximating these rhythmic conditions of individualized spatiotemporal harmony are included in the armament of creativity intervention attempts. [*See* CONDITIONS AND SETTINGS/ENVIRONMENT; CREATIVE CLIMATE.]

C. Instructional Procedures, Methods, Techniques, and Programs

Self-improvement themes in all aspects of being have great cachet in American life. Improvement in creative thinking skills is among the most prized. There is no dearth of interest in or availability of programs, procedures, methods, and techniques from which to choose. They cover a wide spectrum of development levels from infancy to old age. They are packaged in a wide variety of formats such as courses, textbooks, tapes, videos, school curriculum programs, workshops, seminars, training sessions, consulting companies, and the internet. They are as grand as a center for complex adaptive systems populated by Nobelists in Santa Fe, and as humble as a 10-step recipe for boosting creativity emanating from Thailand on the internet. Most are commercially based and lay claim to some form of magic elixir that leads to increased creativity. [*See* ENHANCEMENT OF CREATIVITY.]

Some of the more prominent ones are described as exemplars of those available from the creativity training industry.

1. *School Programs*

Offerings in schools include pre- and inservice workshops or training sessions for teachers and administrators to improve attitudes toward creativity and the improvement of pedagogical skills for teaching creativity. Techniques are emphasized such as balancing open-ended questions with right-answer questions. In addition to question raising, problem sensitivity and problem finding discussion techniques are discussed in the context of an inquiry orientation. Encouragement of and tolerance for creative expressions of students and the development of a creative classroom climate are fostered. Text materials are also available describing strategies that can be used by teachers to develop creativity in their students (e.g., the publication by the Association for Supervision and Curriculum development entitled "How to Develop Student Creativity").

Many of these ideas are embodied in commercially available curriculum sequences. Packaged curricula for the elementary grades, such as the semester-long, Man: A Course of Study (MACOS), are available. MACOS shapes inquiry through raising such questions as "What's human about human beings?" "How did they get to be that way?" "How can we make them more so?" MATCH (Materials and Activities for Teachers and Students) kits involve students in activities such as excavating a waste basket to develop inferencing skills.

The initial school materials offered were the result of the work of E. Paul Torrance. These are well-designed materials in the form of records, workbooks, and teacher guides. Creative thinking activities (e.g., producing drawings and stories) are elicited in science, history, and geography. "Ideabooks" cover grades one through eight. They employ exercises that foster imagination, explore possibilities, promote analogical thinking, encourage curiosity, and other general creative thinking skills and attitudes.

The Productive Thinking Program is also designed specifically for school children in the upper elementary grades. It is intended to develop general creative problem solving abilities through exposure to each of 16 programmed instructional booklets. Each booklet is about an hour in length. They are presented in graphic cartoon form. Each booklet contains a mystery story which has to be solved. Chief characters in the stories are Lila, Jim, and their Uncle John, a local science teacher. Lila and Jim are portrayed as approximating the age of the students for whom the materials are intended. Unbeknown to Jim and Lila, Uncle John is also "Mr. Search," a detective who goes about solving each of the 16 mystery stories. Early on in the stories, Jim and Lila discover that their Uncle John is indeed Mr. Search. They implore him to share with them his problem solving skills as he goes about unraveling the mysteries. Uncle John guides them through problem (mystery) solutions using a number of different techniques. He stresses affective qualities such as valuing thinking, open-mindedness, self confidence in one's thinking ability, the taking of educated chances, and the like. Cognitive abilities used (and taught) by Uncle John include asking relevant questions, defining the problem (mystery), using alternative ways to approach the problem, producing and evaluating quality ideas, and recognizing problem solutions. The underlying notion is that the students will identify with Jim and Lila. As Jim and Lila learn creative problem solving skills from Uncle John, so will the students.

The Purdue Creative Thinking Program is a similar example of a well-designed program of instruction intended to promote divergent thinking abilities (verbal and figural fluency, flexibility, originality, and elaboration) in elementary school students. Initially presented to school children by radio, the success of the program led to more widespread distribution in the form of a series of 34 audio tapes with accompanying printed exercises and teacher manuals.

The program consists of 28 lessons, each having three parts. The first part is a brief presentation directly teaching a principle for improving creative thinking. The second part is an audiotaped story of an American historical event (e.g., explorers, important people and events, statesmen, and recent events). Part three is a series of printed exercises affording the students practice in creative thinking. The exercises encourage student imagination, playfulness, idea generation, seeking of alternative solutions instead of one correct answer, and similar techniques to increase fluency, flexibility, and originality in thinking. In addition to direct instruction in these creative thinking skills, the Purdue Creative Thinking Program teaches language arts skills, listening skills, and social studies skills.

The programs described are illustrative of a host of those available. They are based on the assumption that creative thinking potentials are as modifiable as are other cognitive abilities and affective characteristics. Evaluation research on the effectiveness of these programs shows modest success in reaching the goals of improving inquiry skills, creative problem solving abilities, and divergent thinking components. [*See* EDUCATION.]

2. Other Procedures and Methods

A half century ago Alex Osborn designed an influential group problem solving method termed "brainstorming." It has become one of the most widely used methods for enhancing creativity. Originally developed for improving creative problem solving in an advertising firm, brainstorming has become part of everyday language as an approach to solving seemingly intractable problems. [*See* BRAINSTORMING.]

Brainstorming is based on Osborn's belief that all people have creative potential, but this potential is unrealized as we develop because of the overuse of premature judgment of ideas. Deferment of judgment became one of the first principles of brainstorming. No ideas are criticized during brainstorming. Quantity of ideas is prized. The notion that quantity of ideas breeds quality leads to the second principle, that the more ideas that are generated the greater the probability that some of those ideas will be useful in original problem solution.

A typical brainstorming session consists of a group of people with a selected leader and a recording secretary. The leader states a working definition of the problem and ensures that brainstorming rules are followed. The secretary records all ideas that are generated. The goal is to produce high-quality ideas in a small group, based on the concept that idea generation should be kept separate from the evaluation of the worth of those ideas.

The rules of a brainstorming session, enforced by the leader, include no criticism of ideas (judgment is held in suspended animation); freewheeling (producing wild, funny, or seemingly silly ideas) and flights of fanciful thinking are welcomed; production of a large quantity of ideas is encouraged (quantity breeds quality); and ideational hitchhiking (building on previous ideas through combination and improvement) is sought. The session ends when the group feels that all possibilities have been exhausted. At that point, idea evaluation, as a convergent thinking part of the creative problem solving process, begins.

Brainstorming techniques in various forms are utilized throughout business, industry, education, and government. They are an integral part of the Creative Problem Solving Institute (sponsored by the Creative Education Foundation) in Buffalo, New York, as well as in other venues in the United States and abroad. These institutes have conducted courses and workshops for over a quarter of a century. They employ brainstorming as part of an eclectically based training program developed by Sidney Parnes. Both group techniques (like brainstorming) and individual techniques (like the use of checklists for generating new ideas from old ones) are used across several sessions. Five stages of creative problem solving are followed: fact finding (information gathering about the problem); problem finding (formulating problems and subproblems); idea finding (generating possible solutions); solution finding (evaluating proposed solutions systematically against a criterion); and acceptance finding (idea implementation and selling the solution to others).

Synectics is a more recent extension of brainstorming. It is also a group process used widely in education and management science. William Gordon, founder of this creativity stimulating procedure, is a proponent of "making the strange familiar and making the familiar strange." This is reflected in the term synectics, taken from the Greek word meaning the joining together of different and apparently irrelevant elements. The use of metaphor is important in synectics. Dissociation between things is emphasized. Inspiration is deemphasized in favor of instilling understanding of the underlying processes in creativity. Synectic sessions utilize emotion for idea generation. They are also characterized by greater external direction than brainstorming.

There are two important steps in the synectics process. First, a new problem is transformed into something familiar by the use of metaphor and analogy (i.e., making the strange familiar). Second, new ways of viewing something commonplace are sought through analogy (i.e., making the familiar strange). Participants in a typical synectics group (about six in number, preferably with different backgrounds) are instructed in the use of four types of analogy in a problem solving session: personal analogy (refers to a personal identification with the elements of a problem); direct analogy (refers to a direct comparison of facts, knowledge, and technology of one domain with another); symbolic analogy (refers to the use of impersonal and objective images to describe the problem); and fantasy analogy (refers to the expression of wishes for ideal problem solution through fantasy). Solutions are then translated into more practical terms and reevaluated on more realistic bases.

These analogy mechanisms are intended as psychological tools in creative problem solving. They depend on the conscious suspension of reality. The participant is aware that analogies or solutions violate reality's laws, but engages willingly in the temporary suspension of those laws in the service of creative problem solving.

Many other procedures and methods exist in addition to the ones reviewed. Some are related to the Wallas notion of incubation, letting the unconscious have free reign (e.g., transcendental meditation). Still others are similar to stimulating the flexibility component of divergent thinking (e.g., de Bono's notion of lateral thinking). Many link creativity to problem solving (as do brainstorming and synectics). A further example of such a program is the IDEAL model offered by John Bransford and Barry Stein. IDEAL is an acronym for identity the problem, define and represent the problem, explore possible strategies, act on strategies, and look back and evaluate the effects of activities. Removing blocks to creativity is an essential ingredient of this model.

V. CREATIVITY AND PROBLEM SOLVING: SOME CONCLUSIONS

Variability seems to be an apt watchword for creative processes and people. No one pattern fits all. Different programs, methods, procedures, and techniques work with different degrees of effectiveness for different people. Nowhere is this more evident when creativity is linked to problem solving.

Creativity can be viewed as one form of problem solving. Harnessing creativity (as the "getting of good ideas") to problem solving is one way of adapting it to reality. Thinking about problem solving gives rise to a distinction between well-structured and ill-structured problems. Well-structured problems are those that are clearly defined with all the needed information provided and an available algorithm that guarantees a correct answer. Ill-structured problems are fuzzy (giving rise to a nonpejorative form of "fuzzy thinking or logic" as a respectable approach to problem solving). Not all the needed information is available, there is no algorithm, and no clear answer is demonstrably correct.

Different methods are needed to teach the types of problem solving skills for well- and ill-structured problems. Linear-vertical thinking with an emphasis on convergent thinking skills would seem appropriate for developing skill in solving well-structured problems. It is more likely that skills appropriate to ill-structured problems are those associated with divergent or creative thinking abilities like idea generation, fluency, flexibility, originality, elaboration, problem finding, analogy seeking, and the like.

Many of the problems faced in everyday real life are ill structured. They are human problems, and nontrivial to individuals who face them. This construction reinforces the view that all humans are capable of creativity in some degree in meeting everyday problems— what has been referred to as "little c" creativity. The creativity involved in solving everyday real-life problems of less than heroic proportions helps people make it through the day better and more effectively. It is useful when the mundane problems involved in making a living and dealing with personal-social affairs are encountered. And this is the kind of creativity that seems most amenable to improvement through direct programmatic instruction utilizing the techniques, methods, and procedures discussed.

"Large C" creativity, the special province of special individuals at rare moments in history, seems beyond our control other than in removing blocks from its expression. But there is no reason to believe that Capital C creativity leads to a more fulfilling life than is led by persons possessing small c creativity.

Bibliography

Amabile, T. M. (1983). *The social psychology of creativity.* New York: Springer-Verlag.

Boden, M. (1992). *The creative mind.* London: Basic Books.

Csikszentmihalyi, M. (1996). *Creativity.* New York: Harper Collins.

Dacey, J. (1989). *Fundamentals of creative thinking.* Lexington, MA: Lexington Books.

Gruber, H. (1989). *Creative people at work.* New York: Oxford University Press.

Sternberg, R. (Ed.) (1989). *The nature of creativity.* Cambridge: Cambridge University Press.

Weisberg, R. (1993). *Creativity.* New York: W. H. Freeman.

Teams

Gerard J. Puccio

Center for Studies in Creativity, Buffalo State College

Climate The psychological atmosphere that affects behaviors, attitudes, and feelings at work.

Cognitive Style The way in which people prefer to process information.

Creative Problem Solving A rational process model used to solve problems in new and useful ways.

Facilitator An individual who guides a team through a rational process.

Group Development Stages associated with the various relationship and task activities that occur as a group moves from inception to dissolution.

Team Two or more individuals who join together to perform a specific task.

The use of **TEAMS** is on the rise in organizations. In particular teams are often asked to tackle challenges and problems that require creative thinking. This article ex- amines the nature of creativity in teams. Specifically, it describes individual versus team creativity, group development and the effect of aging on creativity, and impediments to team creativity. The article closes by exploring the impact of psychological diversity and leadership on a team's ability to think in new and useful ways.

I. INTRODUCTION TO TEAMS: A DEFINITION AND RATIONALE

A team is a group of individuals who meet to perform some specific task. Additionally, the following criteria are used to describe a team: (a) Individuals have the authority to become a team if they choose to do so; (b) the group is small enough for its members to interact fully with one another; and (c) the members have decision making power.

With the rise of competition in business and industry, organizations around the world are striving to implement strategies that enhance productivity. One strategy adopted by many organizations is the use of teams. Organizational leaders recognize that when individuals work alone their talents may not be fully used. The isolation of individuals in the workplace generally results in the inability on the part of organizations to capitalize on the synergistic effects of group work. It is believed that teams yield greater output than the combined efforts of individuals working alone. As organizations become more complex in response to the ever-changing world, the individual's influence within organizational life has diminished. Teams offer the resilience, range of skills, abilities, and experience to ensure that creative ideas are supported and eventually brought to fruition. Furthermore, some writers argue that teams avoid duplication of effort, enhance cooperation among individuals, stimulate new ideas, and motivate employees.

Another reason cited for the increased use of teams in organizations has been the desire to enhance employees' involvement at work. Many organizational leaders believe that employees provide greater support to those aspects of work that they have helped to create. Furthermore, teamwork creates more opportunities for employees to participate in creative problem solving and decision making in the workplace. Leaders recognize the value of allowing those who are closest to the problem the opportunity to solve it. Leaders hope that individuals are able to find greater meaning in their work through activities that allow them to solve problems creatively and together.

The purpose of this article is to provide an overview of the nature of teams whose primary purpose is to achieve creative outcomes. The article begins by briefly reviewing research that has compared individual and group creativity. The bulk of the article then focuses on the types of teams used in organizations, the typical development process a team goes through, and the factors that facilitate or inhibit team creativity.

II. INDIVIDUAL VERSUS TEAM CREATIVITY

Creativity in teams has received far less attention than other areas of creativity research, such as the identification of the characteristics of highly creative people or the impact of creativity training and educational programs. As a consequence, there has been little research that compares individual creativity to team creativity. However, much research has examined the advantages of individuals working together against those working alone on general types of tasks. In 1984, Arthur B. VanGundy summarized what is generally known about the superiority of group work as com-

pared to individuals working alone, as well as the advantages of creative problem solving in teams. Van-Gundy's observations about the relative advantages of group work are presented in Table I. Although there are many advantages to teamwork, VanGundy was quick to point out that there are some drawbacks. For example, teams generally take more time to work through a task than would a single individual, may use social pressure to bring about consensus, may make riskier decisions, may engage in unproductive conflict, and may not permit input from all group members.

Research that has specifically examined group creativity has been limited primarily to the validation of one creative problem-solving tool—namely, brainstorming. Within this research a popular area of interest has been the comparison of group brainstorming against individual brainstorming. Brainstorming is a tool used to generate many varied and unusual options. Brainstorming is based on two basic principles: (a) Idea generation is more effective when criticism is eliminated, and (b) more ideas lead to better solutions. Studies of the efficacy of brainstorming typically compare the ideas produced by a team of individuals using brainstorming techniques against the combined ideas of individuals who work alone following the brainstorming principles. The latter is referred to as nominal group brainstorming. The results of the many studies designed to compare real brainstorming groups to

---

TABLE I
Advantages Associated with Groups

Groups
- possess more knowledge
- make fewer mistakes
- develop more unique perspectives on problems
- enhance acceptance and understanding of solutions
- increase members' satisfaction with solutions
- enhance effective implementation of solutions
- make riskier decisions
- generate more diverse and higher-quality ideas
- reject incorrect solutions, check errors, and monitor performance
- arouse greater interest in the task
- are more effective on certain types of problems, such as problems that can be resolved through division of labor or problems with multiple stages and verifiable solutions

nominal brainstorming groups have not yielded conclusive results. One trend that has emerged from research is that nominal groups tend to generate more ideas than real brainstorming groups. In regard to the quality of the output, the conclusions drawn vary from study to study. One quite serious limitation to many of these investigations has been the quality of the brainstorming instructions and training given to the research participants. The tremendous variability in this regard may be one of the reasons why the research has not been conclusive. [*See* BRAINSTORMING.]

Although much of the research in the field of creativity has endeavored to discover what factors predispose individuals to show an above-average amount of creative behavior, the synonymous question in regard to teams has received far less attention. One of the more extensive investigations of team creativity studied top management teams. Results revealed that the most significant predictor of overall innovativeness was the extent to which the work environment supported new ideas, change, creative thinking, and departure from established work practices. In fact 46% of the variance in the overall rating for team innovation was accounted for by this variable. The extent to which team members were able to participate in decision making positively affected the number of innovations produced, and increased levels of participation encouraged members to share more ideas, led to greater levels of cross-fertilization, and enhanced commitment to new ideas. In regard to the radicalness of the innovations implemented by these teams, it was the proportion of innovators on the team that predicted the degree of novelty associated with the change. [*See* INNOVATIONS.]

Diversity also plays a role in team creativity. Teams that are more heterogeneous seem to be better able to develop novel approaches to problems. One research team explored the effect of ethnic diversity among team members on the development of ideas for a realistic problem. They compared the ideas generated by 18 diverse teams against 16 all-Anglo teams. The diverse teams produced ideas that were judged to be significantly more feasible and effective.

Because this research underscores the critical role that the work environment and diversity play in facilitating team creativity, these topics will be explored in more detail later. The next section examines the types of teams formed in organizations.

III. TYPES OF TEAMS

A variety of teams are formed in organizations. Often one of the primary functions of these teams is to solve problems that do not have immediately apparent solutions. Thus, these teams must engage in creative problem solving to be successful. Examples of teams that engage in creative thinking include autonomous work teams, intact work teams, management teams, project teams, special-improvement teams, committees and councils, and shared-decision-making teams.

An autonomous work team refers to a set of individuals who are able to establish many of the parameters for how they will conduct their work. These types of teams emphasize shared problem solving and decision making. Autonomous work teams have control over such matters as establishing their own work standards, schedule, production process, and fund allocation. Often these teams work without a supervisor.

Intact work teams refer to individuals who work together on a daily basis. Generally, these types of teams have a supervisor or a leader.

A management team refers to a manager and his or her staff or direct reports. This might include secretaries, other support staff, technicians, professional staff, and others.

A project team is a set of people who are brought together to work on a specific task and generally for a specified period of time. These types of teams are composed of individuals whose particular expertise or perspectives are perceived to add value to the successful completion of the task. Examples of these types of teams include design teams, procurement teams, product-development teams, and construction teams.

Special-improvement teams generally focus on evaluating present systems to discover methods for improving work. Various labels are used for these kinds of teams, including: quality-improvement teams, cross-functional teams, process-improvement teams, and quality-management teams.

Committees and councils are formed for a host of reasons. Depending on the task, the life span of committees and councils can be short or long. These types of teams might address such issues as performance review, awards, recognition, promotion, and conflict resolution.

Finally, shared-decision-making teams, sometimes called school-improvement teams, specifically refer to teams created to improve teaching and learning in our schools. These teams are composed of a cross-section of stakeholders who are involved in the educational process, such as teachers, administrators, support staff, parents, and sometimes students. The purpose of these teams is to involve all stakeholders in regard to decisions that affect the quality of learning in school districts.

IV. GROUP DEVELOPMENT AND AGING

Teams, like individuals, go through predictable stages of development. A number of models have been articulated to explain the various stages of team development. These stages emerge from the interaction between two primary sets of activities associated with teams: managing relationships among team members and managing tasks assigned to the team.

Using terminology from B. W. Tuckman's model, the first stage is referred to as *forming*. During this initial stage the team members require an orientation in regard to the task and to one another. Before delving into the task, individuals need to explore the anticipated outcomes of their efforts and to clarify goals and objectives. In short, they must come to an understanding as to the nature of the task they were organized to carry out. As a result of this need for clarity and structure, the relationships among the team members are characterized by dependency. Individuals are highly dependent on each other for support and on the leader to provide clear directions. It is during this initial stage that team members, if they do not know each other, become acquainted with one another by testing what interpersonal behaviors are acceptable. The desired outcomes of the first stage of development are commitment to the task and acceptance of the team members.

The second stage, called *storming*, is marked by conflict in regard to both tasks and relationships among team members. At this point individuals often begin to question objectives, authority, or the way in which tasks are carried out. Individuals may resist the formation of group structure as a means of expressing their individuality. As a consequence, interpersonal relationships may be characterized by conflict. Additionally, this tension may also be aimed at the task such that group members resist or challenge demands associated with the task. The goal of this stage is to develop an atmosphere that encourages the expression of varying opinions and ultimately a sense of belonging. This atmosphere should also enable team members to clarify their purpose, as well as the most productive means to achieve their goals.

During the third stage relationships move toward cohesion and group members begin to engage in open communication in regard to the task. This stage is referred to as *norming* and is characterized by cooperation. There is a general positive feeling among team members and a respect for individual differences. Individuals openly share ideas and opinions. There is also an increased willingness to give and receive feedback. This stage is marked by collaboration. As a result, team members become more involved in sharing information and making decisions. Members develop norms to promote harmony, thereby ensuring the team's continuing existence. As a result, individuals openly share different interpretations and thoughts regarding the task.

Tuckman called the fourth stage of group development *performing*. At this point of development the team has well-established interpersonal and group structures. This synergy makes it possible for team members to focus their efforts on the task. To maximize overall effectiveness and efficiency, team roles become more flexible. Task-related activities are characterized by problem-solving efforts, which result in the emergence of solutions that resolve the task.

The final stage of group development is *adjourning*. This stage occurs when the group has realized its goal, reached its lifetime, or when new team members join. Some teams do not reach the adjourning stage but recycle back to the first stage. This is particularly true when a team is assigned a new task. The new task requires orientation to a new set of expectations, which in turn may influence relationships among team members. During the adjourning stage, task behaviors focus on successfully terminating activities associated with the task. Relationship behaviors are concerned with disengagement among team members.

The duration of the team's life affects the pace with which the team moves through the developmental stages. Teams created for short periods of time, such as only a few hours, experience these same stages of development. However, the limited time of their existence generally requires them to reach the problem-solving stage quickly. In such cases the ability to reach the problem-solving stage at a rapid rate is facilitated by the clarity of the task. The more information available to a team in this circumstance, the more quickly it will progress through the necessary step of orientation. Furthermore, since situations that require successful problem-solving quickly are primarily focused on task behaviors, it is possible for team to move more rapidly through norming behavior.

A number of researchers working independently have examined a team's performance over time. Many of these investigators reported a curvilinear relationship between a team's age and its level of performance. In general, this research has shown that a team's performance peaks when the team is between 3 and 4 years old. Afterward the team's performance steadily declines. There are two main reasons attributed to the deterioration in performance. One is that as teams grow older they often narrow their focus and become specialists within their context. The second factor is that with age many teams become less concerned with acquiring new information. In essence, they stop growing.

Performance of some teams can actually increase with age. Research has shown that leadership has a significant impact on whether a team is able to maintain high levels of performance over time. Researchers found that when project managers were able to resolve internal conflict and to keep their teams connected to the organizational objectives, there was a greater likelihood that the team would be successful over time. Additionally, functional managers who kept team members informed of current technology and new sources of information, as well as helped them to approach their tasks with an open mind, contributed significantly to a team's long-term performance. In short, these leadership activities counteracted the negative effects specialization and isolation have on team performance. [*See* LEADERSHIP.]

V. IMPEDIMENTS TO TEAM CREATIVITY

Despite even the best of intentions, teams are not as effective as they may always wish. Creating a team by joining a set of individuals together to pursue a common goal does not automatically yield productive results. Various challenges can prevent a group of individuals from producing a creative solution to a problem. These impediments to team creativity relate to the process used to solve problems creatively, the roles assumed during problem-solving meetings, and the environment in which the team works.

A. Solving Problems Creatively

One of the important activities teams engage in to achieve their goals are meetings. Team meetings are becoming so prevalent in today's organizations that the typical manager and technical professional spend about 25% of their time in meetings. A number of important tasks can be carried out in team meetings. These tasks include developing the team, making decisions, sharing information, and solving problems. Although creative thinking may play an important role in all of these tasks. It is perhaps most crucial when a team endeavors to find a solution to a complex problem.

Meetings provide an opportunity for team members to come together to address a challenge. They create a forum in which members can share information directly, build off of each others' ideas, challenge each others' assumptions, evaluate competing alternatives, and ultimately produce a new and useful solution. Unfortunately a number of obstacles can prevent a team from effectively engaging in these problem-solving pursuits. Ineffective meetings result from five factors: lack of resources, inadequate structure, failure to use rational processes, poor quality of communication, and failure to develop a clear understanding of the task. A number of these factors relate directly to how well the team manages its creative process. The explicit use of a rational process, in contrast to an unstructured approach, significantly improved communication and the quality of the solutions produced by the team. Additionally, the use of an explicit process for solving a problem can also lead to a more structured meeting and a better understanding of the task.

A rational process that has been used to develop creative solutions to complex and ambiguous problems is creative problem solving (CPS). The CPS method, and variations of CPS, have shown the greatest impact on enhancing creative-thinking skills. [*See* ENHANCEMENT OF CREATIVITY.]

Briefly, CPS is a creative process model that allows individuals and teams to structure their thinking. It establishes guidelines for generating options as well as for evaluating alternatives. It provides individuals and teams with structured strategies for producing many diverse and novel options to challenges, as well as strategies for screening, refining, and analyzing options. One version of CPS separates the model into three components or areas of operation. One component is focused on developing a clear understanding of the problem to be addressed. Another component deals with the generation of many ideas to resolve the problem. The third component is aimed at developing promising ideas into workable solutions and then developing a plan to implement the solution.

Contained within the three components are a total of six stages: mess finding, data finding, problem finding, idea finding, solution finding, and acceptance finding. In a recent update to the CPS process, a metacomponent called task appraisal was introduced, which helps individuals determine whether CPS is the appropriate process given their situation. An historical hallmark of the CPS model is that each stage entails a balance between divergent and convergent thinking. Divergent thinking refers to the generation of options and is guided by four rules of which *suspending evaluation* is the key. Convergent thinking refers to evaluating options and is guided by the key principle of *affirmative judgment*. The philosophy behind the separation of these two forms of thinking is to first allow individuals and teams to create a menu of options without restricting their thinking and then to evaluate the options once the fullest range of possibilities has been created. [*See* DIVERGENT THINKING.]

The use of a rational process like CPS can significantly improve a team's ability to resolve complex problems that have no immediately apparent solution. A rational process helps to structure and organize a team's thinking and brings a focus to team problem-solving meetings. It also leads to a more even distribution of input among team members.

B. Clarifying Roles in Problem-Solving Meetings: The Importance of the Facilitator

Another factor that inhibits team creativity is the lack of attention paid to establishing clear roles when en-

gaged in problem-solving activities, particularly roles that reinforce the use of a rational process. A crucial process role that is often overlooked or under appreciated is that of the facilitator. A facilitator is someone who guides the team through a process toward some end goal. A common mistake among teams is that they believe they have the skills to manage themselves through problem-solving tasks and therefore do not engage someone in the formal role of facilitator. Having a facilitator allows the team to focus on the task, while someone else helps the team move through a rational process. Without a facilitator, whose identified role is to consciously monitor the process, it is easy for a team to become entangled in an ineffective process. The facilitator enables a team engaged in problem solving to balance content and process effectively. When group process is monitored, team members can immerse themselves in the content of the task, while the facilitator provides structure for their thinking.

Facilitators can help teams avoid some of the most common problems with meetings. The following are some of the most common complaints about meetings: getting off the subject, time being wasted, no goals or agenda, inconclusive, rambling or digressive discussion, and lack of control on the part of the leader. The facilitator can overcome these challenges by dedicating his or her full attention to managing the process of the meeting. It is generally recommended that the facilitator remain fully focused on the process of managing the meeting and not provide any input into the content of the meeting. An implication of this singular focus in the facilitator's role is that it may be difficult, and often unproductive, for the formal leader of a team to adopt the role of facilitator. This is why many teams either bring in an individual outside of the group to facilitate or appoint a team member who is not the primary decision maker with regard to the task currently being addressed.

The facilitator provides leadership to the team. However, the kind of leadership provided by a facilitator departs significantly from common views of leadership. The controlling leader is described as tell, sell, direct, decide, delegate, solve problems, set goals, and use authority to get things done. The facilitating leader's role is to listen, ask questions, direct group process, coach, teach, build consensus, share goal setting, share in decision making, and empower others to get things done.

Besides the facilitator, two further roles are necessary

for effective teams: client and resource group. The client is the individual or individuals who have ownership of the task to which CPS is being applied. In other words, the client is the chief decision maker regarding the situation being addressed. Others may have a stake in the outcomes or may be influenced by the decisions made by the team, but the client has primary responsibility for implementing the outcomes of the problem-solving meeting. Because the client is accountable for the task, it is recommended that he or she make the critical decisions during the converging phases of the CPS process (i.e., the most critical data to consider, the best statement of the problem, the most promising solutions, etc.). Additionally, because CPS is a rational process that is designed specifically to produce novel approaches to tasks, the client must be seeking imaginative ideas and outcomes. The use of a rational process takes time and energy. Therefore, it is recommended that a client be highly motivated to resolve the task at hand. There is no point in working through the CPS process if the task is a low priority.

The primary responsibility of the resource group is to help the client generate options. The resource group works to produce a broad and diverse set of options for the client to consider. Therefore, the resource group is engaged mainly during the divergent phases of the CPS process. For example, the resource group would help the client to generate many different statements of the problem, ideas to solve the problem, and criteria for selecting the best solution. To help increase the probability that the resource group generates a divergent list of options, it is helpful to have a diverse set of individuals in the resource group (i.e., gender, age, ethnicity, function, experience, level in the organization, personal styles, etc.). If a team has been established for some time, it may be particularly useful to bring in outsiders to act as resource group members. The fresh perspectives introduced by these resource group members may stimulate the creative thinking of the existing team and their lack of experience with the task may yield a novel and useful solution.

C. The Climate for Team Creativity

Many creativity scholars agree that the environment in which an individual works can have a dramatic effect on his or her ability to perform in creative ways. Thus for teams to have the fullest use of the creative potential of their members, they must establish environments that act as a catalyst, rather than an inhibitor, to creative thinking. Göran Ekvall defined climate as the behaviors, feelings, and attitudes that are typical of life in the workplace. The climate in which people work acts as an intervening variable between an organization's resources and its organizational processes, such as problem solving, decision making, and communication. As a result of its impact on these processes, the climate affects individuals' productivity, well-being, and creativity.

Ten dimensions of climate conducive to creative thinking are challenge, freedom, idea support, trust, dynamism, playfulness, debates, conflicts, idea time, and risk taking. In all cases, except for conflict, greater amounts are hypothesized to result in greater levels of creative performance by employees. This hypothesis has been successfully supported by demonstrating that various teams, departments, and organizations with a measurably better climate did in fact produce significantly greater levels of creative outcomes.

Working with a highly innovative Swedish newspaper team, factors that facilitated the development of this team's extremely positive work climate were explored. This all-female team transformed a conventional daily woman's page into a cutting-edge product that attracted many new subscribers to the newspaper. In exploring the essential factors that produced the nurturing climate in which these women worked, nine critical elements were identified, which are described briefly in Table II. It is the nature of these nine factors that determines the extent to which the work climate embodies the 10 dimensions that foster creative performance (challenge, dynamism, trust, playfulness, etc.). Thus, a team concerned about its climate for creative thinking should consider such factors as the nature of its vision, leadership, and strategies.

Teresa Amabile and her colleagues also examined the environment conducive to creative productivity in the workplace and developed a measure called KEYS: Assessing the Climate for Creativity. Her measure was formerly known as the Work Environment Inventory. The conceptual underpinnings to this work was based on a review of relevant research literature and a study conducted with research and development scientists and technicians. The participants in this investigation were asked to recall past projects and then to describe the situation surrounding these projects. Close exam-

TABLE II
Factors That Affect the Work Climate

Factor	Description
Visions and goals	Strongly held images of what a team wishes to achieve
Strategies	The kinds of approaches and processes used to accomplish the team's visions and goals
Leadership	The style, quality, and effectiveness of the leader helps to set the tone for the team
Work setting	The physical set up in which the members of the team work
Individuals	The personality traits, experiences, and background of the members of the team
Type of work	The nature of the work itself
Work organization	How tasks are organized and carried out; how decisions are made
Context	The relationship between the team and the organization as a whole
Values and norms	Commonly held beliefs, assumptions, and practices

TABLE III
Scales Measured by KEYS: Assessing the Climate for Creativity

Scale	Description
Stimulant scales	
Organizational encouragement	Encouragement of risk taking, valuing innovation from all levels of management, evaluating new ideas in a fair and affirmative manner, reward and recognition for creative performance, and the cross-fertilization of ideas that results from participative management and decision making
Supervisory encouragement	Project managers and supervisors who provide goal clarity and engage in open interactions with subordinates; effective leadership prevents a fear that ideas will be negatively criticized
Work group supports	The stimulation of creativity through qualities found within the group, such as diversity of backgrounds, openness to ideas, and a common commitment to the project
Freedom	The amount of autonomy individuals experience in carrying out their work; greater autonomy results in an enhanced sense of ownership and control
Sufficient resources	Belief that the necessary funds, materials, and information are in place to support the team
Challenging work	A belief that projects and tasks are important and therefore provide a source of motivation; work that is intellectually challenging
Obstacle scales	
Organizational impediments	The existence of internal strife, conservatism, and rigid management structures
Workload pressure	The perception that external factors are imposing excessive time pressures to complete tasks and projects

ination of the interviews revealed 10 environmental stimulants to creativity. The content analysis of these interviews yielded two major themes: environmental stimulants and environmental obstacles to creativity.

Through ongoing research Amabile has refined her theory and measure. A recent study tested the validity of the KEYS by comparing the perceptions of the climate in teams that worked on highly creative projects versus teams that were involved in projects that were deemed to be less creative. The KEYS contains six scales that are hypothesized to stimulate creativity and two scales that act as obstacles to creative productivity. Each scale is described briefly in Table III. Results indicated that perceptions of the respective climates in the high- and low-creativity projects were substantially different. In particular, clear differences were found for work group supports, challenging work, organizational encouragement, supervisory encouragement, freedom, and organizational impediments.

Ekvall and Amabile focused primarily on the psychological atmosphere of teams. VanGundy, who also recognized the critical importance of the work envi-

ronment, discussed the influence the physical environment has on employees' ability to engage in creative thinking. He offered the following room features as consideration for teams that wish to engage in group problem solving: aesthetically pleasant, walls painted pastel colors, evenly distributed lighting, and comfortable temperature. VanGundy also suggested that round or square tables, with no more than seven people, be used to facilitate discussions. [*See* CONDITIONS AND SETTINGS/ENVIRONMENT; CREATIVE CLIMATE.]

VI. INDIVIDUAL DIFFERENCES AND TEAMWORK

Another factor that has often been written about in regard to team effectiveness and performance is the diversity of personality styles among team members. As Ekvall observed, the characteristics of the team members themselves can have a dramatic effect on how well teams function. To work together effectively, team members must understand one another. To facilitate this understanding, many organizations have turned to psychological measures to help team members better understand their personalities and consequently how their differences affect the way they work together. Two of the more popular theories that relate to creativity are Jung's theory of psychological type, as measured by the Myers-Briggs Type Indicator (MBTI) and Kirton's cognitive style theory of adaptors and innovators.

Although both theories posit different personality styles, the developers are quick to note that there is no one best type or style of personality. These theories focus attention on the productive use of differences and attempt to help people avoid pejorative views of those who are unlike themselves. Both theories emphasize that all styles have their inherent strengths and weaknesses and that the demands of the situation determines which styles will adapt most easily.

The Myers-Briggs Type Indicator, developed more than 50 years ago to operationalize Jung's theory of psychological type, measures people's preferences in regard to four dimensions. The first dimension examines people's attitudes toward life and classifies them as either extraverted or introverted (EI). Extraverts get their energy from the outer world of people and things, while introverts gain energy from the inner world of ideas. The second dimension examines preferred modes of perception and identifies individuals as sensing or intuitive (SN). Sensing types prefer to work with the details and to take in information through direct experience. Intuitive types, in contrast, prefer to look at the big pic-

ture and to focus on possibilities. The third continuum examines two kinds of judgment, either thinking or feeling (TF). Thinking refers to a preference to base decisions on dispassionate logic, while individuals with a feeling preference take a more personal approach to decisions. The fourth scale is concerned with the way people orient their lives and sorts respondents into the categories of judgment and perception (JP). Those with a judging attitude strive for structure and closure. Conversely, those who prefer perception like to keep things flexible and open. The combination of preferences across these four dimensions produces an individual's MBTI type (i.e., INFJ, ENTP, etc.). In all there are 16 MBTI types.

As mentioned previously, one of the critical functions of teams is to develop creative solutions to complex problems. In examining the four dimensions of the MBTI, characteristically different approaches to problem solving have been identified among the four MBTI dimensions. Extraverts, for example, generally solve problems by talking them through. They need to hear their own thinking out loud and appreciate others input and reactions. Introverts, in contrast, are most effective when they can take input from others and reflect on it. Introverts have the ability to step back and carefully consider the problem before leaping to a solution. Sensing types solve problems best when focusing on the facts and evidence. They like to work on immediate problems for which they can get their hands on. Intuitives on the other hand, prefer to work on problems that are framed within a broad picture. Before tackling the problem, intuitives like to consider all the various perspectives on the given situation. Thinkers are able to approach problem solving in an objective manner. They are able to focus on the implications of any given action and to approach solving the problem through strategic thinking. Feeling types, in contrast, focus on how the problem affects others. They are adept at being sensitive to the interpersonal reactions of others to alternative solutions. Turning to the last dimension, judging types focus on developing a solution. They are able to come to conclusions quickly and to move toward solution implementation. Perceiving types strive to avoid premature closure and remain open to new alternatives. They are flexible thinkers who are able to see an array of potential solutions.

A theory of individual differences that has been

related directly to creativity is Michael J. Kirton's adaptor-innovator work. Kirton developed a theory of cognitive style that posits a continuum that ranges from an adaptive to an innovative style of creativity. Kirton explicitly argued that his theory was unrelated to creative ability. Location along the adaptor-innovator continuum indicates an individual's preferred approach to problem solving, decision making, and creativity. A key distinction between these style preferences is that adaptors approach problems within the current paradigm, while innovators challenge the existing paradigm. Where the adaptor is more likely to initiate change that improves the current system, the innovator is more likely to introduce change that challenges the current system. In a sense the adaptor takes a more incremental and evolutionary approach to change, whereas the innovator takes a more radical and revolutionary approach. Individuals who possess an adaptive preference are described as methodical and conforming and they approach problems in tried and understood ways. In contrast, innovators are described as undisciplined and nonconforming and they approach problems from unsuspected perspectives. [*See* Cognitive Style and Creativity.]

As with the various style orientations identified by the MBTI, Kirton noted that the characteristic adaptor and innovator may possess negative views of the other. However, when working together effectively they bring clear strengths to a team. When collaborating on a team, adaptors provide stability, order, and continuity. Adaptors help to maintain group cohesion through their sensitivity to others. They also provide a solid foundation for riskier ideas. When collaborating, innovators help to challenge set assumptions and accepted theory. Also, innovators introduce periodic radical change that prevents a group from becoming stagnant.

Adaptors and innovators bring different strengths to a team. This is particularly important for teams who are formed to develop creative solutions. Adaptors and innovators describe the characteristics of their creative products in quite different ways. Adaptors tend to describe their products as fulfilling their intended purposes, following accepted and understood rules, being well-crafted, and embodying clear practical applications. Innovators, in contrast, were much more likely to describe their products as new and unusual, attractive, and revolutionary. It would seem that adaptors tend to focus on creating products that are highly use-

ful, whereas innovators tend to focus their attention on developing products that are highly novel. One of the most widely accepted definitions of creativity is that it is the production of ideas that are both novel and useful. By their nature adaptors and innovators seem to develop products that reflect different aspects of this definition. If this is indeed the case, then it would behoove teams to be composed of individuals who represent a range of preferences along Kirton's continuum. This diversity enables teams to unite the respective strengths of adaptors and innovators. Together they may be more likely to develop products that are both highly original and highly useful.

In a study examining the effect of roles adopted by adaptors and innovators, individuals were assigned to different roles on teams based on their Kirton adaption-innovation preference. The two roles involved in the task were planners and implementers. The planners were responsible for creating a plan for completing a puzzle and then communicating this to the implementers who were responsible for assembly. It was hypothesized that teams would be more successful when individuals were assigned to roles that matched their adaptor-innovator preference. Thus, teams that had relatively more adaptive participants in the more structured and detailed-oriented role of planners and the more innovative participants in the less structured role implementers would attain higher levels of success. This hypothesis was supported. Teams with a success rate of greater than 80% were those whose members were assigned to roles consistent with their style preferences. The teams that yielded the lowest rate of success (i.e., 42.9%) were composed of members who were assigned to subteam roles that did not complement their natural preferences (i.e., adaptors as implementers and innovators as planners) and whose subteams were approximately more than one standard deviation apart on the adaptor-innovator continuum. These teams had two strikes against them. First, individuals were assigned to roles that did not match the strengths of their natural preference. Second, communication between the planner and implementer subteams were strained due to large differences in terms of their respective adaptor-innovator preferences. In fact, the performance in these teams was even worse than teams who were randomly formed without consideration for the members' cognitive styles. The randomly formed teams had a success rate of 52%.

As with the primary forms of diversity (gender, age, race, ethnicity, etc.), psychological differences among team members can either be a source of strength or a source of conflict. It is possible that team members with different personality orientations may judge their opposites in a pejorative manner. Two individuals who approach the same problem-solving task in strikingly different ways may judge the other as going about work in the wrong way. Rather than allowing differences to result in clashes of viewpoint, teams must endeavor to use diversity to their creative advantage.

VII. CONCLUSION: LEADERSHIP AS A CRITICAL CATALYST TO TEAM CREATIVITY

A clear theme that emerges from an examination of the various research studies related to team creativity, as well as the literature focused on more applied issues, is that leadership plays a critical role in either facilitating or inhibiting creativity in teams. Much research has shown that the work environment has a significant impact on the extent to which individuals and teams are able to engage in creative thinking. When the factors that help to create the work environment are closely examined, it is leadership that is cited often as the major variable that influences the nature of the environment. In fact, according to Ekvall almost 70% of the variance found in the environment can be attributed to leadership. Leaders set the tone for how supportive the work environment is to creative thinking. Their actions either support others as they begin to play with novel solutions to problems or they can form a psychological atmosphere in which individuals work with fear, situations in which people are unwilling to take risks.

Although the literature points to negative effects of group aging on team creativity, leaders can establish an environment that enables teams to continue to achieve highly creative outcomes over time. The environment established by leaders can prevent teams from isolating themselves from new information or from becoming too narrowly focused on particular problems. The bottom line is that leaders can help teams to continue to grow and to challenge themselves.

It is effective leadership that enables individuals and teams to achieve extraordinary results at work. Individuals who work with effective leaders report feeling more committed, energized, and powerful at work. Five specific practices enable people to become transformational leaders: challenging the process, inspiring a shared vision, enabling others to act, modeling the way, and encouraging the heart. This kind of leadership is called a facilitative style of leadership. The facilitative style of leadership engages people in creative work, and enables others to find meaning in their work. Individuals who emerged as recognized leaders in teams engaged in a creative problem-solving task were those who offered innovative solutions as well as facilitated the creative thinking of others. A truly effective and creative leader employs strategies and develops a work climate that bring out the best in everyone. It is through this kind of leadership that individuals in a team are able to maximize their creative strengths. Without this facilitative style of leadership, the creative potential of teams lies dormant.

Bibliography

Agrell, A., & Gustafson, R. (1996). Innovation and creativity in work groups. In M. A. West (Ed.), *Handbook of work group psychology* (pp. 317–344). Chichester, England: Wiley.
Firestien, R. L. (1996). *Leading on the creative edge: Gaining competitive advantage through the power of creative problem solving.* Colorado Springs, CO: Pinon Press.
Isaksen, S. G., Dorval, K. B., & Treffinger, D. J. (1994). *Creative approaches to problem solving.* Dubuque, IA: Kendall/Hunt.
Kinlaw, D. C. (1993). *Team-managed facilitation: Critical skills for developing self-sufficient teams.* San Diego, CA: Pfeiffer.
Kirton, M. J. (1994). *Adaptors and innovators: Styles of creativity and problem solving* (rev. ed.). London: Routledge.
Kuhn, R. L. (Ed.). (1988). *Handbook for creative and innovative managers.* New York: McGraw-Hill.
Stein, M. I. (1975). *Stimulating creativity: Volume 2: Group Procedures.* San Diego, CA: Academic Press.
Tuckman, B. W., & Jensen, M. A. (1977). Stages of small group development revisited. *Group & Organizational Studies, 2,* 419–427.
VanGundy, A. B. (1984). *Managing group creativity: A modular approach to problem solving.* New York: American Management Association.
West, M. A., & Anderson, N. R. (1996). Innovation in top management teams. *Journal of Applied Psychology, 81,* 680–693.

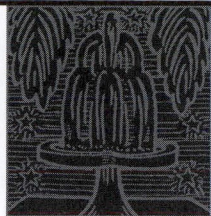

Television and Creativity*

Patti M. Valkenburg

University of Amsterdam

I. Hypotheses on the Impact of Television on Creativity
II. The Research Evidence
III. The Hypotheses Revisited
IV. Epilogue

Arousal Hypothesis Proposes that watching violent programs fosters an active and impulsive behavior orientation, which in turn disturbs the peace and quiet necessary for creative thinking.

Displacement Hypothesis Argues that television viewing hinders creativity because it takes time away from other activities such as reading that may stimulate creativity more than television.

Media Comparison Experiments Experiments in which subjects are presented with stimulus materials in either television (video), radio (audio), or print (written text) format. The text of the stimulus materials is usually kept the same, whereas the presentation modality is varied.

Passivity Hypothesis Claims that television viewing leads to a passive "let you entertain me" attitude in viewers, which in turn undermines the effort necessary for creative thought.

Quasi-experiments Experimental study that does not use random assignment to create the comparisons from which treat-

ment-caused change is inferred. Instead, the comparisons are based on existing groups that may differ from each other in many other ways than the presence or absence of a treatment whose effect is being tested.

Rapid Pacing Hypothesis Argues that the rapid pace of television allows viewers little time to process information or to reflect on what happened previously. Because reflective thinking is necessary for creativity, the viewer's creativity is impaired.

Visualization Hypothesis Claims that television, unlike radio and print, presents viewers with ready-made visual images and leaves them with little room to form their own images, so that they have difficulty generating novel ideas.

*The question whether **TELEVISION** viewing impacts creativity positively or negatively has been debated since the medium became part of everyday life, and there is still no consensus on this issue. Some authors believe that television encourages the viewer's creativity, a view which can be called the* stimulation hypothesis. *Many others, however, argue that television hinders creativity, referred to in this article as the* reduction hypothesis. *This discussion reviews the available research evidence on television's impact on creativity. First, the article presents the different stimulation and reduction hypotheses on the impact of television on creativity that have been proposed in the literature. Next is a review of the research findings on this topic. The final section examines the validity of the different hypotheses.*

* This article is in part adapted from an earlier work by P. M. Valkenburg and T. H. A. van der Voort (1994). "Influence of TV on daydreaming and creativity: A review of research," published in *Psychological Bulletin, 116,* 316–339. Copyright © 1994 by the American Psychological Association. Parts adapted with permission. The reader who is interested in an extended list of references on television and creativity should refer to this paper.

I. HYPOTHESES ON THE IMPACT OF TELEVISION ON CREATIVITY

A. Stimulation Hypothesis

According to the stimulation hypothesis, television enriches the store of ideas from which children can draw. Adherents of the stimulation hypothesis argue that television characters and events are picked up, transformed, and incorporated in the products of children's creativity—their stories, their songs, their dances, their drawings—and that, as a result, the quality or quantity of creative products is improved. [*See* CREATIVE PRODUCTS.]

B. Reduction Hypothesis

The reduction hypothesis has a larger following than the stimulation hypothesis. Five types of reduction hypotheses have been proposed in the literature. In each of them, the reductive effect of television is attributed to a special property of television. The first four reduction hypotheses attribute the reductive effect to some structural characteristic of television, such as its visual nature or its rapid pace. According to the last reduction hypothesis, only a specific type of program hinders the viewer's creativity—namely, action-oriented and violent programs.

1. Displacement Hypothesis

In this hypothesis, the reductive effect of television is a result of the popularity of the medium. Children spend a considerable portion of their free time watching television. The displacement hypothesis assumes that this viewing occurs at the expense of other leisure activities, like reading or listening to the radio, which are thought to stimulate creativity more than television viewing.

2. Visualization Hypothesis

The visualization hypothesis attributes the reductive effect of television on creativity to the medium's visual nature. Television, unlike radio and print, presents viewers with ready-made visual images and leaves them little room to form their own images. When engaged in creative thinking, viewers find it hard to dissociate themselves from the images supplied by television, so that they have difficulty generating novel ideas. [*See* NOVELTY.]

3. Passivity Hypothesis

Adherents of the passivity hypothesis see television as an "easy" medium, requiring little mental effort. With a minimum of mental effort, the viewer consumes fantasies produced by others. According to the passivity hypothesis, this leads to a passive "let you entertain me" attitude that undermines the mental effort necessary for generating creative ideas.

4. Rapid Pacing Hypothesis

The rapid pacing hypothesis attributes television's reductive effect on creativity to the rapid pace of television programs. According to this hypothesis, the viewer is confronted with images that must be instantaneously processed, because scenes are presented in rapid succession. Viewers are thus allowed little time to process the information at their own rate or to reflect on program content. The hypothesis argues that rapidly paced television programs encourage a nonreflective style of thinking. As reflective thinking is a prerequisite for creativity, the development of creativity is impaired.

5. Arousal Hypothesis

This hypothesis does not hold a structural characteristic of television responsible for the reductive effect on creativity. The arousal hypothesis argues that the arousing quality of violent and action-oriented programs fosters a physically active and impulsive behavior orientation, which in turn disturbs the peace and quiet necessary for creativity.

II. THE RESEARCH EVIDENCE

A. Studies Conducted during the Introductory Stage of Television

Two quasi-experimental studies were conducted during the introductory stage of television. In these studies the creativity of children who could already watch television at home was compared to the creativity of children without television. In one study, by H. Himmelweit, A. N. Oppenheim, & P. Vince, the two groups were matched on four criteria: sex, age, intelligence, and social class. Creative capacities of the children as rated by teachers showed no significant differences between children with and without a television set.

In another study, by L. F. Harrison and T. M. Williams, the introduction of television had a negative effect on divergent thinking. Before their town had television, children without a television obtained higher fluency scores on the Alternate Uses test than children with one television channel and children with multiple television channels. Two years after the arrival of television, the fluency scores of the children with no television had fallen to the level of children in the other towns. No television effect was found in the case of a figural test, possibly because figural tasks draw more on visual-spatial skills. It is possible that experience with television stimulates performance on the visual-spatial aspect of figural tasks but also displaces activities that would otherwise stimulate divergent thinking, resulting in an absence of a net effect. [*See* DIVERGENT THINKING.]

B. Correlational Studies

None of the correlational studies reported a positive relationship between television viewing and creativity, and there is little evidence that watching television stimulates creativity. Rather, there are indications of an opposite effect, because the majority of the studies showed a negative relation between amount of television viewing and creativity. Controlling for possible third variables had little effect on the results. More than half of the studies that controlled for third variables still showed a negative relationship between television viewing and creativity (see Table I).

The correlational studies failed to explore whether the television-creativity relationship is sensitive to the

TABLE I
Correlational Studies on the Relationship between Television Viewing and Creativity [a]

Study	Age in years	N	Control variables	Measure of creativity	Direction of the relationship [b]
Furu (1971)	Study I: 10, 13, and 16	1489	Sex, age	Study I: Summed score on Japanese verbal tests of divergent thinking (Sumida)	− (high-TV–low-print group was less creative than low-TV–high-print group; only among older age groups)
	Study II: 10 and 13	647	Sex, age, socioeconomic status, IQ, etc.	Study II: Summed score on Japanese verbal tests of divergent thinking (Sumida)	− (total viewing)
Wade (1971)	14	105	IQ	Summed score on verbal divergent-thinking tests (Guilford)	− (total viewing)
Childs (1978)	8 and 12	121	Sex, age	Verbal and figural divergent-thinking tests (Torrance), scored on	
				• fluency	0 (total viewing)
				• flexibility	0 (total viewing)
				• originality	0 (total viewing)
				• elaboration	0 (total viewing)
Zuckerman, Singer, & Singer (1980)	9–11	167	Sex, age, socioeconomic status, IQ, etc.	Teacher ratings	0 (total viewing) − (fantasy violent programs)
Singer, Singer, & Rapaczynski (1984)	3–4 (Year 0); 8–9 (Year 5)	63	Parenting style, family lifestyle, etc.	Human movement responses to Barron inkblots	− (total viewing) − (realistic action/adventure programs)
Peterson, Peterson, & Caroll (1987)	12 and 13	291	None	Nonstandardized Alternate Uses Test scored on fluency	− (total viewing)

[a] Adapted with permission from P. M. Valkenburg and T. H. A. van der Voort (1994). Influence of TV on daydreaming and creativity: A review of research. *Psychological Bulletin, 116,* 316–339. Copyright © 1994 by the American Psychological Association.

[b] "−" stands for a negative relationship that is significant at least at the 5% level, "+" stands for a positive relationship that is significant at least at the 5% level, and "0" stands for a nonsignificant relationship between television viewing and creativity.

type of programs watched. None of the studies explored for instance the effect of educational children's programming on creativity. After all, it is conceivable that educational children's programs could impact children's creativity in opposite ways than violent and action-oriented programs. The results of some of these studies suggest that children who frequently watch violent programs display less creativity, a result that is in agreement with the arousal hypothesis.

C. Media-Comparison Experiments

Seven experiments were designed to test the visualization hypothesis, which postulates that television is less stimulating for creativity than verbal media because television provides viewers with ready-made images. In all of these media-comparison experiments, children were presented with either a story or a problem. The stories or problems were presented in either television (video), radio (audio), or print (written text) format. The text of the story or problem was usually kept the same, whereas the presentation modality was varied. After the presentation of the stories and problems, children were given a creative task (see Table II).

Six of the experiments in Table II were carried out in the United States, and one was conducted in the Netherlands. In sum, with the exception of one study, all of the U.S. media comparison experiments showed that verbally presented information evoked more novel ideas than did televised information. In these media comparison experiments, the differences in creativity elicited by radio and television were explained with the visualization hypothesis. According to the authors, the television presentations led to fewer novel ideas than did the radio and print presentations because children in the video condition had difficulty dissociating themselves from television images during creative thinking.

However, the results of the media experiments can also be explained in a different way. According to a rival hypothesis, verbal presentations such as radio and print might elicit more novel responses than television presentations, not because verbal presentations are more stimulating for creativity but because they are *remembered less well*. The faulty-memory hypothesis disputes that the superior production of novel ideas after a radio presentation should be attributed to cre-

ativity. According to this hypothesis, the novel ideas produced after radio listening are not creative ideas but merely inventions to fill in holes in a faulty memory.

A part of the faulty-memory hypothesis is that radio information is remembered less well than television information. This assumption is supported by experimental evidence. Several studies have shown that children remember radio information less well than television information. However, to date, none of the media comparison experiments have investigated whether the relatively poor recall of radio information is responsible for the incorporation of more novel ideas in children's responses.

A more recent experiment, summarized at the bottom of Table II, was specifically designed to investigate the faulty-memory hypothesis. Children in two age groups were assigned to think up an ending for an incomplete television or radio story. An extra radio condition was included in which children were exposed twice to the same radio story to stimulate their recall of the radio story. Because there is ample evidence that repetitive stimulus presentation improves recall, the authors expected that double presentation of a radio story would stimulate children's recall. Therefore, the faulty-memory hypothesis was tested by examining whether a double presentation of a radio story would result in fewer novel ideas than a single presentation. In addition, the faulty-memory hypothesis would predict that improved recall should result in a higher quality of novel ideas due to a lower number of irrelevant fabrications. To test these predictions, the number of novel ideas in children's story completions were counted. In addition, the quality of the story completions was assessed by independent judges.

As expected, the double presentation of the radio story improved children's story recall. However, the faulty memory hypothesis did not receive support: In comparison with a single radio presentation, double presentation of a radio story did not lead to fewer novel ideas, nor to stories of a higher quality. Because the faulty-memory hypothesis was not supported, the visualization hypothesis is as yet the only plausible explanation for differences in novel and repetitive ideas following radio presentations. The available research evidence suggests that verbal information is more stimulating to creativity than is television information.

TABLE II
Experimental Comparisons of the Effects of Television, Audio, or Print, on Creativity[a]

Study	Age in years	N	Comparison	Measure of creativity	Main results
Meline (1976)	12 and 13	120	Problem solutions presented via • video • audio • print	Child-produced problem solutions, scored on stimulus freedom (response elements not present in the given information)	*12-year-olds:* • video resulted in fewer stimulus-free solutions than audio • no significant differences between print and audio, and between print and video *13-year-olds:* • video resulted in fewer stimulus-free solutions than print
Kerns (1981)	12 and 16	210	A 6-minute story presented via • video • silent film • audio	Responses to questions, scored on stimulus freedom, fluency, flexibility, and originality	Video resulted in fewer stimulus-free and fewer original responses than silent film, audio, and print
Vibbert & Meringoff (1981)	9–10	60	A 10-minute story presented via • sound film • audio • control (no story)	Content analysis of children's drawings of four selected points in the story	• Film elicited drawings based on pictures in the film, whereas audio drawings more often relied on children's general knowledge and personal experience • Film encouraged children to depict story content in nonconventional ways • Audio elicited conventional drawings similar to those obtained from the control group
Runco & Pezdek (1984)	9 and 12	64	Two 8-minute stories presented via • video • audio	Adaptation of Torrance's Just Suppose Test scored on fluency, flexibility, and originality	No significant media differences in creativity
Greenfield, Farrar, & Beagles-Roos (1986)	7–8; 9–10	48	Two 8-minute stories, interrupted just prior to the end, presented via • video • audio	Children's story completions scored on novel elements not found in the stimulus story	Video resulted in fewer novel elements in the story completions than audio, especially for the more comprehensible story
Greenfield & Beagles-Roos (1988)	7–8; 9–10	192	Two 8-minute stories, interrupted just prior to the end, presented via • video • audio	Children's story completions scored on novel elements not found in the video or audio stimulus	For the more comprehensible story, video resulted in fewer novel elements in the story completions than audio, a finding that held for white children but not for black children
Valkenburg & Beentjes (1997)	7–8; 9–10	64	Two 8-minute stories, interrupted just prior to the end, presented via • video • audio	Children's story completions scored on (a) novelty and quality based on consensus method (b) propositions not found in the video or audio stimulus	Among 7 to 8 year olds, no significant differences in creativity between radio and television stories were found; among 9 to 10 year olds, video resulted in less creative story completions than audio

[a]Adapted with permission from P. M. Valkenburg and T. H. A. van der Voort (1994). Influence of TV on daydreaming and creativity: A review of research. *Psychological Bulletin, 116,* 316–339. Copyright © 1994 by the American Psychological Association.

III. THE HYPOTHESES REVISITED

This final section examines the validity of the stimulation and reduction hypothesis in light of the available research evidence. This section investigates the
assumptions that underlie each hypothesis and analyze
whether these assumptions have been supported by
research.

A. Stimulation Hypothesis

The stimulation hypothesis assumes that television
provides a rich source of ideas from which the individual can draw on when engaged in creative tasks,
which in turn results in an improvement in the quality or quantity of creative products. It is evident that
television, in its role as an information provider, can
enrich the viewer's repertoire of ideas. The media-
comparison experiments have demonstrated, for example, that children who have just seen a television
story incorporate elements from the film in their creative products. However, there is little evidence that
the quality or quantity of creative products is improved
through exposure to television; none of the studies
demonstrated positive relationships between television
viewing and creativity. The only evidence that television fosters the quality of creative products is a finding
that television may stimulate the technical quality of
drawings. Therefore, there is as yet little indication that
the stimulation hypothesis holds true.

The research carried out to date suggests that television's tendency to reduce creativity is much stronger
than television's stimulation effect. The majority of the
correlational studies showed that television viewing
and creativity were negatively related, and in more
than half of the correlational studies the negative relationship remained when possible third variables were
controlled. The quasi-experimental study carried out
during the introductory stage of television that was
least open to methodological criticism showed that
television's arrival resulted over time in a decrease in
creativity. In addition, most experiments that established the short-term effects of exposure to television
suggested that television leads to less creativity than
verbal media.

In summary, each of the different types of research
conducted indicates that television viewing and cre-

ativity are negatively related. However, findings from
the correlational studies do not permit causal interpretations, and the quasi-experimental studies that have
been carried out do not permit conclusive causal interpretations because they did not completely rule out
rival explanations. So although the available research
evidence is in favor of the reduction hypothesis, decisive evidence of a causal relationship between television and creativity is as yet absent.

Furthermore, although there is no evidence that television viewing in general stimulates creativity, there is
some indication that specific types of television programs might foster creative ideas. In a review study of
the impact of television on children's imaginative play,
no evidence was found that television viewing in general stimulates fantasy play either. Nevertheless, it was
found that children's fantasy play could be encouraged
through educational programs that were specifically
designed to foster this kind of play. Similarly, children's creativity might benefit from educational programs meant to foster creativity.

B. Reduction Hypotheses

The *displacement hypothesis* argues that (a) television
viewing takes time from other activities, which (b) are
thought to stimulate creativity more than television
viewing does, (c) with the result that the development
of creativity is hindered.

The first assumption of this hypothesis is supported
by research showing that the arrival of television resulted in a displacement of other media, such as the
cinema, comic books, radio, and books. It has not been
investigated whether the cinema or comic books stimulate creativity more than television viewing. However,
the media comparison experiments suggest that radio
and books do enhance creativity more than television
viewing, a finding that lends support to Assumption b.
Although there is evidence for Assumptions a and b,
whether these assumptions form the basis of television's tendency to reduce creativity has not been directly investigated.

The *visualization hypothesis,* which has been investigated in the media comparison studies, is the only reduction hypothesis that has been directly tested. The
hypothesis is based on three assumptions: (a) Because
the visual medium presents the viewer with ready-

made visual images, television leaves less room for forming one's own images than do verbal media; (b) viewers have difficulty dissociating themselves from television images during thinking; (c) as a result, the development of creativity is impaired.

It is obvious that television viewers do not need to produce their own visualizations, whereas readers and listeners are induced to convert verbal information into their own visual images (Assumption a). Assumption b is supported by media comparison studies that had children draw inferences from a television or radio story. These studies indicated that children who had watched a television story tended to use visual content as a basis for drawing story-related inferences, whereas children who had heard the radio story more often based their inferences on verbal content and information from outside the story, such as personal experience. Finally, Assumption c is supported by the media comparison experiments that suggested that television led to fewer stimulus-free responses than radio or print.

The validity of the *rapid pacing hypothesis* has never been established. Though it is unknown whether the mechanisms proposed by the rapid pacing hypothesis indeed form the foundation of a reductive effect of television on creativity, we may examine whether the available evidence gives reason to believe that these mechanisms operate at all. The rapid pacing hypothesis assumes that (a) television leaves the viewer little time to reflect on the program content because of the medium's rapid pace and continuous movement; (b) reflective thinking therefore decreases; (c) reflective thinking is a condition for creativity; (d) as a consequence of Assumptions b and c, the development of creativity is impaired.

Of course, rapidly paced programs leave children less room for reflection on program content than slowly paced programs (Assumption a). Contrary to Assumption b, there is no evidence that fast-paced programs hinder reflective thinking. Nevertheless, there are some indications that television viewing per se can lead to less reflective thinking and, more specifically, that television may shorten the time people are willing to spend searching for an answer to intellectual problems they are asked to solve. Consistent with Assumption c, there is evidence that reflective thinking is important for creativity. However, whether television-induced decreases

in reflective thinking are responsible for reductions in creativity has not been directly investigated.

The validity of the *passivity hypothesis* has also never been directly investigated. Some studies have however examined the validity of the assumptions on which the passivity hypothesis is based. The passivity hypothesis assumes that (a) the processing of television information requires little mental effort; (b) the low level of mental effort elicited during television viewing leads to a tendency to expend little mental effort in other domains; (c) the viewer consumes fantasies produced by others; (d) creative performance requires mental effort; (e) as a result of Assumptions b, c, and d, the development of creativity is hindered.

Although children in particular are cognitively far from passive while watching television, there is evidence that television viewing requires less mental effort than reading does, lending some support to Assumption a. It has, however, never been investigated whether television viewing leads to a general tendency to expend little mental effort (Assumption b). Of course, television viewers consume fantasies produced by others (Assumption c), but there is little reason to assume that this results in reductions of creativity. People who read a story, listen to a story, or watch a play also consume fantasies produced by others. Nevertheless, it has never been argued that verbal stories or theater hinder the development of creativity. Consistent with Assumption d, there is evidence that creative performances require concentrated mental effort. However, it has never been investigated whether television-induced decreases in mental effort are responsible for reductions in creativity (Assumption e).

Because the validity of the *arousal hypothesis* has also not been directly investigated, the discussion again must be confined to the evidence relevant to the assumptions that underlie this hypothesis. The arousal hypothesis argues that (a) watching action-oriented and violent programs has arousing effects on the viewer; (b) the arousal produced by these programs leads to a restless and impulsive behavioral orientation; (c) creative performance requires one to allow for the peace and quiet needed to give a matter considerable thought; (d) as a result of Assumptions b and c, the development of creativity is hindered.

Violent programs can produce intense arousal in the viewer, a finding that lends support to Assumption a.

Assumption b is supported by research showing that violent programs may increase children's restlessness and impulsivity. Assumption c is confirmed by research showing that an ability to tolerate aloneness with one's thoughts and ideas is important for creative performance.

Although there is evidence in support of Assumptions a, b, and c, whether the mechanisms proposed in these assumptions are responsible for reductions in creativity (Assumption d) has not been directly investigated. It is true that two correlational studies (see Table I) found that watching a lot of violent programs went together with a low level of imagination, but it is unclear whether this relationship resulted from a television-induced impulsive behavioral orientation.

IV. EPILOGUE

In sum, there is evidence that the explanatory mechanisms proposed by the visualization, arousal, and displacement hypotheses actually operate. What remains to be proved, however, is whether these causal mechanisms really are responsible for television-induced decreases in creativity. The assumptions that underlie the rapid pacing and passivity hypotheses have been only partially supported by research, because there are no indications that fast-paced programs hinder reflective thinking or that television leads to a general tendency to expend little mental effort. However, the rapid pacing and passivity hypotheses have also not yet been disproved. There are thus at least three and possibly even five plausible explanations for why television might have reductive effects on creativity. The five explanations are by no means mutually exclusive, and on the basis of the available evidence it is not possible to single out one as the most plausible. Future research should try to unravel which of the theories on television's influence on creativity is the most plausible. Until now, most television research has examined the relation between television viewing and creativity as an input-output process without attempting to explore the mechanisms that underlie this relationship. Only if we know *how* television affects children's creativity is it possible to adequately channel or counteract these effects.

Bibliography

Childs, J. H. (1978). Television viewing, achievement, IQ and creativity. *Dissertation Abstracts International, 39,* 6531A.

Furu, T. (1971). *The function of television for children and adolescents.* Tokyo: Monumenta Nipponica, Sophia University.

Greenfield, P. M., & Beagles-Roos, J. (1988). Radio vs. television: Their cognitive impact on children of different socioeconomic and ethnic groups. *Journal of Communication, 38*(2), 71–92.

Greenfield, P. M., Farrar, D., & Beagles-Roos, J. (1986). Is the medium the message? An experimental comparison of the effects of radio and television on imagination. *Journal of Applied Developmental Psychology, 7,* 201–218.

Harrison, L. F., & Williams, T. M. (1986). Television and cognitive development. In T. M. Williams (Ed.), *The impact of television: A natural experiment in three communities* (pp. 87–142). New York: Academic Press.

Himmelweit, H., Oppenheim, A. N., & Vince, P. (1958). *Television and the child: An empirical study of the effects of television on the young.* London: Oxford University Press.

Kerns, T. Y. (1981). Television: A bisensory bombardment that stifles children's creativity. *Phi Delta Kappan, 62,* 456–457.

Meline, C. W. (1976). Does the medium matter? *Journal of Communication, 26*(3), 81–89.

Peterson, C. C., Peterson, J. L., & Caroll, J. (1987). Television viewing and imaginative problem solving during preadolescence. *Journal of Genetic Psychology, 147,* 61–67.

Runco, M. A., & Pezdek, K. (1984). The effect of television and radio on children's creativity. *Human Communication Research, 11,* 109–120.

Schramm, W., Lyle, J., & Parker, E. (1961). *Television in the lives of our children.* Stanford, CA: Stanford University Press.

Singer, J. L., Singer, D. G., & Rapaczynski, W. S. (1984). Children's imagination as predicted by family patterns and television viewing: A longitudinal study. *Genetic Psychology Monographs, 110,* 43–69.

Valkenburg, P. M., & Beentjes, J. W. J. (1997). Children's creative stories in response to radio and television. *Journal of Communication, 47,* 21–38.

Valkenburg, P. M., & van der Voort, T. H. A. (1994). Influence on daydreaming and creativity: *Psychological Bulletin, 116,* 316–339.

Van der Voort, T. H. A., & Valkenburg, P. M. (1994). Television's impact on fantasy play: A review of research. *Developmental Review, 14,* 27–51.

Vibbert, M. M., & Meringoff, L. K. (1981). *Children's production and application of story imagery: A cross-medium investigation* (Technical Report No. 23). Cambridge, MA: Project Zero, Harvard University. (ERIC Document Reproduction Service No. ED 210 682)

Wade, S. E. (1971). Adolescents, creativity, and media: An exploratory study. *American Behavioral Scientist, 14,* 341–351.

Zuckerman, D. M., Singer, D. G., & Singer, J. L. (1980). Television viewing, children's reading, and related classroom behavior. *Journal of Communication, 30*(1), 166–174.

Time

Mark A. Runco

California State University, Fullerton

Creativity Complex The notion that creativity is a syndrome and is multifaceted.

Future Problem Solving Program in which children practice solving realistic, open-ended problems.

Impulsive Cognitive Style The stable tendency to work quickly. [cf. Reflective Cognitive Style]

Incubation Time away from a problem—at least consciously. The preconscious may continue to work on the problem, with an "ah-ha!" occurring when a solution is found.

Let It Happen Strategies Tactics that involve leaving the problem for a time, allowing incubation and the like to contribute to the problem solving effort.

Old Age Style Intentional changes made by artists, often in the 7th or 8th decades of their lives.

Reflective Cognitive Style The stable tendency to take one's time when working.

Stage Model of Creative Thinking Proposed by Graham Wallas in 1926, with preparation, incubation, illumination, and veri-fication stages. Time is absolutely required by the second stage and probably necessary for the first and fourth as well.

Ten-Year Rule Holds that 10 years, or 10,000 hours, need to be invested into a domain for expertise to develop.

TIME *is related to creative thinking and creative work in numerous ways. In some studies time or some temporal variable is quantified, measured, and perhaps manipulated. In other studies, which are often archival or biographical, the role played by time is included in descriptions of influences or changes in behavior. The present article is an overview of the various approaches to and findings from the study of time and creativity. What may be most important is that there is a broad conception of time as a variable. Also significant is that no over-views or meta-analyses have been conducted with a focus on time. This article is in that sense both unique and exploratory.*

I. TIME IN PERSONAL PROCESSES

Creativity is often defined as a syndrome or complex, the premise being that it is multifaceted. Not surprisingly, then, several different aspects of creative behavior have been connected with time. Time has, for example, been tied to the cognitive bases of creative thinking.

Creative thinking has been defined in associative terms, with the prediction that individuals tend to generate problem solutions in concatenated chains of associations. The first few associations are usually rote, obvious, and unoriginal, but the later and more remote associations become increasingly original. Time is relevant to the associative basis of creative thinking because it takes time for an individual to move through the obvious ideas to find the remote associates. These predictions about remote ideas being original have been repeatedly confirmed.

One of the most commonly cited models of the creative process was proposed in 1926 by Graham Wallas, indicating that problem solving consisted of the four stages of preparation, incubation, illumination, and verification. Incubation implies that some time must elapse. During that time the individual is not consciously working on the problem—but is working on the problem on a preconscious level. The preconscious often succeeds in solving the problem because it encounters fewer constraints than the conscious (and logical) efforts. In 1971 J. P. Guilford claimed that Wallas' description of the stages is primarily designed for problems of great importance—problems that demand a long period of work. Guilford proposed that Wallas' steps are involved in solving ordinary everyday problems, but they are compressed. [*See* EVERYDAY CREATIVITY.]

The need for incubation (and time) was also noted by Sidney Parnes when he distinguished between "make it happen" and "let it happen" strategies for creative problem solving. The former are exemplified by very intentional and systematic tactics, such as working backward (starting with the solution and trying to step back toward the present state) or turning a problem on its head. The latter are exemplified by things like taking a walk or turning to another task; the assumption is that incubation will occur. This in turn assumes that time is useful. [*See* PROBLEM SOLVING.]

Time may be required by one of the most general of the tactics used for creative problem solving: changing one's perspective. Changes of perspective can break a mental set or routine and allow creative insight. Perspectives are often changed literally, by finding another viewpoint or way to represent the problem. A new perspective can also be found simply by taking time away from the problem. Every writer knows that one's own work can be difficult to edit if immersed in it. But if you take time away, editorial work is easier. We become more objective and sensitive to details. The same is true in other areas, where time provides perspective. Unlike incubation, where the preconscious continues to work on the problem, here it is actual and complete time away from the task. [*See* PERSPECTIVES.]

Howard Gruber has described how many seemingly instantaneous and sudden insights are actually protracted and spread out through time. He suggested that insight is *not* a sudden process. Each insight supposedly has a developmental history. This of course is contrary to the popular conception of insights as sudden. The illumination may seem sudden but what led up to it may require that time be invested. [*See* INSIGHT.]

The creative individual may depend on certain cognitive capacities and abilities, such as those mentioned above, but he or she must also be interested in using those capacities or abilities. This interest is described as "intrinsic motivation." If intrinsically motivated, the individual will invest time and effort into a task, problem, or domain. [*See* MOTIVATION/DRIVE.]

II. TIMED TESTS

Creative potential is often estimated with special tasks or tests. When these tasks or tests are administered, special instructions must be given. Otherwise respondents tend to view the tasks as similar to the academic tests most of us have experienced, and when they do that, creativity is a low priority. On academic tests it is important to find the correct answer, spell it correctly, and earn a high grade. When generating original responses to an open-ended task, there may be no correct answer. There may be many appropriate answers, some of which are original and some of which are not, but there is no one correct answer.

For originality on the part of the respondents, grades, conventional answers, and time must be deemphasized in the task instructions. Instead of imposing a time limit, examiners should allow the individual to make the pertinent decisions about investing time and effort for him- or herself. By allowing individuals to decide for themselves how much or little time to allocate to the task, the distinctiveness of divergent thinking (and originality) from convergent thinking is maximized. Performance on the test is determined by the respondent's intrinsic motivation, which often facilitates creative thinking. The flexible time limits also allow the individual to find remote associates and perhaps incubate. [*See* DIVERGENT THINKING.]

There is a common criticism of tests, including tests of creativity, which is the most tenable if they are timed. In the natural environment, creative work may rarely have a timed component, at least one that is similar to that used with tests. If we wish to predict real world creative work, the predictor should require the same tendencies as the criterion behavior. This implies that if creative work in the natural environment is rarely timed, so too should the assessment of creative potential be untimed. The rebuttal to this view is that tests are merely estimates of the potential for real-world creative activity, and that they must have constraints on them to allow them to be used in research and educational settings. [*See* APPENDIX II: TESTS OF CREATIVITY.]

III. CULTURE

Clearly, cultural norms and expectations can limit an individual's creativity. He or she may not think of some possible solutions to a problem because they are taboo within the present culture. Adults in the United States, for instance, may not consider humor or play as contributions to creative work. Work is supposed to be serious rather than fun. Similarly, in the United States there is often pressure to work quickly and to be productive. It may not be easy to tolerate incubation and to appreciate the value of "let it happen" tactics. Time is a valuable commodity and incubation may be seen as a waste of time. One step toward avoiding cultural blocks, like the prejudice against humor, play, and incubation, is simply recognizing that they are imposed by culture rather than absolutes. [*See* CROSS-CULTURAL DIFFERENCES.]

IV. EXPERTISE AS TIME INVESTED

Some domains may require years to develop expertise. Various investigators have suggested that 10 years (or 10,000 hours) need to be invested in a particular domain for expertise to develop. To the degree that expertise is necessary for creative work, this may indeed be a requisite investment. In some areas, expertise may be easier to obtain and require less temporal investment. (These may be domains which depend the least on familiarity with a body of factual information.) What may be surprising is that expertise can sometimes actually inhibit creative insight. Experts sometimes make assumptions that preclude original thinking. They sometimes have invested so much into their area of expertise that they are resistant to considering alternatives. Dean Simonton has described other requisites for high-level achievement. He pointed to three tendencies of eminent persons: They start their careers early, they are productive, and they live a long time. Time is involved in each of these. [*See* EXPERTISE.]

Time is also implied by economic and investment theories of creativity. These use the parallel idea that creative persons tend to invest a great deal into their work. Investments may be temporal. This may sound like another way of saying that expertise takes time to develop, but here it is more that the person concentrates, and frequently, on the task at hand or field of choice. It is possible that investments can work against creative success. In this sense the psychoeconomic theories of creativity support the idea that expertise can sometimes inhibit original thinking. Theoretically, an individual who has invested a great deal in one idea or line of thinking would experience a "depreciation" of his or her knowledge if new lines of thought supplanted the old, and this may lead them to resist new lines of thought. [*See* ECONOMIC PERSPECTIVE ON CREATIVITY.]

V. DEVELOPMENTAL TRENDS AND RATES

Time is often used as a categorical independent variable. This is exemplified in longitudinal studies, where various follow-up assessments are conducted after a particular interval has elapsed. Louis Terman conducted the most famous longitudinal study, though his (gifted) subjects were selected based on IQ and traditional intelligence.

Time is also implied by other developmental

research, where changes depend on maturation and the passing of time. Some longitudinal studies have found discontinuities and changes that would not be apparent with any other research design. Other studies have found continuities. Consider Robert Albert's longitudinal study of exceptionally gifted boys. This investigation has been in progress for approximately two decades. One of the key findings of a recent follow-up assessment was that certain subjects were "cross overs." By this Albert meant that subjects had changed their interest from one domain to another. The change was apparent only because the longitudinal research design allowed a comparison of career interests and general preferences at several points in time. There are also continuities that can be uncovered only with longitudinal research designs. Mihalyi Csikszentmihalyi and Jacob Getzels, for instance, found that art students who invested more time in the preparation of the subject matter were more original—even 18 years later.

Development is a lifelong process, and certain discontinuities appear late in life. Some may facilitate creative work. Many older artists are, for example, less concerned with criticism than they were when younger, and this can allow them to focus on authentic self-expression and experiment in their work. Martin Lindauer and others have found that many of the most creative artists intentionally changed their style as they got older—often in the seventh or eighth decades of their lives. These changes to an "old age style" may have contributed to the artists maintaining a fresh perspective and creative hand. Such changes and perspectives assume that time must pass—the old age style is simply not found in younger individuals. [*See* OLD AGE STYLE.]

Elapsed time is sometimes not the concern. Time can also be used to calculate other indices of development, such as "rate." Rate is the standardization of occurrence as a function of time. Of relevance here are rates of development and rates of creative productivity that reflect individual differences. There is, for instance, evidence that various facets of thought develop at different rates. J. P. Guilford described in detail different kinds of ideational flexibility and how they mature and fail at different rates. Using Guilford's own terms, the "flexibility of classes" is lost at a different rate than is the "flexibility of transformations." Support for this view has been provided by the research on divergent thinking. [*See* FLEXIBILITY.]

VI. ATTRIBUTIONS OF CREATIVITY AND TIME IN INTERPERSONAL PROCESSES

Time is required for some of the social, interpersonal processes that contribute to creative work or are involved in our judgment of it. Many researchers have argued that the attribution of creative ability is most accurate only after a long period has elapsed. That ostensibly gives the judges a better perspective. The need for a long-term perspective is evidenced by the changes that sometimes occur in reputations. Rembrandt, for example, was not the most famous artist of his time, but he is now one of the best known from his era. The work of Gregor Mendel was largely overlooked for 50 years.

An issue arises when eminence is defined in terms of attributions. This involves the question of a creative genius being ahead of his or her time. If the creative genius is ahead of his or her time, he or she might not be recognized. Records might not be kept of his or her work and no attention would be given to it. In fact, necessary resources might not be allocated to the individual because of the lack of appreciation. In that light the creativity might never develop to the level necessary for exceptional achievement. [*See* EMINENCE.]

A second interpersonal issue involves the possibility that immediate temporal constraints can undermine creative work. This was implied earlier, in the discussion of task instructions for assessments of creative potential. It was further intimated by the attributional process that some apply to judgments of creative performance. It can be explained by referring back to the economic theory of creativity, because there time was defined as a resource. Time can be invested in one's training or work. This is an interpersonal dynamic when other persons (e.g., parents, teachers, or supervisors) decide how much time we can invest in our training or work.

VII. TIME AS PERSONAL CONSTRUCT

The research above, noting the inhibitive effects of time constraints, should not be taken to suggest that everyone will be disturbed by deadlines. Some persons work best under pressure. Moreover, time is a function of subjective interpretations, and different people will interpret time periods differently. The subjectivity of time, and the relationship between that interpretive tendency and creativity, is implied by research on "flow." Flow is characterized by a loss of self, and a loss of the awareness of time's passing.

The subjectivity of time and a second connection to creativity is suggested by the ability of certain creative persons to look beyond the present. This tendency is epitomized in the "future problem solving" educational program and in the "proactive creative work" of some creative persons. Proactive creative efforts may allow us to avoid problems, or solve them when they are minor, rather than solving them or dealing with them when they are so large as to be unmanageable.

One part of the subjectivity of time can be explained by "cognitive style." Impulsivity and reflective cognitive styles have, for instance, been isolated, and they differ in terms of how much time is required or used by the individual. Perhaps one individual uses a great deal of time because they are not really aware of its passing. Indeed, that is one of the basic premises of the concept of flow. To the extent that creative insights are often protracted, impulsivity might decrease the likelihood of creative work. [*See* COGNITIVE STYLE AND CREATIVITY.]

VIII. CONCLUSIONS

Time is thus relevant to several cognitive and metacognitive processes that might be involved in some creative thinking. It is related to incubation and necessary for the remote associates that tend to provide original ideas. Time can be used strategically, in "let it happen" tactics, and it may be indicative of investments and intrinsic motivations of creative persons. It should be explicitly deemphasized when using tests of creative potential. The cultural basis of time should be acknowledged, even as specifically associated with creative work, as should the value of time as a resource in most organizational and educational settings.

Time is used in areas of creativity research in addition to what is reviewed in the present article. Gudmund Smith, for example, varies the exposure time in his Creative Functioning tests, and Norbert Jausovec examined heart rates as related to stages in the creative process. The relevance of time is widely recognized and even more varied than the present overview might suggest.

Bibliography

Gruber, H. E. (1993). Creativity in the moral domain: Ought implies can implies create. *Creativity Research Journal, 6,* 3–16.

Gruber, H., & Wallace, D. (Eds.). (1996). Creativity in the moral domain. *Creativity Research Journal* (Special issue).

Heinzen, T. (1993). *Everyday frustration and creativity in government.* Norwood, NJ: Ablex.

Runco, M. A., & Albert, R. S. (Eds.). (in press). *Theories of creativity.* Cresskill, NJ: Hampton Press.

Runco, M. A., & Chand, I. (1994). Problem finding, problem solving, and evaluative thinking. In M. A. Runco (Ed.), *Problem finding, problem solving, and creativity.* Norwood, NJ: Ablex.

Henri-Marie-Raymond de Toulouse-Lautrec-Monfa

1864–1901

Artist

Oil paintings: *Le Cirque Fernando* (1888), *A la Mie* (1891) *Dance at the Moulin Rouge* (1894); Posters: *Le Chat Noir, Le Moulin Rouge, Aristide Bruant, La Goulu and Valentin le Desosse*; Lithographs: *Elles.*

David Pariser

Concordia University, Montreal

HENRI DE TOULOUSE LAUTREC's paintings and prints are linked in spirit and draughtsmanship to the work of artists such as Daumier and Goya. Lautrec's acute rendering of gesture and movement, combined with the fluent vigor with which he disposed of line and color, ensures him a place among great 19th-century graphic artists. As early as 1900, Picasso, on arriving in Paris, paid homage to Lautrec by producing several paintings in Lautrec's style. Lautrec's artistic successors, among them Expressionists such as Beckmann and George Grosz, took a few pages from Lautrec's own book in their scathing portrayals of decadent German city life. More generally, Lautrec's mature style, in which he handled his media roughly and showed small concern for the conventions of Academic painting, makes him a precursor of Modernist painters. In the spirit of these painters, he treated the medium and the technique (i.e., oil painting and lithography) in such a way that the viewer could not evade the artifice of the process and the materials.

Henri de Toulouse-Lautrec, self-portrait c. 1882–1883 from Musée Toulouse-Lautrec, Albi. Used with permission from Giraudon/Art Resource, NY.

I. BACKGROUND

Born into an aristocratic family, Lautrec was afflicted with a glandular disorder that permanently stunted his growth. Yet, even as a sickly child he was noted for his sense of humor and for his intense involvement in the social and visual aspects of life. It was in his large and close-knit family that he acquired amateur drawing skills. As a child he loved to sketch animals, especially equestrian figures and carriages. By his late teens he was taking informal art lessons with a deaf-mute friend, the professional painter of horses Renee Princeteau. Noting the boy's talent, Princeteau advised Lautrec to start taking his art lessons in Paris.

Lautrec studied successively in the workshops of two conservative Parisian painters, Bonnat and Cormon. Even though he was pleasurably challenged by the grind of drawing from plaster casts and nudes, Lautrec never distinguished himself as an academic artist. However, by virtue of living in Paris, Lautrec was exposed to formative cultural influences: the paintings of the Impressionists and Degas (whom he especially admired), Japanese prints, and the disreputable nightlife of Montmartre. It was the habitués and performers in the clubs, theaters, and brothels who became his subject matter. Between 1885 and 1896 he produced most of the oil paintings, lithographs, and posters for which he is famous. The first public successes came with his advertisements for various Montmartre dance halls and "boites a chanson." He made memorable posters of key figures in the nightclub district, such as the balladeer Aristide Bruant and the performers Yvette Guilbert, La Goulou, and Valentin the Boneless. Critics say that Lautrec created a definitive vision of fin-de-siècle Paris, in much the same way that Baudelaire created a verbal description of a slightly earlier Paris. (See Figure 1.)

In 1897 Lautrec confirmed his notorious reputation by publishing a collection of lithographs titled *Elles*. These were based on studies that he had made while living in a brothel. Between 1880 and 1900 he received commissions for advertisements and for illustrations as well as selling his works in a number of galleries in Paris and elsewhere in Europe. His mother supported him financially and emotionally throughout most of his life and was with him when he died in 1901 at the family estate. Relations with his father remained strained up to the end. Alphonse the Count had little

FIGURE 1   Henri de Toulouse-Lautrec, French, 1864–1901, At the Moulin Rouge, oil on canvas, 1893–1895, 123 × 141 cm, Helen Birch Bartlett Memorial Collection, 1928.610. Photograph © 1998, The Art Institute of Chicago. All rights reserved. Used with permission.

respect for his son's "audacious scribbles" (as he called them) and was initially opposed to any posthumous showings of Lautrec's works.

II. METHODOLOGICAL NOTES: THE SYSTEMS VIEW OF CREATIVITY

Some social psychologists wisely advocate a systems approach to the study of creative individuals. These psychologists observe that in addition to intellectual gifts of one sort or another, social and historical circumstances must be propitious for individuals to achieve creative eminence. To put it more simply, if creative individuals are to emerge, they need to be present at a time and place when their special abilities are in demand. Thus, a systems approach to the study of creative people requires the researcher to go beyond a focus on the special qualities of the creator and to include a consideration of the intellectual domain that this person has mastered and the social organization of the field in which the person's work is recognized. For this reason, the discussion of Lautrec that follows suggests both endogenous factors and exogenous factors. The endogenous aspects of his creative activity are those associated with the gifts and afflictions with which he was born. The exogenous features of Lautrec's life include factors such as the happy accident of his birth into a loving and well-to-do family and the historical fact that Lautrec began to produce art at a time when the French Academy of Art was losing its grip on the French art world. What emerges from the discussion that follows is a sketch of his special traits, the luck, the misfortune, and the social and historical circumstances that, taken as a whole, contributed to his emergence as a significant artist.

When we look at Lautrec's life, we can identify several key factors: (a) his precocious gifts as observer and draughtsman; (b) thematic, technical, and emotional continuities between childhood and adult art; (c) the crucial role of emotional and financial support offered by his family; (d) Lautrec's persona as an artist; and (e) the impact of class and historical setting.

A. Lautrec's Precocious Gift for Sure and Vital Line and His Eye for Physical Gesture and Expression

The record of Lautrec's juvenile artistic activity suggests that he fits the profile for childhood giftedness. According to Winner (1996) gifted children possess three key traits: (a) precocious ability in a given discipline or area of knowledge; (b) an intense desire to master a given medium or skill; and (c) the drive to solve problems in their own way, rather than using formulas provided by others. In all respects young Lautrec was a typically gifted child.

1. *Precocious Drawing Ability*

Lautrec's drawings from a young age demonstrate the quality of his rendering skills and the rapidity with which he acquired them. Lautrec's graphic profile (based on his juvenile drawings and paintings) shows that he was a prolific and accomplished draughtsman. In this respect he is like many other visually gifted children who pour out huge quantities of drawings during their early years. It is evident that he possessed a high degree of visuospatial intelligence. About 2500 of Lautrec's drawings and paintings exist that date from

ages 6 to 17. (These drawings were saved for purely sentimental reasons by his doting mother and relatives.) As expected, not all of the drawings are phenomenally accomplished, but a significant number are noteworthy. In some of his earliest drawings of carriages and horses, he demonstrated an unusual mastery of line and movement. His use of sweeping contours to suggest the body of a horse in motion is unusual in the work of a 6-year-old child. As in the drawings of other, less gifted children, we find a mix of accomplished and less skilled drawing performance all in the same picture. Lautrec's sketches of his favorite subject matter—horses—are more accomplished than his renderings of birds—a less favored topic.

An examination of the collected juvenile work reveals the presence of multiple graphic streams. These streams indicate the early emergence of what Gruber and Davis (1989) call "networks of enterprises"—a hallmark of the way that creative individuals work. Among Lautrec's juvenile images one finds life studies, caricatures/broadsides, illustrations, and a visual vocabulary taken from both academic and popular art. Several of these varied approaches can also be found, all in the same work, in some of his adult creations. For example, in *Le Cirque Fernando* (see Figure 2), the sinister ringmaster is flat and cartoonlike, whereas the horse and equestrienne are rendered in a much more plastic manner.

2. *Delight in Mastery*

As a child, Lautrec showed an intense desire to master new problems and to meet representational challenges. The sketches on the margins of his school notebooks and textbooks give us a glimpse of a child struggling successfully with all aspects of rendering: mastery of spatial depth, articulation of limbs, fall of clothing, and the interaction of figures with each other. Although Lautrec's family encouraged him to draw and paint as a form of gentlemanly diversion, he did not receive formal lessons until middle adolescence. Yet sketches from his childhood reveal that he set himself all sorts of impromptu lessons and problems. In one case, we find a set of sketches of what are probably toy circus acrobats perched on the tops of several pages in his French Latin dictionary. (In his letters from the period he mentions his fascination with an American toy circus.) On each of five pages he shows a different tum-

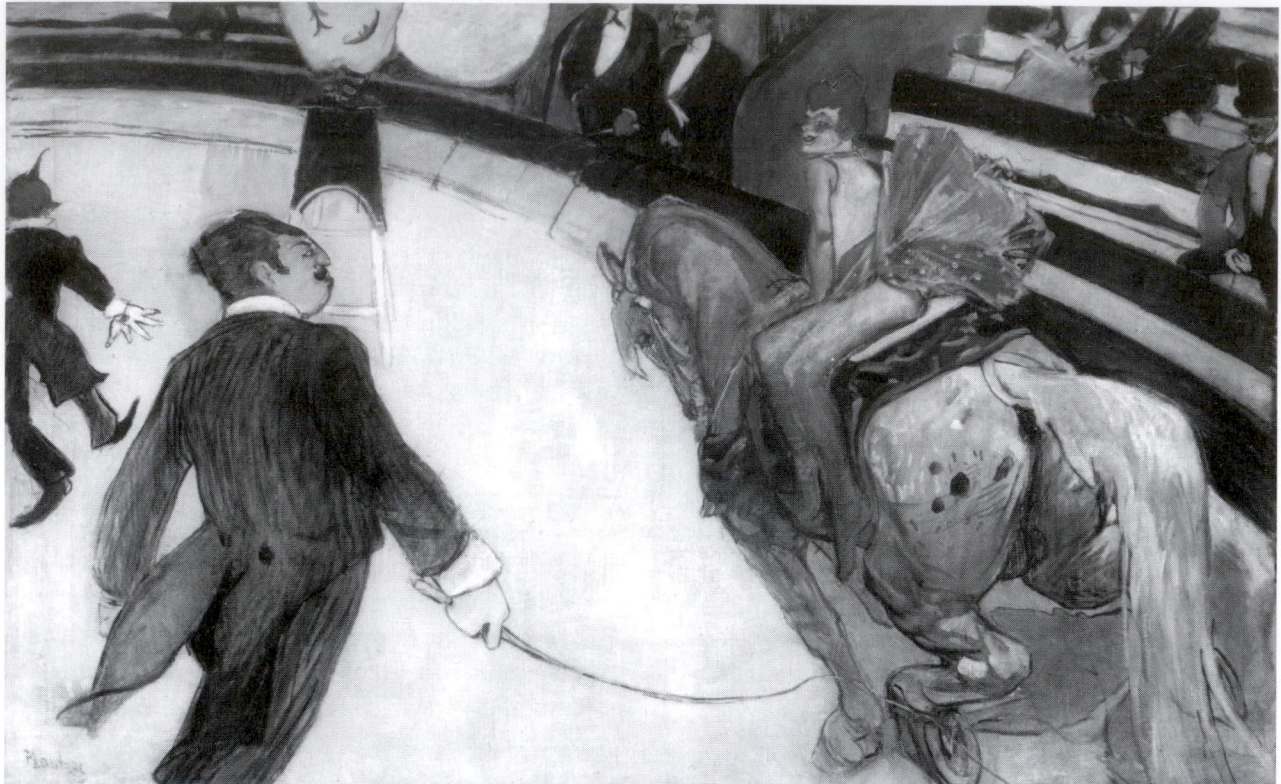

FIGURE 2 Henri de Toulouse-Lautrec, French, 1864–1901, Equestrienne (At the Circus Fernando), oil on canvas, 1887–1888, 100.3 × 161.3 cm, Joseph Winterbotham Collection, 1925.523. Photograph © 1998, The Art Institute of Chicago.

bler or acrobat engaged in gymnastics on a pole. The ink sketches look as though they were all executed in one sitting and demonstrate how well his pen kept up with his prolific imagination. These sorts of drawings are typical of the material from this period and show that he actively pursued visual ideas and schooled himself in drawing. Later in his artistic apprenticeship in Paris, he wrote to his mother that he sorely missed the more demanding artistic standards set by an earlier painting teacher (Bonnat). So even when it came to the drudgery of drawing from casts and nudes, Lautrec enjoyed the technical challenge demonstrating his delight in mastery.

3. Marching to the Beat of a Different Drummer

As a child and adolescent, Lautrec curbed whatever impulses he may have had to arrive at his own solutions to artistic problems. He was not consciously iconoclastic, although one of his fellow students in the Paris studio school noted that even his life studies tended to be more expressive and eccentric than was quite acceptable. However, it was not until he was on the threshold of maturity that his original artistic tendencies showed themselves.

Winner observed that in many instances gifted children do not go on to make significant contributions to the field in which they show such early promise. But, as we know. Lautrec's unusual childhood performance did bear fruit.

B. Three Continuities between Childhood and Adult Art

1. Rapid and Characterful Sketches

Lautrec's early drawings of animals sometimes suffer from an understandable lack of anatomical knowledge. But what they lack in this area they more than make up for in terms of emotional power. In his childhood and adolescent studies of animal expression and motion, Lautrec was developing skills that he was to use throughout his career. Some critics feel that above all, it is this capacity to identify the essential features of expression and gesture that makes Lautrec's images so memorable. Hughes says:

> He would not generalize; every figure acquires a specific energy, and each countenance is its own face, not merely a mask of passion or a symbol of social role. A little bareback rider's squinched up face above the massive churning crupper of a stallion in the Cirque Fernando, 1887–'88; the Cyrano nose and signature black gloves of Yvette Guilbert . . . these images live on as obdurately as the traits of Dickens' characters.

In fact, one can identify some of the sketches that Lautrec made in his schoolbooks and textbooks that prefigure the powerful renderings that were to come from his mature hand one or two decades later. Two examples illustrate this. On page 55 of a school notebook (dated 1875–1880), there is a sketch of a heavily muscled horse with an arched neck. In one of his first mature canvasses, *Le Cirque Fernando* (1888), we find the same horse (see Figure 2). The rear quarters are slightly below eye level, but we can still see the broad back and the equestrienne. Carefully observed anatomy and the characteristically low viewing angle are already present in the schoolboy sketch made 10 to 15 years earlier. Above all, Lautrec's energetic line is plainly there, defining both incarnations of the horse.

An equally compelling instance of the adult use of childhood experimentation with an expressive linear sketch can be found on page 552 of Lautrec's copy of his French Latin dictionary. There we find a drawing of a face made around 1878. The woman is rendered in a few sure lines and the portrait is noticeable for its closed eyes, wide cheekbones, thin lips, flaring nostrils, and high forehead. Her expression is supercilious. In Lautrec's lithograph of Yvette Guilbert, *Linger Longer Lou* (1898), we find a similar effect created by the same means: inflected lines that suggest thin lips, high cheekbones, closed eyes, and flared nostrils. In some of Lautrec's other studies of Yvette Guilbert we find the same blueprint, sketched in late childhood on the back page of his dictionary. It is as though

he learned how to construct a particular expression, which then became part of his stock in trade.

It is plain from an examination of Lautrec's juvenile sketches that his gift for telling characterization based on a masterful control of line was first developed as a schoolboy and that this capacity informed his adult work. It is worth noting that the relationship between Lautrec's childhood work and his mature oeuvre bears out Gardner's (1993) 10-year rule. Gardner's idea is that with many creative individuals it takes a decade between the emergence of a novel idea and its mature expression. This is certainly the case with the two examples cited.

2. A Strong Affinity for Narrative Illustration: Lautrec's Seminal Collaboration with Bruant

Another connection between childhood drawings and adult work is Lautrec's lifelong penchant for narrative and humorous commentary. From his earliest days, Lautrec was a student of the social scene and an inveterate satirist. Forced by circumstances to watch his able-bodied cousins play, he early developed the habit of observation. When he was convalescing at a health spa in the mountains, far away from his cousins, he amused his absent family by sending comic verbal and visual depictions of the hapless guests. A crisis in his uncle's vineyards became the occasion for an illustrated journal outlining the battle waged and won against the vine blight. At the age of 17 Lautrec collaborated with his schoolmate Etienne Devismes in illustrating a maudlin story about an old cavalry mare named Cocotte. Still later, in Paris, it was Lautrec's interest in illustration that led him into his first artistically productive (and commercial) collaboration with Aristide Bruant, cafe owner and balladeer.

Lautrec's affinity for illustration resulted in the development of important stylistic changes in his work. According to Murray (1991), Lautrec's first serious collaboration with Bruant the nightclub singer led the artist to find a visual approach that was for the first time identifiably his own. To create the illustrations, the artist studied popular newspaper drawings. These images supplied him with a repertoire of genre scenes, and some of these were to become Lautrec's stock-in-trade. Murray also suggests that the collaboration with Bruant had a strong influence not only on Lautrec's subject matter but also on the manner in which he chose to depict the singer's lurid stories. Bruant's musical delivery was harsh and unrefined. Some of the same coarseness is reflected in Lautrec's choice of cheap materials (cardboard) and his deliberate lack of technical polish. Thus, Lautrec's business association with Bruant was a truly formative relationship, resulting in his choice of what we now know as Lautrec's typical subject matter and the development of his typical visual treatment. As a result of Lautrec's working relationship with Bruant, his art began to move in the direction of what we, from our perspective, see as a proto-Modern aesthetic.

3. Emotional Distance from His Subject Matter

There is an important emotional continuity between Lautrec's childhood and adult work. This is the consistent psychic distance that he maintained between himself and his subjects. He was doubly distanced from his subjects. This double distance was due to his painful awareness of his physical deformity (something he despairs of in his letters to his family) as well as to his cherished identity as a nobleman. As a child he was fascinated by animals of all sorts. About 40% of the existing drawings that he rendered between the ages of 6 and 19 are of animals alone or of animals with people.) As an adult he was still "at the zoo," but this time he was a disabled nobleman looking at the underclass of Montmartre. It is no coincidence that a couple of critics have noted that Lautrec casts a telling but cold eye on his human subjects. Lautrec himself refers to his prostitute models lolling about "like animals."

It is probably due to his strong identification as an aristocrat that we look in vain to his studies of marginal people for a progressive social commentary. Some images are quite telling. For instance, the highly accomplished drawing of an African man dancing in a bar for the amusement of its clients (_Chocolate Dansant_) carries no special critique of racism. Similarly, in the Dreyfuss affair, Lautrec took no sides at all. And although he illustrated the work of Jewish authors, he had no qualms about contributing illustrations to antisemitic novels as well. Social issues per se did not interest him. What concerned him was solving the formal and technical problems of portraying the inhabitants of the demimonde. Lacking both an aesthetic and a social agenda, he was a voluptuary. If he had a grand project at all, it

was to be the engineer of his own psychological survival—and his art along with his gregarious activities was the principal means he used to achieve this end.

C. The Crucial Role of Emotional and Financial Support Offered by His Family

Theorists have written about the importance of the family as a support system for exceptionally able individuals. It is a common error to believe that genius will out, and that people with exceptional abilities do not need support or instruction. Quite the contrary—children with special abilities require the nurturance and intense support of parents and family. We can see the effect of such support in the case of Lautrec. Although his mother never had much appreciation for his art, she was a selfless and devoted parent. She took charge of his health problems and throughout his life made sure that Lautrec's material needs were supplied. Lautrec's father was another matter. Once it became clear that Henri would never ride to hounds nor look like a gentleman on or off a horse, Alphonse pretty much gave up on his son. There were periods during Lautrec's childhood that his father was not there for almost a year. On the other hand, the rest of the large family was close-knit and took delight in Lautrec's wit and imagination. This family became Lautrec's first audience. And it was the family (particularly his Uncle Charles) that encouraged him in his art.

However, the relationship between Lautrec and his family was by no means idyllic. Throughout his life, Lautrec was very dependent on his mother, and when she grew upset with his drinking and carousing, she abruptly left Paris without informing him. This sudden departure precipitated a psychological episode that ended with Lautrec briefly staying in an asylum. The incident reveals the difficulties that both mother and son experienced in dealing with each other. At the end of his days, Lautrec turned to his mother, who nursed him through his final illness.

Lautrec also may have considered commercial business to be a mark of independence. Even though there were no pressing financial reasons, Lautrec was fascinated by the idea of selling his work and of engaging in the _petit bourgeois_ activity of producing posters and illustrations for trade. The notion of their son as a tradesman must have been at least as unpleasant to his patrician family as the certain knowledge that he was awash in the fleshpots of Paris. But Lautrec pursued his business ventures in Paris, perhaps for several reasons. First, he was not getting anywhere in the academic art world. He did not achieve success in his academic art exams. Thus he was forced to seek another audience for his artwork. Second, the prospect of earning money must have been emblematic of a certain degree of independence. Last, it may have pleased him to tweak his patrician family's sensibilities by threatening to succeed as a businessman.

D. Lautrec's Persona as an Artist

In addition to refining a style and subject matter that was truly Modern in spirit and attack, Lautrec contributed another element to the attributes of the modern artist. He actively constructed a flamboyant private and public life. With his outrageous antics, his notorious drinking and dressing up, he contributed to the stereotype of the artist as a public figure, the bohemian and tormented genius. Like his father, Lautrec was flamboyant. As Frey (1994) points out, both father and son liked to show off (in French *S'afficher*). Lautrec was of course best known for his *affiches*—his posters. The son elaborated his marginality by stressing his physical deformity through wearing odd costumes and by deliberately associating in public with his very tall cousin. He behaved in ways that were calculated to shock and surprise the bourgeoisie (e.g., he spent months painting in a bordello). The prototypical Modern artist (and the Romantic artist before him) was always understood as an obsessed and intense person, one whose behavior was always close to the edge of—and sometimes beyond—the bounds of social convention. One critic has recently suggested that there is a strong parallel between Lautrec's artistic persona, with his entourage of Parisian followers and freeloaders, and the pop artist Andy Warhol's penchant for strikingly odd personal presentation and his retinue of camp followers.

E. The Impact of Class and Historical Setting

This article has already examined the factors that may have charged Lautrec's business venture with psy-

chological meaning. There is little doubt that Lautrec sought recognition from his peers, and when it was not forthcoming from the academic world (one of his studio teachers informed him that his drawings were "atrocious"), Lautrec turned to the world of commercial art. As we know, he achieved a high level of success in this setting, for his posters were so sought after that on some occasions Parisians would rip them down to keep as soon as they were displayed. At the same time that Lautrec was having his public successes, the structure of the French art establishment was changing. Standards for "good art" were in flux and artists organized themselves into alternative settings for the display and sale of work that met with official displeasure. The famous Salon de Refusees (an exhibition by artists of works that had been refused a showing in the French Academy) is an example of the avant-garde community taking matters into its own hands. But, during his lifetime, it was Lautrec's public work and his popular illustrations that helped establish his name. Yet the forces that were then eroding the power of the French academy contributed to the rise of artistic Modernism, and it was the ascendancy of this aesthetic paradigm that assured Lautrec of his immense influence.

III. SUMMARY

Several key features contributed to Lautrec's emergence as an artist of note: (a) his early and sustained fascination with a medium (drawing) for which he showed a precocious affinity; (b) a precocious capacity for close observation and rendering of animal movement and expression, which laid the groundwork for his studies of people; (c) the defining experience of being an intelligent and engaging child, who was often forced to observe the world from the sidelines (this sense of alienation was replaced in adulthood with a painful self-awareness of permanent physical abnormality and of aristocratic class identification); (d) a lifelong delight in entertaining others through dressing up and verbal and visual invention; (e) the emotional and financial support of family members (particularly his mother); (f) ambivalence toward his own family values (i.e., he identified strongly as a nobleman, but at the same time wanted to earn a living in bourgeois fashion as an artist); (g) a formal apprenticeship in the arts, starting with encouragement at the family level and culminating with study in two professional ateliers (this apprenticeship was not crowned with any recognition—his informal activity as a poster maker, illustrator, and frequenter of Montmartre bars was his true apprenticeship as this was the schooling that won him lasting fame; and (h) the luck to develop an unacademic representational style at time when the bastions of French academic art were crumbling.

Bibliography

Gardner, H. (1993). *Creating minds: An anatomy of creativity seen through the lives of Freud, Einstein, Picasso, Stravinsky, Eliot, Graham and Gandhi.* New York: Basic Books.

Gruber, H., & Davis, S. (1989). Inching our way up Mount Olympus: The evolving systems approach to creative thinking. In R. Sternberg (Ed.), *The nature of creativity: Contemporary psychological perspectives* (pp. 243–271). New York: Cambridge University Press.

Hughes, R. (1992). "Cutting Through the Myth," *Time,* March 9, p. 55.

Frey, J. (1994). *Toulouse-Lautrec, a Life.* New York: Viking Books.

Pariser, D. (1995). Lautrec—Gifted child artist and artistic monument: Connections between juvenile and mature work. In Claire Gollomb (Ed.), *The development of artistically gifted children, Selected case studies.* New Jersey: Lawrence Erlbaum Associates Inc. :31–71.

Murray, G. (1991). *Toulouse-Lautrec: The formative years, 1871–1891.* New York: Oxford University Press.

Winner, E. (1996). *Gifted children, Myths and realities.* New York: Basic Books.

Unconscious

Lloyd D. Noppe

University of Wisconsin, Green Bay

Cortical Arousal Level of brain activation, measured physiologically through brain waves, ranging from quiet and unfocused dreaminess to intense and sharp concentration.

Incubation A stage in the creative thinking process in which preliminary problems gestate for an unspecified period of time without conscious attention to their resolution.

Insight Often referred to as illumination or the "aha" experience, a stage in the creative thinking process, following incubation, in which previously unconscious connections become revealed to the conscious mind.

Intuition A vague and anticipatory feeling of an implicit solution to a creative problem that is based on a hunch supported by extensive knowledge and experience in a given domain.

Preconscious A level of arousal that lies between the conscious and the unconscious in which playful, analogical, and combinatory mechanisms function to aid creative thinking.

Primary Process The tendency, according to psychoanalytic theory, to satisfy sexual and aggressive tensions indirectly through imaginative, emotional, and irrational means.

Progression in the Service of the Ego A cognitive style process employed by creative thinkers to facilitate the conscious organization and communication of valued ideas.

Regression in the Service of the Ego A cognitive style processes employed by creative thinkers to delve into the unconscious and interrupt rational constraints on new ideas.

Secondary Process The tendency, according to psychoanalytic theory, to resolve instinctual tensions through the use of logical, realistic, and conscious mechanisms.

Sublimation In psychoanalytic theory, the unconscious displacement or redirection of sexual and aggressive drives into socially acceptable and creative activities.

*Beneath the surface of awareness there are mental processes that affect the flow of creative thought. The **UNCONSCIOUS** has long been believed to facilitate, along with conscious cognitive activity, an individual's creativity. This article examines accounts of the unconscious by creators, the psychoanalytic approach to creativity and the unconscious, critical reaction to such introspection, how similar terms are related to unconscious motivation, a physiological basis for the creative unconscious, and, finally, current cognitive perspectives on this topic.*

I. ANECDOTAL BACKGROUND

At least as far back as the tale of Archimedes in the bathtub, the emergence of a creative solution to a

Copyright © 1999 by Academic Press
All rights of reproduction in any form reserved.

problem, with less than fully conscious attention, has been the subject of both conjecture and awe. How was the ancient Greek scientist, by engaging in a very ordinary activity, able to determine the method for measuring the amount of gold in the king's crown through the displacement of water? Inspiration derived from unconscious sources is presumed to be a primary factor in achieving poetic success, creating an artistic legacy, producing musical compositions, and other inventive or creative accomplishments, as well as in resolving scientific conundrums. The unconscious wellsprings of creative activity are imbued with mystery, reverence, and even fear for their potential disappearance. Creators whose work may depend on a fragile coalition of characteristics and circumstances are wary that the muse may depart, that the guiding spirit or the divine inspiration will leave them barren. There is concern that what may not be easily grasped—the essence of their creative powers—which may not be obvious to conscious exploration, could be easily and inexplicably lost. Perhaps, the creative unconscious represents both to creators and to those who study them simply a summary of what is still beyond our grasp—a more complete analysis of what it means to be creative and how to best actualize the potential for producing creative work.

Accounts of how the unconscious contributes to creative achievement in various fields does not depend exclusively on stories dating back several milennia. Many examples range from the mathematican Poincaré's demonstration of Fuchsian functions, to the chemist Kekulé's discovery of the benzene ring, to Coleridge's poem about Kubla Khan, to Darwin's theory of evolution, to Mozart's musical melodies, to Gutenberg's invention of the printing press. In fact, the classic collection of firsthand reports published by Brewster Ghiselin in 1952 has been one of the most widely cited publications in the creativity literature. These and other descriptions often reveal a strong belief on the part of the creator that subconscious processes are quite involved in the path from dimly perceived to fully formed creative ideas.

The apparent automaticity in creative activity noted by Ghiselin, however, is not to be interpreted as antithetical to conscious processes but instead as a balancing factor that aids in loosening the normal constraints of reality:

[A]utomatic invention, far from being a sign of diminished, imperfectly functioning consciousness, is a healthy activity supplementary to conscious invention and in no way inconsistent with it. The automatic functioning in invention is, rather than an inferior or suspect substitute (or an exalted one), an extension of activity beyond the limited scope of that which is shaped by insight, the conscious activity, which is an observant adjustment of exactly appreciated means to known ends. Something beyond that fully observable conscious construction takes place, to the advantage of consciousness, or of the consciousness able to make use of it. (p. 17)

Examples of the interplay between conscious and unconscious factors from the reports of the creators in Ghiselin's volume include the musician Roger Sessions, who claimed that the composer "is not so much conscious of his ideas as possessed by them [and] often is unaware of his exact processes of thought till he is through with them" (p. 49); the sculptor Henry Moore, who stated that for the artist "the nonlogical, instinctive, subconscious part of the mind must play its part in his work, [but] he also has a conscious mind which is not inactive" (p. 73); and the poet Amy Lowell, who defined the need for "an extraordinarily sensitive and active subconscious personality, fed by, and feeding, a nonresistant consciousness" (p. 110).

II. FREUDIAN ROOTS

Comprehensive psychological elaboration of the relationship of creative thinking to unconscious processing was first explored in the work of Sigmund Freud. Based on his few retrospective studies of the lives of creators such as his 1910 analysis of Leonardo da Vinci, Freud attempted to explain creativity as motivated by the desire to maximize personal gratification. The essential concept that pertains to creativity from a psychoanalytic perspective suggests that the sublimation of tensions resulting from unconscious instinctual drives is responsible for all human progress. Furthermore, sexual and aggressive needs are expressed indirectly through a mechanism that Freud labeled as primary process thinking. In contrast to the more rational, logical, realistic, mature, and clearly conscious secondary process thinking, the primary process is imaginative, irrational, emotional, childlike, and uncontrolled. It is presumed that the creative individual is somehow able to employ primary process thinking to effectively thwart anxieties while engaging in culturally sanctioned behaviors (e.g., writing a song, producing a play, constructing a theory, or inventing a new machine).

Psychoanalytic theory cast a long and dominating shadow over 20th-century efforts to explain the nature of creative thought, particularly in the artistic and literary milieu where the residue of emotional conflict seems to be played out more directly in the works of fiction, composition, and painting. Personality qualities associated with the development of parent-child relationships, disguised by the defensive alterations of the unconscious or in the context of regressive and spontaneous activity, possibly interwoven with elements of neurotic or even psychotic behavior, served as a rich mine to be explored for creative ores. Freud was surely not alone in his approach to untangling the threads of creative motivation; however, his views had serious limitations which led Albert Rothenberg to conclude, in his 1990 treatise titled "Creativity and Madness," that Freud merely replaced "the Platonic idea of possession by an external factor . . . to a factor that is external to awareness [the unconscious]" (p. 50).

Although Rothenberg does not dismiss the value of unconscious influences on creative activity, he did point out that Freud's definition of the unconscious as a kind of repository for creative ideas contradicts the sine qua non of creativity—originality. Is it really possible to create something truly unique if the elements of the achievement already reside in the past, locked away in the unconscious until stimulated by anxiety or insanity? In addition, Rothenberg also questioned how the motivational power of the unconscious to direct creative behavior is commensurate with its distorting functions to alter thought so that it cannot be easily recognized by the conscious. Whatever benefits might be obtained by immersion into the emotional themes and flexible play with material in the unconscious, creative accomplishments ultimately require the unity, organization, and control that must be accessible to awareness.

The key legacy of psychoanalysis is that the distinguishing feature of all creative individuals is their mastery of the ability to utilize the primary process to the degree that ideas can be transformed into meaningful and communicable symbols. Freud himself acknowledged that he did not understand how this actually worked. Standard criticisms of psychoanalytic theory may illuminate why Freud was never able to complete his explication of the creative process. For example, retrospective accounts of creativity do not permit the researcher to actively examine the thoughts or behaviors of the creator. Secondly, the limited sampling and lack of empirical methodology makes generalization extremely difficult. Finally, the heavy emphasis on sexual and aggressive instincts appears to reduce the scope of application from creativity in diverse realms of human achievement.

III. NEOANALYTIC CONCEPTS

Movement away from the orthodox psychoanalytic view, emphasizing creative acts as a result of instinctual drives and the sublimation of anxieties, was fostered by the neoanalytic theorists who stressed the control of primary process thought and its adaptive connections with the secondary processes of the ego. In contrast to describing creativity as a defense mechanism or in terms of coping with frustration, the modifications of Freud's doctrine were to effectively reverse the transcendence of the id over the ego and to allow creative activity to attain a higher priority than sexual or aggressive instincts. The most significant conception forwarded by the neoanalytic tradition was regression in the service of the ego, detailed in 1952 by Ernst Kris. This process consisted of an oscillation between two phases, usually over a lengthy period of time. An inspiration phase involved the breakdown of rational barriers to allow the influence of external, varied ideas and images within the mind. Counterbalancing this process, Kris also postulated an elaboration phase in which the constraints of reality are meaningfully imposed to select and synthesize the critical themes of a problem.

The neoanalytic position engendered a shift from an essentially irrational, unconscious eruption of material controlling the creative process to a somewhat more cognitive approach in which creativity is shaped by reason and critical evaluation.

Lawrence Kubie, another psychoanalyst, suggested in his 1958 book that preconscious processes must mediate between the primary or unconscious level and the secondary or conscious level of thought. He stressed the adaptive and healthy aspect of creative thinking and believed that the playful, analogical, and combinatory mechanisms of the preconscious should not be "anchored either to the pedestrian realities of our conscious symbolic processes or to the rigid symbolic relations of the unconscious" (p. 141). Both Kubie and Kris share with Freud a basic tenet of the psychoanalytic perspective; that is, the source of creative inspiration is not readily accessible to awareness. Whether the emphasis is on the preconscious, a regression to the unconscious, or to the unconscious itself, neoanalytic theorists relegate creative drive to the nonconscious or subconscious realm. The question remains whether this psychoanalytic structural division of consciousness, including the conflict between primary and secondary processes, adequately accounts for the nature of creativity activity.

In his 1993 analysis of the myths associated with creative thinking, Robert Weisberg has suggested that there is little evidence to support any of the versions of psychoanalytic theory. He discounted both primary process thinking and the role of the unconscious as at all significant to creativity. Instead, he argued that creative production is the result of ordinary thought processes, augumented by particular abilities, specific areas of training, and high levels of motivation. Weisberg acknowledged that the neoanalytic approach involves a blend of primary and secondary process thought, but that the "emotionally laden, unconscious associations based on unsatisfied childhood needs are still assumed to be limited to primary process thinking" (p. 31). Thus, the legacy of Freud and his neoanalytic followers was an unfinished portrait of the relationship between affective and cognitive processes in creativity.

IV. INCUBATION, INSIGHT, AND INTUITION

The history of the unconscious in creative thinking is apparently linked to a variety of similar terms that all imply the lack of conscious attention as part of the process in which the creator is able to follow through a sequence from the germ of an idea to its more complete resolution. Three examples of this type of concept include incubation, insight, and intuition, all of which have been discussed widely as representative of the nonconscious components of creativity. Complicating the analysis of such terminology are related words—for instance, *insight* may often be referred to as *illumination*. Although some researchers continue to insist that all creative thinking is based on logical, ordinary, problem-solving processes, and that incubation, insight, and intuition are old myths, many contemporary theorists maintain support for these nonconscious contributions. In her 1996 chapter on affect and cognition, Sandra Russ presented a model that incorporates several elements of primary process thinking, such as adaptive regression and insight abilities, as facilitating factors in creative thought.

Perhaps the earliest well-developed conception of the notion of incubation in the understanding of creative thinking was postulated in 1926 by Graham Wallas. He articulated four stages—preparation, incubation, illumination, and verification—in what was described as a linear process of thought. During the incubation stage, the preliminary ideas of the preparation stage are allowed to gestate for an unspecified period of time while the problem is not pursued consciously. The culmination of the incubation process is the explosive stage of illumination, which is followed by the final, and more prosaic, verification stage. Although Wallas did not really discuss how the process of incubation worked, nor did he recognize the nonlinear possibilities of these stages, later metacognitive theorists, Bonnie Armbruster, for example, did review the self-analysis of several creative thinkers. She concluded in 1989 that "during the incubation stage the interconnected network of flexibly organized knowledge . . . is being restructured into new schemata" and that unconsciously "[c]reative individuals may have a superior metacognitive ability to separate the wheat from the chaff" (p. 179). [*See* INCUBATION.]

Illumination, or insight (the "aha" experience), is the moment when the previously unconscious connections become revealed to the conscious mind. Armbruster again stated that illumination is the "recognition of a mental representation that fulfills, or has the potential of fulfilling, the goal of the creative enterprise" (p. 180). The presumed spontaneity of insightful experiences in creative thinking is undoubtedly exaggerated, embellished by selective memory, frequently divorced from the context of the lengthy preparation leading up to it, and probably far rarer than popular reports would suggest. Nevertheless, the transitions from preparation to incubation to illumination in the creative process do reflect the notion of unconscious, and as of yet not fully identified factors, in the accomplishment of many extraordinary human creations. The concept of insight in problem solving dates back very clearly to the work in the 1930s of the Gestalt psychologists on resolving mental blocks and avoiding the pitfalls of repetitive and routine mental pathways. Yet the recent book titled *The Nature of Insight,* suggests that interest in this area has resurfaced. [*See* INSIGHT.]

Caught between the subconscious wanderings of the incubation stage and the momentary flash of insight or illumination is the sense of creative intuition. In her 1995 review of the intuition concept, Emma Policastro defined it as an implicit form of information processing in which vague and anticipatory perceptions orient and constrain the direction of a creative search. Intuition can be viewed as the unconscious bridge from incubation to insight, and the research team of neurobiologist Antonio Damasio provided evidence in 1997 that the intuitive hunches of people are nonconscious signals that "act as covert biases on the circuits that support processes of cognitive evaluation and reasoning" (p. 1294). Similarly, in his 1988 chance-configuration theory of creative thinking, Dean Keith Simonton suggested that the intuitive genius is characterized by "numerous infraconscious but behaviorally and emotionally active associations" (p. 46) that provide the opportunity for combining appropriate elements in new ways. It is evident that intuition is based on extensive experience and knowledge within a particular domain, somehow connected at a nonconscious level, and yet the explanation of this phenomenon still leaves many unanswered questions. [*See* INTUITION.]

V. BRAIN PHYSIOLOGY

Creative thinking is, of course, ultimately dependent on the functioning of the human brain, conscious or otherwise. Damasio was not the only neurobiologist to speculate about the unconscious as a legitimate realm for conducting scientific research, but he has very clearly postulated a brain mechanism that assists in the solving of problems through a covert examination and preselection of options of which only a few are presented for conscious evaluation. In his 1994 analysis of the fallacy of Cartesian dualism, Damasio cited the views of creative scientists who support the interconnection of reason and emotion. Although the goal of his work is not to discuss creativity per se, the reality of the unconscious is stressed: "It is as if we are possessed by a passion for reason, a drive that originates in the brain core, permeates other levels of the nervous system, and emerges as either feelings or nonconscious biases to guide decision making" (p. 245). It is important to recognize that Damasio is not maintaining that the unconscious is the source of problem solutions, merely that decisions are facilitated by the activation of multiple regions of the brain.

One of the more persistent beliefs in recent decades has been that creative thinking is predominantly a function of the right hemisphere of the brain. In contrast to the logical and conscious processing of the left hemisphere, the right brain is purported to specialize in the emotional and symbolic processing necessary for creativity. However, a number of empirical investigators have concluded that cooperation between both right and left hemispheres is characteristic of the brains of creative thinkers. There is little evidence to conclude that either the unconscious or the primary process be attributed to right hemisphere functioning while conscious and secondary process thinking be relegated to the left hemisphere. There is a common tendency to misconstrue levels of consciousness as particular regions of the brain rather than as a continuum of arousal. Referring to the unconscious as a particular brain structure reflects the 19th century biology that served as the basis for psychoanalytic theory. [*See* SPLIT BRAINS: INTERHEMISPHERIC EXCHANGE IN CREATIVITY.]

Reformulation of the role of the primary process in creative thought has been summarized as a state of defocused attention occuring during a period of relatively low cortical arousal. The connections among different ideas, represented by interneuronal associations, are at the heart of creativity. In states of low cortical arousal, the creator is able to shift easily his or her focus from one node (cluster of neurons) to another. The simultaneous activation of many nodes increases the probability that relationships among them will emerge. In higher states of cortical arousal, more intense focus is placed on a fairly limited number of nodes, decreasing the likelihood that connections will be achieved. Several studies have provided support for these differences in levels of arousal, particularly during the inspiration stage of the creative process. In addition, it has been suggested that creative individuals are more variable in their level of arousal than are uncreative people; perhaps a physiological rewording of the concept of regression in the service of the ego.

Low levels of arousal, whether in dreams, drug-induced states, or everyday reveries, do not necessarily lead to creative achievements with any greater certainty than do the primary process or regression mechanisms forwarded within the psychoanalytic perspective. Therefore, it is neither the amount nor the process of unconscious thought that distinguishes the creative person, but the depth of content related to their field that may better permit "automatic" integration of different ideas. Unconscious automaticity is apt to occur in any individual with respect to relatively trivial insights, whereas the most creative breakthroughs depend on a large repetoire of experience and knowledge that has been established through an extensive network of neuronal interconnections.

VI. CONTEMPORARY COGNITIVE MODELS

Parallel to developments in understanding brain physiology in recent decades has been the explosion of knowledge from cognitive and information processing researchers. It is no surprise that contemporary theorists have attempted to integrate the introspective reports and psychoanalytic processes presumed to be operable in the creative unconscious with the cognitive models that have typically addressed more logical and conscious elements of thought. Probably the earliest effort in this direction was the blind-variation and selective-retention model advocated by Donald Campbell in 1960. He drew an analogy between the evolutionary process of genetic mutation and the almost random combination of ideas that might fuse in the mind of the creative thinker. Dean Keith Simonton elaborated extensively on this approach in 1988 when he proposed his chance-configuration theory in which original work is dependent on a rich but flexible set of associa-

tive connections that provide the context for chance variations. He stated:

> In chance permutations, mental elements evoke other elements by such rare routes that any configuration so generated must be considered an essentially random confluence of psychical events. The appearance of unpredictability is reinforced by the fact that so many of the associative linkages operate at the infraconscious level, making it difficult to reconstruct cognitively the origin of chance configurations. (p. 48)

Previous dismissal of Freudian theory, including references to unobservable phenomena such as the unconscious, had led to isolation and rejection of neo-analytic theorists, resulting in the lack of cooperation in exploring complex notions like creativity. The resurgence of interest in revised perspectives on the unconscious is exemplified by a collection of eight articles on the topic in a 1992 issue of the *American Psychologist*. In the lead article, it was concluded that there is no longer any question about the existence of unconscious processes in human thought, but consensus about how such mechanisms operate has yet to be achieved. Although the current literature on unconscious cognition is much too voluminous to be reviewed here, much of the empirical support for this concept has been produced by John Kihlstrom and Anthony Greenwald. One conclusion reported by the latter in 1995 was that his evidence is consistent with a view of the unconscious that can be supported by the newer parallel distributed network interpretation of the traditional serial information-processing approach. In sum, there appears to be no inherent contradiction between contemporary cognitive research and a significant role for the unconscious in creative thinking.

Excellent illustrations of the renewal of interest by cognitive theorists in the unconscious are the books and edited works of Steven Smith, Thomas Ward, Ronald Finke, and colleagues. In their 1997 collection, titled *Creative Thought,* they defined the field of creative cognition as a "relatively new area of investigation that attempts to characterize creativity in terms of fundamental cognitive processes acting on previously stored knowledge" (p. 4). Chapters in their 1995 book, *The Creative Cognition Approach,* included George Mandler's discussion of the unconscious influences on creativity (particularly the "mind popping" that follows an incubation period), Kenneth Bowers and associates' analysis of the interplay of conscious and unconscious processes in the conceptualization of intuition, and Jonathan Schooler and Joseph Melcher's research, which indicates how the conscious verbalization of thoughts may inhibit the achievement of creative insights. In their other 1995 book, *Creativity and the Mind,* Ward, Finke, and Smith described incubation, intuition, and insight all in terms of the unconscious activation of a network of associations.

A somewhat different angle was suggested by Lloyd Noppe in 1996, drawing on the psychological differentiation theories of Heinz Werner and Herman Witkin, as well as the neo-Piagetian constructive operators model of Juan Pascual-Leone. This model incorporates the cognitive styles of fixity-mobility and field-dependence-independence in an affective-cognitive blending of the primary and secondary processes of regression and progression in the service of the ego. The strategies of creative thinkers are flexible enough to adapt to the demands of complex problems because they effectively balance the combination of executive processing skills with a rich collection of relevant experiences. Creators are systematic and analytic thinkers, but they are also amenable to a relaxed formation of impressions based, at first, on varied elements that may be disconnected and not fully formulated. Regression to unconscious levels of awareness, including sensitivity to the knowledge and issues of one's specific field of creativity, must be coupled with a corresponding progression through a rational and organized set of strategies for communicating the breakthrough.

Mihaly Csikszentmihalyi's 1996 analysis of his interviews with 91 creative individuals provided fresh documentation of the value of the unconscious. Although the methodological ambiguities of introspective self-reports of the creative process still apply, he found frequent reference by these creators to the notions of insight, intuition, and incubation. Csikszentmihalyi distinguished between the psychoanalytic conception of the unconscious, driven by the motivation to achieve resolution of hidden tensions, from cognitive accounts, which posit no predetermined direction, only the potential for attaining useful connections. He further pointed out that irrelevant connections would eventually dissipate, whereas the useful ones would emerge into consciousness. By focusing on the relationship between the conscious and the unconscious, Csikszentmihalyi described a difficult contradiction: "not to miss the message whispered by the unconscious and at the same time force it into a suitable form. The first requires openness, the second critical judgement" (pp. 263–264). If we are not cautious about spilling the water from the bathtub, we may end up throwing out Archimedes with it. Creativity does not flourish without submission to the unconscious components of thought.

Bibliography

Armbruster, B. B. (1989). Metacognition in creativity. In Glover, J. A., Ronning, R. R. & Reynolds, C. R. (Eds.) *Handbook of creativity.* New York: Plenum.

Csikszentmihalyi, M. (1996). *Creativity: Flow and the psychology of discovery and invention.* New York: HarperCollins.

Damasio, A. R. (1994). *Descartes' error: Emotion, reason, and the human brain.* New York: Grosset/Putnam Books.

Ghiselin, B. (1952). *The creative process.* Berkeley: University of California Press.

Kubie, L. S. (1958). *Neurotic distortion of the creative processes.* Lawrence: University of Kansas Press.

Martindale, C. (1990). *The clockwork muse: The predictability of artistic change.* New York: Basic Books.

Ochse, R. E. (1990). *Before the gates of excellence: The determinants of creative genuis.* Cambridge: Cambridge University Press.

Rothenberg, A. (1990). *Creativity and madness: New findings and old stereotypes.* Baltimore, MD: Johns Hopkins University Press.

Russ, S. W. (1993). *Affect and creativity: The role of affect and play in the creative process.* Hillsdale, NJ: Erlbaum.

Simonton, D. K. (1988). *Scientific genius: A psychology of science.* Cambridge: Cambridge University Press.

Smith, S. M., Ward, T. B., & Finke, R. A. (Eds.). (1995). *The creative cognition approach.* Cambridge, MA: Bradford Books.

Sternberg, R. J., & Davidson, J. E. (Eds.). (1995). *The nature of insight.* Cambridge, MA: Bradford Books.

Weisberg, R. W. (1993). *Creativity: Beyond the myth of genius.* New York: W. H. Freeman.

Vincent van Gogh

1853–1890

Artist/painter

Painted *Starry Night*

Richard Brower

Wagner College

VINCENT VAN GOGH *was an artist for 10 years, from 1880 to 1890. As a mature artist, he is known for his distinctive style of undulating lines and bold colors. During his mature phase he was capable of executing works in a rapid fashion, sometimes up to three a day spending less than an hour on each. He spent 9 years of deliberate repetition to evolve his competencies to a level where he could execute rapidly and automatically. In spite of his diverse ways of behaving, van Gogh possessed a remarkable unity of mind and spirit, as can be seen in the many letters—more than 700 of them—that he wrote over a period of 20 years.*

I. CHILDHOOD (1853–1876)

On March 30, 1852, Anna Cornelia Carbentus van Gogh, 33 years old, gave birth to her first child. It was stillborn. Christened Vincent Wilem van Gogh was buried in the graveyard of the local church. Exactly one year later, on March 30, 1853, she gave birth to a healthy male, and he too was named Vincent. As a schoolchild, the young Vincent walked past the local cemetery in which a gravestone bore his name and birthday. Vincent's father, Theodurus van Gogh, was a Protestant pastor at the village of Groot Zundert in

North Brabant in the south of Holland, near the Belgian border. Vincent van Gogh was the firstborn to Anna and Theodurus. They had five more children: Anna Cornelia, Theodorus, Elizabeth Huberta, Cornelis Vincent, and Wilhelmien Jacoba. During his adult years, Vincent would remain close to Wilhelmien, his youngest sister, and extremely close to his younger brother

Vincent van Gogh, self-portrait. Used with permission from Girandon/Art Resource, NY.

and staunch supporter, Theo. The collaboration between Theo and Vincent remains one of the most remarkable interactions in the history of art, and it is difficult to imagine Vincent's creativity without the support of, and feedback from, his younger brother.

Van Gogh came from a relatively unremarkable background. His ancestors had been art dealers, consuls, goldsmiths, preachers, and there had been a sculptor. Other than art dealership, Vincent's family showed no propensity for the type of creativity demonstrated in his work.

Johanna Bonger, Vincent van Gogh's sister-in-law, reported that, as a child, van Gogh had a difficult temper, was often troublesome, and was strongly self-willed. She noted he had a great love for animals and flowers and delighted in collecting things. There was, however, during his childhood, no indication that young Vincent was precocious nor had an unusual talent for art.

On August 1, 1866, van Gogh was apprenticed to a branch of the prominent Paris art dealers Goupil & Cie at The Hague. He was exposed to various works of art and, under the supervision of H. G. Tersteeg, assisted in the sale of paintings, photographs, engravings, lithographs, and reproductions. Van Gogh worked at this apprenticeship until he was fired in 1876 for conducting himself in a manner antithetical to the firm's interests; for one, he would commonly and inappropriately discuss the merits of the works of art with customers, and he frequently talked them out of sales.

II. SEARCHING (1876–1880)

From 1876 until 1880, when van Gogh was 23 to 27 years old, he engaged in multiple activities in the pursuit of a meaningful career. He was variously a teacher, a book dealer, and a minister.

Vincent van Gogh, at the age of 23, four years prior to his decision to become an artist, was an intelligent, enthusiastic book dealer working in Dordrecht, Holland. A fellow lodger wrote of him:

> He was a singular man with a singular appearance into the bargain. He was well made, and had reddish hair which stood up on end; his face was homely and covered with freckles, but changes and brightened wonderfully when he warmed into enthusiasm, which

happened often enough. Van Gogh proved laughter repeatedly by his attitude and behavior—for everything he did and thought and felt, and his way of living, was different from that of others of his age.

In May 1877 van Gogh left Dordecht and his job as a book vendor and went north within Holland to Amsterdam. There he refined his idea of working. Sensing that he was impulsive, he recognized that he needed to exercise patience and discipline and wrote to his brother:

> I have a lot of work to do and it is not very easy, but patience will help me through. I hope to remember the ivy "which stealth on though he wears no wings"; as the ivy creeps along the walls, so the pen must crawl over the paper.

He was referring to the writing he was required to do for his theological studies—he was preparing for an exam he needed to pass for entrance into a university.

Van Gogh outlined his intention to proceed with his theological studies in an ongoing, logical manner and expressed his belief that there were certain commonalities between studying religion and painting: "[G]oing on step by step . . . must lead to a good result. . . . But it takes time. . . . A great deal of study is needed for the work of men like father [a pastor] . . . just as for painting."

Van Gogh started as an artist late. During 1878 to 1880, while he had his job as a lay minister in Belgium, he sketched the miners who made up his congregation. At this time he wrote:

> I still can find no better definition of the word art than this, . . . art is man added to nature . . .—nature, reality, truth, but with a significance, a conception, a character, which the artist brings out in it, and to which he gives expression . . . which he disentangles, sets free and interprets.

He recognized in June 1879 that artistic development involves the conscious quest for novelty, and in this regard wrote, "the artist has put things in a new light . . . all things have become new."

In 1879, van Gogh secured a position as a lay minister with miners in Belgium. As was his custom, he threw himself into this job, giving away his belongings, living on bread and water, and taking sick miners into his own home. His church superiors reprimanded him for his excessive zeal and ultimately he was dismissed. While a minister, he sketched the miners, and it was after his dismissal that he went through a period of existential crisis during which he questioned the direction of his life's work. After several months of soul searching, the answer emerged clearly, and in June 1879 he noted in a letter to his brother Theo that an artist's vocation was a sublime, admirable one. Further, he wrote passionately of his intention to engage in a quest for a distinct style and his belief that a concept for a work precedes the execution of a work. Van Gogh worked as a lay minister with miners. They provided an image for him regarding positive character traits and productive ways of working: "[T]hey are intelligent and quick at their difficult work," he wrote in 1879, "brave and frank." (New York Graphic Society, Letter 129, originally April 1879). He saw his work proceeding by quick actions and slow progress, like the miners with whom he so obviously identified:

[T]hey are short but square-shouldered, with melancholy deep-set eyes. They are skillful at many things, and work terribly hard. They have a nervous temperament—I do not mean weak, but very sensitive. They have an innate, deep-rooted hatred and a strong mistrust of anyone who is domineering. With miners one must have a miner's character and temperament, and no pretentious pride or mastery, or one will never get along with them or gain their confidence.

It was during July 1880, at the age of 27, after being fired from his position as minister, that he wrote to Theo of his intention to become an artist. This begins a collaboration between Vincent and his brother that will last for 10 years until Vincent's death. Theo agreed to send Vincent a monthly allowance in exchange for his artworks.

III. GETTING STARTED (1879–1882)

During the summer of 1880, van Gogh experienced a philosophical and spiritual crisis, and after a period of intense rumination he decided to devote his life to being an artist. At the beginning of his tenure as an artist, he outlined his idea of art:

[A]rt is man added to nature . . . nature, reality, truth, but with a significance, a conception, a character, which the artist brings out in it, and to which he gives expression . . . which he disentangles, sets free and interprets.

In October of 1880 Vincent moved to Brussels to begin art studies; he read books on art and perspective and studied copies from prints, especially Millet. His decision to become an artist was preceded by certain ideas about work: that effective results require commitment and hard work, that to do something with fluency and ease one must spend a great amount of time in preparation, that the miner served as a metaphor for the quick execution of one's actions. Earlier, van Gogh tried executing his sketches in a quick manner. "I am sending you a hasty sketch," he wrote to his brother, "but I . . need to study the . . . masters."

His interest in hard work persisted, and on September 24, 1880, he wrote to Theo that "I am in a rage of work, though for the moment it does not produce very brilliant results." In the same letter he noted the best work is "conscientiously done, with the evident intention of portraying the truth without any straining after effect."

In September 1880, van Gogh wrote of a metaphor that was to guide his work over the succeeding several months: a weaver at a loom. The effective artist and weaver, according to van Gogh, both learned their craft so that the work could be executed unconsciously, with ease and at a cautious, steady, deliberate pace. He wrote, "with his dreamy air, somewhat absent-minded, almost a somnambulist—that is the weaver." During this time, van Gogh rendered more than 36 pictures of weavers at looms. He varied the positions and the lighting, each time seeking the best arrangement of forms.

During his seminal attempts at art in July 1880, van Gogh acknowledged the need to construct and reconstruct a product by first beginning with an initial sketch or rough draft, developing it into a more refined sketch, and again reforming it into a completed work. He wrote, "as the rough draft becomes a sketch, and the sketch becomes a picture—little by little, by working seriously on it, by pondering over the idea, vague at first, over the thought that was fleeting and passing till it gets fixed."

In 1881 he returned to his parents' home in Etten to join Theo and an artist friend Van Rappard. After a brief stay at Etten, he moved to The Hague in 1881 to study with his well-known artist cousin Anton Mauve. He set up his own studio at The Hague, and he met and lived with a reformed prostitute named Clasina Hoornik, nicknamed Sien by him, and her two children. During August of 1881, after concentrating for several months on drawing and multiple media (e.g., charcoal and watercolor), he tried his hand at oil painting for the first time. After some seminal attempts, he decided that his skills were too poorly developed for this demanding medium and returned to the basics, which meant drawing and related media.

During August 1882, he made a second attempt at oil painting after a year of drawing. Again he decided that he was not yet ready for the demands of painting, and he returned to drawing.

Van Gogh's early experimentations with oil painting led to a tube-squeezing insight—the realization that squeezing the paint directly from the tubes opened up possibilities for new effects. It happened when he was painting out-of-doors. He wrote to Theo:

> It struck me how sturdily those little stems were rooted in the ground. I began painting them with a brush, but the surface was so heavily covered, a brush stroke was lost in it—then I squeezed the roots and trunks in from the tube, and molded it a little with the brush. Yes—now they stand there rising from the ground, strongly rooted to it.

As important as the tube-squeezing insight is to van Gogh's mature style, he elected to shelve it, along with all efforts at oil painting, and focused his efforts on drawing and related media, such as pencil drawing and lithography. He believed that oil painting was the most demanding of all media, and to do justice to its demands he believed that he needed to develop his skills for other tasks, such as drawing. "Drawing is the backbone of painting" he was fond of saying. He realized the tube-squeezing insight was valuable. But he had no overall mental structure for style to which it could be adapted. Put aside temporarily, he reactivated it when

other mental structures evolved to more complex levels that were able to accommodate the innovative tube-squeezing insight. The tube-squeezing insight foremost demonstrates that van Gogh's creativity was a combination of long periods of planful work along with spontaneous play and chance events.

Van Gogh went to The Hague, Holland, in December 1881 and left in September 1883. During this 20-month period he wrote approximately one-quarter of his total letters, he redefined his ideas about models, he clarified his notions of love through his romance with Clasina Hoornik, and he rendered a total of 357 existing works, done in multiple media, including pencil, charcoal, chalk, ink, lithography, watercolor, and oil; only 7% of this output was oil painting.

Drawing dominated van Gogh's activities during the first two years of his tenure as an artist. In August 1882 he wrote, "But I have attached great value to drawing and will continue to, because it is the backbone of painting, the skeleton that supports all the rest." He did not address painting seriously until his third and fourth years as an artist; he was very planful to ensure that his drawing skills were acceptable to him before he undertook his adventures at oil painting. He mentioned that "before I began to paint, I had been drawing so much and studied perspective in order to build up the composition of the thing I saw."

When van Gogh began his activities as an artist in 1880, he brought to that experience a wide range of knowledge from previous enterprises, such as knowledge of literature, religion, and teaching. Once firmly committed to art, he subdivided that enterprise into various tasks and purposes, a notion he addressed in the following passage written during October 1884:

> I have bought a very beautiful book on anatomy, *Anatomy for Artists* by John Marshall. . . . I have also what they use at l'Ecole des Beaux-Arts, and what they use in Antwerp. . . . The key to many things is the thorough knowledge of the human body. . . . Besides, I am quite sure that color, that chiaroscuro, that perspective, that tone and that drawing, in short, everything has fixed laws which one must and can study, like chemistry or algebra. This is far from being the easiest view of things, and one who says, "Oh, one must know it all instinctively," takes it very easy indeed. If that were enough! But it isn't enough, for even

if one knows ever so much by instinct, that is just reason to try so hard to pass from instinct to reason.

Van Gogh was addressing multiple issues and multiple activities. Not all of the ideas expressed, such as approaching art like an algebraic equation, were used by him later in the form found here. But leading himself down certain pathways, from which he may retreated or abandoned completely, served a constructive function of having a pattern to reconstruct in his own manner. An initial pattern for reconstruction was provided during this early phase of development by his adoption of classical placements and poses of models resulting from academic influences, from the Holland experiences, and art instruction books.

After 20 months at The Hague, van Gogh decided to move to Drenthe, north within Holland. He left The Hague with vastly improved skills and greatly refined ideas about his working and during his last summer there he noted, "Last year I repeatedly tried to paint figure studies, but the way they turned out made me desperate. . . . [N]ow there is nothing that keeps me from carrying it out, because drawing comes so much more easily to me than last year."

He left The Hague a much better and more confident artist, but still recognized that he had a long way to go to develop an individualized style. "I know that I'll have to make many studies," he told his brother Theo, "therefore a great deal of painting must be done this year, and then there will come more light."

IV. VAN GOGH THE PAINTER (1883–1888)

Experimenting with the interaction between oil and various media was an early preoccupation for van Gogh because he wanted to test the waters. His plan was to eventually tackle and conquer the demanding medium of oil painting on canvas and toward this end he wanted to develop a finely tuned skill for understanding the properties and attributes of oil interacting with other substances. This strategy as part of his overall plan did not go wasted.

Ever looking for the unusual interaction of materials and media, during the spring of 1883, van Gogh rendered a group of drawings that involved the experimentation of the interaction between printer's ink and various media. In regard to this he wrote:

> But now about the drawings. I have done a few with printer's ink, and this week I made some experiments in mixing that printer's ink with white. I found out that it can be mixed in two ways—that is, with the white from the tubes of oil paint and, probably even better, with the ordinary powder zinc with white which can be obtained at any drugstore; it must be diluted with turpentine, which doesn't soak into this paper or cause spots on the black like oil does, because it dries quickly and disappears. One gets much stronger effects working with printer's ink than ordinary ink.

Some of van Gogh's ideas regarding experimentation came from other artists. During May 1882 he wrote, "One can do great things with charcoal soaked in oil, I have seen Weissenbruch do it; the oil fixes the charcoal and at the same time the black becomes warmer and deeper."

In September 1883 van Gogh decided to leave The Hague and go to Drenthe, in northern Holland, for a new "field of action," in his words. He and Sien decided to break up. She returned to prostitution and several years later committed suicide. The breakup caused van Gogh considerable pain, and at Drenthe he wrote, "I often think with melancholy of the woman."

Although his best-known works are paintings, van Gogh proclaimed in June 1883 his early experimentation with charcoal and ink: "[M]y dislike for working with charcoal is disappearing more every day. One reason for this is that I have found a way to fix the charcoal and then work it, for instance, with printer's ink."

Van Gogh engaged in a process of associating and consolidating previously unrelated elements and synthesizing them into a broad, purposeful plan. Van Gogh's broad plan throughout his production was to construct an effective artistic style, based on a notion of action and undulation. He wrote, "I tried to put sentiment into the landscape, and to convey the convulsive, passionate clinging . . . yet . . . half torn quality of the tree, to capture the struggle for life, to faithful to nature."

Van Gogh very strongly believed that a skill for

drawing must be established before advancing to painting. Further, while drawing, he kept in mind the use of drawing as a springboard for skilled painting. In the same letter he wrote, "Though *The Roots* is only a pencil drawing, I have brushed it in with lead pencil and scrapped it off again, as would if I were painting." Scraping a pencil drawing functioned as a cognitive strategy to bridge the skills of drawing and painting. Scraping an oil painting is a method of revision; the artist removes parts that are unsatisfactorily rendered.

One method of revision employed by van Gogh was scraping-and-repainting. In the following passage he describes how he scraped off areas of paint when he was dissatisfied with an effect. He would then repaint the area and, if still not satisfied, scrape and repaint until his intention as achieved. Over time, van Gogh became extremely competent at examining, analyzing, criticizing, and revising his efforts; this is the type of thinking we can call "self-regulation." He established a finely tuned sense of which efforts were poor and which were excellent.

> If I have now painted so many studies in a short time, it is because I work hard, literally working all day, scarcely taking time even to eat or drink. There are little figures in several of the studies. I also worked on a large one and have scraped it off twice, which you perhaps have thought too rash if you had seen the effect; but it was not impatience, it was because I feel I can do better by grinding and trying, and I absolutely want to succeed in doing better, however much time, however much trouble it may cost.

Revision was important to the van Gogh's creative process. He utilized other types of revision in addition to painting-scraping-repainting. Not only would he alter an individual work in an effort to improve its structure, but he would revise a concept by rendering a series of works. His group of sunflower paintings provides an example. He began by painting solitary flowers; then, work by work, introduced two, then three, and so on, until he worked his way toward the magnificent bouquets well known to the public. Revision, thus, is an important aspect of creativity. Effective creators are adept at generating seminal ideas and evolving them into coherent systems.

Van Gogh's use of his studio was an important aspect of his working. He would sketch his subject matter on location, making note of the source of lighting. He wrote, "I enclose a little sketch which I made in the soup kitchen. They sell the soup in a large passage where the light falls from above, through a door to the right."

He would take his initial sketch and use it as a guide to set up the same scene in his studio, positioning models and, by a careful manipulation of the light coming in through the windows (covering some of the windows with curtains), re-create the original scene that was recalled from the sketch. Sketching on location has its advantages and disadvantages. One disadvantage is that the scene is fleeting; people are moving about, and, for the artist, getting accurate details is difficult. A re-creation of the scene in his studio, based on the initial sketch, allowed van Gogh the luxury of attention to details and to careful drawing that was difficult to achieve on location. Further, as can be seen in the following passage, van Gogh drew a backdrop to his models in the studio based on his on-location sketch. He set up the scene in his studio much like a stage manager would arrange the props and actors for a play. He wrote:

> Now I tried to find that same effect in the studio. In the background I put a white screen, and on that I drew the hatch, according to its real position and measurements; I closed the farthest window at the bottom, so that the light falls from P, exactly as in the place itself.

The *P* he refers to is a spot from which the light fell on his models in the studio, replicating the source of light in the original scene. His studio was a transitional arena for him to mediate the source of inspiration and the final work. He added, "You see, when I have the models posing there, I get exactly the same effect as in the real soup kitchen."

Van Gogh consistently made a distinction between *sketches* and *drawings*. A sketch was spontaneous, incomplete, the starting point for further work; a drawing was a finished product. Recreating scenes in his studio allowed him the opportunity to evolve an initial sketch from an ill-defined, seminal idea to a completed drawing. He wrote to Theo, "[T]omorrow I'll have the house filled of people . . . from the neighborhood, and . . . these persons . . . will pose for the drawing of which this is the first rough sketch."

Typical of his attitude toward working with multiple media and executing rapidly during his period at The Hague is the ideas expressed in the following passage, written to his brother Theo during February 1883:

> But I shall have to put up with many more failures, for I believe that in water color much depends on a great dexterity and quickness of touch. One must work in it before it is dry to get harmony, and one hasn't much time for reflection then. So the principal thing is not finishing each one separately, no, one must put down those twenty or thirty heads rapidly, one after the other. Here follow a few curious sayings about water colors: "L'aquarelle est quelque chose de diabolique"; and the other is by Whistler, who said, "Yes, I did that in two hours, but I studied for years to be able to accomplish this in two hours."

This passage highlights several characteristics about van Gogh's ideas for working at that time, 1883. First, he was heavily influenced by James Abbott McNeil Whistler's notion that rapid execution required years of preparation: "Yes, I did that in two hours, but I studied for years to be able to accomplish this in two hours." Whistler, in the mid 1800s, took the well-known art critic John Ruskin to court. Ruskin had accused Whistler of "flinging a pot of paint into the public's face," meaning that the artist had quickly dashed off his works and was trying to pass them off as serious works of art. Whistler, on the stand, pointed out to the court that although he executed the works in a spontaneous, quickly brushed manner, he spent a long time in preexecution training. Van Gogh was very impressed by Whistler's notion that the appearance of spontaneity in art requires arduous preparation. Second, van Gogh was unafraid of failure and of taking risks—and actually thought that failure was necessary as a source of growth. Van Gogh felt that in order to learn, one fails, and then he exclaimed, "Forward—and what the devil do I care if I fail—if I fail, then I'll try again." Third, van Gogh expressed the belief that reflection is most effective when it precedes and follows a work. An artist needs to consider what is going to be done, but also needs to consider what *has* been done so he can decide what to do next. For van Gogh, each work in a group

(such as the 36 weavers) provided inspiration and correction for the next. Fourth, van Gogh believed that a rapidly executed work (based on careful preparation) was aesthetically more expressive and pleasing than one that was not.

Vincent van Gogh loved experimentation. In his quest for a novel artistic style, for example, he used lithographic crayon to do drawings, a use that this type of greasy crayon was not specifically designed for, and he included bread crumbs into the drawings to experiment with various values of tone. As he related to his brother:

> I wrote to Rappard about the crayon yesterday, because I had to write him about various things concerning lithography; and as I wanted to send him a few sketches done with it, I used it for some drawings of our baby, in different positions, and I found it is very well suited to sketching, too. One can bring in demitones by means of bread crumbs.

Van Gogh left The Hague in September 1883 and arrived in Paris 2½ years later. In between he stayed at Drenthe (September to November 1883), Nuenen (December 1883 to November 1885), and Antwerp (November 1885 to February 1886).

During this time he continued working by the principles and ideas established at The Hague, and the culminating work of this period was his monumental *Potato Eaters,* the depiction of peasants sitting about a table having dinner, for which he executed more than 150 studies of heads before rendering the final painting.

Van Gogh moved to Paris to live with his brother Theo in March 1886. Since he was living with his brother, he had no need to write, hence, there is little correspondence during this 2-year period.

V. MATURITY AS AN ARTIST (1888–1890)

Van Gogh decided in 1888 to leave Paris and go to Arles, a small, picturesque town in the south of France, to discover, in his words, "a new light." During his stay at Arles, from February 1888 to May 1889, van Gogh achieved full maturity as an artist and established his own individualized style. He also spent a 2-month period sharing housing and collaborating with Paul Gauguin. During this time, he had the first of seven "attacks" of mental illness during which he severed an artery in his ear; he did not cut off his ear as some people have incorrectly described the famous incident.

More than ever he accelerated his efforts and intentions to work quickly, execute rapidly, and at the same time render effective figures. Van Gogh was ever the one to isolate problems of execution and then work on them tirelessly until he arrived at a solution. He wrote:

> Oh! someday I must manage to do a figure in a few strokes. That will keep me busy all winter. Once I can do that, I shall be able to do people strolling on the boulevards, in the street, and heaps of new subjects. While I have been writing this letter I have drawn about a dozen. I am on the track of it, but it is very complicated because what I am after is that in a few strokes the figure of a man, a woman, a child, a horse, a dog, shall have a head, a body, legs, all in the right proportion.

By 1888 van Gogh had progressed to the point that he would execute a painting in one sitting. "More than once," he wrote, "I have done a size 30 canvas in one day, but then I did not stir from the spot from morning till sunset except to eat a morsel."

Van Gogh worked rapidly, and when his efforts did not please him he would scrape off and repaint sections. In addition, he would add finishing touches, when appropriate, after a painting would dry. Van Gogh worked rapidly and revised by scraping and adding details after drying. A close look at *Starry Night* (at The Museum of Modern Art in New York City) reveals that some of the stars in the sky were painted as part of the original conception and that some were added after the painting had dried. Similarly, if you examine *Pipe with Chair* (executed at Arles), it is evident that the pipe and other details were added after the painting dried.

During September 1888, at Arles, France, van Gogh was faced with a specific problem in regard to painting at night. He was inspired by the contrasting colors, the quality of light, and the overhanging sky with its many glistening stars of a nearby outdoor cafe. Although the subject was well lit and easy to see, the canvas on which he wished to paint was not, and he had difficulty

mixing paints and seeing his palette. He overcame the problem by experimenting with a wide-brimmed hat that had candles secured on it in various positions. What a sight he must have made to the residents of the small town of Arles! Surely, they thought him eccentric at best, and when in December of 1888 he had the first of several epileptic seizures and mutilated his ear, the candle-donning behavior could have added to their notion that he was insane and may have led to their subsequent efforts to encourage him to leave the town. Among their reactions to him after the infamous ear-slicing incident were a petition circulated requesting that he leave and sporadic incidents of the local children taunting him at his window.

Van Gogh closed out the final 14 months of his life at two towns in France, St. Remy (in a mental institution being treated for seizures) and Auvers-sur-Oise. During periods of mental dysfunction, he did not create. In between attacks, he continued developing the ideas about creating he had previously set in motion. In this regard he wrote:

> My work is going very well, I am finding the thing that I have sought in vain for years, and feeling this, I am always thinking of that saying of Delacroix's that you know, namely that he discovered painting when he no longer had any breath or teeth left.

At this point, his powers of rapid execution were refined so that he could quickly execute a rendition of a work by Delacroix in his own individualized style. He wrote, "[I]f you could see me working, my brain so clear and my fingers so sure that I have drawn that *Pieta* by Delacroix without taking a single measurement."

The miner had been, and remained, a stabilizing metaphor for his working style, and he saw himself "like a miner who is always in danger makes haste in what he does."

Van Gogh continued to work purposefully, valiantly between epileptic attacks. In May of 1889, shortly after a psychotic episode, he wrote, "At present all goes well, the whole horrible attack has disappeared like a thunderstorm." He added his observation that his ability to render art firmly and quickly was improving: "I am working to give a last stroke of the brush here with calm and steady enthusiasm."

If there is any doubt that van Gogh was purposeful

regarding his art can be dispelled, I would suggest by his description of his paintings of flowers, writing during May 1889:

> I am doing a canvas of roses with a light green background and two canvases representing big bunches of violet irises, one lot against a pink background in which the effect is soft and harmonious because of the combination of greens, pinks, violets. On the other hand, the other violet bunch (ranging from carmine to pure Prussian blue) stands out against a startling citron background, with other yellow tones in the vase and the stand on which it rests, so it is an effect of tremendously disparate complementaries, which strengthen each other by their juxtaposition.

Van Gogh continued to paint right up until the end. "I have painted . . . vast fields of wheat under troubled skies," he wrote in the summer of 1890, "and I did not need to go out of my way to express sadness and extreme loneliness."

"Well," he stated in his last letter, found unfinished on his person when he shot himself, "the truth is, we can only make our pictures speak." And speak they did and do to countless people of all nations and languages. Van Gogh never wavered from his intention to establish a new visual vocabulary for the expression of universal emotions.

During his adult years, van Gogh wrote copious letters. Most were to his brother Theo, who retained the great majority of them. Conversely, and unfortunately, Vincent did *not* retain the letters sent to him by Theo, so we have essentially a one-way correspondence.

One of the reasons van Gogh's letters are powerful is that they are pure "thinking aloud" materials. He carried paper with him and jotted down his thoughts while he was creating. His writings are not distorted by the passage of time and the haziness of memory that attends it.

Van Gogh wrote many letters to his brother Theo, and to other friends and collaborators. The letters give a firm picture of van Gogh's thinking during critical phases of creativity. They also supply us with a profile

Van Gogh Chronology

1853–1870: Childhood in Holland; firstborn of six children.
1870–1880: Various jobs, including art dealer, lay minister, schoolteacher, book seller.
1880: Makes decision to devote his life to becoming an artist.
1880–1883: Early development as an artist, devotes this period solely to drawing; lives at The Hague and learns from his teacher Anton Mauve.
1883–1886: Moves back with parents at Nuenen; culmination of Dutch period.
1886–1888: Goes to Paris; encounters the Impressionists and palette enlivens; lives rest of his life in France.
1888–1889: Lives at Arles in south of France; collaborates with Gauguin; first attack of mental disturbance (the infamous ear-slicing episode in December 1888).
1889–1890: Voluntarily stays at St. Remy, a mental hospital.
1890: Stays at Auvers; treated by Dr. Gachet; suicide.

of the shifting quality of his moods and of the quality of his emotions toward significant persons, places, and activities. Quotes from his letters were utilized in this work to demonstrate the rich world of emotional and cognitive states he experienced and to show that his ideas provided the basis to produce art.

In his letters, van Gogh reveals the gentleness, love of humanity, and clarity of thought about his art that he maintained throughout his creative process—properties of his personality that are not so apparent in the sensationalistically magnified actions of his brief psychotic behavior.

Bibliography

Hulsker, J. (1984). *The complete van Gogh.* New York: Harrison House.
New York Graphic Society. (1978). *The complete letters of Vincent van Gogh* (Vols. 1–3). Boston: Little, Brown & Co.
Stone, I. (1963). *Lust for life.* New York: Pocket Books. (Original work published 1937)
Treble, R. (1975). *Van Gogh and his art.* New York: Galahad Books.
Winner, E. (1982). *Invented worlds.* Cambridge, MA: Harvard University Press.

Lev Semenovich Vygotsky

1896–1934

Psychologist

Author of *Cultural-Historical Theory of Human Development*

Natalia Gajdamaschko

The University of Georgia, Athens

LEV SEMENOVICH VYGOTSKY has become famous in the scientific world as the creator of the cultural-historical theory of psychology. Born at the end of last century into a Jewish family living in one of the provincial towns of the Russian empire, he is thought by many to be one of the major figures in 20th century psychology. Among L. Vygotsky's major works available in English are Thinking and Speech *(published in 1934; published first in the United States in 1962 as* Thought and Language*),* Tools and Symbols in Child Development *(written in 1930, published first in English in 1978, and in Russia at the end of the 1980s), and* The History of the Development of Higher Psychological Functions *(published in the 1960s). He also wrote a series of articles dealing separately with the development of creativity in childhood and adolescence.*

I. BACKGROUND

Lev Semenovich Vygotsky was born in the town of Orsha, Vytebskaya oblast' (former Mogilev guberniya) in Byelorussia on November 5, 1896 (old calendar style). In 1897 his family moved to the city of Gomel, where Lev Vygotsky spent his childhood and his school

years. Orhsa and Gomel were towns inside of the Pale, a few provinces where Jews were allowed to stay permanently in the Russian Empire. Lev returned to

Lev Semenovich Vygotsky

Gomel after finishing his university education in Moscow in 1917 and stayed there until January 1924.

Vygotsky's early interest in humanities and art was influenced by his family, one of the best educated in town. His father, Semen L'vovich Vygotsky (1896–1931), had graduated from the Commerce Institute in Kharkiv and worked as a banker. A very respected man in the Gomel community, he devoted a lot of time organizing activities in different service organizations, including an educational association that created one of the best public libraries in the city. Family history, recorded by Lev Vygotsky's daughter, Gita Vygodskaya, stresses that the personality of Lev's father was not easy to deal with—he was often stern, but this did not prevent him from being a loving father.

The heart and soul of the family was Cecilia, Lev's mother. At home she upheld an atmosphere of love and care. She was well educated and, like her husband, fluent in several languages. By training, she was a teacher, but she never got a chance to work in school; her whole life was dedicated to raising her eight children and running the household. Lev was the second child in the family.

Lev received his elementary education at home, studying independently and having a tutor for consultation. He passed an exam for the first 5 years of elementary school and entered into a private all-boys secondary school. Lev was a very good student in all subjects, and teachers often commented on his gifted abilities. His favorite subjects were literature and philosophy, both objects of his youthful fascination and involvement. In 1913 Lev graduated with a gold medal from the gymnasium, a secondary school in prerevolutionary Russia that prepared students for the university. With his honored diploma he could have been accepted by any university to study philology, his favorite subject, but for a Jew in prerevolutionary Russia such a course of study would not have been very practical: philology graduates became, in most cases, teachers in public schools, a position not available for Jews. Lev's parents advised him to become a doctor because this would allow him to live outside of the Pale.

Lev was admitted to medical school at Moscow University, but a month later he realized how distant medicine was from his true interests, and he transferred to the law school at the same university. This school opened the way for a career as a lawyer, which would

have allowed him to live outside the boundaries of the Jewish settlements. But his deep interest in the problems of literature, art criticism, philosophy, and the philosophical analyses of art led him, in 1914, without interrupting his education at the law school, to enroll in the Historical-Philosophical Department of Shanyavsky's University. Soon after, however, he become interested in psychology, and he combined his training in law, literature, and history with psychology.

Vygotsky's first publications, written during his student years and recently discovered by his daughter, were devoted to the problems of literary criticism. His student graduation paper "The Tragedy of Hamlet, Prince of Dutch, W. Shakespeare" had an unusual history. It was published 52 years after he wrote it and gained a reputation nationally and internationally as one of the most original and unique analyses of *Hamlet*. Few student graduation papers receive serious attention from the international academic community more than 50 years after they were written.

In 1917, after graduating from both universities, Lev Vygotsky returned to his family in Gomel. According to his daughter and biographer, Gita Vygodskaya (1996), the seven years that Lev Vygotsky spent in Gomel before moving to Moscow were important in his professional and personal development. The time after the Great October Socialist Revolution (1917) and the civil war that followed were very difficult for Lev Semenovich's family, which suffered diseases and the death of two of Vygotsky's brothers. Nevertheless, during this time, Vygotsky was active in teaching in the pedagogical college, managing a theater, and publishing his own journal of literary criticism. Most important, he conducted scientific studies of the psychology of art and the psychology of education, which resulted in his first famous books *The Psychology of Art,* which was written in 1925 but first published in 1965, and *Pedagogical Psychology,* which was published in 1926 then "arrested" (withdrawn from libraries and destroyed) and forbidden for more than 60 years. This book was republished only at the end of the 1980s.

After a very impressive presentation at the Second Psychoneurological Congress in Leningrad in 1924, Lev Vygotsky received an invitation to join the Moscow Institute of Psychology. He accepted the invitation.

During the next 10 years of Lev Vygotsky's career, he built a new psychology, a new approach to the study of human development, and a powerful school of thought. He did all this as a Russian intellectual who was actively involved in building *Soviet psychology,* an effort to revise and reform psychology along Marxist lines and to build a new, objective materialistic psychology. The new Soviet psychology was challenged to address the practical needs of a new regime to form new educational, clinical, and academic systems.

Vygotsky together with his closest friends and colleagues, Alexander Romanovich Luria and Aleksei Nikolaevich Leont'ev, started this enterprise at the time when nobody knew how to build a "new psychology." Vygotsky began by analyzing what he believed to be a "crisis of contemporary psychology." He was very ill and in hospital at the time he wrote a book *The Historical Meaning of the Crisis in Psychology* (this book was finished in 1927 but was not published until 1982). At that time, psychology was divided into different scientific schools. While analyzing the theoretical differences of these schools, Vygotsky concluded that, in reality, two camps existed in psychology. One camp was *objective* psychology, built on the principles of natural sciences. I. M. Sechenov and Ivan Pavlov, and their studies of reflexes, were among the most famous representatives of this camp. The second camp was phenomenological, idealistic, *subjective* psychology. Vygotsky's attempts to unite the contradictory objective and subjective fields resulted in the creation of the cultural-historical theory of human development. From 1924 to 1934 Vygotsky had more than 270 published articles, monographs, and books.

Ironically and tragically, the rise of Stalin's political regime resulted in closer, potentially dangerous scrutiny of Lev Vygotsky and his colleagues as they worked enthusiastically to build a new Marxist psychology. They tried to save their activities by moving from Moscow to Kharkiv (Ukraine), where their situation was not so politicized. Vygotsky spent much of his last 7 years in trains traveling from Moscow to Kharkiv to Leningrad. During this time he worked intensively, knowing that he was terminally ill with tuberculosis.

Vygotsky died prematurely in 1934 at the age of 37. His death spared him from the suffering inflicted on other leading intellectuals by the Stalin regime. His likely fate, if he had lived longer, is indicated by the treatment of his research. His work was banned in the Soviet Union and was preserved only as oral history by his family, colleagues, and friends until it was rehabilitated in 1956.

Despite Stalin's effort to obliterate his research and ideas, and his short, difficult life, Vygotsky is now viewed by many as one of the most influential figures of 20th century psychology and pedagogy. Remarkably, the books and articles he wrote more than 65 years ago continue to inspire and excite new researchers and research, and to influence practitioners.

II. VYGOTSKY PSYCHOLOGY

The efforts of Vygotsky and his colleagues to build a new Soviet psychology led them into diverse areas of investigation. All of these areas were linked to the same core ideas of his theory and were drawn from and tested with empirical studies, many performed with innovative techniques. Because Vygotsky's work on creativity flows from and is closely related to his cultural-historical theory of psychology, it is important to introduce key elements of that theory before discussing how they relate to creativity.

According to Luria, Vygotsky liked to call his approach "instrumental," "cultural" and "historical" psychology. Each term reflected a different feature of a new approach to psychology that Vygotsky proposed to explain the development of higher psychological functions.

The term *instrumental* reflected the fundamental idea of the mediated nature of higher psychological functions. Unlike basic reflexes, which could be analyzed as a simple stimuli-response situation, complex psychological functions incorporate in their structure new elements—internal and external tools—that transform the whole structure of mental functioning. The analysis of tools, which individuals actively use as instruments to modify and master their own behaviors, became a necessary part of Vygotsky's new approach.

The term *cultural* emphasized that aspect of Vygotsky theory that views cultural development as a unique direction in the development of the child, reflecting socially constructed ways in which society organizes the various types of tasks faced by a growing child and the physical and mental tools that society provides to the young child to master those tasks.

The *historical* aspect of Vygotsky's theory is closely connected to the *cultural* aspect. The set of tools provided by a given culture were invented and developed during the long course of human history. Thus, tools like language, arithmetic or algebraic systems, maps, and signs have a long history of development and accumulation of their social influence before they become available as special instruments for a child's individual development. Because the invention and development of cultural tools continues, *historical* also means not only something from the past, but also contemporary aspects of life that are in process of change, linking the past and the future.

The historical method of psychological analysis differs greatly from the traditional methods used in the West. Vygotsky wrote that the concept of historically based psychology is misunderstood by most researchers. For them to study something historically means, by definition, to study some past event, and hence they naively imagine an insurmountable barrier between historic study and the study of the present-day behavioral forms. In Vygotsky's view, to study something historically means to study it in the process of change. That is why he argued that the historical study of behavior is not an auxiliary aspect of theoretical study, but rather forms its very base. In fact, studying something in the process of change is the basic demand of the dialectic method, which is an essential element of Vygotsky's theory.

The *dialectical method,* incorporated by Vygotsky in his work owes much to Hegel's dialectic concept, which was later used by Marx and Engels. The Hegelian dialectic concept views things as in constant change and movement. It is concerned with interrelations and in-teractions. The sources for constant movement and development, the driving force of change, are conflicts and tensions between the contradictory aspects of things. As a result of these conflicts and tensions, development was viewed as constant transformation: nothing can be stable, everything is in a constant process of becoming.

Vygotsky viewed the very essence of psychic development as lying in the change of the *interfunctional structure of consciousness.* He criticized the atomistic and functional models of analysis, which treat psychological processes in isolation while ignoring their interdependence and their organization in the structure of consciousness as a whole. Rejecting methods of research perfected to study separate functions, Vygotsky suggested that psychology's main problem for investigation should be the changing relationships between psychological functions and their developmental changes.

The basic characteristics of Vygotsky's theory are summarized in Table I. As this framework shows, Vygotsky separated higher psychological functions (like creativity) from natural psychological functions, then compared them based on their origins, structure, functioning, and complexity.

As Table I shows, natural psychological functions are genetically inherited (their origin), they are unmediated (their structure), they are involuntary (their way of functioning), and they are isolated from each other (their relation to other mental functions). In contrast, higher mental functions are socially acquired, "instrumental," mediated by social means, voluntarily coconstructed and controlled, and exist as a part of a broad system of functions rather than as separate elements (see Table I).

TABLE I

Main Criteria of Differences between Natural and Higher Psychological Functions

Psychological functions	Origin	Structure	Functioning	Complexity, integration
Natural psychological functions	Mainly inherited	Unmediated, direct	Involuntary	Relatively isolated
Higher psychological functions	Social origins, culturally acquired	"Instrumental," mediated by cultural tools (internal and external), which transform the structure of mental functioning	Actively, voluntarily co-constructed and controlled	Systematic, always exist as part of complex integrated functional systems

III. VYGOTSKY ON CREATIVITY

The starting point for understanding Vygotsky's view of creativity is that he believed that creativity is a higher psychological function. It is one of the complex and multidimensional human characteristics that distinguishes us from animals. Creative imagination is linked to the free processing of elements of our experience, creating their free combinations. It requires an inner freedom of thinking, activity, and cognition that is possible only for "cultural man." Vygotsky stresses that it is freedom of creativity that distinguishes us from animals even more than intellect does.

He characterized creativity as the ability of humans to deal not just with the past or react to the present, but the ability to deal with change and with the future. Such an ability is lacking in animals, children of early age, and primitive humans. They all are unable to act creatively, to reach beyond the concrete situation and free themselves from a total dependency on the present.

Vygotsky viewed imagination and creativity as equal parts of all aspects of cultural life, including artistic, scientific, and technical creativity. In this sense, all that is the work of the human hand, the whole world of culture, was distinguished in his view from the natural world because it is a product of human imagination and creativity based on imagination.

To explore Vygotsky's views on creativity, the framework in Table I is used to structure the remainder of this section. We discuss these key points: (a) creativity has social origins and is culturally and historically determined; (b) creativity has a mediated structure; and (c) creativity exists not as a separate function but as a part of a more complex system, and changes during developmental stages.

A. Social Origins of Creativity

Vygotsky believed that the origins of individual creativity can be found only in the individual's social relationships with the world. Creativity, like all other higher psychological functions, begins in the social environment and then through the process of *internalization* moves from the "outside" into the "inside." His view was the opposite to the Piaget's, who believed that intelligence is started and matured from inside the individual and then is directed from the inside to the outside. Internalization, according to Vygotsky, is a dialectical process that occurs during a child's interaction with others: children watch other people speak, think, or behave in certain ways and thus can learn how to speak, think, or behave this way themselves. A child can learn how to think creatively only by first trying to do it together with other people. After that, the child can then internalize and model what has been done socially at first.

Once the process is internalized, it becomes a property of the inner psyche, even though Vygotsky never drew a real line between the inner and outside because the dialectic nature of internalization is a mechanism of human development. Vygotsky described this basic idea in his theory, which he called the *general law of cultural development,* as follows: Each higher psychological function in child development appears on the stage twice. It is seen first as a social collective activity, an interpsychological function. At the first stage of development, adults are viewed as external agents mediating the contacts that children have with the world. Second it is seen as an individual activity, which is the inner manner of a child's thinking, an intrapsychological function. At the second stage, the tasks that the child initially shared with an adult could be performed alone, they are internalized. As a higher psychological function, creativity follows this pattern in development.

Because Vygotsky believed that a child can acquire abilities for creative thinking through the interaction with adults, there was no doubt for him that creativity, creative thinking, could be enhanced through appropriate teaching. Vygotsky believed that good teaching can lead to the development of a child's creativity if it is based on the principles of the *zone of proximal development.* The concept of the zone of proximal development is a very influential Vygotkian idea. It is defined as the distance between (a) the actual development level of a child, as determined by independent problem solving and (b) the level of the child's potential development, as determined by problem solving carried out under adult guidance or in collaboration with more capable peers.

B. Creativity Has Mediated Structure

As noted earlier, Vygotsky described the cultural development of higher psychological functions as a dialectical process that goes beyond incrementally improving the elementary functions to stimulate fundamental changes in the direction of development. Thus higher psychological functions like creativity are not built *on* (on the top of) the elementary functions, but are separate, new psychological systems.

This radical transformation of the structure and the functioning of higher psychological processes is based on the use of signs, words, symbols, and other cultural tools, which become psychological tools for organizing behavior. The structure of higher psychological processes become mediated and, in some cases, could be flexible, depending on the nature of tools that are used.

According to Vygotsky, creativity as a mediated activity means that creativity as a higher psychological process could have a very different structure, depending on what cultural tools are available at a given moment and which kind of cultural tools a person uses for its mediation. The direction of creativity depends on the tools that are supplied to a given individual, which is determined by the culture and history of the society in which the person lives. Vygotsky argued that it would be a miracle if the imagination could create something from nothing, or if it had another source of creation besides previous experience. He stressed that the creative activity of imagination is found to depend primarily on rich and varied previous experiences. The richer the person's experience, the more material his imagination has at its disposal. Accordingly a child has less imagination than the adult because he or she has less rich and diverse experiences.

Vygotsky wrote that any inventor, even a genius, is always a plant growing at a certain time and in a certain environment. His creativity issues from needs, which are given to him. He operates with the possibilities that exist around him. Because of this, we can trace the historical development of technical areas and the sciences. He stresses that no inventions of scientific discoveries can occur before the materials and psychological conditions necessary for their creation are at hand.

So, Vygotsky viewed creativity as a mediated activity and he attempted the scientific analysis of different types of mediation. He specifically studied symbolic mediation, which is originated during the interaction in child play as a visual, perceptual mediation and then transformed during adolescence into the verbal, symbolic mediation.

C. The Development of Creativity

Rejecting the model of development as the linear, gradual accumulation of small changes, Vygotsky described development as a dialectical transformation that includes both evolutionary and revolutionary changes. He applied this approach to analyze creativity and noted that even though creativity usually appears to be a "catastrophic act," it is actually the result of a very lengthy internal maturation. For Vygotsky, evolutionary changes (maturation) and revolutionary shifts (catastrophic act) in creative behavior were not opposite forms, as could be viewed from the "common-sense" point of view. Instead, he viewed them as mutually dependent forms of the dialectical process of the development of creativity.

Vygotsky argued that creativity, as one of the higher psychological functions, cannot be studied separately without taking into account its relationships with other psychological functions in different stages of the development of the individual. For Vygotsky, the dialectic of the relationships among memory, perception, abstract thinking, and motivation play a major role in the systematic analysis of creativity and imagination and its development.

Vygotsky wrote that creativity as a higher psychological function does not appear suddenly; instead it develops slowly and gradually from more elementary and simple forms to more complex forms at each age level of childhood, which has its own form of creativity. It does not appear by itself in the behavior of the child as a separate psychological function, but it emerges in direct dependence on other forms of activity and other psychological functions.

Vygotsky found that creativity in childhood differs from the creative abilities of adults. The imagination of children is poorer than the imagination of adults. In the process of child development, the imagination also develops, reaching maturity when the child become an adult. He describes child play as the first activity during which creative imagination appears, mediated mainly by perception, memory, and visual thinking. During the same period, a child first becomes aware of differences between reality and imagination and develops the ability to undertake symbolic play. [*See* PLAY.]

In the adolescent stage of development, creativity begins a revolutionary shift that is caused by the appearance of new powerful mediators, inner speech and abstract thinking. At this stage of development, creativity changes due to complex interfunctional connections between imagination and abstract thinking. In Vygotsky words, creativity "is intellectualized." It enters into a system of intellectual activity and begins to play a completely new function in the structure of adolescent personality. From the developmental point of view, argues Vygotsky, imagination in the adolescent is the successor of children's play.

Vygotsky argued that imagination of the adolescent is more creative than a child's fantasy, but it is not productive in comparison with the fantasy of an adult. Only in adulthood does creative imagination and creative thinking reach maturity in the form of artistic, scientific, and technological creativity. [*See* IMAGINATION.]

IV. CONCLUSION

Drawing on his cultural-historical theory of psychology, Vygotsky attempted to analyze creativity from inside of culture and history. He regarded individual creativity as a higher, mediated psychological process, whose origins could be found only in the individual's social relationships with the world. Vygotsky view of

creativity is optimistic: He sees that humans have the ability to develop creativity and to formulate the fundamental laws of its development.

Bibliography

Luria, A. R. (1979). In *The making of mind: A personal account of Soviet psychology.* M. Cole & S. Cole (Eds.). Cambridge, MA: Harvard University Press.

Smolucha, F. (1992) A reconstruction of Vygotsky's theory of creativity. *Creativity Research Journal, 5*(1), 49–67.

Van der Veer, R., & Valsiner, J. (Eds.). (1994). *The Vygotsky reader.* Oxford, England: Blackwell.

Vygodskaya, G. L., & Lifanova, T. M. (1996). *Lev Semenovich Vygotsky.* Moscow: Academia Press, Smusl. [In Russian].

Vygotsky L. S. (1978). In *Mind in society: The development of higher psychological processes.* M. Cole, V. John-Steiner, S. Scribner, & E. Soubermann (Eds.). Cambrige, MA: Harvard University Press.

Vygotsky L. S. (1987). *The collected works of L. S. Vygotsky* (Vol. 1). New York: Plenum.

Vygotsky L. S. (1990) Imagination and creativity during childhood. *Soviet Psychology, 28,* 84–96.

Vygotsky L. S. (1997). *The collected works of L. S. Vygotsky* (Vol. 3). New York: Plenum.

Vygotsky L. S. (1997). *The collected works of L. S. Vygotsky* (Vol. 4). New York: Plenum.

Vygotsky L. S. (1998). Imagination and creativity in the adolescent. In R. W. Reiber (Ed.), *The collected works of L. S. Vygotsky* (Vol. 5). New York: Plenum.

Women and Creativity

Sally M. Reis

University of Connecticut

It's never too late to be what you might have been.

George Eliot

- I. Introduction
- II. Theme One: Personality Characteristics of Creative Women and Internal Barriers to Creativity
- III. Theme Two: Societal Factors That Facilitated or Impeded the Development of Women's Creativity and Why There Are So Few Eminent Female Creators
- IV. Theme Three: Gender Differences in Creativity and the Creative Process
- V. Theme Four: New Initiatives or Research on Issues Relating to Women and Creativity
- VI. Internal and External Barriers to Creative Work in Women
- VII. Conclusion

External Barriers Societal issues relating to families, schooling, environment, and culture that affect the realization of creativity in women.

Historical Views The use of retrospective analyses to investigate how creativity evolved in eminent, creative women.

Internal Barriers Personal obstacles or blocks experienced by creative women related to external blocks such as the way women have been raised and the messages they receive from our culture.

Modern Explanations "Modern" explanations of why there continue to be relatively few eminent women creators.

Research Themes about Women and Creativity Four themes identified by the author emerging from the limited research base on the development of women's creativity.

In examining **WOMEN AND CREATIVITY,** *little written work can be found about highly creative women, the choices they make, and the decisions they face in life. It is clear that most research conducted on creativity and productivity in adult life has concentrated on men. A few researchers have questioned why so few eminent female creators exist and, despite the limited research on highly creative women, some explanations have been offered. Jane Piirto suggested that one reason for the absence of many famous women artists is how intensely they pursue their passions for art. Other research on the creative processes and personalities of creative girls and women has demonstrated that gender stereotyping in childhood, as well as issues in their education, marriage, and family have affected their creative productivity.*

I. INTRODUCTION

It has been noted that male professors produce more creative work in the form of research publications than female professors, and research also indicates that men earn more degrees, produce more works of art, and make more contributions in professional fields. Even in areas such as literature, in which both younger boys and girls believe that females excel, adult men are more productive in their professional accomplishments. For many years, for example, more men than women have been recipients of grants from the National Endowment for the Arts Fellowships in Literature.

The Anonymous Was a Woman Foundation provides ten unrestricted grants each year to female visual artists older than 30 who show creative promise and are at critical junctures in their careers. The title of the foundation, borrowed from Virginia Woolf's book *A Room of One's Own*, is a testimony to female artists in past centuries who may have signed their work "Anonymous" to protest the discouragement they felt about how society and other artists denied them professional respect and recognition. Many art historians and critics believe that women continue to be left out of the inner circles of art and have been systematically excluded from early institutions of art. [*See* ART AND ARTISTS.]

The social and political movement focusing on women during the past 3 decades has provided more of an understanding of the creative roles that women have played in our society and the forces that shape those roles. Unfortunately, a limited research base has focused on the development of women's creativity, which can be classified into four major themes.

II. THEME ONE: PERSONALITY CHARACTERISTICS OF CREATIVE WOMEN AND INTERNAL BARRIERS TO CREATIVITY

The first theme relates to the personality characteristics of highly creative women, the internal blocks that may prevent them from creating, and the study of these characteristics as a means of helping other women with creative potential develop their creativity. Research in this area generally falls under the umbrella of either historical views or more modern explanations. To explore historical issues, researchers use retrospective analyses to investigate how creativity evolved in eminent women. Studies have been conducted, for example, on famous writers, scientists, and artists in an attempt to identify what characterized the lives of talented, creative women of the time, such as the ability to overcome challenges or problems, the need for or absence of support, the opportunity to learn independently in the absence of formal education, and the willingness to live a different life from their peers or counterparts. For example, Herbert Walberg and his associates attempted to identify the early conditions of successful adult females by using a historical analysis of psychological traits and childhood environments. Results suggest that intelligence and environment were correlates in the success of notable women. As girls, notable women were intelligent, hard working, imaginative, and strong willed. Future writers studied were encouraged by their parents, were culturally and financially advantaged, and learned much outside school. In addition, girls who became famous writers were more apt to question assumptions and conventions than were those who became notable artists, scientists, lawyers, and politicians.

Ravenna Helson compared a sample of highly creative women mathematicians with a sample of other female mathematicians. The two groups differed slightly, if at all, on measures of intelligence, cognition, and masculine traits, but creative subjects had more research activity and were highly flexible, original, and rejected outside influence. Half of the creative women were foreign born, and most had fathers who were professional. As compared with creative male mathematicians, the creative women had less assurance, published less, and occupied less prestigious positions. She also found that the many large differences between the creative and comparison subjects in background and personality seemed to indicate that personality characteristics are powerful determinants of creativity of women in mathematics. The traits most characteristic of the creative women seemed to be the following: (a) rebellious independence, introversion, and a rejection of outside influence; (b) strong symbolic interests and a marked ability to find self-expression and self-gratification in directed research activity; (c) flexibility, or lack of constriction, both in general attitudes and in mathematical work. Helson attributed differences in creative productivity between men and women after graduate school to social roles and institutional arrangements. [*See* PERSONALITY.]

III. THEME TWO: SOCIETAL FACTORS THAT FACILITATED OR IMPEDED THE DEVELOPMENT OF WOMEN'S CREATIVITY AND WHY THERE ARE SO FEW EMINENT FEMALE CREATORS

The second theme in research relates to the societal factors that facilitated or became an impediment to the development of women's creativity. Research in this area also generally falls under the umbrella of either historical or more modern explanations. Rhonda Ochse asked why there were so few eminent female creators (scientists, composers, or artists). Researchers who study the history of female achievement have shown that creative works produced by women are often underrated or ignored in history. Historical research indicates that although intellectual stimulation in the home seems to play a major role in the development of creative ability, many girls were typically not encouraged or even allowed to engage in intellectual pursuits. They traditionally received less education than boys and society often denied women access to certain cultural materials and to teachers. In the past, women undoubtedly received little encouragement, stimulation, and access to the tools necessary for building intellectual skills and developing the ability to create something of cultural value. Moreover, females were regarded as less able than males to use their intellectual skills creatively. An important component of this theme is the dilemma faced by women who also have deep urges to create and the constraints placed on their personal lives.

Some authors attempted "modern" explanations of why there continue to be relatively few eminent women creators. These scholars have asked a similar question as posed by the researchers who have offered "historical" views on this matter: Why have we not had more female writers, painters, scientists, sculptors, or artists. One explanation offered is that many women do not perceive themselves as creators, follow their interests into career preparation, or place importance on the works they produce. Moreover, the problem may be further exacerbated even when a women produces an original, creative work of art, as some researchers have found that women are more conscious of criticism and find it more difficult to deal with negative perceptions of their work.

Other explanations of why there were so few eminent women creators have to do with time commitments. Researchers who have offered "historical" explanations about the limited number of women creators argued that women were burdened with family responsibilities, childbearing, and limited educational opportunities. More contemporary researchers argue that women have too many demands on their time, feel guilty if they attempt to do creative work in time that should be spent with their families, or perhaps do not enjoy working alone for long periods of time, which is clearly needed for creative accomplishment. Some researchers have noted that the years in which Lehman found the height of male creative performance to occur also characterize the peak period of women's family responsibilities related to childbearing and raising. Several contemporary researchers have noted that in our society, exceptionally able women experience considerable stress related to role conflict and overload, which may reduce creative urges.

Modern explanations attempt to study highly creative women currently living to investigate the factors enabling them to develop their creativity. For example, in 1991, Karen List and Joseph Renzulli examined the impact of societal influences on the development of creative artists and studied their formal educational experiences, familial support, the role played by mentors, and the artists' views about the development of their own creative processes. Results indicated that despite negative formal educational experiences, the women generally had supportive families and the benefit of at least one influential mentor in their lives. Each woman experienced a strong personal drive to create and the need to share their products with appropriate audiences.

In 1989, Nina Roscher studied a group of 12 highly creative successful women scientists who attributed part of their accomplishments to a role model, whether at high school or in college, or an individual professor or family member who provided encouragement. The majority of the married women attributed their continued success to the encouragement of their spouse, often a scientist, who recognized the sacrifices needed to be successful.

IV. THEME THREE: GENDER DIFFERENCES IN CREATIVITY AND THE CREATIVE PROCESS

A third theme relates to the notion that gender differences exist in creativity and the creative process. A growing number of researchers have called for changes in the paradigm of how we view women and creativity and the need for changes in society that would facilitate the development of creativity in women. It has also been argued that women have made and continue to make many creative contributions that are different from the creative accomplishments made by men and that men's creative accomplishments are valued more by society. [*See* GENDER DIFFERENCES.]

A number of researchers have argued that sex differences exist in creativity among men and women. Some researchers suggest that at least some women perceive creative phenomena differently from men. Because women's experiences and situations in society have been vastly different from men's, one would expect differences in perception to emerge, for perception cannot be separated from learning and experience. As an example, women artists believe that their creative growth from both childbirth and parenting contributes to a creative growth in their artwork.

Joyce VanTassel-Baska studied the lives of Charlotte Brontë and Virginia Woolf to investigate whether the path of a talented female writer is different from that of a male writer, and she identified similarities in the lives and work of Brontë and Woolf related to the complexity of gender-relevant aspects of writing talent over the life span. The influences on eminent women writers she identified dealt with the themes of adversity (obstacles that the women had to overcome in order to realize their potential), autodidactism (dependence on self-learning due to limited or absent formal educational opportunities), and emotional support (need to have mentors to help these gifted women attain their potential). These areas surface in much of the research related to women and the creative process across domains. [*See* BRONTË SISTERS.]

Some researchers pointed out in studies in the 1950s and 1960s that women seemed to be more conservative, conventional, and unlikely to possess the traits most associated with creativity. However, later replication studies found that creative females preferred more complexity than males and that women were more open than males in terms of emotional expression. Perhaps the most controversial issue related to women and the creative process is the claim that there may be a potential mismatch between the single-minded devotion necessary for creative accomplishment in eminent artists and researchers and the desire to balance family and career that appears so frequently in research about creative women.

Still other researchers argue that women's perceptions of the creative process in art as well as other areas have been filtered through male perspectives and the cultural roles developed for women but not by women. Therefore, female writers, artists, scientists, and creators in all domains deal with male conceptions of creativity, which have been accepted as the standard within that domain but may be the standard for male creators.

V. THEME FOUR: NEW INITIATIVES OR RESEARCH ON ISSUES RELATING TO WOMEN AND CREATIVITY

The last research theme involves new initiatives or investigations of issues that have not been well researched, such as the finding that some women's time lines for creative work may occur much later than men's. Studies by Sally Reis published in 1995 indicate that later years for women can be very productive for the development of women's creativity. She found that talent realization in creative women is based upon abilities, personality traits, environmental factors, belief in self, and perceptions about the perceived social importance of the realization of their talent. These studies have also found women's creativity to be more diversified, occurring through different outlets, relative to men, who may pursue a single end goal.

Rena Subotnik and Karen Arnold investigated women in science and found what has been noted in previous research findings—that creative female scientists appear to be motivated largely by deep intellectual engagement and the recognition associated with influential discoveries. They suggested that the degree to which women scientists resemble or differ from this largely male-derived profile has not been extensively researched. As noted, the literature does indicate that a potential mismatch exists between the single-minded devotion to science characteristic of eminent researchers and the desire to balance family and career that appears so prevalently in reports of professional women. [*See* SCIENCE.]

VI. INTERNAL AND EXTERNAL BARRIERS TO CREATIVE WORK IN WOMEN

What types of barriers cause women with high levels of creative potential not to realize their potential? Perhaps their creativity is manifested in ways that are not generally recognized by society. Perhaps our society has a limited view of creativity, which is generally defined according to male standards of creative accomplishment. Many talented women demonstrate their creativity in different ways. Their creativity is seldom applied directly to one aspect of their life; rather, as noted earlier, it is diffused into many directions of work, family, and home. Their creativity may, for example, be demonstrated not only in their work but also in the way they decorate their homes, the meals they prepare, the complicated schedules they plan for their families, the creative ways they stretch the family budget, and even the clothes that they purchase or, sometimes, design and sew. Because many women still assume the primary responsibility of family nurturer and caretaker, many creative energies are directly channeled into their family and home, while their spouse's creative energy is free to be directly applied to his work. Although this nurturing has in the past been directed primarily to child care, people are living longer and the need for care has been shifted to elderly parents. In the early 1970s, for example, only 25% of people in their late 50s had a surviving parent, but by 1980, 40% did, as did 20% of those in their early 60s, and 3% of those in their 70s. The need for care has become most necessary for the oldest people in our society, those over the age of 85, a group that has grown from fewer than 300,000 in 1930 to more than 3 million today. The primary caregivers for these elderly parents are women, and thus the time commitment and responsibilities increase. Completing creative work requires long periods of concentrated effort, which are not available to many women in their peak

work and childbearing years and perhaps not even in their older years. Younger women who have families, of course, simply do not have that kind of time available for their professional work. [*See* BARRIERS TO CREATIVITY AND CREATIVE ATTITUDES.]

A. External Barriers to Creative Productivity in Women

Other external barriers to creativity in women have also been identified. The first set of barriers to female creativity deal with childhood family issues, such as number and sex of siblings, birth order of the siblings, and presence and absence of one or both parents. Other childhood issues include the attitudes of parents toward having and raising girls and boys, including purchasing different stereotypical toys for each gender and decorating rooms differently, with girls' rooms having more dolls and dollhouses and boys' rooms having more vehicles, educational and art materials, and machines. [*See* BIRTH ORDER.]

Parents may also hinder the creative process in their daughters. In a study of young gifted female sculptors, researchers found that it was most important to parents that their daughters be happily married. Parents also hoped that their daughters would be able to do something in which they were interested, finish their education, and become financially secure. If parents are primarily encouraging their talented daughters in these areas, little encouragement may have been given to their creative potential in art.

Mark Runco suggested that two broad personality and cognitive transformations occur in the development of high levels of creativity in persons with high potential. The first is the development of outstanding creative ability during the first 2 decades of life and the second begins in adolescence and entails the transformation of creative abilities into an integrated set of cognitive skills, career-focused interests and values, specific creative personality dispositions, and moderately high ambitions. Accordingly, if parental encouragement of art is regarded as less important than encouragement to marry and have children, a different set of priorities may be embedded in creative females than in males.

Some creative young girls are willful and determined, and Sally Reis found in 1998 that many parents strive to correct the same creative behaviors that are sorely needed as their daughters grow older. Too many parents squelch their daughters' enthusiasm and spirit under the guise of manners.

Kazimierz Dabrowski's personality theories have been applied to gifted individuals. Dabrowski believed that some people display supersensitivities, translated into English as overexcitabilities, in several areas: psychomotor (increased levels of physical activities), intellectual (increased levels of intellectual activities), sensual (expanded awareness), imaginational (high levels of imagination), and emotional (intensified emotions). Highly creative girls may experience some of these overexcitabilities and many have expanded awareness in the sensual, imaginational, and emotional areas. Too strict a behavior code may directly conflict with their emotional nature and could be difficult for parents to enforce and for children to obey. Parents who demand a certain behavior code at all times sometimes dampen some of the passion in their creative spirited daughters. [*See* OVEREXCITABILITIES.]

The primary mixed messages creative girls receive emanate from the interaction of family variables, their parents' relationship, and expectations that their daughters will have certain types of manners and behaviors. Many highly creative girls have problems reconciling messages that have emerged from home and school with their creative potential. Parents often have strict guidelines about manners for their daughters, which include not being too aggressive and acting like a "young lady." Confusion about roles and expectations often results. Being praised for looking like a little doll, being encouraged to consistently "mind their manners," and being told to be polite and ladylike may conflict with the characteristics that are necessary for girls with high creative potential to evolve into women whose creative potential is manifested in adult productivity. These characteristics include the ability to challenge convention, to question authority, and to speak out about things one needs to change. The characteristics found to be associated with older creative women (determination, commitment, assertiveness, and the ability to control their own lives) directly conflict with what some parents encourage as good and appropriate manners in their daughters. The manners taught to some daughters are, of course, influenced by the cultures in which we live. While not wanting to eliminate what is unique to each diverse culture, a discussion of some of the issues related to strict implementation of a code of manners and behavior for girls is warranted.

B. Personal Barriers to Creative Expression in Women

Ravenna Helson, who compared highly creative women with less creative women, found that the more creative women had higher levels of ambition, confidence, a stronger sense of purpose, and greater social energy. They also showed the greatest need to succeed and needed partners and relationships that supported creativity. Because of the way women have been raised and the messages received from our culture, even single women without families may not possess the belief in themselves required for a commitment to highly creative work. Instead, they may be content to work in the background, in a less center-stage position, as implementers of the ideas of others. Female creative work may be directed at lower-profile products. While their male counterparts produce plays, write articles or books, undertake large deals, and are viewed as creative high achievers, many women make conscious or unconscious decisions to work in a more facilitating role, implementing the creative ideas of others.

Another reason why fewer women fulfill their potential to complete professional and creative endeavors is that they have different priorities. Most women face a multitude of important issues that need and deserve their time and attention. People they love more than their work, a sick child or elderly parents who need care, a friend who is in trouble, and many other personal issues cause talented women to make choices about what is most important to them. For many women, having to split time between those they love and their work is a difficult and often wrenching choice.

In 1998, Reis found that the *greatest* conflicts for highly creative women in their 20s, 30s, and 40s concerns the interaction between their career and personal lives. This intensely personal struggle to try to develop their personal talents while they also try to meet the needs of those they love causes gifted women the most conflict, guilt, and pain. Maric Mileva Einstein, Albert's first wife, was a gifted mathematician with extremely high potential who was a fellow classmate at the prestigious Swiss Federal Polytechnic. After she married Albert and had their children, however, her life changed drastically. Friends recalled that she often spent all day cleaning, cooking, and caring for the children and then would busy herself in the evening by proofreading her husband's work and doing mathematical calculations to help him in his writings.

Relationships with children and family are firmly rooted in the lives of highly creative females and are interwoven with their accomplishments. Most women take on the responsibilities for child care, after-school care, summer activities, camps, homework, and other child-related issues. In addition to the responsibilities of children, more recent years have seen an added wrinkle to the complex decisions made by women. Just as many enter the time in which their responsibilities to their children decrease, they struggle to cope with the responsibilities of taking care of aging parents. As Robert Albert wrote in *Genius and Eminence,* "Development is change, but not all change is progressive."

C. Perfectionism

Another reason that women with high levels of creative potential may not pursue creative productive work is that they may possess certain personality traits that often conflict with high-profile creative endeavors. These traits occur in many women, whether they work within or outside of the home, whether they are married or single, and whether or not they have children. One of the most common traits is perfectionism, which causes some girls and women to expend maximum energy at all times, attempting to do everything and do it well. Often, it is not enough to try to be outstanding in work; perfectionistic women also feel they have to strive for a flawless body, a beautiful house, and perfect children. These talented women wear themselves out trying to do everything well, often with minimal help from their spouses, yet despite these accomplishments, they still feel plagued by guilt that they may not have given enough to their husbands, children, home, and career.

D. Changes in Perceptions about Personal Creativity

In a study by Reis, published in 1995, of 67 highly creative, talented women, participants were asked to compare life today with the dreams they held for their future when they graduated from college. Sixty percent indicated they experienced a conflict between the real world and the cultivation and the realization and their own creative talents. Societal expectations often led them *not* to plan a career that was personally satisfying, to put their talents and aspirations on hold while raising their families, and eventually to stop regarding themselves as capable of more creative life than they are currently living. Many respondents indicated that they had not been able to pursue their own creative talents because of the pressures of marriage and family.

In interviews conducted with these creative women, half of the respondents were apologetic when explaining their professional accomplishments. They indicated that they knew their achievements in this particular area might seem "modest," but they were also often defensive, acknowledging how hard it was to accomplish anything given their work and family commitments. The other half of the respondents were proud of what they had accomplished, without reservation.

E. Minimizing Differences

A tendency exists for many females, regardless of their age, to try to minimize their differences. Both young girls and older women have a greater need to be accepted and a need to have people like them. *Defying the Crowd,* the title of a recent book on creativity by Robert Sternberg and Todd Lubart, illustrates a fundamental difference in creative endeavors for women. Defying the crowd is the last thing that many women with high creative potential seek to accomplish. If women either feel different, or are different, most want to minimize differences through quiet work and failing to call attention to themselves. Most talented women I have studied have wanted to create and produce quietly and do their work, preferably in an environment in which their differences do not appear so obvious and they are not singled out. While in school or any environment that enables people to make comparisons, females across the life span hide or mask their abilities so as not to appear too different or to appear as if they are bragging. Parental influences, such as teaching daughters to be modest or polite, seem to confound this issue. In many interviews with young and adolescent gifted girls, they explained that they did not like to share the news of a high grade or a special accomplishment because it would seem as if they were bragging.

F. Selflessness and Subjugation of Creative Talents

Many creative women with firm religious backgrounds and beliefs have grappled with the religious training they received as young children. Throughout their lives, this religious training may conflict with what is required if they are to develop their own talents. Selflessness, modesty, turning the other cheek, and the subjugation of individual pursuits for the good of others are lessons some women learn from their earliest interaction with religious training, and these lessons may conflict with experiences that occur later in life.

Concerns about pursuing one's creative talents being misconstrued as "selfish consideration" have been mentioned repeatedly by many creative women who have been raised with religious beliefs. Many still struggle with their learned beliefs that to pursue their own talents is selfish. Guilt seems intertwined with many women's struggles to understand the relationship between their own talent development and what they learned in their religious training about their responsibilities to those they love. The guilt they feel perhaps explains why selecting work that results in social change or the improvement of the human condition is so important to some talented women with strong religious backgrounds.

G. Self-Doubt, Self-Criticism, and Comparisons

Creative females often compare themselves more, express more doubt about their abilities, and criticize themselves and others more. Unfortunately, this critical nature often extends to withholding support from other women. Several different researchers have found that a lack of confidence in girls seems to increase with females who are more intelligent, and this pattern may continue into midlife. In addition to having less confidence in their own abilities, creative females are also overly critical of themselves, and they listen more to advice given by others, taking it more to heart and often following it. For example, in a study of creative women

artists, several were hesitant to show their art to others because they felt "it wasn't good enough" or feared rejection in some form. This low self-esteem might have affected their creative process and productivity. "Sometimes," one stated, "I make things and hide them because I don't think they're good enough. I'll bring them out and somebody will say they're pretty good and it surprises me. If I get enough positive feedback on a piece, I'll show it somewhere." Several of the women avoided the prospect of having their efforts (and, consequently, their self-confidence and self-esteem) diminished by either having their art rejected in art competitions or ignored by the buying public. Other research has found that women take criticism much more seriously and that women are more influenced by the evaluations they receive than men, perhaps because of differing perceptions of the informative value of those evaluations.

H. Absence of Support for One Another and Loneliness Experienced by Creative Women

In interviews conducted with older and younger creative females, they described their feelings of loneliness. A successful college president, widely acclaimed for her creative contributions, when asked about friendships replied simply, "I have none." Some of the reasons that many talented women had few friends and were often lonely revolve around the extremely limited time they have for friendships. Other reasons involve the ambivalence of other women to highly creative women who achieve. In interview after interview, successful women recounted situations in which their success was viewed negatively by both other women and men. Women who had successful careers often reported that they were pitted against women who stayed at home and worked to raise their children.

I. The Importance of Creative Expression

In research conducted by Robert Kirschenbaum and Sally Reis on creative female artists, participants commented about the process of creating art and how valuable this was for them. Especially for those involved in some aspect of sculpting, the feeling of doing physical work as they created was very gratifying. One woman explained:

> The process of doing art is often more important [than the product] to me because of my feeling that I have to get something out. The act of welding, of fusing metal together, is very important to me. The passion I feel, the violence of creating something with an arc-welder as the sparks fly everywhere, watching the metal heat up, then manipulating it by bending, hammering, and cutting it, gives me feelings that are hard to describe. It's a rich feeling, one of power, I guess.

Several said they preferred making and selling things of their own design, for others' enjoyment, to working in a regular job. One woman, a counselor, said that art is a path to self-discovery and healing; this would appear to be true for all the participants in this study. Another woman explained, "I may not be in the mood to paint, but if I don't do something [artistic], it's like I'm suffering from drug withdrawal. If I don't take care of this creative urge, I feel like I'm going to blow up. I need that high of being creative." When asked about their futures, the goals mentioned by these female artists included being able to keep learning and doing their art, obtaining necessary equipment and materials when the money was available, and completing specific projects in the near future.

VII. CONCLUSION

The accomplishments of some highly creative females and the underachievement of others is a complex issue dependent on many factors, including personal choices and decisions. Our current societal structure virtually eliminates the possibility that many highly creative females who are married and have children can achieve at a similar level as their male counterparts, at least during the time they commit to raising a child and now possibly another: the time needed to care for aging parents. Although the importance of women's contributions to family cannot be underestimated, it is often not enough for highly creative women who want more or who have a sense of destiny about making a difference in the world. Even though our society has a critical need for those who excel in traditionally female

careers, decisions to pursue these careers should be considered by those who have been exposed to the full range of options available to them.

Creative young females should explore careers, further education, and plan and pursue professional opportunities that will challenge their intellect as well as fit into their personal plans for the future. Opportunities should be provided across the life span of talented women to enable them to continue to examine and pursue their personal choices. They should learn to assess and determine whether they are finding the time needed for their own creative development. If they are not able develop their creative talents, they should learn to examine why and be proactive about what is required to help them to realize their potential. One aspect of life that must be reexamined and carefully considered is new models of how adults parent and do daily work, the types of decisions they make about labor and the division of responsibilities, and the ways in which new patterns of family life can evolve in the future.

The exploration and discussion of the personality issues and personal choices facing girls and women with high levels of creative potential should be encouraged. The development of a creative life is intricate and complex. What one young girl regards as an impossible obstacle may be regarded as an intriguing challenge by another. Many creative women interviewed were so negatively influenced by their parents' lack of support for their career preferences that they changed their career plans; a much smaller percentage of women were so angry that their parents tried to steer them away from their dreams that they rebelled and became eminent in their selected areas of endeavor. How the same obstacles differentially affect girls and women provides the fascination of researching their creative accomplishments. Resilience, rebellion, multipotentiality, different cycles of creativity and extremely high achievement in the face of obstacles such as poverty, and a complete absence of support characterize many of the highly creative women studied. Yet, creative women persist. Can this type of persistence, determination, and inner will be learned or is it the result of innate personality traits? Many of the women studied developed these characteristics throughout their lives, and it is precisely this act of development that creates their success—an active, evolutionary success learned throughout their life span. Exploring how and when they develop these characteristics will help both teachers and parents guide creative young females in their journeys.

The unique pattern of the lives of creative women seems almost to defy general theories of human development, yet, some trends have emerged. There is no clear path for creative women because their creativity is intimately connected with relationships to family and friends, and their creative productivity is more diffused than that of their male counterparts. Because relationships are central to women's lives, they cannot be secondary to their work and individual creative attainment. Yet without meaningful work, creative women are not satisfied. Over and over again, in interviews conducted with women at various stages of their lives, they echoed their desire for meaningful work that made a difference.

The realization of the creative potential in women requires effort, conscious decision making, and an understanding that the full range of creative talents in many women may be unrealized in our world today. However, many people never fully understand the creative opportunities denied to girls and women because we live in a world in which our realities and daily experiences reinforce certain roles and obligations for women. It is time for that to change.

Bibliography

Helson, R. (1996). In search of the creative personality. *Creativity Research Journal, 9*(4), 295–306.

Kirschenbaum, R. K., & Reis, S. M. (1997). Conflicts in creativity: Talented female artists. *Creativity Research Journal, 10*(2&3), 251–263.

List, K., & Renzulli, J. (1991). Creative women's developmental patterns through age thirty-five. *Gifted Education International, 7*(3), 114–122.

Ochse, R. (1991). Why there were relatively few eminent women creators. *Journal of Creative Behavior, 25*(4), 334–343.

Piirto, J. (1991). Why are there so few? (Creative women: Visual artists, mathematicians, musicians). *Roeper Review, 13*(3), 142–147.

Reis, S. M. (1995a). Talent ignored, talent diverted: The cultural context underlying giftedness in females. *Gifted Child Quarterly, 39*(3), 162–170.

Reis, S. M. (1995b). Older women's reflections on eminence: Obstacles and opportunities. In K. D. Arnold, K. D. Noble, and R. F. Subotnik (Eds.), *Remarkable women: Perspectives on female talent development* (pp. 149–168). Cresskill, NJ: Hampton Press.

Reis, S. M. (1998). *Work left undone: Compromises and challenges of talented females.* Mansfield Center: Creative Learning Press.

Roscher, N. (1987). Chemistry's creative women. *Journal of Chemical Education, 56*(4), 748–752.

Runco, M. A. (1991). *Divergent thinking.* Norwood, NJ: Ablex.

Simonton, D. K. (1984). Artistic creativity and interpersonal relations across and within generations. *Journal of Personality and Social Psychology, 46,* 1273–1286.

Sloane, K. D., & Sosniak, L.A. (1985). The development of accomplished sculptures. In B. Bloom (Ed.), *The development of talent in young people* (pp. 90–138). New York: Ballantine.

Subotnik, R., & Arnold, K. (1995). Passing through the gates: Career establishment of talented women scientists. *Roeper Review, 13*(3), 55–61.

VanTassel-Baska, J. (1995). As study of life themes in Charlotte Brontë and Virginia Woolf. *Roeper Review, 13*(3), 14–19.

Wallace, T., & Walberg, H. (1995). Girls who became famous literalists of the imagination. *Roeper Review, 13*(3), 24–27.

Virginia (Stephen) Woolf

1882–1941

Novelist and essayist

Author of *To the Lighthouse, The Waves,*
and *A Room of One's Own*

Maria F. Ippolito

Bowling Green, Ohio

*English novelist **VIRGINIA WOOLF** is acclaimed for her innovations in novelistic structure and for a writing style perhaps best represented by her fifth novel,* To the Lighthouse *(1927). Although Woolf considered her nonfiction efforts secondary to her novels, she was a productive and influential essayist. Her best-known essay,* A Room of One's Own *(1929), argues for financial security and independence as essential to women writers. In the preponderance of her essays, Woolf attempted to detail the English novel as re-formed by stream-of-conscious writers such as herself. Plagued by mental illness from childhood, Woolf ended her own life in 1941.*

I. BACKGROUND

Virginia Stephen (Woolf) was born on January 25, 1882, in Victorian England into an upper middle-class family. Her father, Leslie Stephen, was a distinguished literary figure who developed friendships with many members of the literary elite, such as Thomas Hardy and Henry James, childhood acquaintances of Woolf. Some years later, Woolf was a distinguished member of another group of intellectuals that came to be known as the Bloomsbury Group (named for the district in London to which Woolf and her sister and brothers moved

in 1904 after Leslie Stephen's death). The Bloomsbury Group originated when Woolf's older brother invited friends he had made at Cambridge University to the Stephen siblings' residence. Discussions at informal Thursday evening gatherings, which began in 1905,

Virginia Woolf. Used with permission of Frederick R. Koch Collection, The Harvard Theatre Collection, The Houghton Library.

ranged over a number of topics including history, philosophy, art, sexuality, and literature. In addition to Woolf, other well-known members among the original participants in the Bloomsbury Group included Leonard Woolf (her future husband and a novelist, political activist, author of political treatises, editor, and publisher), biographer Lytton Strachey, economist John Maynard Keynes, and novelist E. M. Forster.

To her father's delight, Woolf expressed an interest in becoming a writer during her childhood. Among her first literary efforts was a household newspaper, *The Hyde Park Gate News,* named for the longtime Stephen family residence. This newspaper was a compendium of household events, essays, and Woolf's first fiction efforts, with issues dating from shortly after her ninth birthday until just weeks before her mother's death in early 1895. The passion for writing that began during Woolf's childhood persisted throughout her lifetime. For Woolf, however, writing was a double-edged sword. She characterized writing as a pleasurable, essential, and consuming aspect of her life but, also, as analogous to coal mining, subduing a python, and galloping at fences. Woolf wrote in her diary when she was 39 years old: "I shall never write out all the books I have in my head, because of the strain. The devilish thing about writing is that it calls upon every nerve to hold itself taut" (v. 2, p. 128–129).

The strain of writing that Woolf spoke of was arguably attributable to the task she set herself. Almost without exception, the novels of her contemporaries continued in the realistic/materialistic style of Charles Dickens and Jane Austen—relying on descriptions of what characters said, did, and wore as primary components. In "The Art of Fiction," written the same year as *To the Lighthouse,* Woolf hoped English novelists would "cut adrift from the eternal tea-table and the plausible and preposterous formulas which are supposed to represent the whole of our human adventure. . . . Then the novel . . . might become a work of art" (p. 112).

The novel Woolf envisioned would chart the mental as well as the material lives of the characters. As early as 1908, Woolf recorded in her early journals (published as *A Passionate Apprentice: The Early Journals, 1897–1909*) the intent that her writing reflect "all the traces of the mind's passage through the world and achieve . . . some kind of whole made of shivering fragments" (p. 393). And in "Modern Fiction," Woolf wrote:

> Life is not a series of gig lamps symmetrically arranged; but a luminous halo, a semi-transparent envelope surrounding us from the beginning of consciousness to the end. Is it not the task of the novelist to convey this varying, this unknown, this uncircumscribed spirit, whatever aberration and complexity it may display, with as little mixture of the alien and external as possible? (pp. 154).

Although it was clear to Woolf that the prevalent realistic novel was inadequate, it was, as yet, unclear what novelistic forms might accommodate her new kind of novel and how the English language might be stretched to capture the dynamics of mental processes. Whereas Woolf admired Dorothy Richardson's and James Joyce's efforts to expand the novel to include the workings of the mind, she felt the novels of these authors were limited in that each provided access to the uncontradicted psychology of a single character. Eventually Woolf constructed stream-of-consciousness novels that embodied a shifting chorus of consciousnesses so the reader knows what the characters think of the unfolding events and each other.

She married Leonard Woolf on August 10, 1912. Throughout their 29-year marriage, Leonard was meticulously solicitous of Woolf's health and acted as her editor and sole prepublication critic. He also collaborated with Woolf in the 1917 establishment of the Hogarth Press (named for Hogarth House where the Woolfs resided from 1915 to 1924). The Woolfs' primary intentions were that the press would free Woolf's efforts to re-form the novel from being subject to the approval of established, often conservative, publishers and publish works of literary merit that other publishers declined. The press succeeded in both respects. In England, Woolf's short stories, essays, her third and following novels, and the second and later editions of her first two novels all appeared with the Hogarth Press as publisher. Further, the press published Katherine Mansfield's short story "Prelude," short fiction and nonfiction works by E. M. Forster, the poetry of Robert Graves and Herbert Read, was the first publisher in England of "The Waste Land" and other poems by T. S. Eliot, and was the sole English publisher of all but one of Sigmund Freud's works from 1920 to 1938. The Hogarth Press was also intended to provide Woolf with therapeutic work to fend off or assist her recovery from mental collapse.

Woolf suffered a number of nervous breakdowns, which included alternating periods of debilitating depression and mania with accompanying suicide attempts, violence toward family members and nurses, and hallucinations. It is likely that she suffered from bipolar disorder (manic depression). Woolf's first bout of what she referred to as madness occurred shortly after her mother's death. This and Woolf's subsequent breakdowns, including one shortly after her marriage, were often followed by extended periods of convalescence, with Woolf estimating that she had lost five years of her life to insanity. Woolf's letters to her husband and sister before her suicide indicate she was fearful of impending insanity, from which she might not recover. She committed suicide by drowning herself (having forced a large stone into her coat pocket) in the river near the Woolfs' country home on March 28, 1941.

Woolf's writing legacy includes 10 novels, numerous short stories, a play, a biography, and several volumes of essays. Woolf's first publication—an unsigned review published several days before her 23rd birthday—followed a lengthy writing apprenticeship. Her last novel was completed 1 month before her death (and published posthumously).

II. THE WRITING APPRENTICESHIP

From childhood, Woolf engaged in a self-assigned writing apprenticeship. Her surviving diaries and correspondence document her writing ambitions, practices, and developing philosophy of literature, and they chart the progress of this apprenticeship. Woolf's intent was that her diaries be a place to practice her craft and collect observations she might incorporate in her fiction. A July 30, 1903, entry—which preceded her first publication by several months—recorded her intent that her early journals

> serve for a sketch book; as an artist fills his pages with scraps and fragments . . . so I take up my pen and trace here whatever shapes I happen to have in my

head. It is an exercise—training for hand and eye (pp. 186–187).

Woolf continued to use her diaries to practice her craft, writing on April 20, 1919, by which time she was a well-known essayist and had finished her second novel, that she believed "the habit of writing . . . for my eye only is good practice. It loosens the ligaments" (v. 1, p. 266). In the same entry, Woolf identified her diaries as a receptacle for observations to be used in her fiction; these volumes were

> to resemble some deep old desk or capacious hold-all, in which one flings a mass of odds and ends. . . . I should like to come back . . . and find that the collection had sorted itself and refined itself and coalesced . . . into a mold transparent enough to reflect the light of life and yet steady, tranquil, composed, with the aloofness of a work of art (v. 1, p. 266).

Woolf's writing apprenticeship included a reading program. As was customary for girls of her socioeconomic class, Woolf had little formal education; but she did have access to her father's vast library. Leslie Stephen was enthusiastic about sharing his books with the daughter who would be a writer; although by the time Woolf was 15, her father expressed concern regarding the volume of his daughter's reading. Notations in her early journals indicate that, during a 6-month period, the 15-year old Woolf read 59 volumes of biographies, novels, history, and essays. Woolf regularly tested her ability to grasp the contents of her reading in discussions with her father and, later, with fellow members of the Bloomsbury Group. Clearly, Woolf placed a high value on extracting the essences of the books she read. In a 1926 lecture at a girls' school, published in 1932 as "How Should One Read a Book?," she stated:

> To receive impressions with the utmost understanding is only half the process of reading. . . . We must pass judgment upon these multitudinous impressions; we must make of those fleeting shapes one that is hard and lasting. . . . Continue reading without the book before you. . . . Hold one shadow-shape against another. . . . Read widely enough and with enough understanding to make such comparisons alive and illuminating (pp. 241–242).

As with her diaries and writing, Woolf recognized a connection between her reading program and writing ability. For Woolf, reading enabled familiarity with the possibilities and peculiarities of the English language and an understanding of the relation between author and readers.

Eventually, Woolf's writing ability, her commitment to reading critically, and an acquaintanceship with a journal editor led to her first publication; an unsigned review in the December 14, 1904, issue of *The Guardian.* Woolf's excitement at subsequently becoming a regular contributor to several literary journals quickly gave way to disillusionment. She came to see assigned essays as failing to challenge her intellectually and as taking time away from novel writing. However, she continued to critique what she read informally in her diaries and correspondence and to publish occasional reviews. Woolf also retained a lifelong interest in writing essays for which she could pick the topics, a concession many editors were eventually willing to make, in light of her growing fame as a novelist and critic.

A final aspect of Woolf's writing apprenticeship is her short stories, which she referred to as sketches— akin to the sketches prepared by an artist contemplating a complex painting or the pilot studies of a scientist. While completing her first two novels, *The Voyage Out* (1915) and *Night and Day* (1919), which were primarily materialistic in style, Woolf wrote a number of sketches experimenting with the lyric and essayistic limits of English and the employment of alternative perspectives and revised plot forms. Woolf envisioned her third novel, *Jacob's Room* (1922), as an extension of the techniques and forms developed in three of these sketches. The writing experiments continued; in a July 30, 1925, diary entry, just prior to beginning to write *To the Lighthouse,* Woolf recollected: "My summer's wanderings with the pen have . . . shown me one or two new dodges for catching my flies. I have sat here like an improviser with his hands rambling over the piano" (v. 3, p. 37).

III. THE WRITING OF *TO THE LIGHTHOUSE*

For Woolf, novels frequently originated with a scene. She wrote in "A Sketch of the Past" that

Scenes . . . are not altogether a literary device—a means of summing up and making a knot out of innumerable little threads. . . . A scene always comes to the top; arranged; representative. This confirms me in my instinctive notion . . . that we are sealed vessels afloat upon what it is convenient to call reality; at some moments, without any reason, without an effort, the sealing matter cracks; in floods reality; that is a scene . . . I almost always have to find a scene; either when I am writing about a person . . . or when I am writing about a book (p. 142).

Woolf would later write in "A Sketch of the Past" that the idea for *To the Lighthouse* came

in a great, apparently involuntary, rush. One thing burst into another. Blowing bubbles out of a pipe gives the feeling of the rapid crowd of ideas and scenes which blew out of my mind, so that my lips seemed syllabling of their own accord as I walked (p. 81).

On May 14, 1925, Woolf recorded in her diary the scene from which this novel emerged:

This is going to be fairly short, to have father's character done complete in it, and mother's, and St. Ives, and childhood. . . . But the center is father's character, sitting in a boat, reciting "We perished, each alone," while he crushes a dying mackerel (v. 3, pp. 18–19).

Once one has gotten hold of the scene that is the germ for a work of art, "one must hold the scene . . . in a vise and let nothing come in and spoil it" says the painter who is a character in *To the Lighthouse* (p. 201). The next step for Woolf was to devise a novelistic form appropriate to the germinal scene, a form that would not spoil it.

To the Lighthouse is the story of the Ramsay family at their summer home—not unlike St. Ives where the Stephen family summered until the death of Woolf's mother. Mr. and Mrs. Ramsay are modeled on Woolf's parents. Among the Ramsay's guests are a painter named Lily Briscoe. There are two parallel stories in this novel: the first about a postponed boat trip to the lighthouse and the second about Lily's struggle with the composition of an abstract painting.

The form of *To the Lighthouse* is a three-part structure, which Woolf depicted schematically in her note-book as two rectangles joined by a narrow passageway. Per Woolf's July 20, 1925, diary entry, this novel was to be about a

> father and mother and child in the garden, the death, the sail to the lighthouse. . . . When I begin it I shall enrich it in all sorts of ways, thicken it, give it branches and roots which I do not perceive now. . . . I conceive the book in three parts: 1. at the drawing room window; 2. seven years passed; 3. the voyage (v. 3, p. 36).

The first part of the finished novel, "The Window," records the happenings in and around the Ramsay's summer home. The next day's trip to the lighthouse is canceled because Mr. Ramsay anticipates poor weather; Lily is unable to solve the problems of her painting of Mrs. Ramsay. The second, passageway, part of the novel, "Time Passes," records the passage of 10 years during which Mrs. Ramsay dies. In the third and last part, "The Lighthouse," Mr. Ramsay and his children return to their summer home and Lily Briscoe is again a guest. The trip to the lighthouse finally takes place—with Mr. Ramsay reciting poetry while piloting the boat; meanwhile, Lily Briscoe resumes work on the unfinished abstract painting she abandoned 10 years earlier. The novel ends as the expedition reaches the lighthouse and Lily is able to successfully resolve the problems of her painting.

Once Woolf had settled on the form of her novel, she shifted her attention to its microstructure. For example, Woolf intended that the rhythms of the sea be heard throughout this novel. In *To the Lighthouse: The Original Holograph Draft,* Susan Dick indicated that Woolf began each writing session by rereading what she had written to refresh her memory and "help start a particular rhythm in her mind" (p. 14). Woolf may have also read *To the Lighthouse* aloud to ensure it had the right sound. In *Recollections of Virginia Woolf,* a cook hired by the Woolfs in 1934 recalled hearing Woolf talking to herself while taking a bath:

> When Mr. Woolf saw that I looked startled he told me that Mrs. Woolf always said the sentences out loud that she had written during the night. She needed to know if they sounded right and the bath[room] was a good, resonant place for trying them out. He was so

used to hearing her talk to herself in this way that he did not notice it at all (pp. 155–156).

In *To the Lighthouse* and her other experimental novels, Woolf intended that the words she wrote carry meaning *and* convey atmosphere (e.g., the ever present sound of the sea) and the moods of the characters.

The writing of a provisional draft of *To the Lighthouse* was accomplished between the latter part of 1925 and the fall of 1926. The commitment of the constructed novel to paper initially progressed rapidly. On February 23, 1926, Woolf recorded in her diary:

> At last, at last, after the battle of *Jacob's Room,* that agony—all agony but the end—*Mrs. Dalloway,* I am now writing as fast and freely as I have written in the whole of my life, more so—20 times more so—than any novel yet (v. 3, p. 59).

Perhaps Woolf's ease in writing his novel can be explained. Although she claimed she had to solve the problems of *Jacob's Room* (1922) as she wrote it—because she was initially unsure of her destination—and hoped to plan *Mrs. Dalloway* (1925) more thoroughly, *To the Lighthouse* (1927) was outlined in detail some time before she began to record it. On June 14, 1925, several weeks before she wrote the first words of this novel, Woolf commented on how extensively she had already planned it, fearing she had "thought [it] out perhaps too clearly" (v. 3, p. 29). Curiously, it appears Woolf devoted not less but increasingly more effort to the prewriting planning of each successive experimental novel.

By September 5, 1926, Woolf worried in a diary entry that *To the Lighthouse* might "run too fast and free, and so be rather thin" (v. 3, p. 106). Eight days later on September 13, 1926, Woolf's diary indicated:

> This is the greatest stretch I've put my method to, and I think it holds. By this I mean that I have been dredging up more feelings and character. . . . But . . . until I look at my haul this is only my feeling in process (v. 3, p. 109).

Three days later, on September 16, 1926, the first draft was completed. Now the questions regarding the quality of her "haul" that had crept into preceding diary entries became paramount during revision and rewriting.

Earlier, while working on her previous novel, *Mrs. Dalloway,* Woolf had described revising in her diary as "the dullest part of the whole business of writing, the most depressing and exacting" (v. 2, p. 4). Although she had written *To the Lighthouse* relatively quickly, its revision presented some difficulty. On November 23, 1926, Woolf's diary indicated:

> I am re-doing six pages of *To the Lighthouse* daily. This is not, I think, so quick as *Mrs. D[alloway]*; but then I find much of it very sketchy and have to improvise on the typewriter. . . . My present opinion is that it is easily the best of my books (pp. 117–118).

Leonard Woolf read the revised version on January 23, 1927, and pronounced it a masterpiece; Woolf then completed her revisions in March of 1927.

The publication of *To the Lighthouse* on May 5, 1927, did not represent an end to Woolf's writing experimentation but, rather, the beginning of a whole new series of experiments that culminated in what is perhaps Woolf's most innovative, although not universally critically accepted, novel, *The Waves* (1931). Later she attempted a novel-essay, which was eventually separated into a novel, *The Years* (1937), and a book-length essay, *Three Guineas* (1938).

The development of *To the Lighthouse* was guided by the intuition of a scene. On the heels of this "aha" experience followed a series of incremental discoveries. First, Woolf constructed an appropriate novelistic form. The constructed form was then used to constrain the selection of language to delineate aspects of the scene. Ultimately, the process of revision, a meticulous reconsideration of the multiple problem solutions that constituted earlier drafts of *To the Lighthouse,* served as a final constraint—the last tightening of germinal scene, novelistic form, and language, to ensure integrity of fit. Her creativity encompassed the large moment of the seemingly instantaneous appearance of a unifying scene as well as the innumerable small moments of incrementally evaluating and constructing nested constraints of this scene.

Woolf's novels clearly benefited from the conscious refinement of her writing, reading, and critical skills. Her writing practices indicate that she never completely relinquished her status as an apprentice; she continued to read extensively, challenge her ability to critically evaluate what she read, and practice writing. Woolf's creativity resulted from the interaction of large and small discoveries—a blending of emergent scenes, purposefully developed writing craftmanship, and novelistic forms developed via experimentation—against the backdrop of an enduring passion for her art and a longstanding ambition to re-form the novel to capture the dynamics of mental life.

Bibliography

Hussey, M. (1995). *Virginia Woolf A to Z.* New York: Facts on File.

Ippolito, M. F., & Tweney, R. D. (in press). Virginia Woolf and the journey to *Jacob's Room*: The "network of enterprise" of Virginia Woolf's first experimental novel. *Creativity Research Journal.*

Noble, J. R. (Ed.). (1972). *Recollections of Virginia Woolf.* New York: William Morrow & Company.

Woolf, V. (1919/1953). Modern fiction. In *The common reader* (pp. 150–158). New York: Harcourt Brace & World.

Woolf, V. (1927/1975). The art of fiction. In *The moment and other essays* (pp. 106–112). New York: Harcourt Brace & Company.

Woolf, V. (1932/1984). How should one read a book? In M. A. Leaska (Ed.), *The Virginia Woolf reader* (pp. 233–245). New York: Harcourt Brace Jovanovich.

Woolf, V. (1975, 1977, 1980). *The diary of Virginia Woolf.* Vols. 1–3. 1915–1930 (A. O. Bell, Ed., Vol. 1; A. O. Bell & A. McNeillie, Eds., Vols. 2–3). New York: Harcourt Brace & Company.

Woolf, V. (1982). *To the lighthouse: The original holograph draft.* S. Dick (Ed.). Toronto, Canada: University of Toronto.

Woolf, V. (1985). A sketch of the past. In J. Schulkind (Ed.), *Moments of being* (pp. 64–159). New York: Harcourt Brace & Company.

Woolf, V. (1990). *A passionate apprentice: The early journals, 1897–1909.* M. A. Leaska (Ed.). New York: Harcourt Brace Jovanovich.

William Wordsworth

1770–1850

Poet

Author of *The Prelude, Lyrical Ballads* (co-published with Samuel Taylor Coleridge), and *The Excursion*

Linda R. Jeffrey

Rowan University

WILLIAM WORDSWORTH, English Lake poet, is revered as a major literary figure and early leader of Romanticism. Ranked with Shakespeare and Milton by Coleridge and later by Matthew Arnold, Wordsworth's radical self-consciousness, intense naturalism, interest in the lives and speech of common people, and strong sense of poetic vocation transformed the subsequent development of poetry and poetics. Remembered today as the supreme nature poet, Wordsworth was also a poet, as Keats observed, of human suffering who could "think into the human heart." He was vitally interested in the development of the imagination. As he wrote in his autobiographical masterpiece, The Prelude, *"the mind of man" is "the main region of my song."*

Portrait of William Wordsworth, 1806. Used with permission from The Wordsworth Trust, Dove Cottage.

I. BACKGROUND

Wordsworth was born April 7, 1770, in Cockermouth, a village in the English Lake District, an area whose "craggs, and forest glooms, and opening lakes" inspired in him a deep love for nature. He was the second child of five born to Ann and John Wordsworth who both died by the time that he was 13 years old. After a period of formal education at Cockermouth, Hawkshead, and Cambridge (St. John's College), youthful walking tours on the Continent, and a sojourn in France during the French Revolution that included a love affair resulting in the birth of an illegitimate French daughter, most of his life was spent in his beloved Lake District in the company of his extraordinary sister Dorothy and his exemplary wife Mary and their children.

Although it is probably often the case that a creative person's quality of productivity is uneven, with periods of breakthroughs and exceptional generativity interspersed with dryer, less productive periods, in Wordsworth's case a decline in the quality of the poetry written in his later years has received much critical comment. His early work and youthful democratic zeal have met with much greater contemporary critical approval, whereas the more conservative political views of his mature years have been viewed by some as something approaching a moral lapse. Certainly the poetic creativity of his youth was stunning, and to some extent the mature Wordsworth is doomed by comparison with the romantic figure of the poet as a young man, engaged by the French Revolution, alienated from his unimaginative, stodgy relatives, and in deep passionate communion with nature and sensory experience. Readers and critics alike today may find it harder to admire the mature Wordsworth, worried about the financial responsibility of a large household, imposing upon his children his ideas of what they should do with their lives, and reshaping his poems to be more orthodox. It is ironic that though today Wordsworth's later work is not critically celebrated, in his own time his reputation as a poet increased as he aged. DeQuincy wrote, "Up to 1820 the name of Wordsworth was trampled under foot; from 1820 to 1830 it was militant; from 1830 to 1835 it has been triumphant."

Wordsworth experienced a period of exceptional poetic productivity from 1798 to 1808, including the *annis mirabilis* (1798), in which he and Coleridge published *Lyrical Ballads,* a volume of historic literary significance opening with Coleridge's "Ancient Mariner," and closing with Wordsworth's "Tintern Abbey." In 1800 he published the second edition of *Lyrical Ballads,* including his famous "Preface" in which he defined poetry as "the spontaneous overflow of powerful feelings: it takes its origin from emotion recollected in tranquillity" and argued that poetry should be written in "the real language of men."

Wordsworth's poetry was roundly condemned by the critics for its "low" subject matter and language. Francis Jeffrey, a highly influential critic writing in the *Edinburgh Review,* severely attacked Wordsworth's radical poetic departure and, in response to the 1814 publication of *The Excursion,* issued his famous dismissal, "This will never do." Wordsworth's poetry was also the target of satire. In 1808 *The Simpliciad: A Satirico-didactic Poem* offered "Hints for the Scholars of the New School." *The British Critic* referred to *The Simpliciad* and pronounced this judgment on *Poems, in Two Volumes*: "such flimsy, puerile thoughts, expressed in such feeble and halting verse, we have seldom seen." Wordsworth's task was difficult indeed for he had to create the audience for his poetry of, in the words of the preeminent Wordsworth biographer, Stephen Gill, "the familiar, the homely, and the unregarded."

A. Intimacy, Sorrow, and Creative Work

Close associations and intimate friendships were important throughout Wordsworth's life although he expressed reticence in making new acquaintances. The early deaths of their parents influenced the close bonds between Wordsworth and his four siblings. Upon their mother's death Dorothy was sent to live with her mother's cousin, Elizabeth Threlkeld, and she did not see her brother William again for 9 years.

When they were reunited in young adulthood, William and Dorothy Wordsworth shared a brother-sister intimacy of unique complexity and passionate devotion. He called her "My hope, my joy, my sister, and my friend,/Or something dearer still, if reason knows/a dearer thought, or in the heart of love/There be a dearer name." She refers to him in her journal as "my Beloved" and "my darling." Wordsworth grounded his being and his creative work in the loving domestic community that he and Dorothy, and later Mary Hutchinson, his wife, established. In addition to the emotional support offered by his circle, Wordsworth also found a group of ready helpmates to transcribe his poetry and offer useful criticism. Of fundamental importance to his creative work was their belief in his calling as a poet.

Wordsworth's friendship with the poet Coleridge was among the most important relationships of his life and was central to the development of both poets' creativity. Coleridge described the bond that he felt with William and Dorothy Wordsworth in 1798 as "three persons and one soul." In 1810 Wordsworth became estranged from Coleridge, and although there was a reconciliation of sorts, their intimacy never regained its previous intensity or level of trust. Coleridge thereafter referred to the break in the friendship as one of the greatest sorrows of his life.

Though Wordsworth was blessed with a devoted circle of friends and family, his adult life was not without pain and loss. His brother John's death in 1805 in a shipwreck came as a serious blow. Almost 40 years later Wordsworth's grief over the loss of his brother was still powerfully evident in the 1842 volume, *Elegiac Verses: In Memory of My Brother, John Wordsworth.* In a period of 6 months in 1812, two of Wordsworth's children died: Catherine, aged 3 years, and Thomas, aged 6 years. Wordsworth grieved the loss of his children intensely, expressing his feelings about Catherine, whom he called his "heart's best treasure," in the sonnet, "Surprised by Joy." In the 1812 revisions of *The Excursion,* Wordsworth drew on his own losses to incorporate themes of pain, disillusion, and fear into the character of the Solitary.

Following the deaths of the two children, the Wordsworth household moved to Rydal Mount and rebuilt their domestic security. In the last 20 years of Wordsworth's life, however, the haven of personal stability that had been so important for his productivity was shaken to its roots. Beginning in 1829 his sister Dorothy suffered a series of physical and mental breakdowns, requiring long periods of bedrest and nursing. She developed a dependency on opium and displayed senile dementia resembling Alzheimer's disease. She was nursed at home during her quarter-century decline, which dramatically altered the normal social life of the household that had been so precious to them all. Dorothy outlived Wordsworth, dying in 1855.

Ironically, at the time that public acclaim for his poetry was increasing, the people who had supported his creative work, and served as the sources of his personal stability and strength, began to die. In the last years of his life, Wordsworth was deeply affected by the series of deaths of family members and friends, including the deaths of Mary Wordsworth's sisters, Sara Hutchinson (1835) and Joanna Hutchinson (1843); Edward Wordsworth, a 5-year-old grandson (1845); Christopher Wordsworth, his brother (1846); John Wordsworth, his nephew (1846); Dora Wordsworth Quillinan, Wordsworth's beloved daughter who had married against his wishes (1847); and Hartley Coleridge (1849) to whom he demonstrated a lifelong fatherly protection.

B. Fiscal Survival in the Life of the Poet

Wordsworth struggled to survive financially through much of his life. When their father died, the Wordsworth children had been unable to collect a sizable claim for funds that their father had spent conducting the affairs of his employer, Lord James Lonsdale. Eighteen years of economic dependency on rather unsympathetic relatives elapsed before the claim was settled at the death of Lord Lonsdale.

Modest economic help came to Wordsworth early in his career through an inheritance from Raisley Calvert, whom Wordsworth had nursed until he died from tuberculosis. In *The Prelude* Wordsworth recognized Calvert, along with Dorothy and Coleridge, as having enabled him to realize his destiny as a poet. His financial position finally changed in 1813 when he acquired the position of distributor of stamps, leading Browning to lament, "Just for a handful of silver he left us." He held that position until 1842 when he was given a civil list pension.

II. WORDSWORTH'S ACCOMPLISHMENTS

A. The Organization of Poetic Purpose

The creativity theorist Gruber has suggested that each creative person has particular conceptions of his or her life tasks. This network of enterprise constitutes the person's organization of purpose, defines the working self, and provides a structure that organizes a complex life. Wordsworth had a highly individuated sense of vocation as a poet that he described in *The Prelude.* In the context of his intimate friendships, especially that with Coleridge, he elaborated a plan that occupied his creative efforts for decades. One of the difficulties of his creative life was that his friend Coleridge had aspirations for Wordsworth to be a philosophical poet when his true gifts and vision lay elsewhere. Plans for *The Recluse* were not abandoned until 1838, several years after Coleridge's death. Another difficulty of his poetic career was that for a considerable part of it he did not seek to publish his major poems, which were being revised in manuscript. Hence he faced the dilemma of privately feeling a strong sense of poetic vocation without an accompanying public recognition of that identity.

He had started writing verses as early as 1786 about his "thoughts and images" of the Lake District scenery in which he was raised. While a freshman at Cambridge University he composed a large part of the *An Evening Walk,* completing it in 1789. In 1790 he took a walking tour with his Cambridge friend Robert Jones in France and Switzerland, which is celebrated in *Descriptive Sketches.* In January 1791 Wordsworth took his B.A. degree and went to France, ostensibly to spend a year learning French. During his sojourn in France he wrote much of *Descriptive Sketches,* which was published with *An Evening Walk* in February, 1793, the same month in which England declared war on France. Wordsworth experienced a deep sense of alienation from his own country and was at a loss to plan his personal future during this period. Complicating his personal outlook was his inability to return to France where Annette Vallon had given birth to his child.

In the autumn of 1793, he began work on *Guilt and Sorrow,* his first considerable poetic project. Finished in 1794, a part of it, under the title of *The Female Vagrant,* was printed in the *Lyrical Ballads* in 1798. A revised form was published in 1842. He was occupied with *The Borderers: A Tragedy* in 1795 and 1796. In 1795 he and his sister Dorothy settled at Racedown where Wordsworth began *Margaret, or The Ruined Cottage,* finishing the work at Alfoxden where the Wordsworths moved in 1797 to be near Coleridge at Nether Stowey. In *The Prelude* Wordsworth describes the healing influence of his sister and Coleridge during this period.

Following the September, 1798, publication of the *Lyrical Ballads,* in one of the coldest winters of the 18th century, the Wordsworths spent several lonely months in a provincial town in Germany where he began writing what would later become his great autobiographical poem, *The Prelude.* Far from his beloved English Lake District, he deeply examined the memories of his childhood and took the first tentative steps in a major literary enterprise that would occupy him at intervals for close to 40 years.

In October 1799 he settled in Grasmere and was a permanent resident of the region for the rest of his life, leaving only for an occasional trip to Scotland, London, or the Continent. In 1800 he added a preface to the second edition of *Lyrical Ballads,* and a second volume of poems, including some of his finest works. A third and fourth edition appeared respectively in 1802 and 1805.

In 1804 he married his childhood friend Mary Hutchinson. In 1807 he published the *Poems in Two Volumes,* including the "Ode to Duty" and the "Ode on Intimations of Immortality." These volumes established Wordsworth as a great innovator of poetic form. Indeed, by 1807 arguably much of his greatest work had been completed, including the volumes of 1800 and 1807, *The Prelude,* the *Recluse* fragment, and *Margaret, or the Ruined Cottage.*

An account of Wordsworth's oeuvre is complicated by his habits of revision, often extending over decades, and his rearranging poems for publication. *The Excursion* was published in 1814, followed in 1815 by the first collected edition of his works and *The White Doe of Rylestone.* Five years elapsed before the series of his later works began to be published, including *The River Duddon* and *Miscellaneous Poems* (1820), *Ecclesiastical Sketches* (1822), and *Evening Voluntaries* (1835).

B. The Poet Writing Prose

Although Wordsworth is remembered primarily as a poet concerned with the human relationship to nature, he also wrote at least two prose works of continuing general interest, "Preface to Lyrical Ballads," his statement of poetics, and "A Guide through the District of the Lakes," his tourist handbook to the landscape of his native region.

His political writings include "A Letter to the Bishop of Llandaff," written in 1793 but not published until 1876, *The Convention of Cintra* (1809), and *Two Addresses to the Freeholders of Westmoreland* (1818). Although *The Convention of Cintra* has been criticized as a reactionary nationalistic rejection of Wordsworth's youthful embrace of revolutionary radicalism, the essay is grounded in Wordsworth's view of the potential of human nature and the human heart. Statesmen, he asserted, living in their isolation and artificial world, lack vital knowledge, "a knowledge of human kind." Although Wordsworth's essay had no significant impact on subsequent political decision making or public opinion, and 178 of the 500 copies printed were sold as waste paper, writing the essay provided focus for ideas to be expressed in *The Ruined Cottage,* later a part of *The Excursion.*

III. CONSTRUCTIVE REPETITION AND REVISION

Constructive repetition is a fundamental process in creative work. As Bernstein wrote in *The Unanswered Question,* "the repetitive principle is at the very source of musical art (and of poetry)." Repeated contact with ideas, images, or sounds may enable a creator to discover new meanings and to reorganize and modify previously formulated views or expressions. Revision may be understood in this sense to be one form of constructive repetition.

Writers may differ as to the value that they place on revision in their work process. For many creators, the patience, discipline, and willingness to put time and energy into reworking a creative product are crucial for the accomplishment of their creative goals. By the same token, compulsive revision may become counterproductive in creative work.

Wordsworth was internally driven to revise. Gill has suggested that Wordsworth found the idea of finality unbearable. For Wordsworth to republish a poem without first subjecting it to revision was to him unthinkable. Moreover, multiple fair copies had to be produced as Wordsworth continued to cross out, substitute words and phrases, and interline even as the printing process commenced. One marvels at the patience of Dorothy, Mary, and his daughter Dora who frequently served as his transcribers. Even his son-in-law, Edward Quillinan, was enlisted on occasion as scribe and recorded in his diary his disappointment that "helping Mr. W. to tinker" prevented his partridge shooting. In addition, intense revision put Wordsworth out of sorts and made him irritable and unwell. In an 1840 letter from Salzburg to his wife, he apologized to

his "inestimable fellow-labourer" for his irritable state caused by "overstrained labor."

A. Revision and Elaboration: Microanalysis

Composing is a process that requires, as Vera John-Steiner in *Notebooks of the Mind* has suggested, an ability to synthesize germinal ideas with elaborative structures. The record of Wordsworth's worksheets reflects a work process in which constant revision takes place as the poem is created.

The earliest drafts for *The Prelude* may serve as an example of this process. Unpublished during the poet's life, *The Prelude* took the form of three major versions. The 1799 *Prelude* is the first version. Twenty-four pages of drafts toward Part I of the 1799 *Prelude* are found in a notebook, MS JJ, dating from Wordsworth's trip to Germany. A rich source of information concerning the process of poetic creativity, these drafts are the record of the birth process of a poetic masterpiece.

The 24 pages of drafts contain approximately 420 lines. Only about 26 lines were not later used in the 1799 *Prelude,* for a later version of *The Prelude,* or for some other poem. Wordsworth displayed a frugality with his poetic creation, and apparently found it difficult to discard lines. About 140 lines of Part I first appear in MS JJ, and are included unchanged in the 1799 version.

The Gestalt of Part I of the 1799 *Prelude* emerged in the MS JJ worksheets. Lines composed early in the MS JJ drafts serve as the opening of 1799 *Prelude,* and lines composed toward the end of the drafts became the conclusion of Part I. There are over a hundred revisions in these 24 pages of drafting, mostly instances in which Wordsworth substituted a word, phrase, or line for another. Rarely did he delete material without replacing it.

The 24 pages each vary markedly in the number of revisions that they contain, ranging from 12 to none with an average of about four revisions per page. The number of revisions per page declined as composition proceeded, reflecting an interaction between the poet and his poem. The growing structure of the poem both guided his composition and limited his alternatives.

The MS JJ drafts had been completed in Goslar, Germany, during the winter of 1798–1799. After these drafts were written, the Wordsworths left Goslar, traveling for a period in Germany before returning to England in early May. At Sockburn, the home of Mary Hutchinson who would later marry Wordsworth, Wordsworth began writing again. By the end of 1799, approximately a year after the first MS JJ drafts were composed, Wordsworth completed the two-part *Prelude.*

Gill has offered an account of revisions in other Wordsworth poems, including most of the poems in later editions of the *Lyrical Ballads* and *The Female Vagrant.* Wordsworth changed single words, phrases, and occasionally wrote lines as well as moving stanzas around. He also changed the titles of poems on occasion. Characteristic of Wordsworth's style of revision was a blindness to scale of revision, treating all revision as important.

B. Poems as Living Presences

Writing poetry is a way of thinking. The thinker as poet may revise a previously written poem as his or her thinking changes about an idea or image or experience. In the process of writing, a dialogue between the thinker and his or her written words, as Bruner has described it, may develop. Wordsworth had this kind of relationship, in a sense, a conversation, with his poetic creations. He treated his poems, as Gill has pointed out, not as discrete objects, but rather as "living presences" of a mind that registered its evolution not only in the creation of new work but in the transformation of old work. Although the subtitle of *The Prelude* was

"Growth of a Poet's Mind," the true record of the development of Wordsworth's mind is in the revisions that he made in his poems throughout his long life.

IV. THE FINAL YEARS

In 1843 Wordsworth succeeded Southey as poet laureate at a time in his life when he had, ironically, for the most part stopped writing poetry. In the early 1840s he became an increasingly pious man, identifying himself as a Christian poet, and revising *The Excursion* of 1845 to be an explicitly Christian poem. Preparation of the 1845 volume constituted Wordsworth's last major poetical effort.

To a degree troublesome to Mary Wordsworth who complained of the American visitors, Rydal Mount became a shrine for those seeking the venerable sage, and the tourists came in droves. He continued his lifelong habit of walking, even crossing the Malvern Hill twice in the last year of his life. In his final illness, pleurisy, he was bedridden for a month. In pain and with trouble breathing, he suffered at the last until he died at noon on April 23, 1850.

Bibliography

Gill, S. (1990). *William Wordsworth: A life.* Oxford: Oxford University Press.
Hartman, G. (1987). *Wordsworth's poetry 1787–1814.* Cambridge, MA: Harvard University Press.
Parrish, S. (Ed.). (1977). *The prelude, 1798–1799 by William Wordsworth.* Ithaca, NY: Cornell University Press.

Wilbur and Orville Wright

(Wilbur) 1867–1912 (Orville) 1871–1948

Inventors

Inventors of the first successful powered airplane

Peter L. Jakab

National Air and Space Museum
Smithsonian Institution
Washington, DC

WILBUR AND ORVILLE WRIGHT placed their names firmly in the pantheon of great American inventors with their creation of the world's first successful, powered, heavier-than-air flying machine. The airplane they designed and built in Dayton, Ohio, and flew at Kitty Hawk, North Carolina, on December 17, 1903, inaugurated the aerial age, one of the defining characteristics of 20th century. The Wrights began serious experimentation in aeronautics in 1899 and perfected their craft by 1905. In this short period, with remarkable originality, they defined the essential elements of the problem, conceived creative technical solutions, and built practical mechanical design tools and components that resulted in a viable aircraft. They did much more than simply coax a machine off the ground. They established the fundamental principles of aircraft design that are still in place today. In 1908, they demonstrated their invention publicly in the United States and Europe and became instant international celebrities. By 1910 the Wright Company was manufacturing airplanes for sale and the brothers were on their way to becoming wealthy men. Despite the Wrights' dramatic leap ahead of the rest of the aeronautical community, contemporary experimenters and would-be aviators quickly caught up to the brothers and surpassed their designs. Nevertheless, it was Wilbur and Orville Wright who made the pivotal breakthrough after countless others had failed, and they did so virtually alone. Transport by air of material and people, quickly over great distances, and the military applications of flight technology have had an incalculable economic, geopolitical, and cultural impact all over the globe. The Wright brothers' invention not only solved a long-studied technical problem, but it helped create a new world.

I. BACKGROUND

The Wright brothers were the product of deep midwestern American roots. Several generations on both sides of the family had been early settlers on the Ohio and Indiana frontier. Their father, Milton Wright, was an itinerant minister, a bishop in the Church of the United Brethren in Christ. His calling would take the family to numerous church posts throughout the region. Milton's wife, Susan, already a member of the United Brethren when they met, was a bright, shy, capable woman. She had studied literature at Hartsville

The "moment" of invention. On December 17, 1903, at 10:35 a.m., the Wright *Flyer* lifts off the beach at Kitty Hawk, North Carolina, with Orville Wright at the controls. Wilbur Wright, at right, observes the brothers' triumph. Courtesy of the Library of Congress.

College, though she left 3 months short of graduation. She also possessed considerable mechanical aptitude, a trait passed on to her sons. After a long courtship and lengthy separations due to Milton's missionary travels, he and Susan were married in 1859 to begin a Christian life devoted to the Church. Wilbur and Orville were two of five surviving children borne by Susan Wright. Two older brothers, Reuchlin and Lorin, arrived in 1861 and 1862. Wilbur was next, born on April 16, 1867, near Millville, Indiana. After giving birth to a set of twins that died in infancy, Susan delivered another healthy son, Orville, on August 19, 1871, in Dayton, Ohio. The Wrights' last child, a daughter named Katherine, was born three years to the day after Orville, in 1874.

Despite their frontier heritage, Wilbur and Orville lived and worked in the suburban, middle-class neighborhood of West Dayton, Ohio. They grew up during the early industrialization of America, and by the time they began their aeronautical experiments in the 1890s, they had witnessed the emergence of numerous technologies that would define the modern era. Milton and Susan were stern disciplinarians but warm, loving parents. They encouraged the intellectual curiosity and creative pursuits of all their children. Although neither Wilbur nor Orville received a high school diploma, both were committed to broad learning and were ex-

cellent students. They made good use of the rich family library and supplemented their formal schooling with a great deal of private study. Though technically high school dropouts, such a characterization belies their extensive self-education and strong intellect.

By 1890 Reuchlin and Lorin had moved out and started families of their own, and Susan Wright had succumbed to tuberculosis. The remaining four Wright family members became an extremely close-knit group, all continuing to live in the same household, providing a network of support that carried them through all manner of crises and triumphs. Despite their powerful commitment to family, Wilbur and Orville remained lifelong bachelors and had no children of their own.

As teenagers the Wright brothers showed little direction or focus toward their future. Wilbur's early plans to attend Yale Divinity College were thwarted by a series of health problems and a funk he fell into following the death of his mother. Orville flitted about from one interest to another. The printing trade was an early pursuit that seemed to hold some sustained interest for the younger Wright, and ultimately Wilbur joined him in several small printing business ventures. But it was in 1892, when the brothers opened their first bicycle rental and repair shop, that Wilbur and Orville found a livelihood to support themselves. At ages 25 and 21, they had settled into the comparatively ordinary life of hardworking local businessmen. It was also during this time that the close relationship and teamwork that would be so important to their aeronautical work solidified.

II. CREATIVE METHODOLOGY

The Wright brothers' story always begs the basic question: How did these two modest, seemingly unremarkable bicycle shopkeepers develop such a world-changing invention as the airplane? How were these men, working essentially alone with little formal scientific or technical training, able to solve a problem so complex and demanding as heavier-than-air flight in only a few short years when it had defied better-known experimenters for centuries? In short, why Wilbur and Orville?

On the surface, the fact that the Wrights did invent a successful airplane quickly and with little assistance would suggest that sheer genius had to have been at the core of their achievement. Probing deeper, however, it becomes apparent that there were a number of specific research techniques, innate conceptual skills, and personality traits that came together in a unique way to largely explain why these two men invented the airplane. In short, Wilbur and Orville had a definable inventive method that in very direct terms led them to the secrets of flight. The Wright brothers unquestionably were talented people. They do indeed deserve much of their towering reputation as inventors. But their genius should be understood in terms of the approach they evolved and employed to create the technology of flight, not just the singular act of getting a machine into the air. Examining the Wrights' inventive methodology peels away some of the mystery behind their rapid and startling success and adds even more luster to their accomplishment.

First and foremost, the Wright brothers' approach to mechanical flight was grounded in strict engineering techniques. They did not develop their aircraft using uninformed trial-and-error methods like so many of their contemporaries. Nor did they tackle the problem as scientists. Wilbur and Orville did not set out to discover the theoretical principles of flight in the same sense that Newton or Einstein sought to explain physical phenomenon in nature. The Wrights' work focused explicitly on determining the design features required to make an airplane fly. Indeed, they not only invented the airplane, but they invented aeronautical engineering in the process.

Merged with this basic engineering perspective and its associated practices were a number of conceptual capabilities and approaches present in the Wrights' method that in large measure explain their inventive success. Among the most important was their capacity for developing conceptual models of a problem that could then be transformed into practical hardware. The brothers' considerable ability for turning abstract concepts into workable machinery reveals itself over and over again in their aeronautical work.

Another prominent feature of the Wright brothers' creative thought process was the great extent to which they used mental graphic imagery and nonverbal thought to conceptualize basic structures and mechanisms, even aerodynamic theory. There is invariably a distinct facet of design that is aesthetic in nature, an aspect that results from the maker's particular sense of what will or will not work or what looks right or wrong. Frequently, truly ground-breaking technological innovations are not based solely on articulated scientific or engineering principles, mathematical calculations, or other forms of knowledge that can be expressed verbally. The designer literally has a vision of what the object or structure should look like and how it will work and, in conjunction with verbal forms of knowledge, produces a tangible article based on these nonverbal ideas. Wilbur and Orville's keen facility for nonverbal thought was among the most prevalent and salient aspects of their inventive method.

The Wrights reinforced these innate talents with several sound approaches to technological innovation. They developed a series of gliders and powered airplanes that were based on a single, evolving basic design, modifying only a few factors at a time. This continuity of design allowed them to isolate flaws and capitalize on design successes, and thereby move ahead rapidly. Though seemingly an obvious approach, many of the Wrights' contemporaries jumped from one radical design to another.

Wilbur and Orville also understood that an airplane was not just one invention but numerous inventions all working in concert to produce a workable flying machine. The airplane is a technological system, each component of which, including the pilot, had to be addressed. The Wrights saw no individual component to be more important than any other. Aerodynamics could not be focused on at the expense of structure, propulsion at the expense of control, and so on. The Wrights' unwavering attention to the complete technological system of mechanical flight was crucial to their success.

Technological transfer, drawing concepts and even hardware from seemingly unrelated fields, also played a valuable role in the Wrights' creativity. The most conspicuous example was the bicycle. In addition to utilizing a number of mechanical devices from bicycles, such as sprockets and chain drives, the vehicle was the source of an important conceptual idea regarding flight control. The bicycle is an utterly unstable machine but completely controllable. Intimate familiarity and comfort with this characteristic in bicycles freed the Wrights to think of airplanes in the same way. The Wrights were not bound by the idea that airplanes must be inherently stable, as were so many other aeronautical experimenters of the day. This concept was critical to the development of the brothers' effective control system, a key element of their invention.

No less important to understanding the Wright brothers' creative achievement was their personal relationship and outlook. More than simply a closeness between brothers, they possessed a synergy, sometimes forged through heated yet constructive argument, that produced collaborative solutions to vexing technical problems. Moreover, their closeness with the other members of the family, often serving as protection from what they perceived as a pernicious, untrustworthy outside world, provided a supportive environment. This instilled confidence to reject the theories of well-known and experienced aeronautical researchers when the brothers felt their own ideas were correct.

Finally, when seeking to explain the Wright brothers inventive success, the factor of timing cannot be ignored. They took up the problem of heavier-than-air flight at a propitious moment. By the time the Wrights entered the field, the study of aeronautics had been legitimized by several prominent late-19th century experimenters, and a foundation of aeronautical knowledge was coalescing around their work. Although the Wrights worked alone, they did not operate in isolation of the advancements contributed by their predecessors. Despite the high degree of originality in their work, there is no reason to believe that the Wright brothers would have invented the airplane no matter when they took up the problem.

The creation of any fundamentally new technology is the result of a myriad of unique factors. The airplane is no exception. The elements cited here, however, were central to the Wright brothers' inventive success. This particular combination of engineering techniques and approaches, innate conceptual abilities, and personality traits and circumstances go far toward answering the basic question: Why Wilbur and Orville?

III. INVENTION

The Wright brothers did not possess a lifelong passion for flight when they began their investigations in the late 1890s. Wilbur in particular was casting about for something to quell his restless intellect. The bicycle business furnished an adequate living, but it did not offer the mental rigor the brothers' active minds craved. The airplane quickly became a consuming passion, but at first it was only an outlet for the Wrights' inquisitiveness.

They began with a literature search to acquaint themselves with the work of their predecessors. A letter to the Smithsonian Institution in 1899 was among their initial inquiries. After absorbing the information the Wrights received from the Smithsonian and other sources, they quickly recognized that control of the aircraft was a fundamental problem to be solved, and to their surprise, few experimenters had theretofore given it much thought.

In the fall of 1899 the brothers developed a basic means of lateral control and tested the mechanism with a small 5-ft wingspan biplane kite. The idea would prove to be among their most significant and creative innovations. It would in fact be the central element of their later 1906 patent on the airplane. The idea was also one the more striking illustrations of their creative skills and method.

Of the Wright predecessors who concerned themselves with control at all, some balanced their craft by continually altering the center of gravity of their aircraft by shifting the body weight of the pilot. Others simply tried steering with a rudder similar to how a ship maneuvers in water. Recognizing that the first approach was limited and that the second was technically flawed, the Wrights chose to control their aircraft aerodynamically. They reasoned that if a wing generates lift when presented to an oncoming flow of air, producing differing amounts of lift on either end of the wing would cause one side to rise more than the other. In other words, it would cause the wing to bank. If the pilot could mechanically alter the amounts of lift on either side of the aircraft when and to the degree the pilot chose, the aircraft could be maintained in level flight in the face of wind gusts or other forces and could be turned when desired.

The Wrights achieved this control by a means they termed *wing warping*. To induce the differing amounts of lift on either side of the airplane, the brothers literally twisted, or warped, the wing structure such that one side was presented to the wind at a higher angle than the other, which increased the lift on that side, thereby setting up the bank of the whole craft. Lines were attached to the ends of the wings and manipulated by the pilot via a hip cradle mounted at the center of the wing to induce the warp. The idea was seminal because it contributed to a method of effectively controlling an aircraft in three-dimensional space, and since it was aerodynamically based, it did not limit the size of the aircraft as body weight shifting obviously did. All aircraft continue to use this basic means of lateral control developed by the Wright brothers.

This aspect of the Wrights' work was not only at the heart of their invention, but it is a telling illustration of their creative methodology and thought processes. They adeptly moved from the abstract idea of aerodynamic control to a concrete structural and mechanical means of employing the concept. Wilbur hit upon the idea of warping the wings after serendipitously twisting a bicycle inner tube box in his fingers one day. He noticed that the box could be twisted longitudinally and still maintain its structural form. The Wrights' biplane wing arrangement mirrored the structural cell of the box. This is a powerful example of visual thinking at work in the design process. Further, even though they worked this idea out on small kites and gliders, they kept the goal of a practical airplane in mind and knew they had to conceive something that could be used in a larger, powered vehicle later. All these aspects of the Wrights' development of the the critical wing

warping system demonstrate their creative talents at their finest.

Encouraged by the success of their small wing warping kite, the brothers went on to build and fly two full-size, piloted gliders in 1900 and 1901, testing them on the isolated sand dunes at Kitty Hawk, North Carolina. Although the control system worked well and the structural design of the craft proved sound, the Wrights continued to experience aerodynamic problems with these designs. The gliders simply did not produce the amount of overall lift that their calculations predicted they should. Now at a critical juncture, Wilbur and Orville decided to conduct an extensive series of aerodynamic tests of their wing shapes. They built a small wind tunnel in the fall of 1901 to gather a body of accurate aerodynamic data on which to design their next glider.

The heart of the Wright wind tunnel was the test instruments mounted inside to measure coefficients of lift and drag, the terms in the equations for calculating lift and drag about which the brothers were in doubt. Like the wing warping system, these wind tunnel instruments are striking examples of the Wrights' ingenuity and skill. They were in essence mechanical analogues of the mathematical aerodynamic equations the brothers were using to design their aircraft. They were physically constructed such that all the factors other that the one they wished to investigate dropped out of the readings taken from the instruments. The resulting data could then be used directly to determine the shape and to calculate the size of wings. The ease with which the Wrights incorporated an abstract mathematical relationship into a practical piece of hardware that yielded concrete design information goes to the heart their creative capabilities and approach and their inventive success.

The Wrights' third glider, built in 1902 based on the wind tunnel experiments, was a dramatic success. The lift problems were solved, and with a few more refinements to the control system they were now able to make numerous extended glides. An important element could easily be overlooked—not only had the brothers built a viable flying machine, but they were now able to gain valuable practice in the air; they could teach themselves to fly. This skill would be vital when attempting to fly a heavier, more complex powered airplane later. The Wrights understood that the pilot was yet another component of the overall system that had to work properly to achieve mechanical flight.

Buoyed by the success of their 1902 glider, the Wrights were now convinced they stood at the doorstep of realizing the age-old dream of human flight. During the spring and summer of 1903 they built their first powered airplane. Maintaining the basic continuity of their proven glider design, the only fundamentally new element of the 1903 craft was the application of power. The brothers made a small, 12-horsepower gasoline engine, which was no insignificant achievement. But the truly innovative aspect of the propulsion system was the propellers.

After realizing that marine propeller theory was nearly nonexistent and inapplicable to flight, the Wrights designed an aerial propeller that stands out as one of the most creative aspects of their entire airplane. They reasoned that if a wing moving horizontally in a flow of air produces a vertical lift force, a similar airfoil-shaped structure turned on its side and spun to create the flow of air over the surface would produce horizontal thrust; in essence, they envisioned a rotary wing. The details of actually designing the propeller proved to be quite complex, but this basic concept was sound and revolutionary. All aircraft propellers since have been of the Wright design. Again, it is apparent that Wilbur and Orville's facility to see abstract principles in physical structures and materials, and their mental agility at manipulating these visual forms in their mind's eye, enabled them to create a critical component of the airplane.

By the fall of 1903, with the powered airplane ready for trial, the brothers headed south to their flight test site of Kitty Hawk. Once they had resolved some teething problems with the engine transmission system, the Wrights were ready. After four years of intensive effort, Orville lifted the Wright *Flyer* off the beach at 10:35 a.m., on December 17, for a 12-s flight. They made three more flights that morning, alternating pilots. With Wilbur at the controls, the fourth and last flight covered 852 ft in 59 s. With this long, sustained flight, there was no question the brothers had flown. The aerial age was born.

At the conclusion of this flight, a gust of wind picked up the *Flyer* and cartwheeled it across the beach. Badly damaged, the world's first airplane was never flown again. After bringing their design to practicality with two more powered machines in 1904 and 1905, the Wrights stopped flying entirely for 2½ years to secure their patent, which was granted in 1906, and to try and sell their invention. In the summer of 1908, they demonstrated their creation in the United States and Europe, amazing crowds of observers on every occasion. They were no longer Wilbur and Orville Wright, proprietors of the Wright Cycle Company. They were now the Wright brothers, inventors of the airplane.

Bibliography

Crouch, T. D. (1989). *The bishop's boys: A life of Wilbur and Orville Wright*. New York: W.W. Norton.

Howard, F. (1987). *Wilbur and Orville: A biography of the Wright brothers*. New York: Knopf.

Jakab, P. L. (1990). *Visions of a flying machine: The Wright brothers and the process of invention*. Washington, DC: Smithsonian Institution Press.

McFarland, M. W. (Ed.). (1953). *The papers of Wilbur and Orville Wright* (Vols. 1–2). New York: McGraw-Hill.

Writing and Creativity

Steven R. Pritzker

Luminescent Creativity, Greenbrae, California

I. Techniques
II. Results of the Research
III. Conclusions

than schizophrenia characterized by more mild disturbances in cognition and affect.

Alcoholism A diseased condition of the system, brought about by the continued use of alcoholic liquors.

Depression A psychoneurotic or psychotic disorder marked especially by sadness, inactivity, difficulty in thinking and concentration, a significant increase or decrease in appetite and time spent sleeping, feelings of dejection and hopelessness, and sometimes suicidal tendencies.

DSM The diagnostic and statistical manual issued by the American Psychiatric Association.

Hypomania A mild mania, especially when part of a manic-depressive cycle.

Manic-Depression Characterized either by mania or by depression, or by alternating mania and depression.

Schizaffective Disorder A class of mental disorder characterized by symptoms of schizophrenia and by disturbances in mood that are similar to those in the affective disorders.

Schizophrenia A psychotic disorder characterized by loss of contact with the environment, by noticeable deterioration in the level of functioning in everyday life, and by disintegration of personality expressed as disorder of feeling, thought (as in hallucinations and delusions), and conduct—called also dementia praecox.

Schizotypal Personality Disorder A mental disorder less severe

Storytelling goes back to the earliest days of spoken language. Writing began as a symbolic means to represent oral communication. This article will present an overview of techniques and results from investigations on **WRITING AND CREATIVITY.** *Some creativity researchers have focused on eminent fiction and poetry writers, attempting to determine if they differ from the general population or other eminent creative people. Other researchers have examined specific writers, trying to understand their life and work.*

I. TECHNIQUES

A. Studies of Biographies

Researchers seek generalizations about eminent writers by compiling statistical data using biographies. They compare this data with information about other creative achievers and the general population, looking for any significant differences. Conclusions from these types of studies may apply to writers as a group, but do not indicate the characteristics of any individual writer.

B. Interviews and Assessments of Writers

Researchers interview eminent writers about their work and in some cases give them psychological evaluations and tests. The majority of these studies evaluate the characteristics and mental health of writers.

Other researchers conduct semistructured interviews focusing on a writer's background, career path, motivation, work habits, internal processes, and personal life. When multiple interviews are conducted, connections that indicate similarities and differences between the subjects are usually offered.

C. Case Studies

Researchers prepare case studies about individual writers by studying their life and work. The results presented in this article will not emphasize individual case studies since they are usually complex and vary widely depending on the training, methodology, and perspective of the author.

Study of collaborative creative writing is just the beginning. A combination of interviewing, observation, and evaluation of changes in the work offer insights into the decision-making process as well as the personal dynamics and leadership factors which may encourage or discourage creativity.

1. The Psychobiography

Freud expressed admiration for creative writers who he said were far in advance of everyday people, because they draw on sources which have not yet opened in science. Freud wrote the prototype for the psychobiography, a format in which key psychological elements in an author's life, which theoretically influenced their work, are presented. Psychobiographies are almost always made without the subject's participation. Critics of this methodology complain there is a great deal of unproven speculation involved, as analyses are not based on experiments or independent evidence. It has also been suggested that the psychoanalytic method reduces life to psychological processes, ignoring social, economic or political forces. More recent researchers in creativity such as Howard Gardner, conclude that Freud's characterizations apply to noncreative as well as creative individuals and thus do not distinguish the effective artist or scientist from the banal one.

Others believe that though Freud's work was not scientifically accurate, his method might provide an imaginative look at the mystery of creativity. A few psychoanalysts and psychologists, most notably Albert Rothenberg, worked with writer-clients who allowed them to write about their creative process using aspects of their therapy.

2. The Systems Approach

The evolving systems approach examines the creative person's life in five contexts, including: total body of work, the milieu in which they worked, their family and personal life, and the sociohistorical period in which they lived.

This approach has been used in studying writers by examining their creative process based on different drafts of their work and their own recollections.

II. RESULTS OF THE RESEARCH

A. Biographical Studies

Biographical studies indicate that successful writers came from more turbulent family backgrounds, suffered more emotional instability, had more problems with alcohol, were more suicidal, and had a lower life expectancy than other eminent professionals.

In 1936, E. Baskin studied 123 nineteenth century authors who were mentioned in at least half the standard histories of literature and compared them to 120 eminent scientists. After studying their biographies, she concluded that writers were more likely to come from poor homes, were more prone toward depression and ill health, and died slightly earlier.

Mildred Goertzel, Victor Goertzel, and Ted Goertzel studied the lives of 717 eminent personalities who had two or more biographies written about them since 1962. The Goertzels compared 92 literary figures with other eminent personalities who lived in the 20th century. They found writers were:

1. More likely to be only children (26% versus 17% overall)
2. Tended to be voracious readers (77% versus 48%)
3. Disliked school (52% versus 33%)

4. Came from homes described as very unhappy (67% versus 44%)
5. Had more alcoholic parents (one or both) (11% versus 7%)
6. Were more likely to commit suicide (11% versus 5%)
7. Were more likely to be divorced (42% versus 35%) or never married (25% versus 19%)
8. Were far more likely to be "sexually divergent" (20 of the 21 personalities identified in the study in this category were literary personalities)

Arnold Ludwig examined the lives of 1,004 eminent people who had a biography reviewed in *The New York Times Book Review* between 1960 and 1990. Included in the total were 180 fiction writers, 64 nonfiction writers, and 53 poets. His findings agreed with other studies that poets and fiction writers are more likely to suffer from some form of psychopathology. While 28% of the total sample had any mental disorder in their lifetime, a striking 87% of the poets, 77% of the fiction writers, and 72% of nonfiction writers were identified by Ludwig as pathological at some point in their lives. Writers were also more likely to have fathers, mothers, and siblings with identifiable pathological problems.

Eminent people in general were more likely to commit suicide (4.4%) than the general population, which had an estimated rate of 1.0 to 1.4%. However, 20% of the poets were considered suicides. Fiction writers had an average rate of suicides while nonfiction writers were below average. Ludwig proposed that emotional problems often interfered with creative productivity, but actually improved performance for 16% of eminent creative people by increasing productivity, overcoming writing blocks, and generating new ideas or better performances.

Felix Post, a psychiatrist, reviewed biographies of 291 famous men in a variety of fields, including science, politics, and art. He concluded that depression occurred in 29% of scientists, 31% of artists, 26% of intellectuals, 30% of politicians and 31% of composers, and that depression occurs twice as often in novelists and dramatists. Post also found a higher incidence of alcoholism in writers. In a follow-up study which focused on biographies of 100 American and British writers, he found that 93% of the writers in his sample suffered some psychopathology. However, in contrast to previous researchers, Post found 14% of poets had no disorders, which made them more stable than other writers. The poets did exhibit more depression, bipolar illness, and suicide than prose writers or playwrights.

Summing up, biographical studies offer impressive indications that eminent writers as a group suffer more problems than other eminent creators or the general population. Despite the robustness of the statistics, they must be considered cautiously. Diagnoses have often been made posthumously using loose and inconsistent diagnostic criteria. In many cases the validity of a diagnosis of mental illness, alcoholism, or suicide cannot be verified. In addition, solid statistical evidence of the extent of mental illness, alcoholism, and suicide in the general population is still far from precise. Finally, it is possible writers with dramatic lives and early deaths are more likely to become eminent and have biographies written about them.

B. Interviews and Assessments

1. Psychopathology

Writers, along with other creative artists, have been subject to the speculation that genius and madness are linked. This association has been traced back to Plato's colorful description of poets' "divine madness" as well as Aristotle's claim that all creative people were touched with melancholia. Anecdotal evidence and biographical studies support the notion that mental illness is more common among fiction writers and poets. [*See* Mad Genius Controversy.]

The most comprehensive face to face study of professional writers was analyzed by Frank Barron, who, with other psychologists, interviewed and psychologically tested 30 professional writers nominated by the faculty of the University of California at Berkeley. Also included in this study were 26 "successful and productive" student writers and nonwriters.

Barron tested for the presence of psychopathology by administering the Minnesota Multiphasic Personality Inventory. He found the most eminent writers scored high on scales measuring schizoid, depressive, hysterical and psychopathic tendencies and in terms of femininity of interest pattern. However, these writers also registered higher scores on ego strength, so Barron concluded that while they suffered psychological turmoil, they also possessed more resources to deal with it. He felt this conclusion was reinforced by their social behavior since they presented themselves as clearly effective people with pride and distinctiveness while sometimes showing pain, protest, distance, and withdrawal, as well as being very emotional. Barron's study warrants replication with a contemporary group of writers because his conclusions might vary with subjects who lived in a different time frame.

Nancy Andreason conducted structured interviews with 30 faculty members at the Iowa workshop over a period of 15 years. Her interest was based on the large number of writers who committed suicide in this century. She wanted to determine if these writers or their first-degree relatives had a history of mental illness. Andreason performed a psychiatric diagnosis of both writers and their relatives, comparing them with a matched control group. She concluded that 24 of the 30 writers (80%) suffered from an affective disorder compared to 9 (30%) of the control sample. She diagnosed 13 writers with a bipolar disorder and 11 with a major depressive disorder. In fact, 2 writers committed suicide while the study was taking place. Using the family history method, she also diagnosed the writers as having many more first-degree relatives with affective disorders and creative ability.

Andreason recognized the limitations of her study, including the fact that she was cognizant of the writers and the controls. Also, writers might have more awareness of affective illness both in themselves and in their relatives. She also commented that the degree of illness diagnosed might be exaggerated by the broad definition of bipolar illness in the DSM. It has also been pointed out that Andreason was the sole interviewer and this particular group of writers may have turned to teaching because of depression.

Kay Jamison interviewed 47 British prize-winning writers and artists with a mean age of 53.2 years, asking them if they had been treated for mental illness. She discovered that 38% had been treated for affective illness at some point, 23.4% had taken antidepressants, and 6.4% had been diagnosed as manic-depressive (all poets). She compared this with "normal lifetime rates" of 5% for depression and 1% for manic-depression.

A. M. Ludwig interviewed and compared 59 female writers matched with a control group. He found female writers had higher rates of depression (59% vs. 9%), alcoholism (20% vs. 5%), drug abuse (17% vs.

5%), panic disorder (22% vs. 2%), generalized anxiety (14% vs. 5%) and eating disorders (12% vs. apparently none). Women writers, like men, suffered more bipolar illness and depression, but they also had higher rates of a number of additional psychological disorders. Ludwig found that significantly more women writers came from families with mothers or fathers with psychopathology and that more of these writers were physically or sexually abused as children.

These studies all concluded that fiction writers and poets had much higher rates of psychopathology than other creative professions and the general population. Ludwig suggested that writers demonstrate more psychopathology because writing and poetry rely on a "personal vision" which is based on an internal subjective experience as opposed to science where more stability may be required to do work that has "predictability, replicability, reliability and testability." The arts tolerate eccentric and irrational behavior much more readily than other professions. In fact, the creative writer's uniqueness is his or her stock in trade, and it takes a strong, independent personality to go one's own way. The characteristics that support this kind of abnormality are similar to the traits that characterize psychotic behavior.

There is also the distinct possibility that the characteristics of mental illness can be a detriment or benefit to creativity, depending on the individual case. For example, creative writers and poets may be far more sensitive to their emotions.

Freud felt writers "not far from neurosis" and, "oppressed by excessively powerful instinctual needs," use fantasy to satisfy these needs. This anticipates other researchers who concluded the difference that composes what has been called the thin line between genius and madness is control. This point of view acknowledges that creative people may at times exhibit traits of mental illness, but argues they are essentially healthy because they can make critical judgments about their thoughts and work that would be impossible if they were truly pathological. Other researchers take the opposite position that psychotic thinking is an essential ingredient in creativity.

A third possibility accepts both psychopathology and creativity as ingredients which may vary along a continuum. At times creativity and schizophrenia may be inextricably linked together in varying degrees.

Examples include the poet Holderlin, who was diagnosed as schizophrenic; Strindberg, who had a schizo-affective disorder; and writers who displayed a schizoid or schizothymic temperament, including Baudelaire, Kafka, and Beckett. It may be the schizoid or schizotypal propensities and world view which gave these writers' creative contribution its uniqueness.

Hypomanic traits have been cited as a positive force giving some writers energy, concentration, and confidence which enhanced their work. Depression inspired a small percentage of writers to work harder, perhaps attempting to escape their pain. Other writers such as Edgar Allan Poe used their dark moods as a source for some of their best work.

However, most writers with mental illness paid a heavy price in both their personal and their professional lives. Ezra Pound, Virginia Woolf, and Sylvia Plath spent parts of their lives in mental institutions. Depression and manic-depression hampered the ability of many eminent writers, including Joseph Conrad, Leo Tolstoy, John Ruskin, and Ernest Hemingway. A partial list of writers thought to have serious mental illness problems are listed in Table I.

2. Alcoholism

Alcoholism has been a problem for many accomplished writers, including Nobel prize-winning authors Sinclair Lewis, Eugene O'Neill, and William Faulkner. The generation of American expatriate writers in post-World War I Paris that included Ernest Hemingway and F. Scott Fitzgerald glamorized and romanticized drinking, making it a more sophisticated and respect-

TABLE I
Writers Thought to Have Mental Illness

James Barrie (playwright/fiction)
Charles Baudelaire (poetry/nonfiction)
Honore de Balzac (fiction)
William Blake (poetry/fiction/nonfiction)
Louise Bogan (poetry/nonfiction)
Elizabeth Barrett Browning (poetry)
Robert Browning (poetry/playwright)
Truman Capote (fiction/nonfiction/playwright)
Thomas Carlyle (nonfiction)
Thomas Chatterton (poetry/playwright)
John Clare (poetry)
Samuel Taylor Coleridge (poetry/nonfiction/playwright)
William Collins (poetry)
Joseph Conrad (fiction/playwright/nonfiction)
William Cowper (poetry)
Hart Crane (poetry/playwright/nonfiction)
Charles Dickens (fiction/playwright/nonfiction)
Theodore Dreiser (fiction/nonfiction/poetry/playwright)
F. Scott Fitzgerald (fiction/nonfiction)
Ian Fleming (fiction)
Robert Frost (poetry)
Nikolai Gogol (fiction/playwright)
Graham Greene (fiction/nonfiction/screenplays/playwright)
Ernest Hemingway (fiction/nonfiction)
Friedrich Holderlin (poetry/playwright)
Franz Kafka (fiction/nonfiction)
Charles Lamb (poetry/playwright/nonfiction)
Nathaniel Lee (playwright)
Jack London (fiction)

TABLE I
(Continued)

Robert Lowell (poetry/playwright)
Guy du Maupassant (fiction/nonfiction/poetry)
John Stuart Mill (nonfiction)
Gerard de Nerval (poetry)
Frank O'Connor (fiction/nonfiction/playwright)
Sylvia Plath (poetry/fiction)
Edgar Allan Poe (poetry/fiction/playwright)
Ezra Pound (poetry/nonfiction)
Arthur Rimbaud (poetry)
Theodore Roethke (poetry)
Jean-Jacques Rousseau (nonfiction/fiction/playwright)
William Saroyan (fiction)
Friedrich Schiller (poetry/drama/nonfiction)
Arthur Schopenhauer (nonfiction)
Delmore Schwartz (poetry/fiction/nonfiction)
Anne Sexton (poetry/fiction/nonfiction)
Percy Bysshe Shelley (poetry/fiction/nonfiction/playwright)
Christopher Smart (poetry/nonfiction/librettos)
Edmund Spencer (poetry/nonfiction)
August Strindberg (playwright/fiction/poetry)
Jonathan Swift (fiction/nonfiction/poetry)
Torquato Tasso (poetry/playwright/nonfiction)
Alfred Tennyson (poetry/playwright)
Leo Tolstoy (fiction/nonfiction/playwright)
Virginia Woolf (fiction/nonfiction)

Note: Many authors are classified as having mental illness automatically if they demonstrated heavy use of alcohol or drugs.
Sources: Ludwig, Magill, Prentky, Simonton, and others.

able behavior. Writers who used their drinking experiences for major works include Eugene O'Neill (*The Iceman Cometh*), William Burroughs (*Naked Lunch*), and Malcolm Lowry (*Under the Volcano*).

Andreason concluded that 30% of the creative writers she interviewed at the Iowa workshop had a problem with alcoholism at some point in their lives.

Arthur Rothenberg reviewed biographical and autobiographical data of writers known for their use of alcohol. He found very few did their actual writing or their thinking about writing, while under the influence of alcohol.

In Ludwig's study of the biographies of 34 well-known heavy-drinking writers, artists, and composer-performers, he found that alcohol negatively affected the work of 75%, especially as the drinking continued. Long-term drinking has physiological effects which directly hinder the concentration required of creative individuals. However, Ludwig believed that drinking actually benefited 9% of the subjects. Writers such as Hemingway, O. Henry, Raymond Chandler, and John O'Hara claimed that drinking *improved* the quality of their writing.

Many writers recognized they could not write well while they were drinking. F. Scott Fitzgerald and Ring Lardner said they went on the wagon when they worked.

Anja Koski-Jannes reviewed 60 interviews with prominent Finnish writers who started writing between the 1920s and 1950s. Only 32 writers commented on their use of alcohol while they wrote since this was not a primary question in the interviews. Writers who used alcohol occasionally saw it as an aid in getting started or a stimulus when they were tired. Duplicating results of studies in England and the United States, poets reported more alcohol use than other types of writers. The most heavy use for all writers occurred between writing projects. Immediately after a project was finished, writers reported they felt "empty, depressed and dissatisfied with themselves." They considered going out and drinking as a way to loosen up and relax, make social contacts with other writers, and generate new ideas. Writers also said they used alcohol to dissociate themselves from common concerns, and to facilitate the writing process.

Koski-Jannes suggested that among the reasons writers use alcohol frequently are that the job

is insecure, highly valued but poorly paid (at least in Finland), it is subject to many publicity pressures and conflicting expectations from the reading public, critics and the writer himself. As actual work it is unstable, lonely and at times emotionally highly demanding. Because of the marginality of this profession the identity of the writer is continually at stake. (1985, p. 131)

These comments sum up the hazards of the job mentioned by a number of researchers. However, it does not explain why some writers respond to these pressures by drinking heavily while other writers drink in moderation or abstain.

A few researchers have attempted to determine if alcohol facilitates creative writing under laboratory conditions. There were indications that alcohol significantly increased the number of words produced, which confirms anecdotal accounts of writers who found alcohol an aid in writing. However, these studies did not examine professional writers, so any determination of the quality of thinking under actual working conditions remains unknown. [See ALCOHOL AND CREATIVITY.]

Often the term "depression" is mentioned when it comes to writers who drink, which indicates that it may be used as a form of self-medication. If, in fact, more writers tend to be alcoholics than the general population, it's still not clear if the job makes writers depressed or depressed people are more likely to choose writing as a profession. Since most alcoholic writers were drinking before they started writing, perhaps professional writing was attractive because it allowed the individual the freedom to continue drinking. It is also possible that writing, like alcohol, serves as a way to escape negative feelings. A questionnaire given to writers on just this topic indicated that writers experience positive emotions significantly more often than negative emotions when writing. Furthermore, during the actual writing process, positive emotions tended to intensify, whereas negative emotions resisted change.

3. Drug Use

Ludwig's analysis indicated that poets and fiction writers trail only musicians and theatrical performers when it comes to drug use and abuse. Coleridge wrote about the palace of Kublai Khan while on opium; Keats also tried the drug and described his experience. Al-

TABLE II
Some Writers Thought to Have Committed Suicide

Ryunosuke Akutagawa (fiction)
John Berryman (poetry/nonfiction/fiction)
Truman Capote (fiction/nonfiction/playwright)
Thomas Chatterton (poetry/playwright)
Hart Crane (poetry/playwright/nonfiction)
Sergei Esenin (poetry)
Maxim Gorky (fiction)
Tom Heggen (fiction/playwright)
Ernest Hemingway (nonfiction/fiction)
Heinrich von Kleist (fiction/playwright)
Arthur Koestler (fiction/nonfiction)
Vachel Lindsay (poetry/nonfiction)
Ross Lockridge (fiction)
Jack London (fiction/nonfiction/playwright)
Malcolm Lowry (fiction/poetry)
Lucretius (poetry)
Vladamir Mayakovsky (poetry)
Yukio Mishima (fiction/nonfiction/playwright)
Charlotte Mew (poetry)
Gerard de Nerval (poetry/playwright/nonfiction/fiction)
Cesare Pavese (fiction/poetry/nonfiction)
Sylvia Plath (poetry/fiction)
Anne Sexton (poetry)
Sara Teasdale (poetry)
Marina Tsvetayeva (poetry/playwright/nonfiction)
Virginia Woolf (fiction/nonfiction)
Stefan Zweig (fiction)

Sources: Hendrickson, Ludwig, Magill, Prentky, Simonton, and others.

dous Huxley made no secret of his fondness for mescaline, which he wrote about in *The Doors of Perception*. It's impossible to accurately measure the level of drug use because, aside from the question of legality, some writers might be afraid their reputations would suffer if they publicly admitted they used drugs. As times change, writers' use of alcohol and drugs may change.

Recent studies challenge the popular notion that creatively successful individuals lead excessive life styles. A survey of 22 writers, 27 artists, 12 musicians, and 25 controls about use of cocaine, marijuana, alcohol, etc. found no significant difference in the use of most substances between groups. However, a high rate of heavy use (23%), a small sample, and an even smaller control group preclude any definitive conclusions. [*See* DRUGS AND CREATIVITY.]

4. Suicide

Individuals who have problems with traumatic childhood loss, mental illness, alcoholism, and drug abuse are more likely to commit suicide, so it is not surprising the suicide rate among writers is higher than average. Difficulty with their writing is often a factor contributing to writers' suicides. A partial list of writers who are believed to have committed suicide is in Table II. [*See* SUICIDE.]

5. Life Span

Researchers have concluded the stresses caused by being a professional writer result in a measurably lower life expectancy. A comparison of the age of death of 160 writers with that of 80 members of nine other creative occupations found that writers died at an average age of 61.7 years, which was 8.3 years less than composers and painters. Several hypotheses have been put forward to explain the cause of writers dying at an earlier age:

1. The theory that poets produce their major works at a younger age so they could die at a younger age and still be considered eminent in their field.
2. The differential-resources hypotheses, which suggests the lower financial rewards and standard of living in the literary arts results in a shorter life expectancy.
3. The stimulation-deprivation explanation which posits the meager financial rewards and sensory stimulation found in writing leads to risk-taking behavior elsewhere.

A study by Vincent Cassandro found creative writers living an average of 62 years, which was 3 to 7 years less than contemporaries in other disciplines. Scientists and inventors lived the longest. Cassandro concluded evidence supported the first two hypotheses, but not the third. He also made the logical link between a writer's psychopathology and a lower life expectancy. There was also significant evidence that the more writers diversified, the longer they lived. However, the sample was of subjects born no later than 1800 and thus might not generalize to the 20th century. Similarly, the findings might not apply to less eminent creative people. More in-depth research verifying the actual economic status of the creators studied, the actual cause of death, and the interaction of psychopathology upon these variables could help build knowledge in this area.

C. The Creative Process

1. *Motivation and Personality*

Why do writers write? It has been proposed that mental disturbances contribute to a state of "psychological unease" which generates creative tension that is relieved by constant work, and that creators who do not have emotional problems are able to internally generate this unease. Others have theorized that writing may satisfy a biological drive, a search for meaning, or a means to fame and fortune.

Barron theorized that writers are constantly creating a universe of meaning. This need to find meaning in life may be based on childhoods in which writers felt isolated and unhappy. This theory could explain why so many writers find the act of writing difficult. Creating a world that reveals lasting truths is bound to be frustrating as the writer searches for the right words.

However, despite all the pressures and frustrations, many writers have found great satisfaction in their work. For some, writing provides an escape from the pressures of life, offering a place where he or she is in control. Positive aspects frequently mentioned include the pleasure in discovering more about themselves and making new intellectual and emotional connections, feeling they have a real purpose, communicating with others and sharing their reactions when they find something which represents some underlying "truth" about life, and the enjoyment of working with words. Some individuals found a long-sought sense of identity when they became writers.

Two motivations which have not been explored in depth are fame and fortune. Research in experimental settings has indicated that intrinsic motivation is probably more important and extrinsic motivation may even hinder creativity at times. However, it is probable that in the real world fantasies of celebrity and wealth helped some writers keep working through the lean times. [*See* MOTIVATION/DRIVE.]

Economic necessity motivated some writers. Dostoyevsky produced some of his best work when he needed money. Others took lucrative offers from movie studios. Many famous writers and playwrights, including Fitzgerald and Faulkner, "sold out" to Hollywood where they had no control over their work. Usually they wrote bitterly about the experience.

Fame, once achieved, has been a part of the career fabric for many authors who enjoyed the attention. Ernest Hemingway's macho image helped sell his work while giving him ego gratification. However, fame also creates tremendous pressure. Expectations can become so high that writers become blocked. Writing became especially competitive in the 1920s when writing a great novel was not enough—it had to be a best seller. Today's authors are expected to sell themselves on talk shows and do interviews so they can generate enough publicity to become a "name brand."

The alcoholic problems many writers experience may be exacerbated by the drive for success, prestige, fame and money, and the burden put on the creative self.

2. *Work Habits*

Creative writing may be sparked in many ways (for example, a glimpse of a person or imagining a scene) and inevitably encompasses autobiographical elements. Once the subject is chosen, a few legendary writers can produce work with incredible speed. Isaac Asimov reported he would write at the 90 words a minute he could type, and stated he wrote most nonfiction books in seventy hours. However, most writers struggle finding the form which fulfills their vision. Writers' work habits are as individual and idiosyncratic as their work. Some professional writers discipline themselves by treating writing as a 9–5 job. Others may give themselves a daily quota of words or pages to fill. Some procrastinate until they are faced with a deadline and then put in marathon hours.

Most writing decisions offer a number of choices, so often writers develop different drafts of stories and scenes, learning as they rewrite what works for them and what must be changed. During this evolutionary process their original perceptions may radically shift—a minor character may grow into a central figure, or the theme of a story may go in a completely different direction. Thus the creative process in writing is usually not linear, but rather a series of steps that are repeated over and over as refinements are made. Many writers will look for feedback from one or more trusted sources while the work is in progress. Some writers may complete hundreds of pages and decide the idea does not work at all.

The most constructive work is done in a state of total concentration which almost seems effortless at the time, referred to as "flow." The author must remain open to the message whispered by the unconscious, while at the same time maintaining critical judgment.

3. Writer's Block

A common complaint among both amateur and professional writers is the inability to work known as writer's block. Factors contributing to writer's block are self-doubt, perfectionism, procrastination, unrealistic expectations, and fear of failure. Some strategies suggested for countering blocks include writing anything (even about being blocked), setting up a regular time and place to write, isolating oneself from distractions, stopping writing when there is some momentum left so the work can be continued the following day, going to another project for a while, and using positive self-talk. The fact that even blocked writers may eventually produce important work is exemplified by Karl Marx, who spent 18 years writing the first volume of *Das Kapital*.

4. Collaborative Writing

The act of writing is usually an internal process so it has been difficult to make independent observations of elements that encourage or discourage creativity. Research about collaborative writing, which is very common in television script writing, indicates that specific elements encourage creativity, including the willingness to take risks and providing a safe atmosphere where members of the group build upon each others' ideas. Negatives include unresolved emotional conflict between the writer and supervisors, differences in communication styles, settling quickly on a predictable story, and the tendency of executives to demand massive rewrites generating fear of change and fatigue.

5. Creative Writing in Institutions

Creative writing is used as a tool to help prisoners and patients in mental institutions. Cognitive researchers concluded that creative writing takes tremendous effort and requires a great deal of attention; thus for some troubled people it helps center the thinking process and provides insight into problems. William Sty-

ron and Art Buchwald wrote about their deep depression as a catharsis and with the hope the public would understand more about the debilitating nature of their illness. Political prisoners such as Thomas Paine, John Bunyan, and Daniel Defoe used their time in jail to write books that furthered their own cause. Prisoners committed for other crimes who wrote notable works while in jail include O. Henry, William Penn, Marco Polo, Oscar Wilde, Eldredge Cleaver, and Malcolm X. The Marquis de Sade completed the circuit since he began his writing career in prison and continued it in a mental institution.

III. CONCLUSIONS

Work on writing and creativity has consistently indicated that many writers suffer problems with psychopathology, alcoholism, and drug abuse. The next step is to go beyond the interesting and logical theories proposed for this connection and develop verifiable causal explanations.

Information on the life expectancy of writers needs further investigation. If writing inherently contains occupational hazards, then therapists and creative writing teachers can develop a proactive stance to help some of their clients understand and cope with the stress of the job and deal with their personal demons.

Much of the research has concentrated on eminent writers. Learning more about professional writers who are more "ordinary" can widen our knowledge and possibly lead to training which can encourage creativity.

While a great deal of attention has been paid to dysfunctional writers, the healthy writer (if one exists) is barely represented in the literature. It might prove worthwhile to look closely at the lives of writers with less dramatic histories since they may serve as positive models other writers may emulate.

Bibliography

Andreason, N. C. (1987). Creativity and mental illness: Prevalence in writers and their first degree relatives. *American Journal of Psychiatry, 144*(10), 1288–1292.

Barron, F. (1961). Creative vision and expression in writing and painting. In *The creative person* (pp. II-1–II-19). Berkeley: University of California.

Baskin, E. (1936). A comparison of scientific and literary ability:

A biographical study of eminent scientists and men of letters of the nineteenth century. *Journal of Abnormal and Social Psychology, 31,* 20–35.

Brand, A. G., & Leckie, P. A. (1992). The emotions of professional writers. *The Journal of Psychology, 122,* 421–439.

Brunke, M., & Gilbert, M. (1992). Alcohol and creative writing. *Psychological Reports, 71,* 651–658.

Cassandro, V. J. (1998). Explaining premature mortality across fields of creative endeavor. *Journal of Personality, 66*(5), 805–829.

Goertzel, V., & Goertzel, M. G. (1962). *Cradles of eminence.* Boston: Little, Brown.

Goertzel, M. G., Goertzel, V., & Goertzel, T. G. (1978). *Three hundred eminent personalities.* San Francisco: Jossey-Bass.

Hendrickson, R. (1994). *The literary life and other curiosities.* San Diego: Harcourt Brace.

Jamison, K. R. (1989). Mood disorder and patterns of creativity in British writers and artists. *Psychiatry, 52,* 125–134.

Kaun, D. E. (1992). Writers die young. *Journal of Economic Psychology, 12*(2), 381–399.

Kerr, B., Shaffer, J., Chambers, C., & Hallowell, K. (1991). Substance abuse of creatively talented adults. *Journal of Creative Behavior, 25,* 145–153.

Koski-Jannes, A. (1985). Alcohol and literary creativity: The Finnish experience. *Journal of Behavior, 19,* 120–136.

Lester, D. (1991). Premature mortality associated with alcoholism and suicide in American writers. *Perceptual & Motor Skills, 73,* 162.

Ludwig, A. M. (1995). *The price of greatness: Resolving the creativity and madness controversy.* New York: Guilford.

Post, F. (1994). Creativity and psychopathology: A study of 281 world-famous men. *British Journal of Psychiatry, 165,* 22–34.

Post, F. (1996). Verbal creativity, depression and alcoholism: An investigation of one hundred American and British writers. *British Journal of Psychiatry, 168,* 545–555.

Pritzker, S. (1998). Creative differences: The creative decision-making process in situation comedy writing (Doctoral dissertation, University of Southern California, 1998). *Dissertation Abstracts International.*

Rothenberg, A. R. (1990a). *Creativity and madness.* Baltimore, MD: The Johns Hopkins University Press.

Rothenberg, A. R. (1990b). Creativity, mental health and alcoholism. *Creativity Research Journal, 3,* 179–201.

Sandborn, P. (1995). *Creativity and disease.* New York: Marion Boyers.

Zeitgeist

Leonard Shlain

University of California Medical School, San Francisco

Hemispheric Lateralization The division of labors between the two brain cortical lobes whereby one hemisphere is better suited to process linear, sequential information such as language, arithmetic, and logic and the other hemisphere is better suited to process information that is holistic, simultaneous, and intuitive.

Knossos Staggeringly impressive remains of the palace of Knossus excavated by Arthur Evans in the 1890 on the Isle of Crete. It is the remains of the late Bronze Age Minoan civilization.

Rococo Style of architecture developed in France and characterized by elaborate and profuse ornamentation mimicking scrollwork, foliage, and shellwork.

Spacetime Continuum Fourth-dimensional manifold consisting of the union of the three vectors of space—height, length, and depth—with all three durations of time—past, present, and future. Deduced by Hermann Minkowski in 1908 from studying Einstein's 1905 special theory of relativity.

Synergetic Working together in cooperation.

A conjunction of artistic and scientific creativity can occur within a society without there being active interaction between artists and scientists. Yet, in some mysterious manner, the new forms of art and the innovations in science appear to be related in a noncausal way. The phenomenon is known as a ZEITGEIST.

I. INTRODUCTION

Between 1770 and 1810, German anthropologist Carl Meiners developed the earlier general concept of "the genius of the age" into an academic theory he called *zeitgeist*. Probably aware of Giambattista Vico's work along these lines, Meiners proposed that each age and place had a special mentality determined by its situation, institutions, and technology. In the ensuing centuries the idea of a zeitgeist has changed little. Combining two German words *age* or *period* with *mind* or *spirit,* a zeitgeist encapsulates the spirit of an age.

To describe a phenomenon, however, does not explain it and because a zeitgeist refers principally to times infused with great originality in fields far removed from each other, this peculiar phenomenon begs for some reasonable explanation that can account for individual bursts of creativity across a spectrum of endeavors.

Perhaps an example of a zeitgeist will help bring the concept into focus. Vienna at the turn of the century blossomed into a luxuriant tangle of geniuses each making a significant contribution to their own particular field, but at the same time each of their innovations contained an essence of the others. Architect Adolph Loos, rebelling against the rococo filigree that had come to characterize Hapsburg buildings, initiated a spare new style. Loos defended his work by saying that it was necessary to strip away all the unessentials to understand the structural elements of a building. Ludwig Wittgenstein was at the same time paring language down to its bare essentials. The philosopher attempted to reduce thought to the simplest verbal equations. After many intense years trying to achieve his goal, he concluded in his *Tractatus Eight* that language was inadequate to the task of really saying anything pertinent about reality, so he quit philosophy and became an orderly in a hospital. Sigmund Freud founded psychoanalysis in Vienna, a discipline he felt could be used to study the very foundation of the psyche, while Arthur Schnitzler wrote psychologically insightful dramas using the stage as a means to study the underpinnings of the human personality.

The Viennese positivists such as Ernst Mach were proclaiming that science should only concern itself with what could be proven and in a way reflected the architectural style of Loos in that it tried to jettison all the speculative hypothesis that Mach believed had encrusted science with layers of unproven theories. In art, Vassily Kandinsky was reducing the elements of painting to point and line and in the process proclaimed that art did not need an identifiable image. Kandinsky became the first artist to paint an abstract painting.

Vienna at the turn of the century was enveloped by a zeitgeist. There was some undefined factor that affected a diverse group of innovative individuals to break with the traditions of their respective fields and bring forth entirely new ideas that had as their essence the desire to get to the very heart of the matter. Because it might be too unwieldy to try to examine the wellsprings of creativity for every innovator in their respective fields, perhaps it would make the discussion clearer if we narrow the study to two widely divergent fields: art and physics. Few would disagree that in methodology and temperament the practitioners of each one of these polar opposites are themselves polar opposites.

What connects the two endeavors is that the revolutionary artists' imagery contains crucial insights that underlie the conceptual framework of how society thinks about the world. Later, these insights most often shine through visionary physicists' equations and subsequently change the way the rest of us see the world. But if art embodies these concepts before their formulations filter down from scholarly physics journals, then the artists who give them form cannot possibly have had any conscious knowledge of their development—a proposition artists' writings, lectures, letters, and documented conversations overwhelmingly support. *Art & Physics: Parallel Visions in Space, Time, and Light* presents numerous examples of the concordance between these two endeavors. We must next ask how this is possible. How could so many diverse artists over so many centuries, virtually all of them unaware of what was about to happen in the field of physics, manage to bring forth so many innovative styles of art that spoke directly to the imminent revisioning of physical reality in their times?

Confronted by this baffling phenomenon, most commentators have invoked the condition of the zeitgeist, claiming that some ill-defined quickening in the air precipitates change not just in one field, but across the whole range of human endeavor. They see societies as something like schools of fish that suddenly, all at once, change direction. The manner in which these grand, coordinated movements are choreographed rules out the possibility that one lead fish gives one signal with all the others following. Similarly, no single determinant can be identified as having sparked the complex network of events that led to the artistic and scientific glories of Periclean Athens, the Florence of the Medici, and multiple European capitals around the turn of the 20th century. Unfortunately, the concept of a zeitgeist does not explain how this force that precipitates action at a distance ordinates and propagates. How do the central principles of a new style in art segue across the spectrum of culture, like ripples on a pond, eventually to resonate in the equations of visionary physicists?

II. THE STRUCTURE OF CONSCIOUSNESS

To consider this question, we must roam farther afield, venturing into evolutionary theory, brain lateralization, and mythology. Let us begin by examining our beliefs about the structure of consciousness. To an observer, an animal is conscious if it is moved by moods and feelings and is capable of assessing its present situation in the light of past experience, enabling it to arrive at a response that is more than an instinctive behavior pattern. Somewhere on the evolutionary trail leading from the primate brain, the self-reflective mind emerged in our species. Mind, a striking new development in the history of the planet, is a *self*-conscious reflective epiphenomenon that *knows* that it *knows*. Materialists have claimed that mind is the product of the electromagnetic and electrochemical energy expressed by a complex mechanism they identify as the brain, but our understanding of the connection between mind and brain has always been tenuous. Wilder Penfield, the great neurosurgeon, spent the 1940s and 1950s mapping the regions of the brain, and he was constantly on the lookout for the hiding place of the mind, trying to identify the precise anatomical location that wills action. He never did discover it and was forced to conclude that he could not be sure if brain and mind were as intimately attached as the materialists would have had him believe.

The search for the interface between mind and brain continues to occupy present-day physiologists and philosophers. To date, no satisfactory explanation has been forthcoming for the essential question: What mechanism allows matter to act on mind or—even more troubling—mind on matter.

Most people in Western culture believe that each individual's mind is a distinct, separate entity, that every person's consciousness is integral to the person's physical being. The concept of "I," ends at our skin. Within this waterproof bag the human immune system has at its disposal extreme measures designed to isolate the "I" from its environment, which the system most emphatically perceives as "*not* I." Perhaps because the full panoply of defense mechanisms surrounding "I" stands guard against any possible encroachment, the "I" upholds its individuality devoutly. The sharp demarcation of our physical boundaries naturally reinforces the idea that the mind of each of us is inviolately separate and distinct from all other minds.

Each person's staunchly held belief in the integrity of his or her private being stands in contrast with the more radical proposal for the existence of a *universal mind*. William James, the American philosopher, suggested that a border encircles each individual human mind and keeps it separate from others of its kind. This border permits thoughts and ruminations to which no one else has access, creating the illusion of separateness. He proposed, however, that one segment of the circle was broken, and that through this vent each solitary consciousness is connected with all others in a much larger, all-encompassing, transcendental mind.

James advanced the concept of a "continuum of cosmic consciousness" that existed in a higher dimension and subsumed individual minds. He proposed that this entity was ultimately God. Unfortunately, attaching the word *God* to an idea tends to still discussion among those who are uncomfortable linking religion to philosophy. Therefore, when the Catholic theologian Pierre Teilhard de Chardin proposed a similar theory in the 1940s, he posited the existence of a membrane of consciousness girdling the globe, which he was careful *not* to call God.

In Teilhard de Chardin's scheme, anytime the consciousness of any one individual in the world is raised, the general quality and quantity of *mind* in the world is enhanced. He called this invisible component of the atmosphere the "noosphere," after the archaic Greek word *noos*, which means "mind." Each person, on becoming more aware of his or her life, adds to an ectoplasmic pool of awareness, thus ever so slightly raising its level. While Teilhard de Chardin envisioned a global mind attached to this planet, I would use the term *universal mind* in a less restrictive spatial sense. By universal mind, I mean an overarching, disembodied universal consciousness that binds and organizes the power generated by every person's thoughts. I shall use such a model of a human superconsciousness arising from the joining together of individual minds as the framework to explain how an artist can incorporate ideas into his or her work that have not as yet been discovered by physicists and that are certainly unknown to the general public.

To explore this idea, an example drawn from E. A. Abbott's book *Flatland* might be helpful. When the idea of a fourth dimension began to float about in the late 19th century, Abbott made the concept comprehensible by writing a novel based on analogy. To his two-dimensional Flatlanders the third dimension was as strange and incomprehensible a concept as the fourth dimension was to his three-dimensional readers. In his charming tale, Abbott demonstrates how a visit from a sphere, a three-dimensional figure from solid geometry, is perceived by the square, two-dimensional inhabitants of Flatland. This clever literary device makes it possible for his three-dimensional readers to understand how they might perceive a four-dimensional geometrical object. Abbott's novel concerns only the spatial vectors of geometry and does not take into account the coordinate of time, but his analogy suggests how universal mind could exist in the four dimensions of the space–time continuum and be missed or misperceived by three-dimensional humans.

III. THE ANT AS AN EXAMPLE

How can we conceive of such a higher dimension, a history of human thoughts? For the sake of conjecture, let us interject ourselves into the mental existence of a life form that antedated *Homo sapiens*. For the purpose of our analogy, the ideal form would be one that lived in space but not in time. A social insect, like the ant, provides just such an example because although individual ants maneuver through the three dimensions of space, they apparently have little or no temporal perception. Like Abbott's Flatlanders, they provide a convenient model that allows us to step down one dimensional level so that we can better envision the nature of universal mind as perceived from our limited three vectors of space and three durational states of time.

Ants cannot be self-conscious, because no self-referential thought is possible without the ability to exist in time. An essential prerequisite of self-consciousness is the presence of memory, a neurological apparatus capable of holding the idea of the past so that it can be compared to the present. For all intents and purposes, ants do not possess this attribute—they cannot be aware that they are aware.

Ants cannot be taught to run complex mazes because their memory is extremely limited. Their amazing feats of patience, endurance, and industry are due to an innate behavior program precoded into their nervous systems. They have a very restricted ability to learn from past mistakes and for the most part ants are ruled by instinct, which forbids any variation in response to a particular environmental stimulus. Any specific provocation to an ant will elicit a repetition in its pattern of behavior. Individual insects cannot escape from the brutish totalitarian grip of instinct.

Despite this severe limitation on each individual ant, a curious phenomenon occurs when ants join together in a group. If a few ants are placed in a sandbox, they wander about without apparent purpose, except to engage in a peculiar activity—on meeting one another, they vigorously rub one another's antennae. If more ants are added to the box, this fraternal activity increases in both its intensity and its frequency. Finally, when their sheer numbers reach a critical mass and a queen is present, the milling, chaotic group becomes a single organism with an obvious higher purpose. The ants cease their frenzied socializing and split into specialized groups committed to the task of building a cooperative community. From out of this heap of crawling insects begins to rise a structure of enormous complexity—the mound nest or, as it is more commonly known, the anthill.

All anthills are marvels, but the home of the Brazilian species *Atta* is a veritable Knossos. This structure burrows down into the soil over 6 meters and contains underground chambers for food storage, tunnels whose sole purpose is the air-conditioning of the interior, and complex pathways for soldier ants to quickly come to the defense of the hill. There are subterranean fungus farms and an elaborate queen's throne room.

Sometime during the laborious construction of an anthill, the complex takes on a life of its own, superseding the life of any individual ant. Whereas the average life span of an individual ant can be measured in months, some anthills achieve 15 years. If, during its life span, a person kicks in the side of the mound, more ants will be born in successive generations that specialize in repairing the damage, and fewer born to farm, soldier, or explore.

The hill's self-healing reconstructive capability gradually diminishes, however, and toward the end of its years, it mysteriously begins to decay. The final generations of ants seem dispirited, tired, and disoriented. They no longer show the industriousness and common purpose that characterized ants in the early phase of the hill's development. Tunnels cave in from neglected maintenance, and the complex slowly decays and crumbles during a period of senescence culminating in death. This event goes unnoticed by any individual ant, however, because to notice an event taking place over time a creature must have memory, a basis for comparison. Although one can never know for sure, ants most likely are part of a larger entity whose purpose seems to have been to knit them into a higher level of organization.

But what of the guiding force that organized the ants in the first place? The anthill, created by these individual social insects, seems to have a synergetic life force that permeates the hill and is its true essence. We saw earlier how physicists came to believe that the incorporeal force field is a more essential component of reality than the particulate things suspended in it; so, too, there seems to exist an incorporeal "soul" of the anthill directing the detached particulate ants in stages of its development. Where then does this soul reside? The ants are obviously separated by physical distance and so it would be a tenuous presumption to propose that the life force of the hill existed in the limited ganglionic neurons of each ant. Scientific materialists will quickly point out that the soul is a mirage and the plan for the hill is encoded in the DNA of each individual ant. Although this is the correct scientific answer, is it the complete answer or even the right answer? Can a living organism (one anthill) of 15 years' life span, existing without any physical connection between its parts (the individual ants), be the exclusive product of protein synthesis?

IV. THE SPACE–TIME CONTINUUM

Using this example from an insect's world that lacks the coordinate of time—that is, memory—as a departure point, we can extrapolate into the human sphere where reality includes both space and time, but only as separate coordinates. We humans evolved long after the insects and can perceive another dimension in addition to the three vectors of space. We know what an ant does not: We know our existence in time. Our individual minds can roam leisurely back and forth along a temporal line that includes all three durational states of past, present, and future. Yet, we are in a quandary similar to that of the individual ant. Because of Einstein's and Minkowski's insights, we have learned that there exists another dimension to which we are not

privy because it lies tantalizingly just beyond our perceptual capabilities. As the individual ant is unaware of its existence in time despite belonging to a community that lives on for years after its death, so may we be part of a much larger entity existing in the space–time continuum with an agenda of which we are not aware. The proof that higher dimensions exist has been traced out in the arachnid formulas of the physicist as it was explained in the Flatland fiction of the novelist. When the coordinate of time is added to the vectors of space, mind enters the world. There is nothing to preclude the possibility that some entity of great moment exists in a higher fourth dimension as well.

In *Tertium Organum* (1911), P. D. Ouspensky, a Russian mathematician and philosopher, describes how circumscribed entities existing in two dimensions can be part of a unity in the third dimension. Observe from one side of a pane of frosted glass the prints left by the tips of someone's fingers touching the opposite side. A two-dimensional investigator, counting five separate circles, would conclude that each fingerprint is a separate entity. But we who can appreciate the third dimension of depth, know that the five separate fingerprints belong to one unified object in three dimensions: a hand. We also know that the three-dimensional hand is attached to a being that generates mind when time is added to the vectors of space. By extrapolation, this is exactly the example that illustrates how our separate, individual minds, existing in our limited perceptual apparatus using two coordinates, space and time, could also be part of a universal mind that is a unified entity in the higher dimension of the space–time continuum.

Classical 19th-century physics described a physical world bounded by the distinct, contrasting coordinates of space and time, consisting of combinations of energy and matter. These four cornerstones now stand revealed by relativity and quantum mechanics to be inextricably enmeshed with one another as a unity in the matrix of the space–time continuum.

The one phenomenon that cannot be categorized within Newton's classical framework is mind, yet we know it exists because each of us is aware that someone in there is reading this page. By emphasizing the *relative* frame of reference of the observer, relativity introduced into physics the idea that the position and speed of the mind that is observing and measuring had to be taken into account in the measurement. Quantum mechanical theory went even further and made mind an actual component of the objective world's physical processes by acknowledging the reciprocal nature of observer and observed. Space/time, mass/energy, space–time/mass–energy, and observer/observed are all complementary reciprocal dualities. If the physicist John Wheeler is correct and *mind* and *universe* are but another binary pair that appear in this dimension as separate entities, then most likely they are unified in the space–time continuum. Such a unity would be most appropriately named *universal mind*. A zeitgeist might be a space-and-time manifestation in these artificially limited coordinates of a space–time universal mind.

In our world of divided space and time, the only clues that such a schema existed would be occurrences that cannot be explained by the rules of causality. One such clue would be the puzzling way artists' images seem to anticipate new discoveries about reality. If artists' intuitions are the first intimations of movement in the larger entity of universal mind, artists themselves can be seen to serve the unique function of seers through whom the zeitgeist appears. Visionary artists, able to discern what the rest of us still cannot, embrace and announce through their art the principles emanating from this *spiritus mundi*. It does not matter if the critics and even the artists themselves are unaware of their singular purpose: If the artists' work is truly the apparition of the zeitgeist, it can become evident only in retrospect, as society matures and its members achieve the same vantage point visionary artists occupied decades earlier. Art is the singular harbinger of universal mind.

V. HEMISPHERIC LATERALIZATION AND UNIVERSAL MIND

In the nervous system, the smallest unit is the neuron. When many neurons congregated into an entity as advanced as a mammalian brain, the conditions were present for the first thought. As mammalian brains became increasingly sophisticated, a critical number of thoughts accumulated in *Homo sapiens'* brains, from which there emerged the fantastic, self-reflective mind. (Some researchers suggest that other mammals, such as porpoises, whales, and higher apes, might also be

capable of self-reflection.) Observing this inexorable progression, the next obvious step up the evolutionary scale would seem to be the integration of individual minds to create a giant, towering ectoplasmic brain capable of generating universal mind. Because it is problematical to speak of a mind without reference to a physical brain, perhaps an analogy rooted in experience can be made to conceptualize the universal mind.

The human brain consists of a large number of individual neurons. These neurons cluster together in groupings that perform specialized functions. Each separate region and pathway of the brain is responsible for specific tasks. For example, Broca's area is responsible for language; the visual cortex processes the impulses arriving from the eyes' retinas. Mind seems to emerge from the knitting together of the information gleaned from many of these discretely organized cognitive modules. [*See* BRAIN BIOLOGY AND BRAIN FUNCTIONING.]

Superimposing the template of a single brain that generates a solitary mind on a hypothetical universal brain allows me the framework to speak further about the universal mind. In this model, each member of our entire species plays the role of an individual neuron building the larger brain, much as every ant contributes to the hill. As each neuron is a separate world unto itself, so too is each person, and the physical space between individuals is like the synapses within a colossal brain. In this enlarged model of a hypothetical brain generating universal mind, specialized groups perform the same kinds of specific functions as do neuron clusters within a single human brain.

The features of brain lateralization are the loom on which to weave these theories. The strands of argument I have presented are strengthened by the passage of the shuttle back and forth, intertwining the warp and woof of right and left, space and time, art and physics. The pattern that emerges from the fabric will enhance the connections between universal mind and the fourth-dimensional manifold as well as illuminate the peculiar congruence between artist and physicist.

It has now been more than 80 years since Einstein and Minkowski revealed the interrelationships among space, time, and light. Despite indisputable proof of the existence of the space–time continuum, there has been a dearth of speculations concerning what could possibly exist on this new plane, apart from Einstein's discovery that gravity is due to the curvature of space–time in the fourth dimension. To revert to the anthill analogy once more, a creature that can perceive only space but not time lives in a severely constricted world. The addition of linear time to mammals' mental operations resulted in unique thoughts, and when a critical number of thoughts accumulated in this one species, *Homo sapiens,* something even more ephemeral emerged: the self-reflective mind, capable of comprehending both infinite space and eternal time. The discovery of a fourth dimension should be as momentous for our species as the introduction of the coordinate of time was to lower animals. By extrapolation, I propose that space–time generates universal mind.

If the individual self-reflective mind *knows* that it *knows,* universal mind not only knows that it knows, but it also knows everything, everywhere and anytime. It is in a dimension where all durational states merge so that they can be appreciated simultaneously, and at the speed of light, separate locations in front and back fuse. Universal mind most likely manifests itself in our coordinate system as clairvoyance, and it is known by certain individuals whom the rest of us, still bound by history, would dismiss as cranks and mountebanks.

Universal mind would be the moving force behind our zeitgeist, speaking through the works of revolutionary, right-brained, intuitive artists first, and later through left-brained, visionary, rational physicists. What to our limited perceptual apparatus appears as a movement affecting many fields at once may in fact be a manifestation of universal mind operating in a higher dimension that we can only dimly perceive. In our world we call it a zeitgeist.

Bibliography

Abbott, E. A. (1952). *Flatland: A romance of many dimensions.* New York: Dover.

Argüelles, J. (1975). *The transformative vision.* Boulder, CO: Shambhala.

Jaynes, J. (1977). *The origin of consciousness in the breakdown of the bicameral mind.* Boston: Houghton Mifflin.

Janik, A., & Toulmin, S. (1973). *Wittgenstein's Vienna.* New York: Simon & Schuster.

McLuhan, M. (1964). *Understanding media: The extensions of man.* New York: New American Library.

Ouspensky, P. D. (1970). *Tertium organum: A key to the enigmas of the world.* New York: Vintage.

Teilhard de Chardin, P. (1959). *The phenomenon of man.* New York: Harper & Row.

Zen

Steven R. Pritzker

Luminescent Creativity, Greenbrae, California

Enlightenment A final blessed state marked by the absence of desire or suffering.

Koan A paradoxical question that cannot be answered using ordinary logic.

Mushin The state of "no mind" or "no ego" in which true emptiness is achieved.

Nirvana An advanced state of enlightenment in which desire, frustration, and ignorance are dissipated so absolute silence and stillness reign.

Samadhi The state in which consciousness is stopped and the individual is no longer aware of time, space, and causation.

Satori The moment of enlightenment when one sees into one's own nature.

Zazen Zen sitting meditation.

Zen A Japanese sect of Mahayana Buddhism that aims at enlightenment by direct intuition through meditation.

This article offers a brief description of the history of Buddhism and describes the impact of combining ZEN and creativity. Buddhism originated in India, then migrated to China and Japan. Zen Buddhism was most influential in Japan where it became a significant cultural force inspiring a unique style of creativity in art, poetry, garden design, drama, calligraphy, and other arts. Zen also influenced the ritual tea ceremony as well as swordsmanship, archery, and the martial arts. Zen was a powerful force within Japanese culture because it significantly changed the worldview of the people who studied it.

I. A BRIEF HISTORY OF ZEN BUDDHISM

Prince Guatama was born near the border of Nepal and India in approximately the 6th century B.C. His wealthy father gave him every luxury and kept him protected within the palace walls. When the prince finally left his sheltered life, he was very upset when he encountered sickness, old age, and death. He met a holy man who seemed happy despite the problems that surrounded him, so the prince decided he would seek his own liberation. He became a holy man, wandering the country without finding peace. Finally he vowed to sit on a straw mat under a bodhi tree until he found an answer. He sat there for 6 days. On the morning of the 7th day, he awakened to the morning star and became enlightened.

Prince Guatama became known as The Buddha

745

Tathagata. He developed the Four Noble Truths, which emphasized that life's suffering was engendered by selfish craving that could be overcome through following the eight-fold path of right understanding, purpose, speech, conduct, livelihood, effort, alertness, and concentration. The detachment of a solitary life led to liberation. The ultimate goal was achieving Nirvana, which represented a state of undisturbed peace.

The founder of Zen Buddhism was The Bodhidharma who was the 28th patriarch of Indian Buddhism. He arrived in China about 520 A.D. The Bodhidarma meditated facing a wall for 9 years before becoming a teacher. His teaching was based on the principles of Mahayana Buddhism, which emphasized helping others and concrete experience. His disciples continued teaching in China.

Zen became recognized as a separate branch of Buddhism about 700 A.D. during the time of the patriarch Hui-neng. Hui-neng stressed the concept of emptiness, which minimized the importance of the individual ego in a world where everything and everybody are connected and constantly changing.

Suspicion of language is a basic tenet of Buddhism. The Bodhidharma called for "no dependence on words and letters" but "direct pointing to the real person, seeing into one's nature and attainment of Buddhahood."

Buddha stated that all humans are inherently enlightened; however, there is a need to practice in order to remove the obstacles to experiencing satori. Satori is reached through the study of koans, meditation, and living a purposeful life. "Chop wood, drink water"—concentrate on what is necessary at this moment. It takes most people a great deal of training to calm what is called in India "monkey mind," the constant chatter of thoughts, for even a few moments. Zazen is a form of meditation in which concentration on breathing and calming the mind helps the practitioner lose awareness of the body. The goal is to reach a state where time, space and causation, as the framework of consciousness, drop away.

Koans are a unique method of teaching. The student is assigned a koan—for example, "What is the meaning of Mu?" The individual repeats the koan over and over during meditation until suddenly its truth is revealed. Reaching enlightenment is a long, challenging path for most people. Philip Kapleau suggested that the three essential qualities necessary for enlightenment include (a) strong faith, (b) a strong doubt based on the imperfect state of the individual and the world compared to the idealistic image, and (c) strong determination to dispel this doubt with the whole force of one's energy and will.

Enlightened individuals are encouraged to participate in life. D. T. Suzuki stated that "the object of Zen training consists in making us realize that Zen is our daily experience and that it is not something put in from the outside." The enlightened individual interacts with everybody in a different way because the desire for ego gratification and material things no longer dominate the individual's thinking. Success and failure, happiness and unhappiness all become an accepted part of life.

II. ZEN AND CREATIVITY IN CHINA AND JAPAN

By 800 A.D. Zen was widely practiced in China. Zen's influence on culture was relatively minor. It contributed to Chinese philosophy in the Sung dynasty and a form of 13th century asymmetrical painting called *one corner* that was eventually exported to Japan. This inspired the *thrifty brush* style of Japanese painting that reflected the simplicity of Zen experience. Zen gardens and calligraphy also originated in China, but it was in Japan where Zen had the most impact on culture.

Zen monasteries became the primary source of learning and art for the upper classes in Japan. Creativity was inherent in the teaching practiced by the Zen masters who used improvisational methods specifically tailored to the individual student.

The model of discipline and concentration required in Zen influenced other aspects of life. Training was often done by a master teacher similar to a roshi or Zen teacher. The idea of reaching mushin, a state of "no mind," penetrated the arts in Japan and stimulated creativity in many areas. Mushin represents the highest state of consciousness with no thoughts or judgments clouding the mind. Students practiced calligraphy, painting, or archery until the routine requirements—the moving of the pen or brush or the firing of the bow—could be accomplished automatically without thought. This training took many years because conscious control was not surrendered easily. Students without self-consciousness could completely absorb themselves in the moment, allowing intuition rather than intellect to control their process. When the mind was clear with no duality in the way, true human nature could take over and the artist knew where the brush was supposed to go. Some professions Zen influenced include the following.

A. Architecture and Design

Many great Zen temples began as imperial palaces and castles. They are noteworthy because they reflect and respect the unique beauty of the gardens that surround them.

The Japanese tea room, which originated in the 15th century, is an excellent example of how Zen deeply influenced many aspects of Japanese culture. The tea ceremony is a ritual designed as a diversion from the everyday world. Each tea room is built specifically for the individual tea master.

The ceremony begins with a walk through a garden where stepping stones form an asymmetrical path. The walk through a tea garden is intended to foster recollection and inner peace. The tea room's construction is deliberately delicate, consisting of bamboo supports and thatched roofs. The interior is strikingly simple with a fire pit, tatami mats, and a hanging scroll or some other object of art. Tea ceramics are a Japanese art form. Each item is carefully chosen to be part of a group. After the special tea is brewed and drank, the tea master and guests may discuss each implement or the beauty of nature. Ordinary business matters are left outside in this special world. The simplicity of tea-room decor has influenced the design of functional things, including kitchen implements, floor mats, textiles and common bowls and cups.

B. Calligraphy

Calligraphy originated in China in the 3rd century A.D. The ink (sumi) was mixed using an inkstand to grind an ink block made of lampblack and glue. Sometimes poetry was created spontaneously, which contributed to the development of haiku.

The first Zen calligrapher was Huang T'ing-chien (1045–1105) who became enlightened and recognized this changed the quality of his writing. Dogen Kigen (1200–1253), a legendary Zen master who founded the Soto sect, was a highly skilled calligrapher, and emphasized the importance of meditation.

C. Art

Ashikaga monochrome ink painting began as a natural extension of calligraphy. The black ink can be mixed in various shades that suggest the perception of color. As stated by T. Hoover, the purpose of Zen painting is to penetrate beyond the perceptions of the rational mind, to show nature's essence. The artist paints the enlightenment of the moment, and therefore has no time to labor over each stroke. Absolute concentration is crucial because no retouching can be done. The artist never pauses to evaluate his work. The ink flows in an unending flurry of strokes producing a sense of rhythm, movement, form, and the artist's vision of life's inner music.

This type of painting began in the Sung dynasty in China as a rebellion against conventional art similar to the abstract expressionist movement. Ch'an monks threw ink and rubbed it in by hand or using their hair. Three types of schools emerged. Zenkiga emphasized Zen parables, insight, and practice. Chinz specialized in portraits of well-known Zen teachers.

A third school focused on landscape painting with a very specific set of rules including which items were usually present (mountains, trees, rocks, etc.). Each painting was divided into three tiers that illustrated the scene from different perspectives. These landscapes pioneered concepts that became important in other Zen art including the symbolic use of empty space and emphasis on rocks and trees, which eventually became significant metaphors.

Japanese monks who traveled in China brought Zen painting home in the 13th century. Sesshu Toyo (1414–1481) reinvented the form so that it reflected Zen precepts in its veneration of nature's beauty. He inspired a number of other artists who worked for the next 150 years.

D. Gardening

Zen gardens were also inspired by Chinese models created during the Sung dynasty. The use of rocks, trees, sand, and water were replications of Ashikaga ink landscapes. The idea of depicting a garden as three-dimensional painting inspired the development of perspective and abstraction approximately the same time as Ucello (1397–1495) was doing similar work with painting in Italy.

The Zen garden was designed, like a painting, for viewing with the hope the emotional reaction of the viewer would inspire greater awareness. Excellent examples from the 13th and 14th century are in Kyoto.

War and poverty in the 15th century inspired the creation of stark stone gardens called *kare sansu*. These monochromatic gardens were specifically designed for meditation. They anticipated several art techniques by centuries including the abstract expressionist "symbolic arrangement of mass and space."

E. Haiku

Haiku is a tightly structured poetry format that requires the use of exactly 17 syllables. The poems are written in time to the seasons and often encompass themes about nature. Created in the 14th century, haiku was popularized by the Zen monk Basho (1643–1694). Haikus represent Zen thinking in their absolute absorption in the moment, offering a direct clear unmistakable experience without reference to anything else.

> With every gust of wind,
> The butterfly changes its place
> On the willow

The best haiku are those which arise from the tension between the rigidity of the form and the depth of the poetic feeling.

F. Other Arts

The No drama, developed in the 13th century, used masks, dances and poetry to explore emotional experience. However, because there is no story and very little movement, most untrained Westerners have difficulty appreciating the plays. Like other Zen arts, the purpose is to inspire a profound emotional response. The Japanese puppet theater was also impacted by Zen.

Zen was used to train the samurai in swordsmanship and archery. The Zen archer practiced breathing until it was second nature and the arrow could be released without thought. Intense concentration allowed Zen archers to attain phenomenal accuracy. A Zen mind-set helped warriors overcome fear and respond automatically and unconsciously with deadly accuracy during battles. In 1281, the samurai defeated Kubla Khan's army of more than 100,000 men. Zen also influenced the creation and training in martial arts such as kung-fu, akido, and judo.

Morita therapy, developed in Japan, combined Zen principles with psychotherapy in an effort to get hypochondriac and obsessive-compulsive patients to accept reality.

In business, Zen influenced the design and development of products, the structure of companies and the way business decisions were made. Onda, a Japanese creativity researcher, stated that, compared to Westerners, the Japanese are more tolerant of ambiguity but not as logical. Intuitive thinking is more common, which may be partially based on meditation. [*See* INTUITION.]

III. ZEN IN THE WEST

After World War II, teachers from Japan moved to the United States and Europe establishing Zen centers in major cities and mountain retreats.

A. Beat Zen

Beat Zen was embraced in the fifties by some writers and musicians who felt they were rebelling against American conformity. Alan Ginsberg's poems reached a wide audience, while Jack Kerouac wrote popular semi-autobiographical novels such as *The Dharma Bums*. John Cage developed a form of "music" that used multiple tape recorders and wrote a piano recital where the pianist did not play a note, but a page turner still turned the pages. Drugs, especially marijuana, were identified with beat Zen enthusiasts. Alan Watts felt Kerouac "confused 'anything goes' at the existential level with 'anything goes' on the artistic and social levels." The social responsibility inherent in Zen Buddhism was forgotten.

B. Psychology and Science

Zen has been advocated by a number of psychologists as a valuable tool that can complement traditional therapy. Meditation, mental exercises (koans), and skill training were primary sources of interest. Modern interpretations of this include relaxation exercises, hypnosis, biofeedback, and openness to experience. Alpha biofeedback training may have originated with electro-encephalogram (EEG) monitoring of Zen and Yoga practitioners who have claimed that meditation may create a unique form of consciousness. Researchers found that zazen, when practiced by Monks, created slower breathing patterns and more muscle relaxation.

Carl Jung admired Zen, but felt the states achieved sometimes had delusional elements. Like most Western psychologists, Jung believed in the concept of the self, which could never really know the collective unconscious. This viewpoint contrasted sharply with Buddhist practice, in which the experience of satori awakened and absorbed the unknown self into a world beyond human consciousness. Some theorists criticized the use of Zen in therapy. It has been suggested that Zen's fixation on enlightenment sometimes caused psychological problems, and that Morita-therapy was inappropriate for patients in the West because of its cultural dependence and fondness for simple answers.

Other psychologists felt Zen could help reduce the ego, expand consciousness, and promote self-integration. It was thought that the sudden enlightenment and gradual training in Zen practice were comparable with "insight" and "working through" in psychology. The concept of personal growth inherent in Zen is a cornerstone of psychotherapy, especially notable in the work of Abraham Maslow and Carl Rogers. It was proposed that the psychotherapist could be compared to a Zen martial arts teacher in terms of developing specific teaching techniques and strategies for each client. Morita-therapy has been used by some Western psychologists. Albert Ellis proposed that Zen could be integrated with rational-emotive therapy.

C. Creativity Research

Investigation into creativity confirms the inherent worth of some aspects of Zen training. Some researchers have proposed that there exists a similarity between solving koans and the creative problem-solving model of preparation, incubation, illumination, and evaluation. After preparation and incubation, a solution to a koan or a problem comes suddenly and unexpectedly. Satori is similar to the "Aha" moment in creativity.

Then the viability of the solution must be evaluated. [*See* INCUBATION; INSIGHT.]

A few studies indicate creativity may be facilitated in sitting meditation by freeing perceptions. Other researchers identified a satiation effect, which resulted from focusing on a picture or words with intense concentration. Eventually previous meaning dissolved, which opened the possibility for new perspectives. Creative people have described a similar fixation on a specific melody when composing or a specific object when painting.

This process appears to break down previous belief systems, inhibiting cognition in favor of perception, in the same way that a Zen student must go through deconstruction of his or her belief system before arriving at enlightenment and a true understanding of the world. It is a shift in paradigms that links creativity and Zen. [*See* PARADIGM SHIFTS.]

The evidence that expertise takes 10 years to achieve suggests that the slow learning mentor-student relationship practiced by Zen teachers may be more effective in the long run than some Western techniques. Flow, defined as the feeling of an almost automatic, effortless, yet highly focused state of consciousness, is similar to descriptions of Zen creativity. [*See* EXPERTISE.]

D. Business

The American business community has been exposed to some Zen principles, especially during the 1970s and 1980s when Japanese businesses were thriving and American companies were struggling. Writers, consultants, and teachers gave advice about creative management using Zen principles, while others stressed meditation as a way to relieve stress. Nike had great success using the Zen-tinged slogan "Just do it." A recent movement toward spirituality in business may lead to further interest in Zen within the corporate world.

As vegetarian diets have increased in popularity, some Zen cookbooks have cracked the marketplace. Books about Zen and using Zen have multiplied with training advice and application for a number of fields including education, writing, career planning, and guitar playing.

Zen thinking is part of all the world cultures. As more people in the Western world become interested in Buddhism, it is likely that Zen training and ideas about creativity will work their way into the mainstream of Western society. Examples of public figures who have acknowledged their appreciation of Zen include comedian Garry Shandling, singer-songwriter Leonard Cohen, actress Anne Bancroft, and martial-arts expert Chuck Norris. Professional basketball coach Phil Jackson used Zen principles in coaching the Chicago Bulls to six championships. Peter Matthiessen, a Zen practitioner for many years wrote about his search for inner peace in *The Snow Leopard,* which won the National Book Award in 1979.

IV. CONCLUSION

Zen has influenced both the concept and execution of many different areas involving creativity, especially in Japan. The key aspects that Zen affected include the following:

1. The training for professions, which in many ways interacted and reinforced Zen principles. Each type of training became known as a way to enlightenment. A mentor-master teacher worked with students to make routine aspects automatic and as free of ego as possible. Once the ego was minimized, the mind and body were free so creativity could become natural and spontaneous.

2. An element of deliberate incompleteness that required the audience to use their own life experience to participate in the creative process. The viewer is part of the picture. Zen art is designed to be an experience grasped as a whole, not intellectually analyzed.

3. An appreciation of asymmetry and "happy accidents" that produced distinctive products. The term *wabi* is used to describe the nobility of simplicity and rough edges of Zen products.

4. Increasing awareness and understanding by altering perceptions and forcing the mind to stretch.

5. Emphasis on the nonverbal with only a minimum of words even in haiku and No drama.

Zen art has touched upon almost every aspect of Japanese life and its presence is still felt today. Sensitivity to nature, the awareness of beauty, and the attention to the aesthetic details in life inherent in Japanese culture are a direct legacy of Zen creativity.

Bibliography

Abe, M. (1997). *Zen and comparative studies.* Honolulu: University of Hawaii.

Austin, J. H. (1998). *Zen and the brain.* Boston: MIT Press.

Blackstone, J., & Josipovic, Z. (1995). *Zen for beginners.* New York: Writers and Readers Publishing.

Dumoulin, H. (1990). *Zen Buddhism: A History. Volume 2. Japan.* New York: Macmillan.

Hoover, T. (1977). *Zen culture.* New York: Random House.

Kapleau, P. (1965). *The three pillars of Zen: Teaching, practice, enlightenment.* Boston: Beacon Press.

Kubose, S. K., & Umemoto, T. (1980, March). Creativity and the Zen koan. *Psychologia: An International Journal of Psychology in the Orient, 23*(1), 1–9.

Radford, J. (1976). What can we learn from Zen? A review and some speculations. *Psychologia: An International Journal of Psychology in the Orient, 19*(2), 57–66.

Sekida, K. (1996). *Zen training: Methods and philosophy.* New York: Weatherhill.

Suzuki, D. T. (1959). *Zen and Japanese culture.* New York: Pantheon.

Watts, A. (1957). *The way of Zen.* New York: Pantheon.

Watts, A. (1958). *This is IT and other essays of Zen and spiritual experience.* New York: Pantheon.

Appendix I: Chronology of Events and Significant Ideas and Works on Creativity

Mark A. Runco

California State University, Fullerton

1859	Sir Francis Galton, first cousin to Charles Darwin, published *Hereditary Genius*.
1870	Galton's *British Men of Science* appears.
1876/1958	Charles Darwin's *Autobiography*. Howard Gruber, who refined biographical methods for the study of creative persons, claimed that Darwin's *Autobiography* is "one of the first and maybe the best autobiographies of a creator."
1881	Cesare Lombroso, *The Man of Genius*.
1901	Alfred Binet, author of the first test of mental ability (later revised as the Stanford Binet IQ test) publishes "L'observateur et l'imagination" ["Imagination and the Observer"].
1908	Freud published *Creative Writers and Daydreaming*.
1910	Freud published *Leonardo da Vinci and a Memory of His Childhood*.
1913	Henri Poincaré's *Science and Method* was published. It contained very influential essays and his famous insight about Fuchsian functions. [His *Science and Hypothesis* was published in 1905.]
1917	Wolfgang Köhler, *Mentality of the Apes*. Various demonstrations of insights.
1925	Louis Terman publishes the first volume from his classic longitudinal study, *Genetic Studies of Genius*.
1926	Graham Wallas presents the seminal four-stage model of the creative process, with the preparation, incubation, illumination, and verification stages.
1926	Catherine Cox publishes *Genetic Studies of Genius. Vol. 2: The Early Mental Traits of Three Hundred Geniuses*.
1935/1945	Karl Duncker, *On Problem Solving*. [Reports the famous radiation problem.]
1937	Catherine Patrick's article, "Creative Thought in Artists," appears in the *Journal of Psychology*. [Her "Creative Thought in Poets" appeared in 1935.]
1942	Leta Hollingworth, *Children above 180 IQ*.
1945	Max Wertheimer, *Productive Thinking*.
1945	Jacques Hadamard, *The Psychology of Invention in the Mathematical Field*. Probably the first questionnaire study of mathematicians and an interesting account of Poincaré's famous insight.
1946	Henri Bergson's *The Creative Mind* is published.

1946   Division 10 (Psychology and the Arts) is one of the founding divisions of the American Psychological Association.

1949   Institute for Personality Assessment and Research founded (Berkeley, CA). Barron, MacKinnon, Helson, and many others would conduct significant research on creativity at IPAR.

1950   Guilford published his seminal article, "Creativity," based on his Presidential Address to the American Psychological Association.

1950   Morris I. Stein founded the Center for the Study of Creativity and Mental Health. It was attached to the Psychology Department of the University of Chicago.

1952   Anne Roe's *The Making of a Scientist* is published.

1952   Frank Barron and G. S. Welsh publish the "Figure Preference Test" (later the "Barron-Welsh Art Scale").

1952   Brewster Ghiselin's edited, *The Creative Process*.

1952   Kris describes "regression in the service of the ego" in *Psychoanalytic Explorations in Art.*

1957   Sputnik launched, drawing attention to the need for more emphasis on science, technology, and creativity.

1958   Symposium organized by H. Gruber, M. Wertheimer, and G. Terrell, published in 1962 as *Contemporary Approaches to Creative Thinking.*

1958   Kubie's *Neurotic Distortion of the Creative Process* is published.

1958   Frank Barron's "The Psychology of the Imagination" appears in *Scientific American.*

1959   Maslow tied creativity to self-actualization in "Creativity in Self-Actualizing People." He later concludes that creativity and self-actualization may be inextricable.

196x   Roger Sperry reports significant differences between the two hemispheres of "split brain" patients (*Scientific American*).

1960   Donald Campbell's "Blind Variation and Selective Retention" appears in *Psychological Bulletin.*

1962   Donald MacKinnon's "Nature and Nurture of Creative Talent" is released in the *American Psychologist.*

1962   Goertzel and Goertzel published *Cradles of Eminence.*

1962   Thomas Kuhn presents seminal ideas about paradigms in *The Structure of Scientific Revolutions* (Chicago Univ. Press).

1962   Jerome Bruner defines creativity as "effective surprise" in his article, "The Conditions of Creativity."

1962   Mednick's theory of remote associates is presented in his article, "The Associative Basis of the Creative Process" (*Psychological Bulletin*).

1962   Getzels and Jackson's *Creativity and Intelligence: Explorations with Gifted Students* stirs debate over the distinction between creativity and traditional intelligence.

1963   Calvin Taylor and Frank Barron publish *Scientific Creativity* (proceedings from the Utah Conferences).

1963   Osborn's *Applied Imagination* is published.

1964   Arthur Koestler introduces "bisociation" in his book, *The Act of Creation.*

1965   Michael Wallach and Nathan Kogan published *Modes of Thinking in Young Children*—a huge step for assessment with divergent thinking tests and clarification of the relationship between creativity and traditional intelligence.

1966   E. Paul Torrance publishes the "Torrance Tests of Creative Thinking" (which were previously the "Minnesota Tests of Creative Thinking").

1967   The first issue of the *Journal of Creative Behavior* appears.

1969   Wallach and Wing's *The Talented Student* appears.

1969   Rudolph Arnheim's *Visual Thinking* is published.

1970	P. E. Vernon's collection, *Creativity,* is published by Penguin.
1972	Getzels and Csikszentmihalyi describe the value of problem finding for artists and publish *The Creative Vision.*
1972	Nicholls publishes "Creativity in the Person Who Will Never Produce Anything Original or Useful" in the *American Psychologist.*
1973	Khatena and Torrance's *Thinking Creatively with Sounds & Images* (rev. 1998, Scholastic Testing Service).
1974	Morris Stein publishes two volumes of *Stimulating Creativity.*
1974	Howard Gruber's *Darwin on Man* demonstrates the value of case studies and applies systems thinking to the topic.
1974	E. P. Torrance directed the first Future Problem Solving activities in Athens, GA.
1975	Robert Albert's "Behavioral Definition of Genius" published in the *American Psychologist.*
1975	Dean Keith Simonton revitalizes the historimetric approach to the study of exceptional achievement (*Journal of Personality and Social Psychology*).
1977	Harriet Zuckerman's *Scientific Elite* appears.
1983	Howard Gardner published *Frames of Mind.* It contains the most convincing argument to date for the delineation of domains.
1988	The *Creativity Research Journal* is founded.
1990	The U.S. Patent and Trademark Office publishes their *Inventive Thinking Curriculum Project.*
1990	Creativity Symposium held at Pitzer College in Claremont, CA (proceedings published in M. A. Runco and R. S. Albert's *Theories of Creativity*).
1990	International Working Creativity Research Conference, Center for Creative Studies, State University College of New York at Buffalo (proceedings published in Isaksen et al.'s *Understanding and Recognizing Creativity*).
1990	The first Gustav Theodor Fechner Award was given to Rudolf Arnheim by Division 10 of the American Psychological Association for Outstanding Achievement in Psychology and the Arts. (Since 1990 it has been given annually but called the Rudolf Arnheim Award.)
1992	IBM and PBS Television develop and televise "The Creative Spirit."
1993	Doris Wallace and Howard Gruber edit a special issue of the *Creativity Research Journal* which explicates the need for research on "Creativity in the Moral Domain."
1993	Nobel laureates describe their work in a symposium on scientific creativity at the Royal Society of Medicine, published in a special issue of the *Creativity Research Journal.*
1999	The *Encyclopedia of Creativity* is published by Academic Press.

Bibliography

Bethune, G. W. (1837). *Genius.* Philadelphia: G. W. Mentz & Son.

Cattell, J. (1903). A statistical study of eminent men. *Popular Science Monthly, 62,* 359–377.

Ellis, H. (1904). *A study of British genius.* London: Hurst & Blackett.

Hutchinson, E. D. (1931). Materials for the study of creative thinking. *Psychological Bulletin, 28,* 392–410.

James, W. (1880). Great men, great thoughts, and the environment. *Atlantic Monthly, 46,* 441–459.

Jastrow, J. (1898). Discussion and reports: The psychology of invention. *Psychological Review, 5,* 307–309.

Lombroso, C. (1891). *The man of genius.* London: Walter Scott.

Ribot, T. (1900a, January–June). The nature of the creative imagination. *International Monthly, 1,* 648–675.

Ribot, T. (1900b, January–June). The nature of the creative imagination. *International Monthly, 2,* 1–25.

Royce, J. (1898). The psychology of invention. *Psychological Review, 5,* 113–144.

Appendix II: Tests of Creativity

Mark A. Runco

California State University, Fullerton

*This appendix reviews some of the **TESTS** used to assess creativity. Psychometric issues about many of these tests are given in the* Mental Measurements Yearbooks, Tests in Print, *and various texts on testing. Some tests listed herein were not developed for creativity but either have been adapted to that end (e.g., Tangrams) or have several scales, one of which is directly relevant to creativity or originality (e.g., the Adjective Check List and the California Psychological Inventory). This appendix focuses on tests, inventories, and rating scales.*

Creativity is often assessed with other techniques, such as interviews, open-ended surveys, or a tally of products. Sometimes in the research, nominations are used rather than an instrument with a score. This appendix covers only tests, inventories, and rating scales.

It does not cover all assessments. It is only a partial list of some of the major tests.

I. BIOGRAPHICAL INVENTORIES

Alpha Biographical Inventory of Creativity.
(1968). The Institute for Behavioral Research in Creativity. Salt Lake City, UT.

Biographical Inventory of Creativity: Art and Writing Scales for females; Art-Writing and Math-Science for males.
Schaefer, C. E. (1970). San Diego, CA: Educational and Industrial Testing Service.

II. PERSONALITY

Adjective Check List (ACL). Various scales have been developed to identify creativity and at least four others are relevant (i.e., intellectence-origence).
Gough, H., Heilbrun, A. B. (1983). USA: Consulting Psychologists Press.
See also Domino, G. (1994). *Creativity Research Journal, 7,* 21–34.

California Psychological Inventory (CPI). The CPI is now routinely scored for the Creative Temperament Scale. An older Creative Personality index was scored from the standard scales and an Empathy scale (Creativity = $65.96 + .63Cs - .34Sy - .37Gi - 1.15Cm + .61Em$).
Gough, H. (1975). Palo Alto, CA: Consulting Psychologists Press.

Sixteen Personality Factor Questionnaire. The Cattell 16PF has a creativity index based on a regression formula.

> Cattell, R. B. (1986). USA: Institute for Personality and Ability Testing.

The Myers-Briggs Type Indicator includes Intuitive as one of four primary domains.

> Myers, I. Briggs, & Briggs, K. (1985). Palo Alto, CA: Consulting Psychologists Press.

The NEO Personality Inventory has an openness scale which is reportedly correlated with creativity.

> Costa, P., & McCrae, R. R. (1985). Odessa, FL: Psychological Assessment Resources, Inc.

Overexcitability Questionnaire-II (OEQ II): 50 items, Likert scale, 10 items in each of five forms of overexcitability.

> Falk, R. F., Lind, S., Miller, N. B., Piechowski, M., & Silverman, L. K. (1999). Institute for Study of Advanced Development.

What Kind of Person Are You? is a subtest of the Khatena-Torrance Creative Perception Inventory.

> Khatena, J., & Torrance, E. P. (1976). Bensenville, IL: Scholastic Testing Service.

Creative Behavior Disposition Scale.

> Taylor, I. A., & Fish, R. A. (1979). The Creative Disposition Scale: A Canadian Validation. *Canadian Journal of Behavior Science, 11,* 95–97.

III. RATING INSTRUMENTS AND SOCIALLY VALID MEASURES

Students' Self-Evaluation of Creativity.

> Miller, H. B., & Sawyers, J. K. (1989). A comparison of self and teachers' ratings of creativity in fifth grade children. *Creative Child and Adult Quarterly, 14,* 179–185, 229–238.

The Parental Evaluation of Children's Creativity—Revised.

> Runco, M. A., Johnson, D., & Bear, P. (1993). Parents' and teachers' implicit theories of children's creativity. *Child Study Journal, 23,* 91–113.

Preschool and Kindergarten Interest Descriptor.

> Rimm, S. B. (1983). Watertown, WI: Educational Assessment Service, Inc.

Teacher's Evaluation of Student's Creativity.

> Runco, M. (1984). *Perceptual and Motor Skills, 59,* 711–717.

Scales for Rating the Behavioral Characteristics of Superior Students.

> Renzulli, J. S. (1976). Mansfield Center, CT: Creative Learning Press.

IV. STYLES

Kirton Adaptation-Innovation Inventory (KAI).

> Adaptors and Innovators: A Description and Measure. (1976). *Journal of Applied Psychology, 61,* 622–629.

Creativity Styles Questionnaire.

> Kumar, V. K., Kemmler, D., & Holman, E. (1997). *Creativity Research Journal, 10,* 51–58.

Kaufmann & Martinsen's Assimilator/Explorer measure of styles.

> Martinsen, O. (1993). Insight Problems Revisited: The Influence of Cognitive Styles and Experience on Creative Problem Solving. *Creativity Research Journal, 6,* 435–447.

Your Style of Learning and Thinking

> Torrance, E. P. (1977). *The Gifted Child Quarterly, 21*(4), 563–573.

Creative Problem Solving Inventory.

> Basadur, M., Wakabayashi, M., & Graen, G. B. (1990). *Creative Research Journal, 3,* 22–32.

V. DIVERGENT THINKING AND PROBLEM SOLVING

Divergent Thinking Tests

For preschool children: Multidimensional Stimulus Fluency Measure.

> Broberg, G., & Moran, J., III (1988). *Creativity Research Journal, 1,* 115–121.

J. P. Guilford (1960) relied on Consequences, Alternate Uses, and Plot Titles. He also developed Names for Stories (1971), Plot Titles (1962), Possible Jobs (1963), Seeing Problems (1971).

> Guilford's approach and tests are described in his book.

Guilford, J. P. (1968). *Creativity, Intelligence, and Their Educational Implications.* San Diego, CA: EDITS/Robert Knapp.

Meeker and Meeker (1975) further developed Guilford's ideas about the structure of intellect as part of their test battery for school children.

> Meeker, M. (1987). Meeker Creativity Rating Scale. Vida, OR: SOI Systems.

Wallach and Kogan (1965) used two visual tests (Pattern Meanings and Line Meanings) and three verbal tests (Uses, Instances, and Similarities).

> Wallach, M. A., & Kogan, N. (1965). *Modes of Thinking in Young Children: A Study of the Creativity–Intelligence Distinction.* New York: Holt, Rinehart and Winston.

Multiple Choice Test of Divergent Thinking. Abedi-Schumaker Creativity Test.

> Auzmendi, E., Villa, A., & Abedi, J. (1996). *Creativity Research Journal, 9,* 89–95.

Mark Runco developed divergent thinking tasks to examine "problem generation," one aspect of problem finding, and "real-world" tasks that were predictive of problem solving in the natural environment.

> See Runco's 1994 book *Problem Finding, Problem Solving, and Creativity,* Norwood, NJ: Ablex).

Test for Creative Thinking-Drawing Production
> Urban, K. K. (1991). On the Development of Creativity in Children. *Creativity Research Journal, 4,* 177–191.

Torrance Tests of Creative Thinking
> (e.g., Product Improvement, Ask and Guess, Just Suppose).

Thinking Creatively with Sounds and Word, Sounds and Images, Onomatopoeia and Images
> Torrance, E. P., Khatena, J., & Cunningham, B. F. (1973). Personnel Press.

Thinking Creatively in Action and Movement
> Torrance, J. P. (1974). Georgia Studies

Thinking Creatively About the Future
> Torrance, J. P. (1974).

Torrance Test of Imagination
> Torrance, J. P. (1959). Bureau of Educational Research, University of Minnesota.

Scores: The most common scores from divergent thinking tests are Fluency, Originality, and Flexibility. Guilford also used a remoteness score for Consequences; Runco developed an Appropriateness index; Torrance an elaboration index.

Formulating Hypotheses Test. Quantity and quality of ideas generated when formulating hypotheses, designing methods for measurement, solving problems involving the scientific method, and when evaluating research proposals.

> Frederiksen, N., & Ward, W. C. (1978). *Applied Psychology Measurement, 2*(1), 1–24.

Remote Associates Test. Remote Associates Test: Examiners manual.
> Mednick, S. (1967). Boston: Houghton Mifflin.

Functionally Remote Associates Test.
> Worthen & Clark. (1971). *Journal of Educational Measurement, 8,* 113–123.

Similes

Simile Interpretations.
> Christensen, P. R., Guilford, J. P., & Hoepfner, R. (1963). Orange, CA: Sheridan Psychological Services, Inc.

The Similes test.
> Schaefer, C. (1969). *Similes Manual.* NYC Center for Urban Education.

VI. WORK AND EDUCATIONAL ENVIRONMENT

The Creative Environment Scales: Work Environment Inventory.
> Amabile, T. M., Gryskiewicz, & Nur. D. (1989). *Creativity Research Journal, 2,* 231–253.

Ekvall's Creative (Organizational) Climate Questionnaire.

Swedish Council for Management and Organization. Stockholm, Sweden.

Climate for Creativity.
> Torrance, E. P. (1958). Bureau of Educational Research.

Classroom Climate Questionnaire
> Walberg & Anderson (1968). *Journal of Creative Behavior.*

Technical Audit for Creativity of Organizations.
   Stein, M. I. (1959). Amagansett, NY: Mews Press.

Epstein Creativity Competencies Inventory for Managers. Measures eight competencies that predict managers' ability to elicit creativity in others.
   Epstein, R. (1998). InnoGen. West Chester, PA.

Jones Inventory of Blocks.
   A self-report described in the *Creativity Research Journal* (1991), 4, 303–315.

Creativity Audit for Organizations.
Rickards' creativity audit measures self-report data on three levels: (1) local or team, (2) organizational; and (3) market environment.
   Rickards, T., & Bessant, J. (1980). The creativity audit: Introduction of a new research measure in programs for facilitating organizational change, *R&D Management, 10*(2), 67–75.

VII. COMPETENCIES

Epstein Creativity Competencies Inventory for Individuals. Measures four core competencies that predict creative performance. (Also see Epstein, above.)
   (1998). InnoGen. West Chester, PA.

VIII. AESTHETIC SENSITIVITY

Tests of Aesthetic Sensitivity.
   Frois, J. P., & Eysenck, H. J. (1995). The visual aesthetic sensitivity test applied to Portuguese children and fine art students. *Creativity Research Journal, 8,* 277–284.

IX. PROJECTIVE AND PERCEPTION MEASURES

Creative Functioning Test.
   Smith, G., Carlsson, I., & Andersson, G. (1989). *Creativity Research Journal, 2,* 1–16.

Thematic Apperception Test (TAT). A projective measure often used in clinical assessments of personality. A blank card has been used to assess problem finding tendencies.

Murray, H. (1973). Psychological Corporation, San Antonio, TX.
   (See also Eisenman, R. (1992). *Creativity Research Journal, 5* 175–181.)

Rorschach Psychodiagnostic Technique.
   Rorschach, H. (1954). Australia: Australian Council for Educational Research.

Synesthesia Questionnaire.
   Domino, G. (1989). *Creativity Research Journal, 2,* 17–29.

Khatena Torrance Creative Perception Inventory. Contains two tests of Creative Self-Perceptions: What Kind of Person Are You? and Something about Myself.
   Khatena, J., & Torrance, E. P. (1998). Bensenville, IL: Scholastic Testing Service.

Physiognomic Cue Test.
   Stein, M. (1974). Physiognomic cue test: Test and manual. Amagansett, NY: Mews Press. (*See also* Martindale in *Creativity Research Journal*.)

X. PREFERENCES AND ATTITUDES

Barron Welsh Art Scale. (Originally the Figure Preference Test, 1949). Assumes that the preference for complexity is predictive of creative talent.
   Welsh, G., & Barron, F. (1963). Palo Alto, CA: Consulting Psychologists Press.

Basadur's Attitude Measure. Originally a 14-item self-report, expanded in the 1996 *Creativity Research Journal*. The original version was scored for two scales measuring the preference for ideation and the tendency toward premature closure.

How Do You Think test. A mix of achievements, attitudes, and opinions—with good predictive validity. For younger persons, the Group Inventory for Finding Interests (GIFFT) and the Group Inventory for Finding (creative) Talent (both Ed Assessment Service, Inc.)
   Davis, G. (1975). *Journal of Creative Behavior.*

The Creative Attitude Survey.
   Schaefer, C., & Bridges, C. I. (1970). Development of a creative attitude scale for children. *Perceptual and Motor Skills, 31,* 861–862.

What Kind of Person Are You?
  Khatena, J., & Torrance, E. P. (1976). Bensenville, IL: Scholastic Testing Service.

Eisenman's Preference for Polygons test
  Eisenman, R. (1966). Perceived creativity, set, and preference for simple or complex shapes. *Perceptual and Motor Skills, 22,* 111–114.

XI. CRITERION MEASURES

Instruments in this category are typically thought to assess *actual* creative behavior rather than tendencies or the potential for creativity. Here is a sample of the better known instruments:

Tel-Aviv Activities and Accomplishments Inventory. Three forms: Primary, Adolescent, Adult.
  Milgram, R. (1973, 1998) see her chapter in the book, *Theories of Creativity,* Hampton Press (in press).

Academic, Military, Work, and Leisure Activities subscales.

Arnold Ludwig's Creative Achievement Scale.
  Ludwig, A. (1992). *Creativity Research Journal, 5,* 109–124.

Lifetime Creativity Scales
  Richards, R., Kinney, D. K., & Benet, M. (1988). Developed at McLean Hospital, Belmont, MA and Harvard Medical School.
  Richards, R., Kinney, D., Benet, M., & Merzel, A. (1988). Assessing everyday creativity: Characteristics of the lifetime creativity scales and validation with three large samples. *Journal of Personality and Social Psychology, 54,* 476–485.

XII. ACTIVITY CHECKLISTS

Holland's Checklists of extracurricular and academic activities.

Extracurricular creative activity. Given in the book *The Talented Student.*
  Wallach & Wing (1969). New York: Holt, Rinehart & Winston.

Quality and quantity of activities in seven domains.
  Runco, M. (1986). Divergent thinking and creative performance in gifted and nongifted children. *Educational and Psychology Measurements, 46,* 375–384.

Runco's Ideational Behavior Scale (RIBS). Designed specifically as criterion for divergent thinking tests. The emphasis is on actual behavior involving ideas. Originally 93 items with Likert scale but a 23-item subscale is most reliable.
  Runco, M. *Divergent Thinking and Creative Ideation.* Hampton Press (in press).

XIII. CREATIVE PRODUCTS

Tangrams.
  Domino, G. (1980). Chinese tangrams as a technique to assess creativity. *Journal of Creative Behavior, 14,* 204–213.

Creative Products Semantic Scale (CPSS) contains 55 bi-polar adjective pairs, Likert Scale. Three factors are represented: Novelty, Resolution, and Synthesis.
  Besemer, S., & O'Quin, K. (1989). The development, reliability, and validity of the revised creative product semantic scale. *Creative Research Journal, 2,* 268–278.

XIV. DOMAIN-SPECIFIC MEASURES

Action Preference Test.
  Alter, J. (1989). *Creativity Research Journal, 2,* 184–195.

Manual for Evaluating Performance in Technical Personnel.
  Stein, M. I. (1961). Science Research Associates.

Musical Creativity Test (1971).

Musical Divergent Production test
  Gorder, W. (1976). An investigation of divergent production abilities as constructed of musical ability. *Dissertation Abstracts International, 37,* 171.

Measure of Creative Thinking in Music (version II)
  Webster (1983).

Poetry Writing.
  Kasof, J. (1997). *Creativity Research Journal, 10,* 303–316.

Iowa Inventiveness Inventory.
   Colangelo, N., Kerr, B., Hallowell, K., Huesman, R., & Gaeth, J. (1992). The Iowa Inventiveness Inventory: Toward a measure of mechanical inventiveness. *Creativity Research Journal, 5,* 157–163.

Preconscious Activity Scale
   Holland & Baird (1968). *Journal of Creative Behavior, 2,* 214–223.

Pun Test.
   Karlines (1967). *Journal of Psychology, 67,* 335–340.

Barron Symbol Equivalents Test.
   Barron, F. (1958). *Scientific American*; or (1996). *No rootless flower.* Cresskill, NJ: Hampton Press.

Barron Anagram Test.
   Barron, F. (1958). *Scientific American*; or (1996). *No rootless flower.* Cresskill, NJ: Hampton Press.

Contributors

Gordon Abra
Collaboration and Competition; Sports and Creativity
Department of Sociology
University of Arizona
Tucson, Arizona 85721

Jock Abra
Collaboration and Competition; Sports and Creativity
Department of Psychology
University of Calgary
Calgary, Alberta
Canada T2N 1N4

Andrei G. Aleinikov
Humane Creativity
Mega-Innovative Mind International Institute
Montgomery, Alabama 36106

Judy Alter
Dance
Department of World Arts and Cultures
University of California, Los Angeles
Los Angeles, California 90024

Teresa Amabile
Consensual Assessment; Motivation/Drive
Business Administration
Harvard Business School
Boston, Massachusetts 02163

Don Ambrose
Adaptation and Creativity
Graduate Studies
School of Education and Human Services
Rider University
Lawrenceville, New Jersey 08648

Gretchen Arian
Distribution of Creativity
University of Illinois, Chicago
Chicago, Illinois 60680

Patricia Arlin
Dialectical Thinking: Implications for Creative Thinking
School of Education
California State University, San Bernardino
San Bernardino, California 92407

Karen D. Arnold
Longitudinal Studies
College of Education
Boston College
Chestnut Hill, Massachusetts 02167

John Baer
Domains of Creativity; Gender Differences
Rider University
Lawrenceville, New Jersey 08648

Susan Besemer
Creative Products
Reed Library
State University College, Fredonia
Fredonia, New York 14063

Glenda M. Bogen
Split Brains: Interhemispheric Exchange in Creativity
Pasadena, California

Joseph E. Bogen
Split Brains: Interhemispheric Exchange in Creativity
University of Southern California and University of California, Los Angeles, Los Angeles, California, and California Institute of Technology, Pasadena, California

Richard Brower
Crime and Creativity; van Gogh, Vincent
Wagner College
Staten Island, New York 10301

761

Glen R. Brown
Postmodernism and Creativity
  Kansas State University
  Manhattan, Kansas 66502

David Carson
Counseling
  Department of Family and Consumer Sciences
  University of Wyoming
  Laramie, Wyoming 82071

Corissa Chopp
Families and Creativity
  Department of Psychology in Education
  Arizona State University
  Tempe, Arizona 85287

LeoNora M. Cohen
Adaptation and Creativity
  School of Education
  Oregon State University
  Corvallis, Oregon 97331

Mary Shane Connelly
Leadership
  American Institute for Research
  Washington, DC 20007

Regina Conti
Motivation/Drive
  Department of Psychology
  Colgate University
  Hamilton, New York 13346

Bonnie Cramond
Creativity in the Future
  Department of Educational Psychology
  University of Georgia
  Athens, Georgia 30602

Arthur J. Cropley
Definitions of Creativity; Education
  Psychology Institute II
  University of Hamburg
  20146 Hamburg, Germany

Gerald C. Cupchik
Perception and Creativity
  Division of Life Sciences
  Scarborough College
  University of Toronto
  Scarborough, Ontario
  Canada, M1C 1A4

John S. Dacey
Concepts of Creativity: A History
  Boston College
  Chestnut Hill, Massachusetts 02167

Robert Q. Dana
Drugs and Creativity
  University of Maine
  Orono, Maine 04469

Jeffrey L. Dansky
Play
  Department of Psychology
  Eastern Michigan University
  Ypsilanti, Michigan 48197

Janet Davidson
Insight
  Department of Psychology
  Lewis and Clark College
  Portland, Oregon 97219

Gary Davis
Barriers to Creativity and Creative Attitudes
  University of Wisconsin–Madison,
  Madison, Wisconsin 53706

Peter Derks
Humor
  Department of Psychology
  College of William and Mary
  Williamsburg, Virginia 23187

Lise Deschamps Ostwald
Schumann, Robert
  Peter F. Ostwald Health Program for Performing
    Artists
  University of California, San Francisco
  San Francisco, California 94116

Cora L. Díaz de Chumaceiro
Serendipity
  Universidad Simon Bolivar
  Caracas 1080, Venezuela

Rebecca A. Dodds
Fixation; Incubation
  Department of Psychology
  Texas A&M University
  College Station, Texas 77845

Mattei Dogan
Marginality
  National Center of Scientific Research
  75013 Paris, France

George Domino
Synesthesia
  Department of Psychology
  University of Arizona
  Tucson, Arizona 85721

Gayle Dow
Problem Finding
  California State University
  Fullerton, CA 92834

Stephanie Z. Dudek
Architecture, Modern Western; Art and Aesthetics
  Psychology Clinic
  University of Montreal
  Montreal, Quebec, Canada H3C 3J7

Kevin Dunbar
Science
  Department of Psychology
  McGill University
  Montreal, Quebec
  Canada H3A 2T5

Stephen Durrenberger
Mad Genius Controversy
  College of Medicine
  Department of Psychiatry
  University of Kentucky
  Lexington, Kentucky 40536

Göran Ekvall
Creative Climate
  University of Lund and FA Institute
  16776 Bromma
  Sweden

Alan C. Elms
Freud, Sigmund
  Department of Psychology
  University of California, Davis
  Davis, California 95616

Robert Epstein
Behavioral Approaches to Creativity; Generativity Theory
  United States International University
  San Diego, California 92131

K. Anders Ericsson
Expertise
  Department of Psychology
  Florida State University
  Tallahassee, FL 32306

Barbara Duarte Esgalhado
Pessoa, Fernando
  Department of Psychology
  Duquesne University
  Pittsburgh, Pennsylvania 15203

Giselle B. Esquivel
Diversity, Cultural
  Fordham University
  New York, New York 10023

Daniel Fasko, Jr.
Associative Theory
  Morehead State University
  Morehead, Kentucky 40351

Gregory J. Feist
Autonomy and Independence
  Department of Psychology
  College of William and Mary
  Williamsburg, Virginia 23187

John F. Feldhusen
Giftedness and Creativity; Talent and Creativity
  Purdue University
  West Lafayette, Indiana 47907

David Feldman
Prodigies
  Eliot-Pearson Department of Child Development
  Tufts University
  Medford, Massachusetts 02155

Cameron M. Ford
Business Strategy; Corporate Culture
  Department of Management
  College of Business
  University of Central Florida
  Orlando, Florida 32816

Natalia Gajdamaschko
Vygotsky, Lev Semenovich
  The University of Georgia
  Athens, Georgia 30601

Howard Gardner
Multiple Intelligences
  Project Zero
  Harvard Graduate School of Education
  Cambridge, Massachusetts 02138

Raymond W. Gibbs, Jr.
Metaphors
  Department of Psychology
  University of California, Santa Cruz
  Santa Cruz, California 95064

Gabriella Goldschmidt
Design
  Technion, Israel Institute of Technology
  Technion City, Haifa 32000, Israel

Michael Gorman
Bell, Alexander Graham
  School of Engineering and Applied Science
  University of Virginia
  Charlottesville, Virginia 22903

Amit Goswami
Quantum Theory of Creativity
  University of Oregon
  Institute of Theoretical Sciences
  Eugene, Oregon 97403

Mary Lee Grisanti
Creativity in the Moral Domain
  Developmental and Educational Psychology
  Teachers College, Columbia University
  New York, New York 10027

Howard E. Gruber
Creativity in the Moral Domain; Ensemble of Metaphor;
Evolving Systems Approach; Piaget, Jean
  Department of Human Development
  Teacher's College, Columbia University
  New York, New York 10027

David M. Harrington
Conditions and Settings/Environment
  Department of Psychology
  University of California
  Santa Cruz, California 95064

Thomas E. Heinzen
Proactive Creativity
  Department of Psychology
  William Paterson University
  Wayne, New Jersey 07470

Ravenna Helson
Institute of Personality Assessment and Research;
Personality
  Institute of Personality and Social Research
  University of California, Berkeley
  Berkeley, California 94708

Beth Hennessey
Consensual Assessment
  Wellesley College
  Wellesley, Massachusetts 02481

Michael T. Hertz
Invention
  University of Virginia
  Charlottesville, Virginia 22903

Edward R. Hirt
Mood
  Department of Psychology
  Indiana University
  Bloomington, Indiana 47405

Frederic L. Holmes
Krebs, Hans Adolf
  History of Medicine
  Yale University
  New Haven, Connecticut 06520

John Houtz
Imagery
  Fordham University
  New York, New York 10023

Amy Ione
Multiple Discovery
  Art and Science Writer
  Berkeley, California 94709

Maria F. Ippolito
Woolf, Virginia
  Bowling Green, Ohio 43402

Peter L. Jakab
Wright, Orville and Wilbur
  Aeronautics Division
  National Air and Space Museum
  Smithsonian Institution
  Washington, DC 20560

Norbert Jaušovec
Brain Biology and Brain Functioning; Metacognition
  Univerza v Mariboru
  Pedagoska fakulteta Maribor
  Koroska c. 160
  2000 Maribor
  Slovenia

Linda R. Jeffrey
Wordsworth, William
  Rowan University
  Glassboro, New Jersey 08028

Philip Johnson-Laird
Logic and Reasoning
  Department of Psychology
  Princeton University
  Princeton, New Jersey 08544

Keri Jones
Jungian Theory
  Private Practice
  Long Beach, California 90814

Joseph Kasof
Attribution and Creativity
Department of Psychology and Social Behavior
School of Social Ecology
University of California
Irvine, California 92697

Albert Katz
Psycholinguistics
Department of Psychology
University of Western Ontario
London, Ontario
Canada N6A 5C2

Geir Kaufmann
Cognitive Style and Creativity
Norwegian School of Management
5019 Bergen
Norway

Susan Kavaler-Adler
Sexton, Anne
Object Relations Institute for Psychotherapy and
    Psychoanalysis
New York, New York 10003

Robert T. Keegan
Darwin, Charles Robert
Department of Psychology
Pace University
Pleasantville, New York 10570

Barbara Kerr
Families and Creativity
Department of Psychology in Education
Arizona State University
Tempe, Arizona 85287

Stanley Krippner
Altered and Transitional States; Dreams and Creativity
Saybrook Graduate School
San Francisco, California 94133

Ellen Langer
Aging; Mindfulness
Department of Psychology
Harvard University
Cambridge, Massachusetts 02142

Gaynell Laptosky
Behavioral Approaches to Creativity
United States International University
San Diego, California

Andreas C. Lehmann
Expertise
Institut fur Musikwissenschaft

Martin-Luther-Universitat Halle
D-06114 Halle, Germany

Marc Leman
Music
Institute for Psychoacoustics and Electronic Music
University of Ghent
B-9000 Ghent
Belgium

David Lester
Plath, Sylvia; Suicide
Psychology Program
Richard Stockton College
Pomona, New Jersey 08240

Becca Levy
Aging
Department of Epidemiology and Public Health
Yale University
New Haven, Connecticut 06520

Martin S. Lindauer
Old Age Style
State University of New York
College of Brockport
Brockport, New York 14420

Todd Lubart
Componential Models; Economic Perspective on Creativity
Universite Rene Descartes (Paris V)
Laboratoire Cognition et Developpement
75006 Paris, France

Pavel Machotka
Cezanne, Paul
University of California, Santa Cruz
Santa Cruz, California 95060

István Magyari-Beck
Creatology
Budapest University of Economic Sciences
Budapest, Hungary

Colin Martindale
Art and Artists; Genetics; History and Creativity
Department of Psychology
University of Maine
Orono, Maine 04469

Øyvind Martinsen
Cognitive Style and Creativity
Psychometrics Unit
Department of Psychosocial Science
University of Bergen
5015 Bergen, Norway

Richard E. Mayer
Problem Solving
Department of Psychology
University of California, Santa Barbara
Santa Barbara, California 93106

Robert R. McCrae
Consistency of Creativity Across the Life Span
Gerontology Research Center
National Institute of Aging
Baltimore, Maryland 21224

Robert B. McLaren
Dark Side of Creativity
Department of Child and Adolescent Studies
California State University
Fullerton, California 92834

William Michael
Guilford's View
School of Education
Division of Educational Psychology and Technology
University of Southern California
Los Angeles, California 90089

Arthur I. Miller
Einstein, Albert
Department of Science & Technology Studies
University College London
Gower Street
London WC1E 6BT
England

Mihnea C. Moldoveanu
Mindfulness
Harvard Business School and Department of Psychology
Harvard University
Cambridge, Massachusetts 02142

Martha J. Morelock
Prodigies
Department of Psychology and Human Development
Peabody College
Vanderbilt University
Nashville, Tennessee 37203

Sandra Moriarty
Advertising
School of Journalism and Mass Communication
University of Colorado, Boulder
Boulder, Colorado 80303

Delmont Morrison
Carroll, Lewis
Department of Psychiatry
University of California, San Francisco
San Francisco, California 94143

Shirley Linden Morrison
Dinesen, Isak
College of Notre Dame
Belmont, California 94002

Michael Mumford
Analogies; Heuristics; Leadership
American Institutes for Research
Washington Research Center
Washington, DC 20007

Edward Nȩcka
Memory and Creativity
Institute of Psychology
Jagellonian University
31 007 Krakow, Poland

Jill Nemiro
Acting
California School of Professional Psychology
Organizational Psychology Program
Alhambra, California 91803

Thomas J. Nickles
Paradigm Shifts
Department of Philosophy
University of Nevada, Reno
Reno, Nevada 89509

Lloyd D. Noppe
Unconscious
Department of Human Development
University of Wisconsin–Green Bay
Green Bay, Wisconsin 54311

Dwayne G. Norris
Heuristics
American Institutes for Research
Washington Research Center
Washington, DC 20007

Linda O'Hara
Learning Styles
Department of Psychology
Yale University
New Haven, Connecticut 06511

Karen O'Quin
Creative Products; Humor
Department of Psychology

Buffalo State College
Buffalo, New York 14222

David Pariser
Conventionality; Toulouse-Lautrec, Henri de
Department of Art Education
Concordia University
Montreal, Quebec
Canada H3G 1M8

Sidney J. Parnes
Programs and Courses in Creativity
Buffalo State College
Buffalo, New York 14222

Cathryn Patricola
Imagery
Fordham University
New York, New York 10023

Paul B. Paulus
Group Creativity
Department of Psychology
University of Texas
Arlington, Texas 76019

Kirsten M. Peters
Diversity, Cultural
Fordham University
New York, New York 10023

Michael M. Piechowski
Overexcitabilities
Northland College
Ashland, Wisconsin 54806

Jane Piirto
Poetry; Synchronicity
Ashland University
Ashland, Ohio 44805

Jonathan Plucker
Deviance; Drugs and Creativity; Enhancement of Creativity
Indiana University
Bloomington, Indiana 47405

Emma Policastro
Intuition
Harvard University
Cambridge, Massachusetts 02138

Paige P. Porter
Analogies
AON Consulting
Alexandria, VA 22315

Kimberly Powell
Multiple Intelligences
Project Zero
Harvard Graduate School of Education
Cambridge, Massachusetts 02138

Karl Pribram
Brain and the Creative Act
Center for Brain Research
Radford University
Radford, Virginia 24142

Steven R. Pritzker
Alcohol and Creativity; Writing and Creativity; Zen
Luminescent Creativity
Greenbrae, California 94904

Tony Proctor
Artificial Intelligence; Computer Programs
Independent Lecturer, Writer, and Consultant
Lancashire, England L39 2HG
United Kingdom

Gerard J. Puccio
Teams
Center for Studies in Creativity
Buffalo State College
Buffalo, New York 14222

M. K. Raina
Cross-Cultural Differences; Tagore, Rabindranath
Department of Educational Psychology and Foundations of Education, National Council of Educational Research, and Training
New Delhi 110016, India

Kevin Rathunde
Systems Approach
Department of Family and Consumer Studies
University of Utah
Salt Lake City, Utah 84112

Sally Reis
Women and Creativity
University of Connecticut
Storrs, Connecticut 06269

Ruth Richards
Affective Disorders; Everyday Creativity; Five-Part Typology; Four Ps of Creativity
Saybrook Graduate School, San Francisco, California 94133, University of California, San Francisco, and Harvard Medical School, Cambridge, Massachusetts 02138

Tudor Rickards
Brainstorming; Innovation; Organizations Interested in Creativity
  Manchester Business School
  University of Manchester
  Manchester M15 6PB
  United Kingdom

Richard E. Ripple
Teaching Creativity
  Department of Education
  Cornell University
  Ithaca, New York 14853

Brett A. Robbs
Advertising
  School of Journalism and Mass Communication
  University of Colorado, Boulder
  Boulder, Colorado 80309

Robert Root-Bernstein
Discovery; Productivity and Age
  Department of Physiology
  Michigan State University
  East Lansing, Michigan 48824

Albert Rothenberg
Articulation; Homospatial Process; Janusian Process
  Harvard University
  Cambridge, Massachusetts 02140

Mark A. Runco
Appendix I: Chronology of Events and Significant Ideas and Works on Creativity; Appendix II: Tests of Creativity; Contrarianism; Critical Thinking; Developmental Trends in Creative Abilities and Potentials; Deviance; Divergent Thinking; Economic Perspective on Creativity; Enhancement of Creativity; Flexibility; Fourth Grade Slump; Implicit Theories; Misjudgment; Perspectives; Problem Finding; Self-Actualization; Tactics and Strategies for Creativity; Time
  California State University
  Fullerton, California 92834

Sandra W. Russ
Emotion/Affect
  Psychology Department
  Case Western Reserve University
  Cleveland, Ohio 44106

Stephen Keith Sagarin
Ensemble of Metaphor
  Teacher's College

  Columbia University
  New York, New York 10027

Cathy Sanguinetti
Sexton, Anne
  Independent Writer/Producer
  Wrentham, Massachusetts 02093

Louis A. Sass
Schizophrenia
  Graduate School of Applied and Professional Psychology
  Rutgers, The State University of New Jersey
  Piscataway, New Jersey 08854

R. Keith Sawyer
Improvisation
  Department of Education
  Washington University
  St. Louis, Missouri 63130

David A. Schuldberg
Chaos Theory in Creativity; Schizophrenia
  Department of Psychology
  University of Montana
  Missoula, Montana 59812

Teres Enix Scott
Knowledge
  Hampton University
  Hampton, Virginia 23668

Jay Seitz
Political Science and Creativity
  Department of Political Science and Psychology
  York College
  City University of New York
  New York, New York 10021

Kennon Sheldon
Conformity
  Department of Psychology
  University of Missouri
  Columbia, Missouri 65211

Leonard M. Shlain
da Vinci, Leonardo; Zeitgeist
  California Pacific Medical Center
  San Francisco, California 94115

Dean Keith Simonton
Eminence; Historiometry; Matthew Effects; Shakespeare, William
  Department of Psychology
  University of California, Davis
  Davis, California 95616

Jerome L. Singer
Imagination
Department of Psychology
Yale University
New Haven, Connecticut 06520

Gudmund Smith
Perceptgenesis
Department of Psychology
Lund University
S-22350 Lund, Sweden

Steven M. Smith
Fixation; Incubation
Department of Psychology
College of Liberal Arts
Texas A&M University
College Station, Texas 77845

Becca Solomon
Multiple Intelligences
Project Zero
Harvard Graduate School of Education
Cambridge, Massachusetts 02138

Robert J. Sternberg
Insight; Intelligence; Learning Styles
Department of Psychology
Yale University
New Haven, Connecticut 06511

Patricia D. Stokes
Novelty
Barnard College
Columbia University
New York, New York 10027

Rena Subotnik
Longitudinal Studies
Hunter College
Educational Foundations
New York, New York 10021

Frank Sulloway
Birth Order
Center for Advanced Study in the Behavioral
   Sciences
Stanford, California 94305

Laura Tahir
Shaw, George Bernard
Garden State Youth Correctional Facility
East Windsor, New Jersey 08520

Eugene Taylor
Archival Investigation
Harvard University Medical School
Cambridge, Massachusetts 02140

Warren D. TenHouten
Handwriting and Creativity
Department of Sociology
University of California, Los Angeles
Los Angeles, California 90095

Becky J. Thurston
Curie, Marie Sklodowska; Flexibility
Department of Psychology
University of Hawaii, Hilo
Hilo, Hawaii 96720

Glenn Toplyn
Attention
Mount Sinai School of Medicine
New York, NY 10029

Patti M. Valkenburg
Television and Creativity
Amsterdam School of Communications Research
University of Amsterdam
1012 CE Amsterdam
The Netherlands

Joyce VanTassel-Baska
The Bronte Sisters
Center for Gifted Education
College of William and Mary
Williamsburg, Virginia 23185

Herbert J. Walberg
Distribution of Creativity
University of Illinois, Chicago
Chicago, Illinois 60680

Kate Ward
Eccentricity
Jardine Clinic
Royal Edinburgh Hospital
Edinburgh EH10 5HF
Scotland, United Kingdom

David J. Weeks
Eccentricity
Jardine Clinic
Royal Edinburgh Hospital
Edinburgh EH10 5HF
Scotland, United Kingdom

Michael West
Innovation
  Aston Business School
  University of Aston
  Birmingham B4 7ET
  England

Paul Wink
Self Processes and Creativity
  Department of Psychology
  Wellesley College
  Wellesley, Massachusetts 02481

Bernice Yan
Dialectical Thinking: Implications for Creative Thinking
  Department of Educational Psychology and Special
    Education
  University of British Columbia
  Vancouver, British Columbia
  Canada V6T 1Z4

Tobi Zausner
O'Keeffe, Georgia
  The New School University
  New York, New York 10016

Name Index

Volume numbers are boldfaced, separated from the first page reference with a colon. Subsequent references to the same material are separated by commas.

A

Aalto, A., **1**:86
Abbott, E. A., **2**:743
Abe, M., **2**:750
Abler, W. H., **1**:125, **2**:108
Abra, J., **1**:293, **1**:758, **2**:463, **2**:583
Abraham, F., **1**:266, **1**:268, **1**:272
Abraham, R. H., **1**:272
Achee, J. W., **2**:250
Ackerman, D., **1**:362
Adams, J., **1**:7, **1**:27, **1**:174, **1**:675, **2**:263, **2**:615
Adamson, R., **1**:727
Addams, J., **2**:255
Adler, A., **1**:159, **1**:599
Adler, S., **1**:8
Adorno, T. W., **1**:106, **1**:112
Aeschylus, **1**:2
Aesop, **1**:2
Agor, W., **2**:93
Agrell, A., **2**:649
Agronic, G. S., **2**:79
Alba, J., **2**:62
Albert, R., **1**:322, **1**:468, **1**:732, **2**:128, **2**:240, **2**:259, **2**:371, **2**:431, **2**:663
Aleinikov, A. G., **1**:844
Alexander, C., **1**:233, **1**:529, **1**:535
Alexander, P., **2**:392
Alger, H., **1**:366
Ali, M., **2**:579

Allard, F., **1**:707
Allen, M., **1**:846, **1**:853
Allen, W., **2**:16
Alleyn, E., **1**:3
Allport, G., **1**:690, **1**:693
Almansi, G., **1**:605
Alpaugh, P. K., **2**:463
Alter, J. B., **1**:481
Alto, A., **1**:82
Amabile, T., **1**:6, **1**:7, **1**:133, **1**:160, **1**:163, **1**:180, **1**:295–296, **1**:299, **1**:300, **1**:346, **1**:349, **1**:350, **1**:357, **1**:359, **1**:400, **1**:412, **1**:413, **1**:415, **1**:417, **1**:419, **1**:421, **1**:524, **1**:595, **1**:675, **1**:784, **2**:88, **2**:128, **2**:129, **2**:259, **2**:277, **2**:282, **2**:530, **2**:627, **2**:637
Ambrose, D., **1**:22, **1**:167
Anderson, J. R., **1**:139
Anderson, N., **2**:649
Andreasen, N., **2**:503, **2**:586, **2**:589, **2**:730, **2**:735
Angst, J., **1**:202
Anson, R., **1**:227
Antheil, G., **1**:569
Anthony, D., **1**:800, **1**:805
Aquinas, St. Thomas, **1**:117
Ared, R., **1**:159
Argonic, G. S., **2**:79
Arguelles, J., **1**:509, **2**:743
Arieti, S., **1**:339, **1**:453, **1**:464
Aristodemus, **1**:2
Aristotle, **2**:415
Arlin, P., **1**:552
Arlin, P. K., **2**:568
Armstrong, J., **1**:158
Arnheim, R., **1**:112, **1**:377, **1**:383, **1**:534, **1**:620, **2**:317, **2**:360

Arnold, K., **2**:168, **2**:708
Arnold, K. D., **1**:6
Arnold, M., **2**:412
Aronson, E., **1**:120, **1**:545
Artaud, A., **1**:5, **2**:513
Arwine, A., **1**:202
Asch, S., **1**:430
Ashforth, B. E., **1**:404, **1**:412
Astaire, F., **1**:475
Athenodorus, **1**:2
Au, S., **1**:481
Auden, W. H., **2**:413
Augustine, Saint, **1**:313
Austin, J. H., **2**:750

B

Baars, B., **2**:25
Babbit, I., **2**:602
Bach, J. S., **1**:4, **1**:648
Bachelard, G., **2**:343
Bachelor, P., **1**:797
Backman, E. L., **1**:471
Backtold, L., **1**:161
Bacoche, L., **1**:813
Bacon, F., **1**:6, **1**:316
Bacon, R., **1**:5
Baer, D., **1**:177
Baer, J., **1**:139, **1**:595, **1**:758, **2**:304
de Baif, J. A., **1**:479
Bain, Al., **1**:575
Bakan, D., **2**:15
Baker, J. E., **1**:176, **1**:183, **2**:304
Baker, S., **1**:29
Balanchine, G., **1**:480
Baldwin, J., **2**:138
Baltes, M., **1**:6

Subject Index

Volume numbers are boldfaced, separated from the first page reference with a colon. Subsequent references to the same material are separated by commas.

A

Ability, creativity as, **1**:433
Abstract learning, learning styles and, **2**:597
Abstraction, vs. realism, in work of Georgia O'Keeffe, **2**:309
Acceptance, conformity and, **1**:341
Accommodative thinking, education and, **1**:629
Achievement, personality, creativity as, **2**:364
Actualization, creativity and, **1**:686, **2**:538–539
Actus reus, crime and, **1**:443
Adaptation, **1**:9–22
  accommodation, **1**:9
  assimilation, **1**:9
  chance and, **1**:15–17, **1**:17
  complexity theory, **1**:9
  continuum
    adaptive creative behaviors, **1**:9, **1**:18–21
    creative behaviors, levels of, **1**:18–21
  creative-adaptive styles, **1**:15–16
  creativity, definitions of, **1**:521–522
  definitions, **1**:520–521
  discontinuity, **1**:9, **1**:18–19
  environmental support, **1**:17–18
  equilibrium, **1**:9
  expertise, **1**:15–17

facilitative contenxts, **1**:17–18
  intelligence, **1**:15
  mature creativity, **1**:9
  mundane creativity, **1**:9
  structure, **1**:9
  in systems approach, **1**:698–699
  theoretical perspectives related to, **1**:12–14
Adaptive flexibility, **1**:729
Adolescence, **1**:494–495
Advantage, competitive, business strategies, **1**:235
Advertising, **1**:23–29
  brainstorming, **1**:23
  concept, **1**:24–25
  creative concept, **1**:23
  development of, **1**:23–24
  director, creative, **1**:23
  discipline, **1**:27
  execution and, **1**:23
  ideation process, **1**:25–26
  industry, changing, demands and, **1**:28–29
  portfolio, **1**:23
  visualization, **1**:23, **1**:26–27
Aesthetics, **1**:99–113. *See also* Art
  discovery and, **1**:559
  evolution, **1**:823
  morality and, **1**:431
  response, **1**:108
Affect, **1**:659–668. *See also* Affective disorders
  affective processes, types of, **1**:660–661
  art and, **1**:110–111
  artistic creativity, **1**:667
  cognitive-affective models, **1**:663
  curiosity, **1**:664
  divergent thinking, **1**:659

empirical evidence, **1**:662
  integrative model, **1**:664–666
  intrinsic motivation, **1**:663–664
  mood induction, **1**:659
  neurological processes, **1**:667–668
  play and, **1**:666
  positive effect, **1**:666–667
  pretend play, **1**:659
  primary process, **1**:659, **1**:661–662
  proactive creativity and, **2**:430
  psychoanalytic theory, **1**:661–663
  regression, in service of ego, **1**:662
  resolution, conflict, sublimation and, **1**:662–663
  tension, **1**:664
Affective disorders, **1**:31–44
  acquired immunity, **1**:31, **1**:41–42
  bipolar disorder, **1**:31
    unipolar disorder, distinction, **1**:34
  compensatory advantage, **1**:31, **1**:41
  eminent creativity, **1**:31
  everyday creativity, **1**:31, **1**:39
  genes, **1**:39
  illness, **1**:40–42
  inverted-U effect, **1**:32
  psychological applications, **1**:41
  psychopathology, **1**:41
  resilience, **1**:42–43
  romanticism and, **2**:504
  vs. schizophrenia, **2**:511–512
  suicide and, **2**:586–587
  unipolar affective disorders, **1**:32
Affective functioning, effects of imagery on, **2**:602–604
Affective process
  negative affect, **1**:666–667
  scientific creativity, **1**:667
Age of Enlightenment, **1**:315–316

Simonton model, creative careers, 1:49
Simulation packages software, 1:306
Sinusoidal wave, 1:213
Situational creativity, 2:502–503
Skill, in systems approach, 1:693
Slack, organizational, 2:45
Sleep
 non-REM, 1:597
 REM, 1:598
Sleep terrors, 1:598
Slump, fourth grade, 1:743–744
Social basis of creativity, 2:286–287
Social cognition, 2:143
Social constructivism, 1:669
Social creativity, 1:324
Social domain, creative action in, 1:386–387
Social ecology, 1:147–148
Social entities, creative products, 1:436
Social factors, creativity and, 1:636–637
Social influence
 informational, conformity and, 1:341
 normative, conformity and, 1:341
Social phenomenon, creativity and, 1:518–520
 organizational environment, 1:519–520
 social rules, 1:518
 sociocultural validation, 1:518–519
Social-psychological research, 1:349–351
Social self, 2:541
Social system
 creative personality in, 2:370
 personality, creative personality in, 2:365–366
Societal filters, 1:629
Sociocultural environment, 1:654–656
Sociocultural theories, gender differences, 1:757–758
Sociocultural validation, creativity, definition, 1:511
Sociopathy, 1:173–174
Software, computer, 1:306
 databases, 1:306
 electronic mail systems, 1:306
 simulation packages, 1:306
 spreadsheets, 1:306
Solitude, autonomy and, 1:162
Southwest, Georgia O'Keeffe in, 2:307

Space
 importance of, 1:331
 measures of, 1:647
 negative, positive space, in work of Georgia O'Keeffe, 2:309
Space-time continuum, 2:741–742
Speaking subject, postmodernism, 2:427–428
Special-process view, of insight, 2:57, 2:63–65
Special talent creativity, 1:165
Speciation, aesthetic, 1:828–829
Specificity, domain, 1:591
Speech, metaphor in, 2:210–211
Split brain, 2:571–576
 effects, 2:573
 handwriting, 1:801–805
 interhemispheric transfer, lack of, 2:573
 Leonardo da Vinci, 2:505–508
 strategies, 2:573
Spreadsheet software, 1:306
Stabilization, creativity and, 1:437
Stage of adulthood, personality, creativity and, 2:368
Stakeholder, corporate culture and, 1:385
State space, in chaos theory, 1:259
Statistical distribution, distribution of creativity, 1:573–574
Status expectancy bias, 1:151–153
Stimulants, central nervous system, use of, 1:607
Stimulation hypotheses, regarding television, 2:652
Stimulus equivalence, behavior and, 1:175
Storage, memory, 2:196–197
Strategic vision, corporate culture and, 1:390
Strategy, for creativity, 1:537, 2:611–616
 classifying, 2:612–614
 interpersonal, 2:614–615
Stream of consciousness, 2:14–19, 2:16
 of William James, 1:680. *See also* James, W.
Stress, arousal and, 1:143
Structure
 adaptation and, 1:9
 of language, 2:480–483
Structure-of-intellect model, 1:785, 1:787–791
 behavioral, 1:789

 cognition, 1:789
 convergent production, 1:789
 divergent production, 1:789
 evaluation, 1:789
 figural, 1:789
 Guilford, 2:82–83
 memory, 1:789
 semantic, 1:789
 symbolic, 1:789
Style, aging and, 1:45, 2:311–318
Stylistic extinction, 1:829
Subjective creation, 1:436
 objective creation, relationship, 1:436
Substance abuse, 1:607–611. *See also under* specific substance
 alcohol, 1:608
 depressants, central nervous system, 1:607
 family drug use, 1:610
 hallucinogen, 1:607
 marijuana, 1:609
 stimulants, central nervous system, 1:607
 tobacco, 1:608–609
Subtypes of personality, creative personality, 2:369–370
Suicide, 2:585–589
 affective disorder and, 2:586–587
 attitudes toward, 2:587
 creative writing and, 2:588–589
 Sylvia Plath, 2:390–391
 treatment, 2:588
 women, 2:586
 writers, 2:586, 2:732
Supportive environment, aging and, 1:47
Symbolism, in work of Georgia O'Keeffe, 2:310
Synchronicity, 2:591–596
 in biology, 2:594
 in chaos theory, 2:594–595
 in physics, 2:595
 in psychology, 2:592–594
Synectics, creativity program, 2:474–477
Synesthesia, 2:597–604
Synesthetic processes, 2:358
Synthesis, in dialectical thinking, 1:549
Systems approach, 1:689–693, 2:605–609
 adaptation, 1:698–699
 componential model, 1:297–298
 extrinsic motivation, 1:689, 2:605
 facets, 1:689, 1:691–692, 2:605, 2:607–608

U

Unconscious, **2**:673–680
  brain physiology, **2**:677–678
  cognitive models, **2**:678–679
  collective, Jungian theory, **2**:112–113
  in Freudian theory, **2**:674–675
  intuition, **2**:676–677
  in Jungian theory, **2**:112–113
    individuation, **2**:113–114
    personal unconscious, **2**:112
  neoanalytic concepts, **2**:675
  personal, Jungian theory, **2**:112
  processing, in creativity, **2**:481–482
  role of, **2**:508
Unexpected discoveries, **2**:264–265
Unification, creative, homeospatial processes and, **1**:833
Unpredictability, chaos theory and, **1**:261–262
U. S. Office of Education, **1**:777
Utility, of creativity, **1**:623
Utopian thinking, **1**:427

V

Validation, consensual, **1**:91
Valuation, **1**:449–452
  brainstorming, processes in, **1**:451
  convergent thinking, **1**:449
  educational advantages, **1**:450–451
  vs. evaluation, **1**:451
  research on, **1**:451–452
  varieties of, **1**:450
van Gogh, Vincent, **1**:166, **2**:171, **2**:269, **2**:282, **2**:681–690
Variability, aesthetic, **1**:825
Verbal creativity tests, **2**:486–487
Vernacular, indigenous design and, **1**:525
Vertical thinking, **2**:475

Vinci, Leonardo da. *See* da Vinci, Leonardo
Vision, strategic, corporate culture and, **1**:390
Visionizing, creativity program, **2**:471
Visual arts, multiple discovery, **2**:265–270
Visual memory, in work of Georgia O'Keeffe, **2**:308
Visual outliners software, **1**:304
Visual thinking in design, **1**:533–535
Visualization
  advertising and, **1**:23, **1**:26–27
  television, **2**:652
Vygotskian theory, **1**:669
Vygotsky, Lev, **2**:394, **2**:691–698

W

Wakefulness, dreaming and, **1**:598
Whole brain problem solving, **2**:475
Witkin's field dependence, vs. field independence, learning style, **2**:4
Women, creativity in, **2**:75–76, **2**:699–708
  expression, creative, barriers to, **2**:703–707
    external, **2**:703–704
    internal, **2**:700
    personal, **2**:704–705
  gender differences, in creativity, **2**:702
  perceptions about personal creativity, **2**:705
  perfectionism, **2**:705
  research, **2**:702–703
  self-doubt, **2**:706
  selflessness, **2**:706
  societal factors, **2**:701
  subjugation of creative talents, **2**:706
  suicide in, **2**:586
  support, absence of, **2**:706
Woolf, Virginia, **2**:16, **2**:171, **2**:501, **2**:709–714, **2**:731

Wordsworth, William, **1**:5, **2**:15, **2**:410, **2**:412, **2**:715–720
Work
  environment, **2**:48–49
  habits, of writers, **2**:734
Worldview, dialectical, dialectical thinking, **1**:548–549
  change, **1**:548
  contradiction-resolution, **1**:549
  part-whole relationship, **1**:548
  qualitative transformation, **1**:548
  thesis-antithesis-synthesis, **1**:549
Wright, Wilbur, Orville, **2**:721–726
Writers, suicide in, **2**:586, **2**:732
Writer's block, **2**:734
Writing, **2**:727–736
  alcoholism, in writers, **2**:731–732
  biographical studies, **2**:728–729
  collaborative, **2**:734–735
  creative writing, in institutions, **2**:735
  drug use, in writers, **2**:732
  motivation, **2**:733–734
  psychobiography, **2**:728
  psychopathology, writers, **2**:729–731
  suicide, of writers, **2**:732
  work habits, **2**:734
  writer's block, **2**:734

Z

Zeitgeist, **1**:446–447, **1**:647, **2**:737–744
Zen, **2**:745–750
  in architecture, **2**:747
  in China, **2**:746–748
  in design, **2**:747
  history of, **2**:745–746
  in west, **2**:748–750
    beat zen, **2**:748
    in business, **2**:749–750
    in creativity research, **2**:749
    in psychology, **2**:748–749
    science, **2**:748–749

ISBN 0-12-227077-0

9 780122 270772

90038

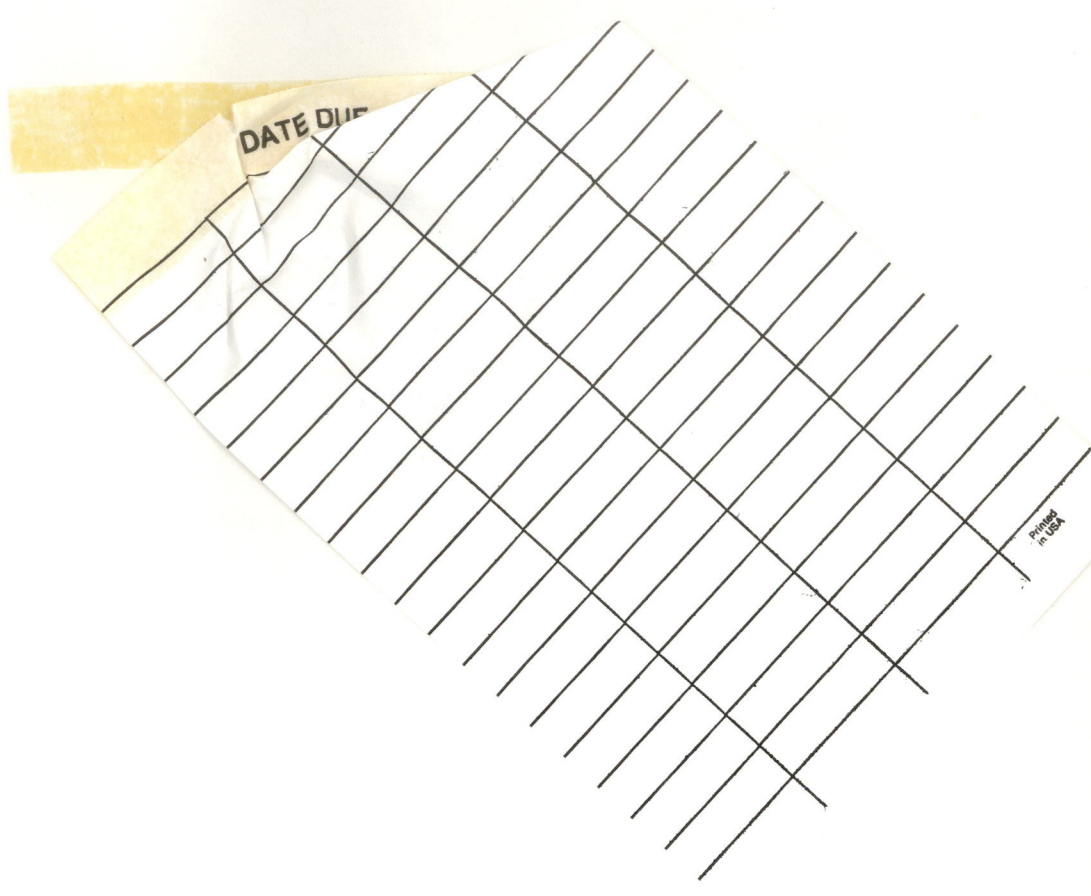

DATE DUE

Printed
in USA